HARRY L. RINKER

The Official® Price Guide To

COLLECTIBLES

HARRY L. RINKER

The Official® Price Guide to

COLLECTIBLES

Second Edition

HOUSE OF COLLECTIBLES

THE BALLANTINE PUBLISHING GROUP • NEW YORK

Important Notice. All of the information, including valuations, in this book has been compiled from the most reliable sources, and every effort has been made to eliminate errors and questionable data. Nevertheless, the possibility of error, in a work of such immense scope, always exists. The publisher will not be held responsible for losses that may occur in the purchase, sale, or other transaction of items because of information contained herein. Readers who feel they have discovered errors are invited to *write* and inform us, so they may be corrected in subsequent editions. Those seeking further information on the topics covered in this book are advised to refer to the complete line of *Official Price Guides* published by the House of Collectibles.

Published by: House of Collectibles
                 The Ballantine Publishing Group
                 201 East 50th Street
                 New York, New York 10022

Distributed by The Ballantine Publishing Group, a division of Random House, Inc., New York, and simultaneously in Canada by Random House of Canada Limited, Toronto.

http://www.randomhouse.com

Manufactured in the United States of America

ISSN: 1094–3862

ISBN: 0–676–60107–3

Cover design by Kristine V. Mills–Noble

Second Edition: September 1998

10 9 8 7 6 5 4 3 2 1

RINKER ENTERPRISES, INC.

HARRY L. RINKER
President

DENA C. GEORGE
Associate Editor

DANA N. MORYKAN
Senior Editor

KATHY WILLIAMSON
Associate Editor

NANCY BUTT
Librarian

VIRGINIA REINBOLD
Controller

RICHARD SCHMELTZLE
Support Staff

ABOUT THE AUTHOR — HARRY L. RINKER

Harry L. Rinker is one of the most forthright, honest, and "tell–it–like–it–is" reporters in the antiques and collectibles field today. He is the King of Collectibles, the last of the great antiques and collectibles generalists.

Rinker is president of Rinker Enterprises, Inc., a firm specializing in providing consulting, editorial, educational, photographic, research, and writing services in the antiques and collectibles field. He also directs the Institute for the Study of Antiques & Collectibles, serving as the principal instructor for its seminars and conferences.

Rinker is a prolific antiques and collectibles writer. Other House of Collectibles titles by Rinker include *Dinnerware of the 20TH Century: The Top 500 Patterns*, *Silverware of the 20TH Century: The Top 250 Patterns*, and *Stemware of the 20TH Century: The Top 200 Patterns*. Rinker also is author of *Price Guide to Flea Market Treasures, Fourth Edition* and *Hopalong Cassidy: King of the Cowboy Merchandisers.* He is co–author with Dana N. Morykan of *Warman's Country, 3RD Edition* and *Garage Sale Manual & Price Guide* and with Norman Martinus of *Warman's Paper.*

"Rinker on Collectibles," a weekly syndicated column, appears in trade and daily newspapers from coast to coast. Often highly opinionated and controversial, it is one of the most widely read columns in the antiques and collectibles trade.

Rinker is a frequent television and radio guest. He often refers to himself as the "national cheerleader for collectibles and collecting." His television credits include "Oprah, NBC–Today Show, ABC–TV Good Morning America," "CNBC–TV Steals and Deals", and "MPT Wall Street Week With Louis Rukeyser." "Whatcha Got," a ninety–second antiques and collectibles daily feature, is distributed to radio stations by the Minnesota News Network. Rinker also does weekly call–in radio shows for KFGO (Fargo, North Dakota) and WIBC (Indianapolis, Indiana).

Each year Rinker lectures and/or makes personal appearances in over a dozen cities across the United States, often sponsored by the Antiques and Collectibles Dealers Association, trade publications, and antiques mall or show promoters. In 1996 Rinker and James Tucker co–founded the National Association of Collectors.

Rinker is a dedicated accumulator, a collector of collections. He is continually adding new items to over 250 different collections. Among collectibles collectors, he is best known for his collections of Hopalong Cassidy memorabilia and jigsaw puzzles, the latter exceeding 5,000 examples.

Rinker and Connie A. Moore, his wife, live at Schtee Fens (Stone Fences), a modern passive solar house in eastern Pennsylvania.

"One great thing about spending time with Harry is that you come away with some great 'Harry' stories. People who have met him trade these stories like bubble gum cards. Each person tries to have the most outrageous story to tell. I brought back some good ones."

Connie Swaim, Editor, Eastern Edition, *AntiqueWeek*

"He was brash, he was iconoclastic, he was funny, and above all, he was thought provoking."

Cheryl York–Cail, *Unravel the Gavel*

ABBREVIATIONS

4to = 8 x 10"
8vo = 5 x 7"
12mo = 3 x 5"
ADS = autograph document signed
adv = advertising or advertisement
ALS = autograph letter signed
AOG = all over gold
AP = album page signed
AQS = autograph quotation signed
C = century
c = circa
cal = caliber
cat = catalog
cov = cover
CS = card signed
d = depth or diameter
dec = decorated or decoration
dj = dust jacket
dwt = penny weight
DS = document signed
ed = edition
emb = embossed
ext = exterior
FDC = first day cover
FH = flat handle
folio = 12 x 16"
ftd = footed
gal = gallon
gf = gold–filled
ground = background
GW = goldware
h = height
HH = hollow handle
hp = hand painted
illus = illustrated, illustration, or illustrator
imp = impressed
int = interior
irid = iridescent

j = jewels
K = karat
l = length
lb = pound
litho = lithograph or lithographed
LS = letter signed
mfg = manufactured, manufacturer, or manufacturing
MIB = mint in box
MIP = mint in package
mkd = marked
MOC = mint on card
opal = opalescent
orig = original
oz = ounce
pat = patent
pc = piece
pcs = pcs
pkg = package or packaging
pp = pages
pr = pair
PS = photograph signed
pt = pint
qt = quart
rect = rectangular
sgd = signed
SP = silver plated
sq = square
SS = sterling silver
ST = stainless
TLS = typed letter signed
unmkd = unmarked
unsgd = unsigned
Vol = Volume
vol = volumes
w = width
wg = white gold
yg = yellow gold
# = number

CONTENTS

INTRODUCTION

Welcome to the second edition of the *Harry L. Rinker The Official Price Guide to Collectibles*. This edition boldly goes where no general collectibles price guide edition has gone before—annual. It is the only starship positioned at the edge of the collectibles universe.

As the 1990s end, there has been a dramatic shift in the antiques and collectibles market. Antique prices are extremely stable. There is no longer a need for an annual antiques price guide. Collectibles are the hot portion of the antiques marketplace in the late 1990s. They are trendy. Collectible pricing is in a constant state of flux. If you fail to keep up with these price shifts annually, you are at a decided disadvantage whether auctioneer, collector, dealer, decorator, or simple enthusiast.

How does the *Harry L. Rinker The Official Price Guide to Collectibles* differ from other general antiques and collectibles price guides? First, it focuses on the heart of today's antiques, collectibles, and desirables market—the period between 1920 and the present. Between 80% and 85% of all the material found at auctions, flea markets, antiques malls, shops, and shows dates from this period. Further, today's collectors are primarily 20th–century collectors.

Each year the percentage of individuals collecting 18th– and 19th–century material compared to the whole grows less and less. While there will always be collectors for this early material, they will need deep pocketbooks. Pre–1920 antiques are expensive. Most post–1920 antiques, collectibles, and desirables are both affordable and readily available.

Second, it is comprehensive. This book is filled with the things with which your parents, you, and your children lived and played. Nothing is missing. You will find furniture, decorative accessories, and giftware along with the traditional character and personality items, ceramics, glass, and toys. It is a complete document of the 20th–century American lifestyle.

Third, because *Harry L. Rinker The Official Price Guide to Collectibles* is now an annual publication, it is capable of responding more quickly to market changes and developments. It contains over one hundred categories not found in its only competitor. Categories are constantly being restructured and reorganized so that they accurately reflect how things are collected in today's antiques and collectibles market.

I will never be accused of complacency because of what this book contains—no same–old, same–old here. Every category is put to the test. If it no longer has collecting validity, it is dropped or merged into a general category. Over a dozen new categories appear for the first time,

another indication of how rapidly the collectibles market changes.

Fourth, over the years I have developed a reputation in the trade for being extremely opinionated and outspoken. I call 'em like I see 'em. I am not a member of the "if you can't say something nice, don't say anything at all" school.

As a reporter, my job is to present the facts and to interpret them. You will not find any artificial price propping in this book. If prices within a category are being manipulated or highly speculative, I spell it out. Whether you agree or not is not the issue. Unlike the good news price guides, the *Harry L. Rinker The Official Price Guide to Collectibles* is designed to make you think.

ANTIQUES, COLLECTIBLES, & DESIRABLES

Harry L. Rinker The Official Price Guide to Collectibles contains antiques, collectibles, and desirables. This being the case, why doesn't this book have a different title? The answer is twofold. When most individuals think of things made in the 20th century, they think of collectibles. People do not like to admit that objects associated with their childhood have become antiques. Further, not everyone, especially manufacturers of contemporary collectors' editions and giftware, separates collectibles and desirables into two different categories. They prefer them lumped together.

What is an antique, a collectible, and a desirable? An antique is anything made before 1945. A collectible is something made between 1945 and the early 1970s. Antiques and collectibles have a stable secondary resale market. A desirable is something made after the mid–1970s. Desirables have a speculative secondary resale market.

As each year passes, the number of people who disagree with my definition of an antique lessens. The year 1945 is an important dividing line. Life in America in 1938 was very different than life in America in 1948. The immediate post–World War II period witnessed the arrival of the suburbs, transfer of wartime technology, e.g., injection molding, into domestic production, television, women in the work force, a global view, and, most importantly, the Baby Boomers.

Today, there are three generations of adult collectors who grew up in the post–1945 time period—those whose childhood (by my definition the period between ages 7 and 14) occurred between 1945 and 1960, between 1960 and the mid–1970s, and between the mid–1970s and the late 1980s. Half of today's population was born after 1960. All they know about John F. Kennedy is what they read in history books. They cannot answer the question: Where were you when you heard JFK was shot?

I used to define a collectible as something made between 1945 and 1962. I have now extended the end date to the early 1970s. The reason is Rinker's Thirty–Year Rule: "For the first thirty years of anything's life, all its value is speculative." It takes thirty years to establish a viable secondary resale market. Some early 1970s objects, especially in vintage clothing, costume jewelry, and movie, music, and television memorabilia, have achieved a stable secondary market. The number is only going to increase.

Will there come a time when I have to move the antique date forward? The answer is yes. I strongly suspect that by 2010, material from the 1950s will definitely be considered antique. However, 2010 is eleven years in the future. In the interim, a collectible remains an object made between 1945 and the early 1970s.

America is a nation of collectors. There are more collectors than non–collectors. However, not everyone collects antiques and collectibles. Many individuals collect contemporary objects ranging from Hallmark ornaments to collectors' edition whiskey bottles. These are the desirables. It is as important to report on the market value of desirables as it is antiques and collectibles.

I do not care what someone collects. All I care about is that they collect. The joy of collecting comes from the act of collecting. I resent those who make value judgments relative to what is and is not worth collecting. I know Avon collectors who are far more caring, willing to share, and knowledgeable of the history and importance of their objects than wealthy collectors whose homes are filled with Colonial period furniture and accessories. There is no room for snobbery in today's collecting community. You will find none in this book.

Manufacturers of desirables market them as collectibles. They are not collectibles as I define the term. Desirables have not stood the test of time. Some undoubtedly will become collectibles and even eventually antiques. However, the vast majority will not. Their final resting place is more likely to be a landfill than a china cabinet or shelf.

Harry L. Rinker The Official Price Guide to Collectibles reports on objects in play, i.e., things that are currently being bought and sold actively in the secondary market. Desirables are as much in play as antiques and collectibles. Hence, they belong in this book.

ORGANIZATION

Categories: Objects are listed alphabetically by category beginning with Abingdon Pottery and ending with Yellow Ware. In the past decade, dozens of collectible subcategories, e.g., Barbie and Star Wars, have evolved as full–blown, independent collecting categories. This book's categories clearly illustrate the manner in which objects are being collected in the late 1990s.

If you have trouble locating an object, check the index. Collectibles are multifaceted, i.e., they can be assigned to more than one category. A 1949 C & O Railroad calendar picturing Chessie and her kittens playing with a toy train would be equally at home in the Advertising Character, Calendar, Cat, Illustrator, Railroad, or Toy Train categories. Such objects have been extensively cross–referenced. Do not give up after checking your first and second classification choices. Most post–1920 objects cross over into six or more collecting categories.

Category Introduction: An object has many values. Financial is only one of them. The pleasure of owning an object and the nostalgic feelings it evokes are others.

It is a proven fact that the more that is known about an object, the more its value increases. It is for this reason that the histories found in this book are more substantial than those found in other general price guides. Every object has multiple stories attached to it—who made it, when it was made, how it was made, how it was used, why it was saved, etc. The histories answer many of these questions.

Occasionally one or two additional pieces of information—collecting tips and/or market trends—are included with the history. You will not find these insider tips in other general price guides. Of all the information found in this book, these may prove to be the most valuable of all.

References: In many cases, you will find the information you seek in this book. What happens when you do not? Where do you turn next? The answer is the references listed in this book.

Each reference listing contains the name of the author, complete title, edition if appropriate, publisher, and publishing date of the book. This information will enable you to purchase the book, locate it at a library, or have the location of a copy researched through interlibrary loan.

Two principal criteria—availability and quality of information, descriptions, and pricing—were used to select the books that are listed. Almost every book listed is still in print. An occasional exception was made for a seminal work in the category.

Unfortunately, the antiques and collectibles field is plagued with price guides that are nothing more than poorly done point–and–shoot priced picture books or whose prices in no way reflect true market values. They are not listed as references in this book even though they are in print.

Accuracy of information is one of the main hallmarks of this book. Nothing is gained by referencing a source that does not adhere to these same high standards. *Harry L. Rinker The Official Price Guide to Collectibles* is designed to earn your trust. Carefully selecting the references is only one example of that commitment.

David J. Maloney, Jr.'s *Maloney's Antiques & Collectibles Resource Directory*, published by Antique Trader Books, is the most important reference book, next to this one of course, in the field. The fourth edition is now available. Buy it. I wear out a copy a year. If you use it properly, so will you.

Periodicals and Newsletters: A list of general antiques and collectibles trade periodicals with full addresses and telephone numbers is part of this book's front matter. The periodicals and newsletters listed within a category relate specifically to that category. They are the first place to turn when looking for further information about that category.

Collectors' Clubs: Collectors' clubs play a vital role in the collecting field. They put collectors in touch with one another. Their newsletters contain information simply not found elsewhere. Their annual conventions allow for an exchange of information and objects. Their membership lists are often a who's who within the category.

Trying to keep track of the correct mailing address for a collectors' club is a full–time job. A club's address changes when its officers change. In some clubs, this occurs annually. The address provided has been checked and double–checked. Hopefully, it is current.

A few individuals and manufacturers have created collectors' clubs as sales fronts. With a few exceptions, e.g., Royal Doulton, these are not listed. The vast majority of clubs listed have an elected board of directors and operate as non–profit organizations.

Reproduction Alert: Reproductions (an exact copy of a period piece), copycats (a stylistic reproduction), fantasy items (in a shape or form that did not exist during the initial period of manufacture or licensing), and fakes (deliberately meant to deceive) are becoming a major problem within the antiques and collectibles field. It would require a book more than double the size of this one to list all the objects that fall within these categories.

Reproduction alerts have been placed throughout the book to serve as a reminder that problems exist more than to document every problem that exists. Do not assume that when no reproduction alert appears, the category is free of the problem. Assume every category has a problem. Make any object you are purchasing prove to you that it is right.

The *Antique & Collectors Reproduction News* (PO Box 12130, Des Moines, IA 50312, annual subscription $32) is a publication devoted to keeping track of current reproductions, copycats, fantasy items, and fakes. Consider subscribing.

Listings: The object descriptions and value listings are the heart and soul of this book. Listings contain the details necessary to specifically identify an object. Unlike some price guides whose listings are confined to one line, this guide sets no limit other than to provide the amount of information needed to do the job right. While this approach results in fewer listings, it raises the accuracy and comprehension level significantly. Better to be safe than sorry.

Each category's listings are only a sampling of the items found in that category. Great care has been taken to select those objects that are commonly found in the market. A few high–end objects are included to show the price range within a category. However, no price guide has value if the list-

ed objects cannot be found or are priced so high few can afford them.

If you do not find the specific object you are seeking, look for comparable objects similar in description to the one that you own. A general price guide's role is to get you into the ballpark and up to the plate. Great care has been taken in each category to provide objects that represent a broad range of objects within a collecting category. Ideally, when looking for a comparable, you should find two or more objects that fit the bill.

The listing format is quick and easy to use. It was selected following a survey of general price guide users. Surprisingly, it allows for more listings per page than an indented system.

Auction Price Boxes: While the values provided in this price guide come from a wide variety of sources, people continually ask, "What does it sell for at auction?" A partial answer to this question is found in the Auction Prices boxes scattered throughout this book.

The assumption is that the highest values are achieved at auction. This is not the case. Dealers purchase a large percentage of objects sold at auction. This is why all auction prices are carefully evaluated and adjusted when necessary before being used in the general listings of this price guide.

The auction boxes are also designed to introduce you to auction houses with which you may not be familiar. There are hundreds of great regional and specialized auction houses conducting catalog sales throughout the United States. I am pleased to help you make their acquaintance.

Index: The index is a road map that shows you the most direct route to the information you are seeking. Take a moment and study it. Like any road map, the more you use it the more proficient you will become.

When researching your object, always start with the broadest general category. If this proves unsuccessful, try specific forms of the object and/or its manufacturer. Remember, because of their multifaceted nature, 20th–century collectibles are at home in multiple categories. Perseverance pays.

Illustrations: Great care has been taken in selecting the illustrations that appear in this book. They are not just fill. Illustrations indicate the type of object or objects commonly found in the category. They come from a variety of sources—auction houses, authors, field photography, and mail and trade catalogs.

This book provides caption information directly beside or beneath the illustration. You do not have to hunt for it in the text listings as you do in some other guides.

The Rinker Enterprise staff works hard to change the illustrations that appear in each edition. This is why you should retain and not discard previous editions of this book. *Harry L. Rinker The Official Price Guide to Collectibles* saved in series becomes a valuable identification and priced picture book to collectibles.

PRICE NOTES

The values in this book are based on an object being in very good to fine condition. This means that the object is complete and shows no visible signs of aging and wear when held at arm's length. If the value is based on a condition other than very good or fine, the precise condition is included in the descriptive listing.

Prices are designed to reflect the prices that sellers at an antiques mall or collectibles show would ask for their merchandise. When an object is collected nationally, it is possible to determine a national price consensus. Most of the objects in this book fall into that category. There are very few 20th–century collectibles whose values are regionally driven. Even racing collectibles, once collected primarily in the South, have gone national.

There are no fixed prices in the antiques and collectibles market. Value is fluid, not absolute. Price is very much of the time and moment. Change the circumstances, change the price. *Harry L. Rinker The Official Price Guide to Collectibles* is a price guide. That is all it is—a guide. It should be used to confirm, not set prices.

Must the original box or packaging accompany an object for it to be considered complete? While some would argue that the answer is yes, especially for post–1980s material, this book is based on the assumption that the box and object are two separate entities. If the price given includes the box, the presence of the box is noted in the description.

Prices represent the best judgment of the Rinker Enterprises staff after carefully reviewing all the available price source information related to the collecting category. It is not required that an object actually be sold during the past year to be listed in this book. If this policy was followed, users would have a distorted view of the market. Sales of common objects are rarely documented. A book based solely on reported prices would be far too oriented toward the middle and high ends of the market.

Instead, each category's listings have been carefully selected to reflect those objects within the category that are currently available in the antiques and collectibles market. Commonly found objects comprise the bulk of the listings. A few hard–to–find and scarce examples are included. These show the category's breadth and price range.

PRICE SOURCES

The values found in this book come from a wide variety of sources—auctions, dealers, direct sale catalogs and lists, field research, the Internet, private individuals, and trade periodicals. All prices are carefully reviewed and adjusted to reflect fair market retail value.

Several criteria are used in deciding what sources to track. All sections of the country must be represented. This is a national, not a regional, price guide. The sources must be reliable. Listings must be specific. Prices must be consistent, not only within the source but when compared to other national price sources. There must be a constant flow of information from the sources. Auctions held by collectors' clubs at their annual conventions are the one exception.

ADVISORS

While not creating a formal Board of Advisors for this second edition, I did request information from experts for a few categories. When the listings in a category are exclusively from this information, I have included their name and address in an "Advisor" heading at the bottom of the category introduction.

However, do not assume for one moment that I lacked or failed to seek advice from hundreds of antiques mall managers, appraisers, auctioneers, authors, dealers, private collectors, show promoters, and others during the preparation of this book. During the twenty–plus years in which I have been actively involved in the antiques and collectibles field, I have established a network of individuals upon whom I can call whenever a question arises. In many cases, my contacts within a collecting category are several individuals strong.

AMERICANA VERSUS INTERNATIONALISM

Americana, defined as things typical of America, is an obsolete term. It should be dropped from our collecting vocabulary.

First, the entire world is rapidly becoming Americanized. American movies, music, and television play as major a role outside as they do inside America. Burger King, Foot Locker, McDonald's, and Toys 'R Us have gone global. Barbie has a far higher worldwide recognition factor than any human personality.

Second, foreign collectors are not content to collect objects produced and licensed in their countries. America is the great mother lode of 20th–century collectibles. When African, European, Far Eastern, or South American collectors want Star Wars memorabilia, they come to America to buy. The role played by foreign buyers in the antiques and collectibles market continues to increase.

Third, thanks to the Internet, most individuals need only turn on their computers to sell and buy collectibles anywhere in the world. The Internet is not limited by international boundaries. It is turning us into world citizens no matter what our personal preferences.

Finally, many "American" goods are manufactured offshore or contain parts that were made abroad. Defining something as being distinctly American is no longer easy. We live in an age when new designs can be copied within days of their appearance. Foreign manufacturers are quick to make products that look like the American form.

Let's delete "Americana" and send it to the trash bin.

BUYER'S GUIDE, NOT A SELLER'S GUIDE

Harry L. Rinker The Official Price Guide to Collectibles is a buyer's guide. Values reflect what someone should expect to pay for an object he wishes to purchase.

This book is not a seller's guide. Do not make a mistake and assume that it is. If you have an object listed in this book and wish to sell it, expect to receive 30% to 40% of the price listed if the object is commonly found and 50% to 60% if the object is harder to find. Do not assume that a collector will pay more. In the 1990s' antiques and collectibles market, collectors expect to pay what a dealer would pay for merchandise when buying privately.

Also, there is no guarantee that you will do better at auction. First, you will pay a commission for selling your goods. Second, dealers buy the vast majority of antiques and collectibles sold at auction. They certainly are not going to resell them for what they paid for them.

The method most likely to result in your selling objects for the values found in this book is to become an antiques dealer. This is not as easy as it sounds. Selling antiques and collectibles is hard work.

There is no one best way to sell antiques and collectibles. All of the above are reasonable choices. Much depends on how much time, effort, and money you wish to expend.

In the final analysis, a good price is one in which the buyer and seller are equally happy. Make as many of your purchases as possible win–win deals. Keep your focus on the object, not the buying and selling process.

COMMENTS INVITED

Every effort has been made to make this price guide useful and accurate. Your comments and suggestions, both positive and negative, are needed to make the next edition even better. Send them to: Rinker Enterprises, Inc., 5093 Vera Cruz Road, Emmaus, PA 18049.

ACKNOWLEDGMENTS

Thanks to everyone who purchased a copy of the first edition of this book. I appreciate your vote of confidence. I pledge my efforts and those of the Rinker Enterprises staff to ensuring that this and future editions of *Harry L. Rinker The Official Price Guide to Collectibles* continue to earn your support and loyalty.

The success of this book relies heavily on cooperation from hundreds of auctioneers, auction houses, collectors, dealers, trade publications' staffs, and others associated with the antiques and collectibles industry. Virtually every request for help was answered. Whenever possible, I have thanked you personally. For those I missed, please accept written thanks until next we talk.

The bridge of the starship *Rinker Enterprises* continues to be manned by the same command crew that piloted the first edition of this book. We explored a number of universes in 1997, one result of which was four new book titles from Rinker Enterprises—*Dinnerware of the 20th Century: The Top 500 Patterns*; *Silverware of the 20th Century: The Top 250 Patterns*; *Stemware of the 20th Century: The Top 200 Patterns*; and *Guide to Games and Puzzles*. We have a number of expeditions as well as visits to some previously explored planets planned for 1998.

This book is a joint effort, as are all Rinker Enterprises' books. Dana Morykan, my Number One, Kathy Williamson, Dena George, and Nancy Butt are the heart and soul of this book. Few employers are able to travel, something I did with increasing frequency this past year, while maintaining the level of confidence that I have in my starship's crew to perform admirably. When you give credit for the quality of the information in this book, be certain to include them as well as me.

With Virginia Reinbold at the financial helm, Rinker Enterprises runs at peak efficiency. Thanks to her, we will be in a position to undertake a few additional journeys in 1998 that are only in the planning stages at the moment. Richard "Cap" Schmeltzle continues to see that our starship is flight worthy.

There will be a third and fourth edition of this book. Thanks to Random House, now part of Bertlesmann AG, and Timothy J. Kochuba, general manager of House of Collectibles, for their commitment to this title and pledge to devote the resources necessary to ensure its long–term growth. As promised in the "Acknowledgments" in the first edition, the gestation period of this second edition was considerably shorter than that of the first.

Kudos to the House of Collectibles team of Randy Ladenheim–Gil (editing), Alex Klapwald (production), Simon Vukelj (marketing), and Patrick Price and Regina Su (public relations). You and those with whom you work are the best support team with which Rinker Enterprises has ever worked. We especially appreciate your willingness to allow us to be part of the decision–making process.

Rinker Enterprises, Inc.   Harry L. Rinker
5093 Vera Cruz Road   Author
Emmaus, PA 18049   June 1998

STATE OF THE MARKET REPORT

In last year's "State of the Market Report" I wrote: "When the history of the 20th–century antiques and collectibles market is written in 2050, the 1990s will be recognized as the decade that produced the profoundest change in the market." Change is the order of the day. The antiques and collectibles marketplace is different today than it was a year ago. All I can say is *viva la différence!* Traditionalists and people with weak hearts are encouraged to direct their efforts elsewhere.

It is a boom time for 20th–century antiques, collectibles, and desirables. While still far from the bull market of the early to mid–1980s when it was impossible to make a mistake, the market continued the slow, steady annual growth that began in the mid–1990s. Each selling season seems better than the last. There is growth everywhere from dealers' profits to the attendance gate at antiques and/or collectibles shows.

The market remains trendy. Growth depends on the ability to respond quickly to changing demands. There still is a limit on how long a collecting category can run hot. Most runs last less than five years, with many petering out in two or three years. Ridiculously high prices, reproductions, and another new collecting trend are key factors in ending runs.

Individuals buying antiques and collectibles for use as decorative accents or conversation pieces, to create a period look, or to recapture part of their childhood (the nostalgia factor) play as vital a role in today's market as do collectors. The general feeling is that collectors buy less than half the antiques and collectibles sold in today's market. This is a positive, not a negative. It is part of the market's natural evolution.

Hurrah for the young collector! They use the objects they buy. The period of putting antiques and collectibles on a shelf and worshipping them is over. Once again, antiques and collectibles are the functional objects they began as and not *objets d'art.* Young collectors understand that they are collecting mass–produced goodies. If something breaks, it can be replaced. They understand that more value is derived from living with antiques and collectibles than buying them as investments.

Buying for investment still dominates the masterpiece (Top 5) and upper echelon (Top 100) objects in most collecting categories. It is a concept that will never completely disappear, especially when so heavily touted by auction houses and the media. As in the past, it plays a far greater role in the antiques than the collectibles sector.

As indicated in the "Introduction," **Harry L. Rinker The Official Price Guide To Collectibles** includes antiques, collectibles, and desirables, a necessity to provide coverage for objects made from 1920 to the present. Collectibles continue to be the hottest of these three key collecting sectors.

This is especially true in antiques malls. Although the shift has probably been gradual, I have never seen as much post–1945 material in antiques malls as I have during this past year. In many malls it comprised more than 75% of the merchandise. Further, discussions with mall management indicate that post–1945 collectibles are the objects that sell best — not good news for antiques.

A significant shift occurred during this past year. Previously, one talked about the post–1945 collectibles market as a single entity. It is now necessary to separate collectibles made between 1945 and the end of the 1950s from those dating from 1960 to the mid–1970s. These have become two very distinct markets. There are major collecting differences between individuals who grew up during the Eisenhower and Johnson presidencies.

There are plenty of signs that the heyday of 1950s collectibles is ending. Price slippage is occurring in many collecting categories. Hopalong Cassidy and Howdy Doody collectibles are tougher and tougher to sell. Look for this trend to continue in the years ahead. Also expect those who deal in 1950s collectibles and grew up with them to deny it. No one likes the idea that they may be old and obsolete. Hey, I grew up in the Fifties.

The Sixties are hot. Stella Show Management Company held its first Sixties Show in March 1998 in New York. Attendance was in the thousands. Scandinavian and Italian glass, designer furniture from Eames, Bertoia, and others, Peter Max licensed items, psychedelic anything, rock 'n roll posters, and polyester vintage clothing are as vital in today's collectibles market as television cowboy hero collectibles and Fiesta ware.

Having trouble accepting this? Here are two things to consider. First, half the people alive today in the United States cannot answer the question: "Where were you when you heard JFK was shot?" They were not born yet. Second, Oldies radio no longer plays tunes from the Fifties. Even Sixties tunes are rare. Oldies radio plays Seventies music. Is Oldies radio a harbinger of things to come for antiques and collectibles? I vote yes.

Serious collector involvement in contemporary collectibles has cooled considerably. Do not be deceived by the current Beanie Baby craze. It is atypical, and a bubble that should burst within the next eighteen to twenty–four months. After being burned by action figure crazes, Mighty Morphin Power Rangers, Tickle Me Elmo, and Barbie, most collectors understand the speculative nature of crazes and the role played in them by market–manipulating manufacturers and greedy toy scalpers. I enjoyed watching the 1997 Holiday Barbie decline from its initial price point of $39.95 in November 1997 to $34.95 in early December to $24.95 a few days before Christmas to $14.95 at Kmart in March 1998.

The collectibles field lost a friend early this year. *Collecting Toys* ceased publication. Kalmbach was unable to find a buyer. *Collecting Toys'* failure is an indication of the growing specialization in the collectibles sector. It tried to serve the entire toy community and failed.

The collectibles market is fragmented and becoming more so. Collectors prefer specialized periodicals, shows, and Internet sites that focus exclusively on their own collecting interests.

Diversity is fine and worth encouraging. So is unity, now more than ever. Federal, state, and local governments are taking a strong interest in the antiques and collectibles trade. Laws are being passed that dramatically affect how business is done. It is time to seek common ground. I encourage everyone to consider joining either the **National Association of Collectors** or the **Antiques and Collectibles Dealers Association**. Information about both is available by calling 1–800–287–7127.

Portions of the antiques and collectibles business, especially publishing and the Internet, have attracted the interest of corporate America. Landmark, a publisher and owner of the Weather Channel, as part of its Landmark Specialty Publications, has created a vertical empire that includes the Antique Trader periodical group, Antique Trader Books, A & C Books (direct book sales), and an Internet site. Its appetite has been whetted, but I doubt satisfied.

Krause Publications, already a major trade publisher in its own right, acquired Books Americana, Chilton Books, including its Wallace–Homestead and Warman imprints, and DBI, greatly strengthening its position in the book sector. Although friendly rivals at the moment, look for the "King of the Hill" competition between Landmark and Krause to intensify.

In a business that prides itself on individualism, is consolidation, especially when driven by corporate America, a positive thing? Authors of specialty book titles are having increased difficulty finding a publisher. There is concern over the potential appearance of cookie cutter editorial in trade periodicals.

For the moment, consolidation is focused primarily in the publishing sector. However, Internet antiques and collectibles sites, antiques malls, and antiques shows offer ripe opportunities.

The number of antiques and collectibles Internet sites continues to grow exponentially. Everyone wants his own site. Chaos reigns. This is an area in dire need of consolidation. Market leaders, such as **www.antiqnet.com** and **www.buycollectibles.com**, are emerging. The next three years should identify the key players. Once that happens, the safest place to be will be under one or more of their umbrellas.

Antique Trove and Brass Armadillo are examples of antiques mall chains. These are mega–malls, consisting of hundreds of dealers and providing a full range of services. Although growing slowly and primarily through the establishment of new malls, acquisition and conversion of existing malls has to be in the planning stages of these chains.

The "antiques mile," a mile or longer stretch of highway containing over a dozen antiques malls or shops, has arrived. Doing business seven days a week, an antiques mile provides buyers with access to a thousand dealers plus. If the antiques mile of Adamstown/Stevens, Pennsylvania, is any indication, this concept works exceptionally well.

Antiques malls have joined the march toward specialization. There are several antiques malls devoted exclusively to toys. The newest arrival is the decorator antiques mall, a mall with objects devoted exclusively to the needs of the interior decorator. Container load–laden, these decorator malls focus on "Look" rather than authenticity. Collectors are advised to stay away rather than be frustrated by their exceptionally high prices.

Several large trade show groups have looked at the antiques show circuit with a view toward acquisition and consolidation. Each walked away, largely because they did not find the profit margins they needed. Existing promoters appear content with what they have created. This is one area in the trade where traditional trade practices will continue well into the first decade of the 21st century.

As recently as a year ago, I said that individuals in the trade over the age of fifty did not have to worry about the computer. They could survive without it. I no longer believe this. Long–term survival depends upon computer literacy.

This past year I conducted an informal show–of–hands survey at my educational seminars and personal appearances asking how many people owned computers and were accessing the Internet. By year's end, the percentge was always above fifty. While this surprised me, I was amazed and pleased that almost everyone was using the Internet. Will the percentage of computer owners reach seventy by the end of 1998? I am betting it will.

Each month the percentage of antiques and collectibles sold on the Internet increases. Some are new sales, most are not. The latter are sales that previously took place at auctions, antiques malls, antiques shows, and through classified advertisements. Dealers are reducing the number of shows they do in favor of selling on the Internet. Many new dealers are selling exclusively on the Internet. Internet auction sites such as **www.ebay.com** are well established. Several live Internet auction sites are in the planning stages.

I am on the Internet. You can visit me at **www.rinker.com.** This is only the beginning. When I write the "State of the Market Report" for the third edition of this book, I expect to report that several Rinker Enterprises data bases, as well as educational seminars, are available via the Internet.

I have seen the future. In fact, I am staring at it. At the moment it is only a 17" screen. In the future, I expect it will engulf an entire wall of my office. I can hardly wait.

AUCTION HOUSES

The following auctioneers and auction companies generously supply Rinker Enterprises, Inc., with copies of their auction lists, press releases, catalogs and illustrations, and prices realized.

Action Toys
PO Box 102
Holtsville, NY 11742
(516) 563-9113
Fax: (516) 563-9182

Sanford Alderfer Auction Co.,
    Inc.
501 Fairgrounds Road
Hatfield, PA 19440
(215) 393-3000
Fax: (215) 368-9055
web: http://www.alderfercompany.com
e mail: auction@alderfercompany.com

American Social History and
    Social Movements
4025 Saline Street
Pittsburgh, PA 15217
(412) 421-5230
Fax: (402) 421-0903

Arthur Auctioneering
RR 2, Box 155
Hughesville, PA 17737
(800) ARTHUR 3

Aston
154 Market Street
Pittston, PA 18640
(717) 654-3090

Auction Team Köln
Breker – Die Spezialisten
Postfach 50 11 19, D-50971
Köln, Germany
Tel: 0221/38 70 49
Fax: 0221/37 48 78
Jane Herz, International Rep
    USA
(941) 925-0385
Fax: (941) 925-0487

Bill Bertoia Auctions
1881 Spring Road
Vineland, NJ 08361
(609) 692-1881
Fax: (609) 692-8697
web: http://bba.ccnj.net
e mail: bba@ccnj.net

Butterfield & Butterfield
220 San Bruno Avenue
San Francisco, CA 94103
(415) 861-7500
Fax: (415) 861-8951

Butterfield & Butterfield
7601 Sunset Boulevard
Los Angeles, CA 90046
(213) 850-7500
Fax: (213) 850-5843

Cards From Grandma's Trunk
The Millards
PO Box 404
Northport, MI 49670
(616) 386-5351

Christie's
502 Park Avenue at 59th Street
New York, NY 10022
(212) 546-1000
Fax: (212) 980-8163
web: http://www.christies.com

Christie's East
219 East 67th Street
New York, NY 10021
(212) 606-0400
Fax: (212)737-6076
web: http://www.christies.com

Christmas Morning
1806 Royal Lane
Dallas, TX 75229-3126
(972) 506-8362
Fax: (972) 506-7821

Cobb's Doll Auctions
1909 Harrison Road
Johnstown, OH 43031-9539
(740) 964-0444
Fax: (740) 927-7701

Collector's Auction Services
RR 2, Box 432 Oakwood Road
Oil City, PA 16301
(814) 677-6070
Fax: (814) 677-6166

Collector's Sales and Service
PO Box 4037
Middletown, RI 02842
(401) 849-5012
Fax: (401) 846-6156
web: www.antiquechina.com
e mail: collectors@antiquechina.com

Copake Auction
Box H, 226 Route 7A
Copake, NY 12516
(518) 329-1142
Fax: (518) 329-3369

Dawson's
128 American Road
Morris Plains, NJ 07950
(973) 984-6900
Fax: (973) 984-6956
web: http://idt.net/~dawson1
e mail: dawson1@idt.net

Dixie Sporting Collectibles
1206 Rama Road
Charlotte, NC 28211
(704) 364-2900
Fax: (704) 364-2322
web: http://www.sportauction.com
e mail: gun1898@aol.com

William Doyle Galleries
175 East 87th Street
New York, NY 10128
(212) 427-2730
Fax: (212) 369-0892
web: www.doylegalleries.com

Dunbars Gallery
76 Haven Street
Milford, MA 01757
(508) 634-8697
Fax: (508) 634-8698
web: http://www.dunnings.com
e mail: dunbar2bid@aol.com

Dunning's
755 Church Road
Elgin, IL 60123
(847) 741-3483
Fax: (847) 741-3589
web: http://www.dunnings.com

Early Auction Co.
Roger and Steve Early
123 Main Street
Milford, OH 45150
(513) 831-4833
Fax: (513) 831-1441

Etude Tajan
37, Rue des Mathurins 75008
Paris, France
Tel: 1-53-30-30-30
Fax: 1-53-30-30-31
web: http://www.tajan.com
e mail: tajan@worldnet.fr

Ken Farmer Auctions & Estates,
    LLC
105A Harrison Street
Radford, VA 24141
(540) 639-0939
Fax: (540) 639-1759
web: http://kenfarmer.com

Fink's Off the Wall Auction
108 East 7th Street
Lansdale, PA 19446
(215) 855-9732
Fax: (215) 855-6325
web: http://www/finksauctions.com
e mail: lansbeer@finksauction.com

Flomaton Antique Auction
277 Old Highway 31
Flomaton, AL 36441

Frank's Antiques
Box 516
Hilliard, FL 32046
(904) 845-2870
Fax: (904) 845-4000

Frasher's Doll Auctions, Inc.
Route 1, Box 142
Oak Grove, MO 64075
(816) 625-3786
Fax: (816) 625-6079

Freeman/Fine Arts Co. of
  Philadelphia, Inc.
1808 Chestnut Street
Philadelphia, PA 19103
(215) 563-9275
Fax: (215) 563-8236

Garth's Auction, Inc.
2690 Stratford Road
PO Box 369
Delaware, OH 43015
(614) 362-4771
Fax: (614) 363-0164

Glass Works Auctions
PO Box 180
East Greenville, PA 18041
(215) 679-5849
Fax: (215) 679-3068
web: http://www.glswrk–auction.com

Greenberg Auctions
7566 Main Street
Sykesville, MD 21784
(401) 795-7447

Marc Grobman
94 Paterson Road
Fanwood, NJ 07023-1056
(908) 322-4176
web: mgrobman@worldnet.att.net

Gypsyfoot Enterprises, Inc.
PO Box 5833
Helena, MT 59604
(406) 449-8076
Fax: (406) 443-8514
e mail: gypsyfoot@aol.com

Hakes' Americana and
  Collectibles
PO Box 1444
York, PA 17405-1444
(717) 848-1333
Fax: (717) 852-0344

Gene Harris Antique Auction
  Center, Inc.
203 South 18th Avenue
PO Box 476
Marshalltown, IA 50158
(515) 752-0600
Fax: (515) 753-0226
e mail: ghaac@marshallnet.com

Norman C. Heckler & Co.
Bradford Corner Road
Woodstock Valley, CT 06282
(860) 974-1634
Fax: (860) 974-2003

The Holidays Auction
4027 Brooks Hill Road
Brooks, KY 40109
(502) 955-9238
Fax: (502) 957-5027

Horst Auction Center
50 Durlach Road
Ephrata, PA 17522
(717) 859-1331

Michael Ivankovich Antiques,
  Inc.
PO Box 2458
Doylestown, PA 18901
(215) 345-6094
Fax: (215) 345-6692
e mail: wnutting@comcat.com

Jackson Auction Co.
2229 Lincoln Street
Cedar Falls, IA 50613
(319) 277-2256
Fax: (319) 277-1252
web: http://jacksonsauction.com

James D. Julia, Inc.
Route 201, Skowhegan Road
PO Box 830
Fairfield, ME 04937
(207) 453-7125
Fax: (207) 453-2502

Gary Kirsner Auctions
PO Box 8807
Coral Springs, FL 33075
(954) 344-9856
Fax: (954) 344-4421

Charles E. Kirtley
PO Box 2273
Elizabeth City, NC 27906
(919) 335-1262
Fax: (919) 335-4441
e mail: ckirtley@erols.com

Henry Kurtz, Ltd.
163 Amsterdam Avenue, Ste 136
New York, NY 10023
(212) 642-5904
Fax: (212) 874-6018

Lang's Sporting Collectables, Inc.
31R Turtle Cove
Raymond, ME 04071
(207) 655-4265

Los Angeles Modern Auctions
PO Box 462006
Los Angeles, CA 90046
(213) 845-9456
Fax: (213) 845-9601
web: http://www.lamodern.com
e mail: peter@lamodern.com

Howard Lowery
3812 W Magnolia Boulevard
Burbank, CA 91505
(818) 972-9080
Fax: (818) 972-3910

Mad Mike
Michael Lerner
32862 Springside Lane
Solon, OH 44139
(216) 349-3776

Majolica Auctions
Michael G. Strawser
200 North Main
PO Box 332
Wolcottville, IN 46795
(219) 854-2859
Fax: (219) 854-3979

Manion's International Auction
  House, Inc.
PO Box 12214
Kansas City, KS 66112
(913) 299-6692
Fax: (913) 299-6792
web: www.manions.com
e mail: collecting@manions.com

Ted Maurer, Auctioneer
1003 Brookwood Drive
Pottstown, PA 19464
(610) 323-1573 or (610) 367-
  5024
web: www.maurerail.com

Wm Morford
RD 2
Cazenovia, NY 13035
(315) 662-7625
Fax: (315) 662-3570
e mail: morf2bid@aol.com

Muddy River Trading Co.
Gary Metz
263 Key Lakewood Drive
Moneta, VA 24121
(540) 721-2091
Fax: (540) 721-1782

New England Absentee Auctions
16 Sixth Street
Stamford, CT 06905
(203) 975-9055
Fax: (203) 323-6407
e mail: neaauction@aol.com

New England Auction Gallery
Debby and Marty Krim
PO Box 2273
West Peabody, MA 01960
(978) 535-3140
Fax: (978) 535-7522
web: http://www.oldtoys.com

Norton Auctioneers of Michigan,
  Inc.
Pearl At Monroe
Coldwater, MI 49036-1967
(517) 279-9063
Fax: (517) 279-9191
e mail: nortonsold@juno.com

Nostalgia Publications, Inc.
21 South Lake Drive
Hackensack, NJ 07601
(201) 488-4536

Richard Opfer Auctioneers, Inc.
1919 Greenspring Drive
Timonium, MD 21093
(410) 252-5035
Fax: (410) 252-5863

Ron Oser Enterprises
PO Box 101
Huntingdon Valley, PA 19006
(215) 947-6575
Fax: (215) 938-7348
web: members.aol.com/ronoserent

Pacific Book Auction Galleries
133 Kearney Street, 4th Floor
San Francisco, CA 94108
(415) 989-2665
Fax: (415) 989-1664
web: www.nbn.com/pba

Past Tyme Pleasures
101 First Street
Suite 404
Los Altos, CA 94022
(510) 484-4488
Fax: (510) 484-2551

Pettigrew Auction Co.
1645 South Tejon Street
Colorado Springs, CO 80906
(719) 633-7963
Fax: (719) 633-5035

Phillips Ltd.
406 East 79th Street
New York, NY 10021
(800) 825-2781
Fax: (212) 570-2207
web: http://www.phillips–auctions.com

Postcards International
PO Box 85398
Hamden, CT 06518
(203) 248-6621
Fax: (203) 248-6628
web: csmonline.com/postcardsint/
e mail: postcrdint@aol.com

Poster Mail Auction Co.
PO Box 133
Waterford, VA 20197
(703) 684-3656
Fax: (540) 882-4765

Provenance
PO Box 3487
Wallington, NJ 07057
(973) 779-8785
Fax: (212) 741-8756

David Rago Auctions, Inc.
333 North Main Street
Lambertville, NJ 08530
(609) 397-9374
Fax: (609) 397-9377

Lloyd Ralston Gallery
109 Glover Avenue
Norwalk, CT 06850
(203) 845-0033
Fax: (203) 845-0366

Red Baron's
6450 Roswell Road
Atlanta, GA 30328
(404) 252-3770
Fax: (404) 257-0268
e mail: rbarons@onramp.net

Remmey Galleries
30 Maple Street
Summit, NJ 07901
(908) 273-5055
Fax: (908) 273-0171
e mail: remmeyauctiongalleries@world
    net.att.net

L. H. Selman Ltd.
761 Chestnut Street
Santa Cruz, CA 95060
(800) 538-0766
Fax: (408) 427-0111
web: http://paperweight.com
e mail: selman@paperweight.com

Skinner, Inc.
Bolton Gallery
357 Main Street
Bolton, MA 01740
(978) 779-6241
Fax: (978) 350-5429

Slater's Americana
1535 North Tacoma Avenue
Suite 24
Indianapolis, IN 46220
(317) 257-0863
Fax: (317) 254-9167

Smith & Jones, Inc.
12 Clark Lane
Sudbury, MA 01776
(978) 443-5517
Fax: (978) 443-2796

R. M. Smythe & Co., Inc.
26 Broadway, Suite 271
New York, NY 10004-1701
(800) 622-1880
Fax: (212) 908-4047

Sotheby's
1334 York Avenue at 72nd Street
New York, NY 10021
(212) 606-7000
web: http://www.sothebys.com

Steffen's Historical Militaria
PO Box 280
Newport, KY 41072
(606) 431-4499

Susanin's
Gallery 228 Merchandise Mart
Chicago, IL 60654
(312) 832-9800
Fax: (312) 832-9311
web: http://www.theauction.com

Swann Galleries, Inc.
104 East 25th Street
New York, NY 10010
(212) 254-4710
Fax: (212) 979-1017

Theriault's
PO Box 151
Annapolis, MD 21404
Fax: (410) 224-2515

Tool Shop Auctions
Tony Murland
78 High Street
Needham Market
Suffolk, 1P6 8AW England
Tel: 01449 722992
Fax: 01449 722683
web: http://www/toolshop.demon.co.uk
e mail: tony@toolshop.demon.co.uk

Toy Scouts, Inc.
137 Casterton Avenue
Akron, OH 44303
(330) 836-0668
Fax: (330) 869-8668

Tradewinds Auctions
PO Box 249
24 Magnolia Avenue
Manchester–by–the–Sea, MA
    01944
(978) 768-3327
Fax: (978) 526-3088

James A. Vanek
7031 Northeast Irving Street
Portland, OR 97213
(503) 257-8009

Victorian Images
PO Box 284
Marlton, NJ 08053
(609) 953-7711
Fax: (609) 953-7768

Tom Witte's Antiques
PO Box 399
Front Street West
Mattawan, MI 49071
(616) 668-4161
Fax: 668-5363

York Town Auction, Inc.
1625 Haviland Road
York, PA 17404
(717) 751-0211
Fax: (717) 767-7729

If you are an auctioneer or auction company and would like your name and address to appear on this list in subsequent editions, you can achieve this by sending copies of your auction lists, press releases, catalogs and illustrations, and prices realized to: **Rinker Enterprises, Inc., 5093 Vera Cruz Road, Emmaus, PA 18049.**

ANTIQUES & COLLECTIBLES PERIODICALS

Rinker Enterprises receives the following general and regional periodicals. Periodicals covering a specific collecting category are listed in the introductory material for that category.

NATIONAL MAGAZINES

*Antique Trader's Collector
    Magazine & Price Guide*
PO Box 1050
Dubuque, IA 52004-1050
(800) 334-7165
web: traderpubs@aol.com

Antiques & Collecting Magazine
1006 South Michigan Avenue
Chicago, IL 60605
(800) 762-7576
Fax: (312) 939-0053
e mail: lightnerpb@aol.com

Collectors' Eye
Woodside Avenue, Suite 300
Northport, NY 11768
(516) 261-4100
Fax: (516) 261-9684

Collectors' Showcase
7134 South Yale Avenue
Suite 720
Tulsa, OK 74136
(888) 622-3446

*Country Accents Collectibles,
    Flea Market Finds*
GCR Publishing Group, Inc.
1700 Broadway
New York, NY 10019
(800) 955-3870

NATIONAL NEWSPAPERS

Antiques and the Arts Weekly
The Bee Publishing Co.
PO Box 5503
Newtown, CT 06470-5503
(203) 426-8036
Fax: (203) 426-1394
web: http://www.thebee.com
e mail: editor@thebee.com

The Antique Trader Weekly
PO Box 1050
Dubuque, IA 52004-1050
(800) 334-7165
Fax: (800) 531-0880
web: http://www.csmonline.com
e mail: traderpubs@aol.com

*Antique Week (Central and
    Eastern Editions)*
27 North Jefferson Street
PO Box 90
Knightstown, IN 46148
(800) 876-5133
Fax: (800) 695-8153
web: http://www.antiqueweek.com
e mail: antiquewk@aol.com

Collectors News
506 Second Street
PO Box 156
Grundy Center, IA 50638
(800) 352-8039
Fax: (319) 824-3414
web: http://collectors-news.com
e mail: collectors@collectors-news.com

Maine Antique Digest
911 Main Street
PO Box 1429
Waldoboro, ME 04572
(207) 832-4888
Fax: (207) 832-7341
web:
    http://www.maineantiquedigest.com
e mail: mad@maine.com

Warman's Today's Collector
Krause Publications
700 East State Street
Iola, WI 54990
(800) 258-0929
Fax: (715) 445-4087
web: www.krause.com
e mail: todays collector@krause.com

REGIONAL NEWSPAPERS

New England

MassBay Antiques
2 Washington Street
PO Box 192
Ipswich, MA 01938
(508) 777-7070

New England Antiques Journal
4 Church Street
PO Box 120
Ware, MA 01082
(800) 432-3505
Fax: (413) 967-6009
e mail: visit@antiquesjournal.com

New England Collectibles
PO Box 546
Farmington, NH 03835-0546
(603) 755-4568
Fax: (603) 755-3990

*New Hampshire Antiques
    Monthly*
PO Box 546
Farmington, NH 03835-0546
(603) 755-4568
Fax: (603) 755-3990

Unravel the Gavel
9 Hurricane Road, #1
Belmont, NH 03220
(603) 524-4281
Fax: (603) 528-3565
web: http://www.the-forum.com/gavel
e mail: gavel96@aol.com

Middle Atlantic States

American Antique Collector
PO Box 454
Murrysville, PA 15668
(412) 733-3968
Fax: (412) 733-3968

New York City's Antique News
PO Box 2054
New York, NY 10159-2054
(212) 725-0344
Fax: (212) 532-7294

*Northeast Journal of Antiques &
    Art*
364 Warren Street
Hudson, NY 12534
(800) 836-4069
Fax: (518) 828-9437

Renninger's Antique Guide
PO Box 495
Lafayette Hill, PA 19444
(610) 828-4614
Fax: (610) 834-1599

Treasure Chest
PO Box 245
North Scituate, RI 02857-0245
(800) 557-9662
Fax: (401) 647-0051

South

The Antique Finder Magazine
PO Box 16433
Panama City, FL 32406-6433
(850) 236-0543
Fax: (850) 914-9007

Antique Gazette
6949 Charlotte Pike
Suite 106
Nashville, TN 37209
(800) 660-6143
Fax: (800) 660-6143

The Antique Shoppe
PO Box 2175
Keystone Heights, FL 32656
(352) 475-1679

*The Antique Shoppe of the
Carolinas*
PO Box 640
Lancaster, SC 29721
(800) 210-7253
Fax: (803) 283-8969

Carolina Antique News
PO Box 241114
Charlotte, NC 28224
(704) 553-2865

Cotton & Quail Antique Trail
205 East Washington Street
PO Box 326
Monticello, FL 32345
(800) 757-7755
Fax: (850) 997-3090

Second Hand Dealer News
18609 Shady Hills Road
Spring Hill, FL 34610
(813) 856-9477

*The MidAtlantic Antiques
Magazine*
Henderson Newspapers, Inc.
304 South Chestnut Street
PO Box 908
Henderson, NC 27536
(919) 492-4001
Fax: (919) 430-0125

*The Old News Is Good News
Antiques Gazette*
41429 West I-55 Service Road
PO Box 305
Hammond, LA 70404
(504) 429-0575
Fax: (504) 429-0576
e mail: gazette@i–55.com

Southern Antiques
PO Drawer 1107
Decatur, GA 30031
(888) 800-4997
Fax: (404) 286-9727

20th–Century Folk Art News
5967 Blackberry Lane
Buford, GA 30518
(770) 932-1000
Fax: (770) 932-0506

Midwest

The American Antiquities Journal
126 East High Street
Springfield, OH 45502
(800) 557-6281
Fax: (937) 322-0294

*The Antique Collector and
Auction Guide*
Weekly Section of *Farm and
Dairy*
PO Box 38
Salem, OH 44460
(330) 337-3419
Fax: (330) 337-9550

Antique Review
PO Box 538
Worthington, OH 43085
(614) 885-9757
Fax: (614) 885-9762

Auction Action News
1404¹/₂ East Green Bay Street
Shawano, WI 54166
(715) 524-3076
Fax: (800) 580-4568

Auction World
101 12th Street South
Box 227
Benson, MN 56215
(800) 750-0166
Fax: (320) 843-3246

The Collector
204 South Walnut Street
PO Box 148
Heyworth, IL 61745-0148
(309) 473-2466
Fax: (309) 473-3610

Collectors Journal
1800 West D Street
PO Box 601
Vinton, IA 52349-0601
(319) 472-4763
Fax: (816) 474-1427
web: http://discoverypub.com/kc

Discover Mid–America
400 Grand, Suite B
Kansas City, MO 64106
(800) 899-9730

Great Lakes Trader
132 South Putnam Street
Williamston, MI 48895
(800) 785-6367
Fax: (517) 655-5380
web: gltrader@aol.com

The Old Times
PO Box 340
Maple Lake, MN 55358
(800) 539-1810
Fax: (320) 963-6499
e mail: oldtimes@lkdllink.net

Three Trails Emporium
PO Box 459
Independence, MO 64051
(816) 254-8600
web: examiner.net

Yesteryear
PO Box 2
Princeton, WI 54968
(920) 787-4808
Fax: (920) 787-7381

Southwest

The Antique Traveler
PO Box 656
109 East Broad Street
Mineola, TX 75773
(903) 569-2487
Fax: (903) 569-9080

Arizona Antique News
PO Box 26536
Phoenix, AZ 85068
(602) 943-9137

Auction Weekly
PO Box 61104
Phoenix, AZ 85082
(602) 994-4512
Fax: (800) 525-1407

West Coast

Antique & Collectables
500 Fensler, Suite 205
PO Box 12589
El Cajon, CA 92022
(619) 593-2930
Fax: (619) 447-7187

Antique Journal
1684 Decoto Road, Ste 166
Union City, CA 94587
(800) 791-8592
Fax: (510) 523-5262

Antiques Today
Kruse Publishing
977 Lehigh Circle
Carson City, NV 89705
(800) 267-4602
Fax: (702) 267-4600

Old Stuff
VBM Printers, Inc.
336 North Davis
PO Box 1084
McMinnville, OR 97128
(503) 434-5386
Fax: (503) 472-2601
e mail: bnm@pnn.com

The Oregon Vintage Times
856 Lincoln #2
Eugene, OR 97401
(541) 484-0049
e mail: venus@efn.org
web: www.efn.org/~venus/antique/
antique.html

West Coast Peddler
PO Box 5134
Whittier, CA 90607
(562) 698-1718
Fax: (562) 698-1500

INTERNATIONAL NEWSPAPERS

Australia

*Carter's Homes, Antiques &
Collectables*
Carter's Promotions Pty. Ltd.
Locked Bag 3
Terrey Hills, NSW 2084
Australia
(02) 9450 0011
Fax: (02) 945-2532
e mail: carters@magna.com.au

Canada

Antique Showcase
Trojan Publishing Corp
103 Lakeshore Road, Suite 202
St. Catherine, Ontario
Canada L2N 2T6
(905) 646-0995
web: http://www.vaxxine.com/trojan/
e mail: bret@trojan.com

Antiques and Collectibles Trader
PO Box 38095
550 Eglinton Avenue West
Toronto, Ontario
Canada M5N 3A8
(416) 410-7620

The Upper Canadian
PO Box 653
Smiths Falls, Ontario
Canada K7A 4T6
(613) 283-1168
Fax: (613) 283-1345
e mail: uppercanadian@recorder.ca

England

Antique Trade Gazette
17 Whitcomb Street
London WC2H 7PL
England

ABINGDON POTTERY

The Abingdon Sanitary Manufacturing Company began manufacturing bathroom fixtures in 1908 in Abingdon, Illinois. The company's art pottery line was introduced in 1938 and eventually consisted of over 1,000 shapes and forms decorated in nearly 150 different colors. In 1945 the company changed its name to Abingdon Potteries, Inc. The art pottery line remained in production until 1950, when fire destroyed the art pottery kiln. After the fire, the company focused once again on plumbing fixtures. Eventually, Abingdon Potteries became Briggs Manufacturing Company, a firm noted for its sanitary fixtures.

Reference: Joe Paradis, *Abingdon Pottery Artware: 1934–1950,* Schiffer Publishing, 1997.

Collectors' Club: Abingdon Pottery Club, 210 Knox Hwy 5, Abingdon, IL 61410.

Ashtray, figural elephant on top, #509, 5½" d	$145.00
Bookends, pr, fern leaf, white, #427, 5½" h	45.00
Bowl, pineapple, #700D, 14¾" l	85.00
Bowl, wreath, #413, 12" d	70.00
Box, blue base, white lid, rose dec, #585D, 4½" d	80.00
Cache Pot, starflower, cameo pink, #559D, 5½" h	30.00
Candleholders, pr, rope dec, #323, 3¾" d	35.00
Candleholders, pr, wreath, #414, 4" d	60.00
Cornucopia, double, #581, 8¼" h	35.00
Flower Boat, fern leaf, #426,13 x 4"	95.00
Jar, pelican, #609D, 6½" h	170.00
Lamp Base, turquoise, swirl shaft, 20½" h	95.00
Pitcher, fern leaf, #435, 8" w	120.00
Planter, Dutch shoe, #655D, 5" l	40.00
Planter, ram, #671, 4" h	35.00
Plate, wild rose, #344, 10 x 12" l	120.00
Range Set, daisy, 3 pcs, #690D	70.00
Salad Bowl, rope dec, #313, 10½" d	70.00
Vase, green, ring handles, #318, 10¼" h	90.00
Vase, star, #463, 7½" h	20.00
Vase, trumpet shape, #597, 9" h	40.00
Wall Pocket, green and yellow ivy dec, #590D, 7" h	60.00
Wall Pocket, triple fern leaf, #435, 8" w	120.00
Wall Vase, match box, cherries dec, #675D, 5½" h	85.00
Window Box, green, white floral dec, #570, 10" l	10.00

Vase, emb ship, green, #494, 1940–46, 10" h, $25.00.

ACTION FIGURES

Early action figures depicted popular television western heroes from the 1950s and were produced by Hartland. Louis Marx also included action figures in several of its playsets from the late 1950s.

Hassenfield Bros. triggered the modern action figure craze with its introduction of G.I. Joe in 1964. The following year Gilbert produced James Bond 007, The Man From U.N.C.L.E., and Honey West figures. Bonanza and Captain Action figures arrived in 1966.

In 1972 Mego introduced the first six superheroes in a series of thirty–four. Mego also established the link between action figures and the movies with its issue of Planet of the Apes and Star Trek: The Motion Picture figures.

The success of the Star Wars figures set introduced by Kenner in 1977 prompted other toy companies to follow suit, resulting in a flooded market. However, unlike many collecting categories, scarcity does not necessarily equate to high value.

References: John Bonavita, *Mego Action Figure Toys With Values,* Schiffer Publishing, 1996; Wallace M. Chrouch, *Mego Toys: An Illustrated Value Guide,* Collector Books, 1995; Paris and Susan Manos, *Collectible Action Figures: Identification & Value Guide, Second Edition,* Collector Books, 1996; Bill Sikora and T. N. Tumbusch, *Tomart's Encyclopedia & Price Guide to Action Figures, Book 1* (1996), *Book 2* (1996), *Book 3* (1997), Tomart Publications; Stuart W. Wells III and Jim Main, *The Official Price Guide to Action Figures,* House of Collectibles, 1997.

Periodicals: *Action Figure News & Review,* 556 Monroe Turnpike, Monroe, CT 06468; *Tomart's Action Figure Digest,* Tomart Publications, 3300 Encrete Ln, Dayton, OH 45439.

Collectors' Club: Classic Action Figure Collector's Club, PO Box 2095, Halesite, NY 11743.

Addams Family, Playmates, Gomez, 1992, MIP	$15.00
Addams Family, Playmates, Lurch, 1992, MIP	15.00
Addams Family, Playmates, Morticia, 1992, MIP	35.00
Addams Family, Playmates, Pugsley, 1992, MIP	20.00
Addams Family, Playmates, Uncle Fester, 1992, MIP	15.00
Advanced Dungeons and Dragons, LJN, Ogre King, 6" h, MOC	60.00
Advanced Dungeons and Dragons, LJN, Strongheart, first series, 4" h, MOC	45.00
Advanced Dungeons and Dragons, LJN, Warduke, 4" h, MOC	45.00
Alien, Kenner, Alien Queen, MOC	25.00
Alien, Kenner, Drake, MOC	15.00
Alien, Kenner, Lt Ripley, MOC	20.00
Alien, Kenner, Panther Alien, MOC	15.00
Allien, Kenner, Queen Face Hugger, MOC	15.00
Batman, Animated Series, Kenner, Infrared Batman, loose	8.00
Batman, Animated Series, Kenner, Joker, MOC	30.00
Batman, Animated Series, Kenner, Mr Freeze, MOC	25.00
Batman Returns, Kenner, Catwoman, loose	15.00
Batman Returns, Night Climber Batman, MOC	30.00
Batman, The Dark Knight, Bruce Wayne, MOC	20.00
Batman, The Dark Knight, Knock–Out Joker, MOC	100.00
Battlestar Galactica, Mattel, Boray, loose	40.00
Battlestar Galactica, Mattel, Cylon Centurian, MOC	45.00
Battlestar Galactica, Mattel, Imperious Leader, loose	15.00
Battlestar Galactica, Mattel, Lucifer, MOC	115.00

Planet of the Apes, Mego, Peter Burke, 8" h, $195.00. Photo courtesy Action Toys.

Best of the West, Marx, Princess Wildflower, c1975, 12" h, MOC **125.00**

Best of the West, Marx, Sam Cobra, c1974, 12" h, MOC.... **125.00**

Best of the West, Marx, Sam Cobra, Quick Draw Action, c1975, 12" h, MOC.............................. **195.00**

Big Jim, Mattel, Torpedo Fist, 1972, MOC **85.00**

Bionic Six, LJN, Dr Scarab, 1986, MIP **10.00**

Bionic Six, LJN, Glove, 1986, MIP..................... **15.00**

Bionic Six, LJN, Madam–O, 1986, MIP **20.00**

Blackstar, Galoob, Vizir–Ice Castle Wizard, MIP **20.00**

Butch Cassidy & The Sundance Kid, Kenner, Butch, MOC **45.00**

Butch Cassidy & The Sundance Kid, Kenner, Sundance, MOC **45.00**

Chuck Norris Karate Kommandos, Kenner, Kimo, 1987, MIP **30.00**

Chuck Norris Karate Kommandos, Kenner, Chuck Norris, Kung–Fu,1987, MIP.............................. **25.00**

Chuck Norris Karate Kommandos, Kenner, Ninja Warrior, 1987, MIP **30.00**

Chuck Norris Karate Kommandos, Kenner, Super Ninja, 1987, MIP... **35.00**

Comic Action Heroes, Mego, Green Goblin, loose **25.00**

Comic Action Heroes, Mego, Green Goblin, MOC......... **75.00**

Comic Action Heroes, Mego, Penguin, MOC **70.00**

C.O.P.S., Hasbro, A.P.E.S., MIP **30.00**

C.O.P.S., Hasbro, Highway, 1st series, MIP.............. **30.00**

C.O.P.S., Hasbro, Koo Koo, 2nd series, MIP **35.00**

C.O.P.S., Hasbro, Nightstick, 2nd series, MIP **25.00**

C.O.P.S., Hasbro, Rock Crusher, 1st series, MIP **30.00**

Defenders of the Earth, Galoob, Flash Gordon, MOC **30.00**

Defenders of the Earth, Galoob, Mandrake the Magician, MOC **30.00**

Dukes of Hazzard, Mego, Bo, 3³/₄" h, MOC **25.00**

Dukes of Hazzard, Mego, Boss Hogg, 3³/₄" h, MOC **30.00**

Dukes of Hazzard, Mego, Cletus, 3³/₄" h, MOC **35.00**

Ghostbusters, Kenner, Slimer, with 3 pcs of food, series 1, 1988 .... **15.00**

Godaikins, Bandai, Bioman, #30021, MIB **110.00**

Indiana Jones, Kenner, Belloq, ceremonial robe, loose **30.00**

Indiana Jones, Kenner, German Mechanic, MOC **45.00**

Indiana Jones, Kenner, Marion Ravenwood, MOC. **195.00**

Indiana Jones, Kenner, Sallah, loose **30.00**

Indiana Jones, Temple of Doom, LJN, Mola Ram, loose ... **50.00**

Inhumanoids, Hasbro, Herc Armstrong, 1986, MOC. **30.00**

Inhumanoids, Hasbro, Redsun, 1986, MIB **30.00**

Lord of the Rings, Knickerbocker, Gollum, loose. **35.00**

Marvel Secret Wars, Mattel, Baron Zemo, MOC **40.00**

Marvel Secret Wars, Mattel, Constrictor, MOC **70.00**

Marvel Secret Wars, Mattel, Falcon, MOC **50.00**

Marvel Secret Wars, Mattel, Iceman, MOC. **75.00**

Marvel Secret Wars, Mattel, Kang, MOC **15.00**

Marvel Secret Wars, Mattel, Spiderman, black, MOC **75.00**

M.A.S.K., Kenner, Gator, 12" h, MIB. **30.00**

M.A.S.K., Kenner, Outlaw, 12" h, MIB **65.00**

M.A.S.K., Kenner, Stinger, 12" h, MIB................. **30.00**

Masters of the Universe, Mattel, Dragstor, MOC **22.00**

Masters of the Universe, Mattel, Fisto, MOC. **25.00**

Masters of the Universe, Mattel, King Randor, MOC **40.00**

Masters of the Universe, Mattel, Man–E–Faces, loose **15.00**

Masters of the Universe, Mattel, Screech, MOC **25.00**

Masters of the Universe, Mattel, Trapjaw, loose. **20.00**

Masters of the Universe, Mattel, Zodiac, loose **25.00**

Micronauts, Mego, Galactic Warrior, loose............... **35.00**

Mighty Morphin Power Rangers, Bandai, Pink Ranger, 1993. .... **10.00**

Monsters, Mego, Dracula, 8" h, MOC **295.00**

Monsters, Mego, Frankenstein, 8" h, MOC **125.00**

Nightmare Before Christmas, Hasbro, Behemoth, MOC **50.00**

Nubia, Mego, 12" h, MIB **90.00**

Pee Wee Herman, Matchbox, with scooter and helmet, 6" h, MOC **40.00**

Planet of the Apes, Mego, Galen, 8" h, MOC **200.00**

Pocket Superheroes, Mego, Superman, MOC **65.00**

Pocket Superheroes, Mego, Spiderman, MOC. **45.00**

Predator, Kenner, Night Storm, MOC **15.00**

Predator, Kenner, Scavage, MOC **25.00**

Princess of Power, Mattel, Bow, MOC **35.00**

Princess of Power, Mattel, Entrapta, MOC. **50.00**

Princess of Power, Mattel, She–Ra, MOC **35.00**

Queen Hippolyte, Mego, 12" h, MIB **95.00**

Rambo, Coleco, Rambo, 1985, MIP................... **15.00**

Robin Hood, Mego, Little John, MIB **125.00**

Robin Hood, Mego, Friar Tuck, MIB **75.00**

Robocop, Kenner, Anne Lewis, MOC **25.00**

Robocop, Kenner, Scorcher, MOC **20.00**

Sectaurs, Coleco, Mantor and Raplor, 1984, MIP **30.00**

Sectaurs, Coleco, Zak and Bitaur, 1984, MIP **25.00**

Silverhawks, Kenner, Bluegrass, with sideman, 1st series, 1986–87, MOC **20.00**

Silverhawks, Kenner, Moon Stryker, with Tail Spin, 2nd series, MOC **20.00**

Silverhawks, Kenner, Stargazer, MOC. **10.00**

Silverhawks, Kenner, Steel Heart, with Rayzor, 1st series, 1986–87, MOC **35.00**

Simpsons, The, Mattel, Bart, 1990, 5" h **5.00**

Six Million Dollar Man, Kenner, Bionic Man with Bionic Grip, MIB **95.00**

Sky Commanders, Kenner, Rollerball with Gen Summit, 1987, MIP....................................... **20.00**

Space 1999, Mattel, Commander Koenig, 10" h, MOC **60.00**

Space 1999, Mattel, Professor Bergman, 10" h, MOC **75.00**

Teenage Mutant Ninja Turtle, Playmates, Michaelangelo, with nunchukus, MOC, $30.00.

Spawn, Todd McFarlane Toys, Angela, 2nd series, MOC 25.00
Spawn, Todd McFarlane Toys, Chapel, 2nd series, MOC 20.00
Spawn, Todd McFarlane Toys, Cy–Gor, 4th series, MOC 45.00
Spawn, Todd McFarlane Toys, Redeemer, 3rd series, MOC . . . 15.00
Spawn, Todd McFarlane Toys, Tremor, 1st series, MOC 25.00
Spiderman, Mego, with web net, 12" h, MOC 95.00
Starsky & Hutch, Mego, Huggy Bear, 8" h, MOC 70.00
Starsky & Hutch, Mego, Starsky, 8" h, MOC 65.00
Starsky & Hutch, Mego, Hutch, 8" h. 70.00
Superheroes, Mego, Hulk, 8" h, MOC 65.00
Superheroes, Mego, Kid Flash, 8" h, MOC 500.00
Superheroes, Mego, Shazam, 8" h, MOC 275.00
Superheroes, Mego, Superman, 8" h, MOC 95.00
Super Knights, Mego, Ivanhoe, 8" h, MIB 95.00
Super Knights, Mego, King Arthur, 8" h, MIB 95.00
Super Knights, Mego, Lancelot, 8" h, loose 45.00
Super Pirates, Mego, Black Beard, 8" h, loose 35.00
Super Pirates, Mego, Jean Lafitte, 8" h, MIB 125.00
Super Pirates, Mego, Long John Silver, 8" h, MIB 125.00
Super Powers, Kenner, Brainiac, MOC 40.00
Super Powers, Kenner, Darkseid, MOC 25.00
Super Powers, Kenner, Green Arrow, MOC 55.00
Super Powers, Kenner, Hawkman, MOC 50.00
Super Powers, Kenner, Kaliback, MOC 30.00
Super Powers, Kenner, Martian Manhunter, MOC 35.00
Super Powers, Kenner, Wonder Woman, MOC 40.00
Swamp Thing, Kenner, Anton Arcane, MOC 20.00
Swamp Thing, Kenner, Dr Deemo, MOC 20.00
Swamp Thing, Kenner, Skin Man, MOC 20.00
Teenage Mutant Ninja Turtles, Playmates, Bebop, Turtle
    Force Fan Club Flyer, 1988, 4¹/₂" h 20.00
Teenage Mutant Ninja Turtles, Playmates, Krang, #5056,
    1989, 4¹/₂" h 15.00
Teenage Mutant Ninja Turtles, Playmates, Rocksteady,
    #5009, 1988, 4¹/₂" h 8.00
Teenage Mutant Ninja Turtles, Playmates, Sewer Sports
    All–Stars, Grand Slammin' Ralph, #5144, 1991 . . . . 5.00
The Tick, Bandai, Bounding Tick, 1st series, 5" h, MOC 15.00
The Tick, Bandai, Dyna–Mole, 1st series, 5" h, MOC 12.00
The Tick, Bandai, Hurling Tick, 2nd series, 5" h, MOC 25.00
The Tick, Bandai, Mucus Tick, 2nd series, 5" h, MOC 30.00

Thundercats, LJN, Captain Shiner, MOC 50.00
Thundercats, LJN, Grune the Destroyer, MOC 35.00
Thundercats, LJN, Snowman, MOC 45.00
Thundercats, LJN, Tuska Warrior, MOC 30.00
Visionaries, Hasbro, Arzon, 1987, MOC 25.00
Visionaries, Hasbro, Cravex, 1987, MOC 30.00
Visionaries, Hasbro, Witterquick, 1987, MOC 30.00
Voltron, Panosh Place, Doom Commander, 1984, MIP 20.00
Voltron, Panosh Place, Hunk, 1984, MIP 15.00
Wonder Woman, Mego, 12" h, MIB 250.00
World Wrestling Federation, Hasbro, Hulk Hogan,
    series 1, MOC 25.00
World Wrestling Federation, Jakks, Diesel, MOC 15.00
World Wrestling Federation, Jakks, Razor Ramon, MOC 15.00
World Wrestling Federation, Jakks, Undertaker, MOC 15.00
World Wrestling Federation, LJN, Adrian Adonis, MOC 35.00
World Wrestling Federation, LJN, Big John Studd, MOC 45.00
World Wrestling Federation, LJN, Bobby Heenan, MOC 40.00
World Wrestling Federation, LJN, Brutus Beefcake, MOC 55.00
World Wrestling Federation, LJN, Hulk Hogan, white
    shirt, MOC 225.00
World Wrestling Federation, LJN, Roddy Piper, MOC 60.00
World Wrestling Federation, LJN, Superfly Snuka, MOC 45.00
World Wrestling Federation, Tag Teams, LJN, Hulk
    Hogan & Hillbilly Jim, MOC 125.00

ADVERTISING

Advertising premiums such as calendars and thermometers arrived on the scene by the 1880s. Diecut point–of–purchase displays, wall clocks, and signs were eagerly displayed. The advertising character was developed in the early 1900s. By the 1950s the star endorser was firmly established. Advertising became a big business as specialized firms, many headquartered in New York City, developed to meet manufacturers' needs. Today television programs frequently command well over one hundred thousand dollars a minute for commercial air time.

Many factors affect the price of an advertising collectible—the product and its manufacturer, the objects or persons used in the advertisement, the period and aesthetics of design, the designer and/or illustrator, and the form the advertisement takes. Almost every advertising item is sought by a specialized collector in one or more collectibles areas.

References: *Advertising & Figural Tape Measures*, L–W Book Sales, 1995; Michael Bruner, *Advertising Clocks: America's Timeless Heritage*, Schiffer Publishing, 1995; Michael Bruner, *Encyclopedia of Porcelain Enamel Advertising*, Schiffer Publishing, 1994; Michael Bruner, *More Porcelain Enamel Advertising*, Schiffer Publishing, 1997; Douglas Collins, *America's Favorite Food: The Story of Campbell Soup Company*, Harry N. Abrams, 1994; Douglas Congdon–Martin, *America For Sale: A Collector's Guide to Antique Advertising*, Schiffer Publishing, 1991; Douglas Congdon–Martin, *Tobacco Tins: A Collector's Guide*, Schiffer Publishing, 1992; Fred Dodge, *Antique Tins: Identification & Values* (1995), *Book II* (1998), Collector Books.

Ted Hake, *Hake's Guide to Advertising Collectibles*, Wallace–Homestead, Krause Publications, 1992; Sharon and Bob Huxford, *Huxford's Collectible Advertising, Second Edition* (1995), *Third Edition* (1997), Collector Books; Jerry Jankowski, *Shelf Life: Modern Package Design 1920–1945*, Chronicle Books, 1992; Jerry Jankowski, *Shelf Space: Modern Package Design 1945–1965*,

Chronicle Books, 1998; Jim and Vivian Karsnitz, *Oyster Cans*, Schiffer Publishing, 1993; Ray Klug, *Antique Advertising Encyclopedia, Vol. 1* (1978, 1993 value update) and *Vol. 2* (1985, 1990 value update), L–W Promotions; *Letter Openers: Advertising & Figural*, L–W Book Sales, 1996; Norman E. Martinus and Harry L. Rinker, *Warman's Paper*, Wallace–Homestead, Krause Publications, 1994; Linda McPherson, *Modern Collectible Tins: Identification & Values*, Collector Books, 1998; Alice L. Muncaster and Ellen Sawyer, *The Black Cat Made Me Buy It!*, Crown Publishers, 1988; Alice L. Muncaster and Ellen Sawyer, *The Dog Made Me Buy It!*, Crown Publishers, 1990; Dawn E. Reno, *Advertising: Identification and Price Guide*, Avon Books, 1993; B. J. Summers, *Value Guide to Advertising Memorabilia*, Collector Books, 1994; David Zimmerman, *The Encyclopedia of Advertising Tins: Smalls and Samples*, published by author, 1994.

Periodicals: *Paper Collectors' Marketplace* (PCM), PO Box 128, Scandinavia, WI 54977; *The Paper & Advertising Collector* (PAC), PO Box 500, Mount Joy, PA 17552.

Collectors' Clubs: Advertising Cup and Mug Collectors of America, PO Box 680, Solon, IA 52333; Antique Advertising Assoc of America, PO Box 1121, Morton Grove, IL 60053; The Ephemera Society of America, PO Box 95, Cazenovia, NY 13035; Inner Seal Club (Nabisco), 4585 Saron Dr, Lexington, KY 40515; Porcelain Advertising Collectors Club, PO Box 381, Marshfield Hills, MA 02051; Tin Container Collectors Assoc, PO Box 440101, Aurora, CO 80044.

REPRODUCTION ALERT

Ashtray, Coney Island, white metal, parachute tower, roller coaster, "Wonder Wheel" ferris wheel, and Statue of Liberty scenes, made in Japan, 1930s, $3^{1}/_{2}$ x 6"... **$25.00**

Ashtray, Mack Trucks, brass, chrome finish, stylized 3–dimensional figural bulldog image attached to center, "Mack" on front collar, mkd "Central Die/Casting & Manufacturing Company, Chigago," 1960s, 6" h **100.00**

Bandanna, Lee, cotton, red, each corner depicts different work clothing outfit, Union Made symbol between each scene, 1930s, 25 x 27"................. **70.00**

Bank, Insty Prints, plastic, smiling boy dressed as wizard holding wand, 1960s, $8^{1}/_{2}$" h **65.00**

Bank, OK Tires, plastic, red, smiling and saluting service dealer image on front, "When Full, Get A New Bank From Your Local O.K. Rubber Welders/Home Of Autofloat Tires" inscription above back coin slot, 1960s, 2 x $3^{1}/_{2}$ x 6" **70.00**

Bank, Oscar Mayer Weinermobile, plastic, hotdog shape, company logo on sides, 1992 Olympic decal on tan plastic base, black wheels, $9^{1}/_{2}$" l **32.00**

Bank, Tootsie Roll, cardboard, figural Tootsie Roll, metal end caps, 1970s, $2^{1}/_{4}$" d, 12" h **10.00**

Bank, TP Thompson Products, ceramic, Indian and teepee, c1950s **150.00**

Biscuit Jar, Alpo, Dan the Dog, ceramic, gray molded fur, white muzzle, black nose, whisker dots, smiling mouthline, "Alpo" on collar, underside mkd "Dan The Dog," Alpo and USA inscriptions, 1960s, 4 x 4 x 8" **75.00**

Bobbing Head, South of the Border, painted wood Mexican figure in yellow sombrero, red letter decal inscription around front, 1960s, $6^{1}/_{4}$" h **100.00**

Fan, Kis–Me Gum Co, Louisville, KY, paper, 10" d, 15" l, $242.00. Photo courtesy Past Tyme Pleasures.

Booklet, French's Bird Seed, Canary Care Booklet, yellow cov, graphics of canary on front, box of bird seed on back, 4–pg insert shows company products for canaries and parrots, ©1928 R T French Co, 44 pgs, $4^{1}/_{4}$ x $6^{1}/_{2}$"...................................... **18.00**

Box, Campfire Marshmallows, red, white, and blue, Boy Scouts toasting marshmallows over campfire scene on lid, housewife frosting cake with marshmallow topping on bottom, 2 recipes and offer for Campfire Recipe Book on panel, 1920s, $1^{1}/_{2}$ x $3^{1}/_{2}$ x $6^{3}/_{4}$" **50.00**

Box, Sen–Sen, "For Horseness Use Sen–Sen," 1920s **45.00**

Calendar, Goodyear, 1935, bear surprising fisherman in river scene, full pad, artist signed Hy Hintermeister, 21 x 12" **25.00**

Calendar, Whistle, 1931, Rolf Armstrong artwork, matted, framed, black and gold highlights, 15 x 32"....... **1,050.00**

Calendar Holder, Yellow Cab, black and white, "Yellow Cab 243–1111," 1950s, 7 x 11".................... **55.00**

Card, Mail Pouch, black and white, center image of laughing baby on blanket, "Just Found His Mail Pouch" at top, "The Poor Man's Friends The Rich Man's Delight" at bottom, 1940s, 2 x $3^{3}/_{4}$" **5.00**

Catalog, Magee Carpet Co, blue cov, black lettering, gold accents, 40 pgs, 1932, $9^{1}/_{4}$ x $12^{1}/_{4}$" **15.00**

Ceiling Light, Kentucky Fried Chicken, glass, metal cap, Colonel Sanders image, ©1969 KFC Corp, $9^{1}/_{2}$" h **100.00**

Centerpiece, Stork Club, wooden, 7" h figural long–beaked white stork, wearing top hat, white lettering, 4" d black base, 1930s **100.00**

Charm, Bell Telephone, plastic, light blue, figural Trimline desk telephone, unmkd, 1960s **10.00**

Cigarette Lighter, York Air Conditioning, plastic insert panel on one side depicts cartoon man in nightgown sleeping in air conditioning, other panels with engraved name of local sales distributor in VA, red, gold, yellow, shades of blue, chrome luster metal case, made in Japan, 1960s **15.00**

Clock, Monad Paints and Varnishes, octagonal, neon, 1940s, 18" d **450.00**

Clock, Westinghouse, "Westinghouse Television Radio" in orange circle below Westinghouse logo **250.00**

Dispenser Barrel, Liberty Root Beer, oak, orig decals, missing refrigeration coils, 1920s, 24" h **350.00**

Dispenser, Mission Grapefruit, goblet style, pot metal base, orig box and promotional paper sign **275.00**

Display, Bright Star Flashlight Battery, replica black, white, red, and gold battery illus on yellow ground, litho tin hanger plate holding 2 actual batteries, "20% More Service," 1930s, 3½ x 4¾" **100.00**

Display, Johnny Walker, composition trademark figure wearing tan hat, gloves, red jacket, white pants, glossy black gold trim boots, holding gold baton in left hand, black wire monocle in right hand, mounted on green wooden base with decal, 1940–50, 10" h **85.00**

Display, Kleenex Tissue, Kimberly–Clark, figural Little Lule in majorette uniform holding box of Kleenex tissues, cone–shaped bottom forms free standing base, 1956, 10" h. **25.00**

Display, Life Savers, 5 scenes with flavors, 1920s **1,500.00**

Display, Roma Wine, painted plaster, waiter whose body forms letter "R" holding yellow bowl, purple and green vineyard scene on yellow and red base, "Roma Wine Company, Fresno, California, America's Largest Selling Wine" in relief, 1950s, 5½ x 14 x 17" **200.00**

Doll, Campbell's Kid, soft rubber, hollow, painted, squeaker sound, 1940–50s, 7" h. **150.00**

Doll, Swanson, penguin, plush, stuffed, black and white, red felt beak, brown plush padded web feet, yellow fringed scarf, "Swanson" printed in red, Acorn Inc tag, made in Korea, 1970s, 20" h **45.00**

Door Push, Cel-Ray, tin, emb, "Cel–Ray" above Dr Brown's Cel–Ray bottle, "Vitamin D Added" below, 1930–40s, 10" h **65.00**

Door Push, Sunbeam Bread, loaf of bread, "Sunbeam Compare It's Batter Whipped," 1950s, 30 x 15". **500.00**

Door Push, Ken–L Ration, blue ground, yellow dog, white and yellow lettering, 1950s. **425.00**

Fan, Campbell's Soup, cardboard, diecut, oversized tomato centered by can of Tomato Soup front illus, tomato image centered by yellow, red, and black picture ad for Campbell Soup kitchens in New Toronto, Canada, listing of 21 soup varieties, 6½ x 9¼", 5½" wooden handle, c1920 . . . . **75.00**

Fan, Ward's Bread, cardboard, diecut, wood handle, fairy tale–like flour mill with verse and Ward Baking Co color illus, 7 x 7" **50.00**

Figure, Belmont Clothes, molded hard rubber, painted, Art Deco style, jockey on horseback, 1930s, 6½" h **200.00**

Figure, Brake Shoe Co, seated dog, painted plaster, yellow–tan and black, gold "Stopper" collar tag, clear acrylic block insert over "American Brakeblok/The Safety Brake Lining/American Brake Shoe Company" on underside, 1960–70s, 2¼ x 2¾ x 3½" **75.00**

Figure, Cleveland National Screw And Mfg Co, Nat, metal, wooden head, 6 sided base, assorted bolts, nuts, screws, and cotter pin nose pcs, chest engraved "NAT," inscribed "Cleveland National Screw And Mfg. Co." on base, 1960s, 4½" h **650.00**

Figure, Hush Puppies, basset hound, vinyl, painted, hollow, white face, black muzzle, brown and black body markings, off–white and green base, brown lettering "Hush Puppies" inscription, Wolverine Shoe Co, 1970s, 8" h **50.00**

Figure, Old Crow, vinyl, hollow, black crow wearing white shirt and red vest, simulated walking stick tucked under one wing, product name incised on

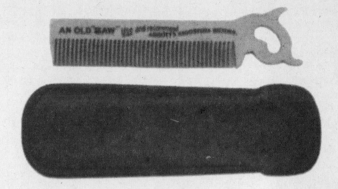

Mustache Comb, Abbotts Angostora Bitters, celluloid, leather carrying case, $66.00. Photo courtesy Past Tyme Pleasures.

front white base, "Kentucky Straight Bourbon Whiskey 86 Proof Distilled And Bottled By The Famous Old Crow Distillery Co., Frankfort, Ky." on rear, 13½" h **75.00**

Figure, Westinghouse Tuff Guy, plaster, gold paint, image of chef with muscular crossed arms with image of woman at stove on shirt, "Westinghouse House Tuff Guy 1952" in relief on base, 5" h. **90.00**

Flier, Borden's Milk, sepiatone, illus, shows various products available by saving milk can coupons, orig 10–coupon certificate stapled at bottom, c1940, 4¼ x 6½" **20.00**

Folder, 1964 Volkswagen Station Wagon, full moon and starry sky above "Spacious" cover design, full color illus inside shows 2 models on one side and profile view on other, 8½ x 9½" **25.00**

Game, Chicklets Gum Village Game, lid shows backs of heads of boy and girl holding balloons looking at village scene, small sketched figure in bottom right corner, contains small boxes of Chicklets, Hasbro, 1959 . . . . . **30.00**

Game, Hawaiian Punch, lid shows sketch of man wearing flowered shirt, fruit drink mascot holding glass of punch, youngsters playing game inset, Mattel, 1978 . . . . . . **12.00**

Game, Revlon's $64,000 Question Quiz Game, lid shows person in booth, "Categories & Questions For Children of All Ages," Lowell, 1955 . . . . **25.00**

Hot Pad, Reddy Kilowatt, cardboard, "My name is Reddy Kilowatt, I keep things cold, I make things hot; I'm, your cheap electric servant. Always ready on the spot," 1940s, 6" d **50.00**

Keychain, Fanta Orange, painted rubber figure, movable hat and head, green hat and body, orange head, smiling white mouthline, small keychain and loop ring inserted in tip of hat, 1960s, 2" h **45.00**

Letter Opener, Lucas Motor Express, Shelbyville, IN, plastic, opener/calendar combination, c1943, 8¾" l **20.00**

Letter Opener, Servel Hermetic Winners Convention 1931, Evansville, IN, plastic, opener/magnifying glass/ruler combination, 7½" l **15.00**

Letter Opener, Wayne Hardware Co, Inc, plastic, metal blade, c1950, 8½" l **10.00**

Match Holder, American Steel Farm Fences, green and white, 1920–30s **40.00**

Night Light, Big Boy, figural, vinyl, orig attached cord and bulb, "Underwriters Laboratories Inc./Portable Lamp" sticker, 1960s, 6½" h **100.00**

Paperweight, Columbia Coal, brown and white cello on weighted metal, mirror insert, coal chunks filling railroad car scene, 1920–30s **25.00**

Paperweight, Flametech, vinyl, red, figural devil with black and white eyes holding metal screw, orig foil stickers with company names on 3 sides, c1970, 7" h **65.00**

Paperweight, Haskell Implement & Seed Co, sepia cello on weighted metal, mirror insert, store building with title above front door scene, 1920s **50.00**

Pencil, Armour's Big Crop Fertilizers, silvered metal, black, white, and red cello wrapper, "Make Every Acre Do Its Best," removable end cap holds stub replacement pencil,1940s **15.00**

Pencil Clip, Hekman's Bakery, red and white, "At Every Meal Eat Hekman's Cookie–Cakes And Crackers," 1920–30s **25.00**

Pencil Clip, Starrett Tools, metal, gold luster, entwined 2 caliper tools trademark with angle measuring tool image, c1920s **20.00**

Pin, Hotpoint, enameled brass, figural Hotpoint character image, red and yellow outfit, green backing, 1930s, ½" h **5.00**

Pinback Button, Campbell's Kid Club, image of Kid as weightlifter, 1930s.............................. **100.00**

Pinback Button, Heinz Ketchup, red and white, black lettering, 1930s **25.00**

Pinback Button, Hostess Cake, red, white, and blue, Hostess silhouette symbol inside heart shape, 1940s **15.00**

Pinback Button, Koester's Bread, red, white, blue, and gold, 1930s **25.00**

Plate, Reddy Kilowatt, smiling Reddy image at left, dark red accent rim, 1950s, 9" d **60.00**

Pocketknife, Chevrolet, silvered metal, pearl–like panel inserts, one with blue Chevrolet logo and "Parts and Accessories" designation, opposite panel with imprint of local dealer, Hammer Brand, 1940s **45.00**

Pocket Mirror, ABC Bread, acetate over textured gold paper, inscribed "Kansas City's Favorite" in red and blue, 1930s... **25.00**

Pocket Mirror, Price & Teeple Piano Co, metal, black and white fabric, young woman seated at player piano, 1920s **50.00**

Pocket Watch, Sundial Shoes, silvered metal case and bezel, clear plexiglass over gold luster, Scotch boy to right of "Time will tell—wear Sundial Shoes," sweep second hand on lower dial face, New Haven Clock Co, 1930s, 1⅞" d case............................. **100.00**

Poster, Bond Bread, "Easter Greetings," 1930–40s, 13 x 38" **110.00**

Poster, Wings Cigarettes, cardboard, easel back, yellow airplane flying over pack of Wings cigarettes, 1940–50s, 20 x 30" **140.00**

Salt and Pepper Shakers, pr, Squirt Co, figural Squirt bottles, green, red and yellow logo on front, yellow plastic cap, 1960s, 4" h **10.00**

Serving Tray, Pepsol, dog illus, 1941, 12" d.............. **60.00**

Shoe Horn, Buster Brown Blue Ribbon Shoes, litho tin, blue and red on white lettering inscription and trademark symbol on top, 1920s, 4¾" h **75.00**

Sign, Alka–Time, tin, green bottle with yellow trim, "Drink Alka–Time" above, "It's Refreshing Anytime" on blue banner across center, "A Good Mixer in Any Company" below, 1930s **325.00**

Left: Scale, KASCO Feeds, metal, debossed lettering, "Weigh the milk, Weigh the feed," 16" h, 4½" w, $143.00. Photo courtesy Collectors Auction Services

Sign, American Red Cross, cardboard, diecut, easel back, 3 dimensional, woman holding world globe with red cross in center, "Serves Humanity" above and below, 1930–40s, 14 x 22" **200.00**

Sign, Armour Franks, tin, boy eating hot dog illus, "Plump, Juicy, Tender!," 1950s, 20 x 26".............. **180.00**

Sign, Beech Nut Mello Fruit Chewing Gum, cardboard, diecut, black woman holding gum pack, "New Mello Fruit Chewing Gum," Extra Mello! Long lasting flavor! Swing to Beech Nut!," 1940–50s, 12 x 10" **10.00**

Sign, Bell Helicopter, porcelain, 2 sided, white ground, blue graphics and lettering, 18" d **2,300.00**

Sign, Birthday Beverage, metal, red, white, and blue, hand holding tilted bottle, 1940s, 9 x 11"............. **50.00**

Sign, The Canton Repository, tin, diecut, black and yellow, "The Canton Repository Daily & Sunday," 1920–30s, 14 x 18" **130.00**

Sign, Carnation Evaporated Milk, tin, blue ground, red, white, and black, 1950s, 12 x 18" **195.00**

Sign, Cheer Up Beverage, tin, owl illus, "Cheer Up, A Delightful Beverage," 1940–50s, 19" sq **550.00**

Sign, Clabber Girl Baking Powder, tin, 2 sided, yellow, red, and black, "Clabber Girl The Double–Acting Baking Powder," 1950–60s, 12 x 34" **60.00**

Sign, Calotabs, tin, emb, man looking in mirror at tongue, "Tongue Coated? You Need Calotabs, We Sell Them—10¢ and 35¢," 1930s, 14 x 20"........... **575.00**

Sign, Dr Morse's Indian Root Pills, cardboard, easel back, diecut, Indian and teepee illus, 1930s, 13½ x 25"... **100.00**

Sign, Drink Texas Punch, tin, emb, yellow, red, 1940s, 9 x 27" **275.00**

Sign, Everess Table Water, cardboard, "Serve Sparkling Everess Table Water On Your Home Menu," 1940s, 36 x 29" **210.00**

Sign, Greyhound Lines, porclain, oval, 2 sided, blue ground, yellow lettering, white greyhound, 1930–40, 21 x 36" **700.00**

Sign, Harrison's, tin, emb, "Harrison's Heart Range Sold Here," 1930–40s, 14" d **135.00**

Sign, Horoscope, porcelain, black, white, and red, "Horoscope, What Do The Stars Foretell?," 1940–50, 12 x 15" **35.00**

Sign, Ilco, aluminum, diecut, figural key, "Keys Made Here," 26½" l **25.00**

Sign, Ladies Rest Room, porcelain, 2 sided, checkerboard pattern rim, 1920–30s, 6 x 12" **250.00**

Sign, Leaf Chewing Gum, tin, yellow, red, green, and white, "Leaf, The Flavor Lingers Longer," 1940–50s **325.00**

Sign, Lux Fire Extinguishing Equipment, porcelain, 2 sided, red, white, and blue, 1940–50, 18 x 13" **525.00**

Sign, Life Savers, porcelain, black ground, red and white lettering, 27 x 60" **2,100.00**

Sign, Merlita Bread, tin, emb, Lone Ranger on horse, 1955, 2 x 3" **350.00**

Sign, Morton Salt, porcelain, product name in white above girl holding umbrella in rain, "When It Rains It Pours" below, 1920–30, 12 x 15" **1,700.00**

Sign, Nabisco, paper, diecut, Santa Claus holding vintage packages of Nabisco products, c1937, 17 x 25" ... **1,000.00**

Sign, Oh Boy Gum, tin, boy holding 4 packs of gum, elf sitting on shoulder, "1¢" in circle, "It's Pure!," 1920–30, 7 x 15" **325.00**

Sign, Palmolive, tin, yellow ground, red, green, black, and white, man and woman, bar of Palomolive soap, "Palmolive's Beauty Plan brings you a younger–looking skin from head to toe," 1940s, 14 x 28" **400.00**

Sign, Penny Scale, tin, turquoise and black, "A Penny Each Day Shows You The Weigh To Health, Scale Tested–U.S. Standard Weights," 1930s, 9 x 10" **20.00**

Sign, Philip Morris, cardboard, easel back, "Come In and Call for Philip Morris," 1940s, 21 x 29" **425.00**

Sign, Piedmont Cigarettes, porcelain, blue ground, white lettering, 1920–30, 30 x 46" **650.00**

Sign, Purity Butter Pretzels, cardboard, diecut, easel back, smiling blonde hair boy carrying giant pretzel, 1930s, 12¼ x 22" **65.00**

Sign, RCA Victor, cardboard, diecut, easel back, blonde woman in green tight sweater and red shorts illus, "RCA Victor Tubes," 1940s, 8 x 9¾" **75.00**

Sign, Red Edge Shovels, man holding shovel, 1940–50, 11 x 18" **85.00**

Sign, R G Sullivan's Cigar, porcelain, red ground, "7–20–4 Cigar" in white, black and yellow trim, 1930–40, 10 x 23" **450.00**

Sign, Red Indian Motor Oils, porcelain, black and red ground, white "Red Indian Motor Oils," center Indian in red, 1920–40, 20 x 20" **2,100.00**

Sign, Samoset Chocolates, tin over cardboard, red "Agency Samoset Chocolates" with arrow through "S" in Samoset, Indian in canoe, 1920s, 9 x 13" **325.00**

Sign, Southern Bell Telephone and Telegraph Co, porcelain, black and white, "Local Long Distance Telphone" on black bell in circle, 18 x 23" **625.00**

Sign, Stroehmann's Sunbeam Bread, tin, red ground, yellow and blue lettering, girl eating piece of bread on left, 1956, 6 x 30" **140.00**

Sign, Tom's, tin, emb, red, white, and blue, food illus, "Time Out for Tom's," 1958, 20 x 28" **260.00**

Sign, TruAde, tin, emb, yellow, red, blue, and white, "Naturally Delicious!, Drink A Better Beverage Not Carbonated," 1954, 18 x 54" **300.00**

Sign, Vicks VapoRub, Vicks jar in upper right, mother rubbing Vicks on child's chest, "Relieves Misery of Colds" **170.00**

Sign, Western Union, porcelain, oval, 2 sided, orig hanging bracket, 21 x 34" **525.00**

Sign, Westinghouse Mazda Lamps, cardboard, easel back, young Jackie Cooper illus, 1930s, 28 x 40" **500.00**

Sign, Wise Potato Chips, cardboard, easel back, color illus, trademark owl and winking white bunny, *Good Housekeeping* magazine and Potato Chip Institute seals with Wise Delicatessen Co copyright on bottom margin, 11 x 14" **50.00**

Sign, Wonder Bread, tin, diecut, 1950s, 20 x 42" **185.00**

Sign, Woodward's Butter Brickle, cardboard, easel back, silver and black, raised inscriptions, "Brastex Sign" back sticker, National Art Works, Covington, KY, 1920–30s, 6 x 9" **25.00**

Spinner Top, Betsy Ross Bread, litho tin, yellow, red lettering, 1930–40s **25.00**

Spinner Top, Tastykake, celluloid, red, white, and blue, Parisian Novelty Co, 1930s **15.00**

Spoon Rest, Handy Flame, ceramic, blue, "Handy Flame" on one side with copyright symbol, c1950s...... **65.00**

Squeeze Toy, Purina Dog Chow Chuck Wagon, vinyl, brown, red and white checkerboard design covered wagon, red and black driver, 2 horses with black reins, white simulated cloud of dust, ©Ralston Purina Co, 1975 .... **30.00**

Telephone, Raid, plastic, figural, painted yellow and green Raid trademark figure, black vinyl antenna sprouts, S C Johnson Co, made in Hong Kong, 1980s, 8½" h **50.00**

Thermometer, Guinness Stout, litho tin, cream, red and green accents, 3" d glass thermometer, c1940s, 9" d **30.00**

Thermometer, Hills Bros Coffee, porcelain, red ground, man in yellow gown drinking coffee, 1920s, 9 x 21".... **275.00**

Thermometer, Listerine, "Listerine the Safe Antiseptic, for Coughs, Colds, Sore Throats, Bad Breath" **550.00**

Left: Thermometer, Muller's Pinehurst Milk, Rockford, IL, wax–coated cardboard, 2½ x 6⅛", $15.00; Right: Tin, Jolly Time Hulless Pop Corn, litho tin, ©1933, 5¼" h, $55.00. Photo courtesy Past Tyme Pleasures.

Thermometer, Ramon's Pills, wood, yellow ground, boy wearing monacle, black top coat, high top hat, red bowtie, carrying bag mkd "The Little Doctor, Ramon's Plus Pills, A Real Laxative" below, 1930–40, 9 x 21".... **210.00**

Tin, Dean's Peacocks Prophylactics, litho tin, hinged lid, peacock in garden setting color scene, product description on underside panel, late 1940s............ **25.00**

Tin, Frontenac Peanut Butter, litho tin, wire bail, ivory, litho title, red and blue illus, gold trim, emb gold lid, 1920s, 3" d, 3¼" h **95.00**

Toy Truck, Baby's Dy–Dee Service, vinyl, squeeze toy, white, company name on each side in red, image of baby as king on top, yellow accents, 1950s, 2½ x 6 x 2¾" **35.00**

Tray, J R B Ise Kream, litho tin, American Art Works, 13" d .. **100.00**

Trolley Sign, Beech Nut Cough Drops, man looking up to pack of cough drops in sky, blue sky, white clouds shaped like old man's face, 1920–30s, 11 x 21" **210.00**

Tumbler, Star–Kist, transparent smoked gray, flaired outer lip, white Charlie the Tuna blowing bubbles, 1970s, 4½" h, price for 5 .... **50.00**

Vehicle, Gray–Line Tour Bus, red, white, blue, "New York's First Air Conditioned Sightseeing Coach," and "Gray–Line Sightseeing Tours" on side, Coca–Cola logo on back, ATC, Japan, 1950–60s, 4 x 14" **300.00**

Whistle, Buster Brown Shoes, litho tin, Buster and Tige color image, yellow border, "Tread Straight Feature" in green, gold flashing on underside, 1930s **45.00**

Whistle, Poll–Parrot Shoes, litho tin, yellow, green and red trademark, Kirchoff Co, 1930s **25.00**

Whistle, Red Goose Shoes, litho tin, yellow ground, red and yellow trademark symbol, Kirchoff Co, 1930s........ **25.00**

Whistle, Skeezix Shoes, litho tin, red and blue image of Skeezix and girlfriend, "Outgrown Before Outworn" in red, made in Germany.......................... **25.00**

ADVERTISING CHARACTERS

Many companies created advertising characters as a means of guaranteeing product recognition by the buying public. Consumers are more apt to purchase an item with which they are familiar and advertising characters were a surefire method of developing familiarity.

The early development of advertising characters also enabled immigrants who could not read to identify products by the colorful figures found on the packaging.

Trademarks and advertising characters are found on product labels, in magazines, as premiums, and on other types of advertising. Character subjects may be based on a real person such as Nancy Green, the original "Aunt Jemima." However, more often than not, they are comical figures, often derived from popular contemporary cartoons. Other advertising characters were designed especially to promote a specific product, like Mr. Peanut and the Campbell Kids.

References: Douglas Collins, *America's Favorite Food: The Story of Campbell Soup Company,* Harry N. Abrams, 1994; Pamela Duvall Curran and George W. Curran, *Collectible California Raisins: An Unauthorized Guide With Values,* Schiffer Publishing, 1998; Warren Dotz, *Advertising Character Collectibles: An Identification and Value Guide,* Collector Books, 1993, 1997 value update; Joan Stryker Grubaugh, *A Collector's Guide to the Gerber Baby,* pub-

lished by author, 1996; Ted Hake, *Hake's Guide to Advertising Collectibles,* Wallace–Homestead, Krause Publications, 1992; Mary Jane Lamphier, *Zany Characters of the Ad World,* Collector Books, 1995; Norman E. Martinus and Harry L. Rinker, *Warman's Paper,* Wallace–Homestead, Krause Publications, 1994; Myra Yellin Outwater, *Advertising Dolls,* Schiffer Publishing, 1997.

Collectors' Clubs: Camel Joe & Friends, 2205 Hess Dr, Cresthill, IL 60435; Campbell Soup Collectors Club, 414 County Lane Ct, Wauconda, IL 60084; Sorry Charlie...No Fan Club For You, 7812 N W Hampton Rd, Kansas City, MO 64152.

REPRODUCTION ALERT

Bud Man, Budweiser Beer, doll, foam rubber, red outfit, blue gloves, boots, bowtie with Budweiser name, Bud Man stickers on chest, 1960s, 18" h **$150.00**

California Raisin, doll, plush, maroon body, white fabric triangular vest dotted in black, stitched tag with ©1988 CALRAB, and "Acme" inscription for Applause, 18" h, 14" d.......................... **70.00**

Charlie Tuna, Star–Kist, doll, cloth, pull string talker, shades of blue, printed lavender sunglasses, open mouth with red tongue, orange cap, orig tag, Mattel, ©1969, 15" h, 12 x 19" display bag **100.00**

Dig 'Em Frog, Sugar Smacks, doll, cloth, green and yellow body, red accents, ©1973 Kellogg's, 8 x 17"........ **20.00**

Elf, Ernie Keebler, watch, chrome luster metal bezel, full color character image, textured black leather band, 1980s..................................... **45.00**

Elsie, Borden's Milk and Cream, Zippo lighter, chrome Elsie image with yellow daisy, Borden copyright and Zippo patent number, orig box, 1950................. **50.00**

Icee Bear, bank, painted vinyl, white body, black accents, red sweater, red, white, and blue cup, coin slot across back shoulders, 5 x 5 x 7½" **45.00**

Iron Fireman, Iron Fireman Co, ashtray, metal, figural, 1940s, 3¾" h **95.00**

Jolly Green Giant, doll, vinyl, 2 shades of green, movable upper torso, Product People, Inc, Minneapolis, 9¼" h, 2½ x 5 x 12" display box, 1970s.............. **75.00**

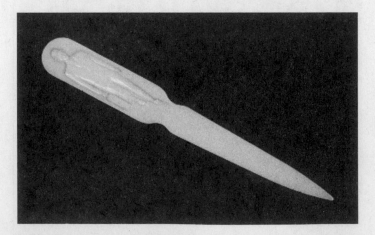

Fuller Brush Man, Fuller Brush Co, letter opener, molded plastic, white, salesman one side, saleswoman other side, 8" l, $18.00.

Little Oscar, Oscar Mayer, doll, inflatable, vinyl, figural Little Oscar wearing white chef outfit with red inscriptions, light yellow mitt hands, 30" h **50.00**

Little Sprout, Green Giant, doll, green soft vinyl, movable head, 1970s, 6" h. **30.00**

Mohawk Tommy, Mohawk Carpet Mills, bank, hard styrofoam, painted, coin slot in head, metal trap, orig sticker, La Della Art Studios, Fox Lake, WI, c1950s, 4 x 6 x 10" **195.00**

Mr Bib, Michelin, figural tape measure, blue plastic, metal metric measuring tape, 1980s, 2¹/₂" h **50.00**

Mr Clean, figure, vinyl, painted, "P&G" copyright on one underside of foot, 1961, 8" h. **100.00**

Mr Peanut, Planters Peanuts, paint book, "The Making Of America," story and illus about "Progress Of America's Industries," ©1938, 32 pgs, 7¹/₂ x 10¹/₂". **25.00**

Nipper, RCA, doll, plush, black bendable ears, applied felt eyes, black vinyl nose, black vinyl collar with silvered brass rivet dec, attached silver foil paper collar inscribed in red "Nipper/Radio Corp. of America," 1960s, 19¹/₂" h. **190.00**

Pillsbury Dough Boy, child's mug, plastic, white, blue eyes, 4¹/₂" h. **15.00**

Poppin' Fresh, Pillsbury, playhouse and dolls, vinyl over cardboard carrying case–type playhouse, 4 soft hollow vinyl finger puppet dolls, Pillsbury Playthings series, ©1974, 3 x 11¹/₂ x 14". **95.00**

Punchy, Hawaiian Punch, watch, Punchy image, watch hands depict extended arm with pointing finger for hour, shorter arm holding product can for minutes, gold flashing luster bezel, black fabric strap, silvered metal buckle, 1970s **50.00**

Reddy Kilowatt, bib, cloth, printed Reddy design, 1950s, 10 x 10" **75.00**

Reddy Kilowatt, Philadelphia Electric Co, blotter, black, white, and tan, "Philadelphia Electric Co" printed in bottom margin beneath 1939 copyright, 3³/₄ x 8¹/₂" **25.00**

Speedy, Alka–Seltzer, figure, vinyl, painted, 1950s, 8" h **700.00**

Sunbeam Girl, Sunbeam Bread, driver's badge, oval, red and white, trademark girl image, bar area for employee name, 1940s. **25.00**

Tony the Tiger, Kellogg's, wristwatch, chromed metal, clear crystal over full color image of Tony the Tiger, 1976 Kellogg copyright, 1³/₈" d **75.00**

Willie the Penguin, Kool Cigarettes, figurine, plaster, painted, Willie with stethoscope around neck, "Dr Kool" inscription on carrying case, ¹/₂" h, 2¹/₂ d base, 1940s. **95.00**

AKRO AGATE

The Akro Agate Company was founded in Ohio in 1911 primarily to manufacture agate marbles. In 1914 the firm opened a large factory in Clarksburg, West Virginia.

Increasing competition in the marble industry in the 1930s prompted Akro Agate to expand. In 1936, following a major fire at the Westite factory, Akro Agate purchased many of Westite's molds. Akro Agate now boasted a large line of children's dishes, floral wares, and household accessories. The company also produced specialty glass containers for cosmetic firms, including the Mexicali cigarette jar (originally filled with Pick Wick bath salts) and a special line made for the Jean Vivaudou Company, Inc.

The Clarksburg Glass Company bought the factory in 1951.

Akro Agate glass has survived the test of time because of its durability. Most pieces are marked "Made in USA" and often include a mold number. Some pieces have a small crow in the mark. Early pieces of Akro made from Westite molds may be unmarked but were produced only in typical Akro colors and color combinations.

References: Gene Florence, *The Collectors Encyclopedia of Akro Agate Glassware, Revised Edition,* Collector Books, 1975, 1992 value update; Roger and Claudia Hardy, *The Complete Line of the Akro Agate,* published by author, 1992.

Collectors' Club: Akro Agate Collector's Club, 10 Bailey St, Clarksburg, WV 26301.

Note: See Children's Dishes for additional listings.

REPRODUCTION ALERT: Reproduction pieces are unmarked.

Chiquita, creamer and sugar, opaque light blue **$35.00**
Chiquita, cup, opaque green **6.50**
Chiquita, cup, transparent cobalt **14.00**
Chiquita, plate, opaque green **8.00**
Chiquita, saucer, opaque yellow **7.00**
Concentric Rib, cup, opaque orange, small **15.00**
Concentric Rib, plate, opaque medium blue, small. **9.00**
Concentric Rib, saucer, opaque white, small **4.00**
Concentric Rib, teapot, open, opaque green, small **8.00**
Interior Panel, plate, opaque green, small. **6.00**
Interior Panel, saucer, opaque blue, small. **6.00**
Interior Panel, teapot, open, opaque pink, small **10.00**
Marbleized, ashtray, orange, shell **7.00**
Marbleized, ashtray, red, 2⁷/₈" sq **8.00**
Marbleized, plate, green, large **13.00**
Marbleized, teapot, oxblood, no lid, small **28.00**
Octagonal, closed handle, plate, green, large. **5.00**
Octagonal, closed handle, saucer, beige, large **4.00**
Octagonal, closed handle, saucer, white, large **4.00**
Octagonal, closed handle, teapot, bright blue, pink lid, large. **21.00**
Octagonal, closed handle, tumbler, green, large **12.00**
Octagonal, open handle, cup, dark green, small. **10.00**
Octagonal, open handle, teapot, bright blue, white lid **24.00**

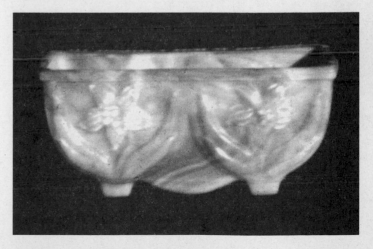

Marbleized, lily planter, oxblood and lemonade, mkd "657," 5¹/₄", $10.00.

Stacked Disc, creamer and sugar, pink **45.00**
Stacked Disc, teapot, cov, pink, blue lid **17.00**
Stacked Disc, tumbler, opaque beige, small **12.00**
Stacked Disc, water pitcher, opaque green, small **10.00**
Stacked Disc and Panel, cup, transparent green **60.00**
Stacked Disc and Panel, pitcher, transparent green **18.00**
Stacked Disc and Panel, plate, opaque yellow, small **12.00**
Stacked Disc and Panel, plate, transparent green, large **21.00**
Stacked Disc and Panel, tumbler, transparent green, 2" **10.00**
Stippled Band, creamer, cobalt, large **35.00**
Stippled Band, cup, topaz, large **18.00**
Stippled Band, cup and saucer, green, large **28.00**
Stippled Band, plate, green, small **12.00**
Stippled Band, plate, topaz, small **7.50**
Stippled Band, teapot, cov, green, small **30.00**
Transparent, cup and saucer, topaz **22.00**
Transparent, plate, green, large **9.00**
Transparent, sugar, cov, green, large **40.00**
Transparent, tumbler, green, 2" **10.00**

ALADDIN LAMPS

Victor Samuel Johnson founded the Western Lighting Company in Kansas City, Missouri, in 1907. The company imported the foreign–made "Practicus" lamp, forerunner and inspiration of the Aladdin lamp.

In 1908 the company became the Mantle Lamp Company of America. In 1909, Johnson introduced the Aladdin lamp, which derived its name from the magic lamp found by Aladdin in *The Arabian Nights*. The success of the first Aladdin model, which utilized a new burner patented by Charles E. Wirth, enabled Johnson to establish and maintain a research and development department to continually improve the Aladdin's performance.

Although the company has diversified and become as well known for its lunch boxes and vacuum bottles as its lamps, Aladdin lamps are still being manufactured today.

References: J. W. Courter, *Aladdin Collectors Manual & Price Guide #17: Kerosene Mantle Lamps*, published by author, 1997; J. W. Courter, *Aladdin Electric Lamps: Collectors Manual & Price Guide #3*, published by author, 1997; J. W. Courter, *Aladdin: The Magic Name in Lamps, Revised Edition*, published by author, 1997.

Collectors' Club: The Mystic Light of the Aladdin Knights, 3935 Kelley Rd, Kevil, KY 42053.

REPRODUCTION ALERT: Tall Lincoln Drape, Short Lincoln Drape, glass and paper shades.

Note: All lamps priced with complete burners.

Model 2, table, plain foot, polished brass **$325.00**
Model 4, parlour, Old English **600.00**
Model 12, hanging, 4 post, parchment shade **250.00**
Model 12, style 1231U, Crystal Vase, pale yellow,
   10 1/4" h **700.00**
Model 12, style 1241, Crystal Vase, variegated tan, 12" h . . . **200.00**
Model 12, style 1250, floor, blue and gold, 1928–29 . . . . . . **200.00**
Model 23, style B–2301, table, solid brass **50.00**
Model A, style 100, table, Venetian, white, 1932–33 . . . . . . **100.00**
Model B, style 105, table, Colonial, green, 1933 . . . . **175.00**
Model B, style 109, table, Cathedral, amber, 1934 . . . . **125.00**

Model B, style 62S, table, Short Lincoln Drape, ruby
   crystal, solitaire base, 1939 . . . . **4,500.00**
Model B, style B–70, table, Solitaire, white moonstone,
   1938 . . . . **2,800.00**
Model B, style B–81, table, Beehive, green, 1937–38 . . . . . . **125.00**
Model B, style B–91, table, Quilt, white moonstone,
   1937 . . . . **300.00**
Model B, style B–97, table, Queen, green moonstone,
   1937–39 . . . . **375.00**
Model B, style B–102, table, Corinthian, green, 1935–36 . . . **100.00**
Model B, style B–121, table, Majestic, rose moonstone,
   1935–36 . . . . **400.00**
Model B, style B–132, table, Orientale, rose gold,
   1935–36 . . . . **225.00**
Model B, style B–291, floor, ivory and gold, 1938 . . . . **200.00**
Model B, style B–400, caboose, brass font **150.00**
Model C, style B–139, table, aluminum font, 1955–63 . . . . . . **40.00**

ALUMINUM, HAND–WROUGHT

The mass production of hand–wrought aluminum decorative accessories is indebted to the inventiveness of Charles M. Hall and Paul T. Heroult. Hall of the United States and Heroult in France, working independently, simultaneously discovered an inexpensive electrolytic reduction process in 1886. Soon after, the price of aluminum dropped from $545.00 per pound to 57¢ per pound.

Aluminum ware's popularity thrived throughout the lean Depression years and into the first years of World War II, when aluminum shortages caused many factories to close. Some resumed production after the war; however, most pieces no longer originated with the artistic craftsman—the Machine Age had arrived. By the late 1960s, decorative aluminum was no longer in fashion.

References: Dannie Woodard and Billie Wood, *Hammered Aluminum: Hand–Wrought Collectibles*, published by authors, 1983, 1990 value update; Dannie A. Woodard, *Hammered Aluminum Hand–Wrought Collectibles, Book Two*, Aluminum Collectors' Books, 1993.

Newsletter: *The Continental Report*, 5128 Schultz Bridge Rd, Zionsville, PA 18092.

Collectors' Clubs: Hammered Aluminum Collectors Assoc, PO Box 1346, Weatherford, TX 76086; Wendell August Collectors Guild, PO Box 107, Grove City, PA 16127.

Ashtray, Everlast, berry sprig **$20.00**
Basket, harvest, flared sides, scalloped handle, 12" **15.00**
Basket, Rodney Kent **35.00**
Bowl, Continental Silverlook, chrysanthemum pattern,
   11 1/4" **15.00**
Bracelet, Wendell August, cuff, pine motif **55.00**
Butler's Tray, with stand, Everlast **110.00**
Candy Dish, unmkd, 3 sections, fruit, thick glass, alu-
   minum cov, pear knob **30.00**
Casserole, Continental **65.00**
Cheese, cov **25.00**
Dish, ftd, Cellini, ball feet, 9" d **5.00**
Dish, oval, Wendell August, basket of apples, 5 x 7" **2.50**
Ice Bucket, Continental, mum, #705 . . . . **85.00**
Ice Bucket, Everlast, bali bamboo **6.00**
Ice Bucket, cov, Lehman, double twisted handles,
   11 1/2" h **15.00**

Casserole, cov, Everlast, rose and forget–me–not, 8¹/₂", $45.00.

Magazine Rack, Arthur Armour, dogwood	5.00
Patio Cart, Everlast	600.00
Pendant, Everlast, flower motif	35.00
Pitcher, Buenilu, ovoid, twisted handle	30.00
Punch Ladle, unmkd, plain handle	45.00
Server, cov, Everlast, #5010, stamped flowers, fluted flange, removable divider, handles, 11"	18.00
Silent Butler, Everlast, scalloped, oval, rose motif	22.00
Silent Butler, Rodney Kent, flower/ribbon handle	45.00
Smoking Stand, Wendell August, pine motif	95.00
Tray, Cellini, curled handles, tile center, 15³/₄"	10.00
Tray, Everlast, Daisy, bar style, tab handles	35.00
Tray, National Silver Co, bird on flowering limb, 11 x 16"	25.00
Tray, Rodney Kent, #425, tulip, 14 x 20"	35.00
Tray, Wendell August, dogwood, #705, 6 x 11³/₄"	2.50

AMERICAN BISQUE

The American Bisque Company, founded in Williamstown, West Virginia in 1919, was originally established for the manufacture of china head dolls. The company soon began producing novelties such as cookie jars, ashtrays, serving dishes, and ceramic giftware.

B. E. Allen, founder of the Sterling China Company, invested heavily in the company and eventually purchased the remaining stock. In 1982 the company operated briefly under the name American China Company. The plant ceased operations in 1983.

American Bisque items have various markings. The trademark "Sequoia Ware" is often found on items sold in gift shops. The Berkeley trademark was used on pieces sold through chain stores. The most common mark found consists of three stacked baby blocks with the letters A, B, and C.

References: Susan and Al Bagdade, *Warman's American Pottery and Porcelain,* Wallace–Homestead, Krause Publications, 1994; Mary Jane Giacomini, *American Bisque: A Collector's Guide With Prices,* Schiffer Publishing, 1994; Lois Lehner, *Lehner's Encyclopedia of U.S. Marks on Pottery, Porcelain & Clay,* Collector Books, 1988.

Bank, Little Audrey	$550.00
Bank, Popeye	400.00
Cereal Bowl, Ballerina Mist	7.50
Cookie Jar, baby elephant	195.00

Cookie Jar, bear with cookie	75.00
Cookie Jar, cat in basket	65.00
Cookie Jar, churn boy	200.00
Cookie Jar, coffeepot, red flowers, bail handle	35.00
Cookie Jar, cookie barrel, brown, mkd "USA"	25.00
Cookie Jar, cowboy boots	115.00
Cookie Jar, granny	135.00
Cookie Jar, kitten and beehive	45.00
Cookie Jar, lady pig	125.00
Cookie Jar, milk can, bell in lid, "After School Snacks"	40.00
Cookie Jar, pig wearing straw hat	55.00
Cookie Jar, potbelly stove, black	35.00
Cookie Jar, rooster	75.00
Cookie Jar, rabbit with hat	125.00
Cookie Jar, sailor elephant	75.00
Cookie Jar, seated horse	165.00
Dinner Plate, Ballerina Mist	7.00
Lamp, Billy the Kid	200.00
Luncheon Plate, Ballerina Mist	5.00
Planter, duck wearing flowered hat, gold	25.00
Planter, wailing kitten	25.00
Planter, parrot, maroon and green	18.00
Planter, rooster	20.00
Salt and Pepper Shakers, pr, butter churns	75.00

ANCHOR HOCKING

The Hocking Glass Company was founded in Lancaster, Ohio in 1905. Although the company originally produced handmade items, by the 1920s the firm was manufacturing a wide variety of wares including chimneys and lantern globes, tableware, tumblers, and novelties. Hocking introduced its first line of pressed glass dinnerware in 1928. Molded etched tableware was released shortly thereafter.

Following the acquisition of several glass houses in the 1920s, Hocking began producing new glass containers. In 1937 Hocking merged with the Anchor Cap and Closure Corporation, resulting in a name change in 1939 to Anchor Hocking Glass Corporation. In 1969 the company became Anchor Hocking Corporation.

References: Gene Florence, *Collectible Glassware From the 40s, 50s, 60s, Fourth Edition,* Collector Books, 1998; Gene Florence, *The Collector's Encyclopedia of Depression Glass, Thirteenth Edition,* Collector Books, 1998; Hazel Marie Weatherman, *Colored Glassware of the Depression Era, Book 2,* published by author, 1974, reprint available.

Note: See Depression Glass and Fire–King for additional listings.

Batter Bowl, Mayfair blue, ribbed	$125.00
Butter Dish, cov, Block, 3 x 5"	50.00
Canister, green transparent, metal lid, 6" h	85.00
Cookie Jar, green transparent, ribbed	50.00
Cup, green transparent, ribbed	5.00
Ice Bucket, clear, tab handles, black, yellow, and red rings	18.00
Juice Tumbler, pink transparent, ribbed	15.00
Measuring Cup, clambroth, 2 cup	135.00
Mixing Bowl, vitrock, red dec, 10¹/₂" d	25.00
Reamer, green transparent, ribbed	20.00
Refrigerator Dish, cov, rect, green transparent, ribbed	25.00
Salt and Pepper Shakers, pr, fired–on yellow, black lettering	25.00
Syrup, cov, green, metal top	35.00
Vase, ribbed, milk glass	8.00

ANIMAL COLLECTIBLES

The hobby of collecting objects depicting one's favorite animal has thrived for years. The more common species have enjoyed long lives of popularity. Cats, dogs, cows, horses, and pigs are examples of animals whose collectibility is well established. Their markets are so stable, in fact, that they merit separate listings of their own.

The desirability of other animals changes with the times. Many remain fashionable for only a limited period of time, or their popularity cycles, often due to marketing crazes linked to advertising.

References: Diana Callow et al., *The Charlton Price Guide to Beswick Animals, Second Edition,* Charlton Press, 1994; Jean Dale, *The Charlton Standard Catalogue of Royal Doulton Animals, Second Edition,* Charlton Press, 1997; Jean Dale, *The Charlton Standard Catalogue of Royal Doulton Beswick Storybook Figurines, Third Edition,* Charlton Press, 1996; Lee Garmon and Dick Spencer, *Glass Animals of the Depression Era,* Collector Books, 1993, out of print; Everett Grist, *Covered Animal Dishes,* Collector Books, 1988, 1993 value update; Herbert N. Schiffer, *Collectible Rabbits,* Schiffer Publishing, 1990; Mike Schneider, *Grindley Pottery: A Menagerie,* Schiffer Publishing, 1996.

Newsletters: *The Glass Animal Bulletin,* PO Box 143, North Liberty, IA 52317; *Jumbo Jargon,* 1002 West 25th St, Erie, PA 16502.

Collectors' Clubs: The Frog Pond, PO Box 193, Beech Grove, IN 46107; The National Elephant Collector's Society, 380 Medford St, Somerville, MA 02145.

Note: See Breyer Horses, Cat Collectibles, Cow Collectibles, Dog Collectibles, Horse Collectibles, and Pig Collectibles for additional listings.

Alligator, toy, windup, native on back, Chein **$300.00**
Bear, bank, celluloid, nightlight and bank. **40.00**
Bird, book, *Audubon Western Bird Guide, Land Water & Game Birds,* Richard H Pough, 1957, 316 pp **15.00**
Bird, pinback button, "Audubon Society," multicolored, bluebird illus, "Indianapolis News" in black lettering, c1920s **15.00**

Chick, chocolate mold, tin, clamp style, hatching from egg, #REI26112, 3" h **20.00**
Deer, Doe, and Fawns, print, litho, Gary Lucy, 1984, 22½ x 17". **85.00**
Duck, cov animal dish, matte purple slag, 4½" **75.00**
Duck, toy, windup, litho tin, Chein **50.00**
Elephant, bank, glass, Lucky Jumbo **100.00**
Elephant, powder jar, figural, transparent green glass, trunk down **125.00**
Elephant, rocking blotter, black **40.00**
Elephant, toy, Flying Elephant, windup, litho tin, gyro attached to trunk, orig box, Yone, 1950s, 6" l **100.00**
Fox, poster, rabid fox in woods, "The Fox Can Transmit Rabies," 1946, 14 x 22". **110.00**
Frog, cookie jar, figural, mkd "2645 USA" **8.00**
Frog, movie poster, *Frogs,* Ray Milland, Sam Elliot, American International, 1972. . . . . **30.00**
Goose, toy, Pleasure Goose, friction, litho tin, beak opens and closes, advances with flapping wings, clicking sounds, orig box, Daito, 1950s, 6" h **130.00**
Hen, candy container, composition, white, sitting on box, 2 colored eggs, wood base, German, 3½" **110.00**
Monkey, toy, Monkey–Dean, dressed as professor, glasses, cap, and cane, windup, plush body, celluloid face, KSK, orig box, 6" h **115.00**
Owl, book, *An Owl Came to Stay,* Clair Rome, Crown Pub, NY, 1980 . . . . **5.00**
Owl, pitcher, cov, china, Edwin M Knowles China Co, 9½" h **40.00**
Owl, salt and pepper shakers, pr, Shawnee. **20.00**
Owl, vase, Knifewood, Weller, 8 ¼" h **150.00**
Panda, ashtray, figural Panda and bamboo across center, China, 4½" h. **15.00**
Parrot, spinner top, metal, diecut, yellow, red, and green, Poll Parrot Shoes adv, c1940s. **30.00**
Polar Bear, print, Midday Moonlight, Fred Machetanz, 1981, 23 x 27" **400.00**
Rabbit, candy container, glass, seated, eating carrot **30.00**
Rabbit, toy, wearing tuxedo and bowtie, windup, litho tin, Chein, 1930, 5" l **140.00**
Rhinoceros, poster, "Facing Troubles Kills Them," purple, brown, and orange, W F Elmes, Mathes Co, Chicago, 1929, 36 x 44" **110.00**
Rooster, chocolate mold, tin, clamp style, stamped "Jaburg 20," 5¾" h **40.00**
Skunk, ashtray, ceramic, figural skunk with fur tail sitting inside bowl shaped tray, "For Little Butts and Big Stinkers" on rim, 4½" h **10.00**
Snake, toy, Jolly Wiggling Snake, windup, litho tin, metal tongue, body wiggles, head turns, orig box, Toplay, Ltd, 7½" l **170.00**
Turkey, candy container, plaster, German, 4" h **30.00**

Horse, ashtray, Art Deco styling, glass, black horse, pink ashtray, $40.00.

ANIMATION ART

To understand animation art, one must understand its terminology. The vocabulary involving animation cels is very specific. The difference between a master, key production, printed or publication, production, and studio background can mean thousands of dollars in value.

A "cel" is an animation drawing on celluloid. One second of film requires over twenty animation cels. Multiply the length of a cartoon in minutes times sixty times twenty–four in order to approximate the number of cels used in a single cartoon strip. The vast quantities of individual cels produced are mind–boggling. While Walt Disney animation cels are indisputably the most sought after, the real bargains in the field exist elsewhere. Avoid limited edition serigraphs. A serigraph is a color print made by the silk screen process. Although it appears to be an animation cel, it is not.

References: Jeff Lotman, *Animation Art: The Early Years, 1911–1954*, Schiffer Publishing, 1995; Jeff Lotman, *Animation Art: The Later Years, 1954–1993*, Schiffer Publishing, 1996.

Periodicals: *Animation Magazine*, 30101 Agoura Ct, Ste 110, Agoura Hills, CA 91301; *In Toon*, PO Box 487, White Plains, NY 10603; *Storyboard Magazine*, 80 Main St, Nashua, NH 03060.

Collectors' Club: Animation Art Guild, Ltd, 330 W 45th St, Ste 9D, New York, NY 10036.

Drawing, graphite, ink, and marker on MGM animation paper, MGM Studio/Chuck Jones Productions, *How the Grinch Stole Christmas*, 1966, sketch of Grinch with horror stricken expression, signed by Chuck Jones in lower right, image size: 4"; sight: 5½ x 6¼". . . **$1,100.00**
Drawing, graphite and colored pencil on paper, Walt Disney Studio, *Peter Pan*, 1953, full figure Tinker Bell, image size: 7"; sight: 8½ x 13" **1,700.00**
Drawing, on graphite paper, Walt Disney, *Mickey Mouse*, Mickey's head, signed by Walt Disney on back of "Irish Traffic Embarkation Card," 6 x 4" **8,000.00**
Drawing, Walt Disney Studio, Bongo, Clara, and W C Fields, *Mother Goose Goes Hollywood*, 1938, 2 drawings of Bongo and Lulubelle nose–to–nose, 2 drawings of Clara Cluck, and 1 drawing of W C Fields as Humpty Dumpty, first 2 blue pencil and paper, second 2 graphite and colored pencil on paper, fifth one graphite on paper, full margins **400.00**
Gouache on Celluloid, applied to print ground, Famous Studios, *Puss N' Boos*, 1954, kittens happily jump out of bag from which Casper has freed them, image size: Casper 5", kittens 2" each; sight: 10 x 12" **700.00**
Gouache on Celluloid, applied to print ground, Warner Bros, *Bugs Bunny*, smiling Bugs leaning forward on his hands, signed by Chuck Jones, image size: 5"; sight: 10¾ x 15" **1,500.00**
Gouache on Celluloid, applied to print ground, Warner Bros, *Foghorn Leghorn*, c1960s, full figure image of rooster in profile, image size: 8"; sight: 9¼ x 14½". **1,200.00**
Gouache on Celluloid, applied to watercolor ground, Fleischer Studios, *Gulliver's Travels*, 1939, 2 Lilliputians attempting to hoist Gulliver's leg up to tie him up, sight: 8½ x 11¼". **1,000.00**
Gouache on Celluloid, applied to watercolor ground, Walt Disney Studio, *Robin Hood*, 1973, Robin Hood battles crocodile, image size: Robin 4", crocodile 7"; sight: 10½ x 14½" **2,800.00**
Gouache on Celluloid, Hanna Barbera Studios, *The Flintstones and Huckleberry Hound*, c1960, 2 cels, multi–level setup of Barney reading to Fred, Barney's head, body and arm on separate levels, Fred's eyes on separate level from rest of him, with cel of Huckleberry Hound dressed like caveman, carrying club over his shoulder, image size: Barney and Fred 3" each, Huck 5"; sight: 7½ x 9½" **800.00**

Gouache on celluloid applied to gouache production background, Warner Bros. Studio, Bugs Bunny, "Sleepytime Pal" and "April – 1946" written on cel at left, image size: 6"; 10 x 11½", $2,070.00. Photo courtesy Sotheby's.

Gouache on Celluloid, Walt Disney Studio, *The Big Bad Wolf*, 1934, Little Red Riding Hood carrying basket and pointing to the left, image size: 5½" **1,000.00**
Gouache on Celluloid, Walt Disney Studio, *Lady and The Tramp*, 1955, full figure Tramp image looking happily to right, image size: 8 x 4½" **1,500.00**
Gouache on Celluloid, Walt Disney Studio, *One Hundred and One Dalmations*, 1961, Lucky and Patch disguised as Labrador Retrievers, applied to printed Disneyland background, gold Disneyland label on back, image size: each puppy 4"; sight: 8 x 10". **1,600.00**
Gouache on Paper, Walt Disney Studio, *Ben and Me*, 1953, Ben Franklin flying kit with key attached, sight: 6 x 8" **460.00**

APPLIANCES

The turn of the century saw the popularity of electric kitchen appliances increase to the point where most metropolitan households sported at least one of these modern conveniences. By the 1920s, innovations and improvements were occurring at a rapid pace. The variations designed for small appliances were limitless.

Some "firsts" in electrical appliances include:

1882   Patent for electric iron (H. W. Seeley [Hotpoint])
1903   Detachable cord (G. E. Iron)
1905   Toaster (Westinghouse Toaster Stove)
1909   Travel iron (G. E.)
1911   Electric frying pan (Westinghouse)
1912   Electric waffle iron (Westinghouse)
1917   Table Stove (Armstrong)
1918   Toaster/Percolator (Armstrong "Perc–O–Toaster")
1920   Heat indicator on waffle iron (Armstrong)
1920   Flip–flop toasters (all manufacturers)
1920   Mixer on permanent base (Hobart Kitchen Aid)
1920   Electric egg cooker (Hankscraft)

1923   Portable mixer (Air–O–Mix "Whip–All")
1924   Automatic iron (Westinghouse)
1924   Home malt mixer (Hamilton Beach #1)
1926   Automatic pop–up toaster (Toastmaster #1h–A–A)
1926   Steam iron (Eldec)
1937   Home coffee mill (Hobart Kitchen Aid)
1937   Automatic coffee maker (Farberware "Coffee Robot")
1937   Conveyance device toaster ("Toast–O–Lator")

References: E. Townsend Artman, *Toasters: 1909–1960: A Look at the Ingenuity and Design of Toast Makers*, Schiffer Publishing, 1996; Linda Campbell Franklin, *300 Years of Kitchen Collectibles, Fourth Edition*, Krause Publications, 1997; Michael J. Goldberg, *Groovy Kitchen Designs For Collectors: 1935–1965*, Schiffer Publishing, 1996; Helen Greguire, *Collector's Guide to Toasters & Accessories*, Collector Books, 1997; Diane Stoneback, *Kitchen Collectibles: The Essential Buyer's Guide*, Wallace–Homestead, Krause Publications, 1994; *Toasters and Small Kitchen Appliances: A Price Guide*, L–W Book Sales, 1995.

Newsletter: *A Toast to You*, PO Box 529, Temecula, CA 92593.

Collectors' Clubs: Electric Breakfast Club, PO Box 306, White Mills, PA 18473; Old Appliance Club, PO Box 65, Ventura, CA 93002.

Note: For additional listings see Fans, Electric and Porcelier Porcelain.

Blender, Kenmore, Model 116–82421, 2 speed, 1951 . . . . . . **$55.00**
Bottle Warmer, Sunbeam, Model B–2, aluminum, black
   Bakelite, rocketship shape, 1956 . . . . **75.00**
Broiler, Royal Master Appliance, Model 1–A, cast ham-
   mered aluminum, well–and–tree platter base, black
   Bakelite handles, AC/DC, 1930s, 20" l **25.00**
Chafing Dish, Manning–Bowman, 4 part, chrome, Art
   Deco style, heating base with high/low plug, hot
   water pot, int cooking pan, and lid, black Bakelite
   handles, 1930s **45.00**
Coffee Maker, Extractolator, chromium plated finish, jet
   black trim, 1934 . . . . **45.00**
Coffee Maker, Farberware, Model 10, chrome, glass,
   painted wood handles, 425 watts, 115 volts,
   1930s **75.00**
Coffee Maker, Silex, Model LE–82, chrome, glass, black
   Bakelite handles, 525 watts, 1935 . . . . **55.00**
Coffee Mill, Kitchen Aid, Hobart Manu Co, Model A–9,
   pot metal base, 115 volts, 1.25 amps, 1937 . . . . **70.00**
Coffee Urn, Universal, #440, 9 cup, nickel plated
   gold lined sugar, creamer, and tray, 1928 . . . . **125.00**
Drink Mixer, Hamilton Beach, white enamel finish, nick-
   el silver cup, AC/DC, 1928 . . . . **90.00**
Egg Cooker, Sunbeam, Model E, handleless, AC, orig
   cardboard insert and tag, 1943, 6½" h **25.00**
Hot Plate, Liberty, #701, steel frame, nickel plated,
   nichrome wire heating elements, 7" d, 4" h **20.00**
Hot Plate, Universal, #986, nickel plated, ebonized
   handle, 1928, 6" d. **20.00**
Iron, Adjust–O–Matic, Westinghouse, nickel body, black
   wood handle, detachable cord **12.00**
Malt Mixer, Gilbert, green painted, crinkle finish over
   cast iron, AC/DC, 1930s **70.00**

Toaster, Protos, chrome plated, 7¼" w, 3" d, 6⅞" h, $35.00.

Mixer, Handywhip, Chicago Electric Mfg Co, 1934,
   9½" h **40.00**
Mixer, Kitchen Aid, Hobart, Model 3–C, with glass bowl,
   1.2 amps, 1950s **60.00**
Percolator, Hotpoint, 9 cup, Grecian panel design, com-
   plete with matching sugar, creamer, and tray, 1930 . . . . . . **125.00**
Popcorn Popper, Kwikway, steel construction, aluminum
   baked enamel finish, hinged lid with holes, 1938 . . . . **30.00**
Popcorn Popper, Knapp Monarch, aluminum, brown
   Bakelite handles **30.00**
Portable Stove, White Cross, black enamel finish,
   nichrome elements, nickel trim, 110 volt, 1930 . . . . **35.00**
Sandwich Grill, Patrician, Bersted Manu Co, Model 326,
   chrome, black painted metal, black Bakelite handles,
   1938. . . . . **50.00**
Toaster, Heat Master, 2 slice, chrome body, black
   Bakelite handle and feet, 1923–35 . . . . **30.00**
Toaster, Fostoria, 4 slice, chrome plated, walnut Bakelite
   handles, nichrome heating element, crumb tray, 1940 . . . . . **50.00**
Toaster, Sunbeam, Model T–1–C, 2 slice, chrome, black
   Bakelite handles and base, 1938 . . . . **45.00**
Toaster, Universal, Model EA–2815, 2 slice, chrome,
   black Bakelite handles, 1944 . . . . **25.00**
Waffle Iron, Dominion, Modern–Mode Sandwich
   Queen, Model 510, chrome, Bakelite handles, 1931 . . . . . . **25.00**
Waffle Iron, Estate Stove Co, #75, porcelain enameled,
   Bakelite switch on cord, wooden handles, 9" d
   base, 6½" h. **50.00**
Waffle Iron, Hotpoint, nickel plated pedestal base, alu-
   minum plates, 1926. . . . . **30.00**

ART POTTERY

Art pottery production was at an all–time high during the late 19th and early 20th centuries. At this time over one hundred companies and artisans were producing individually designed and often decorated pottery which served both utilitarian and aesthetic purposes. Artists often moved from company to company, some forming their own firms.

Condition, quality of design, beauty in glazes, and maker are the keys in buying art pottery. This category covers companies not found elsewhere in the guide.

References: Susan and Al Bagdade, *Warman's American Pottery and Porcelain*, Wallace–Homestead, Krause Publications, 1994; Paul Evans, *Art Pottery of the United States, Second Edition*, Feingold & Lewis Publishing, 1987; David Edwin Gifford, *The Collector's Encyclopedia of Niloak: A Reference and Value Guide*, Collector Books, 1993, out of print; Jeffrey, Sherrie and Barry Hershone, *The Peters and Reed and Zane Pottery Experience*, published by authors, 1992; Ralph and Terry Kovel, *Kovels' American Art Pottery: Collector's Guide to Makers, Marks and Factory Histories*, Crown Publishers, 1993; Jessie Poesch, *Newcomb Pottery: An Enterprise for Southern Women, 1895–1940*, Schiffer Publishing, 1984, out of print; Dick Sigafoose, *American Art Pottery: A Collection of Pottery, Tiles and Memorabilia, 1800–1950*, Collector Books, 1997.

Newsletter: *Pottery Lovers Newsletter*, 4969 Hudson Dr, Stow, OH 44224.

Collectors' Club: American Art Pottery Assoc, PO Box 834, Westport, MA 02790-0697.

Additional Listings: See California Faience, Cowan, Fulper, Potteries: Regional, Rookwood, Roseville, Van Briggle, and Weller.

Brouwer, vase, bottle shaped, flaring cylindrical neck, orange, yellow, and metallic glaze, incised "whalebone/M/Brouwer," 7 x 3½" **$1,200.00**

Buffalo Pottery, candlesticks, electric, Deldare Ware, polychrome town scenes, brown ground, black ink mark "1925," 9¼ x 4¾" **475.00**

Chicago Crucible, vase, four lobed design, closed–in top, frothy matte green glaze, die stamped, 5 x 3½" **300.00**

Chicago Crucible, vase, 2 handled, mottled matte brown and green glaze, die stamped mark, 11 x 5" **475.00**

Clewell, centerbowl, bronze, incised "C.W. CLEWELL/506–216/BKEX–SBEX," 3½ x 10½" **450.00**

Clewell, vase, classical shaped, copper–clad, brown and verdigris patina, incised "Clewell/357–25," 7½ x 4" **300.00**

Clewell, vessel, copper–clad, emb water lilies and lily pads, water textured ground, incised "Clewell," 8 x 8" **2,400.00**

Dedham, bowl, Rabbit pattern, ink stamped, 4¾ x 8" **325.00**

Dedham, plate, center poppy dec surrounded by poppy pods, ink and die stamp, 8½" d **350.00**

Dedham, plate, Horse Chestnut, stamp mark, 9" d **75.00**

Dedham, vase, experimental, by Hugh Robertson, Sang–De–Boeuf glaze, incised "Dedham Pottery/HCR," 5 x 3½" **750.00**

Gregory, Weylande, charger, emb mermaid, fish, and waves design, blue and green crackled glaze, inscribed on bottom "To Dr. Langrock/With Our Deep Appreciation/Waylande Gregory," c1935, 14" d **2,700.00**

Jugtown, candlesticks, pr, corseted, gray speckled semi–gloss glaze, circular mark, 11½ x 4¾" **750.00**

Jugtown, urn, 2 handles, olive green and ochre glaze over bisque brown body, circular mark, 9½ x 7½" **800.00**

Jugtown, vessel, turquoise and red Chinese blue glaze, chip to base, imp mark, 5½ x 6½" **850.00**

Marblehead, tile, tree in forest design, brown and umber, moss green matte ground, mounted, imp ship mark, 6 x 6" **1,300.00**

Marblehead, vase, by Hannah Tutt, cylindrical, incised geometric design, dark green matte on lighter green matte ground, ship mark incised cipher "MT," 8¾ x 4" . . . **850.00**

Marblehead, vase, ovoid, gray matte glaze ext, light blue matte glaze int, ship mark, 9 x 6½" **700.00**

Marblehead, vessel, squat, 2 handles, moss green matte glaze, ship mark, 2¾ x 3¾" **450.00**

Marblehead, wall pocket, semi–circular rim, blue matte glaze, ship mark, 5¾ x 6¾" **400.00**

Moorcroft, creamer and sugar, Pomegranate pattern, ink script mark, sugar 4½ x 4½", 1913–25. . . . . **1,100.00**

Moorcroft, vase, fruit and leaves dec, shaded blue to green ground, ink script mark, 1928–34, 8 x 6". **475.00**

Moorcroft, vase, Pomegranate patten, squeezebag dec, orange and purple fruit on blue ground, some crazing, die stamped "MOORCROFT/MADE IN ENGLAND," ink signature, 9¾ x 6" **850.00**

Newcomb College, bowl, squat, carved paperwhites with swirling green leaves, medium to dark blue ground, imp "NC/AFS/PX41/22," 3 x 5" **850.00**

Newcomb College, jar, temple shape, by Anna Francis Simpson, lily–of–the–valley dec, "NC/SG67/242/AFS" paper label, 1930, 6 x 6" **3,250.00**

Newcomb College, vase, by Leona Nicholson, amber gloss over volcanic matte green glaze, stamped "NC/H," 6" h **500.00**

Newcomb College, vase, by Anna Simpson, carved dark blue and green pine trees and full moon, blue and green ground, imp "NC/JM/AFS/OP391/150," 1925, 11 x 5" **4,000.00**

Newcomb College, vase, carved design, tapering top, stylized leaves dec, mkd "NC/PC93," artist sgd, 8½ x 3½" **1,800.00**

Newcomb College, vessel, squat, by Henrietta Bailey, moon peering through live oaks dec, Spanish moss glaze, short hairline to inside rim, imp "NC/HB/UN26/F," 1933, 3¾ x 5½". **2,600.00**

Niloak, vase, Mission ware, scroddled brown, rust, white, and blue bisque–fired clay, imp "Niloak," 10 x 4¾" **450.00**

North Dakota School of Mines, trivet, circular, dec by Huckfield, dark blue incised flowers, light blue ground, ink stamped, incised "Huck/2773," 5½" d **175.00**

North Dakota School of Mines, vase, by D Obrien, ovoid, molded stylized leaves design, matte brown glaze, circular ink mark "D. Obrien," 8½ x 4¾" **500.00**

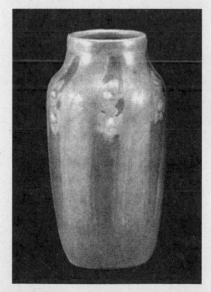

Newcomb College, vase, Sadie Irvine, modeled blue and yellow flowers, green leaves, dark blue ground, imp "NC/SI/19/PL44/JM," repair to rim, 1925, 6½ x 3¼", $1,000.00. Photo courtesy David Rago Auctions.

Overbeck, grotesque figural, large footed strutting rooster, red, white, and brown, incised "OBK," 3¼ x 1¾" **250.00**

Overbeck, vase, stylized white crows, matte blue–gray ground, incised "OBK/E/H," 6 x 6" **3,600.00**

Paul Revere, cup and saucer, demitasse, painted band of bright green trees against blue sky, circular ink stamp, 1928, 5" d saucer **350.00**

Paul Revere, plate, dec by E Brown, center cuerda seca dec, landscape scene, green, blues, and yellow, stamp mark "5–26/E.B/J.M.D.," 1926, 10" d **950.00**

Paul Revere, vase, blue and brown drip glaze, gun–metal brown ground, paper label, 10½ x 5½" **500.00**

Pewabic, bowl, ftd, flared, mottled green and purple glaze, paper label, 2¾ x 5" **300.00**

Pewabic, bud vase, bottle shaped, purple, indigo and celadon iridescent mirrored glaze, circular stamp, 4½ x 4" **1,100.00**

Pewabic, cabinet vase, bottle shaped, turquoise, silver, and red mirrored mottled glaze, circular stamp, 4½ x 2¾" **800.00**

Pewabic, floor vase, ovoid, lustered copper glaze, unmkd, 13 x 7½" **2,000.00**

Pewabic, vase, bottle shaped, iridescent taupe and umber glaze drip over black ground, paper label, 7½ x 4½" **1,800.00**

Pewabic, vase, flat shoulder, mirrored iridescent purple glaze dripping over gold base, circular stamp 10½ x 6½" **2,300.00**

Pewabic, vessel, flat shoulder, celadon and lavender iridescent glaze, paper label, 6¾ x 5½" **1,800.00**

Pewabic, vessel, ridged design, corseted shoulder, mirrored iridescent lavender glaze, hairline to rim, circular stamp, 9½ x 4¾" **600.00**

Pisgah Forest, vase, baluster, metallic brown and cream flowing crystalline glaze, emb mark, 6 x 3¾" **100.00**

Pisgah Forest, vase, bulbous, ivory to amber glaze, blue–gray crystals, raised mark, 1940, 5 x 4½" **450.00**

Saturday Evening Girls, inkwell, rect, green, brown, and blue banded landscape dec, teal blue ground, orig liner and pristine, orig paper label, 2 ¾ x 4" **1,700.00**

Saturday Evening Girls, pitcher, bulbous, cuerda seca dec, band of trees against blue sky, matte green ground, mkd "S.E.G.," 5 x 3½" **500.00**

Saturday Evening Girls, plate, center cuerda seca dec, house in landscape, dark and light blue ground, 1922, 6½" d **500.00**

Saturday Evening Girls, vase, closed–in rim, green and blue banded landscape dec, semi–gloss ground, mkd "S.E.G.L7–22," 8½ x 7" **1,700.00**

Teco, vase, bulbous, mottled light green matte glaze, die stamped, 3 x 3" **200.00**

Teco, vase, classical shaped, buttressed base, matte green glaze, imp "Teco," 9¾ x 5" **1,000.00**

Teco, vase, ovoid, green matte glaze, die stamped "Teco," 4½" h **250.00**

Teco, vessel, tapered, matte green glaze, die stamped "TECO/250," 9½ x 10" **1,300.00**

Wheatley, vase, bulbous, leathery matte green glaze, unmkd, 6 x 6½" **500.00**

Wheatley, vase, tapered, molded peacock, leaves, and heraldic shields design, matte green glaze, die stamped "802/WP," 10 x 8" **1,100.00**

Wheatley, wall pocket, molded leaves and buds dec, green matte glaze, unmkd, 8 x 5¼ x 5½" **650.00**

ASHTRAYS

Ashtrays can be found made from every material and in any form imaginable. A popular subcategory with collectors is advertising ashtrays. Others include figural ashtrays or those produced by a particular manufacturer. It is still possible to amass an extensive collection on a limited budget. As more people quit smoking, look for ashtrays to steadily rise in price.

Reference: Nancy Wanvig, *Collector's Guide to Ashtrays: Identification & Values,* Collector Books, 1997.

Advertising, HER Store, metal, 2 Scottie dogs holding 1939 calendar, 4¼" w **$20.00**

Advertising, Jockey Underwear, center jockey, "100 Years 1976," 8¾" d **12.00**

Advertising, Pizza Hut, glass, center logo, 5" d **6.00**

Advertising, Queen City Dog Training Club, Cincinnati, red dog jumping over fence center, white ground, 5¾" d **5.00**

Advertising, S & H Green Stamps, glass, green lettering in center, 6" l **8.00**

Advertising, UPS, glass, pictures of trucks on rim, "Seventy Years of Progress, 1907–1977," 7½" d **12.00**

Angel, playing stringed instrument, Art Nouveau, brass coating, frogs in relief, 9" l **55.00**

Beer Stein, yellow, drinking verse, 7¾" l **6.00**

Buffalo, metal, gold, painted Buffalo picture center, 3⅜" sq **7.00**

Butterfly, copper, enamel dec, Holland, 3¼" d **30.00**

Clown, Art Deco, playing banjo, 2 rests, 3⅝" l **12.00**

Elephant, bronze, white tusk, sand casting, 6¼" l **55.00**

Fish, figural, chrome plated, Chase, 6¼" l **20.00**

Frog, cloisonné dec, open mouth, brass cells, 3½" h **75.00**

Horseshoe, sterling silver, 2⅞" l **15.00**

Leaf, figural, metal, blue enamel int, 5 rests, 4⅛" l **10.00**

Man Fishing, white ground, shamrock dec on rim, Carringaline Pottery, 5⅜" d **8.00**

Advertising, Fisk Tires, ceramic, different adv each side, $100.00.
Photo courtesy Collectors Auction Services.

Mexican Waterway, brass, emb, Xochimilco, 1976,
6½" d **15.00**
Nude, brass, Art Deco, imp sea animals at side, 2 rests,
France, 7⅜" l **50.00**
Racing Helmet, figural, Penske Racing, 1984 Indy 500
Winner, Mears–Unser, 2 rests, 4⅜" h **30.00**
Sailboat, glass tray, chrome sail, 6⅛" h **15.00**

AUTO & DRAG RACING

The earliest automobile racing occurred in Europe at the end of the 19th century. By 1910, the sport was popular in America as well. The Indianapolis 500, first held in 1911, has been run every year except for a brief interruption caused by World War II. Collectors search for both Formula 1 and NASCAR items, with pre–1945 materials the most desirable.

References: Mark Allen Baker, *Auto Racing: Memorabilia and Price Guide*, Krause Publications, 1996; James Beckett and Eddie Kelley (eds.), *Beckett Racing Price Guide and Alphabetical Checklist, Number 2*, Beckett Publications, 1997; David Fetherston, *Hot Rod Memorabilia & Collectibles*, Motorbooks International, 1996; Jack MacKenzie, *Indy 500 Buyer's Guide*, published by author, 1996.

Periodicals: *Collector's World*, PO Box 562029, Charlotte, NC 28256; *Racing Collectibles Price Guide*, PO Box 608114, Orlando, FL 32860; *TRACE Magazine*, PO Box 716, Kannapolis, NC 28082; *Tuff Stuff's RPM*, PO Box 1637, Glen Allen, VA 23060.

Newsletter: *Quarter Milestones*, 53 Milligan Ln, Johnson City, TN 37601.

Collectors' Clubs: Auto Racing Memories, PO Box 12226, St Petersburg, FL 33733; National Indy 500 Collectors Club, 10505 N Delaware St, Indianapolis, IN 46280; The National Racing Club, 615 Hwy A1A North, Ste 105, Ponte Vedra Beach, FL 32082.

REPRODUCTION ALERT

Autograph, Brett Bodine **$4.00**
Bobbing Head, Bill Elliott, 8" h **35.00**
Comic Book, Hot Rods & Racing Cars, #3, Motormag/
Charlton, Nov 1951 . . . . **45.00**
Comic Book, Hot Rod Racers, #1, Charlton Comics,
Dec 1964 . . . . **30.00**
Comic Book, Legends of Nascar, #2, Richard Petty,
©Vortex **4.00**
Game, Drag Strip, Milton Bradley, 1965 . . . . **25.00**
Game, Wide World of Sports–Auto Racing, Milton
Bradley, 1974 . . . . **15.00**
Golf Badge, 1966 Indianapolis Speedway, 500 Festival
Golf **30.00**
Handbook, *Indy Motor Speedway Brickyard 400 Inaugural Race*, full color illus, center pictures 12
well–known NASCAR drivers, Aug 6, 1994, 12 pp **5.00**
Magazine, *Racing Pictorial*, summer 1965, #1,
Langhorne crash **40.00**
Mug, "Fuel Injection Special," frosted white glass,
applied brass detailed image of "Fuel Injection Special" race car one side, black inscription "1953/ Bill
Vukovich/128.740 mph" other side, girdled by
brass luster metal bands holding wood handle, 5" h **25.00**

Checkered Flag, used at drag strip, $125.00.

Pass, California Stock Car Racing Association, 1950,
2½ x 3¼" **8.00**
Pen Holder, Indianapolis Motor Speedway, metal, gold
luster, horseshoe with center shield design depicting
racing car of 1930s, 2¼ x 2½" **70.00**
Pinback Button, Roosevelt Raceway, race car image, red,
white, and blue, 1930s **35.00**
Pitt Pass Pin, 1951 Indianapolis Speedway, metal, gold
luster, "Borg–WWarner Trophy/The Indianapolis 500
Mile Race," 1951 date above engraved "3518" serial
number, back inscription "Indianapolis Motor
Speedway Corp. 500 Mile Race/Indianapolis" **90.00**
Poster, Auto Races–Bridgewater Grange, red roadster
pursued by black car in background, yellow ground,
c1933, 29 x 42" **170.00**
Program, Indianapolis 500, May 1947 . . . . **95.00**
Shot Glass, Indianapolis Motor Speedway, "Indy 500" on
upper rim, checkered flags, racing cars, winged wheel
symbol illus, c1970s **10.00**
Thermometer, Bobby Labonete, T–Series Racing Plaque **20.00**
Ticket Stub, Daytona 500, 1982 . . . . **4.00**
Ticket Stub, Indy 500, 1936 . . . . **135.00**
Tie Bar, "500 Mile Race/Indianapolis," number "10" race
car image,1950s, 3" w **50.00**
Yearbook, Indianapolis 500, J Parsons cov, 1950 . . . . **50.00**

AUTOGRAPHS

Early autograph collectors focused on signature only, often discarding the document from which it was cut. Today's collectors know that the context of the letter or document can significantly increase the autograph's value.

Standard abbreviations denoting type and size include:

ADS	Autograph Document Signed
ALS	Autograph Letter Signed
AP	Album Page Signed
AQS	Autograph Quotation Signed
CS	Card Signed
DS	Document Signed
FDC	First Day Cover
LS	Letter Signed
PS	Photograph Signed
TLS	Typed Letter Signed

References: Mark Allen Baker, *All Sport Autograph Guide*, Krause Publications, 1994; Kevin Martin, *Signautres of the Stars: A Guide for Autograph Collectors, Dealers, and Enthusiasts*, Antique Trader Books, 1998; Norman E. Martinus and Harry L. Rinker, *Warman's Paper*, Wallace–Homestead, Krause Publications, 1994; Kenneth W. Rendell, *History Comes to Life: Collecting Historical Letters and Documents*, Norman and London: University of Oklahoma Press, 1995; George Sanders, Helen Sanders, and Ralph Roberts, *The Sanders Price Guide to Autographs, 4th Edition*, Alexander Books, 1997; George Sanders, Helen Sanders and Ralph Roberts, *The Sanders Price Guide to Sports Autographs, 2nd Edition*, Alexander Books, 1997.

Periodicals: *Autograph Collector*, 510–A S Corona Mall, Corona, CA 91719; *Autograph Times*, 1125 Baseline Rd, #2-153-M, Mesa, AZ 85210; *The Collector*, PO Box 255, Hunter, NY 12442.

Newsletters: *Autograph Research*, 862 Thomas Ave, San Diego, CA 92109; *Autographs & Memorabilia*, PO Box 224, Coffeyville, KS 67337.

Collectors' Clubs: The Manuscript Society, 350 N Niagara St, Burbank, CA 91505; Universal Autograph Collectors Club, PO Box 6181, Washington, DC 20044.

REPRODUCTION ALERT: Forgeries abound. Signatures of many political figures, movie stars, and sports heroes are machine or secretary signed rather than by the individuals themselves. Photographic reproduction can also produce a signature resembling an original. Check all signatures using a good magnifying glass or microscope.

Andrews Sisters, PS, sepia, close–up, poses in uniform, with hats, each sgd full name on own image, added inscriptions and sentiment, 1946 and other information imprinted on lower white border, 10 x 8".......... **$450.00**
Astaire, Fred, and Ginger Rogers, PS, full dancing pose, black and white, 8 x 10"......................... **675.00**
Barclay, McClelland, orig black India sketch of battleship, inscribed and sgd on lower white area, early 1940s, 5 x 3"................................ **225.00**
Barysnikov, M, playbill for *Metamorphosis*, sgd on blank area on cov.................................... **50.00**

Alan Alda, script from "M*A*S*H" episode 9/3/76, "Dear Sigmund," $200.00. Photo courtesy Collectors Auction Services.

Beard, Daniel, TLS, official Boy Scouts of America stationery, names of members of executive board, national officers, etc, jamboree plans, sgd "Daniel C. Beard/National Scout commissioner/Suffern, N.Y.," 1932.. **295.00**
Bowie, David, PS, black and white, dated "'90," matted, 8 x 10".................................... **125.00**
Craig, Jenny, orig sketch of apple, carrot and grapes beneath "Best Wishes/Jenny Craig," 5 x 3"........... **95.00**
Crosby, Bing, DS, contract with Hope Enterprises, Inc, for radio show for $125.00 for use of his songs not himself in person, green ink signature on lower left, 8 x 10".................................... **450.00**
Dewey, Thomas E, Republican National Convention ticket, Philadelphia, 1948, sgd across center, 5 x 3"...... **95.00**
Eddy, Nelson, PS, sepia, portrait pose, 8 x 10"........... **175.00**
Freleng, Friz, and Henry Mancini, FDC, honoring *The Grand Piano*, black felt tip pen signatures............. **95.00**
Galloway, Marie S, ALS, plain stationery, mentions article she wrote about the Leper Colony, 6 x 9".......... **95.00**
Garland, Judy, DS, bank check, blue ballpoint pen signature, 1966................................. **850.00**
Gibb, Andy, PS, close–up, inscribed "The guys at "Al's," "Best wishes/Andy Gibb," red ink, 8 x 10"........... **250.00**
Hitchcock, Alfred, PS, black and white, profile pose, large black ink full signature across upper left area, 8 x 10", 1966, matted, 11 x 14" overall.............. **695.00**
Houdini, Harry, TLS, personal stationery, letter to Mr W Jones pertaining to being guest at Northport, phone number on lower left area, 1922, 8½ x 5½"......... **1,950.00**
Johns, Jasper, and Leroy Neiman, FDC, commemorating *Fine Arts in America*, sgd front.................... **150.00**
Johnson, R W, TLS, business stationery, red cross beneath company title, November 16, 1971................ **195.00**
Kelly, Emmett, Sr, FDC, *Circus*, penned with green ink "Delavan, WI, 1966"........................... **125.00**
Liberace, orig sketch of piano, 6 x 4".................. **95.00**
Lombardi, Vince, CS, 1959........................ **375.00**
Masaryk, Jan, ALS, personal stationery, New Year wishes, orig envelope, January 15, 1942, 7 x 9"............. **350.00**
Maxim, Hudson, CS, blue ink, "Compliments of Hudson Maxim/Sept. 19–1926," 2 x 2".................... **95.00**
Mead, Margaret, PS, formal portrait pose, sgd name and dated December 6, 1963 in black ink, 8 x 10"...... **295.00**
Menendez, Kitty, ADS, Beverly High School diploma request for Eric Galen Menendez, complete name printed and filled in twice, sgd by Kitty Menendez, dated 9–8–88, 8 x 5"........................... **450.00**
Newley, Anthony, and Cyril Ritchard, program, Playhouse Theatre, *The Roar of the Grease Paint–The Smell of the Crowd*, photo of both on cov, black and white, sgd, dated "1975," 6 x 9".................. **60.00**
Purvis, Melvin, CS, membership card for the Masonic Lodge in Hampton, SC, 1947...................... **150.00**
Pyle, Ernie, TLS, 8 paragraphs to Papa & Auntie, sgd "Ernest" on lower blank in pencil, Belfast, Ireland, July 20, 1942, 8 x 10"............................. **325.00**
Reagan, Ronald, CS, center signature on White House card..................................... **795.00**
Serling, Rod, AP, black ink signature, 3 x 2"............ **350.00**
Thomas, Dave, orig color sketch of hamburger with trimming, penned in black ink "Wendy's Old Fashioned ½ lb Single," sgd "Dave Thomas" beneath, 6½ x 4½".... **175.00**

Thomas, Norman, TLS, The Warren Report, personal stationery, 1967, 8 x 10" **275.00**

The Three Stooges, AP, "Larry, Moe, and Curly" penned in red ink, 1" sq newsphoto of Moe Howard pasted on upper right corner, "3 Stooges" with line drawn beneath penned on upper center area by Larry, matted beneath 10 x 8" black and white character photo, 15 x 19" overall **2,250.00**

Trapp, Maria, FDC, honoring The Sound of Music, 1964. . . . **125.00**

Trump, Donald, typescript, one paragraph titled "The Art Of The Deal/Dealing: A Week In the Life," signature beneath typed quotation, 8 x 10" **45.00**

Vaughn, Sarah, PS, smiling portrait pose, inscribed "To John," black and white, 9 x 10" **250.00**

Wilder, Thorton, ALS, 2 pp, personal stationery, remark actor Frank Craven made to someone in audience while performing a play in New York, sgd on verso "all my regards and very best wishes of the Season. Sincerely yours, Thonton Wilder," orig holograph envelope, Dec 9, 1949, 6 x 7" **495.00**

Wilson, Brian, ADS, bank check, filled in and sgd, matted beneath 10 x 8" black and white Beach Boys photo, 1990, 12 x 16" overall. **250.00**

Wyeth, NC, ALS, personal stationery, orig holograph envelope, 1936, 7 x 7" **1,150.00**

AUTOMOBILES

The Antique Automobile Club of America instituted a policy whereby any motor vehicle (car, bus, motorcycle, etc.) manufactured prior to 1930 be classified as "antique." The Classic Car Club of America expanded the list, focusing on luxury models made between 1925 and 1948. The Milestone Car Society developed a similar list for cars produced between 1948 and 1964.

Some states, such as Pennsylvania, have devised a dual registration system for classifying older cars—antique and classic. Depending upon their intended use, models from the 1960s and 1970s, especially convertibles and limited production models, fall into the "classic" designation.

References: Robert H. Balderson, The Official Price Guide to Collector Cars, Eighth Edition, House of Collectibles, 1996; James T. Lenzke and Ken Buttolph (eds.), 1998 Standard Guide to Cars & Prices: Prices For Collector Vehicles 1901–1990, Tenth Edition, Krause Publications, 1997.

Periodicals: Automobile Quarterly, PO Box 348, Kutztown, PA 19530; Car Collector & Car Classics, 8601 Dunwoody Pl, Ste 144, Atlanta, GA 30350; Cars & Parts, PO Box 482, Sidney, OH 45365; Hemmings Motor News, PO Box 100, Rt 9W, Bennington, VI 05201; Old Cars Price Guide, 700 E State St, Iola, WI 54990.

Collectors' Clubs: Antique Automobile Club of America, 501 W Governor Rd, PO Box 417, Hershey, PA 17033; Classic Car Club of America, 2300 E Devon Ave, Ste 126, Des Plaines, IL 60018; Milestone Car Society, PO Box 24612, Indianapolis, IN 46224; Veteran Motor Car Club of America, PO Box 360788, Strongsville, OH 44136.

Note: Prices are for cars in good condition.

BMW, 1964, Model R 27, 2500 cc **$2,000.00**
Brough, 1956, Goldstar DBD **1,500.00**

Buick, 1939, Century, club coupe, 8 cyl **5,000.00**
Buick, 1942, Roadmaster, sedan, 8 cyl **6,200.00**
Buick, 1954, Skylark, convertible, 8 cyl. **20,000.00**
Buick, 1959, LeSabre, 4 door, hardtop, 8 cyl **2,000.00**
Cadillac, 1946, 60 Special, sedan, V 8 cyl **10,000.00**
Cadillac, 1955, 75 Fleetwood, sedan, V 8 cyl **12,000.00**
Cadillac, 1975, Eldorado, convertible, V 8 cyl **10,000.00**
Chevrolet, 1939, Master 85, 2 door, sedan, 6 cyl **3,000.00**
Chevrolet, 1952, Fastback, 2 door, sedan, 6 cyl **3,000.00**
Chevrolet, 1957, pickup, ½ ton, short bed, 6 cyl **3,500.00**
Chevrolet, 1959, Nomad, 4 door, station wagon, V 8 cyl . . **3,700.00**
Chevrolet, 1964, Corvair Spyder, coupe, 6 cyl turbo **3,000.00**
Chrysler, 1949, New Yorker, sedan, V 8 cyl **3,000.00**
Chrysler, 1959, Saratoga, sedan, V 8 cyl **2,000.00**
Chrysler, 1962, Newport, hardtop, 8 cyl **1,800.00**
DeSoto, 1950, S–14 Custom, 6 passenger station wagon, 6 cyl **4,600.00**
DeSoto, 1958, Firesweep, sedan, 8 cyl **2,000.00**
Dodge, 1950, Coronet, town sedan, 6 cyl **2,750.00**
Dodge, 1963, Polara, 2 door, hardtop, V 8 cyl **1,200.00**
Dodge, 1969, Dart Swinger, hardtop, 8 cyl **2,600.00**
Dodge, 1971, van, ½ ton, 6 cyl **1,500.00**
Fiat, 1972, Model 128, sport. **1,700.00**
Ford, 1950, Custom, 2 door, sedan, V 8 cyl **2,200.00**
Ford, 1954, F–100, rack side, 6 cyl **3,000.00**
Ford, 1962, van, 1 ton, 4 speed, V 8 cyl **3,500.00**
Ford, 1964, Fairlane, sedan, V 8 cyl 260 . . . . **2,000.00**
Ford, 1968, Torino, sedan, V 8 cyl **1,800.00**
Ford, 1972, LTD, convertible, V 8 cyl **5,000.00**
General Motors, 1949, pickup, ¾ ton, 4 speed, 6 cyl. **3,000.00**
General Motors, 1954, tow truck, 1½ ton **3,500.00**
Harley Davidson, 1954, Hummer, 125cc **800.00**
Harley Davidson, 1962, Harley Topper **1,500.00**
Hudson, 1955, Hornet, sedan, V 8 cyl. **1,400.00**
Hudson, 1957, Hornet Super, sedan, 8 cyl. **5,000.00**
Indian, 1947, WLD **1,500.00**
Indian, 1955, Woodsman, 500 cc **1,200.00**
International Harvester, 1963, pickup, ½ ton, V 8 cyl **3,000.00**
Jaguar, XJ6 II, sedan, I–6 . . . . **5,500.00**
Jeep, 1965, Wagoneer, station wagon, V 8 cyl **3,000.00**
Jeep, 1971, Jeepster, convertible, 4 cyl **2,250.00**
Lincoln, 1958, Capri, sedan, V 8 cyl **4,000.00**
Mercedes–Benz, 1971, Model 220D, sedan, 6 cyl **3,000.00**
Mercury, 1962, Comet, station wagon, 6 cyl **2,000.00**
Mercury, 1970, Cyclone GT 428, 2 door, hardtop, V 8 cyl. **3,300.00**
Oldsmobile, 1971, Delta 88, sedan, 8 cyl **1,500.00**
Oldsmobile, 1973, Vista Cruiser, station wagon, V 8 cyl . . . **2,000.00**
Pontiac, 1947, Torpedo, sedan, 8 cyl. **2,500.00**
Pontiac, 1969, Bonneville, station wagon, V 8 cyl **1,750.00**
Studebaker, 1963, pickup, ½ ton, V 8 cyl **3,000.00**
Triumph, 1974, Trident, 750 cc **2,000.00**
Volkswagen, 1974, Thing **4,000.00**

AUTOMOBILIA

Automobilia can be broken down into three major collecting categories—parts used for restoring cars, advertising and promotional items relating to a specific make or model of car, and decorative accessories in the shape of or with an image of an automobile. Numerous subcategories also exist. Spark plugs and license plates are two examples of automobilia with reference books, collectors clubs, and periodicals dealing specifically with these fields.

References: David K. Bausch, *The Official Price Guide to Automobilia,* Steve Butler, *Promotionals 1934–1983: Dealership Vehicles in Miniature,* L–W Book Sales, 1997; House of Collectibles, 1996; Bob Crisler, *License Plate Values: A Guide to Relative Prices of Collectible U.S. Auto License Plates and Their Grading,* 3rd Edition, King Publishing, 1994; David Fetherson, *Hot Rod Memorabilia and Collectibles,* Motorbooks International, 1996; John A. Gunnell (ed.), *A Collector's Guide to Automobilia,* Krause Publications, 1994; Jim and Nancy Schaut, *American Automobilia: An Illustrated History and Price Guide,* Wallace–Homestead, Krause Publications, 1994.

Periodicals: *Car Toys,* 7950 Deering Ave, Canoga Park, CA 91304; *Hemmings Motor News,* PO Box 100, Rt 9W, Bennington, VT 05201; *Mobilia,* PO Box 575, Middlebury, VT 05753; *PL8S: The License Plate Collector's Magazine,* PO Box 222, East Texas, PA 18046.

Collectors' Clubs: Automobile License Plate Collectors Assoc, Inc, PO Box 77, Horner, WV 26372; Automobile Objects D'Art Club, 252 N 7th St, Allentown, PA 18102; Hubcap Collectors Club, PO Box 54, Buckley, MI 49620; Spark Plug Collectors of America, 14018 NE 85th St, Elk River, MN 55330.

Blotter, Cities Service, 1940s, 4 x 9" **$20.00**
Booklet, We Drivers, General Motors, illus, 1935, 36 pgs **5.00**
Can, Simoniz Wax, litho tin, lid shows man waxing family car, 1930s, 4¼" d, 1¾" h. **20.00**
Car Attachment, litho, metal, domed image of Shell Oil symbol under colorful International Code Flags, 1930–40s, 3¼ x 5½". **70.00**
Catalog, Ford Mustang, February 1964, double page foldout, color, first catalog, 1964, 12 pgs, 12 x 11". **80.00**
Coin, commemorative, 1939 Chrysler Anniversary, metal, gold luster, 1924 model on one side under inscription "15 Years Of Progress," other side depicts 1939 model in front of skyscraper spire with inscription "Be Modern/Buy Chrysler" **10.00**

Game, Get That License, "The License Plate Game," Selchow & Richter, 1955 . . . . **30.00**
Gear Shift Knob, akro agate, red and white, 1½" h brass attachment **20.00**
Key Fob, Michelin, plastic, 3 dimensional Michelin Man, silvered metal, 1950–60s, 1¼" h **20.00**
Lapel Stud, brass, blue accents, "Safe Driver Award," upper torso view of male driver, "Green Cross For Safety," "National Safety Council," c1930s **5.00**
License Plate, Cook Islands, #4132, white on dark blue **20.00**
License Plate, Georgia, #MRSHEA, 1970 . . . . **5.00**
Magazine, *The Highway Traveler,* April–May 1937, tourist attraction photos, travel–related ads, Greyhound Management Co, 60 pgs **10.00**
Manual, Buick Dynaflow Drive, color illus, Nov 1948, 7 x 9". **20.00**
Matchcover, "Call A Yellow Cab," orange, black and white, cab in night scene illus on one side, "The Thinking Fellow Calls A Yellow" on other, unused, 1930s. **12.00**
Pinback Button, Studebaker, multicolor, wood–spoked automobile wheel bordered in red with blue and white inscription band at center, 1920s **20.00**
Pocket Mirror, Ford/Lincoln Zephyr, acetate over yellow paper, black lettering, 1930–40s. **20.00**
Postcard, DeSoto, color, 4 door sedan, 1939 . . . . **5.00**
Sign, Champion Spark Plug Service, tin, 1940–50, 10 x 28" **250.00**
Spark Plug, Champion Franklin, ⅞" **20.00**
Spark Plug, Mosler Spitfire, 18 mm **15.00**
Stock Certificate, General Motors Corporation, $1,000 bond, green, vignette with car, truck, and train, 1954 . . . . . **10.00**
Tab, Ford Pinto, litho tin, black, red, white, and blue accent within letter "P" of inscription, 1970s **10.00**

Lunch Box, Volkswagen Van, litho tin, red, beige, and gray, 1960s, 10½" w, 4½" d, $450.00. Photo courtesy Collectors Auction Services.

AUTUMN LEAF

Autumn Leaf dinnerware was manufactured by Hall China Company and issued as a premium by the Jewel Tea Company. The pattern was originally produced between 1933 and 1978. Many other companies produced matching kitchen accessories.

References: Susan and Al Bagdade, *Warman's American Pottery and Porcelain*, Wallace–Homestead, Krause Publications, 1994; Harvey Duke, *The Official Price Guide to Pottery and Porcelain, Eighth Edition*, House of Collectibles, 1995; C. L. Miller, *The Jewel Tea Company: Its History and Products*, Schiffer Publishing, 1994; Margaret and Kenn Whitmyer, *The Collector's Encyclopedia of Hall China, Second Edition*, Collector Books, 1994, 1997 value update.

Collectors' Club: National Autumn Leaf Collectors Club, 62200 E 236 Rd, Wyandotte, OH 74370.

Note: Pieces are in good condition with only minor wear to gold trim unless noted otherwise

DINNERWARE

Baker, French, 2 pt	**$150.00**
Baker, French, 3 pt	20.00
Baker, Ft Pitt, mint, 12 oz	175.00
Ball Jug	45.00
Bread and Butter Plate, 6" d	8.00
Butter Dish, cov, ruffled lid, 1/4 lb	275.00
Butter Dish, cov, ruffled lid, 1 lb	450.00
Cake Plate	25.00
Coffeepot, drip, all china, 4 pcs	325.00
Coffeepot, rayed, metal dripper, 9 cup	90.00
Cookie Jar, rayed	250.00
Creamer and Sugar, rayed, 1930s	65.00
Creamer and Sugar, ruffled, mint, 1940s	50.00
Cream Soup, 2 handled	45.00
Custard, Radiance	8.00
Dinner Plate, 10" d	20.00
Flat Soup	20.00
Gravy Boat	35.00
Grease Bowl, cov	25.00
Luncheon Plate, 8" d	18.00
Mixing Bowls, Radiance, nesting set of 3	95.00

Mug, conic	75.00
Mug, Irish coffee	150.00
Percolator, electric	425.00
Pie Plate	30.00
Platter, oval, 13 1/2" l	40.00
Salad Plate, 7 1/4" d	12.00
Salt and Pepper Shakers, pr, ruffled	35.00
Stack Set, 4 pc	100.00
St Denis Cup and Saucer	45.00
Teapot, Aladdin	75.00
Teapot, Newport 1933	250.00
Tidbit Tray, 3 tier	150.00
Utility Jug, rayed, 2 1/2 pt	35.00
Warmer, oval, mint	175.00
Warmer, round	150.00

MATCHING ACCESSORIES

Cake Safe, pattern on top and sides	**$65.00**
Canister Set, square, tin, 4 pcs	275.00
Clock, electric	525.00
Coffee Dispenser, tin	350.00
Cookbook, Mary Dunbar	25.00
Curtain/Towel	65.00
Fruitcake Tin	15.00
Hot Pad, tin back, 7 1/4" d	15.00
Serving Tray, metal, red border	75.00
Sifter, metal	575.00
Tablecloth, muslin	225.00
Tea Kettle, porcelain	275.00
Tea Towel	65.00
Tray, wood and glass	175.00
Tumbler, banded, 5 1/2" h	45.00
Tumbler, Brockway, 13 oz	50.00
Tumbler, frosted, 3 3/4" h	35.00
Tumbler, Libbey, gold and frost, 10 oz	65.00

AVIATION COLLECTIBLES

Most collections relating to the field of aviation focus on one of four categories—commercial airlines, dirigibles, famous aviators, or generic images of aircraft.

Early American airlines depended on government subsidies for carrying mail. By 1930, five international and thirty–eight domestic airlines were operating in the United States. A typical passenger load was ten. After World War II, four–engine planes with a capacity of 100 or more passengers were introduced.

The jet age was launched in the 1950s. In 1955 Capitol Airlines used British–made turboprop airliners in domestic service. In 1958 National Airlines began domestic jet passenger service. The giant Boeing 747 went into operation in 1970 as part of the Pan American fleet.

References: Lynn Johnson and Michael O'Leary, *En Route: Label Art From the Golden Age of Air Travel*, Chronicle Books, 1993; Norman E. Martinus and Harry L. Rinker, *Warman's Paper*, Wallace–Homestead, Krause Publications, 1994; Ron Smith, *Collecting Toy Airplanes: An Identification & Value Guide*, Books Americana, Krause Publications, 1995; Richard R. Wallin, *Commercial Aviation Collectibles: An Illustrated Price Guide*, Wallace–Homestead, 1990, out of print.

Periodical: *Airliner*, PO Box 521238, Miami, FL 33125.

Bean Pots. Left: 1 handle, 2 1/4 qt, introduced 1960, $467.50; Right: 2 handles, introduced 1936, $192.50. Photo courtesy Gene Harris.

Collectors' Clubs: Aeronautica and Air Label Collectors Club, PO Box 1239, Elgin, IL 60121; CAL/NX211 (Charles Lindbergh), 727 Youn–Kim Parkway South, Columbus, OH 43207; International Miniature Aircraft Collectors Society, PO Box 845, Greenwich, CT 06836; World Airline Historical Society, 13739 Picarsa Dr, Jacksonville, FL 32225.

Ashtray, United Air Lines, metal, silver, blue anodized center, "Fly the friendly skies of United," 4³/₈" d **$20.00**

Bank, cast aluminum, *Spirit of St Louis* replica, "Spirit Of Saving" inscription, black rubber tires, spinning propeller, engraved inscriptions for Mexican bank sponsor on upper wing tips, 8" l, 4" h, 10" wing span, 1920s **400.00**

Belt Buckle, TWA, red enamel initials, Hickok, 1960s **20.00**

Book, *The Fun of It*, Amelia Earhart, 1932 . . . . **260.00**

Book, *Jet–O–Rama*, punch–out picture book, Whitman, 1954, 10 x 14³/₄" **10.00**

Brochure, Eastern Airlines 1958 Annual Report, gold accent cover, black and white pgs, photos, fiscal report, planes, and routes, 28 pgs, 8¹/₂ x 10³/₄" **8.00**

Employee Badge, Goodyear Aircraft, 1930s **65.00**

Fan, BOAC Airlines, paper, polished wood, color illus, gold lettering, "B–O–A–C Speedbird Routes Across The World" slogan in gold lettering, 1970s **15.00**

Flight Schedule, United Airlines, 1962, 24 pgs, 4 x 9" **4.00**

Folder, American Airlines, contains flight information and map, color illus, 1960s, 4 x 9" **4.00**

Medal, "Mohawk Airlines Gold Chip Service," bronze luster, raised profile portraits of pilot and service personnel, reverse inscription "We're On Your Side/ Mohawk" **10.00**

Model, Aero Mini Pan American, diecast metal, orig box, 1970s, 7¹/₄" l **40.00**

Napkin Holder, American Airlines, center "AA" soaring eagle symbol **20.00**

Pin, KLM Junior Pilot, brass, oval, diecut, dark blue enamel backing, 1960s **10.00**

Pinback Button, Friendship International Airport, scene of blue and white fighter planes in WWII era, red inscription on white **10.00**

Playing Cards, "TWA" and plane on back **8.00**

Postcard, Lakehurst Naval Air Station, black and white, photo of US Navy zeppelin above hangar, bottom handwritten inscription, "U.S.S. Los Angeles," reverse inked address and 1928 postmark from Lakehurst, NJ **20.00**

Poster, Colonial Airlines, scene of DC–4 over Bermuda Island, 1950s, 27 x 41" **365.00**

Program, decication of Wright family home, autographed by Orville Wright, 1938 . . . . **1,425.00**

Ring, Bell Air Craft, plastic, 1930–40s **40.00**

Sheet Music, Like An Angel You Flew Into Everyone's Heart, Lindberg photo cov, 1927 . . . . **45.00**

Timetable, United Air Lines, map of US and bi–plane, 1930s **45.00**

AVON

David H. McConnell founded the California Perfume Company in 1886. Saleswomen used a door–to–door approach for selling their wares. The first product was "Little Dot," a set of five perfumes. Following the acquisition of a new factory in Suffern, New York, in 1895, the company underwent several name changes. The trade name Avon, adopted in 1929, was derived from the similarity the Suffern landscape shared with that of Avon, England.

Reference: Bud Hastin, *Bud Hastin's Avon & C.P.C. Collector's Encyclopedia, 14th Edition*, published by author, 1995.

Newsletter: *Avon Times*, PO Box 9868, Kansas City, MO 64134.

Collectors' Club: National Assoc of Avon Collectors, Inc, PO Box 7006, Kansas City, MO 64113.

Baby Shoe Pin Cushion, baby lotion, plastic, white, pink pin cushion, blue bow, 1973–74, 7 oz **$4.00**

Bunny Puff, talc, white plastic rabbit, pink fluffy tail, 1969–72 . . . . **4.00**

Hammer Decanter, Everest or Wild Country After Shave, amber glass, silver top, 2.5 oz, 1978, 8¹/₂" l **5.00**

Howdy Pardners Set, Buckaroo Cologne with 2 pc blue cowboy hat cap, talc, orig box, 1982–83 . . . . **5.00**

Juke Box Decanter, Wild Country After Shave or Sweet Honesty, amber glass, silver top, 4.5 oz, 1977–78 . . . . **8.00**

Jacket Wings, "PAA Stewardess," single wing, gold, 1945, $85.00.

Meadow Bird, pomander, plastic, blue and white, 6" h, $4.00.

Lily of the Valley Scented Pillow, lace, green and white, 1979, 10 x 10" **8.00**

Miss Lollypop Powderette, talc, red plume puff, 1967–68, 3½ oz **10.00**

Nesting Hen, soap, white milk glass, painted beige nest, 4 yellow egg shaped soap, 1973 . . . . **15.00**

Old 99 Soap, figural train, yellow, 1958 . . . . **65.00**

Pick A Daisy Set, soap–on–a–rope, Daisies Won't Tell cream sachet, orig pink and blue box, 1963–64 . . . . **32.00**

Pretty Me Doll, powdered bubble bath, plastic bottle, gold hair, cap, pink neck ribbon, 1969–71, 5 oz, 6½" h **6.00**

Ruler, No Tear Shampoo, plastic, red and white, 1966–67, 8 oz **8.00**

Savona Bouquet Toilet Soap, box of 6 bars, 1932–36 . . . . **70.00**

Strawberry Fair Soap, red soap in yellow plastic basket, green grass, cellophane wrap and bow, 1969–70 . . . . **8.00**

Topsy Turvey Clown, bubble bath, plastic, white and yellow, blue hat, black feet, 1965, 10 oz **15.00**

Volkswagen, Oland or Windjammer After Shave, glass, painted, light blue, plastic cap, 1973–74, 4 oz **5.00**

BANKS

The earliest still banks were made from wood, pottery, gourds, and later, cast iron. Lithographed tin banks advertising various products and services reached their height in popularity between 1930 and 1955. The majority of these banks were miniature replicas of the products' packaging.

Ceramic figural banks were popular novelties during the 1960s and 1970s. The most recent variation of still banks are molded vinyl banks resembling favorite cartoon and movie characters.

References: Don Cranmer, *Collector's Encyclopedia: Toys–Banks*, L–W Book Sales, 1986, 1994–95 value update; Don Duer, *A Penny Saved: Still & Mechanical Banks*, Schiffer Publishing, 1993; Don Duer, *Penny Banks Around the World*, Schiffer Publishing, 1997; Beverly and Jim Mangus, *Collector's Guide to Banks*, Collector Books, 1998; Andy and Susan Moore, *Penny Bank Book: Collecting Still Banks*, Schiffer Publishing, 1984, 1997 value update; Tom and Loretta Stoddard, *Ceramic Coin Banks: Identification & Value Guide*, Collector Books, 1997; Vickie Stulb, *Modern Banks*, L–W Book Sales, 1997.

Newsletters: *Glass Bank Collector*, PO Box 155, Poland, NY 13431; *Heuser's Quarterly Collectible Diecast Newsletter*, 508 Clapson Rd, PO Box 300, West Winfield, NY 13491.

Collectors' Club: Still Bank Collectors Club of America, 4175 Millersville Rd, Indianapolis, IN 46205.

Note: All banks listed are still banks unless noted otherwise.

Abominable Snowman, vinyl, white, full figure snowman, simulated fur, striped umbrella in left arm, Banthrico, Niagara Plastics on trap, c1960s, 7¼" h **$45.00**

Amish Man, Reynolds Toys, edition of 50, 1980 . . . . **130.00**

Barrel, figural, litho tin, "Happy Days," Detroit car dealer promotion, Chein, 1930s **60.00**

Betty Boop, Vandor **25.00**

Bob's Big Boy, adv, figural **25.00**

Bosco, glass bottom, plastic bear lid, 8" h **35.00**

Bozo, plastic, gumball, Hasbro, 1968, 8½" h **45.00**

Buddy Bank, mechanical, glass, 3–D litho tin figure attached to lid, top mkd Buddy Bank," one arm with Marx logo, one hand mkd Shake, Buddy!," other hand mkd "Place Coin Here," Marx, c1950 . . . . **100.00**

Cash Register, litho tin, "Happy Days," Chein, 1930–50s **50.00**

Cash Register, litho tin, "Register Ten Dollars," floral scroll design, Chein, 1948–69 . . . . **40.00**

Cave Girl, painted composition, girl wearing yellow outfit with yellow dots holding white bone, mkd "Japan," 2½ x 4 x 6½", 1960s **25.00**

Coffin, windup, built–in key, black, red, and green, spider webs illus, top skeleton image covered by black felt, green plastic skeleton hand and head, hand reaches out from under felt and pulls coin into slot, head pops up, Yone, Japan, 1960s, 2½ x 6 x 2" **45.00**

Dogpatch Pappy **35.00**

Drinker's Savings Bank, battery operated, Illfelder Co, 9" h, 1960s **90.00**

Elephant, mechanical, litho tin, Chein, 1960s **65.00**

Elephant, walking, Frankoma **25.00**

Garfield, egg **65.00**

Graduation Baby, plastic, smiling brown haired baby boy, wearing mortar board with blue string tassel, holding diploma, Baby World Co, Inc, c1950s, 7½" h **25.00**

Howdy Doody Head, Vandor **45.00**

Hubert Lion, Lefton **35.00**

Humpty Dumpy, litho tin, Humpty Dumpty head on base, Chein, 1930–40 . . . . **95.00**

Kliban Cat, walking, red sneakers, Sigma **90.00**

Lucy, figural, ceramic, Lucy frowning, Italian stamp and ©1963 King Features Syndicate, Inc, missing trap **90.00**

Miss Piggy, Sigma **55.00**

Money Hungry, plastic, spool shape, set of teeth mounted on top, inscribed around sides "Lick Inflation/Money Talks/Put Your money Where Your Mouth Is," Poynter Products, 1975 . . . . **35.00**

Nash's Prepared Mustard, adv, glass, figural "Lucky Joe," tin cap, 1941, 4½" h **35.00**

Old Mother Hubbard, litho tin, book bank, Kirchhof, Volume III, c1930–40s **75.00**

Pig, Franciscan, mkd "USA" **350.00**

Popeye, Vandor **125.00**

Popeye Dime Register, litho tin, King Feature Syndicate, 1929 . . . . **115.00**

Prince Valiant, Dime Register, litho tin, King Features Syndicate, Inc, 2½ x 2½ x ¾", ©1954 . . . . **200.00**

Scooby Doo, plastic, gumball, clear smiling face holding white bone, yellow base, Hasbro, 1968 . . . . **25.00**

Strato Bank, mechanical, cast metal, metallic aqua, 3–D rocketship launches coins, decal on each side of base mkd "Munch, Pa," box mkd "Duro Mold & Manufacturing Inc," 3½" h, 1950s **75.00**

Tootsie Roll, cardboard cylinder, tin ends, 11¼" l, $2.50.

Television, litho tin, brown wood design, black and white screen and accents, mkd on top "Television Co of Baltimore," c1950 .... **30.00**

Tom, Tom the Piper's Son, litho tin, book bank, Kirchhof, c1930s **65.00**

Uncle Wiggly, mechanical, litho tin, Chein, 1931–40s **175.00**

Woody Woodpecker, Applause **30.00**

BARBER SHOP, BEAUTY SHOP & SHAVING

The neighborhood barber shop was an important social and cultural institution in the first half of the 20th century. Men and boys gathered to gossip, exchange business news, and check current fashions. With the emergence of *unisex* shops in the 1960s, the number of barber shops dropped by half in the United States. Today, most men and women patronize the same shops for services ranging from hair cuts to perms to coloring.

References: Ronald S. Barlow, *The Vanishing American Barber Shop*, Windmill Publishing, 1993; Jim Sargent, *Sargent's American Premium Guide to Pocket Knives & Razors...*, 4th Edition, Books Americana, Krause Publications, 1995.

Collectors' Clubs: National Shaving Mug Collectors' Assoc, 320 S Glenwood St, Allentown, PA 18104; Safety Razor Collectors Guild, PO Box 885, Crescent City, CA 95531.

After Shave, Colgate After Shave Lotion, clear glass bottle, red plastic lid, red and white label, black and white lettering, full, 5 oz **$8.00**

Business Cards, The Newest and Most Sanitary Shop in Providence, man cutting hair illus, 6 x 3¼". **10.00**

Catalog, Cuttaraugus Cutlery Co, 1925, 81 pp **75.00**

Catalog, Hudson Beauty Shop Equipment, No. 1 Supplement, Los Angeles, CA, 1938, 8 pp, 5¾ x 8¾" **30.00**

Chair, child's, #107, removable carved horse's head on front, iron, porcelain enamel, hydraulic, Emil J Paidar Co, 1925 .... **2,000.00**

Cologne, Jovan Musk, plastic bottle, silver metal lid, 2 oz, orig box with bar of soap, 3¾ x 2 x ¾" **8.00**

Sign, Dickinson's Witch Hazel, cardboard stand–up, red, yellow, black, and white, 28" h, 19½" w, $95.00. Photo courtesy Collectors Auction Services.

Display, Clix Razor, 3 dimensional, painted wooden barbershop, light–up, "Smooth Shaving Clix Always Clicks," c1930, 17½ x 25½" **800.00**

Hair Cutter, stainless steel cutter, double–edge blade, cutter cleaner brush, orig 7½ x 1⅞ x 1⅛" cardboard box, Playtex **20.00**

Hair Net, Flamingo, woman illus, pink and white envelope, brown and pink lettering, Flamingo Products, Inc, Danvilld, IL, 1958, 6½ x 3½" **3.00**

Hair Tonic, Wildroot, glass bottle, plastic pump lid, gold letters, full, 7 oz, Wildrooot Co, Inc, Buffalo, NY **10.00**

License, framed, c1930 .... **45.00**

Razor, Gillette, metal, made in USA, 2¾ x 1¾ x ¾". **5.00**

Sign, Clairol, cardboard, diecut, easel back, woman's profile upper right, "Amazing Look Magazine Eye Camera age–test proves Clairol helps you look years younger!," 1941, 16 x 21" **10.00**

Sign, Furnald's Hair Brush, paper, 2 women brushing their hair, little girl offers them flowers, 9¾ x 12¾" **200.00**

Sign, Robeson Razor, cardboard, diecut, seated cowboy reading paper, 42 x 26½". **100.00**

Sign, Wildroot, tin, emb "Barber Shop Ask For Wildroot," barber pole illus on right, c1950s, 13½ x 39½". **75.00**

BARBIE

The first Barbie fashion dolls, patented by Mattel in 1958, arrived on toy store shelves in 1959. By 1960, Barbie was a marketing success. The development of Barbie's boyfriend, Ken, began in 1960. Many other friends followed. Clothing, vehicles, doll houses, and other accessories became an integral part of the line.

From September 1961 through July 1972 Mattel published a Barbie magazine. At its peak, the Barbie Fan Club was the second largest girls' organization, next to the Girl Scouts, in the nation.

Barbie sales are approaching the 100 million mark. Annual sales exceed five million units. Barbie is one of the most successful dolls in history.

References: Fashion and Accessories: Joe Blitman, *Barbie Doll and Her Mod, Mod, Mod, Mod World of Fashion*, Hobby House Press, 1996; Joe Blitman, *Francie and Her Mod, Mod, Mod, Mod World of Fashion*, Hobby House Press, 1996; Sarah Sink Eames, *Barbie Doll Fashion, Vol. I: 1959–1967* (1990, 1998 value update), *Vol II: 1968–1974* (1997), Collector Books; A. Glenn Mandeville, *Doll Fashion Anthology and Price Guide, 5th Revised Edition*, Hobby House Press, 1996; Rebecca Ann Rupp, *Treasury of Barbie Doll Accessories: 1961–1995*, Hobby House Press, 1996.

General: Scott Arend, Karla Holzerland and Trina Kent, *Skipper: Barbie's Little Sister*, Collector Books, 1998; J. Michael Augustyniak, *The Barbie Doll Boom*, Collector Books, 1996; J. Michael Augustyniak, *Collector's Encyclopedia of Barbie Doll Exclusives and More: Identification and Values*, Collector Books, 1997; Sibyl DeWein and Joan Ashabraner, *The Collectors Encyclopedia of Barbie Dolls and Collectibles*, Collector Books, 1977, 1996 value update; Robert Gardner, *Fashion Dolls Exclusively International: ID and Price Guide to World–Wide Fashion Dolls*, Hobby House Press, 1997; A. Glenn Mandeville, *Doll Fashion Anthology and Price Guide, 5th Revised Edition*, Hobby House Press, 1996; Paris and Susan Manos, *The Wonder of Barbie: Dolls and Accessories 1976–1986*, Collector Books, 1987, 1996 value update; Paris and Susan Manos, *The World of Barbie Dolls: An Illustrated Value Guide*, Collector Books, 1983, 1998 value update; Marcie Melillo, *The Ultimate Barbie Doll Book*, Krause Publications, 1996; Lorraine Mieszala, *Collector's Guide to Barbie Doll Paper Dolls: Identification and Values*, Collector Books, 1997.

Patrick C. Olds and Myrazona R. Olds, *The Barbie Doll Years: 1959–1996, Second Edition*, Collector Books, 1997; Margo Rana, *Barbie Doll Exclusively for Timeless Creations: 1986–1996, Book III*, Hobby House Press, 1997; Margo Rana, *Barbie Exclusives, Book II: Identification and Values*, Collector Books, 1996; Margo Rana, *Collector's Guide to Barbie Exclusives: Identification and Values*, Collector Books, 1995; Jane Sarasohn–Kahn, *Contemporary Barbie: Barbie Dolls 1980 and Beyond, 1998 Edition*, Antique Trader Books, 1997; Beth Summers, *A Decade of Barbie Dolls and Collectibles, 1981–1991: Identification and Values*, Collector Books, 1996; Kitturah B. Westenhouser, *The Story of Barbie*, Collector Books, 1994.

Periodicals: *Barbie Bazaar*, 5617 6th Ave, Kenosha, WI 53140; *Miller's Barbie Collector*, PO Box 8722, Spokane, WA 99203.

Collectors' Club: Barbie Doll Collectors Club International, PO Box 586, White Plains, NY 10603.

ACCESSORIES

Activity Book, Skipper and Scott Beauty Sticker Fun, 1980. . . . . **$5.00**
Armoire, #2471, Dream Furniture Collection, light pink, 1980. . . . . **35.00**
Book, *Barbie's Fashion Success*, hard cov, 16 chapters, © Random House, 1958 and 1962, 5½ x 8¼" **12.00**
Camera, Super Star Cameramatic Flash Camera, #8503, 1978. . . . . **20.00**
Carrying Case, Barbie and Midge, blue, 1964. . . . . **35.00**
Carrying Case, Miss Barbie, black patent leather, 1963 . . . . . **165.00**
Couch, #0408, Go–Together Furniture, 1964 . . . . **30.00**
Fashion Queen Wig Wardrobe, #1009, 1964 . . . . **250.00**
Game, Barbie's Little Sister Skipper, Mattel, 1964 . . . . **50.00**
Game, The Barbie World of Fashion, Mattel, 1967 . . . . **50.00**
Midge's Wig Wardrobe, #1009, 1964 . . . . **450.00**
Miss Barbie Furniture Set, #4443, Sears, 1964 . . . . **70.00**

Paper Dolls, Pos'n' Barbie, Whitman Pub, #1975, 6 pp, unused, 1972, 7¼ x 15¼", $45.00.

Suburban Shopper, blue striped dress, 1961, $140.00.

Pencil Case, Skipper and Skooter, Standard Plastic, 1966 . . . . **15.00**
Purse Fashion Pak, 1962–63 . . . . **40.00**
Puzzle, Skipper and Skooter, 1965, 100 pcs **15.00**
Recliner and Serving Cart, #1480, Dream Pool Collection, 1969 . . . . **20.00**
Record, *A Happy Barbie Birthday*, #0506, Columbia, 1965 . . . **20.00**

CLOTHING

Arabian Knights, #0733, 6 pc set, 1964–65 . . . . **$145.00**
Campus Hero, #770, 1961–64 . . . . **75.00**
Dr Ken, #793, 1963–65 . . . . **95.00**
Evening Gown, #1005, yellow, 1979 . . . . **15.00**
Hooray for Leather, #1477, leather–type skirt, knit top, shoes, 1969–70 . . . . **55.00**
Hootenanny, #1707, Sew Free Fashions, 1965 . . . . **75.00**
Jazzy Jams, #1967, 1969 . . . . **50.00**
Knit Shirt Fashion Pak, 1963 . . . . **40.00**
Loop Scoop, #1454, 1970 . . . . **80.00**
Picnic Set, #967, 1959–61 . . . . **90.00**
Ski Queen, #948, 1963 . . . . **200.00**
Wild 'N Wonderful, multicolor top and skirt, hot pants, plastic cut–out boots, 1969 . . . . **65.00**

DOLLS, BARBIE

Australian Barbie, #3626, Dolls of the World series, 1992. . . . . **$40.00**
Barbie and the Rockers, #1140, 1985 . . . . **35.00**
Bubblecut Barbie, #850, 1961 . . . . **300.00**
Canadian Barbie, #4928, Dolls of the World series, 1987 . . . . **80.00**
Classique Evening Extravaganza Barbie, #11638, black version, 1993 . . . . **85.00**
Dorothy from Wizard of Oz, #12701, Hollywood Legends series, 1994 . . . . **45.00**
Fashion Queen Barbie, #870, 1962 . . . . **500.00**
Gold Medal Olympic Barbie Skier, #7264, 1974 . . . . **125.00**
Growin' Pretty Hair Barbie, #1144, 1972 . . . . **275.00**
Happy Birthday Barbie, #1922, 1980 . . . . **35.00**
Happy Holidays Barbie, #1429, Happy Holidays Cristalline series, 1992 . . . . **125.00**
Happy Holidays Barbie, #1703, Happy Holidays series, 1988. . . . . **600.00**
Happy Holidays Barbie, #3253, Happy Holidays series, 1989. . . . . **250.00**
Icelandic Barbie, #3189, Dolls of the World series, 1986 . . . **100.00**

Busy Gal, Nostalgic line, #13675, 1995, $30.00.

Italian Barbie, #1602, International Italian series, 1979 . . . . . **185.00**
Italian Barbie, #2256, Dolls of the World series, reissue,
    1992. . . . . **20.00**
Live Action Barbie, #1155, 1970 . . . . **150.00**
Mardi Gras Barbie, #4930, American Beauty series,
    1987. . . . . **100.00**
My First Barbie, #1875, 1982 . . . . **35.00**
Peaches 'n Cream Barbie, #7926, 1984 . . . . **45.00**
Pilgrim Barbie, #12577, American Stories series, 1994 . . . . . . **25.00**
Ponytail Barbie, #850, 1960 . . . . **450.00**
Quick Curl Barbie, #4220, 1972 . . . . **125.00**
Rapunzel Barbie, #13016, Children's Collectors series,
    1994. . . . . **40.00**
Sun Lovin' Malibu Barbie, #1067, 1978 . . . . **20.00**
Swiss Barbie, #7541, International series, 1983 . . . . **110.00**
Talking Barbie, #1115, 1967 . . . . **300.00**
Twist 'N Turn Barbie, #1160, 1967 . . . . **550.00**
Western Jeans Barbie, #5315, 1981 . . . . **45.00**

DOLLS, BARBIE'S FRIENDS

Allan, #1000, 1963 . . . . **$135.00**
Casey, #9000, 1974 . . . . **450.00**
Cool Times Midge, #3216, 1988 . . . . **50.00**
Francie, #1130, 1965 . . . . **450.00**
Growing Up Ginger, #9222, 1975 . . . . **85.00**
Ken, #750, 1961 . . . . **150.00**
Midge, #1080, 1964 . . . . **650.00**
Ricky, #1090, 1964 . . . . **135.00**
Scott, #1019, 1979 . . . . **65.00**
Skipper, #950, 1963 . . . . **125.00**
Skooter, #1040, 1965 . . . . **125.00**
Talking PJ, #1113, 1969 . . . . **200.00**
Talking Stacey, #1125, 1968 . . . . **500.00**
Tutti, #3580, 1965 . . . . **125.00**

PLAYSETS

Barbie Fashion Stage, 1981 . . . . **$65.00**
Barbie's Pool Party, 1973 . . . . **45.00**
Fashion Plaza, 1976–77 . . . . **85.00**
Olympic Ski Village, 1975 . . . . **45.00**

VEHICLES

'57 Chevy, #3561, 1989 . . . . **$70.00**
Barbie's Beach Bus, 1974–77 . . . . **50.00**
Corvette, 1962–63 . . . . **85.00**
Country Camper, #4994, 1971 . . . . **25.00**
Hot Rod, #1460, 1963 . . . . **200.00**
Ten Speeder Bike, 1974–77 . . . . **35.00**

BARWARE

During the late 1960s and early 1970s it became fashionable for homeowners to convert basements into family rec rooms, often equipped with bars. Most were well stocked with both utilitarian items (shot glasses and ice crushers) and decorative accessories. Objects with advertising are usually more valuable than their generic counterparts.

References: Mark Pickvet, *Shot Glasses: An American Tradition,* Antique Publications, 1989; Stephen Visakay, *Vintage Bar Ware Identification & Value Guide,* Collector Books, 1997.

Collectors' Club: International Swizzle Stick Collectors Assoc, PO Box 1117, Bellingham, WA 98227.

Note: See also Breweriana, Cocktail Shakers, and Whiskey Bottles.

Ashtray, Jim Beam, 9½" d **$125.00**
Bottle Opener, figural sailor, cast iron. **65.00**
Clock, Bud Malt Liquor, battery operated, "Now Is The
    Time," exclamation mark on center clock face, 1970s,
    16" d **50.00**
Coaster, Fox Head, Fox Head Brewery, Waukesha, WI,
    red, black, and yellow, 4" d **5.00**
Coaster, Lowenbrau, set of 40, World's Fair, 1964–65 . . . . **25.00**
Cocktail Shaker, Chantilly, metal top, Cambridge **95.00**
Cordial, Caprice pattern, blue, Cambridge, 1 oz **125.00**
Decanter, Cleo pattern, pink, orig stopper, Cambridge **225.00**

Combination bottle opener/shot glass/stirring spoon, Mad Hatter from *Alice in Wonderland*, 1933 Century of Progress souvenir, 9½" l, $45.00.

Glass, Pabst Blue Ribbon, painted labels, 1960s,
6" h, set of 4 . . . . 6.00
Ice Bucket, aluminum, hand wrought, double wall,
beaded edge around lid, Buenilum 30.00
Lamp, table, hula girl, wearing grass skirt, white metal,
motorized hip movement, circular base, 1940s 75.00
Light, hanging, Imported Heineken Beer, 1970, 7 x 10" 10.00
Liquor Set, brass ring holds 4 gold banded glasses, c1950. . . . 18.00
Martini Pitcher, Diana pattern, crystal, Cambridge 750.00
Match Holder, pr, Coors, ceramic 15.00
Mirror, Miller High Life, 1980s 5.00
Pitcher, Seagram's 7, white, emb, red ground 8.00
Shot Glass, Gem City Whiskey, etched design 15.00
Swizzle Stick, figural die, Bakelite, attached to top of
square plastic stick 3.00
Swizzle Stick, figural leaf, black Catalin 5.00
Swizzle Stick, figural palm tree 2.00
Tap Handle, Ballantine Beer, Bakelite knob, enamel
insert, 1940s 45.00
Whiskey Glass, American pattern, crystal, Fostoria,
2½" h 10.00
Wine, Imperial Hunt Scene pattern, emerald green,
Cambridge, 2½ oz. 55.00

BASEBALL CARDS

Baseball cards were originally issued by tobacco companies in the late 19th century. The first big producers of gum cards were Goudey Gum Company of Boston (1933–41) and Gum, Inc. (1939). After World War II, Gum, Inc.'s successor, Bowman, was the leading manufacturer. Topps, Inc. of Brooklyn, New York, followed. Topps bought Bowman in 1956 and monopolized the field until 1981 when Fleer of Philadelphia and Donruss of Memphis challenged the market.

References: James Beckett, *The Official 1998 Price Guide to Baseball Cards, 17th Edition,* House of Collectibles, 1997; James Beckett and Theo Chen (eds.), *Beckett Baseball Price Guide, Number 19,* Beckett Publications, 1997; Allan Kaye and Michael McKeever, *Baseball Card Price Guide, 1997,* Avon Books, 1996; Mark Larson (ed.), *Baseball Cards Questions & Answers,* Krause Publications, 1992; Mark Larson, *Sports Collectors Digest Minor League Baseball Card Price Guide,* Krause Publications, 1993; Mark Larson (ed.), *Sports Collectors Digest: The Sports Card Explosion,* Krause Publications, 1993.

Bob Lemke (ed.), *Sportscard Counterfeit Detector, 3rd Edition,* Krause Publications, 1994; Bob Lemke (ed.), *Sports Collectors Digest, 1998 Standard Catalog of Baseball Cards, 7th Edition,* Krause Publications, 1997; Alan Rosen, *True Mint: Mr. Mint's Price & Investment Guide to True Mint Baseball Cards,* Krause Publications, 1994; Sports Collectors Digest, *1998 Baseball Card Price Guide, 12th Edition,* Krause Publications, 1998; Sports Collectors Digest, *101 Sportscard Investments,* Krause Publications, 1993; Sports Collectors Digest, *Premium Insert Sports Cards,* Krause Publications, 1995.

Periodicals: *Beckett Baseball Card Monthly,* 15850 Dallas Pkwy, Dallas, TX 75248; *Card Trade,* 700 E State St, Iola, WI 54990; *Tuff Stuff,* PO Box 1050, Dubuque, IA 52004.

Bowman, 1948, #8, Phil Rizzuto $80.00
Bowman, 1948, #17, Enos Slaughter 100.00

Bowman, 1949, #60, Yogi Berra 275.00
Bowman, 1949, #133, Aaron Robinson 15.00
Bowman, 1949, common player (145–240) 50.00
Bowman, 1950, #10, Tommy Henrich 65.00
Bowman, 1950, #62, Ted Kluszewski 100.00
Bowman, 1950, complete set (252) 9,000.00
Bowman, 1951, #181, Casey Stengel 75.00
Bowman, 1951, #253, Mickey Mantle 8,200.00
Bowman, 1952, #44, Roy Campanella 225.00
Bowman, 1952, #92, Eddie Waitkus 20.00
Bowman, 1952, #196, Stan Musial 600.00
Bowman, 1953, #10, Richie Ashburn 150.00
Bowman, 1953, #153, Whitey Ford 500.00
Bowman, 1954, common player (1–128) 10.00
Bowman, 1955, #173, Chico Carrasquel 8.00
Bowman, 1989, #126, Bo Jackson 15
Bowman, 1990, complete set (528) 12.00
Donruss, 1981, #228, Reggie Jackson 2.00
Donruss, 1982, #15, George Brett 2.00
Donruss, 1983, #3, Christy Mathewson, Hall of Fame
Heroes Series 50
Donruss, 1983, #279, Cal Ripken 15.00
Donruss, 1983, #586, Wade Boggs 15.00
Donruss, 1983, complete set (660) 90.00
Donruss, 1984, #51, Dave Winfield 5.00
Donruss, 1986, #34, Pete Rose 75
Donruss, 1986, complete set (660) 70.00
Donruss, 1992, #32, Kirby Puckett, Cracker Jack II Series 1.00
Fleer, 1959, #6, Ted Turns Pro, Ted Williams Series 25.00
Fleer, 1960, common player (1–79) 4.00
Fleer, 1961, #4, Cap Anson 4.00
Fleer, 1963, #5, Willie Mays 200.00
Fleer, 1981, #640A, Mike Schmidt 2.00
Fleer, 1982, #229, Nolan Ryan 6.00
Fleer, 1985, #12, Keith Hernandez, Limited Edition
Series 10
Fleer, 1986, #1, Don Mattingly, All–Stars Series 8.00
Fleer, 1989, #3, Jose Canseco, Canseco Slams LA,
World Series 50
Hostess, 1975, #2, Cookie Rojas, Hostess Twinkie Series 1.00
Hostess, 1975, #37, Dave Winfield 20.00
Hostess, 1976, #12, Rick Manning 50

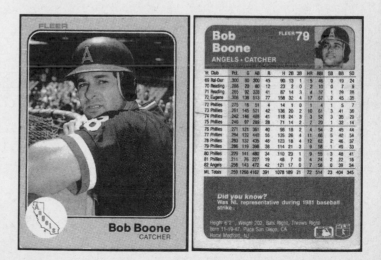

Fleer, 1983, #79, Bob Boone, 8¢.

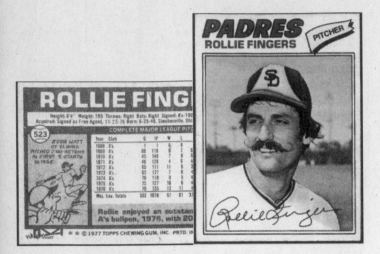

Topps, 1977, #523, Rollie Fingers, $2.00.

Hostess, 1976, #22, Johnny Bench, Hostess Twinkie
Series 12.00
Hostess, 1977, #5, Thurman Munson..................... 4.00
Hostess, 1978, #11, Willie Stargell..................... 3.00
Hostess, 1979, complete set (150) 225.00
Kellogg's, 1970, #32, Reggie Jackson 22.00
Kellogg's, 1971, #6, Gaylord Perry.................... 20.00
Kellogg's, 1972, #16, Bobby Murcer 1.00
Kellogg's, 1974, #42, Cookie Rojas 75
Kellogg's, 1975, #7, Johnny Bench.................... 12.50
Kellogg's, 1976, #18, Greg Luzinski.....................75
Kellogg's, 1977, #14, Steve Garvey 3.00
Leaf, 1948–49, #1, Joe DiMaggio 2,000.00
Leaf, 1960, #41, Ernie Broglio........................ 5.00
Leaf, 1990, #1, Steve Sax 15.00
Leaf, 1992, complete set (528)....................... 15.00
Leaf, 1993, #15, Casey Candaele.........................10
Topps, 1951, #4, Hoot Evers, Current All–Star Series....... 250.00
Topps, 1951, #6, Philadelphia Athletics Team.............. 200.00
Topps, 1952, #Topps, 190, Don Johnson 30.00
Topps, 1953, #76, Pee Wee Reese 175.00
Topps, 1954, #37, Whitey Ford 100.00
Topps, 1955, #19 and #20, Karl Spooner and Jim
Hughes, Double Header Series 40.00
Topps, 1956, #150, Duke Snider 90.00
Topps, 1958, #312, Boston Red Sox Team 15.00
Topps, 1959, #69, Giants Team 25.00
Topps, 1960, #34, Sparky Anderson.................... 18.00
Topps, 1961, #542, Minnesota Twins Team.............. 70.00
Topps, 1962, #15, Norm Cash, Baseball Bucks Series........ 5.00
Topps, 1962, #43, Los Angeles Dodgers Team 8.00
Topps, 1963, complete set (46), Stick–On Insert Series 275.00
Topps, 1964, #109, Rusty Staub 5.00
Topps, 1965, ##39, Jim Fregosi, Embossed Series 75
Upper Deck, 1989, #1, Ken Griffey Jr 75.00
Upper Deck, 1990, #285, Manny Lee.....................05
Upper Deck, 1990, complete set (10), Jackson Heroes
Series 20.00
Upper Deck, 1991, complete set (10), Hank Aaron
Series 7.00
Upper Deck, 1993, #1, Phillie Phanatic, Fun Pac
Mascots Series.................................... 1.50

Upper Deck, 1993, complete set (9), All–Stars Series 18.00
Upper Deck, 1994, #5, Chipper Jones, Fun Pack Series....... 2.00
Upper Deck, 1995, #R9, Matt Williams, Predictor
League Leaders Series 2.50

BASEBALL MEMORABILIA

Baseball traces its beginnings to the mid–19th century. By the turn of the century it had become America's national pastime.

The superstar has always been the key element in the game. Baseball greats were popular visitors at banquets, parades, and more recently at baseball autograph shows. Autographed items, especially those used in an actual game, command premium prices. The bigger the star, the bigger the price tag.

References: Mark Allen Baker, *Sports Collectors Digest Baseball Autograph Handbook, Second Edition,* Krause Publications, 1991; Mark Baker, *Team Baseballs: The Complete Guide to Autographed Team Baseballs,* Krause Publications, 1992; David Bushing, *Sports Equipment Price Guide,* Krause Publications, 1995; David Bushing and Joe Phillips, *Vintage Baseball Glove 1997 Pocket Price Guide, Vol. 1, No. 5,* published by authors, 1997; Douglas Congdon–Martin and John Kashmanian, *Baseball Treasures: Memorabilia From the National Pastime,* Schiffer Publishing, 1993; Mark Larson, *Sports Collectors Digest Complete Guide to Baseball Memorabilia, Third Edition,* Krause Publications, 1996; Mark Larson, Rick Hines, and Dave Platta (eds.), *Mickey Mantle Memorabilia,* Krause Publications, 1993; Roderick A. Malloy, *Malloy's Sports Collectibles Value Guide,* Wallace–Homestead, Krause Publications, 1993; Norman E. Martinus and Harry L. Rinker, *Warman's Paper,* Wallace–Homestead, Krause Publications, 1994; Michael McKeever, *Collecting Sports Memorabilia,* Alliance Publishers, 1996; Tuff Stuff (eds.), *Baseball Memorabilia Price Guide,* Antique Trader Books, 1998; Jim Warren II, *Tuff Stuff's Complete Guide to Starting Lineup: A Pictorial History of Kenner Starting Lineup Figures,* Antique Trader Books, 1997.

Periodicals: *Baseball Hobby News,* 4540 Kearny Villa Rd, San Diego, CA 92123; *Sports Collectors Digest,* 700 E State St, Iola, WI 54990; *Tuff Stuff,* PO Box 1050, Dubuque, IA 52004.

Newsletter: *Diamond Duds,* PO Box 10153, Silver Spring, MD 20904.

Collectors' Clubs: Society for American Baseball Research, PO Box 93183, Cleveland, OH 44101; The Glove Collector, 14057 Rolling Hills Ln, Dallas, TX 54210.

Baseball, Detroit Tigers, sgd, 1936.................. **$1,800.00**
Baseball, New York Yankees, sgd, 1934 .... 3,200.00
Baseball, St Louis Browns, sgd, 1936 .... 500.00
Bat, Louisville Slugger, 125, Joe DiMaggio, facsimile sig-
nature on barrel, c1936–40 .... **12,650.00**
Bat, Louisville Slugger, Karl Spooner, 1955 World Series .. 2,300.00
Batting Glove, Rickey Henderson, Mizuno, sgd 90.00
Book, *Big–Time Baseball,* Ben Olan, history text,
192 pp, 1958 .... 35.00
Bread Label, Fischer Baking, Mel Parnell, #23, Boston
Red Sox, 1952–52, 2³/₄ x 2³/₄"..................... 35.00
Bread Label, National Tea Company, Yogi Berra, #2,
New York Yankees, 1952, 2³/₄ x 2¹/₁₆"................ 180.00

Bread Label, Northland Bread, Mannie Minoso, #18, Chicago White Sox, $2^1/_{16}$ x $2^1/_{16}$" 50.00

Check, sgd by Ty Cobb and Pete Rose, First National Bank of Nevada, May, 2, 1960 .... 2,300.00

Christmas Card, sent by Lou Gehrig from Japan, orig envelope, 1931 .... 1,000.00

Dixie Lid, Chico Carrasquel, Chicago White Sox, blue tint, 1952 .... 40.00

Fan, Pete Rose, diecut, "Ty–Breaker/Cobb Buster" 20.00

Game, Authentic Major League Baseball Game, Sports Games, Inc, 1962 .... 20.00

Game, Electric Baseball, "Jim Prentice Brings You, True To Life Action," 1940s 60.00

Jacket, Brooklyn Dodgers, blue and white, "Dodgers" on front, embroidered "16" near zipper, c1947 ...... 2,000.00

Jersey, Ken Griffey, Jr of Seattle Mariners, sgd, 1989 ..... 3,500.00

Jersey, Orel Hershiser of Los Angeles Dodgers, sgd "Orel Hershiser 1988 Cy Young, 59 scoreless innings," 1988 .. 3,200.00

Magazine, *Baseball Monthly*, March 1962, Vol 1, #1, first edition, BRS Publishing Co, 64 pp 35.00

Photograph, Babe Ruth, sgd "To my friend Rudy Rudd from 'Babe' Ruth, Nov 9, 1926," 8 x 10" 2,000.00

Photograph, Mickey Mantle, Casey Stengel, and Elston Howard, sgd, 1955 World Series, 7 x 9". 1,350.00

Pinback Button, Babe Ruth, Mickey Mantle, and Roger Maris, "The Greatest Home Run Hitters, Shooting For 61 in '61, New York Yankees," 6" d 3,500.00

Poster, "'Babe' Ruth will do some swatting At Lake Oscawano, August 21," c1920s 3,500.00

Press Pin, 1923 World Series, New York 1,350.00

Program, 1936 Major League All Star Game 1,400.00

Program, 1938 World Series, sgd 2,000.00

Ring, New York Mets, 1969 World Champions, sales-man's sample, "Hodges" on side panel 2,500.00

Ring, Karl Spooner, Brooklyn Dodgers, 1955 World Championship 20,500.00

Sheet Music, *Bam, It's Going, Going, Gone*, Cincinnati Reds cov, 1939 .... 65.00

Sign, 1955 World Series Brooklyn Dodgers, Schaefer Beer adv, diecut 2,500.00

Ticket Stub, 1945 World Series, Chicago Cubs and Detroit Tigers, Wrigley Field 20.00

Tray, plastic, Mets, sgd by players, and "property of Ed Kranepool 1969" 850.00

Yearbook, Philadelphia Phillies, 1950 .... 50.00

BASKETBALL CARDS

Muriad cigarettes issued the first true basketball trading cards in 1911. In 1933 Goudey issued the first basketball cards found in gum packs. The era of modern hoop basketball trading cards dates from 1948 when Bowman created the first set devoted exclusively to the sport. By the 1950s Topps, Exhibit Supply Company, Kellogg's, Wheaties, and other food manufacturers joined with Bowman in creating basketball trading cards. Collectors regard the 1957–58 Topps set as the second true modern basketball set.

Today basketball trading card sets are issued by a wide variety of manufacturers. Collectors also must contend with draft card series, special rookie cards, insert or chase cards and super premi-um card sets. Keeping up with contemporary issues is time con-suming and expensive. As a result, many collectors focus only on pre–1990 issued cards.

References: James Beckett, *The Official 1998 Price Guide to Basketball Cards*, 7th Edition, House of Collectibles, 1997; James Beckett and Grant Sandground (eds.), *Beckett Basketball Card Price Guide, No. 7*, Beckett Publications, 1997; Sports Collectors Digest, *1998 Sports Collectors Almanac*, Krause Publications, 1998.

Periodicals: *Beckett Basketball Card Magazine*, 15850 Dallas Pkwy, Dallas, TX 75248; *Sports Cards Magazine & Price Guide*, 700 E State St, Iola, WI 54990.

Fleer, 1961–62, #27, George Lee $15.00

Fleer, 1973–74, #8, Driving Hook, The Shots Series 3.00

Fleer, 1987–88, #1, Kareem Abdul–Jabbar 8.00

Fleer, 1990–91, #1, Charles Barkley, All–Stars Series .... .75

Fleer, 1991–92, #52, Magic Johnson, Tony's Pizza Series 15.00

Fleer, 1992–93, complete set (444) 25.00

Fleer, 1993–94, #2, Jim Jackson, Sharpshooters Series 4.00

Fleer, 1994–95, #1, Mookie Blaylock, Triple Threats Series ...... .25

Fleer, 1995–96, #2, Karl Malone, Towers of Power Series 6.00

Harlem Globetrotters, 1971–72, #8, Mel Davis and Curly Neal, Globetrotters, Cocoa Puffs Series, Fleer 6.00

Harlem Globetrotters, 1971–72, #17, Meadlowlark Lemon, Globetrotters Series, Fleer 6.00

Harlem Globetrotters, 1974, #20, J C Gipson and Granny, Wonder Bread Series. 5.00

Harlem Globetrotters, 1992, #82, City Slickers, Comic Images .... .15

Hoops, 1989–90, #17, Reggie Lewis .... .25

Hoops, 1989–90, complete set (7), Announcers Series 350.00

Hoops, 1990, #4, Moses Malone, Superstars Series .... .40

Hoops, 1991–92, #9, Larry Bird, Prototypes Series 15.00

Hoops, 1995–96, #18, Patrick Ewing, Hoop's Magazine/Mother's Cookies Series, $8^1/_2$ x 11" 4.00

Sky Box, 1990–91, common card (301–423) .... .10

Sky Box, 1990–91, complete set (10), Prototypes Series 100.00

Sky Box, 1991–92, #86, Dennis Rodman, Prototypes Series 30.00

Sky Box, 1992–93, #ST6, Georgia Tech, John Salley and Dennis Scott, School Ties Series .... .40

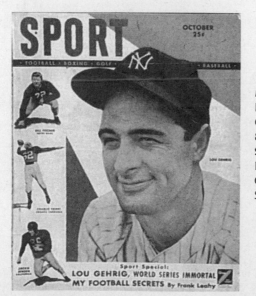

Magazine, *Sport*, Lou Gehrig cov, October 1948, $8^1/_2$ x $10^3/_4$", $20.00. Photo courtesy Collectors Auction Services.

Upper Deck, 1993, #6, Larry Johnson, Behind the Glass series, $3.00.

Topps, 1948, complete set (252), Magic Photos Series **3,500.00**
Topps, 1957–58, #49, Walt Davis **40.00**
Topps, 1969–70, #12, Gus Johnson **15.00**
Topps, 1970–71, common card (1–110), 2¹/₂ x 4¹¹/₁₆". **2.50**
Topps, 1973–74, #80, Wilt Chamberlain **25.00**
Upper Deck, 1990–91, #32, Magic Johnson, Prototypes
   Series **400.00**
Upper Deck, 1991–92, #2, Charlotte Hornets Team, Stay
   in School Series. **6.00**
Upper Deck, 1992–93, #22, Larry Bird, 1981–86 three
   NBA Championships, Larry Bird Heroes Series **1.00**
Upper Deck, 1992–93, complete set (38), MVP
   Holograms Series **25.00**

BASKETBALL MEMORABILIA

The first basketball game was played on a regulation 94 x 50′ court in 1891. James Naismith, physical director of the Y.M.C.A. College, Springfield, Massachusetts, originated the game. Early basketball collectibles relate to high school and college teams.

Professional basketball was played prior to World War II. However, it was not until 1949 and the founding of the United States National Basketball Association that the sport achieved national status. Competing leagues, franchise changes, and Olympic teams compete for collector loyalty.

References: Mark Larson, *Complete Guide to Football, Basketball & Hockey Memorabilia*, Krause Publications, 1995; Roderick Malloy, *Malloy's Sports Collectibles Value Guide: Up–to–Date Prices For Noncard Sports Memorabilia*, Attic Books, Wallace–Homestead, Krause Publications, 1993.

Basketball, 1985 All Star Team, sgd **$3,500.00**
Drawing, Michael Jordan wearing "Bulls 23" uniform,
   color pastel, by Rit LaStarza, sgd by Jordan, 19 x 23". . . **1,800.00**
Figurine, Charles Barkley, Gartlan USA, 1992. . . . . **30.00**
Game, Basketball, Transogram, 1969 . . . . **30.00**
Jacket, John Havilek of Boston Celtics, 1984 Old Timers
   Game, name sgd on inside label **500.00**
Jersey, Jerry West of Los Angeles Lakers, 1973–74 season . . **4,500.00**
Magazine, *All–Pro Basketball Stars*, Julius Erving, 1978 . . . . . . **10.00**
Magazine, *Hoop*, Larry Bird, May 1985 . . . . **8.00**

Pennant, Chris Mulin, Win Craft, 1992. . . . . **4.00**
Plate, Magic Johnson, sgd, Gartlan USA **275.00**
Poster, Willis Reed, 1968–71 . . . . **20.00**
Program, NBA All–Star Game, West vs East in Los
   Angeles, 1972 . . . . **15.00**
Ticket, Detroit, NBA All–Star Game, 1959 . . . . **25.00**
Uniform, Darrall Imhoff, worn in 1960 Olympic Games
   in Rome, sgd **3,000.00**
Yearbook, New Orleans Jazz, 1976–77 . . . . **10.00**

BAUER POTTERY

John Bauer founded the Paducah Pottery in Paducah, Kentucky, in 1885. John Andrew Bauer assumed leadership of the pottery in 1898 following the death of John Bauer. In 1909 the pottery moved its operations to Los Angeles, California.

The company's award winning artware line was introduced in 1913. Molded stoneware vases were marketed shortly thereafter.

In 1931 Bauer Pottery began production of its most popular line—Ring ware. Decorated in brightly colored glazes, it included over a hundred different shapes and sizes in table and kitchen lines. Ring ware proved to be Bauer's most popular and profitable pattern. Other successful lines include Monterey (1936–45), La Linda (1939–59), and Brusche Contempo and Monterey Moderne (1948–61). Increasing competition at home and abroad and a bitter strike in 1961 forced Bauer to close its doors in 1962.

References: Susan and Al Bagdade, *Warman's American Pottery and Porcelain*, Wallace–Homestead, Krause Publications, 1994; Jack Chipman, *Collector's Encyclopedia of Bauer Pottery: Identification & Values*, Collector Books, 1997; Lois Lehner, *Lehner's Encyclopedia of U.S. Marks on Pottery, Porcelain & Clay*, Collector Books, 1988; Mitch Tuchman, *Bauer: Classic American Pottery*, Chronicle Books, 1995.

Newsletter: *Bauer Quarterly*, PO Box 2524, Berkeley, CA 94702.

Brusche Contempo, butter, yellow speck **$20.00**
Brusche Contempo, dinner service, service for 4 plus
   serving pieces, pink speck **95.00**
Brusche Contempo, gravy, pink speck **20.00**
Brusche Contempo, tea set, teapot and four #46 mugs,
   spice green **45.00**
Brusche Contempo, vegetable bowl, indigo brown,
   7¹/₂" d **20.00**
Gloss Pastel Kitchenware, batter bowl, green, 2 qt **55.00**
Gloss Pastel Kitchenware, casserole, in metal holder,
   1 qt **40.00**
Gloss Pastel Kitchenware, coffeepot, individual, canary
   yellow **35.00**
Gloss Pastel Kitchenware, cookie jar, blue, matte **90.00**
Gloss Pastel Kitchenware, jug, 1 qt. **40.00**
Gloss Pastel Kitchenware, mixing bowl, #18, orange. **25.00**
Gloss Pastel Kitchenware, teapot, canary yellow, 8 cup. **55.00**
La Linda, ball jug, ice lip, gray. **95.00**
La Linda, carafe, chartreuse, glossy, wood handle. **20.00**
La Linda, cookie jar, jade **85.00**
La Linda, creamer, turquoise **20.00**
La Linda, cup and saucer, pink, matte **15.00**
La Linda, dinner plate, chartreuse, 9" d **15.00**
La Linda, fruit bowl, canary yellow **10.00**
La Linda, plate, dark brown, glossy, 7¹/₂" d **20.00**
La Linda, plate, ivory, glossy, 9¹/₂" d **10.00**

Ring, mixing bowl, cobalt blue, #24, 7⁵/₈" d, $45.00.

La Linda, ramekin, pink, glossy 7.50
La Linda, shaker, tall, turquoise, glossy. 15.00
La Linda, teapot, olive green, 8 cup 35.00
La Linda, tumbler, burgundy, glossy, metal handle 20.00
Monterey Moderne, berry bowl burgundy 18.00
Monterey Moderne, beverage server, cov, orange–red 125.00
Monterey Moderne, bread and butter plate, Monterey
    blue, 6" d 10.00
Monterey Moderne, chop plate, California orange–red 50.00
Monterey Moderne, chop plate, canary yellow, 13" d 35.00
Monterey Moderne, coffee server, wood handle, 8 cup 35.00
Monterey Moderne, creamer and sugar, midget orange 55.00
Monterey Moderne, fruit bowl, ftd, yellow, 13" d 60.00
Monterey Moderne, gravy boat, canary yellow 33.00
Monterey Moderne, luncheon plate, blue, 9¹/₂" d 12.00
Monterey Moderne, luncheon plate, turquoise, 9¹/₂" d 15.00
Monterey Moderne, platter, canary yellow, 17" l 45.00
Monterey Moderne, salad plate, white, 7¹/₂" d 17.50
Monterey Moderne, soup bowl, blue, 7¹/₂" d 30.00
Monterey Moderne, teapot, cov, canary yellow, 6 cup 65.00
Monterey Moderne, tumbler, orange–red, 9 oz 20.00
Monterey Moderne, vegetable bowl, divided, Monterey
    blue 45.00
Ring, berry bowl, green. 35.00
Ring, berry bowl, orange. 35.00
Ring, berry bowl, yellow 35.00
Ring, bread and butter plate, green 45.00
Ring, bread and butter plate, orange 45.00
Ring, bread and butter plate, yellow 45.00
Ring, butter, oblong, green. 195.00
Ring, creamer, orange 60.00
Ring, cup and saucer, black. 150.00
Ring, cup and saucer, cobalt 85.00
Ring, cup and saucer, yellow 85.00
Ring, dinner plate, green, 9" d 65.00
Ring, dinner plate, light blue, 9" d 65.00
Ring, dinner plate, orange, 9" d 65.00
Ring, dinner plate, yellow 65.00
Ring, pitcher, delphinium, 2 qt. 275.00
Ring, place setting, ivory, 5 pcs 250.00
Ring, punch cup, black 125.00
Ring, salad plate, green, 7" d 50.00
Ring, salad plate, orange, 7" d . , ... 50.00
Ring, saucer, green 25.00

Ring, saucer, light blue 25.00
Ring, saucer, orange 25.00
Ring, sugar, green 85.00
Ring, teapot, orange, 6 cup 125.00
Ring, tumbler, ftd, cobalt. 225.00

BEANIE BABIES

While there is an extremely active secondary resale market for Ty's Beanie Babies, it is highly manipulated and speculative. Prices fluctuate wildly. The Beanie Babies' bubble will burst, as did other contemporary collectibles such as Holiday Barbie, Precious Moments, and Tickle Me Elmo. The only question is when.

Many factors can contribute to the collapse of a speculative secondary market for a contemporary item. Several already are impacting on the Beanie Babies market. Dozens of companies have launched competitive products, e.g., the Idea Factory's Meanies and Walt Disney's cartoon character plush toys. Even Avon has gotten into the act. A general feeling has developed that prices have reached the ridiculous level. Many Beanie Babies advertised in the hundreds of dollars are going unsold. Finally, counterfeits are flooding the secondary market. United States Customs agents in Chicago have seized hundreds of counterfeit examples of high–end Beanie Babies, including 456 examples of Grunt, the red razorback boar. One collector reportedly paid $1,500 for a counterfeit Peanut the Elephant sold on the Internet.

The market is flooded with Beanie Baby price guides. Consider carefully how accurately they reflect the secondary retail market. A few years from now, their only value will be the ability to look nostalgically back on the craze and think "if I had only sold then."

References: Sharon Brecka, *The Beanie Family Album and Collectors Guide,* Antique Trader Books, 1998; Les and Sue Fox, *The Beanie Baby Handbook,* West Highland Publishing, 1997; Peggy Gallagher, *The Beanie Baby Phenomenon, Volume 1: Retired,* published by author, 1997; Rosie Wells, *Rosie's Price Guide for Ty's Beanie Babies,* Rosie Wells Enterprises, 1997.

Note: See page 431 for an **Exclusive Report** on Beanie Babies.

BEATLES

Beatlemania took the country by storm in 1964, the year the Beatles appeared on "The Ed Sullivan Show." Members of the Fab Four included George Harrison, John Lennon, Paul McCartney, and Ringo Starr (who replaced original drummer Pete Best in 1962). The most desirable items were produced between 1964 and 1968 and are marked "NEMS."

The group disbanded in 1970 and individual members pursued their own musical careers. John Lennon's tragic murder in New York City in 1980 invoked a new wave of interest in the group and its memorabilia.

References: Jeff Augsburger, Marty Eck, and Rick Rann, *The Beatles Memorabilia Price Guide, Third Edition,* Antique Trader Books, 1997; Perry Cox and Joe Lindsay, *The Official Price Guide to The Beatles,* House of Collectibles, 1995; Barbara Crawford and Michael Stern, *The Beatles: A Reference and Value Guide, Second Edition,* Collector Books, 1998; Courtney McWilliams, *The Beatles, Yesterday and Tomorrow: A Collector's Guide to Beatles Memorabilia,* Schiffer Publishing, 1997.

Periodicals: *Beatlefan*, PO Box 33515, Decatur, GA 30033; *Good Day Sunshine*, PO Box 1008, Los Angeles, CA 90066; *Instant Karma*, PO Box 256, Sault Ste. Marie, MI 49783; *Strawberry Fields Forever*, PO Box 880981, San Diego, CA 92168.

Collectors' Clubs: Beatles Connection, PO Box 1066, Pinellas Park, FL 34665; Working Class Hero Club, 3311 Niagara St, Pittsburgh, PA 15213.

REPRODUCTION ALERT: Records, picture sleeves, and album jackets have been counterfeited. Sound quality may be inferior. Printing on labels and picture jackets usually is inferior to the original. Many pieces of memorabilia also have been reproduced, often with some change in size, color, design, etc.

Ashtray, glass, black portraits, white ground, unmkd, c1964, 3³/₄ x 3³/₄ x ³/₄" **$100.00**

Binder, vinyl covered cardboard, blue, sepiatone front photo, black facsimile signatures, ©NEMS Enterprises Ltd, 1964, 9¼ x 11¼" **100.00**

Book, *The Beatles*, Pocket Books, Inc, ©1964, 32 pp, 8½ x 10³/₄" **25.00**

Buckle, gold luster, black and white photo insert under clear plastic cov, unmkd, c1964, 2 x 3" **45.00**

Cake Decorations, set of 4, plastic, figural Beatles heads, painted accents, mkd "Hong Kong," c1950, 1½" h **50.00**

Comic Book, Strange Tales, Vol 1, #30, Mar 1965, "Meet The Beatles," Marvel Comics **15.00**

Game, The Beatles Flip Your Wig Game, Milton Bradley, 1964 .... **125.00**

Guitar, plastic, front portrait images and facsimile signatures, head mkd "Beatles Guitar," pocket clip on back, Mastro, c1964, 5¼" h **200.00**

Lunch Bag, vinyl, zippered lid, handle, ©NEMS Enterprises Ltd, Aladdin Industries, Inc, 1965 .... **400.00**

Magazine Article, *Life*, Aug 28, 1964, 7 pp, black and white photos, color cov photo **25.00**

Magazine, *Saturday Evening Post*, color photos, Aug 8–15, 1964 .... **20.00**

Mug, ceramic, white ground, black and white portrait photos, illus suits, black facsimile signatures and name, mkd "England" on bottom, c1964, 4" h **100.00**

Photograph, color, Beatles wearing gray suits, one foot resting on stuffed donkey, facsimile signatures, ©NEMS, 1964, 8 x 10" **20.00**

Pinback Button, "I'm A Official Beatles Fan," litho, red, white, and blue, black and white portrait photos, Green Duck Co, ©1964 NEMS Enterprises Ltd, 4" d **20.00**

Poster, "The Beatles," banner type, black and white photo images on red and white ground, star, musical note, and heart designs, Dell, 18½ x 8½" **50.00**

Poster, "The Beatles/Let It Be," black, white, and yellow, color photos, 1970, 13 x 30" **45.00**

Rug, fabric with portraits of Beatles, guitar, snare drum, and musical notes, "Made In Belgium" stitched tag, c1964, 22 x 34" **200.00**

Soaky, Paul McCartney, ©NEMS Enterprises Ltd, 10" h **100.00**

Thermos, metal, group illus, ©NEMS Enterprises Ltd, Aladdin Industries, Inc, 1965, 6½" h. **200.00**

Ticket, Fox Theater, release of *A Hard Day's Night*, black and yellow, Beatles photo image, 7 PM, Sep 2–3, 1964, 4 x 7½" **70.00**

Ticket, King's Hall, Balmoral, peach paper, Nov 2, 1964, 3³/₄ x 6¼" **150.00**

Ticket, live closed circuit telecast of Washington concert, simultaneously broadcast at Norva Theater, Norfold, VA, orange paper, black text, Sunday, Mar 15, 1964, 2½ x 5½" **75.00**

Toy, The Yellow Submarine, diecast, metal and plastic, revolving periscopes, spring–operated hatches, Corgi, c1968, 2 x 5½" **200.00**

Wrapper, "Beatles Ice Cream Bar," waxed paper, maroon and orange design, offer for "Lucky Beatle Coin," Country Club Ice Cream Co, c1964 .... **20.00**

Lunch Box, litho tin, Aladdin, ©1965 NEMS Enterprises, $235.00. Photo courtesy Collectors Auction Services.

BELLEEK, AMERICAN

The American Belleek era spanned from the early 1880s until 1930. Several American firms manufactured porcelain wares resembling Irish Belleek. The first was Ott and Brewer Company of Trenton, New Jersey, from 1884 until 1893. Companies operating between 1920 and 1930 include Cook Pottery (1894–1929), Coxon Belleek Pottery (1926–1930), Lenox, Inc. (1906–1930), Morgan Belleek China Company (1924–1929), and Perlee, Inc. (1920s–c1930).

Reference: Mary Frank Gaston, *American Belleek*, Collector Books, 1984, out of print.

Bowl, white ware, dragon shaped handles, Lenox artist's palette mark, 13" d **$100.00**

Chocolate Pot, individual, sterling silver overlay, Lenox artist's palette mark, 5¼" h **150.00**

Coffeepot, applied silver with pink floral garlands, thin yellow enamel horizontal lines, Lenox artist's palette mark, 11" h **500.00**

Creamer, blue and pink transfer floral design, wide yellow outer border, gold trim, Coxon mark, 5" h **250.00**

Dinner Plate, small enamel flowers inner border, yellow outer border, Coxon mark, 10½" d **150.00**

Figure, swan, green, Lenox green wreath mark **65.00**

Mask, lady's face, black, Lenox green wreath mark,
7¹/₂" h **175.00**

Perfume, figural rabbit, white, Lenox green wreath mark,
price for pair **525.00**

Plate, Bouquet pattern, gold trim, Coxon mark, 8" d **100.00**

Plate, peacocks and flowers dec, gold trim, Gordon
Belleek mark, 7" d **40.00**

Salt, individual, hp leaf dec, gold trim, 3 ftd, Cook mark,
1³/₄" h, 2¹/₂" d **130.00**

Sugar, cov, single pink flowers and narrow gold lines
border, gold angular handles, gold trim, sq pedestal
base, Lenox green wreath mark, 6" h **130.00**

Talcum Shaker, hp rose garland with blue bow dec, pale
blue ground, gilded top, artist sgd, Lenox artist's
palette mark, 6" h **100.00**

Vase, black top border with multicolored floral design,
gold trim, Perlee mark, 5" h **80.00**

Vase, bulbous, pine cone and branches dec, Lenox
green wreath mark, 8¹/₂" h **55.00**

Vase, hp red and white poppies, gold rim, artist sgd "E.S.
Wilcox," Lenox artist's palette mark, 16" h **300.00**

Vase, hp Springer Spaniel on front, white ground, gold
rim, gold "Hunter Arms Co. First Prize" on back, artist
sgd "Baker," Lenox green wreath mark, 8¹/₄" h **450.00**

BELLEEK, IRISH

Belleek is a thin, ivory–colored, almost iridescent–type porcelain. It was first made in 1857 in county Fermanagh, Ireland. Production continued until World War I, was discontinued for a period of time, and then resumed.

Shamrock is the most commonly found pattern, but many patterns were made, including Limpet, Tridacna, and Grasses. Pieces made after 1891 have the word "Ireland" or "Eire" in their mark. Some are marked "Belleek Co., Fermanagh."

The following abbreviations have been used to identify marks:

1BM	=	1st Black Mark (1863–1890)
2BM	=	2nd Black Mark (1891–1926)
3BM	=	3rd Black Mark (1926–1946)
4GM	=	4th Green Mark (1946–1955)
5GM	=	5th Green Mark (1955–1965)
6GM	=	6th Green Mark (1965–c1980)
B/GM	=	Brown/Gold Mark (1980–present)

References: Susan and Al Bagdade, *Warman's English & Continental Pottery & Porcelain, 2nd Edition,* Wallace–Homestead, Krause Publications, 1991; Richard K. Degenhardt, *Belleek: The Complete Collector's Guide and Illustrated Reference, Second Edition,* Wallace–Homestead, Krause Publications, 1993.

Collectors' Club: The Belleek Collectors' Society, 144 W Britannia St, Taunton, MA 02780.

Ashtray, shamrock horseshoe, 4GM, 4¹/₂" d **$45.00**

Basket, Urne pattern, shamrock, basketweave, green
rope trim, 2BM **500.00**

Breakfast Set, cup, saucer, and plate, Pine Cone pattern,
pink edge, 2BM **350.00**

Creamer, Ampanida pattern, double handle, pink trim,
2BM **225.00**

Creamer, Undine pattern, cob luster, 3BM, 5" h **85.00**

Coffeepot, Shamrock pattern, B/GM, 6¹/₂" h, $250.00.

Creamer and Sugar, Lotus pattern, 3BM **80.00**
Creamer and Sugar, Neptune pattern, 6GM **95.00**
Cup and Saucer, Shell pattern, 3BM **90.00**
Ewer, mask face and emb designs under handle, green,
gold trim, 2BM, 8¹/₂" h **800.00**
Figure, Irish Greyhound, 3BM **620.00**
Figure, Leprechaun, on mushroom, 3BM, 5¹/₂" h **300.00**
Flower Pot, Diamond pattern, 2BM, 3¹/₂" h **145.00**
Jug, Tridacna pattern, pink trim and handle, 2BM, 5¹/₂" h **600.00**
Mug, Shamrock pattern, 3BM, 6" h **100.00**
Plate, Shamrock pattern, 3BM, 8¹/₂" d **50.00**
Salt Shaker, Shell pattern, 3BM **50.00**
Teapot, Neptune pattern, shell feet and finial, green trim,
2BM **300.00**
Tobacco Box, Mask Tea Ware, cob luster, 3BM,
6¹/₂ x 3³/₄" **300.00**
Vase, figural frog, black eye accents, 2BM, 6" h **1,380.00**
Vase, Princess pattern, flowers, yellow, blue, pink, and
white, 2BM **800.00**

BESWICK

James Wright Beswick and his son, John Beswick, are well known for their ceramic figures of horses, cats, dogs, birds, and other wildlife. Produced since the 1890s, figures representing specific animal characters from children's stories, such as Winnie the Pooh and Peter Rabbit, have also been modeled. In 1969 the company was bought by Royal Doulton Tableware, Ltd.

References: Diana Callow et al., *The Charlton Standard Catalogue of Beswick Animals, Second Edition,* Charlton Press, 1996; Diana and John Callow, *The Charlton Standard Catalogue of Beswick Pottery,* Charlton Press, 1997; Harvey May, *The Beswick Price Guide, Third Edition,* Francis Joseph Publications, 1995, distributed by Krause Publications.

Note: See Royal Doulton for further information.

Figure, "Cats Chorus," #LL8, 4³/₄" h **$40.00**
Figure, Christopher Robin, #2395, 4³/₄" h **175.00**

Figure, dog, begging, Beswick backstamp, 4³/₄" h **80.00**
Figure, geese, #820, 4" h, price for pair **40.00**
Figure, goat, #398, 4¹/₂" h **60.00**
Figure, Golden Eagle, #2062, Royal Doulton backstamp,
   9¹/₂" h **175.00**
Figure, kitten, climbing, #1857 . . . . **90.00**
Figure, owl, #2238, 6³/₄" h **80.00**
Figure, panda, #711, 4¹/₂" h **75.00**
Figure, penguin, #800, 2" h **20.00**
Figure, Peter Rabbit, #1098/2, Beatrix Potter, 4¹/₂" h **80.00**
Figure, pheasant, #849, wings up, Beswick backstamp,
   6" h **175.00**
Figure, quarter horse, #2186, 8¹/₄" h **120.00**
Figure, Queen of Hearts, #2490, 4" h **100.00**
Figure, Scottie, #2037, 4¹/₂" h **40.00**
Figure, shepherd boy, 2 sheep under arm, #1124, 6¹/₄" h **300.00**
Figure, Snow White, #1332, 5" h **600.00**
Figure, trout, #2087, 6" h **175.00**
Figure, woman on donkey, #1244, 5¹/₂" h **300.00**
Flask, pheasant, #2208, 3¹/₂" h **20.00**
Jug, "A Midsummer Night's Dream," #1366, 8" h **150.00**
Jug, Jeremy Fisher, #3006, Beatrix Potter, 2³/₄" h **80.00**
Tankard, "Ghost of Christmas Past," #2532 . . . . **60.00**
Wall Plaque, "Don't Worry It May Never Happen,"
   8 x 8³/₄" **300.00**
Wall Plaque, flamingo, #731, 15" l **325.00**
Wall Plaque, horse's head, #807, 7¹/₄ x 6" **100.00**
Wall Plaque, hummingbird, #1023/1, 5³/₄" l **120.00**
Wall Plaque, indian, #282, 7¹/₂" h **150.00**
Wall Plaque, Jemima Puddleduck, #2082, Beatrix Potter,
   6" h **1,500.00**

BICYCLES & RELATED

The bicycle was introduced in America at the 1876 Centennial. Early bicycles were high wheelers with heavy iron frames and disproportionately sized wooden wheels. By 1892 wooden wheels were replaced by pneumatic air–filled tires, which were later replaced with standard rubber tires with inner tubes. The coaster brake was introduced in 1898.

Early high wheelers and safety bikes made into the 1920s and 1930s are classified as antique bicycles. Highly stylized bicycles from the 1930s and 1940s represent the transitional step to the classic period, beginning in the late 1940s and running through the end of the balloon tire era.

References: Jim Hurd, *Bicycle Blue Book*, Memory Lane Classics, 1997; Jay Pridmore and Jim Hurd, *The American Bicycle*, Motorbooks International, 1995; Jay Pridmore and Jim Hurd, *Schwinn Bicycles*, Motorbooks International, 1996; Neil S. Wood, *Evolution of the Bicycle*, Volume 1 (1991, 1994 value update), *Volume 2* (1994) L–W Book Sales.

Periodicals: *Antique/Classic Bicycle News*, PO Box 1049, Ann Arbor, MI 48106; *National Antique & Classic Bicycle*, PO Box 5600, Pittsburgh, PA 15207.

Newsletters: *Bicycle Trader*, PO Box 3324, Ashland, OR 97520; *Classic & Antique Bicycle Exchange*, 325 W Hornbeam Dr, Longwood, FL 32779; *Classic Bike News*, 5046 E Wilson Rd, Clio, MI 48420.

Collectors' Club: Classic Bicycle and Whizzer Club, 35769 Simon Dr, Clinton Twp, MI 48035.

Bicycles

Columbia Goodyear, boy's, c1940, 24" . . . . : **$45.00**
Elgin Robin, brown and cream, c1937 . . . . **2,500.00**
Evel Knievel Tricycle, 1964 . . . . **450.00**
Inland, Pinky–Lee Sports Trike, 1955 . . . . **400.00**
Lindy, decal on down tube, orig airplane front fender
   ornament, Shelby, Ohio, 1929 . . . . **6,500.00**
Monark Tandem, balloon tires, front wheel drum brake,
   headlight, tool bag, book rack, Sweden, c1940s **350.00**
Roadmaster Junior, 1955 . . . . **300.00**
Schwinn Black Phantom, boy's, Limited Edition,
   1995, 26" **1,700.00**
Schwinn Li'l Chick, girl's, blue and white, c1969, 20" **110.00**
Schwinn Varsity, boy's, red and white, c1976, 27" **150.00**
Sears Hydraulic, boy's, 10 speed, apple green, 26" **35.00**
Shelby Flying Cloud, 1947 . . . . **650.00**
Stelber, Bozo Talking Tricycle, plastic battery operated
   mounted Bozo bust on front, rear hubcaps with emb
   stars, plastic red, white, and blue streamers on han-
   dlebars, 1961 . . . . **350.00**
Westfield Compax, c1940, folding, rechromed rims,
   bars, gooseneck, and cranks, orig tires and pedals,
   unused saddle, orig paint, c1940 . . . . **150.00**
Yamaha BMX, 1970s **500.00**

Related

Billhead, Warren Bros Bicycles & Sporting Goods,
   Birmingham, AL, printed black and white, 1927, used **$25.00**
Book, *Bicycling: The Bicycle in Recreation, Competition,
   Transportation*, Nancy N Baranet, London, 1973 . . . . **15.00**
Book, *Fifty Years of Road Riding 1885–1935*, The History
   of the North Road Cycling Club, SH Moxham,
   Bedford, England, dj, c1935 . . . . **115.00**
Book, *The Wonderful Ride*, G T Loher's 1895 coast to
   coast tour on his Yellow Fellow Wheel, Harper & Row,
   San Francisco, orig dj, 1978 . . . . **15.00**
Catalog, Columbia, 1932 . . . . **50.00**

Columbia 3 Star Deluxe, boy's, blue, c1950, 26", $330.00. Photo courtesy Copake Auction.

Generator Kit, "Make–A–Lite," head lamp, generator,
   and tail lamp, Chefford Master Mfg Co, c1940 . . . . **65.00**
Magazine, *The Boneshaker*, Autumn 1955–60, Southern
   Veteran Cycle Club, 21 volumes **55.00**
Motor, Vroom, Mattel, battery operated, 1964 . . . . **45.00**
Photograph, boy and dog with Rollfast Deluxe
   Motobike, framed, c1925, 8 x 10" **55.00**
Pocketknife, Tour de France, brass, c1930. . . . . **155.00**
Racing Medal, engraved "Gentlemen 1943," 2" d **30.00**
Sign, Columbia Built Bicycles, electric, transfer on glass,
   c1940, 25" l, 14" h **460.00**
Sign, Rudge Britain's Best, electric, transfer on plexiglass,
   c1960, 10 ½ x 14". **115.00**
Sign, Schwinn Built Bicycles, Art Deco, electric, transfer
   on glass, c1930, 24 x 10 ½". **500.00**
Siren, Superman, Empire, 1970s **25.00**
Trading Card, Greg LeMond, sgd **35.00**

#1171, *Dan Dunn Secret Operative 48 and the Crime Master*, 1937, $20.00.

BIG LITTLE BOOKS

Big Little Books is a trademark of the Whitman Publishing Company. In the 1920s Whitman issued a series of books among which were Fairy Tales, Forest Friends, and Boy Adventure. These series set the stage for Big Little Books.

The year 1933 marked Big Little Books' first appearance. Whitman experimented with ten different page lengths and eight different sizes prior to the 1940s. Many Big Little Books were remarketed as advertising premiums for companies such as Cocomalt, Kool Aid, Macy's, and others. Whitman also published a number of similar series, e.g., Big Big Books, Famous Comics, Nickel Books, Penny Books, and Wee Little Books.

In an effort to keep the line alive, Whitman introduced television characters in the Big Little Book format in the 1950s. Success was limited. Eventually, Mattel–owned Western Publishing absorbed Whitman Publishing.

References: Bill Borden, *The Big Book of Big Little Books*, Chronicle Books, 1997; Larry Jacobs, *Big Little Books: A Collector's Reference & Value Guide*, Collector Books, 1996; Lawrence F. Lowery, *Lowery's: The Collector's Guide to Big Little Books & Similar Books*, Educational Research and Applications Corp, 1981, out of print; *Price Guide to Big Little Books & Better Little, Jumbo, Tiny Tales, A Fast–Action Story, Etc.*, L–W Books Sales, 1995.

Collectors' Club: Big Little Book Collector Club of America, PO Box 1242, Danville, CA 94526.

#714, *Jackie Cooper Movie Star of "Skippy" and "Sooky"* . . . **$25.00**
#734, *Chester Gump at Silver Creek Ranch* **35.00**
#772, *Erik Noble and the Forty Niners* **20.00**
#1101, *Hairbreadth Harry in Department QT* **25.00**
#1103, *Little Orphan Annie with the Circus* **35.00**
#1108, *Bobby Benson on the H–Bar–O Ranch* **20.00**
#1120, *Little Miss Muffet* **20.00**
#1121, *Frank Merriwell at Yale* **15.00**
#1122, *Scrappy* **45.00**
#1123, *Joe Palooka* **40.00**
#1130, *Apple Mary and Dennie Foil the Swindlers* **20.00**
#1148, *David Copperfield* **15.00**
#1183, *Tom Mix and the Stranger From the South* **30.00**
#1188, *Buck Jones in the Fighting Rangers* **20.00**
#1189, *Mac of the Marines in Africa* **25.00**
#1194, *Buffalo Bill Plays a Lone Hand* **10.00**

#1199, *Perry Winkle and the Rinkeydinks* **25.00**
#1400, *Nancy and Sluggo* **45.00**
#1400, *Red Ryder and Little Beaver on Hoofs of Thunder* **30.00**
#1401, *Just Kids* **25.00**
#1405, *Uncle Wiggly's Adventures* **20.00**
#1408, *Don Winslow and the Giant Girl Spy* **20.00**
#1409, *Buck Rogers vs The Fiend of Space* **65.00**
#1413, *Hal Hardy in the Lost Land of Giants* **25.00**
#1415, *Blondie and Baby Dumpling* **20.00**
#1415, *Kayo and Moon Mullins and the One Man Gang* **25.00**
#1421, *Smokey Stover the Foo Fighter* **40.00**
#1422, *Popeye the Sailor Man* **35.00**
#1425, *Riders of the Lone Trails* **15.00**
#1426, *Walt Disney's Brer Rabbit, Song of the South* **40.00**
#1431, *Mandrake the Magician and the Midnight
   Monster* **35.00**
#1434, *Dick Tracy and the Phantom Ship* **30.00**
#1434, *Donald Duck Forgets to Duck* **45.00**
#1440, *Bugs Bunny in Risky Business* **30.00**
#1441, *Andy Panda in the City of Ice* **20.00**
#1442, *Tillie Toiler and the Wild Man of Desert Island* **45.00**
#1443, *Big Chief Wahoo* **20.00**
#1444, *Mickey Mouse in the World of Tomorrow* **45.00**
#1448, *Air Fighters of America* **20.00**
#1441, *Andy Panda in the City of Ice* **20.00**
#1442, *Ken Maynard and the Gun Wolves of the Gila* **20.00**
#1452, *Tarzan the Untamed* **35.00**
#1453, *Chuck Malloy Railroad Detective on the
   Streamliner* **10.00**
#1456, *Our Gang Adventures* **35.00**
#1461, *Little Orphan Annie in the Movies* **45.00**
#1464, *Dirigible–ZR90 and the Disappearing Zeppelin* **20.00**
#1464, *Flame Boy and the Indians' Secret* **10.00**
#1466, *Pilot Pete Dive Bomber* **15.00**
#1468, *Brick Bradford with Brocco the Mountain
   Buccaneer* **20.00**
#1482, *Detective Higgins of the Racket Squad* **15.00**
#1487, *Blondie, Baby Dumpling and All!* **25.00**
#1491, *Dick Tracy and the Man with No Face* **30.00**
#1495, *Tarzan and the Jewels of Opar* **40.00**
#1498, *Radio Patrol and Big Dan's Mobsters* **20.00**
#1558, *Betty Boop in Miss Gulliver's Travels* **70.00**

BIG LITTLE BOOK TYPES

Today, Big Little Books is often used as a generic term that describes a host of look–alike titles from publishers such as Dell, Engel–Van Wiseman, Lynn, and Saalfield.

References: Larry Jacobs, *Big Little Books: A Collector's Reference & Value Guide*, Collector Books, 1996; Lawrence F. Lowery, *Lowery's: The Collector's Guide to Big Little Books and Similar Books*, Educational Research and Applications Corp, 1981, out of print; *Price Guide to Big Little Books & Better Little, Jumbo, Tiny Tales, A Fast–Action Story Etc.*, L–W Book Sales, 1995.

Dell Fast–Action Story, *Bugs Bunny and the Secret of Storm Island*	**$55.00**
Dell Fast–Action Story, *Tail Spin Tommy and the Airliner Mystery*, ©1938	**25.00**
Engle Van–Wiseman, Five Star Library, *Buck Jones in Rocky Rhodes*, #20, ©1935	**15.00**
Engle Van–Wiseman, Five Star Library, *Rex King of Wild Horses in Stampede*, #12, ©1935	**15.00**
Golden Press, Golden Star Book, *Autumn Tales*, ©1955	**5.00**
Golden Press, Golden Star Book, *Walt Disney's Snow White*, #6076, ©1967	**10.00**
Lynn Book, *Donnie and the Pirates*, #L13, ©1935	**15.00**
Lynn Book, *Victor Hugo's Les Miserables*, #L10, ©1935	**20.00**
Saalfield, *Jumbo Book, Abbie 'an Slats*, #1175, ©1940	**30.00**
Saalfield, *Little Big Book, Chandu the Magician*, #1323, ©1935	**20.00**
Samuel Lowe, *Nevada Jones, Trouble Shooter*, ©1949	**5.00**
Samuel Lowe, *Swap–It Book, Little Tex's Escape*, ©1949	**5.00**
Whitman 710 Series, *Woody Woodpecker Big Game Hunter*, #710–10	**30.00**
Whitman Better Little Book, *Big Chief Wahoo*, #1443, ©1938	**25.00**
Whitman Big Big Book, *Skippy, The Story of*, #4056	**150.00**
Whitman New Little Better Book, *Blondie and Dagwood Some Fun!*, ©1949	**20.00**
Whitman Tiny Tales, *Cowboy Bill*, #2952, ©1950	**10.00**

Whitman 710 Series, Roy Rogers and the Snowbound Outlaws, #701–10, ©1949, $20.00.

BING & GRONDAHL

Frederick Grondahl and brothers Meyer and Jacob Bing founded Bing & Grondahl in 1853 to create replicas of the work of the famed Danish sculptor Thorvaldsen. The company's initial success led to an expansion of its products that included elegant dinnerware, coffee services, and other tabletop products.

In 1895 Harald Bing decided to test the idea of a plate designed specifically for sale during the Christmas season. F. A. Hallin, a Danish artist, created "Behind the Frozen Window" which appeared on a limited edition of 400 plates with the words "Jule Aften" (Christmas Eve) scrolled across the bottom and decorated in the company's signature blue and white motif. While Bing & Grondahl's annual Christmas plate is its most recognized and collected product, collectors have expanded their focus to include the company's figurines, dinnerware, and other desirables.

References: Pat Owen, *Bing & Grondahl Christmas Plates: The First 100 Years*, Landfall Press, 1995, distributed by Viking Import House; Rinker Enterprises, *The Official Price Guide to Collector Plates, Sixth Edition*, House of Collectibles, 1996.

Cake Plate, flying seagulls, blue and white, open handles	**$80.00**
Demitasse Cup and Saucer, multicolored flowers on cup front, gold leaves on body and saucer, blue and gold line rims	**30.00**
Figure, boy playing accordian, #1661SV, 9" h	**180.00**
Figure, cat, #2527, white, 2" h	**50.00**
Figure, chimney sweep, kissing girl, polychrome, 9" h	**350.00**
Figure, dog, white body, gray spots and ears, B & G mark, 6" h	**135.00**
Figure, "Ear Ache," white, B & G mark, 5" h	**30.00**
Figure, girl feeding cat, #1745, "One Drop," 5¼" h	**400.00**
Figure, girl kissing boy, 7" h	**140.00**
Figure, grouse, 7" h	**100.00**
Figure, "Little Mother," #1779	**230.00**
Figure, mandolin player, on stool, #1600, 11" h	**325.00**
Figure, Pekinese dog, #2114, B & G mark, 8" l	**80.00**
Figure, soldier, hiding in tree stump, polychrome, 8¼" h	**350.00**
Gravy Boat, with attached undertray, Seagull pattern, gold trim	**150.00**
Vase, Eskimo pattern, blue–green seal killing scene, blue bands, mkd "B. & G. Denmark," c1925	**1,275.00**

BLACK MEMORABILIA

Black memorabilia is a generic term covering a wide range of materials from advertising to toys made in the image of a black person or featuring an image of a black person in its artwork. The category also includes materials from the era of slavery, artistic and literary contributions by black people, Civil Rights memorabilia, and material relating to the black experience in America.

Much of the material in this category is derogatory in nature, especially pre–1960s material. In spite of or perhaps because of its subject, it is eagerly sought by both white and black collectors.

Interest in Civil Rights memorabilia has increased significantly in the past decade.

References: Douglas Congdon–Martin, *Images in Black: 150 Years of Black Collectibles*, Schiffer Publishing, 1990; Patiki Gibbs, *Black Collectibles Sold in America*, Collector Books, 1987, 1996 value update; Myla Perkins, *Black Dolls: 1820–1991*, Collector Books, 1993, 1995 value update; Myla Perkins, *Black Dolls, Book II: An Identification and Value Guide*, Collector Books, 1995; Dawn E. Reno, *The Encyclopedia of Black Collectibles*, Wallace–Homestead, Krause Publications, 1996; J. P. Thompson, *Collecting Black Memorabilia: A Picture Price Guide*, L–W Book Sales, 1996; Jean Williams Turner, *Collectible Aunt Jemima*, Schiffer Publishing, 1994; Jackie Young, *Black Collectibles: Mammy and Her Friends*, Schiffer Publishing, 1988.

Newsletter: *Lookin Back at Black*, 6087 Glen Harbor Dr, San Jose, CA 95123.

Collectors' Club: Black Memorabilia Collector's Assoc, 2482 Devoe Terrace, Bronx, NY 10468.

Ashtray, ceramic, black boy pushing barrel of ashes, 4" l.... **$40.00**
Badge, cardboard, diecut, litho paper front, Aunt Jemima, "Pancake Days Are Happy Days," 4" d......... 70.00
Book, *Little Brown Koko*, Blanche Hunt, American Colortype Co, 1952, 96 pp 25.00
Comic Book, Clean Fun Starring Sugarfoots Jones, 1944 .... 135.00
Doll, cloth, stuffed, vinyl, Mammy, printed flower dress, white scarf and apron, floral accent bandanna, white underclothes, stitched red fabric shoes, unmkd, c1930s, 17" h 85.00
Game, The Black Experience, cover shows history of black and faces of famous people, Theme Productions, 1971....................... 15.00
Match Holder, diecut cardboard, litho paper, red tin holder, caricature cook image, "Ah Is Yo' Helpful Mandy, Ah Keeps De Home Fires Bright. Yo'll Fine Me Mighty Handy When Yo All Needs A Light," reverse inked 1930 gift inscription, 1½ x 2¾ x 5".............. 75.00
Measuring Cups, set of 4, china, native with exaggerated flat nose, dark fuchsia purple lips, soft yellow ring in each ear, repeated spiral design of gray hair curls on back, black and white accents, various liquid measures mkd on bottom, stamped "Japan," c1950s 200.00
Pinback Button, "Free Angela And All Political Prisoners," black and yellow 10.00

Salt and Pepper Shakers, pr, Mammy and Chef, ceramic, unmkd, $85.00.

Pinback Button, "N.A.A.C.P. 1948," brown, cream lettering 20.00
Pitcher, china, figural black woman with exaggerated features, off-white dotted orange outfit, light blue sleeve cuffs, mkd "Germany," 1930s................ 100.00
Program, Porgy and Bess, 1944 .... 50.00
Sheet Music, *Carolina Mammy*, pink and white, black and white Aunt Jemima photo and inscription "Successfully Sung By Aunt Jemima," 1922, 9 x 12" 20.00
Sign, emb cardboard, diecut, black children with watermelon, c1920 .... 45.00
Tab, Aunt Jemima Breakfast Club, litho tin, diecut, multicolored portrait under red title bar, c1950.......... 15.00
Table Set, Aunt Jemima and Uncle Moses, plastic, 3½" salt and pepper shakers, 3 x 2" cov sugar bowl and creamer, F & F Mold & Dye Works, Dayton, Ohio, 1950s... 70.00
Timer, black chef, sand, double vial, unmkd, 1930s, 3¼" h 70.00
Trivet, metal, relief image of black painted face, open mouth, red painted tongue, wearing white chef's hat, 1930s 45.00

BLUE RIDGE POTTERY

The Carolina Clinchfield and Ohio Railroad established a pottery in Erwin, Tennessee, in 1917. J. E. Owens purchased the pottery in 1920 and changed the name to Southern Potteries. The company changed hands again within a few years, falling under the ownership of Charles W. Foreman.

By 1938 Southern Potteries was producing its famous Blue Ridge dinnerware featuring hand–painted decoration. Lena Watts, an Erwin native, designed many of the patterns. In addition, Blue Ridge made limited production patterns for a number of leading department stores.

The company experienced a highly successful period during the 1940s and early 1950s, the Golden Age of Blue Ridge. However, cheap Japanese imports and the increased use of plastic dinnerware in the mid–1950s sapped the company's market strength. Operations ceased on January 31, 1957.

References: Betty and Bill Newbound, *Collector's Encyclopedia of Blue Ridge Dinnerware* (1994), *Vol. II* (1998), Collector Books; Betty and Bill Newbound, *Southern Potteries, Inc.: Blue Ridge Dinnerware, Revised Third Edition*, Collector Books, 1989, 1996 value update; Frances and John Ruffin, *Blue Ridge China Today*, Schiffer Publishing, 1997.

Periodical: *Blue Ridge Beacon Magazine*, PO Box 629, Mountain City, GA 30562.

Newsletter: *National Blue Ridge Newsletter*, 144 Highland Dr, Blountville, TN 37617.

Collectors' Club: Blue Ridge Collectors Club, 208 Harris St, Erwin, TN 37650.

Cake Plate, maple leaf............................. **$125.00**
Candy Box, Fruits, 6".............................. 95.00
Celery, French Peasant............................. 95.00
Creamer, Carnival 10.00
Cup, Arlington Apple, rope handle................... 4.00
Demitasse Cup and Saucer, Colonial 15.00

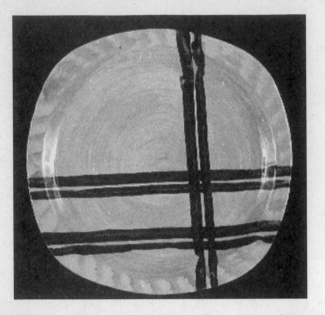

Salad Plate, Piedmont Plaid, Piecrust shape, 7⁷/₈" w, $10.00.

Dinner Plate, Beaded Apple, 10¹/₂" d 7.00
Dinner Plate, Carnival, 9¹/₂" d 15.00
Dinner Plate, Colonial, 9¹/₄" d 15.00
Dinner Service, Country Fair, service for 8 . . . . 75.00
Dinner Service, Rustic Plaid, service for 8 with serving
    pcs 200.00
Flat Soup, Sculptured Grape 22.00
Fruit Bowl, Bluebell Bouquet 4.00
Leaf Relish, Fruit Punch 50.00
Pitcher, chick, 6" 75.00
Pitcher, Sculptured Fruit, 6¹/₂" 60.00
Pitcher, Sculptured Fruit, 7¹/₂" 60.00
Plate, Duplicate Astor, 12" d 35.00
Platter, Turkey and Acorns 75.00
Ramekin, cov, Garden Green, 4³/₄" 45.00
Relish, Spring Shower, T handle 40.00
Salt and Pepper Shakers, pr, Blossom Top 25.00
Salt and Pepper Shakers, pr, Colonial 15.00
Saucer, Beaded Apple 3.00
Saucer, French Peasant 10.00
Sugar, Bluebell Bouquet 8.00
Vase, Delphine 75.00
Vase, Gladys, boot, 8" 65.00

BOEHM PORCELAIN

Edward and Helen Boehm founded The Boehm Studio in 1950. It quickly became famous for its superb hand–painted, highly detailed sculptures of animals, birds, and flowers. Boehm also licensed his artwork to manufacturers of collector plates.

Boehm porcelains are included in the collections of over 130 museums and institutions throughout the world. Many U.S. presidents used Boehm porcelains as gifts for visiting Heads of States.

Reference: Reese Palley, *The Porcelain Art of Edward Marshall Boehm*, Harrison House, 1988, out of print.

Collectors' Club: Boehm Porcelain Society, PO Box 5051, Trenton, NJ 08638.

Red Shouldered Hawk, #40251, 1984, $975.00.

Amanda, with parasol, #10269, 1986 . . . . $750.00
American Bald Eagle, #40185, 1981 . . . . 1,330.00
American Redstart, #40138, 1958 . . . . 1,090.00
Blackburnian Warbler, #40253, 1984 . . . . 965.00
Bluebonnets, #30050, 1980 . . . . 775.00
Calliope Hummingbird, #40319, 1987 . . . . 595.00
Caprice Iris, pink, #30049, 1980 . . . . 725.00
Chicadees, #400–61, 1976 . . . . 1,550.00
Elephant, white bisque, #200–44B, 1985 . . . . 575.00
Fledging Brown Thrasher, #400–72A, 1977 . . . . 680.00
Fledging Great Horned Owl, #479, 1965 . . . . 1,590.00
Hunter, #203, 1952 . . . . 1,400.00
Kirkland's Warble, #40169, 1980 . . . . 890.00
Meg, with basket, #10268, 1986 . . . . 625.00
Orchid, Cymbidium, #30114, 1984 . . . . 625.00
Queen of the Night Cactus, #300–14, 1976 . . . . 895.00
Red Breasted Nuthatch, #40118, 1979 . . . . 925.00
Soaring Eagle, #40296B, 1985 . . . . 960.00
Spanish Iris, #300–29, 1978 . . . . 760.00
Waterlily, #300–10, 1974 . . . . 725.00

BOOKENDS

Theme is the most important consideration when placing a value on bookends. In most cases, the manufacturer is unknown, either because the bookends are unmarked or research information about the mark is unavailable. Be alert to basement workshop examples. Collectors prefer mass-produced examples.

References: Douglas Congdon–Martin, *Figurative Cast Iron: A Collector's Guide*, Schiffer Publishing, 1994; Louis Kuritzky, *Collector's Guide to Bookends: Identification and Values*, Collector Books, 1997; Gerald P. McBride, *A Collector's Guide to Cast Metal Bookends*, Schiffer Publishing, 1997; Robert Seecof, Donna Lee Seecof and Louis Kuritsky, *Bookend Revue*, Schiffer Publishing, 1996.

Collectors' Club: Bookend Collector Club, 4510 NW 17th Pl, Gainesville, FL 32605.

Note: All bookends are priced as pairs.

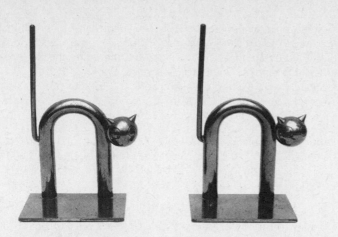

Art Deco Cats, mkd "Chase," 4 x 2¹/₂" base, 7¹/₂" h, $350.00.

Abraham Lincoln, sitting, plated iron, BronzMet, 5 x 5¹/₂" . . . **$60.00**

American Eagle, plated iron, Bradley & Hubbard Mfg
Co, 6 x 4¹/₂" **80.00**

Bowling Ball and Pins, plated iron, 5¹/₂ x 6". **40.00**

Church, painted iron, Champion Hardware Co, ©1931,
5 x 3³/₄" **40.00**

Clipper Ship, glass, crystal, New Martinsville. **125.00**

Eagle, glass, clear, Fostoria **125.00**

Hunter and Huntress, #9928, bronze, Judd Mfg Co,
5³/₄ x 5¹/₂" **25.00**

John Alden and Priscilla, painted iron, Bradley &
Hubbard Mfg Co, 6 x 3³/₄" **100.00**

Lion's Head, bronze, 4¹/₄ x 4¹/₄" **100.00**

Man, muscular pose, Art Deco, bronze, 6 x 5¹/₄" **40.00**

Oil Lamp, double flame, painted iron, Judd Mfg Co,
4¹/₂ x 5". **75.00**

Owl, glass, clear, Fostoria **250.00**

Pirate, plated iron, Littco Mfg Co, 7 x 4¹/₂". **60.00**

Quail, #461, painted iron, Hubley Mfg Co, 5¹/₂ x 5¹/₂". **150.00**

Sailing Ship, #9661, painted bronze, Judd Mfg Co,
5¹/₄ x 4" **100.00**

Tiger and Snake, painted iron, Connecticut Foundry, 1928,
5 x 5" **50.00**

BOOKS

Given the millions of books available, what does a collector do? The answer is specialize. Each edition of this price guide will focus on one or more specialized collecting categories.

This edition focuses on limited edition modern press and illustrated books. Values for many of these titles are determined more by the perceived value of the individuals who illustrated them than they are by the value attached to the press that printed them.

References: Allen Ahearn, *Book Collecting: A Comprehensive Guide*, G. P. Putnam's Sons, 1995; Allen and Patricia Ahearn, *Collected Books: The Guide to Values*, F. P. Putnam's Sons, 1997; *American Book Prices Current*, Bancroft–Parkman, published annually; Ron Barlow and Ray Reynolds, *The Insider's Guide to Old Books, Magazines, Newspapers, Trade Catalogs*, Windmill Publishing, 1995; Ian C. Ellis, *Book Finds: How to Find, Buy and Sell Used and Rare Books*, Berkley Publishing, 1996; *Huxford's Old Book Value Guide, Tenth Edition*, Collector Books, 1998; Marie Tedford and Pat Goudey, *The Official Price Guide to Old*

Books, Second Edition, House of Collectibles, 1997; John Wade, *Tomart's Price Guide to 20th Century Books,* Tomart Publications, 1994; Nancy Wright, *Books: Identification and Price Guide,* Avon Books, 1993.

Periodicals: *AB Bookman's Weekly,* PO Box AB, Clifton, NJ 07015; *Biblio Magazine,* 845 Wilamette St, PO Box 10603, Eugene, OR 97401.

Firsts: *The Book Collector's Magazine,* PO Box 65166, Tucson, AZ 85728; *Book Source Monthly,* 2007 Syosett Dr, PO Box 567, Cazenovia, NY 13035.

Newsletter: *Rare Book Bulletin,* PO Box 201, Peoria, IL 61650.

Collectors' Club: Antiquarian Booksellers Assoc of America, 20 West 44th St, 4th Flr, New York, NY 10036.

Banister, Judith, *Old English Silver,* New York, GP Putnam's Sons, 1965, 287 pp, marks, forgeries, chronological survey of development of English silver from before the Restoration to the machine age, black and white and line illus, 7 x 10". **$40.00**

Berry–Hill, Henry and Sidney, *Antique Gold Boxes: Their Lore and Lure,* New York, Abelard Press, 1953, 223 pp, English and European boxes of the 18th and 19th centuries, black and white illus, 8¹/₂ x 11". **60.00**

Butler, Joseph T, *Candleholders in America, 1650–1900: A Comprehensive Collection of American and European Candle Fixtures Used in America,* New York, Crown Publishers, 1967, 178 pp, black and white illus, 7¹/₂ x 10¹/₂", dj. **50.00**

Chipman, Frank W, *The Romance of Old Sandwich Glass,* Sandwich Publishing Company, 1938, 2nd printing, 7 x 10¹/₂". **60.00**

Clouston, Kate W, *The Chippendale Period in English Furniture,* Weathervane Books, 1975, 224 pp, facsimile of 1897 edition, 200 drawings, 6 x 9", dj **35.00**

Davidson, Marshall B, *Early American Tools,* Olivetti, 1975, 80 pp, black and white illus, 10¹/₂ x 12" **100.00**

Ducret, Siegfried, *Unknown Porcelain of the 18th Century,* Frankfurt am Main, Lothar Woeller Verlag, 1956, 142 pp, 5 tipped–in color and 70 black and white plates, 7 x 10", dj. **150.00**

Gilhespy F Bradshaw, *Crown Derby Porcelain,* Leigh–on–Sea, F Lewis, 1951, 108 pp, edition limited to 600 sgd copies, 108 black and white plates, 7¹/₂ x 10", dj **325.00**

Hammond, Dorothy, *Confusing Collectibles: A Guide to the Identification of Reproductions (with) More Confusing Collectibles, Vol. 2,* 221 pp, Leon, Mid–American Book Co, 1969 and 1972, color and black and white illus, softcover, 47 pp softcover supplement, 7 x 10", 8¹/₂ x 11", dj **75.00**

Holstein, Jonathan, *American Pieced Quilts,* New York, Viking Press, 1973, Makowski 293, 94 pp, color and black and white illus, 6¹/₂ x 6¹/₂", dj **50.00**

Hughes, G Bernard, *Horse Brasses and Other Small Items for the Collector,* London, Country Life Ltd, 1956, 104 pp, color frontispiece and 42 black and white plates, 6¹/₂ x 10", lightly chipped dj. **50.00**

Jacobs, Carl, *Guide to American Pewter,* New York, McBride, 1957, 216 pp, black and white illus, 6 x 9", dj. **40.00**

Jones, John, *Wonders of the Stereoscope*, New York, Alfred A Knopf, 1976, 2 volumes, 126 pp, numerous black and white illus in first volume, volume 2 housing plastic folding stereoscopic viewer and 48 reproduction cards, slipcase, 9¹/₂ x 10¹/₂" **125.00**

Kendrick, A F, *Catalogue of Early Medieval Fabrics*, London, V & A Museum, 1925, 74 pp, 25 black and white plates, ex library copy, rebound in buckram, stamped, 7¹/₂ x 10" **65.00**

Putnam, P A, *Bottled Before 1865*, P A Putnam, 1968, 100 pp, black and white illus, softcover, 8¹/₂ x 11" **45.00**

Roberts, Kenneth, *The Collector's Whatnot*, Boston, Houghton Mifflin, 1923, 147 pp, line illus, 5¹/₂ x 8¹/₂" **75.00**

Watkins, Lura Woodside, *American Glass and Glassmaking*, New York, Chanticleer Press, 1950, 104 pp, 4 color plates and 51 black and white illus, 6¹/₂ x 9", dj **40.00**

AUCTION PRICES

Swann Galleries, Public Auction Sale 1765, September 18, 1997. Prices include a 15% buyer's premium.

Kelley, Charles Fabens and Ch'en Meng–Chia, *Chinese Bronzes From the Buckingham Collection*, Chicago, 1946, 84 plates and photographic illus, 4to, cloth gilt, lightly rubbed **$46.00**

Major, Howard, *The Domestic Architecture of the Early American Republic: The Greek Revival*, Philadelphia & London, 1926, color frontispiece, 256 plates, 4to, cloth gilt, few spots on rear cover, dj, lightly worn **126.00**

Mourlot, Fernand, *Art in Posters: The Complete Original Posters of Braque, Chagall, Dufy, Leger, Matisse, Miro, Picasso*, New York, 1959, profusion of color plates, 4to, cloth, dj, few tears, contents becoming loose in binding **161.00**

Museum of Modern Art, *Ludwig Mies Van Der Rohe: Drawings in the Collection of the Museum of Modern Art, New York*, 31 plates, notes by Ludwig Glaeser, New York, 1969, oblong folio, spiral bound gilt boards, publisher's box **201.00**

Guide, Collector Books, 1997; E. Christian Mattson and Thomas B. Davis, *A Collector's Guide to Hardcover Boys' Series Books*, published by authors, 1996; Diane McClure Jones and Rosemary Jones, *Collector's Guide to Children's Books, 1850 to 1950: Identification & Values*, Collector Books, 1997; Edward S. Postal, *Price Guide & Bibliography to Children's & Illustrated Books*, M. & P. Press, 1994.

Periodicals: *Book Source Monthly*, 2007 Syossett Dr, PO Box 467, Cazenovia, NY 13035; *Mystery & Adventure Series Review*, PO Box 3488, Tucson, AZ 85722; *Yellowback Library*, PO Box 36172, Des Moines, IA 50315.

Newsletters: *The Authorized Edition Newsletter*, RR1, Box 73, Machias, ME 04654; *Martha's KidLit Newsletter*, PO Box 1488, Ames, IA 50010.

Collectors' Clubs: Movable Book Society, PO Box 11645, New Brunswick, NJ 08906; The Society of Phantom Friends, PO Box 1437, North Highlands, CA 95660.

Note: There are numerous collectors' clubs for individual authors. Consult the *Encyclopedia of Associations* at your local library for further information.

Aiken, Joan, *The Whispering Mountain*, Pat Marriott illus, Jonathan Cape, London, 1968, 1st ed **$110.00**

Angelo, Valenti, *Big Little Island*, Valenti Angelo illus, Viking, 1955, 1st ed, 190 pp **20.00**

Ashford, Daisy, *Daisy Ashford Her Book*, Doran, 1920, 1st ed, cloth photo of author set in stamped design, 338 pp **30.00**

Austin, Margot, *Churchmouse Stories*, Margot Austin illus, Dutton, Weekly Reader Book club, 1960 .... **15.00**

Barrie, J M, *Peter Pan in Kensington Gardens*, Arthur Rackham illus, Scribners, 1930/1902, 126 pp **30.00**

Bennett, Charles H., *Bennett's Fables, From Aesop and Others*,   Charles Bennett illus, Viking, 1978, 1st reprint since 1857, dj, 54 pp **12.00**

Best, Herbert, *Bright Hunter of the Skies*, Bernarda Bryson illus, Macmillan, 1961, 1st ed, 164 pp **20.00**

BOOKS, CHILDREN'S

Although children's books date as early as the 15th century, it was the appearance of lithographed books from firms such as McLoughlin Brothers and series books for boys and girls at the turn of the 20th century that popularized the concept. The Bobbsey Twins, Nancy Drew, the Hardy Boys, and Tom Swift delighted numerous generations of readers.

The first Newberry Medal for the most distinguished children's book was issued in 1922. In 1938 the Caldecott Medal was introduced to honor the children's picture book.

Most children's book collectors specialize. Award winning books, ethnic books, first editions, mechanical books, and rag books are just a few of the specialized categories.

References: E. Lee Baumgarten (comp.), *Price Guide and Bibliographic Checklist for Children's & Illustrated Books for the Years 1880–1960, 1996 Edition*, published by author, 1995; David and Virginia Brown, *Whitman Juvenile Books: Reference & Value*

Ingri & Edgar Parin D'Aulaire, *Children of the Northlights*, Viking, ©1962, 39 pp, 8³/₄ x 11⁷/₈", $15.00.

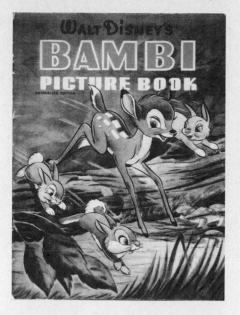

Walt Disney's Bambi Picture Book, Walt Disney Productions, 1941, 16 pp, 9½ x 13", $45.00.

Carroll, Lewis, *The Annotated Snark*, Henry Holiday illus, Simon & Schuster, 1962, 1st ed, 111 pp **30.00**

Cavanah, Frances, *Children of the White House*, Genevieve Foster illus, Rand McNally, 1936, 1st ed, dj, 35 pp **30.00**

Cleary, Beverly, *Ramona and Her Mother*, Morrow, 1979, 6th ed, 208 pp **15.00**

Dr Seuss, *Happy Birthday to You*, Dr Seuss illus, 1959, 52 pp **20.00**

Field, Rachel, *Calico Bush*, Allen Lewis illus, Macmillan, 1931, 1st ed, 213 pp **25.00**

Gavin, Maxwell, *Raven Seek Thy Brother*, Dutton, 1969, 1st ed, 210 pp **20.00**

Herriot, James, *All Things Wise and Wonderful*, St Martins, c1977, 1st ed **25.00**

Ladd, Elizabeth, *Meg's Mysterious Island*, Mary Stevens illus, Morrow, 1963, 1st ed, 218 pp **20.00**

Lenski, Lois, *Flood Friday*, Lois Lenski illus, Lippincott, 1956, 1st ed **30.00**

McKeown, Martha, *Linda's Indian Home*, Binfords, 1956, 1st ed, 79 pp, sgd and inscribed by author **35.00**

Meigs, Cornelia, *The Scarlet Oak*, Elizabeth Orton Jones illus, Macmillan, 1938, 1st ed **25.00**

Molloy, Anne, *Celia's Lighthouse*, Ursula Koering illus, Houghton Mifflin, 1949, 248 pp **25.00**

Ohanian, Phyllis Brown, *Mother Goose, Favorite Nursery Songs*, Marjorie Torrey illus, Random House, 1956, 2nd ed **35.00**

O'Neill, Mary, *Hailstones and Halibut Bones*, Leonard Weisgard illus, Doubleday, 1961, 59 pp **20.00**

Pyne, Mable, *The Little Geography of the United States*, Mable Pyne illus, Houghton Mifflin, 1941, 1st ed, dj, 36 pp **50.00**

Rawlings, Marjorie Kinnan, *The Yearling*, N C Wyeth illus, Scribners, 1961/1938, 405 pp **20.00**

Rogers, Fred, *Mister Rogers' Songbook*, Steven Kellogg illus, Random House, 1970, 59 pp **15.00**

Selden, George, *The Dog That Could Swim Under Water*, Morgan Denis illus, Viking, 1956, 1st ed, 126 pp **25.00**

Sendak, Maurice, *Where the Wild Things Are*, Maurice Sendak illus, Harper, 25th Anniversary Edition, 1988/1963, dj, 37 pp **20.00**

Squires, Elizabeth B, *David's Silver Dollar*, Margot Austin illus, Platt & Munk, c1940 . . . . **25.00**

Tudor, Tasha, *Wings From the Wind*, Tasha Tudor illus, 1955, 1st ed, 96 pp **20.00**

White, Dale, *The Wild–Horse Trap*, Richard Bennett illus, Viking, 1955, 1st ed, 192 pp, sgd by author **30.00**

Wilder, Laura Ingalls, *The Long Winter*, Garth Williams illus, Harper Row, 1940, 335 pp **20.00**

Worm, Piet, *Three Little Horses*, Piet Worm illus, Random House, 1958, 61 pp **20.00**

Yonge, Charlotte, *The Dove and the Eagle's Nest*, Marguerite deAngeli illus, Macmillan, 1926, 1st ed, 294 pp **65.00**

BOTTLE OPENERS

In an age of pull–tab and twist–off tops, many young individuals have never used a bottle opener. Figural openers, primarily those made of cast iron, are the most commonly collected type. They were extremely popular between the late 1940s and early 1960s.

Church keys, a bottle opener with a slightly down–turned "V" shaped end, have a strong following, especially when the opener has some form of advertising. Wall–mounted units, especially examples with soda pop advertising, also are popular.

Collectors' Clubs: Figural Bottle Opener Collectors Club, 3 Avenue A, Latrobe, PA 15650; Just For Openers, PO Box 64, Chapel Hill, NC 27514.

ADVERTISING

Eichler Beer, copper **$5.00**
Pabst Blue Ribbon Brew, bottle shape, 1930s **15.00**
Piels, slide–out, 1930s. **20.00**
Schlitz, wooden, bottle shape, 1939 World's Fair **30.00**
Victory Brewery, slide–out, 1930 . . . . **25.00**

FIGURAL

Clown, white ground, red and black accents, cast iron, 4½ x 4". **$50.00**
Cowboy, playing guitar, cast iron, 5 x 3¾" **100.00**
Do Do Bird, cast iron, cream, black highlights, red beak, 2¾" h **160.00**
Drunk, leaning on palm tree,
Elephant, brass, flat, standing, trunk up, mouth is opener, dark brown, 3 x 2³⁄₁₆" **80.00**
French Girl, leaning on lamp post, box mkd "449 B. O. French–Girl," cast iron, 4½ x 2" **50.00**
Goat, sitting, tan body, gray highlights, yellow curved horn on top of head, green base, Wilton Products, 4¼" h **45.00**
Hitch Hiking Sailor, white uniform, black tie and shoes, white sign with black trim, John Wright Co, 3¾" h **40.00**
Monkey, holding branch at left side, black body, tan chest and face markings, brown branch, John Wright Co, 2½" h **130.00**
Patty Pep, with hands behind head, wearing yellow mini skirt, blue blouse, yellow hat, emb "Women's Weekend '55," mkd "L & L Favors," 4" **400.00**

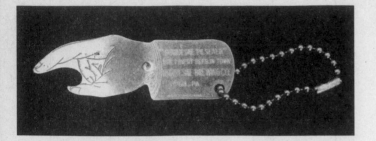

Advertising, pointing hand, aluminum, Duquesne Brewing Co, Pittsburgh, PA, 3³/₄" l, $3.00.

Skull, wall mount, off–white, black, eye sockets, 4¹/₄" h,
  3" w **500.00**
Trout, cast iron, red, orange, and green body, Wilton
  Products, 5" l **80.00**
Winking Boy, cast iron, wall mount, flesh face, red lips
  and freckles, red hair, Wilton Products, 3⁷/₈ x 3⁵/₈" **400.00**

BOTTLES

This is a catchall category. Its role is twofold—to list a few specialized bottle collecting areas not strong enough to have their own category and provide the logical place to find information about bottle references, collectors' clubs, and periodicals.

References: Ralph and Terry Kovel, *The Kovels' Bottles Price List, Tenth Edition,* Crown Publishers, 1996; Jim Megura, *The Official Identification and Price Guide to Bottles, Twelfth Edition,* House of Collectibles, 1997; Michael Polak, *Bottles: Identification and Price Guide, Second Edition,* Avon Books, 1997; Carlo and Dorothy Sellari, *The Standard Old Bottle Price Guide,* Collector Books, 1989, 1997 value update.

Periodical: *Antique Bottle and Glass Collector,* PO Box 180, East Greenville, PA 18041.

Collectors' Clubs: Federation of Historical Bottle Collectors, 88 Sweetbriar Branch, Longwood, FL 32750; Midwest Antique Fruit Jar & Bottle Club, PO Box 38, Flat Rock, IN 47234.

Note: Consult *Maloney's Antiques & Collectibles Resource Directory* by David J. Maloney, Jr., at your local library for additional information on regional bottle clubs.

Barber Bottle, hobnail pattern, opalescent cranberry,
  polished pontil, rolled lip, 1885–1925, 6⁵/₈" h **$80.00**
Barber Bottle, hobnail pattern, yellow, amber tone,
  smooth base, tooled lip, 1885–1925, 7¹/₄" h **60.00**
Barber Bottle, LeVarn's Rose Hair Tonic and Dandruff
  Cure, clear, white, black, and gold label, tooled
  mouth, Mettowee Toilet Specialty Co, Granville, NY,
  1885–1925, 7⁵/₈" h **75.00**
Commerative, Christmas, 1975, blue, Wheaton Glass Co **5.00**
Commemorative, Richard Nixon, green, miniature,
  Wheaton Glass Co **5.00**
Commemorative, Presidents, Ronald Reagan, cobalt
  blue, Wheaton Glass Co **5.00**
Commemorative, Skylab I, frosted, Wheaton Glass Co **15.00**
Flask, reproduction, calabash, emerald green, Jenny–
  Lind Glass Factory **15.00**

Flask, reproduction, ribbed and swirled, amethyst, Emil
  Larson, 4³/₄" h **115.00**
Miniature, Amber Gold Whiskey, 1930 . . . . **70.00**
Miniature, L & G Whiskey, 1931 . . . . **45.00**
Miniature, Eastside Beer, Zobelein's, Los Angeles
  Brewing Co, emb "No Deposit No Return," 1947 . . . . **10.00**

BOYD CRYSTAL ART GLASS

Boyd Crystal Art Glass, Cambridge, Ohio, traces its heritage back to Bernard C. Boyd and Zackery Thomas Boyd, two glass makers who worked for a number of companies in the Cambridge area. In 1964 Elizabeth Degenhart asked Zack Boyd to assume the management of Degenhart Glass. When Zack died in 1968, Bernard assumed leadership of the company.

In 1978, Bernard C. Boyd and his son, Bernard F., purchased Degenhart Glass. Initially working with the 50 molds acquired from Degenhart, the Boyds began making pieces in a host of new colors. Eventually, John Bernard, son of Bernard F., joined the company. Today Boyd Crystal Art Glass has over 200 molds available for its use including a number of molds purchased from other glass companies such as Imperial.

Reference: *Boyd's Crystal Art Glass: The Tradition Continues,* Boyd's Crystal Art Glass, n.d.

Newsletters: *Boyd's Crystal Art Glass Newsletter,* 1203 Morton Ave, PO Box 127, Cambridge, OH 43725; *Jody & Darrell's Glass Collectibles Newsletter,* PO Box 180833, Arlington, TX 76096.

Collectors' Club: Boyd Art Glass Collectors Guild, PO Box 52, Hatboro, PA 19040.

Bell, Santa, olde lyme **$15.00**
Card Holder, grape, primrose. **8.00**
Doll, Louise, golden delight. **10.00**
Figurine, airplane, classic black **15.00**
Figurine, bull dog head, ice green **12.00**
Figurine, Christmas Willie, 1991 . . . . **15.00**
Figurine, Chuckles the Clown, baby blue **10.00**
Figurine, Fuzzy Bear, rosewood **12.00**
Figurine, Joey, leaping pony, persimmon **15.00**
Figurine, owl, heather **10.00**
Figurine, pooch, marigold **10.00**
Figurine, Sammy the Squirrel, cashmere pink **8.00**
Master Salt, swan, lilac, 4¹/₂" h **15.00**
Salt, duck, spinnaker blue **8.00**

Debbie Duck, shasta white, $8.00.

BOY SCOUTS

William D. Boyce is the father of Boy Scouting in America. Boyce was instrumental in transferring the principles of Baden–Powell's English scouting movement to the United States, merging other American organizations into the Scouting movement, and securing a charter from Congress for the Boy Scouts of America in 1916.

Scouting quickly spread nationwide. Manufacturers developed products to supply the movement. Department stores vied for the rights to sell Scouting equipment.

The first national jamboree in America was held in Washington, D.C., in 1937. Patch trading and collecting began in the early 1950s. The Order of the Arrow, national Scouting centers, e.g., Philmont, and local council activities continually generate new collectible materials.

Reference: George Cuhaj, *Standard Price Guide to U.S. Scouting Collectibles*, Krause Publications, 1998.

Periodicals: *Fleur–de–Lis*, 5 Dawes Ct, Novato, CA 94947; *Scout Memorabilia*, PO Box 1121, Manchester, NH 03105.

Collectors' Clubs: American Scouting Traders Assoc, PO Box 210013, San Francisco, CA 94121; National Scouting Collectors Society, 806 E Scott St, Tuscola, IL 61953; World Scout Sealers, 509–11 Margaret Ave, Kitchener, Ontario N2H 6M4 Canada.

Award, brass pendant, inscribed "War Service 1945/Boy Scout Gen Eisenhower Waste Paper Campaign," suspended from metal hanger bar covered by red and white striped fabric ribbon, text on reverse **$45.00**
Calendar, 1957, "High Adventure At Philmont," Norman Rockwell color illus, Brown & Bigelow, 16 x 33" **45.00**
Certificate, Certificate of Appreciation to Den Mother, red and green print and illus, Cub Scouts in various activities, sgd by Cubmaster, dated 1955, 5 x 7" **5.00**
Game, The Boy Scouts Progress Game, Parker Brothers, ©1924–26 . . . . **250.00**
Handbook, Boy Scouts of America, Leyendecker illus cov, March 1937, 506 pp **50.00**
Magazine, *Life*, July 24, 1950, Boy Scout cov **3.50**
Pennant, felt, orange, "Philmont Scout Ranch," black lettering, 8½ x 12½" **15.00**

Photograph, Boy Scout group and leaders demonstrating camp procedures, 1938, 8½ x 6½" **25.00**
Pinback Button, "Pledged To Be First Class For Scout Rodeo," orange and black, white ground, 1930s **20.00**
Pinback Button, "Roosevelt 20th Pilgrimage, Oct 21, 1939," Teddy Roosevelt portrait and "BSA" **45.00**
Registration Card, bi–fold, Norman Rockwell illus, dated Feb 1947, orig envelope, 5 x 4" **20.00**
Tie Bar, brass, official trefoil symbol, c1940s **10.00**
Tie Slide, metal, red ground, blue rim, silver "Boy Scouts Of America–Region 3," 1930s **10.00**
Watch Fob, brass, trefoil within sunburst design, "Atlantic Area Council Patron," c1930s **20.00**

BRASTOFF, SASCHA

In 1948, Sascha Brastoff established a small pottery on Speulveda Boulevard in West Los Angeles. Brastoff's focus was that of designer. Skilled technicians and decorators gave life to his designs.

Brastoff was at the cutting edge of modern design. Figurines were introduced in the early 1950s to a line that included ashtrays, bowls, and vases. In 1953 a new studio was opened at 11520 West Olympic Boulevard. In 1954 production began on the first of ten fine china dinnerware lines.

Although Brastoff left the studio in 1963, the company survived another decade thanks to the inspired leadership of plant manager Gerold Schwartz.

References: Steve Conti, A. Dewayne Bethany and Bill Seay, *Collector's Encyclopedia of Sascha Brastoff: Identification & Values*, Collector Books, 1995; Leslie Piña, *'50s & '60s Glass, Ceramics, & Enamel Wares Designed & Signed by Georges Briard, Sascha B., Bellaire, Higgins...*, Schiffer Publishing, 1996.

Ashtray, jewel bird **$45.00**
Bookends, pr, horse **650.00**
Bowl, Chi Chi Bird, 8" d **65.00**
Box, cov, jewel bird, #020 . . . . **50.00**
Candle Holder, Aztec, 10" h **125.00**
Figure, pelican **400.00**
Figure, rooster, gold with black **750.00**

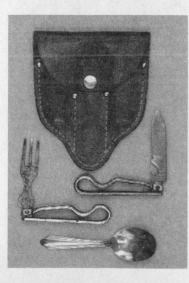

Chow Kit, brown leather case with stamped emblem, folding knife, folding fork, and spoon, $25.00.

Dish, Hawaiian boy playing ukulele, 10" l, $80.00.

Flower Pot, jewel bird, 6" h **75.00**
Pitcher, igloos, Alaska line, 10¹/₂" h **100.00**
Plate, African dancer, teal with black, full signature **650.00**
Plate, pagoda, curled lip, 12" d **85.00**
Salt and Pepper Shakers, pr, Eskimo, Alaska line **40.00**
Sculpture, nude, metal, 6" h **400.00**
Tile, white, rust, and gold leaves, black ground, sgd,
    7 x 9" **100.00**
Vase, jewel bird, F20, 6" h. **45.00**
Vase, rearing stallion, 9¹/₂" h **100.00**

BRAYTON LAGUNA CERAMICS

Durline E. Brayton founded Brayton Laguna, located in South
Laguna Beach, California, in 1927. Hand–crafted earthenware dinnerwares were initially produced. The line soon expanded to
include figurines, flowerpots, tea tiles, vases, and wall plates.

In 1938 Brayton Laguna was licensed to produce Disney figurines. Webb, Durlin's second wife, played an active role in design
and management. A period of prosperity followed.

By the end of World War II, Brayton Laguna ceramics were
being sold across the United States and abroad. In the early and
mid–1960s the company fell on hard times, the result of cheap foreign imports and lack of inspired leadership. The pottery closed in
1968.

Reference: Jack Chipman, *Collector's Encyclopedia of California
Pottery,* Collector Books, 1992, 1995 value update.

Candleholders, pr, seated blackamoors, green, 5" **$20.00**
Cookie Jar, gingham dog, blue and red. **425.00**
Creamer, cat **45.00**
Figure, bride and groom **80.00**
Figure, grouse. **70.00**
Figure, sitting clown **40.00**
Figure, swan **75.00**
Figure, zebra. **75.00**
Flower Holder, Sally, 6¹/₄" h **25.00**
Planter, blackamoor, gold trim **85.00**
Planter, girl and wolfhounds **100.00**
Planter, girl with bonnet and basket **75.00**

**Cookie Jar, gypsy,
$450.00.**

Salt and Pepper Shakers, pr, black peasants, 5" h **30.00**
Salt and Pepper Shakers, pr, calico cat and dog **50.00**
Salt and Pepper Shakers, pr, chubby Dutch kids **85.00**

BREWERIANA

Breweriana is a generic term used to describe any object, from
advertising to giveaway premiums, from bar paraphernalia to beer
cans, associated with the brewing industry. Objects are divided
into pre– and post–Prohibition material.

Breweries were one of the first industries established by early
American settlers. Until Prohibition, the market was dominated by
small to medium size local breweries. When Prohibition ended, a
number of brands, e.g., Budweiser, established themselves nationwide. Advertising, distribution, and production costs plus mergers
resulted in the demise of most regional breweries by the 1970s.

Imported beers arrived in America in the 1960s, often contracting with American breweries to produce their product. In the
1980s and 1990s America experienced a brewing renaissance as
the number of micro–breweries continues to increase.

Collectors tend to be regional and brand loyal. Because of a
strong circuit of regional Breweriana shows and national and
regional clubs, objects move quickly from the general marketplace
into the specialized Breweriana market.

References: George J. Baley, *Back Bar Breweriana: A Guide to
Advertising Beer Statues and Beer Shelf Signs,* L–W Book Sales,
1992, 1994 value update; *Beer Cans: 1932–1975,* L–W Book
Sales, 1976, 1995 value update; Herb and Helen Haydock, *The
World of Beer Memorabilia,* Collector Books, 1997; Bill Mugrage,
The Official Price Guide to Beer Cans, Fifth Edition, House of
Collectibles, 1993; Gary Straub, *Collectible Beer Trays With Value
Guide,* Schiffer Publishing, 1995; Robert Swinnich, *Contemporary
Beer Neon Signs,* L–W Book Sales, 1994; Dale P. Van Wieren,
American Breweries II, East Coast Breweriana Assoc, 1995.

Periodicals: *All About Beer,* 1627 Marion Ave, Durham, NC
27705; *Suds 'n' Stuff,* 4765 Galacia Way, Oceanside, CA 92056.

Collectors' Clubs: American Breweriana Assoc, Inc, PO Box
11157, Pueblo, CO 81001; Beer Can Collectors of America, 747
Merus Ct, Fenton, MO 63026; East Coast Breweriana Assoc, PO
Box 64, Chapel Hill, NC 27514; National Assoc of Breweriana
Advertising, 2343 Met–To–Wee Ln, Milwaukee, WI 53226.

Ashtray, Heineken, ceramic, cup shape, white ground,
    green lettering, 3⁵/₈" l, 2" h **$8.00**
Bank, Coors, aluminum, figural can **5.00**
Bell, Minster Beer, Star Brewing, Minster, OH, porcelain,
    1970s **25.00**
Belt Buckle, Stroh's **5.00**
Bottle, Neuweilers Cream Ale, Neuweiler Brewing,
    Allentown, PA, paper label, 1 qt **5.00**
Bottle, Pabst Extract, orig cap, 1933 . . . . **30.00**
Bottle, Rheingold Extra Dry Lager Beer, Liebmann
    Brewery, New York, NY, paper label, 1 qt **12.00**
Box, Gibbons Beer, Lion, Inc, Wilkes Barre, PA, card-
    board, with dividers, 1940s **5.00**
Calendar, Duke Beer, Duquesne Brewing, Pittsburgh,
    PA, tin, 1960s, 9¹/₂ x 13" **15.00**
Can, Ballantine Bock Beer, Ballantine Brewing Co,
    Newark, NJ, BCU#17/6 . . . . **30.00**

Clock, Fort Pitt, illuminated, glass face and dome, metal body, Pam Clock Co, NY, ©1956, 14½" d, $170.00. Photo courtesy Collectors Auction Services.

Can, Harvard Ale, Harvard Brewing Co, Baltimore, MD **30.00**
Can, Old Bohemian Beer, Eastern Brewing Co, Hammonton, NJ **100.00**
Can, Sunshine Beer, Sunshine Brewing Co, Reading PA **20.00**
Certificate, Burlington Brewing Co, unissued, 1937 . . . . **5.00**
Charm, Budweiser, commemorative, wood, 1876–1976 . . . . . **15.00**
Clock, Lowenbrau, electric, lions hold clock **95.00**
Clock, Schlitz plastic, stained glass effect, 21 x 25" **35.00**
Coaster, Bleser Brewery, Manitowoc, WI, blue, red, and yellow, 4" d **10.00**
Coaster, Standard Ale, Standard Brewing, Rochester, NY, brass, 1930s **40.00**
Coaster, Ye Tabern Brew, Lafayette Brewery, Lafayette, IN, red, yellow, and black, 3" d **6.00**
Display, Falstaff Beer, cardboard and plastic, emb figure **45.00**
Door Push, Old Milwaukee **95.00**
Foam Scraper, plastic, "Koch's, The Smoother Beer" **20.00**
Handkerchief, Coors, 20" sq **5.00**
Light, Bavarian Beer, neon, 2–color, 1950s, 14 x 23¼" **160.00**
Magazine Tear Sheet, Budweiser, full color illus, framed **5.00**
Match Holder, Ballantine, 1939 World's Fair, ceramic **90.00**
Mirror, Kingsbury Pale Beer, Kingsbury Brewing, Sheboygan, WI, reverse glass stand up, 1940s, 8 x 12" **45.00**
Mug, Leisy's Lager Beer, Leisy's Brewing, Cleveland, OH, mini, 1950s **45.00**
Mug, Miller, ceramic, Christmas scene, 6" h **6.00**
Pen Knife, Schlitz, tractor trailer shape, metal, mother–of–pearl handle, 1950 . . . . **45.00**
Pencil Clip, Krueger Beer Ales, red, black, and white **25.00**
Pinback Button, White Seal Beer, "I M 4 R U 2," red and white, 1930s **10.00**
Plate, Miller Beer, "Keep On Rocking," Michigan **25.00**
Poster, Koehler Beer, "Pour a Koehler Collar Today!," repeated design of 3 beer bottles and glasses, 1956, 35 x 23" **25.00**
Recipe Book, C Schmidt & Sons Brewing Co, woman wearing hat and holding glass of beer cov illus, 8 pp **8.00**
Register Light, Michelob Draught Beer, 1950s, 9¾ x 5" **50.00**
Salt and Pepper Shakers, pr, Ballantine Beer, aluminum and cardboard, can shape, c1940 . . . . **25.00**

Sign, Burgermeister, plastic, stand–up, 1940s, 9¼ x 14½" **70.00**
Sign, Chester Pilsener Beer, diecut cardboard, 1930s, 11½ x 5" **50.00**
Sign, Rolling Rock Beer, neon, ©1939, 34" h **115.00**
Sign, Yuengling's Beer, Yuengling Brewing, Pottsville, PA, rubber, plastic feet, 1950s, 13 x 14½" **50.00**
Statue, back bar, Stoney's Beer, Jones Brewing Co, Smithton, PA, hard rubber, 1950s, 12 x 6 x 3" **125.00**
Stein, stoneware, #2035, cobalt blue, colored medallions, Marzy & Remy, c1950, 4" h **45.00**
Sticker, National Bohemian, National Brewing, Detroit, MI, 1960s, 20 x 5" **8.00**
Tap Handle, Budweiser, Anheuser–Busch, Inc, St Louis, MO, lucite basketball **10.00**
Tap Handle, Michelob, Anheuser–Busch, St Louis, MO, horn shape, plastic and chrome **35.00**
Tap Knob, Ballantine, Ballantine Brewing, Newark, NJ, plastic, metal insert, emb on back, 1940s **20.00**
Tap Knob, Fort Pitt, Bakelite, 1940s **15.00**
Thermometer, Lone Star Beer, round, 1958 . . . . **130.00**
Tip Tray, Standard Scranton Beer, Standard Brewing, Scranton, PA, 1930s **55.00**
Tray, Liebmann Valley Export Beer, 1950s, 13¼" **60.00**
Tray, Lucky Lager, 2 sided, 12" d **15.00**

BREYER HORSES

When founded in 1943, the Breyer Molding Company of Chicago manufactured custom designed thermoset plastics. After WWII, the company shifted production to injection molded radio and television housings. As a sideline, Breyer also produced a few plastic animals based on designs sculpted by Christian Hess.

By 1958 the Breyer line contained a barnyard full of animals — cats, cows, dogs, and horses. In 1959 the company introduced its wood–grain finish. By the end of the 1970s the sale of horses accounted for most of the company's business.

Reeves International, a distributor of European collectibles such as Britains and Corgi, acquired Breyer in 1984. Manufacturing was moved to a state–of–the–art plant in New Jersey.

References: Felicia Browell, *Breyer Animal Collector's Guide: Identification and Values,* Collector Books, 1998; Nancy Atkinson Young, *Breyer Molds and Models: Horses, Riders and Animals,* Schiffer Publishing, 1997.

Periodicals: *The Hobby Horse News,* 2053 Dryehaven Dr, Tallahassee, FL 32311; *TRR Pony Express,* 71 Aloha Circle, North Little Rock, AR 72120.

Newsletter: *The Model Horse Trader,* 143 Mercer Way, Upland, CA 91786.

Collectors' Clubs: Breyer Collectors Club, 14 Industrial Rd, Pequannock, NJ 07440; North American Model Horse Show Assoc, PO Box 50508, Denton, TX 76206.

Adios, #50, quarter horse stallion, black, gray speckles **$40.00**
Black Beauty, #89, Dream Weaver **40.00**
Clydesdale Stallion, #80, dapple gray, dark gray mane and tail **150.00**
Family Arabian Mare, #8, Galena, shaded chestnut, dark points, light face **20.00**

Arabian Stallion, Woodgrain Family, #907, $55.00.

Fighting Stallion, #31, alabaster, gray hooves, pink and
gray muzzle **35.00**
Fury Prancer, #40, black Pinto, white mane, black tail
with white tip, gray hooves, black saddle **100.00**
Indian Pony, #175, dark bay Appaloosa, black points,
blanket pattern over hindquarters **50.00**
Lady Roxanna, #425, alabaster, gray points, Artist Series **30.00**
Merrylegs, #3040, Horses Great and Small, palomino,
white mane and tail, gray hooves, shaded muzzle **20.00**
Old Timer, #200, McDuff Old Timer, gray Appaloosa,
blanket pattern, dark points, white hat with red band **25.00**
Pacer, #46, Dan Patch, red bay, black points, star, right
hind coronet, natural hooves, Limited Edition **40.00**
Pony of the Americas, #155, bay/chestnut Appaloosa,
black mane and tail, blanket pattern **30.00**
Proud Arabian Mare, #215, dapple gray, black/dark gray
points and hooves **35.00**
Proud Arabian Stallion, #212, dapple rose gray, rose gray
mane and tail, gray muzzle, knees, hocks, and hooves **40.00**
Quarter Horse Foal, #3045FO, black, bald face, gray
hooves **20.00**
Quarter Horse Gelding, #98, Appaloosa Gelding **40.00**
Shetland Pony, #25, chestnut, flaxen mane and tail **25.00**
Western Pony, #45, alabaster, gray hooves, gold bridle,
black snap–girth saddle **40.00**
Western Prancing Horse, #110, black Pinto, bald face,
gray shaded plastic slip on saddle, gold chain reins **100.00**

BRIARD, GEORGES

Georges Briard, born Jascha Brojdo, was an industrial designer
who worked in a wide range of materials—ceramics, glass, enameled metals, paper, plastic, textiles, and wood. Jascha Brojdo
arrived in Chicago from Poland in 1937. He earned a joint Master
of Fine Arts degree from the University of Chicago and the Art
Institute of Chicago. In 1947 Brojdo moved to New York. Deciding
he needed a designer pseudonym, Brojdo settled upon Georges
Briard, George with an "s" because it sounded French and Briard
for a briard he and his wife saw at a dog show.

Columbian Enamel, Glass Guild (The Bent Glass Company),
Hyalyn Porcelain, and Woodland were among the early clients of
Georges Briard Designs. In the early 1960s Briard designed
Pfaltzgraff's Heritage pattern. In 1965 Briard created sixteen pat-
terns for melamine plastic dinnerware in Allied Chemical's Artisan
line, marketed under the Stetson brand name.

Briard continued to create innovative designs for the houseware
and giftware market through the end of the 1980s. Responding to
changing market trends, many of Briard's post–1960s products
were made overseas.

Reference: Leslie Piña, *'50s & '60s Glass, Ceramics, & Enamel
Wares Designed & Signed by Georges Briard, Sascha B., Bellaire,
Higgins...,* Schiffer Publishing, 1996.

REPRODUCTION ALERT: Do not confuse 1970s' and 80s' Briard
knockoffs, many made in Japan, with licensed Briard products. A
high level of quality and the distinctive Briard signature are the
mark of a Briard piece.

Ashtray, Trée Briard pattern, molded relief lion, 8¼" d **$25.00**
Casserole, cov, Gréen Garden pattern, white ground,
Porcelainite, warming stand **40.00**
Cheese Board, wood, Ambrosia pattern ceramic tile
insert, 16 x 17½" **40.00**
Chip and Dip Plate, Golden Harvest border, white opal
center, 10" sq **25.00**
Clock, green and blue mosaic tile, 12" sq **120.00**
Glass, Teardrop pattern **5.00**
Percolator, Ambrosia pattern, white ground, polychrome
dec, 9¾" h **40.00**
Percolator, Coq D'or pattern, Porcelainite, poly chrome
dec, yellow ground, 8¾" h **40.00**
Plate, Persian Garden pattern, clear aura ground, 11¾" sq . . . **15.00**
Plate, Regalia pattern, teal ground, 5¾" sq **20.00**
Relish Tray, 3 part, Forbidden Fruit pattern, orange and
gold **10.00**
Snack Bowl, Paradise pattern, clear, wood and brass cen-
ter post handle, 7" d, 8" h **15.00**
Tray, Ambrosia pattern, white ground, Porcelainite,
13 x 19" **30.00**

Tray, Sunflower pattern, Glass Guild, $12.00.

BRITISH ROYALTY COMMEMORATIVES

British royalty commemoratives fall into two distinct groups: (1) souvenir pieces purchased during a monarch's reign and (2) pieces associated with specific events such as births, coronations, investitures, jubilees, marriages, or memorials. Items associated with reigning monarchs are the most popular.

Only five monarchs have reigned since 1920 — King George V (May 6, 1910 to January 20, 1936), King Edward VIII (January 20, 1936, abdicated December 10, 1936), King George VI (December 10, 1936 to February 6, 1952), and Queen Elizabeth II (February 6, 1952 to the present).

References: Susan and Al Bagdade, *Warman's English & Continental Pottery & Porcelain, Second Edition,* Wallace–Homestead, Krause Publications, 1991; Douglas H. Flynn and Alan H. Bolton, *British Royalty Commemoratives: 19th & 20th Century Royal Events in Britain Illustrated by Commemoratives, Value Guide With Photographs,* Schiffer Publishing, 1994; Eric Knowles, *Miller's Royal Memorabilia,* Reed Consumer Books, 1994, distributed by Antique Collectors' Club.

Newsletter: *British Royalty Commemorative Collectors Newsletter,* PO Box 294, Lititz, PA 17543.

Collectors' Club: Commemorative Collector's Society, Lumless House, Gainsborough Rd, Winthrope, New Newark, Nottingham NG24 2NR UK.

Bell, Andrew and Fergie, Herbert Pottery, 5½" h, 3" d **$25.00**
Calendar, Diana Fashion Calendar, 1985 .... **10.00**
Doll, Diana, Princess of Wales, vinyl, white fabric wedding gown outfit with simulated fur, rhinestone tiara, 11½" h, orig 3 x 11½ x 15" display box, 1981 .... **75.00**
Magazine, *His Majesty King Edward VIII,* "The Story Of His Life," color cov portrait, sepia photos, 48 pp, c1937, 9 x 12" **20.00**
Pendant, King George VI and Queen Elizabeth 1937 Coronation, metal, crowned profile portraits, fabric ribbon with bar pin fastener **10.00**
Pinback Button, "Queen Elizabeth II Coronation 1953" **10.00**
Plate, Queen Elizabeth II Coronation, china, sepia portrait, Canadian provinces seals border, mkd

"Confederation Series Canada, Approved By The Council Of Industrial Design, Royal Staffordshire Ceramics Burslem England, Clarice Cliff," c1953, 10½" **20.00**
Ribbon Badge, King Edward VIII Coronation, red, white, and blue fabric, red fringed tassel, blue woven portrait, red inscription, 1¼ x 3½" **20.00**
Urn, cov, Charles and Diana's Royal Wedding, china, red gargoyle dragon art with Charles and Diana photo portraits, inscribed below "July 29, 1981 marriage of H.R.H. The Prince Of Wales And Lady Diana Spencer," Sadler, England, 8" h **100.00**

BRUSH–MCCOY POTTERY

The J. W. McCoy Pottery and Brush Pottery joined forces in 1911, resulting in the formation of the Brush–McCoy Pottery. The company produced a wide range of ceramic wares, including cookie jars, garden wares, kitchen wares, novelty planters, and vases.

References: Sharon and Bob Huxford, *The Collector's Encyclopedia of Brush–McCoy Pottery,* Collector Books, 1978, 1996 value update; Martha and Steve Sanford, *The Guide to Brush–McCoy Pottery,* published by authors, 1992; Martha and Steve Sanford, *Sanfords Guide to Brush–McCoy Pottery, Book 2,* published by authors, 1996.

Cookie Jar, Conestoga wagon **$650.00**
Cookie Jar, old shoe **125.00**
Cookie Jar, owl, gray **80.00**
Cookie Jar, panda bear **250.00**
Cornucopia, berries and leaves, 4 x 6" **40.00**
Cuspidor, frog, 7½" h **125.00**
Eggcup, chicken **20.00**
Figure, swan, 1950s **20.00**
Figure, Trojan horse, white, #106, 1930s, 6" **40.00**
Figure, turtle, 7" l **65.00**
Garden Dish, seahorse and waves, #913, 1956, 10" **65.00**
Planter, figural lamb, 1950s **35.00**
Planter, squirrel on log, #206, 1952, 6" **50.00**
Spoon Rest, 2 flowers with faces, #LXZB–4S, 1952, 5 x 5½" **35.00**
Vase, Dutch shoe **25.00**

Mug, Prince William's birth, triple portrait by Lord Snowden, Coronet, 4" h, $25.00.

Vase, Blue Onyx, #050X, 6" h, $175.00.

Vase, Kolorkraft, Amaryllis, blue, 1929, 7½" h 200.00
Vase, oriental motif, 7½" h 40.00
Vase, square, 2 handles, emb poppies, #555, 1948, 7½" h . . . 65.00
Wall Pocket, fish 80.00

BUSINESS & OFFICE MACHINES

Europeans, especially the Germans, are the leading collectors of business and office equipment. In the United States, decorators buy most examples to use as decorative conversation pieces. It is for this reason that adding machines, check writers, dictating machines, and stock tickers machines are the most eagerly sought after types. Novelty and/or functionality are more important value keys than age.

Reference: Thomas F. Haddock, *A Collector's Guide to Personal Computers and Pocket Calculators*, Books Americana, Krause Publications, 1993.

Collectors' Club: Historical Computer Society, 3649 Herschel St, Jacksonville, FL 32205.

Note: See Calculators and Typewriters for additional listings.

Burroughs, adding machine $15.00
Commodore PET 2001, computer, 1 mhz 6502 processor, 32 K ram, 9" video monitor, 73–key keyboard, built–in cassette and 5¼" floppy drive, c1977 . . . . 75.00
Dalton, bookkeeping machine 100.00
Ediphone, Typease typewriter attachment 15.00
F & E, International Dectetive Agency, check writer 25.00
Gem, notecard duplicator 10.00
Golden Gem, adding machine 80.00
Heath Data Systems, dot matrix printer, c1979 . . . . 40.00
Hewlett Packard 85, computer, 8 bit HP processor, 16–K ram, built–in 5" CRT, 92 key keyboard, 200 K integral HP DC–100 data cartridge drive, c1980 . . . . 100.00
Paymaster, check protector 25.00
S & P, checkwriter 100.00
Texas Instruments, adding machine, TI–5045 II, 12 digits, 2–color printing 10.00
Type S, Saving machine, Dictaphone 50.00

CALCULATORS

The first affordable electronic integrated circuit calculator appeared in the early 1970s. Early pocket calculators cost hundreds of dollars. By the early 1980s the price of a basic pocket caluilator was $10 or less. Manufacturers such as HP and Texas Instruments made dozens of different models. First models tend to be the most valuable.

References: Guy Ball and Bruce Flamm, *Collector's Guide to Pocket Calculators*, Wilson/Barnett Publishing, 1997; Thomas F. Haddock, *A Collector's Guide to Personal Computers and Pocket Calculators*, Books Americana, Krause Publications, 1993; W.A.C. Mier–Jadrzejowica, *A Guide to HP Handheld Calculators and Computers, Second Edition*, Wilson/Barnett Publishing, 1996.

Collectors' Clubs: International Assoc of Calculator Collectors (IACC), 14561 Livingston St, Tustin, CA 92780; The Oughtred Society (Slide Rules), PO Box 99077, Emeryville, CA 94662.

Adler 121C, 1974 . . . . $45.00
American L180 . . . . 40.00
APF Electronics Mark V 60.00
Brother 861 . . . . 35.00
Canon LE–80R 55.00
Casio CQ–2 . . . . 45.00
Commodore M55 . . . . 65.00
Emerson SX–4500 . . . . 100.00
Figural, compact, Design Factory, Tokyo 35.00
Figural, computer, credit card size 20.00
Figural, crayon, small, made in China 30.00
Figural, floppy disk, made in China 5.00
Gillette PC–1 . . . . 65.00
Hewlett–Packard 33E 40.00
J C Penney MM3R 35.00
Mattel, J R Ewing Game Calculator 5.00
National Cash Register (NCR), 1844 . . . . 200.00
Panasonic Panac SD–1 . . . . 40.00
Radio Shack 4–in–1 Electronic Game Calculator 15.00
Rockwell 63R, Scientific Slide Rule 40.00
Sanyo CZ–8141, Scientific Calculator 40.00
Sears Digi–matic D–8 . . . . 40.00
Sharp EL–5001, scentific function 45.00
Texas Instruments SR–56, programmable, scientific function 25.00
Toshiba Sc–6100, scientific function 65.00
Toy, dog with bone, slide–open style 20.00
Toy, Fun' N Calc, Radio Shack 23–582 . . . . 20.00
Toy, Little Professor 10.00
Toy, Space–N–Counter 45.00
Toy, Star Trekulator, ST 101A, flashing LEDs, sound effects, c1977 . . . . 75.00
Toy, Mickey Mouse School, Unisonic SH 2013 . . . . 35.00

CALENDARS

The 19th–century printing revolution made calendars accessible to everyone. As the century ended, calendars were a popular form of advertising giveaway and remained so through much of the 20th century. Cheesecake calendars enjoyed a Golden Age between 1930 and the mid–1960s.

In the 1980s, the "art" or special theme calendar arrived on the scene. Moderately expensive when purchased new, they are ignored by most calendar collectors.

Today, calendars are collected because of the appeal of their subject matter, the artwork created by a famous illustrator, or because the year matches the birth year of the purchaser. If the monthly pages remain attached value increases 10% to 20%.

Reference: Norman E. Martinus and Harry L. Rinker, *Warman's Paper*, Wallace–Homestead, Krause Publications, 1994.

Collectors' Club: Calendar Collector Society, 18222 Flower Hill Way #299, Gaithersburg, MD 20879.

REPRODUCTION ALERT

1921, Milton Bradley, color illus $15.00
1925, Hartford Tires, woman wearing blue hat in circle, matted, oak frame 550.00
1925, Peters Cartridge Co, flying mallards above water, 18 x 33" 350.00
1925, Star Brand Shoes, "A Bear Chance," 15½ x 10½" 50.00

1953, Howard L. Ayers Builder and Contractor, full pad, 15 x 23", $15.00.

Trivet, dec in cuenca with dark red, celadon, and yellow basket of fruit, dark blue ground, imp "California Faience," 5¹/₂" d, $225.00. Photo courtesy David Rago Auctions.

1927, Wrigley's Double Mint Gum, 3¹/₂ x 6". 28.00
1932, American Stores, children and 13–star flag 50.00
1933, Gold Dust Washing Powder. 35.00
1933, Keen Kutter 90.00
1936, Brunham Boilers, man on rocker by furnace 35.00
1937, Traveller's Insurance, Currier & Ives illus. 35.00
1939, Johnson Winged Gasoline 18.00
1939, Sunshine Cookies 18.00
1943, Federal Motor Truck Co, 34 x 16". 150.00
1945, California Grocery Store, girl and dog looking up
   at army plane 18.00
1945, How Nong Chinese Herb Co, Oakland, CA,
   10 x 16" 12.00
1946, Evening Star, full figured nude, E Moran, 16 x 33". . . . 175.00
1948, Esquire Glamour Gallery, 8¹/₂ x 12" 40.00
1949, Evinrude, color illus, boat scenes 95.00
1949, Queen Elizabeth II. 35.00
1950, Sweet Sixteen, 8 x 11". 25.00
1950, TWA. 20.00
1951, Arkansas Cotton Oil Co. 25.00
1954, American Airlines 20.00
1966, Union Pacific Rail Road. 8.00

CALIFORNIA FAIENCE

William Bradgon and Chauncey Thomas first manufactured art pottery and tiles in 1916. In 1924 they named their products California Faience.

Most art pottery pieces are characterized by cast molding and a monochrome matte glaze. Some pieces had a high gloss glaze. Plaster molds were used to make the polychrome decorated titles. California Faience also produced a commercial floral line and made master molds for other California potteries.

The company was hard hit by the Depresssion. Bradgon bought out Thomas in the late 1930s. He sold the pottery in the early 1950s, working with the new owners until he died in 1959.

Box, raspberry tile top, cloisonné dec, 1¹/₂ x 4¹/₂ x 3¹/₂" $100.00
Flower Holder, figural, 2 pelicans, turquoise, 6" h. 135.00
Jar, cov, bulbous body, periwinkle blue gloss glaze,
   incised "California Faience," 9¹/₂" h 300.00
Potpourri Jar, oriental shape, yellow matte glaze, incised
   mark, 4¹/₂" h 225.00

Tile, blue peacock on matte ochre ground, incised mark,
   5¹/₄" d 375.00
Tile, flower basket design, matte and gloss glazes,
   mounted and framed, mkd "California Faience" 700.00
Tile, round, stylized green dandelion leaves, red blossoms, sky blue ground, incised mark, 5¹/₂" d 300.00
Vase, multicolored floral band, blue ground, 3" h. 950.00
Vase, relief band with stylized doves, arrowheads, and
   spruce, turquoise glaze, incised mark, c1924, 6¹/₂" h. 375.00

CAMARK POTTERY

Samuel Jack Carnes founded Camark Pottery, Camden, Arkansas, in 1926. The company made art pottery, earthenware, and decorative accessories. John Lessell, previously employed at Weller, and his wife were among the leading art potters working at Camark.

After Carnes sold the plant in 1966, it was run primarily as a retail operation by Mary Daniels. In January 1986 Gary and Mark Ashcraft purchased the Camark Pottery building in hopes of re–establishing a pottery at the site. At the time of the purchase, they stated they did not intend to reissue pieces using the company's old molds.

References: David Edwin Gifford, *Collector's Guide to Camark Pottery: Identification & Values*, Collector Books, 1997; Letitia Landers, *Camark Pottery: An Identification and Value Reference*, *Vol. 1* (1994), *Vol. 2* (1996), Colony Publishing.

Collectors' Club: Arkansas Pottery Collectors Society, PO Box 7617, Little Rock, AR 72217.

Ashtray, sunburst. $15.00
Bowl, pumpkin, small 15.00
Casserole, chicken lid 45.00
Figure, lion. 35.00
Figure, tropical fish, 8¹/₂" h. 50.00
Figure, wistful kitten, black 35.00
Fishbowl Cat, white. 60.00
Fishbowl Stork, white 150.00
Pitcher, bulbous, cat handle, 8¹/₂" h 50.00
Planter, elephant, 11 x 8". 65.00
Planter, rolling pin, N1–51 . . . . 10.00
Planter, rooster 25.00

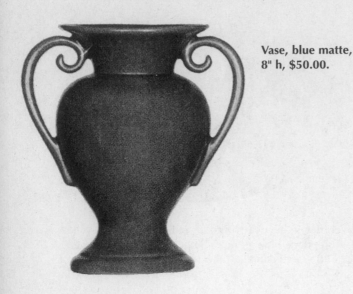

Vase, blue matte, 8" h, $50.00.

Vase, fluted, 7" h..................................30.00
Vase, fan shaped, large 35.00

CAMBRIDGE GLASS

Cambridge Glass, Cambridge, Ohio, was founded in 1901. The company manufactured a wide variety of glass tablewares. After experiencing financial difficulties in 1907, Arthur J. Bennett, previously with the National Glass Company, helped reorganize the company. By the 1930s, the company had over 5,000 glass molds in inventory.

Although five different identification marks are known, not every piece of Cambridge Glass was permanently marked. Paper labels were used between 1935 and 1954.

Cambridge Glass ceased operations in 1954. Its molds were sold. Imperial Glass Company purchased some, a few wound up in private hands.

References: Gene Florence, *Elegant Glassware of the Depression Era, Seventh Edition,* Collector Books, 1997; National Cambridge Collectors, Inc., *The Cambridge Glass Co., Cambridge, Ohio* (reprint of 1930 catalog and supplements through 1934), Collector Books, 1976, 1997 value update; National Cambridge Collectors, Inc., *The Cambridge Glass Co., Cambridge Ohio, 1949 Thru 1953* (catalog reprint), Collector Books, 1976, 1996 value update; National Cambridge Collectors, Inc., *Colors in Cambridge Glass,* Collector Books, 1984, 1997 value update.

Periodical: *The Daze,* PO Box 57, Otisville, MI 48463.

Collectors' Club: National Cambridge Collectors, Inc, PO Box 416, Cambridge, OH 43725.

Ashtray, Caprice, 206, moonlight blue, triangle shape......**$10.00**
Ashtray, Crown Tuscan, ftd..........................15.00
Ashtray Set, stack away, blue.........................35.00
Bon Bon, Rose Point, 3900 ....40.00
Bon Bon, Wildflower, 3900/131, gold encrusted, 2 handled, ftd, 8"...................................25.00
Bouillon and Liner, Cleo, green 35.00
Bowl, Rose Point, 3400, crimped, 4 toed, 12"...........95.00
Bowl, Rose Point, 3900, handled, 4 toed, 12"..........125.00

Butter Dish, Cleo, amber, base only....................15.00
Butter Dish, cov, Rose Point, 3400/52, crystal............190.00
Candle Holder, Rose Point, 3500, 2½".................20.00
Candle Holder, Shell, dolphin, crystal, 4"...............50.00
Candle Holders, pr, Caprice, crystal, triple............145.00
Candle Holders, pr, Diane, 3900/67, crystal, inverted......50.00
Candle Holders, pr, Diane, crystal, keyhole..............50.00
Candle Holders, pr, Rose Point, 3900, 5"...............100.00
Candle Holders, pr, Shell, Windsor blue, toed, 2½".......185.00
Candy Dish, Rose Point, 3121, 4½"....................65.00
Candy Dish, Rose Point, 3121, 6".....................75.00
Champagne, Caprice, moonlight blue, thin 25.00
Champagne, Rondo, low..............................12.00
Champagne, Rose Point, 3121.........................25.00
Cheese Comport, Rose Point, 3500, 6".................65.00
Cigarette Box, Crown Tuscan, flowers, gold trim..........60.00
Cocktail, amber nude stem, crystal bowl, white base 145.00
Cocktail, black nude stem, crystal bowl, white base 125.00
Cocktail, Caprice, blue 50.00
Cocktail, Farber, amber 10.00
Cocktail, Lynbrook 10.00
Cocktail, Rose Point, 3121............................25.00
Cocktail, Rose Point, 3500............................22.00
Comport, nude stem, SS/10 #4, crystal.................125.00
Comport, Rose Point, 3500, 6".........................55.00
Compote, 3120 line, #739 etching.....................45.00
Cordial, Rose Point, 3121.............................75.00
Cordial Set, Farber, chrome plate, 7 pcs................55.00
Cornucopia, Crown Tuscan, small 20.00
Creamer and Sugar, Rose Point, 3400...................50.00
Creamer and Sugar, Rose Point, 3500, individual 45.00
Cruets, oil and vinegar, Farber, 5453, cobalt.............60.00
Cruets, oil and vinegar, Farber, 5453, amethyst, 3 oz 40.00
Cup and Saucer, Caprice, crystal 15.00
Cup and Saucer, Cleo, moonlight blue..................25.00
Cup, Cleo, moonlight blue 20.00
Flower Holder, Shell, crystal, 6".......................25.00
Goblet, Rose Point, 3121, 10 oz 35.00
Iced Tea, Lynbrook, ftd, 12 oz 15.00
Ice Tub, Farber, 2 handled, cobalt 175.00
Ivy Ball, Optic, crystal...............................185.00
Ivy Ball, Optic, crystal, frosted stem...................200.00
Juice Tumbler, Caprice, 300, crystal...................15.00
Mayonnaise, Chantilly, crystal, with liner and 2 spoons......55.00
Mayonnaise, Rose Point, 1532, with ladle and underplate...60.00

Creamer and Open Sugar, Caprice, blue, $35.00.

Mustard, Caprice, moonlight blue, open **45.00**
Oyster Cocktail, Rose Point, 3500 . . . . **45.00**
Parfait, Rose Point, 3121, 5 oz **95.00**
Plate, Blue Willow, amber, 8" d . . . . : **35.00**
Plate, Caprice, blue, 4 ftd, 11" **60.00**
Plate, Caprice, crystal, 6½" d **9.00**
Plate, Caprice, crystal, 8½" d **15.00**
Plate, luncheon, Cleo, green **17.00**
Plate, luncheon, Cleo, moonlight blue **20.00**
Plate, luncheon, Cleo, pink **15.00**
Plate, Rose Point, 3400, 7" d **15.00**
Plate, Rose Point, 3400, 8" d **20.00**
Plate, Rose Point, 3900, 5½" d **12.00**
Plate, Rose Point, 3900, 7" d **15.00**
Platter, Wildflower, 3400/1181, 2 handled, 6". **25.00**
Relish, Apple Blossom, 3400/91, 3 part, green **45.00**
Relish, Rose Point, 3400, 2 part, 2 handled, 8¾" **75.00**
Relish, Rose Point, 3400, 3 part, 3 handled, 8" **45.00**
Relish, Rose Point, 3500, 2 part, 5½" **40.00**
Relish, Rose Point, 3500, 3 part, handled, 6½" **45.00**
Relish, Wildflower, 3400/124, 2 part, 7" **25.00**
Relish, Wildflower, 3500/69, 3 part, 6½" **25.00**
Salt and Pepper Shakers, pr, Caprice, moonlight blue **125.00**
Salt and Pepper Shakers, Chantilly, 3900/1177 . . . . **50.00**
Salt and Pepper Shakers, Diane, 3400, ftd **55.00**
Salt and Pepper Shakers, pr, Rose Point, 3400. . . . . **55.00**
Salt and Pepper Shakers, pr, Wildflower, 3400, ftd **30.00**
Sherbet, Lynbrook, low **10.00**
Sherbet, Rondo, low **10.00**
Sherbet, Rose Point, 3121, low, 6 oz **20.00**
Sherbet, Rose Point, 3500, low, 7 oz **20.00**
Sugar, Rose Point, 3400. . . . . **18.00**
Sugar, Rose Point, 3900. . . . . **20.00**
Tumbler, Caprice, 300, crystal, ftd, 10 oz **15.00**
Tumbler, Rose Point, 1397, ftd, 5 oz. **85.00**
Vase, Caprice, 344, smooth top, amber **100.00**
Water Tumbler, Rose Point, 3121, low, ftd, 10 oz **25.00**
Water Tumbler, Rose Point, 3500, low, ftd, 10 oz **28.00**
Wine, Caprice, 300, crystal, 2½ oz **25.00**
Wine, Rondo, low. **15.00**
Wine, Rose Point, 3121. . . . . **55.00**

CAMERAS & ACCESSORIES

The development of the camera was truly international. Johann Zahn, a German monk, created the first fully portable wood box camera with a movable lens, adjustable aperture, and mirror to project the image in the early 1800s. Joseph Niepce and Louise Daguere perfected the photographic plate. Peter Von Voigtlander, an Austrian, contributed the quality lens. An industry was born.

By the late 19th century, England, France, and Germany all played major roles in the development of camera technology. America's contributions came in the area of film development and marketing.

In 1888 George Eastman introduced the Kodak No. 1, a simple box camera that revolutionized the industry. Model No. 4 was the first folding camera. The Brownie was introduced in 1900.

After World War II, the Japanese made a strong commitment to dominating the camera market. By the 1970s, they had achieved their goal.

Reference: Jim and Joan McKeown (eds.), *Price Guide to Antique and Classic Cameras, 1997–1998, 10th Edition,* Centennial Photo Service, 1997.

Periodical: *Classic Camera,* PO Box 1270, New York, NY 10156.

Collectors' Clubs: American Photographic Historical Society, Inc, 1150 Avenue of the Americas, New York, NY 10036; American Society of Camera Collectors, 7415 Reseda Blvd, Reseda, CA 91335; International Kodak Historical Society, PO Box 21, Flourtown, PA 19301; Leica Historical Society of America, 7611 Dornoch Ln, Dallas, TX 75248; Nikon Historical Society, PO Box 3213, Hammond, IN 45321; The Movie Machine Society, 42 Deerhaven Dr, Nashua, NH 03060; Zeiss Historical Society, 300 Waxwing Dr, Cranbury, NJ 08512.

CAMERAS

Agfa Kamerawerke, Munich, Germany, Agfafles, SLR, Prontor 1–300, c1959 . . . . **$50.00**
Ansco, Binghamton, NY, Buster Brown, MIB. **40.00**
Ansco, Binghamton, NY, Karat, folding, 35mm, c1937 . . . . . . **30.00**
Bell & Howell, Chicago, IL, Eyemo 35mm Motion Picture Camera, 1926 . . . . **100.00**
Bolsley Corporation of America, NY, Bolseyflex, 120 film, green–gray covering, f7.7/80mm lens, made in Germany by Ising for Bolsey, c1954 . . . . **20.00**
Camera Corporation of America, New York, NY, B2, 35mm, 1949–56 . . . . **30.00**
Canon, Tokyo, Japan, IIIA, screw–mount, 1951–53 . . . . **120.00**
Canon, Tokyo, Japan, Canonex, leaf shutter, fixed lens, c1963 . . . . **75.00**
Craig Movie Supply Splicer, chrome and mahogany, 1930s **35.00**
Eastman Kodak Co, Rochester, NY, Anniversary Box Camera, tan box, given away to mark 50th anniversary of Eastman Kodak Co in 1930 . . . . **30.00**
Eastman Kodak Co, Rochester, NY, Boy Scout, 127, green, orig case, 1920s **120.00**
Eastman Kodak Co, Rochester, NY, Pony, 135, Kodak Anaston f4.5 lens, 1950–54 . . . : **10.00**
Eastman Kodak Co, Rochester, NY, Winner, 1988 Olympics, plastic, red, 110 film **5.00**

Sears Roebuck and Co, Tower One Twenty, box camera, 1950s, 2⅞" w, 4⅛" d, 3⅞" h, $8.00.

Ertel Werke, Munich, Germany, Filmette I Movie Camera, 35mm, wood body, hand crank, folding side sportsfinder, Ertel Glaukar f3.¹/₅₀mm lens **750.00**

Fuji, Japan, Fujica Rapid S, streamlined, 16 exp, 24 x 24mm on 35mm rapid cassettes, 40mm lens, c1965 . . . . . . **20.00**

Graflex, The Folmer & Schwing Mfg Co, NY, Graflex, #1A, Kodak Anastigmat f4.5 lens, 116 roll film, 1909–25 . . . . **175.00**

Houghton, London, England, Ensign Autospeed, 120 roll film, FP 5–500, 6 x 6cm format, Aldis f4.5/4" lens, c1933 . . . . **175.00**

Igahee Kamerawerk, Dresden, Germany, Ultrix Auto, folding, Schneider Xenar 70mm f4.5 lens, c1934 . . . . **45.00**

Leitz, Ernst Leitz GmbH, Wetzlar, Leica Standard, 12mm d rewind knob, rotating range finder, nickel lens, black, 1932–48 . . . . **425.00**

Minolta, Chiyoda Kogaku Seiko Co, Ltd, Osaka, Japan, Minolta SR–1S, 1964 . . . . **80.00**

Nikon, Nikon S2, rapid wind lever, crank rewind, 24 x 36mm format, chrome, black dials, 1954–58 . . . . **350.00**

Olympic Camera Works, Japan, Contz F, 35mm, SLR, semi–automatic cocking diaphragm, c1957 . . . . **90.00**

Pentacon, Dresden, Germany, Taxona, 24 x 24mm exposures on 35mm film, Novonar lens, Tempor 1–300 shutter, 1950 . . . . **35.00**

Royal Camera Co, Japan, Royal 35, 35mm RF, f2.8/50mm lens, Copal 1–300 shutter, c1960 . . . . **75.00**

Sears Roebuck & Co, Marvel S–20, 120 film, Art Deco faceplate, c1940 . . . . **5.00**

Toy, Mick–A–Matic, shape of Mickey Mouse's head, 126, meniscus lens in nose, 1969 . . . . **80.00**

Toy, Snoopy Counting Camera, Romper Room, Hasbro **5.00**

Toy, Squirt Pix, Premier Plastics Co, Brooklyn, NY, shoots water, orig box **10.00**

Universal Camera Corp, New York, NY, Minute 16, 16mm subminiature, meniscus lens, c1950 . . . . **85.00**

Vitascope Corp, Providence, RI, Movie Maker, 16mm, hand crank, black crinkle metal body, waist level finder, c1931 . . . . **15.00**

Voiglander & Son, Braunschweig, Germany, Vito, 35mm, folding, c1950 . . . . **30.00**

Zeiss, Carl, Optical Co, Dresden, Germany, Maximar B, folding plate camera, 1940s **80.00**

ACCESSORIES

Album, 35mm SLR shape, holds 24 prints, 3¹/₄ x 5" **$2.00**

Booklet, Brownie Cameras, Nov, 1926, 42 pp, 3 x 4" **10.00**

Booster Meter, Canon **40.00**

Brochure, Kodak Medalist II, c1949, 24 pp **20.00**

Camera Bag, Silver Lens, 35mm camera shape, plastic, c1987 . . . . **5.00**

Catalog, Graflex, 1937, 28 pp **20.00**

Catalog, Kodaks and Brownies, Oct 1938, 36 pp **15.00**

Catalog, Korona, 1926, 52 pp **25.00**

Catalog, Schneider Lens, 1930, 20 pp **20.00**

Drying Rack, wooden, folding, 4 x 5" **5.00**

Exposure Meter, DIN Exposure Calculator, AGFA, aluminum, 1936 . . . . **5.00**

Film Box, Kodak, Verichrome Film Pack, c1933 . . . . **15.00**

Flash, 117A, Canon **35.00**

Lens, FL, 50mm f/1.4, Canon **50.00**

Lens, ML, 42–75 f/3.5–4.5, Yashica **45.00**

Magazine, *Studio Light*, 1917–29, 107 issues **200.00**

Manual, Graflex, service and parts, punched for binder, c1948, 60 pp **15.00**

Manual, Leica Reflex Housing, 1956, 8 pp **5.00**

Rangefinder, Watameter, silver/black, Photopia, 1950s **12.00**

Stereo Viewer, metal, black, hand–held, 1930s **25.00**

TM–1 Quartz Interval Timer, Canon **85.00**

Tote Bag, Canon, Montreal 1976 Olympic insignia **25.00**

Tripod, crown #1, wooden, 1920s **20.00**

Window Display, "Color Experts," glossy, Kodak, 1949, 8 x 10" **30.00**

CANDLEWICK

Imperial Glass Corporation introduced its No. 400 pattern, Candlewick, in 1936. Over 650 different forms and sets are known. Although produced primarily in cyrstal (clear), other colors exist. The pattern proved extremely popular and remained in production until Imperial closed in 1982.

After a brief period of ownership by the Lancaster–Colony Corporation and Consolidated Stores, Imperial's assets, including its molds, were sold. Various companies, groups, and individuals bought Imperial's Candlewick molds. Mirror Images of Lansing, Michigan, bought more than 200. Boyd Crystal Art Glass, Cambridge, Ohio, bought 18.

Reference: Mary M. Wetzel–Tomalka, *Candlewick: The Jewel of Imperial, Book II*, published by author, 1995.

Collectors' Club: The National Candlewick Collector's Club, 275 Milledge Terrace, Athens, GA 30606.

Bowl, 400/183, 3 toed, 6" **$65.00**

Bowl, 400/3F, 5¹/₂" **12.00**

Bowl, 400/75F, shallow, cupped, 11" **37.00**

Bud Vase, 400/107 . . . . **72.00**

Butter Plate, 400/40, 4¹/₂" **9.00**

Canape Plate, 400/7 . . . . **18.00**

Coaster, 4" **5.00**

Cologne, stopper **130.00**

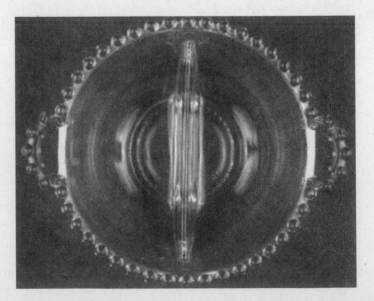

Jelly, 400/52, divided, 2 handled, 6", $20.00.

Compote, 400/45, 4 bead stem **22.00**
Creamer and Sugar, 400/31 .... **30.00**
Cruet Set, 400/7796 .... **135.00**
Deviled Egg Plate **160.00**
Epergne, 400/196 .... **270.00**
Heart Bowl, 400/40/H, handled, 5" **25.00**
Juice Tumbler, 400/19 .... **16.00**
Marmalade Lid **12.00**
Mint, 400/2, ring handle, 6¼" **18.00**
Pastry Tray, 400/149D, 8" **30.00**
Plate, 400/1D, 6" **8.00**
Relish, 400/208, 3 part, 3 toed. **125.00**
Relish, 400/55, 4 part, 8½" **22.00**
Salt and Pepper Shakers, pr, 400/190, ftd **80.00**
Seafood Icer, 400/190 .... **95.00**
Sugar, 6 oz **5.00**
Tray, 400/68D, center handle **40.00**
Tumbler, 400/19, 14 oz **40.00**
Vase, crimped, 8½" h **145.00**
Wine Tumbler, 100/19, ftd, 3 oz. **25.00**

CAP GUNS

The first toy cap gun was introduced in 1870. Cap guns experienced two Golden Ages: (1) the era of the cast iron cap gun from 1870 through 1900 and (2) the era of the diecast metal and plastic cap guns.

Hubley, Kilgore, Mattel, and Nichols are among the leading manufacturers of diecast pistols. Many diecast and plastic pistols were sold as part of holster sets. A large number were associated with television cowboy and detective heroes. The presence of the original box, holster, and other accessories adds as much as 100% to the value of the gun.

References: Rudy D'Angelo, *Cowboy Hero Cap Pistols*, Antique Trader Books, 1997; James L. Dundas, *Cap Guns: With Values*, Schiffer Publishing, 1996; Jerrell Little, *Price Guide to Cowboy Cap Guns and Guitars*, L–W Book Sales, 1996; Jim Schleyer, *Backyard Buckaroos: Collecting Western Toy Guns*, Books Americana, Krause Publications, 1996.

Collectors' Club: Toy Gun Collectors of America, 3009 Oleander Ave, San Marcos, CA 92069.

Big Horn, engraved diecast, metal, revolving cylinder, Kilgore, 1950–60 .... **$70.00**
Cap Pistol, bronze luster white metal, brown marbled woodgrain plastic grips, Daisy bull's–eye emblem and logo, Daisy, 1960s, 9½" l **100.00**
Colt .45, diecast, gold cylinder, ivory grips, bullets, Hubley **120.00**
Cowboy, cap pistol, nickel finish metal, white plastic steer head grips, Hubley **385.00**
Fanner Shootin' Shell, diecast, stag grips, chrome plated, revolving cylinder, Mattel, 1958–65, 9" l **40.00**
Gambler, diecast metal, grained white plastic grips, designed to fire single cap plus potato pellet to be formed by pressing bullet cartridge into common potato, Lone Star, 3½" l, orig box **35.00**
Paladin, stag grips, Halco Cap Gun **400.00**
Pioneer, diecast, nickel finish, engraving, orange–amber swirl grips, Hubley, c1950 .... **75.00**
The Sheriff, cast iron, nickel finish, ivory white plastic insert grips, right grip has raised image of crossed six–shooters and cowboy head, left grip has raised image of horse head, both have inset red cut glass stone, top–loading for roll caps, 1940, J & E Stevens Co, 8½" l, 1¼ x 4½ x 8½" orig box **160.00**
Spitfire, cast iron, silver finish, ivory white plastic grips, each depicting 3 fighter planes, left grip plate opens for loading roll caps, Stevens, 4½" l **75.00**
Wagon Train, antique bronze, revolving cylinder **275.00**

Hopalong Cassidy: Cap Gun, nickel silver finish, ivory plastic grips, Wyandotte, 1950s, $200.00; Holster, brown leather, steer conch, $100.00.

CARLTON WARE

Wiltshow and Robinson produced Staffordshire earthenware and porcelains at the Charlton Works, Stoke–on–Trent, beginning in the 1890s. In 1957 the company's name was changed to Carlton Ware, Ltd.

Black was the background color most often used on the company's wares. During the 1920s the line included pieces decorated with Art Deco designs in brightly enameled and gilt flowers and porcelain vases featuring luster decoration in oriental motifs.

Reference: *Collecting Carlton Ware*, Francis Joseph Publications, 1994, distributed by Krause Publications.

Collectors' Club: Carlton Ware International, PO Box 161, Sevenoaks, Kent Tn15 6GA UK.

Maggie and Jiggs, standing in front of tree, Jiggs' face repaired, 12" h, $121.00. Photo courtesy Collectors Auction Services.

Biscuit Jar, multicolored floral motif, cobalt trim, 9½" h. . . . **$120.00**
Bowl, green ground, applied yellow and brown banana
　feet, 9" d. **50.00**
Bowl, oval, Pink Buttercup **100.00**
Charger, Art Deco girl with hoop skirt and parasol,
　15½" d. **1,500.00**
Dish, hp red tomatoes, green molded cabbage and let-
　tuce ground, 10½" l. **60.00**
Dish, Rouge Royale, orange, green, and blue enameled
　and gilt pagoda scene, maroon ground, raised triangle
　in center, curved border, 9½" d **100.00**
Feeding Dish, 2 children on see–saw center design,
　multicolored, black "Baby's Dish" on rim, 7½" d. **100.00**
Flower Frog, purple irid glaze, 5" h **25.00**
Ginger Jar, cov, Egyptian motif, light blue ground, gilt
　border, c1920, 20" h **215.00**
Mug, man hanging from wooden support scene, cream
　ground, chartreuse handle, reverse "There are several
　Reasons for Drinking," 3¾" h. **40.00**
Mustard, cov, drum shaped, cream, orange base and top,
　black lines and drum sticks on cov, 1¼" h **200.00**
Pitcher, Art Deco, stripes and floral motif, blue, pink,
　and yellow, rose–beige ground, artist sgd, 8" h **300.00**
Salad Set, bowl, fork, and spoon, int and ext multicol-
　ored floral design, beige ground, SP rim **400.00**
Teapot, Blackberry **130.00**
Tea Set, cup and saucer, set of 6, magenta and gilt, scal-
　loped edge, fitted case. **200.00**
Vase, bird and floral motif, gold, enamel, maroon luster
　ground, pearl int, 7" h **245.00**
Vase, Rouge Royale, hp oriental motif, purple trim, gold
　trim, 5⅜" h **350.00**

Bathing Beauty, enamel finish, metallic tinsel bathing
　suit, Midland Doll Co, 1932 . . . . **$35.00**
Broncho Buster, removable hat, Pacini Novelty Statuary
　Co, 1936, 15" h. **60.00**
Bugs Bunny, flat back, c1940, 9¼" h **40.00**
Cat, yellow, wearing black hat, 4 x 9". **10.00**
Colt and Circus Horse, silver tinsel, Pacini Novelty
　Statuary Co, 1936, 8½" h. **20.00**
Dancing Doll, tinsel trim, Pacini Novelty Statuary Co,
　1936, 14" h. **35.00**
Dopey, c1937, 6" h. **45.00**
Eagle, "Victory," 8 x 13". **40.00**
Gorilla, c1940, 6¼" h **12.00**
Indian on Horse, St Louis Art Toy Co, 9 x 10" **30.00**
Kewpie, 12" h. **75.00**
Lady and Dog, floral trim c1935, 11¼" l **15.00**
Lamb, flat back, mkd "Rosemead Novelty Co," c1940,
　7" h **8.00**
Little Red Riding Hood, mkd "Connie Mamat," 1930s,
　14" h **30.00**
Parrot, 5 x 13". **35.00**
Porky Pig, 1940–50, 11" h. **32.00**
Rooster, 8 x 13" **25.00**
Skull, white, black painted hat. **25.00**
Soldier Boy, c1940, 9" h **10.00**
Uncle Sam, standing inside "V," 7 x 14". **35.00**
WWII Dog, 4 x 5". **15.00**

CARNIVAL CHALKWARE

Inexpensive plaster of Paris figurines made from the 1920s through the 1960s are collected under the generic classification of carnival chalkware because they most frequently were given away as prizes at games of chance. Doll and novelty companies produced them in quantity. Cost was as low as a dollar a dozen. While some pieces are marked and dated, most are not.

Reference: *Price Guide to Carnival Chalkware, Giveaways and Games*, L–W Book Sales, 1995.

CARTOON CHARACTERS

The comic strip was an American institution by the 1920s. Its Golden Age dates from the mid–1930s through the late 1950s. The movie cartoon came of age in the late 1930s and early 1940s as a result of the pioneers at the Disney and Warner Brothers studios. The Saturday morning television cartoon matured through the creative energies of Bill Hanna, Joe Barbera, and Jay Ward.

A successful cartoon character generates hundreds of licensed products. Most collectors focus on a single character or family of characters, e.g., Popeye, Mickey Mouse, or the Flintstones.

References: Bill Bruegman, *Cartoon Friends of the Baby Boom Era: A Pictorial Price Guide,* Cap'n Penny Productions, 1993; *Cartoon & Character Toys of the 50s, 60s, & 70s: Plastic & Vinyl,* L–W Book Sales, 1995; Ted Hake, *Hake's Guide to Comic Character Collectibles,* Wallace–Homestead, Krause Publications, 1993; Maxine A. Pinsky, *Marx Toys: Robots, Space, Comic, Disney & TV Characters,* Schiffer Publishing, 1996; Stuart W. Wells III and Alex G. Malloy, *Comics Collectibles and Their Values,* Wallace–Homestead, Krause Publications, 1996.

Newsletter: *Frostbite Falls Far–Flung Flier* (Rocky & Bullwinkle), PO Box 39, Macedonia, OH 44056.

Collectors' Clubs: Dick Tracy Fan Club, PO Box 632, Manitou Springs, CO 80829; Garfield Collectors Society, 7744 Foster Ridge Rd, Memphis, TN 38138; Official Popeye Fan Club, 1001 State St, Chester, IL 62233; Pogo Fan Club, 6908 Wentworth Ave S, Minneapolis, MN 55423.

Note: For additional listings see Disneyana, Hanna–Barbera, Peanuts, Smurfs, and Warner Bros.

Alvin & The Chipmunks, harmonica, plastic, blue and white, Plastic Inject Corp, 1959, 4" l, MOC **$30.00**

Alvin & The Chipmunks, magic slate, Saalfield, 1962 . . . . . . **15.00**

Andy Gump, figure, bisque, jointed, dark blue coat, yellow pants, late 1920s, 4" h. **95.00**

Archies, The, doll, Archie, cloth, orange hair, printed red shirt, orange and black pants, mkd "Archie," c1960 . . . . . **165.00**

Archies, The, figure, Veronica, cloth body, vinyl head, Mattel, 1977, 6½" h **10.00**

Barney Google, bank, figural whiskey jug, Snuffy illus on front, corncob stopper, 4¾" h **50.00**

Barney Google, book, *Barney Google and Spark Plug,* ©1925 Cupples & Leon, #3 of series, black and white comic strip reprints, cardboard cov, 48 pgs, 10 x 10" **75.00**

Barney Google, game, Barney Google an' Snuffy Smith, Milton Bradley, 1963. . . . . **40.00**

Barney Google, sheet music, Barney and Spark Plug cov, 1923. . . . . **25.00**

Beany & Cecil, carrying case, vinyl, red, zippered, red vinyl strap, color illus, Bob Clampett logo, 1961, 8½ x 9". **50.00**

Beany & Cecil, Cecil–in–the–Music–Box, litho metal box, cloth Cecil figure, musical crank handle, Mattel, 1961. . . . . **55.00**

Beany & Cecil, Disguise Kit, 18 different disguise costumes, 24" green plush bendable Cecil figure, orig 10 x 16" window display box, Mattel, 1961 . . . . **60.00**

Beetle Bailey, figure, rubber, complete with working compass, 6 x 4" display card, Toy House, 1963. . . . . **25.00**

Beetle Bailey, Fold–Away–Camp Swampy Playset, fold–open cardboard box, plastic soldiers, jeeps, trucks, and exploding bridge, 5 character figures, MPC, 1964 . . . . **175.00**

Betty Boop, charm, celluloid, tinted colors, brass loop at top, 1930s. **30.00**

Betty Boop, doll, vinyl, jointed, M–Toy, 1986, 12" h **10.00**

Betty Boop, figure, celluloid, hollow, fleshtone, green dress, gold, black, and red accents, movable arms, holding white hoop, c1930, 3" h **130.00**

Betty Boop, mask, stiff paper, diecut, full color, Bob–o–link Shoes, 1930s, 9½ x 9". **125.00**

Blondie, book, *Blondie & Dagwood's Snapshot Clue,* text, cartoons, 1934. . . . . **45.00**

Blondie, game, Blondie and Dagwood's Race for the Office Game, Jaymar, 1950 . . . . **45.00**

Blondie, puzzle, Blondie and Dagwood Interchangeable Blocks, Gaston Manufacturing Co, c1950, orig 7 x 11" box. **65.00**

Bringing Up Father, poster, color graphics of Jiggs and friend in cabaret smoking cigars and watching girls wearing hula skirts, red and black "George McManus' Cartoon Comedy–With Music Bringing Up Father Jiggs, Maggie, Dinty Moore And Others," Harold Poster Co, IL, early 1920s, 20½ x 36¾". **375.00**

Casper the Friendly Ghost, bop bag, vinyl inflatable, Casper and Wendy illus, Doughboy, 1966, 54" h **50.00**

Casper the Friendly Ghost, game, Casper Electronic Adventure Game, Tarco, 1962 . . . . **25.00**

Casper the Friendly Ghost, Rub–A–Pencil Set, box contains 5 coloring books and pencil, Saalfield, 1960. . . . . **45.00**

Cat in the Hat, jack–in–the–box, litho metal box, pop–up Cat in the Hat, musical crank handle, Mattel, 1970. . . . . **55.00**

Cat in the Hat, pinback button, "Cat In The Hat/Happy 30th Birthday," ©1957 Dr Seuss, issued in 1987, 2½" d **20.00**

Chilly Willy, squeeze toy, rubber, 1950s. **25.00**

Dan Dunn, pinback button "I'm Operative 48," issued by Philadelphia Evening Ledger Comics, back paper ad text, 1930s, 1¼" d **75.00**

Dennis the Menace, Mischief Kit, complete with bugs, snake bow tie, replica ink blot, and various tricks, orig 15½" box, Hasbro, 1955 . . . . **50.00**

Dennis the Menace, sheet music, yellow, Dennis holding teddy bear with slingshot and broken toys on floor cov, ©1953 Santly Joy, Inc, 4 pgs **15.00**

Dennis the Menace, Stuff N' Lace Doll, Standard Toycraft, 1950s **35.00**

Dick Tracy, 2–Way Electronic Wrist Radios, set of 2, plastic, battery operated, orig 2½ x 9½ x 13½" box, Remco, c1950. . . . . **125.00**

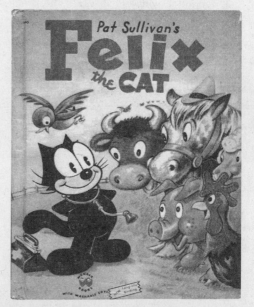

Felix the Cat, Wonder Book, #665, 1953, $12.00.

Dick Tracy, hand puppet, Bonny Braids, soft molded vinyl plastic head, hands, and feet, flannel pajama outfit, baby blanket, orig tag, c1953, 10" h **60.00**

Dick Tracy, hand viewer, Dick Tracy In Movie Style, black and white films, "Turn The Knob And See Dick Tracy In Action," ©1953 . . . . **110.00**

Don Winslow of the Navy, comic book, #50, Oct 1947, Fawcett **20.00**

Dudley DoRight, magic drawing slate, wooden stylus, Saalfield, 1970, 8 x 12" **20.00**

Dudley DoRight, squeeze toy, vinyl, scowling Dick Dastardly in blue overcoat, red aviator hat and gloves, black boots, Lambert Kay ©HBP, Spain, c1970, 4³/₄" **70.00**

Felix the Cat, bowl, china, color Felix image with white cat on fence, "Will You Walk With Felix?" gold accent letters, c1930, 6¹/₂" d **200.00**

Felix the Cat, brochure, Eastman Kodak adv, Kodatoy film projector and theater, black, white, and red Felix, late 1920–30, 5¹/₄ x 8¹/₄" **55.00**

Felix the Cat, card holder, celluloid, diecut, full figure, made in China sticker on bottom, c1930s, 2⁷/₈" h **185.00**

Felix the Cat, flashlight, plastic, color litho paper illus of Felix riding rocket, 5 x 7" display card, Bantamlite, 1960 . . . . **30.00**

Felix the Cat, palm puzzle, silvered tin, German, 1930s, 3" d **100.00**

Felix the Cat, pencil sharpener, figural Felix, metal, painted, c1930s, 1¹/₂" h **200.00**

Felix the Cat, sheet music, Felix singing with ukelele with 2 smiling cats next to him in moonlit street scene cov, sgd "Messmer" at bottom left corner, ©1928 Sam Fox Pub Co, 6 pgs **100.00**

Felix the Cat, target set, litho tin target, plastic pistol, rubber tipped darts, orig window display box, Lido, 1953 . . . . **75.00**

Go–Go Gophers, glass, Pepsi premium, gopher image on front and back, ©Lednardo–TTV, c1970s, 6¹/₄" h **20.00**

Heckle and Jeckle, 3–D Target Game, plastic, emb character image, TV Film Sales, 1958 . . . . **30.00**

Hector Heathcote, game, 4 figures, 64 cards, playing pc, marble cannon ball, instruction leaflet, 17" sq playing board, Transogram, 1963 . . . . **55.00**

Henry, book, comic strip reprint, David McKay Co, 1945, 5¹/₂ x 7" **30.00**

Henry, book, *Henry Goes to a Party*, Wonder Book, #1508, emb cov art and spiral binding, 1955 . . . . **15.00**

Herman and Catnip, kite, cardboard, color illus, Saalfield, 1960 . . . . **20.00**

Joe Palooka, booklet, School Bus Safety Tips, 1950, 3 x 5" **20.00**

Joe Palooka, game, Joe Palooka Boxing Game, Lowell, c1950s **75.00**

Joe Palooka, pinback button, "I Read Joe Palooka Every Day In The Bulletin," full color portrait, dark red ground, 1940s, 1³/₄" d **70.00**

Krazy Kat, book, *Adventures of Krazy Kat and Ignatz Mouse in Koko Land*, #1056, Saalfield, 1934 . . . . **150.00**

Krazy Kat, pin, figural, metal, enameled, rhinestone eyes, 1930s, 1¹/₄" h **35.00**

Li'l Abner, bank, Schmoo, hard plastic, blue, black accents, inscribed "Li'l–Abner–Sez, Woo the Schmoo, with Lucky Money/Make Your Future Bright And Sunny!" on back, orig diecut money bag shaped card, Gould & Co, ©1948, 7" h **65.00**

Li'l Abner, doll, Mammy Yokum, vinyl, cloth outfit, Baby Barry Toy Co, 1957, 13" h **125.00**

Li'l Abner, pin, figural, plaster, red and black accents, late 1940s, 2¹/₄" h **100.00**

Li'l Abner, salt and pepper shakers, pr, plaster, figural Schmoo, one with green bow tie, other with red bow tie, 3¹/₂" h **200.00**

Little Audrey, costume, 1 pc, yellow and red bodysuit, Little Audrey illus and name, plastic mask, Halco, 1960 . . . . **30.00**

The Little King, figure, composition wood, painted, 2¹/₂" h, 1944 . . . . **150.00**

Little Lulu, book, *Little Lulu*, hardcover, Curtis Publishing Co, Rand McNally Co, 1937, 64 pgs **55.00**

Little Lulu, Cartoon–A–Kit, 1948 . . . . **75.00**

Little Lulu, greeting card, full color illus, 1944 Marjory H Buell copyright series, Hallmark, price for set of 4 . . . . **75.00**

Little Lulu, jigsaw puzzle, #5605–25, Lulu and Tubby bouncing on pogo sticks picking apples, Whitman, ©1981 Western Publishing, Inc, orig 8¹/₄ x 10¹/₂ x 3" box **10.00**

Little Lulu, paint book, Little Lulu and Tubby Tom, #684, Whitman, 8¹/₄ x 11¹/₄" **45.00**

Little Nemo, sheet music, *Little Nemo/A Fairy Tale*, red, white, and blue cov illus, 1926 . . . . **55.00**

Mighty Mouse, doll, arms raised in air, stuffed, rubber face, corduroy hands and ears, satin cloth body and cape, vinyl white belt with red accent buckle, orig cloth label with Ideal and CBS logo, 1950s, 14" h **150.00**

Mighty Mouse, squeeze toy, figural, attached red felt cape, Terrytoons, 1950s **75.00**

Moon Mullins, figure, Moon, wood, jointed, orig box, 5" h **120.00**

Moon Mullins, salt and pepper shakers, pr, Moon Mullins and Kayo **20.00**

Mr Magoo, Mr Magoo at the Circus Pop–Up Target Set, 20 x 22" window display box, Knickerbocker, 1956 . . . . . **125.00**

Nancy and Sluggo, doll, Nancy, molded plastic vinyl head, painted accents, stuffed vinyl body, cloth outfit, S & P Doll and Toy Co, 1954, 16" h **175.00**

Pink Panther, flashlight, plastic, Ja–Ru **8.00**

Popeye, toy, windup, riding tricycle, metal and celluloid, Linemar, $550.00.

Pink Panther, Pink Panther & Sons Target Game, Ja–Ru **12.00**

Pogo, book, *Positively Pogo*, 1st ed, Simon & Schuster, ©1957, 190 pgs **25.00**

Pogo, mug, set of 6, plastic, full color character images, ©Walt Kelly, 1950–60, 4⅛" h **55.00**

Popeye, figure, Popeye the Thinker, chalk, 1929, 6" h **95.00**

Popeye, game, Adventures of Popeye Game, Transogram, 1957 . . . . **60.00**

Popeye, harmonica, plastic, red, 5 x 5" illus display card with songs on reverse, Plastic Injector Corp, 1958 . . . . **40.00**

Popeye, pinback button, "I Yam Strong for King Comics," late 1930s **30.00**

Popeye, Popeye Tootin' Bubble Blower, Transogram, 1958. . . . . **50.00**

Popeye, puppet, push button, Popeye and Olive Oyl, orig box, 1940s, price for pr **85.00**

Popeye, sand pail, litho tin, Popeye Under the Sea, color illus, ©1933 T Cohn, Inc, 8" h **40.00**

Popeye, soaky, Brutus, fleshtone face, black beard, red and white painted outfit, 1960s, 10" h **30.00**

Ren & Stimpy, flicker watch, plastic, brown band, "Happy Happy!, Joy Joy!" flicker image on dial, orig illus warranty and case, Bigtime Enterprises, Inc, 1992 . . . . **50.00**

Ren & Stimpy, game, Ren & Stimpy Show Log Cereal Game, Parker Brothers, 1992 . . . . **15.00**

Rocky & Bullwinkle, book, *Make Way For Bullwinkle*, #1363, ©Whitman, 1972, 24 pp **20.00**

Rocky & Bullwinkle, Bullwinkle's Jr Cartoonist Stamp Set, character, alphabet, and numbers stamp pads, litho tin ink pad, Bullwinkle illus on lid, Larami, 1969 . . . . **20.00**

Rocky & Bullwinkle, coloring book, #2261, cover scene of Bullwinkle on bucking horse and Rocky holding camera, Saalfield, 1965 . . . . **25.00**

Rocky & Bullwinkle, figure, Snidley Whiplash, Wham–O, 1972, 5" h **10.00**

Rocky & Bullwinkle, jigsaw puzzle, Rocky and His Friends, Whitman, 1960s, 63 pcs **30.00**

Rocky & Bullwinkle, pinback button, "Hokey Smokes, It's Channel 5," black Bullwinkle silhouette against carnival scene ground, blue and white sticker from Reno Nevada on reverse, 2½" d **10.00**

Rocky & Bullwinkle, soaky, Rocky, painted gray body, green aviator cap, 1960s, 9" H **35.00**

Skippy, Big Little Book, *The Story of Skippy*, Phillips Magnesia Toothpaste premium, ©Whitman, 1934 . . . . **35.00**

Skippy, manual, Good Eyesight Brigade, "Skippy presents Stories of Interesting People who wear glasses," ©1937 . . . . **15.00**

Smitty, Big Little Book, *Smitty Golden Gloves Tournament*, Cocomalt premium, ©Whitman, 1930s **30.00**

Smitty, coloring book, ©McLoughlin Bros, 1931, 10 x 10" **30.00**

Teenage Mutant Ninja Turtles, Mutant Maker Crazy Character Creation Kit, #5695, Playmates, 1990 . . . . **12.00**

Teenage Mutant Ninja Turtles, Pizza Thrower, 1989 . . . . **35.00**

Teenage Mutant Ninja Turtles, Turtle Blimp, green vinyl, 1988, 30" l **30.00**

Tillie the Toiler, coloring book, Tillie the Toiler Magic Drawing and Coloring Book, Gabriel, 1930s, 9 x 12" **35.00**

Underdog, game, Milton Bradley, 1964 . . . . **25.00**

Underdog, thermos, steel, full color, white plastic cup, Universal Vacuum Products, 1974, 7½" h **200.00**

Winky Dink, Winky Dink and You Super Magic TV Kit, Standard Toykraft, Screen Magic, Inc, 1968. . . . . **75.00**

Woody Woodpecker, game, Travel with Woody Woodpecker, Cadaco–Ellis, 1956 Lantz copyright, orig box **80.00**

Woody Woodpecker, pendant watch, metal, gold, full color smiling Woody image with red hands pointing to black numerals, white ground, attached 24" gold accent chain, Endura, ©1972 Walter Lantz Productions, Inc **70.00**

CATALINA POTTERY

The Catalina Pottery, located on Santa Catalina Island, California, was founded in 1927 for the purpose of making clay building products. Decorative and functional pottery was added to the company's line in the early 1930s. A full line of color–glazed dishes was made between 1931 and 1937.

Gladding, McBean and Company bought Catalina Pottery in 1937, moved production to the mainland, and closed the island pottery. Gladding, McBean continued to use the Catalina trademark until 1947.

References: Jack Chipman, *Collector's Encyclopedia of California Pottery, Second Edition*, Collector Books, 1998; Steve and Aisha Hoefs, *Catalina Island Pottery*, published by authors, 1993.

Ashtray, cowboy hat, green **$100.00**

Bowl, bonnet, 10½" d **225.00**

Candle Holders, pr, pedestal base, flared rim, pink, #606 . . . **135.00**

Coaster, yellow **20.00**

Cup and Saucer, green **40.00**

Dessert Bowl, red **18.00**

Figure, fish, #C253 . . . . **25.00**

Lady Head, Carmen Miranda, black, blue, and maroon. **450.00**

Nut Dish, blue **20.00**

Planter, square, green **20.00**

Plate, scalloped edge, blue, 10½" d **35.00**

Salt and Pepper Shakers, pr, flower baskets. **75.00**

Tray, leaf shape, turquoise and coral **60.00**

Tumbler, orange, 4" h **20.00**

Vase, flared, red clay, blue glaze, 6" h **125.00**

Vase, oxblood, 5" h **75.00**

Water Set, carafe and 6 tumblers, red. **250.00**

Wine Decanter, Spanish woman, yellow gloss **265.00**

CATALOGS

There are three basic types of catalogs: (1) manufacturers' catalogs that are supplied primarily to distributors, (2) trade catalogs supplied to the merchant community and general public, and (3) mail–order catalogs designed for selling directly to the consumer. Montgomery Ward issued its first mail–order catalog in 1872. Sears Roebuck's came out in 1886.

A catalog revolution occurred in the 1980s with the arrival of specialized catalogs and select zip code mailing niche marketing. In the 1990s catalogs began appearing on the Internet. Many predict this will make the printed catalog obsolete by the mid-21st century.

References: Ron Barlow and Ray Reynolds, *The Insider's Guide to Old Books, Magazines, Newspapers and Trade Catalogs*, Windmill Publishing, 1995; Norman E. Martinus and Harry L. Rinker, *Warman's Paper*, Wallace–Homestead, Krause Publications, 1994.

1924, Spanjer Bros, Newark, NJ, manufacturers of advertising and decorative woodwork, 60 pp, 7½ x 10".. **$100.00**

1926, Beck Manufacturing Co, Sioux City, IA, 5 illus of oiler showing parts, 8 pp, 2½ x 5½"................. **10.00**

1927, National Cloak & Suit Co, New York, NY, spring and summer catalog, 366 pp, 9 x 11¾"............... **35.00**

1929, Henion & Hubbell, Chicago, IL, catalog B, "H & H" pneumatic water supply systems for supplying water to country residences, 6 x 9"................ **30.00**

1930, Clocks, Blanche M Beal, West Union, IA, Bily Clocks, illus, 16 pp, 6¾ x 9"...................... **45.00**

1931, Bingham Brothers Co, New York, NY, reference book of roller for printing industry, 59 pp, 8¾ x 11¼"..... **25.00**

1933, Butler Brothers, St Louis, MO, 212 pp, 9½ x 13¾".................................... **25.00**

1934, Toys, Metal Cast Products Co, New York, NY, illus, 16 pp, 9½ x 11½"............................ **35.00**

1936, Neidhoefer & Co, Chicago, IL, Mohawk Carpet Mills Distributors, floor coverings, 90 pp, 9½ x 12½"..... **30.00**

1937, Metalware, Atlantic Stamping Co, Rochester, NY, c1937, 27 pp, 8½ x 11"......................... **35.00**

1938, Gordon–Van Tine Co, Davenport, IA, building materials, 72 pp, 8½ x 11½"...................... **40.00**

1939, Amana Society, Amana, IA, 27 pp, 8¼ x 10½"....... **45.00**

1940, Middleton Mfg Co, Milwaukee, WI, 32 pp, 6½ x 9½".................................... **32.00**

1942, Shakespearre Co, Kalamazoo, MI, fishing supplies, 86 pp, 5½ x 8½"........................ **50.00**

1945, Firearms, Stoeger Arms Corp, New York, NY, "The Shooter's Bible No. 36," 512 pp, 8 x 10"............. **45.00**

1953, H L Wild, New York, NY, True Blue catalog #78, woodworking, 74 pp, 8½ x 11".................... **20.00**

1955, Snap–On Tools Corp, Kenosha, WI, 108 pp, 8½ x 11".................................... **20.00**

1956, Standard Electric Supply, Milwaukee, WI, #56, distributors of electrical supplies, etc, 36 pg, 8½ x 11" **30.00**

1961, Kenneth Lynch & Sons, Wilton, CT, #2061, general wholesale catalog, garden ornaments, weather vanes, sundials, bird baths, etc, 136 pp, 11 x 17"........ **45.00**

1962, Sears, Roebuck & Co, Chicago, IL, fall and winter catalog, 1,516 pp, 8¼ x 11".................... **32.00**

1963, Star Band Co, Portsmouth, VA, Halloween, 16 pp, 8½ x 11"................................. **42.00**

Me Buy It!, Crown Publishers, 1988; Alice Muncaster and Ellen Yanow, *The Cat Made Me Buy It*, Crown Publishers, 1984.

Collectors' Club: Cat Collectors, 33161 Wendy Dr, Sterling Heights, MI 48310.

Activity Book, Garfield, sticker album, 7 sticker packets, c1978.. **$5.00**

Ashtray, black and white kitten on top, Lustreware, incised "Made in Japan," 3¼" h.................... **25.00**

Book, *Christmas in Cat Land*, Goyder, Alice, Thomas Y Cromwell, NY, hardcover, 1978.................... **20.00**

Book, *Four Little Kittens*, Rand McNally, 1934 .... **15.00**

Box, ceramic, cat shaped, oriental blue design, pink flowers, mkd "Made in China," 7½" l, 4½" h **65.00**

Calendar, Chesapeake & Ohio Railway, 1957, Chessie illus **75.00**

Cookie Jar, gold colored cat, brown and caramel floral dec, 1930s.................................. **75.00**

Cookie Jar, Kliban's Cat, full figure.................... **135.00**

Doorstop, black cat, probably Albany Foundry Co, mid–1920s, 6¾" h................................ **75.00**

Figure, bisque, straw flower neck dec, redware, 5¾" h **8.00**

Figure, Cats of Character, Danbury Mint, 1986, 4" h........ **15.00**

Figure, Egyptian–style cat, allover small floral pattern, c1920s, 6½" h................................ **40.00**

Figure, glass, arched back cat, Venetian glass, Celleni, 1950s, 11½" h................................ **150.00**

Game, Game of Cat and Mouse, Parker Brothers, 1964 ..... **15.00**

Halloween Lantern, cardboard, cat's head, black, orange tissue paper eyes, nose, and mouth, 2 sided, late 1940s, 11" h.................................. **65.00**

Jigsaw Puzzle, The Robber Kitten, Parker Brothers, 1920s **40.00**

Lithograph, "Susie," kitten between 2 puppies, ©Daily Mirror, Inc, 1940, 8¾ x 12 ¾"................... **15.00**

Match Holder, wood, painted, handmade, 1940s **18.00**

Napkin Holder, ceramic, 3 kittens in basket, 1940s **20.00**

Oil and Vinegar Cruets, pr, 2 black cats, Shafford, 7½" h..... **40.00**

Pillow Cover, cotton, litho, "Don't Forget the Kitty," smoking cat playing banjo....................... **175.00**

CAT COLLECTIBLES

Unlike dog collectors who tend to collect objects portraying a single breed, cat collectors collect anything and everything with a cat image or in the shape of a cat. It makes no difference if an object is old or new, realistic or abstract. Cat collectors love it all.

The popularity of cats as pets increased significantly in the 1980s. Many contemporary 1980s cat collectibles, e.g., Kliban's cats and Lowell Davis porcelains featuring cats, are experiencing strong secondary markets. Remember, this market is highly speculative. Serious cat collectors stick to vintage (pre–1965) cat collectibles that have withstood the test of time.

References: Marbena Jean Fyke, *Collectible Cats: An Identification & Value Guide* (1993, 1995 value update), *Book II* (1996), Collector Books; J. L. Lynnlee, *Purrrfection: The Cat*, Schiffer Publishing, 1990; Alice L. Muncaster and Ellen Sawyer, *The Black Cat Made*

Cookie Jar, Puss 'n Boots, red bow, long tail, Shawnee, 10¼" h, $150.00.

Plate, The Booted Cat, Meissen annual, 1980 . . . . **175.00**
Playing Cards, Chessie, orig box **15.00**
Poster, Ideal Classic adv, Persian cat cuddling up to radi-
   ator heater, Luisa Polo illus, G Ricordi Co, Milan, Italy,
   c1930, 39 x 53" **475.00**
Salt and Pepper Shakers, pr, snow dome bellies, Japan
   paper label, 4¹/₂" h **245.00**
Shot Glass, figural, metal, silver color, 1 oz, 3³/₄" h **30.00**
Toy, stuffed, Steiff, 5" l, 2¹/₂" h, 1945–54 . . . . **45.00**
Toy, windup, Garfield, plastic face, fur covered body,
   plastic feet, 1980. . . . . **8.00**

CERAMIC ARTS STUDIO

Lawrence Rabbett and Ruben Sand founded the Ceramic Arts Studio, Madison, Wisconsin, in January 1941 for the purpose of making wheel–thrown ceramics. During World War II the company began production on a line of high–end molded figurines that were sold in jewelry stores and large department stores. The flood of cheap imported ceramics in the early 1950s led to the demise of the studio in 1955.

Reference: Mike Schneider, *Ceramic Arts Studio: Identification and Price Guide*, Schiffer Publishing, 1994.

Collectors' Club: Ceramic Arts Studio Collectors Assoc, PO Box 46, Madison, WI 53701.

Figure, Dutch love girl, blue **$27.00**
Figure, frisky lamb. **25.00**
Figure, Harry, southern gentleman **50.00**
Figure, Little Boy Blue, striped shirt **30.00**
Figure, panda bear holding cub **85.00**
Figure, Pomeranian **40.00**
Figure, Spaniel puppy **25.00**
Figure, Wing Sang **15.00**
Figures, pr, Gay 90's couple, pastel **150.00**
Figures, pr, Peter Pan and Wendy **125.00**
Figures, pr, Ting–A–Ling and Sung–Tu. **40.00**
Figures, pr, waterman and woman **180.00**
Planter, oriental girl. **18.00**
Salt and Pepper Shakers, pr, mouse and cheese **25.00**
Salt and Pepper Shakers, pr, oriental children **40.00**
Shelf Sitter, Nip, early glaze. **22.00**
Shelf Sitters, pr, birds, Pete and Polly **175.00**

CEREAL BOXES

Ready–to–eat breakfast cereal appeared around 1900. Until the 1930s, most advertising and packaging was targeted toward mothers. The popularity of children's radio programs and their sponsorship by cereal manufacturers shifted the focus to youngsters.

By the 1950s cereal premiums inside the box and cutouts on cereal box backs were a standard feature. Cereal boxes also were used to promote television shows and the personalities and characters that appeared on them. By the early 1970s, cereal manufacturers issued special promotional boxes, many of which featured local and national sports heroes.

As the 1990s come to a close, cereal box prices are highly speculative. Market manipulators are at work. Crossover collectors are paying premium prices for character and personality boxes whose long–term collectibility is uncertain.

References: Scott Bruce, *Cereal Box Bonanza: The 1950's*, Collector Books, 1995; Scott Bruce and Bill Crawford, *Cerealizing America: The Unsweetened Story of American Breakfast Cereals*, Faber and Faber, 1995.

Collectors' Club: Sugar–Charged Cereal Collectors, 5400 Cheshire Meadows Way, Fairfax, VA 22032.

Note: All boxes are in good condition.

Alpha Bits, Post, Archie cutout record, 1970. . . . . **$150.00**
Apple Jacks, Kellogg's, comics on back, 1966. . . . . **30.00**
Banana Frosted Flakes, Kellogg's, Tony on front, 1980s **30.00**
Batman, Ralston, hologram t–shirt offer, 1989. . . . . **10.00**
Cheerios, General Mills, Star Wars poster in box, 1978. . . . . . . **20.00**
Cocoa Pebbles, Post, Bedrock Biker Racer poster in box,
   1987. . . . . **3.00**
Cocoa Puffs, General Mills, aircraft carrier/jet launcher
   toy on front, aircraft carrier cutout on back, 1950s **65.00**
Corn Chex, Party Mix recipe, 1950s. **65.00**
Corn Flakes, Kellogg's, frying pan set offer, 1952 . . . . **20.00**
Donkey Kong Junior, Ralston, baseball card pack, 1984 . . . . . **30.00**
Dunkin' Donuts Cereal, Ralston, back to school kit offer,
   1988. . . . . **10.00**
Froot Loops, Kellogg's, Mattel Fun on Wheels contest,
   1970. . . . . **30.00**
Frosted Flakes, Kellogg's, Tony the Tiger spoon offer, 1965. . . . **40.00**
Golden Grahams, General Mills, roller blade offer, 1980s. **3.00**
Jersey Corn Flakes, multicolored, family eating cereal,
   unopened, 1920s **40.00**
Kix, personalized pencil offer, General Mills. **10.00**
Nerds, Orange 'N Cherry, Ralston, Nerds candy in box,
   bowl offer, 1985 . . . . **20.00**
Quaker Puffed Wheat, No 8 Space Flight to Moon, 1953 . . . **100.00**
Quaker Muffets Shredded Wheat, authentic Civil War
   cannon adv on side panel, 1960s, 3 x 6 x 7" **40.00**
Rice Chex, red check design, 1950s. **65.00**
Shredded Wheat, Kellogg's, baseball ring in box, 1955 . . . . . **100.00**
Sugar Jets, General Mills, 1960s. . . . .
Wheat Honeys, Nabisco, Disney character offer, 1960s **75.00**
Wheaties, General Mills, bowling champion contest,
   1959. . . . . **30.00**

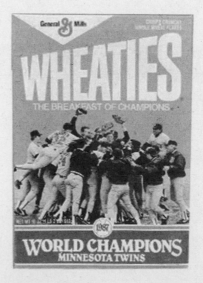

Wheaties, General Mills, 1987 World Champions Minnesota Twins, 18 oz, $10.00.

CHILDREN'S DISHES

Children's dish sets date back to the Victorian era. In the 1920s and 1930s American glass companies manufactured sets of children's dishes in their most popular patterns. Inexpensive ceramic sets came from Germany and Japan. Injection molded plastic sets first appeared in the late 1940s. By the 1950s, miniature melamine plastic sets mimmicked the family's everyday plastic service.

Most children's dish sets were designed to be used by their owners for tea and doll parties. At the moment, collecting emphasis remains on pre–war sets.

References: Maureen Batkin, *Gifts for Good Children Part II: The History of Children's China 1890–1990*, Richard Dennis Publications, n.d., distributed by Antique Collectors' Club; Doris Anderson Lechler, *Children's Glass Dishes, China and Furniture* (1983, 1991 value update), *Vol. II* (1986, 1993 value update), Collector Books; Lorraine Punchard, *Playtime Pottery and Porcelain From The United Kingdom and The United States*, Schiffer Publishing, 1996; Lorraine Punchard, *Playtime Pottery and Porcelain From Europe and Asia*, Schiffer Publishing, 1996; Margaret and Kenn Whitmyer, *Collector's Encyclopedia of Children's Dishes: An Illustrated Value Guide*, Collector Books, (1993, 1995 value update).

Collectors' Club: Toy Dish Collectors Club, PO Box 159, Bethlehem, CT 06751.

CHINA

Betty Boop, tea set, 4 cups and saucers, creamer, sugar, and cov teapot, 2 saucers have chips, Japan	$800.00
Blue Willow, creamer, unmkd, 2" h	18.00
Blue Willow, cup, Occupied Japan, 1³/₄"	15.00
Blue Willow, cup, unmkd, 2¹/₄"	12.00
Blue Willow, grill plate, Japan, 4¹/₄"	60.00
Blue Willow, plate, Occupied Japan, 3³/₄"	12.00
Blue Willow, plate, Occupied Japan, 4³/₄"	21.00
Blue Willow, plate, unmkd, 4¹/₂" d	9.00
Blue Willow, platter, oval, Occupied Japan	48.00
Blue Willow, platter, oval, unmkd, 6¹/₂ x 3³/₄"	35.00
Blue Willow, saucer, Occupied Japan, 3¹/₄"	8.00
Blue Willow, set, 4 cups and saucers, 4 plates, cov teapot, cov sugar, creamer, orig box, Japan, 17 pcs	20.00

Tin, tea set, includes 4¹/₄" d serving plate, 2¹/₄" h cov teapot, two cups, and two 2¹/₂" d saucers, Ohio Art, c1940, $40.00.

Blue Willow, sugar, cov, unmkd, 3¹/₂" h	25.00
Blue Willow, teapot, cov, unmkd, 4" h	50.00
Moss Rose, plate, 4¹/₂" d	3.00
Petit Point Basket, set, Salem China, 9 pcs	60.00
Playtime Rose, platter, 2 cups and saucers, and cov creamer	25.00
Whirly Gig, set, Blue Ridge	500.00

GLASS

Akro Agate, Chiquita, set, cobalt, cov teapot, creamer and sugar, and 6 cups, saucers, and plates	$225.00
Akro Agate, Stippled Band, set, topaz, 17 pcs	295.00
Akro Agate, set, transparent topaz, teapot, creamer, cov sugar, and 4 each cups, saucers and plates, topaz	215.00
Akro Agate, Interior Panel, set, transparent green, large, 21 pcs	225.00
Cameo, water set, cobalt blue	25.00
Cherry Blossom, creamer, delphite	45.00
Cherry Blossom, creamer, pink	50.00
Cherry Blossom, cup and saucer, delphite	40.00
Cherry Blossom, cup and saucer, pink	45.00
Cherry Blossom, plate, delphite	12.00
Cherry Blossom, plate, pink	12.50
Cherry Blossom, saucer, delphite	7.00
Cherry Blossom, saucer, pink	7.00
Cherry Blossom, set, delphite, 14 pcs	300.00
Cherry Blossom, set, pink, 14 pcs	400.00
Cherry Blossom, sugar, delphite	45.00
Circus, cereal bowl, red, Pyrex	15.00
Diamond Quilted, candlesticks, pr, green	25.00
Doric & Pansy, creamer and sugar, pink	75.00
Doric & Pansy, creamer and sugar, teal	100.00
Doric & Pansy, cup and saucer, teal	58.00
Doric & Pansy, plate, teal	12.00
Doric & Pansy, saucer, teal	8.00
Doric & Pansy, set, pink, 14 pcs	275.00
Hex Optic, plate, green, 8"	5.00
Homespun, partial set, 4 plates, 4 saucers, 3 cups, pink	195.00
Laurel, set, red trim, McKee, 14 pcs	350.00
Moderntone Little Hostess, creamer and sugar, pastel pink	30.00
Moderntone Little Hostess, cup, burgundy	13.00
Moderntone Little Hostess, cup, gray	13.00
Moderntone Little Hostess, cup, pastel pink	13.00
Moderntone Little Hostess, cup and saucer, chartreuse	20.00
Moderntone Little Hostess, cup and saucer, gray	19.00
Moderntone Little Hostess, cup and saucer, pastel blue	16.00
Moderntone Little Hostess, cup and saucer, pastel yellow	16.00
Moderntone Little Hostess, plate, gold, 5¹/₄"	12.00
Moderntone Little Hostess, plate, gray, 5¹/₄"	10.00
Moderntone Little Hostess, plate, pastel blue, 5¹/₄"	12.00
Moderntone Little Hostess, plate, pastel green, 5¹/₄"	12.00
Moderntone Little Hostess, plate, pastel pink, 5¹/₄"	12.00
Moderntone Little Hostess, plate, pastel yellow, 5¹/₄"	10.00
Moderntone Little Hostess, plate, turquoise, 5¹/₄"	10.00
Moderntone Little Hostess, saucer, gold	7.50
Moderntone Little Hostess, saucer, gray	5.00
Moderntone Little Hostess, saucer, pastel yellow	6.00
Moderntone Little Hostess, saucer, turquoise	7.00
Moderntone Little Hostess, set, pastel colors	100.00
Moderntone Little Hostess, set, turquoise teapot, other pcs gray, rust, gold, and turquoise	295.00

Pineapple & Floral, creamer and sugar, crystal **13.00**
Radiance, butter dish, crystal, platinum trim. **135.00**
20th Century, set, Hazel Atlas, 14 pcs **85.00**
Wee Branches, creamer and sugar, missing lid **175.00**

CHINTZ CHINA

Chintz patterned goods owe their origin to Indian chintes, fabrics decorated with richly hued flowers and brightly plumed mythical birds that were imported to England from India in the 17th century. Although English Staffordshire potters produced chintz pattern ceramics as early as the 1820s, the golden age of chintz decorated ceramics dates from 1920 through 1940. Although dozens of post–World War II patterns were made, collectors prefer pre–war examples.

References: Linda Eberle and Susan Scott, *The Charlton Standard Catalogue of Chintz, 2nd Edition,* Charlton Press, 1997; Muriel Miller, *Collecting Royal Winton Chintz,* Francis Joseph Publications, 1996, distributed by Krause Publications; Jo Anne Peterson Welsh, *Chintz Ceramics, 2nd Edition,* Schiffer Publishing, 1998.

Collectors' Club: Chintz China Collector's Club, PO Box 50888, Pasadena, CA 91115.

Beeston, coaster **$50.00**
Beeston, plate, 5" sq **58.00**
Butterfly Chintz, plate, Wade Heath, England, 6" **60.00**
Chelsea, compote, ftd **175.00**
Clevdon, butter pat **65.00**
Crocus, tray for creamer and sugar, black **105.00**
English Rose, relish, Grimwade, Royal Winton **200.00**
Evesham, creamer and sugar **150.00**
Festival, condiment set, Crown Ducal. **165.00**
Floral Feast, plate, 8". **100.00**
Floral Garden, jug, 4" h **165.00**
Hazel, demitasse cup **68.00**
Julia, trivet **165.00**

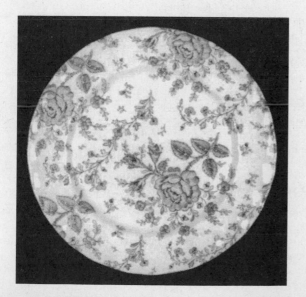

Rose Chintz, dinner plate, Johnson Bros., 9³/₄" d, $15.00.

Kinver, salad bowl, chrome rim **175.00**
Mayfair, bowl, 5" d **45.00**
Morning Glory, dish, canoe shaped **200.00**
Nantwich, butter, cov, square. **190.00**
Pekin, teapot, 2 cup **200.00**
Peony, salt and pepper shakers, pr **65.00**
Richmond, cake stand, 2 tier **150.00**
Richmond, plate, 6" **50.00**
Rose Du Barry, soup bowl, 8" **75.00**
Rosetime, pr salt and pepper shakers and tray. **135.00**
Rosetime, tray for creamer and sugar **85.00**
Royal Brocade, salt and pepper tray **100.00**
Royal Brocade, stacking teapot **500.00**
Shrewsbury, bon bon dish **50.00**
Summertime, butter, cov, square **175.00**
Summertime, cup and saucer. **75.00**
Summertime, plate, 6". **60.00**
Summertime, plate, 8". **95.00**
Summertime, tray for creamer and sugar **95.00**
Sunshine, bud vase **110.00**
Tapestry, jam pot. **110.00**
Welbeck, cake plate, tab handles. **250.00**

CHRISTMAS COLLECTIBLES

The tradition of a month–long Christmas season beginning the day after Thanksgiving was deeply entrenched by the end of the first World War. By the 1930s retailers from small town merchants to large department stores saw Christmas season sales account for 25% and more of their annual sales volume.

Beginning in the 1960s the length of the Christmas season was extended. By the mid–1990s Christmas decorations appeared in many stores and malls the day after Halloween. Today, some Christmas catalogs arrive in mail boxes as early as September.

References: Robert Brenner, *Christmas Past, 3rd Edition,* Schiffer Publishing, 1996; Robert Brenner, *Christmas Through the Decades,* Schiffer Publishing, 1993; Jill Gallina, *Christmas Pins Past and Present,* Collector Books, 1996; Beth Dees, *Santa's Price Guide to Contemporary Christmas Collectibles,* Krause Publications, 1997; George Johnson, *Christmas Ornaments, Lights & Decorations,* 1987, 1998 value update, *Vol. II* (1997), *Vol. III* (1997), Collector Books; Polly and Pam Judd, *Santa Dolls & Figurines Price Guide: Antique to Contemporary, Revised,* Hobby House Press, 1994; Chris Kirk, *The Joy of Christmas Collecting,* L–W Book Sales, 1994, 1998 value update; Mary Morrison, *Snow Babies, Santas and Elves: Collecting Christmas Bisque Figures,* Schiffer Publishing, 1993; Tim Neely, *Goldmine Christmas Record Price Guide,* Krause Publications, 1997; Margaret and Kenn Whitmyer, *Christmas Collectibles; Identification and Value Guide, Second Edition,* Collector Books, 1994, 1996 value update.

Newsletter: *Creche Herald,* 117 Crosshill Rd, Wynnewood, PA 19096.

Collectors' Club: Golden Glow of Christmas Past, 6401 Winsdale St, Minneapolis, MN 55427.

Badge, celluloid, Christmas shopping reminder, paper strip inserted in back indicates remaining shopping days, 1950s. **$15.00**
Bank, Santa, plaster, painted, 1950s, 6½ x 7 x 14" **70.00**

Candy Container, molded plastic face, white mesh body, red fabric hood and arms, silver foil trim on molded red cardboard car, Japan, 1930s, 5^1/$_2$" h, 6" l, $95.00.

Ornament, glass, pine cone, green, Shiny Brite, Japan, 2^5/$_8$" l, $2.00.

Bobbing Head, snowman, composition, painted, blue wood base, "A Rumpus Room Original, Japan" foil label, 1960s, 6" h 70.00

Book, *Rudolph the Red Nosed Reindeer*, premium, author Robert L May, illus by Denver Gillen, soft cov, ©1939 Montgomery Ward & Co, Inc, 32 pp, 7^1/$_2$ x 10^1/$_4$" 70.00

Book, *Santa Claus Book*, L L Stearn's Dept Store, Williamsport, PA giveaway, color illus, 1920s 15.00

Candy Box, cardboard, rect, Santa face on all sides, 1950s 10.00

Candy Container, figural, ground glass covered boot, crepe paper closure, 3" h 35.00

Card Holder, paper, fold–up Santa and reindeer, Hallmark, 1940s 20.00

Catalog, 1934 Ward's Christmas Catalogue, 92 pp 90.00

Charm, Santa with lantern, celluloid, Japan, 1930s 20.00

Color Wheel, for aluminum tree 15.00

Drinking Glass, Rudolph the Red Nosed Reindeer, Rudolph pulling Santa and sleigh over snow covered town below, 1950s, 5" h 20.00

Game, Santa Claus Game, Milton Bradley, 1920–24 . . . . 90.00

Light Bulb, figural, Christmas tree, painted milk glass, Japan 620.00

Light Bulb, figural, man with cello, painted milk glass, Japan 375.00

Light Bulb, figural, snake charmer, painted milk glass, Japan 425.00

Light Set, bubble lights, rocket ship type, Noma 130.00

Light Set, bubble lights, saucer style, Noma 32.00

Light Set, figural, angels playing musical instruments, milk glass, Japan 95.00

Light Set, Snow White and the Seven Dwarfs, Noma, 1938, 6^1/$_4$ x 16^1/$_2$ x 2^1/$_4$" box 400.00

Nativity Set, composition figures, 7" w wooden stable, Japan 3.00

Ornament, Christmas 1978 Heavenly Trio, Schmid, orig box, unused 10.00

Pin, Santa head, plastic, painted, white fur and hair, 1950s 20.00

Pinback Button, "Mellon Christmas Club Button Buddy," c1930s 10.00

Pinback Button, Santa surrounded by white polar bear, brown seal, icebergs, and US flag, sun rays at upper horizon, c1920s 70.00

Postcard, Santa Trio, cloth and cardboard bodies, paper and celluloid faces, Japan, 1950s, 5–7" 50.00

Poster, "Cudahy's Puritan Meat Products," Santa with bag and sleigh bells holding Cudahy products and doll, ©1926, 21 x 42" 190.00

Pull Toy, plastic, Santa in sleigh pulled by 4 reindeer, orig box, 10^1/$_2$" l 85.00

Puzzle, Santa Claus Puzzle Box, 3 litho puzzles in orig box, Milton Bradley, 1924–26 . . . . 100.00

Roly Poly, snowman, plastic, musical, orig wrapping, Japan, 7" h 18.00

Salt and Pepper Shakers, pr, Santa and Mrs Claus, china, gold glitter, rubber stoppers, c1960s, 3^1/$_2$" h 20.00

Sign, "Buy Christmas Seals, For Sale Here," cardboard, TB poster stamp image, Santa with little girl, Edwards & Deutsch Litho Co, Chicago, 1924, 11 x 13^3/$_4$" 95.00

Snow Dome, set of 6, 4 scenes depict Santa Claus activities, 2 scenes depict Nativity scene and group of choir carolers, boxed set, Marx, 1960s 190.00

Soaky, Santa, red and white, Colgate–Palmolive, 1960s 20.00

Squeeze Toy, Santa Claus, rubber, Rempel, Akron, OH, orig box 35.00

Stocking, red felt, drawstring top, "Merry Christmas From Donald Duck, Pluto, Mickey Mouse, Elmer Elephant, Ferdinand, Happy, Dopey, And Doc," c1938, 10^1/$_2$ x 21" 90.00

Tree Topper, figural robot, blown glass, robot standing atop circular base with sparkle stars and moon, "Made In Italy" sticker on back, 1960s, 10^1/$_2$" h 70.00

Toy, windup, celluloid Santa in metal sleigh pulled by prancing reindeer, key missing, 8" l 70.00

CIGAR COLLECTIBLES

Cigars and cigarettes are not synonymous. Cigars have always had an aloofness about them. They were appreciated by a select group of smokers, not the masses. Cigar connoisseurs are as fanatical as wine aficionados concerning the objects of their affection.

The cigar renaissance of the early 1990s has renewed collector interest in cigar collectibles. The primary focus is advertising. Prices remain stable for traditional cigar collectibles such as cutters, molds, and cigar store figures.

References: Tony Hyman, *Handbook of American Cigar Boxes,* Arnet Art Museum, 1979, 1995 value update; Norman E. Martinus and Harry L. Rinker, *Warman's Paper,* Wallace–Homestead, Krause Publications, 1994; Jerry Terranova, *Antique Cigar Cutters and Lighters,* Schiffer Publishing, 1996.

Newsletter: *The Cigar Label Gazette,* PO Box 3, Lake Forest, CA 92630.

Collectors' Clubs: Cigar Label Collectors International, PO Box 66, Sharon Center, OH 44274; International Seal, Label and Cigar Band Society, 8915 E Bellevue St, Tucson, AZ 85715.

Box, Karl Marx, 1939	**$50.00**
Box, Mae West, ftd, black flocking, "Why Don't You Try Me Sometime," 1920s	35.00
Box, Rocky Ford Perfectos, Indian illus, 1920s	15.00
Box, Speaker Joe Puritanos, Joe Canon illus, 1930s	15.00
Box, St Julien, "2 For 5¢," "Superior Over All," 1930s	25.00
Catalog, American Electrical Nov & Mfg Co Ever Ready Portable Electric Cigar Lighters, 1925, 8 pp.	30.00
Cigar, Buster Brown	7.00
Cigar Holder, nickel plated brass, engraved "Edwin Cigar Co., New York" on each side, 1910–30, 5½ x 2½"	15.00
Door Push, Edgeworth Smoking Tobacco, litho tin, c1930s, 4 x 14", price for pair	100.00
Key Chain, Muriel Cigars	10.00
Label, Caesar, 1910–30	125.00
Label, Pinzon, Van Dam Cigar Co, Grand Rapids, 1920–40	20.00
Label, Rudolph Valentino, 1920s, 2½ x 5"	8.00
Label, Storky, bird with cigar, "It Fills the Bill," 1910–30	75.00
Label, Uncle Jake's Nickel Seegar, bearded comical man with cat, 1925	3.00
Lighter, brass, counter model	70.00
Matchcover Holder, metal, red Muriel lady insert, 1920s	12.00
Postcard, Swisher Cigar Factory, Florida, depicts factory operation, unused, 1940s	5.00
Punchboard, Y–B Cigars, 9 punches out, 1930s	10.00
Sign, Admiration Cigars, tin, lady admiring herself in mirror, black, green, and gold, 1920s, 5½ x 7½"	30.00
Sign, Havana Ribbon Cigars, cardboard, Indian Chief illus, 1940–50s, 11½ x 17"	195.00
Sign, Imperial Club 5CTS Cigar, litho tin, emb, cigar box illus, chain hanger, 1920s, 10 x 13¾"	100.00
Sign, White Label 5¢ Cigars, litho tin, emb, chain hanger, c1920s, 10 x 13¾"	100.00
Tin, Camel Cigars	10.00
Tin, White Ash Cigars, H E Snyder portrait, 1928	20.00

CIGARETTE COLLECTIBLES

The number of cigarette smokers grew steadily throughout the 19th century and first two decades of the 20th century. By the 1940s the cigarette was the dominant tobacco product sold in America. In the 1950s cigarette manufacturers were major periodical and television advertisers.

The Surgeon General's Report changed everything. Despite limitations on advertising and repeated non–smoking bans, the cigarette industry has proven highly resourceful in creating public exposure for its product—just watch any televised NASCAR race.

Surprisingly, as the anti–smoking crusade has become stronger, the interest in cigarette collectibles has increased. Cigarette memorabilia, especially advertising dating between 1945 and 1960, is one of the hot collectibles of the 1990s.

References: Douglas Congdon–Martin, *Camel Cigarette Collectibles: The Early Years, 1913–1963,* Schiffer Publishing, 1996; Douglas Congdon–Martin, *Camel Cigarette Collectibles, 1964–1995,* Schiffer Publishing, 1997; Norman E. Martinus and Harry L. Rinker, *Warman's Paper,* Wallace–Homestead, Krause Publications, 1994; Murray Cards International Ltd. (comp.), *Cigarette Card Values: 1994 Catalogue of Cigarette and Other Trade Cards,* Murray Cards International, 1994; Fernando Righini and Marco Papazzoni, *The International Collectors' Book of Cigarette Packs,* Schiffer Publishing, 1998; Neil Wood, *Smoking Collectibles: A Price Guide,* L–W Book Sales, 1994.

Collectors' Clubs: Camel Joe & Friends, 2205 Hess Dr, Cresthill, IL 60435; Cigarette Pack Collectors Assoc, 61 Searle St, Georgetown, MA 01833.

Ashtray, aluminum, Winston, 8½" l	**$8.00**
Ashtray, ceramic, "Smokin' Joe's Racing," white, gold lettering, 5" d	15.00
Ashtray, Winston–Salem adv, bowling pin, 9⅛" h	20.00
Camera, Parliament	12.00
Case, silvered brass, engraved Camel cigarettes pack on cover, 1930s, 2¼ x 3½"	45.00
Charm, Chesterfield Cigarettes adv, plastic, red, paper replica wrapper around 3 sides, Hong Kong, 1970s	10.00
Cigarette Card Album, German, 1950s, complete	50.00
Cigarette Holder, bone, trumpet shape, gold bowl	40.00
Display, cardboard, Mail Pouch Chewing Tobacco, diecut cardboard, standup, parading bass drummer and dog, 1930s	475.00

Clock, Marlboro, Philip Morris, electric, metal, red, white, and black, Ohio Advertising Display Co, Cincinnati, OH, not working, 11" h, 27¾" w, $60.00. Photo courtesy Collectors Auction Services.

Sign, Yellow Cab Cigar, emb litho tin, yellow, black, and white, c1920s, 6¾ x 19⅞", $1,000.00. Photo courtesy William Morford Auctions.

Punchboard Label, litho paper, 8 x 3", $15.00.

Lighter, Ronson, Crown **18.00**

Match Holder, brass, figural turtle, top of shell inscribed "Grand Rapids Brass Co. Souvenir, Grand Rapids, Mich," underside inscribed "Mfgr's Refrigerator & Furniture Hdw.," hinged at tail, oval textured inner lid for match striking, 1920–30s, 1½ x 3 x 5" **100.00**

Paperweight, penguin, Kool adv, white metal, painted, 1930–40s **20.00**

Pinback Button, Kool adv, Willie Penguin surrounded by donkey and elephant symbols, 1930s **20.00**

Poster, Kool Cigarettes, Willie the Penguin wearing military outfit, paper, glossy, full color portrait, 12 x 18" **45.00**

Record, L & M Cigarettes, Christmas, shows L & M TV quartet in Santa suits, Liggett & Meyers Tobacco Co giveaways, orig carton holder **10.00**

Sign, Avalon Cigarettes, paper, full color cigarette pack image, 1930s, 12 x 18" **70.00**

Sign, Philip Morris Cigarettes, paper, bellhop and cigarette pkgs, 1930–40s, 18¼ x 23¼" **75.00**

Thermometer, Chesterfield, 13" l **40.00**

Tin, Muratti's Young Ladies Cigarettes, 1915–30 . . . . **10.00**

Tin, Red Jacket Smoking Tobacco, B Payn's Son's Tobacco Co, Albany, unused, 1930 . . . . **15.00**

CIRCUS ITEMS

The 1920s through the 1940s marked the golden age of the tent circus. The circus trains for Ringling and Barnum and Bailey often exceeded 100 cars. The advent of television marked the beginning of the tent circus' decline. Mergers occurred. Most small circuses simply vanished. Today, the majority of circus performances occur at civic and institution auditoriums, not under the Big Top.

Most circus collectors are individuals who remember attending a circus under canvas. When this generation dies, what will be the fate of circus collectibles? Categories with crossover potential, e.g., lithographed posters, will hold collector interest. Others will vanish just as did the great circuses they document.

Reference: Norman E. Martinus and Harry L. Rinker, *Warman's Paper*, Wallace–Homestead, Krause Publications, 1994.

Collectors' Clubs: Circus Fans Assoc of America, 1544 Piedmont Ave ME, Ste 41, Atlanta, GA 30324; Circus Historical Society, 3477 Vienna Court, Westerville, OH 43081.

Book, *The Fabulous Showman: The Life and Times of P. T. Barnum*, Irving Wallace, illus, hardback, 1959, 279 pp, 5¾ x 8½" **$3.00**

Broadside, Campbell's One Ring Circus, 2 sided, c1920, 11 x 24" **35.00**

Window Card, Ringling Bros. and Barnum & Bailey Circus, litho cardboard, ©1974, 21¼" h, 13¼" w, $40.00. Photo courtesy Collectors Auction Services.

Directory, The Great American Circus Directory, Informative Guide for Agents, Circus & Variety artists, sample issue, illus, 1976, 8 pgs, 9 x 12" **15.00**

Letter, publicity for Ringling Brothers and Barnum & Bailey, press releases and complimentary press tickets, orig envelope, 1939 . . . . **20.00**

Magazine, *The Strange Stories of Gargantua and Toto*, Ringling Circus gorillas articles, c1940, 12 pp, 9 x 12" **25.00**

Poster, "Clyde Beatty in Person," Clyde Beatty–Cole Bros Combined Circus, The World's Largest Circus, multicolor, Roland Butler, lion tamer, 19 x 26" **90.00**

Route Book, Ringling Bros and Barnum & Bailey, The Greatest Show on Earth, red and black cov, clown sitting on elephant illus, black and white, 1946, 61 pp, 8¼ x 5" **15.00**

Transfer, Ringling Bros World's Largest Menagerie, color, 9 x 11¼" **2.00**

CLICKERS

These noisemakers were extremely popular from the early 1930s through the late 1950s. Many were distributed to adults and children as advertising premiums. Those touting a particular beer, hotel, political, or household product were meant for adults. Children delighted in receiving clickers when buying Buster Brown or Red Goose shoes. The Halloween season was responsible for more clickers than any other holiday season.

Buster Brown Shoes, litho tin, emb image of Buster and Tige, 5 star logo, 1920–30s **$45.00**

Gargoyle, red, yellow ground **10.00**

Halloween, litho tin, black and white, orange ground, gargoyle devil holding trident pitchfork with 2 bats, Kirchhof Co, Newark, NJ **10.00**

Owl, red, black ground **10.00**

Pez, litho tin, Pez girl leaning forward to give candy to boy leaning against large package of peppermint Pez candy, English text, mkd "U.S. Zone Germany," c1950s **250.00**

Poll–Parrot Shoes, litho tin, emb, green tint parrot image, 1930s **50.00**

Pez, litho tin, girl bends and hands Pez candy to boy when clicked, 2¹/₂ x 3¹/₂", $250.00. Photo courtesy William Morford Auctions.

Twinkie Shoes, litho tin, multicolor image of Twinkie elf standing on mushroom, inscribed "Made By Hamilton–Brown Shoe Co" **15.00**
V G Pretzels, litho tin, image of clown playing tuba–type instrument shaped like pretzel, Kirchhof, 1930s **15.00**
Weather Bird Shoes, litho tin, yellow, black, and red, Kirchhof, 1930s **15.00**

CLIFF, CLARICE

Clarice Cliff (1899–1972) joined A. J. Wilkinson's Royal Staffordshire Pottery at Burslem, England, in the early 1910s. In 1930 she became the company's art director.

Cliff is one of England's foremost 20th–century ceramic designers. Her influence covered a broad range–shapes, forms, and patterns. Her shape lines include Athens, Biarritz, Chelsea, Conical, Iris, Lynton, and Stamford. Applique, Bizarre, Crocus, Fantasque, and Ravel are among the most popular patterns.

In addition to designer shape and pattern lines, Cliff's signature also appears on a number of inexpensive dinnerware lines manufactured under the Royal Staffordshire label.

References: Susan and Al Bagdade, *Warman's English & Continental Pottery & Porcelain, 2nd Edition,* Wallace–Homestead, Krause Publications, 1991; Leonard R. Griffin and Susan Pear Meisel, *Clarice Cliff: The Bizarre Affair,* Harry N. Abrams, 1994; Pat and Howard Watson, *The Clarice Cliff Colour Price Guide,* Francis Joseph Publications, 1995, distributed by Krause Publications.

Collectors' Club: Clarice Cliff Collector's Club, Fantasque House, Tennis Dr, The Park, Nottingham, NG7 1AE, UK.

REPRODUCTION ALERT: Lotus vases.

Bowl, Bizarre Ware, Fantasque pattern, ftd base, hp abstract landscape design, ink stamp, Newport Pottery, England, 8" d, 4" h **$1,000.00**
Bowl, Bizarre Ware, Fantasque pattern, stepped form, hp floral dec, litho mark, Newport Pottery, England, 9" sq, 41/2" h **950.00**

Dish Set, Bizarre Ware, 36 pcs, Applique pattern, honey glaze, black, orange, and yellow banded dec, six 10" plates, six 9" plates, five 9" plates, five 7" plates, 6 cups, 2 saucers, 2 small bowls, 1 low bowl, 3 platters, stamped and painted marks, Wilkinson and Newport Pottery **750.00**
Honey Jar, Crocus pattern, yellow and orange crocuses in green field dec, bee on cov, ink stamp, Wilkinson, 3" h **350.00**
Jam Jar, Crocus pattern, blue, orange, and lavender dec, green stems, brown ground, ink stamp, Brice Rogers, Wilkinson, 3¹/₄" d, 3¹/₂" h **400.00**
Jug, Secrets pattern, green, yellow, orange, and brown landscape dec, blue water, ink stamp, Newport Pottery, England, 11¹/₂" h **1,100.00**
Jug, Viscaria pattern, green, red, yellow, flowers dec, brown stems, cream ground, ink stamp, Wilkinson, 7¹/₂" h **800.00**
Pitcher, Crocus pattern, blue, orange, and lavender dec, brown–green ground, ink stamp, Wilkinson, 7¹/₂" h **255.00**
Pitcher, My Garden pattern, red, white, and orange floral relief handle, yellow–brown glaze body, ink stamp, Newport Pottery, England, 9" h **250.00**
Plate, Blue Chintz pattern, blue, green, and red flowers dec, ink stamp, Newport Pottery, England, 9" d **215.00**
Plate, Crocus pattern, blue, yellow, and red dec, green ground, 9" d **200.00**
Plate, Inspiration Lily pattern, white flowers with blue stems dec, green ground, ink stamp, Newport Pottery, England, 9" d **745.00**
Toast Rack, Cabbage Flower pattern, green, brown, and orange dec, ink stamp, Newport Pottery, England, 3" h . . . **285.00**
Tureen, orange, black, and yellow banded dec, Newport stamp, 9" w, 8" d, 7" h **400.00**
Vase, Bizarre Ware, Delecia pattern, cubist form, hp dec, litho mark, Newport Pottery, England, 3" d, 7" h . . . **1,300.00**
Vase, Blue Chintz pattern, top and bottom blue, green, and red flower dec, yellow, blue, and green bands outline, ink stamp, Newport Pottery, England, 7³/₄" h **975.00**

Bowl, Crocus pattern, shape #585, Bizarre ware, 5¹/₄" h, $862.50. Photo courtesy Sotheby's Chicago.

Vase, Inspiration pattern, blue and white flowers dec, blue and green ground, ink stamp, Wilkinson, 7¼" h **800.00**

Vase, Lydiat pattern, orange, brown, and yellow flowers dec, black leaves, cream ground, ink stamp, Newport Pottery, England, 8" h. **400.00**

Vase, Windbells pattern, blue and black trees, orange, yellow, and green ground, elongated handle, ruffled rim, ink stamp, Newport Pottery, England, 12½" h **1,265.00**

Vase, Pansies pattern, yellow, blue, red, and purple dec, yellow ground, blue, green, and brown drips, ink stamp, Newport Pottery, England, 4½" d, 10½" h **575.00**

Wall Pocket, Bizarre Ware, Delecia pattern, geometric form, hp dec, litho mark, Newport Pottery, England, 10" l, 3" d, 12" h. **1,800.00**

Wall Pocket, Rhodanthe pattern, double, yellow, brown, and orange flowers dec, ink stamp, Newport Pottery, England, 6½" d **460.00**

CLOCKS

This collecting category is heavily dominated by character alarm clocks, especially those dating from the 1940s and 50s. Strong collector interest also exists for electric and key wind novelty clocks and clocks featuring advertising.

Generic clocks such as mass–produced Big Ben alarm clocks have little or no collector interest. 1920s' and 30s' wood-cased mantel clocks, banjo–style wall clocks, and period 1950s' wall clocks prove the exception.

References: Hy Brown, *Comic Character Timepieces: Seven Decades of Memories*, Schiffer Publishing, 1992; Michael Bruner, *Advertising Clocks: America's Timeless Heritage*, Schiffer Publishing, 1995.

Collectors' Club: National Assoc of Watch and Clock Collectors, Inc, 514 Poplar St, Columbia, PA 17512.

Advertising, Evervess Sparkling Water, light up, parrot with top hat, red, white, and blue, 1940–50s **$350.00**

Advertising, Jefferson Standard Life Insurance Co, light up, Thomas Jefferson illus. **140.00**

Advertising, Keen Kutter, alarm, Big Ben style, paper label dial, 1920s **175.00**

Advertising, Osh Kosh B'Gosh, octagonal, neon, 1930–40 . . . . **575.00**

Advertising, Poly Stamps, round, orig box, 1940–50 . . . . **1,500.00**

Advertising, Purina Chows, light up, red, white, and blue, "Purina Chows Sanitation Products," 1940s **325.00**

Advertising, Red Goose Shoes, light up, 1930–40 . . . . **400.00**

Advertising, Tetley Tea, 1940s, 14" sq **400.00**

Animated, Apollo XI, diecut, red, white, and blue, gold numerals, ivory case, mkd "Lux Clock Mfg Co" **115.00**

Animated, Kit Kat. **30.00**

Character, ET, head raised, battery operated, finger and chest lights up when alarm sounds **120.00**

Character, Popeye and Sweé Pee, alarm, color illus on dial, ivory enameled steel case, Smiths, c1968. . . . . **100.00**

Character, Strawberry Shortcake, alarm, orig box **25.00**

Figural, refrigerator, white metal, GE label, Warren Telechron Co, Ashland, MA, 8½" h **185.00**

Kitchen, musical, drum, red **35.00**

CLOTHES SPRINKLERS

Although steam irons have made it unnecessary, many individuals still sprinkle clothing before ironing. In many cases, the sprinkling bottle is merely a soda bottle with an adaptive cap. However, in the middle decades of the 20th century, ceramic and glass bottles designed specifically for sprinkling were made. Many were figural, a primary reason why they have attracted collector interest.

Cat, marble eyes, American Bisque **$150.00**

Cat, seated, jeweled eyes, 9" h. **85.00**

Cat, stray **75.00**

Chinaman, Cleminson. **25.00**

Chinaman, yellow and green, Cardinal China. **30.00**

Clothespin, ceramic, white, yellow, and pink, smiling face **100.00**

Elephant, fat and squatty, happy face, curled trunk handle **200.00**

Rooster, ceramic, metal and cork stopper, $75.00.

Elephant, plastic, red. **20.00**
Elephant, shamrock on tummy, white and pink, raised
   trunk. **75.00**
Emperor, ceramic **50.00**
Iron, ceramic, Wonder Cave souvenir. **85.00**
Iron, woman ironing decal, white ground, 1950s **40.00**
King, ceramic, Tilso, Japan. **100.00**
Mandarin, flowing pink robe **70.00**
Merry Maid, plastic, hands on hips, made in USA **15.00**
Queen, ceramic, Tilso, Japan **100.00**
Victorian Lady, with purse **120.00**

CLOTHING & ACCESSORIES

Victorian era clothing is passé. Clothing of the flapper era has lost much of its appeal. Forget pre–1945 entirely. Today's collectors want post–1945 clothing.

1960s' psychedelic–era clothing is challenging 1950s' clothing for front position on sellers' racks. No matter what the era, a major key to clothing's value is a design which screams a specific period. Further, collectors want clothing that is ready to wear. Older collectors still love to play "dress up."

Hollywood–, television–, and movie–personality–related and high–style fashion designer clothing is now steady fare at almost every major American auction house. Prices continue to rise. Many buyers are foreign. Paris may be center stage for the contemporary clothing market, but the American collectibles marketplace is the focus of vintage clothing sales.

References: Mary Bachman, *Collector's Guide to Hair Combs*, Collector Books, 1998; Joanne Dubbs Ball and Dorothy Hehl Torem, *The Art of Fashion Accessories*, Schiffer Publishing, 1993; Mark Blackburn, *Hawaiiana: The Best of Hawaiian Design*, Schiffer Publishing, 1996; Maryanne Dolan, *Vintage Clothing: 1880–1980, 3rd Edition*, Books Americana, Krause Publications, 1995; Kate E. Dooner, *A Century of Handbags*, Schiffer Publishing, 1993; Kate E. Dooner, *Plastic Handbags, 2nd Edition*, Schiffer Publishing, 1998; Ray Ellsworth, *Platform Shoes: A Big Step in Fashion*, Schiffer Publishing, 1998; Roseanne Ettinger, *'50s Popular Fashions for Men, Women, Boys & Girls*, Schiffer Publishing, 1995; Michael Jay Goldberg, *The Ties That Bind: Neckties, 1945–1975*, Schiffer Publishing, 1997; Evelyn Haertig, *Antique Combs & Purses*, Gallery Graphics Press, 1983; Kristina Harris, *Vintage Fashions for Women: 1920s–1940s*, Schiffer Publishing, 1996; Kristina Harris, *Vintage Fashions for Women: The 1950s & 60s*, Schiffer Publishing, 1997; Ellie Laubner, *Fashions of the Roaring '20s*, Schiffer Publishing, 1996; Jan Lindenberger, *Clothing & Accessories From the '40s, '50s & '60s: A Handbook and Price Guide*, Schiffer Publishing, 1996; Sally C. Luscomb, *The Collector's Encyclopedia of Buttons*, Schiffer Publishing, 1997.

Gerald McGrath and Janet Meana, *Fashion Buckles: Common to Classic*, Schiffer Publishing, 1997; J. J. Murphy, *Children's Handkerchiefs: A Two Hundred Year History*, Schiffer Publishing, 1998; Peggy Anne Osborne, *Button, Button: Identification and Price Guide, 2nd Edition*, Schiffer Publishing, 1997; Maureen Reilly and Mary Beth Detrich, *Women's Hats of the 20th Century for Designers and Collectors*, Schiffer Publishing, 1997; Trina Robbins, *Tomorrow's Heirlooms: Fashions of the 60s & 70s*, Schiffer Publishing, 1997; Nancy M. Schiffer, *Hawaiian Shirt Design*, Schiffer Publishing, 1997; Desire Smith, *Hats*, Schiffer Publishing, 1996; Desire Smith, *Vintage Style: 1920–1960*, Schiffer

Publishing, 1997; Diane Snyder–Haug, *Antique & Vintage Clothing: A Guide to Dating & Valuation of Women's Clothing, 1850 to 1940*, Collector Books, 1997; Sheila Steinberg and Kate E. Dooner, *Fabulous Fifties: Designs for Modern Living*, Schiffer Publishing, 1993; Joe Tonelli and Marc Luers, Bowling Shirts, Schiffer Publishing, 1998; Debra J. Wisniewski, *Antique & Collectible Buttons: Identification & Values*, Collector Books, 1996.

Newsletter: *The Vintage Connection*, 904 N 65th St, Springfield, OR 97478.

Collectors' Clubs: Antique Comb Collectors Club International, 3748 Sunray Dr, Holiday, FL 34691; The Costume Society of America, PO Box 73, Earleville, MD 21919; National Button Society, 2733 Juno Pl, Apt 4, Akron, OH 44313.

Apron, cotton, half, red, checked design, 1950. . . . . **$5.00**
Apron, cotton, slip–on, embroidered, deep pockets, 1928. . . . **20.00**
Apron, white, lace dec, embroidered "Souvenir of
   France". **15.00**
Ballgown, "soir a chambord," white tulle scattered with
   gold sequins, sewn around draped strapless bodice,
   stripes at back of huge skirt with long pheasant feath-
   ers alternating with bands of taffeta painted to resem-
   ble pheasant feathers, labeled "Pierre Balmain Paris,"
   early 1940s, size 6 . . . . **2,185.00**
Barrette, celluloid, hp, black and red rhinestones **15.00**
Blouse, cotton, crepe, jade green, henna embroidery,
   1920s **200.00**
Blouse, cotton, white, c1940 . . . . **15.00**
Blouse, rayon, padded shoulders, rayon, button back,
   1935–45 . . . . **30.00**
Bonnet, baby's, organdy, embroidered, silk ribbon trim,
   1920s **40.00**
Camisole, cotton, 1924 . . . . **60.00**
Camisole, silk, pink, lace trim **25.00**
Coat, polyester, cotton, large pockets, short, 1960 . . . . **70.00**

Left: **Evening Bag, newsprint motif, Schiaparelli, c1935, $3,105.00.** Photo courtesy William Doyle Galleries.
Right: **Necktie, hand–painted silk, multicolor ground, dark red flowers with rhinestone centers, Van Heusen, 4¼" w, $25.00.**

Coat, steamer blanket, plaid, bright red woven wool, large navy and dark green plaid, red satin lining, Charles James, size 6 .... **19,500.00**

Cocktail Dress, sheath dress, fitted corset bodice, wide scoop neck, fitted black silk draped sleeves, side panniers and bustle back, white satin overlaid black lace underskirt, labeled "Oleg Cassini," 1950s, size 8....... **200.00**

Comb, celluloid, flame shaped, black overlay, hand–set blue stones, Art Deco **40.00**

Comb, celluloid, white, pompadour, 1915–30 .... **30.00**

Dress, black crepe, round neck, padded shoulders, crossed self–tab at front of waist, appliquéd at yoke with red, navy, and green gingham and other plaid cottons, labeled "Adrian Original," early 1940s, size 8–10 .... **3,450.00**

Dress, black satin, flapper style, embroidered pink roses, on waistline, 1925 .... **800.00**

Dress, chiffon, beaded, large bow dec, 1923 .... **1,750.00**

Dress, 2 pc, black wool, long sleeved bodice fastening at slant, black buttons, self–tie neck, turned–back cuffs, black moire taffeta lining, labeled "Christian Dior Paris," c1950, size 6 .... **3,450.00**

Dress, cotton and rayon, V–back, satin bow at waist, back zipper, 1950s **45.00**

Dress, silk, printed, belted, 1926 .... **275.00**

Dress, silk, slip–on, Chinese design trim, wide belt with buckle, 1920s **700.00**

Evening Coat, taffeta, rose, rayon lining, short, 1938....... **150.00**

Evening Dress, rayon crepe, multicolored sketchy flowers print against ivory ground, cutout flower straps, low back, slight train, labeled "Schiaparelli 4 Rue de la Paix Paris model no. 4396," early 1930s, size 4 ..... **2,100.00**

Evening Dress, slip torso of curved bands and tabs of black silk satin, black tulle tiered cutaway skirt, labeled "Tappé Inc. Modes 9 West 57th St. New York," c1930, size 4 .... **700.00**

Evening Dress, strapless, white silk twill, island dancers and swirling ribbons print, shades of purple, turquoise, rose, gray, green, and black, labeled "Pucci," 1950s, size 4 .... **575.00**

Evening Gown, crepe, black, beaded, c1920 .... **80.00**

Evening Gown, organdy, peach, c1930 .... **45.00**

Fan, silk, white, hp, wooden sticks................... **50.00**

Gloves, cotton, hand–stitched accent, wrist length, 1940 .... **10.00**

Gloves, leather **5.00**

Handkerchief, satin, pink, Christmas scene............. **15.00**

Hat, fedora, felt, John Wanamaker, 1930s............. **45.00**

Hat, fur, pillbox, mink, brown netting, brown brocade at crown, 1960s **25.00**

Hat, man's, gray, open crown, fur blend, 1959 .... **30.00**

Hat, straw, jockey type, purple, purple grosgrain ribbon and cloth violets dec, Hale Original, 1940s **45.00**

Hat, tam, felt, black, black feathers on side at front, 1930s... **45.00**

Hat, turban style, velvet, turquoise, 1960s **10.00**

Hatpin, Bakelite, black fluted disc, rhinestone dec, silver accents...................................... **35.00**

Hatpin, brass, knob design, Art Deco, 8½" l............. **95.00**

Hat Stand, velvet and rhinestone covered top, c1920 .... **35.00**

Jacket, apricot velvet, gilt stitched Islamic pattern, short sleeved kimono style, hip length, round faille label "Mariano Fortuny Venise," 1920s, size 6–8 .... **5,450.00**

Jacket, velvet, black, crushed, white silk lining, c1920 ..... **50.00**

Kimono, silk, black damask, red, yellow–green, and white raised embroidered flower design, gold silk lining, 1920s..................................... **500.00**

Necktie, silk, Sak's Fifth Avenue..................... **20.00**

Necktie, wide, red and green, snowflakes design, 1951 ..... **10.00**

Pants Suit, cotton, flesh colored, wide flared leg, scalloped edge, size large, 1960s........................ **25.00**

Prom Dress, pink taffeta, velvet trim, sweetheart neckline, puff sleeves, puff sleeves, 1939............. **165.00**

Purse, Art Deco, black and white, Whiting Davis, 6½ x 3½" **100.00**

Purse, beaded, white, red and turquoise beads, Indian motif, 1920–25 .... **60.00**

Purse, leather, hand tooled, suede lined, 1920s **25.00**

Purse, leather, hand woven, black strap, button fastener, silk–lined, 1932.................................. **50.00**

Purse, rhinestone dec, chain handles, c1930s........... **175.00**

Purse, wooden, box style, leather trim, beads, glass stones, gold braid and painted butterfly dec, contains mirror, Enid Collins, 1966 .... **60.00**

Raincoat, cotton gabardine, hooded, double breasted, 1930s... **75.00**

Shawl, Egyptian, white net, embroidered with brass, rect shape, 1920–30 .... **90.00**

Shirt, man's, rayon, Vargas design, labeled "Vargas Floral Collage, Chemise Et Cie," and "Playboy," 1950–60s **150.00**

Shoes, pr, black patent leather, pump, filigree, scalloped, leather lining **10.00**

Shoes, pr, black patent leather, stiletto heel, pointed toe, bow accent, c1960s **20.00**

Shoes, pr, girl's, black patent leather, Colonial style, slip–on, silver trim, c1930s **30.00**

Skirt, wool flannel, green, back kick–pleat, front pocket, 1950s... **15.00**

Sundress, waffle pique, scoop neck, spaghetti straps, 1950s... **20.00**

Swimsuit, 2 pc, sarong, batik print cotton sateen, halter–style top, blue, early 1960s **10.00**

Swimsuit, skirted, white, green print, 1940............. **30.00**

Tennis Outfit, pleated skirt, loose top, 1930s **50.00**

AUCTION PRICES

William Doyle Galleries, Couture & Textiles auction, June 11 & 12, 1997. Prices include a 15% buyer's premium.

Handbag, Hermès, beige crocodile with gilt–metal gear shaped fittings, sgd, early 1960s **$258.00**

Hat, Hattie Carnegie, natural straw with pearl band trim, labeled, 1940s.......................... **34.00**

Necktie, Salvador Dali, ecru and ruby red and white stylized lilies drawn in black on ruby red ground, sgd "Dali," labeled "C.C. Anderson Fashion Craft Cravats," 1930s **230.00**

Scarf, silk, world newspapers and jounalistic drawings on tobacco ground, 1950s................... **46.00**

Shawl, silver lamé, geometric Deco pattern of triangle bursts and ziggurat shapes on black silk, 1920s, 50" w **345.00**

Shoulder Bag, Gucci, brown grained leather with saddle shaped flap and gilt–metal ornament, sgd, 1970s **57.00**

COALPORT FIGURINES

After completing an apprenticeship at Caughley, Robert Rose established a pottery at Coalport, located in Shropshire's Severn Gorge, England, in 1796. The pottery remained in the Rose family until acquired by the Bruff family in 1853.

In 1923 Cauldon Potteries, located in Stoke–on–Trent, Staffordshire, bought Coalport. In 1926 operations were moved from the Shropshire plant to Staffordshire. In 1936 the Crescent potteries of George Jones & Sons acquired Cauldon/Coalport. In 1958 E. Brian and Company, whose Foley China Works were established in 1850, purchased Coalport, maintaining its identity as a separate company. Coalport became part of the Wedgwood Group in 1967.

Although known primarily for its dinnerware, Coalport produced a line of porcelain figurines between 1890 and the present that rival those of Royal Doulton and Lladro. Each figure has a distinctive name. Many are found in multiple variations. Backstamps play a role in value with examples bearing the earliest backstamp having the highest value. As with Royal Doulton, the figurine's designer also impacts on value.

Reference: Tom Power, *The Charlton Standard Catalogue of Coalport Figurines*, Charlton Press, 1997.

Anne of Green Gables, purple dress, white apron,
 issued 1982, 8¹/₂" h **$385.00**
Barbara Ann, pink and purple, Ladies of Fashion series,
 issued 1988, 8¹/₄" h **350.00**
Carla, light green dress, white hat, Debutante
 Collection, issued 1987–92, 5³/₄" h **125.00**
Christmas Caroller, red and brown, Christmas
 Collection, issued 1987, 8" h **265.00**
Corporal, Royal Horse Artillery 1815, dark blue and gold
 tunic, light blue and brown trousers, Battle of
 Waterloo Collection, issued 1990, 8¹/₂" h **425.00**
Danielle, white dress, green trim, Debutante Collection,
 issued 1982–85, 5" h **165.00**

Heather, emerald green dress, white underskirt, Ladies of Fashion series, style 1, issued 1977–82, 8" h, $300.00.

Denise, pink bodice, white skirt with yellow and red
 flowers, Ladies of Fashion series, issued 1975–77,
 7³/₄" h **325.00**
Fiona, royal blue and white, Ladies of Fashion series,
 issued 1975–79, 8¹/₂" h **250.00**
First Tee, green–blue and yellow, Sporting Collection,
 issued 1984–87, 8" h **395.00**
The Hostess, white floral pattern, Ladies of Fashion
 series, issued 1977–80, 8¹/₄" h **340.00**
I Love Kitty, light blue pajamas, black cat, Children
 Studies series, issued 1980, 4¹/₂" h **280.00**
Katherine Howard, green and beige, Royal Collection,
 issued 1979–92, 8" h **550.00**
Lauren, white and gold, Grosvenor Collection, issued
 1991–93, 8¹/₂" h **285.00**
The News Sheet Seller, jade jacket and cap, black
 trousers and shoes, Character Collection, issued
 1982–85, 7" h **340.00**
Pitti Sing, turquoise and sea green, Gilbert and Sullivan
 series, issued 1979–81, 8" h **550.00**
The Romantic Seventies, woman wearing pink dress
 with white frills, rose–pink flowers, man wearing
 black trousers with red stripe, white jacket with blue
 collar, cuffs, belt and sash, Dancing Years series,
 issued 1982–84, 9" h **500.00**
The Shoe Shine Boy, blue suit, black cap, brown shoe
 box, Old London Streets series, issued 1977, 4¹/₄" h **300.00**

COCA–COLA

John Pemberton, a pharmacist from Atlanta, Georgia, developed the formula for Coca–Cola. However, credit for making Coca–Cola the world's leading beverage belongs to Asa G. Candler. Candler improved the formula and marketed his product aggressively.

The use of "Coke" in advertising first occurred in 1941. Foreign collectors prefer American Coca–Cola items over those issued in their own countries.

Reproduction and copycat items have plagued Coca–Cola collecting for the past three decades. The problem is compounded by Coca–Cola's licensing the reproduction of many of its classic products. Finally, the number of new products licensed by Coca–Cola appears to increase each year. Their sales represent a significant monetary drain of monies previously spent in the vintage market.

References: *B. J. Summers' Guide to Coca–Cola: Identifications, Current Values, Circa Dates,* Collector Books, 1997; Gael de Courtivron, *Collectible Coca–Cola Toy Trucks: An Identification and Value Guide,* Collector Books, 1995; Steve Ebner, *Vintage Coca–Cola Machines, Vol. II, 1959–1968,* published by author, 1996; Bob and Debra Henrich, *Coca–Cola Commemorative Bottles,* Collector Books, 1998; Bill McClintock, *Coca–Cola Trays,* Schiffer Publishing, 1996; Allan Petretti, *Petretti's Coca–Cola Collectibles Price Guide, 10th Edition,* Antique Trader Books, 1997; Allan Petretti and Chris Beyer, *Classic Coca–Cola Serving Trays,* Antique Trader Books, 1998; Al and Helen Wilson, *Wilsons' Coca–Cola Price Guide,* Schiffer Publishing, 1997.

Collectors' Club: Coca–Cola Collectors Club, PO Box 49166, Atlanta, GA 30359.

REPRODUCTION ALERT: Coca–Cola trays.

Apron, bib style, "things go better with Coke," 1960s **$30.00**

Badge, flicker, 1994 World Cup soccer competition, full
color, 1³/₄ x 2³/₄" 10.00

Bank, plastic, figural vending machine, "Play
Refreshed," 1950s 125.00

Banner, "Try Our Coca–Cola 5¢," 1940s 35.00

Billhead, logo, Augusta, GA, 1923, 8¹/₂ x 7" 30.00

Book, *Alphabet Book of Coca–Cola*, 1928 . . . . 60.00

Book Cover, Norman Rockwell illus, 1931 . . . . 12.00

Bookends, pr, bronze, figural bottle, 1963 . . . . 275.00

Boomerang, c1950 . . . . 20.00

Bottle, clear, paper label, diamond design, 1960s 65.00

Bottle, emb "Bottle Pat. D105529," 1937–48 . . . . 2.00

Bottle, emb diamond design, 1960s, 10 oz. 20.00

Bottle and Can Opener, Handy Walden, painted logo,
1960s 65.00

Bottle Holder, red tin label, wire frame, "Enjoy
Coca–Cola While You Shop," 1950s 15.00

Bottle Opener, figural bottle cap, 50th Anniversary, with
presentation box, 1950 . . . . 100.00

Bottle Opener, metal, wall mount, red enamel logo,
c1948–50 . . . . 65.00

Bottle Opener, nude woman, "Early Morn". 175.00

Bottle Opener, sword shape, inscribed "Purity is sealed
in a bottle," 1920–30. . . . . 200.00

Bottle Opener/Ice Pick, 1930s 25.00

Bottle Opener/Shoe Horn, 1930–40s 250.00

Bottle Protector, "So Easy To Serve," 1942 . . . . 2.00

Brochure, Pause For Living, 1957. . . . . 5.00

Calendar, 1931, farm boy sitting under tree with dog,
Rockwell illus 750.00

Calendar, 1933, blacksmith and boy, Frederick Stanley
illus 400.00

Calendar, 1955, "Coke Time". 35.00

Calendar, 1964, "Things go better with coke". 10.00

Can Punch, logo stamped on top, orig package,
Topmaster, 1950s 50.00

Cap, driver's, c1939 . . . . 75.00

Carrier, aluminum, silver colored, red label with white
lettering on both sides, slide handle, holds 6 green
bottles, "Delicious Coca–Cola Refreshing," 1950s. 60.00

Carrier, plastic, 1950s 15.00

Carrier, plywood, holds 24 bottles, 1940 . . . . 125.00

Carrier, strap and cup holder, 1950s. 285.00

Carrier, wood, cut–out handle, 1940 . . . . 150.00

Case, wooden, miniature, 9 glass bottles, some syrup left 50.00

Cigar Band, 1930s. 175.00

Clicker, metal, 1930s. 135.00

Clock, figural can, clock face on top, 1970–80. . . . . 35.00

Clock, plastic, light–up, "Time To Enjoy—Coca–Cola Be
Really Refreshed," 1960s 250.00

Cooler, vinyl, red, Royal Portable Coolers, orig box,
1950s 300.00

Dart Board, 1940–50s 125.00

Dish, aluminum, figural bottles on sides, 1930s 225.00

Display Bottle, plastic, 1953, 20". 400.00

Doll, stuffed, cloth, blue and white striped outfit, red and
white striped hat, 1969, 14" h 100.00

Door Handle, plastic and metal, figural bottle, 1950s 225.00

Door Push, porcelain, "Merci Revenez Pour un
Coca–Cola," red, yellow and white lettering, c1941 . . . . 150.00

Festoon Sign, woman in floppy hat holding glass of
Coke, "Delicious," "Refreshing," 1950 . . . . 750.00

Fly Swatter, plastic, "Coca–Cola Tarboro, NC" on han-
dle, 1960s. 10.00

Game, Anagrams and Letters, 1950s 225.00

Game, Tick–Tack–Toe, Milton Bradley, 1940–50s 185.00

Glass, pewter, c1930s 225.00

Hat Pin, chrome, c1920, 4" l 225.00

Horn, cardboard, Christmas motif, 1940–50s, 7¹/₄" h 200.00

Ice Tongs, aluminum, 1940s, 9" l 250.00

Lighter, figural can, diamond design, 1960s 30.00

Map, North America, 1940s, 36 x 30" 40.00

Menu Board Panel, french fries and Coca–Cola cup,
c1960s, 17" sq 2.00

Menu, cardboard, "Sign of Good Taste," 1950s. 50.00

Music Box, miniature, complete, 1950s 185.00

Necktie, square logos, 1970s. 10.00

Newspaper Advertisement, Katz & Besthoff, full color,
1935, 16 x 22" 30.00

Pencil, mechanical, bottle on end, c1942. . . . . 50.00

Pencil Box, Memphis Bottling Co, c1948, 11" l. 200.00

Pin, routeman's, brass, Indianapolis Bottling Co, c1930,
2¹/₂" h 150.00

Pin, "Safe Driving Award," enameled, 1920s 350.00

Plate, 50th Anniversary, Lenox, 1950s, 10¹/₂" d 475.00

Plate, "Drink Coca–Cola," "Good with food" on rim,
Wellsville China Co, 1940–50s, 6¹/₂" d 350.00

Pocketknife, pearl, corkscrew, Colonial Prov, RI, c1935 . . . . . 75.00

Postcard, 50th Anniversary, Louisville, KY, 1950 . . . . 50.00

Postcard, 1968 World's Fair Coke pavilion, Coca–Cola
Hemisfair 6.00

Poster, seated woman holding basketball, other woman
leaning on soda cooler, 18 x 16" 160.00

Punchboard, 1930s, The Pause That Refreshes, 9¹/₄" sq 750.00

Puzzle, wood, boy sitting on wall, begging dog at feet,
1932. . . . . 500.00

Ruler, plastic, "it's the real thing," 1970 . . . . 3.00

Seltzer Bottle, Hornell, NY, 1940s 165.00

Serving Tray, bottle of Coke setting on brick wall, bird in
birdhouse with flowers, "Delicious, Refreshing,"
and "Coca–Cola" on sides, 1957 . . . . 175.00

Grocery Cart Bottle Carrier, wire frame, $60.00.

String Holder, litho tin, 1930s, 14 x 16", $1,100.00. Photo courtesy Gary Metz's Muddy River Trading Co.

Toy, airplane, styrofoam. 15.00
Toy, dispenser, plastic, Chilton Toys, complete, 1970s. 40.00
Toy, My Dolly Loves A Party, 1950s 200.00
Toy Truck, #171, rubber wheels, Metalcraft, c1932 . . . . 975.00
Toy Truck, plastic, F J Holden Van, Watsonia Food
    Products, Micro Models, 1970s, 4" h 275.00
Tumbler, set of 8, Around the World, orig box 125.00
Uniform Patch, "Your Coca–Cola Salesman," 1950s 8.00
Visor, cardboard, 1960s. 6.00
Whistle, cardboard, figural bottle, 1920s, 3³/₄" h 325.00
Whistle, plastic, "Merry Christmas," "Coca–Cola
    Bottling Co, Memphis, Tenn.," c1950 . . . . 20.00
Whistle, wood, 1920s 150.00
Yo Yo, Kooky Kaps, complete, 1960s 300.00

COCKTAIL SHAKERS

The modern cocktail shaker dates from the 1920s, a result of the martini craze. As a form, it inspired designers in glass, ceramics, and metals.

Neither the Depression nor World War II hindered the sale of cocktail shakers. The 1950s was the era of the home bar and out-door patio. The cocktail shaker played a major role in each. The arrival of the electric blender and the shift in public taste from liquor to wine in the 1960s ended the cocktail shaker's reign.

Reference: Stephen Visakay, *Vintage Bar Ware,* Collector Books, 1997.

Bernard Rice & Sons, silver plated, figural rooster on
    top, 8 matching goblets, 14" h shaker, c1920s. $385.00
Black Lotus Glass, "Call of the Wild," sterling over-
    lay, 4 matching ftd goblets, c1934 . . . . 500.00
Heisey Glass Co, orchid pattern, sterling top and bot-
    tom, small. 225.00

Serving Tray, "Curb Service," waiter serving couple in
    early car, "Drink Coca–Cola" top and bottom, sgd,
    1930. . . . . 235.00
Serving Tray, woman wearing yellow dress and hat, hold-
    ing bottle, 1938. . . . . 60.00
Sign, cardboard, bell shaped, "Sign Of Good Taste,"
    1950s 18.00
Sign, cardboard, cut–out, 4 Cabbage Patch Kids sitting
    with Coke bottle, 1980s. 35.00
Sign, cardboard, "Coke in King Size another great
    Holiday Idea," bottle of Coke with bow around neck,
    1960s, 16 x 27". 30.00
Sign, cardboard, "King Size puts you at your sparkling
    best," 1950s, 7" d 25.00
Sign, cardboard, "Pause...refresh Drink Coca–Cola," bot-
    tle of Coke surrounded by noisemakers and celebra-
    tion scene, 1950, 16 x 27". 150.00
Sign, cardboard, "Thirst Knows No Season Drink
    Coca–Cola All the Year Round," 1920s, 15 x 25". 525.00
Sign, light–up, Harvel Pharmacy, 1956, 28 x 36" 375.00
Sign, porcelain, "Drink Coca–Cola in Bottles," red
    ground, white lettering, 36" d. 265.00
Sign, reverse glass, "Drink Coca–Cola Please Pay
    Cashier," orig chrome frame, Brunhoff, restored,
    1932, 12 x 20". 1,400.00
Sign, tin, coke bottle, emb, raised gray border, 1953,
    18 x 33" 450.00
Sign, tin, diecut, figural bottle, emb, 1933, 12 x 39". 375.00
Sign, tin, "Take a case home Today, Quality Refresh-
    ment," 1950, 19 x 28". 325.00
Soda Fountain Card, 2 couples greeting each other, "A
    Friendly Place to Meet! Drink Coca–Cola," 1950s. 20.00
Stationary Set, tablet and pencil, "Drink Coca–Cola" 8.00
Statue, silver, inscribed "Salesman of the Month" on
    base, 1930s, 6¹/₂" h 600.00
Syrup Container, glass, amber, paper label, 1930s. 425.00
Syrup Container, wood, keg, 1930s, 5 gal. 275.00
Tennis Racket Cover, 1970s 20.00
Thermometer, tin, figural bottle, 1930s, 17" h 385.00
Thermometer, tin, silhouette of woman drinking bottle of
    Coke, 1939, 6¹/₂ x 16". 325.00
Thermometer, outdoor, plastic face, metal base, 1950s,
    4¹/₂ x 5¹/₄". 100.00

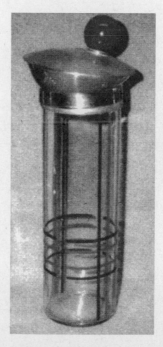

Cocktail Shaker, glass, Tam–O–Shanter, Seymour Products, $220.00. Photo courtesy Norton Auctioneers.

Napier, figural penguin, chrome, beak opens to reveal rubber stopper and pourer, stamped on bottom, "Napier – pat. pending, or pat D – 101559," 1930s, 12" h **1,200.00**

Revere Copper & Brass Co, chrome plated brass, Zephyr shaker, circular tray, and 7 ftd cups with Catalin bases, 1937–41 . . . . **225.00**

Revere Copper & Brass Co, Manhattan Serving Set, designed by Norman Bel Geddes, chrome plate over brass, includes shaker, trays, and set of 2 Revere tumblers, c1937 . . . . **550.00**

West Bend Aluminum Co, Bakelite base and top, 8 matching aluminum goblets and tray, c1933 . . . . **75.00**

West Bend Aluminum Co, Tippler Tumbler, chrome, red plastic top, "Tipple Tips" booklet, ©1934 . . . . **45.00**

West Virginia Specialty Glass Co, Cocktail Set, glass, blue dumbell, ribbed, SS lid and trim, 6 matching goblets, c1935, 13" h **775.00**

West Virginia Specialty Glass Co, Cocktail Set, glass, ruby red ladies slipper, chrome top, removable high heeled chrome slipper, 4 matching goblets with applied sterling rim, 1937, 15½" h **1,155.00**

COINS & CURRENCY

Chances are you have some old coins and currency around the house. Many individuals deposit their pocket change in a large bank or bottle on a daily basis. People who travel return home with foreign change. Most currency exchanges will not convert coinage. Millions of Americans put aside brand new one dollar silver certificate bills when America went off the silver standard.

Condition plays a critical role in determining the value of any coin or piece of currency. If your coins and currency show signs of heavy use, chances are they are worth little more than face value, even if they date prior to World War II. Circulated American silver dimes, quarters, half dollars, and dollars from before the age of sandwich coins do have a melt value ranging from two–and–one¬half to three times face value. In some foreign countries, once a coin or currency has been withdrawn from service, it cannot be redeemed, even for face value.

The first step in valuing your coins and currency is to honestly grade them. Information about how to grade is found in the opening chapters of most reference books. Be a very tough grader. Individuals who are not serious collectors tend to overgrade.

Remember, values found in price guides are retail. Because coin and currency dealers must maintain large inventories, they pay premium prices only for extremely scarce examples.

Coins are far easier to deal with than currency, due to the fact that there are fewer variations. When researching any coin or piece of currency, the reference must match the object being researched on every point.

Allen G. Bergman and Alex G. Malloy's *Warman's Coins & Currency* (Wallace–Homestead, 1995) is a good general reference. It includes the most commonly found material. However, when detailed research is required, use one of the following:

References: American Coins: Coin World (eds.), *The Comprehensive Catalog and Encyclopedia of U.S. Coins, 2nd Edition*, Avon Books, 1998; David Harper (ed.), *1998 North American Coins & Prices, 7th Edition*, Krause Publications, 1997; Thomas E. Hudgeon, Jr. (ed.), *The Official 1998 Blackbook Price Guide of U.S. Coins, 36th Edition*, House of Collectibles, 1998;

Scott A: Travers (ed.), *The Official Guide to Coin Grading and Counterfeit Detection*, House of Collectibles, 1997.

American Currency: Thomas Hudgeons, Jr. (ed.), *The Official 1998 Blackbook Price Guide to U.S. Paper Money, 30th Edition*, House of Collectibles, 1998; Chester L. Krause and Bob F. Lemke, *Standard Catalog of United States Paper Money, 16th Edition*, Krause Publications, 1997.

Foreign Coins: Chester L. Krause and Clifford Mishler, *1998 Standard Catalog of World Coins, 1901–Present*, Krause Publications, 1997.

Foreign Currency: Colin R. Bruce II and George Cuhaj, *1997 Standard Catalog of World Paper Money: Modern Issues (1961 to Present), Volume III, 3rd Edition*, Krause Publications, 1996; Colin R. Bruce II and Neil Shafer (ed.), *Standard Catalog of World Paper Money, Specialized Issues, 7th Edition*, Krause Publications, 1996; Albert Pick, *Standard Catalog of World Paper Money: General Issues, Volume II, 8th Edition*, Krause Publications, 1997.

Periodicals: *Coin World*, PO Box 150, Sidney, OH 45365; *Coin Prices, Coins, Numismatic News*, and *World Coin News* are all publications from Krause Publications, 700 E State St, Iola, WI 54990.

Collectors' Club: American Numismatic Assoc, 818 N Cascade Ave, Colorado Springs, CO 80903.

COLORING BOOKS

Coloring books emerged as an independent collecting category in the early 1990s, due largely to the publication of several specialized price guides on the subject and the inclusion of the category in general price guides.

The McLoughlin Brothers were one of the first American publishers of coloring books. The Little Folks Painting Books was copyrighted in 1885. Although Binney and Smith introduced crayons in 1903, it was not until the 1930s that coloring books were crayoned rather than painted.

When Saalfield introduced its Shirley Temple coloring book in 1934, it changed a market that traditionally focused on animal, fairy tale, and military themes to one based on characters and personalities. It is for this reason that crossover collectors strongly influence the value for some titles.

Beginning in the 1970s, the number of licensed coloring books began a steady decline. If it were not for Barbie, Disney, and G.I. Joe, today's coloring book rack would consist only of generic titles, primarily because the market focuses on a younger consumer. Further, many of today's coloring books are actually activity books.

Reference: Dian Zillner, *Collectible Coloring Books*, Schiffer Publishing, 1992.

Note: Books are unused unless otherwise noted.

Alice in Wonderland Paint Book, Whitman, #1257, 1951 . . . **$25.00**
Animal Alphabet to Color, Saalfield, 1941 . . . . **75.00**
Around the World in 80 Days, Saalfield, #4828, 1957 . . . . . . **20.00**
Baby Huey the Baby Giant Coloring Book, Saalfield, #4536, 1959 . . . . **18.00**
Bambi Paint Book, Whitman, #664, 1941 . . . . **35.00**
Barbie, Watkins–Strathmore, Mattel copyright, 1962/63 . . . . . **15.00**
Bedknobs and Broomsticks Coloring Book, Whitman, #1082, 1971 . . . . **15.00**

Real Cowboys in Action, Merrill #2532, ©1950–1963, $15.00.

Bobby Sherman Paint and Color Album, Columbia Pictures, #5160, 1971 .... **30.00**

Boots and Her Buddies Coloring Book, Saalfield, 1941 ...... **22.00**

Cinderella Paint Book, Whitman, #2092, 1950 .... **25.00**

Deanna Durbin Pictures to Paint, Merrill Publishing Co, #3479, 1940 .... **40.00**

Diana Lynn, Saalfield, #2536, 1946 .... **25.00**

Drowsy Color Book, Whitman, #1041, 1976 .... **5.00**

Dumbo Cut–Out Coloring Book, Project Books, Inc, #F5047, 1953 .... **25.00**

Elsie the Cow, 1957 .... **15.00**

Goodbye, Mr Chips, A Coloring Book, Saalfield, #9569, 1969 .... **15.00**

Joan Carroll Coloring Book, Saalfield, 1942 .... **25.00**

Juliet Jones Coloring Book, Saalfield, #953, 1954 .... **15.00**

Lennon Sisters, Whitman, 1950–60 .... **12.00**

Mary Poppins Coloring Book, Whitman, #1112, 1966 .... **8.00**

One Hundred and One Dalmations, Whitman, #1004, 1960 .... **35.00**

Pinky Lee's Health and Safety Cut–Out Coloring Book, Pocket Books, 1955 .... **15.00**

Raggedy Ann and Andy Mini–Coloring Book, Hallmark, 1974 .... **30.00**

Siggie's Adventures in Color, c1950s **8.00**

Son of Flubber Coloring Book, Whitman, 1963 .... **10.00**

The Fantastic Osmonds, Saalfield, 1973 .... **20.00**

The Valley of Gwangi, A Coloring Book, Saalfield, #9568, 1969 .... **8.00**

Tippee–Toes, Whitman, 1969 .... **15.00**

Tom Terrific with Mighty Manfred the Wonder Dog, Treasure Books, #312, 1957 .... **10.00**

Watergate/Join the Fun/Color the Facts, 1973, 48 pgs, 8 x 11" **25.00**

Young America Coloring Book, Platt and Munk Co, 1928 ..... **8.00**

COMIC BOOKS

The modern comic book arrived on the scene in the late 1930s. Led by superheroes such as Batman and Superman, comics quickly became an integral part of growing up. Collectors classifiy comics from 1938 to the mid–1940s as "Golden Age" comics and comics from the mid–1950s through the end of the 1960s as "Silver Age" comics. The Modern Age begins in 1980 and runs to the present.

Comics experienced a renaissance in the 1960s with the introduction of the Fantastic Four and Spider–Man. A second revival occurred in the 1980s with the arrival of the independent comic. The number of comic stores nationwide doubled. Speculation in comics as investments abounded. A period of consolidation and a bitter distribution rights fight among publishers weakened the market in the mid–1990s and burst the speculative bubble. The comic book market is in recovery as the decade ends.

References: Grant Geissman, *Collectibly MAD: The MAD and EC Collectibles Guide*, EC Publications, 1995; Dick Lupoff and Don Thompson (eds.), *All in Color for a Dime*, Krause Publications, 1997; Alex G. Malloy, *Comics Values Annual, 1998 Edition: The Comics Books Price Guide*, Antique Trader Books, 1997; Robert M. Overstreet, *The Overstreet Comic Book Price Guide, 27th Edition*, Avon Books, Gemstone Publishing, 1997; Robert M. Overstreet and Gary M. Carter, *The Overstreet Comic Book Grading Guide*, Avon Books, 1992; Maggie Thompson (ed.), *Marvel Comics Checklist & Price Guide, 1961–1993*, Krause Publications, 1993; Maggie Thompson and Brent Frankenhoff, *Comic Buyer's Guide 1998 Comic Book Checklist and Price Guide: 1961 to Present*, Fourth Edition, Krause Publications, 1997; Jerry Weist, *Original Comic Art: Identification and Price Guide*, Avon Books, 1993.

Periodicals: *Comics Buyer's Guide*, 700 E State St, Iola, WI 54990; *Comics Source*, PO Box 2512, Chattanooga, TN 37409; *Overstreet's Comic Book Marketplace* and *Overstreet's Advanced Collector*, 1996 Greenspring Dr, Ste 405, Lutherville–Timonium, MD 21093.

Collectors' Club: Fawcett Collectors of America & Magazine Enterprise, Too!, 301 E Buena Vista Ave, North Augusta, SC 29841.

REPRODUCTION ALERT: Publishers often reprint popular stories. Check the fine print at the bottom of the inside cover or first page for correct titles. Also, do not confuse 10 x 13" treasury–sized "Famous First Edition" comics printed in the mid–1970s with original comic book titles.

Note: All comics listed are in near mint condition.

Adventures of Robin Hood, Gold Key, #2, 1974–75 .... **$3.50**

Airboy, Eclipse, 739, 1986–89 .... **1.75**

Alf, Marvel, #5, Alf's Evil Twin, Mar 1988 .... **1.50**

Alien Legion, Marvel, #13, Apr 1984 .... **2.25**

Alien Worlds, Pacific, #3, 1982 .... **3.00**

All Star Squadron, DC, #40, The Real American, 1981–87 .... **1.50**

Amazing Spider–Man, Marvel, #196, Mar 1963 .... **8.00**

American Flagg, First, #8, State of the Union, 1983–88 ...... **2.50**

Animal Man, DC, #6, Hawkman, 1988–95 .... **3.00**

Aquaman, DC, #21, The Fisherman, 1st series, 1962–78 ..... **35.00**

Archie's Madhouse, Archie Publications, #32, 1959–69 ...... **3.50**

Arion, Lord of Atlantis, DC, #5, 1982–85 .... **1.00**

Astonishing Tales, Marvel, #14, Aug 1970 .... **3.00**

Avengers, Marvel, #64, Sep 1963 .... **16.00**

Badger, Capital, 734, 1983 .... **3.00**

Barbie, Marvel, #51, Jan 1991 .... **1.50**

Barney and Betty Rubble, Charlton, #6, 1973–76 .... **7.50**

Batman and the Outsiders, DC, #2, Baron Bedlam, Aug 1983 .... **2.50**

Batman, DC, #290, Skull Dagger, Spring 1940 .... **8.00**

Batman Family, DC, #15, Sep–Oct 1975 . . . . **3.00**
Battle of the Planets, Gold Key, #5, Jun 1979 . . . . **2.50**
Battlestar Galactica, Marvel, #7, Mar 1979. . . . . **2.50**
Beauty and the Beast, Marvel, #3, Jan 1985 . . . . **2.00**
Beetlejuice, Harvey, #1, 1991 . . . . **1.50**
Black Fury, Charlton, #5, May 1955. . . . . **5.00**
Black Lightning, DC, #10, Trickster **2.00**
Black Panther, Marvel, #3, 1st series **3.50**
Blue Beetle, DC, #1, 1986–88. . . . . **1.50**
Bomba, The Jungle Boy, DC, #2, 1967–68 . . . . **10.00**
Brave and the Bold, DC, #103, Metal Men, Aug–Sep
  1955. . . . . **7.00**
Captain Action, DC, #4, Dr Evil, Oct–Nov 1968. . . . . **35.00**
Captain America, Marvel, #146, Apr 1968 . . . . **7.00**
Care Bears, Marvel, #1, Nov 1985. . . . . **1.50**
Casper the Friendly Ghost, Harvey, #160, 1958 . . . . **4.00**
Cave Kids, Gold Key, #7, Pebbles and Bamm Bamm, 1963 . . . . **8.00**
Chamber of Chills, Marvel, #5, Nov 1972 . . . . **3.00**
Checkmate, DC, #10, Apr 1988. . . . . **1.50**
Claw the Unconquered, DC, #10, May–Jun 1975 . . . . **1.00**
Conan the Barbarian, Marvel, #18, Oct 1979 . . . . **12.00**
Courtship of Eddie's Father, Dell, 1970. . . . . **20.00**
Creatures on the Loose, Marvel, #23, The Man–Monster
  Strikes, Mar 1971 . . . . **4.00**
Crossfire and Rainbow, Eclipse, #1, Marx Bros, 1986 . . . . **2.00**
Daredevil, Marvel, #81, Apr 1964 . . . . **12.00**
DC Special, DC, #5, Green Lantern, Oct–Dec 1968. . . . . **5.00**
DC Superstars, DC, #6, Superstars of Space, 1976–78 . . . . **1.50**
Dead of Night, Marvel, #9, Dec 1973 . . . . **3.00**
Defenders, Marvel, #58, Aug 1972 . . . . **4.50**
Dennis the Menace, Fawcett, #16, Fun Fest, 1979–80. . . . . . . **2.00**
Dennis the Menace, Marvel, #1, Nov 1981 . . . . **1.25**
Detective Comics, DC, #472, Hugo Strange, Mar 1937. . . . . **15.00**
Diver Dan, Dell, 1962. . . . . **30.00**
Doctor Fate, DC, #2, New Dr Fate, Jul 1987. . . . . **2.50**
Doomsday, Charlton, 745, Jul 1975 . . . . **5.00**
Dracula, Dell, #8, Nov 1966 . . . . **10.00**
Dr Strange, Marvel, #61, 2nd series **2.50**
Duckman, Topps, #4 . . . . **2.50**
Fantastic Four, Marvel, #279, Nov 1961 . . . . **3.00**
Fantastic World of Hanna–Barbera, Marvel, #2, Dec 1977 . . . . **1.00**
Flash Gordon, Charlton, 1969–70 . . . . **20.00**

Dennis the Menace, Fawcett, #174, Dennis the Menace in Hawaii, 1978, $1.25.

The Flintstones, Charlton, #10, 1970 . . . . **12.00**
Frankenstein, Marvel, #16, The Brute and the Berserker,
  1973–75. . . . . **3.00**
From Beyond the Unknown, DC, #3, Oct–Nov 1969 . . . . . . **15.00**
Fury of Firestorm, DC, #21, Killer Frost, Jun 1982. . . . . **2.00**
Generation X, Marvel, #28 . . . . **2.00**
Gentle Ben, Dell, #3, Feb 1968 . . . . **15.00**
George of the Jungle, Gold Key, #2, Feb 1969 . . . . **30.00**
Ghosts, DC, #81, Unburied Phantom, Sep–Oct 1971 . . . . **3.00**
G I Joe, A Real American Hero, Marvel, #87, Cobra, Jun
  1982. . . . . **1.00**
Godzilla, Marvel, #21, Aug 1977. **4.00**
Golden Comics Digest, Gold Key, #32, Woody
  Woodpecker Summer Fun **6.00**
Green Arrow, DC, #4, 1983. . . . . **3.50**
Green Lantern, DC, #158, Fall 1941 . . . . **2.50**
Gunhawks, Marvel, #4, Oct 1972 . . . . **2.75**
Gunsmoke Western, Marvel, #77, Jul 1963. . . . . **16.00**
Heathcliff's Funhouse, Marvel, #17, Masked Moocher,
  Apr 1985 . . . . **1.00**
The Heckler, DC, #5, 1992–93 . . . . **1.25**
Hook, Marvel, #2, Return to Never Land **1.00**
Hopalong Cassidy, DC, #134, Cast of the Three
  Crack–Shots, Feb 1954 . . . . **50.00**
Hot Wheels, DC, #6, Mar–Apr 1970 . . . . **30.00**
House of Mystery, DC, #249, Hit Parade of Death,
  Dec–Jan 1952 . . . . **8.00**
House of Secrets, DC, #91, The Eagle's Talon, Nov–Dec
  1956. . . . . **12.00**
Human Fly, Marvel, #16, Jul 1987 . . . . **1.75**
Incredible Hulk, Marvel, #427. . . . . **1.50**
Indiana Jones, Further Adventures of, #5, Jan 1983 . . . . **1.50**
Inferior Five, DC, #5, Mar–Apr 1967 . . . . **15.00**
Inhumans, Marvel, #11, Oct 1975 . . . . **2.00**
Iron Fist, Marvel, #8, Nov 1975 . . . . **14.00**
Iron Man, Marvel, #81, May 1968 . . . . **6.00**
Johnny Thunder, DC, #3, Feb–Mar 1973. . . . . **4.00**
Justice, Marvel, #3, Nov 1986 . . . . **1.00**
Karate Kid, DC, #15, Jul–Aug 1978 . . . . **1.25**
Leave It to Binky, DC, #62, Feb–Mar 1948 . . . . **7.50**
Lidsville, Gold Key, #2, Oct 1972 . . . . **7.00**
Li'l Kids, Marvel, #10, Aug 1970 . . . . **4.50**
The Little Mermaid, Marvel, #9 . . . . **1.50**
The Little Stooges, Gold Key, #5, Sep 1972 . . . . **5.00**
Logan's Run, Marvel, #4, Dread Sanctuary, Jan 1977 . . . . **2.00**
Luger, Eclipse, #3, Sharks, 1986–87 . . . . **1.75**
Machine Man, Marvel, #17, Madame Menace, Apr 1978 . . . . . **2.50**
Madballs, Marvel, #1, Sep 1986 . . . . **1.25**
Man From Atlantis, Marvel, #4, Beware the Killer Spores,
  Feb 1978 . . . . **1.25**
Manhunter, DC, #5, 1988–90 . . . . **1.25**
Marvel Chillers, Marvel, #7, Oct 1975 . . . . **2.50**
Marvel Classic Comics, Marvel, #16, Ivanhoe, 1976–78 . . . . . **3.00**
Marvel Two–in–One, Marvel, #37, Matt Murdock and
  Thing, Jan 1974. . . . . **3.00**
MASK, DC, #4, final issue, March 1986 . . . . **1.00**
Masked Man, Eclipse, #6, 1985–88 . . . . **2.00**
Master of Kung Fu, Marvel, #25, special edition, Apr
  1974. . . . . **8.00**
Maze Agency, Comico, #1. . . . . **3.00**
Men of War, DC, #24, The Presidential Peril, Aug 1977 . . . . . **1.25**
Meteor Man, Marvel, #4, Night Thrasher **4.00**
Micronauts, Marvel, #25, 1st series, Jan 1979. . . . . **1.50**
Mighty Morphin Power Rangers, Marvel, #3, Saban's **1.75**

The Mighty Thor, Marvel, #236, Absorbing Man, Mar 1966 . . . . **3.50**
Millenium, DC, #3, Worst Nightmare, Jan 1988 . . . . **1.75**
Misty, Marvel, #2, Dec 1985 . . . . **1.00**
Mod Squad, Dell, #2, 1968–71 . . . . **18.00**
Muppet Babies, Harvey, #1, Return of Muppet Babies. **1.25**
New America, Eclipse, #2, 1987–88 . . . . **1.75**
New Teen Titans, DC, #21, Nov 1980 . . . . **3.00**
Nightcrawler, #2, Nov 1985 . . . . **3.00**
Nightmare on Elm Street, #1, Oct 1989 . . . . **3.00**
Omega Men, DC, #23, Nimbus, Dec 1982 . . . . **1.50**
Our Fighting Forces, DC, #112, What's in It For the
    Hellcats, Oct–Nov 1954 . . . . **10.00**
Plastic Man, DC, #9, 1st series, Joe the Killer Pro,
    Nov–Dec 1966 . . . . **12.00**
Plop, DC, #1, Sep–Oct 1973 . . . . **5.00**
Richie Rich Bank Books, Harvey, #11, 1972–82 . . . . **7.50**
Roger Rabbit, Walt Disney, #10, Tuned–in–Toons, 1990 . . . . . . **2.50**
Sabrina the Teenage Witch, Archie Publications, #5,
    1971–83 . . . . **7.00**
Sarge Steel/Secret Agent, Charlton, #7, 1964–66 . . . . **2.50**
Secrets of Haunted House, DC, #36, Sister Sinister,
    Apr–May 1975 . . . . **1.25**
Steel, The Indestructible Man, DC, #1, Mar 1978 . . . . **1.00**
Strikeforce Morituri, #14, The Horde, Dec 1986 . . . . **1.25**
Sub–Mariner, Marvel, #19, Stingray, May 1968 . . . . **15.00**
Superboy and the Legion of Super Heroes, DC, #233,
    1976–79 . . . . **2.00**
Swamp Thing, DC, #57, 1972 . . . . **2.50**
Tailgunner Jo, DC, Sep 1988 . . . . **1.00**
Tales of the Unexpected, DC, #104, Master of the
    Voodoo Machine, 1956–68 . . . . **30.00**
Tarzan, DC, #207, Apr 1972 . . . . **4.50**
Team America, #8, Hydra, Jun 1982 . . . . **1.25**
Teenage Mutant Ninja Turtles, Mirage, #11, Raphael, 1993 . . . . **2.75**
The Thing, Marvel, #1, Jul 1983 . . . . **2.50**
Thundercats, Marvel, #6, Dec 1985 . . . . **1.50**
Tomb of Dracula, Marvel, #5, Nov 1979 . . . . **3.00**
2001: A Space Odyssey, #7, The New Seed **1.50**
Underdog, Gold Key, #20, Six Million Dollar Dog, Mar
    1975 . . . . **15.00**
Underworld, DC, #2, Dec 1987 . . . . **2.00**
US 1, Marvel, #3, Rhyme of the Ancient Highwayman,
    May 1983 . . . . **1.00**
Vigilante, DC, #4, Oct 1983 . . . . **2.00**
Warlord, DC, #113, Through Fiends Destroy Me, Jan 1976 . . . . **1.75**
Web of Spider–Man, Marvel, #2, Apr 1985 . . . . **8.00**
Weird War Tales, DC, #62, The Grubbers, Sep–Oct 1971 . . . . . **2.00**
Weird Western Tales, DC, #14, Jun–Jul 1972 . . . . **2.50**
Weird Wondertales, Marvel, #12, The Stars Scream
    Murder, Dec 1973 . . . . **2.50**
Werewolf By Night, Marvel, #12, Cry Monster, Sep 1972 . . . . . **6.00**
Wonder Woman, DC, #219, 1st series **2.50**

COMPACT DISCS

CD technology was first introduced in 1982. Although the technology is recent and many compact discs are still available commercially, a dedicated group of CD collectors has emerged.

Collectors focus on three main categories: (1) promotional issues, including CD singles and radio programs on compact discs, (2) limited edition discs, especially those with creative or innovative packaging, and (3) out of print discs. At the moment, American collectors are focused almost exclusively on American manufactured CDs.

As in other emerging collecting categories, prices can vary dramatically. Comparison shopping is advised. Bootleg discs have little to no value. Blues, rock, and pop titles dominate the secondary collecting market. Country and jazz titles follow. Few collectors seek classical titles.

References: Gregory Cooper, *Collectible Compact Disc: Price Guide 2*, Collector Books, 1997; Fred Heggeness, *Goldmine's Promo Record & CD Price Guide*, Krause Publications, 1995; Jerry Osborne and Paul Bergquist, *The Official Price Guide to Compact Discs*, House of Collectibles, 1994.

Periodicals: *DISCoveries Magazine*, PO Box 1050, Dubuque, IA 52004; *Goldmine*, 700 E State St, Iola, WI 54990; *ICE*, PO Box 3043–A, Santa Monica, CA 90408.

AC/DC, *Thunderstruck*, Atco, #3522, diecut gatefold
    hardcover, picture sleeve, 1990 . . . . **$10.00**
Alabama, *Then Again*, RCA, #62059, black logo, rear
    insert, 1991 . . . . **5.00**
Alpert, Herb, *Under a Spanish Moon*, A & M, #17593, 9
    tracks, gatefold cloth cov, 1988 . . . . **15.00**
Bangles, *Everything*, Columbia, limited tour CD, picture
    CD, tour dates on back, 1989 . . . . **30.00**
Blue Magic, *Romeo and Juliet*, Def Jam, #1439, 1989 . . . . **5.00**
Brown, James, *It's Time to Love*, Scott Bros, #75295, 1991 . . . . **8.00**
Bush, Kate, *The Man With the Child in His Eyes*, EMI,
    #79002, 1986 . . . . **25.00**
Carpenter, Karen, *If I Had You*, A & M, #17926 . . . . **12.00**
Cash, Johnny, *The Greatest Cowboy of Them All*,
    Mercury, #360, silk–screened, rear insert, 1990 . . . . **6.00**
Clay, Andrew Dice, *Dice's Greatest Bits From 40 Too
    Long and Other Jems*, Def American, #5631,
    75 tracks, 1992 . . . . **10.00**
Cooper, Alice, *Poison*, Epic, #1665, 1989 . . . . **5.00**
Everly Brothers, *Wake Up Little Susie*, Rhino, #73008,
    1988 . . . . **8.00**
Hendrix, Jimi, *Stages '67–'70*, Reprise, #5194, 8 track
    sampler, 1991 . . . . **20.00**
Jackson, Michael, *Dirty Diana*, Epic, #1110, 1988 . . . . **12.00**
Jethro Tull, *20 Years of Jethro Tull*, Chrysalis, #21655,
    21 tracks **12.00**
John, Elton, *Club at the End of the Street*, MCA, #18303,
    1989 . . . . **5.00**
Judas Priest, *Blood Red Skies*, Columbia, #1249, 1988 . . . . . **8.00**
Kinks, *Entertainment*, MCA, 18168, 1989 . . . . **4.00**
Madonna, *Erotic*, Maverick, #5665, promo,
    silk–screened picture, 1992 . . . . **8.00**
Metallica, *Don't Tread on Me*, Elektra, #8728, silk-
    screened logo, 1991 . . . . **10.00**
Midler, Bette, *Wind Beneath My Wings*, Atlantic, #2615,
    rear insert, 1988 . . . . **5.00**
Milli Vanilli, *Girl I'm Gonna Miss You*, Arista, #9870,
    picture sleeve, 1989 . . . . **10.00**
Nicks, Stevie, *Rooms on Fire*, Modern, #2691, gatefold
    hardcover, picture sleeve, 1989 . . . . **6.00**
Pink Floyd, *Dark Side of the Moon*, 20th anniversary
    edition, 9 tracks, box cover, postcards, 1993 . . . . **20.00**
Pop, Iggy, *High On You*, A & M, #17632, 1988 . . . . **4.00**
Psychedelic Furs, *World Outside*, Columbia, #47303, 10
    tracks, gatefold hardcover, lyric poster, 1991 . . . . **12.00**

Queen, *Breakthru*, Capitol, #79720, 1989 . . . . **10.00**
Ratt, *Lovin' Yous a Dirty Job*, Atlantic, #3495, 1990 . . . . **4.00**
Ren & Stimpy, *Little Eediot!*, Sony, #5473, 2 CD set, 1993 . . . . **15.00**
Rolling Stones, *Rock and a Hard Place*, #73057, 1989 . . . . . . **15.00**
Screaming Trees, *Bed of Roses*, Epic, #2296, silk-
  screened, rear insert, 1991 . . . . **6.00**
Stewart, Rod, *Forever Young*, Warner Brothers, #3169,
  1988 . . . . **6.00**
Streisand, Barbra, *Someone That I Used to Love*,
  Columbia, #73099, 1989 . . . . **8.00**
Styx, *Show Me the Way*, A & M, #75021, silk–screened
  logo on brown, 1990 . . . . **6.00**
Theme From Northern Exposure, soundtrack, MCA,
  #2463, 1992 . . . . **6.00**
U2, *Until the End of the World*, Island, #6704, logo on
  white, 1991 . . . . **10.00**

COMPACTS

Cosmetic use increased significantly in the 1920s as women started playing a major role in the business world. Compacts enabled
a woman to freshen her makeup on the run.

Although compacts are still made today, they experienced a
Golden Age from the mid–1930s through the late 1950s.
Collectors designate compacts manufactured prior to 1960 as
"vintage."

Compacts are found in thousands of shapes, styles, and decorative motifs in materials ranging from precious metals to injection
molded plastic. Decorative theme, construction material, manufacturer, and novelty are four major collecting themes.

References: Roseann Ettinger, *Compacts and Smoking Accessories*,
Schiffer Publishing, 1991; Roselyn Gerson, *Vintage Contemporary
Purse Accessories: Identification & Value Guide*, Collector Books,
1997; Roselyn Gerson, *Vintage Ladies' Compacts*, Collector
Books, 1996; Roselyn Gerson, *Vintage Vanity Bags and Purses: An
Identification and Value Guide*, Collector Books, 1994; Laura M.
Mueller, *Collector's Encyclopedia of Compacts, Carryalls & Face
Powder Boxes: Identification & Values* (1994, 1996 value update)
Vol. II (1997), Collector Books; Lynell Schwartz, *Vintage Compacts
& Beauty Accessories*, Schiffer Publishing, 1997.

Collectors' Club: Compact Collectors, PO Box 40, Lynbrook, NY
11563.

American Maid, figural heart, goldtone, brocade lid,
  c1930 . . . . **$45.00**
Belle, beveled lucite base, goldtone frame, faux burled
  walnut plastic lid plate, case sgd, glued mirror **65.00**
Celma Co, white metal, engine turned domed lid, shield
  monogram cartouche, reverse log, framed mirror,
  pierced celluloid powder screen, 2" d **40.00**
Clarice Jane, goldtone, Red Cross cloisonné emblem,
  black encased enamel, domed saddlebag, puff with
  logo, 2½" d **125.00**
Colgate and Co, pressed powder can, black enamel and
  goldtone, hp woman with fan, acanthus border,
  framed mirror, artist sgd, 2½" d **75.00**
Coty, Flying Colors, spread eagle shape, gilt metal, red,
  white, and blue lipstick tube center, orig presentation
  box, c1940 . . . . **200.00**
Dermetics, goldtone, sunrays and gazelle motif **40.00**

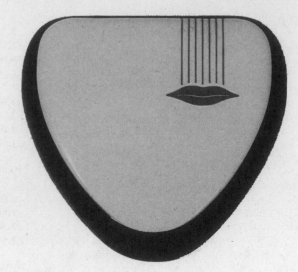

**Unknown Maker, white lid with black trim and red stylized lips,
blue base, interior lipstick, powder, and rouge cases, patent
#D–128–188, 5 x 5", $100.00.**

Elizabeth Arden, loose powder compact, faux sapphires
  and rhinestones pierced lid dec, domed case, case
  sgd, framed mirror, 3⅞" d **150.00**
Evans, compact and cigarette case, bronzed metal,
  engine turned design, white cloisonné disk on lid,
  c1930 . . . . **90.00**
Evans, loose powder pouch compact, white metal, mail
  mesh case, owl face domed enameled lid motif, emb
  floral design, puff with logo, framed mirror, 2½" d **50.00**
Evans, mock tortoise shell over sterling frame, case sgd,
  puff with logo, framed mirror, 3⅞" d **75.00**
J M Fisher, loose powder pendant vanity, white metal,
  multicolored dog motif, crimped link ring chain,
  2¼" d **275.00**
Marie Earle, pressed powder glove compact, goldtone,
  faux carved ivory side panels, quatrefoil motif lid,
  framed mirror **40.00**
Max Factor, vanity case, goldtone, Chevron lid, red logo
  mask, case sgd, framed mirror **55.00**
Prince Matchabelli, vanity case, goldtone, black enam-
  eled lid, crown lid logo, case sgd, puff with logo, top
  hinged double framed mirror **55.00**
Revlon, plastic, mermaid motif, aqua, coin purse clo-
  sure, papers sgd "She Shells," silver lurex aqua
  damask puff, case sgd, glue mirror, 4" d **70.00**
Rex, vanity pouch, mesh, white plastic beads, c1930 . . . . . . **50.00**
Ronson, Art Deco, enamel, brown and white mar-
  bleized, compact/lighter, cigarette case combination,
  c1930–40 . . . . **150.00**
Souvenir, Statue of Liberty **50.00**
Volupté, goldtone, multi shell landscape scene, abalone
  border, flanged, fluted sides, puff with logo, framed
  beveled mirror **100.00**
Wadsworth, Compakit, plastic, camera shape, black,
  front compartment, lipstick and cigarette lighter on
  top, cigarette compartment on bottom, c1940 . . . . **200.00**
Zell Fifth Avenue, goldtone, poodle motif, red cabochon
  stones, lipstick fitted black grosgrain case, 1940–50 . . . . . **125.00**

CONSOLIDATED GLASS COMPANY

The Consolidated Glass Company was founded in 1893, the result of a merger between the Wallace and McAfee Company and the Fostoria Shade & Lamp Company. In the mid–1890s, the company built a new factory in Corapolis, Pennsylvania, and quickly became one of the largest lamp, globe, and shade manufacturers in the United States.

The Consolidated Glass Company began making giftware in the mid–1930s. Most collectors focus on the company's late 1920s and early 1930s product lines, e.g., Florentine, Martele, and Ruba Rombic.

Consolidated closed its operations in 1932, reopening in 1936. In 1962 Dietz Brothers acquired the company. A disastrous fire in 1963 during a labor dispute heralded the end of the company. The last glass was made in 1964.

Reference: Jack D. Wilson, *Phoenix & Consolidated Art Glass: 1926–1980,* Antique Publications, 1989.

Collectors' Club: Phoenix & Consolidated Glass Collectors' Club, PO Box 2847, Edmond, OK 73083.

Biscuit Jar, Florette, light green, satin **$225.00**
Bon Bon, Ruba Rombic, smokey topaz, 6" d **120.00**
Bowl, Dance of the Nudes, dark blue, 8" d **365.00**
Box, cov, Martele Line, Fruit and Leaf, scalloped edge **70.00**
Candlesticks, pr, Martele Line, Hummingbird, oval body,
   jade green, pedestal base, 6³/₄" h **325.00**
Celery Tray, Florette, pink **40.00**
Condiment Set, Florette, light blue cased glass **130.00**
Cup and Saucer, Dance of the Nudes, ruby **250.00**
Decanter, Ruba Rombic, dark green **650.00**
Jug, Catalonian, purple **115.00**
Lamp, Cockatoo, bittersweet, blue, tan, and white **280.00**
Lamp, Love Birds, crystal **350.00**
Luncheon Plate, Dance of the Nudes, light blue, frosted,
   8" d **250.00**
Platter, Dance of the Nudes, clear **400.00**
Puff Box, Lovebirds, blue **100.00**
Snack Set, Martele Line, Five Fruits, pink **40.00**
Sugar, cov, Ruba Rombic **45.00**
Tumbler, ftd, Martele Line, Five Fruits, 5³/₄" h **35.00**
Vase, 700 Line, frosted lining, 6¹/₂" h **150.00**
Vase, Dance of the Nudes, fan **250.00**

CONSTRUCTION TOYS

Childen love to build things. Modern construction toys trace their origin to the Anchor building block sets of the late 19th and early 20th centuries. A construction toy Hall of Fame includes A. C. Gilbert's Erector Set, Lego, Lincoln Logs, and Tinker Toys.

A construction set must have all its parts, instruction book(s), and period packaging to be considered complete. Collectors pay a premium for sets designed to make a specific object, e.g., a dirigible or locomotive.

References: William M. Bean, *Greenberg's Guide to Gilbert Erector Sets, Vol. One: 1913–1932,* Greenberg Books, 1993; William M. Bean, *Greenberg's Guide to Gilbert Erector Sets, Vol. Two: 1933–1962,* Greenberg Books, 1998; Craig Strange, *Collector's Guide to Tinker Toys,* Collector Books, 1996.

Collectors' Clubs: A. C. Gilbert Heritage Society, 16 Palmer St, Medford, MA 02155; Girder and Panel Collectors Club (Kenner), Box 494, Bolton, MA 01740.

Animakers, multicolored wooden blocks fit together to
   make animals, 1945 . . . . **$20.00**
Auburn Rubber, Building Bricks, 1940s **20.00**
Bilt–E–Z, Skyscraper Building Blocks, Scott Mfg,
   Chicago, c1925 . . . . **135.00**
Cozzone Construction Set, #500, electric motor,
   machined metal parts **225.00**
Fisher–Price, Construx, #6331, Mobile Missiles Military
   series, "The Action Building System" **50.00**
Gabriel, Tinkertoy, #30010, 50 pcs **10.00**
A C Gilbert, Ferris Wheel, #10074, 1960 . . . . **100.00**
A C Gilbert, Junior Erector, #4 . . . . **55.00**
A C Gilbert, Lunar Vehicle Set, #10127, 1963 . . . . **50.00**
A C Gilbet, Musical Ferris Wheel, #10072, 1958 . . . . **200.00**
Halsam, American Logs, 1950s **15.00**
Halsam, American Plastic Bricks, #60 . . . . **80.00**
Hasbro/Playskool, Tinkertoy, Hasbro/Playskool, Beginner
   Set, #840, 57 pcs **5.00**
Hasbro/Playskool, Tinkertoy, Super Set, #843 . . . . **10.00**
Ideal, Super City Heliport Set, 1968 . . . . **12.00**
Ideal, Super City Skyscraper Building Set, Ideal, 1960s **140.00**
Kenner, Home Workshop, #1010, motorized, plastic
   lumber, 7 power tools, paints, adhesive, and instruc-
   tion booklet, 1962–63 . . . . **30.00**
Lincoln Logs, #1A, 1920 . . . . **25.00**
Lincoln Logs, #29 . . . . **125.00**
Microrail City, Micropolis, 232 pc set, c1978 . . . . **45.00**
Questor, Tinkertoy, Big Tinkertoy for Little Hands, #104,
   1976 . . . . **20.00**
Questor, Tinkertoy, Little Designer Tinkertoy, #126,
   95 plastic and wooden pcs **15.00**
Spalding, Tinkertoy, Curtain Wall Builder, #640, 123 pcs **35.00**
Spalding, Tinkertoy, Teck Tinkertoy, 113 pcs, 1963 . . . . **15.00**
Strombecker, Bill–Ding Clowns, 1940–50 . . . . **20.00**
Tupper Toys, Build–O–Fun, 1965 . . . . **75.00**
Wannatoy, Construction Kit, 1950s **80.00**

Halsam, American Plastic Bricks, #715, 208 pcs, 15¹/₂" h, $40.00.

COOKBOOKS

The cookbook was firmly entrentched as a basic kitchen utensil by the beginning of the 20th century. *Fannie Farmer's Cookbook* dominated during the first half of the century; *The Joy of Cooking* was the cookbook of choice of the post–1945 generations.

Cookbooks with printings in the hundreds of thousands and millions, e.g., the *White House Cookbook*, generally have little value except for the earliest editions.

Although some cookbooks are purchased by individuals who plan to use the recipes they contain, most are collected because of their subject matter, cover image, and use as advertising premiums. Do not hesitate to shop around for the best price and condition. The survival rate for cookbooks is exceptionally high.

References: Bob Allen, *A Guide to Collecting Cookbooks and Advertising Cookbooks*, Collector Books, 1990, 1995 value update; Mary Barile, *Cookbooks Worth Collecting*, Wallace–Homestead, Krause Publications, 1994; Linda J. Dickinson, *A Price Guide to Cookbooks and Recipe Leaflets*, Collector Books, 1990, 1997 value update; Barbara Jane Gelink, *Collectible Old Cookbooks With Values, Second Edition*, Onento, 1997.

Collectors' Club: Cook Book Collectors Club of America, PO Box 56, St James, MO 65559.

Chiquita Banana's Recipe Book, ©1947, United Fruit Co, $8.00.

Alice Bay Cookbook, J Rousseau, paperback, 247 pgs, 1985. . . . . **$4.00**
An Herb and Spice Cookbook, C Clairborne, 1963, 334 pgs. **16.50**
Baker's Famous Chocolate Recipes, 1950, 112 pgs **7.00**
Better Homes & Gardens Cook Book, ring binder, c1950 . . . . **30.00**
Betty Crocker, Dinner For Two, 1st ed, 1958, 207 pgs. **8.00**
Cake Secrets, Ingleheart, 1921. . . . . **15.00**
Casserole Cookbook, 1968, 124 pgs **7.50**
Cheese Cookbook, Culinary Arts, 1956 . . . . **3.00**
Chef's Secret Cookbook, Szathemary, 1972, 28 pgs. **10.00**
Chinese Cooking with American Meals, 1970, 228 pgs. **6.00**
Chiquita Banana Recipe Book, 1950, 25 pp. **2.00**
Complete Pie Cookbook, Farm Journal, Nichols, 1965, 308 pp, hardbound **2.50**
Cook Book for All Occasions, DeBoth, 1936, 192 pp, hardbound **8.00**
Cookies & More Cookies, L Sumption, 1938 . . . . **5.00**
Cooking School of the Air, General Foods, 1932/1934, 100 pp **8.00**
Cooking with Sour Cream and Buttermilk, Culinary Arts, 1955, 68 pgs, paperback **3.00**
Fannie Farmer Junior Cookbook, Perkins, 1942, 208 pp, hardbound **3.00**
Favorite Recipes of Famous Women, F Stratton, 1925, 119 pp **10.00**
Feeding the Child From Crib to College, Wheatena, 1928, 44 pp **12.50**
The Fish Book Cookbook, published by Woman's World Magazine, Chicago, 1922, 50 pp **8.00**
Fun to Cook Book, Blake, 1955. . . . . **3.00**
Heinz Book of Meat Cookery, 1930, 54 pp, paperback **8.00**
How's and Why's of Cooking, 1936, 252 pp. **6.00**
Joy of Eating Natural Foods, 1962, 363 pp **6.50**
La Cuisine de France, C Turgeon, 1944, 709 pp **12.50**
Monarch Electric Cook Book, 1928, 28 pp, paperback **1.50**

Quaker Woman's Cookbook, E Lea, 1982, 310 pp, hardbound. **8.00**
Quick Gourmet Dinners, Rieman, 1972, 141 pp **6.50**
Recipes and Menus for All Occasions, Frito Co, 1947, 31 pp, paperback **3.00**
Recipes for Van Camps Pureed Fruits & Vegetables, 1930, 31 pp **10.00**
Rumford Fruit Cookbook, 1927, 47 pp, paperback **6.00**
Sally Stokely's Prize Recipes, Stokely Foods, 1935 . . . . **4.50**
Toll House Recipes, R Wakdfidle, 1946, 275 pp. **35.00**
Twentieth Century Cookbook, 1921, 164 pp **18.00**

COOKIE JARS

Although cookie jars existed as a form prior to 1945, the cookie jar's Golden Age began in the late 1940s and ended in the early 1960s. Virtually every American ceramics manufacturer from Abingdon to Twin Winton produced a line of cookie jars. Foreign imports were abundant.

There was a major cookie jar collecting craze in the 1980s and early 1990s that included a great deal of speculative pricing and some market manipulation. The speculative bubble is in the process of collapsing in many areas. Reproductions and high-priced contemporary jars, especially those featuring images of famous personalities such as Marilyn Monroe, also have contributed to market uncertainty. This major market shakeout is expected to continue for several more years.

References: Fred Roerig and Joyce Herndon Roerig, *Collector's Encyclopedia of Cookie Jars, Book I* (1991, 1997 value update), *Book II* (1994, 1997 value update), *Book III* (1997), Collector Books; Mike Schneider, *The Complete Cookie Jar Book*, Schiffer Publishing, 1991; Ellen Supnick, *The Wonderful World of Cookie Jars*, L–W Book Sales, (1995, 1997 value update); Ermagene Westfall, *An Illustrated Value Guide to Cookie Jars*, (1983, 1997 value update), *Book II* (1993, 1997 value update), Collector Books.

Periodical: *Cookie Jar Collectors Express*, PO Box 221, Mayview, MO 64071.

Newsletters: *Cookie Jarrin',* RR #2, Box 504, Walterboro, SC 29488; *Crazed Over Cookie Jars,* PO Box 254, Savanna, IL 61074.

Alpo Dog Biscuits Dog **$60.00**
Apple, California Originals 55.00
Apple, Franciscan 285.00
Archway Cookie Van 40.00
Baby Elephant, American Bisque 195.00
Baby on Lid, green, #561, Abingdon, 11" h 600.00
Bag of Cookies, American Bisque 55.00
Barn, Regal................................... 275.00
Barnum's Apples, McCoy........................ 55.00
Barrel of Apples, Metlox 45.00
Basket of Cookies, American Bisque............. 100.00
Bear, Twin Winton............................ 35.00
Bear, wearing bib, American Bisque............. 75.00
Bear, wearing blue sweater, Metlox 40.00
Bee Hive, McCoy 70.00
Bert and Ernie, California Originals 325.00
Betsy Baker, McCoy 150.00
Big Al, Treasure Craft......................... 50.00
Big Bird Chef, California Originals 100.00
Bo Peep, NAPCO, 1950s 225.00
Boy with Baseball, California Originals 65.00
Brown Bear, California Originals 55.00
Brownie, American Bisque..................... 100.00
Bunny, white, Brush McCoy.................... 150.00
Care Bear, Tenderheart, American Greetings 100.00
Casper, American Bisque 325.00
Cat, white, blue bow, stamped "China" 15.00
Cat in Basket, American Bisque 40.00
Cat's Head, Metlox 125.00
Century 21 House, new......................... 95.00
Chef, American Bisque 100.00
Chef, Red Wing, pink and black specks 165.00
Chilly Willy, McCoy 30.00
Churn, American Bisque 30.00
Clown, APCO................................. 35.00
Clown, Fitz & Floyd 90.00
Coca–Cola Jug, McCoy 65.00
Coffee Grinder, McCoy 40.00
Coffee Mug, McCoy 35.00
Coffeepot, turquoise, McCoy.................. 45.00
Collegiate Owl, American Bisque 85.00
Cookie Monster, California Originals 55.00
Cookie Truck, American Bisque 70.00
Cookies Out of This World, American Bisque ... 300.00
Cookstove, white, McCoy...................... 40.00
Covered Wagon, Brush McCoy 475.00
Cow, cat finial, Brush–McCoy 75.00
Cow Jumped Over the Moon, green, Doranne ... 175.00
Cowboy Boots, American Bisque 200.00
Daisy, Hull 85.00
Dalmation Fireman, Sigma 425.00
Dalmations, McCoy 300.00
Derby Dan, Pfaltzgraff........................ 200.00
Dog in Basket, American Bisque 70.00
Donald Duck, Hoan 45.00
Dove, blue, Fredburg 50.00
Dove, blue and green, Fapco.................. 30.00
Dragon, Doranne 225.00
Drummer Boy, Shawnee, blue stripes 125.00
Dutch Girl, Pottery Guild 75.00
Dutch Girl, tulip, Shawnee 175.00

Hen, Farmyard Follies, Doranne, blue and white, mkd "CJ–100 of U.S.A. Doranne," 10³/₄" h, $75.00.

Dutch Girl, Twin Winton....................... 100.00
Ears of Corn, Metlox 75.00
Eeyore, Disney 750.00
Elf, on log, Twin Winton 35.00
Ernie Muppets, #973, California Originals 60.00
Fairy Godmother, Applause 45.00
Farmer Pig, Treasure Craft 50.00
Feed Bag, American Bisque 100.00
Fern, yellow, Shawnee........................ 65.00
'57 Chevy, Applause 100.00
Fireplace, McCoy 90.00
Floral Plaid, #697D, Abingdon, 8 ½" h. 110.00
Fred Flintstone and Pebbles, Twin Winton...... 300.00
French Girl, Lefton 275.00
French Poodle, American Bisque 145.00
Frog, wearing blue bow tie, Doranne........... 60.00
Gift Box, American Bisque.................... 225.00
Gingerbread Boy, Hull........................ 100.00
Girl Pig, American Bisque 75.00
Goldilocks, Regal 270.00
Goose, green, Doranne 110.00
Grandfather Clock, McCoy 75.00
Granny, yellow, Treasure Craft 75.00
Halo Boy, DeForest.......................... 85.00
Harley Davidson, blue gas tank............... 145.00
Harley Davidson Hog, McCoy................. 400.00
Hen, brown, Fredburg........................ 50.00
Hen, brown, Fredburg........................ 50.00
Hippo, Brush McCoy......................... 400.00
Hobby Horse, #602D, Abingdon, 10 ½" h 280.00
Holly Hobbie, California Originals............. 95.00
House, love birds on top, Lefton 165.00
Humpty Dumpty, Clay Arts 95.00
Humpty Dumpty, wearing cowboy hat, Brush–McCoy 175.00
Humpty Dumpty, Metlox...................... 250.00
Ice Cream Cone, Doranne..................... 60.00
Indian Maiden, American Bisque 250.00
Jack in Box 300.00
Jazz Singer, Clay Arts......................... 195.00
Jug, brown and white, McCoy 30.00
Keebler Elf 50.00
Ken–L–Ration, dog head, plastic, F & F 110.00

Kliban Cat, kiss on cheek 175.00
Koala Bear, McCoy 125.00
Kookie Kettle, bronze, McCoy 25.00
Kraft T Bear 165.00
Lantern, black, McCoy 60.00
Lion, Metlox 450.00
Little Miss Muffet, Abingdon 230.00
Lucky Elephant, decals, gold trim 135.00
M & M's 100.00
Majorette, American Bisque 255.00
Mammy, yellow, McCoy 650.00
Milk Bone Dog House 120.00
Milk Can, McCoy 65.00
Milk Wagon, American Bisque 125.00
Monk, DeForest 85.00
Monk, Treasure Craft 50.00
Monkey, on stump, McCoy 70.00
Monkey, quizzical expression, Maurice of California 100.00
Mouse, N S Gustin 70.00
Mrs Tiggy Winkle, Sigma 450.00
Nabisco Chips Ahoy 85.00
Oaken Bucket, McCoy 45.00
Oriental Woman, Regal 600.00
Owl, #2728, California Originals 15.00
Owl, gray, Brush–McCoy 80.00
Panda, McCoy 45.00
Penguin, Metlox 100.00
Picnic Basket, McCoy 50.00
Pig, wearing straw hat, American Bisque 90.00
Pillsbury Funfetti 40.00
Pineapple, McCoy 90.00
Pinocchio, Metlox 125.00
Potbelly Stove, Treasure Craft 75.00
Pumpkin, #674D, Abingdon, 8" h 420.00
Puss 'n Boots, gold trim, Regal 385.00
Puss 'n Boots, Shawnee 150.00
Quaker Oats, Regal 100.00
Rabbit on Cabbage, Metlox 165.00
Raggedy Ann, Maddux 200.00
Ranger Bear, Twin Winton 55.00
Rooster, black and white, McCoy 85.00

Rooster, Twin Winton 75.00
Safe, bulldog on top, California Originals 110.00
Santa, head, American Bisque 350.00
Scottie Dog, Metlox 185.00
Sheriff Bear, Twin Winton 50.00
Sir Frances Drake, Metlox 15.00
Snoopy, McCoy 160.00
Snowflake, yellow, Shawnee 65.00
Space Cadet, California Originals 95.00
Spaceship, McCoy 150.00
Spool of Thread, American Bisque 210.00
Squirrel, McCoy 90.00
Squirrel on Stump, California Originals 50.00
Strawberry, McCoy 45.00
Sylvester the Cat, Applause 50.00
Teapot, black, McCoy 40.00
Teddy Bear, blue, Metlox 75.00
Three Bears, Abingdon 70.00
Tony the Tiger, head, plastic 100.00
Train, yellow and black, Abingdon 250.00
Train Depot, Hull 75.00
Treasure Chest, Abingdon 195.00
Treasure Chest, Brush–McCoy 125.00
Turtle, sitting, California Originals 40.00
Wilma Flintstone, talking on telephone 600.00
Winnie the Pooh, Disney 110.00
Witch, white, black, and yellow, #692D, Abingdon,
    11 ½" h 1,500.00
Woody Woodpecker, Napco 250.00
World Globe, green, Doranne 125.00
Wren House, McCoy 210.00
Yarn Doll, American Bisque 60.00
Yogi Bear, American Bisque 325.00
Yosemite Sam, McCoy 150.00

COOPER, SUSIE

After a brief stint as a designer at A. E. Gray & Co., Hanley Staffordshire, England, Susie Cooper founded the Susie Cooper Pottery in Burslem in 1932. There she designed ceramics that were functional in shape and decorated with bright floral and abstract designs. It was Cooper who first introduced the straight–sided "can" shape for coffeepots. Eventually Cooper was employed by the Wedgwood Group where she developed several lines of bone china tableware.

Reference: *Collecting Susie Cooper,* Francis Joseph Publications, 1994, distributed by Krause Publications.

Collectors' Club: Susie Cooper Collectors Group, PO Box 7436, London N12 7QF U.K.

Candlesticks, pr, sgraffito dec $200.00
Coffeepot, Dresden Spray 150.00
Coffeepot, geometric design, Kestrel shape 150.00
Coffeepot, Elegance, Falcon shape, cord and ring trans-
    fer print 175.00
Cup, Dresden Spray 30.00
Cup and Saucer, Asterix, Falcon shape 70.00
Cup and Saucer, Lustre Ware 150.00
Cup and Saucer, Orchid 70.00
Dish, divided, hp landscape 90.00
Fruit Bowl, hp florals 180.00

Smiley Pig, yellow bib, floral decals, gold trim, hairline on neck, Shawnee, $99.00. Photo courtesy Gene Harris.

Coffeepot, Kestrel shape, cream, yellow, and black, $150.00.

Rosebud, bean pot, green, 2¹/₂ pt, $25.00.

Fruit Bowl, woodpecker print 120.00
Jug, gray–green, incised leaping rams 100.00
Jug, Paris shape 75.00
Plate, Apple, 9" d 40.00
Plate, Kestrel shape, blue ground, crescent sgraffito dec,
    9" d 280.00
Plate, Printemps, 9" d 45.00
Plate, Tigerlily, 7" d 30.00
Plate, Tree of Life, 8" d 35.00
Teapot, Swansea Spray 125.00
Tureen, cov, with underplate, Crayon Loop 200.00
Tureen, cov, Pear in Pompadour 145.00
Vase, Gloria, Lustre Ware, pear shaped, green and pur-
    ple ground, gold dec 200.00
Wall Plaque, fox, hp 200.00

COORS POTTERY

After J. J. Herold went to work for the Western Pottery Company in Denver in 1912, Adloph Coors and the other investors in the Herold China and Pottery Company, Golden, Colorado, kept the factory open and renamed it the Golden Pottery. In 1920 the name was changed to Coors Porcelain Company.

Initially concentrating on chemical, industrial, and scientific porcelain products, the company introduced a line of household cooking ware known as "Thermo-Porcelain." Six dinnerware lines, Coorado, Golden Ivory, Golden Rainbow, Mello–Tone, Rock-Mount, and Rosebud Cook–N–Serve were added in the 1930s. Dinnerware production ceased in 1941. Although the company produced some utilitarian ware such as ashtrays, ovenware, and teapots after the war, it never resumed its dinnerware production.

References: Carol and Jim Carlton, *Collector's Encyclopedia of Colorado Pottery*, Collector Books, 1994; Robert H. Schneider, *Coors Rosebud Pottery*, published by author, 1984, 1996 value update.

Newsletter: *Coors Pottery Newsletter*, 3808 Carr Place N, Seattle, WA 98103.

Hawthorne, cake knife **$75.00**
Hawthorne, Custard 35.00
Hawthorne, pitcher, cov 95.00
Mello–Tone, baker, 8" d 20.00
Mello–Tone, casserole, 2³/₄ pt, 8" d 35.00
Mello–Tone, cup and saucer 15.00
Mello–Tone, custard 10.00
Mello–Tone, fruit bowl, 5¹/₂" d 6.00
Mello–Tone, plate, 5¹/₄" d 4.00
Mello–Tone, platter, 12" d 20.00
Mello–Tone, sugar shaker 65.00
Mello–Tone, tumbler 35.00
Mello–Tone, water server 150.00
Open Window, cake plate 55.00
Open Window, french casserole 95.00
Rock–Mount, baker, cov, 1²/₃ pt 25.00
Rock–Mount, cereal bowl, 6¹/₄" d 7.00
Rock–Mount, gravy boat 45.00
Rock–Mount, plate, 6¹/₄" d 4.00
Rock–Mount, salt and pepper shakers, pr 15.00
Rock–Mount, sugar 15.00
Rock–Mount, teapot, 6 cup 55.00
Rosebud, baker, oval, shallow, orange, 11¹/₄" 35.00
Rosebud, bowl, handled, blue, small 125.00
Rosebud, creamer, green 50.00
Rosebud, cup, blue 6.00
Rosebud, dinner plate, blue, 9¹/₄" d 20.00
Rosebud, dinner plate, rose, 9¹/₄" d 15.00
Rosebud, honey pot, cov, yellow 225.00
Rosebud, rim soup, maroon 40.00
Rosebud, saucer, orange 9.00
Rosebud, shaker, tapered, green, small glaze crack, 4¹/₂" 10.00
Rosebud, shirred egg, green 20.00
Rosebud, soup bowl, blue, small nick, 8" d 12.00
Rosebud, soup bowl, rose, 8" 25.00
Rosebud, water server, white 250.00
Tulip, casserole, cov, metal holder 130.00
Tulip, pie plate, metal holder 75.00
Tulip, pudding, cov, small 60.00
Tulip, teapot 110.00

COUNTER CULTURE

Counter cultural collectibles are the artifacts left behind by the Beatnik and Hippie culture of the 1960s. These range from concert posters to a wealth of pinback "social cause" buttons.

Some collectors prefer to designate this material as psychedelic collectibles. However, the psychedelic movement was only one aspect of the much broader Counter Culture environment.

Belt Buckle, brass, Peace sign, 2½ x 3"................ **$20.00**
Book Bag, canvas, brown and black peace sign, inscription "Blessed Are The Peacemakers" one one side, 14" sq.. **20.00**
Book, *Steal This Book*, Abbe Hoffman, c1971, Private Editions, NY...................................... **35.00**
Book, *Woodstock 69*, Joseph J Sia, 1970, Scholastic Book Services, 124 pgs............................ **25.00**
Clock, peace symbol face, Westclox, 6½" d.......... **125.00**
Jigsaw Puzzle, Peace, A Committed Jigsaw Puzzle, ©1969 American Publishing Corp, 5½" h unopened can.. **25.00**
Pin, "LO" above "VE" to spell LOVE, sterling silver........ **45.00**
Pinback Button, "Draft Beer Not Students," hand holding beer mug.. **5.00**
Pinback Button, "Kent 25," lettering in 2 shades of red, black outline, yellow ground, "For Kent Legal Defense Fund" on curl...................................... **45.00**
Pinback Button, "Make Love Not War," red, white, and blue, 3½" d.. **35.00**
Pinback Button, "Our Flag, Our Future, Join the New Action Army," dripping American flag with peace symbol raining down on soldier and Vietnamese prisoner, 22 x 23"................................ **60.00**
Pinback Button, "Stop The Bombing! Out Now!," bomber silhouette and target design over faces of Vietnamese woman and child, National Peace Action Coalition initials.................................. **10.00**
Pinback Button, "United We Stand/Divided We Fall," black and white hand under flag with peace symbol, blue lettering, white ground, c1970................ **20.00**
Pinback Button, "Woodstock Anarchist Party," black flag on red ground, c1970............................ **10.00**
Poster, "Peace Now," boy walking in rain under umbrella, 22 x 29", 1968.................................. **45.00**
Poster, "Suppose They Gave A War And Nobody Came," silk–screen black light, letters in text spell "Peace," 22 x 30".. **45.00**
Poster, Woodstock, white dove of peace on red ground, 24 x 36".. **425.00**
Sticker, "Peace"..................................... **2.50**
T–Shirt, cotton, light blue, "Out Now!" on silk–screened peace dove symbol, size extra large, late 60s, early 70s.. **20.00**

COUNTRY WESTERN

This category is primarily record driven—mainly due to the lack of products licensed by members of the Country Western community. There is not a great deal to collect.

Country Western autographed material, other paper ephemera, and costumes have attracted some collectors. Although fan clubs exist for every major singer, few stress the collecting of personal memorabilia.

References: Fred Heggeness, *Goldmine Country Western Record & CD Price Guide*, Krause Publications, 1996; Jerry Osborne, *The Official Price Guide to Country Music Records*, House of Collectibles, 1996.

Newsletter: *Disc Collector*, PO Box 315, Cheswold, DE 19936.

Autograph, Chet Atkins, sgd and dated 1956, 6 x 7"....... **$20.00**
Autograph, Charlie Pride, PS............................ **12.00**
Doll, Dolly Parton, vinyl head, plastic body, jointed, painted eyes, orig gown, mkd "Dolly Parton/Eegee Co/Hong Kong" on back of head, "Goldberger Mfg Co" on back, Eegee, 12" h.......................... **40.00**
Game, Hee Haw, Dooley Fant, Inc, 1975................. **15.00**
Greeting Card, Loretta Lynn, sgd and inscribed............ **12.00**
Letter, Will Carter, typewritten, sgd, c1975.............. **8.00**
Magazine, *Country Music, Country Song Roundup*, Feb 1966, 34 pgs, 9 x 12"............................. **8.00**
Paper Dolls, Hee Haw, Saalfield, #5139, 1971.......... **12.00**
Photograph, Rex Allen, black and white, glossy, sgd, 8 x 10".. **15.00**
Postcard, Cliff Carlisle photo.......................... **4.00**
Poster, Dolly Parton, *Nine to Five*, 20th Century, 1980...... **10.00**
Poster, Loretta Lynn, *Coal Miner's Daughter*, Universal, 1979.. **10.00**
Record, *The Best of Willie Nelson*, Willie Nelson, LP, 1973.. **15.00**
Record, *Dumb Blonde*, Dolly Parton, 45 rpm, 1967...... **10.00**
Record, *Howdee*, Minnie Pearl, LP, 1963.............. **40.00**
Record, *I Walk the Line*, Johnny Cash, LP, soundtrack, Columbia, 1970.................................. **20.00**
Record, Old Betsy, Tex Williams, 45 rpm, Decca.......... **10.00**
Record, *Stars of the Grand Ole Opry*, boxed LP set, RCA Victor, 1967...................................... **30.00**
Record, T V Blues, Grandpa Jones, 78 rpm, 1951........ **18.00**
Record Jacket, Grandpa Jones, LP, sgd................. **35.00**
Record Jacket, Tex Ritter, 78 rpm, double album, sgd, 1946.. **135.00**
Sheet Music, *You're Only a Star*, Gene Autry.............. **4.00**
Songbook Album, Flatt & Scruggs, Hillbilly Park, Newark, OH, sgd by band, July 28, 1963............ **50.00**

Sheet Music, Roy Rogers, *Along The Navajo Trail*, 1942–45, $15.00.

COWAN POTTERY

R. Guy Cowan's first pottery, operating between 1912 and 1917, was located on Nicholson Avenue in Lakewood, Ohio, a Cleveland suburb. When he experienced problems with his gas supply, he moved his operations to Rocky River. The move also resulted in a production switch from a red clay ceramic body to a high–fired porcelain one.

By the mid–1920s Cowan manufactured a number of commercial products including dinnerware, desk sets, and planters. In addition, he made art pottery. In 1931, just a year after establishing an artists' colony, Cowan ceased operations, one of the many victims of the Great Depression.

References: Mark Bassett and Victoria Naumann, *Cowan Pottery and the Cleveland School*, Schiffer Publishing; Tim and Jamie Saloff, *The Collector's Encyclopedia of Cowan Pottery: Identification & Values*, Collector Books, 1994, out of print.

Ashtray, figural ram, 3¼ x 5¼"	**$130.00**
Bookends, pr, elephant, shape #E–2	**400.00**
Bookends, pr, figural boy and girl, matte ivory glaze, imp mark, 6½ x 4 x 3"	**375.00**
Bookends, pr, sunbonnet girl, shape #521, 7½" h	**130.00**
Bookends, pr, unicorn, shape #961, 7" h	**400.00**
Bowl, #B5C, oriental red, custom metal frame	**200.00**
Candelabra, 2 nudes, 8" h	**300.00**
Candlesticks, pr, #734, 1926, 4" h	**30.00**
Decanter, figural Queen of Hearts, cork stopper, crystalline Chinese red glaze, stamp mark, 12 x 4½"	**500.00**
Dessert Cup, set of 4, Colonial shape	**80.00**
Figure, Art Deco, Russian peasant playing tambourine, beige crackled glaze, die stamped, artist sgd, 9½ x 7"	**600.00**
Figure, dancing girl, flower frog base with waves, glossy white glaze, imp mark, 12 x 6 x 3¾"	**850.00**
Figure, nude in contrapposto, flower frog lotus base, glossy white glaze, imp mark, 9 x 4"	**650.00**
Figure, pr, Spanish dancers, polychrome glaze, imp mark, 9 x 6½ x 2"	**2,300.00**
Flower Frog, figural nude, sitting on tree stump, white crackled glaze, imp mark, 14½ x 6"	**2,700.00**

Jar, cov, melon ribbed, blue–green crystalline glaze, imp mark, 5¾ x 5", $220.00. Photo courtesy David Rago Auctions.

Flower Frog, figural·partially clad woman, glossy ivory glaze, imp lozenge mark, paper label, 10 x 4½"	**425.00**
Ginger Jar, cov, shape #584, blue glaze, 10" h	**200.00**
Lamp, figural Aztec base, 13" h	**400.00**
Match Holder, duck, shape #774, 1928, 3½" l	**50.00**
Nut Dish, figural bird, shape #768, 3½" h	**50.00**
Plate, hunting motif	**400.00**
Plate, polo motif, shape #X–48, 11¼" d	**500.00**
Strawberry Jar, shape #SJ–1, 7¾" h	**130.00**
Teapot, cov, Colonial shape, 6" h	**50.00**
Trivet, shape #X–18, 1931, 9¼" d	**100.00**
Urn, cov, shape #V–88, 1930, 13¼" h	**100.00**
Vase, fan, seahorse dec, shape #715–B	**45.00**
Vase, fluted, shape #673, 11¾" h	**125.00**
Vase, squirrel motif, shape #V–19, 8¼" h	**700.00**
Vessel, lustered gray, yellow drip, stamped ink mark, 13 x 5¼" h	**750.00**

COWBOY HEROES

Cowboy Heroes are divided into eight major categories: (1) silent movie cowboys, (2) "B" movie cowboys, (3) "A" movie cowboys, (4) 1950s' and 60s' TV cowboy heroes, (5) Gene Autry, (6) Hopalong Cassidy, (7) The Lone Ranger, and (8) Roy Rogers.

Silent movie cowboys are in the final stages of the last memory roundup. "B" movie cowboys, comprising individuals such as Buck Jones, Ken Maynard, and Tim McCoy, are just down the trail. Reruns of the old "B" westerns have all but disappeared from television—out of sight, out of mind. "A" movie cowboys such as Clint Eastwood and John Wayne have cult followers, but never achieved the popularity of Gene, Hoppy, or Roy.

Currently the market is strong for 1950s' and 60s' television cowboy heroes. The generations that watched the initial runs of Bonanza, Gunsmoke, Paladin, Rawhide, The Rifleman, and Wagon Train are at their peak earning capacities and willing to pay top dollar to buy back their childhood. Prices for common 1950s material have been stable for the past few years.

Gene, Hoppy, The Lone Ranger, and Roy are in a class by themselves. Currently, Hoppy collectibles are the hottest of the four with Roy close behind. Gene and The Lone Ranger are starting to eat dust. Look for a major collecting shift involving the collectibles of these four individuals in the next ten years.

References: Joseph J. Caro, *Hopalong Cassidy Collectibles*, Cowboy Collector Publications, 1997; Lee Felbinger, *The Lone Ranger: Collector's Reference & Value Guide*, Collector Books, 1997; Ted Hake, *Hake's Guide to Cowboy Character Collectibles: An Illustrated Price Guide Covering 50 Years of Movie & TV Cowboy Heroes*, Wallace–Homestead, Krause Publications, 1994; Robert Heide and John Gilman, *Box–Office Buckaroos*, Abbeville Press, 1989; Robert W. Philips, *Roy Rogers: A Biography, Radio History, Television Career Chronicle, Discography, Filmography, Comicography, Merchandising and Advertising History, Collectibles Description, Bibliography and Index*, McFarland & Co, 1995; Harry L. Rinker, *Hopalong Cassidy: King of the Cowboy Merchandisers*, Schiffer Publishing, 1995.

Newsletter: *The Cowboy Collector Newsletter*, PO Box 7486, Long Beach, CA 90807.

Collectors' Club: Westerns & Serials Fan Club, Rte 1, Box 103, Vernon Center, MN 56090.

Note: For information on fan clubs for individual cowboy heroes, refer to *Maloney's Antiques & Collectibles Resource Directory* by David J. Maloney, Jr., published by Antique Trader Books.

Gene Autry, badge, celluloid, "Official Gene Autry Club," center portrait, black, white, and orange, c1940, 1¼" d **$65.00**

Gene Autry, cowgirl outfit, orig box **85.00**

Gene Autry, comic book, Gene Autry Comics, Vol 1, #20, Dell, Oct 1948 .... **18.00**

Gene Autry, pinback button, "Gene Autry's Brand/ Sunbeam Bread," black and white photo, dark blue ground, 1¼" d........................... **35.00**

Gene Autry, sheet music, *No Letter Today*, blue and white cov photo, ©1943, 9 x 12" **12.00**

Buffalo Bill Cody, figure, syroco–type composition and wood, "Buffalo Bill" and 1941 maker's copyright inscribed on base, 6" h **65.00**

Buffalo Bill Cody, pinback button, litho, Cody on horse behind buffalo, black, white, tan, and dark red, Van Brode America Series, #1, biography on back paper, c1950, 1⅜" d **20.00**

Cisco Kid, picture card, stiff paper, glossy black and white photo, facsimile signature, red and white Wards Tip–Top Bread adv on reverse, early 1950s, 3½ x 5½" **20.00**

Cisco Kid, program, souvenir, "Cisco Kid Rodeo," stiff paper folder, glossy, Wrigley Field, Chicago, dated mid–July, 1950s, 8½ x 11" **25.00**

Cisco Kid, tab, litho tin, "Pancho/Weber's Bread/Cisco Kid," red, white, and blue, Pancho wearing bright green hat, 1950s **20.00**

Wyat Earp, Color and Stencil Set, Hugh O'Brian, MIB...... **135.00**

Wyatt Earp, statue, Hartland **35.00**

Hopalong Cassidy, belt, black leather, silver "Hopalong" between metal rivets and stars on center back, early 1950s, 30" l **35.00**

Hopalong Cassidy, camera, metal, box style, black, illus of Hoppy on topper on title plate, Galter Products of Chicago, ©1940 William Boyd, 3 x 4 x 5" **90.00**

Hopalong Cassidy, coloring kit, orig box **30.00**

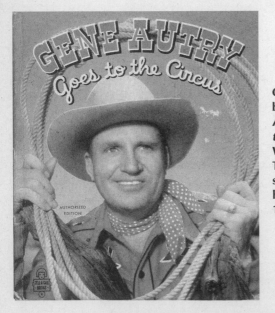

Gene Autry, book, *Gene Autry Goes to the Circus*, Whitman Tell–A–Tale series, 28 pp, hard cov, 1950, $22.00.

Hopalong Cassidy, display, Butter–Nut Bread, figural bread loaf **75.00**

Hopalong Cassidy, doll, cloth, molded vinyl child's face stitched to fabric head, plush hair and chaps, removable black felt hat, yellow hat band inscribed "Hopalong Cassidy," early 1950s, 22" h **190.00**

Hopalong Cassidy, game, Hopalong Cassidy Game, Milton Bradley, 1950 .... **60.00**

Hopalong Cassidy, knife and scabbard, miniature, black vinyl belt loop sheath, "Hopalong Cassidy" inscription, 4" l single blade knife, white plastic handle, mkd "USA," early 1950s **60.00**

Hopalong Cassidy, party plates, set of 6, cardboard, multicolored Hoppy on topper, white ground, orig cellophane shrink wrap, unopened................ **20.00**

Hopalong Cassidy, popcorn pin, litho, bright colors, Hoppy portrait, 5" h **30.00**

Hopalong Cassidy, radio, red and silver, Arvin **125.00**

Hopalong Cassidy, record, *Square Dance Hold Up*, LP, set of 2 .... **75.00**

Hopalong Cassidy, waste can....................... **95.00**

Hopalong Cassidy, woodburning kit, orig box........... **200.00**

Davy Crockett, archery set, 46" strung wood bow, 7 feathered wood arrows, paper target sheet, Rollin Wilson Co, orig box, 1950s **45.00**

Davy Crockett, belt buckle, silvered metal, rounded, raised border, Old Betsy rifle, inscription, brown leather belt, simulated alligator texture, 1½ x 3" **35.00**

Davy Crockett, clock, pendulum, MIB **125.00**

Davy Crockett, clothing, complete outfit, orig box **100.00**

Davy Crockett, coonskin cap, simulated brown fur, brown vinyl crown insert with dark gold Crockett image, brim with stapled price tag, unused............ **35.00**

Davy Crockett, glass, white, frosted, brown portrait both sides, Ritchey's Milk, mid–1950s, 5" h **35.00**

Davy Crockett, gun, plastic, flintlock, brown, silver accents, gold "Davy Crockett" lettering on side, raised pirate ship on handle, c1955, 10½" l **30.00**

Davy Crockett, hat, straw........................ **30.00**

Davy Crockett, lunch box, steel, full color illus, silver gray ground, green trim, American Thermos, 1955–56..... **90.00**

Davy Crockett, planter, souvenir, china, figural young Davy, bear, tree stump, inscribed "Davy Crockett Birthplace/Limestone Tenn" in gold on back of tree stump, c1950, 3½ x 6 x 5"..................... **25.00**

Davy Crockett, playset, Davy Crockett At the Alamo, Marx, late 1950s **600.00**

Davy Crockett, ring, plastic **20.00**

Davy Crockett, Thermos, steel, color illus on sides, plastic cap, American Thermos, c1955–56, 8½" h........... **40.00**

Lone Ranger, flashlight, signal siren **65.00**

Lone Ranger, game, The Lone Ranger Game, 18½" sq board, 4 colored metal rearing horses, 2 red plastic markers, 8 metal markers, Parker Brothers, 1938, orig 5 x 7½" box **60.00**

Lone Ranger, mask, molded black fabric, starched, elastic head string, 1950s, 3½ x 6½" **25.00**

Lone Ranger, model, Tonto, #183, plastic, 8–pp comic book, instructions, backdrop mural, ©1974 Aurora Products Corp, unopened **35.00**

Lone Ranger, palm puzzle, litho tin frame, checkerboard design, full color Lone Ranger scene, 4 small metal balls, clear glass cov, "Guard Gold Panners" series, #5, c1940, ½ x 3½ x 5"........................ **25.00**

Hopalong Cassidy, binoculars, Galter Products Co, Chicago, IL, Hoppy and Topper decals on black ground, $35.00.

Lone Ranger, pinback button, "Lone Ranger Silver Bullet Award," celluloid, center bullet, red, white, and blue, red inscription on silver ribbon, issued by Lone Ranger Family Restaurants, c1970, 2¼" d **25.00**

Lone Ranger, ring, Six Shooter **125.00**

Lone Ranger, token, premium, "The Lone Ranger Seventeenth Anniversary 1933–1950," silvered brass, Lone Ranger and Tonto on reverse, inscribed "The Lone Ranger Lucky Piece," 1¼" d **30.00**

Ken Maynard, cigar band, diecut, black and white photo, emb, red, gold, and black design, 1930s, 1 x 3". . . . **20.00**

Ken Maynard, lobby card, red, white, blue, flesh, and brown, Universal, 1933, 14 x 22". **50.00**

Red Ryder, belt buckle, silvered brass, cowboy on bron-co, name spelled twice in rope script, 1940s, 2" sq **35.00**

Red Ryder, gloves, child's, black, white gauntlet, fringed, black title and illus, early 1940s. **40.00**

Red Ryder, Little Beaver Archery Set, cardboard target, 1951. . . . . **35.00**

Red Ryder, pop gun, double barrel, Daisy, 1950s **75.00**

Rin Tin Tin, canteen, Nabisco premium, plastic, textured, black cap, brown vinyl carrying strap, "Official Rin Tin Tin 101st Cavalry" raised inscription, ©1955 Screen Gems Inc, orig box, 7" h **70.00**

Rin Tin Tin, game, The Adventures of Rin Tin Tin, Transogram, 1955 . . . . **40.00**

Rin Tin Tin, playset, Rin Tin Tin at Fort Apache, #3627, 2½" h plastic figures, tin fort, Marx, 1950s, orig box, unused **450.00**

Rin Tin Tin, ring, brass, raised portrait, 2 ink pads under hinged lid, c1930 . . . . **85.00**

Roy Rogers & Dale Evans, action figure, Dale Evans and Buttermilk, Hartland Plastics, 8" h **130.00**

Roy Rogers & Dale Evans, badge, tin, star, silver finish, "Roy Rogers/Deputy," 1950s **35.00**

Roy Rogers & Dale Evans, bank, figural horseshoe, metal and plastic, wall mount, Roy Rogers and Trigger Savings Bank. **85.00**

Roy Rogers & Dale Evans, book, *Favorite Western Stories*, orig box **95.00**

Roy Rogers & Dale Evans, charm bracelet, silver link, 4 black and white photos in clear plastic disks, Roy in one disk, other stars in remaining disks, c1950, 6" l **60.00**

Roy Rogers & Dale Evans, comic book, Roy Rogers Comics, Vol 1, #17, Dell, file copy issue, May 1949 . . . . . . **80.00**

Roy Rogers & Dale Evans, harmonica, white plastic and silvered metal, Roy Rogers' Riders, "Good Luck" and "King of the Cowboys" on engraved paltes, 1950s, 4½" l **40.00**

Roy Rogers & Dale Evans, hat, felt, black, inscribed "Queen Of The West" **55.00**

Roy Rogers & Dale Evans, holster, cartridge belt, rhine-stone dec **65.00**

Roy Rogers & Dale Evans, neckerchief, gold synthetic, Roy portrait printed on ends, rope script name, 1950, 5½ x 35". **55.00**

Roy Rogers & Dale Evans, playing cards, complete deck **55.00**

Roy Rogers & Dale Evans, playset, Roy Rogers Fix–It Chuckwagon and Jeep, Ideal, plastic, orig box **125.00**

Roy Rogers & Dale Evans, thermos, litho metal, Double R Bar Ranch, red plastic cap, 1950s, 8½" h **35.00**

Tom Mix, bar pin, premium, "Tom Mix Sharpshooters Award," heckerboard fabric, white plastic dayglow horseshoe hanger, c1945 . . . . **100.00**

Tom Mix, cereal bowl, china, white, "Hot Ralston Cereal For Straight Shooters" illus and inscription repeated around rim, checkerboard and T–M Bar Ranch symbol int, ©1982 Ralston Purina, 5½" d **35.00**

Tom Mix, comic book, Ralston premium, #3, Jan 1941 . . . . . **60.00**

Tom Mix, compass, Straight Shooter, Ralston **65.00**

Tom Mix, dixie lid, brown and white, photo, "Miracle Rider" rim inscription, 1935, 2¼" d **25.00**

Tom Mix, manual, Ralston premium, *Life of Tom Mix*, revised 1st ed, 24 pp, orig envelope, 1933, 5 x 7". **75.00**

Tom Mix, sheet music, *The Old Spinning Wheel*, Straight Shooters cov photo, ©1933 . . . . **30.00**

Tom Mix, tobacco card, Orami cigarettes pack insert, black and white photo, #350, series D, Germany, c1930, 1½ x 2" **10.00**

John Wayne, arcade card, 1950s **2.00**

John Wayne, lobby card, *Blood Alley*, John Wayne and Lauren Bacall, Warner Brothers, 1955 . . . . **25.00**

John Wayne, mug, china, "Good Luck" signature, blue, gray, black, and yellow design, stamped "Ketchum Originals" on base, *McQ* movie issue, 3¼" h **30.00**

Roy Rogers, frame tray puzzle, Frontiers, Inc, 1952, $18.00.

John Wayne, poster, *Rooster Cogburn*. **40.00**
John Wayne, tablet, color photo and facsimile signature
   on cov, c1950, 5¹/₂ x 9" **30.00**
Wild Bill Hickok, Breakfast Game Score Card, Kellogg's
   cereal boxes and messages from Guy Madison and
   Andy Devine on front, mid–1950s, 8 x 10". **25.00**
Wild Bill Hickok, game, Wild Bill Hickok's The Calvary
   and The Indian Game, Built–Rite **50.00**
Wild Bill Hickok, pinback button, "Wild Bill Hickok,"
   brown photo, pink ground, 1950s, ⁷/₈" d **20.00**

COW COLLECTIBLES

Cow collectors came in from the pasture in the late 1980s, the result of a shift in decorating motif preferences from ducks to cows in Country magazines.

The category is completely image driven. Few collect only a specific breed. Contemporary items are just as popular and desirable as are vintage examples.

Collectors' Club: Cow Observers Worldwide, 240 Wahl Ave, Evans City, PA 16033.

Bank, tin, Press My Tail Moo Cow, c1940. . . . . **$35.00**
Booklet, Trip to the Moon, Elsie, 1950s **15.00**
Box, Enterprise Butter, 2 cows illus, 1952, 2¹/₂ x 2¹/₂ x
   4¹/₂" **3.00**
Box, Greer's Moo Girl Creamery Butter, Sutherland
   Paper Co, Kalamazoo, MI, 1925, 1 lb. **3.50**
Box, Pine Grove Dairy, Cow Butter, cows in pasture,
   1940s, 2¹/₂ x 2¹/₂ x 5". **3.00**
Coloring Book, Elsie, 1957 . . . . **15.00**
Cookie Cutter, tin, missing handle, 4¹/₂" l **5.00**
Cookie Jar, figural Elsie bust, barrel shaped, Pottery
   Guild, 11¹/₂" h. **225.00**
Doll, Elsie, plush, 12" h. **40.00**
Envelope, grazing cows, DeLaval Cream Separator adv,
   1932. . . . . **35.00**
Game, Elsie, Selchow Righter, 1941. . . . . **70.00**

Sign, Spring Valley Dairy, painted metal, green and black on white ground, 12" h, 18" w, $154.00. Photo courtesy Collectors Auction Services.

Glass, Aunt Elsie, brown illus, 1930–40, 3¹/₂" h. **25.00**
Milk Bottle, Hillcrest Farms, cow illus, ¹/₂ pt **15.00**
Pinback Button, Ayshires, US outline background, stand-
   ing cow, maroon and white, 1940s. **15.00**
Pinback Button, Guernsey's Rich Inheritance, yellow,
   brown, and white, 1930–40 . . . . **18.00**
Sheet Music, *Cowbelles*, 1922. . . . . **5.00**
Sugar, figural Elmer, china, 1930–40 . . . . **40.00**
Thermometer, wood, Socony Vacuum Sanilac Cattle
   Spray, 1920s, 19" h **100.00**
Toy, cow, Fisher–Price, #132 . . . . **20.00**
Toy, Milky the Marvelous Milking Cow, plastic, Kenner,
   ©1977 General Mills Fun Group, orig box, unused. **45.00**
Toy, Walking Cow, windup, plush, built–in key, movable
   head, walks forward, mooing sound, orig box, TN,
   Japan, 1960s. **775.00**

CRACKER JACK

Cracker Jack arrived on the scene at the 1893 World's Columbian Exposition in Chicago when F. W. Rueckhaim, a pop store owner, introduced his world famous mixture of popcorn, peanuts, and molasses. The mix was not called "Cracker Jack" until three years later. The 1908 song, *Take Me Out to the Ball Game*, created national recognition for Cracker Jack.

The first prize in the box appeared in 1912. In the past 85 years plus, over 10,000 different prizes have made an appearance. New examples are being discovered every year. Today's prizes, with the exception of the magnifying glass, are made primarily from paper. The Borden Company, owner of Cracker Jack, buys prizes in lots of 25 million and keeps several hundred in circulation at one time.

References: Ravi Piña, *Cracker Jack Collectibles*, Schiffer Publishing, 1995; Larry White, *Cracker Jack Toys*, Schiffer Publishing, 1997.

Collectors' Club: Cracker Jack Collector's Assoc, 108 Central St, Rowley, MA 01969.

Badge, cast metal, 6 point star, silver, 1931 . . . . **$35.00**
Baseball Card, set of 2, full color photo, #6 Mickey
   Mantle, #13 Willie Mays, ©Borden, Inc and Topps
   Chewing Gum, 1982. . . . . **20.00**
Bird, plastic, green **7.00**
Book, *Birds We Know*, miniature **45.00**
Booklet, Cracker Jack Riddles, Rueckheim Bros &
   Eckstein, black and white illus, 40 pgs **25.00**
Bookmark, litho tin, diecut, brown Spaniel, c1930, 2¹/₂" l **20.00**
Coin, aluminum, emb, "Honest Old Abe," "The Great
   Emancipator," and "Join Cracker Jack Mystery Club"
   on reverse. **5.00**
Corn Popper, 14" handle, c1930 . . . . **60.00**
Disguise Glasses, paper, hinged, with eyeballs, 1933 . . . . **6.00**
Figurine, Smitty, stand–up, litho tin, diecut, 1930s, 1¹/₃" h **45.00**
Game, Cracker Jack Toy Surprise Game, Milton Bradley,
   1976. . . . . **22.00**
Iron–On Transfer, patriotic figure, 1939 . . . . **32.00**
Lapel Stud, oval, dark finish white metal, Sailor Jack and
   dog raised illus, inscribed "Me For Cracker Jack,"
   c1930. . . . . **35.00**
Magnifying Glass, swing–out clear plastic loop lens,
   green plastic case, c1960. . . . . **8.00**
Mask, "Cracker Jack" on front, c1960, 8¹/₂ x 10". **15.00**

Top, litho tin, 1930s, $18.00.

Plate, tin, silvered, c1930, 1¾" d 35.00
Premium, baseball bat 95.00
Puzzle, 2 pc, wire nail, 1940s 20.00
Radio, plastic, Borden Co, c1970 . . . . 45.00
Rocket, metal, litho, red, white, and blue 20.00
Rocking Horse, figural, cast metal 8.00
Sand Picture, cardboard, c1930 . . . . 45.00
Sign, full color, diecut, girl, dog, and product, 1930s,
   7 x 11" 300.00
Sled, silvered tin, mkd, c1930s, 2" l 35.00
Spinner Top, litho tin, red, white, and blue, 1930s 50.00
Toy, lion in cage, litho tin, diecut, inscribed "Cracker
   Jack Shows" on roof, late 1930s 60.00
Whistle, tin, mkd "Cracker Jack," c1930 . . . . 25.00

CRACKLE GLASS

Crackle glass, a glass–making technique that results in a multiple–fractured surface appearance, dates back to the 16th century. Martin Bach of Durand Glass is credited with reintroducing the concept in the late 1920s.

Crackle glass achieved widespread popularity in the late 1930s and was produced into the 1970s. Over 500 glass companies made crackle glass. Bischoff Glass, Blenko Glass, Hamon Glass, Kanawha Glass, Pilgrim Glass, Rainbow Art Glass, and Vogelsong Glass are just a few.

References: Judy Alford, *Collecting Crackle Glass*, Schiffer Publishing, 1997; Stan and Arlene Weitman, *Crackle Glass: Identification and Value Guide* (1996), *Book II* (1997), Collector Books.

Collectors' Club: Collectors of Crackle Glass, PO Box 1186, Massapequa, NY 11758.

Beaker, crystal, olive green leaves, Blenko, 9½" h $100.00
Bud Vase, amberina, Kanawha label, 7¾"" h 65.00
Bud Vase, orange, 8" h 40.00
Candlestick, apricot, 10½" h 50.00
Candy Dish, amberina, Kanawha, 3" h 40.00
Creamer, emerald green, drop over handle, Pilgrim, 3¾" h . . . 30.00
Cruet, amberina, pulled back handle, Rainbow, 6½" h 45.00

Cruet, sea green, Pilgrim, 6" h 40.00
Cup, light sea green, drop over handle, 2½" h 25.00
Decanter, amberina, Blenko, 1970, 8½" h, price for pair **150.00**
Decanter, charcoal, blue tint, Blenko, 11¾" h 75.00
Glass, topaz, 6¾" h 35.00
Goblet, olive green, 5¾" h 50.00
Jug, amberina, drop over handle, Blenko, 8¼" h 80.00
Jug, dark blue, drop over handle, 6" h 50.00
Ladle, crystal, amethyst hook handle, Blenko, 15" l 150.00
Liqeur Glass, topaz, drop over handle, Pilgrim, 4" h 40.00
Miniature Jug, blue, drop over handle, Pilgrim, 4" h 30.00
Miniature Jug, teal green, drop over handle, Pilgrim, 4" h 30.00
Miniature Pitcher, lemon lime, drop over handle,
   Pilgrim, 3¾" h 25.00
Miniature Pitcher, olive green, drop over handle,
   Pilgrim, 3¼" h 30.00
Miniature Pitcher, tangerine, pulled back handle,
   Pilgrim, 3¾" h 30.00
Pitcher, crystal, drop over handle, 12¼" h 75.00
Pitcher, Tangerine, drop over handle, Blenko, 13¼" h 100.00
Syrup Pitcher, blue, pulled back handle, Kanawha, 6" h 50.00
Vase, blue, Pilgrim, 5" h 45.00
Vase, crystal, rosettes, Blenko, 7" h 75.00
Vase, crystal, Blenko, 8" h 100.00
Vase, double neck, olive green, Blenko, 4" h 50.00
Vase, ftd, crimped top, jonquil, Blenko, 7¼" h 100.00
Vase, smoke gray, 5½" h 60.00
Wine Bottle, figural fish, topaz, green eyes, 15" l 75.00

CREDIT CARDS & TOKENS

The charge coin, the forerunner of the credit card, first appeared in the 1890s. Each coin had a different identification number. Charge coins were made in a variety of materials from celluloid to German silver and came in two basic shapes, geometric and diecut. The form survived until the late 1950s.

Metal charge plates, similar to a G.I.'s dog tag, were issued from the 1930s through the 1950s. Paper charge cards also were used. Lamination of the cards to prolong use began in the 1940s.

The plastic credit card arrived on the scene in the late 1950s.

In the 1980s pictorial credit cards became popular. Individuals applied for credit just to get the card. The inclusion of holigrams on the card for security purposes also was introduced during the 1980s. Today institutions from airlines to universities issue credit cards, many of which feature a bonus program. Little wonder America has such a heavy credit card debt.

Reference: Lin Overholt, *The First International Credit Card Catalog, 3rd Edition*, published by author, 1995.

Newsletter: *Credit Cards & Phone Cards News*, PO Box 8481, St Petersburg, FL 33738.

Collectors' Clubs: Active Token Collectors Organization, PO Box 1573, Sioux Falls, SD 57101; American Credit Card Collectors Society, PO Box 2465, Midland, MI 48640; American Vecturist Assoc, PO Box 1204, Boston, MA 02104; Token & Medal Society, Inc, 9230 SW 59th St, Miami, FL 33173.

CARDS

Air Travel, 1981 . . . . $5.00
American Airlines, Mar 1986 . . . . 6.00

American Express, "The Executive Money Card, gold,
  card changes color when rotated, 1972 . . . . **50.00**
ARCO, Atlantic Richfield Co, 1976 . . . . **4.00**
Bank Americard, account number in tan area. **15.00**
Bell System, high gloss paperboard, dime holder, 1964. . . . . . **15.00**
Carte Blanche, gold, blue on gold, 1973 . . . . **40.00**
Carte Blanche, blue on white, gold border **7.50**
Champlin, "A great name in the Great Plains," gas pump
  island drawing, 1967. . . . . **12.00**
Chevron National, attendants servicing car, 1967 . . . . **20.00**
Choice, 1984 . . . . **4.00**
Diners Club, colored blocks, blue top, 1967 . . . . **45.00**
Diners Club, red top, expires Nov 30, 1962 . . . . **55.00**
Eastern, Oct 1984 . . . . **7.50**
Esso, "Happy Motoring," waving attendant, 1966 . . . . **15.00**
Frederick's of Hollywood, "Fabulous Hollywood
  Fashions" **17.50**
Goodyear, blimp illus **7.50**
Hotels Statler, paperboard, 1952 . . . . **45.00**
International Credit Card, sailing ship log, 1960 . . . . **30.00**
Macy's, "It's smart to be thrifty," red star **5.00**
Mastercard, pre–hologram, cardholder photo on back **6.00**
Mastercharge, cardholder photo on back, early 1970s **60.00**
Neiman Marcus, commemorative, 75th anniversary **15.00**
Playboy Club International, gold, Jan 1979. . . . . **6.00**
Uni–Card, 1970s. **10.00**
Zollinger Harned, Allentown, red on white. **10.00**

TOKENS

Abraham & Strauss, A & S, hat shaped **$15.00**
Chemin De Fer Club, France, silver, 1930s. **18.00**
Conrad's, Boston, MA, round, irregular, gold plated, pic-
  ture of store. **25.00**
Knights of the Golden Eagle, Washington, brass **20.00**
McDonald's, Redwood City and Menlo Park, wooden,
  50 cent, white metal **12.50**
Pay Toilet, American Sanitation Lock Co **3.00**
Pocahontas Pioneer Garage, Philadelphia, oval, white
  metal, Indian profile in high relief **18.00**
Nathan Snellenberg, NS & Co, round, irregular **10.00**
Strawbridge & Clothier, arrowhead shaped. **20.00**
R H White, Boston, MA, pear shaped, white metal, inter-
  locking script **20.00**

CROOKSVILLE POTTERY

Founded in 1912, the Crooksville Pottery, Crooksville, Ohio, made
semi–porcelain dinnerwares and utilitarian household pottery.
Their decal decorated "Pantry–Bak–In" line was extremely popular
in the 1930s and 40s.

The company's semi–porcelain dinnerware line was marketed as
Stinhal China. Most pieces are not marked with a pattern name.
Check the reference books. The company ceased operations in
1959, a victim of cheap foreign imports and the popularity of
melamine plastic dinnerware.

References: Harvey Duke, *The Official Price Guide to Pottery and
Porcelain, Eighth Edition,* House of Collectibles, 1995; Lois Lehner,
Lehner's Encyclopedia of U.S. Marks on Pottery, Porcelain & Clay,
Collector Books, 1988.

Apple Blossom, bean pot, $25.00.

Apple Blossom, Pantry–Bak–In, casserole, cov **$18.00**
Apple Blossom, Pantry–Bak–In, pie baker **15.00**
Dartmouth, cookie jar **45.00**
Dartmouth, bowl, 7³/₈" d **10.00**
Dartmouth, gravy **15.00**
Dartmouth, mixing bowl, 9" d **12.00**
Dartmouth, syrup jug **25.00**
Dawn, casserole **20.00**
Dawn, saucer **2.00**
Euclid, casserole, 4" d **12.00**
Euclid, creamer. **5.00**
Euclid, pie baker, 10" d **12.00**
Harmony, creamer **5.00**
Harmony, saucer. **2.00**
Ivora, butter dish. **22.00**
Ivora, creamer, new style. **5.00**
Ivora, soup bowl. **10.00**
Ivora, teapot **25.00**
Provincial Ware, casserole. **20.00**
Provincial Ware, plate, 6" d. **1.50**
Provincial Ware, sugar **8.00**
Quadro, casserole. **20.00**
Quadro, gravy. **12.00**
Quadro, saucer. **1.50**
Silhouette, mixing bowl, lipped, 6" d **12.00**
Silhouette, oatmeal canister, 6¹/₂" h **45.00**
Silhouette, pickle tray **10.00**
Silhouette, plate, Provincial Ware, 9" d **10.00**
Silhouette, plate, Quadro, 8" d **8.00**
Silhouette, salad bowl, round, emb petal style, 9¹/₂" d **30.00**

CYBIS

Boleslaw Cybis, a professor at the Academy of Fine Art in Warsaw,
Poland, and his wife, Marja, came to the United States in 1939 to
paint murals in the Hall of Honor at the New York's World Fair.
Unable to return to Poland after war broke out, the couple
remained in the United States and opened an artists' studio to create porcelain sculpture.

After a brief stint in New York, the studio moved to Trenton, New Jersey. Sculptures were produced in a variety of themes ranging from the world of nature to elegant historical figures.

Autumn, 1972	$200.00
Ballerina Recital, 1985	300.00
Bear, 1968	400.00
Beavers, Egbert and Breuster, 1981	335.00
Bluebirds, nestling, 1978	260.00
Buffalo, 1968	180.00
Clarissa, 1986	200.00
Country Fair, 1972	200.00
Cybis Holiday, 1984	150.00
Dandy Dancing Dog, 1977	300.00
Dormouse, Maximillian, 1978	145.00
Dormouse, Maxine, 1978	225.00
Duckling, baby brother, 1962	140.00
Easter Egg Hunt, 1972	200.00
Heavenly Angels Ornament, 1987	400.00
Holiday Ornament, 1985	100.00
Huey, The Harmonious Hare, 1986	275.00
Independence Celebration, 1972	200.00
Jody, 1985	300.00
Kitten Chantilly, 1984	210.00
Kitten Tabitha, 1975	150.00
Lullaby Blue, 1986	175.00
Lullaby Ivory, 1986	175.00
Lullaby Pink, 1986	175.00
Madonna Lace and Rose, 1960	300.00
Merry Christmas, 1972	200.00
Nativity, Merry, 1964	350.00
Pierre the Performing Poodle, 1986	300.00
Pinto, 1972	250.00
The Pond, 1972	200.00
Rabbit, Muffet, 1976	140.00
Raffles Raccoon, 1965	365.00
Recital, 1985	300.00
Rhinoceros, Monday, 1985	145.00
Sabbath Morning, 1972	200.00
Seal, Sebastian, 1976	225.00
The Seashore, 1972	200.00
Spring, 1972	200.00
Squirrel, Mr Fluffy Tail, 1965	345.00
Summer, 1972	200.00
Windy Day, 1972	200.00
Winter, 1972	200.00

CZECHOSLOVAKIAN WARES

The country of Czechoslovakia was created in 1918 from the Czech and Solvak regions of the old Austro–Hungarian Empire. Both regions were actively involved in the manufacture of ceramics and glass.

Czechoslovakian ceramics and glassware were imported into the United States in large numbers from the 1920s through the 1950s. Most are stamped "Made in Czechoslovakia." Pieces mirrored the styles of the day. Czechoslovakian Art Deco glass is stylish, colorful, and bright. Canister sets are one of the most popular ceramic forms.

By 1939, Czechoslovakia had fallen under the control of Germany. The country came under communist influence in 1948. Communist domination ended in 1989. On January 1, 1993,

Czechoslovakia split into two independent states, the Czech Republic and the Slovak Republic.

References: Dale and Diane Barta and Helen M. Rose, *Czechoslovakian Glass & Collectibles,* 1992, 1995 value update, *Book II,* 1997, Collector Books; Ruth A. Forsythe, *Made in Czechoslovakia,* Richardson Printing Corp, 1982, 1994–95 value update; Ruth A. Forsythe, *Made in Czechoslovakia, Book 2,* Antique Publications, 1993, 1995–96 value update; Diane E. Foulds, *A Guide to Czech & Slovak Glass, 2nd Edition,* published by author, 1993, 1995 value update, distributed by Antique Publications; Robert and Deborah Truitt, *Collectible Bohemian Glass: 1880–1940,* B & D Glass, 1995, distributed by Antique Publications.

Collectors' Club: Czechoslovakian Collectors Guild International, PO Box 901395, Kansas City, MO 64190.

Bank, Scottie, black, white accents, 4³⁄₈" h	$50.00
Basket, ceramic, handled, orange with blue rim, 5" h	5.00
Basket, pottery, brown, Art Deco panels, colored balls, 5" h	50.00
Bell, figural man's head, comical, brown hair finial handle, 5" h	35.00
Bowl, mottled color, cased, 4¹⁄₂" d	55.00
Bowl, peasant design, Mrazek, 3" d	30.00
Candlestick, handled, blue and yellow flowers, green leaves, black outline, cream ground, 4¹⁄₂" h	30.00
Card Holder, hanging basket, glass beads, 12 x 7¹⁄₂"	75.00
Chamberstick, ceramic, cream, blue and brown floral design, 6" h	20.00
Condiment Set, canister and spicer jars, set of 14, orange, magenta, rust, green, and yellow floral bands, black borders, irid ground	325.00
Console Bowl, glass, ftd, black, orange trim, sgd	100.00
Creamer, checkerboard body, red and blue, orange luster rim bands, 3" h	5.00
Creamer, figural cat, white with blue and red accents, 1940s	10.00
Creamer and Sugar, figural swans	90.00
Dresser Set, 3 pc, enameled floral design	30.00
Figure, bulldog, frosted glass, 3" h	35.00
Honey Pot, cov, enameled design, blue base, 5" h	75.00

Bowl, glass, oval, flared, opal green with 3 applied black feet and black rim wrap, attributed to Michael Powolny, 10¹⁄₂" d, 5" h, $287.50. Photo courtesy Skinner's.

Jardiniere, pottery, cattails on side, figural kingfisher
  perched on edge, 5" d, 4¹/₄" h 115.00
Perfume Bottle, clear, cut, 3" h 95.00
Pin Tray, Art Nouveau style, bust of woman in relief, 7" l 35.00
Pitcher, Coin Dot pattern, blue, 3³/₄" h 55.00
Pitcher, floral pattern, Mrazek, 4" h 50.00
Plate, white ground, red trim, mkd, 7" d 4.00
Rose Bowl, vaseline base color, wave dec pattern,
  iridized finish, Loetz, 4" d 65.00
Spoon, center Blue Delft porcelain windmill illus, dec
  handle and bowl edge, 5" l 45.00
Tea Kettle, earthenware, carved and polychrome dec,
  stamp and imp Eleanor mark, c1925, 6¹/₄" h 220.00
Toothpick Holder, black and green design, orange
  ground, cased, 2¹/₄" h 30.00
Trivet, man on camel center scene, gold and cobalt bor-
  der, 7¹/₂" d 45.00
Vase, bulbous ovoid body, incised dec, intertwining
  vines and pendent cluster of grapes between geometric borders incised dec, shades of green, brown, tan,
  purple, and pink, mkd "Czechoslovakia, Amphora,
  813," c1925 . . . . 1,725.00
Vase, cobalt, green and red ground, Serpent, 10" h 45.00
Vase, glass, amethyst, gilded poppies and leaves overlay,
  gold bands on top and bottom, orig paper label, 10" h . . . 120.00
Vase, glass, fan shaped, blue, yellow threading at top,
  9¹/₄" h 230.00
Vase, green irid glass, funnel shaped, Rusticana pattern,
  Loetz, 7¹/₄" h 160.00
Vase, green veining on yellow ground, orange stripes at
  neck, 12" h 185.00
Vase, polychromed floral patterns, matte and gloss
  glazes, ink stamped "Made in Czecho–Slovakia
  Amphora," 16" h 440.00
Vase, pottery, square, marbelized Art Deco design,
  Coronet, 7" h 10.00
Wall Pocket, bird and fruit dec 40.00

AUCTION PRICES

Czechoslovakian wares sold by Pence Auction Company in
conjunction with the Czechoslovakian Collector's Guild
International Convention held May 3, 1997. Prices include a
5% buyer's premium.

Basket, black cased glass with silver mica flakes,
  greenish int, 8¹/₂" h $168.00
Bowl, ceramic lustre with flower frog, 6" d 7.50
Centerpiece, Alien pottery, mkd "Made in
  Czechoslovakia," 4¹/₂" h 50.00
Figure, doctor holding needle, glass, orig paper
  label, 8¹/₂" h 147.00
Globe, Kralik, clambroth glass with blue and green
  flame pattern, 8" h 136.50
Pitcher, ceramic, Erphila, hp orange poppy 89.25
Rose Bowl, Kralik, glass, ftd, clear with enamel dec,
  5" h 52.50
Vase, Alien Deco, pottery, airbrushed, gray, gold,
  and black, 8" h 57.75
Vase, crackle glass, ruby with red pulls, 9" h 115.50
Vase, glass, red and yellow swirl pattern, black
  enamel dec, 8¹/₂" h 68.25
Vase, Loetz, green iridized glass, tree bark design,
  trefoil top, 5" h 294.00

DAIRY COLLECTIBLES

The mid–20th century was the Golden Age of the American dairy
industry. Thousands of small dairies and creameries were located
throughout the United States, most serving only a regional market.

Dairy cooperatives, many of which were created in the 1920s
and 30s, served a broader market. Borden pursued a national marketing program. Elsie, The Borden Cow is one of the most widely
recognized advertising characters from the 1940s and 50s.

Reference: Dana Gehman Morykan and Harry L. Rinker,
Warman's Country Antiques & Collectibles, Third Edition,
Wallace–Homestead, Krause Publications, 1996.

Newsletters: *Creamers,* PO Box 11, Lake Villa, IL 60046; *The
Udder Collectibles,* HC73 Box 1, Smithville Flats, NY 13841.

Collectors' Clubs: Cream Separator Assoc, Rte 3, Box 189,
Arcadia, WI 54612; National Assoc of Milk Bottle Collectors, Inc,
4 Ox Bow Rd, Westport, CT 06880.

Badge, clerk's, celluloid, bar pin fastener back, Borden's
  Evaporated Milk can with wrapper partly removed
  exposing inner coupon of chinaware illus, "Free Gifts
  For Coupons," 3¹/₂" d $25.00
Badge, Elsie, celluloid, pinback, oval, cream, Elsie and
  green sprig of Christmas holly scene, red lettering,
  "Try Our Egg Nog," 1950s, 1³/₄ x 2³/₄" 75.00
Charm, Elsie, plastic, white, replica pocket watch, clear
  plastic dome over raised head Elsie image, red
  tongue, yellow daisy collar, printed hour numerals,
  brown time hands, 1950s 25.00
Clock, Cloverlake Dairy Foods, light–up, double bubble,
  green clover leaf center 375.00
Lamp, china, figural Elsie holding Beauregard on lap
  with opened book, ©Borden Co, 1948, 3¹/₂ x 4 x 10" 200.00
Palm Puzzle, tin frame, clear plastic over 2 black and
  white milk glasses image, recessed for capturing tiny
  ball, red lettered inscription "June Is Dairy Month,"
  post–1950s 25.00

Bottle Cap, Dutch Mill Dairy, 1⁵/₈" d, 20¢

Pin, Elsie, figural, plastic, white, raised relief, color accents, 1940s **50.00**

Pinback Button, Borden's Golden Crest Milk, red, white, and blue, product name in gold, 1930–40s **25.00**

Pinback Button, Farm Maid Milk, red, white, and blue, "Junior Member," serial number, 1930s **15.00**

Pinback Button, Gridley Milk Did It Club, celluloid, achievement and rank buttons, blue, white, and gold, 1930s, price for six **25.00**

Ring, Elsie, plastic, gold luster, clear plastic dome center over Elsie head image with name and Borden Co copyright, 1950s **20.00**

Salt and Pepper Shakers, pr, Elsie and Elmer, 3¹/₂" h Elsie wearing dress hat with fuchsia simulated feather plume, 4" h Elmer as chef, 1940s **100.00**

Sign, Biltmore Dairy Products, tin, yellow ground, blue lettering, "Supreme in Quality," 1961, 2 x 3" **300.00**

Sign, Carnation Milk, porcelain, diecut, red, green, and white, 1950s, 22 x 23" **425.00**

Sign, Coble Milk, tin, emb, black ground, yellow, red, and white, comical milk carton looking up at large milk carton, "Reach For Me!," 1953, 15 x 24" **300.00**

DAVID WINTER COTTAGES

David Winter, born in Caterick, Yorkshire, England, is the son of Faith Winter, an internationally recognized sculptor. Working from his garden studio located at his home in Guildford, England, Winter created his first miniature cottage in 1979.

David Winter Cottages received the "Collectible of the Year" award from the National Association of Limited Edition Dealers in 1987 and 1988 and was named NALED "Artist of the Year" in 1991. In 1997 Enesco signed an agreement with David Winter to manufacture David Winter Cottages and operate the David Winter Cottages Collectors' Guild.

The secondary market for David Winter miniature cottages is as strong (perhaps stronger) in England. Be cautious of English price guides that provide a straight conversion from pounds to dollars in their price listings. Taste and emphasis among collectors differs between England and the United States.

References: *Collectors' Information Bureau Market Guide & Price Index, Fifteenth Edition,* Collectors' Information Bureau, 1997, distributed by Krause Publications; John Hughes, *The David Winter Cottages Handbook,* Kevin Francis Publishing, 1992; Mary Sieber (ed.), *1998 Collector's Mart Magazine Price Guide to Limited Edition Collectibles,* Krause Publications, 1997.

Collectors' Club: Enesco David Winter Cottages Collectors Guild, 225 Windsor Dr, Itasca, IL 60143.

The Apothecary Shop, Heart of England, 1985 .... **$50.00**

Bishopsgate, Castle Collection, 1995 .... **150.00**

Black Bess Inn, Collecters Guild Exclusive, 1988 .... **145.00**

Blossom Cottage, May, British Traditions, 1990 .... **45.00**

Brooklet Bridge, Cameos Collection, 1992 .... **15.00**

Burn's Reading Room, January, British Traditions, 1990 ..... **35.00**

The Cat and Pipe, English Village Collection, 1994 .... **50.00**

Crystal Cottage, English Village Collection, 1994 .... **50.00**

Drover's Cottage, In the Country, 1982 .... **35.00**

Edna, Bugaboos, 1989 .... **45.00**

Friar Tuck's Sanctum, New Sherwood Forest Collection, 1995 .... **45.00**

Hogmanay, Dickens Christmas Carol Collection, 1988, $100.00.

Harbour Master's Watch House, Seaside Boardwalk, 1995 .. **125.00**

Harvest Barn, October, British Traditions, 1990 .... **55.00**

Irish Round Tower, Irish Collection, 1992 .... **70.00**

Little Market, Centere of the Village, 1980 .... **55.00**

Lock Keepers Cottage, Midlands Collection, 1988 .... **80.00**

Market Day, Cameos Collection, 1992 .... **15.00**

Mothers Cottage, Celebration Cottages Collection, 1995 ..... **65.00**

Mr Fezziwig's Emporium, Dickens Christmas Carol Collection, 1990 .... **95.00**

Oscar, Bugaboos, 1989 .... **45.00**

The Plucked Ducks, Collectors Guild Exclusive, 1990 .... **65.00**

Pudding Cottage, April, British Traditions, 1990 .... **80.00**

Rochester Castle, Castle Collection, 1996 .... **190.00**

Single Oast, Regions Collection, 1981 .... **55.00**

Sleeping Beauty Castle, Disneyana, 1993 .... **565.00**

Squires Hall, Landowners Collection, 1985 .... **80.00**

Sweet Dreams, Porridge Pot Alley Collection, 1995 .... **75.00**

Sweetheart Haven, Celebration Cottages Collection, 1994 ... **55.00**

Willow Gardens, Garden Cottages of England, 1995 .... **225.00**

The Wine Merchant, Centere of the Village, 1980 .... **75.00**

Wreckers Cottage, Masterpiece Collection, 1996 .... **225.00**

DECORATIVE ACCESSORIES

Design style plays a major role in today's collecting world. The period look is back in vogue as collectors attempt to recreate the ambiance of the particular period, e.g., Art Deco or the 1950s.

This emphasis on "the look" has created value for a wide range of tabletop decorative pieces, from stylish cigarette boxes to table lamps. Fabrics, wallpaper, and other products that cry "period" are eagerly sought. Most items are purchased for use as accent pieces. Buyers incorporate them in their home decor and use them. Value is as much about pizzazz as it is collectibility.

References: Tony Fusco, *Art Deco: Identification and Price Guide, 2nd Edition,* Avon Books, 1993; Mary Frank Gaston, *Collector's Guide to Art Deco, Second Edition,* Collector Books, 1997; Anne Gilbert, *40's and 50's Designs and Memorabilia: Identification and Price Guide,* Avon Books, 1993; Anne Gilbert, *60's and 70's Designs and Memorabilia: Identification and Price Guide,* Avon Books, 1994; Robert Heide and John Gilman, *Popular Art Deco: Depression Era Style and Design,* Abbeville Press, 1991; Richard

Horn, *Memphis: Objects, Furniture & Patterns*, Simon and Schuster, 1986; Jan Lindenberger, *Collecting the 50s & 60s*, 2nd Edition, Schiffer Publishing, 1997; Madeleine Marsh, *Miller's Collecting the 1950's*, Millers Publications, 1997, distributed by Antique Collectors' Club; Paula Ockner and Leslie Piña, *Art Deco Aluminum: Kensington*, Schiffer Publishing, 1997; Leslie Piña, *'50s & '60s Glass, Ceramics & Enamel Wares: Designed & Signed by George Briard, Sascha B., Bellaire, Higgins...*, Schiffer Publishing, 1996.

Periodical: *Echoes Magazine*, PO Box 155, Commaquid, MA 02637.

Collectors' Clubs: Chase Collectors Society, 2149 W Jibsail Loop, Mesa, AZ 85202; International Coalition of Art Deco Societies, One Murdock Terrace, Brighton, MA 02135.

Art Deco, bun warmer, Russell Wright, spun aluminum, spherical, plastic bail handle and knob **$85.00**
Art Deco, clock, Westclox, yellow Bakelite, flashing light and alarm, 1940s 100.00
Art Deco, desk set, American, double inkstand, pen holder, 2 letter openers, and rocking blotter, striped black and green Bakelite with chrome accents, 1920s 750.00
Art Deco, picture frame, chrome, black enameled geometric design, 3 x 12" 45.00
Art Deco, smoking stand, top with sliding doors for smoking supplies, 3 columns leading from top to circular base, 1930s, 22" h 225.00
Art Deco, tea set, Chase, cov teapot, cov sugar, creamer, and tray, spherical ftd bodies, ivory Bakelite handles, stamped "Chase," 8½" h teapot 165.00
Art Deco, vase, Jaffa, tapered glass, cylindrical body flanked on either side with 3 tiers of stylized foliage, 12½" h 3,225.00
Modern, desk clock, Moon Crest, brushed copper, rect, digital, foil decal, 4" h, 8½" l 110.00
Modern, floor lamp, Lanel, brushed chrome with mushroom shaped frosted glass globe, unmkd, 57" h, 14" d globe 650.00

Art Deco, table lamp, black iron figure, wrapped fiberglass shade, wood base, 16 x 12 x 8", $192.50. Photo courtesy David Rago Auctions.

Modern, desk clock, electric, glass and chrome, blue mirrored face, silver balls for numerals, mkd on motor "Gilbert Rohde for Herman Miller," c1935, 6½" h, $770.00. Photo courtesy David Rago Auctions.

Modern, vase, Pillin, bottle shaped, polychrome figures of woman, girl, and deer, gray ground, sgd "Pillin," 14" h, 4" d 650.00
Modern, wall sculpture, in the style of Harry Bertoia, blue, white, and green small enamel panels on irregular abstract brass wire grid, 38 x 54" 300.00
Modern, wool pile hooked area rug, design by Henri Matisse, black and olive borders, colorful abstract panel in coral, yellow, black, and blue, sgd "H. Matisse" in pile, 3 x 5' 700.00
Modern Streamlined, cocktail set, Chase, cocktail shaker and ice bucket, chrome with black enameled lines, imp "Chase," 11 1/2" h cocktail shaker 100.00
Modern Streamlined, table top radio, Spartan, Sparks–Wittington Co, MI, designed by Walter Teague, round front, mirrored glass and chrome, circular dial surrounded by circle of chrome, 3 horizontal bands, 1930s 2,500.00
1930s, cake and sandwich server, Chase, chrome, 3 round tiers, yellow Bakelite handle, imp "Chase," 8" d, 12" h 100.00
1930s, figure, dancer, bronze and ivory, after a model by B Callender, standing woman with raised arm wearing foliate patterned costume, raised on stepped onyx base, 17" h 4,500.00
1930s, lamp, electric, glass, 3 sockets on 3–forked pedestal base patterned with birds in flight, 10½" h 2,750.00
1930s, vase, Longwy, Primavera, circular pillow shape, incised medallion of dark blue stylized Medusa, gray crackled glaze, ink mkd, 12" h, 9" w 450.00
1940s, ottoman, flattened spherical shape, vinyl, radiating color panels joined with piped seams, 34" d, 18" h . . . 150.00
1940s, tea towel, cotton, Mexican man and burrow, red, yellow, green, and white 5.00

1950s, candy dish, sgd "Erica," square, turned up sides, stylized brown and black birds on white ground **15.00**

1950s, ceiling light fixture, Western motif glass shade with bucking broncos, wagon wheels, horseshoes, and branding symbols **60.00**

1950s, hamper, Pearlwick, steel reinforced, rose colored fibre cover, dec metal panel on arched front, vinyl cov pearl top, 26" h **25.00**

1950s, planter, wood bucket planter with brass bands, bentwood bail handle, and eagle dec, 3 turned splayed legs, 19½" h **25.00**

1950s, smoking stand, bronze finish metal stand with fluted column and emb base, amber glass ashtray, 28" h **30.00**

1950s, tablecloth and 4 napkins, Bates, ivory rayon damask, chrysanthemum pattern, 54 x 72" tablecloth **20.00**

1950s, thermometer/wall plaque, chalk, poodle in bathtub **15.00**

1950s, umbrella stand, wire frame with metal leaf dec, conical plastic insert with gold spatter on pink ground **20.00**

1950s, wall lamp, maple, nautical motif, lacquered brass wheel spokes, 8" paper parchment shade **18.00**

1950s, waste basket, metal, poodle holding parasol, line–drawn shops in background, pink ground **15.00**

1960s, box, Vohann of California, ceramic, rect, yellow, stylized green and yellow flowers on lid, 8" l, 3½" w **15.00**

1960s, canister set, wood, hp roster dec, set of 4 . . . . **35.00**

1960s, hanging planter, burwood, sphere with cutout Florentine leaf design, 36" gold tone chain, 11" d **10.00**

1960s, lava lamp, electric, blue and yellow, 15" h **50.00**

1960s, pillow, Norman Norell, silk and satin with black and white "N" pattern and Norell logo, orig label, 22" sq **250.00**

1960s, poster, Peter Max, peace symbols, 24 x 36" **250.00**

1960s, table radio, General Electric, rect antique white plastic case, red trim, center tuning dial, built–in antenna, push button on/off switch. **20.00**

1960s, wall plaques, set of 4, syroco, Danish Modern design with turquoise and brown flowers depicting 4 seasons, diamond shaped walnut frames, 14¾" h **20.00**

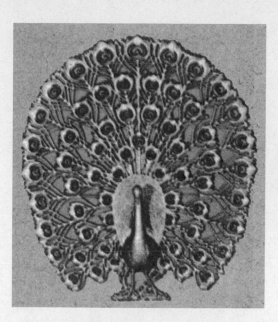

1970s, wall plaque, peacock, burwood, metal gold finish, 30" w, 34" h, 5½" d, $20.00.

1970s, bank, figural hippopotamus, papier–mâché, pink and yellow flower dec on green body **8.00**

1970s, candle holders, wrought–iron stands with scroll-work ornamentation, red, blue, and gold glass votive candle holders, graduated heights, set of 3 . . . . **12.00**

1970s, figure, Treasure Craft, bull, ceramic, wood stain finish, 6½" h, 14" l **10.00**

1970s, figures, pr, Lane, Spanish dancers, man and woman, avocado glaze **18.00**

1970s, pile area rug, Axis, France, abstract geometric design of black lines and blue, red, and black polygons on charcoal gray ground, cloth label, 78" sq **825.00**

1970s, pillow, pink cotton, tufted with rhinestones **35.00**

1970s, record rack, Maurice Duchin, brass plated wire frame, 2 shelves, holds 200 LPs, 14" w, 27" h **10.00**

1970s, scatter rug, acrylic/modacrylic pile, printed zebra skin shape, Safari Collection, 48" l, 27" w **15.00**

1970s, sculpture, flowers, wire stems and leaves, multi-color glass petals, plastic base, 10½" h **20.00**

1970s, telephone, plastic, desk model, turquoise **30.00**

DEGENHART GLASS

John and Elizabeth Degenhart directed the operation of Crystal Art Glass, Cambridge, Ohio, from 1947 until 1978. Pressed glass novelties, such as animal covered dishes, salts, toothpicks, and paperweights were the company's principal products.

Boyd Crystal Art Glass, Cambridge, Ohio, purchased many of the company's molds when operations ceased. Boyd continues to manufacture pieces from these molds in colors different from those used by Degenhart. Most are marked with a "B" in a diamond.

Collectors' Club: Friends of Degenhart, Degenhart Paperweight and Glass Museum, Inc, 65323 Highland Hills Rd, PO Box 186, Cambridge, OH 43725.

REPRODUCTION ALERT: Although most Degenhart molds were reproductions themselves, many contemporary pieces made by Kanawha, L. G. Wright, and others are nearly identical.

Animal Dish, cov, hen, amber **$35.00**

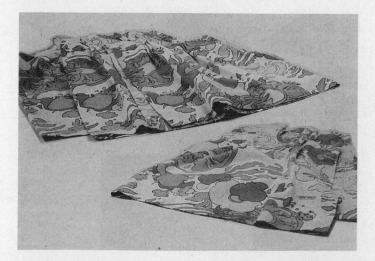

1960s, curtain panels, Peter Max, multicolored printed cotton, French pleats, stamped "Peter Max," 26 x 28" panel, price for 16 panels, $385.00. Photo courtesy David Rago Auctions.

Animal Dish, cov, hen, sapphire blue.	20.00
Animal Dish, cov, lamb, cobalt blue	40.00
Animal Dish, cov, robin, bloody Mary	90.00
Animal Dish, cov, turkey, amber	35.00
Baby Shoe, milk glass	15.00
Bicentennial Bell, canary.	15.00
Bicentennial Bell, Elizabeth's Lime Ice	15.00
Boot, Texas, peach	12.00
Candy Dish, cov, Wildflower, pink.	25.00
Candy Dish, cov, Wildflower, twilight blue.	25.00
Creamer and Sugar, Texas, emerald green.	50.00
Cup Plate, Heart and Lyre, cobalt blue	15.00
Gypsy Pot, Blue Jay.	20.00
Hand, amethyst.	8.50
Hand, frosty jade	15.00
Hat, Daisy and Button, amethyst	8.00
Hat, Daisy and Button, blue milk glass.	12.00
Jewelry Box, baby green	25.00
Jewelry Box, heliotrope.	35.00
Jewelry Box, light chocolate creme	35.00
Jewelry Box, old lavender	25.00
Miniature Pitcher, jade	20.00
Owl, amberina	35.00
Owl, Crown Tuscan.	40.00
Owl, frosty jade	45.00
Owl, ivory	30.00
Owl, seafoam	35.00
Owl, sunset	25.00
Owl, yellow	35.00
Paperweight, double tree.	80.00
Paperweight, gear shift knob	125.00
Paperweight, hp plate	75.00
Paperweight, multicolored.	75.00
Paperweight, red flower.	65.00
Pooch, fawn	20.00
Pooch, slag, caramel custard	25.00
Portrait Plate, crystal, 1974	35.00
Priscilla, amber.	75.00
Priscilla, blue and white	90.00
Priscilla, jade green.	100.00
Salt, Daisy and Button, amethyst	15.00
Salt, Star and Dewdrop, Henry's blue.	18.00
Salt, Star and Dewdrop, sapphire blue	18.00

Salt and Pepper Shakers, pr, birds, amberina.	25.00
Salt and Pepper Shakers, pr, birds, antique blue	20.00
Skate, green, orig decal.	30.00
Slipper, Daisy and Button, taffeta.	20.00
Tiger, lavender blue.	30.00
Tomahawk, persimmon	30.00
Toothpick Holder, Baby, gold.	8.00
Toothpick Holder, Baby or Tramp Shoe, bluebell.	15.00
Toothpick Holder, Baby or Tramp Shoe, opaque blue	18.00
Toothpick Holder, Basket, sparrow slag	15.00
Toothpick Holder, Beaded Oval, old lavender.	20.00
Toothpick Holder, Beaded Oval, teal	18.00
Toothpick Holder, Bird, persimmon	15.00
Toothpick Holder, Colonial Drape and Heart, clear.	15.00
Toothpick Holder, Daisy and Button, dichromatic.	25.00
Toothpick Holder, elephant head, amber	20.00
Toothpick Holder, Forget–Me–Not, dogwood	25.00
Toothpick Holder, Forget–Me–Not, hetherbloom.	20.00
Toothpick Holder, Gypsy Pot, blue fire.	15.00
Toothpick Holder, Heart, opaque glass, blue.	35.00
Tray, hand shaped, Bittersweet.	15.00
Wine, taffeta.	40.00

DEPRESSION GLASS

Depression Glass is a generic term used to describe glassware patterns introduced and manufactured between 1920 and the early 1950s. Most of this glassware was inexpensive and machine made.

In its narrow sense, the term describes a select group of patterns identified by a group of late 1940s and early 1950s collectors as "Depression Glass." Many price guides dealing with the subject have preserved this narrow approach.

Many manufacturers did not name their patterns. The same group of individuals who determined what patterns should and should not be included in this category also assigned names to previously unidentified patterns. Disputes occurred. Hence, some patterns have more than one name.

References: Gene Florence, *Collectible Glassware From the 40s, 50s & 60s...*, *Fourth Edition*, Collector Books, 1998; Gene Florence, *Collector's Encyclopedia of Depression Glass*, *Thirteenth Edition*, Collector Books, 1998; Gene Florence, *Elegant Glassware of the Depression Era*, *Seventh Edition*, Collector Books, 1997; Gene Florence, *Kitchen Glassware of the Depression Years: Identification & Values*, *Fifth Edition*, Collector Books, 1995, 1997 value update; Gene Florence, *Very Rare Glassware of the Depression Years*, *Third Series* 1993, 1995 value update, *Fourth Series* 1995 and *Fifth Series* 1997, Collector Books; Ralph and Terry Kovel, *Kovel's Depression Glass & American Dinnerware Price List*, *Fifth Edition*, Crown, 1995; Carl F. Luckey, *An Identification & Value Guide To Depression Era Glassware*, *Third Edition*, Books Americana, Krause Publications, 1994; Naomi L. Over, *Ruby Glass of the 20th Century*, Antique Publications, 1990, 1993–94 value update; Hazel Marie Weatherman, *Colored Glassware of the Depression Era*, *Book 2*, published by author, 1974, available in reprint.

Periodical: *The Daze*, PO Box 57, Otisville, MI 48463.

Collectors' Clubs: National Depression Glass Assoc, PO Box 8264, Wichita, KS 67209; 20–30–40 Society, Inc, PO Box 856, La Grange, IL 60525.

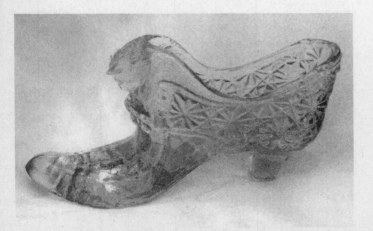

Kat Slipper, Daisy & Button pattern, pink, $40.00.

REPRODUCTION ALERT: Reproductions (exact copies) of several patterns are known. In other cases, fantasy pieces have been made from period molds in non–period colors. Few of these reproductions and fantasy pieces are marked.

The Daze distributes a list of these reproductions and fantasy items. Send a self–addressed, stamped business envelope along with a request for a copy.

Dogwood, MacBeth–Evans, cup, thin, pink	$12.00
Dogwood, MacBeth–Evans, dinner plate, 9¼" d, pink	30.00
Dogwood, MacBeth–Evans, fruit bowl, monax	70.00
Dogwood, MacBeth–Evans, luncheon plate, 8" d, pink	7.00
Dogwood, MacBeth–Evans, saucer, green	8.00
Dogwood, MacBeth–Evans, sugar, ftd, pink	15.00
Homespun, Jeannette, butter, cov, crystal	60.00
Homespun, Jeannette, cereal bow, closed handles, 5" d, pink	28.00
Homespun, Jeannette, dinner plate, 9¼" d, pink	16.00
Homespun, Jeannette, iced tea tumbler, 12½ oz, 5⅜" h, crystal	30.00
Homespun, Jeannette, saucer, crystal	4.00
Homespun, Jeannette, sugar, ftd, pink	9.50
Homespun, Jeannette, water tumbler, flared top, 8 oz, 4⅛" h, crystal	20.00
Jubilee, Lancaster, cake tray, 2 handles, pink	65.00
Jubilee, Lancaster, candlesticks, pr, yellow	185.00
Jubilee, Lancaster, creamer, pink	35.00
Jubilee, Lancaster, creamer, yellow	17.50
Jubilee, Lancaster, cup, yellow	12.00
Jubilee, Lancaster, fruit bowl, flat, 11½" d, pink	195.00
Jubilee, Lancaster, juice tumbler, ftd, 6 oz, 5" h, yellow	95.00
Jubilee, Lancaster, lucheon plate, 8¾" d, yellow	12.00
Jubilee, Lancaster, mayonnaise set, yellow	265.00
Jubilee, Lancaster, salad plate, 7" d, yellow	13.00
Jubilee, Lancaster, saucer, yellow	4.00
Jubilee, Lancaster, sugar, pink	30.00
Jubilee, Lancaster, sugar, yellow	17.50
Jubilee, Lancaster, tray, 2 handles, 11" l, yellow	45.00
Jubilee, Lancaster, water tumbler, 10 oz, 6" h, yellow	33.00
Mayfair, Federal, cereal bowl, 6" d, crystal	9.50
Mayfair, Federal, creamer, ftd, crystal	10.50

Newport, Hazel Atlas, cup and saucer, cobalt, $20.00.

Mayfair, Federal, platter, oval, 12" l, crystal	17.00
Mayfair, Federal, tumbler, 9 oz, 4½" h, crystal	13.00
Mayfair, Federal, salad plate, 6¾" d, amber	7.00
Mayfair, Federal, sauce bowl, 5" d, crystal	6.50
Miss America, Hocking, celery tray, 10½" l, pink	35.00
Miss America, Hocking, comport, pink	30.00
Miss America, Hocking, cup, pink	22.00
Miss America, Hocking, cup and saucer, pink	35.00
Miss America, Hocking, platter, 12" l, pink	35.00
Miss America, Hocking, salad, 8½" d, pink	30.00
Miss America, Hocking, sherbet, pink	15.00
Miss America, Hocking, vegetable bowl, oval, 10" l, pink	35.00
Newport, Hazel Atlas, berry bowl, 4¾" d, amethyst	15.00
Newport, Hazel Atlas, cereal bowl, 5¼" d, cobalt	37.50
Newport, Hazel Atlas, luncheon plate, 8½" d, amethyst	12.00
Newport, Hazel Atlas, salt and pepper shakers, pr, amethyst	40.00
Newport, Hazel Atlas, sugar, amethyst	13.00
Newport, Hazel Atlas, tumbler, 9 oz, 4½" h, amethyst	35.00
Patrick, Lancaster, console bowl, yellow	80.00
Patrick, Lancaster, creamer, yellow	37.50
Patrick, Lancaster, saucer, pink	20.00
Patrick, Lancaster, sugar, pink	75.00
Patrick, Lancaster, water goblet, yellow	67.50
Petalware, MacBeth–Evans, cereal bowl, 5¾" d	9.00
Petalware, MacBeth–Evans, creamer, pink	8.00
Petalware, MacBeth–Evans, cup and saucer, monax	9.00
Petalware, MacBeth–Evans, cup and saucer, pink	9.00
Petalware, MacBeth–Evans, dinner plate, 9" d, pink	14.00
Petalware, MacBeth–Evans, dinner plate, 9¼" d, monax	12.00
Petalware, MacBeth–Evans, mustard, with underplate, open, cobalt	10.00
Petalware, MacBeth–Evans, plate, 6" d, pink	2.50
Petalware, MacBeth–Evans, plate, 8" d, pink	5.00
Petalware, MacBeth–Evans, platter, pink	20.00
Petalware, MacBeth–Evans, sherbet, ftd, monax	10.00
Petalware, MacBeth–Evans, sherbet, ftd, pink	10.00
Petalware, MacBeth–Evans, sugar, pink	7.00
Pineapple & Floral, #618, Indiana, ashtray, 4½" d, crystal	17.50
Pineapple & Floral, #618, Indiana, cereal bowl, 6" d, amber	20.00
Pineapple & Floral, #618, Indiana, cream soup, crystal	20.00
Pineapple & Floral, #618, Indiana, cup, crystal	10.00

Homespun, Jeannette, creamer, ftd, pink, $10.00.

Pineapple & Floral, #618, Indiana, salad plate, 8³/₈" d,
crystal..8.50
Pineapple & Floral, #618, Indiana, sandwich plate,
11¹/₂" d, amber..15.00
Pineapple & Floral, #618, Indiana, tumbler, 8 oz, 4¹/₄" h,
amber..22.00
Pyramid, Indiana, berry bowl, 4³/₄" d, green..............18.00
Pyramid, Indiana, creamer, pink.........................23.00
Pyramid, Indiana, pitcher, green.......................200.00
Pyramid, Indiana, tray, crystal.........................15.00
Queen Mary, Hocking, berry bowl, 4¹/₂" d, pink...........6.00
Queen Mary, Hocking, berry bowl, 8³/₄" d, crystal.......10.00
Queen Mary, Hocking, bowl, 4¹/₂ x 1¹/₂", pink............5.00
Queen Mary, Hocking, bowl, deep, crystal................6.00
Queen Mary, Hocking, bowl, handled, 4¹/₂" d, pink.......5.00
Queen Mary, Hocking, bowl, small, 4" d, crystal.........4.00
Queen Mary, Hocking, butter, cov, crystal...............25.00
Queen Mary, Hocking, celery dish, 5 x 10", crystal......11.00
Queen Mary, Hocking, cereal bowl, 6" d, pink............23.00
Queen Mary, Hocking, creamer, oval, pink................7.50
Queen Mary, Hocking, creamer, pink.....................18.00
Queen Mary, Hocking, cup, small, pink...................8.00
Queen Mary, Hocking, cup, large, crystal................5.50
Queen Mary, Hocking, cup, large, pink..................10.00
Queen Mary, Hocking, dinner plate, 9³/₄" d, crystal.....18.00
Queen Mary, Hocking, juice tumbler, 5 oz, 3¹/₂" h, pink...10.00
Queen Mary, Hocking, plate, 6" d, pink..................6.50
Queen Mary, Hocking, plate, 6⁵/₈" d, crystal............4.00
Queen Mary, Hocking, plate, 6⁵/₈" d, pink...............7.50
Queen Mary, Hocking, relish tray, 3 part, 12", crystal...9.00
Queen Mary, Hocking, sandwich plate, 12" d, crystal.....9.00
Queen Mary, Hocking, saucer, crystal....................2.50
Queen Mary, Hocking, serving bowl, 6" d, crystal........7.00
Queen Mary, Hocking, sherbet, flat, pink...............10.00
Queen Mary, Hocking, sherbet, low, 5³/₄", pink.........10.00
Queen Mary, Hocking, sugar, oval, pink..................7.50
Queen Mary, Hocking, tumbler, 5 oz, 3¹/₂" h, pink......10.00
Queen Mary, Hocking, tumbler, 9 oz, 4" h, pink.........14.00
Ring, Hocking, cup, crystal.............................15.00
Ring, Hocking, decanter and stopper, crystal............28.00
Ring, Hocking, decanter, black bands, crystal...........35.00

**Rose Cameo,
Belmont Tumbler Co,
tumbler, ftd, 5" h,
green, $22.00.**

Ring, Hocking, sandwich plate, crystal..................10.00
Ring, Hocking, server, green center handle, crystal......32.00
Ring, Hocking, shaker, crystal..........................12.00
Ring, Hocking, sugar, ftd, gold trim, crystal............5.50
Rose Cameo, Belmont Tumbler Co, berry bowl, 4¹/₂" d,
green..10.00
Rose Cameo, Belmont Tumbler Co, bowl, straight sides,
6" d, green...22.00
Sharon/Cabbage Rose, Federal, berry bowl, 5" d, amber....5.00
Sharon/Cabbage Rose, Federal, berry bowl, 5" d, green...13.00
Sharon/Cabbage Rose, Federal, berry bowl, 5" d, pink....10.00
Sharon/Cabbage Rose, Federal, bread and butter plate,
6" d, amber...4.00
Sharon/Cabbage Rose, Federal, bread and butter plate,
6" d, pink..6.00
Sharon/Cabbage Rose, Federal, butter dish, cov, amber...45.00
Sharon/Cabbage Rose, Federal, butter dish, cov, pink....50.00
Sharon/Cabbage Rose, Federal, cake plate, ftd, 11" d,
amber..20.00
Sharon/Cabbage Rose, Federal, cake plate, ftd, 11¹/₂" d,
pink...35.00
Sharon/Cabbage Rose, Federal, candy dish, cov, amber....42.00
Sharon/Cabbage Rose, Federal, candy dish, cov, pink.....50.00
Sharon/Cabbage Rose, Federal, creamer and sugar, ftd,
pink...45.00
Sharon/Cabbage Rose, Federal, creamer and sugar,
open, amber..15.00
Sharon/Cabbage Rose, Federal, creamer, ftd, green.......20.00
Sharon/Cabbage Rose, Federal, cream soup, green.........50.00
Sharon/Cabbage Rose, Federal, cream soup, 5" d, amber...25.00
Sharon/Cabbage Rose, Federal, cup, green................18.00
Sharon/Cabbage Rose, Federal, cup, pink.................15.00
Sharon/Cabbage Rose, Federal, cup and saucer, green.....25.00
Sharon/Cabbage Rose, Federal, dinner plate, 9¹/₂" d,
amber..10.00
Sharon/Cabbage Rose, Federal, dinner plate, 9¹/₂" d,
green..20.00
Sharon/Cabbage Rose, Federal, dinner plate, 9¹/₂" d, pink...16.50
Sharon/Cabbage Rose, Federal, fruit bowl, 10¹/₂" d,
amber..15.00
Sharon/Cabbage Rose, Federal, fruit bowl, 10¹/₂" d, green....35.00
Sharon/Cabbage Rose, Federal, jam jar, pink............250.00
Sharon/Cabbage Rose, Federal, pitcher, ice lip, 80 oz,
pink..150.00
Sharon/Cabbage Rose, Federal, platter, amber............18.00
Sharon/Cabbage Rose, Federal, platter, oval, 12¹/₂" l,
green..28.00
Sharon/Cabbage Rose, Federal, salad plate, 7¹/₂" d,
amber..12.00
Sharon/Cabbage Rose, Federal, salt and pepper shakers,
pr, amber...35.00
Sharon/Cabbage Rose, Federal, salt and pepper shakers,
pr, green...72.00
Sharon/Cabbage Rose, Federal, saucer, pink.............10.00
Sharon/Cabbage Rose, Federal, sherbet, ftd, amber.......10.00
Sharon/Cabbage Rose, Federal, sugar, cov, amber.........30.00
Sharon/Cabbage Rose, Federal, sugar, open, pink.........12.00
Sharon/Cabbage Rose, Federal, tumbler, thick, 9 oz,
4¹/₈" h, pink...35.00
Sharon/Cabbage Rose, Federal, tumbler, thin, 4¹/₈" h,
amber..28.00
Spiral, Hocking, berry bowl, 4³/₄" d, green..............5.00
Spiral, Hocking, creamer, ftd, green....................7.50
Spiral, Hocking, platter, 12" l, green..................25.00

Windsor, Jeannette, pitcher, 52 oz, 6³/₄" h, pink, $30.00.

DINNERWARE

This is a catchall category. There are hundreds of American and European dinnerware manufacturers. Several dozen have their own separate listing in this book. It is not fair to ignore the rest.

This category provides a sampling of the patterns and forms from these manufacturers. It is designed to demonstrate the wide variety of material available in the market, especially today when individuals are buying dinnerware primarily for reuse.

References: Susan and Al Bagdade, *Warman's American Pottery and Porcelain,* Wallace–Homestead, Krause Publications, 1994; Jo Cunningham, *The Best of Collectible Dinnerware,* Schiffer Publishing, 1995; Jo Cunningham, *The Collector's Encyclopedia of American Dinnerware,* Collector Books, 1982, 1998 value update; Harvey Duke, *The Official Price Guide to Pottery and Porcelain, Eighth Edition,* House of Collectibles, 1995; Joanne Jasper, *Turn of the Century American Dinnerware: 1880s to 1920s,* Collector Books, 1996; Lois Lehner, *Lehner's Encyclopedia of U.S. Marks on Pottery, Porcelain & Clay,* Collector Books, 1988; Raymonde Limoges, *American Limoges: Identification & Value Guide,* Collector Books, 1996; Harry L. Rinker, *Dinnerware of the 20th Century: The Top 500 Patterns,* House of Collectibles, 1997.

Spiral, Hocking, salt and pepper shakers, pr, green	32.50
Spiral, Hocking, saucer, green	2.00
Spiral, Hocking, sherbet plate, 6" d, green	2.00
Spiral, Hocking, sugar, ftd, green	7.50
Tulip, Dell, candle cup, blue	20.00
Tulip, Dell, cup, blue	14.00
Tulip, Dell, cup and saucer, blue	18.00
Tulip, Dell, plate, 6" d, blue	7.00
Tulip, Dell, plate, 7¹/₂" d, blue	12.00
Windsor, Jeannette, ashtray, pink	35.00
Windsor, Jeannette, berry bowl, 4¹/₄" d, pink	35.00
Windsor, Jeannette, butter dish, cov, clear	15.00
Windsor, Jeannette, butter dish, cov, pink	55.00
Windsor, Jeannette, cake plate, clear	8.00
Windsor, Jeannette, cake plate, ftd, 13¹/₂" d, pink	28.00
Windsor, Jeannette, cereal bowl, 5¹/₂" d, pink	25.00
Windsor, Jeannette, chop plate, 13⁵/₈" d, green	35.00
Windsor, Jeannette, console bowl, 12¹/₂" d, pink	125.00
Windsor, Jeannette, creamer, clear	4.00
Windsor, Jeannette, creamer, green	18.00
Windsor, Jeannette, cream soup bowl, green	35.00
Windsor, Jeannette, cup and saucer, green	15.00
Windsor, Jeannette, dinner plate, 9" d, clear	6.00
Windsor, Jeannette, dinner plate, 9" d, green	20.00
Windsor, Jeannette, dinner plate, 9" d, pink	15.00
Windsor, Jeannette, nappy, 8¹/₂" d, green	30.00
Windsor, Jeannette, nappy, 8¹/₂" d, pink	55.00
Windsor, Jeannette, pitcher, 16 oz, clear	15.00
Windsor, Jeannette, platter, oval, 11¹/₂" l, green	25.00
Windsor, Jeannette, platter, oval, 11¹/₂" l, pink	18.00
Windsor, Jeannette, salt and pepper shakers, pr, green	45.00
Windsor, Jeannette, sandwich tray, handled, 4 x 9", green	25.00
Windsor, Jeannette, sherbet, cone, pink	10.00
Windsor, Jeannette, sherbet, round, green	4.00
Windsor, Jeannette, tray, handled, pink	22.00
Windsor, Jeannette, tray, divided, 8¹/₂" sq, pink	170.00
Windsor, Jeannette, tumbler, flat, 5 oz, 3¹/₄" h, green	30.00
Windsor, Jeannette, tumbler, ftd, 5" h, clear	10.00
Windsor, Jeannette, tumbler, ftd, 4" h, pink	15.00

American Limoges, Casino, cereal bowl, hearts	$15.00
American Limoges, Casino, creamer and cov sugar	45.00
American Limoges, Casino, cup and saucer, clubs	15.00
American Limoges, Casino, dinner plate, spades	18.00
American Limoges, Casino, platter, diamonds	45.00
American Limoges, Casino, sugar, diamonds	15.00
American Limoges, Triumph, chop plate, 11"	12.00
American Limoges, Triumph, cup and saucer	5.00
American Limoges, Triumph, eggcup	10.00
American Limoges, Triumph, gravy	12.00
American Limoges, Triumph, plate, 6¹/₂" d	1.00
American Limoges, Triumph, plate, 9" d	8.00
American Limoges, Triumph, platter, 11"	10.00
American Limoges, Triumph, soup bowl, 8¹/₄"	10.00
American Limoges, Triumph, vegetable bowl, 8³/₄" d	15.00
Canonsburg Pottery, Georgelyn, cup and saucer	5.00
Canonsburg Pottery, Georgelyn, plate, 9" d	7.00
Canonsburg Pottery, Keystone, creamer	4.00
Canonsburg Pottery, Keystone, cup	4.00
Canonsburg Pottery, Keystone, plate, 9" d	8.00
Canonsburg Pottery, Keystone, platter, 11"	10.00
Canonsburg Pottery, Priscilla/Washington Colonial, gravy	12.00
Canonsburg Pottery, Priscilla/Washington Colonial, plate, 9" d	5.00
Canonsburg Pottery, Priscilla/Washington Colonial, sugar	8.00
Canonsburg Pottery, Spartan, dish, 5¹/₄"	2.00
Canonsburg Pottery, Spartan, plate, 6¹/₄" d	1.00
Canonsburg Pottery, Spartan, saucer	1.00
Canonsburg Pottery, Westchester, casserole	20.00
Canonsburg Pottery, Westchester, creamer	4.00
Canonsburg Pottery, Westchester, sugar	8.00
Castleton, Empire Blue, place setting	100.00
Castleton, Jade, place setting	120.00
Castleton, Lace, place setting	150.00
Castleton, Rose, place setting	125.00
Continental Kilns, Square, cup and saucer	5.00
Continental Kilns, Square, plate, 9¹/₂" d	7.00
Continental Kilns, Square, platter, 13¹/₂"	12.00
Continental Kilns, Square, tumbler, square	12.00

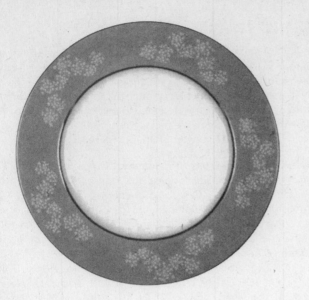

Castleton, Lace, dinner plate, 10³/₄" d, price for 5–pc place setting, $150.00.

Cronin China, Zephyr, creamer 4.00
Cronin China, Zephyr, cup and saucer 5.00
Cronin China, Zephyr, plate, 9" d. 7.00
Cronin China, Zephyr, salad bowl, 9¹/₂" d 15.00
Cronin China, Zephyr, platter, 11¹/₂" 10.00
W S George, Argosy, cup and saucer 5.00
W S George, Argosy, gravy liner 6.00
W S George, Argosy, plate, 6¹/₈" d 1.00
W S George, Argosy, sugar 8.00
W S George, Argosy, casserole. 20.00
W S George, Argosy, plate, 6¹/₄" d 1.00
W S George, Basketweave, creamer. 4.00
W S George, Basketweave, eggcup 10.00
W S George, Basketweave, grill plate, 10" 8.00
W S George, Basketweave, platter, 11" l 10.00
W S George, Bolero, cup and saucer 5.00
W S George, Bolero, gravy, round, double lipped,
  handled 12.00
W S George, Bolero, creamer 4.00
W S George, Bolero, plate, 8" d. 4.00
W S George, Bolero, sugar 8.00
W S George, Cape Cod, cup and saucer 5.00
W S George, Cape Cod, plate, 9" d 8.00
W S George, Elmhurst, cup and saucer 5.00
W S George, Elmhurst, demitasse cup 10.00
W S George, Elmhurst, gravy. 12.00
W S George, Elmhurst, plate, 6" d 1.00
W S George, Elmhurst, plate, 9" d 8.00
W S George, Elmhurst, platter, 13" 12.00
W S George, Fleurette, creamer. 4.00
W S George, Fleurette, cup and saucer 5.00
W S George, Fleurette, gravy. 12.00
W S George, Fleurette, plate, 9" d 8.00
W S George, Georgette, creamer 5.00
W S George, Georgette, cup and saucer. 5.00
W S George, Georgette, demitasse cup and saucer 13.00
W S George, Georgette, dish, 6¹/₂". 3.00
W S George, Georgette, plate, 6¹/₂" 1.00
W S George, Georgette, plate, 9¹/₄" d 8.00

W S George, Georgette, platter, 13" l 12.00
W S George, Lido, butter dish 20.00
W S George, Lido, creamer 4.00
W S George, Lido, cup and saucer. 5.00
W S George, Lido, eggcup. 10.00
W S George, Lido, plate, 6¹/₂" 1.00
W S George, Lido, plate, 9¹/₄" d 8.00
W S George, Lido, platter, 13¹/₄" d 12.00
W S George, Lido, sugar 8.00
Irouois, Carrara Modern, cup and saucer 8.00
Iroquois, Carrara Modern, creamer 10.00
Iroquois, Carrara Modern, gravy. 15.00
Iroquois, Carrara Modern, plate, 6¹/₂" d 5.00
Iroquois, Carrara Modern, shaker, pr 12.00
Iroquois, Impromptu, condiment dish, metal handle 20.00
Iroquois, Impromptu, cup, low, 2¹/₄". 4.00
Iroquois, Impromptu, saucer, low cup 1.00
Iroquois, Impromptu, soup bowl, coupe, 7¹/₄". 10.00
Iroquois, Impromptu, sugar 8.00
Iroquois, Informal, butter, rect, ¹/₄ lb. 15.00
Iroquois, Informal, creamer 4.00
Iroquois, Informal cup and saucer 5.00
Iroquois, Informal, plate, 6¹/₂" d 1.00
Iroquois, Informal, plate, 8" d 5.00
Iroquois, Informal, vegetable bowl, divided, 11" l 10.00
Iroquois, Inheritance, cup and saucer. 5.00
Iroquois, Inheritance, dish, 8" 3.00
Iroquois, Inheritance, plate, 10¹/₂" d 10.00
Iroquois, Inheritance, salad bowl, 10" 15.00
Iroquois, Intaglio, creamer. 4.00
Iroquois, Intaglio, cup and saucer 12.00
Iroquois, Intaglio, plate, 6⁵/₈" d 1.00
Iroquois, Intaglio, plate, 8¹/₂" d 4.00
Iroquois, Intaglio, platter, 15¹/₄" 15.00
James River, Cascade, cup and saucer 5.00
James River, Cascade, creamer. 4.00
James River, Cascade, dish, 6" 2.00
James River, Cascade, plate, 6¹/₄" 1.00
James River, Cascade, plate, 9¹/₂" 5.00
James River, Cascade, relish. 10.00
Sebring, Aristocrat, cup and saucer 5.00
Sebring, Aristocrat, dish, 5¹/₂". 2.00
Sebring, Aristocrat, gravy. 12.00
Sebring, Aristocrat, plate, 9". 5.00
Sebring, Aristocrat, shaker, pr. 8.00
Sebring, Barbara Jane, butter dish 20.00
Sebring, Barbara Jane, demitasse cup 10.00
Sebring, Barbara Jane, soup bowl, 9" 10.00
Sebring, Barbara Jane, eggcup 10.00
Sebring, Barbara Jane, plate, 6¹/₄" d 1.00
Sebring, Barbara Jane, plate, 8" d. 4.00
Sebring, Corinthian, cup and saucer 5.00
Sebring, Corinthian, gravy. 12.00
Sebring, Corinthian, plate, 9" d 5.00
Sebring, Corinthian, soup bowl, 8". 10.00
Sebring, Doric, casserole. 20.00
Sebring, Doric, cup and saucer 5.00
Sebring, Doric, demitasse cup 10.00
Sebring, Doric, gravy. 12.00
Sebring, Doric, plate, 7" d. 4.00
Sebring, Gadroon, butter dish 20.00
Sebring, Gadroon, casserole, oval 20.00
Sebring, Gadroon, cup and saucer. 5.00
Sebring, Gadroon, creamer 4.00

Stetson, Heritage Ware, Cynthia pattern, Ionic shape, bread and butter plate, hp red and blue flowers, 6¹/₈" d, c1950, $2.00.

Sebring, Gadroon, cream soup cup **12.00**
Sebring, Gadroon, demitasse cup and saucer **12.00**
Sebring, Gadroon, eggcup. **10.00**
Sebring, Gadroon, plate, 6¹/₄" d **1.00**
Sebring, Gadroon, plate, 8" d **5.00**
Sebring, Pegasus, creamer **4.00**
Sebring, Pegasus, cup and saucer. **5.00**
Sebring, Pegasus, gravy **12.00**
Sebring, Pegasus, plate, 10" d **10.00**
Sebring, Pegasus, platter, 11" **10.00**
Sebring, Trojan, cup and saucer **5.00**
Sebring, Trojan, dish, 5¹/₄" **2.00**
Sebring, Trojan, plate, 6" d **1.00**
Sebring, Trojan, plate, 9" d **5.00**
Sebring, Trojan, sugar **8.00**
Stetson, Airflow, creamer. **5.00**
Stetson, Airflow, cup and saucer **5.00**
Stetson, Airflow, onion, cov. **12.00**
Stetson, Airflow, plate, 6¹/₄" d. **1.50**
Stetson, Airflow, salad bowl, 8¹/₂" d **15.00**
Stetson, Annette, casserole. **20.00**
Stetson, Annette, cup and saucer **5.00**
Stetson, Annette, dish, 5¹/₄" **2.00**
Stetson, Annette, platter, 11" **10.00**
Stetson, Heritage Ware, Cynthia pattern, Ionic shape,
    casserole. **20.00**
Stetson, Heritage Ware, Cynthia pattern, Ionic shape,
    creamer **4.00**
Stetson, Heritage Ware, Cynthia pattern, Ionic shape,
    cup and saucer **5.00**
Stetson, Heritage Ware, Cynthia pattern, Ionic shape,
    platter, 11" **10.00**
Stetson, Heritage Ware, Cynthia pattern, Ionic shape,
    sugar **8.00**
Stetson, Oxford, creamer. **4.00**
Stetson, Oxford, gravy. **12.00**
Stetson, Oxford, plate, 7¹/₄" d **4.00**
Stetson, Oxford, salad bowl, 9" **15.00**
Stetson, Oxford, vegetable bowl, 8" **10.00**

DIONNE QUINTUPLETS

Annette, Cecile, Emilie, Marie, and Yvonne Dionne were born on May 28, 1934, in rural Canada between the towns of Corbeil and Callander, Ontario. Dr. Dafoe and two midwives delivered the five girls. An agreement to exhibit the babies at the Chicago World's Fair led to the passage of "An Act for the Protection of the Dionne Quintuplets" by the Canadian government.

The Dafoe Hospital, which served as visitor viewing center for thousands of people who traveled to Canada to see the Quints, was built across the street from the family home. The Quints craze lasted into the early 1940s. Hundreds of souvenir and licensed products were manufactured during that period. Emile died in August 1954 and Marie on February 27, 1970.

Reference: John Axe, *The Collectible Dionne Quintuplets*, Hobby House Press, 1977, out of print.

Collectors' Club: Dionne Quint Collectors, PO Box 2527, Woburn, MA 01888.

Blotter, cardboard, sepia photo, NEA Service, 1935,
    4 x 9" **$20.00**
Book, *The Dionne Quintuplets Growing Up*, 1935,
    8¹/₂ x 11". **40.00**
Box, Dionne Pops, Vitamin Candy Co, Providence, RI,
    1936, 4 x 10¹/₂ x 1" **125.00**
Calendar, 1936, Watch Us Grow **18.00**
Calendar, 1938, Brown & Bigelow Co, color illus,
    unused, 8 x 11³/₄" **30.00**
Dish, chrome plated, Quints names and faces engraved
    along edge **35.00**
Doll, set of 5, composition, molded, curly hair, swivel
    head, jointed arms and legs, Ralph A Freundlich,
    1935. . . . . **350.00**
Fan, cardboard, multicolored, Stonington Furniture Co
    adv, 1936 . . . . **40.00**
Lobby Card, "Five Of A Kind," color, girls playing piano,
    1938, 11 x 14" **70.00**
Magazine Cover, *Life*, May 17, 1937 . . . . **50.00**
Magazine Cover, *Look*, Oct 11, 1938, Dr Dafoe. **5.00**
Magazine, *Dionne Quints/Pictorial Review*, Feb 1937,
    Karo Syrup adv with Quints **15.00**
Paper Doll, Merrill, #3488, uncut, 1935. . . . . **175.00**

Story Booklets, paper, black and white photos, both sgd in front by mother, ©1936, 9⁷/₈" h, 9¹/₂" w, price for pair, $60.00. Photo courtesy Collectors Auction Services.

Photo, color, framed, ©NEA Service, 1935, 10 x 12".......**25.00**
Pinball Game, Place the Quintuplets in the Carriage,
    green tin frame, 3½ x 5".........................**20.00**
Plate, china, 3 tinted color photos, red trim, 7¼" d........**75.00**
Sign, cardboard, Quints with tea set, 11 x 16"........**60.00**
Souvenir, tray, china, irid tan, soft brick pattern, colorful
    maple leaf, Quint figures on edge, mkd "Souvenir of
    Callander," late 1930s, 2 x 3½"..................**100.00**

DISNEYANA

The Disney era began when *Steamboat Willie*, Walt Disney's first animated cartoon, appeared on theater screens in 1928. The success of Walt Disney and his studio are attributed to two major factors: (1) development of a host of cartoon characters, feature–length cartoons, and feature movies enjoyed throughout the world, and (2) an aggressive marketing and licensing program.

European Disney and Disney theme park collectibles are two strong growth areas within Disneyana. Be especially price conscious when buying post–1975 Disneyana. Large amounts have been hoarded. The number of licensed products increased significantly. Disney shopping mall stores and mail–order catalog sales have significantly increased the amount of new material available. In fact, products have been created to be sold exclusively through these channels. It is for this reason that many Disneyana collectors concentrate on Disney collectibles licensed before 1965.

References: Bill Cotter, *The Wonderful World of Disney Television: A Complete History*, Hyperion, 1997; Robert Heide and John Gilman, *Disneyana: Classic Collectibles 1928–1958*, Hyperion, 1994; Robert Heide and John Gilman, *The Mickey Mouse Watch: From the Beginning of Time*, Hyperion, 1997; David Longest and Michael Stern, *The Collector's Encyclopedia of Disneyana*, Collector Books (1992, 1996 value update); R. Michael Murray, *The Golden Age of Walt Disney Records, 1933–1988: Price Guide for Disney Fans and Record Collectors*, Antique Trader Books, 1997; Maxine A. Pinsky, *Marx Toys: Robots, Space, Comic, Disney & TV Characters*, Schiffer Publishing, 1996; Dave Smith, *Disney A to Z: The Official Encyclopedia*, Hyperion, 1996; Michael Stern, *Stern's Guide to Disney Collectibles, First Series* (1989, 1992 value update), *Second Series* (1990, 1995 value update), *Third Series* (1995), Collector Books; Tom Tumbusch, *Tomart's Illustrated Disneyana Catalog and Price Guide, Condensed Edition*, Wallace–Homestead, 1990, out of print.

Periodicals: *Storyboard Magazine*, 80 Main St, Nashua, NH 03060; *Tomart's Disneyana Digest*, 3300 Encrete Ln, Dayton, OH 45439.

Collectors' Clubs: National Fantasy Club For Disneyana Collectors & Enthusiasts, PO Box 19212, Irvine, CA 92713; The Mouse Club, 2056 Cirone Way, San Jose, CA 95124.

Alice in Wonderland, figure, china, signature style
    1960 Disney copyright on bottom, 6" h...........**$18.00**
Alice in Wonderland Magic Picture Kit Set, set of 4, Jiffy
    Pop, 1974..**12.00**
Alice in Wonderland Sewing Kit, plastic, 7" sewing
    machine, 5" doll, Hasbro, 1951...................**40.00**
Babes in Toyland, figure, soldier, holding bugle, plastic,
    hp, black, white, and red outfit, Marx, 1961, 3" h......**15.00**
Bambi, figure, Thumper, Hagen–Renaker, 1950s, 1¼" h.....**75.00**

Bambi, lamp, open upright storybook, plastic Bambi and
    Thumper figures on front, Dolly Toy Co, c1950,
    12" h...**55.00**
Cinderella Molding Set, Model Craft, 1950s..............**55.00**
Cinderella, serving set, Gus and Jaq, creamer, pitcher,
    and sugar bowl, 1960s............................**60.00**
Daisy Duck, figure, ceramic, hp, Daisy wearing blue
    and pink outfit, 1960s...........................**50.00**
Disneyland, ashtray, china, white, gold accents, multi-
    colored landscape, castle in front, river in foreground,
    underside rim stamped "Disneyland Copyright Walt
    Disney Productions," 1960s, ¾" h, 5" d...........**12.00**
Disneyland, camera, plastic, "18 Pictures Of Disney-
    land," 1950s.....................................**75.00**
Disneyland, pennant, red felt, white logo, late 1950s,
    28" l..**18.00**
Disneyland, salt and pepper shakers, pr, china, figural
    coffeepots, white, gold accents, top handle, orig stop-
    pers, multicolored Disneyland castle on one side,
    Victorian woman and Main Street police officer on
    other side, late 1950s, 2" h.....................**35.00**
Disneyland, souvenir guide book, glossy paper, 1961,
    28 pp, 8 x 11½"..................................**45.00**
Disneyland Card Game, deck of 44 cards, instructions,
    clear plastic case, Whitman, 1964................**30.00**
Disneyland Melody Player, paper rolls, 1950s...........**15.00**
Disneyland Target Game, black plastic gun, 33 suction
    cup darts, litho tin target, Hasbro, unused, 1960s......**50.00**
Donald Duck, bank, glass jar, front color label, blue and
    yellow tin lid, Nash–Underwood, 1950s, 2½ x 4¾"......**75.00**
Donald Duck, crayon box, tin, Donald Duck and
    Mickey Mouse illus, Transogram, 1946.............**40.00**
Donald Duck, magic slate, "Air Raid Game," 1950s........**15.00**
Donald Duck, mask, cardboard, blue hat, orange bill,
    elastic strap, 1950s.............................**25.00**
Donald Duck, roly–poly, vinyl, black, white, yellow,
    and blue, chimes, 1970s, 6" d, 11" h.............**20.00**
Dumbo, squeeze toy, Dell, 1950s......................**30.00**
Goofy, Bump 'N Go Action Lawn Mower, plastic figure
    pushing silver handled lawn mower, Illfelder, 1980s.....**50.00**

Mickey Mouse, pull toy, Mickey Mouse Safety Patrol, #733, Fisher–Price, $375.00.

Jungle Book, Bagheera, Disneykin, plastic, hp, 1967 . . . . **30.00**

Jungle Book, Mowgli's Hut Mobile, Baloo and King Louis figures, Multiple Toymakers, 1968, 2 x 3 x 3" **50.00**

Lady and the Tramp, doll, Tramp, stuffed, hard plastic eyes and mouth, Schuco, 1955, 8" h **70.00**

Mary Poppins, figure, bendable, Gund, 1964, 11½" h **40.00**

Mary Poppins Needlepoint and Frame Set, 3 pre–colored tapestry canvases, yarn, needles, 3 white styrofoam frames, Hasbro, 1965, MIB **60.00**

Mickey Mouse, bank, vinyl, figural, wearing black jacket, white shirt, orange bow tie, and red pants, movable arm and head, orig cardboard tags and price sticker on ear, 1970s, 6½" h **25.00**

Mickey Mouse, doll, Talking Mickey, red shirt, green pants, Mattel, 1976 . . . . **15.00**

Mickey Mouse, jeep, tin litho, blue, folding windshield, Mickey litho on hood, Jiminy Cricket litho on sides, black rubber wheels, 1950–60 . . . . **250.00**

Mickey Mouse, Mousegetar, black plastic, white plastic front, 1960s, 30" l **72.00**

Mickey Mouse, Nestled Rattle Blocks, 5 stiff cardboard blocks, full color paper labels, orig brown shipping box, Gabriel Industries, 1950s **65.00**

Mickey Mouse, pull toy, Mickey Mouse Puddle Jumper, Fisher–Price, 1953 . . . . **60.00**

Mickey Mouse, push puppet, Drummer Mickey, Kohner, 1950s **100.00**

Mickey Mouse, radio with microphone, yellow, attached 2–dimensional Mickey Mouse figure, 1970s **25.00**

Mickey Mouse, riding toy, Mickey Mouse Bus Lines, "Walt Disney Stars," 1960s, 19½" l **150.00**

Mickey Mouse, soaky, red cap, 1960s, 7" h **15.00**

Mickey Mouse, spinning top, Mickey Mouse, litho tin, Chein, 1950s **70.00**

Mickey Mouse, Talking Alarm Clock, hard plastic, orange and blue plastic train engine on front, figural Mickey attached at top, color sticker on front grill, orig box, Bradley Time, 1970s **60.00**

Mickey Mouse Bump–N–Go Spaceship, litho tin, battery operated, clear dome, 6 flashing lights, rotating antenna, Matsudaya, 1980s **50.00**

Mickey Mouse Club Bow and Arrow Set, 1955 . . . . **25.00**

Mickey Mouse Club Drum, Walt Disney Productions **115.00**

Mickey Mouse Club, projector, hard plastic, gray, Mickey Mouse Club sticker on side, 16 mm black and white films, Stephens Products, 1950s, 7½" h **85.00**

Mickey Mouse Club, soaky, girl Mouseketeer, wearing red and white outfit, orange bow in hair, 1960s **45.00**

Mickey Mouse Doctor's Office, Hassenfield, 1951 55 . . . . . **92.00**

Mickey Mouse Rhythm Band, orig box, Emenee **65.00**

Minnie Mouse, marionette, wood and composition, 1950s, 13" h **170.00**

101 Dalmatians, key chain, plastic, black and white flicker shows dalmatian when piece is moved, reverse with inscription and place to fill in name and address, silver link chain, 1961 . . . . **30.00**

101 Dalmatians, record, *Dalmatian Plantation/Cruella DeVille*, 45 rpm, color paper sleeve, 1962 . . . . **15.00**

101 Dalmatians, squeeze toy, Lucky, Dell, 7" h **12.00**

Peter Pan, doll, stuffed, plush, green body, vinyl head and arms, green felt jacket, brown felt shoes, gold elastic belt, Ideal, 1950s **55.00**

Peter Pan, hand puppet, Captain Hook, Gund **20.00**

Peter Pan, sewing cards, Whitman, 1952 . . . . **20.00**

Walt Disney Character Pictorial Map of the United States, frame tray, Jaymar #2734, ©Walt Disney Productions, $18.00.

Pinocchio, Disneykins, Pinocchio, Geppetto, Jiminy Cricket, Figaro, and Blue Fairy, complete with accessories, MIB **50.00**

Pinocchio, squeeze toy, Cleo, Sun Rubber, 1940s **70.00**

Pluto, car, plastic, Pluto sitting in white and red Mercedes Benz, "30" on hood, boxed, Elm Toys, 1960s, 2" l **45.00**

Pluto, soaky, ©Walt Disney Production, 1965, 8½" h **18.00**

Sleeping Beauty, clock, hard plastic, white front rim, red numerals, translucent green back, Phinney–Walker, Japan, 1957 . . . . **50.00**

Sleeping Beauty, plate, glazed white ceramic, gold rim, Sleeping Beauty's castle with multicolored Alpine scene, purple accents, gold "Disneyland," stamped "Disneyland Copyright Walt Disney Productions," Japan sticker, red ribbon for hanging, c1950s, 4" d **12.00**

Sleeping Beauty Magic Paint Set, Whitman **40.00**

Snow White, doll, Dopey, cloth, Gund, 12" h **50.00**

Snow White, figurine, ceramic, hp, seated Snow White with bluebird resting on back of her hand, 1960s, 4¾" h **6.00**

Snow White, marionette, Dopey, Peter Puppet Playthings, 1952 . . . . **100.00**

Snow White, pin, Happy, painted wood, 1940s **25.00**

Three Little Pigs, ramp walker, plastic, worker pig holding trowel with Big Bad Wolf tied up in front of him, Marx, 1950s **80.00**

Walt Disney's Character Mini–Mold Set, rubber molds, molding powder, paint, and brushes, Yankee Homecraft Corp, 1966, MIB **25.00**

Walt Disney's Nautilus Expanding Periscope, paper covered cardboard body, green plastic end caps, "Inspired By 20,000 Leagues Under The Sea," Pressman Toy Corp, c1954, 30" l **45.00**

Winnie the Pooh, magic slate, Western Publishing, 1965 . . . . **35.00**

Winnie the Pooh, snow globe, musical, 5½" h **25.00**

Zorro, figure, plastic, Zorro on stallion, black, flexible vinyl accessories, 1958, 11" h **250.00**

Zorro Action Set, hat, mask, whip, lariat, pistol, 2 fencing foils, and sheath knife, Marx, c1957 . . . . **65.00**

DOG COLLECTIBLES

There are over 100 breeds of dogs divided into seven classes: herding, hounds, non–sporting, sporting, terriers, toy breeds, and working dogs. The first modern dog show was held in Newcastle, England, in 1859. The recording of bloodlines soon followed.

Unlike other animal collectors, dog collectors are breed specific. A Scottie collector is highly unlikely to own a Boxer collectible. In most cases, these collections mate with the breed of dog owned by the collector. Finally, dog collectors demand that the collectibles they buy closely resemble their pet. The fact that the collectible portrays a German Shepherd is not enough. It must remind them specifically of their pooch.

References: Edith Butler, *Poodle Collectibles of the 50's & 60's*, L–W Book Sales, 1995; Candace Sten Davis and Patricia Baugh, *A Treasury of Scottie Dog Collectibles*, Collector Books, 1998.

Newsletters: *Collectively Speaking!*, 428 Philadelphia Rd, Joppa, MD 21085.

Collectors' Clubs: Canine Collectibles Club, 736 N Western Ave, Ste 314, Lake Forest, IL 60045; Wee Scots, PO Box 1597, Winchester, VA 22604.

Airedale, figure, carved wood, 2 pups on chain	**$35.00**
Beagle, figure, Boehm, 1984	**225.00**
Bulldog, figure, bisque, 5½" h	**50.00**
Bulldog, hood ornament, Mack Trucks	**25.00**
Cocker Spaniel, bottle opener, figural, front paw up, cast iron, off–white body with black patches, John Wright Co, 2¾" h, 3¾" l	**55.00**
Dalmatian, Penny, Enesco, large	**50.00**
Poodle, powder jar, glass, iridescent	**24.00**
Scottie, ashtray, metal, dog sitting aside tree shaped tray, 2¾" h	**25.00**
Scottie, bookends, pr, metal, c1929	**85.00**
Scottie, charm, plastic, white, c1940s	**10.00**
Scottie, pencil set, cardboard case, snap closure on front, brown textured paper covering with 2 emb Scottie dogs design, int sliding drawer, contains pencils, eraser, and ruler, American Pencil Co, 1930s, 5¾ x 9¾ x 1½"	**20.00**
Scottie, pinback button, "Texaco Scottie," 2 Scottie dogs, black and white, red and black lettering, 1930s	**45.00**
Scottie, powder jar, transparent pink glass	**30.00**
Scottie, rocking blotter, jade	**40.00**
Scottie, tie bar, black dog on pearl–like backing, silver accents, Swank, 1930–40s	**15.00**
Scottie, tip tray, Black & White Scotch adv	**30.00**
St Bernard, rug, wool, lap	**195.00**

Greyhound, hood ornament, cast bronzed metal, "Florida 5" on red fabric blanket, 6⅛" l, 2⅞" h, $20.00.

DOLL HOUSES & FURNISHINGS

Handmade doll house furniture falls into the realm of miniatures. Miniatures are exact copies of their larger counterparts. Depending on the accuracy of detail, material used, and recognition of the maker, these miniatures can quickly jump into the hundreds of dollars. Miniature collectors tend to look down on machine–made material.

Petite Prince, Plastic Art Toy Corporation, Tootsietoy, and Renwal are just four of hundreds of major manufacturers of machine–made doll house furniture. Materials range from wood to injection molded plastic. This furniture was meant to be used, and most surviving examples were. The period packaging and its supporting literature can double the value of a set.

References: Jean Mahan, *Doll Furniture, 1950s–1980s: Identification & Price Guide*, Hobby House Press, 1997; Dian Zillner, *American Dollhouses and Furniture From the 20th Century*, Schiffer Publishing, 1995; Dian Zillner and Patty Cooper, *Antique and Collectible Dollhouses and Their Furnishings*, Schiffer Publishing, 1998.

Periodicals: *Doll Castle News*, PO Box 247, Washington, NJ 07882; *Miniature Collector*, Scott Publications, 30595 Eight Mile, Livonia, MI 48152; *Nutshell News*, PO Box 1612, Waukesha, WI 53187.

Collectors' Clubs: Dollhouse & Miniature Collectors, PO Box 16, Bellaire, MI 49615; National Assoc of Miniature Enthusiasts, PO Box 69, Carmel, IN 46032.

DOLL HOUSES

Bungaloo, litho tin, Marx, c1950s	**$75.00**
Cape Cod, litho tin, clapboard and gray stone, red roof, 3 dormers, 1 chimney, 5 windows, 21 x 15", Meritoy, 1949	**190.00**
Colonial Dollhouse, litho tin, Playsteel, 1948	**200.00**
Country Cottage, #800, Wolverine, 1980s	**40.00**
Miniature Dollhouse, #95, litho tin, complete with 28 pcs of plastic furniture, Ohio Art, 3 x 8½ x 5¼"	**75.00**
Princess Patti, Ideal	**120.00**
Ranch House, litho tin, T Cohn, 1950s	**75.00**
Ranch House, with side porch, litho tin, Marx, 1960s	**65.00**
Spanish Two–Story, litho tin, 1 patio, T Cohn, 1948	**150.00**
Suburban, litho tin, Marx, c1950s	**110.00**
Three–Story, #0250, 5 rooms, spiral staircase, 2 figures, complete with instructions, Fisher–Price, 1970s	**45.00**
Two–Story, with Disney nursery, litho tin, Marx, 1950	**145.00**

FURNISHINGS

Accessory Set, #1427, complete with 20 figures, playground equipment, swimming pool, Marx, 1950s, MIB	**$160.00**
Baby Carriage, #115, molded baby, Renwal	**25.00**
Baby Push Cart, #87, Renwal	**15.00**

Bathroom Set, #253, sink, toilet, shower stall,
Fisher–Price **3.00**
Bathroom Scale, #10, Renwal **10.00**
Bathtub, Plasco. **8.00**
Breakfast Bar, Plasco **10.00**
Buffet, Plasco **10.00**
Chair, metal, Tootsietoy, c1920, price for pair **25.00**
Coffee Table, Plasco **5.00**
Coffee Table, Young Decorator, Ideal **10.00**
Crib, Young Decorator, Ideal **25.00**
Deluxe Refrigerator, Renwal, #24 . . . . **35.00**
Diaper Pail, Young Decorator, Ideal **20.00**
Doctor with Bag, #44, Renwal. **45.00**
Family, #265, mom, dad, 2 girls, Fisher–Price. **2.00**
Floor Lamp, Young Decorator, Ideal **20.00**
Garbage Can, #64, Renwal **15.00**
Garden Set, 4 chairs, umbrella table, sun lounge,
refreshment table, and fountain, Plasco **140.00**
Grandfather Clock, folding screen, Petite Princess, Ideal,
MIB **45.00**
Hamper, Renwal, #T98 . . . . **10.00**
Ironing Board, folding, cast iron, Kilgore, c1930. . . . . **20.00**
Kitchen Set, sink, stove, refrigerator, table, and
4 chairs, Renwal, MIB **140.00**
Kitchen Stool, #12, Renwal **10.00**
Linen Cabinet, 4 towels, Princess Patti, Ideal **60.00**
Little Princess Bed, Petite Princess, Ideal. **45.00**
Living Room Set, couch, club chair, lady's chair, fire-
place, 2 end tables, 2 table lamps, floor lamp, coffee
table, floor radio, piano, and piano bench, Renwal **150.00**
Mother, #43, Renwal. **25.00**
Nursery Set, #257, crib, dresser, rocking horse, and baby
figure, Fisher–Price **3.00**
Nursery Set, night stand, chest, bathinette, cradle crib,
table lamp, playpen, carriage, and highchair, Renwal,
MIB **140.00**
Patio Set, #259, redwood chair, chaise lounge, grill, and
dog, Fisher–Price. **2.00**

Piano, #L74, Renwal **20.00**
Playpen, #118, Renwal **5.00**
Policeman, #44, Renwal **50.00**
Radio/Phonograph, #18, Renwal **20.00**
Refrigerator, Renwal, #K66 . . . . **10.00**
Refrigerator, Young Decorator, Ideal **25.00**
Rolling Tea Cart, Petite Princess, Ideal, complete with
wine bottle and 3 wine cups **25.00**
School Desk, #33, Renwal. **15.00**
Sewing Machine, #89, Renwal. **40.00**
Sideboard, #D55, Renwal **10.00**
Sink, Plasco **8.00**
Sink, Princess Patti, Ideal **50.00**
Sink, Young Decorator, Ideal **20.00**
Stove, Plasco **5.00**
Swing, #19, Renwal **30.00**
Table, metal, c1920, Tootsietoy **25.00**
Tea Cart, metal, Tootsietoy, c1920 . . . . **25.00**
Teeter–Totter, #21, Renwal. **15.00**
Telephone, #288, Renwal **10.00**
Television Set, Plasco, MIP **30.00**
Television Set, Young Decorator, Ideal **50.00**
Twin Bed, Plasco **5.00**
Twin Bed. #81, Renwal **5.00**
Twin Bed, Young Decorator, Ideal **20.00**
Umbrella Table, Plasco **15.00**
Vacuum Cleaner, #37, Renwal. **20.00**
Vanity, metal, Tootsietoy, c1920 . . . . **25.00**
Wing Chair, Plasco **5.00**

DOLLS

The middle decades of the 20th century witnessed a number of major changes in doll manufacture. New materials (plastic), technology (injection molding), and manufacturing location (the Far East) all played a major role in revolutionizing the industry by the mid–1960s.

Hard, then soft plastic dolls dominated the market by the mid–1950s. Barbie arrived on the scene in 1959. The Cabbage Patch doll was the marketing sensation of the 1970s.

Doll manufacturers are quick to copy any successful doll. Horsman's Dorothy looked surprisingly like Effanbee's Patsy doll. Cosmopolitan's Ginger could easily be mistaken for Vogue's Ginny. Even with a single manufacturer, the same parts were used to make a variety of dolls. Barbie and her friends borrowed body parts from each other.

While condition has always played a major role in doll collecting, it became an obsession in the 1980s, particularly among collectors of contemporary dolls. MIB, mint–in–box, gave way to NRFB, never–removed–from–box.

More and more collectors, especially those under the age of forty–five, are focusing on 1950s and 60s dolls. Many values have doubled in the past five years.

References: J. Michael Augustyniak, *Thirty Years of Mattel Fashion Dolls*, Collector Books, 1998; John Axe, *Effanbee: A Collector's Encyclopedia, 1949 Present, Second Edition*, Hobby House Press, 1994; John Axe, *Tammy and Her Family of Dolls: Identification and Price Guide*, Hobby House Press, 1995; Joseph Bourgeois, *Collector's Guide to Dolls in Uniform*, Collector Books, 1995; Carla Marie Cross, *Modern Doll Rarities*, Antique Trader Books, 1997; Linda Crowsey, *Madame Alexander: Collector's Dolls Price*

Living Room Set, Nancy Forbes "Dream House" Furniture #171, American Toy & Furniture Co, wood, 7 pcs, $50.00.

Guide #23, Collector Books, 1998; Jan Foulke, *12th Blue Book Dolls & Values*, Hobby House Press, 1995; Beth C. Gunther, *Crissy & Friends: Collector's Guide to Ideal's Girls*, Antique Trader Books, 1998; Dawn Herlocher, *200 Years of Dolls: Identification and Price Guide*, Antique Trader Books, 1996; Judith Izen, *Collector's Guide To Ideal Dolls: Identification & Value Guide*, Collector Books, 1994; Judith Izen and Carol Stover, *Collector's Guide to Vogue Dolls: Identification and Values*, Collector Books, 1998.

Polly Judd, *Cloth Dolls of the 1920s and 1930s*, Hobby House Press, 1990; Polly and Pam Judd, *Composition Dolls: 1909–1928, Volume II*, Hobby House Press, 1994; Polly and Pam Judd, *Composition Dolls: 1928–1955*, Hobby House Press, 1991; Polly and Pam Judd, *European Costumed Dolls*, Hobby House Press, 1994; Polly and Pam Judd, *Glamour Dolls of the 1950s & 1960s: Identification and Values, Revised Edition*, Hobby House Press, 1993; Polly and Pam Judd, *Hard Plastic Dolls I, Third Revised Edition*, Hobby House Press, 1993; Polly and Pam Judd, *Hard Plastic Dolls II, Revised*, Hobby House Press, 1994; Michele Karl, *Composition & Wood Dolls and Toys: A Collector's Reference Guide*, Antique Trader Books, 1998; Sean Kettelkamp, *Chatty Cathy and Her Talking Friends*, Schiffer Publishing, 1998; Kathy and Don Lewis, *Chatty Cathy Dolls*, Collector Books, 1994.

A. Glenn Mandeville, *Alexander Dolls Collector's Price Guide, 2nd Edition*, Hobby House Press, 1995; A. Glenn Mandeville, *Ginny: An American Toddler Doll, 2nd Revised Edition*, Hobby House Press, 1994; A. Glenn Mandeville, *Madame Alexander Dolls Value Guide*, Hobby House Press, 1994; A. Glenn Mandeville, *Sensational '60s Doll Album*, Hobby House Press, 1996; Marjorie A. Miller, *Nancy Ann Storybook Dolls*, Hobby House Press, 1980, available in reprint; Patsy Moyer, *Doll Values: Antique to Modern, Second Edition*, Collector Books, 1998.

Patsy Moyer, *Modern Collectible Dolls: Identification & Value Guide* (1997), *Vol. II* (1998), Collector Books; Myla Perkins, *Black Dolls: 1820–1991*, Collector Books, 1993, 1995 value update; Myla Perkins, *Black Dolls, Book II, An Identification and Value Guide*, Collector Books, 1995; Susan Nettleingham Roberts and Dorothy Bunker, *The Ginny Doll Encyclopedia*, Hobby House Press, 1994; Patricia R. Smith, *Collector's Encyclopedia of Madame Alexander Dolls, 1965–1990*, Collector Books, 1991, 1997 value update; Patricia R. Smith, *Modern Collector's Dolls, Seventh Series* (1995), *Eighth Series* (1996), Collector Books; Evelyn Robson Strahlendorf, *The Charlton Standard Catalogue of Canadian Dolls, 3rd Edition*, Charlton Press, 1997.

Periodicals: *Doll Reader*, 741 Miller Dr SE, Ste D2, Harrisubrg, PA 20175; *Dolls—The Collector's Magazine*, 170 Fifth Ave, 12th Floor, New York, NY 10010; *Doll World*, 306 E Parr Rd, Berne, IN 46711.

Collectors' Clubs: Cabbage Patch Kids Clubs, 1027 Newport Ave, Pawtucket, RI 02862; Cabbage Patch Kids Collectors Club (company sponsored), PO Box 714, Cleveland, GA 30528; Chatty Cathy Collectors Club, PO Box 140, Readington, NJ 08870; Dawn Dolls Collectors Club, PO Box 565, Billings, MT 59103; Ginny Doll Club (company sponsored), Corporate Dr, Grantsville, MD 21536; Ginny Doll Club, PO Box 338, Oakdale, CA 95361; Ideal Toy Co Collector's Club, PO Box 623, Lexington, MA 02173; Liddle Kiddles Klub, 3639 Fourth Ave, La Crescenta, CA 91214; Madame Alexander Doll Club (company sponsored), 208 Terrace Dr, Mundelein, IL 60060; United Federation of Doll Clubs, 10920 N Ambassador Dr, Kansas City, MO 64153.

Note: Prices listed are for dolls in excellent condition, unless otherwise noted.

American Character Toy Company, Baby Tiny Tears, hard plastic head, rubber body, molded hair, orig clothes, 1950, 15" h **$90.00**

American Character Toy Company, Bottletot, cloth body, composition arms, holds bottle, mkd "Petite/America's Wonder Baby Doll," 20" h **175.00**

American Character Toy Company, Chuckles, vinyl head and body, rooted blonde saran hair, painted brown eyes, closed mouth, elastic strung legs, mkd "Amer. Doll & Toy Co/1961/copyright," 23" h **150.00**

American Character Toy Company, Graduate, 1–pc vinyl body, orig cap and gown, 1960, 21" h **50.00**

American Character Toy Company, Margaret–Rose, vinyl head, arms, and legs, rooted blonde hair, plastic body, 17" h **50.00**

American Character Toy Company, Tiny Tears, hard plastic head, curly rooted hair, vinyl body, sun suit, wood and plastic bathinette, c1955, 11" h **85.00**

American Character Toy Company, Toodle–Loo, magic foam plastic body, rooted blonde synthetic hair, painted brown eyes, closed mouth, magic foam body, fully jointed, mkd "American Doll & Toy Co," 1961, 18" h **175.00**

Appalachian Artworks, Inc, Xavier Roberts, orig Cabbage Patch, Anna Ruby, 1989 . . . . **300.00**

Appalachian Artworks, Inc, Xavier Roberts, orig Cabbage Patch, Mitzi, circus outfit, 1991 . . . . **150.00**

Arranbee, Baby Donna, hard plastic head, cloth body, latex arms and legs, molded hair, 1959, 17" h **45.00**

Arranbee, Little Dear, rooted hair, blue sleep eyes, stuffed vinyl body, c1956, 8" h **80.00**

Arranbee, My Dream Baby, bisque neck, cloth body, rubber hands, wearing baby dress, mkd "AM German 351/4," 9" h **275.00**

Arranbee, Nanette, vinyl, orig skating outfit, 1953, 14" h, MIB **115.00**

Arranbee, So Big, composition head and limbs, cloth body, 1936 . . . . **55.00**

American Character, baby doll, vinyl head, hard plastic body, rooted curly brown hair, orig blue dress and bonnet, mkd "American Character Doll Corp.," 23" h, $50.00.

Effanbee, Baby Winkie, #2423, orig bottle and box, $25.00.

Arranbee, Taffy, plastic, socket head, brunette saran wig, blue eyes, straight walker legs, blue striped satin skirt, white organdy blouse, ruffled sleeves, straw hat, 1954, 23" h. 175.00

Cameo Doll Company, Margie, composition head, molded painted hair, painted eyes, nose, and mouth, wooden segmented spool–like body, undressed, c1929, 10" h. 250.00

Cameo Doll Company, Miss Peeps, black, vinyl, inset eyes, mkd "Cameo" on head, "Cameo Doll Products/Strombecker Corp" on tag, 1973, 19" h. 35.00

Cameo Doll Company, Plum, 1–pc latex body, painted hair, sleep eyes, mkd "Cameo," 18" h 175.00

Cameo Doll Company, Black Scootles, composition, molded hair, painted eyes, smiling closed mouth, jointed at neck, shoulders, and hips, wrist tags, 13" h 725.00

Character, Mama Bear, cloth, stuffed 75.00

Character, Little Doggie, cloth, stuffed, Saalfield 100.00

Coleco, Cabbage Patch, cowgirl, vinyl head, cowgirl outfit, 16" h. 85.00

Cosmopolitan Doll Company, Emily, hard plastic head, blonde wig, cloth body, composition arms and legs, 1949, 25" h. 60.00

Cosmopolitan Doll Company, Ginger, vinyl head, rooted blonde hair, closed mouth, plastic body, arms, and legs, bride outfit, 1956, 7½" h 35.00

Cosmopolitan Doll Company, Little Miss Ginger, vinyl head, rooted ash blonde hair, closed mouth, hard plastic body, high heel feet, mkd "Little Miss Ginger" on head, 1956, 7½" h 20.00

Cosmpolitan Doll Company, Merri, plastic, rooted blonde hair, high heel feet, red gown, white fur trim, mkd "AE1406/41," backward "AE" on lower back, 1960, 14" h. 20.00

DeHetre, Terre, Punkin, 1988 DOTY award 155.00

Deluxe Topper, Dancing Dawn 30.00

Eegee Doll Company, Buster, vinyl head and arms, molded hair, plastic body, mkd "1959/Eegee," 17" h 25.00

Eegee Doll Company, Gemette, vinyl head and arms, rooted brown hair, plastic body, mkd "Eegee 1963/11" on back, 15" h 15.00

Eegee Doll Company, Newborn Baby Doll, vinyl head, arms, and legs, cloth body, mkd "Eegee Co/173," 1963, 16" h. 20.00

Eegee Doll Company, Playpen Baby, vinyl head, rooted blonde hair, nurser, plastic body, mkd "13/14AA/Eegee Co," 1967, 14" h 15.00

Eegee Doll Company, Schoolgirl, vinyl head, hard plastic body, jointed knees, orig blouse and jumper, 1957, 10½" h 20.00

Eegee Doll Company, Tina, vinyl head, rooted blonde hair, closed mouth, hard plastic body, jointed knees, walker, mkd "S" on head, 1959, 11" h 15.00

Effanbee Doll Corporation, Dy–Dee Baby, hard plastic, head, molded hair, open mouth, nurser, applied rubber ears, 1950, 11" h. 80.00

Effanbee Doll Corporation, First Patsy, composition, molded hair, painted eyes, mkd "Effanbee/Patsy," c1926, 14" h 650.00

Effanbee Doll Corporation, Fluffy, 1954, 8" h 40.00

Effanbee Doll Corporation, Half Pint, vinyl head, rooted hair, jointed, 1966, 11" h 70.00

Effanbee Doll Corporation, Lovums, composition swivel head, painted hair, blue tin sleep eyes, cloth body, composition limbs, redressed, c1930, 27" h 100.00

Effanbee Doll Corporation, Mae West, vinyl, fully jointed, 1982, 18" h. 100.00

Effanbee Doll Corporation, Mickey, vinyl head and body, painted features, molded football helmet, mkd on head and back, 1956, 11" h 45.00

Effanbee Doll Corporation, Sweetie Pie, composition, 10" h, MIB 350.00

Effanbee Doll Corporation, Twinkie, vinyl, molded hair, nurser mouth, mkd "Effanbee 1959," 15" h 45.00

Effanbee Doll Corporation, Wizard of Oz, set of 6, 50th Anniversary 125.00

Fisher–Price, Audrey, #0203, vinyl face, cloth body 45.00

Hasbro, Amanda, Sweet Dreams, stuffed gingham head and body, yarn hair, black felt eyes, button nose, embroidered smile, orchid print dress, eyelet lace trimmed night cap, 1974, 17" h 15.00

Georgene Novelties Co, Raggedy Ann, cloth, 15" h, $300.00.

Hasbro, Choo Choo Charlie, soft vinyl head, rooted hair, painted eyes, bean bag body, mkd "Copyright 1972 Quaker City Chocolate 7 Conf'y Co, Inc," 9" h 20.00

Hasbro, Junior Miss Sewing Kit, jointed arms, includes orig box with doll patterns, material, dresses to sew, and sewing implements, c1948, 7½" h 25.00

Hasbro, Little Miss No Name, vinyl head, rooted hair, plastic eyes, hard plastic body, jointed, burlap dress, 1965, 15" h 140.00

Hasbro, Mama Cass, vinyl, 4½" h, 1967 . . . . 30.00

Horsman Doll Company, Baby Dimples, cloth body, composition arms and legs, blue steel sleep eyes, open mouth, lace outfit, c1928, 16½" h 115.00

Horsman Doll Company, Bye–Lo, vinyl head, arms and legs, molded straight hair, painted eyes, cloth body, christening outfit, mkd "Horsman Doll/1972" on head, 14" h, MIB 50.00

Horsman Doll Company, Cindy walker, hard plastic head and body, sleep eyes, open mouth, 2 teeth, redressed in lace, 1950s, 21" h 65.00

Horsman Doll Company, Emmett Kelly Jr, vinyl head, cloth body, movable mouth, 24" h, 1979 . . . . 65.00

Ideal Toy Corporation, Baby, composition head, lower arms, and legs, molded hair, flirty eyes, closed mouth, mkd "Ideal Doll," c1938, 18" h 175.00

Ideal Toy Corporation, Baby Coos, hard plastic head, molded and painted light brown hair, blue sleep eyes, open/closed mouth, rubber body, c1950, MIB, 13½" h . . . 150.00

Idea Toy Corporation, Baby Giggles, vinyl head, arms, and legs, rooted hair, blue eyes, plastic body, 1965, 16" h, MIB 45.00

Ideal Toy Corporation, Baby Plassie, hard plastic head and body, molded hair, sleep eyes with lashes, open mouth with teeth, cry voice, 1949, 16" h 80.00

Ideal Toy Corporation, Betty Jane, composition, lashed sleep eyes, open mouth, teeth, jointed neck, shoulders, and hips, orig clothes, mkd "Ideal 18," 1953, 18" h 200.00

Ideal, Miss Revlon, vinyl, jointed rooted honey blonde hair, pierced pearl earrings, high heel feet, mkd "Ideal Doll/VT 10⅛"," 10⅛" h, $150.00.

Ideal Toy Corporation, Boopsie, plastic, painted molded hair, side glancing sleep eyes, jointed, wearing diaper, 1950–55 . . . . 15.00

Ideal Toy Corporation, Butterick Sew–Easy Designing Set Mannequin, plastic, molded blonde hair, Butterick patterns and sewing accessories, 1953, 14" h 35.00

Ideal Toy Corporation, Cinnamon, plastic, vinyl, rooted red hair, mkd "1971/Ideal Toy Corp GH–12–H 183/Hong Kong," 12" h 35.00

Ideal Toy Corporation, Crown Princess, vinyl, rooted hair, orig outfit, 1957, 10½" h 100.00

Ideal Toy Corporation, Diana Ross, ©Motown, Inc, molded hard plastic body, vinyl face and arms, gold glitter dress, orig box with The Supremes picture, ©Motown, Inc, 19" h 100.00

Ideal Toy Corporation, Goody Two Shoes, vinyl, rooted blonde hair, blue sleep eyes, blue dress, 2 pr of shoes, walks, battery operated, 1965, 19" h 100.00

Ideal Toy Corporation, Harmony, vinyl, sleep eyes, open–closed mouth, 1972, 19" h 200.00

Ideal Toy Corporation, Jet Set, Chelsea, vinyl head, rooted long straight hair, poseable polyurethane body, mod–style outfit, earrings, strap shoes, 1967, 24" h 45.00

Ideal Toy Corporation, Johnny Play Pal, vinyl, molded hair, blue sleep eyes, purple and white check outfit, booties, 1959, 24" h 250.00

Ideal Toy Corporation, Kissin' Thumbelina, vinyl head and limbs, soft body, pull–string action, 1971 . . . . 50.00

Ideal Toy Corporation, Kit 'N Kaboodle, vinyl head and hands, rooted blonde hair, soft body, blue overalls, red and white check shirt, rides plastic pony, 1984–85, 14" h 25.00

Ideal Toy Corporation, Magic Lips, vinyl head and limbs, rooted dark blonde or brown saran hair, blue sleep eyes, 3 lower teeth, open mouth, stuffed pink vinyl oilcloth body, flocked organdy dress, rayon slip, panties, plastic button shoes, toothbrush, bottle and curlers, press her back she closes her lips, released she opens mouth with cooing sound, says "mama," 1955–56, 23" h 85.00

Ideal Toy Corporation, Mary and Her Lamb, cloth, stuffed, mask face, yellow yarn hair, short dress, organdy apron, bonnet, white shoes and socks, carrying stuffed lamb, 1944 . . . . 50.00

Ideal Toy Corporation, Mary Hartline, hard plastic, blonde nylon glued wig, blue sleep eyes with lashes, dark eyeshadow, fully jointed, majorette outfit, 1952, 16" h 200.00

Ideal Toy Corporation, Miss Revlon, bride, 18" h 45.00

Ideal Toy Corporation, Mitzi, vinyl, rooted Saran hair, painted eyes, closed mouth, jointed neck and shoulders, 1965, 11¾" h 25.00

Ideal Toy Corporation, New Pepper, soft vinyl head and arms, rooted blonde hair, painted side glancing eyes, 3 painted lashes, freckles, soft plastic legs and body, red and white fringed playsuit, 1965, 9¼" h 30.00

Ideal Toy Corporation, Pam's Pram, plastic baby doll in plastic carriage, painted hair and features, painted diaper, doll cries and moves arms and legs when carriage is pushed, 1954, 8 x 8¼ x 4¼" 25.00

Ideal Toy Corporation, Patty Playpal, vinyl head, hard vinyl jointed body, orig clothes, 36" h 150.00

Ideal Toy Corporation, Playtime Tubsy, vinyl head and body, rooted hair, battery operated, 1968, 18" h **45.00**

Ideal Toy Corporation, Posin' Cricket, vinyl head and body, rooted auburn hair, brown sleep eyes, painted teeth, growing hair, swivel waist, orig orange check dress, 1971, 15½" h **55.00**

Ideal Toy Corporation, Pretty Curls, soft vinyl, rooted nylon hair, painted eyes, orig hair styling kit, 1981–82, 12½" h **20.00**

Ideal Toy Corporation, Rub–a–Dub Dolly, Tugboat Shower, vinyl, rooted hair, painted eyes, movable arms and legs, 1974–78, 17" h. **30.00**

Ideal Toy Corporation, Saralee, brown, vinyl head and limbs, molded hair, brown sleep eyes with lashes, stuffed cotton body, cries when tilted, organdy dress, cotton slip, 1951–53, 17" h **200.00**

Ideal Toy Corporation, Smokey Bear, cloth, 1950s. **65.00**

Ideal Toy Corporation, Sparkle Plenty, hard plastic head, yellow yarn hair, 1 pc latex body, mkd "Made in USA/Pat No 2252077," 1947, 15" h **55.00**

Ideal Toy Corporation, Tammy, vinyl head and arms, rooted hair, painted side glancing eyes, plastic body and legs, orig outfit, 1962, 12" h **40.00**

Ideal Toy Corporation, Ted, vinyl head and arms, molded painted light brown hair, painted brown eyes, plastic legs and body, 1963, 12½" h. **50.00**

Ideal Toy Corporation, Tickletoes, hard plastic head and shoulder plate, molded hair, sleep eyes, cry voice, latex arms and legs, 1950, 19" h **65.00**

Ideal Toy Corporation, Tippy Tumbles, vinyl head and arms, rooted hair, painted eyes, plastic body, battery operated, stands on head and flips over, pocketbook–style battery pack, 1977, 6½" h **40.00**

Ideal Toy Corporation, Twins in Basket, boy and girl, vinyl head and limbs, rooted saran hair, sleep eyes, cloth body, boy with open mouth wearing cotton romper, girl with pouty mouth wearing silk dress, flannel basket with organdy skirt, 1963–64, 14" h. **40.00**

Ideal Toy Corporation, Upsy Dazy, vinyl head, rooted blonde hair, painted eyes, soft foam body, hard arms and flat spindle hands, hard plastic red cap, doll somersaults with mechanism, 1973, 15" h **30.00**

Ideal Toy Corporation, Velvet, vinyl head, frosted blonde hair, hair grow feature, plastic body and legs, mkd "1969/Ideal Toy Corp," 16" h **15.00**

Knickerbocker, Annie, Aileen Quinn, vinyl, fully jointed, 1982, 6" h. **10.00**

Knickerbocker, Raggedy Andy, orig clothes and tags, 1970s, 15" h **25.00**

Knickerbocker, Raggedy Ann, orig clothes and tags, 1970s, 15" h **25.00**

Knickerbocker, Robbie, rag, shirt, blue jeans, 9" h, MIB **15.00**

Knickerbocker, Sunbonnet Doll, May, vinyl, painted eyes, mkd "K.T.C./Made in Taiwan/1975," 7" h **6.50**

LJN, Boy George, hard plastic, soft vinyl head, hat, microphone and posing stand, orig box, made in China, 12" h **30.00**

LJN, Brooke Shields, black and white sweat shirt, stretch pants, hair brush, ring and posing stand, MIB **50.00**

Madame Alexander Doll Company, Alexander–kins, Wendy, hard plastic, synthetic wig, sleep eyes, closed mouth, jointed at neck, shoulder, and hips, orig ballerina outfit, 1953, 7½" h **250.00**

Madame Alexander, plastic, jointed arms and legs, blonde hair, blue net over blue satin dress, mkd "Alex" on back, 7½" h, $300.00.

Madame Alexander Doll Company, Beth, Little Women Series, 1951 . . . . **325.00**

Madame Alexander Doll Company, Billy, hard plastic, bending knees walker, brunette wig, 1–pc red and white suit, red tie, 1960, 8" h. **400.00**

Madame Alexander Doll Company, Cinderella, hard plastic, 1950, 10" h. **250.00**

Madame Alexander Doll Company, Cousin Grace, hard plastic, blonde synthetic wig, blue sleep eyes, closed mouth, bent knee walker, straw picture hat, orig clothes, c1956, 7½" h **675.00**

Madame Alexander Doll Company, David and Dianna, wagon, FAO Schwarz, 8" h, MIB **145.00**

Madame Alexander Doll Company, Fairy Princess, composition head, jointed neck, jointed arms and legs, orig blonde mohair wig, brown sleep eyes, real lashes, closed mouth, white satin gown, silver slippers, c1950, 18" h. **165.00**

Madame Alexander Doll Company, Little Genius, hard plastic swivel head, molded and painted hair, sleep eyes, open mouth, vinyl body, orig clothes, c1958, 8" h **165.00**

Madame Alexander Doll Company, Mary Ellen, hard plastic, rooted nylon hair, smiling mouth, pink blush on cheeks, jointed walker, mkd "MME ALEXANDER" on head, 31" h **700.00**

Madame Alexander Doll Company, Muffin, pink flannel head and body, yellow yarn wig, blue felt eyes, pink floral print cotton dress with tag, c1975, 14" h, MIB **85.00**

Madame Alexander Doll Company, Netherlands Boy, International Series, hard plastic, straight legs, 1975, 8" h, MIB **80.00**

Madame Alexander Doll Company, Pinkie Baby, composition head and limbs, molded hair, sleep eyes, rosebud mouth, cloth body, white organdy christening gown and ruffled bonnet, clover wrist tag, c1937, 22" h, MIB **400.00**

Madame Alexander Doll Company, Shari Lewis, hard plastic and vinyl body, jointed, synthetic dark blond wig, blue sleep eyes, real upper lashes, painted lower lashes, pierced ears, 21" h **900.00**

Marx, First Love, poseable, baby powder scent, 1970s,
16" h **40.00**

Mattel, Baby First Step, vinyl, 1960s, 18" h. **30.00**

Mattel, Baby Walk 'N Play, plastic, vinyl, rooted yellow
hair, painted eyes, 2 upper teeth, battery operated,
mkd "1967 Mattel Inc/Hong Kong" on head, 11" h **12.00**

Mattel, Buffy and Mrs Beasley, vinyl head, blonde pony-
tails, painted blue eyes, plastic body, pull string talker,
c1969, 10½" h, MIB **125.00**

Mattel, Cathy Quick Curl, complete with brush and
comb, 15" h **55.00**

Mattel, Charmin' Chatty, orig clothes, 1961, 24" h **60.00**

Mattel, Cheerful Tearful, vinyl head and body, orig
clothes, 1966, 12" h **35.00**

Mattel, Debby Boone, 10" h **45.00**

Mattel, Doug Davis Spaceman, vinyl, dark brown hair,
posable, mkd "Mattel Inc/1967/Hong Kong" on head,
6" h **10.00**

Mattel, Liddle Kiddles, Anabelle Autodiddle, hat, car,
and pusher, 1968, 3" h **30.00**

Mattel, Liddle Kiddles, Heather Hiddlehorse, 4" h. **65.00**

Mattel, Liddle Kiddles, Lolli Lemon, 2" h **45.00**

Mattel, Liddle Kiddles, Louise Locket **15.00**

Mattel, Liddle Kiddles, Orange Blossom Kologne, bottle,
doll stand, 1969, 3" h **20.00**

Mattel, Liddle Kiddles, Santa Kiddle, 1969, 3" h **35.00**

Mattel, Liddle Kiddles, Telly Viddle, 3½" h **50.00**

Mattel, Live Action Christie, viny, 1970s, MIB. **85.00**

Mattel, Marie Osmond, hard plastic body, movable vinyl
arms and head, pink dress, white shoes, orig box with
unused contents, 30" h **300.00**

Mattel, Talking Baby Tenderlove, 1 pc, inset scalp, rooted white hair, painted eyes, open mouth, nurser, pull
string talker, mkd "677K/1969 Mattel Inc/Mexico" on
head, 16" h **12.00**

**Remco, Snugglebun, plastic, rooted ash blonde hair, orig red flan-
nel pajamas, mkd "1/Remco Ind. Inc./©1965" on head, plastic
accessories, $30.00.**

Mego, Cher, 12" h, 1976 . . . . **45.00**

Mollye Dolls, International Doll Company, Business
Girl, hard plastic, blonde wig, business suit, 17" h **125.00**

Mollye Dolls, International Doll Co, Martha
Washington, hard plastic, hand painted face, white
mohair wig, 8" h **50.00**

Remco, Baby Laugh a Lot, vinyl, with rocker, 16" h **75.00**

Remco, Heidi, vinyl, red plastic case, 1965, 5" h **40.00**

Remco, Laurie Partridge, vinyl and plastic, 1973, 19" h **100.00**

Remco, Lisa Littlechap, 1964. . . . . **25.00**

Richwood, Sandra Sue, sleep eyes with molded lashes,
closed mouth, jointed arms and legs, ski outfit, 8" h **130.00**

Sun Rubber, Betty Bows, rubber, molded hair, blue sleep
eyes, full jointed, drinks and wets, mkd "Betty
Bows/copyright The Sun Rubber Company/Barberton,
OH USA/34A," c1953, 11" h **35.00**

Sun Rubber, Sun–Dee, black, lasiloid vinyl, nurser, mkd
"Sun–Dees/Sun Rubber 1956," 17" h **45.00**

Sun Rubber, Tod–L–Lee, vinyl, molded hair, closed
mouth, jointed at neck, painted sunsuit, shoes, and
socks, mkd "Sun Rubber Co," 1956, 10" h **30.00**

Virga, Virga Walking Doll, plastic, jointed arms, 1950s **60.00**

Vogue Dolls, Baby Dear, composition, bent limbs, 1961,
12" h **40.00**

Vogue Dolls, Betty Jane, composition, braided pigtails,
bent right arm, red plaid woven cotton dress, white
eyelet trim, "Vogue Dolls, Inc" on tag, 1947, 12" h. **85.00**

Vogue Dolls, Brickette, rooted hair, strawberry blonde,
sleep eyes, polka dot dress, straw hat, 1979–80, 18" h **65.00**

Vogue Dolls, Crib Crowd Baby, hard plastic, blonde synthetic ringlets wig, painted eyes, curved baby legs,
orig tagged dress, rubber pants, c1949, 7½" h. **425.00**

Vogue Dolls, Ginny, Bride, soft vinyl head, rooted hair,
hard plastic body, 1963, 8" h **55.00**

Vogue Dolls, Ginny, Country Fair, walker, floral print
gown, black bodice, flowered straw hat, straw basket,
1959. . . . . **265.00**

Vogue Dolls, Ginny, Nun, moving eyes, mkd "Vogue"
on head, and "Vogue Doll" on back, 1950–53, 8" h **150.00**

Vogue Dolls, Ginny, Southern Belle, soft vinyl head,
rooted hair, hard plastic body, bendable knees, striped
skirt, straw hat, 1957 . . . . **85.00**

Vogue Dolls, Ginny, Springtime, walking mechanism,
mkd "Ginny" on back, "Vogue Dolls, Inc. Pat.
Pending., Made in USA," 1954, 8" h **70.00**

Vogue Dolls, Ginny, Star Brite, vinyl, rooted brown hair,
large side glancing eyes with stars, long lashes, 1964,
17" h **35.00**

Vogue Dolls, Ginny, Valentine, hard plastic, molded
hair, mohair wig, painted eyes, 1948–50, 8" h **125.00**

Vogue Dolls, Hansel and Gretel, hard plastic, blonde
mohair wigs, blue sleep eyes, jointed at neck, shoulders, and hips, orig clothes, The Vogue Doll Family
booklet, ©1958, mkd "Ginny/Vogue Dolls, and
"Hansel/Vogue Dolls," 7" h, price for pair. **325.00**

Vogue Dolls, Hug A Bye Baby, pink pajamas, 22" h, MIB **45.00**

Vogue Dolls, Jill, bride, hp, 1958, 10" h. **50.00**

Webster, Mary Hortence, Flapper Doll, composition,
cloth, black wig, painted eyes, off–the–shoulder
gown, pearl necklace, 1925, 28" h. **275.00**

Wellings, Norah, Pajama Bag Doll, velvet head, dark
skin tone, mohair wig, painted features, pajama bag
body, felt shoes, orig sticker on foot, c1928, 19" h **100.00**

DOORSTOPS

Prior to the 1920s, the three–dimensional, cast–metal figural doorstop reigned supreme. After 1920, the flat–back, cast–metal doorstop gained in popularity. By the late 1930s, it was the dominant form being manufactured. Basement workshop doorstops, made primarily from wood, were prevalent from the 1930s through the mid–1950s. By the 1960s the doorstop more often than not was a simple plastic wedge.

Crossover collectors have a major influence on value. Amount of surviving period paint also plays a critical role in determining value.

Beware of restrikes. Many period molds, especially those from Hubley, have survived. Manufacturers are making modern copies of period examples.

References: Jeanne Bertoia, *Doorstops: Identification and Values*, Collector Books, 1985, 1996 value update; Douglas Congdon–Martin, *Figurative Cast Iron: A Collector's Guide*, Schiffer Publishing, 1994.

Collectors' Club: Doorstop Collectors of America, 1881–G Spring Rd, Vineland, NJ 08630.

Note: All doorstops listed are cast iron unless otherwise noted.

Advertising, Eureka Steel Co, flower basket, blue,
6 x 4¹/₂" **$100.00**
Black Bellhop, carrying satchel, facing sideways,
orange–red uniform and cap, 7¹/₂" h **375.00**
Black Man, playing saxophone, white pants, red jacket,
6⁷/₈" h **425.00**
Cape Cottage, blue roof, fenced garden, flowers, path,
sgd "Eastern Specialty Mfg Co 14," 5³/₄" h **135.00**
Dutch Boy, full figure, hands in pocket, blonde hair, blue
jumpsuit and hat, red belt and collar, brown shoes,
11" h **395.00**
Elephant, pulling coconut out of palm tree, natural color,
14" h **145.00**
French Girl, holding skirt out at sides, hat, sgd "Hubley
23," 9" h **125.00**

Birds of Paradise, cast iron, green, blue, cream, beige, and black, 7" h, $137.50. Photo courtesy Collectors Auction Services.

German Shepherd, Hubley **110.00**
Goldenrods, natural color, sgd "Hubley 268," 7¹/₈" h **225.00**
Golf Caddy, carrying brown and tan bag, white, brown
knickers, red jacket, 8" h **475.00**
Guitar Player, flat back, red jacket with green trim and
waistband, yellow hat and pants, brown guitar,
11⁷/₈" h **335.00**
Horse, jumping fence, jockey, sgd "Eastern Spec Co
#790," 7⁷/₈" h **325.00**
House, woman walking up front stairs, grapevines, sgd
"Eastern Spec Co," 6" h **165.00**
Huckleberry Finn, floppy hat, pail, stick, Littco Products
label, 12¹/₂" h **410.00**
Lighthouse, flat back, white, red window and door trim,
green rocks, black path, 14" h **250.00**
Log Mill, brown, tan roof, white path, green bushes,
6¹/₄" h **225.00**
Mammy, red dress, blue kerchief with white dots, white
apron, sgd "Hubley 327," 8¹/₂" h **150.00**
Mary Quite Contrary, yellow dress and socks, blue hat,
green watering can, "Littco Products" label, 11³/₈" h **545.00**
Owl, sitting on books, polychrome, Eastern Specialty
Mfg Co, 9¹/₂ x 6" **300.00**
Parrot, sitting in ring, 2 sided, heavy gold base, sgd
"B & H," 13³/₄" h **210.00**
Peacock, stylized design, colorful, 5³/₄ x 9" **100.00**
Penguin, head up, Taylor Cook, ©1930, 9¹/₂ x 6" **1,000.00**
Persian Cat, sitting, gray, light markings, sgd "Hubley"
inside casting, 9¹/₂" h **145.00**
Police Dog, dark bronze finish, 10" h **55.00**
Popeye, pipe in mouth, blue pants, black and red shirt,
white hat, sgd "Hubley, 1929 King Features Syndicate,
Made in USA," 9" h **1,000.00**
Puss in Boots, flat back, head sticking out of boot, sgd
"Creations Co 1930" **400.00**
Rabbit, sitting on hind legs, tan, green grass, detailed
casting, sgd "B & H 7800," 15¹/₄" h **485.00**
Ringmaster, hands behind back, red jacket, green pants,
top hat, 10¹/₂" h **1,000.00**
Rooster, standing, 2 sided, 13 x 10" **500.00**
Squirrel, siting on stump eating nut, brown and tan, 9" h . . . **185.00**
Texas, name spelled in center star, longhorn at gate,
10 x 10¹/₄" **500.00**
Three Kittens, in wicker basket, sgd "M Rosenstein,
c1932, Lancaster, PA," 7" h **350.00**
Three Puppies, in basket, natural colors, sgd "Copyright
1932 M Rosenstein, Lancaster, PA, USA," 7" h **325.00**
Whistling Boy, flat back, hands in tan knickers, yellow
striped baggy shirt, 2 rubber stoppers, sgd "B & H,"
20¹/₄" h **1,350.00**
Wicker Basket, ivory, rose, natural flowers, handle with
bow, sgd "Hubley 121," 11" h **135.00**
Woman, bronze, Art Deco, standing and holding out
skirt, clinging gown, 7 x 9" **175.00**

DRINKING GLASSES, PROMOTIONAL

The first promotional drinking glasses date from 1937 when Walt Disney licensed Libbey to manufacture a set of safety edge tumblers featuring characters from *Snow White and the Seven Dwarfs*. The set was sold in stores and used by food manufacturers for promotional product packaging. In the early 1950s Welch's sold its jelly in jars featuring Howdy Doody and his friends.

The first fast–food promotional glasses appeared in the late 1960s. Gasoline stations also found this premium concept a good trade stimulator. The plastic drinking cup arrived on the scene in the late 1980s. A decade later, they have become collectible.

A never–out–of–the–box appearance is the key value component for any promotional drinking glass, whether made from glass or plastic. Regional collecting preferences affect value. Beware of hoarding. Far more examples survive in excellent to mint condition than most realize.

References: Mark Chase and Michael Kelly, *Collectible Drinking Glasses: Identification & Values*, Collector Books, 1996; John Hervey, *Collector's Guide to Cartoon & Promotional Drinking Glasses*, L–W Book Sales, 1990, 1995 value update.

Periodical: *Collector Glass News*, PO Box 308, Slippery Rock, PA 16057.

Collectors' Club: Promotional Glass Collectors Assoc, 3001 Bethel Rd, New Wilmington, PA 16142.

1939 Disney All Star Parade, The Ugly Duckling	**$45.00**
1964–65 New York World's Fair Unisphere, juice glass, sponsored by US Steel	**6.00**
American Winter Scene, Currier & Ives, Kraft cheese container, 1970s	**2.50**
Apollo 11, July 1969, Marathon Oil Co	**3.00**
Archies, "Betty and Veronica Give A Party," Welch's, 1973	**1.50**
Barney, white letters, Pepsi, MGM, 1975	**6.00**
Boris Badenov, Holly Farms Fried Chicken & Seafood, 1975	**70.00**
Care Bears, Cheer Bear, Pizza Hut, 1983	**1.00**
Casper, Pepsi–Cola, 1970s, 5" h	**12.00**
E T, "I'll be right there," Pizza Hut, 1982	**3.00**
Family Circus, Wyler's	**1.50**
Flintstone Kids, Pizza Hut, 1986, set of 4	**16.00**
Holly Hobbie, Simple Pleasures, "Fill your day with happiness," Coca–Cola	**5.00**
Jefferson, Thomas, Libbey Presidential series, 1940–50s	**6.00**
Jewel Tea Old Time Series, Jewel Tea Jelly, set of 3	**12.00**
"Love is...," *Los Angeles Times*, 1970s	**3.00**

Batman Returns, McDonald's, plastic, frisbee disc top, 1992, 7" h, $1.00.

Laurel and Hardy, smoke colored, black paint, silver band, "Wrong Again," Arby's Actors series, 1979	**6.00**
National Flag Foundation, Washington's Cruisers	**3.00**
New York Times Headlines, Limited Edition, "Columbia Returns: Shuttle Era Opens," Wendy's, 1981	**4.00**
Old Time Songs, Big Top Peanut Butter, 1950s	**3.00**
Pac–Man, Arby's, 1980	**3.00**
Rattlesnake, "Don't Tread On Me," Revolution at Sea—series V, National Flag Foundation, Anchor Hocking, 1974–76	**7.00**
"The Riverboat," Armour Peanut Butter Transportation series, 1950s	**4.00**
Road Runner, plastic, 1966 copyright	**3.00**
Rockwell, Norman, Coca–Cola	**4.50**
Rockwell, Norman, *Saturday Evening Post* cover, "No Swimming," Arby's, 1980s	**3.00**
Rockwell, Norman, *Saturday Evening Post* cover, Country Time Lemonade mail premium, set of 4	**28.00**
Schmoos, Pappy Yokum/Schmoos, green, ©1949 UFS	**15.00**
Snidley Whiplash, static pose, Pepsi–Cola, 5" h	**10.00**
Snoopy, plastic, "Civilization is Overrated!," McDonald's, 1983	**6.00**
Superman to the Rescue, Polaner's TV Treat Pure Concord Grape Jam, 1964	**30.00**
Twelve Days of Christmas, Pepsi–Cola, 16 oz, 1976	**2.00**
World War II Victory, cocktail, Auxiliary fireman	**8.00**
Ziggy, "Try to have a nice day," Hardee's, ©1979 Universal Press Syndicate	**6.00**

DRUGSTORE COLLECTIBLES

Product type (e.g., laxative), manufacturer (such as Burma Shave), and advertising display value are three standard approaches to drugstore collectibles. Unlike country store collectors, whose desire it is to display their collections in a country store environment, few drugstore collectors recreate a pharmacy in their home or garage.

Emphasis is primarily on products from the first two–thirds of the 20th century. Few individuals collect contemporary chain drugstore, e.g., CVS, memorabilia. Dental and shaving items are two subcategories within drugstore collectibles that are currently seeing value increases.

References: Al Bergevin, *Drugstore Tins & Their Prices*, Wallace–Homestead, Krause Publications, 1990; Patricia McDaniel, *Drugstore Collectibles*, Wallace–Homestead, Krause Publications, 1994.

Newsletter: *The Drug Store Collector*, 3851 Gable Lane Dr, #513, Indianapolis, IN 46208.

Baby Powder, Playtex, Drug Div, International Latex Corp, Playtex Park, Dover, DE, cardboard cylinder, metal bottom, plastic shaker top, gold, white, and blue, pink and blue letters, 1948, 6 oz	**$10.00**
Book, *American Drug Index*, Charles O Wilson, Ph D, and Tony Everett Jones, M S, J P Lippincott Co, Philadelphia and Montreal, hardcover, 650 pp	**10.00**
Book, Pfizer Laboratories Price Schedule, Pfizer Laboratories, Chas Pfizer & Co, Inc, Brooklyn, NY, Jan 5, 1954, illus, hardcover	**12.00**
Bottle, Child's Witch Hazel, paper label, 1928, 16 oz, 8" h	**18.00**

Condom Tin, Chariots, Goodwear Rubber Co, litho tin, 2¹/₈ x 1⁵/₈ x ¹/₈", $198.00. Photo courtesy Wm Morford Auctions.

Bottle, Olafin Cod Liver Oil, 1935, 16 oz, 8" h 12.00
Bottle, Walgreen Tar Soap Shampoo, barber screw cap, 1920, 12 oz, 7¹/₂" h 15.00
Box, Peau–Doux Shaving Cream, yellow, red, and black, orig 4 oz tube, 1938, 7¹/₂" h 12.00
Bracelet, copper, Walgreen building, 1933–34 Chicago World's Fair souvenir 45.00
Canister, Calonite Powder, cardboard, Research Labs, vertical round, orange and blue, 1920, 3 oz, 4" h 22.00
Canister, Peau–Doux Golf Balls, sleeve of 3, green box, 1938. . . . . 75.00
Canister, tin, Salted Peanuts, vertical cylinder, orange, cream and black, 1935, 16 oz, 4¹/₂" h 35.00
round, yellow and brown, 1925, 3" h 15.00
Coin, Walgreen building, copper colored, 1933–34 Chicago World's Fair souvenir, 2¹/₂" d 40.00
Condom Tin, Caravan, litho tin, rect, camel caravan in desert, multicolor, Tiger Skin Rubber Co, NY, 2¹/₈ x 1⁵/₈" 135.00
Condom Tin, Carmen Brand, litho tin, round, pin–up image of woman with red shawl and fan, yellow ground, 1⁵/₈" d 185.00
Condom Tin, De–Luxe Blue–Ribbon, litho tin, rect, German Shepherd head on ribbon, American Hygienic Co, Baltimore, MD, 50¢, 2¹/₈ x 1³/₄ x ¹/₄ 800.00
Condom Tin, Double–Tip, litho tin, rect, woman in bathing suit, red, white, and blue, Department Sales Co, NY, 2³/₁₆ x 1⁵/₈" 825.00
Condom Tin, Gold–Pak, litho tin, rect, black and white, "Liquid Latex, 3 For $1.00," Crown Rubber Co, Akron, OH, 2 x 1¹/₂" 450.00
Condom Tin, Kamels, litho tin, rect, camel and palace, black and white, Frank Aaronoff, NY, 2¹/₄ x 1³/₄" 135.00
Condom Tin, L E Shunk, litho tin, rect, LES logo and "Genuine, Liquid, Latex" on green, white, and red band, 2¹/₈ x 1³/₄" 90.00
Condom Tin, Napoleons, litho tin, rect, crossed sabers and hat, fleur–de–lis border, Valentine Labs, Chicago, IL, 1⁷/₈ x 1⁵/₈ x ³/₈" 325.00
Condom Tin, Nutex, litho tin, rect, red and white on blue ground, Nutex Corp, Philadelphia, PA, 2³/₁₆ x 1⁵/₈ x ¹/₄" . . . 935.00
Condom Tin, Peacock, litho tin, round, multicolor peacock, white ground, 1⁵/₈" d 275.00

Condom Tin, Ramses, litho tin, rect, white ground, Egyptian motif bands, 2³/₄ x 1⁷/₈" 85.00
Condom Tin, Silver Star, lihto tin, rect, shooting star, black and white, Silver Star Rubber Co, NY, 2³/₁₆ x 1⁵/₈ x ¹/₄" 900.00
Condom Tin, Three Knights, litho tin, rect, 3 knights on horseback, black and white, Goodwear Rubber Co, NY, 2¹/₈ x 1⁵/₈" 165.00
Condom Tin, Trojan–Enz, litho tin, rect, silhouette Trojan head, black and white lettering, white and red ground, Youngs Rubber Co, 2¹/₈ x 1⁵/₈ x ¹/₄" 325.00
Cooper Creme, Whittaker Labs, Inc, Peekskill, NY, "the original creme—since 1934," yellow tube, yellow and black box, 75 grams 10.00
Disposable Diaper Pads, box of 30, Chix Baby Products Division, Chilcopee Mills, Inc, New York, NY, 1958, orig 7¹/₂ x 6¹/₂ x 16¹/₂" box 12.00
Drink Shaker, aluminum, Art Deco style, 1933–34 World's Fair souvenir, 11" h 75.00
Heat 'N Serve Baby Dish, General Electric, 3 sections, electric, detachable cord, bunny illus in middle section, orig 12 x 6 x 2¹/₂" box 18.00
Napkin, souvenir, lists 4 Walgreen store locations at 1933–34 World's Fair, 4¹/₂" sq. 15.00
Pocket Mirror, Walgreen's Green Bay store opening, 1938. . . . . 60.00
Sign, backboard type, Malted Milk, 1938, 45 x 25 x 3". . . . 400.00
Tin, aspirin, Walgreen Brand, rect flat, orange and brown, 24 tablets, 1938. . . . . 22.00
Tin, Carrel Paislay's Talcum Powder, vertical rect oval, litho, 1940, 3 oz, 4³/₄" h 30.00
Tin, Golden Crown Tennis Balls, cylinder, sleeve of 3, 1938, 8" h. 75.00
Tin, Hygienic Baby Talc, vertical oval, litho, white, black, and red, 1932, 4 oz 75.00
Tin, Milk of Magnesia Tablets, light blue and cream, 1945. . . . . 12.00
Tin, Quick–Strip Bandages, 1940 . . . . 12.00
Tin, Styptic Powder, Peau–Doux Brand, vertical oval, litho, yellow and red, 1938, 1¹/₂ oz, 2³/₄" h 45.00
Tin, Valentine Throat Lozenges, Orlis, orange and cream, flat, 1940 . . . . 12.00

Talcum Powder Tin, White Witch, 5¹/₄" h, $99.00. Photo courtesy Past Tyme Pleasures.

Tin, Walgreen Malted Milk, litho tin, 1935, 25 lb,
    13 x 9½ x 9½" **125.00**
Toiletry Kit, Peau–Doux brand, includes talc, styptic
    powder, and shaving cream, red box, 1938............ **125.00**
Toy, truck, Walgreen Delivery Truck, white and red, 7" l **75.00**
Toy, truck, Walgreen Ice Cream, white, blue letters,
    1950, 20½ x 7 x 4" **200.00**

EASTER COLLECTIBLES

Easter collectibles are the weak sister when it comes to holiday collectibles. The number of collectors is a far cry from those of Valentine, Halloween, or Christmas memorabilia.

Focus is primarily on objects related to the secular side of this important religious holiday. Rabbit (Easter Bunny), chicken, decorated eggs, and Easter baskets head the list of desired objects. While plenty of two–dimensional material exists, most collectors focus primarily on three–dimensional objects.

References: Juanita Burnett, *A Guide to Easter Collectibles,* Collector Books, 1992, out of print; Pauline and Dan Campanelli, *Holiday Collectibles: A Price Guide,* L–W Books, 1997; H. N. Schiffer, *Collectible Rabbits,* Schiffer Publishing, 1990.

Basket, metal, round, 1940s........................ **$15.00**
Book, *The Tale of Peter Rabbit,* Edna M Aldredge and
    Jessie F McKee, Harter Publishing Co, 1931 .... **18.00**
Box, candy, cardboard, egg shaped, chick emerging
    from egg illus, yellow, purple flowers, 1940s **20.00**
Candy Container, papier–mâché, rabbit with basket,
    German, 1950s, 4¾" h **38.00**
Cookie Cutter, bunny, plastic, red, 1970–80s **1.50**
Decoration, paper, honeycomb, bunny in basket, 1940s..... **30.00**
Eggcup, china, duck, rabbit, chick, mkd "Japan," price
    for 8–pc set **40.00**
Egg Dye Packet, PAAS, 1930–40 .... **10.00**
Figure, chick, cotton, 1940s........................ **5.00**
Figure, chick, pulling wicker cart, Avon, 1990 .... **10.00**
Figure, chick, wearing red coat, composition, mkd
    "Germany," 5½" h **38.00**
Figure, rabbit, celluloid, sitting, floppy ears, radish in
    mouth, Japan, 3" h............................ **30.00**
Figure, rabbit, white, metal, mkd "Germany," price for
    set of 4 .... **45.00**
Greeting Card, mechanical, bunny drink soda, soda
    flows through straw, 1920s **8.00**

Toy, Mechanical Bumpty Bunny Cart, windup, litho tin, bunnies pushing egg cart, orig box, 8¼" l, 4¾" h, $75.00.

Postcard, "Easter Greetings," boy and girl carrying flowers, emb, early 20th C **5.00**
Record, *Easter Parade,* illus sleeve, colorful, 1957, mint **15.00**
Toy, egg shaped, rabbit dec, musical, side crank handle,
    Mattel, 1950s **25.00**
Toy, egg shaped, rabbit dec, pip squeak, Grand Toys,
    1960s..................................... **8.00**
Toy, windup, plastic rabbit on metal motorcycle, 1970s **35.00**

EDWIN KNOWLES

In 1900 Edwin M. Knowles founded the Edwin M. Knowles China Company. The company's offices were located in East Liverpool, Ohio, the plant in Chester, West Virginia. Products included dinnerware, kitchenware, specialties, and toilet wares.

In 1913 the company opened a plant in Newell, West Virginia. Harker Pottery purchased the Chester plant in 1931. Knowles continued production at the Newell plant until 1963.

Collectors focus primarily on the company's dinnerware. Three of its popular patterns are: Deanna (introduced 1938); Esquire (1956–1962); and Yorktown (introduced in 1936).

In the 1970s the Bradford Exchange bought the rights to the Knowles name and uses it for marketing purposes as a backstamp on some limited edition collector plates. These plates are manufactured offshore, not in America.

References: Susan and Al Bagdade, *Warman's American Pottery and Porcelain,* Wallace–Homestead, Krause Publications, 1994; Harvey Duke, *The Official Identification and Price Guide to Pottery and Porcelain, Eighth Edition,* House of Collectibles, 1995; Lois Lehner, *Lehner's Encyclopedia of U.S. Marks on Pottery, Porcelain & Clay,* Collector Books, 1988.

Alice Ann, bowl, oval, 9" d **$10.00**
Alice Ann, bowl, round, 8½" d **15.00**
Alice Ann, casserole **20.00**
Alice Ann, cup **4.00**
Alice Ann, demitasse cup **10.00**
Alice Ann, plate, 6¼" d **1.50**
Alice Ann, saucer **3.00**
Alice Ann, soup bowl, 7½" d........................ **10.00**
Arcadia, bowl, oval, 9" d **10.00**
Arcadia, creamer **4.00**
Arcadia, cup and saucer **5.00**
Arcadia, plate, 9¼" d **8.00**
Beverly, bowl, round, 9½" d **15.00**
Beverly, coaster. **8.00**
Beverly, cream soup cup **12.00**
Beverly, dish, 5¼" d **2.50**
Beverly, gravy liner **6.00**
Beverly, plate, 7½" d............................. **4.00**
Beverly, salt and pepper shakers, pr **8.00**
Beverly, soup bowl, lug handle, 6¾" d.................. **8.00**
Beverly, teapot **25.00**
Deanna, bowl, 36s **7.50**
Deanna, cake plate, lug handle, 11" d **10.00**
Deanna, coaster **8.00**
Deanna, demitasse cup **10.00**
Deanna, eggcup, double **10.00**
Deanna, plate, 10" d.............................. **10.00**
Diana, cup and saucer **5.00**
Diana, dish, 5" d. **2.00**
Diana, plate, 9" d **7.50**

Tia Juana, bowl, 9¼", $15.00.

Diana, soup bowl, 8" d 10.00
Esquire, cereal bowl, Queen Anne's Lace, 6¼" d 10.00
Esquire, cup and saucer. 12.50
Esquire, fruit dish, ftd, 5½" h 6.00
Esquire, jug, 2 qt 85.00
Esquire, plate, 8¼" d 8.00
Esquire, platter, Solar, 16" l 30.00
Esquire, soup bowl, ftd, 6¼" d 10.00
Esquire, teapot, Botanica 95.00
Hostess, creamer. 4.00
Hostess, cup and saucer 5.00
Hostess, dish, lug handle, 6½" d 4.00
Hostess, plate, 7" sq 5.00
Marion, cup and saucer 5.00
Marion, dish, 5¼" d 2.50
Marion, plate, 10" d 10.00
Marion, platter, 13¾" d 12.00
Potomac, bowl, 36s 7.50
Potomac, creamer. 4.00
Potomac, cup and saucer 5.00
Potomac, demitasse cup 10.00
Potomac, plate, 6¼" d 1.00
Potomac, plate, 9¼" d 7.50
Potomac, platter, 11½" d 10.00
Potomac, salt and pepper shakers, pr 8.00
Roslyn, bowl, oval, 9" d 10.00
Roslyn, cup and saucer 5.00
Roslyn, plate, 9⅛" d 7.50
Roslyn, platter, 11" d 10.00
Sylvan, creamer 4.50
Sylvan, cup and saucer 5.00
Sylvan, plate, 9" d 7.50
Tia Juana, luncheon plate, 9½" d 8.00
Tia Juana, mixing bowl 35.00
Tia Juana, platter. 15.00
Tia Juana, shaker. 12.00
Tia Juana, soup, flat, 8" d 20.00
Utility Ware, custard, 5 oz. 4.00
Utility Ware, leftover, 4" 6.00

Utility Ware, mixing bowl, 8" d 10.00
Utility Ware, pie baker, 9½" d 10.00
Williamsburg, cake plate, lug handle, 10" d 10.00
Williamsburg, cup and saucer 5.00
Williamsburg, dish, lug handle, 5¼" d 2.00
Williamsburg, plate, 6" d 1.50
Williamsburg, plate, 9¼" d 7.50
Yorktown, bowl, round, 9" d 18.00
Yorktown, cup and saucer 8.00
Yorktown, demitasse cup 12.00
Yorktown, dish, 6" d 4.00
Yorktown, plate, 8" d 6.00
Yorktown, platter, 15" d 20.00
Yorktown, salt and pepper shakers, pr 10.00
Yorktown, soup bowl, coupe, 8" d 12.00

EGGBEATERS

Kitchen collecting is becoming specialized. A new collecting category often evolves as the result of the publication of a book or formation of a collectors' club. In this instance, eggbeaters became a separate category as the result of the publication of a checklist book on the subject.

Learn to differentiate between commonly found examples and those eggbeaters that are scarce. Novelty and multipurpose beaters are desired. American collectors are expanding their collecting horizons by seeking out beaters from Canada and Europe.

Reference: Don Thornton, *Beat This: The Eggbeater Chronicles,* Off Beat Books, 1994.

A & J, metal, wood handle, Full Vision Beater, orig metal
 container, 10" h **$30.00**
A & J, metal, wood handle, High Speed Center Drive,
 11½" h 10.00
A & J, metal, "Lady Bingo #72," 10¾" h 15.00
A & J, metal, wood handle, pat Oct 9, 1923, 13½" h 15.00
Aurelis, metal, wood handle, Master Egg Beater, 11½" h 300.00
Benson, aluminum, The Benson Beater, 12" h 95.00
Busscraft of Hollywood, plastic, 12" h 60.00
Cyclone, cast iron, 11½" h 75.00
Dazey Churn & Mfg, #60, 6 qt 100.00
Dover, standard, cast iron, 10" h 45.00
EKCO, black handle, bell shaped dashers, 10¾" h 5.00
EKCO, plastic side handle, 11½" h. 5.00
EKCO, One Hand Beater, 10" h 7.00
Henderson Corp, The Minute Maid, heart shaped dash-
 ers, 11½" h 120.00

Edlund Co, Burlington, VT, stainless steel blades, red painted wood handle, $5.00.

Konvex, bowl shaped dasher, 12" h 90.00

Maynards, Master Mixer, #N88, red plastic handles,
  nylon dashers, 11" h 25.00

Maynards, yellow plastic handles, 11" h 15.00

Perfection, cast iron, propeller shaped dashers, 10" h 200.00

Stuber & Kuck Co, Biltrite Egg Beater, wavy dashers,
  10¹/₂" h 30.00

Talpin, Betty Talpin Egg Beater, wood handle, 5³/₄" h 45.00

Talpin, Light Running, D–handle, 11" h 50.00

Toy, Bird Bird, Wilton Woodridge, 10" h 10.00

White and Hallock, Whippit, 13¹/₂" h 20.00

ERTL

Fred Ertl, Sr., founded Ertl, the world's largest manufacturer of toy farm equipment, in 1945. The company has licenses from most major manufacturers. Located in Dyersville, Iowa, Ertl also manufactures a line of promotional banks, promotional trucks, and toys ranging from airplanes to trucks.

Ertl makes many of its toys in a variety of scales. It also has a line of limited edition, highly detailed models designed for direct sale to the adult collector market. When researching an Ertl toy be certain you are looking in the right scale and quality categories.

Collectors' Club: Ertl Collectors Club, PO Box 500, Dyersville, IA 52040.

Note: All toys listed are in very good condition. Banks are in mint condition.

Bank, #1350UO, 1913 Model T Van, Hershey's Milk
  Chocolate, brown body, trim, 1990 . . . . $25.00

Bank, #2115, 1926 Mack Truck, Publix #2, white body
  and tires, green spokes, 1985 . . . . 100.00

Bank, #9017, horse and carriage, Chicago Tribune,
  black, 1989 . . . . 55.00

Bank, #9218, 1913 Model T Van, Canadian Province,
  Alberta, white body, brown trim, 1986 . . . . 30.00

Bank, #9275, 1926 Mack Truck, RCA #3, white body,
  red trim, 1987 . . . . 40.00

Bank, #9377, step van, Little Debbie #1, white on white,
  1987 . . . . 90.00

Bank, #9681, step van, Delaval, white, 1989 . . . . 110.00

Bank, Allied Van Lines, orange body, black top and running boards, white rubber tires, mkd "Replica Ford 1917 Model T Van," 6" l, 2¹/₂" h, $20.00.

Bank, #9701, 1917 Model T Van, 4–H Clubs of America,
  white, 1988 . . . . 30.00

Bank, #9776, 1937 Ford Tractor Trailer, Allied Van Lines
  #4, orange body, black trim, 1988 . . . . 65.00

Bank, #9883, 1918 Runabout, Dyersville Historical
  Society, red body, black trim, 1988 . . . . 35.00

Case "L" Tractor 60.00

Ford 7500 Backhoe 55.00

Hydraulic Dump Truck #1645 . . . . 30.00

Iron Horse Van 50.00

John Deere 400 Bulldozer 30.00

John Deere Tilt Bed 135.00

Loadstar Tilt Bed, green/gray 125.00

Mobile Tanker 60.00

Transtar Rowe Furniture Truck 40.00

Velveeta Semi 35.00

FANS, ELECTRIC

While hundreds of companies made electric fans, the market was mostly dominated by Emerson Electric, General Electric, and Westinghouse Electric. Other collectible manufacturers include Berstead Manufacturing, Hunter–Century Gilbert, Menominee, Peerless, Robbins & Meyers, and StarRite/Eskimo.

Montgomery Ward, Sears, Singer, and Western Electric never manufactured electric fans. They put their brand names on fans made by others. Polar Cub electric fans were made for the five–and–dime store trade.

Electric fan collecting came of age in the 1990s. Currently, the focus is primarily on desk fans made prior to 1960. The market for large ceiling fans, with the exception of those of unusual design, is still primarily reuse.

Reference: John M. Witt, *Collector's Guide to Electric Fans*, Collector Books, 1997.

Collectors' Club: American Fan Collectors Assoc, PO Box 5473, Sarasota, FL 34277.

REPRODUCTION ALERT: Beware of assembled fakes. Unscrupulous individuals assemble fictitious fans by using parts from several different fans. Buy only from sellers willing to provide a money–back, no–questions–asked guarantee.

Note: All fans listed are in excellent condition.

Berstead Manufacturing, Model 1005, Eskimo, star
  formed guard, cast–iron blade, non–oscillating,
  c1947, 10" $15.00

Dominion, Art Deco style, shield shaped guard,
  cast–iron base, black wrinkle paint finish, 1940, 10" 30.00

Emerson, Model 444A, black, gold painted blades,
  2 speed, 1926, 8" 30.00

Emerson, Model 5250–F, Silver Swan, sheet–steel body,
  polish chrome front screen, cast–metal base, 1940, 10" . . . 150.00

Emerson, Model 77648–TE, dark metallic brown,
  3–speed switch at base, 1958, 16" 30.00

Emerson, Model 71666, steel blades and guard,
  1923–32, 12" 50.00

General Electric, Model 236327, Whiz, polished brass
  blades, glossy hunter green finish, 1–speed toggle
  switch in base, c1924, 9" 35.00

General Electric, Model F125107, steel body, 1947, 10" 15.00

Western Electric, #6100, cast iron and metal, 13¹/₂" h, 10" d, $70.00. Photo courtesy Collectors Auction Services.

Gilbert, Art Deco style, chrome plated guard, blades, and motor housing, cast–iron base, black wrinkle finish, c1936, 12" **75.00**

Knapp–Monarch, non–oscillating, brown wrinkle finish, 1940, 9" **15.00**

Polar Cub, stamped steel blades, motor housing, and base, non–oscillating, c1925, 10" **15.00**

StarRite, Art Deco style, octagonal guard, polished brass blades, lime green gloss finish, 3–speed slide switch, c1933, 10" **55.00**

Westinghouse, Model 165D3, cast aluminum base, plastic blades, 3–speed, c1955, 16" **25.00**

Westinghouse, Model 420550–A, Whirlwind, cast–iron base, 1–speed slide switch, c1922, 9" **25.00**

FAST–FOOD COLLECTIBLES

McDonald's dominates the field. In fact, it has become so important that it has its own category. If you have a McDonald's fast–food collectible, look under "M."

Each year dozens of new fast–food franchises are launched. Each year dozens of fast–food franchises fail. Collectors focus primarily on collectibles from those which have achieved national success. National fast–food chains do regional promotions. Collectors' club newsletters are the best way to keep up with these and the premiums that result.

All the major fast–food franchises have gone international. Collectors also are hopping aboard the international bandwagon. Many American collections now contain examples from abroad.

References: Ken Clee and Susan Hufferd, *Tomart's Price Guide to Kid's Meal Collectibles (Non–McDonald's)*, Tomart Publications, 1994; Gail Pope and Keith Hammond, *Fast Food Toys, 2nd Edition*, Schiffer Publishing, 1998.

Arby's, figure, Little Miss Helpful, 1981 .... **$2.00**

Arby's, figure, Tweety Bird, dressed like elf, 1989 .... **4.00**

Arby's, glass, Monopoly Collector Series, Free Parking, 1985 .... **6.00**

Arby's, mini disk, plastic, Ranger Smith, blue, 1993 .... **1.00**

Arby's, mug, Pittsburgh Steelers, Steelers 50 Seasons Gold Cup, 5¹/₂" h **4.00**

Arby's, pencil topper, Looney Tunes, 1988 .... **5.00**

Arctic Circle Drive Inn, Acey, glass, "Enjoy Coca–Cola" on front, "At Your/Arctic Circle" on reverse, black, white, and plum stained glass and filigree design, 5¹/₂" h **4.00**

A & W, iron–on decals, sheet, Root Beer Bear and A & W logo, 1977 .... **2.50**

Big Boy, activity book, *Adventures of the Big Boy*, #241, full color, May 1977, 7 x 10" **20.00**

Big Boy, figure, soft rubber **10.00**

Big Boy, glass, Big Boy 50th Anniversary, red, white, black, and gold, 6¹/₄" h **3.00**

Big Boy, Big Boy Mistic Slate, 1970s, 2³/₄ x 3³/₄" **25.00**

Big Boy, pinback button, litho, symbol trademark, orange, white, and brown, 1960s, 1¹/₈" d **15.00**

Burger King, booklet, Cruisin' Rules Fun Book, 1987 .... **5.00**

Burger King, calendar, 20 Magical Years, 1992 .... **4.00**

Burger King, Crayola marker, 1982 .... **2.00**

Burger King, cup, plastic, Gargoyles transformation cup, 1995 .... **3.00**

Burger King, doll, Glow–in–the–Dark Trolls, Jaws, 1993 ..... **3.00**

Burger King, figure, Archie in red jalopie, 1991 .... **3.00**

Burger King, figure, Beetlejuice, The Charmer, 1990 .... **2.00**

Burger King, game, Burger King Championship Checkers, "Official Guiness Book of World Records Challenge," commemorative limited edition, 1988 .... **10.00**

Burger King, glass, Have It Your Way Collector's Series 1776–1976, Liberty Bell, red lettering **5.00**

Burger King, Life Savers Freaky Fellas, 1992 .... **2.50**

Burger King, magic kit, 1992 .... **1.00**

Burger King, pencil top eraser, Burger King bust, 1979 ...... **1.00**

Burger King, pencil topper, Alvin, 1987 .... **3.00**

Burger King, puzzle, frame tray, full color, 1973, 8¹/₂ x 10" **10.00**

Burger King, watch, Nightmare Before Christmas, Halloweentown, 1993 .... **4.00**

Burger King, water bottle, Teenage Mutant Ninja Turtles Bike Gear, 1991 .... **2.00**

Carl's Jr, book, *Just Me and My Dad*, Mercer Mayer, Little Critter Books, Golden Look–Look Book, Western Publishing, 1986 .... **3.00**

Carl's Jr, cassette tape, *The Velveteen Rabbit*, 1989 .... **4.00**

Carl's Jr, flying disk, Beach Creatures Series, 1990 .... **2.50**

Carl's Jr, ice pop maker, Happy Star, 1987 .... **4.00**

Carl's Jr, magnet, hot dog, 1988 .... **3.00**

Carl's Jr, mini volleyball, Camp California Series, 1992 .... **2.50**

Carl's Jr, sand pail/mold, plastic, snap–on white handle, 1986 .... **2.00**

Carl's Jr, Star Gazers telescope, 1988 .... **3.00**

Chuck E Cheese, coin holder **1.00**

Chuck E Cheese, doll, cloth, plush, 13" h **15.00**

Chuck E Cheese, figure, bendable **10.00**

Chuck E Cheese, hackeysack ball **4.00**

Chuck E Cheese, purse **1.00**

Chuck E Cheese, yo yo **1.50**

Dairy Queen, beach ball, inflatable, Dairy Queen logo **3.00**

Dairy Queen, bloom ball, 1994 .... **1.00**

Dairy Queen, card game, ABC Flash Cards, Creative Child, 1993 .... **1.00**

Dairy Queen, Christmas Ornament, oval, Dennis the Menace with candy cane, clear, gold accent, 1994 .... **2.00**

Dairy Queen, figure, wagon, red, black, and white, 1991, 4" l plus handle 3.00

Dairy Queen, noise maker, plastic cylinder, iridescent colors, 3" l, 1993 .... 2.00

Dairy Queen, whistle, figural ice cream cone, 1991 .... 2.00

Denny's, Flintstones Fun Squirter, 1991 .... 2.00

Denny's, Jetsons Space Card, 1992 .... 1.00

Denny's, stencils, sealife 1.00

Domino's Pizza, bookmark, 1989 .... 8.00

Domino's Pizza, figure, noid, rubber, bendable, 1988, 7" h 10.00

Domino's Pizza, game, Domino's Pizza Delivery Game, Wortquest USA, Inc, 1989 .... 10.00

Domino's Pizza, glass, frosted design and logo, 4¹/₈" h 2.00

Dunkin' Donuts, action figure, Captain Planet Series, 1992 .... 5.00

Dunkin' Donuts, figure, Beach Munchkin, 1989 .... 6.00

Hardee's, activity book, The Presidents Activity Fun, 1992 ..... 2.00

Hardee's, bookmark, Nicktoons, 1994 .... 3.00

Hardee's, car, Mello Yello #51, Days of Thunder Series, Matchbox, 1990 .... 4.00

Hardee's, figure, California Raisins, Waves Weaver, 1988 ..... 3.00

Hardee's, figure, Cruiser, Speed Bunnies Series, 1994 .... 2.00

Hardee's, Ghostbusters siren, 1989 .... 2.00

Hardee's, straw slider, Where's Waldo, 1991 .... 3.00

Hardee's, stuffed toy, Pound Puppies, 8" l, 1986 .... 4.00

International House of Pancakes, doll, cloth, Chocolate Chip Charlie, 1992 .... 6.00

International House of Pancakes, figure, Pancake Kid, Bonnie Blueberry, 1992 .... 3.00

Jack–in–the–Box, ball, clear, colored, Jumbo Jack disk inside, 1¹/₂" d 2.00

Jack–in–the–Box, figure, bendable, Ollie O Ring, 1991 .... 5.00

Jack–in–the–Box, miniature yo yo, character sticker on front, 1" d 2.00

Kentucky Fried Chicken, bank, plastic, figural Col Sanders holding bucket of chicken, 1977, 8" h 20.00

Kentucky Fried Chicken, doll, Col Sanders, Canada, 13" h 28.00

Kentucky Fried Chicken, mini disk, 4" d 3.00

Little Caesars, doll/finger puppet, stuffed, Meatsa Meatsa Man, 1990, 5" h 5.00

Little Caesars, flip flyer, 1993–94 .... 4.00

Little Caesars, secret ring, red and yellow 1.00

Long John Silver, card game, Go Fish, 1989 .... 6.00

Long John Silver, telescope, paper scene, Orange Sea Watcher, 1990 .... 2.50

Long John Silver, water squirter, rubber, 4 different characters, 2" h 3.00

Nathan's Famous Hot Dogs, figure, Franksters 5.00

Pizza Hut, comic book, X–Men, #1, Rogue and Gambit, Marvel Comics, mkd "Marvel Collector's Edition," 1993 .... 1.00

Pizza Hut, compass, Young Indiana Jones Chronicles, 1994 .... 2.00

Pizza Hut, cookie cutter, plastic, figural pizza 3.00

Pizza Hut, cup, plastic, Eureeka's Castle Series 1.50

Pizza Hut, figure, bendable, Aliens Series, 1980s 8.00

Pizza Hut, glass, Puffball Popple, "Steppin' out for fun!," 1986 .... 3.00

Pizza Hut, pinback button, "Book It" 3.00

Pizza Hut, pinback button, The Land Before Time Series, 1988 .... 3.00

Pizza Hut, puppet, rubber, Eureka's Castle 5.00

Pizza Hut, ruler, plastic, Garfield, 1992 .... 2.00

Pizza Hut, sunglasses, Back to the Future Series, Solar Shades, 1989 .... 3.00

Roy Rogers, figure, batting helmet, baseball team logo, 1992 .... 1.00

Roy Rogers, figure, Critters Series, plastic, painted eyes, 3" h 3.00

Roy Rogers, magnet, Be A Sport, price for set of 4 .... 22.00

Roy Rogers, secret decoder pen, 1988 .... 4.00

Sambo, stuffed toy, wearing chef's hat, fuzzy beard, felt facial features, 7" h 10.00

Subway, Doodle Top Jr 1.00

Subway, figure, Tom on skateboard, Tom & Jerry Series, 1994 .... 2.00

Subway, pencil topper, Coneheads 3.00

Subway, ring, Captain Planet, 1993 .... 3.00

Taco Bell, coloring card, When You Grow Up Series, 1992 .... 2.00

Taco Bell, finger puppet, Lowly Worm, rubber, 1993, 2" h 4.00

Taco Bell, poster, Wally Mammoth, Dinosaur Days Series, 1994 .... 1.50

Taco Bell, watch, Congo the Movie Series, 1995 .... 4.00

Wendy's, bowling game, 6 pcs, 1994 .... 1.00

Wendy's, box, Definitely Dinosaurs!, 1988 .... 2.00

Wendy's, Bristle Blocks, Playskool, 1987 .... 4.00

Wendy's, Dino Jam Pinball, 1992 .... 2.00

Wendy's, figure, Charlie, All Dogs Go to Heaven Series, 3 x 3¹/₄" 2.00

Wendy's, fun flyer ring, plastic, 3¹/₂" d 1.25

Wendy's, glass hanger, frog, 1993 .... 1.00

Wendy's, Gobots, Tonka, 1986 .... 4.00

Wendy's, Krazy Straw, 1984 .... 4.00

Wendy's, maze game, Sea Turtle, mkd "1993 Wendy's Int'l China," 1993 .... 1.50

Wendy's, mug, ceramic, red, white, and black trademark, 1970s 4.00

Wendy's, puppy stickers, sheet, 9 x 3³/₄" 5.00

Wendy's, stickers, glow–in–the–dark, reusable, 1993 .... 2.00

Burger King, record album, *The Many Faces of Alf*, 33¹/₃ rpm, cardboard, premium offer on back, 5³/₄" d, 1987, $3.00.

Tony's Pizza, cloth doll, Zippy, $8.00.

Decade, Glass Press, 1996; Margaret and Kenn Whitmeyer, *Fenton Art Glass, 1907–1939: Identification and Value Guide*, Collector Books, 1996.

Periodical: *Glass Messenger*, 700 Elizabeth St, Williamstown, WV 26187.

Collectors' Clubs: Fenton Art Glass Collectors of America, Inc, PO Box 384, Williamstown, WV 26187; National Fenton Glass Society, PO Box 4008, Marietta, OH 45750.

Aqua Crest, epergne, hobnail, 3 trumpet, small	**$115.00**
Aqua Crest, saucer, 6"	**12.00**
Aqua Crest, vase, 4½"	**25.00**
Aqua Crest, vase, triangular, 4"	**30.00**
Blue Opalescent, bowl, Hobnail, DC, 10"	**60.00**
Blue Opalescent, cat slipper, Hobnail	**30.00**
Blue Opalescent, compote, Hobnail	**50.00**
Blue Opalescent, console set, Diamond Lace, 3 pcs	**125.00**
Blue Opalescent, fan vase, Hobnail, 6½"	**42.00**
Blue Opalescent, oil cruet, Hobnail, orig stopper	**38.00**
Cranberry Opalescent, bowl, Hobnail, 10½"	**85.00**
Cranberry Opalescent, creamer, Coin Dot, #1924, 4"	**75.00**
Cranberry Opalescent, creamer, Dot Optic, 4"	**75.00**
Cranberry Opalescent, vase, Hobnail, 4½"	**50.00**
Cranberry Opalescent, vase, miniature, ftd, Hobnail	**30.00**
Cranberry Opalescent, water pitcher, Coin Dot, #1353	**250.00**
Cranberry Opalescent, water pitcher, Dot Optic	**250.00**
Emerald Crest, compote, 6"	**38.00**
Emerald Crest, compote, DC	**35.00**
Emerald Crest, fan vase, 4½"	**23.00**
French Opalescent, basket, Hobnail, 4½"	**40.00**
French Opalescent, bonbon, Hobnail	**15.00**
French Opalescent, boudoir lamp, Coin Dot	**225.00**
French Opalescent, cake stand, Diamond Lace, low	**75.00**
French Opalescent, candlesticks, pr, Hobnail, low	**50.00**
French Opalescent, cologne bottle, no stopper, Hobnail	**25.00**
French Opalescent, oil cruet, Hobnail, orig stopper	**35.00**
French Opalescent, punch cup, Hobnail	**12.00**
French Opalescent, vase, miniature, clover top, Hobnail	**30.00**
French Opalescent, water tumbler, Hobnail, 4¼"	**20.00**
Peach Crest, bowl, orig label, 13"	**85.00**
Peach Crest, bowl, ruffled, 6"	**18.00**
Peach Crest, top hat	**42.00**
Peach Crest, vase, jack-in-the-pulpit, 8½"	**75.00**
Ruby, juice, flat, Georgian	**14.00**
Ruby, juice tumbler, Georgian	**14.00**
Ruby, salt and pepper shakers, pr, ftd, Georgian	**80.00**
Ruby, sherbet, Plymouth	**25.00**
Ruby, water goblet, Georgian	**25.00**
Ruby, water goblet, Georgian	**10.00**
Silver Crest, banana bowl, high	**75.00**
Silver Crest, banana bowl, low, ftd	**50.00**
Silver Crest, basket, low, 7"	**30.00**
Silver Crest, bowl, center handle, ruffled, violets in the snow, 8"	**35.00**
Silver Crest, bowl, ribbed, 11"	**50.00**
Silver Crest, bowl, ruffled, 13"	**45.00**
Silver Crest, cake plate, handled, ftd, 13"	**40.00**
Silver Crest, nut dish, ftd	**17.00**
Silver Crest, plate, 8½"	**28.00**
Silver Crest, relish, 2 part	**55.00**
Silver Crest, relish, heart shape, handled	**30.00**
Silver Crest, salt and pepper shakers, pr, ftd	**110.00**

Wendy's, Tom Thumb Plant Starter Kit, 1987	**4.00**
Wendy's, water bottle, Tricky Tints Series, 12 oz, 1992	**1.50**
Wendy's, water colors, figural hamburger case	**1.00**
White Castle, ballpoint pen, bendable, full color cut–out foam Castle Land character head on top, 1993	**1.50**
White Castle, baseball, rubber, pink, emb cartoon hamburger figure, 1993	**1.50**
White Castle, bow biter, plastic, 6 different characters, 1989	**4.00**
White Castle, soccer ball, mkd "White Castle/Castle Meal Wilson Stuffs," 1991	**3.00**

FENTON GLASS

The Fenton Art Glass Company, founded by Frank L. Fenton in 1905 in Martins Ferry, Ohio, originally offered decorating services to other manufacturers. By 1907 the company had relocated to Williamstown, West Virginia, and was making its own glass.

The company's first products included carnival, chocolate, custard, and opalescent glass. Art glass and stretch glass products were introduced in the 1920s. Production of slag glass began in the 1930s. Decorating techniques ranged from acid etching to hand painting.

Through the 1970s, Fenton marked its products with a variety of paper labels. The company adopted an oval raised trademark in 1970. Recently a date code has been added to the mark.

References: Robert E. Eaton, Jr. (comp.), *Fenton Glass: The First Twenty–Five Years Comprehensive Price Guide 1995*, Glass Press, 1995; Robert E. Eaton, Jr. (comp.), *Fenton Glass: The Second Twenty–Five Years Comprehensive Price Guide 1995*, Glass Press, 1995; Fenton Art Glass Collectors of America (comp.), *Fenton Glass: The Third Twenty–Five Years Comprehensive Price Guide 1995*, Glass Press, 1995; William Heacock, *Fenton Glass: The First Twenty–Five Years*, O–Val Advertising Corp. [Antique Publications], 1978; William Heacock, *Fenton Glass: The Second Twenty–Five Years*, O–Val Advertising Corp. [Antique Publications], 1980, William Heacock, *Fenton Glass: The Third Twenty–Five Years*, O–Val Advertising Corp. [Antique Publications], 1989; James Measell (ed.), *Fenton Glass: The 1980s*

Burmese, vase, wasited cylinder shape, mkd "Hand Painted by B. Montgomery," 7¹/₂" h, $50.00.

Silver Crest, top hat basket, handled, 5"	45.00
Silver Crest, torte plate, 16"	50.00
Silver Crest, vase, bell bottom	85.00
White Milk Glass, banana stand, low ft, Hobnail	40.00
White Milk Glass, basket, Hobnail, 12"	50.00
White Milk Glass, bowl, DC, Hobnail, 8"	30.00
White Milk Glass, butter, cov, Hobnail, ¹/₄ lb	35.00
White Milk Glass, candy jar, cov, ftd, Hobnail	40.00
White Milk Glass, cat slipper, Hobnail	12.00
White Milk Glass, juice pitcher, Hobnail	40.00
White Milk Glass, mustard, cov, wood paddle, Hobnail	35.00
White Milk Glass, punch set, plain edge, Hobnail, #3527	400.00
White Milk Glass, punch set, octagonal, Hobnail, #3820	500.00

FIESTA

Homer Laughlin began production of its Fiesta line in 1936. Frederick Rhead was the designer. Concentric bands of rings were the only decorative motif besides color. Dark blue, light green, ivory, red, and yellow were the first five colors. Turquoise followed a year later.

Fiesta was restyled in 1969. Antique gold, turf green, and mango red (really the old red retitled) were introduced. These changes were not enough to save Fiesta. Production ceased in 1973.

Wishing to capitalize on the tremendous secondary market interest in Fiesta, Homer Laughlin reintroduced Fiesta in 1986. Several new colors made their appearance at that time.

References: Sharon and Bob Huxford, *Collectors Encyclopedia of Fiesta, Eighth Edition,* Collector Books, 1998; Jeffrey B. Snyder, *Fiesta: Homer Laughlin China Company's Colorful Dinnerware,* Schiffer Publishing, 1997.

Collectors' Clubs: Fiesta Club of America, PO Box 15383, Machesney Park, IL 61115; Fiesta Collectors Club, PO Box 471, Valley City, OH 44280.

Chartreuse, dessert, 6" d	$50.00
Chartreuse, mug	90.00
Chartreuse, plate, 10" d	50.00
Cobalt, cake lifter, Kitchen Kraft	195.00

Cobalt, candles, pr, bulb	125.00
Cobalt, casserole, cov, Kitchen Kraft, 8¹/₂" d	110.00
Cobalt, compartment plate, 12" d	75.00
Cobalt, cup and saucer, after dinner	95.00
Cobalt, fork, Kitchen Kraft	225.00
Cobalt, juice tumbler	45.00
Cobalt, relish, side	55.00
Cobalt, spoon, Kitchen Kraft	170.00
Cobalt, tea cup, flat bottom	100.00
Dark Green, cream soup	95.00
Dark Green, plate, 10" d	65.00
Dark Green, sauce boat	90.00
Gray, chop plate, 13" d	95.00
Gray, deep plate	50.00
Gray, eggcup	175.00
Gray, mug	95.00
Green, coffeepot base, after dinner	175.00
Green, cup and saucer, after dinner	85.00
Green, eggcup	50.00
Green, fork, Kitchen Kraft	115.00
Green, juice tumbler	30.00
Green, mixing bowl, #4	200.00
Green, pitcher, ice lip	135.00
Green, relish center	55.00
Green, relish side	50.00
Green, salt shaker, mkd	60.00
Green, teapot, large	225.00
Ivory, candles, pr, bulb	125.00
Ivory, chop plate, 13" d	45.00
Ivory, cream soup	60.00
Ivory, juice tumbler	45.00
Ivory, mixing bowl, #4	225.00
Ivory, mug, mkd	125.00
Ivory, relish center	60.00
Ivory, relish side	55.00
Ivory, relish, 6 colors, cobalt center	350.00
Ivory, relish, 6 colors, red center	350.00
Ivory, spoon, Kitchen Kraft	175.00

Cobalt, fruit bowl, 11³/₄" d, $485.00.

Turquoise, ashtray, unmkd, 5⁷/₁₆" d, $30.00.

Medium Green, creamer	110.00
Medium Green, cup and saucer	65.00
Medium Green, cup and saucer, inside rings	95.00
Medium Green, deep plate	135.00
Medium Green, plate, 6" d	35.00
Medium Green, plate, 9" d	65.00
Medium Green, platter	175.00
Medium Green, salad, individual	145.00
Medium Green, salt shaker	95.00
Red, bowl, 5¹/₂" d	25.00
Red, coffeepot, after dinner	725.00
Red, creamer, individual	350.00
Red, cream soup	75.00
Red, mixing bowl, #1	275.00
Red, relish side	65.00
Red, tea cup, flat bottom	100.00
Red, teapot, large	285.00
Rose, cream soup	95.00
Rose, juice tumbler	65.00
Rose, mug	95.00
Turquoise, bowl, 5¹/₂" d	22.00
Turquoise, bud vase	95.00
Turquoise, candles, pr, bulb	110.00
Turquoise, casserole, cov	135.00
Turquoise, creamer, stick handle	115.00
Turquoise, cup and saucer, after dinner	115.00
Turquoise, marmalade	325.00
Turquoise, mixing bowl, #4	220.00
Turquoise, pitcher, disk	110.00
Turquoise, pitcher, ice lip	195.00
Turquoise, relish base	50.00
Turquoise, relish center	60.00
Turquoise, salt and pepper shakers, pr, both mkd	135.00
Turquoise, teapot, large	275.00
Turquoise, teapot, medium	150.00
Turquoise, water tumbler	75.00
Yellow, bowl, 4³/₄" d	20.00
Yellow, candles, pr, bulb	100.00
Yellow, casserole, cov	130.00
Yellow, coffeepot lid	125.00
Yellow, creamer, individual	75.00
Yellow, cream soup	40.00
Yellow, juice pitcher	40.00
Yellow, mixing bowl, #2	140.00
Yellow, plate, 10" d	25.00
Yellow, relish center	55.00
Yellow, teapot lid, medium	95.00

FIGURAL PLANTERS & VASES

Initially collected as a form by individuals collecting products of a specific maker, figural planters evolved as a collecting category unto itself in the mid–1990s. Figural baby planters are a major sub-category. Lady head vases command their own category.

Most generic examples and pieces whose design and shape do not speak to a specific time period have little value. Crossover collectors, especially those seeking animal, black, and vehicle images, skew value.

References: Kathleen Deel, *Figural Planters*, Schiffer Publishing, 1996; Betty and Bill Newbound, *Collector's Encyclopedia of Figural Planter & Vases: Identification & Values*, Collector Books, 1997.

Note: Refer to specific manufacturers for additional listings.

PLANTERS

Angel, pink robe, gold trim, 10¹/₂" h	$20.00
Angel, wings spread, hands together, blue, unmkd, 6" h	8.00
Asian Girl, squatting next to large bowl with emb dec, blue, black, and yellow, Suzi Singer, 7 x 8"	100.00
Baby and Pillow, blue, Hull, #92	32.00
Baby Block and Bunny, American Art Potteries, 6" h	8.00
Baby Carriage and Dog, blue, 22K gold trim, "What About ME?" on base, McCoy, 8" l	20.00
Baby Scale, Made in Japan, 6¹/₂" h	9.00
Baby Shoe, blue, Stanford Ware	5.00
Baby Shoes, pr, white ground, pink laces, blue accent, 3¹/₄" h	10.00
Balinese Girl, holding bucket, Royal Copley, 8¹/₄" h	25.00
Bandanna Duck, Hull, #76	30.00
Bassinet, blue, ruffled design, "Congratulations," Stanford Pottery, 7¹/₂" l	10.00
Bassinet, white, pink ribbon, 3¹/₄ x 5"	5.00
Beagle and Cart, Made in Japan, 6¹/₂" l	7.00
Bear and Bee Hive, 4³/₄" h	10.00
Bird With Ribbed Pot, Shawnee, USA 502	12.00
Box Turtle, McCoy, #740, 4¹/₄ x 8¹/₂"	12.00
Boy, low stump, Shawnee, USA 532	25.00
Buddha, Shawnee, USA 524	25.00
Bunny, eyes closed, McCoy, 9" l	15.00
Camel, reclining, Niloak, 3¹/₄ x 5¹/₂"	40.00
Canoe, "Davy Crockett" on side, American Bisque, 8¹/₂" l	55.00
Cat, Royal Copley	32.00
Cat, seated, white, red and white gingham bow on neck, glass eyes, mkd "Taiwan," 5 x 8"	8.00
Cat, seated, red ribbon and gold bells around neck, mkd "T4808" inside bell, 5³/₄" h	8.00
Cat and Cello, Royal Copley sticker, 7⁷/₈" h	60.00
Caterpillar, yellow, mkd "Floraline, USA," #0416, 14" l	15.00
Cat in Watering Can, Made in Japan, 5¹/₄" h	7.00
Cherub, mkd "Made in Japan," 5" h	8.00
Cherubs, with basket, white, unmkd, 7¹/₂" l	12.00
Child, sitting, knees up, blue cap, yarn hair, 5¹/₂" h	15.00
Children and Shoe, Shawnee, USA 525	25.00
Cocker Spaniel, lying down, Shawnee, 8¹/₄" l	12.00
Cocker Spaniel with Vase, Robinson–Ransbottom Co, #13020, 6¹/₄" h	12.00
Conch Shell, applied snails, Ebb Tide Line, Hull, 1954, 15³/₄" l	90.00

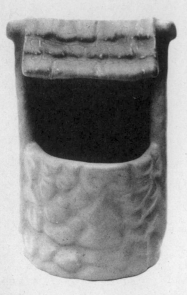

Wishing Well, Niloak, Ozark Dawn II, low relief, 8" h, $35.00.

Covered Wagon, horse and rider, #02341, 10" l **18.00**

Cow, reclining, white bow and bell around neck, Japan, 5¹/₂" l **5.00**

Dachshund, mouth open, RELPO, 7¹/₂" l **7.00**

Deer, standing, yellow, Shawnee **10.00**

Dog, Freeman McFarlin **22.00**

Dog and Shoe, sand finish on dog, brown shoe and accents, imp "Hound Dog Shoe Co" on bottom, Haeger, 7¹/₂ x 10" **25.00**

Donkey and Basket, #722, Shawnee **25.00**

Donkey and Cart, black, gold, and pink trim, 7" l **7.00**

Dove, hole for hanging, McCoy, mkd "LCC, USA, 1620," 7¹/₄ x 12" **20.00**

"Down by the Old Mill Stream," McCoy, 7³/₄" l **20.00**

Duck, Art Deco shape, McCoy **40.00**

Duckling, Kay Finch **40.00**

Ducks, green, Hull, medium size **35.00**

Dutch Boy, carrying buckets, green and white, stamped "Made in Japan," 4" h **7.00**

Dutch Girl, carrying buckets, 6¹/₄" h **9.00**

Eagle, wings spread, brown, white, yellow, green base, 11" l **20.00**

Elephant, trunk raised, blue and pink glaze, 7³/₄" h **15.00**

Elephant, wicker, button eyes, glass container inside, 5¹/₂" h **6.00**

Elf and Shoe, green, Shawnee, USA 765 . . . . **25.00**

Farmer Boy, Hull, #91 . . . . **15.00**

Fawn and Stump, Shawnee, USA 535 . . . . **15.00**

Fox on Log, rabbit and green leaves dec, 9" l **15.00**

Frog, hand on chin, Brush, 10" l **50.00**

Girl, holding kitten, De Lee Art **90.00**

Girl, leaning on barrel, Royal Copley, 6¹/₄" h **15.00**

Girl, pink dress, holding hat, Lefton, 8" h **12.00**

Girl and Mandolin, Shawnee, USA 576 . . . . **30.00**

Giraffe, #521, Shawnee **25.00**

Golfer, 6¹/₄" h **10.00**

Grand Piano, McCoy, 6" l **15.00**

Grist Mill, green, #769, Shawnee **15.00**

Horse and Jockey, green base, 12" l **25.00**

Horse, rearing, Shawnee, 6" h **18.00**

Humpty Dumpty, sitting on wall, 5³/₄" h **12.00**

Kewpie, sitting by stump, 5¹/₂" h **6.00**

Kitten and Basket, white, applied floral dec, Lefton, #1923, 4 x 5" **12.00**

Kitten in Cradle, bow at neck, Royal Copley, 7¹/₂" l **45.00**

Kittens in Basket, stamped "Japan," 5¹/₄ x 5³/₄" **15.00**

Lamb, standing, eyes closed, white, pink, green, yellow, black accents on face, American Bisque, 10³/₄" l **35.00**

Lion, brown and white, black accents, McCoy, 14¹/₄" l **18.00**

Long Billed Duck, McCoy, 7" l **8.00**

Lovebirds, face to face, 11¹/₄" l **12.00**

Mexican, standing by tree, stamped "Japan," 5¹/₂" h **7.00**

Mortar and Pestle, black, gold trim, 6¹/₂" h **7.00**

Oak Leaf Bowl, applied frogs, 5 x 7³/₄" **12.00**

Oaken Bucket and Pump, INARCO, 5¹/₄" h **9.00**

Oriental and Umbrella, Shawnee, USA 701 . . . . **18.00**

Oriental Boy, NAPCO, Japan sticker, 4 x 4¹/₂" **10.00**

Oriental Girl and Pot, Royal Copley, 5¹/₂" h **10.00**

Paddleboat, "Lorena," mkd "Bi–Centennial Project of Zanesville Area Chamber of Commerce, 1976," McCoy, 8³/₄" l **20.00**

Parrot, Hull, #60 . . . . **30.00**

Parrot, sitting on stump, Czechoslovakian, 5¹/₂" h **35.00**

Peasant, with flower cart, Hull, #61 . . . . **25.00**

Pelican, open mouth, 6 x 7³/₄" **8.00**

Persian Cat with Bowl, Hull, c1940s, 7¹/₂" h **30.00**

Pipe and Hat, Lefton, #H5959 . . . . **15.00**

Pipe, brown, gold trim, 4¹/₂ x 8¹/₂" **8.00**

Puppy with Ball of Yarn, Hull, 6 x 7³/₄" **25.00**

Rabbit, sitting, blue, black eyes and accent, Stanford Pottery, 5¹/₂" l **12.00**

Rabbit with Carrot, matte white, McCoy **65.00**

Rocking Horse, blue, white accents, "Ride A Cock Horse" on one side, "To Banbury Cross" on other side, McCoy, c1955 . . . . **20.00**

Rocking Horse, pink, Stanford Ware, 6¹/₄ x 7¹/₂" **10.00**

Rolling Pin, hp floral dec, Clinchfield Artware Pottery, c1945, 14" l **10.00**

Rooster, bending down, multicolored, Royal Copley, 7³/₄" h **30.00**

Sailor Boy and Boat, Haeger, 7" h **8.00**

Scottie, sitting, brown, white, and black, pink mouth, 5¹/₂" h **6.00**

Seashell, seated elf, 6 x 6¹/₂" **8.00**

Siamese Cats, Hull, #63 . . . . **60.00**

Sneaker, white ground, gold trim, 6" l **10.00**

Spinning Wheel with Dog and Cat, McCoy, c1953 . . . . **18.00**

St Francis, mkd "INARCO, Japan," 12" h **12.00**

Swan, white, gold accents, Stanford Pottery, 4³/₄" **12.00**

Train, black, gold trim, Stanford Pottery, 9" l **15.00**

Train, Santa and holiday dec, gold trim, 5³/₈ x 6³/₄" **12.00**

Tree Trunk, green shamrock dec, Irish Beleek green mark, 6" h **150.00**

Twin Shoes, aqua, McCoy **12.00**

Two Donkeys, flirty eyes, 6" h **9.00**

US Mail Stagecoach, green, gold wheels, Lane & Co, 1952, 11¹/₂" l **70.00**

Wagon Wheel, McCoy, 8¹/₄" h **20.00**

Watering Can, floral dec, white ground, pink trim, mkd "A Tele–gift (c) 1985, Made in Korea," 10¹/₂" l **6.00**

Whale, black, 5 x 9" **10.00**

Whippet, black, 15" l **15.00**

Wild West Rodeo, McCoy, 7¹/₂" l **25.00**

Wren, sitting on tree stump, Royal Copley **18.00**

Zebra, standing, 5¹/₂" h **10.00**

Gazelle, Haeger, #3386, unmkd, 12¹/₈" h, $25.00.

VASES

Bird in Flight, Frankoma	**$25.00**
Boot, yellow, Shawnee, 4¹/₂" h	10.00
Bowling Ball and Pins, black, white, and red, brown base, 5³/₈" h	10.00
Cat, black and white, pink bow, green eyes, Royal Copley, 8¹/₄" h	18.00
Cowboy Boot, McCoy	40.00
Donkey and Basket, Shawnee, #722	25.00
Elmer Fudd, American Pottery, 7"	95.00
Fan, white, Abingdon	20.00
Open Book, "Thinking of You," floral dec, 4³/₄ x 6¹/₄"	10.00
Peacock, yellow and green, Hull, #73, 11"	30.00
Poodle with Vase, begging, white, black eyes and nose, Royal Copley, 7¹/₄" h	20.00
Squirrel, gold trim, 10" h	15.00
Squirrel, Haeger	45.00
Stallion, rearing, Sascha Brastoff, 9¹/₂" h	95.00
Stump, climbing bears, 6⁵/₈" h	8.00
Swan, glass, white and aventurine vetri atrina, applied black eye and bill, orig foil label, Made in Italy, Aureliano Toso, 1950, 4 x 10¹/₂"	400.00
Tree, squirrel sitting on limb, white ground, gold dec, incised "430," 8" h	12.00
Unicorn with Vase, leaf dec, Hull, 10" h	55.00
Watering Can and Vase, mkd "R. R. P. Roseville, Ohio," #1302, 4 x 5³/₄"	10.00
Whale, Venetian smoked glass, applied murine eyes, c1920, 7³/₄ x 10"	150.00

FIGURINES

Figurines played a major role in the household decorating decor between the late 1930s and the early 1960s. Those with deep pockets bought Boehm, Lladro, and Royal Doulton. The average consumer was content with generic fare, much of it inexpensive imports, or examples from a host of California figurine manufacturers such as Kay Finch and Florence Ceramics.

Animals were the most popular theme. Human forms came next. Subject matter and the ability of a piece to speak the deco-

rative motifs of a specific time period are as important as manufacturer in determining value.

Note: Refer to specific manufacturers and animal categories for additional listings.

CERAMIC

Abingdon, peacock, #416, 1937–38, 7" h	**$50.00**
Abingdon, seated nude, antique white, 7" h	300.00
Barnware, Hansel and Gretel	34.00
Beswick, foal	85.00
Beswick, Hereford calf	75.00
Brush, reclining frog	75.00
Brush, turtle	65.00
Brad Keeler, cockatoo	55.00
Brad Keeler, flamingos, pr, one head up, one head down	70.00
Brayton Laguna, calf, brown	85.00
Brayton Laguna, child holding doll	125.00
Brayton Laguna, Donald Duck, prone	285.00
Brayton Laguna, lady holding hat and basket	75.00
Brush Pottery, reclining frog, 10" l	80.00
Camark Pottery, lion	40.00
Ceramic Arts Studio, alligator	50.00
Ceramic Arts Studio, Blythe, black and white	90.00
Ceramic Arts Studio, Colonial man	30.00
Ceramic Arts Studio, Inky Skunk	25.00
Ceramic Arts Studio, Little Boy Blue	30.00
Clay Sketches, cockatoo	25.00
DeLee, Annabelle	45.00
DeLee, Daisy	45.00
DeLee, Dutch boy	32.00
Frankart, elephant	275.00
Gilner, baseball boy	65.00
Gilner, football boy	65.00
Haeger, Indian girl with basket	25.00
Haeger, panther, 12" l	20.00
Homer Laughlin, Harlequin cat, yellow	195.00
Homer Laughlin, Harlequin donkey, mauve	275.00
Homer Laughlin, Harlequin duck, maroon	275.00
Homer Laughlin, Harlequin duck, yellow	195.00
Homer Laughlin, Harlequin fish, yellow	250.00
Homer Laughlin, Harlequin lamb, mauve	325.00
Homer Laughlin, Harlequin penguin, spruce	275.00
Howard Pierce, owl, brown tones, 8" h	85.00
Italy, lady, mkd "Italy"	22.00
Josef Originals, Birthstone Girl, December	25.00
Kay Finch, kitten, Muff	85.00
Kay Finch, rooster and hen, pr, #4844 and #4843	185.00
Kaye, girl, pink and blue, buff flower holder, unmkd, 8"	36.00
Keene, At The Beach, Wide Eyed Kids	125.00
Keene, My Kitty, Wide Eyed Kids	150.00
Keene, Watching, Wide Eyed Kids	125.00
Kreiss, oriental man and woman, pr	25.00
Lladro, swan, porcelain	160.00
Maddux of California, double cockatoos	100.00
Maddux of California, Siamese Cat, sgd	40.00
Pacific Clay, nude, holding feather, 15¹/₂" h	55.00
Roselane, boy with dog, brown and white	20.00
Roselane, giraffe, stylized, glossy gray	20.00
Roselane, owl	20.00
Rosemeade Pottery, swan, aqua, 5" h	40.00
Rosemeade Pottery, wolfhound, white, blue spots	135.00
Royal Doulton, elephant, #HN2644	95.00

Kay Finch, western burro, #4769, $125.00.

Shawnee, Pekingese 65.00
Shawnee, tumbling bear 60.00
Sorcha Boru, blue bird 100.00
Sorcha Boru, "Little Eva," polychrome glaze, artist sgd,
    6" h 100.00
Sorcha Boru, little girl between large flowers, artist sgd,
    6" h 225.00
Walker Pottery, comical horse, brown and white, 4¹/₂" 10.00
Will–George, dachshund, stamp mark, 9" l 50.00
Will–George, flamingos, pr, sgd 200.00

GLASS

Alfred Barbini, bird, purple, gold leaf base, 5¹/₂" h . . . . . . $ 75.00
Alfred Barbini, fish, aqua, gold leaf base, 6¹/₄" h 75.00
American Glass Co, Boxer Dog, clear 50.00
Archimede Seguso, dancer, black, pink and blue gold
    foil skirt, unmkd, 13 x 4¹/₂" 800.00
Baccarat, shark, clear 110.00
Baccarat, wild boar, clear 155.00
Barovier, peasant workers, pr, green, white, and black
    pasta glass, gold foil, unmkd, c1935, 11¹/₂ x 11" 600.00
Barovier, seahorse, clear, applied green spiral, murrine
    eyes, gold foil, unmkd, 11 x 4" 350.00
Boyd Crystal Art Glass, pony, chocolate 30.00
Cambridge, bird, crystal satin 25.00
Cambridge, draped lady, light emerald, 8¹/₂" h 100.00
Cambridge, frog, crystal satin 20.00
Cenedese, Alfredo Barbini, bear, vetri scavo, 5³/₄ x 11" 825.00
Degenhart, Priscilla, ivory, 1976 . . . . 65.00
Duncan & Miller, donkey and peasant, clear 425.00
Duncan & Miller, dove, clear 165.00
Duncan & Miller, duck, crystal 55.00
Duncan & Miller, fat goose, clear 275.00
Duncan & Miller, swan, opalescent blue, 6¹/₂" leaf 95.00
Duncan & Miller, swan, opalescent pink, 6¹/₂" leaf 95.00
Duncan & Miller, swordfish, clear 150.00
Fenton, alley cat, dusty rose iridized 65.00
Fenton, alley cat, electric blue iridized 95.00
Fenton, alley cat, Stiegel green iridized 50.00
Fenton, alley cat, twilight blue iridized 50.00
Fenton, fawn, Burmese 38.00
Fenton, fawn, rosalene with hp flowers 42.00

Fenton, fish, blue 15.00
Fenton, fish, pink 15.00
Fenton, happy cat, Burmese 65.00
Fenton, hen on nest, amethyst carnival, large 65.00
Fenton, hen on nest, amethyst carnival, small 35.00
Fenton, puppy, cobalt iridized with hp flowers 28.00
Fenton, raccoon, ruby iridized 22.00
Fenton, unicorn, ruby iridized 22.00
Fostoria, commemorative pelican, cobalt blue, 1989 . . . . . . 100.00
Fostoria, doe, blue, 4¹/₂" h 35.00
Fostoria, goldfish, 4" l 125.00
Fostoria, Madonna, clear 55.00
Fostoria, mermaid, clear, 11¹/₂" h 100.00
Fostoria, penguin, topaz, 4⁵/₈" h 100.00
Fostoria, sea horse, clear, 8" h 90.00
Haley, fawn, sitting, clear, 6" h 12.00
Haley, horse, jumping, clear, hollow base 45.00
Haley, robin, on stump, clear, 6" h 10.00
Haley, 3 ducks swimming, clear, 9¹/₂" l 35.00
Heisey, angelfish, clear 110.00
Heisey, gazelle, clear 1,500.00
Heisey, goose, wings up, clear 125.00
Heisey, kicking colt, clear 175.00
Heisey, mallard, wings half up, clear, 4¹/₂" h 85.00
Heisey, plug horse, clear 115.00
Heisey, Scottie, clear, 3" h 75.00
Heisey, Sealyham Terrier, clear 135.00
Heisey, sparrow, clear 145.00
Heisey, standing colt, clear 95.00
Imperial, bird, clear, sgd "Virginia B. Evans," 1949, 5" h 150.00
Imperial, owl, gloss jade green slag 85.00
Imperial, owl, gloss purple slag 75.00
Imperial, owl, white milk glass 48.00
Imperial, Terrier, amethyst carnival, 3¹/₂" h 40.00
Moser Glass Co, bear, sitting, tawny 10.00
Moser Glass Co, cat, sitting, chocolate, 3" h 6.50
Murano, horse head, clambroth, foil label, 8 x 10¹/₄ x 3" 110.00
New Martinsville, baby bear, sun colored 35.00
New Martinsville, baby chicks 45.00

Heisey, show horse, clear, 1948–49, 7³/₈" h, $100.00.

New Martinsville, eagle, 8" h. **65.00**
New Martinsville, gazelle, leaping, crystal, frosted base **45.00**
New Martinsville, German Shepherd, amethyst, frosted
     base, 5⅛" h. **140.00**
New Martinsville, hen. **75.00**
New Martinsville, Janice swan, 12". **50.00**
New Martinsville, mama bear **225.00**
New Martinsville, polar bear **50.00**
New Martinsville, pony, clear, oval base, 12" h. **60.00**
New Martinsville, rabbit, large, 2½' h **250.00**
New Martinsville, squirrel, eating nut. **35.00**
New Martinsville, squirrel on base. **45.00**
New Martinsville, standing piglet. **145.00**
New Martinsville, starfish, clear. **35.00**
New Martinsville, swan, cobalt blue **35.00**
New Martinsville, tiger, clear **150.00**
New Martinsville, wolfhound, 7" h **75.00**
New Martinsville, woodsman **125.00**
Paden City, bunny, ears down, pink **150.00**
Paden City, pony, long legs, light blue, 12" h **100.00**
Paden City, rooster, head down, clear. **75.00**
Tiffin, cat, black satin, raised bumps, 6¼" h **95.00**
Unknown Maker, pony, white, applied red mane, 5 x 3". . . . **125.00**
Viking, duck, vaseline **15.00**
Vistosi, spherical bird, orange, applied red prunts and
     murrine eyes, 8 x 6" **1,000.00**
Westmoreland, bird, flying, amber marigold. **20.00**
Westmoreland, butterfly, green mist **18.00**
Westmoreland, cat on lacy base, white milk glass. **135.00**
Westmoreland, robin on twig nest, ftd, ruby **95.00**

FINCH, KAY

After over a decade of ceramic studies, Kay Finch, assisted by her husband Braden, opened her commercial studio in 1939. A whimsical series of pig figurines and hand–decorated banks were the company's first successful products.

An expanded studio and showroom located on the Pacific Coast Highway in Corona del Mar opened on December 7,1941. The business soon had forty employees as it produced a wide variety of novelty items. A line of dog figurines and themed items were introduced in the 1940s. Christmas plates were made from 1950 until 1962.

When Braden died in 1963, Kay Finch ceased operations. Freeman–McFarlin Potteries purchased the molds in the mid–1970s and commissioned Finch to model a new series of dog figurines. Production of these continued through the late 1970s.

References: Devin Frick, Jean Frick and Richard Martinez, *Collectible Kay Finch*, Collector Books, 1997; Mike Nickel and Cindy Horvath, *Kay Finch: Art Pottery*, Schiffer Publishing, 1997; Frances Finch Webb and Jack R. Webb, *The New Kay Finch Identification Guide*, published by authors, 1996.

Ashtray, #6085, oriental shape, cobalt glaze, 10½" d **$90.00**
Ashtray, #6103, shell, pale pink matte, 9" d **45.00**
Bowl, #4657, square, scalloped edges, 10". **75.00**
Bowl, #5187, flat top, sea foam glaze, 11½ x 5½" **75.00**
Bowl, #5980, petal bowl, dark brown glaze, 17 x 11". **135.00**
Candy Cane Tumbler, #5702, zombie style, white with
     barber pole stripes, red luster, 12 oz, 5 x 2½" d **20.00**
Cane Vase, #T509A, cane, carnelian glaze, 1949, 8"
     section **25.00**

Plate, #4634, Corral pattern, prancing horse, $75.00.

Colossal Jar, #5560, sand matte, 34" **275.00**
Cup and Saucer, Blue Daisy. **120.00**
Figure, bird, #806, woodtone, Freeman–McFarlin
     Potteries, 3 x 5½" **55.00**
Figure, Banty Hen, #4843, brown and gold, 3½" **95.00**
Figure, bird, #825, Freeman–McFarlin Potteries. **40.00**
Figure, choir boy, kneeling, #211, yellow hair, 5½". **150.00**
Figure, Mr. Bird, #453, applied leaves, brown, 4½" **45.00**
Figure, peasant girl, Scandie, #126, 5" **155.00**
Garden Seat, #5730, glossy purple, 15 x 17" **200.00**
Lotus Fountain Stand, #6005, sand matte, 11 x 5½" **90.00**
Mug, Santa, white **95.00**
Pencil Vase, tapered, lavender sand matte, 1958, 3¾ x
     3¼" **55.00**
Planter, #6030, book and lamb, Baby's First, California
     Line **100.00**
Plate, #4750, hp rooster and hen, 10½" d **95.00**
Plate, #5381, bas relief vegetables, turquoise, 8¾" d. **50.00**
Shell, #510, lined with pale turquoise slip, 4½" **40.00**
Shell, #5406, rosy pink, 4" **15.00**
Snack Tray with Cup, #5107, rooster motif, 2 tone **50.00**
Stein, applied marlin handle **200.00**
Vase, #508, slip dec philodendron, 3 x 3" **65.00**
Wall Piece, Ancestor Man, #5775, turquoise **275.00**
Wall Piece, Eagle, #5902, white matte, 25 x 10". **300.00**
Wall Piece, Starfish, #5670, turquoise luster and gold, 8" . . . **200.00**
Wall Piece, Wall Pocket, #5803, carnelian, 9½ x 8 x 5" **200.00**

FIREARMS & ACCESSORIES

Many Americans own firearms, whether a .22 plunking rifle or pistol or a 12–gauge shotgun for hunting. The vast majority were inexpensive when purchased, bought for use and not investment, and have only minor secondary value in today's market. Many firearms sold on the secondary market are purchased for reuse purposes.

Recent federal statutes have placed restrictions on the buying and selling of certain handguns and rifles on the secondary market. Check with your local police department to make certain you are in compliance with state and federal laws before attempting to sell any weapon.

Collector interest in firearm advertising, prints, ammunition boxes, and other firearm accessories has increased significantly in the last decade. Auctioneers such as Dixie Sporting Collectibles (1206 Rama Rd, Charlotte, NC 28211) and Langs (31R Turtle Cove, Raymond, ME 04071) hold several specialized catalog sales each year in this field.

References: Robert H. Balderson, *The Official Price Guide to Antique and Modern Firearms, Eighth Edition,* House of Collectibles, 1996; Robert H. Balderson, *The Official Price Guide to Collector Handguns, Fifth Edition,* House of Collectibles, 1996; John Ogle, *Colt Memorabilia Price Guide,* Krause Publications, 1998; Russell and Steve Quetermous, *Modern Guns Identification & Values, Eleventh Edition,* Collector Books, 1997; Ned Schwing, *Standard Catalog of Firearms, 8th Edition,* Krause Publications, 1998; John Walter, *Rifles of the World,* Krause Publications, 1998.

Periodicals: *Gun List,* 700 E State St, Iola, WI 54990; *Military Trader,* PO Box 1050, Dubuque, IA 52004; *The Gun Report,* PO Box 38, Aledo, IL 61231.

Collectors' Club: The Winchester Arms Collectors Assoc, PO Box 6754, Great Falls, MT 59406.

Note: Prices are for firearms in very good condition.

FIREARMS

Handgun, Colt, Model L, 38 ACP caliber, 4¹/₂" barrel, semi–automatic action, exposed hammer, 7–shot clip magazine, blued finish, checkered hard rubber grips **$475.00**

Handgun, Ruger Blackhawk 357 Magnum, single action, 6–shot cylinder, ejector rod under barrel, blued finish, checkered hard rubber or walnut wood grips, pre–1961 . . . . **150.00**

Handgun, Webley & Scott, 1911 Model Single Shot, 22 caliber, 4¹/₂" or 9" barrel, manual operation slide to chamber cartridge action, exposed hammer, blued finish, checkered hard rubber grips, adjustable sight **300.00**

Rifle, Browning BL–22 Grade I, 22 caliber, 20" blued barrel, lever action, short throw lever, exposed hammer, tubular magazine, walnut straight grip stock and forearm, barrel band, adjustable folding rear sights **200.00**

Rifle, Colt Courier, 22 caliber, 19¹/₂" l blued barrel, semi–automatic action, 15–shot tubular magazine, plain walnut straight grip stock and forearm, barrel band, open rear sights, hooded ramp front, 1960–70s **100.00**

Rifle, Remington, Model 552, A Speedmaster, 22 caliber, 21" and 23" round tapered barrel, semi–automatic, hammerless, side ejection, 20–shot tubular magazine, plain 2–pc pistol grip stock, semi–beavertail forearm, buttplate, notched adjustable rear sight, bead front sight **150.00**

Rifle, Winchester, Model 67, 22 caliber, 27" blued barrel, bolt action, single shot, plain walnut 1–pc semi–pistol grip stock, fluted forearm **90.00**

Shotgun, Harrington & Richardson, Model 400, 12, 16, and 20 gauge, 28" full choke barrel, slide action, hammerless, 5–shot tubular magazine, blued finish, semi–pistol grip stock and grooved slide handle, 1950–60s **140.00**

Shotgun, Kessler Lever Matic, 12, 16, and 20 gauge, 26", 28", and 30" full choke barrel, lever action, 3–shot magazine, blued finish, checkered walnut straight stock and forearm, recoil pad, 1950s **150.00**

Shotgun, Remington, Model 870 Express, 12, 20, 28, or .410 gauge, 20", 21", 25", 26", or 28" ventilated rib barrel, slide action, hammerless, side ejection repeating, 4–shot tubular magazine, blued finish, checkered hardwood or synthetic pistol grip stock and forearm, 1987 . . . . **180.00**

ACCESSORIES

Ammunition Box, Peters Target Loads, 12 gauge, empty **$5.00**

Ammunition Box, Winchester Ranger Super Skeet Load, 20 gauge, #9 shot, quail and clay target on front, partial box **95.00**

Book, *From Trigger to Target,* handbook on shooting and loads, red and yellow cover, 1930, 24 pp **15.00**

Booklet, Super–X, The Long Range Load, Charles Askins, 1932 . . . . **22.00**

Calendar, Winchester, 1930, cowboy dressed in cowhide looking at prairie, 26 x 15" **620.00**

Catalog, Colt Revolvers & Automatic Pistols, tri–fold, 1953 . . . . **10.00**

Catalog, Kennebec Supply Co, Lynn, MA, High Grade Fire Arms & Accessories, illus, 1929–30 . . . . **60.00**

Catalog, Stevens Rifles and Shotguns, #40, illus, 1940, 30 pp **25.00**

Catalog, Winchester, World's Standard Guns and Ammunition **15.00**

Cleaning Kit, Outers Rifle Cleaning Kit, complete, 1950s **60.00**

Display, Peters Cartridge Co, diecut cardboard, stand–up, "Peters the Old Timer's standby," running deer and bullet images, 1930, 14 x 18" **75.00**

Handbook, *Colt's Police Revolver Hand Book,* illus, 1920s, 48 pp **25.00**

Holster, Iver Johnson, model 303–M, for 4" gun **35.00**

Sign, Remington UMC 22 Cal Repeating Rifle, cardboard, full color, duck hunter, 1930s, 9 x 13" **150.00**

Pinback Button, Peters, hunter and duck, ⁷/₈" **d, $99.00.** Photo courtesy Past Tyme Pleasures.

FIRE–KING

Fire–King is an Anchor Hocking product. Anchor Hocking resulted from the 1937 merger of the Anchor Cap Company and Hocking Glass Corporation, each of which had been involved in several previous mergers.

Oven–proof Fire–King glass was made between 1942 and 1976 in a variety of patterns including Alice, Fleurette, Game Bird, Honeysuckle, Laurel, Swirl, and Wheat, and body colors such as azurite, forest green, jadeite, peach luster, ruby red, and white. Non–decorated utilitarian pieces also were made.

Housewives liked Fire–King because the line included matching dinnerware and ovenware. Anchor Hocking's marketing strategy included the aggressive sale of starter sets.

Anchor Hocking used two methods to mark Fire–King—a mark molded directly on the piece and an oval foil paper label.

References: Gene Florence, *Anchor Hocking's Fire–King & More*, Collector Books, 1998; Gene Florence, *Collectible Glassware From the 40s, 50s, 60s, An Illustrated Value Guide*, Fourth Edition, Collector Books, 1998; Gene Florence, *Kitchen Glassware of the Depression Years*, Fifth Edition, Collector Books, 1995, 1997 value update; Gary Kilgo et al., *A Collectors Guide to Anchor Hocking's Fire–King Glassware*, 2nd Edition, published by authors, 1997; April M. Tvorak, *Fire–King*, Fifth Edition, published by author, 1997.

Newsletter: *The Fire–King News*, PO Box 473, Addison, AL 35540.

Collectors' Club: The Fire–King Collectors Club, 1406 E 14th St, Des Moines, IA 50316.

Ovenware, Sapphire, roaster, cov, 10³/₈", $75.00.

22 K Gold, bowl, 4⁷/₈"	$3.50
22 K Gold, creamer	5.00
22 K Gold, cup	3.00
22 K Gold, dinner plate	6.00
22 K Gold, saucer	1.50
22 K Gold, sugar, open	5.00
Black Dot, bowl, 9¹/₂" d	45.00
Black Dot, grease jar, cov	48.00
Black Dot, mixing bowl, nesting set of 3	95.00
Black Dot, salt and pepper shakers, pr	60.00
Golden Anniversary, bowl, 4⁷/₈" d	4.50
Golden Anniversary, creamer	5.50
Golden Anniversary, cup	4.00
Golden Anniversary, dinner plate	7.00
Golden Anniversary, saucer	2.00
Golden Anniversary, sugar, open	5.50
Golden Shell, bowl, 4³/₄"	5.00
Golden Shell, bowl, 7⁵/₈"	8.00
Golden Shell, bowl, 8¹/₂"	10.00
Golden Shell, creamer	5.00
Golden Shell, cup	3.00
Golden Shell, plate, 10"	8.00
Golden Shell, saucer	2.00
Golden Shell, sugar, cov	8.00
Golden Shell, sugar, open	4.00
Golden Shell Swirl, creamer and sugar, ftd	7.00
Golden Shell Swirl, cup and saucer	5.00
Golden Shell Swirl, dessert bowl, 4³/₄"	2.00
Golden Shell Swirl, flat soup, 7⁵/₈" d	6.00
Golden Shell Swirl, plate, 7¹/₂"	3.00
Golden Shell Swirl, plate, 9" d	5.00

Jadeite, after dinner cup and saucer, orig label	80.00
Jadeite, Ball pitcher, orig label	280.00
Jadeite, bowl, crimped, label, 8"	65.00
Jadeite, cup, square	7.00
Jadeite, eggcup	21.00
Jadeite, shaving mug	24.00
Jadeite, skillet, 2 spout, orig small label	105.00
Ovenware, Sapphire, casserole, individual, 10 oz	12.00
Ovenware, Sapphire, cereal bowl, 5¹/₂"	17.00
Ovenware, Sapphire, coffee mug	22.00
Ovenware, Sapphire, custard cup, 5 oz	3.25
Ovenware, Sapphire, custard cup, 6 oz	4.00
Ovenware, Sapphire, hot plate, tab handles	22.00
Ovenware, Sapphire, loaf pan, 9 x 5"	16.00
Ovenware, Sapphire, measuring bowl, 16 oz	25.00
Ovenware, Sapphire, nurser, 4 oz	8.50
Ovenware, Sapphire, pie plate, 9" d	7.00
Peach Lustre, bowl, 4⁷/₈" d	5.00
Peach Lustre, bowl, 8¹/₄"	10.00
Peach Lustre, creamer	5.50
Peach Lustre, cup	4.00
Peach Lustre, dinner plate	7.00
Peach Lustre, salad plate	5.00
Peach Lustre, saucer	2.50
Peach Lustre, sugar	5.50
Red Dot, grease jar, cov	45.00
Red Dot, mixing bowls, nesting set of 4	95.00
Red Dot, salt and pepper shakers, pr	55.00
Soreno, bowl, avocado, 4³/₄"	2.50
Soreno, butter, cov, avocado	9.00
Soreno, creamer, avocado	3.50
Soreno, cup, avocado	2.50
Soreno, juice tumbler, amber	3.00
Soreno, pitcher, aquamarine	15.00
Soreno, pitcher, avocado, 65 oz	10.00
Soreno, plate, avocado, 10"	4.00
Soreno, plate, avocado, 5⁷/₈"	4.00
Soreno, saucer, avocado, 5³/₄"	1.00
Soreno, shaker, avocado	3.50
Soreno, snack plate, 10"	5.00
Soreno, sugar, cov, avocado	6.00
Soreno, tumbler, avocado, 12 oz	3.00
Soreno, water tumbler, amber	3.00

Turquoise, mixing bowl, 1 qt, $15.00

Turquoise, cereal bowl, 4½" d 15.00
Turquoise, cup and saucer 6.00
Turquoise, cup, sq 2.75
Turquoise, mug 7.50
Turquoise, plate, 9" d 8.50
Turquoise, saucer, sq 1.00
Turquoise, sherbet plate 9.00
Turquoise, soup bowl, 7" d 18.00
Turquoise, vegetable bowl, 8" 11.00

FISHER–PRICE

Irving L. Price, a retired F. W. Woolworth executive, Herman G. Fisher, previously with Alderman–Fairchild Toy Company, and Helen M. Schelle, a former toy store owner, founded Fisher–Price Toys in 1930. The company was headquartered in East Aurora, New York. Margaret Evans Price, a writer and illustrator of children's books and wife of Irving Price, was the company's first artist and designer.

Toys made prior to 1962 are marked with a black and white rectangular logo. Plastic was introduced for the first time in 1949.

The company remained in private hands until acquired by the Quaker Oats Company in 1969.

Reference: John J. Murray and Bruce R. Fox, *Fisher–Price, 1931–1963: A Historical, Rarity, Value Guide*, Books Americana, Krause Publications, 1991.

Collectors' Club: Fisher–Price Collectors Club, 1442 N Ogden, Mesa, AZ 85205.

Note: Prices listed are for toys in excellent condition.

Adventure People Set, #0377, Astro Knight, complete **$8.00**
Bonny Bunny Wagon, #318 . . . . 50.00
Bunny Engine, #703 . . . . 80.00
Butch the Pup, #333 . . . . 80.00
Car and Camper, #686, 5 pcs 55.00
Change–A–Tune Carousel, #170 . . . . 45.00
Corn Popper, #788 . . . . 55.00
Creative Block Wagon, #161 . . . . 80.00

Cry Baby Bear, #711 . . . . 45.00
Cuddly Cub, #719 . . . . 25.00
Dinkey Engine, #642 . . . . 55.00
Double Screen TV Music Box, #196 . . . . 35.00
Drummer Boy, #0634 . . . . 55.00
Farmer in the Dell TV Radio, #166 . . . . 40.00
Ferry Boat, #932 . . . . 30.00
Fire Truck, #630 . . . . 55.00
Fisher–Price Choo–Choo, #215 . . . . 90.00
Frisky Frog, #154 . . . . 25.00
Gabby Duck, #767 . . . . 85.00
Happy Hauler, #732 . . . . 45.00
Happy Hippo, #151 . . . . 70.00
Huffy Puppy Train, #999 . . . . 80.00
Husky Dump Truck, #145 . . . . 50.00
Jack–n–Jill TV Radio, #50 . . . . 50.00
Jiffy Dump Truck, #156 . . . . 35.00
Jolly Jumper, #450 . . . . 80.00
Katie Kangaroo, #158 . . . . 35.00
Katy Kackler, #140 . . . . 85.00
Kitty Bell, #499 . . . . 100.00
Lady Bug, #658 . . . . 50.00
Little People Main Street, #2500 . . . . 45.00
Lunch Kit, #557, plastic, barn shape, red, white, and
    green 45.00
Milk Wagon, #131 . . . . 60.00
Mother Goose Music Cart, #784 . . . . 100.00
Movie Viewer, #461, crank handle 8.00
Music Box Movie Camera, #919, 5 picture disks, plays
    "This Old Man" 45.00
Musical Ferris Wheel, #969 . . . . 55.00
Musical Push Chime, #722 . . . . 55.00
Musical Sweeper, #225 . . . . 70.00
Musical Tick Tock Clock, #997 . . . . 50.00
Patch Pony, #0616 . . . . 55.00
Perky Penguin, #786 . . . . 35.00
Peter Pig, #479 . . . . 65.00
Picture Disk Camera, #112, complete with 5 picture
    disks 45.00
Pinky Pig, # 695 . . . . 75.00
Play Family Camper, #944, complete with 4 figures and
    accessories 80.00
Play Family Farm, #915, first version, masonite base,
    complete with plastic animals, 4 wooden figures, and
    accessories 35.00
Play Family Fun Jet, #183 . . . . 20.00
Play Family Houseboat, #985 . . . . 45.00
Play Family Lacing Shoe, #136, complete 55.00
Play Family Merry–Go–Round, #111, plays "Skater's
    Waltz" 45.00
Play Family Sesame Street Clubhouse, #937 . . . . 70.00
Pocket Radio, #768, plays "Happy Birthday" 20.00
Pop 'N Ring, #809 . . . . 70.00
Prancing Pony, #617 . . . . 45.00
Pudgy Pig, #478 . . . . 60.00
Quacky Family, #799 . . . . 65.00
Queen Busy Bee, #444 . . . . 55.00
Rattle Ball, #682 . . . . 35.00
Rock–A–Stack, #627 . . . . 30.00
Rolling Bunny Basket, #310 . . . . 70.00
Roly Raccoon, #172 . . . . 20.00
Sesame Street Music Box TV, #114, plays "People in Your
    Neighborhood" 15.00
Sleepy Sue, #495 . . . . 50.00

Bunny Bell Cart, #604, 1954, $80.00.

Smokie Engine, #642	45.00
Snoopy Sniffer, #181	55.00
Stake Truck, #649	85.00
Suzie Seal, #460	45.00
Talk–Back Telephone, #747	75.00
Teddy Bear Zilo, #777	55.00
Ten Little Indians TV Radio, #159	55.00
Three Men in a Tub, #0142	25.00
Toot Toot Engine, #641	50.00
Tote–A–Tune Radio, #795, plastic, plays *"Over The Rainbow"*	6.00
Tuggy Turtle, #139	80.00
Whistling Engine, #617	85.00
Wobbles, #130	55.00
Woodsey's Log House, #960	45.00
Zoo, #0916, complete with 6 figures and accessories	40.00

FISHING

The modern fishing lure (plug) evolved at the end of the 19th century. Wood was used primarily for the body until replaced by plastic in the mid–1930s. Hundreds of lures, many with dozens of variations, are known to exist.

As lures became more sophisticated so did reels and rods. Improvement occurred in two areas—material and mechanism. Each improvement led to demand for more improvement. Drags and multiplying gears were added to reels. The split bamboo rod was eventually challenged by the modern graphite rod.

Serious collectors only buy examples in virtually unused condition and with their period packaging when possible. The high end of the market has become very investment focused. Many collectors are turning to licenses, paper ephemera, and secondary equipment in an effort to find affordable items within the category.

References: Ralf Coykendall, Jr., *Coykendall's Complete Guide to Sporting Collectibles*, Wallace–Homestead, Krause Publications, 1996; Carl F. Luckey, *Old Fishing Lures and Tackle: Identification and Value Guide, Fourth Edition*, Books Americana, Krause Publications, 1996; Dudley Murphy and Rick Edmisten, *Fishing*

Lure Collectibles: An Identification and Value Guide to the Most Collectible Antique Fishing Lures, Collector Books, 1995; Donald J. Peterson, *Folk Art Fish Decoys*, Schiffer Publishing, 1997; Harold E. Smith, *Collector's Guide to Creek Chub Lures & Collectibles*, Collector Books, 1997; Donna Tonelli, *Top of the Line Fishing Collectibles*, Schiffer Publishing, 1997; Karl T. White, *Fishing Tackle Antiques and Collectibles*, Holli Enterprises, 1995.

Periodical: *Fishing Collectibles Magazine*, 2005 Tree House Ln, Plano, TX 75023.

Newsletter: *The Fisherman's Trader*, PO Box 203, Gillette, NJ 07933.

Collectors' Clubs: American Fish Decoy Assoc, 624 Merritt St, Fife Lake, MI 49633; National Fishing Lure Collectors Club, 22325 B Drive S, Marshall, MI 49068; Old Reel Collectors Assoc, 849 NE 70th Ave, Portland, OR 97213.

Book, *Bait Casting*, Wm C Vogt, 1st ed, 1928, 104 pp	**$15.00**
Book, *Salt Water Fishing*, Van Campen Heilner, illus, c1946	**18.00**
Boot Jack, fish shape, open foot shaped slot for boots	**75.00**
Calendar, Bristol Steel Rod Co adv, 1935, 14 x 18"	**55.00**
Catalog, Harley–Wickham Co, Erie, PA, Harley's Catalog of Sporting Supplies, #51, c1930	**40.00**
Catalog, H D Folsom Arms Co, New York, NY, #45, illus, c1935, 240 pp	**50.00**
Catalog, South Bend Co, What Tackle and When, black and white and color photos, 1931, 76 pp, 5 x 7"	**60.00**
Catalog, Weller Deluxe Tackle, punched for binder, 1963, 89 pp, 8 x 10½"	**20.00**
Creel, Ed Cumings, Flint, MI, whole willow, fly fisher's landlocked salmon creel, orig sliding wooden latch, curved back, leather and web harness, J F Anderson 1937 patent #2,085,564, 13" l	**100.00**
Creel, reversed white birch, lashed construction, center hole, dyed images of grouse, rabbit, leaves, and foxes, fox on lid, leather strap	**135.00**
Creel, split willow, offset hole with emb metal fish head latch, rattan hinges and lid reinforcing back	**82.00**

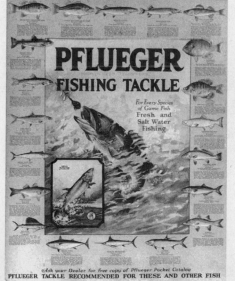

Poster, Pflueger Tackle, cardboard, 1926, $550.00. Photo courtesy Lang's Sporting Collectables.

Creel, wicker, sliding peg latch, leather harness mkd
"L.L. Bean Freeport, Maine" **100.00**
Decoy, ice spearing, green–gray, Oliver Reigstad, 7" l **65.00**
Game, Magnetic Fish Pond, Milton Bradley, 1942 . . . . **10.00**
License, 1960, pink, black printing, 2½ x 4" **4.00**
Lure, CCBC, sucker, wood, glass eyes, natural blue suck-
er scales, belly age lines, minor chips, c1932 . . . . **335.00**
Net, aluminum, folding, triangular shape, belt clip, 24"
handle, mkd "Hardy" **82.00**
Net, collapsible boat net, 47" cane handle, brass fittings,
Wm Mills & Sons **115.00**
Poster, United Airlines adv, fisherman casting rod illus,
airliner overhead, Jos Binder illus, c1953, 25 x 40" **300.00**
Reel, Coxe, Model #25–2, bait casting, nickel silver reel,
cross bolt construction, mkd leather case, orig box
with papers, late 1940s **115.00**
Reel, Shakespeare, Model FK, 1740 Free Spool
Tournament, jeweled nickel silver **82.00**
Rod, Hardy Deluxe, split bamboo fly, brown wraps, alu-
minum tube, 1941, 9" l, 3:2 size **135.00**
Rod, Salmon Deluxe, fly rod, 9½ ft, 3 pc, 2 tip, agate
stripper and tip top guide, German silver ferrules,
screw up–locking reel seat, removable extension butt **300.00**
Rod, Hurd, Super Caster Handle Reel and Rod, check-
ered walnut handle, click switch, push button brake
and drag adjustment, orig vinyl case **165.00**
Rod, Mills, trout rod, 8 ft, 3 pc, 2 tip, red wraps and
screw down–locking reel seat, orig bag and tube **550.00**
Rod, Orvis, Rocky Mountain Spinning Rod, 6½ ft, 3 pc,
1 tip, "Charles F. Orvis Co" paper label **330.00**
Rod, Payne, trout rod, 9 ft, 3 pc, 2 tip, screw up–locking
reel seat, orig bag and tube **550.00**
Rod, F E Thomas, Bangor, ME, salmon rod, removable
extension butt, 10 ft, 3 pc, 2 tips, orig bag and tube **110.00**
Wall Plaque, wood, carved and painted trout mounted
on oval plaque, sgd "M. Schutte – 1937" on front and
back **275.00**

AUCTION PRICES

Fishing reels sold by Lang's Sporting Collectables, Inc., on
March 22, 1997. A buyer's premium of 13% (discounted to
10% for payment by cash or check) was charged. Prices reflect
the 10% buyer's premium.

Coxe, Model #25–2, bait casting reel, late 1940s,
nickel silver, cross bolt construction, no–tools
take apart, new in marked leather case
and box with papers **$115.50**
Farlow, single action salmon reel, "The Ambassa-
dor," back plate drag adjustment, strong click,
very good condition, 4" d, ¾" w **82.50**
Heddon, Pal P–41, bait casting reel, 1950s, black
plates, jeweled bearing caps, new in box with
booklet, bag, and retailer hanging tag **92.50**
J B Moscrops Patent—Manchester, fly reel, brass,
some orig black finish, both foot ends filed, one
foot end shortened, otherwise very good condi-
tion, 3⅛" d, 1" w **55.00**
Orvis Magnalite Multiplier, fly reel, multiplying reel
with exposed rim and drag switch, good condi-
tion, 3⅛" d, ⅞" w **55.00**
Shakespeare, 1740 Free Spool Tournament reel,
Model FK, jeweled nickel silver, old silk tourna-
ment line, excellent condition **82.50**

FLASHLIGHTS

The flashlight owes its origin to the search for a suitable bicycle
light. The Acme Electric Lamp Company, New York, NY, manufactured the first bicycle light in 1896. Development was rapid. In
1899 Conrad Hubert filed a patent for a tubular hand–held flashlight. Two years later, Hubert had sales offices in Berlin, Chicago,
London, Montreal, Paris, and Sydney.

Conrad Hubert's American Eveready company has dominated
the flashlight field for the past century. National Carbon purchased
the balance of the company in 1914, having bought a half–interest in it in 1906. Aurora, Chase, Franco, and Ray–O–Vac are other
collectible companies.

Collectors focus on flashlights from brand name companies,
novelty flashlights, and character licensed flashlights.

References: L–W Book Sales, *Flashlights Price Guide*, L–W Book
Sales, 1995; Stuart Schneider, *Collecting Flashlights*, Schiffer
Publishing, 1997.

Collectors' Club: *Flashlight Collectors of America*, PO Box 4095,
Tustin, CA 92681.

Advertising, Schlitz, plastic, figural bottle, 2 D batteries **$9.00**
Ashflash, 3–color, rear blinker, 1955, 9" l **25.00**
BMG, Girl Scouts, yellow switch and top, 1969, 7½" l **5.00**
Bond, tubular, metal, 1930s **15.00**
Bright Star, Trafficmaster, 1939, 7" l **15.00**
Burgess, Snaplite, Art Deco style, 1930s **45.00**
Burgess, #446, 3–cell pre–focused spotlight, orig box,
1950, 9" l **10.00**
Character, Captain Ray–O–Vac, red, "Leader of Light,"
1055, 7½" l **35.00**
Character, Zorro, pocket, Bantam Lite, 1946, 3¼" l **10.00**
Eveready, #2602, aluminum, 1925, 5½" l **20.00**
Eveready, #2604, tubular, black painted brass case, nick-
el ends, small bulls–eye lens, 2 D batteries, 1924 . . . . **18.00**
Eveready, #6993, vest pocket, nickel plated, cigarette
case type, 2 C batteries, 1929 . . . . **20.00**
Eveready, penlight, yellow, silver, 1960 . . . . **10.00**
Eveready, tubular, plastic, 1950s **4.00**

**H. J. Ashe Co, Hopalong Cassidy, Morse
Code on back, red and silver, $60.00.**

Eveready, Wallite, wall hung, black hammer tone, oval, 1931 . . . . 30.00

Franco, tubular, triple switch, 1920 . . . . 45.00

Tiffany, sterling silver flashlight and chain, 1 AA battery, 1966 . . . . 50.00

Toy, half size kerosene lantern shape, 2 D batteries, Linemar, Japan 20.00

Toy, figural ray gun, blue, red trigger, Ideal, 8" l 20.00

FLATWARE

Flatware refers to forks, knives, serving pieces, and spoons. There are four basic types of flatware: (1) sterling silver, (2) silver plated, (3) stainless, and (4) Dirilyte.

Sterling silver flatware has a silver content of 925 parts silver per thousand. Knives have a steel or stainless steel blade. Silver plating refers to the electroplating of a thin coating of pure silver, 1,000 parts silver per thousand, on a base metal such as brass, copper, or nickel silver. While steel only requires the addition of 13% chromium to be classified stainless, most stainless steel flatware is made from an 18/8 formula, i.e., 18% chromium for strength and stain resistance and 8% nickel for a high luster and long–lasting finish. Dirilyte is an extremely hard, solid bronze alloy developed in Sweden in the early 1900s. Although gold in color, it has no gold in it.

Most flatware is purchased by individuals seeking to replace a damaged piece or to expand an existing pattern. Prices vary widely, depending on what the seller had to pay and how he views the importance of the pattern. Prices listed below represent what a modern replacement service quotes a customer.

Abbreviations used in the listings include:

FH	Flat Handle	SS	Sterling Silver
HH	Hollow Handle	ST	Stainless Steel
SP	Silver Plated		

References: Frances M. Bones and Lee Roy Fisher, *Standard Encyclopedia of American Silverplate,* Collector Books, 1998; Maryanne Dolan, *American Sterling Silver Flatware, 1830's–1990's: A Collector's Identification & Value Guide,* Books Americana, Krause Publications, 1993; Tere Hagan, *Silverplated Flatware, Revised Fourth Edition,* Collector Books, 1990, 1998 value update; Richard Osterberg, *Sterling Silver Flatware for Dining Elegance,* Schiffer Publishing, 1994; Dorothy T. Rainwater, *Encyclopedia of American Silver Manufacturers, Third Edition Revised,* Schiffer Publishing, 1986; Replacements, Ltd., *Stainless Steel Flatware Identification Guide,* Replacements, Ltd., n.d.; Harry L. Rinker, *Silverware of the 20th Century: The Top 250 Patterns,* House of Collectibles, 1997.

Dansk, Fjord, SS, fork $40.00
Dansk, Fjord, SS, iced tea spoon, 9½" 35.00
Dansk, Fjord, SS, knife 40.00
Dansk, Fjord, SS, serving fork, 9⅛" 90.00
Dansk, Fjord, SS, teaspoon 30.00
Gorham, Buttercup, SS, butter spreader, HH, modern ST blade, 6¼" 35.00
Gorham, Buttercup, SS, cold meat fork, 8⅛" 130.00
Gorham, Buttercup, SS, cream soup, round bowl, 6¼" 50.00
Gorham, Buttercup, SS, demitasse spoon, 4⅛" 35.00
Gorham, Buttercup, SS, salad spoon, ST bowl, 11¼" 45.00

Gorham, Buttercup, SS, tablespoon, 8⅜" 85.00
Gorham, Buttercup, SS, tongs, 4⅝" 65.00
Gorham, Celeste, SS, butter knife, HH, 7" 30.00
Gorham, Celeste, SS, carving knife, ST blade, 10¾" 60.00
Gorham, Celeste, SS, cheese knife, ST blade, 7½" 35.00
Gorham, Celeste, SS, cocktail fork, 5¾" 25.00
Gorham, Celeste, SS, cold meat fork, 8⅝" 70.00
Gorham, Celeste, SS, gravy ladle, 6¾" 70.00
Gorham, Celeste, SS, salt and pepper shakers, pr, 3" 200.00
Gorham, Celeste, SS, sugar spoon, 6¼" 32.00
Gorham, Chateau Rose, SS, butter spreader, HH, paddled ST blade, 6⅛" 27.00
Gorham, Chateau Rose, SS, fork, 7⅞" 55.00
Gorham, Chateau Rose, SS, jelly spoon, 6¼" 40.00
Gorham, Chateau Rose, SS, knife, HH, New French blade, 9" 40.00
Gorham, Chateau Rose, SS, tablespoon, 8½" 70.00
Gorham, Greenbrier, SS, carving fork, ST tines, 8⅝" 55.00
Gorham, Greenbrier, SS, cream sauce ladle, 5¼" 45.00
Gorham, Greenbrier, SS, iced tea spoon, 7⅝" 40.00
Gorham, Greenbrier, SS, knife, HH, modern blade, 9⅝" 45.00
Gorham, Greenbrier, SS, pickle fork, short handle, 5⅞" 30.00
Gorham, Greenbrier, SS, pie server, ST blade, 10¼" 60.00
Gorham, Greenbrier, SS, teaspoon, 5 o'clock, 5⅝" 22.00
International, Blossom Time, SS, bonbon spoon, 5" 40.00
International, Blossom Time, SS, butter spreader, FH, 5⅞" 25.00
International, Blossom Time, SS, carving knife, ST blade, 10½" 60.00
International, Blossom Time, SS, demitasse spoon, 4¼" 22.00
International, Blossom Time, SS, gravy ladle, 6½" 80.00
International, Blossom Time, SS, jelly spoon, 6½" 30.00
International, Blossom Time, SS, lemon fork, 4⅝" 25.00
International, Blossom Time, SS, tomato server, 8" 90.00
International, Blossom Time, SS, youth fork, 7" 35.00
International, Courtship, SS, butter serving knife, FH, 7⅛" 40.00
International, Courtship, SS, carving fork, ST tines, 8⅝" 70.00
International, Courtship, SS, carving set, 2 pc, ST blade 140.00
International, Courtship, SS, casserole serving spoon, 8¾" 120.00
International, Courtship, SS, cold meat fork, 9" 90.00

Gorham, Buttercup, SS: Fork, 7½", $60.00; Knife, 8¾", $40.00; Teaspoon, 5⅞", $25.00.

International, Courtship, SS, cream sauce ladle, 5¹/₂" 45.00
International, Courtship, SS, fork, 7¹/₄" 45.00
International, Courtship, SS, gravy ladle, 6¹/₈" 85.00
International, Courtship, SS, lemon fork, 4⁵/₈" 32.00
International, Courtship, SS, knife, HH, New French
    blade, 9¹/₈" 35.00
International, Courtship, SS, pie server, ST blade, 9⁷/₈" 70.00
International, Courtship, SS, sugar tongs, 4¹/₈" 60.00
Kirk Stieff, Corsage, SS, bacon fork, 8¹/₄" 120.00
Kirk Stieff, Corsage, SS, butter spreader, HH, modern ST
    blade, 5⁷/₈" 30.00
Kirk Stieff, Corsage, SS, cold meat fork, 7⁵/₈" 85.00
Kirk Stieff, Corsage, SS, cream soup spoon, round bowl,
    6¹/₂" 50.00
Kirk Stieff, Corsage, SS, iced tea spoon, 7¹/₂" 40.00
Kirk Stieff, Corsage, SS, sugar spoon, 6¹/₈" 40.00
Kirk Stieff, Corsage, SS, tablespoon, 7³/₄" 30.00
Kirk Stieff, Old Maryland Engraved, SS, carving knife, ST
    blade, 10³/₈" 80.00
Kirk Stieff, Old Maryland Engraved, SS casserole serving
    spoon, 8³/₈" 130.00
Kirk Stieff, Old Maryland Engraved, SS, cheese knife, ST
    blade, 7¹/₈" 55.00
Kirk Stieff, Old Maryland Engraved, SS, mayonnaise
    ladle, 5¹/₂" 55.00
Kirk Stieff, Old Maryland Engraved, SS, pie server, ST
    blade, 9¹/₂" 80.00
Kirk Stieff, Old Maryland Engraved, SS, sugar spoon,
    shell shaped bowl, 6¹/₄" 50.00
Oneida, Damask Rose, SS, butter serving knife, HH, 6³/₈" 30.00
Oneida, Damask Rose, SS, cocktail fork, 5¹/₂" 25.00
Oneida, Damask Rose, SS, cream sauce ladle, 5¹/₂" 40.00
Oneida, Damask Rose, SS, dessert spoon, 6⁵/₈" 35.00
Oneida, Damask Rose, SS, jelly spoon, 6³/₈" 30.00
Oneida, Lady Hamilton, SP, butter spreader, FH, 6¹/₂" 12.00
Oneida, Lady Hamilton, SP, carving set, 2 pc, large, ST
    blade 120.00
Oneida, Lady Hamilton, SP, casserole serving spoon,
    9³/₈" 35.00
Oneida, Lady Hamilton, SP, demitasse spoon, 4¹/₂" 12.00

Top: Reed & Barton, Marlborough, SS, fork, 7¹/₄", $45.00.
Bottom: Wallace, Grand Colonial, SS, fork, 7¹/₄", $40.00.

Oneida, Lady Hamilton, SP, grapefruit spoon, round
    bowl, 7" 12.00
Oneida, Lady Hamilton, SP, grille knife, HH, modern
    blade, 8¹/₂" 12.00
Oneida, Lady Hamilton, SP, knife, HH, modern blade,
    9³/₈" 15.00
Oneida, Lady Hamilton, SP, pickle fork, short handle, 6" 17.00
Oneida, Lady Hamilton, SP, soup spoon, oval bowl, 7¹/₂" 17.00
Oneida, Modern Baroque, SP, butter spreader, HH, pad-
    dled ST blade, 6³/₄" 17.00
Oneida, Modern Baroque, SP, casserole serving spoon,
    shell shaped bowl, 8⁷/₈" 40.00
Oneida, Modern Baroque, SP, dessert spoon, 6⁷/₈" 15.00
Oneida, Modern Baroque, SP, gravy ladle, 7¹/₂" 27.00
Oneida, Modern Baroque, SP, infant spoon, 5¹/₂" 15.00
Oneida, Modern Baroque, SP, knife, HH, modern blade,
    8⁵/₈" 17.00
Oneida, Modern Baroque, SP, sugar spoon, shell shaped
    bowl, 5³/₄" 15.00
Oneida, Modern Baroque, SP, tablespoon, 8¹/₂" 22.00
Oneida, Modern Baroque, SP, teaspoon, 5 o'clock, 5¹/₂" 7.00
Reed & Barton, Marlborough, SS, butter spreader, FH,
    5⁷/₈" 30.00
Reed & Barton, Marlborough, SS, carving knife, ST
    blade, 10³/₈" 70.00
Reed & Barton, Marlborough, SS, cheese server, ST
    blade, 6⁷/₈" 50.00
Reed & Barton, Marlborough, SS, cocktail fork, 5¹/₂" 30.00
Reed & Barton, Marlborough, SS, knife, HH, New
    French blade, 9¹/₈" 40.00
Reed & Barton, Marlborough, SS, salad fork, 6¹/₈" 45.00
Reed & Barton, Marlborough, SS, sugar tongs, 4⁵/₈" 65.00
Reed & Barton, Marlborough, SS, tomato server, 7³/₄" 110.00
Towle, Candlelight, SS, boullion spoon, round bowl,
    5¹/₈" 40.00
Towle, Candlelight, SS, butter spreader, FH, 5⁷/₈" 25.00
Towle, Candlelight, SS, carving fork, ST tines, 8¹/₂" 40.00
Towle, Candlelight, SS, cocktail fork, 5³/₄" 25.00
Towle, Candlelight, SS, cold meat fork, 7⁷/₈" 90.00
Towle, Candlelight, SS, cream soup spoon, round bowl,
    6¹/₄" 40.00
Towle, Candlelight, SS, gravy ladle, 6³/₄" 90.00
Towle, Candlelight, SS, jelly spoon, 6¹/₂" 40.00
Towle, Candlelight, SS, knife, New French blade, 8³/₄" 30.00
Towle, Candlelight, SS, salad fork, 6³/₈" 35.00
Towle, Candlelight, SS, salad set, 2 pc, wooden bowl,
    10³/₄" 80.00
Towle, Candlelight, SS, sugar spoon, 5⁷/₈" 30.00
Towle, Candlelight, SS, sugar tongs, 4" 55.00
Wallace, Grand Colonial, SS, bar knife, 9¹/₄" 40.00

Oneida, Damask Rose, SS, left to right: Salad fork, 6¹/₂", $30.00; Fork, 7⁵/₈", $50.00; Knife, 8⁷/₈", $30.00; Soup spoon, 7", $35.00; Teaspoon, $25.00.

Wallace, Grand Colonial, SS, bonbon spoon, 5".......... 45.00
Wallace, Grand Colonial, SS, butter spreader, FH, 6" 27.00
Wallace, Grand Colonial, SS, carving set, 2 pc, ST blade ... 110.00
Wallace, Grand Colonial, SS, casserole serving spoon,
   ST bowl, 9³/₄" 45.00
Wallace, Grand Colonial, SS, cheese server, ST blade,
   6¹/₂" 40.00
Wallace, Grand Colonial, SS, cocktail fork, ⁵/₈"......... 30.00
Wallace, Grand Colonial, SS, cream sauce ladle, 5¹/₂".... 45.00
Wallace, Stradivari, SS, demitasse spoon, 3⁷/₈" 22.00
Wallace, Grand Colonial, SS, fruit knife, ST blade, 6⁷/₈"...... 40.00
Wallace, Grand Colonial, SS, fruit spoon, 5⁷/₈" 40.00
Wallace, Grand Colonial, SS, pickle fork, short handle,
   5¹/₂" 35.00
Wallace, Grand Colonial, SS, pizza cutter, ST blade, 8" 40.00
Wallace, Grand Colonial, SS, soup spoon, oval bowl,
   6⁷/₈" 45.00
Wallace, Grand Colonial, SS, steak knife, 9⁷/₈" 40.00
Wallace, Stradivari, SS, butter spreader, FH, 6".......... 27.00
Wallace, Stradivari, SS, carving set, 2 pc, ST blade 120.00
Wallace, Stradivari, SS, cocktail fork, 5¹/₂" 30.00
Wallace, Stradivari, SS, cream sauce ladle, 5¹/₂" 45.00
Wallace, Stradivari, SS, fork, 7¹/₈"................. 40.00
Wallace, Stradivari, SS, jelly spoon, 6³/₄" 45.00
Wallace, Stradivari, SS, lemon fork, 5¹/₂"............. 35.00
Wallace, Stradivari, SS, pie server, ST blade, 10"........ 45.00
Wallace, Stradivari, SS, sugar spoon, 6" 32.00
Wallace, Stradivari, SS, tablespoon, 8¹/₂".............. 90.00
Wallace, Violet, SS, butter spreader, HH, paddled ST
   blade, 6"...................................... 32.00
Wallace, Violet, SS, iced tea spoon, 7⁵/₈"............. 50.00
Wallace, Violet, SS, knife, HH, modern blade, 9" 55.00
Wallace, Violet, SS, pickle fork, short handle, 5⁵/₈" 35.00
Wallace, Violet, SS, pie server, ST blade, 10³/₈" 85.00
Wallace, Violet, SS, teaspoon........................ 35.00

FLORENCE CERAMICS

Florence Ward of Pasedena, California, began making ceramic objects as a form of therapy in dealing with the loss of a young son. The products she produced and sold from her garage workshop provided pin money during the Second World War.

With the support of Clifford, her husband, and Clifford, Jr., their son, Florence Ward moved her ceramics business to a plant on the east side of Pasadena in 1946. Business boomed after Ward exhibited at several Los Angeles gift shows. In 1949 a state–of–the–art plant was built at 74 South San Gabriel Boulevard, Pasadena.

Florence Ceramics is best known for its figural pieces, often costumed in Colonial and Godey fashions. The company also produced birds, busts, candle holders, lamps, smoking sets, and wall pockets. Betty Davenport Ford joined the company in 1956, designing a line of bisque animal figures. Production ended after two years.

Scripto Corporation bought Florence Ceramics in 1964 following the death of Clifford Ward. Production was shifted to advertising specialty ware. Operations ceased in 1977.

Reference: Doug Fouland, *The Florence Collectibles: The Era of Elegance,* Schiffer Publishing, 1995.

Collectors' Club: Florence Collector's Club, PO Box 122, Richland, WA 99352.

Julie, 7¹/₄" h, $125.00.

Ashtray, shell shape.................................. $25.00
Bowl, shell shape, 11¹/₂" d 80.00
Cigarette Box 75.00
Figurine, Angel 75.00
Figurine, Annabel 400.00
Figurine, Ballerina Wood Nymph...................... 140.00
Figurine, Birthday Girl.............................. 125.00
Figurine, Cherub Clock 700.00
Figurine, Chinese Girl............................... 50.00
Figurine, Clarissa................................... 100.00
Figurine, Darlene 200.00
Figurine, Eve....................................... 145.00
Figurine, John Alden and Priscilla, pr 450.00
Figurine, Joy 90.00
Figurine, Lady Diana................................ 320.00
Figurine, Lady Pompadore 400.00
Figurine, Laura 115.00
Figurine, Margaret.................................. 320.00
Figurine, Nancy 95.00
Figurine, Story Book Hour 750.00
Flower Holder, Beth 35.00
Flower Holder, Emily................................ 35.00
Flower Holder, Mimi 35.00
Frame, Provincial Rose dec, 4 x 5".................... 95.00
Vase, cornucopia, pink 70.00
Wall Plaque, oval, gray, white, and green.............. 80.00

FOLK ART

The definition of folk art is fluid, defined by what subcategories contemporary collectors decide are in or out at any given moment. Simply put, folk art is trendy. Edie Clark's "What Really Is Folk Art?" in the December 1986 issue of *Yankee* continues to be one of the most insightful pieces yet written on the subject.

The folk art craze struck with a vengeance in the early 1970s. Auction houses hyped folk art ranging from quilts to weathervanes as great long–term investments. Several market manipulators cornered then touted the work of contemporary artists. The speculative bubble burst in the late 1980s when the market was flooded and excellent reproductions fooled many novice buyers.

Reference: Chuck and Jan Rosenak, *Contemporary American Folk Art: A Collector's Guide,* Abbeville Press, 1996.

Newsletter: *Folk Art Finder,* One River, Essex, CT 06426.

Collectors' Club: Folk Art Society of America, PO Box 17041, Richmond, VA 23226.

Candlestick, figural man, arms raised, carved wood, carved signature "Rev H.L. Hayes 1971 W.Va.," 10¼" h $110.00

Cane, wood, carved and painted, Elisha Baker, ivory, red, gold, and black, Elvis' head, guitars, musical notes, and hound dog carved images, extended handle 6" from back of cane, 1986, 38¾" 165.00

Decoy, seagull, head turned to left, hollow, carved bill detail, glass eyes, orig paint, inscribed "Made by Steve, Painted by Lem, Ward Bro, 1966, Crisfield, Md., Lem Ward, Steve Ward" 1,025.00

Figural Group, black couple, Dave Hardy, Quakertown, Bucks County, PA, carved and painted, black woman wearing orange kerchief, green blouse, brown skirt and white apron holding basket of vegetables, black man wearing white hat, blue jean overalls and white shirt holding bowl of vegetables, each standing on grassy base, initialed and dated "DNH '91," 10" and 11" h 175.00

Figure, birds, set of 4, carved and painted pine wood, David Ellinger, PA, stylized, carved wing detail, painted red, 1 with yellow wings, other with blue wings, 2 painted green with red and black detail, each with wire legs on rectangular wood stands, 4¾" to 3½" l 1,380.00

Figure, gooney bird, carved and painted wood, stylized, painted black with orange, blue, and yellow details, chip carved wings, rectangular base, 6⅜" h 500.00

Figure, pig dog, carved and painted wood, gray over pink, black trim, 20th C, 13" l 175.00

Figure, pyramid with 6 figures, carved, unpainted poplar, glued and wire nailed to base, rocking motion, carved signature "Rev Hayes 1988 W.Va" on base, 6½" l, 8¾" h 55.00

Figure, raccoon, carved wood, Noah Kinney, colored with paint and marker in brown, red, black, and green, marker sgd on base "Noah Kinney," 8¾ x 17" base, 12¼" h overall 900.00

Whirligig, carved and polychrome painted wood, policeman, hat with tin bill and gold painted badge, dome tack buttons, gold painted cutout tin badge, multiple paint layers, 20th C, 22" h, $440.00. Photo courtesy Jackson's Auctioneers & Appraisers.

Figure, "Snake Handling Preacher," carved wood and paint, Ronald Cooper, royal blue, white, peach, brown, and black, applied twig hair, blue plastic doll eyes, titled, sgd, and dated, "1989," 27½" h 440.00

Figure, spotted cat, carved and painted wood, Earnest Patton, black, spots of brown, blue, white, and yellow, green eyes, legs are separately carved pieces of wood, sgd and dated, "1989," 4¼ x 11½", 8⅛" h overall 110.00

Figure, squirrel, sitting on tree stump, brown stain, carved wood, 20th C, 5" h.......................... 30.00

Garden Stake, wood cutout, black boy fishing, painted, c1950, 28" h.. 60.00

Painting, colored pencil and pen on paper, "Tammy," applied chip carved wood pcs frame with traces of old gold paint, sgd "Tammy 1880 S.L.J.," framed 19½" w, 23¼" h 300.00

Painting, pastel and ballpoint pen on paper, green and shades of brown and light blue, sgd "S.L. Jones 92," matted, molded wood frame with chair rail construction with cross corner assembly, 17½" w, 10¾" h 220.00

Painting, pen and ink and watercolor on paper, red, yellow, and black fantailed rooster beneath arched tulip, David Ellinger, c1950, 4¼ x 3¾" 750.00

Painting, polychrome paint on artist board, "The Magic Numbers," yellow, orange, red, peach, and shades of blue, narrow edged white mat, molded black frame, titled, sgd, and dated, "1989," framed 17¼" w, 21½" h 50.00

Redware, flowerpot, I S Stahl, Bally, PA, brown and ochre ground, manganese and slip dec, horizontal ruffled rim above tapering line incised body, inscribed on underside "Made by IS Stahl. Bally 1–12 1937 17–A," 2½" h 575.00

Redware, plates, set of 3, Lester Breininger, Robesonia, PA, sgraffito dec, large charger with bird on branch with tulips on yellow ground, plate with parrot, and plate with leaves, each inscribed "Robesonia, Pa, 1970, L. B. Breininger," "1970," and "L. B. 1977" respectfully, 3¾" d to 12¾" d 287.00

Sewer Tile Art, jar, ovoid, molded Art Deco designs, 19" h ... 55.00

Walking Stick, bird, "Schtockschnitzler" Simmons, carved and polychromed, red bird with yellow beak

Diorama, carved and painted wood, miniature animals on base, sgd "Frank Riddle," dated "1924," PA, $210.00. Photo courtesy Aston Macek.

and eye, black wing and tail detail, perched on green mound over tapered shaft fitted with metal tip, 38½" l **1,840.00**

FOOD MOLDS

The earliest food molds were ceramic and cast–iron molds used for baking. Today most collectors think of food molds in terms of the cast–iron candy molds, tin chocolate molds, and pewter ice cream molds used in factories, candy shops, and drugstores throughout the first half of the 19th century. Many of these chocolate and pewter molds were imported from Germany and Holland.

A substantial collection of Jell–O and post–1960 metal and plastic molds can be assembled with a minimum of effort and expenditure. Collector interest in these items is minimal.

Beware of reproduction chocolate molds. They appeared long enough ago to have developed a patina that matches some period molds.

Bread, Wheat Stick Pan #27, Griswold, c1925 . . . . **$200.00**
Cake, Santa, "Hello Kiddies," Griswold 550.00
Chocolate, 2 eggs, alligatored relief design, 3¼" h 35.00
Chocolate, boy and bicycle, 2 part, 8¾" h 375.00
Chocolate, circus peanuts, tray type, 105 cavities,
  28 x 13" 50.00
Chocolate, tin, elephant, 3 cavities 75.00
Chocolate, tin, hen, folding, 2 part, 2½" h 105.00
Chocolate, turkey, tray type, 8 cavities, 14 x 10" 45.00
Food, tin, lion, oval, 5¼" l 45.00
Ice Cream, cupid with circle, 4" d 25.00
Ice Cream, cupid with heart, 4" h 60.00
Ice Cream, pewter, basket, individual, replaced hinge
  pins 18.00
Ice Cream, pewter, potato, 4" h 65.00
Ice Cream, playing cards with diamond, mkd "E & Co,
  NY" 25.00
Ice Cream, ship, 2 qts 225.00
Ice Cream, steamboat 90.00
Maple Candy, foliage and fruit design, 2 part, 5½ x 8" 28.00
Patty, cast iron, heart, Griswold 55.00

Butter, yellow ware, grape design, minor chips overall, 3½" h, 7" w, 8" l, $49.50. Photo courtesy Collectors Auction Services.

Pottery, grapes and leaf center design, oval, Wedgwood
  Creamware **110.00**
Pottery, Turk's Head, redware, swirled fluting, brown
  sponged rim, 9" d 45.00

FOOTBALL CARDS

Although football cards originated in the 1890s, the 1948 Bowman and Leaf Gum sets mark the birth of the modern football card. Leaf only produced cards for two seasons. The last Bowman set dates from 1955.

Topps entered the field in 1950 with a college stars set. It produced a National Football League set each year between 1956 and 1963. Topps lost its National Football League license to the Philadelphia Gum Company for the 1964 season. Topps produced only American Football League cards between 1964 and 1967. Topps recovered the ball in 1968 when it once again was licensed to produce National Football League cards. It has remained undefeated ever since.

Football cards remain a weaker sister when compared to baseball cards. Many felt the collapse of the baseball market in the mid–1990s would open the door for a strong surge in the collectibility of football cards. This has not happened.

References: James Beckett, *The Official 1998 Price Guide to Football Cards, 17th Edition,* House of Collectibles, 1998; James Beckett and Dan Hitt (eds.), *Beckett Football Price Guide, No. 14,* Beckett Publications, 1997; Sports Collectors Digest, *1998 Sports Collectors Almanac,* Krause Publications, 1998.

Periodicals: *Beckett Football Card Magazine,* 15850 Dallas Pkwy, Dallas, TX 75248; *Sports Cards,* 700 E State St, Iola, WI 54990; *Tuff Stuff,* PO Box 1637, Glen Allen, VA 23060.

Note: Prices listed are for cards in near mint condition.

Bowman, 1948, #2, Larry Olsonoski **$20.00**
Bowman, 1950, #138, Howie Livingston 20.00
Bowman, 1951, common player (1–144) 18.00
Bowman, 1951, #51, Ed Sprinkle 20.00
Bowman, 1952, #16, Frank Gifford, large 450.00
Bowman, 1953, #71, Thurman McGraw 25.00
Bowman, 1954, #32, Elroy Hirsch 30.00
Bowman, 1991, complete set (561) 5.50
Fleer, 1960, common card (1–132) 4.00
Fleer, 1961, #8, Joe Fortunato 5.00
Fleer, 1963, #23, Cookie Gilchrist 35.00
Fleer, 1973, #10, quarterback, Pro Bowl Scouting Report 4.00
Fleer, 1974, #3, Chuck Bednarik, Fleer Hall of Fame 1.25
Fleer, 1976, #34, Dallas Cowboys, The Big Return, Fleer
  Team Action 7.50
Fleer, 1990, complete set (400) 3.50
Leaf, 1948, #11, Terry Brennan, Notre Dame 25.00
Leaf, 1949, #17, Bob Mann 24.00
Leaf, 1949, #90, Jack Jacobs 24.00
Pacific, 1981, #1, O J Simpson, Pacific Legends 2.50
Pacific, 1981, #28, Lynn Swan, Pacific Legends 55
Pacific, 1991, #2, Andre Reed, Pacific Picks the Pros 1.40
Pacific, 1992, #3, Michael Irvin, Pacific Prototypes 4.50
Pacific, 1994, #8, Trent Dilfer, Pacific Knights of the Gridiron . . 5.50
Philadelphia, 1964, #13, Baltimore Colts 4.00
Philadelphia, 1965, #57, Detroit Lions 3.50
Philadelphia, 1966, #69, Alex Karras 10.00

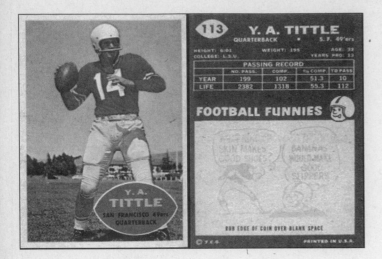

Topps, 1960, #113, Y. A. Tittle, $24.00.

Philadelphia, 1967, #88, Roman Gabriel 4.00
Pinnacle, 1991, #1, Warren Moon 20
Pinnacle, 1992, #193, Steve Bono 55
Pinnacle, 1993, #15, Dan Marino, Pinnacle Men of Autumn . . . 1.80
Pinnacle, 1993, #14, Irv Smith, Pinnacle Rookie 3.50
Pinnacle, 1994, #21, Jim Kelly 10
Score, 1989, #2, Bo Jackson 25
Score, 1990, #3, Barry Sanders, Score Hot Card 2.30
Score, 1991, #7, Boomer Esiason 07
Score, 1992, #46, William Perry 05
Score, 1993, common card (1–26), Score Dream Team 25
Topps, 1950, #9A, Al Burnett, Rutgers, felt back 40.00
Topps, 1951, #49, Don McRae, Wildcats, Topps Magic 18.00
Topps, 1955, #13, Aaron Rosenberg, USC 7.25
Topps, 1957, #149, Ronnie Knox 7.00
Topps, 1961, #48, Frank Ryan 3.00
Topps, 1963, common card (1–170) 2.50
Topps, 1964, #24, Yale, Topps Pennant Stickers 25.00
Topps, 1967, #131, Speedy Duncan 4.50
Topps, 1970, #1, Fran Tarkenton, Topps Super 12.00
Topps, 1971, #80, Mike Curtis 1.00
Topps, 1981, complete set, (528) 250.00
Ultra, 1991, complete set (300) 5.50
Ultra, 1992, common card (1–450) .04
Ultra, 1993, #10, Steve Young, Ultra All–Rookies 11.50
Ultra, 1994, #4, Jerry Rice, Ultra Touchdown Kings 11.50

FOOTBALL MEMORABILIA

Football memorabilia divides into two distinct groups, professional and collegiate, and two distinct categories, equipment and paper ephemera. Collectors of professional football memorabilia far outnumber collectors of collegiate memorabilia. Equipment collectors exceed the number of collectors of paper ephemera.

The category is heavily post–1970 driven, due to availability, and regional in nature. Collectors want game–related material. Team logo material licensed for sale in sports shops has minimal to no appeal.

References: John Carpentier, *Price Guide to Packers Memorabilia*, Krause Publications, 1998; Roderick A. Malloy, *Malloy's Sports Collectibles Value Guide: Up–to–Date Prices for Noncard Sports*

Memorabilia, Attic Books, Wallace–Homestead, Krause Publications, 1993; Jim Warren II, *Tuff Stuff's Complete Guide to Starting Lineup,* Antique Trader Books, 1997.

Periodical: *Sports Collectors Digest,* 700 E State St, Iola, WI 54990.

Autograph, Terry Bradshaw, sgd football **$30.00**
Book, *How Champions Play Football*, paperback, 1948,
　98 pp 10.00
Bookends, pr, cast iron, Knute Rocke, raised portrait,
　incised inscription "The Rock Of Notre Dame," early
　1930s 150.00
Booklet, Football Book Schedules & Information, Hires
　Root Beer premium, college and professional teams,
　1940 . . . . 15.00
Cigarette Lighter, San Francisco 49ers Super Bowl SVI,
　silvered metal and plastic 25.00
Coin, Johnny Unitas, Salada 100.00
Comic Book, Football Thrills, Red Grange Story,
　Approved Comics, 1952 . . . . 150.00
Football, Spalding, white, sgd by New York Giants team,
　1960 . . . . 185.00
Football, Wilson, sgd by Cleveland Browns team, 1962 . . . . 350.00
Game, ABC Monday Night Football, Aurora, 1972 . . . . 40.00
Game, O J Simpson's See Action Football Game, Kenner,
　1974 . . . . 40.00
Game, Super Sunday Football, Hasbro, 1973 . . . . 30.00
Jersey, Dan Marino of Miami Dolphins, autograph on
　front 2,000.00
Magazine, *Sports Illustrated*, Aug 17, 1970, Joe Namath 8.00
Magazine, *Stanley Woodward's Football*, 1953 . . . . 4.00
Nodder, Cleveland Browns, square base 65.00
Pennant, felt, New York Giants, stadium design, white
　inscription, National Football League insignia lower
　left, dark blue ground, red trim, late 1960s 20.00
Photograph, sgd by New York Giants, 1965, 20 x 16" 230.00
Pinback Button, Rockne of Notre Dame, photo, black
　and white, 1930s 15.00
Poster, O J Simpson, 1968–71 . . . . 85.00
Press Pin, Super Bowl XV, 1980, Oakland and
　Philadelphia 175.00

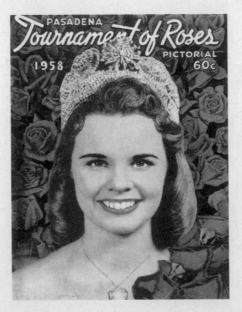

Program, 1958 Pasadena Tournament of Roses, 28 pp, 8¼ x 11", $10.00.

Program, American Football Conference Division,
Miami and Kansas City, 1971 . . . . **30.00**

Program, National Football Conference, Dallas and
Cleveland, 1967 . . . . **75.00**

Program, Philadelphia Inquirer Charities 8th Annual
Classic, Eagles vs Packers, Municipal Stadium,
Sep 13, 1945 . . . . **20.00**

Puzzle, Roman Garbiel, action scene, full color photo,
American Publishing Corp, 300 pcs, 5½" h cardboard
canister, 1972 . . . . **15.00**

Shoes, pr, worn by Dan Marino of Miami Dolphins,
autograph on sides **630.00**

Stadium Cushion, vinyl, stuffed, red, NFL team names
and mascot illus, orig tag, unused, 11 x 16" **18.00**

Ticket Stub, Super Bowl 1, 1966 Green Bay and Kansas
City **125.00**

Yearbook, Naval Academy, Roger Staubach's junior and
senior year, 1965 . . . . **75.00**

Baroque,
candy dish,
marigold,
4¾" h, 5½" d,
$30.00.

FOSTORIA

The Fostoria Glass Company broke ground for a glass factory in Fostoria, Ohio, on January 1, 1888. Within six months the factory was producing a line of glass bottles, shakers, and utilitarian wares. By 1891 Fostoria relocated to Moundsville, West Virginia.

Fostoria's stemware and tableware included a wide variety of products in crystal and colors designed to compete actively against Cambridge, Heisey, and Westmoreland. Fostoria changed with the times. When pressed and needle–etched glass fell from favor, the company turned to plate and master etchings. The role of color was increased. When teas and luncheons were replaced by brunches and cocktail parties, Fostoria added new patterns, shapes, and forms. Fostoria marketed aggressively, especially to the post–1945 bridal market.

Fostoria purchased Morgantown Glass in 1965, moving its operations to Moundsville in 1971. In 1983 Lancaster Colony Corporation purchased Fostoria. The Moundsville factory closed in 1986.

References: Gene Florence, *Elegant Glassware of the Depression Era, Seventh Edition,* Collector Books, 1997; Ann Kerr, *Fostoria: An Identification and Value Guide of Pressed, Blown & Hand Molded Shapes,* Collector Books, 1994, 1997 value update; Ann Kerr, *Fostoria, Volume II: Identification & Value Guide to Etched, Carved & Cut Designs,* Collector Books, 1997; Milbra Long and Emily Seate, *Fostoria Stemware: The Crystal For America,* Collector Books, 1995; Leslie Piña, *Fostoria Designer George Sakier,* Schiffer Publishing, 1996; Leslie Piña, *Fostoria: Serving the American Table 1887–1986,* Schiffer Publishing, 1995; Harry L. Rinker, *Stemware of the 20th Century: The Top 200 Patterns,* House of Collectibles, 1997.

Periodical: *The Daze,* PO Box 57, Otisville, MI 48463.

Collectors' Clubs: Fostoria Glass Collectors, Inc, PO Box 1625, Orange, CA 92668; Fostoria Glass Society of America, PO Box 826, Moundsville, WV 26041.

American, crystal, ashtray, 2⅜" **$8.00**
American, crystal, bonbon, 7" **8.00**
American, crystal, bowl, 1 handle, 4½" sq **5.00**
American, crystal, butter dish, round **110.00**

American, crystal, cake plate, metal handles, 9" **55.00**
American, crystal, cake plate, 2 handled, 10" **32.00**
American, crystal, candle holders, pr, 3" **18.00**
American, crystal, celery bowl, oblong, 10" l, 2" h **20.00**
American, crystal, comb tray, oval, 10½ x 5" **45.00**
American, crystal, compote, cov, 9" h **25.00**
American, crystal, console bowl, tri–corner, 11" **28.00**
American, crystal, creamer, 9½" **15.00**
American, crystal, crescent salad plate **110.00**
American, crystal, cruet, no stopper **20.00**
American, crystal, cup and saucer **10.00**
American, crystal, dinner plate, 9½" **20.00**
American, crystal, relish, 3 part, 11" **40.00**
American, crystal, relish, 3 part, 6 x 9" **35.00**
American, crystal, salt and pepper shakers, pr, straight,
pewter tops **60.00**
American, crystal, sandwich plate, 10½" **15.00**
American, crystal, tray, oval, 10½" **40.00**
American, crystal, vase, square base, ftd, 9" **50.00**
American, crystal, vegetable bowl **27.00**
American, crystal, wedding bowl, small **25.00**
American, crystal, whiskey **15.00**
American, crystal, wine **14.00**
Colony, crystal, bonbon, 3 ftd, 7" **12.00**
Colony, crystal, bonbon, triangular, 3 ftd, 7" **15.00**
Colony, crystal, bowl, flared, 11" **30.00**
Colony, crystal, candle holder, 3½" **8.00**
Colony, crystal, candle holders, pr, 2 light, 6½" **50.00**
Colony, crystal, relish, oval **12.00**
Colony, crystal, sherbet **9.00**
Colony, crystal, sugar, 3½" **5.00**
Fairfax, ashtray, 2375, green, 2½" **10.00**
Fairfax, ashtray, pink, 4" **17.00**
Fairfax, bonbon, 2375, blue **20.00**
Fairfax, candlesticks, pr, 2394, yellow, 2" **28.00**
Fairfax, candy, cov, 2331, 3 part, pink **65.00**
Fairfax, creamer and sugar, individual, black **38.00**
Fairfax, shaker, rose **30.00**
Fairfax, sherbet, 5299, high, blue **20.00**
Fairfax, tumbler, 4095, ftd, pink, 2½ oz **28.00**
Fairfax, tumbler, 5299, ftd, blue, 9 oz **20.00**
Fairfax, water goblet, 6202, pink **25.00**
Fairfax, whipped cream bowl, blue **18.00**

Fairfax, window vase, 2373, with frog, pink **85.00**
Navarre, crystal, bowl, flared, 12" **50.00**
Navarre, crystal, cake plate, handled **45.00**
Navarre, crystal, champagne **25.00**
Navarre, crystal, compote, 4³/₄" **30.00**
Navarre, crystal, sherbet, 6106, high **20.00**
Navarre, crystal, sherbet, 6106, low **18.00**
Navarre, crystal, torte plate, 14". **50.00**
Navarre, crystal, vase, flared, flat, 5" **100.00**
Navarre, crystal, water tumbler, ftd, 10 oz **20.00**
Versailles, bowl, topaz, 5" **15.00**
Versailles, chop plate, blue, 14". **75.00**
Versailles, dinner plate, topaz, 10¹/₂" d **70.00**
Versailles, juice tumbler, topaz, ftd. **15.00**
Versailles, luncheon plate, pink, 8³/₄" **22.00**
Versailles, oyster cocktail, topaz **25.00**
Versailles, relish, 2 part, blue. **18.00**

FRANCISCAN

Gladding, McBean and Company, Los Angeles, developed and produced the Franciscan dinnerware line in 1934. The line includes a variety of shapes, forms, and patterns. Coronado, El Patio, Metropolitan, Montecito, Padua, and Rancho are solid color dinnerware lines.

The Franciscan hand–painted, embossed patterns of Apple, Desert Rose, and Ivy dominated the secondary collecting market in the 1980s and early 1990s. Today collectors are seeking out some of the more modern Franciscan decaled patterns such as Oasis and Starburst.

References: Delleen Enge, *Franciscan: Embossed Handpainted,* published by author, 1992; Delleen Enge, *Plain and Fancy Franciscan Made in California,* published by author, 1996; Lois Lehner, *Lehner's Encyclopedia of U.S. Marks on Pottery, Porcelain & Clay,* Collector Books, 1998; Harry L. Rinker, *Dinnerware of the 20th Century: The Top 500 Patterns,* House of Collectibles, 1997; Jeffrey B. Snyder, *Franciscan Dining Services,* Schiffer Publishing, 1997.

Collectors' Club: Franciscan Collectors Club, 8412 5th Ave NE, Seattle, WA 98115.

Apple, bowl, 5¹/₄" **$12.00**
Apple, bowl, 6". **15.00**
Apple, butter, cov, ¹/₄ lb, stain on lid **30.00**
Apple, creamer and sugar, cov, small **65.00**
Apple, creamer, large **20.00**
Apple, cup and saucer **12.00**
Apple, cup and saucer, after dinner **30.00**
Apple, plate, 6¹/₂" **6.00**
Apple, plate, 8¹/₂" **18.00**
Apple, plate, 10¹/₂" **22.00**
Apple, saucer **5.00**
Apple, sugar, open, large. **18.00**
Apple, sugar, open, small **20.00**
Arcadia Gold, place setting **100.00**
Arcadia Green, place setting **100.00**
Coronado, bread and butter plate **9.00**
Coronado, cereal bowl **25.00**
Coronado, cup and saucer. **24.00**
Coronado, fruit bowl. **18.00**
Coronado, plate, 9". **18.00**

Apple, compote, 4" h, 5" d, $65.00.

Coronado, salad plate **18.00**
Coronado, sugar, cov **25.00**
Daisy, bread and butter plate. **5.00**
Daisy, butter, cov **35.00**
Daisy, cereal bowl **12.00**
Daisy, child's dish **30.00**
Daisy, creamer **15.00**
Daisy, cup and saucer. **5.00**
Daisy, fruit bowl **10.00**
Daisy, gravy, fast stand **35.00**
Daisy, juice tumbler **18.00**
Daisy, plate, 10" **14.00**
Daisy, platter, 14" **45.00**
Daisy, platter, 19" **65.00**
Desert Rose, butter, cov, ¹/₄ lb **45.00**
Desert Rose, candlesticks, pr **75.00**
Desert Rose, celery dish **30.00**
Desert Rose, cookie jar **300.00**
Desert Rose, cup and saucer **15.00**
Desert Rose, dinner plate, 10¹/₂". **18.00**
Desert Rose, grill plate **75.00**
Desert Rose, jam jar, cov **85.00**
Desert Rose, luncheon plate, 9¹/₂" **12.00**
Desert Rose, milk pitcher. **90.00**
Desert Rose, platter, oval, 12" **40.00**
Desert Rose, platter, oval, 14" **48.00**
Desert Rose, platter, round, 13¹/₂". **85.00**
Desert Rose, salad plate, 8". **8.00**
Desert Rose, salt shaker and pepper mill **245.00**
Desert Rose, sandwich plate, 11¹/₂" **50.00**
Desert Rose, sherbet, ftd **25.00**
Forget Me Not, dinner plate, 10" **20.00**
Forget Me Not, fruit bowl **22.00**
Forget Me Not, platter, 14" **95.00**
Forget Me Not, salad plate, 8" **16.00**
Forget Me Not, vegetable bowl, round **45.00**
Fresh Fruit, baking dish, square **195.00**
Fresh Fruit, cereal bowl **18.00**
Fresh Fruit, cup and saucer **18.00**
Fresh Fruit, mug, 7 oz **25.00**
Fresh Fruit, salad plate. **22.00**

Fresh Fruit, dinner plate, 10" d, $30.00.

Bookends, 8¹/₂ x 5¹/₂", $200.00.

Fresh Fruit, tile	65.00
Ivy, bowl, 8¹/₄"	45.00
Ivy, gravy boat	45.00
Ivy, place setting	90.00
Ivy, platter, oval, 13"	60.00
Ivy, soup bowl, ftd, 5¹/₂"	30.00
Ivy, vegetable, 2 part	55.00
Renaissance Grey, place setting	115.00
Renaissance Platinum, place setting	130.00
Silver Pine, place setting	95.00
Wild Flower, bread and butter plate	50.00
Wild Flower, cereal bowl	145.00
Wild Flower, luncheon plate	125.00
Wild Flower, salad plate	120.00
Wild Flower, saucer	25.00
Woodside, place setting	95.00

FRANKART

Arthur Von Frankenberg founded Frankart, New York, New York, in the mid–1920s. The company mass–produced a wide range of aquariums, ashtrays, bookends, lamps, and vases throughout the 1930s. Frankart nudes are the most desired pieces.

Frankart pieces were cast in white metal. Finishes include bronzoid, cream, French, gun–metal, jap, pear green, and verde. Pieces are usually marked with "Frankart, Inc.," and a patent number or "pat. appl. for." Beware of the possibility of a mismatched ashtray when buying a standing figural.

Ashtray, nude acrobatic figure balancing 3" d glass ball shaped container on toes, 12" h	$365.00
Ashtray, nude kneeling on cushion, holding 3" d removable pottery ashtray, 6" h	220.00
Bookends, pr, fawns, step base, mkd, 6" h	80.00
Bookends, pr, horse heads, flowing manes, 5" h	45.00
Bookends, pr, woman's head, step base, mkd, 6" h	175.00
Candlesticks, pr, figural nudes standing on tiptoes, holding candle cup over heads, 12¹/₂" h	365.00
Cigarette Box, nudes back to back supporting removable green glass box, 8" h	425.00

Lamp, figural nude, kneeling before 4" d crystal bubble ball, 8" h	585.00
Lamp, figural nude, standing, holding 6" round crackled rose glass globe, 18" h	400.00

FRANKOMA

John Frank, a ceramics instructor at Oklahoma University, established Frankoma in 1933. In 1938 he moved his commercial production from Norman to Sapulpa. When a fire destroyed the plant in 1939, he rebuilt immediately.

A honey–tan colored clay from Ada was used to make Frankoma pieces prior to 1954. After that date, the company switched to a red brick clay from Sapulpa. Today some clay is brought into the plant from other areas.

Fire again struck the Sapulpa plant in September 1983. By July 1984 a new plant was opened. Since the early molds were lost in the fire, new molds were designed and made.

References: Phyllis and Tom Bess, *Frankoma and Other Oklahoma Potteries*, Schiffer Publishing, 1995; Gary V. Schaum, *Collector's Guide to Frankoma Pottery 1933 Through 1990: Identifying Your Collection Including Gracetone*, L–W Book Sales, 1997.

Collectors' Club: Frankoma Family Collectors Assoc, PO Box 32571, Oklahoma City, OK 73123.

Aztec, creamer and sugar, cov, #7A&B, prairie green	$40.00
Batter Pitcher, #87, desert gold, Ada, 1 qt	30.00
Bookends, pr, Mountain Girl, 5³/₄" h	75.00
Bowl, slender, #45, desert gold, Sapulpa, 12" d	30.00
Bud Vase, crocus, #43, prairie green, Sapulpa	15.00
Christmas Card, The Franks, 1960	55.00
Cornucopia, #222, desert gold, Ada, 12"	20.00
Decanter, Fingerprint, stopper, 2 qt	35.00
Gracetone, dinner plate, pink champagne	15.00
Jug, honey, #833, brown satin, Sapulpa	15.00
Jug, juice, #90, no stopper, 1942 mark	75.00
Lazybones, mug, #4M, 16 oz	5.00
Lazybones, trivet	30.00

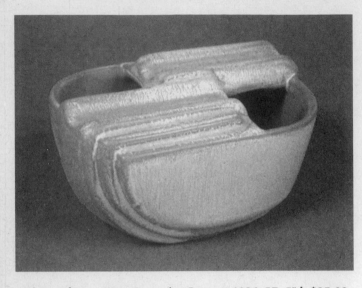

Cigar Ashtray #455, Pompeian Bronze, 1934–57, 5" l, $35.00.

American Legion Globe, white milk glass globe, red, green, and gold etched lettering, repainted, repaired chips and crack at base, 12¹/₂" h, 10" w, $187.00. Photo courtesy Collectors Auction Services.

Lazybones, vegetable bowl, #4N, prairie green. **10.00**
Match Holder, #89A, royal blue. **40.00**
Mug, elephant, gold and white, 1973. . . . . **50.00**
Plainsman, baker and warmer, #5W, prairie green, 3 qt **15.00**
Plainsman, mug, #5M, desert gold, 16 oz. **10.00**
Plainsman, salad plate, #5G, desert gold, 8". **5.00**
Plainsman, soup cup, #4SC, brown satin **8.00**
Plainsman, vegetable bowl, #4N, prairie green. **10.00**
Planter, duck, #208A, prairie green **12.00**
Plate, Jesus the Carpenter, 1971. . . . . **20.00**
Vase, fan, #19, prairie green, Sapulpa **30.00**
Vase, swan, #228, prairie green, Sapulpa **15.00**
Wagon Wheel, dessert bowl, #94XO, desert gold, Ada **8.00**
Wagon Wheel, luncheon plate, #94F, desert gold, Ada,
   9" d **10.00**
Wagon Wheel, pitcher, #94D, desert gold, Sapulpa **25.00**
Wagon Wheel, platter, #94Q, prairie green, Sapulpa. **15.00**
Wagon Wheel, sugar, miniature, #510, prairie green,
   Ada **10.00**
Westwind, chili bowl, #6X, prairie green, 14 oz. **5.00**
Westwind, teapot, cov, #6J, brown satin, 2 cup **12.00**

FRATERNAL & SERVICE ORGANIZATIONS

Benevolent and fraternal societies from the Odd Fellows to the Knights of Columbus continued to play a major role in American life through the first two–thirds of the 20th century. Local service clubs such as the Lions and Rotary established themselves as a major force in community life in the 1920s and 30s. Their golden age spanned the 1950s and 60s. Increasing workplace and family demands have cut heavily into membership. Membership has stabilized at best in most clubs. In many cases, the average age of club members is well above 50.

American Legion, ashtray, metal, Grandpromenade–
   Chicago center seal, 1952, 4" d **$8.00**
Benevolent & Protective Order of the Elks, badge,
   Chicago 56th Annual Reunion, 1920 . . . . **15.00**
Detroit Lodge No 34, watch fob, bronze, 1926. . . . . **18.00**

Independent Order of Odd Fellows, certificate,
   8 vignettes, 1927. . . . . **10.00**
Lion's Club International, badge, International Conven-
   tion, 1954. . . . . **10.00**
Masonic, book, *Mackey's Revised Encyclopedia of
   Freemasonry*, 2 vol, illus, 1,217 pp, 1929 . . . . **55.00**
Masonic, catalog, Henderson–Ames Co, lodge supplies,
   1924, 104 pp **50.00**
Masonic, medal, Sesqui, hanging from celluloid pin,
   1926. . . . . **18.00**
Masonic, shaving mug, 1953 . . . . **40.00**
Masonic, tape measure, celluloid, round, symbols,
   c1920. . . . . **15.00**
Order of Eastern Star, plate, commemorative, Birming-
   ham, AL, Oct 1927 . . . . **20.00**
Order of Eastern Star, plate, Old Bellaire Chapter, #375,
   1957. . . . . **20.00**
Shriner, bust, Atlantic City, 1927 . . . . **125.00**
Shriner, letter opener, 32nd emblem, c1920 . . . . **20.00**
Shriner, nodder, composition, man wearing tuxedo and
   maroon shrine hat, c1960, 7" h **20.00**
Shriner, paperweight, Syria Temple, Pittsburgh/Atlantic
   City Pilgrimage, 1924, 2¹/₂ x 4" **25.00**
Shriner, vase, Limoges, 1921 . . . . **48.00**

FRUIT JARS

The canning of fruits and vegetables played a major role in the American household until the late 1950s. Canning jars were recycled year after year. Jars utilizing zinc lids and rubber–sealed metal lids are extremely common. These jars usually sell for about 50¢.

Do not assume the date on a jar indicates the year the jar was made. In almost every case, it is a patent date or the founding date of the company that made the jar.

References: Douglas M. Leybourne, Jr., *The Collector's Guide to Old Fruit Jars, Red Book No. 8*, published by author, 1997; Jerry McCann, *The Guide to Collecting Fruit Jars: Fruit Jar Annual, Vol. 3–1998*, Phoenix Press, 1997; Bill Schroeder, *1000 Fruit Jars: Priced and Illustrated, 5th Edition*, Collector Books, 1987, 1996 value update.

Newsletter: *Fruit Jar Newsletter*, 364 Gregory Ave, West Orange, NJ 07052.

Collectors' Clubs: Ball Collectors Club, 22203 Doncaster, Riverview, MI 48192; Federation of Historical Bottle Collectors, Inc, 88 Sweetbriar Branch, Longwood, FL 32750; Midwest Antique Fruit Jar & Bottle Club, PO Box 38, Flat Rock, IN 47234.

Anderson Preserving Co, clear, metal lid, qt $75.00
Atlas E–Z Seal, aqua, glass lid, wire bail, handmade, pt 10.00
Atlas Special, blue, zinc lid, pt 25.00
Atlas Strong Shoulder Mason, clear 1.00
Ball, Eclipse, Wide Mouth, clear, glass lid, wire bail, qt 2.50
Ball Freezer Jar front, Pat. Pend. reverse, clear, smooth
  lip, beaded neck seal, c1947–52, 24 oz 4.00
Ball, Ideal, aqua, glass lid, wire bail, pt 2.00
Ball, Ideal, clear, qt 3.00
Ball, Mason, emb backwards "s", zinc lid, qt 4.00
Ball, Mason's Patent 1858, green, qt. 5.00
Brockway Clear–Vu Mason, metal lid, clear, ½ pt 2.50
Calcutt's, clear, glass screw lid, handmade, qt 35.00
Crown Mason, clear, zinc lid, qt 1.50
Crystal Mason, The, clear, zinc lid, pt. 8.00
Diamond Fruit Jar Improved Trademark, clear, pt 2.50
Double Safety, pt 5.00
Dunkley, clear, hinged glass lid, qt. 5.00
Easy Vacuum Jar, clear, glass lid, wire clamp, qt 25.00
Flaccus Bros, clear, cylindrical, steer's head, ground
  mouth, glass lid. 50.00
Franklin Fruit Jar, aqua, glass lid, qt 3.50
Gem 1908, clear, glass lid, screw band 6.00
Genuine Mason, aqua, qt 12.00
Globe, green, glass lid, lever bail, pt 30.00
Heroine, The, aqua, glass lid, screw band, qt 30.00
I G Co, aqua, wax seal, qt. 25.00
Independence Jar, clear, cylindrical, ground mouth,
  glass lid, qt. 40.00
Johnson & Johnson, NJ, amber, glass lid, qt 20.00
Kentucky L G Co, green wax seal, qt 55.00
Kerr, "Self–Sealing" Trademark Reg Pat, Pat Aug 31,
  1915, clear, smooth lip Mason, beaded neck, 2 pc
  metal lid, qt 2.00

Kline, blue, glass stopper reads "AR Kline Pat Oct 27
  1863," qt 30.00
Knight Packing Co, clear, smooth lip Mason, beaded
  neck seal, qt 4.00
Leotric, aqua, glass lid, wire bail, ½ gal 10.00
Longlife Mason Front, Fruit Medallion reverse, clear, pt. 1.00
Lutz & Schramm Co, clear, smooth lip closure, paneled,
  pt 2.00
Lyon Jar, clear, cylindrical, emb "Patented Apr 10 1900,"
  ground mouth. 2.50
Mallinger, clear, zinc lid, qt. 4.00
Mansfield Improved Mason, light green, glass lid,
  screw band, qt 15.00
Mason Fruit Jar, clear, smooth lip, beaded neck seal, qt. 4.00
Mason, Iron Cross, blue, qt 12.00
Mason, Mason's VII, 1858 . . . . 28.00
Mason, Root, aqua, zinc lid, qt 4.00
Mrs Chapin's Salad Dressing Boston Mass, clear, smooth
  lip, old–style lightning seal, pt 6.00
Newmark Special Extra Mason Jar, clear, zinc lid, pt. 10.00
Norge, clear, glass lid, metal band, qt 10.00
Pacific SF Glass Works, aqua, glass lid, screw band, qt 30.00
Pappy, clear, smooth lip, metal screw lid, tapered, pt 8.00
Pearl, aqua, handmade, emb "The Pearl," qt. 25.00
Perfect Seal, clear, rubber seal, qt 3.00
Presto Wide Mouth, clear, glass lid, wire bail, ½ pt. 2.50
Pure–Food Products, smooth lip, Evans St Louis, qt. 3.00
Red Mason's Patent Nov 30th 1858, aqua, zinc lid, pt 10.00
Samco Genuine Mason, clear, zinc lid, 3 gal 15.00
Smalley's Royal Trade Mark Nu–Seal, clear, glass lid,
  wire bail, ½ pt 15.00
Societe, clear, smooth lip, lightning dimple neck seal, qt 2.00
Standard, aqua, wax seal, qt 20.00
Sterling Mason, clear, ribbed sides, smooth lip, beaded
  neck seal 2.00
Sure Seal Made for L Bamberger, blue, qt. 12.00
Swayees Improved Mason, amber, qt 38.00
Swift & Company, Copyright 1908, clear, "Reg. U. S. Pat.
  Off. U. S. A." in center on lid, smooth lip glass lid, 2
  wide side clamps, neck tie wire, pt 4.00
Texas Mason, clear, qt. 5.00
Universal, clear, zinc lid, qt. 5.00
Vacuum, clear, smooth lip glass lid, metal clamp 4.00
Weir, As You Like It, horseradish trademark, minor
  roughness inside lid. 50.00
Whitney Mason, Pat'd 1858, aqua, zinc lid, qt 20.00
Woodbury, aqua, glass lid, metal clip. 25.00
Woodbury Improved (monogram), aqua, cylindrical,
  ground mouth, qt 35.00
Young's, Pat May 27, 1902, stoneware, brown neck,
  metal clamp lid. 20.00

Ball Ideal, aqua, 1 qt, $5.00.

FRY GLASS

H. C. Fry Glass, Rochester, Pennsylvania, operated between 1901 and 1933. After an initial production period making Brilliant cut glass, the company turned to manufacturing glass tableware.

Pearl Oven Glass, a heat–resistant opalescent colored glass, was patented in 1922. Most pieces are marked with "Fry" and a model number. For a two–year period, 1926–27, H. C. Fry produced Foval, an art glass line. Its pieces are identified by their pearly opalescent body with an applied trim of jade green or Delft blue. Silver overlay pieces are marked "Rockwell."

Reference: The H. C. Fry Glass Society, *The Collector's Encyclopedia of Fry Glassware,* Collector Books, 1990, 1998 value update.

Collectors' Club: H. C. Fry Glass Society, PO Box 41, Beaver, PA 15009.

REPRODUCTION ALERT: Italian reproductions of Foval, produced in the 1970s, have a teal blue transparent trim.

Au Gratin, Oven Ware, oval, clear, 9" d **$30.00**
Baking Dish, 6 x 10" **30.00**
Butter Dish, cov, Pearl Oven Ware **65.00**
Cake Plate, Sunnybrook pattern, emerald **48.00**
Canape Plate, cobalt blue center handle, 6¼" d, 4" h **160.00**
Casserole, cov, round, 4½" **95.00**
Cream Soup, with underplate, Oven Ware, 2 handles **40.00**
Cruet, Foval, cobalt blue handle, orig stopper **115.00**
Cup and Saucer, Foval Pearl **65.00**
Custard, etched floral design, clear **20.00**
Fingerbowl, Rose, etched band **80.00**
Jug, #DE 2, Grape pattern **95.00**
Lemonade, Foval Pearl, jade handle, #9416 . . . . **135.00**
Meatloaf, cov, emb grape on lid, clear, 9" **40.00**
Platter, Pearl Oven Ware, etched rim **20.00**
Platter, well and tree, opalescent, metal holder, wood
    handles **200.00**
Reamer, canary, fluted **200.00**
Teapot, cov, #2002, individual, jade green handle,
    spout, and finial **250.00**
Trivet, metal rim, 8" d **30.00**
Tumbler, Crackle, green handle, 5¼" h **65.00**
Tumbler, Diamond Optic, ftd, pink, 4¼" **25.00**
Tumbler, Icicle, green handle **60.00**
Vase, #456, Delft connector, 8" h **225.00**
Vase, reeded design, crystal and black **135.00**
Water Pitcher, Foval, alabaster body, jade green base and
    handle **275.00**
Wine, Diamond Optic, twisted stem, pink, 5½", price
    for set of 10 . . . . **355.00**

FULPER

Fulper Art Pottery was made by the American Pottery Company, Flemington, New Jersey, beginning around 1910 and ending in 1930. All pieces were molded. Pieces from the 1920s tend to be of higher quality due to less production pressures.

Pieces exhibit a strong Arts and Crafts and/or oriental influence. Glazes differed tremendously as Fulper experimented throughout its production period.

References: John Hibel et al., *The Fulper Book,* published by authors, n.d.; Ralph and Terry Kovel, *Kovel's American Art Pottery: The Collector's Guide to Makers, Marks and Factory Histories,* Crown Publishers, 1993.

Collectors' Club: Stangl/Fulper Collectors Club, PO Box 583, Flemington, NJ 08822.

REPRODUCTION ALERT

Artichoke Bowl, leopard's skin crystalline flambé glaze,
    unmkd, 8¼ x 3¾" h **$350.00**
Bowl, blue drip glaze, beige and green int, 9½" d **20.00**

Bowl, flaring rim, leopard skin crystalline glaze, vertical
    ink racetrack marks, 2" h, 5" d, price for set of 6 . . . . **425.00**
Bowl, small, famille rose crystalline glaze, vertical race–
    track ink mark **45.00**
Bud Vase, 4 sided, 4', ivory and clear flambé glaze,
    unmkd, 8¼" h **350.00**
Bud Vase, squat base, cat's eye flambé glaze, vertical
    rect ink mark, 5¼ x 3¾" **150.00**
Cabinet Vase, dark brown and gray matte crystalline
    glaze, vertical rect ink mark, 4" h, 3" w **375.00**
Centerpiece Bowl, ftd, lotus shaped, mirrored black
    glaze, incised vertical mark, 6 x 11" **325.00**
Effigy Bowl, cat's eye flambé glaze, int forming peacock
    feather effect, ext in mustard matte and brown, verti-
    cal rect ink mark, 7½" h **750.00**
Effigy Bowl, frothy butterscotch flambé glaze over mus-
    tard matte, speckled dark brown matte glaze base, 3
    squat figurines supporting flat, curl rimmed bowl,
    early ink mark, 7½ x 10¾" **800.00**
Grecian Urn, 2 handles, cobalt and periwinkle blue
    glaze, ink racetrack mark, 10¾ x 6" **200.00**
Urn, 4 sided, tapering, black and silver cucumber crys-
    talline green flambé glaze, imp geometric dec, early
    ink mark, 8 x 4" **475.00**
Vase, 4 sided, tapering, imp geometric dec, black and
    silver cucumber crystalline green flambé glaze, 8" h **475.00**
Vase, baluster shaped, raised dots on shoulder, mirrored
    black to copperdust crystalline flambé glaze, unmkd,
    7" h, 4½" w **600.00**
Vase, bottle shaped, silvery Flemington green glaze,
    early ink mark, 5 x 3½" **375.00**
Vase, bulbous, elephant's breath flambé glaze, collar
    rim, early Prang mark, 4¼ x 6¼" **450.00**
Vase, bullet shaped, 3 handles, mahogany and ele-
    phant's breath flambé glaze, early ink mark, 6½ x 4½" . . . **550.00**
Vase, ovoid, 2 handled, green to cobalt crystalline flam-
    bé glaze, incised racetrack mark and paper label,
    7¾" h **350.00**
Vessel, 2 angular buttressed handles, leopard skin
    crystalline glaze, vertical rect ink mark, 6½" h, 8" w **550.00**
Vessel, bell pepper shaped, cat's eye to Chinese blue
    flambé glaze, vertical rect ink mark, 4¼" h **350.00**

Cabinet Vase, ovoid, sheer blue and ivory flambé glaze on matte mustard base, rect ink mark, 3¾ x 3¾", $192.50. Photo courtesy David Rago Auctions.

FURNITURE

The furniture industry experienced tremendous growth immediately following World Wars I and II as America's population ballooned and wartime advances in materials and technology were applied to furniture. Furniture was made in a variety of grades, making the latest styles available to virtually every income level.

Beginning in the 1920s, the American popular taste tended to go in two directions, Colonial Revival and upholstered furniture. Colonial Revival furniture divides into two distinct groups: (1) high–style pieces that closely mirrored their historic counterparts, and (2) generic forms that combined design elements from many different styles in a single piece. Large numbers of upholstered pieces utilized frames that drew their inspiration from English and European revival styles. Buyers with a modern bent fell in love with the Art Deco and Streamlined Modern styles.

While leading designers such as Charles Eames experimented with new materials and forms prior to World War II, it was after the war that modern furniture reached the mass market. Colonial Revival gave way to Early American; upholstered furniture veered off in a sectional direction. Many trendy styles, e.g., tubular, Mediterranean, and Scandinavian, survived less than a decade.

In the post–1945 period designers shifted their focus from household furniture to office and institutional furniture. Design became truly international as English and European design studios replaced America as the major influence for style change.

American tastes became traditional and conservative again in the mid–1970s. Colonial Revival styles made a strong comeback. Modernism was out, except among a select few in large metropolitan areas. Today, many people desiring a modern look are buying pieces manufactured from the mid–1940s through the early 1960s.

Collectors pay a premium for furniture made by major manufacturers based on designs by internationally recognized furniture designers. Name counts heavily, even in mass–produced furniture.

Style Chronology:

Craft Revival 1900–1940
Colonial Revival (High Style and Generic) 1915–1940
International 1920s
Art Deco 1925–1935
Streamlined Modern 1930s/early 1940s
Contemporary/Post–War Modernism . . . .late 1940s/early 1960s
Early American 1950s–1960s
Neo–Modernism and Pop 1960s
Craft Revival 1970s–present
Colonial Revival 1970s–present
Memphis 1980s

References: *American Manufactured Furniture, Furniture Dealers' Reference Book*, reprint by Schiffer Publishing, 1988, 1996 value update; Richard and Eileen Dubrow, *Styles of American Furniture: 1860-1960*, Schiffer Publishing, 1997; *Fine Furniture Reproductions: 18th–Century Revivals of the 1930s and 1940s From Baker Furniture*, Schiffer Publishing, 1996; Oscar Fitzgerald, *Four Centuries of American Furniture*, Wallace–Homestead, Krause Publications, 1995; Philippe Garner, *Twentieth–Century Furniture*, Van Nostrand Reinhold, 1980, out of print; Cara Greenberg, *Mid–Century Modern: Furniture of the 1950s*, Crown Publishers, 1995; *The Herman Miller Collection: The 1955/1956 Catalog*, Schiffer Publishing, 1998 reprint; *Indiana Cabinets With Prices*, L–W Book Sales, 1997; Emyl Jenkin, *Emyl Jenkin's Reproduction Furniture: Antiques for the Next Generation*, Crown Publishers, 1995; David P. Lindquist and Caroline C. Warren, *Colonial Revival Furniture With Prices*, Wallace–Homestead, Krause Publications, 1993; Karl Mang, *History of Modern Furniture, Translation*, Harry N. Abrams, 1979, out of print.

Leslie Piña, *Classic Herman Miller*, Schiffer Publishing, 1998; Leslie Piña, *Fifties Furniture*, Schiffer Publishing, 1996; *Popular Furniture of the 1920s and 1930s*, Schiffer Publishing, 1998; Harry L. Rinker, *Warman's Furniture*, Wallace–Homestead, 1993, out of print; Steve Rouland and Roger W. Rouland, *Heywood–Wakefield Modern Furniture*, Collector Books, 1995, 1997 value update; Klaus–Jurgen Sembach, *Modern Furniture Designs: 1950–1980s*, Schiffer Publishing, 1997; Penny Sparke, *Furniture: Twentieth–Century Design*, E. P. Dutton, 1986, out of print; Robert W. and Harriett Swedberg, *Collector's Encyclopedia of American Furniture, Vol. 2*, Collector Books, 1992, 1996 value update; Robert W. and Harriett Swedberg, *Collector's Encyclopedia of American Furniture, Vol. 2*, Collector Books, 1992, 1996 value update; Robert W. and Harriett Swedberg, *Furniture of the Depression Era*, Collector Books, 1987, 1996 value update.

Art Deco, Airline desk, Fletcher Aviation Co, Pasadena, triangular walnut top and conforming case with 6 drawers, recessed metal base, label, refinished, c1940, 72" w, 46" d, 29" h **$2,300.00**
Art Deco, armchair, attributed to Donald Deskey, U–shaped form, walnut trim, green velvet reupholstery, 33" w, 32" d, 26" h **525.00**
Art Deco, armchair, Belgium, oak frame, reupholstered seat, back, and sides in red leatherette with brass studs, 30" w, 30" d, 36" h **750.00**
Art Deco, armchair, custom made, stainless steel frame with shaped arms ending in rolled hand–holds, similarly rolled feet, red fabric upholstered back and seat, c1933, 20" w, 24" d, 41" h **1,800.00**

Art Deco, vanity and stool, attributed to Norman Bel Geddes, yellow enameled metal and chrome, glass shelf, 49 x 30¼ x 17", $770.00. Photo courtesy David Rago Auctions.

Art Deco, chest of drawers, Baker Furniture Co, Kem Weber designer, light maple, 5 drawers with concave handles in orig blue lacquer, vertical metal trim, c1930s, 44" w, 20" d, 44" h...................**3,250.00**

Art Deco, china cabinet, attributed to Donald Deskey, walnut and black lacquer, aluminum trimmed pulls, 2 doors, green lacquered int with 2 shelves, high stretcher base with sq legs and U–shaped stretchers, 38" w, 16" d, 57" h.........................**825.00**

Art Deco, coffee table, veneer cube on black plinth base, overhanging plate glass top, refinished, 36" sq, 19" h..**550.00**

Art Deco, dining table, Hastings, Walter Dorwin Teague designer, rect top with lift sides in bookmatched figured walnut veneer, black lacquer and faux painted wood base with aluminum supports, unmkd, 1930s, 54" w, 28" d, 30' h........................**250.00**

Art Deco, display cabinet, rosewood veneer, illuminated chartreuse lacquered int, top door with 3 octagonal beveled glass windows above fluted base with 1 door, 25" w, 14" d, 72" h, price for pair.................**3,000.00**

Art Deco, end table, 2–tier construction, shaped walnut top and base shelf, chrome U–shaped support and lamp arm, refinished, 20" w, 14" d, 43" h............**110.00**

Art Deco, serving cart, cube form, chrome plated steel frame, sliding glass doors and sides, 30" w, 17" d, 30" h...**1,000.00**

Art Deco, side table, in the style of Ruhlmann, single drawer cabinet, bird's–eye maple veneer with marquetry banding and ivory–like inlay on fluted legs, Bakelite feet and drawer pull, unmkd, 15" w, 16" d, 29" h...**350.00**

Art Deco, vanity, Herman Miller, Gilbert Rohde designer, 2–toned veneer with zigzag design, asymmetrical case with 2 drawers and 2 doors, brushed chrome handles, 1933 World's Fair label, refinished, 50" w, 16" d, 22" h.....................................**650.00**

Colonial Revival, Pre–War, armchair, Chippendale style, Martha Washington, mahogany frame, worn finish, gold striped upholstery, 38" h....................**250.00**

Colonial Revival, Pre–War, bed, Regency style, inlaid rosewood upholstered headboard, conforming footboard, shaped framework, brass inlay and mounts, double mattress size, 56" h.....................**500.00**

Colonial Revival, Pre–War, bedroom suite, generic, 5 pcs, bed, dresser, dressing table, bench, and poster bed, bed with burl walnut veneered headboard, oak broken arch pediment, center urn finial, burl walnut and oak panel on footboard, dresser with plain cut walnut veneer top and sides, 2 outside shaped mirrors flank center arched and engraved mirror, arched and diamond molding on drawer fronts, dressing table with plain cut walnut veneer on top and sides, mirror shaped like dresser but larger in size, bench with turned and scrolled hardwoods, velvet upholstered sides and seat................................**1,500.00**

Colonial Revival, Pre–War, cabinet, generic, figured walnut veneer panels and drawer front, solid walnut back rail, 3 curly maple overlay shield designs, selected hardwood frame, bulbous turned front legs, H–stretcher base, 1920s, 38 x 14 x 65"..............**300.00**

Colonial Revival, Pre–War, card table, Hepplewhite style, mahogany, inlaid, D–shaped top, drop leaves, minor wear, 19" w, opens to 38" w, 38" d, 31" h........**500.00**

Colonial Revival, stand, shaped gallery, base drawer, c1925, $165.00. Photo courtesy Jackson's Auctioneers & Appraisers.

Colonial Revival, Pre–War, chest of drawers, Hepplewhite style, solid mahogany, inlay on drawers and back rail, 2 small drawers over 2 long drawers, eagle brasses, 1920s, 42 x 19 x 38"................**500.00**

Colonial Revival, Pre–War, chifferobe, generic, burl walnut, burl mahogany, bird's–eye maple, and Macassar striped ebony veneers, shaped scalloped pediment over 2 shaped doors over 2 drawers, molded cornice, int with 3 small drawers over 3 long drawers, ring turned bulbous feet, 59" h......................**300.00**

Colonial Revival, Pre–War, china cabinet, Chippendale style, walnut veneer breakfront, scrolled broken pediment, center urn finial, pair of glazed doors and panels, long drawer over 2 cupboard doors, 44 x 15 x 76"...**850.00**

Colonial Revival, Pre–War, china cabinet, generic, bird's–eye maple and zebrawood veneers, marquetry on front of drawer and cabinet, oval crest with inlay and scrolled foliate motif, double arched doors with mullions, shelved int, lower drawers, shaped pediment with carved center urn finials.................**450.00**

Colonial Revival, Pre–War, desk, Chippendale style, block front, solid walnut case, walnut veneered slant front lid, fitted int, paw feet, 32 x 18 x 42"............**750.00**

Colonial Revival, Pre–War, desk, Governor Winthrop style, mahogany veneer, solid mahogany slant front, fitted int with 2 document drawers, shell– carved center door, serpentine front, 4 long drawers, brass pulls and escutcheons, 1920s.........................**600.00**

Colonial Revival, Pre–War, desk, Jacobean style, carved oak, 9 dovetailed drawers, applied foliage scrolls and lion heads, pullout writing surface, worn blue felt covering, rope carved legs, old soft legs, 51 x 28½ x 40¾"...**750.00**

Colonial Revival, Pre–War, desk, Spinet style, solid mahogany, hinged front, fitted int with drawers and pigeonholes, cylindrical reeded legs, 33 x 21 x 39".......**450.00**

Colonial Revival, Pre–War, dining chairs, generic, set of 6, mahogany, Cupid's bow crest, pierced splat, slip seat, cabriole legs joined by box stretcher............**750.00**

Colonial Revival, Pre–War, dining table, Queen Anne style, mahogany, console table shape, pullout frame, 2 shaped leaves, worn finish, 66" l extended, 39 x 30½"...**750.00**

Colonial Revival, Pre–War, drop leaf table, Charak, Tommi Parzinger designer, Hepplewhite style, mahogany with inlaid design of concentric squares in birch, refinished, label, closed size 20" w, 36" d, 29" h, open size 66" w, 36" d **1,500.00**

Colonial Revival, Pre–War, night stand, generic, walnut veneer, drawer over blind cupboard door, applied beaded molding around drawer, reeded trumpet legs, 5" sq top **75.00**

Colonial Revival, Pre–War, Pembroke table, Hepplewhite style, Grand Rapids, plain cut mahogany veneer top and drop leaves, figured mahogany drawer front, solid base, medallion inlay, sq tapering legs, 17 x 15 x 22" **300.00**

Colonial Revival, Pre–War, rocker, Windsor style, Colonial Furniture Co, Grand Rapids, MI, comb back, birch, mahogany finish, turned legs, 21 x 17 x 27½" h from seat to top of back **250.00**

Colonial Revival, Pre–War, secretary/bookcase, Governor Winthrop, bookcase with broken pediment, center urn finial, molded cornice, pair of glazed doors, shelved and fitted int with slant front, 3 graduated drawers, oval brasses, ball and claw feet, 33" w, 80" h **1,000.00**

Colonial Revival, Pre–War, secretary/bookcase, Sheraton style, Luce Furniture, Grand Rapids, MI, veneered, broken pediment with fretwork, urn finial, pair of glazed arched mullioned doors, slant front with fitted int, frieze of 2 drawers over 2 long drawers, tapered sq legs and feet **650.00**

Colonial Revival, Pre–War, settee, William and Mary style, loose cushions, turned baluster legs and stretcher, 48" l **800.00**

Colonial Revival, Pre–War, sewing stand, generic, Priscilla type, painted red, dark trim, floral decal, turned rod–type handle, 13 x 11 x 25" **85.00**

Colonial Revival, Pre–War, sewing stand, Martha Washington style, solid mahogany, 3 drawers, shaped ends, ring–turned legs, 28 x 14 x 29" **350.00**

Colonial Revival, Pre–War, sideboard, Chippendale style, mahogany, central bow front of 2 drawer frieze over 2 deep drawers, flanked by wine drawer, central section flanked by drawers over curved cupboard, whole raised on cabriole legs ending in ball and claw feet, 46 x 18 x 40½" **1,500.00**

Colonial Revival, Pre–War, sideboard, Federal style, Landstrom Furniture Co, mahogany, serpentine front, molded top edge, 2 drawers flanked by doors, sq tapering legs, 116 x 22 x 37" **750.00**

Colonial Revival, Pre–War, side chair, Queen Anne style, walnut veneer, vase splat, slip upholstered seat, modified cabriole legs, 1920s **125.00**

Colonial Revival, Pre–War, side chair, Queen Anne style, walnut veneer slat, walnut stained hardwood frame, pressed cane seat, French legs, 1920s, 27" h **85.00**

Colonial Revival, Pre–War, smoking stand, generic, straight cut walnut veneer, rect top, figured walnut veneered door, painted William and Mary style base, 18 x 11 x 30" **150.00**

Colonial Revival, Pre–War, table, Duncan Phyfe style, drop leaf, mahogany stained and veneered, 16" l D–shaped leaves, brass casters on outswept reeded legs, 41 x 24 x 30" **350.00**

Colonial Revival, Pre–War, vanity, generic, walnut, Chippendale–style swing mirror, reeded mirror supports, mahogany veneered front, central drawer flanked by sections with small drawer over blind cupboard door, reeded trumpet feet, casters, 48" w, 20" d **250.00**

Colonial Revival, Pre–War, wing chair, Queen Anne style, Kittinger, Williamsburg reproduction, pink striped silk upholstery, 49" h **2,500.00**

Contemporary, armchair, Herman Miller, George Nelson designer, swag leg, white fiberglass seat and back, black enameled metal base with 4 legs, label, 29" w, 19" d, 31" h **750.00**

Contemporary, armchair, Widdicomb, T H Robsjohn–Gibbings, walnut, black wool upholstery, arched crest and legs, 27" w, 29" d, 33" h, price for pair **925.00**

Contemporary, Barcelona chairs, pr, Knoll, Ludwig Mies van der Rohe designer, stainless steel frame, tufted dark brown leather cushions, 30" w, 30" d, 30" h **2,500.00**

Contemporary, bedroom suite, Heywood–Wakefield, Riviera, 4–drawer chest with hanging mirror, 2 end tables, 2 twin bed headboards, champagne finish, branded mark, 50" w chest **950.00**

Contemporary, bench, attributed to Edward Wormley, slatted walnut top, molded walnut plywood legs, unmkd, 59" l, 19" d, 13" h **275.00**

Contemporary, bench, Knoll, Florence Knoll designer, tufted green leather seat, chrome frame, 62" w, 18" d, 17" h **700.00**

Contemporary, bench, Knoll, Harry Bertoia designer, walnut slatted top, wrought–iron Y–form legs, label, 72" w, 18½" d, 15" h **750.00**

Contemporary, Bird chair and ottoman, Knoll, Harry Bertoia designer, vivid blue wool fabric cover on black wire grid frame with flexible rubber shock–mounts, label, 39" w, 34" d, 39" h chair, 24" w, 17" d, 17" h ottoman **1,000.00**

Contemporary, "C" chair, Artek, Alvar Aalto designer, wide molded wood arms in natural walnut, seat and back reupholstered in textured white fabric, c1950s, 30" w, 31" d, 27" h **2,500.00**

Contemporary, student desk, Conant Ball, Russel Wright designer, single pedestal, 3 drawers, recent finish, 29½ x 40 x 22½", **$192.50.** Photo courtesy David Rago Auctions.

Contemporary, LCM chair, Herman Miller, Charles Eames designer, molded birch plywood seat and back, chrome frame, 22" w, 24" d, 27" h **450.00**

Contemporary, chest of drawers, James Mont designer, rect, plinth base, 3 drawers, green lacquer with sand-blasted and pickled oak front, c1946, 46" w, 20" d, 34" h **3,200.00**

Contemporary, coffee table, Johnson Furniture Co, Paul Frankl, rect cork top in cream lacquer, dark mahogany Greek key shaped base, top refinished, 1940s, 84" w, 21" d, 12" h **1,500.00**

Contemporary, credenza, George Nelson designer, wal-nut veneered cabinet with doors and drawers, steel chrome legs, 80" w, 18" d, 27" h **275.00**

Contemporary, desk, Herman Miller, George Nelson designer, rect, chrome frame, walnut formica top with raised letter rack, 2–drawer pedestal, label, 54" w, 30" d, 40" h **1,200.00**

Contemporary, desk, Singer & Sons, Geo Ponti designer, rect walnut top on 4 sq tapering legs with brass caps, suspended medial section with 4 drawers and bookshelf in back, refinished, 51" w, 26" d, 29" h. **4,000.00**

Contemporary, dinette table, Knoll, Isamu Noguchi designer, circular black laminated top, chrome wire struts, plastic coated metal base, label, 36" d, 29" h **1,200.00**

Contemporary, dining chairs, pr, Nathan Lerner design-er, plywood construction, plaid fabric upholstery, Chicago Bauhouse design, c1940, 16" w, 19" d, 30" h . . . **500.00**

Contemporary, dining chairs, set of 6, Dunbar, Edward Wormley designer, 2 armchairs and 4 side chairs, dark mahogany frames, caned back and arm supports, seats reupholstered in off–white patterned fabric, 25" w, 18" d, 33" h **650.00**

Contemporary, dining chairs, set of 6, Plycraft, Norman Cherner designer, 2 armchairs, 4 side chairs, molded walnut plywood, label, 25" w, 22" d, 31" h armchair, 17" w, 22" d, 31" h side chair **3,200.00**

Contemporary, dining table, Dunbar, Edward Wormley designer, rect maple veneer top set in bleached mahogany frame, sq legs with carved feet, 2 leaves, 66" w, 44" d, 29" h **285.00**

Contemporary, dining table, Herman Miller, Charles Eames designer, rect white laminated plywood top, folding chrome legs, 54" w, 34" d, 29" h **650.00**

Contemporary, Popsicle Stick dining table, Knoll, Hans Belman designer, circular birch top, black ebonized wood tripod base, refinished, c1952, 48" d, 28" h **2,200.00**

Contemporary, dining table, Widdicomb, R H Robsjohn–Gibbings designer, circular patterned wal-nut veneer top, dowel legs with U–shaped stretchers and 2 leaves, refinished, 48" d, 29" h. **1,750.00**

Contemporary, Eiffel Tower chairs, Herman Miller, Charles Eames designer, fiberglass shell, blue fabric upholstery, zinc struts, white plastic feet, mkd, 25" w, 18" d, 31" h, price for set of 6 . . . . **825.00**

Contemporary, folding screen, Herman Miller, Charles Eames designer, 6 molded ash plywood sections, can-vas hinges, 72" w, 68" h **3,000.00**

Contemporary, Grasshopper chair, Knoll, Eero Saarinen designer, 1–pc construction, bentwood frame, seat and back reupholstered in black wool, 27" w, 32" d, 34" h, refinished **925.00**

Contemporary, magazine stand, Dunbar, Edward Wormley designer, ebonized wood, 5 shelves, increasing in size from top to base, trestle feet, label, 28" w, 15" d, 24" h **1,500.00**

Contemporary, occasional table, Johnson Furniture Co, Paul T Frankl designer, 2 tier, rect, cork top, dark mahogany Greek key base, 36" w, 33" d, 24" h **350.00**

Contemporary, Planner Group cabinet, Paul McCobb, light maple, 3 drawers, stainless steel ring pulls, splayed dowel legs, 36" w, 18" d, 33" h **450.00**

Contemporary, serving cart, Calvin, Paul McCobb designer, rect terrazzo top, brass frame with 2 doors and shelves in bleached mahogany, label, 36" w, 19" d, 29" h. **825.00**

Contemporary, settee, Knoll, Warren Platner designer, wire frame, wrap–around upholstered seat and back in charcoal wool, 68" w, 29" d, 32" h **1,320.00**

Contemporary, shelving unit, Herman Miller, Charles Eames designer, ESU 400, primary color masonite panels in zinc angle iron frame with white fiberglass sliding doors and black laminated drawers, c1952, 47" w, 17" d, 58" h **13,000.00**

Contemporary, sideboard, Thaden/Jordan, 2 doors and drawer cabinet in birch plywood construction, mold-ed birch legs, 49" w, 18" d, 55" h **225.00**

Contemporary, sofa, Dunbar, Edward Wormley designer, dark mahogany frame, tufted seat and back, reuphol-stered in black and white pattern fabric, 39" w, 28" d, 28" h **1,200.00**

Contemporary, stool, Calvin, Paul McCobb designer, sq white vinyl cushion, brass base with 4 legs and X–form stretcher, 20" sq top, 16" h, price for pair **450.00**

Contemporary, Surfboard table, Herman Miller, Charles Eames designer, elliptical laminated plywood top, black wire cage base, top relaminated, base repaint-ed, label, 89" w, 30" d, 12" h **1,500.00**

Contemporary, tub chair, Heywood–Wakefield, sculp-tural form, reupholstered turquoise wool fabric, blond wood frame, 20" w, 30" d, 30" h **150.00**

Craftsman, loveseat and ottoman, George Nakashima designer, walnut, flaring dowel legs, 1960s, 51" w loveseat, 24" sq ottoman, $3,300.00. Photo courtesy David Rago Auctions.

Contemporary, vanity and stool, Herman Miller, George Nelson designer, leather wrapped cabinet with attached mirror and central lighted surface flanked by 2 lift–top compartments, birch legs, stool with cream upholstered seat and splayed birch legs, 48" w, 20" d, 57" h vanity, 22" w, 16" d, 17" h stool. 700.00

Craftsman, Conoid storage unit, George Nakashima, natural edge black wanut plank top over 2 sliding doors with vertical spindles against stretched linen, 4 inside drawers, c1970, 80" w, 17½" d, 29½" h 950.00

Early American, commode (table), solid maple, autumn brown finish, rect top, single drawer, false front with 2 drawers over 2 drawers, shaped skirt, slightly splayed baluster turned legs, 26 x 21 x 23". 40.00

Early American, rocker, Beacon Hill, maple frame, finished in Salem (light maple), removable cushions padded with cotton liners, mint green oval motif cotton print cover, ruffled skirt, 25 x 24 x 34" 65.00

Early American, sofa, Chippendale style, Harmony House, upholstered in medium gold tweed fabric, 2 back Serofoam plastic foam cushions with shaped tops, 2 reversible cushions on seat, padded arms and wing sides, pleated shirt, 85 x 37 x 36" 100.00

International Modern, china cabinet, Herman Miller, Gilbert Rohde designer, mahogany, glass sides and sliding doors above 2 doors in maidou burl veneer, rosewood plinth base, brushed chrome pulls, 34" w, 15" d, 58" h 2,500.00

International Modern, Laverne International, Erwin & Estelle Laverne designers, rect chrome steel frame, woven tan leather seat, 49" w, 21" d, 14" h 1,000.00

Memphis, dining table, circular top with abstract design, attached shelving on chrome and metal legs 1,250.00

Neo–Modern, Easy Edges chaise lounge and ottoman, Frank Gehry designer, corrugated cardboard and masonite construction, freeform design, 24" w, 40" d, 30" h chair, 18" w, 30" d, 15" h ottoman 9,250.00

International Modern, chest of drawers, Herman Miller, Gilbert Rohde, bird's eye maple and mahogany, Bakelite pulls, c1938, 36 x 43 x 18", price for asymmetrical pair, $5,610.00. Photo courtesy David Rago Auctions.

Neo–Modern, Tongue chairs, Artifort, Pierre Paulin designer, curved and undulating sculptured form, psychedelic fabric cover, c1967, 25 x 33 x 35", price each, $1,100.00. Photo courtesy David Rago Auctions.

Neo–Modern, Marilyn sofa, Gufram, Studio 65 designer, distributed by Stendig, lips form, red nylon stretch fabric, label, c1970, 84" w, 32" d, 32" h. 1,875.00

Neo–Modern, Terraza sofa, Ubald Klaug designer, distributed by Stendig, 2–pc sculptural form, black leather, label, c1960s, 60" w, 36" d, 27" h sections 4,500.00

1950s, chest of drawers, generic, box–like appearance, 5 identical drawers, valance skirt, block leg, 18 x 17 x 44". 85.00

1950s, desk and chair, generic, ranch style, oak, rect top, 3 dovetailed drawers to left, drawer beneath writing surface, block and ring legs to right, ox yoke hardware, chair with bowed back slats, plank seat, turned splayed front legs, double stretchers on sides, single stretchers in front, 44 x 16 x 32". 100.00

1950s, dining cart, Yugoslavia, removable serving tray with legs over single shelf within collapsible frame on wheels, 36" w, 20" d, 32" h 175.00

1950s, end table, generic, stepped, walnut finished hardwood frame and legs, rect top, splayed round tapered legs, stepped–back shelf raised on 2 spindles on each end, 16 x 24 x 21" 50.00

1950s, lounge chairs, pr, upholstered form with floating back on wood U–shaped legs, 33" w, 26" d, 25" h, needs reupholstering 875.00

1950s, sofa, generic, Harmony House (Sears), rectilinear form, hardwood frame, walnut finished legs, orange plastic cover, spring seat base, cotton felt padded button back, welt trim, 68 x 27 x 30" 150.00

1950s, telephone stand, generic, wrought metal, 2 wire grill shelves, pinched paper clip–style side supports, bronze lacquer finish, 12½ x 12 x 17" 15.00

1960s, dinette set, generic, table and 6 chairs, table with 2 leaves and high pressure plastic top in wood–grain pattern, tapered black antique finished frame and legs, pillow back chairs with vinyl plastic covers in abstract tree motif on block grid ground 150.00

1960s, dinette table, ebonized wood popsicle stick shaped base, circular glass top, 48" d, 29" h 775.00

1960s, dining table, generic, high pressure plastic top in wood–grain pattern, bronze plated metal tapered block legs, 2 leaves, 42 x 84". 150.00

1950s, "pouf" ottomans, graduated sizes, color panels joined with piped seams, largest ottoman is 19" d, 15" h, price for all 3, $402.50. Photo courtesy David Rago Auctions.

1960s, stereo chair and ottoman, white fiberglass, egg shaped chair with black and white wool fabric int and loose black vinyl cushion, matching fiberglass footstool with black vinyl cushion, 36" w, 30" d, 50" h chair, 19" w, 16" d, 11" h footstool **750.00**

Scandinavian, dining chairs, Finsven, Sweden, Alvar Aalto designer, stacking design, birch plywood seat and back on birch frame, stamped, c1940s, 19" w, 19" d, 31" h, price for set of 6 .... **1,750.00**

Scandinavian, dining armchairs, Johannes Hansen, Hans Wegner designer, teak, brown and blue woven fabric seat cushions, branded mark, 25" w, 19½" d, 30" h, price for set of 6 .... **2,500.00**

Scandinavian, dining table, Artek, Alvar Aalto designer, rect mahogany plywood top, molded birch legs, 2 leaves, 51" w, 36" d, 29" h **1,100.00**

Scandinavian, Safari sling chair, Rod Rasmusen, tilting back, ash frame, strap leather armrests, brown sling leather seat, paper label, 22½" w, 23" d, 32" h **375.00**

Streamlined Modern, armchair, Russel Wright designer, bent maple frame, fabric upholstered seat and back cushions, refinished, 27" w, 34" d, 30" h **850.00**

Streamlined Modern, breakfront, Heritage Henredon, Frank Lloyd Wright designer, mahogany, upper section with 8 open shelves flanking cabinet door with 4 glass panels, base with 10 drawers in varying sizes with recessed handles, Taliesin design to edges, script signature, 65" w, 20" d, 83" h **2,750.00**

Streamlined Modern, coffee table, Quigley & Co, Samuel Marx designer, arched form, covered in patterned parchment, c1941, 24" w, 16" d, 16" h **8,250.00**

Streamlined Modern, end table, Herman Miller, Gilbert Rohde designer, amoeba shaped ¾" glass top, 3 cylindrical lucite legs with brass caps, 29" w, 18" d, 18" h, price for pair **2,500.00**

Streamlined Modern, Morris chair, H Wakefield, Gilbert Rohde designer, walnut, adjustable back, drop–in seat cushion, 1930s, 27" w, 34" d, 28" h **300.00**

Streamlined Modern, sling sofa, Troy Sunshade, Gilbert Rohde designer, tubular and flat band chrome construction, rocking seat, channeled back, needs reupholstering, 1930s, 48" w, 39" d, 31" h **7,000.00**

AUCTION PRICES

Modern furniture sold by Treadway Gallery, Inc., on November 23, 1997. Prices include a 10% buyer's premium.

Contemporary, bedroom suite, Herman Miller, Gilbert Rohde designer, 2 chests, 2 night stands, and double bed with headboard and footboard, no rails, black lacquer and walnut finish, refinished, label, very good condition, 48" w, 19" d, 33" h chests, 15" w, 11" d, 26" h night stands, 46" w, 33" h headboard **$715.00**

Contemporary, credenza, George Nelson designer, walnut veneered cabinet with doors and drawers on steel chrome legs, fair condition, 80" w, 18" d, 27" h **275.00**

Contemporary, ottoman, Dunbar, Edward Wormley designer, circular form in orig orange fabric, label, excellent condition, 24" d, 16" h **319.00**

Contemporary, rocker, Herman Miller, Charles Eames designer, vivid blue fiberglass shell on zinc struts, birch runners, mkd, excellent condition, 25" w, 27" d, 27" h..................... **715.00**

Contemporary, stacking stools, Artek, Alvar Aalto designer, circular laminated birch top on molded birch legs, 1 with red top, good condition, 16" d, 17" h, price for set of 3 .... **467.50**

Scandinavian, dining set, table and 4 side chairs, Finn Juhl, mfg by Bovirke, 1953, rect rosewood top with 2 pop–up leaves on oval teak legs, chairs with sculptured back and seat in rosewood on teak frame, stamp mark, very good condition, 59" w, 35" d, 29" h table, 20" w, 21" d, 29" h chair................................... **1,870.00**

Streamlined Modern, bed, Heritage Henredon, Frank Lloyd Wright designer, upholstered back in orig blue satin fabric set in mahogany frame with Taliesin design to border, orig finish, unsgd, excellent condition, twin size, 40" w, 38" h, price for pair **110.00**

Scandinavian, rope lounge chair, Getama, Hans Wegner designer, enameled steel frame, strung with flag line, attached pillow headrest, unmkd, 1949, 41" w, 48" d, 31½" h, $4,730.00. Photo courtesy David Rago Auctions.

GAMBLING COLLECTIBLES

Gambling collectibles divide into two basic groups, those associated with gambling casinos and saloons and gaming materials designed for private "back room" use. Casino material further subdivides into actual material and equipment used on the gambling floors and advertising giveaways and premiums.

Gambling supply houses located throughout the country sold gambling paraphernalia to casinos, saloons, and private individuals through catalogs. Many of the items were "gaffed," meaning fixed in favor of the owner. Obviously, the general public was not meant to see these catalogs.

Gaming tables and punchboards dominated the 1980s collecting market. Gambling chips are today's hot collectible.

Reference: Leonard Schneir, *Gambling Collectibles: A Sure Winner*, Schiffer Publishing, 1994.

Collectors' Club: Casino Chips & Gaming Tokens Collectors Club, PO Box 63, Brick, NJ 08723.

Note: See Punchboards and Slot Machines for additional listings.

Arcade Game, 1¢ Draw, counter top type, 5 play, orig
   graphics, wood and metal case, c1930, 10 x 15 x 6".... **$400.00**
Ashtray, Carl Giudici's Mint Casino, Sparks, Nevada,
   glass, clear, 3⅝"................................. 3.00
Ashtray, MGM Grand Hotel, glass, clear, red center with
   lion illus, 4½" d 8.00
Ashtray, Riverboat Casino, Reno, Nevada, glass, clear,
   square, 3⅝"....................................... 2.00
Ashtray, Sands Hotel, smoked glass, brown name and
   hotel picture, yellow center, "Las Vegas, NV," 4" d 6.50
Bottle, figural slot machine, Barney's, red, 9 x 9" 15.00
Cheating Device, weighted dice, always total 12, set
   of 3 .... 35.00
Dice, celluloid, red, white spots, round corners, set of 5,
   1", MIB 50.00
Game, Casino Electronic Pinball, Marx, skill and action
   game, includes instant total Score–O–Meter, 1971 .... 30.00

Gaming Token, aluminum, Dunes Oasis, Las Vegas, free slot play, 4½" d, $2.00.

Gaming Token, 1967 Sterling $5 .... 12.00
Gaming Token, Proofs 1965–69 .... 15.00
Pharo Dealing Box, metal, cutout top reveals corner
   index, c1920.................................... **450.00**
Pocket Watch, Crown and Anchor, pointer lands on
   crown, anchor, or suit sign, painted metal dial, c1920.... **225.00**
Poker Chip Box, wood, rect, woodburned dec, banner
   inscribed "Good Luck" above horse head framed by
   horseshoe and cards, fitted int, 1920, 7 x 10 x 2" 30.00
Poker Chips, inlaid, 4 crosses **4.00**
Punchboard, The National Game, c1920, 4½ x 6" 40.00

GAMES

This category deals primarily with boxed board games. The board game achieved widespread popularity in the period from 1890 to 1910. After modest sales in the 1920s, board games increased in popularity in the 1930s and experienced a second golden age from the late 1940s through the mid–1960s. Television and movie licensing played a major role in board game development. As a result, crossover collectors frequently skew market values.

Generic board games such as Monopoly have little value except for the earliest editions. The same holds true for games geared to children aged 4 to 8, e.g., Candyland, Go to the Head of the Class, etc. Generic board games dominate toy store shelves in the 1990s. Disney and a few mega–movie licensed games are the exceptions.

References: Mark Cooper, *Baseball Games: Home Versions of the National Pastime 1860s–1960s*, Schiffer Publishing, 1995; L–W Book Sales, *Board Games of the 50's, 60's, and 70's With Prices*, L–W Book Sales, 1994; Rick Polizzi, *Baby Boomer Games*, Collector Books, 1995; Harry L. Rinker, *Antique Trader's Guide to Games & Puzzles*, Antique Trader Books, 1997; Desi Scarpone, *Board Games*, Schiffer Publishing, 1995; Bruce Whitehill, *Games: American Boxed Games and Their Makers, 1822–1922, With Values*, Wallace–Homestead, Krause Publications, 1992.

Periodicals: *Toy Shop*, 700 E State St, Iola, WI 54990; *Toy Trader*, PO Box 1050, Dubuque, IA 52004.

Collectors' Clubs: American Game Collectors Assoc, 49 Brooks Ave, Lewiston, ME 04240; Gamers Alliance, PO Box 197, East Meadow, NY 11554.

Note: Unless noted otherwise, prices listed are for complete games in mint condition.

A–Team, Parker Brothers, 1984 .... **$12.00**
Acquire, 3M, 1968 .... 15.00
Addiction, Createk, 1968 .... 5.00
Aero–Chute Target Game, American Toy Works, c1930s 65.00
Alee–Oop, Royal Toy, 1937 .... 20.00
Arrest and Trial, Transogram, 1963.................... 35.00
Assembly Line, The Game of, Selchow & Righter, 1960s 30.00
Auto Bridge, Auto Bridge Co, 1948 .... 10.00
Bamboozle, Milton Bradley, 1962 .... 35.00
Bandersnatch, Mattel, 1968........................ 15.00
Battleship, Milton Bradley, 1967 .... 40.00
Beat the Clock Game, Lowell, 1954................... 60.00
Big Town, Milton Bradley, 1962...................... 35.00
Captain Kidd Junior, Parker Brothers, 1926 .... 75.00
Chess Checkers Backgammon Acey–Deucy, Transogram,
   1960.. 10.00

Gettysburg, Avalon Hill, 1958, $25.00.

Clue, John Waddington Ltd, 1949 . . . . **50.00**
Dating Game, The, Hasbro, 1967. . . . . **20.00**
Dig, Parker Brothers, ©1940 . . . . **35.00**
Eddie Cantor's Automobile Game "Tell It to the Judge,"
    Parker Brothers, 1930s. **30.00**
Egg Race Game, Ideal, 1968 . . . . **18.00**
Exciting New Game of the Kennedy's, Transco, 1962 . . . . . . **60.00**
Farmer Electric Maps, J M Farmer, ©1938. . . . . **45.00**
Feeley Meeley, Milton Bradley, 1967 . . . . **15.00**
Finance, Parker Brothers, 1956 . . . . **10.00**
Five Spot, Bradley's, Milton Bradley, 1931 . . . . **15.00**
Giant Barrel of Monkeys, Lakeside, 1969. . . . . **15.00**
Go Back, Milton Bradley, 1967 . . . . **12.00**
Hickety Pickety, Parker Brothers, 1924 . . . . **40.00**
Holly Hobbie Wishing Well Game, Parker Brothers,
    1976. . . . . **12.00**
Image, 3M, 1972 . . . . **10.00**
India Bombay, Cutler & Saleeby, #4023, c1920 . . . . **30.00**
Intercept, Lakeside, 1978. . . . . **15.00**
Jack and Jill Jacks Game, Hasbro, 1966 . . . . **15.00**
Jeopardy, Milton Bradly, 1st ed, 1964. . . . . **12.00**
Jig Race, Game Makers, 1940s **30.00**
Jollytime Dominoes, Milton Bradley, 1955 . . . . **12.00**
Jumping D J Surprise Action Game, Mattel, 1962 . . . . **35.00**
King of the Hill, Schaper, 1964 . . . . **15.00**
Komissar, Selchow & Righter, 1966 . . . . **25.00**
Krull, Parker Brothers, 1983. **10.00**
Leaping Lena, Parker Brothers, 1920s. **95.00**
Let's Make a Deal, Milton Bradley, 1964 . . . . **35.00**
Life, The Game of, Milton Bradley, 1960s. **12.00**
Little Boy Blue, Cadaco–Ellis, 1955 . . . . **15.00**
Mad Magazine Card Game, Parker Brothers, 1980 . . . . **10.00**
Magnetic Fish Pond, Milton Bradley, 1942 . . . . **10.00**
Man–Chu, US Playing Card Co, 1923 . . . . **20.00**
Marble Maze, Hasbro, 1966 . . . . **15.00**
Marline Perkins' Zoo Parade, Cadaco–Ellis, 1955 . . . . **25.00**
Monopoly, Charles Darrow, 1933–34, made prior to
    Parker Brothers purchasing rights to game from
    Darrow **3,000.00**
Monopoly, Parker Brothers, 1957 . . . . **15.00**

Monopoly, Parker Brothers, Deluxe Edition, 1960s–70s **15.00**
Monopoly, Parker Brothers, German Edition, 1992 . . . . **10.00**
Monopoly, Parker Brothers, Popular Edition, 1950 . . . . **20.00**
Monopoly Junior, Parker Brothers, 1990 . . . . **8.00**
Mouse Trap Game, Ideal, 1963 . . . . **35.00**
Movie Land Keeno, Wilder Mfg, ©1929 . . . . **95.00**
Mr Bug Goes to Town, Milton Bradley, #4310, 1955 . . . . . . **35.00**
Mumbly Peg, American Toy Airship Co, c1920s **20.00**
National Velvet Game, Transogram, 1961 . . . . **35.00**
NBC Peacock Game, Selchow & Righter, 1966–67 . . . . **25.00**
Northwest Passage!, Impact Communications, 1969 . . . . **22.00**
O J Simpson's See–Action Football Game, Kenner, 1974 . . . . **40.00**
Old Hogan's Goat, Whitman, #3938, ©1939 . . . . **20.00**
Ouija, William Fuld, 1920. . . . . **15.00**
Ouija, Parker Brothers, 1970s **10.00**
Parcheesi, Selchow & Righter, Popular Edition, 1946. . . . . . . **20.00**
Park & Shop, Milton Bradley, 1950s. **40.00**
Paul Wing's Spelling Bee, Milton Bradley, ©1938 . . . . **35.00**
Peeko, Watkins–Strathmore, 1964 . . . . **10.00**
Perfection, Lakeside, 1979. . . . . **10.00**
Peter Coddle's Trip to New York, Parker Brothers, Nickel
    Edition, c1920s **10.00**
Philco Vance, Parker Brothers, 1937. . . . . **65.00**
Pinhead, Remco, 1959 . . . . **25.00**
Pirate and Traveler, Milton Bradley, 1953 . . . . **25.00**
Pit, Parker Brothers, 1930s. **8.00**
Poor Jenny, The Game of, Alderman–Fairchild, ©1927 . . . . . **65.00**
Price Is Right, Lowell, 1958. . . . . **35.00**
Pro Draft, Parker Brothers, 1974. . . . . **20.00**
Puzzling Pyramid, Schaper, 1959. . . . . **15.00**
Quick Wit, Parker Brothers, 1938. . . . . **15.00**
Quiz Kids Own Game Box, Parker Brothers, ©1940 . . . . **20.00**
Radio Game, Milton Bradley, c1926 . . . . **75.00**
Raggedy Ann, Milton Bradley, 1954 . . . . **25.00**
Revlon's $64,000 Question Junior Quiz, Lowell, 1955 . . . . . . **25.00**
Ring My Nose, Milton Bradley, c1926–28 . . . . **45.00**
Ripcord, Lowell, 1962. . . . . **55.00**
Risk!, Parker Brothers, Original Edition, 1959 . . . . **20.00**
Rock 'Em Sock 'Em Robots, Marx, 1966. . . . . **125.00**
Romper Room Magic Teacher, Bar–Zim, 1960s. **20.00**
Rook, Parker Brothers, 1936 . . . . **8.00**
$ale of the Century, Milton Bradley, 1969 . . . . **15.00**

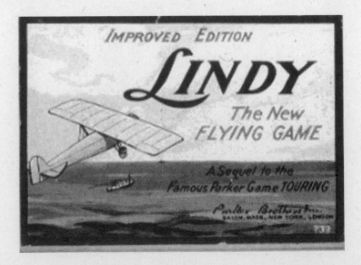

Lindy, Parker Brothers, card game, ©1927, $25.00.

Laverne and Shirley, Parker Brothers, 1977, $15.00.

Scoop, Waddington, British version, 1955 . . . . **30.00**
Seven–Up Game, Transogram, 1961. . . . . **15.00**
Skee Ball, Eldon, 1963 . . . . **30.00**
Skittle–Bowl, Aurora, 1969 . . . . **25.00**
Sorry!, Parker Brothers. **12.00**
Stratego, Milton Bradley, Original Edition, 1961 . . . . **20.00**
Three Men in a Tub, Milton Bradley, c1935–36. . . . . **35.00**
Tiddly Winks, Walt Disney's, Whitman, 1963 . . . . **10.00**
Touring, Parker Brothers, 1955. . . . . **5.00**
Treasure Island, Stoll & Edwards Co, 1923 . . . . **45.00**
Truth or Consequences, Gabriel, 1955. . . . . **30.00**
Tumble Bug, Schaper, 1950s **15.00**
Twister, Milton Bradley, 1966. . . . . **15.00**
Uncle Wiggily Game, Milton Bradley, 1954 . . . . **20.00**
United States Geographical Lotto, Statler Mfg, c1930s **20.00**
What's My Name?, Jay Mar Specialty, c1940 . . . . **35.00**
White Glove Girl, American Publishing Corp, 1966 . . . . **15.00**
Who?, Parker Brothers, 1951 . . . . **30.00**
Whodunit?, Cadaco–Ellis, 1959 . . . . **20.00**
Wizzer Wheel, Walt Disney's Official Mousketeer, Ideal,
    1964. . . . . **25.00**

GAS STATION COLLECTIBLES

Many of today's drivers no longer remember the independently owned full–service gas station where attendants pumped your gas, checked your oil, and cleaned your windshield. Fortunately, collectors do. Many are recreating golden age (1930s through the 1960s) versions of the independent gas station in their basements and garages.

While pump globes and oil cans remain the principal collecting focus, gasoline station advertising, uniforms, and paper ephemera have all become hot collecting subcategories in the 1990s. Road maps, especially those issued prior to the Interstate system, double in value every few years.

References: Scott Anderson, *Check the Oil*, Wallace Homestead, Krause Publications, 1986; Mark Anderton and Sherry Mullen, *Gas Station Collectibles*, Wallace–Homestead, Krause Publications, 1994; Robert W. D. Ball, *Texaco Collectibles*, Schiffer Publishing, 1994; Scott Benjamin and Wayne Henderson, *Gas Pump Globes: Collector's Guide to Over 3,000 American Gas Globes*, Motorbooks International, 1993; Scott Benjamin and Wayne Henderson, *Oil Company Signs: A Collector's Guide*, Motorbooks International, 1995; Scott Benjamin and Wayne Henderson, *Sinclair Collectibles*, Schiffer Publishing, 1997; Mike Bruner,

Gasoline Treasures, Schiffer Publishing, 1996; Todd P. Helms, *The Conoco Collector's Bible*, Schiffer Publishing, 1995; Rick Pease, *Filling Station Collectibles*, Schiffer Publishing, 1994; Rick Pease, *Service Station Collectibles*, Schiffer Publishing, 1996; B. J. Sommers and Wayne Priddy, *Value Guide to Gas Station Memorabilia*, Collector Books, 1995; Sonya Stenzler and Rick Pease, *Gas Station Collectibles*, Schiffer Publishing, 1993; Michael Karl Witzel, *Gas Station Memories*, Motorbooks International, 1994.

Periodical: *Mobilia*, PO Box 575, Middlebury, VT 05753.

Newsletter: *Petroleum Collectibles Monthly*, 411 Forest St, La Grange, OH 44050.

Collectors' Club: International Petroliana Collectors Assoc, PO Box 937, Powell, OH 43065.

Activity Book, Shell Oil Animal Jungle Book, ©1937,
    10 x 10½" **$45.00**
Ashtray, Exxon, ceramic, white, "Exxon Image 75" with
    tiger image below "National Championship Team
    Member June 1975," 6¾" d **20.00**
Ashtray, Gulf, clear glass, blue name on orange center,
    3½" sq **15.00**
Ashtray, Texaco Service, glass, Texaco logo and name
    and services of local dealer in York, PA, red and green
    decal on bottom, 1930–40s, 4½ x 4½". **20.00**
Bank, Sinclair Gasoline, tin, figural gas pump, 4" d. **35.00**
Bank, Thermo Anti–Freeze, litho tin, snowman holding
    thermometer and product can, "Fill Up—Or Freeze
    Up!," 1940s, 2¾" h **45.00**
Baseball, Ashland/Valvoline "Powerful Partners," white
    sponge rubber, regulation size, red "Ashland
    Detergent Gasolines, World's First Valvoline Motor
    Oil," 1930s **45.00**
Bottle, Shell Oil, glass, ribbed design and raised logo,
    1 qt, 15" h. **65.00**
Buckle, Atlantic Oil, metal, silver luster, emb Atlantic
    logo, red enamel backing, initials "KAT". **35.00**
Calendar, Tydol–Veedol, 1941, cowboy scene, "The
    Homeward Trail," Tydol gasoline and Veedol motor oil
    logo and imprint for local dealer, 8½ x 15". **20.00**

Bank, Esso Fat Man, plastic, light blue, minor damage to chest decal, 5" h, $110.00. Photo courtesy Wm. Morford Auctions.

Calendar Card, Socony, red, white, and blue, "Socony Motor Oils" symbols and 1929 monthly calendar on one side, "Socony Special Gasoline" inscription and 1930 monthly calender on other side, Standard Oil Co, NY, 2¼ x 3¾" **20.00**

Can, Cities Service Koldpruf Anti–Freeze, tin, logo and penguin, 1957–65 .... **40.00**

Clock, "Bardahl Service Station," electric, detective and Bardahl slogan on face, 15 x 15" brass frame, ©1959 Pam Clock Co, 1950s **195.00**

Game, Standard Oil Checkers, 1938, 14" sq. **90.00**

Gas Globe, Special **150.00**

Keychain Tag, Amrix Motor Oil, plastic **10.00**

License Plate Attachment, Tydol Oil & Gasoline, litho tin, diecut, 4½ x 7" **50.00**

Map, Esso, Eastern US Road Map, District of Columbia, 1938. .... **5.00**

Mechanical Pencil, Phillips 66, plastic, gold luster metal, orange and black logo and Texas dealership imprint, 1940–50s **20.00**

Mechanical Pencil, Texaco, metal and plastic, star logo and dealer info in red and blue, "The Texaco Company," 1930s **20.00**

Playing Cards, Standard Oil, white circle center with name, dark red, gold border **2.50**

Puzzle, Champion Spark Plug, figural plastic spark plug joined by knotted cord to plastic slogan bar, "Better By Far For Every Car," 2¾" h **10.00**

Radio, Sinclair, pump shape **35.00**

Sign, Indian Gasoline, porcelain, green, blue, white, red, yellow, and black, 1940, 8 x 12" **920.00**

Sign, Perfect Circle Piston Rings, emb tin, pig sitting in car, "Don't drive an Oil Hog! Install Perfect Circle," 1940s, 19 x 25". **675.00**

Sign, Power–Lube Motor Oil, porcelain, 2 sided, blue ground, yellow lettering, tiger, 1920–30, 20 x 28" **1,050.00**

Sign, Socony Motor Oil, porcelain, 2 sided, red, white, and blue, 1930s, 8 x 12" **525.00**

Sign, Texaco Havoline Motor Oil, enamel on steel, dark blue, yellow, white, and red, yellow Havoline can, 17 x 10", c1950s **190.00**

Sign, Tydol Flying A Gasoline, porcelain, white, red, and black, flying "A" logo, 10" d **250.00**

Thimble, Sinclair Oils, plastic, butterscotch swirl ground, black dinosaurs and stars. **4.00**

Tie Bar, AC Spark Plugs, gold luster metal spring clip, raised spark plug on pearl–like oval backing, 1950s **20.00**

Truck, Mobilgas, litho tin, friction, red, white, blue, and cream, "Mobilgas" on sides and doors, Pegasus images, Linemar, 1950s, 1¼ x 3 x 1" **45.00**

Tumblers, set of 4, Phillips 66, red triangles on white panel repeated three times on each 5" h glass, 3 x 5 x 12½" cardboard display carton, "At Your Service" on carton, 1960s. **20.00**

Upholstery Brush, Atlantic Gasoline, emb brass, service station scene, inscribed "Atlantic Gasoline Puts Pep In Your Mouth," 1920s. **25.00**

Yardstick, Gulf Oil, folding, Gulf Oil products text, 1950s. **10.00**

AUCTION PRICES

Gas Station Collectibles sold by Collectors Auction Services on May 10, 1997. Prices include a 10% buyer's premium.

Calendar, Atlantic Petroleum, 1941, 28¾" h, 16" w ... **$49.50**

Child's Hat, Imperial Esso, paper, dealer giveaway, 22¾" l **22.00**

Gas Globe, Flying A Gasoline, rect, 2 milk glass inserts, 6" h, 14½" w, 6½" d **467.50**

Knife, Esso Standard Oil, metal, gas pump shape, paint loss to lettering, 2⅞" l **60.50**

Lamp, Amoco, plastic and metal, electric, working condition, 18¼" h, 8½" d **148.50**

License Plate, Mobilgas, emb tin, yellowing, paint chips and scratches, 7" h, 11¼" w **132.00**

Pin, Gulf Merit Award, enameled metal, some cracks and chips, 1" h, ⅞" w **66.00**

Poster, Super Shell, linen backed, minor staining, 32½" h, 57" w **198.00**

Pump Sign, Time Super Gasoline, porcealin, scratches and soiling, 14" h, 9¼" w **467.50**

Salt and Pepper Shakers, pr, Texaco, plastic, "Fire Chief" salt, "Sky Chief" pepper, orig box, minor decal cracking, 2¾" h, 1" w, ¾" d **71.50**

Sign, Socony Motor Gasoline, porcelain, 2–sided flange, some wear, 24⅛" h, 2" w **880.00**

Thermometer, Shell, porcelain, "Pat. Mar. 16, 1915," minor water stain, 27" h, 7" w **3,850.00**

Gas Globe, Sinclair, plastic, 13½" d, $192.50. Photo courtesy Collectors Auction Serivces.

GEISHA GIRL

Geisha Girl is a generic term used to describe Japanese export ceramics made between the 1880s and the present whose decoration incorporates one or more kimono–clad Japanese ladies. Most collectors focus on pre–1940 ware. Geisha Girl ceramics made after 1945 are referred to as "modern" Geisha Girl.

Reference: Elyce Litts, *The Collector's Encyclopedia of Geisha Girl Porcelain,* Collector Books, 1988, out of print.

REPRODUCTION ALERT: Be alert for late 1970s' and early 1980s' Geisha Girl reproductions in forms ranging from ginger jars to sake sets. These contemporary pieces have red borders. Other telltale characteristics include lack of detail, very bright gold highlights, and a white porcelain body.

Czechoslovakian ceramic manufacturers also copied this ware in the 1920s. Some are marked "Czechoslovakia" or have a false Chinese mark. Many are unmarked. Decal decoration was used extensively. However, the real clue is in the faces. The faces on Czechoslovakian Geisha do not have a strong oriental look.

Bowl, Geisha in Sampan E, octagonal, red–orange, gold
  buds, Nippon, 9½" d $43.00
Celery Set, Porch, small rect master and 5 salts,
  red–orange and gold, Torri Nippon, price for 5–pc set 35.00
Chocolate Cup and Saucer 15.00
Chocolate Pot, Parasol and Lesson, butterfly and floral
  ground, blue and gold 100.00
Cocoa Pot, cov, rust 60.00
Cup and Saucer, Kite A 12.00
Demitasse Set, 15 pcs, child's, Parasol C, pot, creamer
  and sugar, 6 cups and saucers 65.00
Dresser Set, Porch, rect tray, powder jar, and hair receiv-
  er, modern, price for 3–pc set 25.00
Eggcup, Long–Stemmed Peony, orange. 5.00
Eggcup, squat 12.00
Hair Receiver, Geisha in Sampan, square, red, mkd "t't'
  Japan". 18.00
Hatpin Holder, Long–Stemmed Peony 30.00
Mint Dish, leaf shaped 25.00
Mustard Pot, Bamboo Trellis, blue, scalloped 25.00
Nut Bowl, Porch, master, cobalt blue, Torri Nippon. 25.00
Olive Dish, Mother and Son C, oval, red–orange, Kutani,
  7" l 25.00
Pitcher, child's, Parasaol B, red, 3⅝ x 1¾" 15.00
Plate, Chinese Coin, 6" d 15.00
Salt and Pepper Shakers, pr, Visiting with Baby, individ-
  ual, bulbous, blue and gold 20.00
Salt, Temple A, pedestal, floral and turquoise border,
  mkd 25.00
Sugar Bowl, Flower Gathering B, gold lacing, green 15.00
Teapot, Ikebana in Rickshaw, cobalt blue, gold. 35.00
Vase, Bamboo Trellis, basket, green handle, brown
  footrim, 8½" 75.00

Plate, Bamboo Tree, 7¼" d, $10.00.

G.I. JOE

Hasbro introduced G.I. Joe at the February 1964 American International Toy Fair in New York. Initially, this 12–inch poseable figure was produced in only four versions, one for each branch of the military.

A black G.I. Joe joined the line in 1965, followed by a talking G.I. Joe and female nurse in 1967. The G.I. Joe Adventure Team introduced this all–American hero to civilian pursuits such as hunting and deep sea diving. The 1976 Arab oil embargo forced Hasbro to reduce G.I. Joe's size from 12 to 8 inches. Production stopped in 1977.

Hasbro reintroduced G.I. Joe in 1982 in a 3¼–inch format. In 1994 Hasbro resumed production of the 12–inch figure, targeted primarily toward the adult collector market. Action Man, G.I. Joe's British equivalent, was marketed in the United States during the 1996 holiday season.

Collectors concentrate on pre–1977 action figures. Collecting interest in accessories, especially those with period boxes, continues to grow.

References: John Marshall, *GI Joe and Other Backyard Heroes*, Schiffer Publishing, 1997; John Michlig, *GI Joe: The Complete Story of America's Favorite Man of Action*, Chronicle Books, 1998; Vincent Santelmo, *The Complete Encyclopedia to GI Joe*, 2nd Edition, Krause Publications, 1997; Vincent Santelmo, *The Official 30th Anniversary Salute to GI Joe, 1964–1994*, Krause Publications, 1994.

Periodical: *GI Joe Patrol*, PO Box 2362, Hot Springs, AR 71914.

Collectors' Clubs: GI Joe Collectors Club, 12513 Birchfalls Dr, Raleigh, NC 27614; GI Joe: Steel Brigade Club, 8362 Lomay Ave, Westminster, CA 92683.

ACCESSORIES

Action Pilot Accessory Pack, #7811, parachute $90.00
Action Pilot Helmet. 25.00
Action Pilot Sand Bags, #7508. . . . . 65.00
Adventure Team Black Bomb Disposal Box. 20.00
Adventure Team Long Range Reconnaisance Set,
  unused, MOC 100.00
Adventure Team Night Surveillance Set, #7335, unused 175.00
Adventure Team Pick Ax 15.00
Adventure Team Seismograph, #7319–6, 1973, unused,
  MOC 75.00
Combat Man's Equipment Case, complete 45.00
Combat Mess Kit, #7509 . . . . 70.00
Crutch 15.00
Footlocker, no tray, Irwin 20.00
Game, GI Joe Action Team Let's Go Joe Game, 1966,
  MIB 160.00
Landing Signal Paddle, loose 20.00
Life Raft, missing one oar holder 10.00
Machine Gun, no tri–pod 25.00
Marine Paratroopers Small Arms Set, #7706, complete,
  loose. 100.00
Marine Pup Tent, with stakes 35.00
Navy Attack Life Jacket, #7611, loose. 30.00
Navy Machine Gun Set, #7618, MIP 125.00
Scuba Fins, pr 15.00
Scuba Mask, orange 15.00

G.I. Joe Official Space Capsule and Authentic Space Suit, Hasbro, #8020, 1966, $125.00.

Scuba Tank 25.00
Super Joe Helipak, 1977, MIB 60.00
Super Joe Magna Tools, #7538, unused, MIB 48.00
Super Joe Sonic Scanner, #7538, 1977, unused 48.00

ACTION FIGURES

Action Marine, loose, with dog tags $125.00
Action Pilot, #7800, 1964, 12" h 85.00
Action Sailor, #7600, 1964, 12" h 135.00
Astronaut, silver space suit, 12" h 165.00
Cobra Commander, 1983, 3³/₄" h, MIP 12.00
Downtown, 3³/₄" h, MIP 12.00
Dress Marine, black 50.00
Eagle Eye Land Commander, #7275, MIP 100.00
Sea Adventurer, #7281, 12" h, MIB 175.00
Super Joe, #7503, 1977, MIP 75.00
Talking Commander 200.00
US Navy Serviceman, black 35.00
West Point Cadet, 12" h 200.00

CLOTHING

Adventure Team Copter Rescue Jumpsuit and
    Binoculars, #7308–6 . . . . $30.00
Adventure Team Jungle Survival Jacket 20.00
Adventure Team Pith Helmet 25.00
Adventure Team Volcano Jumpsuit 20.00
Air Force Dress Uniform Set, #7803, missing tie, with
    doll, loose 300.00
Air Vest, loose 20.00
Dangerous Climb Outfit, green jumpsuit, climbing rock,
    and rope, MIP 50.00
Dress Cap 20.00
Dress Parade Set, with doll, #7710 . . . . 225.00
Fatigue Cap 10.00
Fatigue Shirt, #7714, MIP 30.00
Japanese Imperial Soldier Outfit, Nambu pistol, top and
    pants only 60.00
Jumpsuit, orange 20.00
Pilot Dress Cap 15.00
Sailor Cap 15.00

PLAYSETS

Future Fortress, Sears, 1980s, MIB $80.00
Mobile Command Center, #6006, 1980s, MIB 65.00
Secret Mountain Outpost, #8040 . . . . 75.00
Tactical Battle Station, #6003, MIB 45.00
Toxic Laboratory, #6146, MIB 20.00

VEHICLES

Action Sea Sled, Irwin, 1970–73 . . . . $45.00
Adventure Team Underwater Explorer, loose 35.00
Air Chariot 45.00
Big Trapper, #7498, no action figure, 1976 . . . . 185.00
Chopper Cycle, #59114, Sears, 1970–73, MIB 45.00
Cobra, F.A.N.G. 25.00
Dragon Fly XH–1, #4025 . . . . 55.00
Jet Fighter Plane, #5396, Irwin, 1967 . . . . 350.00
Rapid Fire Motorcycle, #6073–1 . . . . 30.00
Shark's Surprise Set, #7980, complete with frogman
    figure, 1967, MIB 525.00
Stinger Night Attack Jeep, #6055, complete with Cobra
    officer, 1980s 45.00

GIRL SCOUTS

Juliette Gordon Low of Savannah, Georgia, began the Girl Scout movement in 1912. It grew rapidly. The 1928 Girl Scout manual suggested selling cookies to raise money. Today the annual Girl Scout cookie drive supports local troops and councils.

Girl Scout collectibles enjoy limited collector interest. There is a ready market for flashlights and pocketknives, primarily because they cross over into other collecting fields.

Book, *The Girl Scouts Rally*, Katherine Keene Galt,
    Saalfield, 1921 . . . . $15.00
Calendar, 1954, 8¹/₂ x 10" 15.00
Camera, Official Girl Scout, folding, Kodak, c1929 . . . . 65.00
Catalog, Spring 1947, scouting equipment, illus, full
    color cover photo, 40 pp, 8¹/₂ x 11¹/₂" 25.00
Charter, paper, textured tan, dark brown inscription and
    design, inked signatures, dated January 1921,
    9 x 14³/₄" 22.00

Kutmaster, pocketknife, clear plastic over red handle, locking blade, $25.00.

Diary, Girl Scout, black silhouette on orange cover,
1929, 3¼ x 5¼" **12.00**
Doll, Brownie, vinyl, rooted brown hair, open/close
glass eyes, painted features, movable arms and legs,
dark brown felt fabric outfit, orange ribbon neckerchief, brown vinyl belt, dark khaki elastic fabric stockings, brown vinyl shoes, ©Effanbee 1965, 8¼" h **45.00**
First Day Cover, *50 Years of Girl Scouting,* Burlington, VT,
July 24, 1962 cancel, Ken Boll cachet **4.00**
Handbook, *Girl Scout Handbook,* 4th ed, 1st printing,
1933 . . . . **5.00**
Kerchief, Brownie, yellow, turquoise, and brown, com-
pass point motif, 1940–50 . . . . **25.00**
Manual, Scouting for Girls, 1920, 557 pp **20.00**
Ring, SS, center ⅜" miniature official Girl Scout emblem,
1930s **15.00**
Thermos, metal, red and green striped, white logo, plas-
tic cup, Aladdin. **60.00**
Tray, wood, trefoil design, 1940s **12.00**

GLASS SHOES

Glass shoe is a generic term for any figural shoe (or slipper, boot, ice skate, etc.) made of glass, ceramic, or metal. Some examples are utilitarian in nature, e.g., the Atterbury shoe night lamp or the ruby glass cocktail shaker in the shape of a leg and foot wearing a metal sandal. Most were made for purely decorative purposes.

Shoes were extremely popular during the Victorian era, when household bric–a–brac from toothpick holders to pincushions to salt cellars were made in the form of footwear. Once the glass shoe entered the form vocabulary, it never went out of production. There was a lull during the Depression, when few families had money for non–essential items.

Several contemporary glass companies including Boyd, Degenhart, Fenton, and Moser have reproduced early designs and introduced new ones. Thanks to several new books on the subject, glass shoes are enjoying a collecting renaissance.

References: Earlene Wheatley, *Collectible Glass Shoes: Including Metal, Pottery Figural & Porcelain Shoes,* Collector Books, 1996, 1998 value update; Libby Yalom, *Shoes of Glass, 2,* Antique Publications, 1998.

Collectors Club: Miniature Shoe Collectors Club, PO Box 2390, Apple Valley, CA 92308

Baby Bootee, clear, paperweight, Waterford, c1986 . . . . **$85.00**
Baby Shoe, Boyd Crystal Art Glass, Bermuda slag **15.00**
Baby Shoe, frosted, hollow sole, c1930 . . . . **35.00**
Boot, crystal, wrinkled, lace dec, c1930. . . . . **25.00**
Boot, Fenton, Hobnail, white, with logo. **15.00**
Boot, Guernsey, white milk glass, commemorative of
Elvis Presley's death, c1984 . . . . **15.00**
Boot, western motif, applied handle, green, c1950 . . . . **35.00**
Boot, wrinkled, star under heel, "Los Angeles 1936"
etched across foot, green **35.00**
Cat Slipper, Degenhart, Bermuda slag **15.00**
Cat Slipper, Fenton, Hobnail, amberiana **20.00**
Cat Slipper, Fenton, Hobnail, royal blue. **18.00**
Cat Slipper, Fenton, Hobnail, white **12.00**
Man's Slipper, dark amber, c1920s. **40.00**
Shoe, Fenton, with lid, Hobnail, white. **45.00**

Skate Boot, Degenhart, blue, beaded top edge, introduced 1967, 4⅛" h, $30.00.

Shoe, Guernsey Glass Co, Cambridge, OH, Daisy and
Button, lavender **10.00**
Slipper, crystal, "Georgian Crystal Tutbury LTD" paper
label. **25.00**
Slipper, Moser Glass Co, frosted, Rose slipper #117 . . . . **10.00**
Slipper, souvenir, scalloped border at opening, flashed
red, gilded lettering, c1920 . . . . **65.00**
Slipper, spun glass, yellow band around opening form-
ing a bow, light blue **45.00**
Slipper, stippled, Cuban heel, bow, light blue, c1930 . . . . **35.00**
Slipper, white milk glass, beaded dec, squatty heel **40.00**

GOEBEL

Franz and William Goebel, father and son, founded the F. D. & W. Goebel Porcelain Works near Coburg, Germany, in 1879. Initially, the firm made dinnerware, utilitarian ware, and beer steins. Marx–Louis, William's son, became president in 1912. He introduced many new porcelain figurine designs and added a pottery figurine line. Franz Goebel, son of Marx–Louis, and Dr. Eugene Stocke, his uncle, assumed control of the company in 1929.

Franz Goebel is responsible for making arrangements to produce the company's famous Hummel figurines. During World War II, Goebel concentrated on the production of dinnerware. Following the war, the company exported large quantities of Hummels and other figurines. Today Goebel manufactures high quality dinnerware, limited edition collectibles, the popular Hummel figurines, and figurine series ranging from Disney characters to Friar Tuck monks.

This category consists of Goebel's non–Hummel production.

Collectors' Club: Friar Tuck Collectors Club, PO Box 262, Oswego, NY 13827; Goebel Networkers, PO Box 396, Lemoyne, PA 17043.

Note: See Limited Editions and Hummel Figurines for additional listings.

Creamer, Friar Tuck, 5¹/₂" h, $30.00.

Beer Mug, figural Friar Tuck, 8" h **$250.00**

Creamer, figural clown's head, blue, red hearts, imp
mark. **60.00**

Doll, Alice, #901212, Victoria Ashlea Original, B Ball,
Goebel of North America, 1987 . . . . **130.00**

Doll, Kate, #911353, Bob Timberlake Dolls, B Ball,
Goebel of North America, 1996. . . . . **190.00**

Doll, Melvin Bumps, #911617, Dolly Dingle, B Ball,
Goebel of North America, 1995. . . . . **95.00**

Doll, Monique, #912455, Victoria Ashlea Original, Tiny
Tot School Girls, K Kennedy, Goebel of North
America, 1994 . . . . **45.00**

Doll, Sophia, #912173, Victoria Ashlea Original, B Ball,
Goebel of North America, 1987. . . . . **35.00**

Figurine, A Child's Prayer, Charlot Byj Blondes, C Byj,
Goebel of North America, 1968. . . . . **45.00**

Figurine, bathing girl, sitting on scalloped shell, double
crown mark, 3" h. **130.00**

Figurine, Ben the Blacksmith, Co–Boy, G Skrobek,
Goebel of North America, 1981. . . . . **75.00**

Figurine, bird, olive green, black, brown, cream, and
blue, 2³/₄" h. **35.00**

Figurine, Central Park Sunday, #664–B, Americana
Series, R Olszewski, Goebel of North America, 1985 . . . . . **50.00**

Figurine, dog, seated Boxer, 4¹/₂" h. **65.00**

Figurine, First Degree, Charlot Byk Redheads, C Byj,
Goebel of North America, 1972. . . . . **80.00**

Figurine, Historical Display, #943–D, Historical Series, R
Olszewski, Goebel of North America, 1988 . . . . **60.00**

Figurine, Hummingbird, #697–P, Pendants, R
Olszewski, Goebel of North America, 1990 . . . . **150.00**

Figurine, kitten, paper label. **40.00**

Figurine, Madonna, praying, #HM147, stylized bee
mark, 11¹/₂" h **25.00**

Figurine, owl, 3¹/₂" h **25.00**

Figurine, poodle, black, 11¹/₂" h. **8.00**

Figurine, Prince Charming, #179–P, Disney Series,
Goebel of North America, 1991. . . . . **90.00**

Figurine, Snow Holiday, #635–P, miniature, Children's
Series, R Olszewski, Goebel of North America, 1985 . . . . . **75.00**

Jug, figural cardinal, stylized bee mark, 4" h **175.00**

Mug, figural Great Dane head, brown, black trim, 1¹/₂" h **45.00**

Mustard Pot, figural Friar Tuck, stylized bee mark, 3³/₄" **75.00**

Ornament, Angel Bell, with clarinet, white bisque,
Goebel of North America, 1976. . . . . **5.00**

Salt and Pepper Shakers, pr, Disney's Flower, orig label. **125.00**

Salt and Pepper Shakers, pr, figural Friars, #SB153/1,
2³/₄" h **30.00**

Trinket Box, cat lying on back finial. **35.00**

GOLDSCHEIDER POTTERY

In 1885 Frederich Goldscheider founded the Goldscheider Porcelain and Majolica Factory. The firm had a factory in Pilsen and decorating shops in Carlsbad and Vienna. Regina Goldscheider and Alois Goldscheider, her brother–in–law, managed the firm from 1897 until 1918. Walter and Marcel, Regina's sons, managed the firm in the 1920s. The factory produced high–style figurines and decorative accessories during the Art Nouveau and Art Deco periods.

During World War II, the family relocated its operations to Trenton, New Jersey. When the war ended, Marcel Goldscheider moved the company to England's Staffordshire district where it continues to make bone china figures and earthenware.

Bust, gray and blue, USA and Everlast mark, 5³/₄" h. **$15.00**

Figure, Art Deco Terrier, orange, 4³/₄" h. **55.00**

Figure, black man wearing brown suit, with top hat and
cane, sitting on rock, 14¹/₈" h **325.00**

Figure, flying duck, molded by E Straub, 13" h **100.00**

Figure, German Shepherd, sitting, mkd "Goldscheider,
Wein," 6" h, 9" l **175.00**

Figure, Juliet with Doves, 12¹/₄" h. **225.00**

Figure, Madonna, sgd, 9" h **65.00**

Figure, Old Virginia, sgd "Peggy Porcher," 8¹/₂" h. **125.00**

Figure, pr, black sailor and girl, #7958 . . . . **850.00**

Figure, woman with muff, plumed hat, incised "BCV,"
8¹/₂" h **90.00**

Music Box, Colonial Girl, 7" h. **100.00**

Wall Mask, Art Deco woman's face, curly brown hair,
red lips, aqua scarf, 11¹/₄" h **190.00**

Wall Mask, girl, curly green hair, red lips, black mask,
13¹/₂" h **365.00**

GOLF COLLECTIBLES

Golf roots rest in 15th–century Scotland. Initially a game played primarily by the aristocracy and gentry, by the mid–19th century the game was accessible to everyone. By 1900, golf courses were located throughout Great Britain and the United States.

Golf collectibles divide into four basic groups: (1) golf books, (2) golf equipment, (3) items associated with a famous golfer, and (4) golf ephemera ranging from tournament programs to golf prints. Golf collecting has become highly specialized. There are several price guides to golf balls. There is even a price guide to golf tees.

References: Chuck Furjanic, *Antique Golf Collectibles: A Price and Reference Guide,* Krause Publications, 1997; John F. Hotchkiss, *500 Years of Golf Balls: History & Collector's Guide,* Antique Trader Books, 1997; John M. Olman and Morton W. Olman, *Golf Antiques & Other Treasures of the Game, Expanded Edition,* Market Street Press, 1993; Beverly Robb, *Collectible Golfing Novelties,* Schiffer Publishing, 1992; Shirley and Jerry Sprung,

Decorative Golf Collectibles: Collector's Information, Current Prices, Glentiques, 1991.

Periodical: *Golfiana Magazine,* 222 Leverette Ln, #4, Edwardsville, IL 62025.

Newsletter: *U.S. Golf Classics & Heritage Hickories,* 5407 Pennock Point Rd, Jupiter, FL 33458.

Collectors' Clubs: Golf Collectors Society, PO Box 20546, Dayton, OH 45420; Logo Golf Ball Collector's Assoc, 4552 Barclay Fairway, Lake Worth, FL 33467; The Golf Club Collectors Assoc, 640 E Liberty St, Girard, OH 44420.

Autograph, Gary Player, CS **$15.00**
Autograph, Harry Vardon, ALS, framed and glazed, 1931 . . . **125.00**
Badge, press, Chicago Area Golf Tournament, 1950–60 . . . . . **12.00**
Bag, leather, purporting to belong to 1964 British Open
  Champion Tony Lema **50.00**
Bag Towel, 1980 US Open **6.50**
Ball, 13 assorted, unmkd, 1930–50 . . . . **4.00**
Book, *A New Way to Better Golf,* Alex J Morrison, 1931 . . . . . **35.00**
Book, *How to Hit a Golf Ball,* Slammin Sammy Snead,
  1950, 74 pp **12.00**
Book, *The Curious History of the Golf Ball,* John S
  Martin, 1968 . . . . **155.00**
Bottle, figural golf bag, clear, orig painted dec, 3¼" h **35.00**
Calendar, John C Larkin Insurance Co, Byreon Nelson's
  Winning Golf, 1951 . . . . **18.00**
Club, iron, wood shaft, Hagen concave wedge, 1930 . . . . . . **115.00**
Club, wood, steel shaft, McGregor Tourney 693W driver,
  c1953 . . . . **115.00**
Cookbook, Golfer's, Iarrobino, 1968, 91 pp **3.00**
Decanter, ceramic, figural golfer, plays *"How Dry I Am,"*
  Japan, 1960–70 . . . . **35.00**
Figure, celluloid, diecut, woman golfer in back swing
  position, green and white checked skirt, red sweater,
  yellow cap, black shoes, brown club, tube attached to
  back, 1930s, 3" h **35.00**
Game, Arnold Palmer's Indoor Golf, Marx, 1968 . . . . **80.00**
Game, Let's Play Golf, Burlu Enterprises, 1968 . . . . **35.00**
Lighter, figural golf bag **45.00**
Magazine, *Golf Digest,* 12 issues, 1963 . . . . **15.00**
Magazine, *Sports Illustrated,* Crosby Golf Tournament,
  Jan 23, 1961 . . . . **5.50**
Magazine Cover, *Life,* Ben Hogan, Aug 8, 1955, auto-
  graphed, framed **200.00**
Magazine Tear Sheet, Wescott Soles, The Gathering
  Place of Fashion, May 1927, woman swinging golf
  club, framed **25.00**
Medal, Royal Aberdeen, weekly handicap, 1937 . . . . **125.00**
Movie Poster, *Follow the Sun,* Ben Hogan autograph,
  framed, 1951 . . . . **350.00**
Pitcher, Tanqueray Gin, Bob Hope Desert Classic, 1972,
  7" h **25.00**
Playing Cards, Zweifel Card Golf, orig box, 1932 . . . . **25.00**
Postcard, woman golfer, pyrography, 1930–40 . . . . **5.00**
Print, Blackheath Golfers, framed, c1950 . . . . **150.00**
Program, First Annual Fort Worth Open Golf
  Championship, Glen Garden Country Club, Fort
  Worth, TX, 1945 . . . . **100.00**
Puzzle, Richfield Gasoline, Goofy Golf, #1, A Swiss–itu-
  ation, golfer shooting from eagle's nest, paper enve-
  lope with golf lessons, 1930s **25.00**

Sheet Music, *The Caddy,* Dean Martin and Jerry Lewis,
  1953 . . . . **20.00**
Stereoview, The Embryo Golfer, A C Co, 1925 . . . . **15.00**
Tobacco Card, Harold Gillies, Will's Cigarettes, #6,
  1930 . . . . **50.00**
Tobacco Card, T P Perkins, Churchmann's Cigarettes,
  caricature illus, 1928 . . . . **10.00**
Tray, brass, center golfer illus, Wallace Trophy, 1920s,
  10" d **45.00**
Whiskey Jug, Jim Beam, Bing Crosby 30th Clambake **40.00**

GONDER POTTERY

After a distinguished ceramic career working for American Encaustic Tiling, Cherry Art Tile, Florence Pottery, and Ohio Pottery, Lawton Gonder purchased the Zane Pottery, Zanesville, Ohio, in 1940 and renamed it Gonder Ceramic Arts. The company concentrated on art pottery and decorative accessories. Gonder hired top designers and sculptors to create his products. Gonder's glazes were innovative.

In 1946 Gonder expanded his Zanesville plant and purchased the Elgee Pottery to produce lamp bases. Elgee burned in 1954; operations were moved to Zanesville. Hurt by the flood of cheap foreign imports, Gonder sold his business in 1975 to the Allied Tile Company.

Many Gonder pieces have a double glaze and a pink interior. Most pieces are marked GONDER or GONDER USA in a variety of ways and are numbered. Some pieces were marked with a paper label.

Reference: Ron Hoopes, *The Collector's Guide and History of Gonder Pottery,* L–W Books, 1992.

Collectors' Club: Gonder Collectors Club, 917 Hurl Dr, Pittsburgh, PA 15236.

Basket, L–19, twisted handle, brown, 9" h **$45.00**
Bowl, ribbed, yellow, 6½" d **10.00**

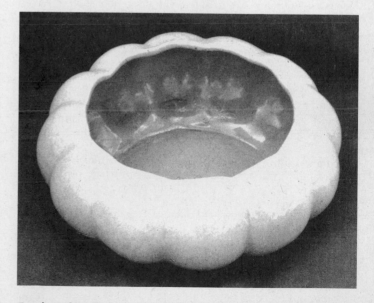

Bowl, melon shape, turquoise ext, pink int, imp "E–12/Gonder/ U.S.A.," 7" d, $20.00.

Candle Holders, pr, J–56, Crescent Moon, white, 6½" h **35.00**
Coffeepot, La Gonda **55.00**
Cookie Jar, round, sleeping dog on lid **50.00**
Cornucopia, turquoise and brown, 7" h **15.00**
Creamer, La Gonda **6.00**
Cream Soup Cup, La Gonda, lug handle **10.00**
Cup, La Gonda, round **6.00**
Ewer, #508, shell shape, green and brown, 14" h **85.00**
Ewer, Shell and Star, green, 13" h **50.00**
Figure, elephant **45.00**
Figure, panther, #217, 15" l **115.00**
Figure, horse's head, 13" l **75.00**
Flower Frog, swirl, blue and brown **20.00**
Ginger Jar, round **30.00**
Salt and Pepper Shakers, pr, La Gonda **15.00**
Saucer, La Gonda **5.00**
Tea Set, 3–pc set, teapot, cov, creamer and sugar, cov,
    brown mottled **25.00**
Television Lamp, seagull, flying over yellow waves,
    black, 12" h **75.00**
Vase, #868, emb flowers **25.00**
Vase, E–49, dark green and brown **18.00**
Vase, H–14, cornucopia, green and brown, 10" h **25.00**
Vase, H–47, 2 swans on base **18.00**
Vase, H–56, handles, green **25.00**
Vase, H–74, rectangular, yellow, 8½" h **20.00**
Wall Pocket, bird and grapes dec **55.00**

GRANITEWARE

Graniteware is a generic term used to describe enamel–coated iron or steel kitchenware. Originating in Germany, the first American graniteware was manufactured in the 1860s. American manufacturers received a major market boost when World War I curtailed German imports.

Graniteware is still being manufactured today. Older examples tend to be heavier. Cast–iron handles date between 1870 and 1890; wood handles between 1900 and 1910.

This market experienced a major price run in the early 1990s as dealers raised their prices to agree with those published by Helen Greguire. At the moment, the category as a whole appears to be greatly overvalued.

References: Helen Greguire, *The Collector's Encyclopedia of Graniteware: Colors, Shapes & Values*, (1990, 1994 value update), *Book 2*, (1993, 1997 value update), Collector Books; Dana Gehman Morykan and Harry L. Rinker, *Warman's Country Antiques & Collectibles, Third Edition*, Wallace–Homestead, Krause Publications, 1996.

Collectors' Club: National Graniteware Society, PO Box 10013, Cedar Rapids, IA 52410.

Bacon Platter, brown and white swirl **$195.00**
Baking Pan, blue and white swirl, small **95.00**
Bowl, blue and white mottled, blue–gray int, 6" d **45.00**
Butter Dish, cobalt and white mottled **195.00**
Chocolate Dipper, tubular handle, gray **155.00**
Coffee Boiler, chrysolite swirl **175.00**
Coffeepot, blue and white swirl **95.00**
Colander, blue and gray swirl **75.00**
Custard, cobalt and white swirl **65.00**
Double Boiler, cobalt and white swirl, Brilliant Belle **295.00**

Boiler, black and white speckled, Quaker Oats, minor chips, 8¼" h, $121.00. Photo courtesy Collectors Auction Service.

Dust Pan, gray speckled **100.00**
Funnel, gray, Acme **40.00**
Gravy Boat, blue and white mottled **195.00**
Jelly Roll Pan, blue and white swirl **40.00**
Mixing Bowl, blue and white mottled, white int, 11½" d **95.00**
Mug, blue and white mottled, white int, cobalt blue trim,
    2¾" d **95.00**
Pitcher and Bowl Set, gray **125.00**
Soup Ladle, blue and white mottled, white int, 14⅞" l **60.00**
Teapot, gooseneck spout, cream and green, 8½" w **75.00**
Tumbler, blue and white mottled, 5" d **65.00**

GREETING CARDS

The modern greeting card originated in the middle of the 15th century in the Rhine Valley of medieval Germany. Printed New Year greetings gained in popularity during the 17th and 18th centuries. Queen Victoria's interest in holiday and special occasion cards helped establish the sending of greeting cards as a regular event.

Louis Prang, a color lithography printer, was one of the first American manufacturers of greeting cards. The post–1945 era witnessed the growth of a number of card manufacturers who eventually would dominate the industry. The Hall Brothers (Joyce C., Rollie, and William), Kansas City postcard distributors and publishers, began printing greeting cards in 1910. Fred Winslow Rust established Rust Craft Company. Cincinnati's Gibson Art Co. entered the greeting card field. Arthur D. and Jane Norcross formed a mutual partnership in 1915.

Although greeting cards are collected primarily by event or occasion, a growing number of collectors seek specialized type cards, e.g., diecut or mechanical. Holiday and specialized collectors represent the principal buyers of greeting cards in the 1990s.

Reference: Ellen Stern, *The Very Best From Hallmark: Greeting Cards Through the Years*, Harry N. Abrams, 1988, out of print.

Birthday, Hopalong Cassidy, photo pinback button insert . . . **$35.00**
Birthday, Star Trek, "This is your Captain speaking...Have
    a far–out birthday," Random House, 1976 . . . . **15.00**

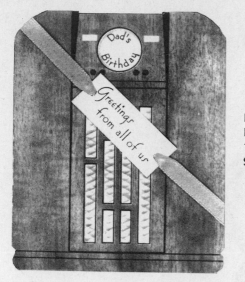

Birthday, bifold, Buzza Craftacres, 1940s, 4³/₈ x 5¹/₂", $7.00.

Christmas, Breyer Ice Cream, c1920 . . . . **20.00**
Christmas, Captain Marvel, 1941 . . . . **30.00**
Christmas, fold–out, Santa on inside, pictures to trace
    inside, "Merry Christmas," 1930s **3.00**
Christmas, house shape, Santa with tree inside,
    "Christmas Greetings In My House," 1930s **3.00**
Christmas, L G Kelly–Miller Bros Circus, pr, 3 color,
    4 pp, early 1940s, 5 x 7" **20.00**
Christmas, Santa cutout, poem inside, "Christmas
    Greetings," 1930s **3.50**
Christmas, Woody Woodpecker surrounded by other
    Lantz characters, Lantz facsimile signature, c1950,
    11 x 15¹/₂" **75.00**
Greeting, Dagwood carrying greeting card on front,
    Dagwood washing dishes inside, Hallmark, 1939,
    5 x 6" **12.50**
Greeting, Universal monsters, includes record, set of
    3 different cards, Buzza, 1963 . . . . **45.00**
Mother's Day, Cracker Jack, diecut, puppy, c1940 . . . . **45.00**
Thanksgiving, family seated at table, mid–20th C **3.00**

GRISWOLD

In the mid–1860s Matthew Griswold entered into partnership with John and Samuel Selden, his brothers–in–law, to establish a company to manufacture hardware in Erie, Pennsylvania. In 1873 the company was known as the Selden & Griswold Manufacturing Company. Matthew Griswold bought out the Selden family interests in 1884.

In 1914, Marvin Griswold, one of Matthew's sons, became company president and was instrumental in making Griswold a leader in the manufacture of cast–iron cookware. Following Marvin's death in 1926, Roger Griswold, a son of Matthew Griswold, Jr., assumed the company's helm. He was responsible for the company's manufacturing commercial electrical appliances.

Ely Griswold, Roger's brother, assumed control following Roger's death in 1944. The company was sold to a group of New York investors in 1946.

McGraw Edison Company, Chicago, purchased Griswold in 1957. Six months later, the Housewares Division and the Griswold trade name was sold to the Wagner Manufacturing Company,

Griswold's major competitor. Wagner operated the company as a separate division, dropping "Erie, Pa." from the trademark.

In 1959 Wagner sold Griswold to Textron, Inc., of Providence, Rhode Island, which operated the company under its subsidiary, Randall Company. In August 1969, the General Housewares Corporation acquired all rights to Griswold and Wagner. Cast–iron cookware is still made at the Sidney, Ohio, plant.

References: John B. Haussler, *Griswold Muffin Pans*, Schiffer Publishing, 1997; David G. Smith and Charles Wafford, *The Book of Griswold & Wagner: Favorite Piqua, Sidney Hollow Ware, Wapak*, Schiffer Publishing, 1995; *Griswold Cast Iron, Vol. 1* (1993, 1997 value update), *Vol 2.* (1995), L–W Book Sales.

Newsletter: *Kettles 'n' Cookware*, Drawer B, Perrysville, NY 14129.

Collectors' Club: Griswold & Cast–Iron Cookware Assoc, Drawer B, Perrysville, NY 14129.

Ashtray, block logo, 1930s **$75.00**
Ashtray, square **35.00**
Coffee Mill, Grand Union Tea Co, burnt orange enamel,
    orange trim, 10³/₄" h. **400.00**
Danish Cake Pan, mkd "Griswold No 31, 963," 9" d **150.00**
Drip Coffee Maker, aluminum, block logo, c1934, 6 cup **75.00**
French Deep Fat Fryer, with basket, c1950s **45.00**
Fruit & Lard Press, #110, tin, gray, wood slats, 10 qt **150.00**
Gem Pan, #3, variation 1 . . . . **240.00**
Gem Pan, #15 . . . . **135.00**
Griddle, #7, mkd #7, 1077," 1930s **35.00**
Griddle, bail handle, #10, block logo, c1925–40 . . . . **125.00**
Griddle, wood handle, #9, mkd "651," and "Griswold"
    on handle, c1920 . . . . **100.00**
Kettle, cov, flat bottom, #8, block logo, 7 qts **200.00**
Lemon Squeezer, #7, japanned, aluminum cups, mkd
    "Classic 7," 10⁵/₈" **100.00**
Mail Box, black, lid mkd "No. 1 Griswold 382," c1930,
    5¹/₂ x 10¹/₂" **150.00**
Sadiron, handle, Griswold–Erie **100.00**
Skillet Cover, glass, clear, logo on knob, 9¹/₂" sq **50.00**
Smokers Kettle, #773 . . . . **65.00**
Tea Kettle, Colonial design, iron, slant logo, 5 qt **250.00**
Tea Kettle, flat bottom, aluminum, 3 qts **100.00**
Tite–Top Baster, cov, #6, applied handle, c1920 . . . . **225.00**
Waffle Iron, #8, finger hinge **125.00**

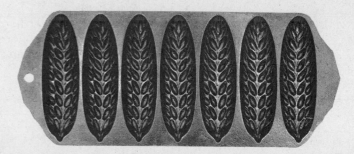

Wheat and Corn Stick Pan, #2700, "No. 2700, Griswold, Wheat & Corn Stick Pan Erie, PA., U.S.A. Pat. No. 73,326, 632," c1925, 13¹/₂ x 5³/₄", $325.00.

Waffle Iron, #8, mkd "No.8/Victor/Pat. Appl'd For," ball
 hinge, c1940 . . . . **100.00**
Waffle Iron, #8, hearts pattern, ball hinge, mkd "Western
 Importing Co, Minneapolis & New York, " c1920–30 . . . . . **75.00**

GUNDERSON

Robert Gunderson purchased the Pairpoint Corporation, Boston, Massachusetts, in the late 1930s and operated it as the Gunderson Glass Works until his death in 1952. Operating as Gunderson–Pairpoint, the company continued for only five more years.

In the 1950s, the Gunderson Glass Company produced a wide range of reproduction glassware. Its peachblow–type art glass shades from an opaque faint pink tint to a deep rose.

Robert Bryden attempted a revival of the firm in 1970. He moved the manufacturing operations from the old Mount Washington plant in Boston back to New Bedford.

Butter Dish, cov, peachblow, scalloped edge, applied
 finial, c1960, 9" d, 5" h **$400.00**
Compote, Camelia Swirl, bubble ball connector, clear
 base, bell tone flint, 6" h **475.00**
Compote, glossy, orig paper label, 3" h **150.00**
Cordial, amberina, set of 10 . . . . **365.00**
Creamer and Sugar **420.00**
Cup and Saucer, peachblow, applied white reeded han-
 dle, applied foot, c1940 . . . . **265.00**
Decanter, pedestal base, deep rose shading to white,
 orig stopper, 9½" h **550.00**
Jug, bulbous, applied white loop handle acid finish,
 4½" h **450.00**
Mug, peachblow, dec, orig paper label, c1970 . . . . **125.00**
Sugar, open, ftd **65.00**
Vase, classic shape, applied serpentine handles, square
 base, 8½" h **165.00**
Vase, peachblow, satin, applied ribbon and acorn at
 neck, 5½" h **250.00**

HAEGER POTTERIES

In 1871 David H. Haeger established a brick yard on the banks of the Fox River in Dundee, Illinois. He was succeeded in 1900 by Edmund H. Haeger, his son. Edmund introduced an art pottery line in 1914. Within a short period of time, Haeger became a leading manufacturer of artware, characterized by a lustrous glaze and soft glowing pastels. The company built and operated a complete working pottery at the 1933–34 Chicago World's Fair.

The company introduced its Royal Haeger line in 1938. The Royal Haeger Lamp Company was formed in 1939, the same year the company purchased the Buckeye Pottery building in Macomb, Illinois, for manufacturing its art line for the florist trade.

In 1954 Joseph F. Estes, Edmund's son–in–law, assumed the presidency. Nicholas Haeger Estes and Alexendria Haeger Estes, son and daughter of Joseph, continue the family tradition.

Reference: David D. Dilley, *Haeger Potteries*, L–W Book Sales, 1997.

Collectors' Club: Haeger Pottery Collectors of America, 5021 Toyon Way, Antioch, CA 94509.

Vase, #424, green agate glaze, 14" h, $10.00.

Ashtray, #162, boomerang **$10.00**
Ashtray, R–632, leopard, 8½" **25.00**
Bookends, pr, R–132, ram, 9" **30.00**
Bowl, R–737, petunia **10.00**
Candle Holders, pr, R–1208, butterfly, 6½" **15.00**
Candle Holder, R–968, starfish **10.00**
Candlestick, cornucopia **10.00**
Candy Dish, R–431, calla lilly, 7½" **18.00**
Candy Dish, R–685, horse head, 7" **25.00**
Figure, R–233, pouter pigeon, 7" **20.00**
Figure, R–401, hen **15.00**
Figure, R–413, kneeling fawn, 7½" **12.00**
Figure, R–683, panther, 18" **50.00**
Figure, #702, polar bear **55.00**
Figure, R–711, Chinese musician **22.00**
Figure, R–736, Dachshund **50.00**
Figure, R–898, seated cat, 6" **20.00**
Fish Bowl Stand, R–656, mermaid **25.00**
Flower Bowl, daisy **15.00**
Flower Frog, R–104, standing deer **18.00**
Flower Frog, R–125, bird in flight **65.00**
Planter, R–719, fish, small **18.00**
Planter, R–754, donkey cart **12.00**
Planter, R–834, turtle **15.00**
Table Lamp, cabbage rose **30.00**
Table Lamp, mare and foal **55.00**
Table Lamp, mermaid **55.00**
Vase, R–186, Bird of Paradise **25.00**
Vase, R–246, double cornucopia **15.00**

HALL CHINA

In 1903 Robert Hall founded the Hall China Company in East Liverpool, Ohio. Taggert Hall, his son, became president following Robert's death in 1904. The company initially made jugs, toilet sets, and utilitarian whiteware. Robert T. Hall's major contribution to the firm's growth was the development of an economical, single–fire process for lead–free glazed ware.

Hall acquired a new plant in 1930. In 1933 the Autumn Leaf pattern was introduced as a premium for the Jewel Tea Company.

Other premium patterns include Blue Bonnett (Standard Coffee Company), Orange Poppy (Great American Tea Company), and Red Poppy (Grand Union Tea Company).

The company launched a decal–decorated dinnerware line in 1933. Hall's refrigerator ware was marketed to the general public along with specific patterns and shapes manufactured for General Electric, Hotpoint, Montgomery Ward, Sears, and Westinghouse.

Hall made a full range of products, from dinnerware to utilitarian kitchenware. Its figural teapots in the shape of Aladdin lamps, automobiles, etc., are eagerly sought by collectors.

References: Susan and Al Bagdade, *Warman's American Pottery and Porcelain,* Wallace–Homestead, Krause Publications, 1994; Harvey Duke, *The Official Price Guide to Pottery and Porcelain, Eighth Edition,* House of Collectibles, 1995; Margaret and Kenn Whitmyer, *The Collector's Encyclopedia of Hall China, Second Edition,* Collector Books, 1994, 1997 value update.

Collectors' Club: Hall Collector's Club, PO Box 360488, Cleveland, OH 44136.

Note: See Autumn Leaf for additional listings.

Blue Blossom, ball jug, #3 . . . . **$95.00**
Blue Blossom, casserole, round, #76 . . . . **40.00**
Blue Blossom, casserole, Sundial, #1 . . . . **50.00**
Blue Blossom, jug, Five Band, 1½ pt **50.00**
Blue Bouquet, bean pot, New England, #4 . . . . **100.00**
Blue Bouquet, ball jug, #3 . . . . **80.00**
Blue Bouquet, bread and butter plate, D–style, 6" d **5.50**
Blue Bouquet, cereal bowl, D–style, 6" d **12.00**
Blue Bouquet, creamer, Boston **10.00**
Blue Bouquet, custard, thick rim **12.00**
Blue Bouquet, dinner plate, D–style, 9" d **15.00**
Blue Bouquet, jug, Radiance **60.00**
Blue Bouquet, leftover, rect **50.00**
Blue Bouquet, sugar, cov, Boston **18.00**
Blue Garden, jug, 1½ pt **70.00**
Cameo Rose, butter dish, ¼ lb **5.00**
Cameo Rose, creamer **7.50**
Cameo Rose, dinner plate, 9¼" d **10.00**
Cameo Rose, flat soup, 8" d **10.00**
Cameo Rose, fruit bowl, 5¼" d **5.00**

Heather Rose, pie baker, $20.00. Photo courtesy Morykan Auctioneers.

Cameo Rose, gravy and underplate 30.00
Cameo Rose, platter, oval, 11¼" 15.00
Cameo Rose, saucer 1.00
Cameo Rose, tidbit tray, 3 tier 35.00
Casual Living, bean pot, brown 15.00
Century Fern, gravy 12.00
Century Sunglow, creamer 6.50
Coffeepot, Blue Bouquet, Kadota 185.00
Coffeepot, Camelia, no drip 85.00
Coffeepot, French, canary yellow, flower, 4 cup 40.00
Coffeepot, Globe, canary yellow, gold decal 85.00
Coffeepot, Hollywood, Monterrey, green 60.00
Coffeepot, New York, 12 cup, marine blue 40.00
Coffeepot, New York, canary yellow 30.00
Coffeepot, New York, Red Poppy 110.00
Coffeepot, Orange Poppy 65.00
Coffeepot, Springtime, coffee server 50.00
Coffeepot, Terrace, white, green, and platinum 22.50
Coffeepot, Waverly, aluminum basket 35.00
Crocus, bean pot, New England, #4 . . . . 100.00
Crocus, cake plate 30.00
Crocus, casserole, Radiance 30.00
Crocus, creamer, Medallion 60.00
Crocus, cup, St Denis 35.00
Crocus, custard 15.00
Crocus, dinner plate, D–style, 10" d 35.00
Crocus, flour shaker, handled 15.00
Crocus, French baker, fluted 20.00
Crocus, jug, cov, Radiance, #3 and #4 . . . . 60.00
Crocus, leftover, Zephyr 175.00
Crocus, mixing bowl 50.00
Crocus, platter, oval, D–style, 13¼" 35.00
Crocus, tidbit, D–style, 3 tier 55.00
Crocus, vegetable bowl, D–style, 9¼" d 30.00
Fantasy, ball jug, #2 . . . . 100.00
Five Band, casserole, red, 8" d 30.00
Five Band, jug, ivory, 5" h 18.00
Game Bird, coffee mug 15.00
Game Bird, creamer 15.00
Game Bird, fruit bowl, 5½" d 7.50
Game Bird, saucer 3.00
Game Bird, sugar, cov 30.00
Golden Glo, bean pot, #4 . . . . 90.00
Heather Rose, cake plate 15.00
Heather Rose, flat soup, 8" d 12.00
Heather Rose, jug, rayed 15.00
Heather Rose, platter, oval, 13¼" d 15.00
Heather Rose, sugar, cov 15.00
Homewood, bowl, Radiance, 6" d 12.00
Homewood, drip jar, Radiance 20.00
Homewood, fruit bowl, D–style, 5½" d 6.00
Homewood, salt and pepper shakers, pr, handled 20.00
Homewood, saucer, D–shape 1.00
Monticello, dinner plate 8.00
Monticello, fruit bowl 8.00
Monticello, plate, 7" d 6.00
Monticello, platter, oval, 15½" 18.00
Monticello, saucer 1.00
Monticello, vegetable, cov 25.00
Mount Vernon, cereal bowl, E–style, 6¼" d 6.00
Mount Vernon, dinner plate, E–style, 9¼" d 4.50
Mount Vernon, sugar, cov, E–style 1.00
Mums, casserole, Radiance 32.00
Mums, cereal bowl, D–style, 6" d 8.00

Mums, creamer, New York 15.00
Mums, cup, D–style 25.00
Mums, dinner plate, D–style, 9" d 12.00
Mums, drip jar, open, Kitchenware, #1188 . . . . 35.00
Mums, gravy, D–style 22.00
Mums, jug, Kitchenware, Simplicity 30.00
Mums, salt and pepper shakers, pr, handled 30.00
Mums, saucer, D–style 2.00
No. 488, butter, Zephyr, 1 lb 425.00
No. 488, creamer, Meltdown 30.00
No. 488, creamer, New York 18.00
No. 488, dinner plate, D–style, 9" d 12.00
No. 488, drip jar, cov, Radiance 22.00
No. 488, French baker, Kitchenware 20.00
No. 488, fruit bowl, D–style, 5½" 5.50
No. 488, leftover, square 70.00
No. 488, platter, oval, D–style, 11¼" d 20.00
No. 488, shaker, Teardrop 15.00
No. 488, sugar, cov, modern 20.00
Orange Poppy, ball jug, #3 . . . . 60.00
Orange Poppy, bean pot, New England, #4 . . . . 100.00
Orange Poppy, bowl, Radiance, 6" d 10.00
Orange Poppy, bread and butter plate, C–style, 6" d 6.00
Orange Poppy, cake plate 22.00
Orange Poppy, canister, Radiance 275.00
Orange Poppy, casserole, cov, oval, 9" l 55.00
Orange Poppy, cereal bowl, C–style, 6" d 12.00
Orange Poppy, cup, C–style 15.00
Orange Poppy, drip jar, cov, Radiance 18.00
Orange Poppy, flat soup, C–style, 8½" d 18.00
Orange Poppy, salt and pepper shakers, pr, handled 50.00
Orange Poppy, salt and pepper shakers, pr, range size 45.00
Orange Poppy, saucer, C–style 2.50
Pastel Morning Glory, ball jug, #3 . . . . 75.00
Pastel Morning Glory, bowl, Radiance, 6" d 10.00
Pastel Morning Glory, cereal bowl, D–style, 6" d 12.00
Pastel Morning Glory, creamer, New York 12.00
Pastel Morning Glory, dinner plate, D–style, 10" d 30.00
Pastel Morning Glory, drip jar, cov, Radiance 22.00
Pastel Morning Glory, drip jar, open, #1188 . . . . 30.00
Pastel Morning Glory, pie baker 25.00

Pastel Morning Glory, saucer, D–style 3.00
Pastel Morning Glory, saucer, St Denis 6.00
Primrose, cake plate 6.50
Primrose, cereal bowl, 6¼" d 4.50
Primrose, creamer 7.50
Primrose, jug, Rayed 25.00
Primrose, pie baker 20.00
Primrose, sugar, cov 15.00
Red Poppy, bowl, Radiance, 9" d 15.00
Red Poppy, cereal bowl, D–style 10.00
Red Poppy, creamer, modern 12.00
Red Poppy, cup, D–style 10.00
Red Poppy, dinner plate, D–style, 9" d 9.00
Red Poppy, drip jar, cov, Radiance 15.00
Red Poppy, gravy, D–style 25.00
Red Poppy, jug, Daniel, #4 . . . . 45.00
Red Poppy, pie baker 25.00
Red Poppy, salad bowl, 9" d 15.00
Red Poppy, saucer, D–style 2.00
Red Poppy, teapot, New York 90.00
Serenade, ball jug, #3 . . . . 55.00
Serenade, bowl, Radiance, 7½" d 15.00
Serenade, cereal bowl, D–style, 6" d 6.50
Serenade, creamer, New York 15.00
Serenade, fruit bowl, D–style 5.00
Serenade, gravy, D–style 30.00
Serenade, salad bowl, 9" d 15.00
Serenade, saucer, D–style 2.50
Silhouette, ball jug, #3 . . . . 90.00
Silhouette, bowl, Medallion, 6" d 12.00
Silhouette, bowl, oval, D–style 25.00
Silhouette, casserole, Medallion, 6" d 15.00
Silhouette, dinner plate, D–style, 9" d 15.00
Silhouette, mug 35.00
Silhouette, salad bowl, 9" d 15.00
Silhouette, salt and pepper shakers, pr, 5 bands 30.00
Silhouette, saucer, D–style 1.50
Silhouette, saucer, St Denis 10.00
Springtime, cake plate 15.00
Springtime, cereal bowl, 6" d, D–style 8.00
Springtime, custard 5.00
Springtime, flat soup, D–style, 8½" d 12.00
Springtime, jug, Radiance, #6 . . . . 20.00
Springtime, platter, oval, D–style, 13¼" 22.00
Teapot, Airflow, turquoise, gold trim 75.00
Teapot, Aladdin, black, gold trim 90.00
Teapot, Aladdin, cobalt blue, gold trim, oval infusor 110.00
Teapot, Aladdin, Daffodil, gold trim 45.00
Teapot, Aladdin, royal blue, gold trim 60.00
Teapot, Aladdin, Wildflower, oval lid and insert 90.00
Teapot, Aladdin, yellow, gold trim, round infusor 55.00
Teapot, Boston, Addison, gray, 4 cup 50.00
Teapot, Boston, cobalt blue, gold trim, 2 cup, gold wear 20.00
Teapot, Boston, delpfth, gold, 6 cup 30.00
Teapot, Cleveland, emerald green 70.00
Teapot, Flare–Ware, white with gold 35.00
Teapot, French, cobalt blue, 1 cup 80.00
Teapot, Hollywood, maroon, 6 cup 30.00
Teapot, Hook Cover, cadet blue 30.00
Teapot, Imperial, canary yellow 50.00
Teapot, Los Angeles, emerald green, no lid, 6 cup 20.00
Teapot, Los Angeles, stock brown, gold trim 30.00
Teapot, New York, Red Poppy 75.00
Teapot, Ohio, brown with gold, 6 cup 170.00

Teapot, Los Angeles, cobalt, standard gold, 6 cup, $29.50. Photo courtesy Gene Harris.

Wildfire, gravy boat, D–style, gold trim, 9" l, $20.00.

Teapot, Parade, yellow, gold trim 40.00
Teapot, Star, turquoise, gold trim 40.00
Teapot, Streamline, Chinese red 175.00
Teapot, Streamline, cobalt, gold trim 100.00
Teapot, Sundial, yellow, gold trim 55.00
Teapot, Windshield, emerald green, gold trim, no lid 35.00
Teapot, Windshield, maroon 40.00
Teapot, Windshield, maroon, gold trim. 40.00
Tulip, bread and butter plate, D–style, 6" d 4.00
Tulip, creamer. 15.00
Tulip, fruit bowl, D–style, 5¹/₂" d 10.00
Tulip, gravy, D–style 25.00
Tulip, mixing bowl, 6" d 28.00
Tulip, saucer, D–style 1.50
Tulip, saucer, St Denis. 8.00
Tulip, sugar, cov 25.00
Wildfire, cereal bowl, D–style, 6" d 12.00
Wildfire, creamer and sugar. 50.00
Wildfire, eggcup 50.00
Wildfire, flat soup, D–style, 8¹/₂" d 15.00
Wildfire, jug, Radiance, #5 . . . . 35.00
Wildfire, pie baker 25.00
Wildfire, platter, oval, 13¹/₄" 30.00
Wildfire, tidbit, 3 tier, D–style 90.00
Wild Poppy, baker, oval. 45.00
Wild Poppy, bowl, Radiance, 7¹/₂" d. 20.00
Yellow Rose, bowl, Radiance, 6" d. 10.00
Yellow Rose, cereal bowl, D–style, 6" d 6.50
Yellow Rose, cup, D–style 25.00
Yellow Rose, dinner plate, D–style, 9" d 8.00
Yellow Rose, gravy, D–style 30.00
Yellow Rose, onion soup 35.00
Yellow Rose, saucer, D–style 1.50
Yellow Rose, sugar, cov, Norse. 25.00

HALLMARK

In 1913 brothers Joyce and Rollie Hall launched a firm to sell Christmas cards. The line soon expanded to all types of holiday cards. In January 1913, a fire destroyed their entire stock of valentines. Undaunted, the Halls purchased a Kansas City engraving firm a year later and began printing and marketing Hallmark cards. Within two years, Hallmark cards were sold nationwide.

Following World War II, Hallmark launched a major expansion. In 1948 Norman Rockwell became the first "name" artist to appear on Hallmark cards. Hallmark's Plans–A–Party line was introduced in 1960. Playing cards appeared a year later. Hallmark introduced

a Cookie Cutter line in the early 1960s, its Keepsake Christmas Ornament line in 1973, and its Merry Miniature line in 1974.

Hallmark is a leader in preserving its company's heritage. The Hallmark Historical Collection is one of the finest company archives in America.

References: *Collector's Value Guide: Hallmark Keepsake Ornaments: Secondary Market Price Guide and Collector Handbook,* Collector's Publishing, 1997; Rosie Wells (ed.), *The Ornament Collector's Official Price Guide for Past Years' Hallmark Ornaments and Kiddie Car Classics, 12th Edition,* Rosie Wells Enterprises, 1998.

Periodical: *The Ornament Collector,* 22341 E Wells Rd, Canton, IL 61520.

Newsletter: *Hallmarkers,* PO Box 97172, Pittsburgh, PA 15229.

Collectors' Club: Hallmark Keepsake Ornament Collectors Club, PO Box 412734, Kansas City, MO 64141.

Cookie Cutter, plastic, Snoopy sitting on pumpkin **$75.00**
Doll, The Yuletide Romance Barbie, Special Edition,
   1996. . . . . 45.00
Figurine, 1935 Steelcraft airplane by Murray, E Weirick,
   Hallmark Galleries, 1996. . . . . 50.00
Figurine, Bunny Pulling Wagon, Tender Touches, E Seale,
   Hallmark Galleries, 1990. . . . . 25.00
Figurine, Christmas Bunny Skiing, Tender Touches,
   E Seale, 1991 . . . . 18.00
Figurine, Father Bear Barbequing, Tender Touches,
   E Seale, Hallmark Galleries, 1991 . . . . 20.00
Figurine, Mice in Rocking Chair, Tender Touches,
   E Seale, Hallmark Galleries, 1988 . . . . 20.00
Greeting Card, Easter, Donald Duck, diecut, flocked
   body, 1942 . . . . 25.00
Ornament, Baby's First Christmas, 1978 . . . . 65.00
Ornament, Bell, acrylic, 1977 . . . . 50.00
Ornament, Bicentennial '76 Commemorative, 1976 . . . . 45.00
Ornament, Christmas Tree, acrylic, 1979 . . . . 70.00
Ornament, Dove, acrylic, 1978 . . . . 125.00
Ornament, Elf, 1973 . . . . 25.00
Ornament, Little Girl, 1974 . . . . 20.00

Ornament, Betsey's Country Christmas, Keepsake Series, 2nd issue, 1993, $18.00.

Ornament, Mickey Mouse, satin, 1977 . . . . **65.00**
Ornament, Mother's Love, glass, 1978 . . . . **45.00**
Ornament, Peanuts, satin, 1978 . . . . **60.00**
Ornament, Praying Angel, Little Trimmers, 1976 . . . . **85.00**
Ornament, Santa, reissue, 1976 . . . . **25.00**
Ornament, Snowflake, Holiday Highlights, 1979 . . . . **40.00**
Ornament, Snowgoose, glass, 1974 . . . . **25.00**
Ornament, Soldier, 1973 . . . . **25.00**

HALLOWEEN

Halloween collectors divide material into pre– and post–1945 objects. Country of origin—Germany, Japan, or the United States—appears to make little difference. Image is everything. The survival rate of Halloween collectibles is extremely high. Currently, Halloween is second only to Christmas in respect to popularity among holiday collectors.

References: Pamela E. Apkarian–Russell, *Collectible Halloween*, Schiffer Publishing, 1997; Dan and Pauline Campanelli, *Halloween Collectibles: A Price Guide*, L–W Books, 1995; Stuart Schneider, *Halloween in America: A Collector's Guide With Prices*, Schiffer Publishing, 1995.

Newsletters: *Boo News*, PO Box 143, Brookfield, IL 60513; *Trick or Treat Trader*, PO Box 499, Winchester, NH 03470.

Candle, figural pumpkin **$10.00**
Candy Container, Jack–O'–Lantern, composition, orange, black trim, early 20th C **75.00**
Candy Cups, cat, owl, and pumpkin, 4" d, price for set of 3 . . . . **15.00**
Clicker, litho tin, smiling Jack–O'–Lantern, black and white Halloween motif, leaves, and 2 black cats, orange ground, Kirchof, 1950–60s **12.00**
Costume, Captain Kid Pirate Set, Lido **30.00**
Costume, Centurian Ace McCloud, Ben Cooper, 1982 . . . . . . **15.00**
Costume, clown, homemade, baggy, yellow and black, trimmed in bells, matching pointed hat, 1940s **8.00**
Costume, H R Puf–n–Stuf, Collegeville, 1971 . . . . **75.00**
Costume, Jet Man, Ben Cooper, 1950s **45.00**

Costume, Sesame Street, Oscar the Grouch, Ben Cooper, $20.00.

Costume, Little Audrey, 1 pc, yellow and red bodysuit with Little Audrey illus and name, plastic mask, Halco, 1960 . . . . **30.00**
Costume, MAD, Alfred E Neuman, Collegeville, 1960, MIB **350.00**
Costume, Star Trek, Mr Spock, 1967 . . . . **55.00**
Costume, The Outer Limits, monster illus, polyester, mask, Collegeville, 1964 . . . . **75.00**
Decoration, owl, diecut, emb paper, 9 x 13½" **30.00**
Decoration, witch, stand–up, USA, 10" h **15.00**
Fan, black cat, orange tissue, made in Germany, 1920 . . . . . . **25.00**
Favor, witch and broom, composition head, pipe cleaner body, 1950, 3" h **6.00**
Figure, black cat, wire neck, 7" h **35.00**
Figure, Pumpkin Man, wire neck, 5½" h **22.00**
Game, Superstition, board game, box cover shows house, moon, trees, and cemetery, Milton Bradley, 1977 . . . . **15.00**
Horn, wooden, cat face, black and orange, mkd "Czecho–Slavakia," 4" h **18.00**
Lantern, papier–mâché, devil's head, 2–tone red, paper insert behind cut–out eyes and mouth, wire bail handle, made in Germany, 7" h **100.00**
Mask, elephant, black and gray **5.00**
Mask, luminous, gauze **30.00**
Noisemaker, litho tin, pumpkins, mkd "T Cohn, USA" **5.50**
Pinback Button, Halloween symbols, yellow, black, and white, 1930s, 1½" d **25.00**
Shot Glass, black cats, black and orange **15.00**
Snowdome, figural, brown owl, outstretched wings, scarecrow, orange ground **20.00**

HANNA–BARBERA

William Denby Hanna was born on July 14, 1910, in Melrose, New Mexico. A talent for drawing landed him a job at the Harman–Ising animation studio in 1930. Hanna worked there for seven years.

Joseph Roland Barbera was born in New York City in 1911. After a brief stint as a magazine cartoonist, Barbera joined the Van Beuren studio in 1932 where he helped animate and script Tom and Jerry.

The year 1937 was a magic one for Hanna and Barbera. MGM was organizing a new cartoon unit. Barbera headed west, Hanna moved across town. In 1938 Hanna and Barbera were teamed together. Their first project was Gallopin' Gals. By 1939 the two were permanently paired, devoting much of their energy to Tom and Jerry shorts. Between 1939 and 1956, they directed over 200 Tom and Jerry shorts, winning several Oscars in the process.

Twenty years after joining MGM, Hanna and Barbera struck out on their own. Their goal was to develop cartoons for television as well as theatrical release. The success of Huckleberry Hound and Yogi Bear paved the way for The Flintstones, one of the most successful television shows of the 1960s.

In 1966 Taft Communications purchased Hanna–Barbera Productions for a reported 26 million dollars. Hanna and Barbera continued to head the company.

Hanna–Barbera Productions produced over 100 cartoon series and specials. In several cases, a single series produced a host of well–loved cartoon characters. Some of the most popular include Atom Ant, Auggie Doggie and Doggie Daddy, The Flintstones, Huckleberry Hound, The Jetsons, Jonny Quest, Magilla Gorilla,

Peter Potamus, Penelope Pitstop, Quick Draw McGraw, Ricochet Rabbit, Ruff and Reddy, Space Ghost, Top Cat, and Yogi Bear.

References: Joseph Barbera, *My Life in 'Toons: From Flatbush to Bedrock in Under a Century*, Turner Publishing, 1994; Bill Hanna, *A Cast of Friends*, Taylor Publishing, 1996.

Atom Ant, Atom Ant Play Fun, punch–out cardboard pcs, Whitman, 1966, orig 9 x 12" box **$45.00**
Banana Splits, doll, Drooper, General Mills, 12" h **55.00**
Banana Splits, Numbered Pencil Color Set, Hasbro, 1969. . . . . **75.00**
Flintstones, Bamm Bamm Bubble Pipe, Transogram, 1963. . . . . **25.00**
Flintstones, Bamm Bamm Color Me Happy, Transogram, 1963. . . . . **60.00**
Flintstones, bubble bath, Pebbles, 24 powdered soap packets, orig box with pop–up display lid, Roclar, 1963. . . . . **85.00**
Flintstones, car, battery operated, Remco, 1964 . . . . **175.00**
Flintstones, chalk box, includes 12 colored chalk sticks, Advance Crayon, 1960s. **20.00**
Flintstones, doll, Barney, Ideal **35.00**
Flintstones, doll, Pebbles, Ideal **100.00**
Flintstones, The Flintstones Stone Age Game, Transogram, 1961 . . . . **40.00**
Flintstones, Mechanical Shooting Gallery, 1962 . . . . **250.00**
Flintstones, pull toy, Bamm Bamm and Pebbles sitting on Stone Age cart, Transogram, 1963 . . . . **70.00**
Hanna–Barbera Give–A–Show Projector, battery operat-ed, 16 color slide strips, Kenner, 1963 . . . . **45.00**
Huckleberry Hound, bank, plastic, figural Huckleberry Hound wearing top hat, 1960, Knickerbocker, 10" h **30.00**
Huckleberry Hound, car, friction, litho tin, Huckleberry Hound riding go–cart, Linemar, 1960s **240.00**
Huckleberry Hound, Flicker Picture Toy TV, plastic, Vari–Vu, Kohner, 1960s **50.00**
Huckleberry Hound, Huckleberry Hound Western Game, Milton Bradley, 1959 . . . . **30.00**
Huckleberry Hound, pencil case, Hasbro, 1960 . . . . **25.00**
Impossibles, magic slate, Watkins–Strathmore, 1969. . . . . . . **25.00**
Jabber Jaws, lunchbox, vinyl, 1977 . . . . **30.00**

Jetsons, toy, Jetson's Hopping Astro, Linemar/HB, litho tin, 4" l, $3,375.00. Photo courtesy New England Auction Gallery.

Jetsons, activity book, The Jetsons Color–By–Number, Whitman, 1963, 11 x 13" **45.00**
Jetsons, game, Jetsons Fun Pad, Milton Bradley, 1963 . . . . . . **65.00**
Jetsons, toy, windup, litho tin, Rosie, Marx, 1962 . . . . **325.00**
Jonny Quest, Crayon By Number and Stencil Set, Transogram, 1965 . . . . **125.00**
Magilla Gorilla, coloring book, Whitman, 1964 . . . . **35.00**
Magilla Gorilla, pull toy, vinyl Magilla on yellow plastic wagon, Ideal, 1964 . . . . **25.00**
Mr Jinks, doll, Knickerbocker, 13" h **50.00**
Mush Mouse, pull toy, Ideal, 1964. **25.00**
Peter Potamus, bank, #4096–4, book style, 1964 . . . . **75.00**
Peter Potamus, figure, Twistables, soft vinyl, poseable, Ideal, 1964, MIB **50.00**
Pixie and Dixie, Punch–O Punching Bag, Kestral, 1959, 18" h **15.00**
Punkin' Puss, playing cards, Whitman, 1960s. **20.00**
Quick Draw McGraw, lamp shade, stiff paper, Quick Draw and friends in western desert scene, 1960, 9" d **40.00**
Quick Draw McGraw, Moving Target Game, Knickerbocker, 1960s **130.00**
Ricochet Rabbit, game, Ricochet Rabbit and Droop Along Coyote, Ideal, 1964 . . . . **295.00**
Ricochet Rabbit, pull toy, vinyl, Ricohet on plastic wagon, 1964, 5" h. **45.00**
Ruff and Ready, doll, Reddy, plush, 15" h. **95.00**
Scooby Doo, game, Scooby Doo...Where Are You?, Milton Bradley, 1973. . . . . **20.00**
Scooby Doo, soap, figural, orig box, Hewitt, unused, 1977. . . . . **20.00**
Top Cat, TV Tinykins, plastic, TV with Top Cat under clear plastic bubble, 3½ x 5½" display card, 1961 . . . . . . **40.00**
Yakky Doodle and Chopper, coloring book, #1836, Watkins–Strathmore, 1962. . . . . **25.00**
Yogi Bear, camera, black plastic, black, instruction sheet, Hong Kong **50.00**
Yogi Bear, doll, stuffed, vinyl face, Knickerbocker, 1959, 10" h **55.00**
Yogi Bear, game, Yogi Bear Presents, Snagglepuss Fun At the Picnic Game, Transogram, 1961 . . . . **40.00**
Yogi Bear, roly poly, hard vinyl, Irwin Toys, 1975, 7½" **50.00**
Yogi Bear, Yogi Bear Score–A–Matic Ball Toss, Transogram, 1960 . . . . **45.00**

Huckleberry Hound, Huck & Yogi Bath Soap, 2 figural soap bars, c1960, $75.00. Photo courtesy Wm. Morford Auctions.

HARKER POTTERY

The Harker Pottery Company traces its heritage back to Benjamin Harker, Sr., who established a pottery in East Liverpool, Ohio, in 1840. The company experienced a number of reorganizations during the 19th century. The George S. Harker Company was incorporated as the Harker Pottery in 1898. In 1930 the firm moved its production facilities from East Liverpool to Chester, West Virginia.

Harker made a variety of household dinnerware, kitchenware, and utilitarian ware. In addition, Harker produced premium and souvenir items. Harker's kitchenwares include Bakerite (introduced in 1935), HotOven (introduced in 1926), and Sun Glow (introduced in 1937). Harker's Gadroon, a dinnerware shape line, is one of the company's best-known products.

Harker's intaglio dinnerware lines included patterns by famous designers such as George Bauer, Paul Pinney, and Russel Wright. Wright's White Clover was introduced in the 1950s.

The Jeannette Glass Company purchased Harker Pottery in 1969. It made reproduction Rebekah-at-the-Well teapots and Toby jugs. Harker ceased operations in 1972.

References: Susan and Al Bagdade, *Warman's American Pottery and Porcelain,* Wallace–Homestead, Krause Publications, 1994; Neva W. Colbert, *The Collector's Guide to Harker Pottery USA,* Collector Books, 1993, out of print; Harvey Duke, *The Official Price Guide to Pottery and Porcelain, Eighth Edition,* House of Collectibles, 1995.

Amy, bean pot $12.00
Amy, bowl, 5½" d. 5.00
Amy, bread and butter plate, 6¼" d 5.50
Amy, pepper shaker. 12.50
Amy, pie baker 20.00
Amy, rolling pin 95.00
Birds and Flowers, utility plate, 12" d. 15.00
Cameoware, berry bowl 4.00
Cameoware, bowl, 5" d. 7.00
Cameoware, bread and butter plate, 6" d 5.50
Cameoware, cake server 12.00
Cameoware, custard, 6 oz 5.00
Cameoware, dinner plate, 10" d. 10.00
Cameoware, drip jar, Skyscraper 15.00

Countryside, scoop, $20.00.

Cameoware, mixing bowl, 9". 15.00
Cameoware, platter, 11" 25.00
Cameoware, saucer. 4.50
Cameoware, syrup jug, Ohio, ½ pt 15.00
Colonial Lady, bread and butter plate. 8.00
Colonial Lady, cake plate 25.00
Colonial Lady, pie baker 15.00
Colonial Lady, rolling pin 125.00
Colonial Lady, salt and pepper shakers, pr 25.00
Colonial Lady, server. 30.00
Colonial Lady, soup bowl 22.00
Countryside, pie server 18.00
Deco–Dahlia, cake lifter 30.00
Deco–Dahlia, spoon, red. 18.00
Deco–Dahlia, utility plate, 12" d 20.00
Ivy, cup 3.00
Ivy, fruit bowl, plain, 5" d 3.00
Ivy, pitcher, Regal shape, 7" h 32.00
Ivy, soup bowl, oval, plain. 2.50
Laurelton, bread and butter plate. 5.00
Laurelton, creamer and sugar, cov 15.00
Laurelton, cup and saucer 6.50
Laurelton, dinner plate 8.00
Laurelton, luncheon plate 5.00
Laurelton, soup bowl 10.00
Lemon Tree, dinner plate. 6.50
Mallow, bowl, 5" d 20.00
Mallow, coffeepot 25.00
Mallow, custard 2.50
Mallow, jug, cov 25.00
Mallow, lard jar, cov 22.00
Mallow, rolling pin 100.00
Mallow, serving spoon 25.00
Mallow, utility plate, lifter, and spoon set, Virginia ... 35.00
Melrose, salad bowl, Oriental Poppy 9.00
Modern Tulip, pie baker, Modern Age 15.00
Modern Tulip, utility plate, Modern Age, 11" 10.00
Monterey, cheese plate, Zephyr 35.00
Monterey, coffeepot, Zephyr, aluminum brewer 50.00
Monterey, utility plate, Virginia, 12". 30.00
Newport, creamer and sugar 5.00
Pansy, cereal bowl. 15.00
Pansy, dinner plate 15.00
Petit Point Rose, batter bowl 60.00
Petit Point Rose, cake plate 15.00
Petit Point Rose, casserole, cov 20.00
Petit Point Rose, coffeepot 40.00
Petit Point Rose, dinner plate. 6.50
Petit Point Rose, mixing bowl 30.00
Petit Point Rose, pie baker. 15.00
Petit Point Rose, rolling pin 95.00
Petit Point Rose, serving spoon 20.00
Red Apple, bowl, 4" d. 8.00
Red Apple, cereal bowl. 7.00
Red Apple, creamer and sugar, cov 25.00
Red Apple, custard 10.00
Red Apple, deep plate, handled, 7". 7.00
Red Apple, pie lifter 30.00
Red Apple, plate, square, 6⅝". 7.00
Red Apple, platter, 14" 15.00
Red Apple, saucer. 3.00
Red Apple, serving plate, 12" d 20.00
Red Apple, sugar, no lid 10.00
Red Apple, vegetable bowl, 9" d 30.00

HAVILAND CHINA

There are several Haviland companies. It takes a detailed family tree to understand the complex family relationships that led to their creations.

David and Daniel Haviland, two brothers, were New York china importers. While on a buying trip to France in the early 1840s, David Haviland decided to remain in that country. He brought his family to Limoges where he supervised the purchase, design, and decoration of pieces sent to America. In 1852, Charles Field Haviland, David's nephew, arrived in France to learn the family business. Charles married into the Alluaud family, owner of the Casseaux works in Limoges. Charles Edward and Theodore Haviland, David's sons, entered the firm in 1864. A difference of opinion in 1891 led to the liquidation of the old firm and the establishment of several independent new ones. [Editor's note: I told you it was complicated.]

Today, Haviland generally means ceramics made at the main Casseaux works in Limoges. Charles Edward produced china under the name Haviland et Cie between 1891 and the early 1920s. Theodore Haviland's La Porcelaine Theodore Haviland was made from 1891 until 1952.

References: Mary Frank Gaston, *Haviland Collectables & Objects of Art*, Collector Books, 1984, out of print; Gertrude Tatnall Jacobson, *Haviland China: Volume One* (1979), *Volume Two* (1979), Wallace–Homestead, out of print; Harry L. Rinker, *Dinnerware of the 20th Century: The Top 500 Patterns*, House of Collectibles, 1997.

Collectors' Club: Haviland Collectors Internationale Foundation, PO Box 802462, Santa Clarita, CA 91380.

Autumn Leaf, bread and butter plate, 6³/₈"	**$8.00**
Autumn Leaf, creamer, 2¹/₂"	35.00
Autumn Leaf, cup, flat, 2"	15.00
Autumn Leaf, dinner plate, 10¹/₄"	15.00
Autumn Leaf, fruit bowl, 5"	10.00
Autumn Leaf, luncheon plate, 8⁵/₈"	12.00
Autumn Leaf, platter, oval, 11¹/₄"	50.00
Autumn Leaf, salad plate, 7¹/₂"	12.00
Autumn Leaf, sugar, cov	40.00
Autumn Leaf, vegetable, oval, 9¹/₂"	15.00
Delaware, creamer	30.00
Delaware, demitasse cup and saucer	16.00
Delaware, dinner plate	15.00
Delaware, gravy, attached underplate	75.00
Delaware, luncheon plate, 8" sq	15.00
Delaware, platter, oval, 11⁵/₈"	45.00
Delaware, salad plate, 7¹/₂"	12.00
Delaware, saucer	5.00
Delaware, sugar, cov	40.00
Delaware, vegetable, oval, 9⁵/₈"	45.00
Montmery, cereal bowl, coupe, 6¹/₄"	12.00
Montmery, dinner plate	15.00
Montmery, gravy, attached underplate	90.00
Montmery, luncheon plate, 8⁵/₈"	18.00
Montmery, platter, oval, 11¹/₄"	127.00
Montmery, saucer, 2"	8.00
Montmery, sugar, cov	50.00
Montmery, teapot, no lid	100.00
Pasadena, bread and butter plate, 6¹/₂"	8.00
Pasadena, cream soup and saucer	28.00

Pasadena, dinner plate, $15.00.

Pasadena, cup, ftd, 2²/₄"	**20.00**
Pasadena, dinner plate	15.00
Pasadena, flat soup, 7⁷/₈"	15.00
Pasadena, fruit bowl, 5"	10.00
Pasadena, platter, oval, 14¹/₈"	65.00
Pasadena, salad plate, 7⁵/₈" d	10.00
Pasadena, vegetable, oval, 9⁵/₈"	50.00
Varenne, chop plate, 12³/₄"	90.00
Varenne, creamer	30.00
Varenne, cup and saucer, flat, 2¹/₈"	25.00
Varenne, fruit bowl, 5¹/₈"	10.00
Varenne, salad plate	12.00
Varenne, soup bowl, coupe, 7¹/₂"	20.00
Varenne, sugar, cov	45.00
Varenne, vegetable, oval, 9³/₄"	60.00

HAZEL ATLAS GLASSWARE

Hazel Atlas resulted from the 1902 merger of the Hazel Glass Company and the Atlas Glass and Metal Company, each located in Washington, Pennsylvania. The company's main offices were located in Wheeling, West Virginia.

The company was a pioneer in automated glassware manufacture. A factory in Clarksburg, West Virginia, specialized in pressed glassware and achieved a reputation in the late 1920s as the "World's Largest Tumbler Factory." Two factories in Zanesville, Ohio, made containers, thin–blown tumblers, and other blown ware. Washington and Wheeling plants made containers and tableware, the latter including many of the Depression–era patterns for which the company is best known among collectors.

Continental Can purchased Hazel–Atlas in 1956. Brockway Glass Company purchased the company in 1964.

References: Gene Florence, *Collectible Glassware From the 40s, 50s, 60s...*, *Fourth Edition*, Collector Books, 1998; Gene Florence, *Kitchen Glassware of the Depression Years, Fifth Edition*, Collector Books, 1995, 1997 value update.

Note: See Depression Glass for additional listings.

Ashtray, Dutch boy and girl, match holder center,
   1920s, 5³/₄" d. $30.00
Aurora, cereal bowl, 5¹/₂" d 18.00
Aurora, plate, 6¹/₂", cobalt 15.00
Aurora, saucer, cobalt 6.00
Coaster, cobalt, ruffled, price for set of 4 . . . . 40.00
Colonial Block, bowl, crystal. 6.00
Colonial Block, butter lid, pink 32.00
Colonial Block, bowl, 7", green 15.00
Colonial Block, goblet, crystal 9.00
Colonial Block, goblet, green. 11.00
Colonial Block, sherbet, crystal 6.00
Criss Cross, creamer, pink 35.00
Criss Cross, lemon reamer, green 20.00
Criss Cross, pitcher, 54 oz, crystal 100.00
Criss Cross, tumbler, 9 oz, crystal. 25.00
Criss Cross, water bottle, 32 oz, crystal 18.00
Florentine #1, creamer, green 15.00
Florentine #1, cup, green 10.00
Florentine #1, cup and saucer, green 18.00
Florentine #1, dinner plate, 9" d, green 25.00
Florentine #1, luncheon plate, 8" d, green 14.00
Florentine #2, ashtray, 5¹/₂", green 27.00
Florentine #2, comport, ruffled edge, 3¹/₂", crystal. . . . 25.00
Florentine #2, cream soup, 4³/₄", green. 15.00
Florentine #2, cup and saucer, crystal 8.50
Florentine #2, cup and saucer, green 15.00
Florentine #2, dinner plate, 10" d, crystal. 18.00
Florentine #2. luncheon plate, 8¹/₂" d, green 9.00
Florentine #2, salt and pepper shakers, pr, green 42.00
Florentine #2, saucer, green. 5.00
Florentine #2, sherbet, 6", yellow. 6.00
Florentine #2, sugar, yellow. 10.00
Florentine #2, tumbler, 5 oz, 4", green 18.00
Florentine #2, vase, 6", crystal 35.00
Moderntone, bread and butter plate, 6", cobalt. 5.00
Moderntone, creamer, cobalt. 12.00
Moderntone, cream soup, handled, amethyst 20.00
Moderntone, cup and saucer, cobalt 18.00
Moderntone, custard, cobalt 20.00
Moderntone, dinner plate, 9", cobalt 24.00
Moderntone, luncheon plate, 8", cobalt 14.00
Moderntone, nappy, 5", amethyst. 24.00

Pebbletone, snack set, crystal, $6.00.

Moderntone, nappy, 5", cobalt. 25.00
Moderntone, salad plate, 7", cobalt 15.00
Moderntone, saucer, cobalt 5.00
Moderntone, sherbet, cobalt 12.00
Moderntone, sugar, cobalt. 10.00
New Century, dinner plate, 10" d, green. 12.00
New Century, tumbler, 5 oz, 3¹/₂", cobalt 10.00
Newport, saucer, white 1.00
Royal Lace, bowl, ruffled, 10" d, green. 165.00
Royal Lace, bowl, ruffled edge, 10" d, pink 100.00
Royal Lace, bowl, straight edge, 10" d, cobalt. 110.00
Royal Lace, bread and butter plate, cobalt 15.00
Royal Lace, butter, cov, cobalt 800.00
Royal Lace, console bowl, ruffled edge, pink 95.00
Royal Lace, cookie jar, cov, cobalt 450.00
Royal Lace, creamer, cobalt. 60.00
Royal Lace, cream soup, cobalt 48.00
Royal Lace, cup and saucer, cobalt 50.00
Royal Lace, cup and saucer, pink. 30.00
Royal Lace, dinner plate, cobalt. 48.00
Royal Lace, pitcher, straight sides, cobalt 225.00
Royal Lace, pitcher, straight sides, green. 185.00
Royal Lace, platter, pink 55.00
Royal Lace, salt and pepper shakers, pr, cobalt 390.00
Royal Lace, sherbet, metal holder, cobalt 40.00
Royal Lace, sugar, open, cobalt 50.00
Royal Lace, tumbler, 9 oz, green 32.00
Royal Lace, tumbler, 9 oz, pink 25.00
Royal Lace, tumbler, 10 oz, green 155.00

HEISEY GLASS

In April 1896, Augustus H. Heisey opened a sixteen–pot glass furnace in Newark, Ohio. Eventually the plant expanded to three furnaces and employed over 700 people.

Early production was limited to pressed ware and bar and hotel ware. In the late 1890s, Colonial patterns with flutes, scallops, and panels were introduced.

George Duncan Heisey, a son of Augustus H., designed the famous "Diamond H" trademark in 1900. The company registered it in 1901. In 1914 blown ware was first manufactured. Not content with traditional pulled stemware, the company introduced fancy pressed stemware patterns in the late 1910s.

Edgar Wilson, another son of Augustus H., became president in 1922 following Augustus' death. He was responsible for most of the colored Heisey glass. While some colored glass was made earlier, the first pastel colors and later deeper colors, e.g., cobalt and tangerine, were manufactured in quantity in the 1920s and 30s. By

Criss Cross, refrigerator dish, cobalt lid, crystal base, 1936–38, $25.00.

the time of Edgar Wilson's death in 1942, colored glassware had virtually disappeared from the market.

T. Clarence Heisey, another son of Augustus, assumed the presidency of the company. Shortages of manpower and supplies during World War II curtailed production. Many animal figures were introduced in the 1940s. An attempt was made to resurrect colored glass in the 1950s. Increasing production costs and foreign competition eventually resulted in the closing of the Heisey factory in December 1957.

The Imperial Glass Corporation of Bellaire, Ohio, bought the Heisey molds in 1958. Only a small number were kept in production, primarily those of patterns Heisey had in production when it ceased operations. Some pieces still carried the Heisey mark. In January 1968, Imperial announced it would no longer use the Heisey mark.

References: Neila Bredehoft, *The Collector's Encyclopedia of Heisey Glass, 1925–1938,* Collector Books, 1986, 1997 value update; Gene Florence, *Elegant Glassware of the Depression Era, Seventh Edition,* Collector Books, 1997; Frank L. Hahn and Paul Kikeli, *Collector's Guide to Heisey and Heisey By Imperial Glass Animals,* Golden Era Publications, 1991, 1994 value update; Harry L. Rinker, *Stemware of the 20th Century: The Top 200 Patterns,* House of Collectibles, 1997.

Collectors' Club: Heisey Collectors of America, Inc, 169 W Church St, Newark, OH 43055.

Lariat, vase, crystal, price for pair, $38.50. Photo courtesy Jackson's Auctioneers & Appraisers.

Carcassonne, cocktail, ftd, sahara, 3 oz	**$28.00**
Carcassonne, sherbet, crystal	20.00
Carcassonne, sherbet, sahara	25.00
Colonial, celery, 12", crystal	35.00
Colonial, custard cup, flared, mkd, crystal	10.00
Colonial, plate, 4³/₄", crystal	5.00
Colonial, plate, scalloped edge, 6", crystal	10.00
Colonial, punch cup, crystal	5.00
Crystolite, bowl, shallow, 10¹/₂" sq, crystal	95.00
Crystolite, candle blocks, pr, round, crystal	40.00
Crystolite, candy, swan, crystal	33.00
Crystolite, cheese stand, 5¹/₂", crystal	20.00
Crystolite, coupe plate, 7¹/₂", crystal	30.00
Crystolite, cup and saucer, crystal	25.00
Crystolite, dessert nappy, 5³/₈", crystal	15.00
Crystolite, gardenia bowl, oval, 12", crystal	40.00
Crystolite, goblet, #5003, crystal	28.00
Crystolite, jug, ice lip, ¹/₂ gal, crystal	125.00
Crystolite, leaf nappy, 5", crystal	20.00
Crystolite, leaf relish, 4 part, 9", crystal	42.00
Crystolite, mustard, cov, with #10 paddle, crystal	47.00
Crystolite, oil cruet, orig stopper, 3 oz, crystal	30.00
Crystolite, plate, 7", crystal	15.00
Crystolite, punch bowl, ¹/₂ qt, crystal	90.00
Crystolite, relish, divided, 6 sided, crystal	35.00
Crystolite, relish, oval, 5 part, crystal	45.00
Crystolite, salad plate, 8¹/₂", crystal	20.00
Crystolite, sherbet, #5003, crystal	16.00
Crystolite, sugar, crystal	30.00
Danish Princess, cocktail, 3¹/₂ oz, crystal	45.00
Danish Princess, cordial, 1 oz, crystal	65.00
Danish Princess, water, 9 oz, crystal	32.00
Danish Princess, wine, 2¹/₂ oz, crystal	55.00
Empress, creamer and sugar, dolphin ft, sahara	46.00
Empress, cup and saucer, sahara	34.00

Empress, plate, alexandrite, 8"	64.00
Empress, plate, sahara, 7" sq	18.00
Empress, plate, sahara, 8" d	13.00
Lariat, bowl, 12", crystal	40.00
Lariat, bowl, oval, floral cut, 13" l, crystal	36.00
Lariat, candle holders, pr, 2 light, crystal	45.00
Lariat, candlestick, low, crystal	20.00
Lariat, cigarette box, cov, crystal	48.00
Lariat, plate, 8", crystal	12.00
Lariat, plate, 13" d, crystal	45.00
Lariat, plate, floral cut, 14", crystal	48.00
Lariat, punch bowl, liner, cups, and ladle, crystal	250.00
Lariat, relish, oval, 2 part, 2 handled, 11", crystal	40.00
Lariat, salad bowl, 10¹/₂", crystal	40.00
Orchid, bowl, crimped, 12", crystal	80.00
Orchid, butter, cov, round, crystal	145.00
Orchid, cake plate, ftd, crystal	225.00
Orchid, candy jar, cov, seahorse handle, crystal	275.00
Orchid, celery vase, 12", crystal	50.00
Orchid, champagne, crystal	25.00
Orchid, cigarette holder, ftd, crystal	16.00
Orchid, creamer and sugar, crystal	70.00
Orchid, cup and saucer, crystal	55.00
Orchid, jelly bowl, ftd, crystal	40.00
Orchid, oil cruet, crystal	175.00
Orchid, plate, 7¹/₄", crystal	18.00
Orchid, relish, 3 part, round, crystal	42.00
Orchid, saucer, crystal	15.00
Orchid, sugar, individual, crystal	35.00
Orchid, tumbler, ftd, 12 oz, 7³/₄", crystal	60.00
Orchid, water goblet, crystal	48.00
Plantation, compote, 5", crystal	45.00
Plantation, creamer and sugar, ftd, crystal	65.00
Plantation, relish, 3 part, 11", crystal	85.00
Plantation, tumbler, ftd, 5 oz, crystal	36.00
Ridgeleigh, ashtray, square, small, crystal	10.00
Ridgeleigh, cigarette holder, round, crystal	15.00
Ridgeleigh, coaster, crystal	5.00
Ridgeleigh, creamer, crystal	20.00
Ridgeleigh, creamer and sugar tray, crystal	20.00
Ridgeleigh, mustard, cov, crystal	50.00

Recessed Panel, candy jar, cov, mkd, crystal, $35.00.

Rose, candlesticks, pr, 3 light, crystal 325.00
Rose, candy, seahorse, tall, crystal 250.00
Rose, cocktail, 4 oz, crystal 40.00
Rose, cracker plate, 12", crystal 130.00
Rose, iced tea, 12 oz, crystal 65.00
Rose, juice tumbler, ftd, 5 oz, crystal 45.00
Rose, plate, 14", crystal 37.00
Rose, relish, 3 part, 11", crystal 75.00
Rose, sherbet, crystal 30.00
Rose, water goblet, 9 oz, crystal 48.00
Victorian, champagne, crystal 11.50
Victorian, cocktail, crystal 12.00
Victorian, punch cup, mkd, 5 oz, crystal 9.00
Victorian, sherbet, crystal 15.00
Victorian, water, mkd, crystal 24.00
Victorian, wine, crystal 16.00

AUCTION PRICES

Heisey glass sold at All Heisey Benefit Auction held April 18 and 19, 1997, at the Apple Tree Auction Center, Newark, Ohio. Prices do not include a 5% buyer's premium which was waived for payment made by cash, money order, or approved check.

Cathedral, 1413, vase, 8" $70.00
Crystolite, 1503, torte plate, mkd, 13" 65.00
Duquesne, goblet, tangerine bowl, 9 oz 210.00
Fancy Loop, 1205, toothpick, emerald 120.00
Fandango, 1201, cruet, faceted stopper, 4 oz 50.00
Fish Bookends, pr, 1554 . . . . 230.00
Galaxy, 8005, sherbet, flamingo, mkd, 6 oz 5.00
Lariat, 1540, basket, no loops, 7" 100.00
Narrow Flute, 393, cocktail, 2 oz 35.00
Pineapple & Fan, 1255, cracker jar, cov, #3 . . . . 135.00
Pleat & Panel, 1170, cruet, flamingo, 3 oz 65.00
Recessed Panel, 465, candy dish, cov, red flash,
  mkd 110.00
Ridgeleigh, 1469, centerpiece, mkd, 8" 65.00
Sunburst, 343, cake salver 120.00
Wabash, 3350, cordial, mkd, 1 oz 30.00
Zodiac, 1590, creamer and sugar 125.00

HESS TRUCKS

Hess Oil and Chemical Corporation of Perth Amboy, New Jersey, introduced its first toy truck in 1964. The Hess Tank Trailer, with operating headlights and taillights and a fillable cargo tank with drainer hose, sold for $1.29, batteries included. It was reissued, unchanged, in 1965.

These promotions were so well received that vehicles have been distributed annually ever since. Available for initial purchase only at Hess service stations, these limited edition plastic toys are known for their quality construction. Each was issued complete with batteries and instructions in a sturdy cardboard box with superb graphics.

Reference: Michael V. Harwood, *The Hess Toy Collector*, FSBO, 1991.

Note: Prices listed for Hess Trucks MIB.

1964, B–Model Mack Tanker **$1,900.00**
1968, Tanker Truck 650.00
1969, Amerada Hess Truck 2,500.00
1970, Red Pumper Fire Truck 675.00
1972, Split Window Tanker 375.00
1975, Box Trailer 385.00
1976, Box Trailer, with barrels 400.00
1977, Tank Truck, large label 175.00
1978, Tank Truck, small label 185.00
1980, Training Van 375.00
1982–83, bank, "First Hess Truck" 125.00
1984, Tank Truck Bank 85.00
1985, First Hess Truck Bank 125.00
1986, Ladder Fire Truck, red 100.00
1987, 19–Wheeler Truck with Barrels 70.00
1988, Race Car Transporter 70.00
1989, Ladder Fire Truck with Siren 60.00
1990, Tanker Truck with Horn 45.00
1991, Semi–Tanker Truck 30.00
1992, 18–Wheeler and Racer, green and white, silver accents, race car fits in back of trailer, working head and taillights, boxed, 3½" h, 4" l 25.00
1994, Rescue Car 20.00
1995, Hess Truck and Helicopter 20.00

1988, Race Car Transporter, MIB, $70.00.

HI–FI EQUIPMENT

1950s and 60s Hi-Fi equipment is now collectible. Vacuum tube–type amplifiers, pre–amplifiers, AM–FM tuners, and receivers are sought. Look for examples from Acrosound, Altec, Eico, Fisher, McIntosh, Marantz, and Western Electric. Some American and English record turntables and speakers are also collectible. Garrard and Thorens are two leading brand names.

Prices reflect equipment in working order. If a piece of equipment does not work, it has parts value only, usually $25 or less. Because collectors restore equipment, unused tubes in their period boxes have value, albeit modest.

Amplifier, Acrosound UL–II, Ultra Linear, stereo, 60
watts, EL34 output tubes **$120.00**
Amplifier, Eico, HF–87, stereo, 70 watts, EL34 output
tubes **75.00**
Amplifier, Harmon Kardon, Citation II, stereo, 120 watts,
KT88 output tubes **100.00**
Amplifier, Marantz, 2, mono, 40 watts, EL34 output
tubes, meter **200.00**
Amplifier, McIntosh, C–20, pre–amplifier, mono, 60
watts, 6550 output tubes **100.00**
Pre–amplifier, Marantz, 7–C, stereo, tubes, wood case,
metal knobs **250.00**
Record Turntable, Thorens TD124, 4 speeds, belt drive,
wooden base **25.00**
Stereo Receiver, Fisher, AM/FM, 800C, 50 watts, walnut
case **75.00**
Stereo Tuner, Fisher, FM1000, FM only, wooden case **75.00**
Vacuum Tube, Amperex EL34, output, made in France or
Holland, new **3.00**

HIGGINS GLASS

Michael Higgins and Frances Stewart Higgins were actively involved in designing and decorating glass in their Chicago studio by the early 1950s. Between 1958 and 1964, the couple worked in a studio provided for them by Dearborn Glass, an industrial glass company located outside Chicago. Pieces were mass produced. A gold signature was screened on the front of each piece before the final firing. During the period with Dearborn, the Higgins developed new colors and enamels for their double–layered pieces and experimented with weaving copper wire into glass, fusing glass chips to create crystalline forms, and overlaying colors onto glass panels.

After leaving Dearborn, the Higgins established a studio at Haeger. In 1966 they re–established their own studio. During the late 1960s and early 1970s, the Higgins manufactured large quantities of glass plaques, often framed in wood. In 1972 they purchased the building in Riverside, Illinois, that currently serves as their studio. Pieces made after 1972 have an engraved signature on the back. When they retire, the Higgins plan to close their studio rather than allow a successor to continue.

Reference: Donald–Brian Johnson and Leslie Piña, *Higgins: Adventures in Glass,* Schiffer Publishing, 1997.

Note: Unless stated otherwise, all pieces have a gold signature.

Ashtray, blue and gray ray, 7 x 10" **$44.00**
Ashtray, blue and yellow ray, inside signature, 10 x 14". **82.00**
Ashtray, blue checkerboard, 7 x 10" **82.00**

Tray, blue scroll, gold signature, 10¹/₂" sq, $93.50. Photo courtesy Jackson's Auctioneers & Appraisers.

Ashtray, clocks in smoked glass, 10 x 14" **82.00**
Ashtray, red sawtooth, rolled over edge, 8¹/₂" **50.00**
Ashtray, white, green pulled feathers, 14 x 10" **65.00**
Bowl, blue spike, 12" d **135.00**
Bowl, blue with fried eggs, 8¹/₂" d **88.00**
Bowl, 3 ftd, white with green pulled feathers, 13¹/₂" d **110.00**
Bowl, ftd, 5 corner, red, bird and birdcage, etched sig-
nature, 8¹/₂ x 8" **165.00**
Bowl, green bush with berries, Stickman, etched sig-
nature, 7" sq **115.00**
Bowl, green, orange, and blue check with bubbles, 9" h **110.00**
Bowl, low, blue and green fried egg, Stickman, 10" sq **165.00**
Bowl, orange spike, 8¹/₂" d **55.00**
Bowl, pink blob, etched signature, 6" d **50.00**
Bowl, with sauce well, green with blue and orange lat-
tice, inside signature, 12" d **170.00**
Box, cov, hardwood, orange ray lid, 7¹/₂ x 4" **66.00**
Condiment, 3 part, orange, green, and red rays, gold
swirl decor, Stickman and gold signature, 7 x 19" d **77.00**
Charger, chartreuse and white stripes, gold seaweed,
orig paper label, 17" d **105.00**
Charger, fall season, etched signature, 15" d **550.00**
Charger, red lattice and plume, etched Francis Higgins
signature, 13" d **110.00**
Charger, summer season, etched signature, 15" d **550.00**
Charger, winter season, etched signature, 15" d **550.00**
Charger, yellow and chartreuse ray, 17" d **165.00**
Dish, 3 ftd, blue pulled feather, 8¹/₂" d **82.00**
Dish, 3 ftd, daisies, 8¹/₂" d **110.00**
Hanging Planter, red feather, 7¹/₂" d **110.00**
Plate, amber and gold pulled scroll, etched signature,
6¹/₂" d **55.00**
Plate, chartreuse and white stripes, gold seaweed,
8¹/₂" d **55.00**
Plate, green, orange, and red fire flower, etched signa-
ture, 6¹/₂" d **16.00**
Plate, red and orange spike, 7¹/₂" d **38.00**
Tray, black and chartreuse triangles, Michael Higgins
etched signature with Stickman, 7" sq **176.00**

Tray, divided, turquoise dot ray, Stickman signature,
7 x 14" **77.00**
Tray, keys and locks, 3½ x 7½" **38.00**
Tray, orange and green dot ray, Stickman and gold sig-
nature, 5 x 10" **82.00**
Tray, orange, red, and avocado ray, orig label, 14" sq **93.00**
Tray, red orange and avocado ray, gold spiral dec,
Stickman and gold signature, 14 x 7" **60.00**
Tray, turquoise dot rays, Stickman and gold signature,
10" sq **82.00**
Tray, yellow and chartreuse ray, gold spiral dec, 14 x 17" **65.00**
Wall Pocket, orange and red ray, inside signature, 10" h **132.00**

HOCKEY CARDS

The first hockey cards were three cigarette sets produced between 1910 and 1913. Four candy card sets and one cigarette set were issued in the 1920s. In the 1930s Canadian chewing gum manufacturers, e.g., World Wide Gum Company, offered hockey cards as a premium.

The modern hockey card dates from the 1950s. Parkhurst issued hockey card sets between 1951 and 1964, the exception being the 1956–57 season. Topps produced its first hockey card set in 1954. Topps sets focused on American teams; Parkhurst on Canadian teams. Starting with the 1964–65 season, Topps issued card sets that included players from all teams in the National Hockey League. O–Pee–Chee, a producer of card sets in the 1930s, re–entered the market in 1968.

There were five major card sets for the 1990–91 season: Bowman, O–Pee–Chee Premier, Pro Set, Score, and Upper Deck. Like trading cards for other sports, current hockey card sets contain special feature cards. This is one collectible that is equally at home in either Canada or the United States.

References: James Beckett, *Beckett Hockey Card Price Guide & Alphabetical Checklist No. 7*, Beckett Publications, 1997; James Beckett, *Official Price Guide to Hockey Cards 1998, 7th Edition*, House of Collectibles, 1997; Sports Collectors Digest, *1998 Sports Collectors Almanac*, Krause Publications, 1998.

Periodicals: *Beckett Hockey Monthly*, 15850 Dallas Pkwy, Dallas, TX 75248; *Sports Cards Magazine & Price Guide*, 700 E State St, Iola, WI 54990.

Note: Prices are for cards in good condition.

Donruss, 1993–94, #1, Mario Lemieux, Elite Series **$32.00**
Donruss, 1993–94, #15, Todd Harvey, Canadian World
Juniors Series .... **.80**
Donruss, 1993–94, #195, Martin Brodeur .... **.40**
Donruss, 1994–95, Ice Masters Series, complete set (10) **12.00**
O–Pee–Chee, 1933–34, #7, Walter Galbraith, Series A **20.00**
O–Pee–Chee, 1934–35, #71, Cecil Dillon, Series B **20.00**
O–Pee–Chee, 1935–36, #79, Lynn Patrick, Series C **50.00**
O–Pee–Chee, 1936–37, #124, Harvey Jackson, Series D **85.00**
O–Pee–Chee, 1937–38, #135, Jimmy Fowler, Series E **15.00**
O–Pee–Chee, 1939–40, #9, Reg Kelly, regular issue **7.50**
O–Pee–Chee, 1940–41, common card (126–150) **15.00**
O–Pee–Chee, 1968–69, #127, Norman Larson, regular
issue **15.00**
O–Pee–Chee, 1969–70, #22, Gerry Cheevers, Boston
Bruins, regular issue **4.50**
Parkhurst, 1951–52, common player **35.00**

Parkhurst, 1952–53, #51, George Armstrong **140.00**
Parkhurst, 1953–54, #26, Doug Harvey **90.00**
Parkhurst, 1955–56, common player **5.50**
Parkhurst, 1961–62, common player **3.00**
Parkhurst, 1962–63, 23, Bruch MacGregor **3.00**
Parkhurst, 1991–92, complete set (475) **40.00**
Score, 1990–91, #1, Wayne Gretzky, regular issue **1.00**
Score, 1990–91, #32, Mark Fitzpatrick, Young Superstars
Series .... **.05**
Score, 1991–92, Bobby Orr Collector Cards, Bobby Orr,
Scoring Leader **15.00**
Score, 1991–92, Score Canadian, complete set (660) **6.00**
Topps, 1958–59, #52, Alex Delvecchio, regular issue **7.50**
Topps, 1959–60, Bobby Hull, regular issue **135.00**
Topps, 1960–61, #8, Cy Denneny, regular issue **3.00**
Topps, 1961–62, 40, Bronco Horvath, Chicago Black
Hawks, regular issue **3.00**
Topps, 1967–68, #90, Rod Gilbert, New York Rangers,
regular issue **4.50**
Topps, 1972–73, Garry Unger, regular issue .... **.30**
Upper Deck, 1990–91, #24, Alexander Mogliny **4.00**
Upper Deck, 1991–92, #57, Brian Mullen, San Jose
Sharks .... **.05**
World Wide Gum, 1933–34, #12, Nels Stewart **100.00**
World Wide Gum, 1933–34, #22, Ace Bailey **80.00**
World Wide Gum, 1933–34, #30, Bill Cook **55.00**
World Wide Gum, 1933–34, #32, Art Chapman **22.50**
World Wide Gum, 1933–34, #50, Bill Thoms **32.50**
World Wide Gum, 1933–34, #65, Cooney Weiland **75.00**

HOCKEY MEMORABILIA

Hockey memorabilia focuses primarily on professional hockey teams. Although the popularity of college hockey is growing rapidly and Canada's Junior Hockey is deeply entrenched, professional teams have generated almost all licensed collectibles.

Collecting is highly regionalized. Most collectors focus on local teams. Even with today's National Hockey League, there is a distinct dividing line between collectors of material related to American and Canadian teams.

Superstar collecting is heavily post–1980 focused. Endorsement opportunities for early Hockey Hall of Famers were limited. Collectors want game–related material. Logo licensed merchandise for sale in sports shops has minimal or no appeal.

Reference: Roderick Malloy, *Malloy's Sports Collectibles Value Guide: Up–to–Date Prices for Noncard Sports Memorabilia*, Attic Books, Wallace–Homestead, Krause Publications, 1993.

Autograph, Sid Able, unlined card, 5 x 3" **$4.00**
Autograph, Hobey Baker, PS, 8 x 10" **55.00**
Figurine, Brett Hull, Gartlan USA, mini **80.00**
Figurine, Mario, Lemieux, Salvino Sports Legends **275.00**
Game, All–Pro Hockey, Ideal, 1969 .... **20.00**
Game, Blue Line Hockey, 3M, 196 .... **30.00**
Game, The VCR Hockey Game, Interactive VCR Games,
1987 .... **12.00**
Hockey Stick, Bernie Parent **200.00**
Jersey, Brian Leetch **75.00**
Magazine, *Hockey Today*, Ideal Sports, 1978–79 .... **12.00**
Magazine, *Official NHL Guide*, 1960–61 .... **55.00**
Magazine, *Sports Illustrated*, April 7, 1969, St Louis
Hockey cov **6.50**

Nodder, Boston Bruins, 1960s, 4½" h, MIB. **45.00**
Nodder, Detroit Redwings, 1960s, 4½" h, MIB **45.00**
Nodder, San Diego Gulls, composition, caricature sea
   gull head, Sports Specialities **150.00**
Plate, Bobbie and Brett Hull, Gartlan USA, 8½" d **45.00**
Poster, Gordie Howe, *Sports Illustrated*, 1968–71 . . . . **35.00**
Skates, Trevor Kidd **195.00**
Yearbook, New Jersey Devils, 1982–83 . . . . **10.00**
Yearbook, Toronto Maple Leafs, 1981–82, 50th
   Anniversary. **8.00**

HOLIDAY COLLECTIBLES

Holiday collectibles can be broken down into three major periods: (1) pre–1940, (2) 1945 to the late 1970s, and (3) contemporary "collector" items. Crossover collectors, e.g., candy container collectors, skew the values on some items.

   This is a catchall category for those holiday collectibles that do not have separate category listings. It includes Fourth of July and Thanksgiving collectibles. Look elsewhere for Christmas, Easter, Halloween, and Valentines.

Reference: Pauline and Dan Campanelli, *Holiday Collectables: A Price Guide*, L–W Book Sales, 1997.

Periodical: *Pyrofax Magazine*, PO Box 2010, Saratoga, CA 95070.

Newsletters: *St Patrick Notes*, 10802 Greencreek Dr, Ste 703, Houston, TX 77070; *The Phoenix* (fireworks), 44 Toner Rd, Boonton, NJ 07005.

Birthday, party hat, Sweet Sixteen, crown type, card-
   board, silver, glitter dec, 1930 . . . . **$5.00**
Fourth of July, bank, figural Liberty Bell, carnival glass **10.00**
Fourth of July, bottle opener, Uncle Sam, cast iron, paint-
   ed, early 20th C **35.00**
Fourth of July, Coca–Cola bottle carrier, July Fourth,
   6 box wrapper, c1935 . . . . **70.00**
Fourth of July, fan, woman in sailor hat saluting, red and
   white striped ground, c1940 . . . . **15.00**
Fourth of July, flag, 48 stars, wooden stick **2.00**
Fourth of July, horn, litho tin, flags and bells dec **10.00**
Fourth of July, pinback button, Fire Department of Forest
   City issue, red, white, and blue, 1930s **25.00**
Fourth of July, pipe, white, figural Uncle Sam in red,
   white, and blue hat, made in Japan, 1950s **25.00**
Fourth of July, tablecloth, printed red, white, and blue
   flags and Libery Bell, Dennison **10.00**
Mother's Day, pinback button, pink carnations, green
   stems, black and white, Gimbels Mother's Day
   Reminder, 1940–50 . . . . **15.00**
New Year's Day, book, children's, *Miss Flora McFlimsey
   and the Baby New Year*, Lothrop, Lee & Shepard, dj,
   1951. . . . . **25.00**
New Year's Day, menu, New Year's Eve, Fountainbleu,
   Miami Beach, litho paper, 1957 . . . . **10.00**
New Year's Day, noisemaker, figural champagne bottle,
   wood, dated 1929, 4½" h **45.00**
New Year's Day, party hat, cone shape, cardboard, crepe
   paper dec, cutout silver foil, 1928 . . . . **15.00**
New Year's Day, photograph, New Year's Eve party,
   Copacabana Night Club, New York City, New York,
   framed, 1948 . . . . **35.00**

Thanksgiving, planter, figural turkey, Relpo #5293, Japan, gold foil label, $15.00.

New Year's Day, postcard, "Happy New Year," emb,
   baby surrounded by flowers, German. **5.00**
President's Day, bookends, pr, bronzed metal, Abraham
   Lincoln standing by chair, early 20th C. **110.00**
President's Day, calendar, The Lincoln Calendar, 1921,
   ribbon closure, Lincoln quotes printed in red, white,
   and blue, 7 x 9½" **35.00**
President's Day, candy container, George Washington
   bust, Germany. **275.00**
President's Day, centerpiece, honeycomb tissue, George
   Washington chopping down cherry tree, Beistle, 9" d **65.00**
President's Day, postcard, Washington and Lincoln. **20.00**
St Patrick's Day, banner, cloth, stenciled, 1930s **75.00**
St Patrick's Day, book, *Festival Book*, American
   Tissue Mills of Holyoak, MA, 1930, party instructions **125.00**
St Patrick's Day, candy container, figural top hat, made in
   Japan **55.00**
St Patrick's Day, cigar box, The Irishman, c1940–50s. **15.00**
St Patrick's Day, nut cup, crepe paper, double frill, green
   and white, cardboard shamrock. **5.00**
St Patrick's Day, pinback button, green shamrock,
   American flag, 1930s. **15.00**
Thanksgiving, advertising trade card, "Thanksgiving
   Greetings," Acme Stove Co adv, emb, 1936 . . . . **7.00**
Thanksgiving, candy container, figural turkey, composi-
   tion, German, c1920–30s **125.00**
Thanksgiving, candy container, figural roasted turkey,
   pressed cardboard, c1920–20s, 4½" l. **95.00**
Thanksgiving, costume, Pilgrim, handmade, 1940s. **15.00**
Thanksgiving, decoration, cardboard, diecut, turkey,
   1950s, 8" h **45.00**
Thanksgiving, napkin, Pilgrims and Indians print, cello-
   phane package, 1940s. **5.00**
Thanksgiving, nut cup, printed cardboard, turkey and
   pumpkins, tab and slot construction. **8.00**
Thanksgiving, postcard, pilgrims and turkey **15.00**
Thanksgiving, puzzle, Thanksgiving, Jig of the Week, #8,
   diecut cardboard, 300 pcs, 1932, orig box **15.00**
Valentine's Day, box, greeting cards, 1950 . . . . **15.00**
Valentine's Day, cookie cutter, plastic, heart shape **3.00**
Valentine's Day, decoration, honeycomb tissue, cupids
   motif, Beistle. **55.00**

HOLT–HOWARD

A. Grant Holt and brothers John and Robert J. Howard formed the Holt–Howard import company in Stamford, Connecticut in 1948. The firm is best known for its novelty ceramics, including the Cat and Christmas lines and the popular Pixie Ware line of condiment jars. Designed by Robert J. Howard and produced between 1958 and the early 1960s, these ceramic containers proved to be so successful that knock–offs by Davar, Lefton, Lipper & Mann, M–G, Inc., and Norcrest quickly found their way into the market. Kay Dee Designs purchased Holt–Howard in 1990.

Authentic Pixieware is easily identified by its single–color vertical stripes on a white jar, flat pixie–head stopper (with attached spoon when appropriate), and condiment label with slightly skewed black lettering. An exception is three salad dressing cruets which had round heads. All pieces were marked, either with "HH" or "Holt–Howard," a copyright symbol followed by the year "1958" or "1959," and "Japan." Some pieces may be found with a black and silver label.

Reference: Walter Dworkin, *Price Guide to Holt–Howard Collectibles and Related Ceramic Wares of the '50s & '60s,* Krause Publications, 1998.

Ashtray, Santa	$25.00
Bud Vase, rooster	20.00
Candle Climber, pr, yellow bird, with candle holders	100.00
Candle Climbers, pr, bluebird, with candle holders, orig pkg	100.00
Candle Climbers, pr, Christmas pixie, with candle holders, orig pkg	100.00
Candle Holders, pr, angel, orig pkg	75.00
Candle Holders, pr, figural rooster	20.00
Candleholders, pr, Santa in car	15.00
Coffeepot, rooster, emb	70.00
Cookie Jar, figural cat's head	40.00
Cottage Cheese Crock, Kozy Kitten	200.00
Double Eggcup, figural rooster	15.00
Instant Coffee Hot Pot, electric, ceramic	75.00
Juice Pitcher Set, 6 mugs, Santa winking	55.00
Kerosene Lamp, miniature, with glass globe	50.00
Letter Holder, Kozy Kitten	200.00

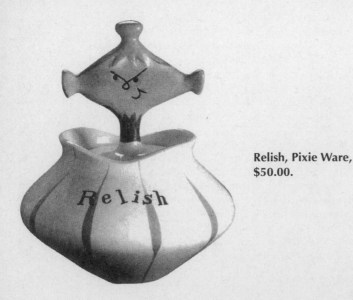

Relish, Pixie Ware, $50.00.

Letter Holder, pheasant	65.00
Mayonnaise, Pixie Ware, winking head finial	50.00
Mug, rooster, emb	15.00
Nativity Scene, 2 x 4 x 2" wood stable with 4 figures	75.00
Pin Box, cat, tape measure comes out of mouth	175.00
Planter, deer and fawn, gold bow	25.00
Plate, rooster, emb, 8½" d	10.00
Salt and Pepper Shakers, pr, apple slice	15.00
Salt and Pepper Shakers, pr, Kozy Kitten	65.00
Salt and Pepper Shakers, pr, mice in baskets	35.00
Spoon Rest, figural rooster	30.00
Vase, Santa sled and chimney	75.00
Vases, pr, Kozy Kitten	375.00
Wall Pocket, cat's head	35.00

HOMER LAUGHLIN

In 1870 Homer and Shakespeare Laughlin established two pottery kilns in East Liverpool, Ohio. Shakespeare left the company in 1879. The firm made whiteware (ironstone utilitarian products). In 1896 William Wills and a group of Pittsburgh investors, led by Marcus Aaron, purchased the Laughlin firm. The company expanded, building two plants in Laughlin Station, Ohio, and another in Newall, West Virginia. A second plant was built in Newall in 1926.

Cookware, dinnerware, and kitchenware were the company's principal products. Popular dinnerware lines include Fiesta, Harlequin, Rhythm, Riviera, and Virginia Rose.

References: Joanne Jasper, *The Collector's Encyclopedia of Homer Laughlin China: Reference & Value Guide,* Collector Books, 1993, 1997 value update; Richard G. Racheter, *Collector's Guide to Homer Laughlin's Virginia Rose: Identification & Values,* Collector Books, 1997.

Newsletter: *The Laughlin Eagle,* 1270 63rd Terrace S, St Petersburg, FL 33705.

Note: See Fiesta for additional listings: See Figurines for Harlequin animals.

Dogwood, mixing bowls, nesting set of 3	$130.00
Epicure, casserole, individual, pink	36.00
Epicure, creamer, pink	16.00
Epicure, sugar, pink	16.00
Hacienda, cereal bowl, 6"	40.00
Harlequin, ashtray, basket, gray	90.00
Harlequin, ashtray, basket, rose	65.00
Harlequin, ashtray, saucer, red	90.00
Harlequin, ball jug, mauve	75.00
Harlequin, ball jug, red	75.00
Harlequin, ball jug, spruce	95.00
Harlequin, ball jug, turquoise	55.00
Harlequin, ball jug, yellow	60.00
Harlequin, berry bowl, individual, rose	8.00
Harlequin, berry bowl, individual, turquoise	7.00
Harlequin, bread and butter plate, gray, 6"	5.00
Harlequin, bread and butter plate, red, 6"	6.00
Harlequin, butter, cov, maroon	100.00
Harlequin, butter base, maroon	50.00
Harlequin, candlesticks, pr, mauve	495.00
Harlequin, casserole, cov, chartreuse	240.00
Harlequin, casserole, cov, maroon	215.00
Harlequin, casserole, cov, spruce	215.00

Eggshell Theme, pattern C48N5, dinner plate, floral decal center, emb fruit and vine border, 10" d, $12.00. Photo courtesy Morykan Auctioneers.

Harlequin, casserole, cov, turquoise 165.00
Harlequin, cream soup, gray 25.00
Harlequin, cream soup, rose 20.00
Harlequin, cream soup, yellow 20.00
Harlequin, creamer, high lip, mauve 375.00
Harlequin, creamer, individual, green 125.00
Harlequin, creamer, individual, rose 35.00
Harlequin, creamer, turquoise 12.00
Harlequin, creamer and sugar, cov, blue 30.00
Harlequin, cup, gray 10.00
Harlequin, cup, red 8.00
Harlequin, cup, rose 9.00
Harlequin, cup, turquoise 7.00
Harlequin, cup, yellow 7.00
Harlequin, cup and saucer, maroon 10.00
Harlequin, cup and saucer, medium green 13.00
Harlequin, cup and saucer, turquoise 9.50
Harlequin, cup and saucer, yellow 9.50
Harlequin, cup and saucer, after dinner, maroon 195.00
Harlequin, cup and saucer, after dinner, red 130.00
Harlequin, cup and saucer, after dinner, spruce 195.00
Harlequin, deep plate, maroon 35.00
Harlequin, deep plate, medium green 125.00
Harlequin, dinner plate, gray, 10" 30.00
Harlequin, dinner plate, mauve, 10" 30.00
Harlequin, dinner plate, rose, 10" 25.00
Harlequin, dinner plate, spruce, 10" 40.00
Harlequin, dinner plate, turquoise, 10" 25.00
Harlequin, dinner plate, yellow, 10" 25.00
Harlequin, eggcup, mauve 12.00
Harlequin, eggcup, rose 12.00
Harlequin, jug, gray, 22 oz 95.00
Harlequin, luncheon plate, medium green, 9" 20.00
Harlequin, luncheon plate, 9", rose 30.00
Harlequin, luncheon plate, turquoise, 9" 12.00
Harlequin, luncheon plate, yellow, 9" 25.00
Harlequin, marmalade base, green 195.00

Harlequin, marmalade base, yellow 160.00
Harlequin, marmalade lid, turquoise 170.00
Harlequin, nappy, medium green 195.00
Harlequin, nut dish, rose 95.00
Harlequin, oatmeal, 36s, medium green 45.00
Harlequin, pitcher, rose, 22 oz 95.00
Harlequin, pitcher, spruce, 22 oz 125.00
Harlequin, pitcher, turquoise, 22 oz 75.00
Harlequin, pitcher, yellow, 22 oz 65.00
Harlequin, Service pitcher, yellow 60.00
Harlequin, sugar, cov, gray 45.00
Harlequin, sugar, cov, maroon 45.00
Harlequin, sugar, cov, mauve 25.00
Harlequin, sugar, cov, red 12.00
Harlequin, syrup, red 395.00
Harlequin, syrup, spruce 470.00
Harlequin, syrup lid, yellow 185.00
Harlequin, teapot, dark green 290.00
Harlequin, teapot, gray 185.00
Harlequin, teapot, maroon 195.00
Harlequin, teapot, mauve 115.00
Harlequin, teapot lid, mauve 95.00
Harlequin, teapot lid, rose 65.00
Harlequin, teapot lid, spruce 95.00
Harlequin, tumbler, rose 75.00
Harlequin, tumbler, maroon 48.00
Mexicana (Mexicali), gravy 45.00
Mexicana (Mexicali), plate, 10" d 52.00
Mexicana (Mexicali), platter, 13¼" 65.00
Riviera, batter jug, green 225.00
Riviera, butter dish, cov, green, ¼ lb 185.00
Riviera, butter dish, cov, ivory, ½ lb 155.00
Riviera, butter dish, cov, turquoise, ¼ lb 320.00
Riviera, butter dish, cov, yellow, ¼ lb 185.00
Riviera, casserole, cov, green 95.00
Riviera, casserole, cov, mauve 110.00
Riviera, casserole, cov, yellow 110.00
Riviera, casserole, green 165.00
Riviera, casserole, ivory 125.00
Riviera, casserole, mauve 185.00
Riviera, casserole, red 165.00
Riviera, casserole, yellow 165.00
Riviera, cup and saucer, after dinner, ivory 95.00
Riviera, dinner plate, green, 10" 95.00

Harlequin, demitasse cup and saucer, medium green, $100.00.

Riviera, dinner plate, yellow, 10" 85.00
Riviera, juice pitcher, mauve 350.00
Riviera, juice pitcher, yellow 175.00
Riviera, juice tumbler, green 85.00
Riviera, juice tumbler, ivory 95.00
Riviera, oatmeal bowl, green 85.00
Riviera, platter, oblong, ivory, gold decal, 15" 50.00
Riviera, salad plate, cobalt, 7" 50.00
Riviera, salad plate, ivory, gold decal 12.00
Riviera, soup bowl, ivory, gold decal 20.00
Riviera, syrup, red 295.00
Riviera, syrup lid, red 90.00
Riviera, teapot, cov, ivory 225.00
Riviera, tumbler, handled, ivory 270.00
Virginia Rose, butter, cov. 45.00
Virginia Rose, creamer 4.00
Virginia Rose, gravy 6.50
Virginia Rose, salt and pepper shakers, pr 10.00

HORSE COLLECTIBLES

Objects shaped like a horse or featuring an image of a horse are everywhere. Most collectors specialize, e.g., collectors of carousel horses. Horse–related toys, especially horse–drawn cast–iron toys, are bought and sold within the toy collecting community.

References: Jan Lindenberger, *501 Collectible Horses: A Handbook and Price Guide,* Schiffer Publishing, 1995; Jim and Nancy Schaut, *Horsin' Around Horse Collectibles,* L–W Book Sales, 1990, out of print.

Note: For additional listings see Breyer Horses.

Bank, cast iron, standing horse with saddle, Grey Iron
    Casting Co, 1928, 4¹/₄" h $275.00
Big Little Book, *Gene Autry, Cowboy Detective,* #1409,
    1946. .... 12.00
Book, *The Original Mr Ed,* Bantam, 1963 .... 14.00
Bookends, pr, rearing horse, glass, L E Smith, 8" h 100.00
Brush, leather back, soft bristles, 1930s 15.00
Calendar, 1950, Dodge Stables and Castleton Farm 45.00

Bookends, pr, deep red with black highlights, unmkd, 9¹/₂" h, 6¹/₂" w, $30.00.

Decanter, Man O'War, Ezra Brooks, 1969 .... 25.00
Doorstop, racehorse, Virginia Metalcrafters, 1949 .... 150.00
Figure, plastic, brown horse with black western saddle,
    Hartland, 7" 25.00
Figure, plastic, Sir Galahad, black, horse and rider,
    1950s, 12¹/₂" 60.00
Game, Cowboy Roundup, Parker Brothers, 1952 .... 25.00
Game, My Little Pony, Milton Bradley, 1988. .... 7.00
Horseshoe, plastic, "Hopalong Cassidy Bar 20 Ranch,"
    5¹/₄ x 6" 12.50
Magazine, *Saddle & Bridle,* 1931 .... 5.00
Photograph, black and white racehorse, c1920, 1¹/₄" 15.00
Pin, figural donkey, "Vote Democratic," 1960s 10.00
Pinback Button, Trigger, litho tin, 1953, ⁷/₈" 10.00
Puzzle, Old Dobbin Scroll Puzzle, diecut cardboard,
    15 pcs, 1920s, set of two 7¹/₂ x 10¹/₄" puzzles 12.00
Rocking Horse, metal springs, Made in England, c1930s,
    36" h 175.00
Salt and Pepper Shakers, pr, 2 donkeys, 1 sitting, 1 kick-
    ing, Japan, 1950s. 15.00
Sign, porcelain, Budweiser Clydesdales illus, 1920s 135.00
Toy, windup, cowboy and horse, c1930 .... 55.00

HORSE RACING

Items associated with Hall of Fame horses, e.g., Dan Patch and Man O'War, bring a premium. Paper ephemera, e.g., postcards and programs, and drinking glasses are two strong areas of focus. A program was issued for the first Belmont Stakes in 1867, the first Preakness Stakes in 1873, and the first Kentucky Derby in 1875. Kentucky Derby glasses date back to 1938, Preakness glasses to 1973, Belmont glasses to 1976, and Breeders Cup glasses to 1985. Pins were introduced at the Kentucky Derby in 1973 and at other major stakes races in the 1980s.

References: *Bill Friedberg's Pictorial Price Guide & Informative Handbook Covering "Official" Kentucky Derby, Preakness, Belmont, Breeder's Cup Glasses and Much More,* published by author, 1996; Roderick A. Malloy, *Malloy's Sports Collectibles Value Guide: Up–to–Date Prices for Noncard Sports Memorabilia,* Attic Books, Wallace–Homestead, Krause Publications, 1993.

Collectors' Club: Sport of Kings Society, 1406 Annen Ln, Madison, WI 53711.

Ashtray, china, Kentucky Derby and Belmont Stakes win-
    ner $15.00
Badge, Budweiser Million, color illus, Aug 1982, 3" d 8.00
Felt Pennant, Derby Day, red, white lettering, 1939, 18" l 15.00
Game, Cavalcade, board game, Selchow & Righter,
    1950s 40.00
Game, Magic Race, board game, Habob, 1940s 70.00
Glass, Belmont Stakes, "The Big Apple of Racing," 1976 ..... 75.00
Glass, Kentucky Derby/Churchill Downs, frosted, 1964 ..... 10.00
Glass, Kentucky Derby, "Kentucky Derby Gold Cup,"
    1952. .... 135.00
Glass, Preakness, horse and large daisies, 1991 .... 10.00
Magazine, *Sports Illustrated,* Hialeah Horse Race, Feb
    28, 1955. .... 10.00
Nodder, composition, jockey holding saddle with yel-
    low and blue blanket, sq red base, stamped Japan,
    1962, 6¹/₂" h 60.00
Pass, Florida Jockey Club, 1926 .... 25.00

Tin, Dan Patch Cut Plug, litho tin, red and black on yellow ground, bail handles, minor light wear, 4¼ x 7 x 4½", $231.00. Photo courtesy Wm. Morford Auctions.

Photograph, black and white racehorse, c1920. . . . . 15.00
Pin, Breeders Cup, 1988 . . . . 10.00
Pin, Kentucky Derby, enamel, 1989 . . . . 3.50
Pinback Button, Pimlico Preakness, horse head illus,
   multicolored, white ground, blue lettering, 1960s,
   1¾" d 15.00
Plate, Kentucky Derby Series, Nearing Finish, Reed and
   Barton, 1972. . . . . 115.00
Program, Belmont Stakes, 1936 . . . . 325.00
Program, Preakness Stakes, 1952 . . . . 250.00

HOT WHEELS

Automobile designer Harry Bradley, Mattel designer Howard Newman, Mattel Chairman Elliot Handler, and R & D chief Jack Ryan were the principal guiding forces in the creation of Hot Wheels. The creative process began in 1966 and culminated with the introduction of a diecast metal 16–car line in 1968. Hot Wheels were an immediate success.

Initially, cars were produced in Hong Kong and the United States. Mattel continually changed styling and paint motifs. Copies of modern cars were supplemented with futuristic models. Since the cars were meant to be raced, Mattel produced a variety of track sets. A Hot Wheels licensing program was instituted, resulting in Hot Wheels comic books, lunch kits, etc. In the 1980s Mattel did a number of Hot Wheels promotions with McDonald's and Kellogg's. In 1993 Mattel introduced a reproduction line focused toward the adult collector market. In 1997 Mattel acquired Tyco, bringing Hot Wheels and Matchbox under one roof.

References: Bob Parker, *The Complete Book of Hot Wheels*, Schiffer Publishing, 1995; Michael Thomas Strauss, *Tomart's Price Guide to Hot Wheels*, 2nd Edition, Tomart Publications, 1997.

Newsletter: *Hot Wheels Newsletter*, 26 Madera Ave, San Carlos, CA, 94070.

ACCESSORIES

2 Way Super Charger **$50.00**
12 Car Rally Case Wheel, 1968. . . . . **10.00**
15th Anniversary Belt Buckle Pack, includes
   '67 Camaro and Long Shot, 1983, MOC. **75.00**
Alpine Mountain Adventure Sto & Go, 1988 . . . . **15.00**
Automatic Lap Counter **15.00**
Daredevil Loop. **15.00**
Dash & Crash Speedway **20.00**
Dual Lane Road Runner Set. **40.00**
Full Curve Accessory Pak. **12.00**
Game, Hot Wheels Wipe–Out Race Game, Mattel, 1968 . . . . **25.00**
Hot Birds Collector's Case, with planes, vinyl carrying
   case with handle, snap closure, contains three 1¼" l
   diecast metal "Hot Birds," 1970 . . . . **50.00**
Hot Curves Race Action Set, includes 2 cars, 1969 . . . . **45.00**
Hot Wheels Military Machines Gift Pack, 1976, box only . . . **250.00**
Hot Wheels Super Chromes Gift Pack, 1976, box only **150.00**
Inside Track Sto & Go Race Set, box only. **20.00**
Jump Ramp Accessory Pak. **12.00**
Pop–Up House & Car Port, box only, 1968. . . . . **35.00**
Snake Mountain Challenge **20.00**
Stunt Action Set, 1969. . . . . **50.00**
Thundershift 500, includes 2 cars. **60.00**
Watch, silvered metal case, red, white, and yellow cen-
   ter dial, Hot Wheels logo, black and white checkered
   design hands, second hand with diecut design of
   2 vehicles, black leather band, Mattel, 1970s **200.00**

CARS

3 Window 6'34, red, 1987, MOC **$35.00**
Alien, dark blue, MOC. **10.00**
Alive 55, red, 1973. . . . . **200.00**
American Victory, light blue, 1974–75, MOC **35.00**
A–OK, red, 1982, MOC **55.00**
Army Funny Car, white, 1979, MOC **55.00**
Baja Breaker, gray, 1977–78, MOC **12.00**
Bugeye, fluorescent green, MOC **60.00**
CAT Dump Truck, yellow. **5.00**
Cement Mixer, brown, 1970 . . . . **35.00**
Chevy Monza, green, 1975 . . . . **500.00**
Classic Cord, blue, 1971 . . . . **300.00**
Classic Cord, lime green, 1971 . . . . **300.00**
Construction Crane, yellow, MOC **12.00**
Custom T–Bird, metallic blue, 1968, MOC. **150.00**

U.S.A. Builder Set, dock, ferry, bridge and tollgate, classic auto dealer, and fast–food restaurant, MIB, $20.00.

Dare Devil Loop Pack **15.00**
Dodge Omni 024, metallic blue, M **5.00**
Firebird Funny Car, magenta **6.00**
Fire Chaser, red, MOC **8.00**
Fire Engine, red, 1971 . . . . **35.00**
Flat Fendered '40, red, 1982, MOC **45.00**
Frito Lay Van, 1984, MOC **125.00**
Funny Money, gray, 1972, MOC **250.00**
GMC Motor Home, gold chrome, 1979 . . . . **600.00**
Greased Gremlin, red, M. **20.00**
Hare Splitter, white, orange tire rack, made in Malaysia **6.00**
The Heroes, Captain America, white, 1979, MOC **55.00**
The Heroes, Human Torch, black, 1979, MOC **55.00**
The Heroes, The Invisible Hulk, yellow, 1979, MOC. **55.00**
The Heroes, Silver Surfer, chrome, 1979, MOC **55.00**
The Heroes, The Thing, blue, 1979, MOC. **55.00**
Hot Ones Stamper Pack, MOC. **40.00**
Indy Eagle, brown, MOC. **50.00**
Khaki Kooler, olive, 1976, MOC **35.00**
King Kenny Funny Car, gray, 1992, M **4.00**
Leapin' Demons Chase Set, box only **45.00**
Lotus Turbine, blue, MOC **35.00**
Mighty Maverick, dark blue, 1975, MOC **65.00**
Mongoose II, blue, 1971 . . . . **95.00**
Mongoose & Snake Wild Wheelie Set **350.00**
Motocross Team, white, red and blue striping, 1979 . . . . **7.00**
Moving Van, blue and white, 1970 . . . . **35.00**
Moving Van, red and gray, 1970 . . . . **35.00**
Neet Streeter, maroon, 1979, MOC **50.00**
Olds 442, lime gold, 1971. . . . . **450.00**
Olds 442, magenta, 1971 . . . . **450.00**
Police Cruiser, 1973 . . . . **80.00**
Racer Rig, red, 1971 . . . . **85.00**
Racing Team Delivery Truck, yellow, red, white, and
   black, 1981–82, MOC. **50.00**
Ratmobile, Speed Demons, white **3.00**
Real Riders Pack, Green Pavement Pounder, Jeep
   Scrambler, Baja Breaker, and Blazin' Bug, 1985, MOC **75.00**
Red Baron, 1973, MOC **120.00**
Rock Buster, yellow, 1976, M **22.00**
Rocketank, tan, 1988, M **4.00**
Scene Machines, Rescue Squad, red, 1979, MOC. **95.00**
S'Cool Bus, yellow, 1971. . . . . **175.00**
Short Order, pink, 1973, MOC. **300.00**
Sir Rodney Roadster, green, 1975. . . . . **500.00**

Peterbilt, yellow body, silver tank, 1979, $6.00.

Sizzlin' Six Set, includes 6 cars with matching collector's
   buttons, MIP **250.00**
Sky Show Plane, blue, no stickers, 1970, M **50.00**
Sky Show Truck, lime gold, complete with ramp and
   stickers, 1970 . . . . **250.00**
Space Van, gray, 1979, M **40.00**
Stage Fright, brown, 1978, MOC **35.00**
Street Eater Motorcycle, yellow, MOC **160.00**
Street Rodder, black, 1981, MOC **45.00**
Sugar Caddy, blue, 1971, MIP **95.00**
Suzuki Quad Racer and Trailbuster, Wacky Warehouse
   Limited Edition, Kool–Aid promo, price for 2 . . . . **15.00**
Torino Stocker, black, 1984, MOC **35.00**
Torino Tornado, yellow, 1984, MOC **35.00**
Turbotrax Mach 1, white Fiero, 1986 . . . . **25.00**
Ultra Hots Stamper Pack, includes black Corvette
   Stingray, red Front Runnin' Fairmont, and yellow
   Datsun 200–SX, 1981, MOC **75.00**

HULL POTTERY

In 1905 Addis E. Hull purchased the Acme Pottery Company, Crooksville, Ohio, and changed its name to the A. E. Hull Pottery Company. By 1917, Hull's lines included art pottery for gift shops and florists, kitchenware, novelties, and stoneware.

Tile production helped the company weather the economic difficulties of the Depression. Hall's Little Red Riding Hood kitchenware arrived in 1943 and remained in production until 1957.

A 1950 flood and fire destroyed the company's plant. Two years later the company returned as the Hull Pottery Company. It was during this period that Hull added a new line of high–gloss glazed ceramics and developed Floraline and Regal, its product lines for the floral industry. The plant closed in 1986.

Hull's early stoneware is marked with an "H." Matte pieces contain pattern numbers. Series numbers identify Open Rose/Camellia pieces (100s), Iris (400s), and Wildflower (W plus a number). Many Hull pieces also are marked with a number indicating their height in inches. Pieces made after 1950, usually featuring the high–gloss glaze, are marked "hull" or "Hull" in a script signature.

References: Barbara Loveless Glick–Burke, *Collector's Guide to Hull Pottery, The Dinnerware Lines: Identification and Values,* Collector Books, 1993; Joan Gray Hull, *Hull: The Heavenly Pottery, Fifth Edition,* published by author, 1997; Brenda Roberts, *The Collectors Encyclopedia of Hull Pottery,* Collector Books, 1980, 1997 value update; Brenda Roberts, *The Companion Guide to Roberts' Ultimate Encyclopedia of Hull Pottery,* Walsworth Publishing, 1992; Brenda Roberts, *Roberts' Ultimate Encyclopedia of Hull Pottery,* Walsworth Publishing, 1992.

Newsletters: *The Hull Pottery News,* 466 Foreston Place, St Louis, MO 63119; *Hull Pottery Newsletter,* 11023 Tunnell Hill NE, New Lexington, OH 43764.

Collectors' Club: Hull Pottery Assoc, 4 Hilltop Rd, Council Bluffs, IA 51503.

Note: See Little Red Riding Hood for additional listings.

Blossom Flite, basket, T–44, 8½" h **$90.00**
Blossom Flite, cornucopia, T–8, 10½" l **90.00**
Blossom Flite, pitcher, Cinderella Kitchenware, 29, 16 oz **45.00**

Mirror Brown, pie baker, #566, mkd "Hull Oven Proof U.S.A.," 9³/₈" d, $6.00.

Blossom Flite, planter, 10¹/₂" l **100.00**
Blossom Flite, vase, T–7, handled, 10¹/₂" h **55.00**
Bouquet, grease jar, Cinderella Kitchenware, 24, 32 oz **50.00**
Bouquet, pitcher, Cinderella Kitchenware, 29, 32 oz **55.00**
Bouquet, teapot, Cinderella Kitchenware, 26, 42 oz **150.00**
Bow Knot, basket, B–25, 6¹/₂" h **330.00**
Bow Knot, bowl, B–18, 5³/₄" d **165.00**
Bow Knot, candle holder, B–17, 4" h **125.00**
Bow Knot, console bowl **300.00**
Bow Knot, cornucopia, B–5 . . . . **165.00**
Bow Knot, double cornucopia, B–13–13, pink and blue **285.00**
Bow Knot, ewer, B–1, 5¹/₂" h **195.00**
Bow Knot, jardiniere, B–18 . . . . **200.00**
Bow Knot, teapot **495.00**
Bow Knot, vase, B–3 . . . . **185.00**
Bow Knot, vase, B–10, 10¹/₄" h **350.00**
Bow Knot, wall pocket, pitcher, B–26 . . . . **265.00**
Butterfly, ashtray, B–3, 7" d **40.00**
Butterfly, basket, B–13 . . . . **130.00**
Butterfly, bonbon, B–4 . . . . **45.00**
Butterfly, bud vase, B–1, 6¹/₄" h **25.00**
Butterfly, pitcher, B–15 . . . . **185.00**
Butterfly, serving tray, B–23, matte white and turquoise,
    gold trim, 11¹/₂" d **100.00**
Butterfly, teapot, B–18 . . . . **140.00**
Butterfly, vase, #814, 10¹/₂" **95.00**
Butterfly, vase, B–9, 9" h **45.00**
Butterfly, window box, 12³/₄ x 4³/₄" **50.00**
Calla Lilly, bowl, 500–32, 8" d **125.00**
Calla Lilly, candle holder, 2¹/₄" h **100.00**
Calla Lilly, console bowl, 590–33, 4 x 13" **180.00**
Calla Lilly, cornucopia, 570/33, 8" h **125.00**
Calla Lilly, ewer, 506, 10" h **425.00**
Calla Lilly, vase, 520/33, 6¹/₂" h **75.00**
Camelia, candleholders, pr, doves, 6¹/₂" h **90.00**
Capri, flower bowl, C–47, round, 5¹/₄ x 8" **40.00**
Capri, pitcher, C–87 . . . . **75.00**
Capri, planter, C–81, twin swan **80.00**
Continental, vase, C–53, 8¹/₂" h **40.00**
Cookie Jar, barefoot boy **400.00**

Cookie Jar, Debonair, Kitchenware, O–8, 8³/₄" h **125.00**
Crestone, creamer, turquoise, 8 oz **15.00**
Crestone, custard, turquoise **8.00**
Dogwood, candle holder, 512, 3³/₄" h **130.00**
Dogwood, ewer, 520, 4³/₄" h **150.00**
Ebb Tide, basket, E–11, 16¹/₂" h **200.00**
Ebb Tide, candle holder, E–13, 2³/₄" h **30.00**
Ebb Tide, console bowl, E–12 . . . . **150.00**
Ebb Tide, creamer, E–15 . . . . **45.00**
Ebb Tide, sugar, cov, E–16 . . . . **45.00**
Ebb Tide, vase, E–2, twin fish, 7" h **65.00**
Imperial, planter, praying hands, F–475, 6" l **65.00**
Iris, bowl, 412, rose, 4" d **70.00**
Iris, bud vase, 410, 7¹/₂" h **100.00**
Iris, candle holder, 411, 5" h **130.00**
Iris, rose bowl, 412, 4" h **120.00**
Magnolia, basket, 10, matte, 10¹/₂" h **200.00**
Magnolia, creamer, 24, matte, 3³/₄" h **65.00**
Magnolia, double cornucopia, 6, matte, 12" h **200.00**
Magnolia, teapot, H–20, 6" h **500.00**
Magnolia, vase, 6¹/₄" h **65.00**
Mardi Gras/Granada, ewer, 31, 10" h **150.00**
Mardi Gras/Granada, planter, 204, 6" h **45.00**
Open Rose, cornucopia, 101, 8¹/₂" h **170.00**
Open Rose, hanging basket, 132, 7" h **200.00**
Orchid, bookends, pr, 316, 7" h **1,350.00**
Orchid, bowl, 314, 13" d **300.00**
Orchid, bud vase, 309, 8" h **165.00**
Orchid, candle holder, 315, 4" h **140.00**
Orchid, console bowl, 314, 13" h **375.00**
Orchid, jardiniere, 310, 6" h **100.00**
Orchid, vase, 309, 8" h **165.00**
Parchment & Pine, basket, S–3, green **75.00**
Parchment & Pine, coffeepot, S–15 . . . . **125.00**
Parchment & Pine, creamer and sugar, green **50.00**
Parchment & Pine, planter, S–5, scroll, 10¹/₂" h **90.00**
Parchment & Pine, teapot, S–11, green **75.00**
Parchment & Pine, vase, S–1, 6" h **20.00**
Poppy, bowl, 608, 4³/₄" d **75.00**
Poppy, jardiniere, 603, 4³/₄" h **70.00**
Poppy, pitcher, 610, 13" h **650.00**
Poppy, wall pocket, 609, 9" h **350.00**
Rosella, vase, R–1, 5" h **40.00**
Rosella, wall pocket, R–10, 6¹/₂" h **150.00**
Royal, basket, W–9, 8³/₄" h **65.00**

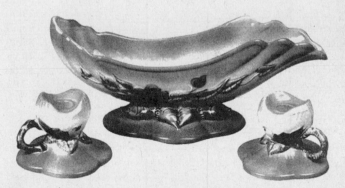

Woodland, console set, 14" W–29 console bowl and pair of 3¹/₂" W30 candle holders, green and chartreuse, $154.00. Photo courtesy Collectors Auction Services.

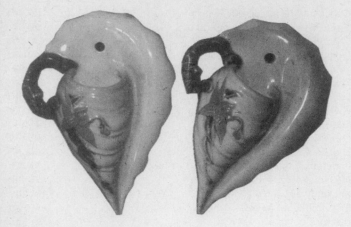

Woodland, wall pockets, W–13, 7¹/₂" h, price for pair, $121.00.
Photo courtesy Collectors Auction Services.

Serenade, ashtray, S–23	95.00
Serenade, vase, W–4	55.00
Sunglow, casserole, cov, 51	50.00
Sunglow, flowerpot, 97, 5¹/₂" h	35.00
Sunglow, vase, 91, 6¹/₂" h	40.00
Sunglow, wall pocket, 82, whisk broom, 8¹/₂" h	65.00
Thistle, vase, 51, 6¹/₂" h	110.00
Tokay/Tuscany, candy dish, 8¹/₂" d	95.00
Tokay/Tuscany, console bowl, 1, 6¹/₂" h	35.00
Tokay/Tuscany, cornucopia, 1, 6¹/₂" l	30.00
Tropicana, pitcher, 56, 13¹/₂" h	550.00
Tropicana, vase, T–53, flat sided, 8¹/₂" h	385.00
Water Lily, cornucopia, L–7, 6¹/₂" l	75.00
Water Lily, jardiniere, L–24, 8¹/₂" h	200.00
Water Lily, pitcher, L–3, 5¹/₂" h	55.00
Water Lily, vase, L–15	55.00
Wildflower, ewer, 63, 4¹/₂" l	95.00
Wildflower, jardiniere, 64, 4" h	70.00
Wildflower, pitcher, W–2, 5¹/₂" h	70.00
Wildflower, teapot, 72, 8" h	800.00
Wildflower, vase, 60, 6¹/₄" h	85.00
Woodland, basket, W–9	245.00
Woodland, bowl, glossy, W–29	110.00
Woodland, candleholder, pr, W–30	50.00
Woodland, console bowl, W–10, 11" h	45.00
Woodland, console bowl, dawn rose, W–29, 14"	295.00
Woodland, cornucopia, W–10	130.00
Woodland, hanging basket, W–17, 7¹/₂" h	150.00
Woodland, jardiniere, W–7	75.00
Woodland, pitcher, W–3, 5¹/₂" h	40.00
Woodland, vase, W–18, gloss, post 1950	55.00
Woodland, wall pocket, shell, W–13	75.00

HUMMEL FIGURINES

Berta Hummel, a German artist, provided the drawings that were the inspiration for W. Goebel's Hummel figurines. Berta Hummel, born in 1909 in Massing, Bavaria, Germany, enrolled at age eighteen in the Academy of Fine Arts in Munich. In 1934 she entered the Convent of Siessen and became Sister Maria Innocentia.

W. Goebel, Rodental, Bavaria, produced its first Hummel figurines in 1935. John Schmid of Schmid Brothers, Randolph,

Massachusetts, secured American distribution rights. When Goebel wished to distribute directly to the American market in 1967, the two companies and Berta Hummel's heirs became entangled in a lawsuit. A compromise was reached. Goebel would base its figurines on drawings made by Berta Hummel between 1934 and her death in 1964. Schmid was given the rights to produce pieces based on Hummel's pre–convent drawings.

A Hummel figurine must have the "M. I. Hummel" legend on its base and a Goebel trademark. If either is missing, the figurine is not a Goebel Hummel. Seven different trademarks are used to identify the production period of a figurine:

Trademark 1	Incised Crown Mark	1935–1949
Trademark 2	Full Bee	1950–1959
Trademark 3	Stylized Bee	1957–1972
Trademark 4	Three Line Mark	1964-1972
Trademark 5	Last Bee Mark	1972–1980
Trademark 6	Missing Bee Mark	1979–1990
Trademark 7	Current/New Crown Mark	1991–Present

References: Ken Armke, *Hummel: An Illustrated Handbook and Price Guide*, Wallace–Homestead, Krause Publications, 1995; Carl F. Luckey, *Luckey's Hummel Figurines & Plates, 11th Edition*, Krause Publications, 1997; Robert L. Miller, *The No. 1 Price Guide to M. I. Hummel: Figurines, Plates, More…, Sixth Edition*, Portfolio Press, 1995.

Collectors' Clubs: Hummel Collectors Club, 1261 University Dr, Yardley, PA 19067; M. I. Hummel Club, Goebel Plaza, PO Box 11, Pennington, NJ 08534.

A Fair Measure, 345, trademark 6	$250.00
Angel Duet, 261, trademark 4	220.00
Angelic Song, 144, trademark 3	175.00
Angel Serenade with Lamb, 83, trademark 2	300.00
Apple Tree Boy, 142/I, trademark 6	240.00
Apple Tree Girl, 141/3/0, trademark 1	275.00
Art Critic, 318, trademark 6	265.00
The Artist, 304, trademark 4	250.00
A Stitch in Time, 255, trademark 4	275.00
Auf Wiedersehen, 153/0, trademark 1	450.00
Baker, 128, trademark 1	375.00
Baking Day, 330, trademark 5	245.00
Band Leader, 129, trademark 4	200.00
Barnyard Hero, 195, trademark 2	525.00
Bashful, 377, trademark 4	850.00
Big Housecleaning, 363, trademark 5	270.00
Bird Watcher, 300, trademark 6	200.00
Birthday Serenade, 218/2/0, trademark 3	225.00
Blessed Event, 333, trademark 4	325.00
Boots, 143/0, trademark 4	200.00
Boy with Toothache, 217, trademark 3	250.00
Brother, 94/I, trademark 3	320.00
The Builder, 305, trademark 4	250.00
Busy Student, 367, trademark 3	650.00
Carnival, 328, trademark 4	225.00
Chicken Licken 385, trademark 4	850.00
Chick Girl, 56/B, trademark 3	200.00
Christmas Angel, 301, trademark 3	5,000.00
Cinderella, 337, new style, trademark 5	270.00
Coquettes, 179, trademark 3	275.00
Eventide, 99, trademark 3	400.00
Farewell, 65/I, trademark 3	320.00

Farm Boy, 66, trademark 2	420.00
Favorite Pet, 361, trademark 4	275.00
Feathered Friends, 344, trademark 3	2,500.00
Flower Vendor, 381, trademark 5	220.00
Flying Angel, 366, trademark 5	120.00
Follow the Leader, 369, trademark 5	1,100.00
For Mother, 257, trademark 3	200.00
Friends, 136/I, trademark 4	225.00
Gay Adventure, 356, trademark 5	195.00
Globe Trotter, 79, trademark 2	375.00
Going Home, 383, trademark 6	280.00
Going to Grandma's, 52/0, trademark 2	375.00
Good Friends, 182, trademark 2	275.00
Good Hunting, 307, trademark 6	220.00
Good Shepherd, 42/0, trademark 5	240.00
Goose Girl, 47/3/0, trademark 5	155.00
Happy Birthday, 176/I, trademark 3	345.00
Happy Days, 150/2/0, trademark 2	245.00
Happy Pastime, 69, trademark 4	150.00
Happy Traveler, 109/0, trademark 2	200.00
Heavenly Lullaby, 262, trademark 4	200.00
Hello, 124/0, trademark 3	250.00
The Holy Child, 70, trademark 3	200.00
Home From Market, 198, trademark 2	325.00
Homeward Bound, 334, trademark 4	650.00
Joyous News, 27/3, trademark 3	500.00
Kiss Me, 311, trademark 5	250.00
Knitting Lesson, 256, trademark 3	525.00
Latest News, 184, trademark 2	400.00
Let's Sing, 110, trademark 2	275.00
Little Cellist, 89/1, trademark 1	400.00
Little Drummer, 240, trademark 2	200.00
Little Goat Herder, 200/0, trademark 3	225.00
Little Guardian, 145, trademark 2	220.00
Little Pharmacist, 322, trademark 4	240.00
Little Scholar, 80, trademark 5	200.00
Little Tailor, 308, trademark 4	250.00
Little Thrifty, 118, trademark 3	170.00
Lost Sheep, 68, trademark 2	325.00
Lost Stocking, 374, trademark 5	135.00

Max and Moritz, 123, trademark 2	320.00
Mother's Darling, 175, trademark 3	250.00
Mother's Helper, 133, trademark 2	275.00
Mountaineer, 315, trademark 4	220.00
On Holiday, 350, trademark 5	1,200.00
Playmates, 58/0, trademark 3	200.00
Postman, 119, trademark 2	190.00
Ring Around the Rosie, 348, trademark 5	2,500.00
School Boy, 82/2/0, trademark 1	285.00
School Girls, 177/I, trademark 5	1,100.00
Serenade, 85, trademark 2	650.00
She Loves Me, She Loves Me Not, 174, trademark 1	475.00
Sister, 98/2/0, trademark 3	170.00
Spring Cheer, 72, trademark 2	280.00
Spring Dance, 353/1, trademark 6	500.00
Star Gazer, 132, trademark 3	250.00
Street Singer, 131, trademark 3	200.00
Sweet Greetings, 352, trademark 6	200.00
Sweet Music, 186, trademark 1	375.00
Telling Her Secret, 196/0, trademark 3	350.00
To Market, 49/3/0, trademark 2	230.00
Trumpet Boy, 97, trademark 2	180.00
Umbrella Boy, 152/0A, trademark 4	550.00
Waiter, 154, trademark 2	420.00
Watchful Angel, 194, trademark 3	375.00
Wayside Harmony, 111/1, trademark 4	275.00
Weary Wanderer, 204, trademark 2	350.00
We Congratulate, 220, trademark 3	175.00
Which Hand?, 258, trademark 3	650.00
Worship, 84/0, trademark 1	300.00

HUMMEL LOOK–ALIKES

If imitation is the most sincere form of flattery, Berta Hummel and W. Goebel should feel especially honored. Goebel's Hummel figurines have been stylistically copied by ceramic manufacturers around the world.

A Hummel look–alike is a stylistic copy of a Goebel Hummel figurine or a completely new design done in an artistic style that mimics that of Berta Hummel. It does not require much of an alteration to avoid infringing on a design patent. These copycats come from a host of Japanese firms, Herbert Dubler (House of Ars Sacra), Erich Stauffer (Arnat Imports), Decorative Figures Corporation, Beswick, and Coventry Ware.

Reference: Lawrence L. Wonsch, *Hummel Copycats With Values*, Wallace–Homestead, 1987, out of print.

Singing Lesson, 63, trademark 5, $115.00.

Apple Tree Boy, HC–142, Japan	$30.00
April Shower, U8561, Erich Stauffer	22.00
Baker, "Leftons Exclusives Japan" foil label	22.00
Boots, HC–143, "Royal Sealy Japan" foil label	25.00
Chick Girl, HC–57C, mkd "#614 made by Lucille Morrison Princeton Kentucky"	35.00
Culprits, HC–56, Taiwan	15.00
Dancing Time, 55/1556, Erich Stauffer	35.00
Good Friends, HC–182, Popware, Spain	35.00
Happiness, HC–86A, mkd "The Strummer SH1A," Napco label	22.00
Junior Doctor, S8543, Erich Stauffer	25.00
Latest News, HC–184, "Leftons Exclusives Japan" foil label	45.00
Life on the Farm, 8394, Erich Stauffer	15.00

Little Mender, U8536, Erich Stauffer. **30.00**
Merry Wanderer, HC–7, Coventry Ware **25.00**
Picnic, 55/972, Erich Stauffer. **12.00**
Sore Thumb, 55/1550, Erich Stauffer **18.00**

HUNTING

Hunting came into its own as a major collecting category in the 1980s. The initial focus was on hunting advertising and paper ephemera, e.g., books, calendars, and catalogs. Examples from firms such as DuPont, Peters Cartridge Company, Remington, and Winchester command premium prices.

Collectors also have identified a group of illustrators whose hunting scenes and images have become highly desirable. Look for works by G. Muss Arnolt, Phillip Goodwin, Lynn Bogue Hunt, and Edmund Osthaus. Beware of the limited edition hunting prints issued in the 1970s and 80s. The secondary market is volatile—more will decline than rise in value over the next decade.

Hunting licenses and ammunition boxes currently are two hot subcategories. Even some post–1945 decoys have joined the collectible ranks.

References: Ralf Coykendall, Jr., *Coykendall's Complete Guide to Sporting Collectibles*, Wallace–Homestead, Krause Publications, 1996; Gene and Linda Kangas, *Collector's Guide to Decoys*, Wallace–Homestead, Krause Publications, 1992; Jim and Vivian Karsnitz, *Sporting Collectibles*, Schiffer Publishing, 1992; Carl F. Luckey, *Collecting Antique Bird and Duck Calls: An Identification and Value Guide, 2nd Edition*, Books Americana, Krause Publications, 1992; Bob and Beverly Strauss, *American Sporting Advertising, Volume 2*, L–W Book Sales, 1992.

Periodical: *Sporting Collector's Monthly*, PO Box 305, Camden Wyoming, DE 19934.

Collectors' Clubs: Call & Whistle Collectors Assoc, 2839 E 26th Place, Tulsa, OK 74114; Callmakers & Collectors Assoc of America, 137 Kingswood Dr, Clarksville, TN 37043.

Ammunition Box, Dominion Cartridge Co, .22 gauge,
    partial box **$10.00**
Ammunition Box, Remington Arrow Express, 12 gauge,
    empty. **110.00**
Ammunition Box, Union Metallic Cartridge Co,
    16 gauge, green paper label, 2–pc, 20 pk, empty **450.00**
Book, *Fur Trapping: A Book of Instructions; To Trap,
    Snare, Poison & Shoot*, 1934, illus, 180 pp **15.00**
Book, *The Art of Hunting Big Game in America*, New
    York, 1st ed, 1967 . . . . **25.00**
Calendar, Hercules Powder Company, 1921,
    "Outnumbered," hunter, dog, and porcupine,
    Goodwin **200.00**
Calendar, Winchester Arms Co, hunter holding calendar
    pages, 1930 . . . . **325.00**
Catalog, The Archers Company, Fine Bows and Arrows,
    Pinehurst, NC, 1932, 32 pp **25.00**
Catalog, Colt Handbook and Catalog, color, 1972,
    32 pp, 11 x 8¹/₂" **23.00**
Catalog, LL Bean, Inc, Spring 1938, orig envelope and
    return order envelope, 60 pp, 7¹/₂ x 8¹/₂". **40.00**
Catalog, Parker Guns, flying geese on cov, 1930, 32 pp **80.00**

**Sign, diecut litho standup, Western Ammunition, 12¹/₂ x 20¹/₄",
$385.00.** Photo courtesy Past Tyme Pleasures.

Decoy, Canadian Goose, wood and cork block, wood
    head, glass eyes, old worn paint, 23" l **150.00**
Decoy, Canvasback Drake, Bill Goenne, CA, branded
    "WRG," glass eyes, orig paint, 18¹/₂" l. **75.00**
Decoy, owl, confidence decoy, papier–mâché, glass
    eyes, orig white and black paint, 14¹/₄" h **125.00**
Decoy, Pintail Drake, Al Wragg and Doug Burdell,
    Canada, carved wing and tail, glass eyes, orig paint,
    c1960, 17" l **75.00**
Decoy, Shorebird, root head, whittled, shot scars, old
    dark finish, 6¹/₂" h **150.00**
Envelope, Remington Autoloading Shotgun, rifle and fly-
    ing geese illus, dated Oct 27, 1923 in pencil,
    Brocket and Strong, Windham, NY, unused. **50.00**
Hatchet, True Temper, orig paper tag, 11" l overall **15.00**
Knife, Remington, 10th Anniversary Bullet Knife, orig tin
    box with sleeve, 1992 . . . . **65.00**
Letter, Remington Game Loads, 1924, 8¹/₂ x 11". **25.00**
License, Junior, waterproof tagboard, blue, black letters
    and numbers, 1963 . . . . **6.00**
License, metal, non–resident, orig leather pouch, 1936. . . . . . **40.00**
License, resident's, Ohio, 1944 . . . . **5.00**
Magazine, *Hunter, Trader, Trapper*, Aug 1923, 7 x 9" **8.50**
Rifle, Winchester Model 1894, .32, 40 cal, full maga-
    zine, 26" barrel **690.00**
Sign, cardboard, "Western Xpert Shells/Popular Prices
    Top Quality," rabbit and quail illus, 18 x 7¹/₂". **8.00**
Sign, cardboard, white, black lettering, "No Gunning or
    Trespassing, Private Property, No Entering or Hunting
    Allowed," Pennsylvania law, 1943, 10 x 13". **30.00**

ICE CREAM COLLECTIBLES

The street ice cream vendor dates from the 1820s. In 1846 Nancy Johnson invented the hand–cranked ice cream freezer, a standard household fixture by the mid–1850s. The urban ice cream garden arrived on the scene in the middle of the 19th century.

The ice cream parlor was superseded by the drugstore soda fountain in the 1920s and 30s. Improvements in the freezer portions of refrigerators, the development of efficient grocery store freezers, and the spread of chain drugstores in the 1950s, 60s, and 70s slowly lessened the role of the local drugstore soda fountain.

Ice cream collectibles fall into two basic groups: (1) material from the dairy industry, and (2) ice cream and soda fountain items. Beware of reproductions, reputed "warehouse" finds, and fantasy items.

Reference: Wayne Smith, *Ice Cream Dippers,* published by author, 1986, out of print.

Collectors' Club: National Assoc of Soda Jerks, PO Box 115, Omaha, NE 68101; The Ice Screamers, PO Box 465, Warrington, PA 18976.

Cone Holder, metal, wall mount, 7 x 5 x 5", $80.00. Photo courtesy Wm. Morford Auctions.

Badge, International Association of Ice Cream Manufacturers Convention, gold, blue, black, and white, 1930s $30.00

Book Cover, Breyers Ice Cream, spaceship and planets illus, 16 x 22" 35.00

Booklet, White Mountain Ice Cream 25.00

Carton, Batman Ice Cream, Slam–Bang Banana Marshmallow, unused, 1966, unused. 50.00

Change Tray, Velvet Ice Cream, oval, young woman eating ice cream 275.00

Menu Clip, Fairmont Ice Cream, 1930–40, 2³/₄" 15.00

Milk Shake Machine, Gilchrist, orig cup, c1926 . . . . 65.00

Mold, egg, mkd "E & Co, NY," 2³/₄" d 25.00

Mold, King of Hearts, mkd "E–920" 35.00

Mold, lady's shoe, 5³/₄" l 25.00

Mold, Santa and Reindeer 65.00

Mold, ship, 2 qt 225.00

Pinback Button, Good Humor Safety Club, blue, white, and orange, 1930s, ⁷/₈" d 20.00

Pinback Button, Hi–Hat Ice Cream Soda 10¢, McCrory's, c1940, 2¹/₄" d 15.00

Pinback Button, National Ice Cream Week, blue and white, 1930s 20.00

Pinback Button, Semons Ice Cream, red, white, and gold, black lettering, 1¹/₄" d 15.00

Pinback Button, Spreckels Milk/Cream/Ice Cream, crowing rooster, yellow ground, black lettering, 1930–40, 1¹/₈" d 25.00

Playing Cards, Dolly Madison Quality Checked Selected Ice Cream, red, white, and blue, yellow ground 5.00

Scoop, silvered metal, mechanical, wooden handle, spring action trigger lever, patented Feb 17, 1925, 12¹/₂" l 200.00

Scoop Rest, Hendlers Ice Cream, brass, molded, inscribed "Friendship Of Hendlers The Velvet Kind," 1930–40 . . . . 45.00

Serving Tray, Furnace Ice Cream, girl holding serving tray, 1920s 150.00

Serving Tray, Merringan's Ice Cream, 2 children eating ice cream under beach umbrella, 1925 . . . . 300.00

Sign, Blue Ridge Velvet Ice Cream, porcelain, "Curb Service Blue Ridge Velvet Ice Cream A Health Food," 1940s, 20 x 28" 225.00

Sign, Country Club Ice Cream, cardboard, "Country Club Ice Cream" above 8 different flavors, 1950s, 10 x 20" 260.00

Sign, Dairy Queen, tin, different Dairy Queen products, Coca–Cola cup upper right, 1950–60s, 22 x 28" 250.00

Sign, Empress Ice Cream, metal, yellow, blue, and white, 1950–60s, 28 x 44" 80.00

Sign, Jersey Ice Cream, tin, c1940, 16 x 34" 40.00

Sign, Mello Ice Cream, tin, 2 sided, yellow, red, and blue, "For Goodness' Sake! Eat Mello Ice Cream," 1957, 2 x 3" 250.00

Sign, Polar Ice Cream, tin, emb, polar bear eating ice cream, "Eat Polar Ice Cream That Velvet Kind," 1920s, 14 x 20" 800.00

Sign, Smith's Ice Cream, tin, emb, boy eating dish of ice cream, 1920–30 . . . . 1,200.00

Spoon, Breyer's Ice Cream 45.00

Straw Jar, glass, red, metal lid, 1950s 175.00

Thermometer, Abbottmaid Ice Cream, orig label, 1920–30, 2 x 6¹/₄" 40.00

Thermometer, Puritas Ice Cream, cardboard, c1923, 12¹/₂" h 35.00

Tumbler, Sealtest Ice Cream, red label, 5¹/₄" h 10.00

Whistle, Dairy Queen, cone shape 15.00

Whistle, Puritan Dairy Ice Cream, litho tin, yellow, black lettering, 1930–40s 25.00

AUCTION PRICES

Ice cream serving trays sold by Gary Metz's Muddy River Trading Company on October 31 and November 1, 1997. Prices do not include the buyer's premium of 10% for payment by cash or check or 15% for credit card payment.

Arctic Ice Cream, round, polar bear, minor dents, light wear $975.00

Bellevue Ice Cream, Green Bay, WI, round, ice cream party with 10 children and puppy, some marks and outer rim edge chipping 675.00

Imperial Ice Cream, round, blue tones, mother and 2 children, minor dents 500.00

Purity Ice Cream, rect, 5 children at table eating ice cream, light dents and scratches, minor paint chipping, 1924 . . . . 700.00

Sanitary Ice Cream, round, Haskell Coffin artwork, woman serving ice cream, minor chips, light rim wear 500.00

Velvet Ice Cream, rect, Kinnett's girl with polar bear rug, rim rubs at outer corners 375.00

ILLUSTRATORS

The mass–market printing revolution of the late 19th century marked the advent of the professional illustrator. Illustrators provided artwork for books, calendars, magazines, prints, games, jigsaw puzzles, and a host of advertising and promotional products.

Illustrator art breaks down into three major categories: (1) original art, (2) first strike prints sold as art works, and (3) commercially produced art. While the first two categories are limited, the third is not. Often images were produced in the hundreds of thousands and millions.

Magazines, more than any other medium, were responsible for introducing the illustrator to the general public. Norman Rockwell's covers for *Boy's Life* and *The Saturday Evening Post* are classics. Magazine covers remain one of the easiest and most inexpensive means of collecting illustrator art.

References: Patricia L. Gibson, *R. Atkinson Fox, William M. Thompson: Identification & Price Guide*, Collectors Press, 1995; Don Kurtz, *Alphonse Mucha: An American Collection*, Collectors Press, 1997; Rick and Charlotte Martin, *Vintage Illustration: Discovering America's Calendar Artists, 1900–1960*, Collectors Press, 1997; Rita C. Mortenson, *R. Atkinson Fox: His Life and Work*, L–W Book Sales, 1994; Norman I. Platnick, *Coles Phillips: A Collector's Guide*, published by author, 1997; Jo Ann Havens Wright, *The Life and Art of William McMurray Thompson, American Illustrator...*, published by author, 1995.

Newsletters: *Calendar Art Collectors' Newsletter*, 45 Brown's Ln, Old Lyme, CT 06371; *The Illustrator Collector's News*, PO Box 1958, Sequim, WA 98382; *The Philip Boileau Collectors' Society Newsletter*, 1025 Redwood Blvd, Redding, CA 96003.

Collectors' Clubs: Arthur Szyk Society, 1294 Sao Paula Ave, Placentia, CA 92670; The Harrison Fisher Society, 123 N Glassell, Orange, CA 92666; Hy Hintemeister Collector's Group, 209 Homevale Rd, Reisterstown, MD 21136; International Rose O'Neill Club, PO Box 668, Branson, MO 64616; R. A. Fox Society, PO Box 358, Janesville, IA 50647.

Note: For additional listings see Nutting, Wallace; Parrish, Maxfield; Rockwell, Norman; and Pin–Up Art, Postcards and Prints.

Adams, Neal, drawing, pen and ink on paper, cov artwork for Justice League of America #61, matted, 1968, 15 x 10" **$880.00**
Becker, Charlotte, calendar, baby print, 1931 . . . . **25.00**
Bisel Peat, Fern, magazine cover, *Children's Play Mate*, Apr 1943 . . . . **5.00**
Bontecou, Lee, etching, #133/144, lower right pencil signature, dated 1967, 26 x 17 1/8" **300.00**
Brangwyn, Frank W, pencil etching, "Ditchling," 1921, sgd, 12 x 15 3/8" **175.00**
Brown, Sam, magazine tear sheet, sgd, *Collier's*, Carter Inx Products, Dec 18, 1926, 10 x 13" **12.00**
Browne, Tom, postcard, American baseball series, green ground **10.00**
Burd, Clara, book, *An Old Fashioned Girl*, Louisa M Alcott author, Winston, 1928, 342 pp, 1st ed, dj **30.00**
Cady, Harrison, book, *Lightfoot the Deer*, Thornton W Burgess author, Little, Brown, & Co, 1921, 205 pp, 1st ed **95.00**

Cady, Harrison, watercolor with graphite and blue pen on paper, On the Beach at Pelican Bay, framed, sgd, and inscribed **495.00**
Christy, Earl, magazine cover, *The American Magazine*, Dec 1923 . . . . **12.00**
Christy, Howard, Chandler, poster, "If You Want to Fight—Join The Marines," 1943, 30 x 41" **575.00**
Coffin, Haskell, magazine cover, *The Farmer's Wife*, c1923 . . . . **10.00**
Coffin, Haskell, sheet music cover, *Land of My Dreams*, c1922 . . . . **10.00**
DeVorss, Dilly, calendar, Draped in Silver Fox, salesman's sample, 16 x 33" **65.00**
Goldberg, Y E, jigsaw puzzle, Sailing Off Block Island, wood, hand cut, 512 pcs, Glencraft/Glendex, 1960s, orig box **45.00**
Hintermeister, Hy, jigsaw puzzle, The Birth of Our Country, Ben Franklin at hearthside, c1920, 80 pcs, 13 x 9" **20.00**
Kaufer, E McKnight, poster, American Airlines—East Coast, 1948, 30 x 30" **250.00**
Kingham, Doug, print, Spirit of July 4th 1976, #451/500, litho, titled on reverse, matted and framed, 20 1/2 x 31 3/4" **100.00**
Marshall, Carol, book, *Hooray for Lassie*, Marion Borden author, Whitman Tell–A–Tale Book, 1964 . . . . **5.00**
McMein, Neysa, magazine cover, sgd, *McCalls*, 1930 . . . . . . **12.00**
Phillips, Cole, magazine tear sheet, Community Plate, "Flapper Girl," full page, color, 1923 . . . . **10.00**
Price, Norman, calendar, sgd, De Laval Separator, Story of John & Mary, orig mailer, 1930 . . . . **150.00**
Sendak, Maurice, book, *The Bee–man of Orb*, Frank R. Stockton author, Holt, Rinehart & Winston, 1964, 46 pp, 1st ed, dj, sgd by illus **100.00**
Thompson, T N, calendar, Studio Sketches, spiral bound, 1952 . . . . **50.00**
Thorne, Diana, book, *Who Goes to the Wood*, Fay Inchfawn author, Winston, 1952, 229 pp **12.00**
Thorne, Diana, jigsaw puzzle, *Woman's Home Companion*, seated cat knocking apart puzzle of dog, Aug 1993 . . . . **25.00**
Twelvetrees, Charles, magazine cover, sgd, *Capper's Farmer*, 1930s **12.00**

Harrison Cady, magazine cover, *People's Home Journal*, Peter Rabbit, Apr 1926, 14 x 10 3/8", $132.00. Photo courtesy Wm. Morford Auctions.

Usobal, magazine cover, sgd, *McCall's*, Mar 1921 . . . . **8.00**
Vallejo, Boris, calendar, Tarzan, color litho, orig card-
board mailer, Ballantine Books, 1978, 13 x 24½" **65.00**
Wrightson, Bernie, painting, watercolor on paper, captioned "Jason's in the Basement...With Daddy," mat-
ted and framed, 1969, 11¼ x 8¾" **1,210.00**
Wyeth, N. C., poster, "Buy War Bonds," Uncle Sam lead-
ing battle, 1942, 14 x 22" **125.00**

IMPERIAL GLASS

In 1901 a group of investors founded the Imperial Glass Company. Production began on January 13, 1904 and was mass–market directed, e.g., jelly glasses, tumblers, and tableware. Imperial's success was guaranteed by one of its first orders, approximately 20 different items to be supplied to almost 500 F. W. Woolworth stores. McCrory and Kresge were also major customers.

Between 1910 and 1920 Imperial introduced a number of new glassware lines. "Nuart" iridescent ware was followed by "Nucut" crystal, a pressed reproduction of English cut glass pieces which sold well as a premium and was widely distributed by The Grand Union Tea Company. In the 1950s, "Nucut" was reintroduced as "Collectors Crystal."

Imperial declared bankruptcy in 1931 but continued to operate through court–appointed receivers. Imperial Glass Corporation, a new entity, was formed during July and August of 1931. In 1937 Imperial launched Candlewick, its best selling line.

In 1940 Imperial acquired the Central Glass Works. It proved to be the first of a number of acquisitions, including A. H. Heisey and Company in 1958 and the Cambridge Glass Company in 1960.

In 1973, Imperial became a subsidiary of Lenox Glass Corporation. In 1981 Lenox sold the company to Arthur Lorch, a private investor, who in turn sold it to Robert Stahl, a liquidator, in 1982. In October 1982 Imperial declared bankruptcy. Consolidated–Colony, a partnership of Lancaster Colony Corporation and Consolidated International, purchased Imperial in December 1984. Most of the company's molds were sold. Maroon Enterprises of Bridgeport, Ohio, purchased the buildings and property in March 1985.

References: Margaret and Douglas Archer, *Imperial Glass: 1904–1938 Catalog*, reprint, Collector Books, 1978, 1995 value update; National Imperial Glass Collectors' Society, *Imperial Glass Encyclopedia, Vol I: A – Cane* (1995), *Vol II: Cape Cod – L* (1998), Antique Publications; Harry L. Rinker, *Stemware of the 20th Century: The Top 200 Patterns*, House of Collectibles, 1997.

Collectors' Club: National Imperial Glass Collectors Society, PO Box 534, Bellaire, OH 43906.

Note: See Candlewick for additional listings.

Beaded Block, bowl, iridescent, 7½" **$30.00**
Beaded Block, creamer, crystal **15.00**
Beaded Block, lily bowl, iridescent, 6" **75.00**
Beaded Block, relish, iridescent, 9" **30.00**
Beaded Block, sugar, blue opalescent **42.00**
Beaded Block, sugar, crystal **16.00**
Cape Cod, baked apple **10.00**
Cape Cod, bowl, #160/62B, handled, 7½" **28.00**
Cape Cod, bread and butter plate, #1D, 6¼" **6.00**
Cape Cod, butter dish, cov, 160/144 . . . . **32.00**

Beaded Block, creamer, ftd, pink, $12.00.

Cape Cod, cake stand, #160/67D **40.00**
Cape Cod, champagne, #1602, 6 oz, crystal **9.00**
Cape Cod, champagne, #1602, green **18.00**
Cape Cod, claret, #1602, azalea **35.00**
Cape Cod, coaster, crystal **8.00**
Cape Cod, cocktail, #1602, 3½ oz, crystal **8.00**
Cape Cod, compote, #160/45, 4¼", crystal **28.00**
Cape Cod, compote, ftd, 7", crystal **40.00**
Cape Cod, creamer and sugar, #30, crystal **24.00**
Cape Cod, juice tumbler, #1602, ftd, crystal **14.00**
Cape Cod, juice tumbler, #1602, ftd, green **15.00**
Cape Cod, marmalade, #160/89, 4 pcs, crystal **45.00**
Cape Cod, mint dish, #160/192, divided, crystal, 8½" **195.00**
Cape Cod, old fashioned tumbler, crystal, 7 oz **15.00**
Cape Cod, oyster cocktail, #1602, crystal **12.00**
Cape Cod, parfait, #1602, crystal **12.00**
Cape Cod, pepper mill, crystal **25.00**
Cape Cod, pitcher, #160/24, crystal, 60 oz **100.00**
Cape Cod, pitcher, crystal, 40 oz **55.00**
Cape Cod, plate, #1608D, flat, crystal, 14" **50.00**
Cape Cod, plate, #1608V, cupped, crystal, 13½" **35.00**
Cape Cod, plate, crystal, 6½" **5.00**
Cape Cod, plate, crystal, 7½" **8.00**
Cape Cod, plate, depressed center, crystal, 7½" **25.00**
Cape Cod, relish, #160/102, 5 part, 11" **65.00**
Cape Cod, relish, 4 part, 9½" **35.00**
Cape Cod, salad plate, #160/5D, 8" **8.00**
Cape Cod, salt and pepper shakers, pr, #160/116, crystal **20.00**
Cape Cod, salt and pepper shakers, pr, #160/117, crystal **24.00**
Cape Cod, saucer, crystal **3.00**
Cape Cod, sherbet, #1602, low, crystal **6.00**
Cape Cod, whiskey, #1602, crystal **15.00**
Cape Cod, wine, #1602, crystal, 3 oz **10.00**
Crocheted, bowl, ftd, 10" d, 7¼" h, crystal **35.00**
Crocheted, cake plate, ftd, 12", crystal **38.00**
Crocheted, compote, 7⅛" h, 10⅜" d, crystal **35.00**
Katy, berry bowl, blue opalescent, flat rim **30.00**
Katy, bowl, blue opalescent, #749B, 9¼" **125.00**
Katy, bowl, blue opalescent, low, 8" **65.00**

Katy, bowl, green opalescent, #749B, 9"................**125.00**
Katy, candle holder, blue opalescent, duo................**125.00**
Katy, candle holder, green opalescent, duo................**98.00**
Katy, cereal bowl, blue opalescent, deep................**65.00**
Katy, cereal bowl, blue opalescent, flared................**60.00**
Katy, mayonnaise and liner, blue opalescent................**120.00**
Katy, plate, blue opalescent, open lace, 9½"................**65.00**
Katy, soup bowl, blue opalescent................**85.00**
Katy, tumbler, blue opalescent................**62.00**
Katy, vase, green opalescent, #743N, 5½"................**65.00**
Mount Vernon, cocktail................**8.00**
Mount Venon, punch set................**150.00**
Mount Vernon, sherbet, low................**7.00**
Nuart, ashtray, mkd................**20.00**
Nuart, berry bowl, tab handles, mkd, 4½" d................**18.00**
Nuart, vase, bulbous, iridescent green, 7" h................**135.00**
Nucut, bowl, mkd, 7½" d................**25.00**
Nucut, compote, 5½" d................**25.00**
Nucut, creamer................**20.00**
Nucut, fern dish, brass lining, mkd, 8" l................**40.00**
Nucut, tumbler, flared rim, molded star................**18.00**
Reeded (Spun), iced tea tumbler, teal, 12 oz................**20.00**
Reeded (Spun), pitcher, teal, ice lip, 90 oz................**95.00**
Reeded (Spun), vanity jar, pink, 7⅝"................**95.00**

INSULATORS

The development of glass and ceramic insulators resulted from a need created by the telegraph. In 1844 Ezra Cornell obtained the first insulator patent. Armstrong (1938–69), Brookfield (1865–1922), California (1912–16), Gayner (1920–22), Hemingray (1871–1919), Lynchburg (1923–25), Maydwell (1935–40), McLaughlin (1923–25), and Whitall Tatum (1920–38) are the leading insulator manufacturers.

The first insulators did not contain threads. L. A. Cauvet patented a threaded insulator in the late 1860s. Drip points were added to insulators to prevent water from accumulating and creating a short. A double skirt kept the peg or pin free of moisture.

Insulators are collected by "CD" (consolidated design) numbers as found in N. R. Woodward's *The Glass Insulator in America*. The numbers are based upon the design style of the insulator. Color, name of maker, or lettering are not factors in assigning numbers. Thus far over 500 different design styles have been identified.

References: John and Carol McDougald, *Insulators: A History and Guide to North American Glass Pintype Insulators*, *Volume 1* (1990), *Volume 2* (1990), *Price Guide* (1995), published by authors; Marion and Evelyn Milholland, *Glass Insulator Reference Book*, 4th Revision, published by authors, 1976, available from C. D. Walsh (granddaughter).

Periodical: *Crown Jewels of the Wire*, PO Box 1003, St Charles, IL 60174.

Collectors' Club: National Insulator Assoc, 1315 Old Mill Path, Broadview Heights, OH 44147.

Note: Insulators are in near mint/mint condition unless otherwise noted.

CD 102, bar/diamond, medium olive green................**$5.00**
CD 106, star, olive green................**10.00**
CD 121, California A–007, purple................**20.00**

CD 121, diamond, purple................**15.00**
CD 121, McLaughlin 16, emerald green................**12.00**
CD 121, New England Tel & Tel, blue aqua................**3.00**
CD 121, pleated skirt 1899, aqua with green wisps................**24.00**
CD 121, W G M Co, dark royal purple................**22.00**
CD 122, Hemingray #16, green................**15.00**
CD 122, McLaughlin 16, light citron................**100.00**
CD 123, E C & M Co, flat–top style, cobalt................**800.00**
CD 124, Hemingray 4, aqua jade swirl................**135.00**
CD 126.4, W E Mfg Co, Patent 1871, teal................**250.00**
CD 133, B G M Co, sun colored amethyst................**75.00**
CD 133, Star, skinny dome, 2 tone, aqua with olive swirls................**20.00**
CD 134, American Ins Co, emb base, light blue................**15.00**
CD 134, patent 1871, clear................**40.00**
CD 135, Chicago Diamond, emb shoulder, blue aqua................**65.00**
CD 145, Grand Canyon, blue/lavender................**150.00**
CD 145, H G Co, petticoat, emerald................**175.00**
CD 145, star, aqua................**2.00**
CD 151, Natco, H G Co, peacock blue................**445.00**
CD 154, Dominion #42, orange amber................**25.00**
CD 154, Whitall Tatum #1, purple................**15.00**
CD 162, California, dark plum purple................**28.00**
CD 162, California, purple................**90.00**
CD 162, Gayner 36–190, aqua................**2.00**
CD 162, Hemingray 19, dark cobalt................**165.00**
CD 162.4, no name, dark purple................**75.00**
CD 164, H G Co, green milk................**30.00**
CD 164, Maydwell 20, white milk, some swirls................**15.00**
CD 164, N E G M, olive green................**24.00**
CD 168, Hemingray D510, gold carnival................**30.00**
CD 169.1, Whitall Tatum #5, light blue................**5.00**
CD 175, Hemingray 25, aqua................**22.00**
CD 178, Cal Santa Ana, purple................**110.00**
CD 178, no name, dark aqua................**8.00**
CD 214, Nacionales, red amber................**75.00**
CD 230, Hemingray D–152, carnival................**15.00**
CD 235, Agee, purple, type 2................**20.00**
CD 251, N E G M, co pat 1890, glossy blue aqua................**34.00**
CD 257, Hemingray #60, light green, amber in ears................**20.00**
CD 258, Cable, dark aqua................**20.00**
CD 260, California, sage green................**55.00**

CD 151, H.G. Co., Petticoat, smooth base, apple green, $275.00.

CD 280, Prism, aqua. **30.00**
CD 297, #16, dark yellow olive green **52.00**
CD 326, Pyrex #453, dark carnival **125.00**
CD 420, C C G, medium amber **18.00**
CD 575, L'Electro Verre, emerald **125.00**
CD 734, McMicking, aqua **50.00**
CD 735, Mulford, bright aqua, no UPRR **275.00**
CD 1038, Cutter, medium emerald green **200.00**
CD U–408A, no name, New Lexington, glossy taffy **395.00**

IRONS

The modern iron resulted from a series of technological advances that began in the middle of the 19th century. Until the arrival of the electric iron at the beginning of the 20th century, irons were heated by pre–heating a slug put into the iron, burning solid or liquid fuels or by drawing heat from a heated surface such as a stove top.

Pre–electric irons from the late 19th and early 20th centuries are common. Do not overpay. High prices are reserved for novelty irons and irons from lesser known makers.

H. W. Seeley patented the first electric iron in 1882. The first iron, a General Electric with a detachable cord, dates from 1903. Westinghouse introduced the automatic iron in 1924 and Edec the steam iron in 1926. Electric irons are collected more for their body design than their historical importance or age. Check the cord and plug before attempting to use any electric iron.

References: David Irons, *Irons By Irons*, published by author, 1994; David Irons, *More Irons By Irons*, published by author, 1997.

Newsletter: *Iron Talk*, PO Box 68, Waelder, TX 78959.

ATC, Japan, travel, electric, c1950, 6³/₄" l **$25.00**
Belgium, electric, round, small pointed toe, c1950, 5¹/₈" d **250.00**
W Bersted Mfg Co, Fostoria, electric, heat indicator, c1925, 7¹/₂" l. **40.00**
Brock Snyder Mfg Co, Royal, electric, wood handle **15.00**
Chicago Electric Mfg Co, Handy Hot, Streamline, electric, heat indicator, c1925, 7¹/₂" l **40.00**
Chief Electrics, Inc, Winsted CT, Air Flow, electric, heat indicator, c1930, 7⁷/₈" l **25.00**
Wm Cissel Mfg Co, Louisville, KY, electric, steam, c1940, 7" l **40.00**
M A Cuming & Co, NY, hat, 2–pc crown, tin top, wood bottom, c1925, 7" l **300.00**
Detroit Appliance, Inc, Pyrex, electric, white, c1940, 7¹/₂" l **750.00**
Dominion Electrical Mfg Co, Minneapolis, MN, Domino Aristocrat, electric, green porcelain, c1925, 6¹/₂" l **125.00**
Empire Electrical Co, Cincinnati OH, steam press, electric, 10³/₈" l **25.00**
European, charcoal, rear chimney, damper in spout, hinged at back, c1925, 8" l **60.00**
Gabrifer, electric, self–contained trivet, c1940 . . . . **125.00**
General Electric, Automatic Iron, orig box, c1950, 7¹/₂" l **15.00**
General Electric, Steam–O–Matic, electric, cast aluminum, 1930s. **20.00**
George Mfg Co, Youngstown, OH, Fiery Feather, electric, folding, orig box, c1950, 6³/₄" l **40.00**
Graetzor, electric, white porcelain, c1925, 7³/₄" l **85.00**

Grand Mfg Co, Los Angeles, CA, Electrical Puff Iron, electric, 11" h **400.00**
Hoover Co, North Canton, OH, The New Hoover Iron, orig box, post–1950, 7¹/₂" l. **15.00**
Hot Point, Heat–O–Matic, orig box, c1925, 6⁷/₈" l **25.00**
KM Gad–A–Bout, travel, electric, heat indicator, c1950, 7³/₄" l **40.00**
Knapp Monarch Co, St Louis, Flat Work Ironer, round, c1935, 5⁷/₈" d **175.00**
Lucas Holder Ltd, Coventry, Smoothie, travel, electric, orig box, c1950, 3³/₈" l. **85.00**
Prilect Traveling Iron, electric, orig tin box, c1925, 4⁷/₈" l **85.00**
Prilect Universal, travel, electric, changeable voltage, post–1960, 5³/₄" l. **60.00**
Proctor, Never Lift Delux, electric, c1950, 7" l **60.00**
Proctor and Schwartz Electric Co, Philadelphia, PA, Proctor Speed Iron, electric, c1940, 7" l **40.00**
Proctor Electric Co, Champion Automatic Speed Iron, electric, brown Bakelite handle **20.00**
Round Iron Co, Detroit USA, electric, round, Model K, c1940, 8" d **250.00**
Silex Co, Hartford, CT, Silex, electric, steam, c1925, 9¹/₄" l **25.00**
Star–Lite, Japan, travel, electric, orig box, c1960, 7" l **25.00**
Steam Electric Corp, electric, aluminum surface, c1925, 9¹/₈" l **25.00**
Sunbeam, orig tin box, c1920, 5³/₈" l **40.00**
Toy, Music Box Iron, Fisher–Price, plastic, paper litho, rolling eyes, 1960s **12.00**
Toy, Playtime Toys, plastic, red body, metal base plate, black plastic handle,1954 . . . . **2.00**
Toy, Sunnie Miss Iron, Ohio Art, metal litho top, plastic handle, metal base plate **2.00**
Toy, Wolverine, electric, 1950s **30.00**
Universal Stroke Sav–R, orig tab, c1950, 9" l **15.00**
Velvet Steam, French, c1930 . . . . **250.00**
Waring Corp, NY, Aluron, electric, porcelain, white, orig box, c1940, 7¹/₄" l **60.00**
Williams Corp, Detroit, Eureka, Cordless Automatic, electric, c1950, 7¹/₂" l **60.00**
WTC, Japan, travel, electric, c1930, 6" l **25.00**

FADA, wireless, with trivet, c1930, 7³/₈" l, $125.00.

JEANNETTE GLASS

The Jeannette Glass Company, Jeannette, Pennsylvania, was founded in 1898. Its first products were glass jars, headlight lenses, and glass brick, known as sidewalk tile. The company supplied glass candy containers to other firms during the 1920s.

Jeannette introduced pressed table and kitchenware in the 1920s. Popular Depression era patterns include Adam (1932–34), Cherry Blossom (1930–39), Cube (1929–33), Doric (1935–38), Doric and Pansy (1937–38), Hex Optic (1928–32), Homespun (1939–49), Iris and Herringbone (1928–32, 1950s, and 1970s), Swirl (1937–38), and Windsor (1936–46).

The company continued to thrive in the post–World War II era. Anniversary (1947–49, late 1960s to mid–1970s), Floragold (1950s), Harp (1954–1957), Holiday (1947 through mid–1950s), and Shell Pink Milk Glass (1957–1959) were among the most popular patterns. The popularity of Iris was so strong it easily made the transition from pre–war to post–war pattern.

In 1952 Jeannette purchased the McKee Glass Corporation, enabling the company to expand into the production of heat resistant and industrial glass.

The Jeannette Glass Company ceased operations in the mid–1980s.

References: Gene Florence, *Collectible Glassware From the 40s, 50s, 60s...*, Fourth Edition, Collector Books, 1998; Gene Florence, *Collector's Encyclopedia of Depression Glass, Thirteenth Edition*, Collector Books, 1998.

Note: For additional listings see Depression Glass and Kitchen Glassware.

Drippings Jar, cov, delphite, $120.00.

Adam, ashtray, 4¹/₂", green	$25.00
Adam, bowl, 7³/₄", d, green	32.00
Adam, bread and butter plate, 6" d, green	30.00
Adam, cake plate, ftd, green	30.00
Adam, candy, cov	120.00
Adam, casserole, bottom, green	42.00
Adam, cereal bowl, pink	40.00
Adam, coaster, green	20.00
Adam, cup and saucer, green	30.00
Adam, dessert bowl, 4³/₄", green	20.00
Adam, dinner plate, 9" d, green	35.00
Adam, ice tea tumbler, 5¹/₂", green	55.00
Adam, platter	35.00
Adam, platter, oblong, green	32.00
Adam, salad plate, 7³/₄", green	15.00
Adam, salt and pepper shakers, pr, pink	75.00
Adam, saucer, green	6.00
Adam, sherbet, ftd, green	35.00
Adam, water tumbler, 4¹/₂", green	28.00
Ashtray, butterfly, crystal	7.00
Ashtray, cowboy hat, delphite	22.00
Cherry Blossom, berry bowl, individual, 4³/₄", green	15.00
Cherry Blossom, berry bowl, master, 8¹/₂" d, pink	42.00
Cherry Blossom, bowl, 8¹/₂" d, pink	45.00
Cherry Blossom, bowl, handled, 9" d, pink	40.00
Cherry Blossom, bread and butter plate, 6" d, green	5.00
Cherry Blossom, cake plate, ftd, green	42.00
Cherry Blossom, cake plate, ftd, pink	28.00
Cherry Blossom, creamer and sugar, cov, green	45.00
Cherry Blossom, creamer and sugar, cov, pink	50.00
Cherry Blossom, cup and saucer, child's, delphite	47.00

Cherry Blossom, cup and saucer, delphite	24.00
Cherry Blossom, cup and saucer, pink	22.00
Cherry Blossom, dinner plate, pink	20.00
Cherry Blossom, grill plate, pink	30.00
Cherry Blossom, ice tea tumbler, flat, pattern at top, pink	60.00
Cherry Blossom, juice tumbler, flat, pattern at top, pink	25.00
Cherry Blossom, pitcher, flat, 42 oz, green	60.00
Cherry Blossom, pitcher, pattern at top, pink	60.00
Cherry Blossom, platter, oval, 11" l, green	20.00
Cherry Blossom, sandwich tray, pink	25.00
Cherry Blossom, sherbet, green	15.00
Cherry Blossom, salad plate, 7" d, green	20.00
Cherry Blossom, water tumbler, pattern at top, pink	20.00
Doric, berry bowl, pink	11.00
Doric, cake plate, ftd, pink	20.00
Doric, candy dish, cov, pink	38.00
Doric, dinner plate, green	22.00
Doric, dinner plate, pink	12.00
Doric, relish, with inserts, pink	82.00
Doric, sherbet, ftd, delphite	7.00
Doric, sugar and creamer, cov, pink	42.00
Doric, sugar, cov, pink	30.00
Doric, tumbler, 4¹/₂", 9 oz, green	125.00
Doric, water tumbler, flat, pink	60.00
Floral, berry bowl, green, small	25.00
Floral, coaster, green	12.00
Floral, cup, green	14.00
Floral, dinner plate, pink	20.00
Floral, ice tea tumbler, green	175.00
Floral, ice tea tumbler, pink	55.00
Floral, juice tumbler, ftd, green	25.00
Floral, platter, oval, pink	18.00
Floral, salad plate, green	15.00
Floral, salad plate, pink	20.00
Floral, salt and pepper shakers, pr, pink	45.00
Floral, saucer, pink	10.00
Floral, sherbet, ftd, pink	18.00
Floral, sherbet, green	20.00
Floral, tumbler, 4¹/₄", green	22.00
Floral, water tumbler, ftd, pink	25.00
Iris, bowl, beaded edge, 4¹/₂" d, iridescent	14.00
Iris, bowl, ruffled edge, 9¹/₂" d, iridescent	10.00
Iris, butter, cov, iridescent	55.00

Iris, coaster, crystal **110.00**
Iris, creamer, iridescent **10.00**
Iris, cup, iridescent **15.00**
Iris, demitasse cup and saucer, crystal **240.00**
Iris, dinner plate, 9" d, iridescent **50.00**
Iris, goblet, 8 oz, 5¹⁄₂" h, crystal **25.00**
Iris, goblet, ftd, plain, 3 oz, 6" h, iridescent **30.00**
Iris, iced tea tumbler, crystal **42.00**
Iris, pitcher, crystal **40.00**
Iris, sandwich plate, iridescent **38.00**
Iris, sherbet, ftd, 2¹⁄₂", crystal **30.00**
Iris, sherbet, ftd, 4", crystal **25.00**
Iris, sherbet, low, crystal **30.00**
Iris, sherbet, low, 2¹⁄₂" h, iridescent **15.00**
Iris, sugar, cov, iridescent. **30.00**
Iris, tumbler, ftd, 6" h, iridescent **19.00**
Iris, vase, crimped, 9" h, iridescent. **30.00**
Iris, water goblet, crystal **30.00**
Iris, water tumbler, crystal **22.00**
Iris, wine goblet, crystal. **20.00**
Swirl, candlesticks, pr, ultramarine **42.00**
Swirl, candy, open, 3 ftd, ultramarine. **15.00**
Swirl, candy base, ultramarine. **45.00**
Swirl, cereal bowl, ultramarine **15.00**
Swirl, console bowl, ultramarine **25.00**
Swirl, creamer, ftd, ultramarine **15.00**
Swirl, creamer and sugar, ultramarine **25.00**
Swirl, cup and saucer, ultramarine **20.00**
Swirl, ice tea tumbler, ultramarine **142.00**
Swirl, lug soup, ultramarine. **42.00**
Swirl, salad bowl, 9" d, ultramarine **22.00**
Swirl, sandwich plate, 12" d, ultramarine **22.00**
Swirl, sherbet, ultramarine. **20.00**
Swirl, tumbler, ftd, 9 oz, ultramarine **42.00**
Swirl, vase, ftd, 8¹⁄₂" h, ultramarine **22.00**

JEWELRY

Jewelry divides into two basic groups: precious and non–precious (a.k.a., costume after 1920). This category focuses on precious jewelry. While collected, most precious jewelry is purchased to be worn or studied.

U.S. custom laws define antique jewelry as jewelry over one hundred years old. Estate or Heirloom jewelry is generally assumed to be over twenty–five years old.

Craftsmanship, aesthetic design, scarcity, and current market worth of gemstones and the precious metal are the principal value keys. Antique and period jewelry should be set with the cut of stone prevalent at the time the piece was made. Names (manufacturer, designer, or both) also play a major role in value.

Be extremely cautious when buying jewelry. Reproductions, copycats (stylistic reproductions), fantasies (non–period shapes and forms), and fakes abound. Also be alert for married and divorced pieces.

References: Ed Aswad and Michael Weinstein, *The Art and Mystique of Shell Cameos: Identification and Value Guide*, 2nd Edition, Krause Publications, 1997; Lillian Baker, *Art Nouveau & Art Deco Jewelry: An Identification & Value Guide*, Collector Books, 1981, 1997 value update; Howard L. Bell, Jr., *Cuff Jewelry: A Historical Account for Collectors and Antique Dealers*, published by author, 1994; Jeanenne Bell, *Answers to Questions About*

1840–1950 Old Jewelry, Fourth Edition, Books Americana, Krause Publications, 1996; Monica Lynn Clements and Patricia Rosser Clements, *Cameos: Classical to Costume*, Schiffer Publishing, 1998; Lodovica Rizzoli Eleuteri, *Twentieth–Century Jewelry: Art Nouveau to Modern Design*, Electa, Abbeville, 1994.

Arthur Guy Kaplan, *The Official Identification and Price Guide to Antique Jewelry, Sixth Edition*, House of Collectibles, 1990, reprinted 1994; Penny Chittim Morrill and Carol A. Beck, *Mexican Silver: 20th–Century Handwrought Jewelry and Metalwork*, Schiffer Publishing, 1994; Ginger Moro, *European Designer Jewelry*, Schiffer Publishing, 1995; Dorothy T. Rainwater, *American Jewelry Manufacturers*, Schiffer Publishing, 1988; Christie Romero, *Warman's Jewelry, 2nd Edition*, Krause Publications, 1998; Nancy N. Schiffer, *Silver Jewelry Treasures*, Schiffer Publishing, 1993; Sheryl Gross Shatz, *What's It Made Of?: A Jewelry Materials Identification Guide, Third Edition*, published by author, 1996; Doris J. Snell, *Antique Jewelry With Prices, Second Edition*, Wallace–Homestead, Krause Publications, 1997.

Periodicals: *Gems & Gemology*, Gemological Inst of America, 5355 Armada Dr, Carlsbad, CA 92008; *Jewelers' Circular Keystone/Heritage*, 201 King of Prussia Rd, Wayne, PA 19089.

Collectors' Clubs: American Society of Jewelry Historians, Box 103, 1B, Quaker Ridge Rd, New Rochelle, NY 10804; National Cuff Link Society, PO Box 346, Prospect Heights, IL 60070; Society of Antique & Estate Jewelry, Ltd, 570 Seventh Ave, Ste 1900, New York, NY 10018.

Bangle Bracelet, 14K yg and diamonds, hinged, floral pattern, pierced openwork design, top half bead set with 3 round old mine cut diamonds **$975.00**
Bracelet, SS and enamel, geometric design links with black and multicolored enamel, sgd "Margot de Taxco" **485.00**
Bracelet, SS, fancy links, T–bar closure, French hallmarks . . . **485.00**
Bracelet, wg–topped 14K yg, rectangular pierced links, 7¹⁄₂" l **85.00**
Brooch, 14K gold, multicolored, parrot's head, textured feathers and diamond set eyes, boxed. **860.00**

Brooch, cabochon sapphire in diamond set scroll frame, platinum mount, 1.50 cts approx total weight, 14.5 x 11.8 mm, $1,610.00. Photo courtesy Skinner, Inc.

Brooch, 14K yg, 3 flowers, citrine, tourmaline, and amethyst, faceted gemstone leaves, centered by round diamond 230.00

Brooch, 14K yg, lady's slipper, Art Nouveau, round old European–cut diamond, transparent green enamel highlights, mkd "Bippart, Griscom & Osborne" 430.00

Brooch, 14K yg, seated cat, green eye accents 400.00

Brooch, 18K yg, bird in flight holding fish in its beak, red stone eye accent 250.00

Brooch, clover shape, 4 smokey topaz petals, center diamond, diamond set stem, 14K yg mount 485.00

Brooch, painted blue flower bouquet, rhinestone accents, Chanel, 1930s 600.00

Brooch, SS and enamel, man and woman seated with child framed in foliate and scroll motifs, colored stone, blue and white accents, suspending 2 similar smaller plaques with enamel and pearl drops 345.00

Brooch, SS, centered by faceted quartz within large circular frame, thistle and foliate goldtone accents, Scottish. 85.00

Brooch, SS, free–form design, Spratling 345.00

Charm Bracelet, 14K yg, paper clip link chain, 17 charms, pop–up devil in a can, cocktail, vintage car, keys, flashlight, "park here for love" sign, hallmarks 632.00

Cuff Bracelet, SS, free–form stepped design, Gayle Saunders hallmark. 170.00

Cuff Links, 14K yg, fox and hound, 2 sided, red stone eyes 430.00

Earrings, pr, 18K yg and diamonds, textured free–form design centered by 2 diamond sprays 345.00

Earrings, pr, 14K yg and ruby, stylized flowers with ruby accented sprays. 285.00

Necklace, 18K yg, spherical fancy links, suspended heart shaped locket with star set diamonds, 10K yg mount. 460.00

Necklace, freshwater pearl, 3 strands, 44" l 115.00

Necklace, graduating faceted amethyst beads, size range from 5.30 to 15.30 mm, 14K yg clasp, 19" l 430.00

Necklace, jade, 7 round and octagonal jade plaques with naturalistic carvings, 14K gold fancy link chain with applied foliate motifs, 16½" l 920.00

Necklace, jade, carved Buddha accented with diamond set 14K wg necklace, suspended from graduating bead necklace, diamond set clasp, 18" l 632.00

Pendant, gilt silver, scroll form design, gem set blister pearls and faceted amethysts, polychrome enamel highlights, Austro–Hungarian 285.00

Pin, blue and white enamel flower centered by pearl, textured gold leaves, scalloped oval frame, 14K yg mount. 285.00

Ring, 14K gold, cabochon cut dyed blue stone on gold band, English hallmarks 200.00

Ring, 18K gold and silver, interlocking halves design, Zolotas hallmark, size 5¾ 172.00

Ring, 18K gold, kinetic cylinders within concave navette form, sgd "Pol Bury 3/30," French hallmarks, c1970 . . . . 1,150.00

Ring, 18K yg, opal and diamonds, centered by oval cabochon cut opal, brilliant cut and single cut diamond highlights 315.00

Ring, cabochon cut emerald framed in diamonds, 14K wg and yg mount 430.00

Ring, cabochon cut jade in pierced engraved 18 K yg mount 290.00

Ring, navette shaped with diamonds, Art Deco, pierced platinum mount. 690.00

Ring, SS, stylized buckle, sgd "Hermes, Paris," size 5 . . . . . . 258.00

Stickpin, 14K yg, turtle form, half pearls, and demantoid garnet, mkd "Riker Brothers," handkerchief holder 285.00

Suite, SS, bracelet and earrings, cabochon cut white discs in floral and foliate openwork frames, sgd "N. E. From, Denmark" 170.00

Watch Chain, 14K yg, curb link chain suspending a book form charm, small chain and small plaque, 16" l . . . 285.00

JEWELRY, COSTUME

Prior to World War I, non–precious jewelry consisted of inexpensive copies of precious jewelry. This changed in the 1920s when Coco Chanel advocated the wearing of faux jewelry as an acceptable part of haute couture. High–style fashion jewelry continued to exercise a strong influence on costume jewelry until the middle of the 20th century.

During the 1930s costume jewelry manufacture benefited from developments such as more efficient casting machines and the creation of Bakelite, one of the first entirely synthetic plastics. Material shortages during World War II promoted the increased use of ceramics and wood. Copper, plastic novelty, and rhinestone crazes marked the 1950s and 60s.

Because of this category's breadth, collectors and dealers focus on named manufacturers and designers. A maker's mark is not a guarantee of quality. Examine pieces objectively. This is a very trendy category. What is in today may be out tomorrow. Just ask anyone who collected rhinestone jewelry in the early 1980s.

References: Lillian Baker, *Fifty Years of Collectible Fashion Jewelry: 1925–1975*, Collector Books, 1986, 1997 value update; Lillian Baker, *100 Years of Collectible Jewelry, 1850–1950*, Collector Books, 1978, 1997 value update; Lillian Baker, *Twentieth–Century Fashionable Plastic Jewelry*, Collector Books, 1992, 1996 value update; Joanne Dubbs Ball, *Costume Jewelers: The Golden Age of Design, Second Edition*, Schiffer Publishing, 1997; Dee Battle and Alayne Lesser, *The Best Bakelite and Other Plastic Jewelry*, Schiffer Publishing, 1996; Vivienne Becker, *Fabulous Costume Jewelry: History of Fantasy and Fashion in Jewels*, Schiffer Publishing, 1993; Jeanenne Bell, *Answers to Questions About Old Jewelry, 1840–1950, Fourth Edition*, Books Americana, Krause Publications, 1996.

Matthew Burkholz, *The Bakelite Collection*, Schiffer Publishing, 1997; Matthew L. Burkholz and Linda Lictenberg Kaplan, *Copper*

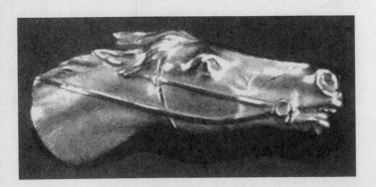

Pin, 14K yg, 3.60 dwt, $345.00. Photo courtesy Skinner, Inc.

Art Jewelry: A Different Luster, Schiffer Publishing, 1992; Deanna Farneti Cera, *Costume Jewelery*, Antique Collectors' Club, 1997; Maryanne Dolan, *Collecting Rhinestone Jewelry, Third Edition*, Books Americana, Krause Publications, 1993; Roseann Ettinger, *Forties & Fifties Popular Jewelry*, Schiffer Publishing, 1994; Roseann Ettinger, *Popular Jewelry: 1840–1940, Second Edition*, Schiffer Publishing, 1997; Roseann Ettinger, *Popular Jewelry of the '60s, '70s & '80s*, Schiffer Publishing, 1997; Sandy Fichtner and Lynn Ann Russell, *Rainbow of Rhinestone Jewelry*, Schiffer Publishing, 1996.

Jill Gallina, *Christmas Pins: Past and Present*, Collector Books, 1996; S. Sylvia Henzel, *Collectible Costume Jewelry, Third Edition*, Krause Publications, 1997; Sibylle Jargstorf, *Baubles, Buttons and Beads: The Heritage of Bohemia*, Schiffer Publishing, 1991; Sibylle Jargstorf, *Glass in Jewelry: Hidden Artistry in Glass*, Schiffer Publishing, 1991; Lyngerda Kelley and Nancy Schiffer, *Costume Jewelry: The Great Pretenders, Revised Edition*, Schiffer Publishing, 1996; Lyngerda Kelley and Nancy Schiffer, *Plastic Jewelry, Third Edition*, Schiffer Publishing, 1996; J. L. Lynnlee, *All That Glitters*, Schiffer Publishing, 1986, 1996 value update; Fred Rezazadeh, *Costume Jewelry: A Practical Handbook & Value Guide*, Collector Books, 1997.

Christie Romero, *Warman's Jewelry, 2nd Edition*, Krause Publications, 1998; Nancy N. Schiffer, *Costume Jewelry: The Fun of Collecting*, Schiffer Publishing, 1988, 1996 value update; Nancy N. Schiffer, *Rhinestones!, 2nd Edition*, Schiffer Publishing, 1997; Cherri Simonds, *Collectible Costume Jewelry*, Collector Books, 1997; Harrice Simons Miller, *Costume Jewelry: Identification and Price Guide, Second Edition*, Avon Books, 1994; Sheryl Gross Shatz, *What's It Made Of?: A Jewelry Materials Identification Guide*, published by author, 1991; Nicholas D. Snider, *Sweetheart Jewelry and Collectibles*, Schiffer Publishing, 1995.

Collectors' Club: Vintage Fashion & Costume Jewelry Club, PO Box 265, Glen Oaks, NY 11004.

Brooch, Christmas tree, green, red, crystal, amber, and pink rhinestones, Weiss, 2³/₈" h, $85.00.

Ankle Bracelet, double heart plaque, 10¹/₂" l	**$32.00**
Bangle Bracelet, Bakelite, butterscotch, plain	**20.00**
Bangle Bracelet, Bakelite, red, laminated black polka dots, c1930	**275.00**
Bangle Bracelet, plastic, neon, multihinged, 1¹/₂" w	**45.00**
Bracelet, cabochon and enamel pastel, Trifari	**25.00**
Brooch, Bakelite, red heart, dangling berries on red stems, c1935, 2¹/₂" w	**265.00**
Brooch, gold–plated white metal, plastic, molded green sail, boat bottom and ocean waves, Hattie Carnegie, c1960	**125.00**
Charm Bracelet, antique silver tone, oriental coin charms, Napier	**125.00**
Charm Bracelet, Bakelite, 5 amber colored charms including horse head, horseshoes, and boots, suspended from gilded link chain, c1940	**250.00**
Charm Bracelet, SS, desk, typewriter, poodle, piano, guitar, heart, key, pennant, turtle, and zodiac disc, 1960s	**35.00**
Choker, gold plated, Art Deco, rose, diamond cut clear rhinestones, prong set, 1940s	**110.00**
Choker, gold plated, flower and ribbon motif, amethyst and clear chaton cut rhinestones, Coro	**125.00**
Clip, Bakelite, carved daisies, brown	**40.00**
Clip, pr, celluloid, carved multicolored flower	**45.00**
Cuff Links, pr, SS, 6 guns with revolving barrels, mother–of–pearl handles, c1945	**100.00**

Earrings, pr, Bakelite, dice, ivory and rhinestone, screw back	**35.00**
Earrings, pr, chrome plated, covered wagons, turning wheels, screwbacks	**35.00**
Earrings, pr, marbelized glass stones, Christian Dior, 1950s	**40.00**
Earrings, pr, plastic, disc, spangles, clear, large	**25.00**
Earrings, pr, porcelain, round drops, Delft	**28.00**
Earrings, pr, silver tone, tassel, Monet, 3¹/₄" l	**25.00**
Lapel Button, Bakelite, horse head, brown	**65.00**
Lapel Watch, ice cube suspended from gold filled bow pin, Avalon, 1940s	**100.00**
Necklace, chromium plated, fringe style, simulated teardrop pearls, clear chaton cut rhinestones	**85.00**
Necklace, fan shaped segments, white, Sam Niello	**85.00**
Necklace, guilded brass, figural turtle pendant, plastic shell, movable legs, head, and tail, yellow glass eyes, twisted gold plated rope chain, 1970s	**50.00**
Necklace, figural pewter perfume bottle with swirl designs, silver tone chain, mkd "Goldette," 1960s	**75.00**
Necklace, silver tone metal chains, aqua and smoky gray glass beads, ball and tassel center accent, mkd "W. Germany"	**40.00**
Pendant, Cartier style, Trifari	**45.00**
Pin, Bakelite, butterfly	**45.00**
Pin, Celluloid, carved flower, coral	**25.00**
Pin, figural dancer, Sam Niello	**40.00**
Pin, plastic, bird, pearl–like finish	**25.00**
Pin, plastic, profile of black woman, purple turban and ruff	**45.00**
Pin, rhinestones, flower, Weiss	**35.00**
Pin, SS, butterfly, Hobe	**50.00**
Pin, SS and moonstone, flower, Coro	**50.00**
Ring, amber, dome, embedded ant, size 7¹/₂	**35.00**
Suite, bracelet, brooch, earrings, and ring, silver tone base metal, smoky glass and pink rhinestones, Sarah Coventry	**175.00**
Suite, necklace and earrings, pr, gilded brass, faux pear shaped topaz	**115.00**
Suite, necklace and earrings, pr, gilded brass, floral motif, aquamarine, emerald, amethyst, and clear rhinestones	**75.00**
Sweater Guard, rhinestones, silver colored metal mount	**30.00**

JOHNSON BROTHERS

In 1883 three brothers, Alfred, Frederick, and Henry Johnson, purchased the bankrupt J. W. Pankhurst Company, a tableware manufactory in Hanley, Staffordshire, England and established Johnson Brothers. Although begun on a small scale, the company prospered and expanded.

In 1896, Robert, a fourth brother, joined the firm. Robert, who lived and worked in the United States, was assigned the task of expanding the company's position in the American market. By 1914 Johnson Brothers owned and operated five additional factories scattered throughout Hanley, Tunstall, and Burslem.

Johnson Brothers continued to grow throughout the 1960s with acquisitions of tableware manufacturing plants in Hamilton, Ontario, Canada, and Croydon, Australia. Two additional English plants were acquired in 1960 and 1965.

Johnson Brothers became part of the Wedgwood Group in 1968.

References: Mary J. Finegan, *Johnson Brothers Dinnerware: Pattern Directory & Price Guide,* published by author, 1993; Harry L. Rinker, *Dinnerware of the 20th Century: The Top 500 Patterns,* House of Collectibles, 1997.

Coaching Scenes, cereal bowl, small nick	**$30.00**
Coaching Scenes, cup and saucer	9.00
Coaching Scenes, dinner plate	9.00
Coaching Scenes, fruit bowl, 5⅛"	9.00
Coaching Scenes, gravy boat and underplate	45.00
Coaching Scenes, plate, 6"	4.00
Coaching Scenes, plate, 7¾"	12.00
Coaching Scenes, teapot, cov	30.00
Coaching Scenes, vegetable bowl, small nick, 8"	25.00
Friendly Village, bread and butter plate	3.00
Friendly Village, cereal bowl, coup, 6⅛"	5.00
Friendly Village, chop plate, 12¼"	35.00
Friendly Village, coaster	12.00
Friendly Village, creamer and sugar, cov	34.00
Friendly Village, dessert plate, 7" d	3.00
Friendly Village, gravy boat stand	10.00

Friendly Village, milk pitcher	30.00
Friendly Village, relish, 3 part	40.00
Merry Christmas, place setting	60.00
Old Britain Castles, blue, bread and butter plate, 6¼" d	8.00
Old Britain Castles, blue, cup and saucer	12.00
Old Britain Castles, blue, platter, oval, 11¾" l	30.00
Old Britain Castles, blue, salad plate, 7⅞" d	12.00
Old Britain Castles, blue, vegetable, oval, 8¾" l	20.00
Olde English Country Side, bread and butter plate	3.00
Olde English Country Side, cereal bowl	5.00
Olde English Country Side, coaster	12.00
Old English Country Side, gravy boat stand	10.00
Old English Country Side, plate, square	8.00
Old English Country Side, vegetable bowl, oval	20.00
Provincial, bread and butter plate, 7" d	10.00
Provincial, coffeepot, cov	75.00
Provincial, creamer	25.00
Provincial, cup and saucer	20.00
Provincial, dinner plate	20.00
Provincial, sugar, cov	28.00

JOSEF FIGURINES

When Muriel Joseph George could no longer obtain Lucite during World War II for her plastic jewelry, she used clay to fashion ceramic jewelry. George loved to model, making a wide variety of serious and whimsical figures for her own amusement.

In 1946 Muriel and her husband, Tom, made their first commercial ceramic figures in their garage. The printer misspelled Joseph, thus inadvertently creating the company's signature name Josef. Despite the company's quick growth, early 1950s' cheap Japanese imitations severely undercut its market.

In 1959 Muriel, Tom, and George Good established George Imports. Production was moved to the Katayama factory in Japan. Muriel created her designs in America, sent them to Japan with production instructions, and approved samples. Once again, the company enjoyed a period of prosperity.

In 1974 the company became George–Good Corporation. When Muriel retired in 1981, George Good purchased her interest in the company. Muriel continued to do design work until 1984. In 1985 George Good sold the company to Applause, Inc.

References: Dee Harris, Jim and Kaye Whitaker, *Josef Originals: Charming Figurines With Price Guide,* Schiffer Publishing, 1994; Jim and Kaye Whitaker, *Josef Originals: A Second Look,* Schiffer Publishing, 1997.

Newsletter: *Josef Original Newsletter,* PO Box 475, Lynnwood, WA 98046.

America, Little Internationals	**$30.00**
Angel, with paddle and ball	25.00
Baby on Pillow, with kitten	25.00
Birthday Girl, "15"	30.00
Boy, holding flowers	25.00
Buying a New Hat, A Mother's World, 7½" h	100.00
Bridesmaid, Bridal Party	25.00
Carol, 4¼" h	50.00
Caroline, Colonial Days, 9½" h	110.00
Cho Cho, 10¾" h	110.00
Church Belle	25.00
Claudia, 5¾" h	70.00
Dinner for Two, 8" h	100.00

Old Britain Castles, blue, dinner plate, 9⅞" d, $15.00.

Mary Ann, yellow dress, green stones, paper labels and ink stamped signature, 3¹/₂" h, $18.00.

Gibson Girls	100.00
Gigi, 7" h	100.00
Girl, holding dog, Little Pets, 5¹/₄"	35.00
Girl, reading book, Morning, Noon, and Night	45.00
Girl, with puppy, An Arm Full of Love	25.00
Girl, with tea set, Make Believe	35.00
Girl, yellow bonnet and dress, Magnolia	65.00
Holly	30.00
Ireland, Little Internationals	30.00
Lady, holding parasol, pink dress, 8" h	100.00
Little Tutu	35.00
Mama, playing accordion, lime green dress	85.00
Mary Lou, First Formal	45.00
Melinda	35.00
Miss America	25.00
Moon Beam, Flower Sprites, 3³/₄"	30.00
Nun, rosary holder	25.00
October, Birthstone Doll	25.00
Party Dress, Sweet Sixteen, 7¹/₂" h	100.00
Pennies From Heaven	25.00
Penny, Musicale	65.00
Pitty Sing, red hat	45.00
Portraits, Ladies of Song, 4³/₄" h	40.00
Puppy Love	25.00
Say Your Prayers, Little Commandments, 3³/₄" h	25.00
Sunday, Days of the Week	35.00
Tea Time	35.00
Wee Ching, with dog	40.00

JUKEBOXES

A jukebox is an amplified coin–operated phonograph. The 1940s and early 1950s were its golden age, a period when bubble machines ruled every teenage hangout from dance hall to drugstore. Portable radios, television's growth, and "Top 40" radio were responsible for the jukebox's decline in the 1960s.

Pre–1938 jukeboxes were made primarily of wood and resemble a phonograph or radio cabinet. Wurlitzer and Rock–Ola, whose jukeboxes often featured brightly colored plastic and animation units, made the best of the 78 rpm jukeboxes of the 1938–1948 period. The 45 rpm jukebox, made famous by the tele-

vision show *Happy Days*, arrived on the scene in 1940 and survived until 1960. Seeburg was the principal manufacturer of these machines. Beginning in 1961, manufacturers often hid the record mechanism. These machines lack the collector appeal of their earlier counterparts.

References: Michael Adams, Jürgen Lukas, and Thomas Maschke, *Jukeboxes*, Schiffer Publishing, 1995; Jerry Ayliffe, *American Premium Guide to Jukeboxes and Slot Machines, Gumballs, Trade Stimulators, Arcade, 3rd Edition*, Books Americana, Krause Publications, 1991; Scott Wood, *A Blast From the Past Jukeboxes: A Pictorial Price Guide*, L–W Book Sales, 1992.

Periodicals: *Always Jukin'*, 221 Yesler Way, Seattle, WA 98104; *Antique Amusements, Slot Machines & Jukebox Gazette*, 909 26th St NW, Washington, DC 20037; *Coin–Op Classics*, 17844 Toiyabe St, Fountain Valley, CA 92708; *Gameroom Magazine*, PO Box 41, Keyport, NJ 07735; *Jukebox Collector*, 2545 WE 60th Court, Des Moines, IA 50317.

AMI A, complete, unrestored	$2,000.00
AMI C	1,500.00
AMI D–80, restored	1,400.00
AMI G–200, choice	2,800.00
Packard Pla–mor, restored	5,500.00
Rock–Ola 1428	4,500.00
Rock–Ola 474 Sybaris	650.00
Rock–Ola 1422, restored	3,000.00
Rock–Ola 1436 Fireball 120	1,500.00
Rock–Ola 1438, complete, wallbox and stepper	3,500.00
Rock–Ola 1448	1,600.00
Rock–Ola 1455	1,300.00
Rock–Ola 1465	1,500.00
Rock–Ola CM–39, with stand, restored	5,500.00
Rock–Ola Commando, with bowl, restored	16,500.00
Rock–Ola, countertop	2,000.00
Rock–Ola Princess 1493, orig, complete with records	1,400.00
Seeburg 100–B, choice	3,200.00
Seeburg 100–C	2,500.00
Seeburg 148	1,500.00
Seeburg 201, original	2,500.00

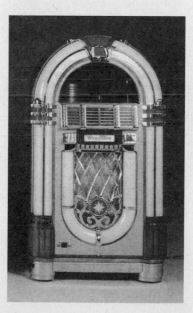

Wurlitzer 1015, 1946–47, 59¹/₂" h, $6,900.00. Photo courtesy Sotheby's.

Seeburg 222. . . . . **1,200.00**
Seeburg AQ–160 . . . . **1,150.00**
Seeburg Classic **1,600.00**
Seeburg DS–100 . . . . **950.00**
Seeburg JL, restored **2,950.00**
Seeburg KD–200 . . . . **2,000.00**
Seeburg Model A **750.00**
Seeburg, Q–160 . . . . **400.00**
Seeburg Regal **1,200.00**
Seeburg STD–2 Entertainer **750.00**
Seeburg V–200 . . . . **3,000.00**
Victory. **7,500.00**
Wurlitzer 61 . . . . **4,000.00**
Wurlitzer 750, 1941 . . . . **5,175.00**
Wurlitzer 800, complete. **5,500.00**
Wurlitzer 850, 1941 . . . . **12,500.00**
Wurlitzer 1015, unrestored, complete, original **6,500.00**
Wurlitzer 1080. . . . . **7,500.00**
Wurlitzer 1100, unrestored, complete, original **3,800.00**
Wurlitzer 2000, complete, original **5,500.00**

KEMPLE GLASS

In May 1945 John E. and Geraldine Kemple leased two buildings in East Palestine, Ohio, for the purposes of manufacturing tabletop glassware. They acquired many old molds from the 1870–1900 era along with molds from the Mannington Art Glass Company of West Virginia and McKee Glass.

During its twenty five years of operation (1945–1970), Kemple Glass produced a large number of "Authentic Antique Reproductions." Concerned that purchasers not confuse its products with period pieces, Kemple initially used milk glass for its restrikes from earlier molds. Color was added to the line in 1960, again in shades that make Kemple's products easy to distinguish from earlier examples. Kemple Glass was marked either with a paper sticker or the letter "K," an addition made to earlier molds whenever possible.

Kemple Glass moved to the old Gill Glass Works in Kenova, West Virginia, following a fire at its East Palestine plant in 1956. When John E. Kemple died in 1970, the company was sold and production ended in Kenova. Today, many of the Kemple molds are in the possession of Wheaton Industries, Millville, New Jersey.

Reference: John R. Burkholder and D. Thomas O'Connor, *Kemple Glass: 1945–1970*, Glass Press, 1997.

Animal Dish, cov, cat, split rib base, green **$55.00**
Ashtray, pony and cart, colored **25.00**
Butter, cov, Aztec **35.00**
Butter, cov, Lace & Dewdrop **45.00**
Cake Plate, Moon & Star Variant, 12" d **35.00**
Candlestick, Moon & Star Variant. **35.00**
Candy, cov, ftd, Ivy–in–Snow **25.00**
Celery, flared, Ivy–in–Snow **30.00**
Chalice, Yutec. **65.00**
Compote, ftd, Moon & Star Variant **35.00**
Cordial, Aztec, 1 oz, amberina **15.00**
Creamer and Sugar, Toltec **45.00**
Creamer, Blackberry **55.00**
Creamer, Lace & Dewdrop **25.00**
Cruet, Sunburn **65.00**
Ewer, Rainbow, tipped spout **30.00**
Figurine, Colonial Lady, milk glass **65.00**

Animal Dish, cov, rooster No. 4, split rib base, amberina, 5¹/₂" h, $60.00.

Figurine, pheasant, amber **85.00**
Hankie Box, cov, Scroll with Flower **28.00**
Hat, Lace & Dewdrop **15.00**
Match Holder, Indian Chief, milk glass **65.00**
Nappy, Bontec, handled, 5" **18.00**
Plate, Cabbage Leaf, 7" d **25.00**
Plate, Lacy Heart, 6" d **25.00**
Plate, maple leaf, 8" d **25.00**
Plate, Mary and Child, yellow **55.00**
Plate, Panel Peg, George Washington, 7" d **20.00**
Plate, Shell & Club, 7" d **25.00**
Powder Box, Fleur–de–Lis **18.00**
Punch Set, 14 pcs, bowl, foot, and 12 cups, Yutec **275.00**
Salt and Pepper Shakers, pr, Yutec **18.00**
Sherbet, Lace & Dewdrop **18.00**
Toothpick, Gypsy Kettle. **25.00**
Tumbler, Blackberry **45.00**
Tumbler, V–Cane & Daisy, 8 oz **18.00**
Vase, Champion, ruffled mouth **35.00**
Vase, Lacey Heart **30.00**

KEWPIES

Rose Cecil O'Neill (1876–1944) created the Kewpie doll. This famous nymph made its debut in the December 1909 issue of *Ladies' Home Journal.* The first doll, designed in part by Joseph L. Kallus, was marketed in 1913. Kallus owned the Cameo Doll Company; Geo. Borgfelt Company owned the Kewpie production and distribution rights.

Most early Kewpie items were manufactured in Germany. American and Japanese manufacturers also played a role. Composition Kewpie dolls did not arrive until after World War II.

O'Neill created a wide variety of Kewpie characters. Do not overlook Ho–Ho, Kewpie–Gal, Kewpie–Kin, Ragsy, and Scootles.

Kewpie licensing continues, especially in the limited edition collectibles area.

References: John Axe, *Kewpies: Dolls & Art of Rose O'Neill & Joseph L. Kallus,* Hobby House Press, 1987, out of print; Cynthia Gaskill, *The Kewpie Kompanion: A Kompendium of Kewpie Knowledge,* Gold Horse Publishing, 1994.

Newsletter: *Traveler,* PO Box 4032, Portland, OR 97208.

Collectors' Club: International Rose O'Neill Club, PO Box 668, Branson, MO 65616.

Doll, Cameo, #1230, vinyl, jointed head, arms, and legs, green dress, AMSCO, Milton Bradley, $25.00.

Carnival Statue, plaster, painted, 3½ x 7"	$30.00
Coloring Book, Christmas	25.00
Doll, black, flange neck, cloth body, 12" h	500.00
Doll, celluloid, painted eyes, jointed shoulders, 2" h	60.00
Doll, composition head and body, painted eyes, 8" h	250.00
Doll, Kuddle Kewpie, cloth, plush body, mask–type Kewpie face, cloth label mkd "Kruegar" or "King Pat. number 1785800," 10" h	250.00
Doll, plush body, vinyl face, painted features, Knickerbocker, 1964, 6" h	50.00
Doll, vinyl, molded and painted hair, side glancing eyes, orig clothing, mkd "Jesco," 9" h	80.00
Figure, bisque, holding parasol and suitcase, c1930, 2½" h	250.00
Figure, celluloid, black, movable arms, Japan, c1930	75.00
Lamp Base, plaster, painted, 3" brass bulb socket, 7" h	75.00
Letter Opener, pewter, Kewpie finial, 7" l	40.00
Paper Dolls, Kewpie–Kin, Saalfield, ©1967	40.00
Perfume Vial, china, Kewpie wearing headphones, Goebel of Germany, c1930, 2¼" h	75.00
Pin Box, cov, Kewpie with foot in air, mkd "Goebel," 2½" d	450.00
Postcard, Victory Ice Cream, full color illus, 1920, 3 x 5½"	25.00
Teacup, china, white, color illus, c1920, 2¼" h	65.00
Wedding Cake Top, bride and groom	40.00

KEYS & KEY CHAINS

People collect keys and key chains more for their novelty than any other reason. Because they are made in such quantities, few examples are rare. Most collectors specialize, focusing on a specific subject such as automobile, hotel, presentation keys ("Key to the City"), railroad, etc.

Beware of fantasy keys such as keys to the Tower of London, a *Titanic* cabin, or a Hollywood movie star's dressing room.

References: Don Stewart (comp.), *Antique Classic Marque Car Keys: United States 1915–1970, Second Edition*, published by author, 1993; Don Stewart (comp.), *Standard Guide to Key Collecting, 3rd Edition*, published by author, 1990.

Collectors' Clubs: Key Collectors International, 1427 Lincoln Blvd, Santa Monica, CA 90401; License Plate Key Chain & Mini License Plate Collectors, 888 Eighth Ave, New York, NY 10019.

KEYS

Cabinet, steel, Art Deco, 2" l	**$6.00**
Car, Corvair, gold plated, colored enamel	**22.50**
Car, De Soto, gold plated	**13.00**
Car, Ford, glove and rear deck, Hurd, 1935–48	**3.00**
Car, Mercury, ignition and door, Hurd, 1939–48	**5.50**
Car, Rambler, gold plated, center "R"	**18.00**
Car, Studebaker, ignition and door, Hurd, 1949–52	**5.50**
Door, bronze, Keen Kutter bow	**5.50**
Hotel, steel bit, hotel name and room number on bow	**4.50**
Presentation, copper plated, Key to the City, 1933 Chicago World's Fair, Hall of Science	**15.00**

KEY CHAINS

Aluminum, inscribed "Keep Me And Never Go Broke," "Parts Boys, Auto Specialty Co" on back, 1946 penny insert, 1½" h	**$10.00**
Emb Copper, Chrysler, Airflow, return to owner inscription on back, 1934	**20.00**
Gold Finish, Coca–Cola adv, bottle shape, c1950	**15.00**
Leather, Dodge, enameled logo	**12.00**
Metal, brass finish and chain, John F Kennedy, diecut initials	**15.00**
Plastic, dayglow, figural Dutch Boy, holding brushing behind back, c1940s	**30.00**
Plastic, ivory, P F Sneakers, premium, animal tooth shape, logo and antelope head dec, built–in siren whistle, sun dial, and alphabet code, 1960s	**25.00**

KITCHEN COLLECTIBLES

Collectors are in love with the kitchen of the 1920s and 30s. A few progressive collectors are focusing on the kitchens of the 50s and 60s. Color and style are the two collecting keys. Bright blue, green, and red enamel handled utensils are in demand, not for use but to display on walls. Everything, from flatware to appliances, in Streamline Modern and Post–War Modern design styles is hot. Do not overlook wall clocks and wall decorations. There are even individuals collecting Tupperware.

References: Linda Campbell Franklin, *300 Years of Housekeeping Collectibles*, Books Americana, Krause Publications, 1992; Linda Campbell Franklin, *300 Years of Kitchen Collectibles, Fourth Edition*, Krause Publications, 1997; Michael J. Goldberg, *Groovy Kitchen Designs for Collectors: 1935–1965*, Schiffer Publishing, 1996; Jan Lindenberger, *Black Memorabilia for the Kitchen: A Handbook and Price Guide*, Schiffer Publishing, 1992; Jan Lindenberger, *The 50s and 60s Kitchen: A Collector's Handbook & Price Guide*, Schiffer Publishing, 1994; Barbara Mauzy, *Bakelite in the Kitchen*, Schiffer Publishing, 1998; Barbara Mauzy, *The Complete Book of Kitchen Collecting*, Schiffer Publishing, 1997.

Dana Gehman Morykan and Harry L. Rinker, *Warman's Country Antiques & Collectibles, Third Edition*, Wallace–Homestead, Krause Publications, 1996; Ellen M. Plante, *Kitchen Collectibles: An Illustrated Price Guide*, Wallace–Homestead, Krause Publications, 1991; Diane W. Stoneback, *Kitchen Collectibles: The Essential Buyer's Guide*, Wallace–Homestead, Krause Publications, 1994; Don Thornton, *Apple Parers*, Off Beat Books, 1997; April M. Tvorak, *A History and Price Guide to Mothers-in-the-Kitchen*, published by author, 1994.

Newsletters: *Cast-Iron Cookware News*, 28 Angela Ave, San Anselmo, CA 94960; *Cookies*, 9610 Greenview Ln, Manassas, VA 20109; *Kettles 'n' Cookware*, Drawer B, Perrysburg, NY 14129; *Piebirds Unlimited*, 14 Harmony School Rd, Flemington, NJ 08822.

Collectors' Clubs: Cookie Cutter Collectors Club, 1167 Teal Rd SW, Dellroy, OH 44620; International Society for Apple Parer Enthusiasts, 17 E High, Mount Vernon, OH 43050; Jelly Jammers, 110 White Oak Dr, Butler, PA 16001; Kollectors of Old Kitchen Stuff, 501 Market St, Mifflinburg, PA 17844; Pie Bird Collectors Club, 158 Bagsby Hill Ln, Dover, TN 37058.

Note: See Advertising, Appliances, Cookbooks, Cookie Jars, Egg Beaters, Fire-King, Food Molds, Fruit Jars, Graniteware, Griswold, Kitchen Glassware, Pyrex, Reamers, Wagner Ware, Yellow Ware, and individual glass and pottery categories for additional listings.

Batter Jug, cov, ring, dark blue, Bauer. **$95.00**
Blender, Waring, enameled body, Bakelite lid, 1950s **15.00**
Bread Box, rect, graniteware, green and white, hinged
   lid, 19" l **95.00**
Booklet, Arm & Hammer Baking Soda, Successful
   Baking For Flavor & Texture, 1938, 38 pp **8.00**
Booklet, Kerr Glass, Home Canning Book, National
   Nutrition Edition, 1954, 56 pp **9.00**
Box, Aunt Sally Quick Cooking Oats, 1940s **55.00**
Box, Castile Soap, Oletyme Products, Indianapolis, IN,
   castle illus, 3 bars **7.00**
Broiler, chrome, dome shape, Manning Bowman, 1940s **25.00**
Bread Board, maple, round, matching knife **45.00**
Broom Holder, tin, DeLaval adv **42.00**
Calendar, Doe Wah Jack, Round Oak Stove, 1922, 10¹⁄₂
   x 20" **175.00**

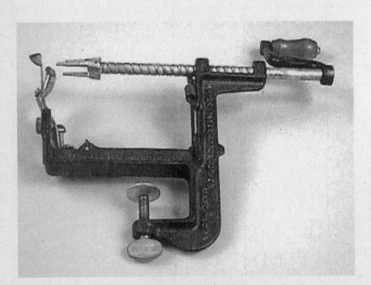

Apple Peeler, White Mountain Freezer, table clamp, mkd "Apple Parer, Corer, Slicer, Made in USA, White Mountain Freezer, Inc.," painted green, red wood knob, 11" l, $35.00.

Candle Holders, Howdy Doody and Friends, figural, set
   of 7, unopened **35.00**
Canister, ivory, earthenware, Brush. **25.00**
Canister Set, plastic, sq, red container, white name and
   lid, price for set of 4 . . . . **15.00**
Catalog, Majestic Electric Refrigerator, color photos,
   1930s, 15 pp. **8.00**
Catalog, National Enameling and Stamping Co, Mil-
   waukee, cooking ware, 1920–30 . . . . **20.00**
Catalog, Springfield Home Appliances, 1953, 96 pp **6.00**
Clock, tin, electric, Dutch children on face **25.00**
Coaster, set of 8, Autumn Leaf accessory **45.00**
Coffee Grinder, Kitchen Aid, Model A–9, Hobart, Troy,
   OH, cream colored cast base, clear glass jar contain-
   er with screw–off top, 1936 . . . . **60.00**
Coffeepot, Flavo Matic, West Bend, gold colored alum-
   minum, silo shape, 1950s **30.00**
Cookbook, *Alaga Syrup*, 1920s, 15 pp **5.00**
Cookbook, *My Better Homes and Gardens Cook
   Book*,1930 . . . . **35.00**
Cookbook, *Pennsylvania Dutch Cook Book of Fine Old
   Recipes*, 1936 . . . . **5.00**
Cookie Cutter, tin, heart, crimped diamond **30.00**
Cookie Cutter, tin, peacock **60.00**
Cookie Jar, Mandy, ceramic, ©Omnibus Japan, 1980 . . . . . . **175.00**
Corn Cob Holders, plastic ears of corn shaped handles,
   metal fork–type holder, price for pr **1.00**
Deep Fryer, Fri–Well, Dormeyer, 1952 . . . . **30.00**
Donut Master, recipes, orig box, 1940s **20.00**
Egg Cooker, Sunbeam, 4 pcs, cast aluminum and
   chrome, egg trivet, poaching insert, body, and lid with
   plastic measure **30.00**
Flyer, Westinghouse Automatic Range adv, color illus,
   c1920 . . . . **7.00**
Food Cooker, Eureka Portable Oven, Eureka Vacuum
   Cleaner Co, Detroit, MI, Art Deco, cream painted
   body, black edges, movable sides reveal hotplates on
   chrome surfaces, fitted int wire racks, front controls,
   1930s, 15 x 13 x 19" **80.00**
Food Cooker, Nesco Electric Casserole, National Enamel
   & Stamping Co, Inc, Milwaukee, WI, cream colored
   body, green enamel lid, 3–prong plug, early 1930s,
   9" d **25.00**
Fruit Jar Funnel, graniteware, gray and white, strap handle . . . **22.00**
Fry Pan, Futuramic Automatic Skillet Casserole, Century
   Enterprises, Inc, flying saucer shape, copper clad steel
   body, copper colored aluminum lid **50.00**
Hot Plate, Samson United Corp, white porcelain enam-
   el, 1950s **15.00**
Jello Mold, ftd, emb, Phoenix glass **8.00**
Juicer, Vita–Juicer, Kold King Dist Corp, Los Angeles,
   Hoek Rotor Mfg Co, Reseda, CA, 3 parts: base motor,
   container, and fitted lid, cream painted cast metal,
   lock groove and lock down wire handle, aluminum,
   pusher, 1930s, 10" h **35.00**
Knife Sharpener, Handy Hannah, red and cream body,
   1930s, 4¹⁄₂" d **10.00**
Mayonnaise Ladle, flat bottom, blue. **18.00**
Measuring Spoon, Monibak Ground Coffee adv, tin **12.00**
Mixer, Mary Dunbar Handymix, Chicago Electric Mfg
   Co, 1930s **30.00**
Mug, Dad's Root Beer, glass. **30.00**
Napkin Ring, Bakelite, round carved rings, orig box,
   price for set of 6 . . . . **85.00**

Sifter, painted, decal dec, 5⅝" h, 4⅜" d, $5.00.

KITCHEN GLASSWARE

Depression Glass is a generic term for glass produced in the United States from the early 1920s through the 1960s. Depression Glass patterns make up only a fraction of the thousands of glass patterns and types produced during this period.

Kitchen Glassware is a catchall category for inexpensive kitchen and table glass produced during this period. Hundreds of companies made it. Hocking, Hazel Atlas, McKee, U.S. Glass, and Westmoreland are a few examples.

Kitchen glassware was used on the table and for storage. It usually has a thick body, designed to withstand heavy and daily use. The category is dominated by storage glass and utilitarian items prior to 1940. Following World War II, tabletop glass prevailed. Kitchen glassware was a favored giveaway premium in the 1950s and early 1960s.

References: Gene Florence, *Kitchen Glassware of the Depression Years*, *Fifth Edition*, Collector Books, 1995, 1997 value update.

Newsletter: *Knife Rests of Yesterday & Today*, 4046 Graham St, Pleasanton, CA 94566.

Note: For additional listings see Depression Glass, Fire–King, Pyrex, Reamers, and individual glass company categories.

Pastry Blender, wire and metal, wood handle, 1924	5.00
Popcorn Popper, Rapaport Bros, Inc, Chicago, IL, aluminum, red knob, chrome handles, sq black base, metal legs, 1920s, 5½" h	25.00
Potato Ricer, steel, red trim 1940s	20.00
Pudding Mold, tin	20.00
Reamer, duck, 2 pc, multicolored, Japan, 2¾"	30.00
Recipe Box, metal, blue, includes recipes	10.00
Roaster, Sunbeam, chrome lid, Bakelite handles, 1952	40.00
Roaster, Heet–Wel, Welco, Inc, 1950s	40.00
Rolling Pin, yellow ware	200.00
Salt and Pepper Shakers, pr, Campbell Kids, F & F Mold and Die Works adv	35.00
Sandwich Grill, Samson United Co, wood handles	40.00
Sign, Pillsbury Cake Mixes, Art Linkletter illus, full color, 1950s, 11½ x 22"	20.00
Skillet, Wagner, #5	20.00
Spoon, Tums adv, "Tums for the Tummy," long handle	15.00
Spoon Rest, yellow ware, "Berea, Kentucky"	45.00
Strawberry Jar, Bird of Paradise, #4, brown and beige, McCoy, 1950	32.00
String Holder, chalkware, cat	25.00
Tea Kettle, chrome, Sunbeam	50.00
Tin, Gustav A Mayer Champagne Wafers, c1935	10.00
Tin, Up to Date Pure Candy, 5 lb, 1920–50	15.00
Tin, Unicy Marshmallows, Brandle & Smith, Philadelphia, 1920–30	15.00
Toaster, Fostoria, McGraw Electric Co, 1950s	40.00
Toothpick Holder, donkey pulling cart, china, Occupied Japan	8.00
Waffle Iron, Manning Bowman & Co, chrome, white Bakelite handles, 1924	50.00
Waffle Iron, Fostoria, McGraw Electric Co, 1941	35.00
Waffle Iron/Hot Cake Griddle, Majestic Electric Appliance Corp, San Francisco, CA, 8" round reversible plates, top pierced tower with Bakelite cap serves as foot for use as double grill, nickel body, brown Bakelite front swing handle, 1920s	45.00
Water Pot, Hurri–Hot Electri–Cup, Dormeyer, electric, chrome body, automatic, 1950s	10.00
Whipper, Dorby, Model E, black Bakelite handle, chrome motor, measured Vidrio glass, 1940s	25.00

Batter Bowl, yellow transparent, slick handled, US Glass	**$30.00**
Batter Jug, pink, Cambridge	75.00
Butter, cov, Criss Cross, crystal, Hazel Atlas, 2 lb	15.00
Canister, crystal, Dutch decal, Hocking	15.00
Canister, green transparent, smooth, metal lid, Hocking	35.00
Canister, sq, Jeannette, 48 oz, 5½" h	30.00
Casserole, green transparent, Pyrex	12.00
Casserole, pink floral dec, Fire–King, 1 qt	10.00
Cheese Dish, green, Kraft	22.00
Coffee Canister, green transparent, emb, Jeannette	110.00
Creamer, Criss Cross, clear, Hazel Atlas	16.50
Cruet, clambroth, frosted, chicken decal	12.00
Cruet, pink, Hazel Atlas	35.00
Cup, green transparent, ribbed, Hocking	7.00
Custard, cov, McKee, 24 oz	22.50
Drawer Knob, crystal, ribbed	9.00
Drawer Knob, peacock blue	15.00

Measuring Cup, fired–on red, Hazel Atlas, 2 cup, $40.00.

Egg Separator, clambroth 55.00
Flour Canister, crystal 40.00
Flour Shaker, Skating Dutch, Hazel Atlas 12.50
Food Mixer, Criss Cross, baby face on side 40.00
Grease Jar, yellow, Hocking 30.00
Ice Bucket, Hex Optic, green, reamer top, Jeannette 40.00
Ice Bucket, pink, sterling bear dec 35.00
Ice Bucket, yellow, Fenton 125.00
Ice Tea Tumbler, Louie, Federal 5.00
Knife, Air–Flo, green 75.00
Knife, Candlewick, 8¹/₂" l 75.00
Knife, crystal, Pinwheel 15.00
Knife, Three Leaf, crystal 15.00
Knife, Three Star, crystal, orig box 25.00
Mayonnaise Ladle, crystal, ribbed handle 7.00
Measuring Cup, 3 spout, green, Hazel Atlas 30.00
Measuring Cup, blue, Fire–King, 2 spout, 16 oz 22.50
Measuring Cup, caramel, 2 spout 85.00
Measuring Cup, green, Hocking, 2 cup 15.00
Measuring Cup, jadeite, Jeannette, ¹/₃ cup 12.00
Measuring Cup, jadeite, Jeannette, 1 cup 25.00
Measuring Cup, jadeite, Jeannette, 2¹/₂ cups 20.00
Measuring Cups, set of 4, Jeannette 125.00
Measuring Pitcher, pink, slick handle, US Glass 40.00
Meat Platter, Glasbake 10.00
Milk Pitcher, Chevron, cobalt 20.00
Milk Pitcher, pink, Hazel Atlas 25.00
Mixing Bowl, cobalt blue, Hazel Atlas, 7³/₄" 40.00
Mixing Bowl, cobalt blue, Hazel Atlas, 9⁵/₈" 55.00
Mixing Bowl, Restwell, cobalt, Hazel Atlas, 6¹/₂" 30.00
Mixing Bowl, Restwell, green, Hazel Atlas, 5³/₄" 20.00
Mixing Bowl, set of 4, Federal 38.00
Mustard Jar, white, hp dec 25.00
Napkin Holder, green clambroth, Serv–All 150.00
Napkin Holder, white, Paden City, Party Line 45.00
Oil and Vinegar, green transparent, Cambridge 75.00
Oil and Vinegar, pink, Heisey 35.00
Pepper Shaker, custard, McKee 12.50
Pepper Shaker, jadeite, Hocking 20.00
Pie Plate, sapphire blue, Fire–King, 9" d 8.00
Pretzel Jar, pink, Hocking 65.00
Punch Ladle, crystal 28.00
Reamer, Criss Cross, crystal, Hazel Atlas 10.00
Reamer, green transparent, ribbed, Hocking 15.00

Refrigerator Dish, cov, amber, rect, Federal, 4 x 8" 12.50
Refrigerator Dish, cov, blue, McKee 28.00
Refrigerator Dish, cov, green, floral lid, Jeannette 20.00
Refrigerator Dish, cov, jade, McKee 12.00
Refrigerator Dish, cov, yellow transparent, Hazel Atlas 30.00
Refrigerator Jar, cov, green transparent, oval, Hocking, 7" . . . 25.00
Rolling Pin, brown, light amber 145.00
Rolling Pin, clambroth white, screw–on wood handles 100.00
Rolling Pin, peacock blue, wooden handle 250.00
Salad Set, fork and spoon, blue and crystal 25.00
Salad Set, fork and spoon, crystal, Art Deco handle 25.00
Salt and Pepper Shakers, pr, blue, Jeannette 70.00
Salt and Pepper Shakers, pr, Dots, McKee 30.00
Salt Box, crystal, round, diamond, short, Hocking 25.00
Salt Box, jadeite, McKee 75.00
Scoop, blue 45.00
Shaker, emb "Salt," green, Hazel Atlas 38.00
Shaker, emb "Sugar," green, Hazel Atlas 85.00
Spoon, peacock blue 22.50
Stack Set, 3 part, green, Hazel Atlas 70.00
Straw Holder, cobalt blue 250.00
Sugar Shaker, green, Lancaster Glass 150.00
Sugar Shaker, pink, Heisey 75.00
Sugar Shaker, light jade, Jeannette 55.00
Sundae Dish, green transparent, Paden City 18.00
Syrup Jug, amber, Cambridge 50.00
Syrup Pitcher, pink, Hazel Atlas 45.00
Tea Canister, blue, Jeannette, 20 oz 125.00
Tea Kettle, clambroth, Glasbake 25.00
Tom & Jerry Mug, custard 12.00
Towel Bar, jadeite, 17" l 25.00
Tumbler, Criss Cross, crystal, Hazel Atlas, 9 oz 25.00
Tumbler, custard, McKee 10.00
Trivet, round, Pyrex, 9" d 12.00
Utility Pan, sapphire blue, Fire–King, 8¹/₈ x 12¹/₂" 20.00
Water Bottle, blue, 64 oz 55.00
Water Bottle, Criss Cross, crystal, Hazel Atlas, small 18.00
Water Bottle, cov, clear, Anchor Hocking 12.00
Water Bottle, green transparent, ribbed, Hocking 25.00
Water Bottle, Royal Ruby, Hocking 75.00

KOREAN WAR

The Korean War began on June 25, 1950, when North Korean troops launched an invasion across the 38th parallel into South Korea. The United Nations ordered an immediate cease–fire and withdrawal of the invading forces. On June 27 President Harry Truman ordered U.S. Forces to South Korea to help repel the North Korean invasion. The United Nations Security Council adopted a resolution for armed intervention.

The first American ground forces arrived in Korea on July 1, 1950. General Douglas MacArthur was named commander of the United Nations forces on July 8, 1950. The landing at Inchon took place on September 15, 1950. U.S. troops reached the Yalu River on the Manchurian border in late November.

On November 29, 1950, Chinese Communist troops counterattacked. Seoul was abandoned on January 4, 1951, only to be recaptured on March 21, 1951. On April 11, 1951, President Truman relieved General MacArthur of his command. General Matthew Ridgway replaced him. By early July a cease–fire had been declared, North Korean troops withdrew above the 38th parallel, and truce talks began. A stalemate was reached.

Refrigerator Dish, cov, pink, Federal, 8" sq, $35.00.

On November 29, 1952, President–elect Dwight Eisenhower flew to Korea to inspect the United Nations forces. An armistice was signed at Panmunjom by the United Nations, North Korea, and Chinese delegates on July 27, 1953.

References: Richard J. Austin, *The Official Price Guide to Military Collectibles, Sixth Edition,* House of Collectibles, 1998; Ron Manion, *American Military Collectibles Price Guide,* Antique Trader Books, 1995.

Periodical: *Military Trader,* PO Box 1050, Dubuque, IA 52004.

Ammunition Belt, canvas, olive drab web, 6 pocket,
  metal fittings, mkd "US" and dated 1952 . . . . **$25.00**
Badge, North Korea, Victory Over Japan, silvered round
  badge with victory design hanging from blue, white,
  and red ribbon **55.00**
Badge, South Korea, Air Gunner, silver, stylized wings
  flanking target, jet in center **20.00**
Flight Trousers, nylon, dark blue, detachable suspenders,
  knit cuffs, size 32 . . . . **45.00**
Helmet, Navy, aviator's, gold finish, ridged top pattern,
  pilot wing decal on front, boom mike on right,
  padded leather and web restraints int **85.00**
Lead Soldiers, set of 18, models of American Army of
  Korean War, 1" h **15.00**
Lighter, souvenir, brushed silver finish, engraved and
  painted designs **20.00**
Parka and Liner, olive drab, built–in hood, zipper and
  snap closure front, button–in liner, 1951 dated
  Quartermaster markings **20.00**
Patch, Army, 1st Corps, bullion design, black felt base,
  2³/₈" d **20.00**
Patch, Army, 40th Division, bullion sunburst design,
  square blue felt base **25.00**
Patch, souvenir, "Returned from Hell," shield shape,
  embroidered designs, black wool base, Korean made **25.00**
Plaque, USAF, 5th Air Force, oak, hp center emblem,
  "5th Air Force" above "Korea" **50.00**
Scarf, souvenir, silk, green, embroidered multicolored
  dragon pattern and "Seoul Korea/1952" **10.00**
Wrist Compass, brass case, plastic lens, floating pointer,
  leather strap **40.00**

K. T. & K. CALIFORNIA

Homer J. Taylor established K. T. & K. California pottery in Burbank, California, in 1937. The son of one of the original founders of the Knowles, Taylor & Knowles pottery in East Liverpool, Ohio, he served as president of that company after his father's death in 1914. Following Knowles, Taylor & Knowles' closing, Homer moved to Burbank and started his own company.

K. T. K. California produced decorative accessories such as figural planters, vases, and wall pockets. "K. T. K. Calif" was incised on all items. "Hand Made" was sometimes included in the mark.

Reference: Mary Frank Gaston, *Collector's Encyclopedia of Knowles, Taylor & Knowles China: Identification & Values,* Collector Books, 1996.

Bowl, diamond shape, scalloped border, applied bow
  and ribbon handle **$50.00**
Bowl, pear and leaves dec, sgd "M" on base, 6" d **40.00**

Cornucopia Vase, blue, 7¹/₂" h, $85.00.

Candle Holders, pr, bow dec, mottled chartreuse brown,
  3" h **80.00**
Creamer and Sugar, open, applied floral dec, yellow
  monochrome finish **50.00**
Creamer and Sugar, open, mottled chartreuse brown,
  mkd "KTK Cabaña Calif" **45.00**
Dutch Shoe, 4" l **40.00**
Planter, duck, applied bonnet, initialed "E" **50.00**
Sugar, open, petal and floral dec **25.00**
Vase, cornucopia, abstract design on body and base,
  1937–1948 mark **80.00**
Vase, square, incised abstract leaf design, 5¹/₂" sq **40.00**
Wall Pocket, hat shape, applied bow dec, 9" w **35.00**
Wall Pocket, pr, figural women's faces, fancy headress,
  mottled glaze, 7³/₄" l **125.00**

LADY HEAD VASES

The lady head vase craze began in the early 1940s and extended through the early 1960s. They were just one of hundreds of inexpensive ceramic novelties made by American and foreign manufacturers, primarily Japanese, in the period immediately following World War II.

Although designated lady head vase, the category is broadly interpreted to include all planters and vases in the shape of a human head.

References: Kathleen Cole, *The Encyclopedia of Head Vases,* Schiffer Publishing, 1996; Mike Posgay and Ian Warner, *The World of Head Vase Planters,* Antique Publications, 1992; Mary Zavada, *Lady Head Vases,* Schiffer Publishing, 1988, 1996 value update.

Collectors' Club: Head Vase Society, PO Box 83H, Scarsdale, NY 10583.

Atlas, white hair, straw hat with pink ribbon, pink dress
  with white and gold trim, pearl earrings and necklace,
  paper label, 6" h **$50.00**
Betty Lou Nichols, nun **95.00**
Brinn's, #2TP–2444, long streaked hair, wearing "Love"
  choker and shirt with stars, 7¹/₂" h **80.00**

Napco, #C7494, black hat, gray bow and dress, pearl earrings and necklace, silver foil label, 6" h, $60.00.

LALIQUE

René Lalique (1860–1945) began his career as a designer and jewelry maker. His perfume flacons attracted the attention of M. Francois Coty. Coty contracted with Lalique to design and manufacture perfume bottles for the company. Initially, the bottles were made at Legras & Cie de St. Dennis. In 1909 Lalique opened a glassworks at Combs–la–Ville. Lalique acquired a larger glassworks at Wingen–sur–Moder in Alsace–Lorraine in 1921 and founded Verrerie d'Alsace René Lalique et Cie.

Although René was not involved in the actual production, he designed the majority of the articles manufactured by the firm. Lalique glass is lead glass that is either blown in the mold or pressed. There are also combinations of cutting and casting and some molded designs were treated with acids to produce a frosted, satiny effect. Lalique blown wares were almost all confined to stemware and large bottles. Glass made before 1945 has been found in more than ten colors, including mauve and purple.

Early pieces were of naturalistic design—molded animals, foliage, flowers, or nudes. Later designs became stylized and reflected the angular, geometric characteristics of Art Deco.

Each piece of Lalique glass is marked on the bottom or near the base. It is often marked in several places, in block letters and in script. Marks include: R. LALIQUE FRANCE (engraved and sandblasted block and script); LALIQUE FRANCE (diamond point tool, engraved, sandblasted block and script); and LALIQUE (engraved). The "R" was deleted from the mark following René's death in 1945. Collectors prefer pre–1945 material.

Lalique closed its Combs–la–Ville factory in 1937. The factory at Wingen–sur–Moder was partially destroyed during World War II. Lalique made no glass between 1939 and 1946. Production resumed after the war. In 1965 Lalique made its first limited edition Christmas plate, ending the series in 1976. Marc Lalique and his daughter, Marie–Claude Lalique, have contributed a number of new designs. The company still produces pieces from old molds.

Reference: Robert Prescott–Walker, *Collecting Lalique Glass*, Francis Joseph Publications, 1996, distributed by Krause Publications.

Collectors' Club: Lalique Collectors Society, 400 Veterans Blvd, Carlstadt, NJ 07072.

REPRODUCTION ALERT: Beware of the Lalique engraved signature and etched mark applied to blanks made in Czechoslovakia, France, and the United States.

Enesco, religious, paper label, 5¾" h	25.00
Florence Ceramics, young lady, brown curls, wearing bonnet and caped coat, 7" h	60.00
Hull, #204, wearing babushka, 6" h	100.00
Inarco, #1064, wide brimmed hat, 4½" h	65.00
Inarco, #E1062, black gloved hand holding closed fan, pearl earrings, 1963, 6" h	55.00
Inarco, #E1756, Lady Aileen, 1964, 5½" h	60.00
Inarco, #E6730, clown, 5½" h	50.00
Japan, girl with brown braided pigtails, holding parasol, 5" h	60.00
Lee Wards, flowered hat, white hair with gold highlights, turquoise dress, paper label, 6½" h	40.00
Lee Wards, Geisha, paper label, 5" h	40.00
Lefton, #2900, wide brimmed hat, eyes closed, hands at cheek, paper label, 6" h	75.00
Margo, blue and white plaid dress, 6" h	45.00
Marti of Hollywood, Art Deco woman, blonde hair, green hair ribbon, flowers on shoulder, 9½" h	395.00
Napco, #C4414A, 6" h	75.00
Napco, #C4818, 1960, 6¾" h	85.00
Napco, #C6439, pearl earrings, green globed hand, flowered neckline, 7½" h	55.00
Napco, #C8494, young woman, long blonde hair, green hair ribbon, green dress with white collar, pearl earrings, paper label, 7" h	145.00
Relpo, #2012, orange and white cap and dress, 6" h	75.00
Relpo, #A916, Santa, orig flowers, 5" h	18.00
Relpo, #K1612, green hair bow, pearl earrings and necklace, green dress with white ruffled collar, 7½" h	145.00
Relpo, #K1335, powdered wig, 8" h	100.00
Relpo, #K1817, 5½" h	65.00
Reubens, #4137, blonde hair in pigtails, 7" h	90.00
Samson Import, #5359, baby with blanket over head, 1966, 7½" h	35.00
Shawnee, #896, Polynesian, 5½" h	85.00
Sonsco, teenager, black hair bow, turquoise and black dress, 4" h	25.00
Unmarked, girl holding poodle, 6" h	75.00
Unmarked, Uncle Sam, green glaze, 6½" h	100.00
UOAGCO China, infant, wearing pink, 5" h	40.00

Ashtray, Chien, opalescent green, dog pattern, c1926	**$690.00**
Ashtray, Vezelay, amber glass, Art Deco style, c1924	**460.00**
Atomizer, Perles, clear and frosted, gilt metal top, c1926	**460.00**
Bowl, Champs Elysees, clear and frosted, leaf pattern, designed by Marc Lalique, 1956	**1,035.00**
Bowl, Oursin and Veronique, opalescent, c1928, price for 2	**460.00**
Bowl, Pinsons, clear and frosted, bird pattern, designed by René Lalique, 1937, 9½" d	**460.00**
Bowl, Yeso, opalescent green, applied fish dec, designed by Marie–Claude Lalique, 1976	**747.00**
Box, cov, Rambouillet, clear and frosted, 2 exotic birds pattern, c1924	**400.00**
Brooch, Cabochon Lilas, opalescent, modern metal back, c1920	**230.00**

Vase, Jaffa, Art Deco design, 3 tiers of stylized foliage, c1937, 12½", $3,220.00. Photo courtesy William Doyle Galleries.

Center Bowl, Bamako, clear and green glass, applied salamanders on rim, designed by Marie–Claude Lalique, 8¾" d.................................. **800.00**

Center Bowl, Deux Moineaux Monquers, clear and frosted, applied sparrows dec, designed by René Lalique, 1930, 16" d......................... **1,092.00**

Champagne Glasses, Champagne Ange, clear and frosted, Angel of Rheims pattern, designed by Marc Lalique, 1948, price for 7 .... **920.00**

Clock, Quatre Perruches, clear and frosted, parakeets pattern, 1920 .... **1,840.00**

Cocktail Shaker, Thomery, clear and frosted, c1928 ...... **1,840.00**

Compact, aluminum, sepia patina, for Roger et Gallet, 1922... **258.00**

Dressing Mirror, Bouton De Roses, oval, clear and frosted, rosebuds pattern, chromium plated easel mount, 9½" h **800.00**

Figure, Cygne Tete Baisee, swan, swimming with head down, clear and frosted, orig flower holder, designed by Marc Lalique, c1944, 14" l................... **2,300.00**

Figure, Motif Ara, cockatoo, clear and frosted, designed by Marc Lalique, c1953, 11" h................... **920.00**

Figure, Pigeon Bruges, clear glass, designed by René Lalique, 1932, 11½" l........................... **345.00**

Ice Bucket, cov, Antilles, clear and frosted, silvered metal rim, designed by Marc Lalique, c1965, 10¼" h ... **800.00**

Jardiniere, St Hubert, clear and frosted, Art Deco gazelles and foliage handles, c1927 .... **460.00**

Paperweight, Chrysis and Tet D' Aigle, clear and frosted, price for set of 2 .... **745.00**

Pendant, Panier De Fruits, clear and frosted, basket of fruit pattern, c1922 .... **300.00**

Perfume Bottle, Chypre, clear and frosted, Art Deco style, made for D'Orsay, c1927 .... **800.00**

Perfume Bottle, Imprudence, clear, Art Deco style, made for Worth, orig display packaging, c1938 .... **690.00**

Perfume Bottle, Sans Adieu, green glass, Art Deco style, ebonized wood and silvered metal stand, made for Worth, c1929 .... **630.00**

Pitcher and Tumblers Set, Chene, clear and frosted, oak leaves pattern, 2 matching tumblers, designed by Marc Lalique, c1950............................. **1,265.00**

Plate, Martigues, opalescent, fish dec, c1920............ **3,450.00**

Plate, Rosace, opalescent, Art Deco style, c1930 .... **747.00**

Table Ornament, Groupe Luzembourg, clear and frosted, 3 cherubs, designed by Rene' Lalique, c1936 .... **747.00**

Vase, Bagatelle, clear and frosted, birds pattern, designed by Rene' Lalique, 1939, 6¾" h.............. **402.00**

Vase, Corinthe, clear and frosted, Art Deco style, c1933.... **460.00**

Vase, Mesanges, clear and frosted, bird pattern, designed by Rene' Lalique, c1931, 12½" h **1,092.00**

Vase, Saint Marc, opalescent, fantail pigeons pattern, c1939 .... **1,725.00**

Vase, Soudan, opalescent, Art Deco style, c1928 .... **345.00**

LAMPS

Kerosene lamps dominated the 19th century and first quarter of the 20th century. Thomas Edison's invention of the electric light bulb in 1879 marked the beginning of the end of the kerosene lamp era.

The 1930s was the Age of Electricity. By the end of the decade electricity was available throughout America. Manufacturers and designers responded quickly to changing styles and tastes. The arrival of the end table and television as major pieces of living room furniture presented a myriad of new design opportunities.

Most lamps are purchased for reuse, not collecting purposes. Lamps whose design speaks to a specific time period or that blend with modern decor have decorative rather than collecting value. Decorative value is significantly higher than collecting value.

With the broad lamp category, there are several lamp groups that are collected. Aladdin lamps, due primarily to an extremely strong collectors' club, are in a league of their own. Other collecting subcategories include character lamps, figural lamps, novelty, motion or revolving lamps, student lamps, Tiffany and Tiffany–style lamps, and TV lamps.

References: *Electric Lighting of the 20s–30s, Vol. 1* (1994, 1998 value update), *Vol. 2*, L–W Book Sales, 1994, 1998 value update, L–W Book Sales (ed.), B*etter Electric Lamps of the 20's & 30's*, L–W Book Sales, 1997; L–W Book Sales (ed.), *Quality Electric Lamps: A Pictorial Price Guide*, L–W Book Sales, 1992, 1996 value update; Nadja Maril, *American Lighting: 1840–1940*, Schiffer Publishing, 1995; Leland & Crystal Payton, *Turned On: Decorative Lamps of the 'Fifties*, Abbeville Press, 1989.

Newsletter: *Light Revival*, 35 W Elm Ave, Quincy, MA 02170.

Note: For additional listings see Aladdin, Motion Lamps, and Television Lamps.

Boudoir, ceramic, figural French poodle, pink, circular base, pink paper shade **$25.00**

Ceiling, globe form, transparent white glass, irregular orange band of rolled glass, orig chrome fitting, Venini, c1960, 18" d **150.00**

Character, Popeye, ceramic, spinach can with raised figures, King Features, 1975......................... **155.00**

Desk, Angle Poise, black enamel, adjustable, sq weighted base, flaring shade, c1950, George Cardwardine **400.00**

Desk, brass arm, copper base, green glazed ceramic shade, imp and printed marks, Wedgwood, c1933, 15" h **275.00**

Figural, fish, jumping over waves, ceramic, carousel beaded shade **195.00**

Left: Table Lamp, plastic, red dome shade, white translucent column on blue cube base, 25" h, $35.00.
Right: Hanging Lamp, ovoid shaped glass shade with thin vertical stripes, Venini, c1960, 14¹/₂" h, $220.00. Photo courtesy David Rago Auctions.

Figural, jai alai basket, chrome and plastic, bright
   orange, Lamperti, 13" h 150.00
Figural, light bulb, oversized bulb with metal cage,
   c1960. . . . . 145.00
Figural, Statue of Liberty, plastic, Econolite, 1957, 11" h 75.00
Floor, brushed chrome base and stand, mushroom
   shaped frosted glass shade, Lanel, 57" h 600.00
Floor, chrome, 4–sided shaft, no shade, Donald Deskey,
   c1935. . . . . 350.00
Floor, chrome, arched, black rect base, spherical shade,
   60 x 48" 225.00
Floor, chrome, vertical pole off–centered on circular
   base, Art Deco style, orig drum shade, Rembrandt
   Lamp Co, c1935, 56" h 250.00
Floor, enameled metal, 4 rotating spherical metal
   shades, Vico Magistretti, 90" h 500.00
Floor, interlocking chrome squares and rectangles on
   painted wood base, c1970, 62¹/₂" h 50.00
Floor, yellow and white enameled steel barbell shape,
   pivots on circular Lucite base, 56" h. 275.00
Hanging, ovoid, thin vertical stripes, Venini, c1960. . . . . . . 200.00
Hanging, red, blue and clear acanne glass, matte finish,
   Fratelli Toso, 14 x 6" 250.00
Hanging, yellow, white, brown, and aqua stripes, Venini,
   12 x 10" 200.00
Lava, bottle shaped, Lava Simplex Corp, c1968 . . . . 75.00
Table, ceramic bulbous vessel base, stylized native war-
   riors in turquoise against white crackle ground,
   Gambone/Italy trademark, 18¹/₂" h 900.00
Table, ceramic base with oval indentations and 2 men
   in bright harlequin costumes, spotty yellow, Marcello
   Fantoni, 15" h 750.00
Table, cordinato oro glass, red, Barovier & Toso, unmkd,
   13" h 100.00

Table, red metal conical shaped shade, tubular brass
   base, c1958, 14¹/₂ x 8 x 16". 175.00
Table, Tiffany style, gilded white metal frame, emb flow-
   ers and leaves, tapered cylindrical base and domed
   shade with caramel slag glass panels, circular base,
   double socket lamp with night light in base 325.00
Table, white and clear sommerso glass, controlled bub-
   bles, Seguso, 10" h 250.00
Wall, metal, eggshell colored semi–spherical shade,
   walnut wall mount, adjustable, Greta Von Nessen,
   c1950, 18 x 15" 255.00

LEFTON CHINA

George Zoltan Lefton was the driving force behind Lefton China, a china importing and marketing organization. Following World War II, Lefton, a Hungarian immigrant, began importing giftware made in the Orient into the United States.

Until the mid–1970s Japanese factories made the vast majority of Lefton China. After that date, China, Malaysia, and Taiwan became the principal supply sources.

Most Lefton pieces are identified by a fired–on trademark or a paper label. Numbers found on pieces are item identification numbers. When letters precede a number, it is a factory code, e.g., "SL" denotes Nippon Art China K.K.

References: Loretta DeLozier, *Collector's Encyclopedia of Lefton China* (1995) and *Book II* (1997), Collector Books; Ruth McCarthy, *Lefton China*, Schiffer Publishing, 1998.

Collectors' Club: National Society of Lefton Collectors, 1101 Polk St, Bedford, IA 50833.

Ashtray, Forget–me–Not floral dec, #4080 . . . . **$25.00**
Ashtray, swan, dark green, gold rose dec, #954 . . . . **35.00**
Bookends, pr, poodle **55.00**
Bowl and Cup, child's, cat, #3553 . . . . **45.00**
Butter, cov, Bossie the Cow, #6514 . . . . **22.00**
Cake Plate, "25th Anniversary," #1130. . . . . **12.00**
Compote, wheat design, #112, latticed edge and base **30.00**
Condiment Relish, onion head. **46.00**
Cookie Jar, bluebird. **325.00**
Cookie Jar, girl's head, #1692 . . . . **150.00**
Creamer and Sugar, Dutch, #2698. **75.00**
Creamer and Sugar, girl's head **60.00**
Creamer and Sugar, grape **65.00**
Creamer and Sugar, rose chintz, #794 . . . . **25.00**
Cup and Saucer, "Happy Anniversary," #2425, chintz,
   gold trim. **15.00**
Cup and Saucer, floral pattern, #912 . . . . **45.00**
Figurine, baby with squirrel, #3056 . . . . **18.00**
Figurine, Christmas Girl, #6604. . . . . **8.00**
Figurine, snow babies, #4405, 3" h, price for 3 . . . . **40.00**
Figurine, Suzette, #5744 . . . . **135.00**
Matchbox Holder, daisy, #5402 . . . . **20.00**
Mug, Teddy Roosevelt, #2191 . . . . **35.00**
Nite Lite, little girl praying, #6626 . . . . **30.00**
Pitcher, violet design, gold trim **25.00**
Planter, cat, polka dot tie, #5741 . . . . **15.00**
Planter, girl, holding bonnet, #6094. . . . . **18.00**
Planter, fish, #709 . . . . **22.00**
Planter, rose dec, gold trim, #414 . . . . **45.00**
Plate, Eastern Star, #105 . . . . **12.00**

Planter, Blue Bird, #4867, foil label, 7¹/₄" h, 9" l, $20.00. Photo courtesy Morykan Auctioneers.

Plate, rose motif, plastic handle, #939 . . . . 40.00
Salt and Pepper Shakers, pr, Dutch Boy and Girl, #3207 . . . . . 15.00
Salt and Pepper Shakers, pr, pink poodles, #104 . . . . 32.00
Teapot, girl's head 115.00
Teapot, grape, #2663 . . . . 95.00
Teapot, stacking, 3 pc, #985 . . . . 120.00
Tidbit Tray, Golden Wheat, #20231 . . . . 20.00
Vase, cornucopia, lilacs and stones, #158 . . . . 60.00
Vase, fruit, #7363, 7¹/₂" h 45.00
Vase, pitcher shape, white bisque, applied flowers,
 #1772 . . . . 50.00
Wall Plaque, mermaid playing harp, 8¹/₂" 75.00

LENOX

In 1889, Walter Scott Lenox and Jonathan Coxon, Sr., founded the Ceramic Art Company in Trenton, New Jersey. Lenox acquired sole ownership in 1894. In 1906 he formed Lenox, Inc.

Lenox gained national recognition in 1917 when President Woodrow Wilson ordered a 1,700 piece dinner service. Later, Presidents Franklin D. Roosevelt and Harry S. Truman followed Wilson's lead. First Lady Nancy Reagan ordered a 4,732–piece set of gold embossed bone china from Lenox in 1901. According to Eric Poehner, the Lenox craftsman who did much of the work, each raised golden seal in the center of the Reagan service plates took two–and–one–half to three hours to hand paint.

During the last two decades, Lenox, Inc., has expanded, acquiring Art Carved, Inc., H. Rosenthal Jewelry Corporation, Imperial Glass Corporation, and many other companies. Operating today as Lenox Brands, the company is a multimillion–dollar enterprise producing a broad range of tabletop and giftware.

References: Susan and Al Bagdade, *Warman's American Pottery and Porcelain,* Wallace–Homestead, Krause Publications, 1994; Collector's Information Bureau, *Collectibles Market Guide & Price Index, 15th Edition,* Collector's Information Bureau, 1997, distributed by Krause Publications; Harry L. Rinker, *Dinnerware of the*

20th Century: The Top 500 Patterns, House of Collectibles, 1997; Harry L. Rinker, *Stemware of the 20th Century: The Top 200 Patterns,* House of Collectibles, 1997.

Note: For additional listings see Limited Edition Collectibles.

Amethyst, bread and butter plate, 6¹/₂" d **$8.00**
Amethyst, cup and saucer, ftd, 3¹/₈" **8.00**
Amethyst, dinner plate, 10³/₄" d **15.00**
Amethyst, salad plate, 8¹/₄" d **12.00**
Amethyst, vegetable, oval, 9¹/₂" **15.00**
The Autumn, luncheon plate **40.00**
The Autumn, place setting **175.00**
Ballad, cup **6.00**
Ballad, dinner plate **12.00**
Ballad, sugar, no lid **18.00**
Blue Breeze, butter cov, ¹/₄ lb **20.00**
Blue Breeze, dinner plate **15.00**
Blue Breeze, pepper shaker **10.00**
Blue Breeze, saucer **6.00**
Blue Ridge, cream soup and saucer **65.00**
Blue Ridge, place setting **125.00**
Blue Ridge, soup bowl **45.00**
Castle Garden, place setting **175.00**
Dewdrops, cup and saucer **12.00**
Dewdrops, dinner plate **15.00**
Dewdrops, salad plate **12.00**
Dewdrops, salt shaker and pepper mill **20.00**
Essex Maroon Smith, place setting **180.00**
Fair Lady, bread and butter plate, 6³/₈" d **6.00**
Fair Lady, cup and saucer, ftd, 3" h **15.00**
Fair Lady, dinner plate **15.00**
Fair Lady, salad plate, 8¹/₈" d **12.00**
Fire Flower, baker, rect, 15³/₈" d **35.00**
Fire Flower, cup and saucer **12.00**
Fire Flower, dinner plate **15.00**
Fire Flower, pepper mill **5.00**
Hancock, bread and butter plate, 6¹/₂" d **6.00**
Hancock, cup, ftd, 2³/₄" h **6.00**
Hancock, dinner plate, 10¹/₂" d **12.00**
Hancock, salad plate, 8¹/₂" d **10.00**
Hancock, vegetable, oval, 9³/₄" d **40.00**
Harvest, place setting **125.00**
Harvest, soup bowl **45.00**
Holiday, ashtray **15.00**
Holiday, cup and saucer, ftd **15.00**
Holiday, fruit bowl, 5¹/₄" **15.00**
Holiday, relish tray, pierced **20.00**
Holiday, salad bowl, 9¹/₂" d **12.00**
Kingsley, fruit bowl **45.00**
Kingsley, place setting **160.00**
Kingsley, soup bowl **65.00**
Ming, fruit bowl **38.00**
Ming, place setting **135.00**
Poppies on Blue, bread and butter plate **6.00**
Poppies on Blue, cup and saucer, flat, 2³/₄" **12.00**
Poppies on Blue, fruit bowl, 5¹/₄" **10.00**
Poppies on Blue, salad plate, 8¹/₂" d **12.00**
Poppies on Blue, spoon holder **8.00**
Princess X576, cup and saucer, demitasse **48.00**
Princess X576, place setting **150.00**
Quakertown, casserole, cov, 6³/₈" d **30.00**
Quakertown, creamer **10.00**
Quakertown, dinner plate **15.00**

Poppies on Blue: cup, $10.00; oval vegetable bowl, $25.00; oval platter, $35.00.

Quakertown, saucer 2.00
Rhodora, fruit bowl 46.00
Rhodora, place setting 175.00
Temple Blossom, bread and butter plate, 6³/₈" d 6.00
Temple Blossom, cup and saucer, ftd, 2¹/₂" 10.00
Temple Blossom, dinner plate, 10⁷/₈" d 15.00
Temple Blossom, salad plate, 8¹/₂" d 12.00
Westfield, place setting 140.00
Windsong, bread and butter plate, 6³/₈" d 6.00
Windsong, demitasse cup and saucer 30.00
Windsong, dinner plate, 10³/₄" d 15.00
Windsong, salad plate, 8¹/₈" d 12.00

L. E. SMITH GLASS

L. E. Smith Glass began when Lewis E. Smith, a gourmet cook, needed glass jars for a mustard he planned to market. Rather than buy jars, he bought a glass factory in Mt. Pleasant, Pennsylvania, and made them himself. Smith remained active in the company from 1908 through 1911. He is credited with inventing the glass top for percolators, the modern–style juice reamer, the glass mixing bowl, and numerous other kitchen implements.

Smith sold his interest in L. E. Smith Glass in 1911. The company continued, making automobile lenses, cookware, fruit jars, kitchenware, novelties, and tableware. Black glass was a popular product in the 1920s and 30s. Giftware and tableware products remain the company's principal focus today.

References: Lee Garmon and Dick Spencer, *Glass Animals Of the Depression Era,* Collector Books, 1993, out of print; Marlena Toohey, *A Collector's Guide to Black Glass,* Antique Publications, 1988.

Ashtray, duck, black, 6¹/₂" l **$12.00**
Aquarium, green, King–Fish, 10" h 250.00
Bean Pot, cov, Greek Key, black, silver dec 65.00
Bean Pot, cov, silver daisy dec, black 65.00
Bonbon, Mt Pleasant, green, 7" 15.00
Bookends, pr, horse head, clear 45.00
Bowl, amethyst, #77 . . . . 10.00
Bowl, delphite, 9¹/₄" d 60.00
Bowl, ftd, Lace Renaissance, scalloped edge, black 45.00
Bowl, Romanesque, 10¹/₂" d 40.00
Bread and Butter Plate, Melba, amethyst, 6" d 5.00

Cake Plate, Mt Pleasant, pink, 10¹/₂" d 20.00
Cake Plate, Romanesque 35.00
Candlesticks, pr, by Cracky, green 15.00
Candlesticks, pr, Mt Pleasant, black 15.00
Candlesticks, pr, Romanesque, pink 10.00
Casserole, cov, Melba, 9¹/₂" l 15.00
Cologne Bottle, Colonial, black 30.00
Console Bowl, 3 ftd, black 30.00
Cookie Jar, black 75.00
Cookie Jar, transparent green 100.00
Cordial Tray, black, #381 . . . . 10.00
Creamer, Homestead, pink 5.00
Creamer, Mt Pleasant, black 15.00
Creamer, Mt Pleasant, pink 20.00
Cup and Saucer, Melba, pink 5.00
Cup and Saucer, Mt Pleasant 24.00
Dinner Plate, Mt Pleasant, scalloped edge, pink, 8" d 6.00
Dresser Set, 7 pcs, crystal, Hobnail, black stoppers, lid,
    and tray 50.00
Fern Bowl, black 25.00
Fern Bowl, 3 ftd, Greek Key, black 20.00
Figure, dog, Scottie, frosted 50.00
Figure, goose, black 20.00
Figure, reclining camel, crystal, 4¹/₂" h 55.00
Figure, rooster, black 15.00
Figure, squirrel, holding nut 30.00
Figure, swan, white opaque, small 15.00
Flower Pot, black, silver floral dec, 4" h 8.00
Fruit Bowl, ftd, 2 handles, black 25.00
Grill Plate, black 8.00
Grill Plate, cobalt 10.00
Grill Plate, pink 10.00
Jardiniere, 3 ftd, black, silver dec 45.00
Lamp, frosted shade with Scottie dec 90.00
Mayonnaise, 3 ftd, Mt Pleasant, black 30.00
Nut Tray, handled, Mt Pleasant, black 20.00
Parfait, Soda Shop 5.00
Plate, 2 handles, Do–Si–Do, black 20.00
Plate, 3 ftd, Mount Pleasant 40.00
Plate, Mt Pleasant, black, 8" d 20.00
Plate, Romanesque, octagonal, 5¹/₂" 5.00
Rose Bowl, Mt Pleasant, rolled edges, cobalt blue 18.00
Salad Bowl, scalloped edges, black 20.00
Salad Tray, Mt Pleasant, 2 handles 50.00
Salt and Pepper Shakers, pr, Snake Dance, 3¹/₂" h 50.00
Sandwich Server, Mt Pleasant, cobalt 40.00

Bowl, cobalt, 8¹/₄" d, $50.00.

Saucer, Mt Pleasant, 6½" d	10.00
Sherbet, Romanesque, plain top	8.00
Soda Glass, crystal, ribbed, jumbo	6.50
Sugar, cov, Do–Si–Do	8.00
Sugar, cov, Homestead	5.50
Tray, Mt Pleasant, black	20.00
Tumbler, ftd, Mt Pleasant, black	22.00
Urn, ftd, 2 handles, emb, black, 8½" h	40.00
Vase, ftd, 2 handles, fancy crimped top, black	70.00
Vase, ftd, 2 handles, flared top, black, 7¼" h	50.00
Vase, Romanesque, fan shape	40.00
Water Dispenser, cobalt	350.00
Water Goblet, Moon 'n Star, amberina	18.00
Window Box, double ridge, dancing ladies, black	30.00
Wine, Moon 'n Star, amberina	15.00

LIBBEY GLASS

The Libbey Glass Company traces its origins to the New England Glass Company, founded in 1818 in Boston. In 1888 New England Glass moved to Toledo, Ohio, to be nearer a better fuel source. The company became the Libbey Glass Company in 1892, named for the family that managed it for several decades.

Financial difficulties arising from the move ended when Libbey began producing light bulbs. The company also manufactured a brilliant cut glass line. By the 1920s, Libbey introduced an art glass line (amberina, pomona, peachblow, etc.) and a hotel and restaurant line. In 1925 Libbey acquired the Nonik Glassware Corp., a major tumbler manufacturer.

In 1933, under the direction of Douglas Nash, Libbey re-emphasized its fine glass lines. It also acquired the H. C. Fry Company. In 1935 Owen–Illinois Glass Company purchased Libbey Glass, then billed as the "world's largest producers of glass containers." Owen–Illinois established a separate division and continues to manufacture products using the Libbey name.

References: Carl U. Fauster (comp.), *Libbey Glass Since 1818: Pictorial History & Collector's Guide*, Len Beach Press, 1979, out of print; Bob Page and Dale Fredericksen, *A Collection of American Crystal: A Stemware Identification Guide for Glasonbury/Lotus, Libbey/Rock Sharpe & Hawkes*, Page–Fredericksen Publishing, 1995; Kenneth Wilson, *American Glass 1760–1930; The Toledo Museum of Art*, 2 vols., Hudson Hills Press and The Toledo Museum of Art, 1994.

Cocktail, Silhouette, clear bowl, black kangaroo silhouette in stem	$125.00
Cordial, 3002 Line, crystal, 4³/₁₆" h	15.00
Cordial, American Prestige	40.00
Cordial, Nob Hill, crystal	8.00
Cordial, Rock Sharpe, 3005 Line, Arctic Rose, crystal, 4¹¹/₁₆" h	20.00
Cordial, Silhouette, Greyhound pattern, black, 4" h	200.00
Drinking Glass, Gulliver's Travels, Libbey Classics	10.00
Drinking Glass, Moby Dick, Libbey Classics	10.00
Drinking Glass, Robin Hood, Libbey Classics	10.00
Drinking Glass, Tom Sawyer, Libbey Classics	10.00
Iced Tea, Galway	18.00
Luncheon Plate, Galway	18.00
Sherbet, Silhouette, clear bowl, black monkey silhouette in stem	90.00
Water Goblet, Galway	18.00

Water Goblet, Rapture	20.00
Wine, Silhouette, clear bowl, black cat silhouette in stem, sgd, 7" h	125.00

LIBERTY BLUE

In 1973 the Grand Union Company, a retail supermarket chain based in New Jersey, commissioned Liberty Blue dinnerware to be offered as a premium in grocery stores throughout the eastern United States. Ironically, though intended to celebrate America's independence, the dinnerware was produced in Staffordshire, England.

Liberty Blue dinnerware, introduced in 1975, portrayed patriotic scenes in blue on a white background. It combined several elements of traditional Staffordshire dinnerware while remaining unique. The Wild Rose border was reproduced from a design dating back to 1784. Original engravings depicted historic buildings and events from the American Revolutionary period.

Liberty Blue is easy to identify. Most pieces contain the words "Liberty Blue" on the underside and all are marked "Made in England." The back of each dish also contains information about the scene illustrated on it.

Reference: Harry L. Rinker, *Dinnerware of the 20th Century: The Top 500 Patterns*, House of Collectibles, 1997.

Berry Bowl	**$5.00**
Bread and Butter Plate	4.00
Butter, cov	50.00
Cereal Bowl	12.00
Coaster	12.00
Coaster, boxed set of 4	60.00
Creamer	20.00
Cup and Saucer	9.00
Dessert Bowl	6.00
Gravy Boat and Liner	50.00
Luncheon Plate	15.00
Mug	14.00
Mugs, boxed set of 4	60.00

Dinner Plate, 10" d, $9.00.

Nappy, 5"	3.75
Pitcher	135.00
Place Marker, boxed set of 4	100.00
Place Setting, 5 pcs.	30.00
Platter, 12"	45.00
Platter, 14"	75.00
Salad Plate	12.00
Salt and Pepper Shakers, pr	35.00
Saucer	2.00
Soup Bowl	30.00
Soup Tureen	250.00
Sugar, cov.	30.00
Teapot, cov.	150.00
Vegetable, cov	150.00
Vegetable, open, oval	35.00
Vegetable, open, round	45.00

LIGHTERS

The cigarette lighter became established during the first quarter of the 20th century. By the 1920s it enjoyed a prominent place in most American homes, even those of non–smokers who kept a lighter handy for guests.

Well–known manufacturers include Bowers, Dunhill, Evans, Marathon, Parker, Ronson, and Zippo. Well over a thousand different manufacturers produced lighters. Although the principal manufacturing centers were Japan and the United States, there was at least one lighter manufacturer in every industrialized country in the 20th century.

Collectors shy away from lighters in less than average condition. It is important that the sparking or lighting mechanism works, whether it be flint, liquid fuel, or gas. Repairing a lighter to working order is accepted among collectors.

References: James Flanagan, *Collector's Guide to Cigarette Lighters,* Collector Books, 1995; David Poore, *Zippo: The Great American Lighter,* Schiffer Publishing, 1997; Stuart Schneider and George Fischler, *Cigarette Lighters,* Schiffer Publishing, 1996; Neil S. Wood, *Collecting Cigarette Lighters* (1994) and *Vol. II* (1995), L–W Book Sales.

Collectors' Clubs: On the Lighter Side, International Lighter Collectors, PO Box 3536, Quitman, TX 75783; Pocket Lighter Preservation Guild & Historical Society, 380 Brooks Dr, Ste 209A, Hazelwood, MO 63042.

Advertising, Coors Beer, figural bowling pin, KEM.	$10.00
Advertising, Denver Police Union, butane, red, with holder, Bic Pen Corp, c1978	5.00
Advertising, Lucky Strike, chromium, painted, c1950	10.00
Advertising, Skelly Oil, brass, red logo and inscription, white ground, 3" l	18.00
Advertising, Zippo, 60th anniversary, chromium, tin gilt box, c1992.	20.00
Colibri, silver lift arm, pocket model, c1937.	75.00
Evans, brass, figural egg.	20.00
Evans, brass, floral dec, gold trim, c1940	25.00
Evans, gold toned brass, figural apple, hinged lid, c1950s. . . .	20.00
Figural, beer stein, ceramic, Germany, c1958	25.00
Figural, bottle, chromium, paper label, KEM, Inc, c1948.	10.00
Figural, camel, metal, c1930	25.00
Figural, double barrel pistol, chromium, butane, Japan	15.00
Figural, Dutch Shoe, hp, Holland, c1940	15.00

Advertising, Honda Ski–Doo, Barlow Automatic Lighter, red, black, and yellow on silver, orig box, minor scratches and soiling, Japan, 1³/₄" h, 2" w, $11.00. Photo courtesy Collectors Auction Services.

Figural, eight ball, plastic, table model	10.00
Figural, horse head, brown, ceramic, table model, Japan.	20.00
Figural, jockey on horse, table model.	35.00
Figural, penguin, SP, c1960	40.00
Figural, ship, chromium, red plastic detail, table model, Occupied Japan	40.00
Figural, stove, brass, c1950	10.00
Figural, television, Swank, c1960.	15.00
Musical, brass, plays *On the Atchinson, Topeka, and the Santa Fe,* Crown, c1940s	45.00
Occupied Japan, 2 pc, chromium, cornucopia on platter, c1949.	40.00
Occupied Japan, chromium lift arm, mother–of–pearl inlays, table model	60.00
Occupied Japan, Penciliter, chromium, Bakelite, 1949	40.00
Parker, chromium, ribbed, table model, c1930s	25.00
Pereline, miniature, brass, attached chain, c1950s	5.00
Perfecto, chromium, 2¹/₂" h	25.00
Ronson, Crown, SP, table model, c1936.	25.00
Ronson, Diana, SP, table model, c1950	15.00
Ronson, Tabourette, chromium and leather, c1929	90.00
Zippo, Corinthian, chronium, table model, c1960	25.00
Zippo, Moderne, chromium, table model, c1966	30.00

LIMITED EDITION COLLECTIBLES

In 1895 Bing and Grondahl produced its first Christmas plate. Royal Copenhagen followed in 1908 and Rosenthal in 1910. Limited edition art prints, many copies of Old Masters, were popular in the 1920s and 30s.

In the late 1960s and extending through the early 1980s, Americans eagerly purchased large quantities of limited edition bells, eggs, mugs, ornaments, plates, and prints. Many came with a "Certificate of Authenticity," in reality a meaningless document.

With production runs often exceeding 100,000 units, very few of these issues were truly limited. Many individuals purchased them as investments rather than for display. The speculative limited edition bubble burst in the mid–1980s. Today, the vast majority of limited edition collectibles issued between the late 1960s and the early 1980s sell for less than 50¢ on the dollar.

Limited edition collectibles is a broad category. Not all items are numbered. In some cases, limited means produced for a relatively short period of time.

Currently, prices are stable or slowly rising on a few select pieces—those that collectors have identified as desirable or whose image crosses over into other collecting categories.

References: *Collectibles Price Guide & Directory to Secondary Market Dealers, Eighth Edition*, Collectors' Information Bureau, 1998, distributed by Krause Publications; Collector's Information Bureau, *Collectibles Market Guide & Price Index, 15th Edition*, Collectors' Information Bureau, 1997, distributed by Krause Publications; Rinker Enterprises, *The Official Price Guide to Collector Plates, Sixth Edition*, House of Collectibles, 1996; Mary Sieber (ed.), *Price Guide to Limited Edition Collectibles*, Krause Publications, 1997.

Periodicals: *Collector Editions*, 170 Fifth Ave, 12th Floor, New York, NY 10010; *Collector's Bulletin*, 22341 East Wells Rd, Canton, IL 61520; *Collectors Mart Magazine*, 700 E State St, Iola, WI 54990; *The Treasure Trunk*, PO Box 13554, Arlington, TX 76094.

Collectors' Club: International Plate Collectors Guild, PO Box 487, Artesia, CA 90702.

Note: In addition to company–sponsored collectors' clubs, there are numerous collectors' clubs for specific limited edition collectibles. Consult *Maloney's Antiques & Collectibles Resource Directory* by David J. Maloney, Jr., at your local library for further information.

Bell, Norman Rockwell Museum, Checking His List, 1982, 6¹/₂" h, $45.00.

Bell, Anri, Christmas, Juan Ferrandiz Musical Christmas Bells Series, 1976 . . . . **$80.00**

Bell, Anri, The Christmas King, Wooden Christmas Bells, J Ferrandiz, 1980. . . . . **18.00**

Bell, Artists of the World, Festival of Lights Series, T DeGrazia, 1980 . . . . **85.00**

Bell, Enesco, Here Comes the Bride—God Bless Her, Memories of Yesterday Series, M Attwell, 1990 . . . . **25.00**

Bell, Fenton Art Glass, Flying Geese, Artist Series, D Johnson, 1985 . . . . **15.00**

Bell, Fenton Art Glass, Gentle Fawn, Mother's Day Series, L Everson, 1981 . . . . **25.00**

Bell, Fenton Art Glass, Going Home, Christmas Series, D Johnson, 1980. . . . . **30.00**

Bell, Fenton Art Glass, Hobby Horse, Childhood Treasure Series, L Everson, 1984. . . . . **15.00**

Bell, Fenton Art Glass, Smoke 'N Cinders, Designer Series, M Dickinson, 1984. . . . . **55.00**

Bell, Fenton Art Glass, Studebaker, American Classic Series, M Dickinson, 1986. . . . . **50.00**

Bell, Fenton Art Glass, Winter on Twilight Blue, M Reynolds, 1992. . . . . **30.00**

Bell, Goebel/Hummel, Letter to Santa Claus, MI Hummel, 1990 . . . . **50.00**

Bell, Gorham, Winter Wonderland, Currier & Ives Mini Bells, 1983 . . . . **15.00**

Bell, Kirk Stieff, Annual Bell 1977, Musical Bells **75.00**

Bell, Lance, John Adams, Hudson Pewter Bicentennial Bells, 1974 . . . . **100.00**

Bell, Lenox, Angel Bell, crystal, 1988. . . . . **45.00**

Bell, Lenox, Deck the Halls, Songs of Christmas Series, china, 1992 . . . . **50.00**

Bell, Olde World Christmas, Santa Bell, 1st ed, E M Merck, 1988 . . . . **10.00**

Bell, Reed & Barton, Little Shepherd, Yuletide Bell, 1982 . . . . **12.00**

Bell, Reed & Barton, Noel Musical Bell, 1981 . . . . **45.00**

Bell, River Shore, Garden Girl, Rockwell Children Series II, N Rockwell, 1978 . . . . **40.00**

Bell, Roman, Inc, Adoration, Masterpiece Collection, F Lippe, 1979 . . . . **20.00**

Bell, Schmid, Merry Mouse Medley, Disney Annuals, 1987. . . . . **15.00**

Bell, Schmid, Sacred Journey, Berta Hummel Christmas Bells, B Hummel, 1976 . . . . **25.00**

Cottage, Fraser International, Balmoral Castle, The British Heritage Collection, I Fraser, 1991 . . . . **135.00**

Cottage, Fraser International, Honey Cottage, Classic Cottage Collection, I Fraser, 1994. . . . . **40.00**

Cottage, Honeymoon Cottage, Countryside in Miniature Collection, I Fraser, 1988. . . . . **25.00**

Cottage, Lilliput Lane, Ltd, Cherry Cottage, English Cottages, D Tate, 1990. . . . . **45.00**

Doll, Ashton–Drake, Goldilocks, Heroines From the Fairy Tale Forests Series, D Effner, 1989 . . . . **80.00**

Doll, Ashton–Drake, Little Sherlock, Born to Be Famous Series, K Barry–Hippensteel, 1989 . . . . **70.00**

Doll, Attic Babies, Christmas Baggie Bear, M Maschino, 1991. . . . . **20.00**

Doll, The Collectibles, Ashley, Yesterday's Child Series, P Parkins, 1986 . . . . **275.00**

Doll, Department 56, Mr & Mrs Fezziwig, Heritage Village Doll Collection, 1988, price for 2 . . . . **170.00**

Doll, Dolls by Jerri, Yvonne, J McCloud, 1986 . . . . **500.00**

Doll, Dynasty Doll, Faith, 1990 . . . . **100.00**

Doll, Georgetown Collection, Katie, Little Loves Series, B Deval, 1989. . . . . **140.00**

Doll, Gorham, Jennifer, Childhood Memories Series, D Valenza, 1991. . . . . **95.00**

Doll, Gorham, Sitting Pretty, Pillow Baby Dolls, L Gordon, 1993 . . . . **35.00**

Doll, H & G Studios, Dorothea, B Burke, 1992 . . . . **395.00**

Doll, Hallmark Galleries, Emma, Victorian Memories, J Greene, 1992 . . . . **25.00**

Doll, Hamilton Collection, Danielle, Through the Eyes of Virginia Turner, 1992 . . . . **95.00**

Doll, Hamilton Collection, He Won't Bite, Bessie Pease Gutmann Doll Collection, 1989 . . . . **135.00**

Doll, Ladie and Friends, black girl with basket, The Little Ones at Christmas Series, BK Wisber, 1990 . . . . **25.00**

Doll, Lenox, Stefan, Ellis Island Dolls, P Thompson, 1991 . . . . **150.00**

Doll, Sarah's Attic, Country Girl, Heirlooms From the Attic Series, 1988 . . . . **25.00**

Doll, Seymour Mann, Inc, Marcey, 1989 . . . . **90 00**

Doll, The Wimbledon Collection, Linda, Hobby Horse Set, G & G Wolf, 1991 . . . . **90.00**

Figurine, All God's Children, Amy, M Holcombe, 1987 . . . . . . **25.00**

Figurines, All God's Children, Mitzi, Ragbabies Series, M Holcombe, 1995 . . . . **30.00**

Figurines, American Artists, Rearing Black Stallion, F Stone, 1987 . . . . **175.00**

Figurine, Angel Gabriel, Nativity Series, J Byers, 1989 . . . . . . **150.00**

Figurine, Anri, Drummer Boy, Shepherds of the Year Series, J Ferrandiz, 1979, 3" **250.00**

Figurine, Anri, Forever Yours, J Ferrandiz, 1988 . . . . **250.00**

Figurine, Anri, Golden Sheaves, J Ferrandiz, 1986, 3" **125.00**

Figurine, Anri, Mickey Skating, Disney Woodcarving Series, 1991, 2" **125.00**

Figurine, Anri, To Market, Ferrandiz Woodcarvings Series, J Ferrandiz, 1982, 3" **115.00**

Figurine, Armani, Doves with Vase, Wildlife Series, G Armani, 1993 . . . . **375.00**

Figurine, Armani, Esmerelda, Gypsy Series, G Armani, 1994 . . . . **200.00**

Figurine, Armani, Julie, Society Members Only, G Armani, 1993 . . . . **125.00**

Figurine, Armani, Summertime, Lady on Swing, Yesteryears Series, 1994 . . . . **450.00**

Figurine, Artaffects, Crazy Horse, The Chieftains Series, G Peerillo, 1983 . . . . **200.00**

Figurine, Artaffects, Nez Perce War Pony, The War Pony Series, G Perillo, 1983 . . . . **175.00**

Figurine, Artists of the World, My First Horse, DeGrazia: Goebel Miniatures, R Olszewski, 1985 . . . . **145.00**

Figurine, Artists of the World, Shepherd's Boy, Nativity Collection, T DeGrazia, 1919 . . . . **135.00**

Figurine, Artists of the World, Wondering, T DeGrazia, 1984 . . . . **220.00**

Figurine, Band Creations, Inc, October, Best Friends, Angels of the Month Series, Richards/Penfield, 1993 . . . . . . **10.00**

Figurine, Barn Owl, Little Night Owls Series, DT Lyttleton, 1990 . . . . **45.00**

Figurine, Best Friends, Snowbabies Series, 1986 . . . . **115.00**

Figurine, Birthday Party, Little Cheesers/Springtime in Cheeserville Collection, C Thammavongsa, 1994 . . . . **22.00**

Figurine, Boyds Collection, Wilson at the Beach, The Bearstone Collection, GM Lowenthal, 1994 . . . . **25.00**

Figurine, Brandywine Collectibles, Antiques Shop, Hometown V Series, M Whiting, 1992 . . . . **20.00**

Figurine, Byers' Choice, Ltd, Spirit of Christmas Present, 2nd ed, Dickens Series, J Byers, 1988 . . . . **275.00**

Figurine, Calabar Creations, Between Chores, Little Farmers Series, P Apsit, 1993 . . . . **40.00**

Figurine, Creart, Mourning Dove, American Wildlife Series, Nelson, 1995 . . . . **130.00**

Figurine, Department 56, Ashbury Inn, Dickens' Village Series, 1991 . . . . **60.00**

Figurine, Department 56, Bisque Lamb, small, Easter Collectibles, 1991 . . . . **20.00**

Figurine, Department 56, Corner Store, Original Snow Village Collection, 1981 . . . . **230.00**

Figurine, Department 56, Down the Hill We Go, Snowbabies Series, 1987 . . . . **20.00**

Figurine, Department 56, Snow Babies, Icy Igloo, 1989 . . . . . **35.00**

Figurine, Department 56, Variety Store, Christmas in the City Series, 1988 . . . . **135.00**

Figurine, Duncan Royale, Uncle, History of Class Entertainers Series, P Aposit, 1987 . . . . **350.00**

Figurine, Enesco, Best Is Yet to Come, The, Cherished Teddies Series, P Hillman, 1995 . . . . **12.00**

Figurine, Enesco, Cleaning House, M Humphrey Bogart, 1988 . . . . **55.00**

Figurine, Enesco, Dawn, Pretty Please Mama, Miss Martha's Collection, M Holcombe, 1991 . . . . **50.00**

Figurine, Enesco, Who Ever Told Mother to Order Twins?, Memories of Yesterday Series, M Attwell, 1991 . . . . **30.00**

Figurine, Flambro Imports, Ringmaster, Emmett Kelly Jr Members Only Figurines, 1993 . . . . **125.00**

Figurine, Franklin Mint, The Nurse, N Rockwell, 1976 . . . . . **175.00**

Figurine, Ganz, Cowsey Jones & the Cannonbull Express, Cowtown Collection, C Thammavongsa, 1994 . . . . **25.00**

Figurine, Geo Zoltan Lefton Company, The Stone House, 1988 . . . . **45.00**

Figurine, Gorham, Babysitter, N Rockwell, 1987 . . . . **75.00**

Figurine, Hamilton Collection, Rose, American Garden Flowers, D Fryer, 1987 . . . . **75.00**

Figurine, Museum Collections, Inc., Christmas Prayers, 1985, 5" h, $65.00.

Figurine, Kaiser, Screech Owl, Birds of America Collection, W Gawantka, 1976 .... **175.00**

Figurine, Lalique Society of America, Enchantment, M C Lalique, 1993 .... **395.00**

Figurine, Lance Corportion, Rise and Shine, Chilmark Pewter Horses Series, B Rodden, 1977 .... **200.00**

Figurine, Lenox, Belle of the Ball, American Fashion Series, 1986 .... **95.00**

Figurine, Lenox, Blue Jay, Garden Birds Series, 1986........ **45.00**

Figurine, Lenox, Western Horse, Carousel Animals Series, 1991 .... **150.00**

Figurine, Lenox, Wood Duck, Porcelain Duck Collection, 1991 .... **45.00**

Figurine, PenDelfin, Buttons, PenDelfin Family Collectors Club, 1994 .... **30.00**

Figurine, Reco International, Mr Cool, Clown Figurines, J McClelland, 1988 .... **35.00**

Figurine, River Shore, Grandpa's Guardian, N Rockwell, 1982 .... **195.00**

Figurine, Schmid, Company's Coming, Davis Cat Tales Series, L Davis, 1982 .... **225.00**

Figurine, Schmid, Brer Coyote, Davis Uncle Remus Series, L Davis, 1981 .... **500.00**

Ornament, Anri, Heavenly Drummer, Ferrandiz Woodcarvings, J Ferrandiz, 1988 .... **225.00**

Ornament, Artaffects, Christmas Cactus, G Perillo, 1986..... **50.00**

Ornament, Artists of the World, Christmas Prayer, T De Grazia, 1991....................................... **75.00**

Ornament, Bing & Grondahl, Christmas Eve at the Farmhouse, E Jensen, 1985 .... **20.00**

Ornament, Bing & Grondahl, Coming Home for Christmas, Christmas in America Series, J Woodson, 1993... **30.00**

Ornament, Bing & Grondahl, Santa's Gifts, Santa Claus Series, 1993 .... **35.00**

Ornament, The Cat's Meow, Grayling House, F Jones, 1985... **40.00**

Ornament, Cazenovia Abroad, Standing Angel, 1968 .... **70.00**

Ornament, Department 56, Scrooge, 1986............... **35.00**

Ornament, Department 56, Snowbaby Adrift Lite–Up, Clip–On, Snowbabies Series, 1987................... **100.00**

Ornament, Department 56, Snowbirds, set of 8 .... **20.00**

Ornament, Department 56, Steeple Church, Village Light–Up Ornaments, 1986 .... **135.00**

Ornament, Enesco, Baby's First Christmas, Memories of Yesterday Series, M Attwell, 1988.................... **25.00**

Ornament, Enesco, Carousel Horse, Treasury of Christmas Ornaments, 1983......................... **20.00**

Ornament, Goebel/Hummel, Celestial Musician, M I Hummel, 1993 .... **110.00**

Ornament, Goebel/Hummel, Flying High, M I Hummel, 1988... **125.00**

Ornament, Hamilton Collection, Angel of Charity, Christmas Angels Series, S Kuck, 1994 .... **20.00**

Ornament, Hand & Hammer, Alice, De Matteo, 1991....... **40.00**

Ornament, Kirk Stieff, Governors Palace, Colonial Williamsburg Series, D Bacorn, 1992................. **10.00**

Ornament, Lenox China, Starburst, 1984 .... **65.00**

Ornament, Lenox Collections, Cat, Christmas Carousel Series, 1989 .... **20.00**

Ornament, Old World Christmas, Boy in Yellow Sweater, E M Merck, 1985............................... **14.00**

Ornament, Orrefors, Reindeer, 1986 .... **40.00**

Ornament, Reed & Barton, Holly Ball, SP, 1976 .... **50.00**

Ornament, Schmid, Cat in Boot, Lowell Davis Country Christmas Series, L Davis, 1984 .... **60.00**

Ornament, Swarovski America, Ltd, Wreath, Holiday Etching, 1988 .... **50.00**

Ornament, Towle Silversmiths, Angel Medallion, 1991 ...... **45.00**

Ornament, Waterford Wedgwood USA, Waterford Crystal Ornament, 1979 .... **80.00**

Plate, Anri, Christmas in Ireland, J Malfertheiner, 1975 ...... **85.00**

Plate, Anri, Mother and Child, J Ferrandiz, Ferrandiz Mother's Day Series, 1973 .... **150.00**

Plate, Anri, Sailing, Father's Day Series, 1976 .... **100.00**

Plate, Artaffects, Arapaho Nation, America's Indian Heritage Series, G Perillo, 1988 .... **35.00**

Plate, Artaffects, A New Love, Bessie's Best Series, Bessie Pease Gutmann, 1984 .... **65.00**

Plate, Belleek Pottery, Celtic Cross, 1971 .... **50.00**

Plate, Bing & Grondahl, Birds and Chicks, Mother's Day Series, H Thelander, 1970 .... **45.00**

Plate, Bing & Grondahl, Christmas Eve at the Capital, Christmas in America Series, J Woodson, 1990 .... **50.00**

Plate, Bing & Grondahl, Christmas Letters, Ove Larsen, 1940... **215.00**

Plate, Bing & Grondahl, Santa's Journey, Santa Claus Collection, Hans H Hansen, 1991 .... **75.00**

Plate, Delphi, '68 Comeback Special, Elvis Presley: In Performance Series, B Emmett, 1990 .... **50.00**

Plate, Enesco, Merry Christmas Deer, Christmas Love Series, S Butcher, 1988 .... **80.00**

Plate, Fenton Art Glass, Printer, American Craftsman Carnival Series, 1971........................... **60.00**

Plate, Fenton Art Glass, Romeo and Juliet, Valentine's Day Series, carnival glass, 1972....................... **25.00**

Plate, Franklin Mint, American Bald Eagle, Birds Series, Richard Evans Younger, 1973 .... **145.00**

Plate, Franklin Mint, Asia, Butterflies of the World Series, 1977–79.. **275.00**

Plate, Franklin Mint, Catching a Trout, Currier & Ives Series, 1977–79................................... **45.00**

Plate, Pemberton & Oakes, Childhood Friendship Series, Beach Break, 1986, D. Zolan, $50.00.

Plate, Franklin Mint, Stealing a Kiss, Mark Twain Series, Yves Beaujard, 1977 . . . . **45.00**

Plate, Franklin Mint, Teenagers Together, Rockwell American Sweethearts Series, N Rockwell, 1977 . . . . . . **160.00**

Plate, Frankoma Pottery, God's Chosen Family, Christmas Series, Joniece Frank, 1987 . . . . **25.00**

Plate, Gartlan USA, Yogi Berra, M Taylor, 1989 . . . . **135.00**

Plate, W S George, Let the Children Come Unto Me, Blessed Are the Children Series, W Rane, 1990. . . . . **45.00**

Plate, W S George, The Lord's My Shepherd, Beloved Hymns of Childhood Series, Cicely Mary Barker, 1988 . . . . **40.00**

Plate, W S George, The Old Hand Pump, Country Nostalgia Series, M Harvey, 1989. . . . . **50.00**

Plate, Goebel/Hummel, Auf Wiedersehen, M I Hummel, Anniversary Plate, 1985 . . . . **250.00**

Plate, Goebel/Hummel, Little Sweeper, The Little Homemakers Series, M I Hummel, 1988 . . . . **60.00**

Plate, Goebel/Hummel, Robin, Wildlife Series, 1974 . . . . . . **65.00**

Plate, Gorham, 1776 Plate, Bicentennial Series, china, 1972. . . . . **35.00**

Plate, Gorham, April Fool's Day, N Rockwell, 1978 . . . . **50.00**

Plate, Gorham, Christmas March, Moppets Christmas Series, 1973 . . . . **35.00**

Plate, Gorham, Winter Camp, Encounters, Survival and Celebration Series, J Clymer, 1983 . . . . **70.00**

Plate, Dave Grossman Creations, Balloon Girl, Margaret Keane, 1976 . . . . **40.00**

Plate, Dave Grossman Creations, Friday's Child, Children of the Week Series, Barbard, 1980 . . . . **40.00**

Plate, The Hamilton Collection, Irish Setters, Classic Sporting Dogs Series, B Christie, 1990 . . . . **50.00**

Plate, The Hamilton Collection, Abraham Lincoln, American Civil War Series, D Prechtel, 1990 . . . . **60.00**

Plate, The Hamilton Collection, Mischief Makers, Country Kitties Series, G Gerardi, 1989 . . . . **45.00**

Plate, The Hamilton Collection, Moody Blues, Elvis Remembered Series, S Morton, 1989 . . . . **85.00**

Plate, The Hamilton Collection, Trophy Bass, Angler's Prize Series, M Susinno, 1991 . . . . **40.00**

Plate, The Hamilton Collection, The Reward, Child's Best Friend Series, Bessie Pease Gutmann, 1985 . . . . **60.00**

Plate, Haviland, Two Turtle Doves, Christmas Series, R Hetreau, 1971. . . . . **45.00**

Plate, Haviland and Parlon, Cardinals, Songbirds Series, 1980. . . . . **90.00**

Plate, Edna Hibel Studios, Camellia, Flower Girl Annual, E Hibel, 1988 . . . . **165.00**

Plate, E Hibel Studios, Colette and Child, Mother and Child Series, E Hibel, 1973 . . . . **460.00**

Plate, E Hibel Studios, A Tender Moment, Nordic Families Series, E Hibel, 1987 . . . . **95.00**

Plate, Edwin M Knowles, All Wrapped Up: Himalayans, Cat Tales Series, A Brackenbury, 1988. . . . . **45.00**

Plate, Edwin M Knowles, Caught in the Act—The Golden Retriever, Field Puppies Series, L Kaatz, 1987 . . . . . **40.00**

Plate, Edwin M Knowles, The Singing Lesson, Backyard Harmony Series, J Thornbrugh, 1991 . . . . **35.00**

Plate, Lenox, Colonial Virginia, Colonial Christmas Wreath Series, 1981 . . . . **90.00**

Plate, Lynell, Cradle of Love, Norman Rockwell's Mother's Day Series, N Rockwell, 1980 . . . . **40.00**

Plate, Lynell, Old Country Inn, Betsy Bates Annual, 1979 . . . . **45.00**

Plate, Pemberton and Oakes, Colors of Spring, Childhood Discoveries Series, miniature, D Zolan, 1990. . . . . **40.00**

Plate, Pemberton and Oakes, The Dreamer, Moments Alone Series, R Bentley, 1980 . . . . **45.00**

Plate, Pemberton and Oakes, Summer Suds, Adventures of Childhood Series, D Zolan, 1989 . . . . **30.00**

Plate, PenDelfin, Mother With Baby, J Heap **150.00**

Plate, Reco International, Family With Puppy, Arta Mother's Day, 1973 . . . . **70.00**

Plate, Reco International, Just Daydreaming, Childhood Almanac Series, S Kuck, 1985 . . . . **45.00**

Plate, Reco International, Snowy Village, Furstenberg Christmas Series, 1972. . . . . **20.00**

Plate, Reed and Barton, Red–Shouldered Hawk, Audubon Series, 1971 . . . . **75.00**

Plate, River Shore, Founder's Day Picnic, Little House on the Prairie Series, E Christopherson, 1985. . . . . **40.00**

Plate, Royal Copenhagen, The Good Shepherd, Christmas Series, Hans H Hansen, 1957. . . . . **125.00**

Plate, Royal Copenhagen, Mother Cat and Kittens, Motherhood Series, Sven Vestergaard, 1983 . . . . **45.00**

Plate, Royal Doulton, A Brighter Day, All God's Children Series, L DeWinne, 1979 . . . . **75.00**

Plate, Schmid, Bicentennial, Peanuts Special Edition, C Schulz, 1976. . . . . **30.00**

Plate, Schmid, Little Fishermen, Berta Hummel's Mother's Day Series, B Hummel, 1973 . . . . **35.00**

Plate, Schmid, Nativity, B Hummel, 1973. . . . . **60.00**

Plate, Schmid, Peter and the Wren, Country Christmas Annual, L Davis, 1989. . . . . **75.00**

Stein, Anheuser–Busch, Inc, 1992 Winter Olympics **85.00**

Stein, Anheuser–Busch, Inc, Grizzly, Endangered Species Series, B Kemper, 1993 . . . . **30.00**

Plate, Royal Copenhagen, Christmas Series, Going Home for Christmas, 1973, Kai Lange, $27.00.

LINENS, LACE, CROCHET WORK & OTHER EMBROIDERED HOUSEHOLD TEXTILES

Linen is now a generic term used for any household covering made from cotton, lace, linen, man–made fibers, or silk. Linens experienced two golden ages, the Victorian era and the 1920s–30s. Victorian ladies prided themselves on their household linen handwork of delicate stitchery, lace insertions, fine tucking, and ruffles.

Lace divides into bobbin, embroidered, needlepoint, and machine made (also includes chemical and imitation lace). Machine–made lace dates to the first quarter of the 19th century. By 1840 technology had reached the point where machines were able to produce an imitation lace that was indistinguishable from most handmade laces.

Inexpensive mass–produced linens arrived at the turn of the century. Women turned to pre–stamped embroidery kits. The popularity of bridge and formal dining in the period following World War I brought with it a renewed interest in linens.

Today the vast majority of linens are manufactured in China, Europe, and the United States. Collectors feel modern examples lack the intricate handwork and freshness of design associated with pre–1945 linens.

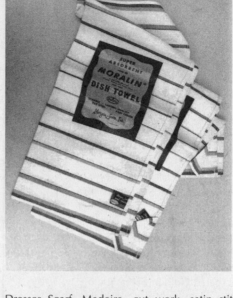

Dish Towels, linen, price each, $1.00.

References: Maryanne Dolan, *Old Lace & Linens Including Crochet: An Identification and Value Guide*, Books Americana, Krause Publications, 1989; Frances Johnson, *Collecting Antique Linens, Lace, and Needlework*, Wallace–Homestead, Krause Publications, 1991; Frances Johnson, *Collecting Household Linens*, Schiffer Publishing, 1997; Elizabeth M. Kurella, *Everybody's Guide to Lace and Linens*, Antique Trader Books, 1997; Elizabeth Scofield and Peggy Zalamea, *20th–Century Linens and Lace: A Guide to Identification, Care, and Prices of Household Linens*, Schiffer Publishing, 1995.

Periodical: *The Lace Collector*, PO Box 222, Plainwell, MI 49080.

Collectors' Club: International Old Lacers, PO Box 481223, Denver, CO 80248.

Antimacassar Set, filet crochet, nautical motif, center ship, anchors on arm pcs, c1930 .... **$18.50**

Blanket Cover, white seersucker, machine bound, c1935, double size **18.00**

Bolster Case, white linen, embroidered white flowers garland, center script letter "P", crocheted edging, open ends, c1920 .... **50.00**

Bridge Set, organdy, light yellow, linen appliquéd flowers on outer edge, hemstitched around appliqués and border, 4 matching napkins, 34 x 34" **50.00**

Cocktail Napkins, set of 6, linen, bunch of grapes shape, lavender and green, 6 x 8" **30.00**

Cocktail Napkins, set of 8, cotton, light yellow, embroidered elephant on one corner, fringed ends, c1930 .... **7.50**

Crib Sheet, white muslin, embroidered animals, light blue top band, matching pillowcase, c1930–40, 48 x 54" **45.00**

Dinner Napkins, set of 6, white linen, double damask, chrysanthemum pattern, hand–rolled edges, 24" sq **25.00**

Doily, white linen center, 2 hand–tatted rows of medallions, c1920, 25" d **35.00**

Dresser Scarf, Alencon lace, floral and medallion designs, ecru, machine made, c1930, 14" w, 48" l **40.00**

Dresser Scarf, Madeira, cut work, satin stitch, hand embroidered, filet lace borders on 4 sides, pointe lace insets each end, c1930 .... **30.00**

Fingertip Towels, pr, linen, one blue, other pink, embroidered yellow roses and green leaves, fringed ends, 9 x 14" **15.00**

Handkerchief, set of 3, white cotton, bright colored floral pattern, c1935 .... **10.00**

Hand Towel, white linen, embroidered orange and blue oriental designs on each end, hand tied fringe, 18 x 24" **10.00**

Luncheon Napkins, set of 4, white Swiss linen, embroidered flower basket on one end, c1920, 14" sq **12.00**

Pillowcases, pr, white muslin, embroidered, girl in full skirt holding flowers, crocheted edge, made from stamped kit, c1930 .... **18.50**

Place Mats, set of 8, white cotton, Battenberg, lavish corners and edging, matching napkins, c1940 .... **75.00**

Runner, white cotton, hand–drawn Chinese work, 16 x 50" **18.00**

Sheet, white muslin, 3" w filet crochet rose motif insert, c1920, double size **15.00**

Tablecloth, crocheted, tobacco string, filet lace sq motifs, c1930–40, 72 x 58" **50.00**

Tablecloth, printed cotton, black children and adults eating watermelon scene, machine hemmed, c1935, 54 x 53" **50.00**

Tablecloth, white cotton, colorful appliquéd linen flowers, crochet edges, 6 matching napkins, c1930, 54 x 56" **35.00**

Tablecloth, white cotton, printed multicolored cross–stitched Amish motif, 52" sq. **25.00**

Tablecloth, white, printed multicolored strawberries dec, 50" sq **25.00**

Tablecloth, white, printed multicolored floral and fruit dec, c1940, 56 x 66" **25.00**

Tête–A–Tête Set, mat and 2 matching napkins, linen, pale blue, embroidered pink roses and vines on 2 corners, c1940 .... **25.00**

Vanity Set, 3 pcs, white muslin, embroidered floral cross–stitched design, white machine–made Cluny–type lace border, c1920–30 .... **25.00**

LITTLE GOLDEN BOOKS

The first Little Golden Books were published in September 1942. George Duplaix and Lucile Olge of the Artist and Writers Guild, a company formed by Western Printing & Publishing in the 1930s to develop new children's books, and Albert Leventhal and Leon Shimkin of Simon & Shuster developed Little Golden Books.

The key to the success of Little Golden Books was their price, 25¢. Within the first five months, 1.5 million copies were printed. Simon & Shuster published the books, the Artists and Writers Guild produced them, and Western Printing and Lithographing printed them. By the 10th anniversary (1952), over 182 million copies had been sold, 4 million of which came from sales of The Night Before Christmas.

The first Walt Disney title was published in 1944. Many of the titles issued in the 1950s and 60s were direct tie–ins with TV shows, especially westerns and Saturday morning cartoons. In 1958 Western Printing and Lithographing and Pocket Books purchased the rights to Little Golden Books from Simon & Shuster. A Golden Press imprint was introduced. Eventually Western bought out Pocket Books and created Golden Press, Inc.

Little Golden Books are identified by a complex numbering system that experienced several changes over the years. Many titles have remained in print for decades. Value rests primarily in first printing examples in near mint condition. If the book contained a dust jacket or any other special feature, it must be intact for the book to have any retail market value.

References: Norman E. Martinus and Harry L. Rinker, *Warman's Paper,* Wallace–Homestead, Krause Publications, 1994; Steve Santi, *Collecting Little Golden Books, Third Edition,* Krause Publications, 1998.

Newsletter: *The Gold Mine Review,* PO Box 209, Hershey, PA 17033.

Collectors' Club: Golden Book Club, 19626 Ricardo Ave, Hayward, CA 94541.

Note: Prices listed are for books in mint condition.

#3, *The Alphabet From A–Z,* 1942, 42 pp. **$20.00**
#8, *The Poky Little Puppy,* 1942, 42 pp **20.00**
#12, *This Little Piggy Counting Rhymes,* 1942, 42 pp **20.00**
#16, *The Golden Book of Flowers,* 1943, 42 pp **15.00**
#22, *Toys,* 1945, 42 pp. **15.00**
#25, *The Taxi That Hurried,* 1946, 42 pp **18.00**
#31, *Circus Time,* 1948, 42 pp **15.00**
#36, *The Saggy Baggy Elephant,* 1947, 42 pp **15.00**
#41, *The New Baby,* 1948, 42 pp **18.00**
#47, *The Three Bears,* 1948, 42 pp **18.00**
#51, *The Seven Sneezes,* 1948, 42 pp **15.00**
#54, *Pat–A–Cake,* 1948, 28 pp **10.00**
#58, *What Am I?,* 1949, 28 pp. **10.00**
#60, *Guess Who Lives Here,* 1949, 42 pp **15.00**
#65, *Gaston and Josephine,* 1949, 42 pp **15.00**
#69, *Bobby and His Airplanes,* 1949, 42 pp **12.00**
#73, *Little Yip and His Bark,* 1950, 42 pp **12.00**
#74, *The Little Golden Funny Book,* 1950, 42 pp **10.00**
#81, *Duck and His Friends,* 1949, 28 pp **10.00**
#83, *How Big?,* 1950, 24 pp **8.00**
#90, *My Little Golden Dictionary,* 1949, 56 pp. **10.00**
#93, *Brave Cowboy Bill,* 1950, 42 pp. **15.00**

#97, *Little Benny Wanted a Pony,* 1950, 42 pp **25.00**
#101, *The Little Golden ABC,* 1951, 28 pp. **6.00**
#104, *Just Watch Me,* 1975, 24 pp. **4.00**
#107–72, *Quints "The Cleanup,"* 1990, 24 pp **3.00**
#108, *Two Little Gardeners,* 1951, 28 pp **10.00**
#108–46, *Grover's Own Alphabet,* 1978, 24 pp. **2.00**
#110, *A Day at the Beach,* 1951, 28 pp **15.00**
#110–59, *Pound Puppies "Pick of the Litter,"* 1985,
    24 pp **3.00**
#115, *My Home,* 1971, 24 pp. **4.00**
#118, *The Train to Timbuctoo,* 1951, 28 pp **15.00**
#111–49, *Bisketts in Double Trouble,* 1984, 24 pp **4.00**
#123, *Happy Birthday,* 1952, 42 pp. **25.00**
#129, *Tex and His Toys,* 1952, 28 pp **25.00**
#128, *Mister Dog,* 1952, 28 pp **20.00**
#134, *Seven Little Postmen,* 1952, 28 pp **12.00**
#137, *Puss 'n Boots,* 1952, 28 pp. **8.00**
#142, *Frosty the Snowman,* 1951, 28 pp **8.00**
#148, *The Ginghams Backward Picnic,* 1976, 24 pp. **4.00**
#148, *Uncle Wiggily,* 1953, 28 pp **15.00**
#149, *Indian Indian,* 1952, 28 pp **8.00**
#153, *Thumbelina, 1953,* 28 pp. **10.00**
#158, *The Christmas Story,* 1952, 28 pp **8.00**
#160, *Donny and Marie, The Top Secret Project,* 1977,
    24 pp **5.00**
#161, *Topsy Turvy Circus,* 1953, 28 pp **10.00**
#174, *Bible Stories of Boys and Girls,* 1953, 28 pp **6.00**
#175, *Where Will All the Animals Go?,* 1978, 24 pp **4.00**
#184, *Birds,* 1973, 24 pp. **5.00**
#188, *Hi Ho! Three in a Row,* 1954, 28 pp **18.00**
#193, *Paper Doll Wedding,* 1954, 28 pp **35.00**
#202, *Little Indian,* 1954, 28 pp. **10.00**
#204, *The Three Bears,* 1965, 24 pp **4.00**
#204–54, *The Store Bought Doll,* 1983, 24 pp **2.00**
#211–45, *Little Golden Book of Jokes and Riddles,* 1983,
    24 pp **2.00**
#214, *Linda and Her Little Sister,* 1954, 28 pp **20.00**
#227, *The Twins,* 1955, 28 pp **25.00**
#232, *Little Red Riding Hood,* 1972, 24 pp **4.00**
#238, *5 Pennies to Spend,* 1955, 28 pp **12.00**
#249, *The Animal Gym,* 1956, 24 pp **10.00**

#453, *Top Cat,* **1962, 24 pp, $15.00.**

#260, *Little Golden Book of Dogs*, 1952, 24 pp **7.00**
#264, *Richard Scarry's Just For Fun*, 1960, 24 pp **6.00**
#270, *The Sky*, 1956, 24 pp. **7.00**
#278, *Captain Kangaroo and the Panda*, 1951, 24 pp **10.00**
#280, *Little Golden Paper Dolls*, 1951, 24 pp **30.00**
#285, *How to Tell Time*, 1957, 24 pp. **15.00**
#287, *Cleo*, 1957, 24 pp **10.00**
#296, *Brave Eagle*, 1957, 24 pp **12.00**
#298, *My Christmas Book*, 1957, 24 pp **15.00**
#302–56, *Little Lost Kitten*, 1951, 24 pp **1.00**
#307–56, *The Elves and the Shoemaker*, 1983, 24 pp **1.00**
#308, *Jack's Adventure*, 1958, 24 pp **8.00**
#308–57, *How Things Grow*, 1986, 24 pp **2.00**
#314, *Pussy Willow*, 1951, 24 pp. **10.00**
#316, *Monster at the End of this Book*, 1971, 24 pp. **6.00**
#322, *Four Little Kittens*, 1957, 24 pp. **5.00**
#329, *The Animals' Merry Christmas*, 1958, 24 pp **15.00**
#333, *Baby Farm Animals*, 1958, 24 pp **6.00**
#342, *Exploring Space*, 1958, 24 pp **7.00**
#349, *Animal Alphabet*, 1958, 24 pp **10.00**
#360, *Party in Shariland*, 1958, 24 pp **15.00**
#369, *Little Golden Picture Dictionary*, 1959, 24 pp **5.00**
#373, *Airplanes*, 1953, 24 pp **6.00**
#375, *The Chipmunk's Merry Christmas*, 1959, 24 pp. **8.00**
#384, *Happy Birthday*, 1960, 24 pp. **12.00**
#388, *Our Flag*, 1960, 24 pp **6.00**
#396, *Animal Quiz*, 1960, 24 pp **6.00**
#404, *Baby Looks*, 1960, 24 pp **15.00**
#408, *Rocky and His Friends*, 1960, 24 pp. **15.00**
#413, *Chicken Little*, 1960, 24 pp **6.00**
#417, *Loopy De Loop Goes West*, 1960, 24 pp. **12.00**
#424, *My Little Golden Book of Jokes*, 1961, 24 pp **6.00**
#428, *Home For a Bunny*, 1961, 24 pp **8.00**
#438, *The Little Red Hen*, 1973, 24 pp **4.00**
#443, *Puff the Blue Kitten*, 1961, 24 pp **15.00**
#446, *Bozo the Clown*, 1961, 24 pp **10.00**
#452–8, *Rudolph The Red–Nosed Reindeer Shines
  Again*, 1982, 24 pp **1.00**
#456, *The Golden Egg Book*, 1962, 24 pp **7.00**
#459–8, *The Biggest, Most Beautiful Christmas Tree*,
  1985, 24 pp **1.00**
#461, *Pick Up Sticks*, 1962, 24 pp. **10.00**
#469, *My Puppy*, 955, 24 pp **8.00**
#471, *Tommy's Camping Adventure*, 1962, 24 pp. **10.00**
#473, *Nurse Nancy*, 1958, 24 pp. **25.00**
#478, *The ABC Christmas*, 1962, 24 pp **15.00**
#480, *Tommy Visits the Doctor*, 1969, 24 pp **6.00**
#488, *Gay Purr–ee*, 1962, 24 pp **18.00**
#492, *Supercar*, 1962, 24 pp **20.00**
#496, *Colors Are Nice*, 1962, 24 pp. **5.00**
#503, *Corkey's Hiccups*, 1973, 24 pp **6.00**
#514, *Thumbelina*, 1953, 24 pp **6.00**
#519, *The Little Red Hen*, 1954, 24 pp **4.00**
#522, *Jamie Looks*, 1963, 24 pp. **15.00**
#527, *The Romper Room Exercise Book*, 1964, 24 pp. **8.00**
#533, *Animal Dictionary*, 1960, 24 pp **5.00**
#539, *Cave Kids*, 1963, 24 pp **16.00**
#548, *The Little Engine That Could*, 1954, 24 pp **8.00**
#552, *We Like Kindergarten*, 1965, 24 pp **6.00**
#562, *Good Little Bad Little Girl*, 1965, 24 pp **18.00**
#567, *Play With Me*, 1967, 24 pp **8.00**
#570, *Things in My House*, 1968, 24 pp **4.00**
#574, *So Big*, 1968, 24 pp. **10.00**
#578, *When I Grow Up*, 1968, 24 pp **5.00**

#582, *The Wonderful School*, 1969, 24 pp **5.00**
#584, *Animal Counting Book*, 1969, 24 pp **4.00**
#587, *Charlie*, 1970, 24 pp **6.00**
#594, *1, 2, 3, Juggle With Me*, 1970, 24 pp **4.00**
#595, *Christmas Carols*, 1946, 24 pp **4.00**
#599, *Let's Visit the Dentist*, 1970, 24 pp **5.00**
#600, *Susan in the Driver's Seat*, 1973, 24 pp **8.00**

LITTLE GOLDEN BOOK TYPES

Competitors quickly rose to challenge Little Golden Books. Wonder Books, part of a publishing conglomerate that included Random House, arrived on the scene in 1946. Rand McNally published its first Elf Books in September 1947 and a Hanna–Barbera Character Series between 1975 and 1977.

Golden Press also produced variations of its successful Little Golden Book line. Giant Little Golden Books arrived in 1957, followed by the Ding Dong School Book series in 1959.

Note: Prices are for books in mint condition.

Big Golden Book, *The Animals' Merry Christmas*, 1950,
  32 pp **$15.00**
Big Golden Book, *Caroline at the Ranch*, 1961, 28 pp **30.00**
Big Golden Book, *David and Goliath*, 968, 28 pp. **8.00**
Big Golden Book, *The Golden Book of Words*, 1974,
  24 pp **5.00**
Big Golden Book, *The Happy Rabbit*, 1963, 28 pp. **18.00**
Big Golden Book, *Never Talk to Strangers*, 1967, 20 pp **15.00**
Carry Me Book, *My Doctor Bag*, 1977, 24 pp **5.00**
De Luxe Golden Book, *The Epic of Man*, 1962, 176 pp **10.00**
Ding Dong School Book, *Dressing Up*, #206, 1953 . . . . **8.00**
Ding Dong School Book, *Mr. Meyer's Cow*, #220, 1955 . . . . **8.00**
Eager Reader, *Boo and the Flying Flews*, #803, 1974. . . . . . **2.00**
Eager Reader, *Monster! Monster!*, #808, 1974 . . . . **2.00**
Eager Reader, *The Pet in the Jar*, #801, 1974 . . . . **2.00**
Giant Golden Book, *Cub Scouts*, 1959, 56 pp **15.00**
Giant Golden Book, *Dogs*, #5008, 1957, 56 pp **12.00**
Giant Sturdy Book, *Baby Farm Animals*, 1958. . . . . **10.00**
Giant Sturdy Book, *Baby's Mother Goose*, 1958, 22 pp **15.00**
Golden Activity Book, *Colors*, #A28, 1959, 20 pp **10.00**
Golden Activity Book, *Stop and Go*, #A8, 1957, 20 pp **15.00**

Wonder Book, *A Surprise for Mrs. Bunny*, #601, 1953, $6.00.

Golden Book, *Adventures of Ookpik*, 1968, 28 pp **10.00**
Golden Book, *Brontosaurus: The Thunder Lizard*, 1983,
  32 pp **5.00**
Golden Book Land, *Tawny Scrawny Lion Saves the Day*,
  1989, 24 pp **2.50**
Golden Forty–Niner, *Presidents of the United States*,
  1956, 30 pp **5.00**
Golden Fun–to–Learn, *School Days*, 1954, 48 pp **8.00**
Golden Funtime Book, *Cars and Trucks*, coloring book **5.00**
Golden Funtime Book, *Nurse Nancy*, stick–um book. **20.00**
Golden Fuzzy Book, *The White Bunny and His Magic
  Nose*. **15.00**
Golden Hours Library, *Big Little Book*, 1962, 24 pp **4.00**
Golden Melody Book, *People in Your Neighborhood*,
  1984, 24 pp **5.00**
Happy Book, *ABC*, 1963, 24 pp **4.00**
Happy Book, *I Am a Puppy*, 1970, 24 pp **5.00**
Land Series, *Shy Little Kittens Secret Place*, regular back
  cov. **2.00**
Lift and Look Books, *Saggy Baggy Elephant and the New
  Dance*, 1985, 24 pp **5.00**
Little Silver Book, *Jerry at School*, 1950, 24 pp **4.00**
Look and Learn Library, *Fun with Words*. **10.00**
My Golden First Learning Library, *The Book of L*, c1965 . . . . . . **1.50**
Play and Learn Book, *Raggedy Ann* **4.00**
Pop–Up Book, *The Fox and the Hound*, 1981, 22 pp **20.00**
Read–It–Yourself Book, *A Dog's Life*, 1964, 32 pp **3.00**
Sniff It Book, *What! No Spinach*, 1981, 12 pp **8.00**
Sturdy Shape Book, *This Is My House*, c1980 . . . . **4.00**
Tiny Golden Book, *The Little Leopard and His Fat
  Stomach* **3.00**
Touch and Feel Book, *The Telephone Book*, 1961, 20 pp **5.00**

LITTLE RED RIDING HOOD

Design Patent #134,889, June 29,1943, for a "Design for a Cookie Jar," was granted to Louise Elizabeth Bauer of Zanesville, Ohio, and assigned to the A. E. Hull Pottery Company. This patent protected the design for Hull's Little Red Riding Hood line, produced between 1943 and 1957.

Hull and the Royal China and Novelty Company, a division of Regal China, made the blanks. Decoration was done almost exclusively at Royal China. Because the pieces were hand painted, many variations in color scheme have been discovered.

REPRODUCTION ALERT: Be alert for Little Red Riding Hood cookie jar reproductions. The period piece measures 13" h; the Mexican reproduction is shorter.

Butter, cov **$375.00**
Canister, blank **600.00**
Cereal Canister. **1,000.00**
Coffee Canister **400.00**
Cracker Jar **690.00**
Creamer and Sugar, open **210.00**
Creamer and Sugar, side pour **325.00**
Dresser Jar **625.00**
Grease Jar, yellow wolf. **1,000.00**
Hot Chocolate Mug **2,000.00**
Match Holder **475.00**
Milk Pitcher, front pour **325.00**
Mustard, with spoon **375.00**
Popcorn Canister **2,200.00**

Pretzel Canister **2,200.00**
Salt and Pepper Shakers, pr, large. **165.00**
Salt and Pepper Shakers, pr, small **90.00**
Spice Jar, cinnamon. **700.00**
Spice Jar, nutmeg **700.00**
String Holder **2,500.00**
Teapot **300.00**
Teapot, cov **325.00**
Toothbrush Holder **75.00**
Wall Bank **2,700.00**

LLADRO PORCELAINS

In 1951 José, Juan, and Vincente Lladró established a ceramics factory in Almacera, Spain. Each was educated at the Escuela de Artes y Oficios de San Carlos. José and Juan focused on painting and Vincente on sculpting. The Lladró brothers concentrated on the production of ceramic figurines, initially producing diminutive ceramic flowers.

In 1953 the brothers built a kiln that could produce temperatures sufficient to vitrify porcelain. With it, they began to make porcelain pieces in styles duplicating those of Dresden and Sevres. In 1955 they opened a shop in Valencia, and in 1958 began construction of a factory in the neighboring town of Tavernes Blanques.

In 1985 the company organized the Lladró Society, a collectors' club. Rosa Maria Lladró assumed the presidency of the Society in 1995. She, along with her sister Marie Carmen, and her cousins, Rosa and Juan Vicente, represent the second generation of the Lladró family to become involved in the business.

References: Collectors' Information Bureau, *Collectibles Market Guide & Price Index, 15th Edition*, Collectors' Information Bureau, 1997, distributed by Krause Publications; Glenn S. Johnson, *The Lladro Collection Reference Guide*, Clear Communications, 1996.

Collectors' Club: Lladro Collectors Society, 1 Lladro Dr, Moonachie, NJ 07074.

Figurine, Angel with Child, 1969 . . . . **$110.00**
Figurine, Baby Jesus, 1971. . . . . **70.00**
Figurine, Barn Owl, 1987 . . . . **175.00**

Figurine, rabbit, natural pastel colors, mkd, 4¹/₂" l, $100.00.

Figurine, Bashful, 1978 . . . . **150.00**
Figurine, Cow, 1969 . . . . **90.00**
Figurine, Donkey, 1969 . . . . **100.00**
Figurine, Ducklings, 1974 . . . . **150.00**
Figurine, Duck Pulling Pigtail, 1978 . . . . **275.00**
Figurine, Iris with Vase, Capricho, 1987 . . . . **375.00**
Figurine, Monk, 1977 . . . . **145.00**
Figurine, Nestling Crane, 1989 . . . . **115.00**
Figurine, Oriental, 1974 . . . . **100.00**
Figurine, Polar Bear, white, 1972 . . . . **75.00**
Figurine, Prayerful Moment, blue, 1988 . . . . **100.00**
Figurine, Praying Angel, 1969 . . . . **80.00**
Figurine, School Days, 1988 . . . . **500.00**
Figurine, Shepherdess with Goats, L1001M, 1969 . . . . **450.00**
Figurine, Swan, spread wings, 1984 . . . . **120.00**
Figurine, Tumbling, 1991 . . . . **135.00**
Figurine, Walk with Father, 1991 . . . . **40.00**
Figurine, Waiting in the Park, 1978 . . . . **450.00**
Plate, Caroling, Christmas Series, 1971 . . . . **30.00**
Plate, Cherubs, Christmas Series, 1975 . . . . **60.00**
Plate, Kiss of the Child, Mother's Day Series, 1971 . . . . **75.00**
Plate, Mother and Child, Mother's Day Series, 1975 . . . . **55.00**
Plate, Snow Dance, Christmas Series, 1979 . . . . **80.00**

LOTTON, CHARLES

Charles Gerald Lotton (born October 21, 1935) is a contemporary glass artist. In 1970 Lotton built a small glass studio behind his house in Sauk Village, Illinois. In June 1971 Lotton sold his first glass to C. D. Peacock, a downtown Chicago jeweler.

A chance meeting with Dr. Ed McConnell during a visit to Corning, New York, resulted in a meeting with Lillian Nassau, a leading New York City art glass dealer. Paul Nassau, Lillian's son, and Lotton signed an exclusive five–year contract in 1972. Lotton leased a former lumber yard in Lansing, Illinois, to serve as his studio. In 1975 he built a new studio in Lynwood, Illinois, eventually building a glassworks behind his home in Crete, Illinois, in 1982.

By 1977 Lotton had achieved a national reputation and wanted the freedom to sell glass directly to his own distributors. Lotton glass is sold through a number of select retailers and at antiques shows. The four Lotton children, Daniel, David, John, and Rachel, are all involved with some aspect of glassmaking.

Reference: D. Thomas O'Connor and Charles G. Lotton, *Lotton Art Glass*, Antique Publications, 1990, out of print.

Ball, iridescent mandarin yellow, blue luster leaf and
   vine design **$150.00**
Bottle, mandarin red, long neck, flared lip **250.00**
Bowl, cobalt blue, multi floral print **450.00**
Bowl, sunset, rolled–out lip, white pulled fern design **150.00**
Cabinet Vase, iridescent coral, lily pad dec. **100.00**
Chalice, ftd, mandarin red **150.00**
Chalice, ftd, mandarin red, blue pulled thread design **150.00**
Lamp, miniature, sunset, white pulled feather design **300.00**
Paperweight, cobalt blue, pink and multicolored floral
   design. **75.00**
Paperweight, cobalt blue, pink flowers **75.00**
Perfume Bottle, selenium red, pink atomizer. **75.00**
Persian Water Sprinkler, mandarin red, blue luster pulled
   feather design **300.00**
Rose Bowl, cobalt blue, gold zipper pattern **150.00**

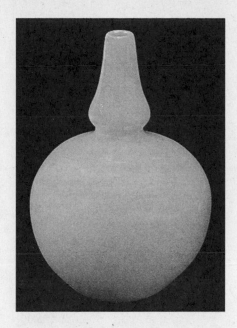

Vase, Mandarin Yellow, 1984, $200.00.

Sculpture, free–form, mandarin red, black swirls
   throughout **200.00**
Vase, bing cherry, black luster pulled feather desgin **250.00**
Vase, floral print, aqua ground. **500.00**
Vase, lime green, drop leaf pulled feather desgin **200.00**
Vase, mandarin red, rolled–out lip, black luster veiled
   threading **200.00**
Vase, mandarin red, silver dec **150.00**
Vase, mandarin yellow, rolled out lip **250.00**
Vase, multicolored floral print, green mottled print
   ground **500.00**

LUNCH BOXES

A lunch kit is comprised of a lunch box and a thermos. Both must be present for the unit to be complete.

Although lunch kits date back to the 19th century, collectors focus on the lithographed tin lunch kits made between the mid–1930s and the late 1970s. Gender, Paeschke & Frey's 1935 Mickey Mouse lunch kit launched the modern form. The 1950s and early 1960s was the lunch kit's golden age. Hundreds of different kits were made, many featuring cartoon, movie, and television show images. Aladdin Company, Landers, Frary and Clark, Ohio Art, Thermos/King Seeley, and Universal are among the many companies who made lunch kits during the golden age.

This market went through a speculative craze that extended from the late 1970s through the early 1990s at which point the speculative bubble burst. Prices have dropped from their early 1990s high for most examples. Crossover collectors, rather than lunch kit collectors, are keeping the market alive in the late 1990s.

References: Larry Aikins, *Pictorial Price Guide to Metal Lunch Boxes & Thermoses*, L–W Book Sales, 1992, 1996 value update; Larry Aikins, *Pictorial Price Guide to Vinyl & Plastic Lunch Boxes & Thermoses*, L–W Book Sales, 1992, 1995 value update; Allen Woodall and Sean Brickell, *The Illustrated Encyclopedia of Metal Lunch Boxes*, Schiffer Publishing, 1992.

Periodical: *Paileontologist's Report*, PO Box 3255, Burbank, CA 91508.

Collectors' Club: Step Into the Ring, 829 Jackson St Ext, Sandusky, OH 44870.

Note: Prices listed reflect boxes with thermos, both in near mint condition.

Action Jackson	$125.00
Addams Family	60.00
Airline National	30.00
America on Parade	45.00
Animal Friends	25.00
Atom Ant	55.00
Auto Race	35.00
Basket Weave	25.00
Batman	85.00
Battle Star Galactica	40.00
Beany & Cecil, carry bag	35.00
Betsy Clark, yellow	25.00
Beverly Hillbillies	85.00
Bionic Woman	35.00
Black Hole	65.00
Bonanza, green	85.00
Bonanza, brown	75.00
Bond XX Secret Agent	95.00
Brave Eagle	65.00
Cabbage Patch Kids	15.00
Campus Queens	60.00
Canadian Train	35.00
Captain Astro	145.00
Care Bear Cousins	10.00
Cartoon Zoo	195.00
Chitty Chitty Bang Bang, 1968	60.00
Clash of Titans	25.00
Close Encounters	55.00
Daniel Boone, #84	95.00
Denim Diner, dome	35.00
Denim, vinyl	30.00
Disney School Bus, dome	75.00
Doctor Doolittle	35.00

Gene Autry, Universal Landers, Frary & Clark, $275.00. Photo courtesy Auction Services.

Dukes of Hazzard, plastic	25.00
Dynomutt	45.00
Fall Guy	20.00
Family Affair	40.00
Fat Albert, old style	35.00
Fat Albert	55.00
Flying Nun	60.00
Fox and the Hound	10.00
Fraggle Rock, plastic, 1987	15.00
Gentle Ben	125.00
Get Smart	110.00
Ghostbusters	20.00
Gomer Pyle	195.00
Gremlins	30.00
Grizzly Adams, dome	100.00
Gunsmoke, 1972	95.00
Hair Bear Bunch	45.00
Happy Days	75.00
Heathcliff	15.00
Hector Heathcote	110.00
He–Man Masters of the Universe	15.00
Holly Hobbie, vinyl, 1982	30.00
Hot Wheels, plastic, 1984	25.00
Huckleberry Hound	110.00
Hunchback of Notre Dame	15.00
James Bond 007	125.00
Jungle Book	65.00
Jr Miss	25.00
Kellogg's Corn Flakes, plastic, 1985	30.00
Kiss, 1977	75.00
Knight Rider	20.00
Kroft Super Show	45.00
Kung Fu	85.00
Lancelot Link	110.00
Land of the Giants	110.00
Last Starfighter	20.00
Laugh–In	85.00
Lawman	75.00
Little Red Riding Hood	65.00
Lone Ranger, #230	40.00
Magic Kingdom	55.00
Major League Baseball	75.00
Mary Poppins	40.00
Mickey Mouse, figural head	20.00
Mighty Mouse, 1984	30.00
Mork & Mindy, plastic, dome, orange	20.00
Muppet Babies	15.00
Muppet Movie, 1979	22.00
NFL Football, plastic	30.00
Partridge Family	55.00
Peanuts, #282, 1980	25.00
Peter Pan Peanut Butter, plastic, 1984	40.00
Phantom	12.00
Pickle, figural, plastic	20.00
Pink Panther & Sons	25.00
Psychadelic, dome	195.00
Rambo	20.00
Rat Patrol	120.00
Return of the Jedi, tin	25.00
Robin Hood	135.00
Rose Petal Place	45.00
Rough Riders	45.00
Sesame Street	15.00
Smokey Bear and Minnesota T–Wolves	15.00

Space: 1999	**20.00**
Speedy Buggy	**45.00**
Star Trek The Next Generation, dome	**20.00**
Star Wars, Ewok	**20.00**
Star Wars Return of the Jedi	**20.00**
Strawberry Shortcake, vinyl, 1980	**35.00**
Street Hawk	**135.00**
Superfriends	**65.00**
Super Heroes	**55.00**
Super Powers	**40.00**
S. W. A. T., plastic, dome	**30.00**
Tarzan	**95.00**
Tazmanian Devil, 3–D	**20.00**
Thunder Cats	**18.00**
Tom Corbett, litho tin	**295.00**
Treasure Chest, dome	**125.00**
Voyage to the Bottom of the Sea	**225.00**
Wagon Train	**55.00**
Waltons	**55.00**
Washington Redskins	**165.00**
Welcome Back Kotter	**55.00**
Wild Wild West	**195.00**
Woody Woodpecker	**20.00**
Yogi and Friends	**110.00**

MADE IN JAPAN

Prior to 1921, objects made in Japan were marked NIPPON or MADE IN NIPPON. After that date, objects were marked JAPAN or MADE IN JAPAN.

Although MADE IN OCCUPIED JAPAN was the primary mark used between August 1945 and April 28, 1952, some objects from this period were marked JAPAN or MADE IN JAPAN.

This is a catchall category for a wide range of ceramic, glass, and metal items made by Japanese manufacturers for export to the United States. Many were distributed by American import companies who designed the products in America, had them manufactured in Japan, and marketed them in the United States.

Reference: Carol Bess White, *Collector's Guide to Made in Japan Ceramics* (1994, 1996 value update), *Book II* (1996), *Book III* (1998), Collector Books.

Note: See Occupied Japan for additional listings.

Ashtray, figural clown sitting on edge with legs spread, opalized tray, 3" h	**$30.00**
Ashtray, figural frog playing banjo, black clubs tray, red accents	**15.00**
Bookends, pr, sleeping Mexican, multicolored, 4¼" h	**25.00**
Bowl, swimming swan in pond scene, hp trim, 7½" w	**25.00**
Cache Pot, Dutch boy and girl with basket, Goldcastle, 6" h	**20.00**
Candleholder, chamberstick style, multicolored floral motif, yellow ground	**30.00**
Candy Dish, applied handle, multicolored floral dec, pink rim and handle, 8¾" l	**20.00**
Cigarette Box, applied cat with arched back, multicolored luster,	**30.00**
Condiment Set, sugar, cov, salt and pepper shakers, pr, and 9" w tray, dark blue and light blue, gold trim	**40.00**
Dish, cov, floral dec, Moriyama Ware, 9½" d	**30.00**
Figurine, baby and bunny in basket	**15.00**

Figurine, mkd "AX2749A," Napco, foil label, 5¼" h, $5.00.

Flower Frog, 2 blue birds on stump, ivy and berries dec, 5¾" h	**20.00**
Match Holder, winking man, 5" h	**25.00**
Nut Cup, oriental woman, holding flowers	**18.00**
Pitcher, multicolored floral motif, mkd "Shofu," 5" h	**35.00**
Plate, souvenir, different states	**8.00**
Relish, divided, multicolored floral motif, white ground, reed handle, 11½" w	**45.00**
Ring Tray, man in top hat and cane, woman with dog, "Just Married"	**15.00**
Salt and Pepper Shakers, pr, lily pad and frog with open mouth, mkd "Made In Japan"	**15.00**
Teapot, hp, multicolored stripe motif, 5" h	**25.00**
Vase, tulip shape, multicolored, 6" h	**25.00**

MAGAZINES

In the early 1700s general magazines were a major source of information. Literary magazines such as *Harper's* became popular in the 19th century. By 1900 the first photo–journal magazines appeared. Henry Luce started *Life*, the prime example, in 1932.

Magazines created for women featured "how to" articles about cooking, sewing, decorating, and child care. Many were devoted to fashion and living a fashionable life. Men's magazines were directed at masculine skills of the time, such as hunting, fishing, and woodworking. "Girlie" titles became popular in the 1930s and enjoyed a golden age in the 1950s and 60s.

Popular magazines, such as *Collier's, Life, Look,* and *Saturday Evening Post,* survive in vast quantities. So do pulps. Value is driven primarily by cover image, content, and advertisements.

Many magazines are torn apart and the pages sold individually. The key value component for these "tear sheets" is subject matter. As a result 99% plus are purchased by crossover collectors. Except for illustrator collectors, crossover collectors care little if the tear sheet features a drawing or photograph. The most desirable tear sheets are in full color and show significant design elements.

References: Ron Barlow and Ray Reynolds, *The Insider's Guide to Old Books, Magazines, Newspapers, Trade Catalogs,* Windmill Publishing, 1995; David K. Henkel, *Magazines: Identification and*

Price Guide, Avon Books, 1993; Denis C. Jackson, *Men's "Girlie" Magazines: The Only Price Guide: Newstanders, 4th Edition*, TICN, 1994; Denis C. Jackson, *Old Magazines: The Price Guide & Identification Guide, 4th Edition*, TICN, 1997; Norman E. Martinus and Harry L. Rinker, *Warman's Paper*, Wallace–Homestead, Krause Publications, 1994; *Old Magazine Price Guide*, L–W Book Sales, 1994, 1997 value update; Lee Server, *Danger Is My Business: An Illustrated History of the Fabulous Pulp Magazines: 1896–1953*, Chronicle Books, 1993.

Periodical: *PCM (Paper Collectors' Marketplace)*, PO Box 128, Scandinavia, WI 54977; *Pulp & Paperback Market Newsletter*, 5813 York Ave, Edina, MN 55410.

Newsletters: *The Illustrator Collector's News*, PO Box 1958, Sequim, WA 98392.

Air Progress, Nov, 1941	$15.00
Amazing Stories, Oct 1930	30.00
American Builder, 1925	12.00
American Detective, 1930s	5.00
American Family, Jul 1952 to Aug 1953, each	5.00
American Gun, Vol 1, 2, and 3, 1961	48.00
American Lady, Sep 1938, Vol 1, #1	15.00
Antiques Magazine, 1947–60, 18 bound vol	150.00
Apple Pie, Mar 1975, Vol 1, #1	10.00
Architectural Digest, Los Angeles, Vol 14, #1, 1934–35	15.00
Avant Garde, 11 issues, 1969–71	44.00
Avon Fantasy Reader, Feb 1947	15.00
Baker Street Journal, Vol 2, #1–4, 1947	150.00
Bedtime Story, Vol 1, #1, 1932	35.00
The Big Story, Vol 1, #1, Oct 1951	22.00
Black Book Detective, 1940s	25.00
Blue Book Magazine, Mar 1939	25.00
Box Office Barometer, 1946–56	8.00
Cartoon Humor, Vol 1, #1, Jan 1939	20.00
Circus, 1940s	8.00
Colliers, KKK, Oct 9, 1948	8.00
Complete Detective Cases, Oct 1951	9.00
Coronet, Masters Of Mystery issue, Feb 1956	25.00
Disney Magazine, 1960s	7.00
Dynamic Science Fiction, Dec 1952	5.00
Esquire, Lenny Bruce, Nov 1960	6.00
Eye Magazine, Vol 1, #1, May 1949	15.00
Family Circle, 1968	4.00
Fashion Digest, 1930–40s	2.00
Filmland, James Dean, Sep 1956	25.00
Follies Magazine, 1959	5.00
Follies Magazine, 46 issues, 1962–69	125.00
Front Page Detective, 1940–50s	3.00
Game Breeder, 1930s	4.00
Gourmet, 1940–60s	3.00
Green Magazine, 1940s	7.00
Harper's Bazaar, Aug 1930	10.00
Hollywood Magazine, Dec 1940	12.00
Home & Field, 1930–40s	2.00
House and Garden, Sep 1927	12.00
Infinity Science Fiction, Nov 1955	6.00
Intimate Detective Stories, Mar 1943	8.00
Jack and Jill, 1940–50s	2.00
Kenyon Review, 1944–45	10.00
Ladies Circle, 1960s	2.00
Liberty, Donald Duck cov, May 1942	12.00
Life, Rudolph Valentino, Jun 20, 1938	35.00

Life, Lucille Ball and Desi Arnaz, Apr 6, 1953	10.00
Life, Hemingway article, Dec 16, 1960	25.00
Life, Paul McCartney, Apr 16, 1971	12.00
Literary Digest, Aug 13, 1932	8.00
Look Magazine, Basil Rathbone, Oct 29, 1946	20.00
Look Magazine, last issue, Oct 19, 1971	10.00
The Magazine Antiques, 28 bound vol, 1947–60	150.00
McCall's, Jul 1931	20.00
Mechanix Illustrated, 1960–80s	1.00
Mercury Mystery Book, Mar 1956	45.00
Dr Miles New Weather Almanac, 1942	5.00
Modern Brewery Age, 1930s	3.00
Motion Picture Herald, 1940s	10.00
Movie Family Album, 1965	10.00
Movie World, Elvis Presley, May 1959	30.00
Mystery Book Magazine, Aug 1946	10.00
New Masses, 1931–46	8.00
New West, 1946	4.00
Nugget, Betty Brosmer, Nov 1955	20.00
Office Magazine, Vol 1, #1, Feb 1926	20.00
Outdoor America, Apr 1931	7.00
The Outsider, #1 and #2, 1961–62	35.00
Parabola, Winter 1981	20.00
Penthouse, 1980s	20.00
People Magazine, 42 issues, 1947–77	3.00
Photoplay Magazine, 1950s	10.00
Pictorial Review, 1930s	10.00
Playmate, 1950s	5.00
Poetry Magazine, Dec 1968	3.00
Popular Mechanics, Anniversary issue, Jan 1956	156.00
Professional Art Quarterly, Rockwell Kent articles, Jun 1936	10.00
Quick Magazine, Vol 1, #1, Oct 1964	15.00
Ring Magazine, 1920s	8.00
Ringmaster, Vol 1, #1, May 1936	30.00
Rolling Stone, 1970–80s	8.00
Science & Technology International, 1962–69	6.00
Scientific Monthly, 1920s	5.00
Screen Guide, Sep 1946	10.00
Screen Land, 1960s	6.00
Show Magazine, 1940–60s	5.00
Sky Fighters, 1933–43	15.00
Songs & Words, Sep 1954	15.00

Saturday Evening Post, Vol. 235, No. 8, Oct 27, 1962, J. Williamson cover illus, $5.00.

Space Journal, Summer 1957	20.00
Spinning Wheel, 1950–70s	6.00
Sporting Goods Journal, 1930s	6.00
Startling Stories, Jan 1939	5.00
Suspense, 1951	5.00
Terror Tales, 1934–41	45.00
Tip–Off, Apr 1958	15.00
Travel, 1926	12.00
True Confessions, 1935–50s	5.00
True Story, May 1933	15.00
US Camera, Fall 1938	35.00
US News & World Report, 1940–66	2.00
Vanity Fair, Nov 1929	40.00
Virginia Quarterly, 1920s	4.00

MARBLES

Marbles divide into three basic types: (1) machine–made clay, glass, and mineral marbles, (2) handmade glass marbles made for use, and (3) handmade glass marbles made for display. Machine–made marbles usually sell for less than their handmade counterparts, comic strip marbles being one of the few exceptions. Watch for modern reproduction and fantasy comic strip marbles.

The Akro Agate Company, Christensen Agate Company, M. F. Christensen & Son Company, Marble King Company, Master Marble Company, Peltier Glass Company, and Vitro Agate/Gladding–Vitro Company are some of the leading manufacturers of machine–made marbles. Today, collector emphasis is on marble sets in their period packaging.

Handmade marbles are collected by type—Bennington, china (glazed and painted), china (unglazed and painted), clay, end of day, Lutz, mica, sulfide, and swirl—and size. Over a dozen reproduction and fantasy sulfide marbles have appeared during the last decade.

Many contemporary studio glassblowers have made marbles, often imitating earlier styles, for sale to the adult collector market. These marbles show no signs of wear and have not been tested in the secondary resale market. Any value associated with these marbles is highly speculative.

References: Robert Block, *Marbles: Identification and Price Guide, 2nd Edition*, Schiffer Publishing, 1998; Everett Grist, *Antique and Collectible Marbles: Identification and Values, Third Edition*, Collector Books, 1992, 1996 value update; Everett Grist, *Everett Grist's Big Book of Marbles*, Collector Books, 1993, 1997 value update; *Everett Grist's Machine Made and Contemporary Marbles, Second Edition*, Collector Books, 1995, 1997 value update; Dennis Webb, *Greenberg's Guide to Marbles, Second Edition*, Greenberg Books, 1994.

Collectors' Clubs: Marble Collectors Society of America, PO Box 222, Trumbull, CT 06611; National Marble Club of America, 440 Eaton Rd, Drexel Hill, PA 19026.

Akro Agate, blue oxblood	**$55.00**
Akro Agate, corkscrew, 2 color	1.00
Akro Agate, egg yoke, oxblood	100.00
Akro Agate, lemonade corkscrew	10.00
Akro Agate, limeade oxblood	18.00
Akro Agate, milky oxblood	12.00
Akro Agate, popeye corkscrew, purple/yellow	45.00
Akro Agate, popeye corkscrew, red/yellow	12.00

Akro Agate, slag	1.00
Akro Agate, transparent or translucent corkscrew	6.00
Christensen Agate Co, American agate or bloodie	35.00
Christensen Agate Co, cobra	600.00
Christensen Agate Co, swirl	30.00
Christensen M F & Son	60.00
Christensen M F & Son, flame swirl, 2 color	50.00
Marble King, bumblebee	1.00
Marble King, Girl Scout	6.00
Marble King, Spiderman, blue/red	150.00
Marble King, watermelon	200.00
Peltier Glass Co, Christmas tree	50.00
Peltier Glass Co, patch with adventurine	20.00
Unknown Manufacturer, bullet mold	15.00
Unknown Manufacturer, common patch or swirl	.25
Unknown Manufacturer, wire pull	10.00
Vitro Agate/Gladding–Vitro Co, all red	.25
Vitro Agate/Gladding–Vitro Co, conqueror	1.00
Vitro Agate/Gladding–Vitro Co, victory	2.00

MATCHBOX

In 1947 Leslie Smith and Rodney Smith, two unrelated Navy friends, founded Lesney (a combination of the first letters in each of their names) in London, England. Joined by John Odell, they established a factory to do die casting.

In 1953, Lesney introduced a miniature toy line packaged in a box that resembled a matchbox. The toys quickly became known as "Matchbox" toys. The earliest Matchbox vehicles had metal wheels. These were eventually replaced with plastic wheels. In 1969 the Superfast plastic wheel was introduced. Slight variations in color and style occurred from the beginning due to paint and parts shortages. In 1956 the Models of Yesteryear series was introduced, followed in 1957 by Major Packs.

Matchbox toys arrived in the United States in 1958 and achieved widespread popularity by the early 1960s. Mattel's Hot Wheels arrived on the scene in 1968, providing Matchbox with a major competitor. Matchbox revamped its models through the 1970s and added the "1–75" numbering system. "Nostalgia" models were introduced in 1992.

In 1982 Universal Group bought Lesney. Production was moved to the Far East. In 1992 Tyco Toys bought Universal Group. In 1997 Mattel, owner of Hot Wheels, Matchbox's biggest rival, acquired Tyco.

References: Dana Johnson, *Matchbox Toys: 1948–1996, Second Edition*, Collector Books, 1996; Charlie Mack, *The Encyclopedia of Matchbox Toys: 1947–1996*, Schiffer Publishing, 1997; Nancy Schiffer (comp.), *Matchbox Toys, Revised*, Schiffer Publishing, 1995.

Collectors' Clubs: Matchbox Collectors Club, PO Box 977, Newfield, NJ 08344; Matchbox U.S.A., 62 Saw Mill Rd, Durham, CT 06422; The Matchbox International Collectors Assoc, PO Box 28072, Waterloo, Ontario, Canada N2L6J8.

1904 Spyker, Y16–A4	**$50.00**
1906 Rolls Royce Silver Ghost, Y10–C1	30.00
1910 Benz Limousine, Y3–B19	70.00
1911 Daimier, Y13–B2	40.00
1912 Packard Landaulet, Y11–B2	40.00
1913 Cadillac, Y6–C3	60.00

1914 Stutz, Y8–C2 .... **40.00**

Aston Martin DB2 Saloon, 53–A, metallic light green, 2½" l, 1958............................. **30.00**

Aston Martin Racing Car, 19–C, metallic green, metal steering wheel, wire wheels, black plastic tires, 2½"" l, 1958 .... **30.00**

Atlantic Trailer, 16–B, orange body, 8 gray plastic wheels, 3½" l, 1957 .... **50.00**

Atlas Truck, 23–E, metallic blue cab, silver interior, orange dumper, red and yellow labels on doors, 3" l, 1975... **8.00**

Beach Buggy, 30–E, pink, yellow paint splatters, clear windows, 2½" l, 1970 .... **4.00**

Bedford Ambulance, 14–C, 2⅝" l, issued 1963........... **18.00**

Beford Low Loader, 27–B, green cab, tan trailer, silver grille, 4 gray wheels on cab, 2 wheels on trailer, 3¾" l, 1959............................. **50.00**

Bluebird Dauphine Trailer, 23–B, green body, gray plastic wheels, left rear side door opens, 2½" l, 1960 .... **130.00**

BMR Racing Car, 25D–1 .... **15.00**

Boat and Trailer, 9–C, white hull, blue deck, clear windows, 5 spoke wheels on trailer, 3¼" l, 1966............. **6.00**

Cattle Truck, 37–D, yellow body, gray plastic box with fold–down rear door, black plastic wheels, green tinted windows, 2¼" l, 1966......................... **10.00**

Cement Mixer, 3–A, blue body, rotating barrel, orange metal wheels, 1⅝" l, 1953 .... **35.00**

Chevrolet Impala Taxi Cab, 20–C, yellow body, ivory or red interior and driver, 3" l, 1865 .... **15.00**

Claas Combine Harvester, 65–C, red body, yellow plastic rotating blades and front wheels, black plastic front tires, solid rear wheels, 3" l, 1967 .... **10.00**

Commer Lyons Maid Ice Cream Truck, 47–B, 1–75 series, blue body, white plastic vendor, 2⁷⁄₁₆" l, 1963 ...... **35.00**

DAF Tipper Container Truck, 46C–2 .... **13.00**

Daimler Bus, 74–B, double deck, white plastic interior, 4 black plastic wheels, 3" l, 1966.................. **15.00**

Dodge Crane Truck, 63–C, yellow body, green windows, 6 black plastic wheels, rotating crane cab, 3" l, 1968 ..... **10.00**

Double Decker London Bus, 5–A, 1–75 series, gold radiator, 2" l, 1954 .... **60.00**

Dragon Wheels Volkswagen, 43–E, light green body, amber windows, silver interior, "Dragon Wheels" on side in orange on black, 2¹³⁄₁₆" l, 1972 .... **8.00**

Drott Excavator, 58–B, red or orange body, movable front shovel, green rubber treads, 2⅝" l, 1962........... **50.00**

D–Type Jaguar, 41–A, dark green body, yellow interior, unpainted base, ¹³⁄₁₆" 1957...................... **30.00**

Duke of Connaught Locomotive, Y14–A1 .... **150.00**

Evening News Van, 42A–3........................ **120.00**

Excavator, 24B–2............................. **45.00**

Ferrari Berlinetta, 51B–2 .... **15.00**

Ferret Scout Car, 61A–1......................... **35.00**

Fiat, red, 56B–3 .... **80.00**

Fire Station, MF–1A, 9¾" l, issued 1963............... **50.00**

Foden Concrete Truck, 21–D, orange/yellow body, rotating barrel, green tinted windows, 8 plastic wheels, 3" l, 1968 .... **5.00**

Ford Capri, 54–D, ivory interior and tow hook, clear windows, 5–spoke wide wheels, 3" l, 1971 .... **4.00**

Ford Customline Station Wagon, 31–A, yellow body, no windows, with or without red painted tail lights, 2⅝" l, 1957............................... **30.00**

Ford Fairlane Fire Chief Car, 59–B, 2⅝" l, issued 1963 ...... **20.00**

Ford Galaxy Police Car, 55–C, 1–75 series, white body, bubble light, driver, 2⅞" l, 1966.................. **30.00**

Ford Model A Van, blue, Champion Spark Plugs adv, 3" l, 1982 .... **10.00**

Ford Model A Van, Kellogg's Corn Flakes adv, MB38, cereal premium, distributed in United Kingdom, Denmark, and France, 3" l, 1982 .... **10.00**

Ford Tractor, diecast metal, blue and yellow, yellow wheels, black tires, 2" l, 1967 .... **25.00**

Formula 5000, 36–F, orange body, silver rear engine, 3" l, 1975 .... **8.00**

Fowler "Big Lion" Showman's Engine, Y–9–A, issued 1958.. **80.00**

Galaxie Fire Chief Car, 59–C **30.00**

Greyhound Bus, 66–C, silver body, white plastic interior, clear or dark amber windows, 6 black plastic wheels, 3" l, 1967 .... **35.00**

Honda Motorcycle and Trailer, diecast metal, metallic blue and green, yellow trailer, red "Honda" decal, 3" l, 1967 .... **25.00**

Jeep, 72–B **20.00**

Jennings Cattle Truck, M7A–1 .... **120.00**

John Deere Tractor, diecast metal, green, yellow steering wheel and wheels, black tires, 2" l, 1960s **25.00**

LeMans Bentley, Y5–1 .... **85.00**

Leyland Site Office Truck, 60–C, 1–75 Series, superfast wheels, 1970, 2½" l **15.00**

Lincoln Continental, 56B–1...................... **10.00**

Lomas Ambulance, 64B–1 .... **20.00**

Lotus Racing Car, 60B–1 .... **22.00**

Maserati, yellow, 52A–4 .... **125.00**

Massey Harris Tractor, 4–B, 1–75 Series, attached driver, no fenders, 1⅝" l............................. **60.00**

Mercedes Truck, 1E–1 .... **12.00**

Mercer 1913 Raceabout, Y7–B2.................... **45.00**

Military Ambulance, 63A–1...................... **65.00**

Milk Delivery Van, 29–A **50.00**

Opoel Diplomat, 44C–1 .... **16.00**

Quarry Truck, 6A–1........................... **60.00**

Race Car Transporter, M6B–1..................... **75.00**

Race N Rallye Set, G4B–3 .... **225.00**

Refrigerator Truck, 1D–1, 1–75 Series **12.00**

Refuse Truck, 15–C **20.00**

Road Roller, 1–A1............................ **125.00**

Speed Kings/Hot Fire Engine, #K–53, red, silver, plastic firemen figures, removable ladder, 1975, MIB **15.00**

Swamp Rat Airboat, 30–F, 1976, $6.00.

MATCHCOVERS

Joshua Pusey, a Philadelphia lawyer who put ten cardboard matches into a plain white board cover, is credited with inventing the matchcover. In 1892 he sold 200 to the Mendelson Opera Company, which hand–printed the cover with its advertisement.

Binghamton Match Company, Binghamton, New York, made the first machine–made matchcover for the Piso Company of Warren, Pennsylvania. Only one example survives, owned by the Diamond Match Company.

Matchcovers dating prior to the early 1930s are scarce. The modern collecting craze dates from the Chicago Century of Progress World's Fair of 1933–34. The matchcover's golden age began in the mid–1940s and extended through the early 1960s.

The introduction of the throw–away lighter in the mid–1960s and rising production costs ended the matchcover era. The per unit cost of diecut matchcovers today falls in the seven to eight cents range. Given this, matchcovers lost their appeal as a free giveaway.

The 1990s saw matchcover prices soar. The $1,000 barrier was broken. Many of these higher prices are being paid by crossover, not matchcover collectors. Trading, usually on a one for–one–basis, remains the principal form of exchange among collectors.

References: Norman E. Martinus and Harry L. Rinker, *Warman's Paper,* Wallace–Homestead, Krause Publications, 1994; Bill Retskin, *The Matchcover Collector's Price Guide, 2nd Edition,* Antique Trader Books, 1997.

Collectors' Clubs: Rathkamp Matchcover Society, 1359 Surrey Rd, Vandalia, OH 45377; The American Matchcover Collecting Club, PO Box 18481, Asheville, NC 28814.

Note: Prices are for matchcovers in mint or near mint condition.

Amusement Park, "Dorney Park, Allentown, Pennsylvania, The Natural Spot & Rides" on front, "Dorney Park, The Natural Spot, Allentown, Penna" on back, "Phone 6583 Allentown" on saddle **$5.00**

Comic, "Fruity Acres Sanitarium, Screwball Rd., Fruitville, N. Y." on front, "Your Daze Go By Faster at Fruity Acres..." on back, "Phone PSycho 341 Q" on saddle, Metalart Co, 1958 . . . . 3.00

Display, 21–Feature, "Club Charles Where The Fun Begins" and dancer on front, int club scene on back, "Ace of Clubs," top hat, stick, and champagne glass on display, "Club Charles" on center stick, dancer on other sticks, Lion Match. 12.00

Features, "Churchills Restaurant Cafe" and propeller on front, Airlines Terminal building on back, each contoured stick is figural liquor bottle labeled "Gin, Wine, Champagne, Rye, Scotch," Churchill's Restaurant across bottom of sticks, 20–strike size, Lion Match 10.00

Features, Eleanor Shop, Portsmouth, VA, garment and word "Blouses, Slips, Robes, Skirts," or "Sweaters" on each stick, Lion Match. 10.00

Features, Longchamps Restaurant, New York City, chef on each stick with "Longchamps" across all sticks, orange and white, 20–strike size, Lion Match 12.00

Features, Lucky Sticks, "Flemington Glass Company, Inc, Flemington, New Jersey" on front, "Factory Showrooms" and wine glass on back, play instructions inside, 21 sticks each with card symbols for different poker hand on each stick, Lion Match. 10.00

Features, Olympic Club, emblem with aviator's wings on front, "San Francisco" on saddle, aerial view of clubhouse and "The Olympic Club at Lakeside" on back, line drawing of club int on inside, 2 men golfing with clubhouse in background across sticks, Lion Match **12.00**

Features Type, Trainer's Seafood, heart and "Trainer's" on front, lobster, fish, crab, and "Trainer's Seafood at its best" on back, seafood illus on sticks, mfg by Harry R Dubbs, Allentown, PA 10.00

Girlie, Faiman's Cafe adv on front, girlie and "Station WOW" on back, "We Never Sleep" on saddle 6.00

Midget, "Blue Mirror Cocktail Lounge 1817 N. Charles St." and champagne glass on front, same on back with "Balto., MD.," "Air Conditioned" on saddle, Lion Match. 5.00

Midget, Doc's Cocktail Lounge, "Doc's" on front, blank saddle, "Doc's Cocktail Lounge 1817 N. Charles St. Baltimore" and drawing of 2 men leaning against lamppost on back, name and address on inside, white on blue, Lion Match 5.00

Midget Type, "The Brass Rail Bar & Cocktail Lounge Cor. 3rd at Central Great Falls, Mont" on front, "Great Falls' finest" on saddle, "Brass Rail, The Best at Popular Prices," and int restaurant scene on back, blank int, white on green, Diamond Match. 6.00

Military, Marines, USMC crest on front, "Camp Lejune, North Carolina" on back, blank saddle, blank inside, orange on olive drab, Diamond Match 5.00

Patriotic, Bond Bread Navy Plane Set, Wildcat Fighter, Lion Match, 1942 . . . . 8.00

Patriotic, Disney/Pepsi–Cola Set, type I, 2nd Signal Armored Battalion, No. 23, Indian playing with tank, 10 lines of inside type, gray, National Match, 1942 . . . . 10.00

Patriotic, "For Safety, Buy Defense Bonds, Stamps" and minuteman on front, "Own a Share in America" on saddle, "A Safe Investment for a Safe America, Buy Defense Bonds, Stamps" with eagle and shield on back, blank inside, Universal Match. 6.00

Printed Sticks, Yonadi's Homestead Restaurant Golf Club, full color photo of building front and back, printed sticks with red "Yonadi's Homestead" and coat of arms, Universal Match. 8.00

40 Strike, Bow–Wow Bon Bons, "A Treat For Your Dog!" on saddle, Universal Match, $4.00. Photo courtesy Morykan Auctioneers.

Display, 21–Feature, "Club Charles 'Where The Fun Begins'" and dancer on front, int club scene on back, Ace of Clubs display, "Club Charles" on center stick, dancers across other sticks, Lion Match, $15.00. Photo courtesy Morykan Auctioneers.

Railroad, "Western Pacific Feather River Route" on front, "The Exposition Flyer" on back, blank saddle, "Fast and Dependable Freight and Passenger Service" inside, black and white, Diamond Match **6.00**

Ten Strike, "Arcade Bar" and cocktail glass on front, "Lower Arcade, Carew Tower" and cocktail glass on back, blank saddle, "In Cincinnati it's the Arcade Bar, Lower Arcade, Carew Tower" inside, Universal Match **5.00**

Transportation, Greyhound Bus, "See This Amazing America, Best go Greyhound" with outline of US and bus on front, "Reservations may be made through Postal Telegraph" on saddle, "Cool Vacations Start Here, Aboard an air–conditioned Greyhound" and bus on back, Postal Telegraph Services info inside **10.00**

21–Feature, Gurney's Inn, Montauk, LI, NY, dark blue cov, plain front, gold nautical symbol and "1926–1976" and "50 years of gracious hospitality" on back, white "Gurney's Inn" across dark blue sticks, 30–stick size **8.00**

21–Feature, "Red Lion Inn, Hackensack, New Jersey" on front, red lion logo on back, red lion logo across center 3 sticks, Lion Match **12.00**

MCCOY POTTERY

In 1910 Nelson McCoy, with his father's (J. W. McCoy) support, founded the Nelson McCoy Sanitary Stoneware Company, to manufacture crocks, churns, and jugs. Early pieces were marked on the side with a stencil of a clover within a shield with an "M" above. By the mid–1920s, the company also made molded artware in forms ranging from jardinieres to vases.

In 1933 the company became the Nelson McCoy Pottery. Products included cookware, dinnerware, floral industry ware, gardenware, kitchenware, and tableware.

In 1967 Mount Clemens Pottery, owned by David Chase, purchased the company. Some pieces were marked "MCP" on the bottom. In 1974 Chase sold McCoy to Lancaster Colony Corporation, which added its logo to the bottom. Nelson McCoy, Jr., served as president under the Mount Clemens and Lancaster Colony Corporation ownership until 1981. After being sold to Designer Accents in 1985, operations at McCoy ceased in 1990.

References: Bob Hanson, Craig Nissen, and Margaret Hanson, *McCoy Pottery: Reference & Value Guide,* Collector Books, 1997; Sharon and Bob Huxford, *The Collectors Encyclopedia of McCoy Pottery,* Collector Books, 1980, 1997 value update; Martha and Steve Sanford, *Sanfords Guide to Pottery by McCoy,* Adelmore Press, 1997.

Newsletter: *The NM Express,* 3081 Rock Creek Dr, Broomfield, CO 80020.

REPRODUCTION ALERT: Nelson McCoy Pottery Company reproduced many of its original pieces.

Ashtray, hands, leaf dec, yellow, 1941	**$6.50**
Ashtray, raised pheasant design center, 9" d	30.00
Bank, Bowery Savings Bank, treasure chest.	37.00
Basket, hanging, butterfly, white.	145.00
Batter Set, Butter, Batter, and Syrup, price for 3.	30.00
Bean Pot, cov, brown	8.00
Bean Pot, cov, Suburbia Ware, 1964, 2 qt	15.00
Bookends, pr, birds, 6" h	95.00
Bowl, ftd, green drip over onyx, 5 x 6½"	35.00
Cat Feeder, late 1930s.	25.00
Cereal Bowl, brown drip	20.00
Cookie Jar, chipmunk, 1959–62.	80.00
Cookie Jar, churn, 1961.	25.00
Cookie Jar, Dalmatians on rocking horse, 1962.	300.00
Cookie Jar, ear of corn, 1969	100.00
Cookie Jar, elephant, sitting, 1943	110.00
Cookie Jar, "Fortune Cookie," Chinese lantern, 1967.	50.00
Cookie Jar, kitten on basket, 1956–69	45.00
Cookie Jar, lollipops, 1958–60.	45.00
Cookie Jar, rooster, 1950s	75.00
Cookie Jar, smiling boy, 1960s.	45.00
Cookie Jar, teepee, 1957–59	200.00
Corn Dish, brown, 9 x 3¼"	10.00
Creamer, dog, green, 1950s.	25.00
Creamer, Ivy	25.00
Creamer, Sunburst Gold, 1957.	15.00
Cup, brown drip, 8 oz.	5.00
Decanter, astronaut.	48.00
Dresser Organizer, eagle	25.00
Fernery, hobnail, 1940	8.00
Figure, angel fish, double, green	285.00
Figure, baseball glove	8.00
Figure, deer	12.00
Figure, fish	10.00
Figure, goat, stretch, white matte	65.00
Figure, lamb, white	25.00
Flower Holder, elephant, coral.	20.00
Flower Holder, swan, yellow	55.00
Flower Pot, emb flowers, attached base, pink, 1940	5.00
Flower Pot, lotus motif	10.00
Flower Pot, smiley face	4.50
French Casserole, 1 pt, 1948	10.00
Grease Jar, cabbage, 1954.	30.00
Jardiniere, flying birds motif, 7½" h	25.00
Jug, frosted blue, 1967	6.00

Cookie Jar, Mammy, imp script "McCoy," 10¹/₂" h, $100.00.

Lamp, western boots **34.00**
Mug, Campbell's Kids **12.00**
Mug, El Rancho, 10 oz **30.00**
Mug, Suburbia Ware, 1964 . . . . **6.00**
Pitcher, butterfly, blue, 10" h **100.00**
Pitcher, cloverleaf dec, 1940s **18.00**
Pitcher, elephant, 1940s **35.00**
Pitcher, emb cloverleaves, 1948. . . . . **18.00**
Pitcher, water lily, 1935 . . . . **15.00**
Planter, basket, lattice, 1957 . . . . **22.00**
Planter, black cat face, 5 x 6". **25.00**
Planter, lion, 1940. . . . . **15.00**
Planter, Liberty Bell, green, 10 x 8¹/₄" **170.00**
Planter, sprinkling can, white, rose decal **6.50**
Planter, trivet base, 1953 . . . . **12.00**
Planter, turtle **15.00**
Planter, wagon, green, yellow wheels, umbrella **55.00**
Planter, zebra, 1956 . . . . **30.00**
Platter, fish shape, brown drip, 18" l. **35.00**
Reamer, 8" d. **35.00**
Relish Set, Lazy Susan. **35.00**
Salt and Pepper Shakers, pr, cabbage, 1954 . . . . **10.00**
Salt and Pepper Shakers, pr, cucumber and mango, 1954 . . . . **20.00**
Soup Bowl, brown drip **6.00**
Spoon Rest, butterfly, 1953 . . . . **35.00**
Spoon Rest, penguin, 1953 . . . . **15.00**
Strawberry Pot, #2, yellow. **30.00**
Sugar, cov, Sunburst Gold, 1957 . . . . **18.00**
Tankard, pig, leaves and berries, 1940s **12.00**
Teapot, 1950s. **12.00**
Urn, butterfly, green **18.00**
Vase, butterfly, blue. **45.00**
Vase, cornucopia, green **12.00**
Vase, fan, chartreuse and green leaves, 15" h **8.00**
Vase, hand, white, 6¹/₂" h. **55.00**
Vase, ripple ware, green, bright pink rim trim, 1950,
   7" h **5.00**
Wall Pocket, butterfly, white, 7 x 6" **175.00**
Wall Pocket, flower, rustic, 1946 . . . . **10.00**
Wall Pocket, leaves and berries, 7" h **125.00**
Wall Pocket, violin, aqua, gold trim, 10¹/₄" h. **125.00**

MCDONALD'S

In 1948 Dick and Mac McDonald opened their first limited menu, self–service McDonald's drive–in restaurant in San Bernadino, California. They began franchising their operation as the Speedee Service System in 1952. In 1955 Ray Kroc became a franchising agent for the McDonald brothers and opened his first McDonald's restaurant in Des Plaines, Illinois.

The 100th McDonald's restaurant opened in 1959 and the 200th in 1960. In 1961 Kroc bought out the McDonald brothers and launched the All American Meal of a hamburger, french fries, and milkshake. The Golden Arches replaced the Speedee logo in 1962. The first "Ronald McDonald," Willard Scott, made his debut in Washington, D.C.'s Cherry Blossom Parade in 1963. The Happy Meal dates from 1977. Toys were introduced in 1982.

By 1983, McDonald's had 7,000 restaurants in the United States and additional restaurants in thirty–one foreign countries. McDonald's has continued to build new restaurants around the world. Promotional tie–ins with movies, television shows, and major toy products have proven highly successful. By 1994, the 15th anniversary of the Happy Meal, McDonald's was serving 25 million customers daily in 70 countries.

References: Gary Henriques and Audre DuVall, *McDonald's Collectibles: Identification and Value Guide,* Collector Books, 1997; Terry and Joyce Losonsky, *McDonald's Happy Meal Toys Around the World,* Schiffer Publishing, 1995; Terry and Joyce Losonsky, *McDonald's Happy Meal Toys in the U.S.A.,* Schiffer Publishing, 1995; Meredith Williams, *Tomart's Price Guide to McDonald's Happy Meal Collectibles, Revised Edition,* Tomart Publications, 1995.

Newsletter: *Collecting Tips Newsletter,* PO Box 633, Joplin, MO 64802.

Collectors' Club: McDonald's Collectors Club, 255 New Lenox Rd, Lenox, MA 01240.

Alarm Clock, windup, 2 silver bells, metal round shape
   ringer, red case, brass feet, mkd "Robertshaw
   Controls, Luxtime Division Lebanon, Tenn, USA,"
   4¹/₂" d **$50.00**
Bank, diecast, delivery van, Ronald McDonald on side,
   1992 Christmas Greetings **35.00**
Baseball, white, red stitching, 1989 . . . . **3.00**
Beach Ball, Grimace scenes, 1986. . . . . **2.00**
Boat, Fry Kids Ferry, 1987 . . . . **2.50**
Book, *Berenstain Bears Attic Treasure,* 1990 . . . . **2.00**
Book, *Tale of Flopsy Bunnies,* Peter Rabbit, 1988 . . . . **10.00**
Button, Hamburglar, plastic, clip–on, Olympic Sports,
   1988. . . . . **3.00**
Car, Archie sitting, New Archies, 1988 . . . . **4.00**
Car, Cargo Climber Van, Mighty Mini's, 1990. . . . . **3.00**
Car, Corvette, white, red stripe, Barbie/Hot Wheels, 1990 . . . . **12.00**
Car, Fraggle Rock, 1988 . . . . **2.50**
Character Glass, Happiness Hotel Bus, 1981 . . . . **2.00**
Character Glass, Miss Piggy riding motorcycle, 1981 . . . . **2.50**
Comb, plastic, Ronald McDonald . . . . **.75**
Comic Book, McDonaldland Comic Book, #101, 1976. . . . . . . **25.00**
Cookie Cutter, plastic, Fry Kid on unicycle, 1987 . . . . **5.00**
Cup Holder, dark blue, orig package **2.50**
Doll, Hamburglar **20.00**
Figure, Baloo the Bear, windup, Jungle Book, 1989 . . . . **3.00**

Figure, Barney, Flintstone Kids, 1988 . . . . **3.25**
Figure, Changeables, Robocakes, 1988 . . . . **2.50**
Figure, farmer, Old McDonald's Farm. **3.00**
Figure, Flounder water squirter, Little Mermaid, 1989 . . . . **3.00**
Figure, Kissyfur Lennie/Hog, 1985 . . . . **6.00**
Figure, Raggedy Ann, with swing, 1989 . . . . **5.00**
Figure, safari rhino, Safari Adventure Meal, 1980 . . . . **1.00**
Figure, Simon, with movie camera, Alvin and the
    Chipmunks, 1990 . . . . **4.00**
Figure, Skull, Runaway Robots, 1988. . . . . **5.00**
Figure, Snoopy's Hay Hauler, Peanuts, 1989. . . . . **2.50**
Figure, Stegosaurus, Dinosaur Days, Diener Industry, 1981 . . . . **2.00**
Figure, whale, Undersea Series, raised head and tail,
    mkd "Diener," 1980 . . . . **1.00**
Fireman Happy Hat, molded plastic, red, Ronald
    McDonald, 1990. . . . . **4.50**
Happy Meal Box, Bedtime, pillow fight, 1988 . . . . **2.50**
Happy Meal Box, Bigfoot, 1987. . . . . **3.00**
Happy Meal Box, Funny Furry Friends, 1989 . . . . **1.50**
Happy Meal Box, Little Mermaid. **3.00**
Happy Meal Box, Olympic Sports '86, Hilarious
    Hurdles, 1988. . . . . **3.00**
Happy Meal Box, Stomper Mini 4 x 4's, Jalopy Jump,
    1986. . . . . **3.00**
Happy Meal Pail, Halloween, McPunkin, 1986 . . . . **1.00**
Happy Meal Pail, Treasure Hunt, plastic, sand sifter lid,
    red rake, 1986 . . . . **4.00**
Harmonica, McDonaldland Band, red, 1986 . . . . **2.50**
Lego, sea eagle seaplane, Lego Motion, orig package,
    1989. . . . . **3.00**
Lunch Box, plastic, blue, Ronald in school house, On
    the Go, 1988 . . . . **3.00**
Magazine, *McDonaldland Fun Times*, 1984 to present **2.00**
Magni Finder, hidden case trick with Ronald McDonald,
    Birdie, and Fry Guy, 1983 . . . . **7.00**
Music Box, figural restaurant, plays "Good Times/Good
    Taste" theme when front door is opened, orig package **18.00**
Pin, 1984 Olympics, brass, red, yellow, blue, and white,
    inscribed "Ronald and Sam," 1⅞" w. **3.00**
Pinback Button, "I Guarantee It's Fast" **2.00**
Record, *One Million Dollar Menu*, 1988 . . . . **5.00**
Ring, plastic, Hamburglar, 1977. . . . . **3.00**
Soccer Ball, red and yellow, 1989 . . . . **3.00**

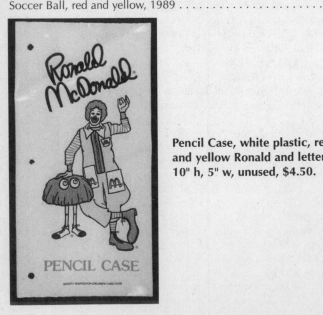

Pencil Case, white plastic, red and yellow Ronald and lettering, 10" h, 5" w, unused, $4.50.

Sport Bottle, green, red basketballs **2.25**
Stuffed Animals, Sea World of Texas Whale, black and
    white, 1988 . . . . **5.00**
Tote Bag, Hamburglar, fabric, red, pale blue vinyl edge,
    "Ronald McDonald Tote Bags" tag with 1982 copy-
    right **18.00**
T–Shirt, *Batman Returns* **10.00**
Visor, cloth, patch on front **1.50**
Wallet, wrist type, Capt Crook, plastic, green, bracelet
    with compartment to carry coins **1.00**
Watering Can, red and yellow, Ronald, Little Gardener,
    1989. . . . . **2.00**
Whistle, Tootler. **2.00**

MCKEE GLASS

McKee and Brothers was founded in Pittsburgh, Pennsylvania, in 1853. In 1888 the factory moved to Jeannette, Pennsylvania. The company reorganized in 1903, renaming itself the McKee Glass Company. It manufactured a wide range of household and industrial glassware. McKee introduced its Glasbake line in the 1910s.

The company is best known for its crystal pressed patterns, Depression glass kitchenware, and opaque ware. Tableware lines in color were first made in the early 1920s. Many older clear patterns, e.g., Aztec and Rock Crystal Flower, became available in color. Between 1923 and the late 1930s, new colors were added to the line each year. The popularity of the colorful opaque ware, made between 1930 and 1940, helped the company weather the hard times of the Depression.

In 1951 Thatcher Glass Company purchased McKee, selling it in 1961 to the Jeannette Glass Corporation. Upon purchasing McKee, Jeannette Glass Corporation closed the manufacturing operations at its plant and moved them to the McKee factory.

References: Gene Florence, *Kitchen Glassware of the Depression Years, 5th Edition,* Collector Books, 1995, 1997 value update; Gene Florence, *Very Rare Glassware of the Depression Years, Fifth Series,* Collector Books, 1997.

Note: For additional listings see Kitchen Glassware and Reamers.

Baker, Skokie green, oval, 7" l **$16.00**
Batter Bowl, 7" d, Seville yellow **24.00**
Batter Jug, crystal **30.00**
Batter Jug, red **115.00**
Beater Bowl, with spout, 6½", jadeite. **21.00**
Bowl, jadeite, 9" **30.00**
Bowl, 4¼" d, Seville yellow. **14.00**
Butter, cov, Chalaine blue **75.00**
Butter, cov, Seville yellow **65.00**
Casserole, cov, 10½" l, pearl **50.00**
Cereal Canister, cov, round, custard **50.00**
Coffee Canister, cov, square, Skokie green **165.00**
Condiment Set, "Cinnamon," "Ginger," "Nutmeg," cus-
    tard, metal lids, orig rack **50.00**
Custard Cup, Skokie green **5.00**
Daisy and Button, clock, tambour shape, 8" h, 7" w,
    Skokie green **65.00**
Decanter Set, decanter and 6 whiskey glasses, pink, ring
    dec. **115.00**
Dots, butter dish, cov, 1 lb, red on white **35.00**
Dots, mixing bowl, 9" d, red on white **35.00**
Drip Jar, cov, spout, 3½" h, custard **18.00**

Egg Beater Bowl, Skokie green........................ **10.00**
Eggcup, custard................................. **15.00**
Eggcup, French ivory............................. **5.00**
Flour Shaker, square, Skokie green................ **25.00**
Flower Band, bowl, 9¹/₂" d, Skokie green **18.00**
Frizz Bowl...................................... **38.00**
Glasbake, measure, 1 cup, white.................... **40.00**
Glasbake, tea kettle, crystal...................... **15.00**
Laurel, berry bowl, 4³/₄", jade green.................. **6.50**
Laurel, candlestick, pr, French ivory................. **35.00**
Laurel, cereal bowl, 6" d, French ivory............... **10.00**
Laurel, cheese dish, cov, French ivory **50.00**
Laurel, creamer, short, jade green **10.00**
Laurel, cup, French ivory.......................... **7.00**
Laurel, dinner plate, white opal, 9¹/₈" d **15.00**
Laurel, grill plate, scalloped edge, jade green, 10³/₄" d **12.00**
Laurel, platter, 8 x 11", Skokie green............... **15.00**
Laurel, salad plate, 7¹/₄" d, Poudre blue **14.00**
Laurel, salt and pepper shakers, pr, jade green **60.00**
Laurel, sherbet, Skokie green...................... **12.00**
Laurel, soup bowl, French ivory..................... **35.00**
Laurel, sugar, short, French ivory **9.00**
Laurel, tumbler, flat, 12 oz, 5" h, French ivory **50.00**
Measuring Cup, 4 cup, Skokie green **35.00**
Measuring Pitcher, 2 cup, Skokie green **40.00**
Mixing Bowl, white, red ship dec.................... **18.00**
Nappy, Seville yellow **7.50**
Reamer, French ivory............................. **50.00**
Reamer, grapefruit, Seville yellow **175.00**
Reamer, pointed top, jadeite **45.00**
Reamer, Seville yellow **165.00**
Refrigerator Dish, cov, 4 x 5", Seville yellow............. **35.00**
Refrigerator Dish, cov, 8 x 5", Skokie green **16.00**
Refrigerator Dish, cov, white, red ship dec.............. **18.00**
Rock Crystal, bonbon, scalloped edge, red............. **60.00**
Rock Crystal, bread and butter plate, scalloped edge,
   6" d, red **15.00**
Rock Crystal, bowl, 4" d, crystal.................... **15.00**
Rock Crystal, bowl, 9¹/₄" d, milk glass, orig label.......... **55.00**
Rock Crystal, bowl, scalloped edge, 4" d, crystal **10.00**

Rock Crystal, bread and butter plate, scalloped edge,
   red, 6" d **20.00**
Rock Crystal, butter lid, crystal..................... **135.00**
Rock Crystal, cake stand, green.................... **50.00**
Rock Crystal, candlestick, 8¹/₄" h, ruby **65.00**
Rock Crystal, candy dish, cov, ftd, crystal............. **60.00**
Rock Crystal, celery bowl, 12" l, crystal............... **28.00**
Rock Crystal, champagne, ftd, 6 oz, crystal **16.00**
Rock Crystal, cheese and cracker set, ruby **160.00**
Rock Crystal, cocktail, ftd, 3¹/₂ oz **20.00**
Rock Crystal, comport, amber **50.00**
Rock Crystal, cordial, 1 oz........................ **25.00**
Rock Crystal, creamer and sugar, ftd, crystal........... **40.00**
Rock Crystal, cup, crystal, 7 oz **18.00**
Rock Crystal, dinner plate, plain edge, 9" d, crystal......... **18.00**
Rock Crystal, dinner plate, scalloped edge, 10¹/₂" d,
   crystal **40.00**
Rock Crystal, goblet, crystal....................... **20.00**
Rock Crystal, jelly, ftd, scalloped edge, red, 5" h........ **52.00**
Rock Crystal, oil cruet, stopper, 6 oz, crystal **95.00**
Rock Crystal, parfait, ftd, low, crystal, 3¹/₄ oz **25.00**
Rock Crystal, pitcher, scalloped edge, 1 qt, crystal **165.00**
Rock Crystal, punch bowl stand, crystal **195.00**
Rock Crystal, salad bowl, scalloped edge, 8" d, crystal **35.00**
Rock Crystal, sandwich server, crystal **30.00**
Rock Crystal, saucer, red **22.00**
Rock Crystal, server, red, center handle **130.00**
Rock Crystal, sugar, cov, crystal.................... **30.00**
Rock Crystal, sundae, ftd, 6 oz, crystal............... **15.00**
Rock Crystal, vase, cornucopia, crystal............... **60.00**
Rock Crystal, vase, ftd, crystal, 11 oz **60.00**
Rock Crystal, whiskey, 2¹/₄" h...................... **15.00**
Rock Crystal, wine **40.00**
Rolling Pin, Chalaine blue **375.00**
Snack Tray, jadeite.............................. **30.00**
Tom and Jerry, bowl, custard **50.00**
Tom and Jerry, mug, scroll red trim **2.00**
Tom and Jerry, punch bowl set, bowl and 6 mugs, cus-
   tard....................................... **150.00**
Tom and Jerry Set, serving bowl, 12 cups, red on white..... **100.00**
Towel Bar, Skokie green **25.00**
Water Dispenser, cov, Skokie green, 4" h, orig spigot **90.00**
Water Dispenser, cov, white........................ **100.00**

**Sugar Shaker, Ships, red
on white, $20.00.**

MEDICAL ITEMS

Doctors are the primary collectors of medical apparatus and instruments. Most collect material that relates to their medical specialty. Medical apparatus and instruments are sold by specialist dealers or auctions. This is why so little medical material is found at flea markets and antiques malls, shops, and shows.

Office furniture, especially large wooden storage cabinets with unusual drawer configurations, are popular in the general antiques marketplace. The same holds true for wall charts, ranging from the standard eye examination chart to those dealing with anatomy.

Pharmaceutical items divide into two groups: (1) items used by druggists to prepare medicines and (2) packaging associated with over–the–counter and doctor–prescribed medications. There is little added value if the contents are intact. In fact, most collectors prefer that they are not.

Collectors' Club: Medical Collectors Assoc, Montefiore Medical Park, 1695A Eastchester Rd, Bronx, NY 10461.

Note: See Drugstore for additional listings.

Book, *Mould Guide for Trubyte New Hue Teeth*, The
Dentist's Supply Company of New York, American,
1920s **$125.00**
Bottle, W H Bull's Vegetable Worm Syrup, W H Bull
Medicine Co, St Louis, MO, orig cardboard box, full
syrup bottle **20.00**
Capsule Filler, Sharpe and Dohme, chrome, instruction
book, orig wood box, 8 x 16" **150.00**
Chemist's Scale, brass and steel, oak box with drawers,
glazed top and sides, Becker's Sons, Rotterdam **225.00**
Dental, Dissolving Cups, set of 2, porcelain, for anes-
thesia, Novol, flared, int line measures, twisted wire
holder, paper on monocaine tabs, orig box, c1940 . . . . **48.00**
Quack Body Roller, Art Deco, green Bakelite ribbed
molded handles, shiny graduated metal end pcs,
black rubber grooved roller, orig box, c1930 . . . . **75.00**
Rectal Medicine, The Inside Story, Medicone Co, NY,
tan, red, full professional sample packet, 1950s **5.50**
Sign, Pepto Bismol, figural bottle, diecut cardboard, red
and black lettering **50.00**
Sleep Goggles, 2 oval Bakelite cups, emb dark green
lenses, elastic strap, "Non Flam–Porta–made in
England," c1930s **15.00**

MELMAC

Thermosetting plastics, principally melamine resins, were used to make dinnerware. Melamine resins result from the interaction of melamine and formaldehyde. A chemical reaction creating permanent hardness occurs when thermosetting plastics are heated.

Melmac is a trade name of American Cyanamid. Like Kleenex and Xerox, it soon became a generic term describing an entire line of products.

The first plastic dinnerware was used in cafeterias, hospitals, restaurants, and other institutional settings. Melamine dinnerware's popularity waned in the early 1960s. Repeated washing caused fading and dullness. Edges chipped, knives scratched surfaces, and foods left stains. Pieces placed too close to heat discolored or scarred. Many early 1960s designs were too delicate. Pieces actually broke. The final death blow came from the import of inexpensive Asian and European ceramic dinnerware in the late 1960s and early 1970s.

Reference: Gregory R. Zimmer and Alvin Daigle, Jr., *Melmac Dinnerware*, L–W Book Sales, 1997.

Collectors' Club: Melmac Collectors Club, 6802 Glenkirk Rd, Baltimore, MD 21239.

Note: Price listed for Melmac in mint condition.

ABC Manufacturing Co, cup, yellow **$1.00**
Air Flite, salad plate, green **2.00**
Apollo Ware, serving bowl **4.00**
Aztec, cup and saucer, turquoise **2.00**
Aztec, cereal bowl, blue **2.00**
Aztec, creamer and sugar, pink **4.00**
Aztec, dinner plate, mustard yellow **2.00**
Aztec, salad bowl, gray **2.00**
Aztec, serving bowl, divided, mustard yellow **4.00**
Boonton, butter, cov, stone gray **10.00**

Watertown, Lifetime ware, designed by Jon Hedu, introduced 1947: Black creamer, $4.00; cups, Caribbean blue and white, price each, $2.00.

Boonton, casserole, cov, pewter gray **20.00**
Boonton, cereal bowl, cranberry red **5.00**
Boonton, gravy boat, powder blue **6.00**
Boonton, jug, cov, seafoam green **20.00**
Boonton, mixing bowl, tawny buff **8.00**
Boonton, salad tongs, cranberry red **12.00**
Boonton, tidbit tray, 3 tier, forest green **15.00**
Boontonware, cup and saucer, powder blue **3.00**
Boontonware, serving dish, oblong, tawny buff **8.00**
Branchell, dinner plate, Golden Grapes **4.00**
Branchell, dinner plate, Sweet Talk **4.00**
Branchell, fruit bowl, glade green **3.00**
Branchell, gravy boat, glow copper **6.00**
Branchell, salad plate, spray lime **4.00**
Branchell, soup bowl, cov, charcoal **5.00**
Branchell, vegetable, divided, mist gray **8.00**
Branchell Royale, salt and pepper shakers, turquoise **6.00**
Branchell Royale, tumbler, glow copper, 6 oz **10.00**
Brookpark Arrowhead, cup, black **2.00**
Brookpark Arrowhead, dinner plate, divided, burgundy **4.00**
Brookpark Arrowhead, sugar, cov, turquoise **6.00**
Brookpark Arrowhead, tidbit tray, 2 tier, Town and
Country **12.00**
Brookpark Modern Design, cup and saucer, Tropicana **3.00**
Debonaire, cereal bowl, white **2.00**
Debonaire, dinner plate, rust red **2.00**
Debonaire, serving bowl, pink **4.00**
Debonaire, tumbler, turquoise, 10 oz **6.00**
Flite Lane, bread and butter plate, green, brown flecks **1.00**
Flite Lane, dinner plate, red–orange **2.00**
Flite Lane, tumbler, yellow, brown flecks, 6 oz **6.00**
Fostoria, bread and butter plate, Golden Twilight **3.00**
Fostoria, cereal bowl, gray **7.00**
Fostoria, relish tray, sky blue **15.00**
Fostoria, serving bowl, Blue Meadow **15.00**
Fostoria, serving bowl, divided, gray **15.00**
Fostoria, sugar, cov, harvest yellow **12.00**
Harmony House, bread and butter plate, chartreuse **2.00**
Harmony House, butter, cov, spice beige **10.00**
Harmony House, casserole, cov, Catalina **20.00**
Harmony House, dinner plate, Avalon, blue **4.00**
Harmony House, salt and pepper shakers, pr, bronze green . . . **6.00**

Holiday, creamer, white, brown flecks **5.00**
Holiday, dinner plate, turquoise, brown flecks **4.00**
Holiday, fruit bowl, yellow, brown flecks **3.00**
Holiday, serving bowl, divided, red, brown flecks. **8.00**
Imperial Ware, creamer, dark green **5.00**
Imperial Ware, dinner plate, speckled turquoise **4.00**
Imperial Ware, salad plate, speckled yellow **4.00**
Lucent, cup and saucer, pale yellow **8.00**
Lucent, dinner plate, white **6.00**
Lucent, serving bowl, divided, April in Paris **15.00**
Mallo–Ware, creamer, light green **1.00**
Mallo–Ware, dinner plate, avocado **2.00**
Mallo–Ware, gravy boat, Moonglow **5.00**
Mallo–Ware, salt and pepper shakers, pr, yellow **4.00**
Mallo–Ware, soup bowl, beige **3.00**
Mar–Crest, creamer and sugar, turquoise **4.00**
Mar–Crest, dinner plate, yellow. **2.00**
Mar–Crest, serving bowl, divided, pastel blue. **4.00**
Mar–Crest, tumbler, pink, 10 oz. **7.00**
Monte Carlo, cup and saucer, mustard yellow **2.00**
Monte Carlo, dinner plate, mustard yellow. **2.00**
Prolon, cup and saucer, Cadence. **3.00**
Prolon, dinner plate, Ponderosa. **4.00**
Prolon, salad plate, Grant Crest **4.00**
Prolon, salt and pepper shakers, Florence. **6.00**
Restraware, fruit bowl **1.00**
Royalon, bread and butter plate, purple. **1.00**
Royalon, dinner plate, Aristocrat **2.00**
Royalon, soup bowl, San Marino. **3.00**

METLOX

In 1927 T. C. Prouty and Willis, his son, established Metlox Pottery, Manhattan Beach, California, primarily for the purpose of making ceramic outdoor signs. When business declined during the Depression and T. C. died in 1931, Willis converted the plant to the production of ceramic dinnerware. Brightly colored California Pottery was the company's first offering. Between 1934 and the early 1940s, Metlox produced its Poppytrail line of kitchenware and tableware. In 1936 the company adopted the poppy, California's state flower, as its trademark.

Designer Carl Romanelli, who joined Metlox in the late 1930s, created Metlox's miniature line and the Modern Masterpiece line that included bookends, figural vases, figurines, and wall pockets.

The company shifted to war production during the early 1940s. California Ivy, Metlox's first painted dinnerware, was introduced in 1946. That same year, Willis Prouty sold Metlox to Evan Shaw, owner of American Pottery, Los Angeles, a company under contract to Disney for ceramic figurines. Production of Disney figurines continued until 1956. In the 1960s and 70s, Metlox made Colorstax (solid color dinnerware), cookie jars, and Poppet (stoneware flower holders and planters).

In 1958 Metlox purchased Vernon Kiln. The company's Vernon Kiln division made artware in the 1950s and 60s, American Royal Horses, and Nostalgia, a scale model carriage line.

Shaw died in 1980. His family continued the business for another decade, ending operations in 1989.

References: Carl Gibbs, Jr., *Collector's Encyclopedia of Metlox Potteries,* Collector Books, 1995; Harry L. Rinker, *Dinnerware of the 20th Century: The Top 500 Patterns,* House of Collectibles, 1997.

Antique Grape, coffee canister. **$75.00**
Antique Grape, coffeepot, cov **80.00**
Antique Grape, compote **80.00**
Antique Grape, dinner plate **25.00**
Antique Grape, flour canister. **95.00**
Antique Grape, platter, oval, 12¹/₂" l **25.00**
Antique Grape, salt and pepper shakers, pr **30.00**
Antique Grape, sugar canister **85.00**
Antique Grape, tea canister **65.00**
Antique Grape, vegetable, 8¹/₂" d **40.00**
Blue Danube, coaster **5.00**
California Confetti, fruit bowl **12.00**
California Confetti, place setting **50.00**
California Confetti, soup bowl **22.00**
California Ivy, creamer **17.00**
California Ivy, dinner plate, 10³/₈" d **15.00**
California Ivy, pitcher, 9¹/₄" h **60.00**
California Ivy, serving bowl, round. **40.00**
California Provincial, bread tray, 9³/₄" d **40.00**
California Provincial, coffeepot, cov. **120.00**
California Provincial, condiment shakers, pr. **40.00**
California Provincial, flour canister **105.00**
California Provincial, lug soup. **25.00**
California Provincial, luncheon plate, 9" d **20.00**
California Provincial, salad plate, 7¹/₂" d **15.00**
California Provincial, salt and pepper shakers, pr **30.00**
California Provincial, sugar canister **95.00**
California Provincial, tea canister. **75.00**
California Strawberry, canister, large. **25.00**
California Strawberry, canister, small **15.00**
California Strawberry, coffeepot, cov **60.00**
California Strawberry, creamer. **20.00**
California Strawberry, dinner plate. **6.00**
California Strawberry, gravy, fast stand **20.00**
California Strawberry, lug cereal bowl, 7" d **12.00**
California Strawberry, pitcher, 4¹/₂" h **30.00**
California Strawberry, platter, 11". **15.00**
California Strawberry, vegetable, 8" d **30.00**
Colonial Homestead, coffeepot, cov. **120.00**

Homestead Provincial, dinner plate, oatmeal, 10" d, $15.00.

Colonial Homestead, teapot, cov, chip inside lid 50.00
Della Robbia, butter, cov, ¼ lb 70.00
Della Robbia, creamer 25.00
Della Robbia, cup and saucer 15.00
Della Robbia, dinner plate. 15.00
Della Robbia, luncheon plate, 9" 22.00
Della Robbia, mug 20.00
Della Robbia, plate, 7½" 12.00
Della Robbia, salt and pepper shakers, pr, 4½" 85.00
Della Robbia, saucer. 5.00
Della Robbia, sugar, cov 35.00
Della Robbia, teapot, cov 100.00
Homestead Provincial, bread and butter plate, blue 5.00
Homestead Provincial, bread server, blue. 35.00
Homestead Provincial, bread server, oatmeal 50.00
Homestead Provincial, butter, cov, blue 50.00
Homestead Provincial, casserole, cov, hen lid, 9", blue. 20.00
Homestead Provincial, cereal bowl, oatmeal 14.00
Homestead Provincial, chicken lid, oatmeal color, 5½". 75.00
Homestead Provincial, chop plate, oatmeal 55.00
Homestead Provincial, cocoa mug, blue 18.00
Homestead Provincial, coffee canister, blue 60.00
Homestead Provincial, coffee pot, cov, blue. 95.00
Homestead Provincial, coffee pot, cov, oatmeal 95.00
Homestead Provincial, creamer, cov, blue 25.00
Homestead Provincial, cruets, oil and vinegar, blue,
    wood tray 100.00
Homestead Provincial, cup and saucer, blue 16.00
Homestead Provincial, cup and saucer, oatmeal 16.00
Homestead Provincial, cup, blue. 7.00
Homestead Provincial, cup, oatmeal 10.00
Homestead Provincial, flour canister, blue 75.00
Homestead Provincial, fruit bowl, blue 8.00
Homestead Provincial, fruit bowl, oatmeal. 12.00
Homestead Provincial, gravy, blue, 1 pt 20.00
Homestead Provincial, lug soup, blue 20.00
Homestead Provincial, lug soup, oatmeal. 22.00
Homestead Provincial, luncheon plate, blue. 20.00
Homestead Provincial, mug, oatmeal. 22.00
Homestead Provincial, relish, divided, handle, blue 60.00
Homestead Provincial, rim soup, blue, 8½" 20.00
Homestead Provincial, salad bowl, blue, 11" 60.00
Homestead Provincial, salad plate, blue. 12.00
Homestead Provincial, salt and pepper shakers, pr, blue 25.00
Homestead Provincial, salt and pepper shakers, pr, han-
    dled, oatmeal 28.00
Homestead Provincial, saucer, blue 5.00
Homesteaad Provincial, shaker, blue 12.00
Homestead Provincial, soup bowl, blue 16.00
Homestead Provincial, sugar canister, blue. 60.00
Homestead Provincial, sugar, cov, blue 25.00
Homestead Provincial, tea canister, blue 50.00
Homestead Provincial, turkey platter, blue 250.00
Homestead Provincial, vegetable, cov, blue 40.00
Homestead Provincial, vegetable, open, blue, 8" d 23.00
La Mancha Gold, dinner plate. 12.00
La Mancha Gold, platter, 11¾" l 25.00
Nasturtium, bread and butter plate, 6" 2.50
Nasturtium, salad plate, 7" 3.00
Nasturtium, cup and saucer. 5.00
Nasturtium, gravy boat and stand. 22.00
Nasturtium, butter dish, oval 22.00
Nasturtium, coffee set, coffeepot, creamer, and sugar 70.00
Poppytrail, Aztec, platter, oval, 13" l. 45.00

Provincial Blue, bread and butter plate 8.00
Provincial Blue, chop plate, 12". 35.00
Provincial Blue, cup and saucer. 18.00
Provincial Blue, salad plate 12.50
Provincial Blue, vegetable, 10" 35.00
Red Rooster, casserole, small 75.00
Red Rooster, coffee canister. 65.00
Red Rooster, cup and saucer 17.00
Red Rooster, eggcup 20.00
Red Rooster, flour canister 75.00
Red Rooster, sugar canister 70.00
Red Rooster, tea canister 60.00

MILK BOTTLES

Hervey Thatcher is recognized as the father of the glass milk bottle. Patents are one of the best research sources for information about early milk bottles. A. V. Whiteman received a milk bottle patent as early as 1880. Patent recipients leased or sold their patents to manufacturers. The golden age of the glass milk bottle spans from the year 1910 to 1950.

Milk bottles are collected by size: gill (quarter pint), half pint, ten ounces (third of a quart), pint, quart, half gallon (two quarts), and gallon.

Paper cartons first appeared in the early 1920s and 30s and achieved popularity after 1950. The late 1950s witnessed the arrival of plastic bottles. Today, few dairies use glass bottles.

References: John Tutton, *Udderly Beautiful: A Pictorial Guide to the Pyroglazed or Painted Milk Bottle,* published by author, no date; John Tutton, *Udderly Delightful: Collecting Milk Bottles & Related Items,* published by author, 1994.

Newsletter: *The Udder Collectibles,* HC73 Box 1, Smithville Flats, NY 13841

Collectors' Club: National Assoc of Milk Bottle Collectors, Inc, 4 Ox Bow Rd, Westport, CT 06880.

B & C Dairy, Pasteurized Milk, Phone 166, Havre, MT,
    "Those who know choose B & C," black ground, little
    boy pouring from giant bottle for little girl,
    tall, round, pyroglazed, 1 qt $42.00
Bridgeman–Russell, Hancock, MI, Purity Brandy Pasteur-
    ized Milk & Cream, emb, tall, round 9, 1 qt 38.00
Chestnut Farms Dairy, Washington, DC, emb logo,
    ribbed shoulder and neck, 1 pt 25.00
Cloverleaf Dairy, Everett, WI, "You can whip our cream
    but you can't beat our milk," large clover leaf, tall,
    round, green pyroglaze, 1 qt 38.00
Columbia Dairy, Columbia, SC, "Drink Columbia
    Dairies Milk, Columbia, SC," and "Eat Columbia
    Dairies Ice Cream Homemade for Home Trade,
    Columbia, SC," round, green pyroglaze, ½ pt 20.00
Elnog Dairy, Coastesville, PA, "It Whips" on cream top,
    emb, round 4, 1 qt 35.00
Ennes Dairy, H Zupke, Greeley, CO, round, black
    pyroglaze, 1 qt 45.00
Farmers Cooperative Creamery, Fairmont, MN, "For
    Health Milk," round, red pyroglaze, 1 qt. 55.00
Forest Hill Dairy, Memphis, TN, "Cream Top Milk It's
    Pasteurized," cream top, round, blue pyroglaze, ½ pt 50.00
Frasure–Brown, Logan, OH, emb, ½ pt 25.00

Bangor Sanitary Dairy, Bangor, PA, emb, ¹/₂ pt, $12.00.

Freeman's Milk, Best by Test, "A Healthy Nation is a Strong Nation, Milk the Nation Builder," outline of US map with Uncle Sam drinking glass of milk, heavy red ground, tall, round, pyroglazed, 1 qt 75.00

Garden Farm Dairy, Denver, CO, "Polar Bear Ice Cream, made by Garden Farm Dairy, Denver," emb, rising sun, icebergs, and polar bears, orange and blue pyroglaze, ¹/₂ pt................................... 48.00

Himes Dairy, Eaton, OH, 1 qt 45.00

Lueck Dairy, Liverpool, NY, cow bellowing "Good Morning," "Better quality and service, visit our Ice Cream Bar," orange pyroglaze, 1 pt 38.00

Model Dairy, Huron, SD, "Taste the Difference" banner with Guernsey cow's head, "A Delicious Drink, A Nutritious Food, Pasteurized," tall, round, red pyroglaze, 1 qt 78.00

New England Creamery Co, Livermore Falls, ME, "New England Milk," Jersey cow's head, tall, round, black pyroglaze, 1 qt 32.00

Poinsettia Dairy Products, Florida, ¹/₂ pt 15.00

Racy Creamery, Knoxville, TN, bowling pin shape, emb, full length ribs, 1 pt.................................. 28.00

Ridgeview Farms, Finer Dairy Products, Chicago, IL, "Food Fights Too, use it wisely," "Plan all meals for Victory" in shield, and "Balance your meals with Milk" at bottom, woman serving platter of food, tall, round, pyroglazed, 1 qt 65.00

Riverview Dairy Farm, Rock Hills, SC, round, ¹/₂ pt......... 20.00

Rock Castle Dairy, Guernsey Milk, Lynchburg, VA, cow's head on front, barn on back, round, green pyroglaze, 1 qt 45.00

Ross Corner Dairy, Derry, NJ, large script "R," cow's head on label, orange pyroglaze, 1 pt................. 32.00

Sardis Creamery, Sardis, MI, Grade A Pasteurized, emb, round 9, 1 qt....................................... 35.00

Selected Dairies, Inc, Winston–Salem NC, round, red pyroglaze, 1 qt 35.00

Supreme Dairy, Peru, IL, "Baby's Choice," baby in crib with bottle, tall, round, blue pyroglaze................ 24.00

Terry Dairy Co, Little Rock, AK, Pasteurized Milk & Cream, emb, tall, round 9, 1 qt 35.00

Topaz Dairy, Hastings, NE, "Topaz Cottage good with any salad" and cottage cheese salad, Grade A Pasteurized Milk and Sweet Cream Butter, tall, round, red pyroglaze, 1 qt 42.00

Valley Gold, "Albuquerque's Favorite Milk, Both defend your home Against all Enemies, Against Ill–Health," milkman carrying tray of bottles, marching side by side with armed infantrymen, tall, round, red pyroglaze, 1 qt 55.00

White Way Pure Milk Co, Decatur, AL, round, 1 pt......... 20.00

MILK GLASS

Opaque white glass, also known as milk glass, enjoyed its greatest popularity in the period immediately prior to World War I when firms such as Atterbury, Challinor–Taylor, Flaccus, and McKee made a wide range of dinnerware, figural, household, kitchenware, and novelty forms. Despite the decline in popularity of milk glass during the 1920s, several manufacturers continued its production, especially for kitchenware and decorative novelty items.

Milk glass enjoyed a brief renaissance extending from the early 1940s through the early 1960s. Most milk glass offered for sale in today's market dates after 1940 and was produced by Fenton, Imperial, Kemple, and Westmoreland.

References: Everett Grist, *Covered Animal Dishes*, Collector Books, 1988, 1993 value update; Betty and Bill Newbound, *Collector's Encyclopedia of Milk Glass*, Collector Books, 1995.

Collectors' Club: National Milk Glass Collectors Society, 46 Almond Dr, Hershey, PA 17033.

Note: For more information and additional listings see Fenton, Imperial, Kemple, and Westmoreland.

Ash Receiver Tray, emb cigar and matches, white, 8¹/₄" l, 3¹/₂" w....................................... $45.00

Ashtray, grape, white, painted floral dec.................. 2.50

Bud Vase, hand held–torch, white, ³/₄" h, price for 2 .... 30.00

Candy Container, suitcase, tin closure, white 65.00

Cardholder, terrier, white............................. 35.00

Compote, cactus, white, 5⁵/₈" h 5.00

Compote, open hand, white 35.00

Creamer and Sugar, cov, cord and tassel, white 30.00

Creamer and Sugar, cov, strawberry, white 80.00

Creamer and Sugar, cov, swan, orig paint, white........ 70.00

Cup, swan, white 17.50

Dish, cov, artichoke, white 50.00

Dish, cov, American Hen, "Patent Applied For," white, 6¹/₂" l 45.00

Dish, cov, British Lion, white 150.00

Dish, cov, chick and eggs, round lacy base, mkd "patd Aug 6, 1889," white 225.00

Dish, cov, covered wagon, 5–ribbed frame, white, 6" l 190.00

Dish, cov, crawfish, finial, octagonal base, tab handles, white 200.00

Dish, cov, cruiser ship, white.......................... 25.00

Dish, cov, dog, pointing, possibly Flaccus, standing in grassy field, white, 6⁵/₈" l 325.00

Dish, cov, duck on wavy base, orig paint, white 200.00

Dish, cov, Easter egg, rabbit finial, white, 4³/₄" l 225.00

Dish, cov, elephant, walking, white 250.00

Dish, cov, hen on basket, master salt, 2 handles, white **10.00**
Dish, cov, monkey on grass mound, leaf and scroll base,
    white, 6¼" l **1,800.00**
Dish, cov, Moses in the Bullrushes, white, 5½" l **300.00**
Dish, cov, turtle, knobby shell lid, white, 9½" l **230.00**
Eggcup, chick, light blue **20.00**
Eggcup, chick, orig paint, white **20.00**
Hen on Nest, black, 5½" l **70.00**
Jar, cov, Queen Victoria, white, 8" h **80.00**
Jar, cov, Scottie dog lid, white **50.00**
Lady's Shoe, blue, gold floral dec **15.00**
Match Safe, Bible, blue **25.00**
Match Safe, butterfly, white **25.00**
Match Safe, Fleur–De–Lis, blue **30.00**
Match Safe, hanging, Indian Chief, white **60.00**
Mug, child's, bird and wheat, white **5.00**
Mug, child's, duck and swan, white **20.00**
Mug, bird and wheat, light pink **2.00**
Mug, cat with mouse, purple marble slag **5.00**
Mug, elk, white **10.00**
Mustard, steer head, tongue spoon, orig paint, white **175.00**
Pin Box, cov, horseshoe, white **40.00**
Pincushion, heart, orig paint, white **1.00**
Pin Dish, bird center, white, 4½" d **25.00**
Pin Tray, cov, girl with doll, white **40.00**
Pin Tray, cov, lion, white, 4¾ x 3½" **10.00**
Pitcher, grazing cows, white **80.00**
Plate, 3 kittens, white **15.00**
Plate, ABC border, white **35.00**
Plate, Angel and Harp, white, gold paint, 7½" l **7.50**
Plate, Easter Chicks, white **25.00**
Plate, Easter Greetings, horseshoe shape with rabbit and
    emerging chick, orig dec, white **60.00**
Plate, gothic border, central relief bust of William
    McKinley, orig gold dec, white, 9¼" d **110.00**
Plate, keyhole border, white **3.00**
Plate, open lattice border, gooseberry, dec, white,
    10½" d **10.00**

Plate, open lattice edge, floral painted center, white,
    10½" d **20.00**
Plate, rabbit and horseshoe, white **12.50**
Platter, notched, painted floral dec **25.00**
Salt, double, leaf design, perching bird handle, white,
    5½" l **50.00**
Salt, master, duck, light blue **15.00**
Salt, master, flying fish, white, orig paint dec, 4⅝" l **120.00**
Salt, master, turtle, blue **70.00**
Salt and Pepper Shakers, pr, bird, handled, white **75.00**
Salt and Pepper Shakers, pr, boy with hat, white **190.00**
Salt and Pepper Shakers, pr, Isabella, orig dec, white **1,400.00**
Salt and Pepper Shakers, pr, owl, white **300.00**
Salt and Pepper Shakers, pr, rabbit, white **60.00**
Shaker, acorn, white **25.00**
Shaker, boy with hat, white **190.00**
Shaker, Columbus, white **450.00**
Sprinkler, white **30.00**
Syrup, open, floral painted, white **20.00**
Toothpick, frog with shell, white **50.00**
Toothpick, snake, blue stain design **25.00**
Tray, lion, handled, white, 5" w, 9" l **15.00**
Tray, scroll border, Alvord, IN souvenir, white **20.00**
Tumbler, actress head, white **25.00**
Vase, corn, white, gold dec, 4½" h **10.00**

MODEL KITS

Model kits break down into three basic types: (1) wood, (2) plastic, and (3) cast resin. Scratch–built wooden models, whether from magazine plans or model kits, achieved widespread popularity in the 1930s. Airplanes were the most popular form. Because of the skill levels involved, these were built primarily by teenagers.

England's 1/72 Frog Penguin kits of the mid–1930s were the first plastic model kits. After 1945, manufacturers utilized the new plastic injection molding process developed during World War II to produce large quantities of plastic model kits. Automobile model kits quickly replaced airplanes as the market favorite.

Model kits are sold by scale with 1/48, 1/72, and 1/144 among the most common. By the 1960s, some model kit manufacturers introduced snap–together models. The 1970s oil crisis significantly reduced production. However, the market fully recovered by the mid–1980s. While vehicles still dominate model kit sales, monster and other personality kits have gained in popularity.

Resin model kits are designed for the adult market. Gruesome monsters, scantily dressed women, and fantasy creatures abound.

Box art influences the value of a model kit, especially when the cover art is more spectacular than the assembled model. Surprisingly, collectors prefer unassembled models. If the model is assembled, its value declines by 50% or more.

References: Bill Bruegman, *Aurora: History and Price Guide, 3rd Edition,* Cap'n Penny Productions, 1996; Gordon Dutt, *Collectible Figure Kits of the 50's, 60's & 70's: Reference and Price Guide,* Gordy's Kit Builders Magazine, 1995; Thomas Graham, *Greenberg's Guide to Aurora Model Kits,* Kalmbach Books, 1998; Rick Polizzi, *Classic Plastic Model Kits: Identification & Value Guide,* Collector Books, 1996.

Collectors' Clubs: International Figure Kit Club, PO Box 201, Sharon Center, OH 44274; Kit Collectors International, PO Box 38, Stanton, CA 90680.

Dish, cov, resting camel, $220.00. Photo courtesy Gene Harris.

Visible V8 Engine, Renwal Blueprint Models, #802, 16 x 22 x 3", $35.00.

The Amazing Spiderman, Aurora, 1966, MIB **$375.00**

Archie's Car, Aurora, 1969, MIB **25.00**

Baron Von Richtoffen's Fokker DR–1 Triplane, metallic red, ¼ scale, air battle illus and news clipping with photo of Richtoffen on right side of box, Aurora, 1964 . . . . **20.00**

Batmobile Power Racer, motorized, AMT/Ertl, 1989 . . . . **65.00**

Brother Rat Fink, Revell, BIB **60.00**

Chance Vought F8U–1 Crusader Jet, Aurora, 1957 . . . . **20.00**

Chinese Mandarin, Aurora, MIB. **35.00**

Cobra and Lola Model Racing Car Set, Monogram, two ¹/₂₄ scale model race car shells, one blue Cobra, other green Lola, Tiger chassis, complete with tools, decals, X–acto oiler, trigger finger control, book of racing tips, 15 x 8" box, 1960s **50.00**

Creeping Crusher, Lindberg, MIB **60.00**

Daddy the Way–Out Suburbanite, Hawk, 1963, MIB **80.00**

Deep Sea Lobster, Superior Plastics, Inc, 1962, MIB **25.00**

Dodge Dart 440, Revell, Metalflake Custom Car, 1962, MIB **50.00**

Dr Deadly, Aurora, MIB. **75.00**

Ed "Big Daddy" Roth's Mr. Gasser Model, Revell, 1963 . . . . . **70.00**

Evel Knievel's Sky Cycle, Addar, MIB **55.00**

Flying Battle Plane Kit, Joe Ott Mfg Co, 1950s, MIB **30.00**

Frantic Cats, Hawk, 1965, MIB **80.00**

Gigantic Wasp Model Kit, Fundimensions, 8" wingspan, 1975, MIB. **30.00**

Gotha Bomber, Aurora, 1958, MIB. **25.00**

Hawk Silly Surfers, "Beach Bunny Catchin' Rays," missing instruction sheet, 1964. . . . . **50.00**

Hogan's Heroes Jeep, MPC, MIB **95.00**

The Incredible Hulk, MPC, 1978, MIB **50.00**

Indian Warrior, Pyro, MIB **65.00**

James Bond Aston Martin DB5, Airfax, 1965. . . . . **100.00**

Jaws, Addar, MIB. **100.00**

Joe Cool, Monogram, MIB **95.00**

Knight Rider Car, Knight 2000, MPC, MIB **50.00**

Krimson Terror, Lindberg, MIB **60.00**

Laurel & Hardy '25 T Roadster, AMT, MIB **45.00**

Mad Mangler, Lindberg, 1965 . . . . **50.00**

Meat Wagon, 37 Packard ambulance, Aurora, 1965 . . . . **60.00**

Mork & Mindy Jeep, Monogram, 1979, MIB. **30.00**

Monkee Mobile, Blue Printer Reissue Kit, Ertl. **85.00**

Night Crawler Wolfman Car, MPC, MIB **130.00**

1932 Skid–Doo, 1963, Aurora, MIB **30.00**

Paul Springfield "Bulldog," Pyro Plastics, 1960, MIB **25.00**

Planet of the Apes, Caesar, Addar, MIB. **50.00**

Prehistoric Scenes, "Tar Pit," complete with tree, vulture, and rhinoceros, Aurora, MIB **75.00**

Pushmi–Pullu, Aurora **75.00**

Rawhide Cowpuncher, 10" Gil Favor figure, Pyro Plastics, orig box,1958. . . . . **70.00**

Red Night of Vienna, Aurora, 1957, MIB **75.00**

Russian T–34 Tank, Revell, 1958, MIB **50.00**

Saber Tooth Tiger, Aurora, 1972, MIB **25.00**

Sick Cycle, Lindberg, MIB **100.00**

Silver Knight of Augsberg, Aurora, 1956, MIB. **50.00**

Sikorsky HO4S–1Helicopter, Revell, 1960, orig box **15.00**

Space: 1999 Eagle 1, MPC, 1975. **25.00**

Star Wars Darth Vader Van, MPC, 1977, MIB **25.00**

Star Wars Artoo–Detoo Van, MPC, MIB **25.00**

Superboy, Aurora, MIB **100.00**

Superman, Aurora, reissue, 1978 . . . . **45.00**

Vanguard at Cape Canaveral, Adams, 1958, MIB **75.00**

Walt Disney's Haunted Mansion, "Grave Robbers' Rewards," 1974, MPC, MIB **60.00**

Walt Disney's Peter Pan's Pirate Ship, Revell, 1969, MIB **75.00**

Weird–Ohs Endsville Eddie, 1963, MIB **75.00**

WWI British SE–5 Scout Airplane, Aurora, 1963 . . . . **25.00**

MONROE, MARILYN

Marilyn Monroe was born Norma Jean Mortenson in Los Angeles, California, on June 1, 1926. An illegitimate child, Marilyn spent her early years in a series of foster homes. She was only 16 when she married Jim Doughtery on June 19, 1942. While Jim was in the Merchant Marines, a photographer discovered Marilyn. She soon found work with the Blue Book Modeling Studio.

After a brief flirtation with the movies in 1947–48, Marilyn found herself without a contract. Her life changed dramatically after Tom Kelley's "Golden Dreams" photograph appeared in magazines and calendars across the nation in 1950. By March, Marilyn had signed a seven–year film contract with MGM. In 1953 *How to Marry a Millionaire* and *Gentlemen Prefer Blondes* turned Marilyn into a superstar. *Bus Stop* (1956), *Some Like It Hot!* (1959), and *The Misfits* (1961) are considered among her best films.

Divorced from Doughtery, Marilyn married Joe DiMaggio in January 1951. Divorce followed in October 1954. Her marriage to Arthur Miller in June 1956 ended in 1961 following an affair with Yves Montand. The threat of mental illness and other health problems depressed Marilyn. She died on August 5, 1962, from an overdose of barbiturates.

References: Denis C. Jackson, *The Price & ID Guide to Marilyn Monroe, 3rd Edition*, TICN, 1996; Dian Zillner, *Hollywood Collectibles: The Sequel*, Schiffer Publishing, 1994.

Collectors' Club: All About Marilyn, PO Box 291176, Los Angeles, CA 90029.

Arcade Card, Premier **$100.00**

Book, *Marilyn*, Norman Mailer, hard cov, 1973, 270 pp **55.00**

Book, paperback, *Seven Year Itch*, 1955 . . . . **28.00**

Limited Edition Collectors Plate, Marilyn Monroe Collection, "Seven–Year Itch," Delphi, 1990, $80.00.

Calendar, 1954, glossy nude photo 150.00
Calendar, 1956, 4 full color photos, 8 x 14" 200.00
Calendar, Dec 1955, cardboard, full color photo,
    Golden Dreams pose, red ground, 8 x 14" 125.00
Cologne Spray, 1983, MIB 45.00
Doll, Tristar, 11½" h 45.00
Lamp, figural, orig Vandor label 80.00
Lobby Card, *The Seven–Year Itch*, #8, 1955 . . . . 40.00
Magazine, *Fans Star Library* 15.00
Magazine, *Marilyn Monroe Pin–Ups*, black and white
    and full color photos, 1953, 32 pp 70.00
Magazine, *Movie Life*, black and white Monroe pictori-
    al, Dec 1956 . . . . 12.00
Magazine, cover story, *Focus*, color, Nov 1955 . . . . 7.50
Magazine, cover story, *Laff*, listed as Jean Norman, Aug
    1946 . . . . 75.00
Magazine, cover story, *Life*, Nov 9, 1959 . . . . 25.00
Magazine, cover story, *Silver Screen*, Feb 1943 . . . . 35.00
Movie Press Book, *Bus Stop*, Monroe cov, 96 pp, 6 x 8" 45.00
Newspaper, headline edition, Aug 6, 1962, "Marilyn
    Monroe Dies" 20.00
Paper Dolls, Saalfield, #158610, uncut 150.00
Photograph, color, Monroe wearing yellow 2–pc outfit,
    A Sheer copyright, late 1950s 25.00
Playing Cards, Golden Dreams portrait, c1955 . . . . 75.00
Postcard, *Bus Stop*, French version 20.00
Poster, *Facciamo L'Amore*, 20th Century Fox 20.00
Poster, *Let's Make It Legal*, 20th Century Fox, 1951 . . . . . . 150.00
Poster, *River of No Return*, 1954, 22 x 28" 100.00
Press Book, *Bus Stop*, Monroe cov, British promotional,
    96 pp, 6 x 8" 45.00
Record Jacket, *Some Like It Hot*, Ascot, 1964 . . . . 75.00
Sheet Music, *Bus Stop*, 1956 . . . . 30.00
Sheet Music, *My Heart Belongs to Daddy*, 1938 . . . . 30.00
Sheet Music, *When Love Goes Wrong* from *Gentlemen
    Prefer Blondes*, Jane Russell and Marilyn Monroe
    color photo cov, 1953 . . . . 35.00
Snowdome, plastic, red, mkd "Koziol" 30.00

MONSTERS

Animal monsters played a major role in the movies from the onset. King Kong is the best known of the pre–1945 genre. The Japanese monster epics of the 1950s introduced Godzilla, a huge reptile monster. Godzilla, his foes, and imitators are all very collectible. The 1950s also saw the introduction of a wide range of animal monsters with human characteristics, e.g., the Creature From the Black Lagoon and numerous werewolf variations.

Early film makers were well aware of the ability of film to horrify. Dracula, Frankenstein, and the Mummy have been the subjects of dozens of films.

The Addams Family and The Munsters introduced a comedic aspect to monsters. This was perpetuated by the portrayal of monsters on Saturday morning cartoon shows. The chainsaw–wielding mentally deranged villains of the 1960s to the present are a consequence of this demystification of the monster.

After a period of speculation in monster material from the mid–1980s through the early 1990s, market prices now appear to have stabilized.

Reference: Dana Cain, *Collecting Monsters of Film and TV*, Krause Publications, 1997.

Periodical: *Toy Shop*, 700 E State St, Iola, WI 54990.

The Addams Family, coloring book, #4591, Saalfield,
    1965 . . . . $25.00
The Addams Family, doll, Uncle Fester, plastic body,
    vinyl head, holding frog in one hand, 1964,
    Remco, 4½" h 120.00
The Addams Family, lunch box, steel, based on cartoon
    series, King–Seeley Thermos Co, 1970s 45.00
The Addams Family, mask, Morticia, Ben Cooper, 1960s 25.00
The Addams Family, model kit, Addam's Family House,
    Aurora, reissue, MIB 25.00
Bride of Frankenstein, costume, Collegeville, 1980 . . . . 50.00
Bride of Frankenstein, keychain/flashlight, 3" h, MOC 20.00
Creature From the Black Lagoon, costume, Ben Cooper,
    1973, M 50.00
Creature From the Black Lagoon, figure, Remco, 8" h,
    1980 . . . . 125.00
Creature From the Black Lagoon, model kit, Glow
    Monster, Aurora 95.00
Creature From the Black Lagoon, Monster Motionette,
    Telco Toys, battery operated, 16" h, MIB 125.00
Dark Shadows, model kit, Barnabas Vampire Van, MPC,
    1969 . . . . 130.00
Dracula, costume, Ben Cooper, 1963 . . . . 100.00
Dracula, doll, Traveler, 1985, 18" h 80.00
Dracula, figure, Remco, 8" h 40.00
Dracula, flicker ring, silver base, 1960s 50.00
Dracula, Mix 'n' Mold Figure Maker Set, MIB 40.00
Dracula, model kit, Monsters of the Movies, Aurora, MIB . . . 325.00
Dracula, Monster Motionette, battery operated, 16" h,
    Telco Toys, MIB 100.00
Frankenstein, bop bag, inflatable, MIB 40.00
Frankenstein, costume, Ben
    Cooper, 1973 . . . . 25.00
Frankenstein, doll, Blushing Frankenstein Mod Monster,
    battery operated, plastic body, vinyl head, hands, and
    feet, cloth outfit, gold colored chain link necklace
    with pendant, TN/Japan, 11" h, 1960s 400.00

Godzilla, toy, battery operated, remote control, tin, walks, opens mouth, growls, breathes smoke, moves arms, eyes and mouth light up, Bullmark, Japan, 1960s, 10" h, $450.00.

Frankenstein, figure, poseable, cloth costume, glow–in–
the–dark, Remco, 1978 . . . . 30.00
Frankenstein, model kit, Aurora, MIB 430.00
Godzilla, figure, Mattel, 1977, 19" h 25.00
Godzilla, model kit, Aurora, assembled 90.00
Godzilla, movie poster, *Godzilla vs. The Smog Monster*,
1972. . . . . 40.00
King Kong, bank, molded plastic, hollow, black, red, and
white, AJ Renzi Corp, c1970, 16" h 25.00
Madame Tussaud, model kit, Chamber of Horrors
"Guillotine," Aurora, orig box, 1964 . . . . 650.00
Mr Hyde, model kit, Monsters of the Movies Kit, Aurora,
MIB 75.00
Mummy, model kit, Mummy's Chariot, Aurora, reissue,
MIB 25.00
Munsters, bank, figural Grandpa Munster, vinyl, Remco,
1964. . . . . 80.00
Munsters, costume, Herman Munster, #209, flannel,
black pants, mask with artificial hair, Ben Cooper,
1964. . . . . 30.00
Munsters, doll, Herman, Remco, 1964, 6½" h 100.00
Munster's, model kit, Munster's Koach and Grandpa's
Dragula, Ertl, reissue, price for pr 125.00
Nightmare on Elm Street, Freddy Fright Squirter, LJN,
1989, MIB. 30.00
Nightmare on Elm Street, Freddy Kruger Electronic Scare
Stick, Marty Toys, MOC 50.00
Outer Limits, jigsaw puzzle, Milton Bradley, 1964,
100 pcs. 45.00
Phantom of the Opera, model kit, Aurora 300.00
Vampirella, model kit, Aurora 75.00
Wolfman, Mix 'n' Mold Figure Maker Set, MIB 50.00
Wolfman, model kit, Glow Monster Kit, 1972, Aurora,
MIB 80.00
Wolfman, Monster Motionette, battery operated, 16" h,
Telco Toys, MIB 100.00
Wolfman, pencil sharpener, UP Co, molded, plastic,
green, 3" h, 1960s 25.00

MORGANTOWN GLASS

In 1903 the Morgantown Glass Works (West Virginia), founded in 1899, changed its name to the Economy Tumbler Company which became the Economy Glass Company in 1924. It marketed its products under the "Old Morgantown" label. In 1929 the company reassumed it original name, Morgantown Glass Works.

Morgantown eventually expanded its line to include household and kitchen glass. The company also made blanks for decorating firms. Morgantown is known for several innovative design and manufacturing techniques, e.g., ornamental open stems, iridization, and application of gold, platinum, and silver decoration.

The company became a victim of the Depression, closing in 1937. In 1939 glassworkers and others associated with the company reopened it as the Morgantown Glassware Guild. In 1965 Fostoria purchased the company and continued to produce most of the Morgantown patterns and colors, marketing them under a Morgantown label. Fostoria closed the plant in 1971. In 1972 Bailey Glass Company purchased the factory and used it primarily to make lamp globes.

References: Gene Florence, *Elegant Glassware of the Depression Era, Seventh Edition*, Collector Books, 1997; Jerry Gallagher, *A Handbook of Old Morgantown Glass, Vol. I*, published by author, 1995.

Collectors' Clubs: Morgantown Collectors of America, 420 1st Ave NW, Plainview, MN 55964; Old Morgantown Glass Collectors' Guild, PO Box 894, Morgantown, WV 26507.

Adonis, water goblet, crystal **$40.00**
American Beauty, #7565, wine, astrid, crystal, 2 oz 65.00
American Beauty, cocktail, pink, 3¼ oz 60.00
American Beauty, tumbler, crystal, 10 oz, 3 ¼". 45.00
Annarose, #1500, plate, Bramble Rose etch, 8⅓" d 35.00
Art Modern, champagne, green 50.00
Art Modern, water goblet, crystal/black 65.00
Art Modern, water goblet, Le Mons, crystal/black 85.00
Art Modern, water goblet, star cut, crystal/black 85.00
Art Modern, whiskey, ftd, crystal/black 85.00
Astrid, #7565, champagne, Anna Rose, American
Beauty etch, 6 oz 37.50
Avalon, #7638, goblet, Venetian green, peacock optic,
9 oz 37.50
Ballerina, #7630, goblet, zaure, Elizabeth etch, 10 oz. 80.00
Barton, #9935, candle holders, pr, peach opaque, 5" h 75.00
Catherine, #26, bud vase, Jade green, enameled floral
dec, crimped rim, 10" h. 175.00
Chanticleer, figural, cocktail, blue 35.00
Chanticleer, figural, cocktail, crystal. 25.00
Chanticleer, figural, cocktail, red 48.00
Chanticleer, figural, cocktail, smoke. 35.00
Contessa, candle holders, pr, steel blue, 4½" h 55.00
Cynthia, #7659, goblet, crystal, Somoma etch, 10 oz 60.00
Fairway, #14½, candy jar, cov, India black, crystal golf
ball finial, 22 oz 150.00
Galaxy, cordial, #7668, crystal, Mayfair etch, 1½ oz. 40.00
Golf Ball, candle holders, pr, Spanish red and crystal,
2 styles 155.00
Golf Ball, champagne, Ritz blue 45.00
Golf Ball, champagne, red. 35.00
Golf Ball, cocktail, red 35.00
Golf Ball, cocktail, Stiegel green 35.00

Reamer and
Pitcher, green,
$225.00.

MORTON POTTERIES

Morton, Illinois, was home to several major potteries, all of which trace their origins to six Rapp Brothers who emigrated from Germany in 1877 and established the Morton Pottery Works.

American Art Potteries (1945–1961), Cliftwood Art Potteries (1920–1940), Midwest Potteries, the continuation of Cliftwood (1940–44), Morton Pottery Company (1922–1976), and Morton Pottery Works, also known as Morton Earthenware Company (1877–1917), were all founded and operated by Rapp descendants.

These companies produced a variety of art, household, novelty, and utilitarian pottery. Morton Pottery Company specialized in kitchenwares, novelty items, and steins. In the 1950s they made a variety of TV lamps ranging from animal figures to personality, e.g., Davy Crockett. Under contract to Sears Roebuck, they produced some of the Vincent Price National Treasures reproductions. The American Art Pottery produced a line of wares marketed through floral and gift shops.

Reference: Doris and Burdell Hall, *Morton's Potteries: 99 Years, 1877–1976, Volume II*, L–W Book Sales, 1995.

Golf Ball, sherbet, red	35.00
Golf Ball, water goblet, cobalt	45.00
Golf Ball, water goblet, red	45.00
Golf Ball, wine, cobalt	60.00
Golf Ball, wine, red	45.00
Golf Ball, wine, red	55.00
Heirloom, #7604½, goblet 14K topaz, Adonis etch, 9 oz	65.00
Jockey, figural, champagne, amber	58.00
Kimball, #7643, ivy bowl, Stiegel green, crystal Golf Ball stem and ft, 4" h	70.00
Leora, #7858, candy jar, cov, Ritz blue, crystal foot and finial, 5½" h	160.00
Melon, #20069, water set, pitcher and 6–11 oz tumblers, alabaster, Ritz blue trim	650.00
Mexicano Lomax, dinner plate, ice, 9"	45.00
Mexicano Lomax, high ball tumbler, ice, 12 oz, 5"	15.00
Mexicano Lomax, ockner pitcher, seafoam	150.00
Mexicano Lomax, pitcher, ice	150.00
Mexicano Lomax, plate, 6", ice	18.00
Mexicano Lomax, plate, ice, 7"	25.00
Monroe, #7690, champagne, red/crystal	35.00
Monroe, #7690, goblet, Golden Iris, 9 oz	70.00
Monroe, #7690, wine, old amethyst, 3 oz	95.00
Old English, #7678, cocktail, Stiegel green, 3½ oz	30.00
Old English, #7678, iced tea, amethyst, 13 oz	45.00
Old English, #7678, wine, cobalt	65.00
Palm Optic, vase, squat, #59, 6", aquamarine	135.00
Paragon, #77943½, goblet, crystal, India black stem, 5½ oz	80.00
Plantation, #8445, champagne, cobalt	120.00
Plantation, cocktail, cobalt	110.00
Plantation, cordial, cobalt	175.00
Plantation, water goblet, cobalt	135.00
Plantation, water goblet, red	65.00
Plantation, wine, cobalt	165.00
Sunrise Medallion, champagne, #7664, crystal	95.00
Sunrise Medallion, finger bowl, ftd, crystal	45.00
Urn, #86½, candy jar, cov, Bristol blue opaque, crystal lid, 6" h	40.00
Venus, #7577, goblet, Anna rose, Palm Optic, 9 oz	40.00
Wallace, martini pitcher and 5 glasses	55.00

American Art Potteries, bowl, inverted umbrella shape, gold bisque, bronze spatter, 5" d	$10.00
American Art Potteries, compote, ftd, dark green bisque, high gloss spatter, 10" d	15.00
American Art Potteries, creamer and sugar, stylized flowers, blue, peach spray glaze, 3" h	20.00
American Art Potteries, demitasse cup and saucer, stylized flower on cup, flat bottom on saucer, gray, pink spray glaze, 3" h	15.00
American Art Potteries, hen and rooster, black spray glaze, price for pr	30.00
American Art Potteries, planter, fish, purple, pink gray glaze, 5" h	15.00
American Art Potteries, vase, bulbous, blue, encircled by molded pink blossoms, 12½" h	30.00
Cliftwood Art Potteries, beer set, pitcher and 6 steins, barrel shape, yellow	100.00

Morton
Potteries, lady
head vase,
white, 7½" h,
$80.00.

Cliftwood Art Potteries, candlesticks, pr, chocolate drip
glaze, sq base, 11" h **50.00**
Cliftwood Art Potteries, creamer, chocolate drip glaze,
4" h, 3" d **35.00**
Cliftwood Art Potteries, flower insert, turtle, #1,
blue–mulberry drip glaze, 4" l **12.00**
Cliftwood Art Potteries, pretzel jar, cov, barrel shape,
emb lettering, green. **60.00**
Cliftwood Art Potteries, reclining cat, cobalt blue glaze,
4¹⁄₂" l **25.00**
Cliftwood Art Potteries, refrigerator bowl, cov, nesting set
of 3, burgundy **40.00**
Cliftwood Art Potteries, sweetmeat bowl, sq, green lid,
yellow drip **50.00**
Cliftwood Art Potteries, teapot, globe, blue–mulberry
glaze, matching ftd trivet, 8 cup **80.00**
Cliftwood Art Potteries, wine decanter, spherical shape,
molded swirl design, mottled green glaze, matching
stopper, 6¹⁄₂" h. **25.00**
Midwest Potteries, Afghan Hound, white, gold dec, 7" h **35.00**
Midwest Potteries, bear, brown spray glaze, 6 x 10" **30.00**
Midwest Potteries, female dancer, Art Deco, white, gold
dec, 8¹⁄₂" h **25.00**
Midwest Potteries, flying seagull, 14K gold, 12" h **40.00**
Midwest Potteries, stylized heron, blue, green, yellow
spray glaze, 22" h **22.00**
Midwest Potteries, flower bowl, deep, flat, turquoise,
11" d **15.00**
Morton Pottery, bank, bulldog, brown **16.00**
Morton Pottery, bookends, pr, eagles, natural **40.00**
Morton Pottery, deer with antlers, white, 5 h **7.50**
Morton Pottery, grass grower, Jolly Jim **20.00**
Morton Pottery, kangaroo, burgundy, 2¹⁄₂" h **6.50**
Morton Pottery, swordfish, yellow, 5" h. **7.50**
Morton Pottery, planter, Mother Earth Line, banana. **3.00**
Morton Pottery, planter, rabbit with umbrella, pink
blouse, egg planter, 9¹⁄₂" h **12.00**
Morton Pottery, vase, crane in bamboo thicket, white **35.00**
Morton Pottery, wall pocket, teapot shape, white, red
apple dec, 6¹⁄₂" h. **12.00**

MOTION LAMPS

A motion lamp is a lamp with animation, usually consisting of a
changing scene, which is activitated by the rising heat from the
lamp's bulb. There are three basic types: (1) stationary exterior
cylinder, revolving interior cylinder, (2) revolving exterior cylinder,
stationary interior cylinder; and (3) revolving shade.

Motion lamps first appeared in the 1920s. They disappeared in
the early 1960s. Econolite Corporation (Los Angeles, California),
L. A. Goodman Manufacturing Company (Chicago, Illinois),
Ignition Company (Omaha, Nebraska), Rev-O-Lite (Brunswick,
New Jersey), and Scene in Action Company (Chicago, Illinois)
were the principal manufacturers.

References: Bill and Linda Montgomery, *Animated Motion Lamps:
A Price Guide,* L–W Book Sales, 1991; Sam and Anna Samuelian,
Collector's Guide to Motion Lamps, Collector Books, 1998.

Note: All lamps are plastic unless noted otherwise.

Airplanes, Econolite, 1958, 11" h. **$55.00**
Antique Auto, wood and glass, Econolite, 1953, 10" h **35.00**

Hopalong Cassidy,
Bar–20 Ranch, red
plastic shade and
base, Econolite,
$275.00.

Butterfly, LA Goodman, 1957, 9" h **50.00**
Christmas tree, red, paper, Econolite, 1952, 10" h. **35.00**
Fireplace, burning logs, Econolite, 1958, 11" h. **45.00**
Forest Fire, Econolite, wood and glass, 1953, 10" h. **30.00**
Fountain of Youth, Econolite, 1950, 11" h. **35.00**
Hawaiian Scene, Econolite, 1959, 11" h. **40.00**
Indian Maiden, sitting on wall, plaster, Gritt, Inc, 1920s,
11" h **55.00**
Mill Scene, Econolite, 1956, 11" h. **40.00**
Mother Goose, Econolite, 1948, 11" h. **55.00**
Mountain Waterfall, LA Goodman, 1956, 11" h **45.00**
Mountains and Waterfalls, LA Goodman, 1956, 11" h **35.00**
Niagara Falls, Rev–O–Lite, 1930s, 10" h. **85.00**
Night Before Christmas, Econolite, 1953, 12" h **40.00**
Oriental Scene, plastic, LA Goodman, 1957, 11" h **35.00**
Sailboats in Water, plastic, LA Goodman, 1954, 14" h **40.00**
Seattle World's Fair, Econolite, 1962, 11" h. **55.00**
Train, plastic, L A Goodman, 1957, 11" h. **40.00**
Tropical Fish, Econolite, 1954, 11" h **45.00**
Waterskiers, Econolite, 1958, 11" h **70.00**

MOVIE MEMORABILIA

This category includes material related to movies and the individuals who starred in them. Movie collectibles divide into two basic
groups, silent and sound era. With the exception of posters, material from the silent era is scarce and collected by only a small number of individuals.

Prior to the 1960s movie licensing was limited. Most collectibles
are tied to media advertising and theater promotions. This changed
with the blockbuster hits of the 1970s and 80s, e.g., the *Star Wars*
series. Licensing, especially in the toy sector, became an important
method of generating capital for films.

Many collectors focus on a single movie personality. Regional
association plays a major role. Many small communities hold
annual film festivals honoring local individuals who went on to
fame and glory on the silver screen.

Two–dimensional material abounds. Three–dimensional material is scarce. Pizzazz is a value factor—the greater the display
potential, the higher the price.

In the 1980s movie studios and stars began selling their memorabilia through New York and West Coast auction houses. Famous props, such as Dorothy's ruby glass slippers from *The Wizard of Oz*, broke the $10,000 barrier.

References: Anthony Curtis, *Lyle Film & Rock 'n' Roll Collectibles*, The Berkley Publishing Group, 1996; Tony Fusco, *Posters: Identification and Price Guide, Second Edition*, Avon Books, 1994; Ephraim Katz, *The Film Encyclopedia, 2nd Edition*, Harper Collins, 1994; Norman E. Martinus and Harry L. Rinker, *Warman's Paper*, Wallace–Homestead, Krause Publications, 1994; Robert Osborne, *65 Years of The Oscar: The Official History of The Academy Awards*, Abbeville, 1994; Christopher Sausville, *Planet of the Apes: Collectibles*, Schiffer Publishing, 1998; Jay Scarfone and William Stillman, *The Wizard of Oz Collector's Treasury*, Schiffer Publishing, 1992.

Moe Wadle, *The Movie Tie-In Book: A Collector's Guide to Paperback Movie Editions*, Nostalgia Books, 1994; Jon R. Warren, *Warren's Movie Poster Price Guide, 4th Edition*, American Collectors Exchange, 1997; Dian Zillner, *Hollywood Collectibles*, Schiffer Publishing, 1991; Dian Zillner, *Hollywood Collectibles: The Sequel*, Schiffer Publishing, 1994.

Periodicals: *Big Reel*, PO Box 1050, Dubuque, IA 52004; *Collecting Hollywood Magazine*, PO Box 2512, Chattanooga, TN 37409; *Movie Advertising Collector*, PO Box 28587, Philadelphia, PA 19149.

Note: For additional listings see Animation Art, Autographs, Disneyana, Marilyn Monroe, Posters, Shirley Temple, Star Trek, and Star Wars.

Almanac, Motion Picture, 1945 . . . . **$12.00**
Arcade Card, Leslie Howard, 1930s **4.00**
Autograph, Ray Bolger, PS **85.00**
Autograph, Deborah Kerr, PS, movie scene, color, 8 x 10" **20.00**
Autograph, Kathleen Turner, PS, color, 8 x 10" **35.00**
Book, *A Dictionary of the Cinema*, Peter Graham, paperback, Louise Brooks cov, 1964 . . . . **15.00**
Book, *Hollywood and the Great Fan Magazines*, M Levin, NY, 1st ed, 1970 . . . . **5.00**
Book, *The Land of Oz*, Frank Baum, John R Neill illus, ©1932, dj **65.00**
Brochure, *Judy Garland Community Sing*, Oct 21, 1942 live performance, 4 pp, 7 x 10", with 7 x 9" RKO Palace Theatre booklet advertising Garland in "Two–a–Day" all–star variety show, 1951 . . . . **60.00**
Brochure, *Let's Go to the Movies*, #62, Reed Publishing, black and white photos, 4 x 6", 48 pp **12.50**
Certificate, A Loving Tribute to the Memory of Rudolph Valentino, multicolored Valentino photo, 1926, 7 x 11" **15.00**
Check, sgd by Errol Flynn, 1941 . . . . **35.00**
Check, sgd by Cary Grant, 1966 . . . . **25.00**
Christmas Stocking, *ET*, cotton **15.00**
Cigarette Card, Clark Gable, #46, Park Drive Cigarettes **25.00**
Cocktail Napkins, Groucho Marx, 1955 De Soto adv and comic scenes, orig box **35.00**
Cookbook, Yul Brynner, 1st ed, dj, 1983 . . . . **18.00**
Cup and Saucer, brown and white 20th Century Fox logo **20.00**
Display, *Ghostbusters*, stand–up **32.00**
Film, *The King and I*, 16 mm, cinemascope, 2 tins with show's logo **450.00**

Flyer, Charlie Chaplin in his Greatest Comedy, 8 x 11" **20.00**
Game, Around The World In 80 Days, Transogram, 1957 . . . . **35.00**
Game, Dune, Avalon Hill, 1979 . . . . **12.00**
Game, The Game of Hollywood Stars, Whitman, 1955 . . . . . . **10.00**
Game, Movie Land Keeno, Wilder Mfg, 1929 . . . . **95.00**
Game, Terminator 2 Judgement Day, Milton Bradley, 1990s **10.00**
Greeting Card, Clint Eastwood, 1959 . . . . **20.00**
Insert, *Three Little Words*, Fred Astaire, Vera Mills, 1950 . . . . **25.00**
Insert, *Up Goes Maisie*, Ann Southern, 1946 . . . . **20.00**
Jigsaw Puzzle, Oliver Twist, Jaymar, orig box, 1968, 100 pcs. **25.00**
Legal Files, *Miracle on 34th Street*, 20th Century Fox, copy infringement, 1947–48 . . . . **45.00**
Letter, Olivia De Haviland, TLS, discussing meeting with Jean Harlow, autographed photo, 1983 . . . . **50.00**
Lighter, Bette Davis, Dunhill, gold, inscribed "Bette" on lid, orig emb leather case **2,000.00**
Lobby Card, *Miss Tatlock's Millions*, Robert Stack, Dorothy Wood, framed, 1948 . . . . **40.00**
Lobby Card, set of 8, *Berlin Express*, RKO Radio Pictures, 1948 . . . . **50.00**
Lobby Card, set of 8, *The Hindenberg*, George C Scott, 1975 . . . . **20.00**
Lobby Card, *Rawhide Rangers*, Johnny Mack Brown, Universal **15.00**
Lobby Card, *Teenage Monster* **20.00**
Lobby Card, *Yogi Bear*, 1964 . . . . **20.00**
Magazine, *Motion Picture*, Jun 1974, Robert Wagner and Natalie Wood cov **8.00**
Magazine, *Screenland*, Feb 1966, Hayley Mills and Peter Noone cov **10.00**
Magazine, *Screen Stories*, Oct 1951, Van Johnson, and June Allyson cov **12.50**
Movie Folder, *Son of the Sheik*, Valentino **25.00**
Movie Prop, *Road to Hong Kong*, fish, hp, battery operated, price for 3 . . . . **690.00**
Photograph, Carole Lombard, automatic pen signature, Paramount Pictures promo, 1938 . . . . **6.00**
Pin, Lana Turner, diamond, figural angel **690.00**
Playbill, *Laffing Room Only*, Olsen and Johnson, 1945 . . . . . . **6.00**
Postcard, Jane Wyman, handwritten, sgd, early 1940s **40.00**

Sheet Music, Joan Crawford, "Always and Always," *Mannequin*, 1937, 9 x 12", $12.00.

Poster, *Back to Bataan*, RKO Radio, John Wayne, linen, 1945, 41 x 81" 460.00
Poster, *Charlie McCarthy Detective*, Universal, Edgar Bergen, 1939, 27 x 41" 200.00
Poster, *Cover Girl*, Columbia, Rita Hayworth, Gene Kelly, linen, 1944, 27 x 41" 550.00
Poster, Dorothy Lamour, wearing sarong, Royal Crown Cola adv, 1940s, 19 x 36" 35.00
Poster, *Giant*, Warner Bros, James Dean, Elizabeth Taylor, Rock Hudson, linen, 1956, 27 x 41" 520.00
Poster, *Empire Strikes Back*, Mark Hamill 27 x 41" 28.00
Poster, *The Great Lie*, Warner Bros, Bette Davis, 1941, 27 x 41" 320.00
Poster, *The High and the Mighty*, John Wayne, 27 x 41" 75.00
Poster, *House on Haunted Hill*, Allied Artists, Vincent Price, 1958, 27 x 41" 700.00
Poster, *The Man Who Knew Too Much*, Jimmy Stewart, linen, 1956, 41 x 81" 230.00
Poster, *Old Overland Trail*, Rex Allen, 1952, 27 x 41" 95.00
Poster, *Sleeping Beauty*, Buena Vista, 1959, 22 x 28" 115.00
Poster, *Springfield Rifle*, Gary Cooper, c1952, 14 x 22" 45.00
Poster, *Willard*, 1971 .... 7.50
Press Book, *Girl Happy*, Elvis Presley, 1965 .... 20.00
Press Book, *The Caine Mutiny*, Humphrey Bogart, 18 pp 18.00
Press Book, *Julius Caesar*, Marlon Brando, 16 pp 15.00
Press Book, *La Parisienne*, Brigitte Bardot, "Oh That Bardot!," 8 pp 75.00
Program, *Gone With the Wind*, 1939 .... 100.00
Record Sleeve, Jayne Mansfield, posed on bed wearing negligee, 1950s 18.00
Sheet Music, *As Time Goes By*, Bogart, Bergman, and Henreid cov, *Casablanca*, 1942 .... 100.00
Sheet Music, *I'll Sing You a Thousand Love Songs*, Clark Gable cov 10.00
Sheet Music, *Let's Face the Music and Dance*, Fred Astaire and Ginger Rogers cov, *Follow the Fleet*, 1935 .... 10.00
Sheet Music, *Wait and See*, Judy Garland photo cov, 1945 .... 5.00
Sheet Music, *Wooden Heart*, Elvis Presley in army uniform cov 7.50
Souvenir Book, *Lawrence of Arabia*, Peter O'Toole 15.00
Souvenir Book, *The Sea Hawk*, Milton Sills, silent version 50.00
Stein, *Butch Cassidy*, Jesse James boot, mkd "Ceramarte," 1981 .... 85.00
Window Card, *On the Waterfront*, Marlon Brando, 1954, 14 x 22" 125.00

MOXIE

During the height of its popularity, 1920 to 1940, Moxie was distributed in approximately 36 states and even outsold Coca-Cola in many of them. It became so popular that moxie, meaning nervy, became part of the American vocabulary.

Moxie is the oldest continuously produced soft drink in the United States. It celebrated its 100th birthday in 1984. It traces its origin to a Moxie Nerve Food, a concoction developed by Dr. Augustin Thompson of Union, Maine, and first manufactured in Lowell, Massachusetts.

Moxie's fame is due largely to the promotional efforts of Frank Morton Archer, an intrepid entrepreneur endowed with a magnificent imagination. Archer created an advertising campaign as famous as the soda itself. Scarcely an event occurred in the first half of the 20th century that Archer did not exploit. The famous World War I "I Want You For The U.S. Army" Uncle Sam poster has

a striking resemblance to the Moxie man pointing at his viewers and commanding them to "Drink Moxie."

Many firms attempted to play upon the Moxie name. Hoxie, Noxie, Proxie, Rixie, and Toxie are just a few. Most of these spurious products were produced in limited quantities, thus making them a prime find for collectors.

Moxie is still produced today, not in New England but Georgia. However, its popularity remains strongest in the Northeast.

Reference: Allan Petretti, *Petretti's Soda Pop Collectibles Price Guide*, Antique Trader Books, 1996.

Collectors' Club: New England Moxie Congress, 445 Wyoming Ave, Millburn, NJ 07041.

Banner, pilgrim holding carton at left, Indian with carton at right, "Mad About Moxie For Thanksgiving" $30.00
Baseball, Moxie League, 1950–60 .... 70.00
Booklet, A New Moxie Company, 1928 .... 65.00
Bottle Bag, waiter holding tray, "Drink Moxie" in circle, 1920s 30.00
Bottle Carrier, cardboard, "Original Moxie," 6 bottle, 1940 .... 10.00
Bottle Carrier, cardboard, 2 bottle, 1940s 12.00
Bottle Carrier, cardboard, 6 bottle, 1950s 5.00
Bottle Display, carousel shape, 1950s 125.00
Bottle Display, "Enjoy A Lift The Healthful Drink Moxie," 2 bottle, 1940s 125.00
Bottle Opener, bowling pin shape, 1930s 10.00
Bottle Opener, "Drink Moxie 100%" 35.00
Can, aluminum, pull tab, Diet Moxie, Mad About Moxie, 12 oz 25.00
Cap, Moxie logo, 1930s 30.00
Dispenser, glass, 1940s 200.00
Doll, 1920s 300.00
Fan, 2–sided, "When the Heat Waves Go Astray," 1950s 45.00
Fan, girl sitting on man's lap, 1924, 8" 40.00
Fan, woman looking in pocket mirror, 1925, 8" 45.00
Lighter, 1930s 175.00
Sheet Music, *Moxie Songs*, 1921 .... 125.00
Sign, diecut cardboard, "Drink Moxie Distinctively Different," boy pointing finger, 1930, 15 x 26" 350.00
Sign, diecut cardboard, "Drink Moxie Never...Sticky Sweet," man pointing finger, 1950s, 8½ x 11" 75.00

Sign, flange, painted metal, red, yellow, and black with white lettering, scratches, paint chipping, 9" h, 18" w, $154.00. Photo courtesy Collectors Auction Services.

Sign, diecut cardboard, "The Swing is to Moxie," woman
on swing, 1930s, 26 x 40" **500.00**
Sign, diecut cardboard, " You Need Moxie," oval, 1940s,
9¹/₂ x 15¹/₂" **175.00**
Sign, tin, "Drink Moxie," 1930s, 6¹/₂ x 19" **125.00**
Sign, tin, Hall of Fame, 1930s, 19 x 54" **385.00**
Thermometer, glass, outdoor, "Drink Moxie It's Always A
Pleasure...To Serve You," 1950s **100.00**
Thermometer, tin, "Ya Gotta Have Moxie," boy wearing
boxing globe holding bottle, 1970s **65.00**

MUSICAL INSTRUMENTS

Most older musical instruments have far more reuse than collectible value. Instrument collecting is still largely confined to
string and wind instruments dating prior to 1900. Collectors simply do not give a toot about brass instruments. The same holds true
for drums unless the drum head art has collectible value.

Celebrity electric guitars is the current hot musical instrument
collecting craze. They are standard offering at rock 'n roll auctions
held by leading New York and West Coast auction houses. In the
1980s a number of individuals began buying guitars as investments. Prices skyrocketed. Although the market has appeared to
stabilize, it should still be considered highly speculative.

From the 1890s through the 1930s, inexpensive student violins
marked with a stamp or paper label featuring the name of a
famous violin maker—Amati and Stradivarius are just two examples—were sold in quantity. They were sold door to door and by
Sears Roebuck. The advertisements claimed that the owner would
have a violin nearly equal in quality to one made by the famous
makers of the past. The cheap model sold for $2.45, the expensive
model for $15. If cared for and played, these student violins have
developed a wonderful, mellow tone and have a value in the $150
to $200 range. If damaged, they are $30 to $40 wall hangers.

References: S. P. Fjestad (ed.), *Blue Book of Guitar Values, Third
Edition*, Blue Book Publications, 1996; George Gruhn and Walter
Carter, *Electric Guitars and Basses: A Photographic History*, Miller
Freeman Books, GPI Books, 1994; Paul Trynka (ed.), *The Electric
Guitar: An Illustrated History*, Chronicle Books, 1993.

Periodicals: *Concertina & Squeezebox*, PO Box 6706, Ithaca, NY
14851; *Vintage Guitar Magazine*, PO Box 7301, Bismarck, ND
58507.

Collectors' Club: American Musical Instrument Society, RD 3, Box
205–B, Franklin, PA 16323.

Banjo, 10" head, 11 high frets, snake–skin head, aluminum hoop, fancy cutouts in aluminum resonator
and armrest, torn head, c1950 . . . . **$50.00**
Banjo, tenor, Gibson, 17 fret neck, hardshell case, 1920s . . . **275.00**
Banjo, tenor, William L Lange, NY, laminated walnut pot
and resonator, spruce top, laminated walnut neck,
rosewood fingerboard with pearl inlay, sgd at peg
head "Paramount, Tenor Harp II, Wm L Lange," c1922 . . . **430.00**
Banjo, Wondertone, S S Steward, walnut, marquetry
inlay, 1920s. **190.00**
Cornet, Carl Fisher Cornet, silver, modified shepherd's
crook, orig mouthpiece, flat spring missing, no case **95.00**
Cornet, Standard (Vega), Boston, silver, pitch change
crook, double split, short lead pipe, mouthpiece **135.00**

Harmonica, Hohner Pocket Pal, $10.00.

Cornet, Wurlitzer, American, silver, 6 crooks and "C"
crook, orig case with accessories **300.00**
Guitar, Gibson, Inc, Kalamazoo, MI, Model ES125, elec-
tric, 1 pc laminated maple back, mahogany sides and
neck, laminated maple top, rosewood fingerboard
with pearl eyes, yellow–brown finish, 1957 . . . . **632.50**
Guitar, C F Martin, Nazareth, PA, Model R–18, arch top,
2 pc mahogany back and sides, carved medium grain
spruce top, mahogany neck, rosewood fingerboard
with inlaid pearl eyes, gold–brown sunburst color finish, with case, stamped internally "C F Martin & Co
est 1833" with "C F Martin & Co, Nazareth PA
67003" decal, 1937. . . . . **621.50**
Harmonica, Japan, miniature, 1,000,000 $ Baby,
4 holes, cardboard box **20.00**
Mandolin, Gibson Mandolin Guitar Co, Kalamazoo, MI,
1 pc maple back and sides, bound wide grain top,
cedar neck with ebony fingerboard inlaid with pearl
eyes, labeled "Gibson Mandolin Style A, Number
551102 Is Hereby Guaranteed," c1920. . . . . **520.00**
Ukelele, C F Martin and Co, Nazareth, mahogany back,
top, and side bound in faux ivory, rosewood fingerboard, stamped internally "C.F. Martin & Co.,
Nazareth PA.," orig case and book, c1939 . . . . **632.00**
Violin, 1 pc bird's–eye maple back and ribs, narrow curl
scroll, brown varnish, labeled "L. Prokop, Vyroba
Hudebnich Nastroju, V Chrudimi 1941" **575.00**
Viola, 2 pc irregular curled back, ribs and scroll, orange–
brown varnish, labeled "Jacobus Hornsteiner," 1947 . . . . . **865.00**
Violin, Adolph Adler, Dresden, Amati copy, 2 pc back,
medium to dark brown color, some edge wear, 1923 . . . . **350.00**
Violin, 2 pc light irregular curled back and ribs, plain
scroll, brown varnish, labeled "Giovanni Pistucci,
Napoli 1924, Copia Giuseppe Gagliano" **345.00**
Violin, American, 2 pc narrow curl back and ribs, plain
scroll, brown varnish, labeled "K. Trimintzos,
September 18, 1934," with bow and case. **550.00**
Violin, Bohemian, Ladislav Prokop, Chrudim, 1 pc irreg-
ular curled back and ribs, plain scroll, orange–brown
varnish, labeled "L. Prokop Vyroba Hudebnich
Nastroju V Chrudimi 1945" **375.00**
Violin, John Juzek Workshops, 2 pc narrow back curl
and ribs, narrow curl scroll, red–brown varnish,
labeled "John Juzek Violin Maker In Prague 1925
Made Czechoslovakia," sgd by maker, with case and
2 bows **630.00**
Violin, John Justice Hull, PA, 2 pc back, orange–brown
varnish, labeled "Made by John Justice Hullin
Kingston, Pa. 1926/USA" **750.00**
Violin, Karl Hofner, German, 2 pc broad irregular curled
back, ribs and scroll, brown varnish, labeled "Karl
Hofner, Bubenreuty 1992" **315.00**

MUSIC BOXES

Antoine Favre, a Swiss watchmaker, made the first true music box in 1796. The manufacture of music boxes was largely a cottage industry until Charles Paillard established a factory in Sainte–Croix, Switzerland, in 1875.

The golden age of the music box was from 1880 to 1910. A cylinder or disc music box occupied a place of importance in many Victorian–era parlors. The radio and record player eventually replaced the parlor music box.

Although novelty music boxes date to the Victorian era, they enjoyed increased popularity following World War II. In the case of the novelty box, the musical portion is secondary to the shape of the box itself. This category focuses primarily on these boxes.

Collectors' Club: Musical Box Society International, 12140 Anchor Lane SW, Moore Haven, FL 33471.

Acrobat, bank, green plastic, Gorham, 7½" h **$18.00**
Bear, hand carved, spin with hand **65.00**
Big Bird and Snowman, limited edition, Gorham, 7" h **24.00**
Box, 3 tunes, children feeding swan, litho on cov, tune
   sheet on bottom, Swiss, Manivelle, 3 x 3 x 5" **80.00**
Box, Santa, white, plays "Jingle Bells," 2½" h **8.00**
Cardinal, ceramic, 6½" h. **18.00**
Cathedral, white plastic, stained glass windows, plays
   "Silent Night," c1950, 15" h. **35.00**
Christmas Tree Stand, revolving, Germany **65.00**
Clock, plays "Hickory Dickory Dock," Mattel, 1952 . . . . **30.00**
Coffee Grinder, 3" **30.00**
Cyclist, bank, red plastic, Gorham, 7½" h **18.00**
Dog, Nipper, ceramic, 12" **45.00**
Doll, drum major, blue uniform, plays "Cecile," 15" **100.00**
Dove, ceramic **18.00**
Easter Egg, red and yellow plastic, wood knob crank,
   plays "Here Comes Peter Cottontail" **12.00**
Easter Egg, tin **15.00**
Elvis Presley, plays "Love Me Tender". **60.00**
Ferris Wheel, cardboard, moving, c1940, MIB **15.00**
Man, leaning against lamppost, cast iron, plays "How
   Dry I Am," NY City souvenir **18.00**

Merry–Go–Round, lamp, c1950, 6½". **30.00**
Owl, ceramic, 6" h **20.00**
Peter Rabbit, limited edition, Anri **100.00**
Powder Box, metal, silver, litho cov, c1940, 3½ x 4½" **25.00**
Raggedy Ann, limited edition, Schmid, 1981 . . . . **20.00**
Santa Claus, movable head, 14" h **35.00**
Scarecrow, limited edition, Enesco, large, orig certificate . . . **195.00**
Snowball, glass, Mr and Mrs Santa, green wood base **10.00**
Stein, porcelain, diamond dec, 5" h **35.00**
Three Little Pigs, Jaymar **48.00**

NAPKIN LADIES

A napkin lady is a ceramic or wooden figure with slits in her skirt into which folded paper napkins can be placed. They were a popular kitchen tabletop decorative accessory from the late 1940s through the end of the 1950s.

Betsons, Holt–Howard, and Kreiss & Company imported ceramic napkin ladies from Japan. In addition to these imports, American firms such as California Originals (Manhattan Beach and Torrance, California) made them. Napkin ladies also were a popular product of ceramic hobby/craft classes with blanks provided by companies such as the Holland Mold Company (Trenton, New Jersey). Most wooden napkin ladies originated in Sweden.

Multifunctional napkin ladies are also known. One example features a hat candle holder, a bell clapper in the skirt, and an attached pair of young girl salt and pepper shakers. Male examples exist, but are scarce.

California Originals, Spanish Dancer, basket on head
   holds toothpicks, napkin slits in rear of skirt **$35.00**
Holland Mold Co, Rosie, #H–132 . . . . **30.00**
Holt–Howard, cocktail version, complete with 5 rice
   paper napkins, 1958 . . . . **35.00**
Japan, pink and yellow dress, hp eyes, stamped "Japan,"
   9¼" h **25.00**
Japan, wood, "Napkins" on round base, paper label,
   11½" h **15.00**
Kreiss & Co, pink dress with gold trim, hp flowers on
   bodice, matching hat, red hair, jeweled eyes, ceramic
   bell clapper on chain inside skirt, hat forms candle
   holder, 10½" h **50.00**
Kreiss, green dress. **50.00**
Kreiss & Co, Mardi Gras, jewels missing on eyes **30.00**
Kreiss & Co, 4¾" h salt and pepper girls peeking from
   behind skirt, toothpick tray, 9¾" h **50.00**
Servy–Etta, wood, red skirt, matching hat with silver
   accents, 11¾" h **18.00**
Unknown Maker, blue and white dress, 1940s **27.00**
Unknown Maker, wood, Jamaican woman, bowl of fruit
   on head, jointed arms **20.00**

Santa on Drum, plastic, cardboard, and fabric, plays "Jingle Bells," windup, rings bell, Taiwan, 9" h, $10.00.

NAZI ITEMS

Anton Drexler and Adolf Hitler founded The National Socialist German Workers Party (NSDAP) on February 24, 1920. The party advocated a 25–point plan designed to lift the German economy and government from the depths of the Depression.

When the Beer Hall Putsch failed in 1923, Hitler was sentenced to a five–year prison term. Although serving only a year, he used that time to write *Mein Kampf*, a book that became the NSDAP manifesto.

During the early 1930s the NSDAP grew from a regional party based in Southern Germany to a national party. Hitler became Reich's chancellor in 1933. Following the death of President von Hindenberg in 1934, Hitler assumed that title as well.

Nazi items are political items, not military items. Do not confuse the two. Although the Wehrmacht, the German military, was an independent organization, it was subject to numerous controls from the political sector. Nazi memorabilia were popular war souvenirs. Large quantities of armbands, daggers, flags, and copies of *Mein Kampf* survive in the United States.

References: Richard J. Austin, *The Official Price Guide to Military Collectibles, Sixth Edition,* House of Collectibles, 1998; Gary Kirsner, *German Military Steins: 1914 to 1945, Second Edition,* Glentiques Ltd, 1996; Ron Manion, *German Military Collectibles Price Guide,* Antique Publications, 1995.

Periodical: *Military Trader,* PO Box 1050, Dubuque, IA 52004.

Ashtray, ceramic, white, brown Hitler profile, gilt stripe, 3 rests, mkd "CKW Buringia" **$145.00**
Banner, red cotton, sewn printed swastika on white circle, wire rings, 2¹⁄₂ x 8" **150.00**
Book, *Hitler,* Hans Diebow and Kurt Goeltzer, biography, photos, saluting Hitler cov illus, dj, 1931 . . . . **230.00**
Book, *Mein Kampf,* Adolf Hitler, small format, blue cloth cov with emb golden party eagle, Hitler portrait in front, hardback, 1934 . . . . **100.00**
Bookplate, dark brown and sepia tone, pointed wing eagle on wreath/swastika design imposed over oak leaf with acorn, banner above "Ex Libris" "Adolf Hitler" below, 3¹⁄₂ x 4" **185.00**
Cufflinks, pr, NSDAP, black swastika on white center, red enamel border, black leather case with gold border outline, white satin lid lining and black velvet base. **175.00**
Figurine, plaster, hp, skunk body with Hitler's head, 5" h. . . . **150.00**
Fork, SS, 3 tines, stamped "A H" and "BSF 800," 5" l **400.00**
Glass, Czechoslovakian lead crystal, pre–1939 rampant lion with crown engraved and frosted in golden yellow oval, rounded fluted base, walls of glass rising upward and outward, flashed base with encircling concave discs, flashed stripe rim with engraved patriotic slogan in script, dated 1938, made for Nazi Party **160.00**
Gravy Boat, attached underplate, German Labor Front, porcelain, white, blue stripe around rim, mkd with Deutsche Arbeitsfront logo and "Hutschenreuther Lelb" **25.00**
Insignia, armband, Kyffhauserbund, blue wool body, bevo Nazi kyffhauserbund shield, 30 x 55 mm bronze wreath and rayed oval badge with monument center. **50.00**
Magazine, *Time,* Nazi cov, Gen Field Marshall Fedor Von Bock, 1942 . . . . **35.00**
Necklace Pendant, cut–out swastika, border ring **25.00**
Newspaper, *Daily Journal–Gazette,* Nazis Open Aerial Battle, Aug 12, 1940 . . . . **3.00**
Newspaper, *Deutsche Studenten Zeitung,* for students by NSDAP, Hitler's victory in Saarland, Jan 24 and Jan 31, 1934 issues. **45.00**
Pennant, NSDAP, triangular, painted swastika, 2 sided, 54" l, 11" h **35.00**
Plate, wood, painted Munich emblem center, crests of 5 cities around edge, Munich insignia crested with Nazi flag, 8³⁄₄" d **20.00**

Medal, Iron Cross, 2nd Class, $23.00.

Pocket Calendar, Hitler youth, gray cloth cov with mobile swastika and 1934, hardback **75.00**
Postcard, Hitler profile, Condor Legion 1939 Berlin cancellation, no stamp, unused **20.00**
Ring, SS, crossed swords, helmet, and swastika. **55.00**
Serving Tray, SS, swastika in wreath, stamped "Gebr Heppo 90" **100.00**

NEW MARTINSVILLE/VIKING GLASS

The New Martinsville Glass Manufacturing Company was founded by Mark Douglass and George Matheny in New Martinsville, West Virginia, in 1901. The company's products included colored and plain dishes, lamps, and tumblers. John Webb, a cousin of the famous English glass maker Thomas Webb, joined the firm in December 1901. Within a brief period of time, New Martinsville was making Muranese, a direct copy of Peachblow.

After being destroyed by a major fire in 1907, the glasshouse was rebuilt and production was resumed in 1908. Harry Barth joined the firm in May 1918. He and Ira Clarke guided the company through the difficult years of the Depression. R. M. Rice and Carl Schultz, two New Englanders, bought New Martinsville Glass in July 1938.

New Martinsville Glass Company was renamed Viking Glass in 1944. Post–1945 product lines included handmade cut and etched giftware, novelties, and tableware. Most pieces were marked with a paper label reading "Viking." In 1951 Viking purchased a number of Paden City and Westmoreland molds.

Viking purchased the Rainbow Art Glass Company, Huntington, West Virginia, in the early 1970s, and continued production of its "Rainbow Art" animal figurines.

Kenneth Dalzell, former head of the Fostoria Glass Company, purchased the Viking Glass Company in mid–1986. After closing the plant for renovations, it was reopened in October 1987. The company's name was changed to Dalzell–Viking Glass. Dalzell–Viking, using models in Viking's inventory, reintroduced animal figurines and other items, often using non–period colors.

Reference: James Jeasell, *New Martinsville Glass: 1900–1944,* Antique Publications, 1994.

Georgian, goblet, ruby **$12.00**
Georgian, sherbet, ruby **8.50**
Janice, bonbon, 2 handled, 6" d, 4" h, crystal **15.00**
Janice, bowl, flower with crimps, 5½" d, crystal **18.00**
Janice, bowl, oval, 11", crystal **40.00**
Janice, candlesticks, pr, 4536, 2 light, blue **125.00**
Janice, celery, 11" d, crystal **15.00**
Janice, compote, low, blue **18.00**
Janice, cup and saucer, ruby **24.00**
Janice, fruit bowl, ruffled, 12", blue **80.00**
Janice, jam jar, cov, 6" h, blue **40.00**
Janice, mayonnaise, round, crystal **10.00**
Janice, mustard, blue **75.00**
Janice, plate, 2 handle, 7" d, crystal **5.00**
Janice, platter, oval, 13" l, crystal **28.00**
Janice, salad plate, 8", ruby **16.00**
Janice, salt and pepper shakers, pr, red **60.00**
Janice, sugar, 6 oz, crystal **8.00**
Janice, swan bowl, crystal, large **50.00**
Janice, tumbler, 12 oz, crystal **8.00**
Janice, vase, 3 ftd, 8", black **115.00**
Janice, vase, flared, 3 ftd, 8" h, crystal **45.00**
Meadow Wreath, bowl, 3 ftd, 10½" d **28.00**
Meadow Wreath, candlesticks, pr, double **20.00**
Meadow Wreath, compote and underplate, 11" d plate **38.00**
Prelude, relish, 5 part, 13" **45.00**
Mildred/Host Master, cake plate, 14" d, amber **25.00**
Mildred/Host Master, creamer and sugar, amethyst **35.00**
Mildred/Host Master, cup and saucer, amethyst **17.00**
Mildred/Host Master, cup and saucer, ruby **15.00**
Mildred/Host Master, cup, cobalt **15.00**
Mildred/Host Master, goblet, 6¼" h, cobalt blue **25.00**
Mildred/Host Master, ice tub, 5½", ruby **55.00**
Mildred/Host Master, pilsner, 7¾", pink **35.00**
Mildred/Host Master, plate, 8½", amethyst **16.00**
Mildred/Host Master, tumbler, 9 oz, ruby **10.00**
Moondrops, ashtray, ruby **35.00**
Moondrops, bread and butter plate, amber **6.00**
Moondrops, bread and butter plate, ruby **10.00**
Moondrops, butter, cobalt, metal lid **75.00**
Moondrops, candy dish, 8" d, smoke **20.00**
Moondrops, celery, boat shape, 11" l, blue **25.00**
Moondrops, cocktail, 4", ruby **22.00**
Moondrops, cordial, 3", amber **35.00**
Moondrops, creamer, ruby, large **20.00**
Moondrops, creamer and sugar, ruby **35.00**
Moondrops, cream soup, 4¼" d, amethyst **30.00**
Moondrops, cup, ruby **16.00**
Moondrops, cup and saucer, amber **12.00**
Moondrops, cup and saucer, cobalt **20.00**
Moondrops, cup and saucer, pink **20.00**
Moondrops, cup and saucer, ruby **20.00**
Moondrops, decanter, orig stopper, 8½", amber **55.00**
Moondrops, dinner plate, amber **15.00**
Moondrops, dinner plate, ruby **30.00**
Moondrops, goblet, 5 oz, blue **20.00**
Moondrops, luncheon plate, amber **12.00**
Moondrops, mayonnaise, red **45.00**
Moondrops, platter, oval, 12" d, red **30.00**
Moondrops, powder jar, 3 ftd, blue **165.00**
Moondrops, salad plate, 8", pink **12.00**
Moondrops, salad plate, 8", ruby **15.00**
Moondrops, sherbet, 2⅝", amber **15.00**
Moondrops, soup bowl, pink **45.00**

Janice, cruet, blue,
$80.00.

Moondrops, soup, ruby **60.00**
Moondrops, sugar, amber, large **8.00**
Moondrops, sugar, individual, emerald green **10.00**
Moondrops, sugar, ruby, large **18.00**
Moondrops, tumbler, 5⅛", amber **18.00**
Moondrops, tumbler, 5 oz, 5⅛", cobalt **22.00**
Moondrops, tumbler, 3⅝", ruby **18.00**
Moondrops, vegetable, oval, amber **25.00**
Moondrops, vegetable, oval, ruby **45.00**
Moondrops, whiskey, handled, 2¾", amber **11.00**
Moondrops, whiskey, handled, 2¾", pink **15.00**
Moondrops, wine, metal stem, 2⅞", cobalt **25.00**
Oscar, pitcher, pink **125.00**
Oscar, tumbler, 9 oz, amber **12.00**
Prelude, cake stand, ftd, 11" d, crystal **45.00**
Radiance, bonbon, ftd, 6" d, amber **15.00**
Radiance, candlesticks, pr, 2 light, amber **60.00**
Radiance, cheese and cracker set, red **48.00**
Radiance, cruet, individual, amber **30.00**
Radiance, decanter, handled, orig stopper, cobalt blue **175.00**
Radiance, ladle, amber **85.00**
Radiance, mayonnaise, 3 pc set, amber **30.00**
Radiance, relish, 3 part, blue **62.00**
Radiance, salt and pepper shakers, pr, amber **40.00**
Radiance, salt and pepper shakers, pr, crystal **7.50**
Radiance, salt and pepper shakers, pr, red **22.00**
Radiance, torte plate, Prelude etching, 18" d **75.00**
Radiance, vase, 12" h, amber **45.00**

NEWSPAPERS

Newspapers are collected first for their story content and second for their advertising. Volume One, Number One of any newspaper brings a premium because of its crossover value. Beware of assigning too much value to age alone; 18th–century and 19th–century newspapers with weak story content and advertising are frequently framed and used for decorative purposes.

A newspaper must be complete and have a minimal amount of chipping and cracking to be collectible. Newsprint, commonly used after 1880, is made of wood pulp and deteriorates quickly without proper care. Pre–1880 newsprint is made from cotton and/or rag fiber and survives much better. If only the front page of a 20th–century headline newspaper survives, value is reduced by 40% to 50%. Banner headlines, those extending across the full page, are preferred. Add a 10% to 20% premium to headline newspapers from the city where the event occurred.

Two of the most commonly reprinted papers are the January 8, 1880, *Ulster Country Gazette*, announcing the death of George Washington, and the April 15, 1865, issue of the *N.Y. Herald*, announcing Lincoln's death. If you have one of these papers, chances are you have a reprint.

References: Ron Barlow and Ray Reynolds, *The Insider's Guide to Old Books, Magazines, Newspapers, Trade Catalogs*, Windmill Publishing, 1995; Norman E. Martinus and Harry L. Rinker, *Warman's Paper*, Wallace–Homestead, Krause Publications, 1994.

Periodical: *PCM (Paper Collectors' Marketplace)*, PO Box 128, Scandinavia, WI 54977.

Collectors' Club: Newspaper Collectors Society of America, 6031 Winterset, Lansing, MI 48911.

1921, Aug 3, *Nashville Tennessean*, Black Sox Acquitted By Jury **$25.00**
1923, Aug 3, *San Franciscan Journal*, President Harding Dies Of Stroke Executive Passes Without Warning **50.00**
1926, Jun 29, *Stockton Independent*, CA, general news **10.00**
1927, *Galveston Daily News*, Babe Ruth's 60th Homerun **82.00**
1927, Jun 20, *Riverside Daily Press*, CA, general news **5.00**
1928, Aug 25, *Daily Argus Leader*, SD, Saloons. **7.00**
1929, Jun 30, *Eastern Argus*, Portland, ME, general news **6.00**
1929, *Nashville Tennessean*, Ruth's Wife Dies In Fire **11.00**
1929, Jun 6, *Washington Observer*, Al Capone Indicted **15.00**
1929, Nov 29, Bird Flies To The South Pole **10.00**
1931, May 18, *St Paul Dispatch*, MN, Stunt Aviator Killed In Crash **7.00**
1931, Oct 17, Al Capone Sentenced For 11 Years On Tax Evasion **22.00**
1933, Apr 4, *Pittsburgh Sun–Telegraph*, Akron Breaks To Pieces: 73 Dead **12.00**

1934, Jul 23, *Newport News*, Dillinger Killed **180.00**
1937, May 6, Hindenburg Crashes In Flames **40.00**
1938, Jun 22, *Chicago American*, Max Schmeling vs Joe Lewis **15.00**
1940, Apr 9, *Minneapolis Times Tribune*, Hitler Seizes Norway. **6.00**
1941, Dec 8, *Roanoke World News*, Pearl Harbor Attacked **20.00**
1941, Dec 8, *San Francisco Chronicle*, Pearl Harbor Attack **55.00**
1944, May 30, *Honolulu Advertiser*, Yanks Lunge On Rome **5.00**
1944, Nov 7, Roosevelt Wins 4th Term **10.00**
1945, Aug 15, *New York Daily News*, War With Japan Ends **15.00**
1945, *CBI Roundup*, Only Japs Left, VE Day. **9.00**
1945, Jan 13, *St Paul Pioneer Press*, Amelia Earhart Lands At Oakland **10.00**
1945, *Los Angeles Times*, European War Ends. **31.00**
1948, Nov 3, *Chicago Daily Tribune*, Dewey Defeats Truman. **500.00**
1948, Babe Ruth's Death **100.00**
1948, Nov 11, *Panama American*, Prince Charles Born **16.00**
1951, Apr 10, Truman Relieves MacArthur Of His Command. **8.00**
1954, May 17, Court Bans School Segregation **10.00**
1956, Jul 27, *San Francisco Examiner*, Andrea Doria Sinks. **15.00**
1962, Feb 21, Garden Grove, CA, *The News*, John Glenn In Space Flight. **10.00**
1964, Johnson/Goldwater Election **5.00**
1967, Superbowl I **12.00**
1968, Jun 6, *Williamsport Gazette*, Robert Kennedy Killed **17.00**
1968, Apr 5, Martin Luther King Slain **15.00**
1977, Aug 17, *Commercial Appeal*, Memphis, TN, Elvis Presley Dies **25.00**
1977, Oct 15, *San Francisco Examiner*, Bing Crosby Dies **12.00**
1982, Mar 7, *San Francisco Chronicle*, John Belushi Dies **10.00**
1982, Aug 30, *Peninsula Times Tribune*, Palo Alto, CA, Ingrid Bergman Dies **15.00**
1986, Jan 28, Challenger Explodes. **5.00**

1969, Jul 21, *New York Times*, Vol. 118, #40,721, Man Walks On Moon, $38.00.

NODDERS & BOBBIN' HEADS

A nodder consists of two separate molded parts. A pin is used as the fulcrum to balance one piece on the other. A true nodder works by gravity, a counterbalance weight attached to the fulcrum located in the base piece. Eventually, electrical, frictional, mechanical, and windup mechanisms were used. While bisque nodders are the most common, nodders were made from almost every medium imaginable.

Most nodders are characterizations, often somewhat grotesque. Buddhas, 18th–century courtiers, ethnic and professional types, cartoon figures, and animals are just a few examples. Most collectors specialize, e.g., nodding salt and pepper shakers or holiday theme nodders.

Bobbin' heads have no weight. Their motion comes from a spring or other mechanism inside their head. While most individuals think of bobbin' heads in respect to the Beatles, Peanuts, and Sports Mascot series from the 1960s, papier–mâché cartoon and holiday figures date from the early decades of the 20th century.

Reference: Hilma R. Irtz, *Figural Nodders: Identification & Value Guide*, Collector Books, 1997.

Collectors' Club: Bobbin' Head National Club, PO Box 9297, Daytona Beach, FL 32120.

Aikman, Troy, 1990s	$40.00
Basketball Player, composition, holding basketball, round gold base, "Millersville" sticker, 1960s, 7" h	22.00
Beetle Bailey	140.00
Berra, Yogi	45.00
Bozo the Clown	230.00
Chinese Kissing	8.00
Crockett, Davey	160.00
Democratic Donkey, papier–mâché, wearing suit, carrying flag, Japan	45.00
Elephant, Alex Ceramics	20.00
Georgia Tech, Berco Products, Inc	15.00
Green Bay Packers, gold base, Merger Series, 1968	70.00
Houston Colts, composition, painted, round green base, Japan, orig box, ©1962, 6" h	75.00
Irish Boy, bisque, Germany	35.00
Kansas City Athletics, composition, painted, white round base with decal, 1960s, 4¹⁄₂" h	100.00
Knott's Berry Farm, CA	65.00
Joe Kool, miniature	30.00
Lennon, John	130.00
Mammy Yokum	85.00
Man, gold base, "Let's Twist" decal, Japan sticker, c1960, 4¹⁄₂"	75.00
Maris, Roger	75.00
Nixon For President	75.00
Oakland Athletics, composition, painted, gold base with decal, ©Sports Specialties, 6¹⁄₂" h	35.00
Osmond, Donny	75.00
Phantom of the Opera, 6" h	80.00
Planters Peanuts, orig box	125.00
Policeman, Japan	18.00
Santa, celluloid, 2 dimensional, tin base, mkd with "K" inside bell, Japan, 7" h	350.00

NON–SPORT TRADING CARDS

Tobacco insert cards of the late 19th century are the historical antecedents of the modern trading (bubble gum) card. Over 500 sets, with only 25 devoted to sports, were issued between 1885 and 1894. Tobacco cards lost popularity following World War I.

In 1933 Indian Gum marketed a piece of gum and a card inside a waxed paper package, launching the era of the modern trading card. Goudey Gum and National Chicle controlled the market until the arrival of Gum, Inc., in 1936. In 1948 Bowman entered the picture, followed a year later by Topps. The Bowman–Topps rivalry continued until 1957 when Topps bought Bowman.

Although Topps enjoyed a dominant position in the baseball trading card market, Frank Fleer Company and Philadelphia Chewing Gum provided strong competition in the non–sport trading card sector in the 1960s. Eventually Donruss also became a major player in the non–sport trading card arena.

Non–sport trading cards benefited from the decline of the sport trading card in the early 1990s. Fueled by a strong comic book store market, many companies issued non–sport trading card sets covering a wide range of topics from current hit movies to pin–up

girls of the past. Dozens of new issues arrived each month. As the 1990s end, the craze appears to be over. High prices, too many sets, and the introduction of chase and other gimmick cards have had a negative impact. Secondary market value for these post–1990 sets is highly speculative, a situation not likely to change within the next ten to fifteen years.

References: Christopher Benjamin, *The Sport Americana Price Guide to Non–Sports Cards: 1930–1960, No. 2*, Edgewater Books, 1993, out of print; Christopher Benjamin, *The Sport Americana Price Guide to Non–Sports Cards: 1961–1992, No. 4*, Edgewater Books, 1992, out of print; Norman E. Martinus and Harry L. Rinker, *Warman's Paper*, Wallace–Homestead, Krause Publications, 1994.

Periodicals: *Non–Sport Update*, 4019 Green St, PO Box 5858, Harrisburg, PA 17110; *Tuff Stuff's Collect*, PO Box 569, Dubuque, IA 52004; *The Wrapper*, 1811 Moore Ct, St Charles, IL 60174.

Collectors' Club: United States Cartophilic Society, PO Box 4020, St Augustine, FL 32085.

Bowman, Frontier Days, 1953, 128 cards	$200.00
Bowman, Jets, Rockets, Spacemen, 1951, 108 cards	875.00
Bowman, US Presidents, 36 cards	55.00
Donruss, Addams Family, 1964, 66 cards	60.00
Donruss, All–Pro Skateboard, 1978, 44 sticker cards	6.00
Donruss, BMX, 1984, 59 cards	5.00
Donruss, Combat, Series I, 1964, 66 cards	55.00
Donruss, Dallas, 1981, 56 cards	5.00
Donruss, Dukes of Hazzard, 1980, 66 cards	3.50
Donruss, Flying Nun, 1968, 66 cards	55.00
Donruss, Green Hornet, 1966, 44 cards	50.00
Donruss, Kiss, 1st, 1978, 66 cards	35.00
Donruss, Osmonds, 1973, 66 cards	30.00
Fleer, Casper, 1960, 66 cards	175.00
Fleer, Dragon's Lair, 1984, 63 stickers, 30 rub–off games	10.00
Fleer, Gong Show, 1979, 66 cards, 10 stickers	5.00
Fleer, Here's Bo, 1981, 72 cards, 12 posters	5.00
Fleer, My Kookie Klassmates, 1968, 20 cards, 9 autograph	
Fleer, stamp sheets	15.00

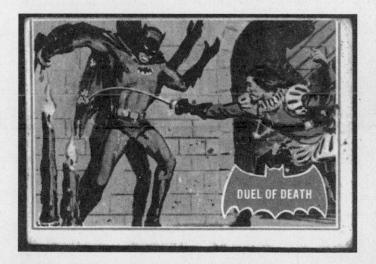

Topps, Batman–2nd Series, Robin Puzzleback, #41A, 1966, $4.00.

Fleer, Three Stooges, 1966, 66 cards 80.00
Fleer, Yule Laff, 1960, 66 cards 55.00
Goudey Gum, Auto License Plates, 1937, 36 cards 150.00
Goudey Gum, Sea Raiders, 1933, 48 cards 850.00
Goudey Gum, Sky Birds, 1941, 24 cards 175.00
Gum, Inc, Bring 'Em Back Alive, 1938, 100 cards 250.00
Gum, Inc, History of Aviation, 1936, 10 cards 150.00
Gum, Inc, Movie Stars, 1939–42, 19 cards 175.00
Gum, Inc, Superman, 1940, 48 cards 1,100.00
Gum, Inc, Wild West Series, 49 cards 350.00
Leaf, Foney Ads, 1960, 72 cards 75.00
Leaf, Good Guys & Bad Guys, 1966, 72 cards 50.00
Leaf, Star Trek, 1967, 72 cards 550.00
Philadelphia Chewing Gum Co, Daktari, 1967, 66 cards 20.00
Philadelphia Chewing Gum Co, Green Berets, 1966, 66
  cards 40.00
Philadelphia Chewing Gum Co, James Bond, 1965, 66
  cards 55.00
Philadelphia Chewing Gum Co, Tarzan, 1966, 66 cards 40.00
Philadelphia Chewing Gum Co, Wild West Series, #46 . . . . . . 4.00
Shelby Gum, Fighting Planes, 1930s, 24 cards 175.00
Shelby Gum, Hollywood Screen Stars, 40 cards 650.00
Shelby Gum, Humpty Dumpty Up–to–Date, 24 cards 225.00
Topps, Alf, 1987, 22 cards, 18 stickers 8.00
Topps, Astronauts, 1963, 55 cards 50.00
Topps, Bay City Rollers, 1975, 66 cards 20.00
Topps, Brady Bunch, 1970, 88 cards 150.00
Topps, Casey & Kildare, 1962, 110 cards 95.00
Topps, Close Encounters, 1978, 66 cards, 11 stickers 3.50
Topps, DC Comic Book Folders, 1966, 44 cards 150.00
Topps, Desert Storm Victory, 1991, 88 cards, 11 stickers 15.00
Topps, Fighting Marines, 1953, 96 cards 350.00
Topps, Flags of the World–Parade, 1949, 100 cards 100.00
Topps, Funny Valentines, 1959, 66 cards 55.00
Topps, Grease, Series I, 1978, 66 cards, 11 stickers 3.00
Topps, Johnson vs Goldwater, 1964, 66 cards 45.00
Topps, Look 'N See, 1952, 135 cards 550.00
Topps, Marvel Comics, 1979, 33 cards 25.00
Topps, Roger Rabbit, 1988, 132 cards, 22 stickers 25.00
Topps, Star Trek, 1976, 88 cards, 22 stickers 220.00
Topps, Terminator 2, 1991, 44 stickers 5.00
Topps, Wacky Packages, 1990, 55 stickers 12.00

NORITAKE AZALEA

Azalea is a Noritake hand–painted china pattern first produced in the early 1900s. Because the pieces are hand painted, subtle variations are common.

The Larkin Company, Buffalo, New York, used Azalea as one of its "Larkin Plan" premiums. In 1931 Larkin billed it as "Our Most Popular China." Some Azalea accessory pieces appeared in Larkin catalogs for three or four years, others for up to nineteen consecutive years. Azalea decorated glass and other coordinating items were made, but never achieved the popularity of the dinnerware.

Note: All items listed are china, unless otherwise noted. For additional information see Noritake China.

Bonbon, 6¼" d **$50.00**
Bouillon Cup and Saucer 25.00
Bowl, 3 ball feet, 4½" 115.00
Bread and Butter Plate 6.00
Butter, cov, round 50.00

Vegetable Bowl, cov, gold finial, $375.00.

Butter Pat, 3¼" d 12.00
Butter Tub 35.00
Cake Plate, glass hp, 10½" d 45.00
Cake Plate, handled, 9¾" d 55.00
Candlesticks, pr, glass, hp 40.00
Casserole, cov, round 125.00
Casserole, cov, round, gold finial 500.00
Celery Dish, closed handle, 10" l 300.00
Cheese and Cracker Set, glass, hp 70.00
Compote, 2¾" 55.00
Condiment Tray 20.00
Cranberry Bowl, 5¼" d 35.00
Creamer and Sugar, cov 40.00
Creamer and Sugar, gold finial 125.00
Cup and Saucer 20.00
Demitasse Cup and Saucer 125.00
Dinner Plate 20.00
Eggcup 55.00
Fruit Bowl 12.00
Grapefruit Bowl, 4½" d 120.00
Gravy Boat 45.00
Lemon Dish 30.00
Luncheon Plate, 8½" d 20.00
Marmalade, with underplate and spoon 150.00
Mayonnaise Set, 3 pcs 45.00
Milk Jug, worn gold 95.00
Mustard, cov, no spoon 30.00
Olive Dish, 7⅛" d 5.00
Platter, oval, 11¾" d 50.00
Platter, oval, 16¼" d 425.00
Relish, oval, 11¾" d 50.00
Salad Bowl, 9½" d 50.00
Salad Plate 8.00
Salt and Pepper Shakers, pr, bulbous, 3" h 35.00
Snack Plate and Cup 45.00
Soup Bowl, 7½" d 25.00
Spoon Holder, 8" l 5.00
Sugar, cov, ... 30.00
Syrup, cov, with underplate 125.00
Teapot, gold finial 445.00
Toothpick Holder 100.00
Vase, fan, ftd 125.00
Vinegar 100.00
Whipped Cream Ladle 10.00
Whipped Cream, with underplate, no ladle 15.00

NORITAKE CHINA

Ichizaemon Morimura, one of the founders of Noritake, established Morimura–kumi, a Japanese exporting company located in Tokyo in 1867. An import shop was also founded in New York to sell Japanese traditional goods. In 1904 he founded Nippon Toki Kaisha Ltd., the forerunner of Noritake, in Nagoya, Japan.

The Larkin Company, Buffalo, New York, was one of the principal distributors for Noritake China in the 1920s. The Azalea, Braircliff, Linden, Modjeska, Savory, Sheriden, and Tree in the Meadow patterns were utilized as Larkin premiums.

The factory was heavily damaged during World War II and production was greatly reduced. The company sold its china under the "Rose China" mark between 1946 and 1948 because the quality did not match that of earlier Noritake China. High quality was achieved once again by early 1949.

Noritake Company was established for selling tableware in the United States. Over the next thirty years, companies were created in Australia, Canada, the United Kingdom, Sri Lanka, Guam, the Philippines, and Ireland for the manufacture and distribution of Noritake products.

In 1956 Noritake began an expansion program that eventually resulted in a full line of tabletop products. Crystal glassware joined the line in 1961, earthenware and stoneware dinnerware and accessories in 1971. The company's name was changed to Noritake Company, Ltd. in 1981.

Close to 100 different Noritake marks have been identified. Most pieces are marked with "Noritake," a wreath, "M," "N," or "Nippon."

References: Aimee Neff Alden, *Collector's Encyclopedia of Early Noritake*, Collector Books, 1995; Joan Van Patten, *Collector's Encyclopedia of Noritake* (1984, 1997 value update), *Second Series* (1994), Collector Books; Harry L. Rinker, *Dinnerware of the 20th Century: The Top 500 Patterns*, House of Collectibles, 1997.

Collectors' Club: Noritake Collectors' Society, 145 Andover Pl, West Hempstead, NY 11552.

Note: For additional listings see Noritake Azalea and Noritake Tree in the Meadow.

175/16034, bouillon and saucer	$10.00
175/16034, bowl, round, handle, 7"	35.00
175/16034, bowl, square, handled, 6³/₄"	30.00
175/16034, bowl, square, handled, 9¹/₄"	75.00
175/16034, bread and butter plate, 6¹/₂"	7.00
175/16034, bread tray, 13"	75.00
175/16034, butter tub	50.00
175/16034, cake plate	35.00
175/16034, cereal bowl	20.00
175/16034, cup	10.00
175/16034, dinner plate, 10"	19.00
175/16034, fruit bowl	8.00
175/16034, gravy	45.00
175/16034, luncheon plate, 8³/₄"	11.00
175/16034, platter, 11³/₄"	35.00
175/16034, relish, 8¹/₂"	20.00
175/16034, salad plate, 7¹/₂"	9.00
175/16034, salt and pepper shakers, individual	10.00
175/16034, shaker, bell, 3"	10.00
175/16034, spoon holder	55.00
175/16034, twin relish, loop handle, 8¹/₄"	35.00

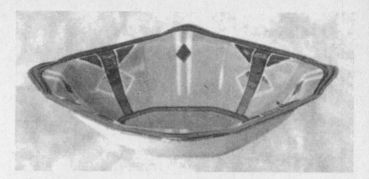

Bowl, Art Deco style, diamond shaped, silver–gray, blue, red, and white on green ground, 1920–30s, 3¹/₈" h, $55.00.

175/16034, vegetable bowl, cov, round	60.00
Blue Moon, cereal bowl	18.00
Blue Moon, creamer	20.00
Blue Moon, fruit bowl	12.00
Blue Moon, gravy	40.00
Blue Moon, plate setting, 5 pc	50.00
Blue Moon, platter, 13¹/₂"	65.00
Blue Moon, salt and pepper shakers, pr	18.00
Blue Moon, soup bowl	18.00
Blue Moon, vegetable bowl, rect, 9³/₄"	35.00
Blue Moon, vegetable bowl, round, 8¹/₂"	40.00
Crest, bread and butter plate, 6¹/₄" d	8.00
Crest, fruit bowl, 5⁵/₈" d	10.00
Crest, platter, oval, 16¹/₈" l	80.00
Crest, salad plate, 7¹/₂" d	10.00
Crest, sugar, cov	35.00
Crest, teapot, cov	100.00
Crestmont, butter, cov, ¹/₄ lb	40.00
Crestmont, cereal bowl, lug, 6³/₄" d	12.00
Crestmont, creamer	20.00
Crestmont, demitasse cup and saucer	20.00
Crestmont, gravy boat	40.00
Crestmont, platter, oval, 11³/₄" l	40.00
Crestmont, salt and pepper shakers, pr	35.00
Crestmont, vegetable, oval, 11¹/₂" l	30.00
Edgewood, dinner plate, 10¹/₂" d	25.00
Edgewood, platter, oval, 11³/₄" l	60.00
Edgewood, salt and pepper shakers, pr	35.00
Edgewood, vegetable bowl, oval, 10" l	45.00
Embrace, #2755 Floral Design, dinner service, 14" platter, 10" oval vegetable bowl, creamer and cov sugar, 8 each 10¹/₂" dinner plates, 8¹/₄" salad plates, 6¹/₄" bread and butter plates, cups, and saucers, 45 pcs	175.00
Glenwood, bread and butter plate, 6¹/₄" d	8.00
Glenwood, cereal bowl, lug, 6³/₄" d	20.00
Glenwood, creamer	30.00
Glenwood, dinner plate, 10¹/₂" d	20.00
Glenwood, gravy boat	60.00
Glenwood, salad plate, 8³/₈" d	12.00
Glenwood, sugar, cov	40.00
Margot, #5605 White Rose Design, dinner service, gravy boat with liner, two 10" oval vegetable bowls, creamer and cov sugar, 14" platter, 9 each 10¹/₂" dinner plates, 6¹/₄" bread and butter plates, and cups, 10 each 8¹/₄" salad plates and saucers, 8 each 5¹/₂" bowls, 62 pcs	195.00
Melissa, creamer	15.00

Melissa, demitasse cup and saucer	10.00
Melissa, dinner plate, 10½" d	15.00
Melissa, salad plate, 8¼" d	8.00
Melissa, saucer	5.00
Rapport, butter, cov	25.00
Rapport, cereal bowl	12.00
Rapport, coffeepot	65.00
Rapport, creamer	15.00
Rapport, cup and saucer	15.00
Rapport, fruit bowl	9.00
Rapport, gravy	30.00
Rapport, place setting, 5 pc	45.00
Rapport, platter, oval, 14½"	55.00
Rapport, soup bowl	12.00
Rapport, sugar, cov	20.00
Rapport, vegetable, oval, 9½"	25.00
Rosemarie, creamer	15.00
Rosemarie, dinner plate, 8¼" d	15.00
Rosemarie, gravy boat, attached underplate	25.00
Rosemarie, salad plate, 8¼" d	8.00
Rosemarie, sugar, cov	15.00
Rosemarie, teapot, cov	55.00
Rothschild, bud vase, 6⅞" h	40.00
Rothschild, chop plate, 11⅜" d	75.00
Rothschild, cup and saucer	25.00
Rothschild, pie server, stainless blade	35.00
Rothschild, sugar, cov	40.00
Royal Orchard, bread and butter plate, 6¾" d	8.00
Royal Orchard, casserole, cov	120.00
Royal Orchard, creamer	32.00
Royal Orchard, dinner plate, 10⅝" d	20.00
Royal Orchard, mug	18.00
Royal Orchard, relish	18.00
Sedan, vegetable, cov	16.00

NORITAKE TREE IN THE MEADOW

Tree in the Meadow is another popular hand–painted Noritake pattern. The basic scene includes a meandering stream (usually in the foreground), a peasant cottage, and a large tree. Muted tones of brown and yellow are the principal colors.

Noritake exported the first Tree in the Meadow pieces to the United States in the early 1920s. Several different backstamps were used for marking purposes. The Larkin Company distributed the pattern in the 1920s and 30s.

Note: For additional listings see Noritake China.

Ashtray, 5¼" d	**$30.00**
Berry Set, bowl with pierced handles, 6 small bowls, price for 7 pcs	70.00
Bread and Butter Plate, 6½" d	10.00
Bread Tray	45.00
Cake Plate, 7½" sq	25.00
Celery Dish, 12" l	35.00
Centerpiece Bowl, 7½" d	100.00
Coffeepot, cov	185.00
Condiment Set, mustard pot, ladle, salt and pepper shakers, tray	40.00
Demitasse Cup and Saucer	35.00
Dinner Plate, 8½" d	15.00
Dish, pierced handles, blue luster border	40.00
Humidor, cov	375.00

Salt and Pepper Shakers, pr, mkd "Made in Japan," $30.00.

Lemon Dish, center ring handle, 5½" d	15.00
Luncheon Plate, 8½" d	15.00
Mug	100.00
Nappy	15.00
Relish, divided	48.00
Salad Plate, 7½" d	12.00
Sugar Shaker	30.00
Tea Set, teapot, creamer, cov sugar, 6 cups and saucers, price for set	135.00
Toothpick Holder, fan shape, 7"	75.00
Wall Plaque, 8½" l	75.00

NUTCRACKERS

Lever–action cast–iron nutcrackers, often in the shape of animals, appeared in the mid–19th century. As with eggbeaters and other mechanical household devices, the nutcracker attracted the attention of hundreds of inventors between 1880 and 1950.

Nutcracker designs mirrored the popular design styles of each era. Art Deco and 1950s–era nutcrackers and sets are eagerly sought by collectors. Beginning in the 1960s, wooden nutcrackers from Germany's Erzgebirger region began flooding the American market. They were primarily decorative, not functional. Still a favorite of the giftware industry, especially as a Christmas gift, these Erzgebirger–style figures are now being made around the world, especially in the Far East, and from a wide variety of material. Buy modern examples because you like them, not as investments. The long–term investment potential for a nutcracker made after 1980 is extremely speculative.

References: Judith Rittenhouse, *Ornamental and Figural Nutcrackers: An Identification and Value Guide*, Collector Books, 1993; James Rollband, *American Nutcrackers: A Patent History and Value Guide*, Off Beat Books, 1996.

Collectors' Club: Nutcracker Collectors' Club, 12204 Fox Run Dr, Chesterland, OH 44026.

Alligator, brass	**$25.00**
Cat, nickel covered brass, 4½" l	45.00
Dog, cast iron, bronze finish	45.00

Eagle, brass... **28.00**
Elephant, orig paint, c1920, 5" h **70.00**
Fish, olive wood **20.00**
Girl, wearing hoop skirt, brass, screw type **110.00**
Jester, head, brass **75.00**
Parrot, brass, 15½" l **15.00**
Pliers Type, cast iron, Torrington...................... **4.00**
Ram, wood, carved, glass eyes, 8½" l. **65.00**
Rooster, brass **28.00**
Sailor and Lady, brass, kisses when handles squeeze
    together **65.00**
Skull and Crossbones, cast iron, 6" l. **85.00**
Squirrel, aluminum **20.00**
Whippet, running, bronze, 3¾" h. **75.00**

NUTTING, WALLACE

Wallace Nutting was born in 1861 in Rockingham, Massachusetts. He attended Harvard University and the Hartford Theological Seminary and Union Theological Seminary in New York. In 1904 Nutting opened a photography studio in New York. Within a year, he moved to Southby, Connecticut and opened a larger studio. His pictures sold well. In 1907 he opened a branch office in Toronto, Canada. By 1913 Nutting's operation was located in Framingham, Massachusetts. Business boomed. At its peak, Nutting employed over 200 colorists, framers, salesmen, and support staff.

Nutting took all his own pictures. However, printing, coloring, framing, and even signing his name were the work of his employees. Over 10,000 photographs in an assortment of sizes have been identified.

In the 1920s when the sale of pictures declined, Nutting explored a host of other business opportunities. His books, especially the *States Beautiful and Furniture Treasury* series, were the most successful.

Wallace Nutting died on July 19, 1941. His wife continued the business. When Mrs. Nutting died in 1944, she willed the business to Ernest John Donnelly and Esther Svenson. In 1946, Svenson bought out Donnelly. In 1971 Svenson entered a nursing home and ordered the destruction of all of the Nutting glass negatives. A few were not destroyed and are in the hands of private collectors.

References: Michael Ivankovich, *Collector's Guide to Wallace Nutting Pictures: Identification & Values,* Collector Books, 1997; Michael Ivankovich, *The Alphabetical & Numerical Index to Wallace Nutting Pictures,* Diamond Press, 1988; Michael Ivankovich, *The Guide to Wallace Nutting Furniture,* Diamond Press, 1990; *Colonial Reproductions* (reprint of 1921 catalog), Diamond Press, 1992; Wallace Nutting (reprint of 1915 catalog), Diamond Press, 1987; Wallace Nutting, *Wallace Nutting General Catalog, Supreme Edition* (reprint of 1930 catalog), Schiffer Publishing, 1977; Wallace Nutting, *Windsors* (reprint of 1918 catalog), Diamond Press, 1992.

Collectors' Club: Wallace Nutting Collector's Club, PO Box 22475, Beachwood, OH 44122.

Book, *The Clock Book,* 1st ed, 1924 .... **$30.00**
Book, *Furniture Treasury,* Vol I–II **10.00**
Book, *Massachusetts Beautiful,* 1st ed, 1923............. **25.00**
Book, *Pathways of the Puritans,* 2nd ed, 1931 .... **25.00**
Book, *Virginia Beautiful,* 2nd ed, 1935, dj **25.00**
Print, Almost Ready.................................. **60.00**

Print, Auspicious Entrance, An **70.00**
Print, Awaiting a Guest **150.00**
Print, Birch Grove **40.00**
Print, Birch Strand................................... **55.00**
Print, Blossoms at the Bend **35.00**
Print, Blossom Valley................................. **90.00**
Print, Bonnie Dale **45.00**
Print, Bonnie May **35.00**
Print, Call of the Road, The **60.00**
Print, Canal Road, The. **180.00**
Print, Cluster of Zinnias, A. **300.00**
Print, Colonial Home Room, A **80.00**
Print, Coming Out of Rosa, The **90.00**
Print, Concord Banks **65.00**
Print, Connecticut Blossoms **40.00**
Print, Cup That Cheers, The **90.00**
Print, Decked As a Bride **75.00**
Print, Durham.. **50.00**
Print, Enticing Waters **55.00**
Print, Feminine Finery **15.00**
Print, Fine Effect, A **120.00**
Print, Floral, miniature................................ **230.00**
Print, Foot Bridge and Ford **240.00**
Print, From the Mountain. **130.00**
Print, Fruit Luncheon, A............................... **170.00**
Print, Grafton Windings............................... **40.00**
Print, Hint of September, A **65.00**
Print, Hollyhock Cottage **40.00**
Print, Home Charm **140.00**
Print, Home Hearth................................... **95.00**
Print, Honeymoon Windings **15.00**
Print, In Tenderleaf **60.00**
Print, Into the West **40.00**
Print, Lane to Uncle Jonathan's, The.................. **80.00**
Print, Larkspur....................................... **150.00**
Print, Lingering Water **15.00**
Print, Litchfield Minster **85.00**
Print, Little River, A **30.00**
Print, Main Coast Sky, A **180.00**
Print, Maple Sugar Cupboard, The **60.00**
Print, Meandering Battenkill, The **45.00**
Print, Memories of Childhood **140.00**
Print, Natural Bridge, miniature....................... **35.00**
Print, Nest, The **140.00**
Print, Newton October, A **35.00**
Print, October Splendors **60.00**
Print, Old Home, The **260.00**
Print, Path of Roses, A **270.00**
Print, Pilgrim Daughter, A **100.00**
Print, Pine Landing **75.00**
Print, Plymouth Curves **80.00**
Print, Quilting Party, The **85.00**
Print, Reeling the Yarn **130.00**
Print, Sallying of Sally, The. **150.00**
Print, Shadowy Orchard Curves **75.00**
Print, Slack Water **40.00**
Print, Southern Puritan, A **350.00**
Print, Spanning the Glen **1120.00**
Print, Spring Pageant, A **75.00**
Print, Street Border, A **220.00**
Print, Tea for Two **130.00**
Print, Three Chums **150.00**
Print, Untitled English Cottage **45.00**
Print, Walk Under the Buttonwood, A **60.00**

Print, Waterside Convention, A 25.00
Print, Way Through The Orchard, The................. 110.00
Print, Way It Begins, The 180.00
Print, What a Beauty! 280.00
Print, Witch Water................................... 75.00

David Davidson, Otter Cap Falls, 13 x 16", $100.00. Photo courtesy Michael Ivankovich Auction Company.

AUCTION PRICES

Wallace Nutting prints sold by Michael Ivankovich Auction Company on September 13, 1997. Prices include a 10% buyer's premium.

A Main Coast Sky, 13 x 16" **$350.00**
An Oak Palm Drive, 12 x 16"................... 350.00
An Old Drawing Room, 12 x 16" 45.00
Birch Brook, 13 x 16" 85.00
Fleur–de–Lis and Spirea, 13 x 16". 620.00
His First Letter, 10 x 16"...................... 160.00
Inside the Gate, 13 x 16" 190.00
LaJolla, 13 x 16" 70.00
Mary's Little Lamb, 13 x 16". 210.00
The Mills at the Turn, 13 x 17" 200.00
There's Rosemary!, 12 x 15".................... 300.00

NUTTING–LIKE PHOTOGRAPHS

The commercial success of Wallace Nutting's hand–colored, framed photographs spawned a series of imitators. David Davidson (1881–1967), Charles Higgins (1867–1930), Charles Sawyer (born 1904) and his Sawyer Picture Company, and Fred Thompson (1844–1923) are only a few of the dozens of individuals and businesses that attempted to ride Nutting's coattails.

Most of these photographers followed the same procedure as Nutting. They took their own photographs, usually with a glass plate camera. Prints were made on special platinum paper. Substitute paper was used during World War I. Each picture was titled and numbered, usually by the photographer. A model picture was colored. Colorists then finished the remainder of the prints. Finally, the print was matted, titled, signed, and sold.

References: Carol Begley Gray, *The History of the Sawyer Pictures*, published by author, 1995; Michael Ivankovich, *The Guide to Wallace Nutting–Like Photographers of the Early 20th Century*, Diamond Press, 1991.

Bicknell, JC, Camp Vassar, 13 x 15" **$45.00**
Bicknell, JC, Leafy Birches, 7 x 9" 30.00
Davidson, David, Bennington Garden, 12 x 15" 30.00
Davidson, David, Birches, The, miniature, 4 x 5" 15.00
Davidson, David, Blossom Lane, 12 x 15" 35.00
Davidson, David, Christmas Day, 12 x 16" 160.00
Davidson, David, Close Framed Boats, 12 x 16" 140.00
Davidson, David, Golden Sunset, 13 x 16". 65.00
Davidson, David, Homeward Bound, 4 x 6" 45.00
Davidson, David, McDermott Falls, 5 x 7" 50.00
Davidson, David, Merry Meeting River, 12 x 15" 55.00
Davidson, David, Rosemary Club, 8 x 10" 40.00
Garrison, JM, Desert Verbenas & Primroses, 8 x 10" 35.00

Gibson, Mirrored Trees, 11 x 14" 10.00
Higgins, Charles R, Apple Blossom Lane, 7 x 11" 25.00
Higgins, Charles R, By the Fireside, 9 x 13" 90.00
Higgins, Charles R, November Sunset, A, 10 x 16" 10.00
Higgins, Charles R, Winding Stair, A, 7 x 14" 35.00
Hodges, Rough Pasture, A, 3 x 4".................... 40.00
Lamson, Moonlight, 8 x 14". 40.00
Lamson, Pine Sentinel, 8 x 10" 30.00
Lamson, Woods, The, 4 x 5" 25.00
Sawyer, Charles, Echo Lake, Franconia Notch, 16 x 20" 50.00
Sawyer, Charles, Gosport Church, 4 x 5" 90.00
Sawyer, Charles, Lake Willoughby, 4 x 5"............... 50.00
Sawyer, Charles, Majestic Nature, 7 x 9" 45.00
Sawyer, Charles, Meadow Stream, The, 12 x 20"........... 80.00
Sawyer, Charles, Mount Washington in October, 5 x 6"...... 55.00
Sawyer, Charles, Old Man of the Mountains, 5 x 7" 35.00
Sawyer, Charles, October Vista, 8 x 10" 60.00
Thompson, Florence, Difficult Lesson, A, 8 x 10" 60.00
Thompson, Florence, Ye Old Time Call, 7 x 9" 100.00
Thompson, Fred, Fireside Fancy Work, 16 x 20" 140.00
Thompson, Fred, Friendly Birches, 11 x 16" 35.00
Thompson, Fred, Silhouette, 2 x 3".................... 210.00
Thompson, Fred, Toiler of the Sea, 13 x 16" 525.00
Thompson, Fred, Triple Seascape Grouping, 3 x 8" 110.00
Villar, Day Dreams, 11 x 14"........................ 35.00
Villar, Puff or Two, A, 11 x 14"...................... 75.00

OCCUPIED JAPAN

America occupied Japan from August 1945 until April 28, 1952. World War II devastated the Japanese economy. The Japanese ceramics industry was one of the first to be revitalized. Thousands of inexpensive figurines and knickknacks were exported to the United States and elsewhere in the late 1940s and 1950s.

Not all products made in Japan between 1946 and April 1952 are marked "Occupied Japan." Some pieces simply were marked "Japan" or "Made in Japan." However, collectors of Occupied

Japan material insist that "Occupied" be found in the mark for an item to be considered a true Occupied Japan collectible.

Beware of Occupied Japan reproductions, copycats, fantasy pieces, and fakes. Period marks tend to be underglaze. They will not scratch off. Rubber–stamped fake marks will. The marks on recent reproductions are excellent. Shape, form, color, and aging characteristics are now the primary means of distinguishing period pieces from later examples.

References: Florence Archambault, *Occupied Japan For Collectors*, Schiffer Publishing, 1992; Gene Florence, *The Collector's Encyclopedia of Occupied Japan Collectibles, First Series* (1976), *Second Series* (1979), *Third Series* (1987), *Fourth Series* (1990), *Fifth Series* (1992), (1996 value update for series I–V), Collector Books; Anthony Marsella, *Toys From Occupied Japan*, Schiffer Publishing, 1995; Lynette Palmer, *Collecting Occupied Japan*, Schiffer Publishing, 1997.

Collectors' Club: The Occupied Japan Club, 29 Freeborn St, Newport, RI 02840.

Ashtray, china, Florida souvenir, state shaped, black "Florida" lettering, gold trim. **$12.00**
Ashtray, metal, playing card suits **18.00**
Ashtray, reticulated border with roaring dragon motif, clear view depicts life and times of silkworm, 5³/₈" d **35.00**
Basket, china, floral dec, miniature **4.00**
Bookends, pr, colonial couple **15.00**
Bookends, pr, emb wood, sailing ships. **75.00**
Box, cov, hen on nest **50.00**
Candlesticks, pr, colonial man and woman. **28.00**
Celery Tray, rect, fan shaped handles, 8¹/₂" l **8.00**
Children's Dish Set, Blue Willow, 2 place settings. **35.00**
Cigarette Dispenser, inlaid wood, spring–operated sliding drawer dispenses cigarette into bird's beak **55.00**
Cigarette Set, plated metal, cov box, with Scottie dog, matching lighter **20.00**
Clock, bisque, double feature, colonial dancing couple atop floral encrusted case, 10¹/₂" h **250.00**
Cologne Bottle, glass, pink **18.00**
Compass, pocket watch shape. **20.00**
Creamer, figural, cow **25.00**

Teapot, bisque, 2³/₄" h, $12.00.

Demitasse Set, coffepot, sugar bowl, creamer, saucer, and 3 cups, translated script "Black like the devil, hot like hell, pure like an angel, sweet like love: Recipe of Rareecand" **40.00**
Dish, china, fish shape **10.00**
Doll House Furniture, china, couch, white, pink roses, 3" l **15.00**
Figure, bisque, black shoeshine boy, 5³/₄' h. **40.00**
Figure, bisque, cherub with horn **25.00**
Figure, celluloid, bunny, pulling cart **28.00**
Figure, celluloid, Hula dancer, MIB **120.00**
Figure, celluloid, swan **10.00**
Figure, ceramic, bird, 2" h. **10.00**
Figure, ceramic, cowgirl, 6" h **65.00**
Figure, ceramic, man and woman, 6" h **35.00**
Figure, china, elf, standing behind log **15.00**
Figure, china, Santa, 6¹/₂" h **65.00**
Figure, porcelain, woman, lavender and yellow dress **20.00**
Grouping, porcelain, Chinese couple, woman playing stringed instrument, man peacefully watching while smoking pipe, 4¹/₂" h, 5³/₄" l **30.00**
Honey Jar, bee hive, bee finial. **25.00**
Incense Burner, porcelain, cobalt blue, floral dec, gold trim **20.00**
Jewelry Box, metal, 12 drawers **12.00**
Lantern, owl motif, 4¹/₂" h **35.00**
Lighter, metal, figural, pistol, pearl grips **15.00**
Lobster Dish, cov **18.00**
Mask, paper, Halloween theme **12.00**
Mug, china, figural boy handle **14.00**
Mug, purple grapes, brown ground, 4" h **10.00**
Necklace, plastic, figural charms, sports motif, 25" l **75.00**
Nut Dish, metal, floral border, 6" d **15.00**
Ornament, Christmas Star **10.00**
Pencil Holder, cat shape **4.00**
Pin Tray, metal, NY City souvenir. **4.00**
Planter, ceramic, zebra **6.00**
Planter, china, baby booties, blue trim **8.00**
Planter, porcelain, figural shoe, floral dec. **20.00**
Plate, silvered metal, pierced scalloped rim, 4¹/₂" d **15.00**
Platter, Blue Willow, oval, 14" l **18.00**
Powder Jar, cov, Wedgwood style, blue and white, 3" d. **15.00**
Reamer, strawberry shape, red, green leaves and handle, 3³/₄" h **65.00**
Rolling Pin, wood **45.00**
Salt and Pepper Shakers, pr, porcelain, black chefs **30.00**
Salt and Pepper Shakers, pr, figural, tomatoes. **6.00**
Tape Measure, celluloid, pink pig **15.00**
Tea Set, ceramic, teapot, creamer, and cov sugar, base mkd "Sango China, Made in Occupied Japan" **30.00**
Toby Mug, Uncle Sam. **25.00**
Toy, windup, celluloid, boy on tin tricycle **70.00**
Toy, windup, celluloid, South Seas native, grass skirt, 6" h **50.00**
Toy, windup, tin, car, "Baby Pontiac," orig box **65.00**
Toy, windup, tin, ice cream vendor, litho tin cart, celluloid boy, 1930s, 4" h **100.00**
Vase, bisque, figural, 3 maidens with flowing skirts, 6¹/₂" h **65.00**
Vase, ceramic, figural, boy reading book, Hummel type, 5¹/₄" h **25.00**
Wall Pocket, ceramic, colonial couple with baskets hanging out window **30.00**
Wall Pocket, porcelain, Art Deco style, lady with hat, 5" h . . . **35.00**

OCEAN LINER COLLECTIBLES

This category is devoted to collectibles from the era of the diesel–powered ocean liner, whose golden age dates between 1910 and the mid–1950s. It is dominated by legendary companies, e.g., Cunard and Holland–American, and ships, e.g., *Queen Elizabeth* and *Queen Elizabeth II*. Many World War II servicemen and women have fond memories of their voyage overseas on a fabulous ocean liner.

Collectors focus primarily on pre–1960 material. Shipboard stores sold a wide range of souvenirs. Printed menus, daily newspapers, and postcards are popular. The category is very much fame driven—the more famous, the more valuable.

References: Karl D. Spence, *How to Identify and Price Ocean Liner Collectibles*, published by author, 1991; Karl D. Spence, *Oceanliner Collectibles* (1992), *Vol. 2* (1996), published by author; James Steele, *Queen Mary*, Phaidon, 1995.

Advertising Display, *Mediterrano Americhe*, easel back, Riccobaldi artwork, 1927	$150.00
Ashtray, *Holland Lines*, hammered aluminum	7.00
Ashtray, *Princess*, Glass, Swedish	10.00
Baggage Tag, *Canadian Pacific*, engraved vessel, c1930	3.00
Book, *Rigby's Book of Model Ships*, punch–out, unused, ©1953	50.00
Booklet, *Independence*, American Export Lines, itinerary and deck plan inserts, Gala Springtime Cruise, 1966	22.00
Booklet, *White Star Line Sailing List*, 1933	40.00
Bottle Opener, *RMS Queen Mary*, floating ship in handle	28.00
Card, White Star Line, *Georgia* ship illus, log abstract on reverse, 1933	20.00
Coffee Tin, Bremen Coffee, *Bremen* at sea on front panel, litho tin, 1930s	50.00
Cruise Book, *Scythia*, 1929	32.00
Deck Plan, *MV Westerdam*, colorful, 1950	18.00
Deck Plan, *SS Manhattan*, 10 pp	50.00
Game, Ocean to Ocean Flight Game, Wilder Mfg Co, c1927	65.00
Key Chain, *Carnival*, ship photo, lucite case	2.50
Letter Opener, *HMS Liverpool*, silver, enamel dec, 1921	65.00
Letterhead, *Empress of Australia I*, Round the World Cruise, 1929–30	2.00
Log, Lykes bros, *SS Ripley*, New Orleans to Calcutta, 1938	8.00
Magazine, *Life*, Andrea Doria Sinks, Aug 6, 1956	12.00
Menu, *Europea*, colorful, 1931	22.00
Menu, *SS City of Omaha*, Christmas 1940	5.00
Menu, *SS Oakwood*, American Export Lines, Christmas 1939	5.00
Menu, *USS Maryland*, Dec 25, 1927	10.00
Pamphlet, Ward Line, New York and Cuba Mail Steamship Co, 1926, 24 pp	15.00
Passenger List, *Aquitania*, 1937	15.00
Pinback Button, Carnival Cruises	4.00
Playing Cards, Carnival Cruises	5.00
Postcard, *Andrea Doria*	20.00
Poster, *SS Washington*, 1933, 25 x 30"	150.00
Program, *Queen of Bermuda*, Feb 7, 1959	18.00
Radio Message Form, *RMS Queen Mary*, Cunard White Star Line, transmits to and from, 8½ x 9½" folder, unused	7.50

Sign, American Line/Red Star Line, litho metal, adv and general offices on back, 3" h, 12" l, $253.00. Photo courtesy Collectors Auction Services.

Stationary, *Queen Mary*, Cunard Line, notepaper, envelope, color portrait, line and ship name, 5 x 7"	12.00
Stein, *TS Bremen*, Caribbean cruise, china, cobalt blue, hinged top, 1950s	20.00
Ticket Folio, Cunard Line, c1928	50.00

PADEN CITY GLASS

The Paden City Glass Manufacturing Company, Paden City, West Virginia, was founded in 1916. David Fisher, formerly president and general manager of the New Martinsville Glass Company, headed the company. When he died in 1933, Sam Fisher, David's son, assumed the presidency.

Initially the company produced pressed lamps, tableware, and vases. Later the company expanded its lines to include hotel and restaurant glassware. The company also acted as a jobber, doing mold work for other glass companies.

Color was one of Paden City's strong points. It offered a wide range of colored glasswares, e.g., amber, blue, cheriglo, dark green, ebony, mulberry, and opal. Thus far over 35 etchings have been identified as being done at Paden City.

In 1949 Paden City purchased the fully automated American Glass Company, continuing production of ashtrays, containers, and novelties. The American Glass acquisition proved disastrous. Paden City Glass ceased operations in 1951.

References: Gene Florence, *Very Rare Glassware of the Depression Years, Fifth Series*, Collector Books, 1997; Dick Spencer, *Glass Animals of the Depression Era*, Collector Books, 1993, out of print.

Ardith, cup, yellow	$50.00
Ardith, gravy boat, green	80.00
Ardith, mayonnaise, ftd, black	58.00
Ardith, water set, pitcher and 6 tumblers, green	595.00
Black Forest, bowl, rolled edge, green, 11¾"	300.00
Black Forest, bowl, rolled edge, ruby, 11¾"	250.00
Black Forest, cup, ruby	120.00
Black Forest, ice bucket, pink	200.00
Black Forest, tumble up pitcher, pink	650.00
Crows Foot, candlesticks, black, sterling etch	175.00
Crows Foot, console set, bowl and candlestick, black, 12" bowl	300.00
Crows Foot, cream soup, amber	10.00
Crows Foot, creamer, amber	10.00
Crows Foot, creamer, ruby	15.00
Crows Foot, cup and saucer, amber	10.00
Crows Foot, cup and saucer, ruby	12.00

Crows Foot, plate, amber, 8½"	7.00
Crows Foot, plate, ruby, 6" sq	5.00
Crows Foot, saucer, ruby	5.00
Crows Foot, sugar, amber	10.00
Crows Foot, sugar, ruby	15.00
Crows Foot, tumbler, flat, black	100.00
Crows Foot, vase, flared, ruby, 11½"	150.00
Cupid, compote, pink	325.00
Cupid, ice tub, green	350.00
Cupid, mayonnaise and liner, green	250.00
Gadroon, bowl, #881, cobalt, 8"	85.00
Gadroon, mayonnaise, #881, cobalt, 4⅝"	35.00
Gazebo, cake stand, pedestal base, crystal	65.00
Hotcha, cup and saucer, ruby	12.00
Hotcha, plate, ruby, 6"	7.00
Hotcha, plate, ruby, 9"	24.00
Lela Bird, compote, green, tall	65.00
Orchid, bowl, 2 handled, ruby	250.00
Orchid, candlesticks, pr, ruby	250.00
Orchid, compote, ruby, 6⅝"	160.00
Orchid, compote, yellow, 6⅝" h	70.00
Orchid, console bowl, ruby	225.00
Orchid, mayonnaise and liner, yellow	160.00
Orchid, plate, ruby, 10" sq	85.00
Party Line, cone tumbler, green, 5¾"	6.00
Party Line, cup, pink	8.00
Party Line, malt glass, green	8.00
Party Line, serving bowl, green	12.00
Party Line, soda tumbler, green, 7"	10.00
Party Line, speakeasy cocktail shaker, green	95.00
Peacock and Wild Rose, bowl, ftd, pink, 9"	175.00
Peacock and Wild Rose, cake plate, low, ftd, pink	175.00
Peacock and Wild Rose, compote, green, 6¼" h	125.00
Peacock and Wild Rose, ice tub, green, 4¾"	215.00
Peacock and Wild Rose, plate, ftd, crystal, 10½"	75.00
Peacock and Wild Rose, tray, oval, ftd, green, 11" l	200.00
Peacock and Wild Rose, vase, elliptical, green	350.00
Peacock and Wild Rose, vase, green, 10"	215.00
Peacock and Wild Rose, vase, green, 12"	250.00
Peacock and Wild Rose, vase, pink, 10"	250.00
Penny Line, candlesticks, pr, amber	30.00
Penny Line, soda tumbler, green, 7" h	20.00
Penny Line, speakeasy cocktail shaker, with spout, green	95.00
Penny Line, tumbler, green, glass, 5¾" h	9.00
Penny Line, vase, ftd, amber	25.00

Bak–Serv, carafe, cov, ceramic lid, wooden handle	$25.00
Bak–Serv, casserole, curl finial, 1½ qt	20.00
Bak–Serv, casserole underplate, sq	5.00
Bak–Serv, custard	5.00
Bak–Serv, fruit bowl, ftd	20.00
Bak–Serv, jug, ftd	15.00
Bak–Serv, mixing bowl, 7" d	10.00
Bak–Serv, pie baker, 9"	10.00
Bak–Serv, teapot, Rose Marie, irid green/yellow	30.00
Blue Willow, chop plate, 12¾" d	15.00
Blue Willow, plate, 9" d	10.00
Blue Willow, saucer	1.50
Caliente, dinner plate, cobalt	10.00
Caliente, pitcher, orange	20.00
Caliente, serving plate, 13" d, tangerine	20.00
Caliente, teapot, blue	28.00
Elite, bread and butter plate, 6½" d	1.50
Elite, chop plate, 12¾" d	15.00
Elite, creamer	5.00
Elite, gravy boat	12.00
Elite, soup bowl	10.00
Elite, sugar	8.00
Elite, vegetable bowl, oval	35.00
Far East, creamer	5.00
Far East, soup bowl	5.00
Highlight, chop plate	40.00
Highlight, creamer	18.00
Highlight, cup and saucer	25.00
Highlight, dinner plate	20.00
Highlight, sugar	32.00
Highlight, vegetable bowl, oval	35.00
Manhattan, bread and butter plate, 6" d	1.50
Manhattan, casserole	20.00
Manhattan, creamer	4.00
Manhattan, gravy boat	12.00
Manhattan, platter, 12½"	12.00
Manhattan, saucer	1.50
Manhattan, vegetable bowl, oval, 9"	10.00
New Virginia, bread and butter plate	1.50

PADEN CITY POTTERY

Paden City Pottery, located near Sisterville, West Virginia, was founded in 1914. The company manufactured high quality, semi–porcelain dinnerware. The quality of Paden City's decals was such that their ware often was assumed to be hand painted.

The company's Shenandoah Ware shape line was made with six different applied patterns. Sears Roebuck featured Paden City's Nasturtium pattern in the 1940s. Bak–Serv, a 1930s kitchenware line, was produced in solid colors and with decal patterns. Paden City also made Caliente, a line of single–color glazed ware introduced in 1936. Russel Wright designed the company's Highlight pattern, manufactured in five colors between 1951 and 1952.

Paden City Pottery ceased operation in November 1963.

Reference: Harvey Duke, *The Official Price Guide to Pottery & Porcelain, Eighth Edition*, House of Collectibles, 1995.

Patio, Shell Crest shape, 1938. Clockwise from top: chop plate, covered casserole, creamer, covered sugar, salt and pepper shakers, cup and saucer. See individual listings for prices.

New Virginia, creamer. 4.00
New Virginia, dinner plate. 10.00
New Virginia, salad plate. 4.00
New Virginia, teapot 25.00
Papoco, casserole 20.00
Papoco, creamer 5.00
Papoco, saucer 1.00
Papoco, sugar 8.00
Patio, berry bowl. 3.00
Patio, casserole, cov 20.00
Patio, creamer. 6.00
Patio, cup and saucer 10.00
Patio, dinner plate 7.00
Patio, platter, oval 10.00
Patio, salt and pepper shakers, pr 12.00
Patio, sugar, cov 8.00
Regina, casserole, cov 20.00
Regina, cup 5.00
Regina, dinner plate, 10" d 10.00
Regina, salad bowl, 9". 15.00
Regina, soup bowl, 8" d 10.00
Regina, sugar 8.00
Regina, vegetable bowl, oval, 9" l 10.00
Sally Paden, casserole 20.00
Sally Paden, cup and saucer 5.00
Sally Paden, plate, 9¹/₄" d. 8.00
Sally Paden, platter, 11¹/₂" l 10.00
Shell Crest, bread and butter plate, 6¹/₄" d 2.50
Shell Crest, casserole, ftd. 30.00
Shell Crest, chop plate, 12¹/₂". 20.00
Shell Crest, cream soup cup 15.00
Shell Crest, cream soup saucer 8.00
Shell Crest, cup and saucer 8.00
Shell Crest, gravy boat. 15.00
Shell Crest, platter, oval, 14¹/₂". 20.00
Shell Crest, salad bowl, 9" d 18.00
/Shell Crest, salt and pepper shakers, pr 12.00
Shell Crest, soup bowl. 12.00
Shenandoah, creamer 5.00
Shenandoah, gravy boat 12.00
Shenandoah, platter, oval, 13¹/₂". 12.00
Shenandoah, sugar 8.00
Shenandoah, teapot 30.00

PAINT BY NUMBER SETS

Paint By Number sets achieved widespread popularity in the early 1950s. They claimed to turn rank amateurs into accomplished painters overnight. Virtually every generic scene, from a winter landscape to horse or clown portraits, was reduced to an outlined canvas with each section having a number that corresponded to one of the paints that came with the set.

Craft House Corporation (Toledo, Ohio), Craft Master (Toledo, Ohio, a division of General Mills), and Standard Toykraft (New York, New York) were among the leading manufacturers. Hassenfeld Brothers (Hasbro) did a number of licensed sets, e.g., Popeye and Superman.

Contemporary licensed paint by number sets, sometimes employing acrylic crayons rather than paint, can be found in today's toy stores. Rose Art Industries makes many of them.

Banana Splits Paint By Number Set, Hasbro, 1969 . . . . $85.00
Batman Paint By Number Set, Hasbro, 1965. . . . . 130.00

Tom Sawyer Paint By Numbers, Standard Toykraft, $20.00.

Crusader Rabbit, Rosebud Art Co, 1950s 50.00
Davy Crockett Magic Paint with Water Pictures, Artcraft,
    1950s 150.00
Dennis the Menace Paint Set, crayons, paints, brush,
    and trays, Pressman, 1954 . . . . 40.00
Dick Tracy Sparkle Paints, Kenner, 5 glitter paints, brush-
    es, 6 pictures, 1963 . . . . 40.00
Disneyland Oil Paintings By Numbers, Hassenfeld
    Brothers, 5 pictures, oil paints, and brush,
    unused, orig box, 1960s 25.00
Flintstones Oil Painting By Numbers Set, Hasbro, 1966. . . . . . 65.00
Hashimoto–San Paint By Number Set, Transogram, 1964. . . . . 75.00
Jonny Quest Paint By Number Set, Transogram, 1965 . . . . . . 130.00
Li'l Abner, Gem Colors Co, contains 26 circular water
    paint tablets affixed to illus display inlay, 2 water trays,
    6 crayons, brush, and 5 x 5" color booklet, 1948 . . . . 50.00
Popeye Paint By Number Set, Hasbro, 1981 . . . . 10.00
Sleeping Beauty Magic Paint Set, Whitman. 50.00
Tales of Wells Fargo Paint By Number Set, Transogram,
    1959. . . . . 45.00
Winky Dink Paint Set, Pressman, pre–numbered sketch-
    es, water paint tiles, crayons, brush, and water tray,
    boxed, 1950s 75.00
Zorro Paint By Number Set, Hasbro, canvas, oil paints 40.00

PAIRPOINT

The Pairpoint Manufacturing Company, a silver plating firm, was founded in New Bedford, Massachusetts, in 1880. In 1894 Pairpoint merged with Mount Washington Glass Company and became Pairpoint Corporation. The company produced a wide range of glass products, often encased in silver–plated holders or frames.

In 1938 the Kenner Salvage Company purchased Pairpoint, selling it in 1939 to Isaac N. Babbitt. Babbitt reorganized the company and named it the Gundersen Glass Works. Robert Gundersen, a master glass blower at Pairpoint, guided the new company.

When Gundersen died in 1952, Edwin V. Babbitt, president of National Pairpoint Company, a manufacturer of aluminum windows, chemical ordinance, glass, and toys, purchased Gundersen Glass Works and renamed it Gundersen–Pairpoint Glass Works. The company made a full line of plain and engraved lead crystal.

In 1957 old equipment and a decline in sales forced a closure. Robert Bryden was assigned the task of moving the plant from New Bedford to Wareham, Massachusetts. The Wareham plant closed in February 1958.

Desiring to fill existing orders, Bryden leased facilities in Spain and moved Pairpoint there. In 1968 Bryden, along with a group of Scottish glassworks, returned to Massachusetts. In 1970 Pairpoint opened a new, two–pot factory in Sagamore, Massachusetts.

When Bryden retired in 1988, Robert Bancroft bought the company. Production of lead crystal glass continues.

References: Edward and Sheila Malakoff, *Pairpoint Lamps,* Schiffer Publishing, 1990; Leonard E. Padgett, *Pairpoint Glass,* Wallace–Homestead, 1979, out of print; John A. Shumann III, *The Collector's Encyclopedia of American Art Glass,* Collector Books, 1988, 1996 value update.

Collectors' Club: Pairpoint Cup Plate Collectors, Box 52D, East Weymouth, MA 02189.

Box, cov, raised gold rococo scrolls, reverse on lid with
  3 Palmer Cox Brownies playing cards, Pairpoint–
  Limoges log, 5" l, 3¹/₂" w, 2¹/₂" h **$750.00**
Bud Vase, amethyst, clear bubble ball connector, orig
  label, 5¹/₂" h **100.00**
Calling Card Receiver, clear bubble ball connected to
  base, engraved floral dec, 5" d **110.00**
Candlesticks, pr, silver and brass wash, imp mark, 11" h **210.00**
Centerpiece Bowl, cut and engraved stylized floral dec,
  12" d **50.00**
Champagne, Flambo, crystal, 5¹/₈" h. **40.00**
Chocolate Pot, cream ground, gold trim and scrolls,
  white floral dec, sgd "Pairpoint Limoges 2500 114,"
  10" h **685.00**
Compote, amber, engraved floral design, 6" d. **70.00**
Creamer and Sugar, Crown Milano, purple aster sprays,
  blue, rose, and green leaves, gold ribbons, gold
  washed metal fittings, glass cov on sugar, sgd
  "Pairpoint–2052/140" **1,250.00**
Desk Lamp, 4 ribbed reverse painted panels with butter-
  flies, brass fittings, slender brass candlestick base, circular foot, base stamped "Pairpoint Mfg Co C3020,"
  12" h, 8¹/₂" shade. **900.00**
Dresser Jar, cov, clear green ground, clear finial, cran-
  berry cov, orig label, 4" h. **110.00**
Mustache Cup and Saucer, quadruplate, engraved
  flowers **60.00**
Perfume Bottle, crystal, controlled bubbles, 5¹/₂" h **44.00**
Pitcher, amberina, applied ruby handle, 8¹/₂" h **165.00**
Salt, master, clear, controlled bubbles **80.00**
Tumbler, clear ground, black and white polar bear dec,
  5¹/₄" h. **70.00**
Urn, ruby red, rolled edge, colorless paperweight con-
  nection with controlled bubbles, Pairpoint/
  Gunderson, 10¹/₂" h. **90.00**
Vase, trumpet shape, cobalt blue **190.00**

PAPERBACK BOOKS

The mass–market paperback arrived on the scene in 1938. Selling for between 15¢ and 25¢, the concept was an instant success. World War II gave paperback book sales a tremendous boost. Hundreds of publishers rushed into the marketplace.

The mid–1940s through the end of the 1950s was the golden age of paperback books.

Price is a key factor in dating paperback books. Collectors focus on titles that sold initially for 75¢ or less. Huge collections still enter the market on a regular basis. Further, many paperbacks were printed on inexpensive pulp paper that has turned brown and brittle over time. Although books in excellent condition are difficult to find, they are available.

Most collections are assembled around one or more unifying themes, e.g., author, cover artist, fictional genre, or publisher.

References: Gary Lovisi, *Collecting Science Fiction and Fantasy,* Alliance Publishing, 1997; Norman E. Martinus and Harry L. Rinker, *Warman's Paper,* Wallace–Homestead, Krause Publishing, 1994; Kurt Peer, *TV Tie–Ins: A Bibliography of American TV Tie–In Paperbacks,* Neptune Publishing, 1997; Dawn E. Reno, *Collecting Romance Novels,* Alliance Publishers, 1995; Lee Server, *Over My Dead Body: The Sensational Age of the American Paperback: 1945–1955,* Chronicle Books, 1994; Moe Wadle, *The Movie Tie–In Book: A Collector's Guide to Paperback Movie Editions,* Nostalgia Books, 1994.

Periodical: *Paperback Parade,* PO Box 209, Brooklyn, NY 11228.

Note: Prices listed are for paperback books in fine conditon.

Andrews, Robert Hardy, *Great Day in the Morning,* Ace
  Books, 1957 . . . . **$3.75**
Anthony, Piers and Robert E Margroff, *The Ring,* Ace
  Books, 1968 . . . . **2.50**
Barry, Joe, *The Third Degree,* Prize Mystery **6.00**
Bliss, Tip, *The Broadway Butterfly Murders,* Checkerbook **15.00**
Boltar, Russell, *Woman's Doctor,* Ace Books, 1956 . . . . **6.00**
Bosworth, Allan R, *Border Roundup,* Bantam Books, 1947 . . . . **3.00**
Burroughs, Edgar Rice, *Tarzan and the Lost Empire,* Ace **4.00**
Carter, Nick, *Death Has Green Eyes,* Vital Book **6.00**
Cellini, Benevenuto, *The Autobiography of Cellini,* Boni
  Book. **4.00**
Christie, Agatha, *Murder At the Vicarage,* Dell, 1961 . . . . **3.00**
Cochran, Hamilton, *Windward Passage,* Ace Books, 1957 . . . . **3.75**
Cushman, Dan, *Tall Wyoming,* Dell, 1957 . . . . **3.00**

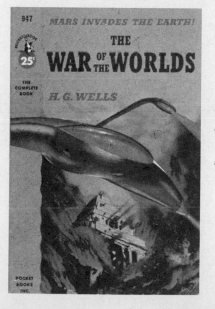

Wells, H. G., *The War of the Worlds,* Pocket Books, #947, 1953, $12.00.

Davidson, David, *The Steeper Cliff,* Bantam Books, 1950 . . . **300.00**
Dean, Dudley, *The Diehards,* Gold Medal, 1956 . . . . **5.00**
Dickson, Carter, *The Peacock Feather Murders,* Berkley,
   1963. . . . . **3.75**
Duncan, David, *Beyond Eden,* Ballantine Books, 1955 . . . . . . **6.00**
Finney, Jack, *The Body Snatchers,* Dell. **10.00**
Fox, Gardner F, *Woman of Kali,* Gold Medal. **4.00**
Gaddis, Peggy, *Intruders in Eden,* Belmont Books, 1966 . . . . . . **2.50**
Galus, Henry, *Unwed Mothers,* Monarch **5.00**
Goodis, David, *Cassidy's Girl,* Gold Medal, 1955 . . . . **17.50**
Grey, Zane, *Nevada,* Bantam. **3.50**
Gruber, Frank, *The Buffalo Box,* Bantam Books, 1946 . . . . . . **3.00**
Hamilton, Donald, *Death of A Citizen,* Gold Medal, 1963 . . . . **4.00**
Harmon, Jim, *The Great Radio Heroes,* Ace A Series,
   Ace Books, 1968. . . . . **2.00**
Holmes, J R, *This Is Guam,* Pacific Press, 1953 . . . . **6.50**
Horner, Lance, *Rogue Roman,* Gold Medal **3.00**
Howard, Mark, *A Time For Passion,* Dell, 1960 . . . . **3.00**
Hubbard, L Ron, *Return to Tomorrow,* Ace. **6.00**
Hunter, John, *West of Justice,* Ballantine Books, 1954 . . . . **4.00**
Jacobs, Bruce, *Baseball Stars of 1955,* Lion Library **5.00**
Kipling, Rudyard, *Captain Courageous,* Bantam Books,
   1946. . . . . **3.00**
Kurtzman, Harvey, *The Mad Reader,* Ballantine Books,
   1954. . . . . **10.00**
Lyon, Dana, *I'll Be Glad When You're Dead,* Quick
   Reader **5.00**
Mooney, Booth, *Here Is My Body,* Gold Medal, 1958 . . . . **5.00**
Neumann, Alfred, *Strange Conquest,* Ballantine Books,
   1954. . . . . **3.75**
Ozaki, Milton K, *Case of the Deadly Kiss,* Gold Medal,
   1957. . . . . **6.00**
Patch, Virgil Franklin, *Man the Beast and the Wild, Wild
   Women,* Dell, 1962. . . . . **2.50**
Patten, Lewis B, *Gunsmoke Empire,* Gold Medal, 1955 . . . . . . **5.00**
Prather, Richard S, *Strip For Murder,* Gold Medal, 1964 . . . . . . **2.50**
Ransom, Stephen, *Death Checks In,* Mystery Novel
   Classic, 1945 . . . . **3.75**
Robinson, Ray, *Baseball Stars of 1961,* Pyramid **2.50**
Scholz, Jackson, *Fighting Coach Comet* **2.50**
Scott, Tarn, *Don't Let Her Die,* Gold Medal, 1957. . . . . **6.00**
Sinclair, Gordon, *Bright Path to Adventure,* Harlequin **9.00**
Stern, Bill, *Bill Stern's Favorite Boxing Stories,* Pocket
   Books. **3.00**
Thomas, T T, *I, James Dean,* Popular Library **6.00**
Uris, Leon, *Battle Cry,* Bantam. **3.00**
Wright W, *Life and Loves of Lana Turner,* Wisdom Hosue **2.00**

PAPER DOLLS

Paper dolls were used as advertising and promotional premiums. *Good Housekeeping, Ladies' Home Journal,* and *McCall's* are just a few of the magazines that included paper doll pages as part of their monthly fare. Children's magazines, such as *Jack and Jill,* also featured paper doll pages.

The first paper doll books appeared in the 1920s. Lowe, Merrill, Saalfield, and Whitman were leading publishers. These inexpensive stiffboard covered books became extremely popular. Celebrity paper dolls first appeared in the 1940s. Entertainment personalities from movies, radio, and television were the primary focus.

Most paper dolls are collected in uncut books, sheets, or boxed sets. Cut sets are valued at 50% of the price of an uncut set if all dolls, clothing, and accessories are present.

Many paper doll books have been reprinted. An identical reprint is just slightly lower in value. If the dolls have been redrawn, the price is reduced significantly.

References: Norman E. Martinus and Harry L. Rinker, *Warman's Paper,* Wallace–Homestead, Krause Publications, 1994; Lorraine Mieszala, *Collector's Guide to Barbie Doll Paper Dolls: Identification & Values,* Collector Books, 1997; Mary Young, *Tomart's Price Guide to Lowe and Whitman Paper Dolls,* Tomart Publications, 1993.

Newsletter: *Paper Doll News,* PO Box 807, Vivian, LA 71082.

Collectors' Club: Original Paper Doll Artist Guild, PO Box 14, Kingsfield, ME 04947.

Note: Prices listed are for paper doll books and sets in unused condition.

Ann Sothern, #4407, Saalfield, 1956 . . . . **$35.00**
Archies, Whitman, 1969 . . . . **30.00**
Baby Betsy, 1967 . . . . **8.00**
Baby Dears, Saalfield, #4418. . . . . **10.00**
Baby Doll, Samuel Lowe, 1957 . . . . **12.00**
Baby Sparkle Plenty, Saalfield, #1510, 194 . . . . **50.00**
Beauty Contest, Lowe, #1026, 1941. **65.00**
Bewitched, Samantha, Magic Wand, 1965 . . . . **65.00**
Bride and Groom, Merrill, 1949 . . . . **20.00**
Buster Brown, Navy suit, outfits, 2 hats, 12" h. **175.00**
Candy Stripers, Saalfield, 1973 . . . . **8.00**
Carmen Maranda, Saalfield, #1558 . . . . **12.00**
Carnation Ice Cream, 1955 . . . . **12.50**
Children of America, Saalfield, #2335 . . . . **10.00**
Dodi From "My Three Sons," Artcraft, 1972 . . . . **50.00**
Dolls of Other Lands, Watkins, 1968 . . . . **12.00**
Donna Reed, Merry Mfg Co, 1964. . . . . **80.00**
Doris Day, Whitman, 1952 . . . . **30.00**
Dutch Treat, Saalfield, 1961. . . . . **12.00**
Flying Marvels, 1945. . . . . **5.00**
Flying Nun, Saalfield, 1968 . . . . **75.00**
Girls in the War, Samuel Lowe, 1943. . . . . **20.00**
Green Acres, Whitman, 1967, M **75.00**
Harry the Soldier, Lowe, #1074. . . . . **8.00**

Elaine and Vicki, Saalfield, #6309:100, $12.00.

Hedy Lamarr, Merrill, 1942 . . . . **4.00**
Hee–Haw, Artcraft, 1971 . . . . **50.00**
June Bride, Stephens Co, 1946 . . . . **18.00**
Laugh–In, Saalfield, 1969 . . . . **55.00**
Lennon Sisters, Whitman, #1979 . . . . **45.00**
Little Ballerina, Whitman, 1969 . . . . **12.00**
Little Kitten to Dress, Samuel Lowe, 1942 . . . . **12.00**
Little Miss America, Saalfield, #2358 . . . . **50.00**
Majorette Paper Dolls, #2760, 1957 . . . . **6.00**
Mother and Daughter, 1950s **18.00**
Mrs Beasley Paper Doll Fashions, Whitman, 1972 . . . . . . **50.00**
Munsters, Whitman, 1966 . . . . **70.00**
Nanny and the Professor, Artcraft, #4283 . . . . **20.00**
Natalie Wood, Whitman, 1957, unused **50.00**
Paper Dolls Around the World, Saalfield, 1964 . . . . **12.00**
Patchy Annie, Saalfield, 1962 . . . . **4.00**
Patty Duke, Whitman, 1964 . . . . **15.00**
Petticoat Junction, Whitman, #1954, 1964 . . . . **60.00**
Princess Diana, Golden Book, 1985 . . . . **20.00**
Roy Rogers and Dale Evans Cut–Out Dolls, Whitman,
     1954 . . . . **70.00**
School Friends, Merrill, 1955–60 . . . . **15.00**
Susan Dey Paperdolls, Saalfield, 1972 . . . . **25.00**
Trixie, Lowe Co, 1961, unused **25.00**
Trudy in Her Teens, Merrill, 1943 . . . . **115.00**
Twiggy, Whitman, 1967 . . . . **30.00**
Wedding Party, Saalfield, #2721, 1951 . . . . **15.00**

PAPER EPHEMERA

This is a catchall category. Maurice Richards, author of *Collecting Paper Ephemera*, defines ephemera as the "minor transient documents of everyday life," i.e., material destined for the wastebasket but never quite making it.

Ephemera collecting has a distinguished history, tracing its origins back to English pioneers such as John Bagford (1650–1716), Samuel Pepys (1633–1703), and John Seldon (1584–1654). The Museum of the City of New York and the Wadsworth Athenaeum, Hartford, Connecticut, are two American museums with outstanding ephemera collections. The libraries at Harvard and Yale also have superior collections.

It is wrong to think of ephemera only in terms of paper objects, e.g., billhead, bookplates, documents, tickets, etc. Many three–dimensional items also have a transient quality to them. Advertising tins and pinback buttons are two examples.

References: Norman E. Martinus and Harry L. Rinker, *Warman's Paper*, Wallace–Homestead, Krause Publications, 1994; Gordon T. McClelland and Jay T. Last, *Fruit Box Labels*, Hillcrest Press, 1995; Craig A. Tuttle, *An Ounce of Preservation: A Guide to the Care of Papers and Photographs*, Rainbow Books, 1995; Gene Utz, *Collecting Paper: A Collector's Identification & Value Guide*, Books Americana, Krause Publications, 1993.

Periodicals: *Bank Note Reporter*, 700 E State St, Iola, WI 54990; *PCM (Paper Collectors' Marketplace)*, PO Box 128, Scandinavia, WI 54977, *Paper & Advertising Collector (P.A.C.)*, PO Box 500, Mount Joy, PA 17552.

Collectors' Clubs: American Society of Check Collectors, PO Box 577, Garrett Park, MD 20896; Fruit Crate Label Society, Rt 2, Box 695 Chelan, WA 98816; Society of Antique Label Collectors, PO

Box 412, Rapid City, SD 57709; The Citrus Label Society, 131 Miramonte Dr, Fullerton, CA 92365; The Ephemera Society of America, Inc, PO Box 95, Cazenovia, NY 13035.

Note: For additional listings see Advertising, Autographs, Cigar Collectibles, Photographs, Postcards, and Posters.

Billhead, Ball Bros Co, "Makers of fruit jars," Muncie,
     IN, vignettes of jars, printed, black and white, 1931 . . . . . **$15.00**
Billhead, F M Bohannon Tobacco Mfg, Winston–Salem,
     NC, Chew Foot Prints Tobacco, woman on bench, fac-
     tory vignettes, printed black and white, 1927 . . . . **20.00**
Billhead, W A Brown Tobacco, Martinsville, VA, "Manf
     of Fine Henry County Plug & Twist Tob. W. A. Browns
     Log Cabin Gold Medal Mild Chew," cabin
     and medals vignette, printed black and white, 1923 . . . . . . **15.00**
Billhead, Larus & Brother co, Mfg of Tobacco,
     Richmond, VA, 2 different Edgeworth Tobacco tins,
     vignettes in blue and white, 1928 . . . . **15.00**
Billhead, Southern Fireworks Co, "Manf & dist. fireworks
     & decorations," Savannah, GA, printed black
     and white, 1923 . . . . **20.00**
Bill of Sale, Bentley Auto, 1926 . . . . **2.00**
Blotter, Kellogg's Rice Krispies, color **8.00**
Bond, Consolidated Edison Co, NY, $1,000, high wing
     radial engine plane vignette, brown border, coupons,
     issued, 1929 . . . . **45.00**
Bond, Toledo, St Louis & Western Railroad, engraved
     pink $5,000 gold bond with ornate train vignette,
     1924 . . . . **18.00**
Booklet, *Art of Ventriloquism, The,* Johnson & Smith Co,
     Detroit, 1930s, 32 pp **10.00**
Booklet, *Freakshow Pitchbook,* 1940s **10.00**
Booklet, *History of the 2 Headed Girl,* 1970s **10.00**
Booklet, *Lest We Forget,* US Navy, 1940s **5.00**
Booklet, *Roulette Gaming Guide,* Thunderbird Hotel
     adv, 1961 . . . . **6.00**
Booklet, William Simon Brewery, Buffalo, NY, driver's
     ledger booklet of container slips, unused, c1930,
     15 pp **10.00**
Brochure, The Alaska Line, browntone photos, c1930 . . . . . . **25.00**
Business Card, Gray National Telegraph Co, NY, 1939 . . . . . . **5.00**
Certificate, Boy Scout Merit Badge, 1936 . . . . **6.00**
Certificate, Certificate of Organization of Oak Park
     Republican Committeemen's Organization, State of
     Illinois, Office of Secretary of State, engraved, Mar 5,
     1937, 8½ x 14" **25.00**

Blotter, Morton's Salt adv, color, 3¼ x 6¼", $5.00.

Poster, Winchester adv, "Winchester Cartridge Shop," WWII–era motivational poster, 22 x 14", ⅝" tear in upper margin, $209.00. Photo courtesy Wm. Morford Auctions.

Check, Carter's Warehouse, Plains Mercantile Co, sgd by Rosalyn S Carter, 1968. . . . . **22.00**

Check, First National Bank of Nevada, filled in and sgd Tyrus R Cobb, cancellation mark, 1945 . . . . **100.00**

Check, Hudson Trust Co, NY, sgd by Enrico Caruso **45.00**

Check, Sonoma Vineyards, L M Martinia Grape Products, Kingsburg, CA, 1939, canceled **8.50**

Court Document, Cochin Government in Hindi, multi–page, currency size copy fee revue, 1930s **12.00**

Diecut, Santa, "A Very Merry Christmas," full color, 1924 . . . . **15.00**

Flyer, Farm, new idea manure spreader, 12 part fold–out, illus, early 1940s. **10.00**

Flyer, Van Briggle Art Pottery Co, order form, full color building illus, 2 part, fold–out, orig envelope, Dec 1947, 8 x 9" **45.00**

Flyer, The William Tell Line, price of flour, etc, from the mill of The Ansted & Beuk Co, Springfield, OH, Mar 1923. . . . . **25.00**

Label, Air Port Whiskey, red tri–motor plane, c1940 . . . .**75**

Label, Forest City Strawberries, berries in glass bowl illus, 1920s. **2.00**

Label, Palm Springs Soda, silver Art Deco design, black and gold ground, dated 1935. . . . .**50**

Label, Uncle Remus Syrup, 1924. . . . . **3.00**

Letter, Herbert Hoover letterhead, letter of thanks, Jun 28, 1943. . . . . **125.00**

Letter, Office of the Minority Leader, House of Representatives, sgd "Joseph W Martin, Jr," Dec 30, 1949. . . . . **9.00**

Letter, Hyman G Rickover, Father of Nuclear Navy, on Atomic Energy committee letterhead, reporting expenses for reimbursement to the Baruch Foundation for services incurred, 1967. . . . . **140.00**

Letter, US General James Gavin, Winter Park, FL, on personal letterhead, typed, sgd, 1985 . . . . **25.00**

Letterhead, United States Cigar Co, York, PA, 1933 . . . . **8.50**

License, fishing, Liberty Bell illus, red, white, and blue, 1976, 2½ x 3". **10.00**

License, marriage, Paul W Swavely and Shirley E Kerr, First Brethren Church, Montgomery County, Pottstown, PA, Aug 24, 1946 . . . . **8.00**

Luggage Label, Yellowstone National Park, full color. **3.00**

Luggage Tag, Greyhound Lines, diecut **10.00**

Map, American Airlines System Map, fold–out, 1950s. **20.00**

Map, Riverside County, CA, issued by Chamber of Commerce, 1920s, 19 pp **30.00**

Menu, Lehigh Valley Railroad, dinner, tugboat photo cov, 1950–60 . . . . **5.50**

Pass, Sturgeon Bay Transit, 1946 . . . . **5.00**

Premium, Quaker Oats, "Deed of Land for Klondike Big Inch Land Co, Inc," 1954, mint **20.00**

Program, Lincoln Center, "Philharmonic Hall," 1962–71, 15 issues **30.00**

Program, Newport Jazz Festival, Neiman cov, 1970s. **10.00**

Stamp, adv, Northern Pacific Railway 1848–1948 . . . . **5.00**

Stock Certificate, ABC Brewing Corporation, green, ornamental engraving, 1934 . . . . **10.00**

Stock Certificate, Canada Southern Railway, engraved with 1880s steam train vignette, issued, 1940s **20.00**

Stock Certificate, Northampton Brewing Corporation, orange, engraved, 1934 . . . . **20.00**

Stock Certificate, New York Railways, engraved trolley vignette, issued and cancelled, c1920s. **18.00**

Stock Certificate, Pittsburgh, McKeesport & Youghiogheny Railroad, engraved green certificate with mine int vignette, 1930s. **20.00**

Ticket, Wasworth Transfer Co, bus fare **3.00**

Ticket, Gene Autry and Champion, Hawkins Stadium, Albany, NY, Aug 21–22, 1959 . . . . **45.00**

Ticket, Mike Douglas Show, Douglas portrait, printed black and white, 1980. . . . . **5.00**

Ticket, Gary Lewis and the Playboys, Albany Armory, 195 Washington Avenue, Albany, NY, Friday, Feb 18, 1966 . . . . **15.00**

Ticket, The Lone Ranger and Lassie, Hawkins Stadium, Menands, NY, Fri, Jun 21, c1950s **35.00**

Ticket, World's Columbian Expo for Chicago Day, Oct 9, 1983. . . . . **10.00**

Ticket Booklet, NY World's Fair 1939, combination souvenir tickets, 2–25¢ tickets for money off at entrance, 2 removed **10.00**

Window Card, Voigts Royal Flour adv, red, white, and black, 1910s, 11 x 4". **2.50**

Yearbook, "The Airman," Sampson Air Force Base, Nov 25–Dec 6, 1955 . . . . **30.00**

Yearbook, Green Bay Packers, Fred Carr and Terry Bradshaw cov, 1976 . . . . **8.00**

PAPERWEIGHTS

The paperweights found in this category divide into three basic types: (1) advertising, (2) souvenir or commemorative, and (3) contemporary glass. Advertising paperweights were popular giveaway premiums between 1920 and the late 1950s. Cast–iron figural paperweights are the most eagerly sought.

Souvenir paperweights are valued highest by regional collectors. Most were cheaply made. Many are nothing more than a plastic disk with information stenciled on the top or a colored photograph applied to the bottom. No wonder collector interest is limited.

Paperweights enjoyed a renaissance in the 1970s and 80s. Baccarat, Perthshire, and Saint Louis are leading contemporary manufacturers. Many studio glassmakers, e.g. Ray and Bob Banford, Paul Stankard, and Victor Trabucco, make paperweights.

References: Andrew H. Dohan, *Paperweight Signature Canes: Identification and Dating*, Paperweight Press, 1997; Monika Flemming and Peter Pommerencke, *Paperweights of the World, 2nd Edition*, Schiffer Publishing, 1998; John D. Hawley, *The Glass*

Menagerie: A Study of Silhouette Canes in Antique Paperweights, Paperweight Press, 1995; Paul Hollister, Jr., *The Encyclopedia of Glass Paperweights,* Paperweight Press, 1969; Sibylle Jargstorf, *Paperweights,* Schiffer Publishing, 1991; Lawrence H. Selman, *All About Paperweights,* Paperweight Press, 1992.

Collectors' Clubs: International Paperweight Society, 761 Chestnut St, Santa Cruz, CA 95060; Paperweight Collectors Assoc, Inc, PO Box 1263, Beltsville, MD 20704.

Advertising, AMR Insurance Group, Neard, NJ, 100th
   Anniversary, brass, 1946 . . . . **$8.00**
Advertising, Crane Co, 40th Anniversary, bronze medal,
   1930. . . . . **10.00**
Advertising, Fageol Safety Coach, lead replica of c1920s
   bus, inscription on both sides. **20.00**
Advertising, Lehigh Foundries, cast iron, round, 1947 . . . . . . **12.00**
Advertising, North River Insurance Co, 100th
   Anniversary, brass, round, 1922, 3³/₄" d **50.00**
Advertising, National Cash Register, figural, cast iron,
   orig paint **50.00**
Advertising, National Molasses Co, figural railroad car,
   bronzed white metal, c1950, 5" l **25.00**
Advertising, Raleigh Cigarettes, Sir Walter Raleigh bust,
   white metal, painted, c1950, 4¹/₂" h **80.00**
Advertising, Superior Stove & Range Co, cast iron **35.00**
Advertising, Texaco, brass, figural anvil **12.00**
Advertising, Westinghouse, Tough Guy, composition,
   1952, 4¹/₂" h **75.00**
Advertising, Wurtz Auto Garage, Degenhart **55.00**
Commemorative, American Bicentennial, Whitefriars,
   central US flag formed from millefiori canes and rods,
   resting on blue and white 6–pointed star canes, sgd
   with blue and white date/signature cane with silhouette of robed friar and bicentennial commerative
   dates, 5 and 1 faceting. **500.00**
Commemorative, Prince Charles and Lady Diana
   Spencer, etched portraits, purple ground, Caithness,
   3" d **175.00**
Commemorative, Queen Elizabeth II, 1953 coronation,
   sulphide, cameo on red and white jasper ground,
   5 and 1 faceting, sgd and dated **465.00**
Contemporary, Banford, Bob, 6 ruby cherries with yel-
   low stems, brown branch with green leaves, set on
   parallel strips of white latticinio filigree, signature
   cane, 2⁷/₈" d **500.00**
Contemporary, Ebelhare, Drew, stardust canes, spaced
   pale pink, yellow, and blue, white, stave basket, white
   stardust carpet, signature cane, sgd and dated, 2⁵/₁₆" d **175.00**
Contemporary, J Glass, amethyst fantasy flower, 3 flow-
   ers with black millefiori centers and green stems, pr of
   opening buds, opaque black ground, STA signature
   cane, 2¹¹/₁₆" d. **250.00**
Contemporary, Kaziun, Charles, chrysanthemum, yellow
   spiked flower, green leaves, ftd crystal pedestal, com-
   plete K signature cane, 2¹/₂" h. **775.00**
Contemporary, Kaziun, Charles, miniature cabbage
   roses, ruby, yellow, and blue roses, emerald green
   leaves, translucent amethyst ground, 14K gold K sig-
   nature on base, 1¹⁵/₁₆" **650.00**
Contemporary, Manson, William, butterfly, complex
   millefiori wings, green aventurine body, and orange
   eyes, green and white cog cane garland, black
   ground, 2³/₄" d **275.00**

Advertising, Bell System C & P Telephone Company and Associated Companies, cobalt blue glass, 3¹/₂" h, 3¹/₄" d, $121.00. Photo courtesy Collectors Auction Services.

Contemporary, Saint Louis, blue and white carpet
   ground, pistachio, turquoise, and pink cog/quatrefoil
   cane set in sea of turquoise and white cog canes, sig-
   nature/date cane, 2⁷/₈" d **275.00**
Contemporary, Tarsitano, Debbie, fuchsia blossom, pink
   and cobalt petals, yellow stamens, curved stem with
   green leaves, star–cut ground, signature cane, 2¹/₄" d **450.00**
Contemporary, Whittemore, Francis, lily of the valley,
   cluster of white bell shaped blossoms with yellow stamens, leafy stem, translucent ruby ground, signature
   cane, 2¹/₂" d **415.00**
Contemporary, Ysart, Paul, double clematis, yellow
   striped amethyst petals, complex stardust cane center,
   green leaves, blue and white jasper ground, signature
   cane, 3" d **450.00**

PARRISH, MAXFIELD

Maxfield Parrish was born in Philadelphia on July 25, 1870. Originally named Frederick Parrish, he later adopted his mother's maiden name, Maxfield, as his middle name.

Parrish received his academic training at Haverford College and the Pennsylvania Academy of Fine Arts, and spent a brief period as a pupil of Howard Pyle at Drexel. His first art exhibit was held at the Philadelphia Art Club in 1893; his first magazine cover illustration appeared on an 1895 issue of *Harper's Bazaar.* He soon received commissions from *Century Magazine, Collier's, Ladies' Home Journal, Life,* and *Scribners.* In 1897 Parrish was elected to the Society of American Artists.

Parrish established a studio, The Oaks, in Cornish, New Hampshire. He painted a large number of works for advertisements, book illustrations, and calendars. He is best known for the work he did between 1900 and 1940.

Maxfield Parrish died on March 30, 1966.

References: Erwin Flacks, *The Maxfield Parrish Identification & Price Guide, Second Edition,* Collectors Press, 1995; *Maxfield Parrish: A Price Guide,* L–W Book Sales, 1993, 1996 value update.

Game, Soldier Ten Pins, Parker Bros., c1921, $1,870.00. Photo courtesy Wm. Morford Auctions.

Advertisement, Jell–O, 1923, 9¹/₂ x 6¹/₂" **$45.00**

Blotter, cardboard, ink split billboard blocking out scenic view, 3¹/₂ x 6" **450.00**

Book, *Emerald Storybook*, Duffield, 1924................ **75.00**

Book, *Golden Treasury of Songs & Lyrics*, Duffield, 1926.... **150.00**

Calendar, "Ecstasy," Edison/Madza adv, cropped and framed, 1930 .... **675.00**

Game, Soldier Ten Pins, Parker Brothers, heavy cardboard, Parrish soldiers on wooden bases, orig wooden "bowling" balls, orig box, c1921, 11¹/₂ x 19¹/₂ x 1³/₄" **1,700.00**

Magazine Cover, *You and Your Work*, Tranquility, May 13, 1944 .... **45.00**

Magazine Tear Sheet, *House & Garden*, Jello–O, "Polly Put The Kettle On," 1923 .... **75.00**

Poster, "Buy Products Not Advertised On Our Roadside," 1939... **600.00**

Print, Dreaming, 1928, 6 x 10" **175.00**

Print, The Lute Players, 1924, 6 x 10"................ **125.00**

Print, When Day Is Dawning, 1954, 13 x 17", orig frame ... **200.00**

AUCTION PRICES

Maxfield Parrish items sold by Wm Morford Auctions on May 30, 1997. Prices include a 10% buyer's premium.

Calendar, "Contentment," 1928 Edison Mazda, 2 women sitting on sunlit rocks, deep purple and bright pink mountains behind them, full calendar pad, framed and matted in modern frame, large . **$1,925.00**

Calendar, "Reveries," 1927 Edison Mazda, 2 women in garden sitting next to raised pool, full pad, framed and matted in modern metal frame, 8¹/₂ x 19¹/₈" **660.00**

Cigar Box Label, Old King Cole Cigars, stone litho emb image of Old King Cole, c1920s, 6¹/₂ x 10" ... **165.00**

Matchcover, Old King Cole design on back, adv for King Cole Bar at St Regis Hotel, NY **121.00**

Menu, Broadmoor Hotel, Colorado Springs, CO, heavy textured stock, fancy gold tassel, 8 x 9³/₄" image, 14¹/₂ x 10¹/₂" menu **264.00**

Pocket Calendar, 1921, "Jack Spratt," Swift's Premium Ham adv, 3¹/₂ x 1³/₄"................. **330.00**

PATRIOTIC COLLECTIBLES

Uncle Sam became a national symbol during the Civil War. His modern day appearance resulted from drawings by Thomas Nast in *Harper's Weekly* and portraits by the artist, James Montgomery Flagg. Uncle Sam played a major role in military recruiting during World Wars I and II.

Other important symbols of American patriotism include Columbia and the Goddess of Liberty, the eagle, the flag, the Liberty Bell, and the Statue of Liberty. Today they are most prevalent during national holidays, such as Memorial Day and the Fourth of July, and centennial celebrations. They often appear subtley in print advertising and television commercials.

References: Gerald E. Czulewicz, Sr., *The Foremost Guide to Uncle Sam Collectibles*, Collector Books, 1995; Nicholas Steward, *James Montgomery Flagg: Uncle Sam and Beyond*, Collectors Press, 1997.

Collectors' Club: Statue of Liberty Collectors' Club, 26601 Bernwood Rd, Cleveland, OH 44122.

Eagle, banner, red, white, and blue eagle and shield, United We Stand, Charles Coiner, 1941, 17 x 123" **$300.00**

Eagle, chocolate mold, tin, clamp style, wings spread, shield at chest, "LIBERTY" above, #JAB 10, 4 ¹/₂" h **55.00**

Eagle, cookie cutter, tin, 6¹/₂" l **85.00**

Eagle, poster, NRA Code, Motor Vehicle Maintenance Trade, red, white, and blue, eagle symbol, Coiner, c1934, 11 x 14" **100.00**

Eagle, poster, Pledge of the Soldier of Supply, eagle and flag, Zarv, 1943, 34 x 43" **175.00**

Eagle, program, Democratic National Convention, eagle on cov, 1948, 80 pp **45.00**

Flag, bandanna, silk, flag and wreath with 36 stars, 22 x 25" **110.00**

Flag, game, Games of the Nations, Heroes of America, flag illus cov, Paul Educational Games, c1920s **25.00**

Flag, pin, Our Country's Flag, 1930s **15.00**

Flag, poster, "Long May It Wave," 1942, 41 x 31" **150.00**

Flag and Shield, paper clip, celluloid, red, white, and blue, steel spring clip, center inscription in shield "The Grand Rapids Furniture Record," 1922 .... **10.00**

Flag and Shield, poster, "Let's All Pull Together," full color, 1943, 29 x 40".................................. **125.00**

Liberty Bell, badge, Liberty Bell with FDR and Garner, red fabric ribbon, 1936, 4¹/₂" l **60.00**

Liberty Bell, bank, pot metal and wood, brown, mkd "USA, 1947," 4¹/₂" h **30.00**

Liberty Bell, jar, glass, clear, metal lid with flag and black letters, emb "Liberty Cherries Jar 1776–1976," 6 x 6¹/₂" **8.00**

Liberty Bell, poster, "What So Proudly We Hailed," full color, Liberty Bell and tourists, quote on bottom, c1943, 16 x 20" **75.00**

Liberty Bell, tablecloth, printed red, white, and blue flags and Liberty Bell, Dennison.................... **10.00**

Liberty Bell, tape measure, The Sesqui–Centennial International Exposition, Philadelphia, 1776–1926, full color Independence Hall, flags, and Liberty Bell **80.00**

Statue of Liberty, poster, "New York—The Wonder City of the World—New York Central Lines," Statue illuminated from below at night, panorama of nighttime cityscape in background, Adolph Treidler, c1930, 27 x 41" **350.00**

Uncle Sam, sheet music, *Any Bonds Today?*, National Defense program theme song, ©1941, 6 pp, 9 x 12", $15.00.

Statue of Liberty, tie slide, Boy Scout, emb brass, detailed raised Statue, scroll banner at base, c1930, 1¼ x 2" 22.00

Statue of Liberty, watch, commemorative, quartz, orig box and papers, 1986 .... 50.00

Uncle Sam, book, *Uncle Sam's Story Book*, Wilhelmina Harper, 1944.................................... 35.00

Uncle Sam, game, Yankee Doodle, Cadaco–Ellis, 1940...... 25.00

Uncle Sam, paper dolls, Uncle Sam's Little Helpers Paper Dolls, Ann Kovach, 1943 .... 15.00

Uncle Sam, ornament, pressed tin, Uncle Sam Keepsake Ornament, Hallmark, 1984 .... 25.00

Uncle Sam, postcard, bust of Uncle Sam front, story of Samuel Wilson on back, Yankee Colour Corp, 1966 ...... 10.00

Uncle Sam, poster, "Jap...You're Next! Buy Extra Bonds," Uncle Sam rolling up sleeves, James Montgomery Flagg, 1945, 13 x 20" 225.00

George Washington, plate, #258, clear, Washington Bicentennial, bust of Washington, star border, stippled ground, 1732–1932, 8" d 50.00

George Washington, sheet music, *Father of the Land We Love*, George Washington illus, James Montgomery Flagg artist, ©1931 .... 6.00

Collectors' Club: Peanuts Collector Club, 539 Sudden Valley, Bellingham, WA 98226.

Book, *Charlie Brown Talking Storybook*, Speak Up, cardboard, vinyl pages, Mattel, 1971 .... $110.00

Bubble Bath, figural Lucy, wearing red dress and beanie, Avon. 8.00

Candle Holders. composition, Linus sucking thumb and holding blanket, brass insert cup, Hallmark Candles sticker, 1970s, 7½" h 25.00

Character Glass, McDonald's, Camp Snoopy, "Civilization Is Overrated" 2.00

Clock, Snoopy chasing butterfly, 1958 .... 38.00

Costume, Charlie Brown, Collegeville 15.00

Costume, Pigpen, Hungerford Plastics, 1958, 8½" h 85.00

Doll, Dress Me Belle, pink dress with blue dots, Knickerbocker, 1983 .... 35.00

Doll, Linus, Ideal, 1976................................. 75.00

Doll, Peppermint Patty, Ideal, 1976 .... 40.00

Figure, Beagle Scout in bus, diecast, Hasbro, 1983.......... 5.00

Figure, Lucy, vinyl, smiling, yellow dress, red accents, yellow hat, black shoes, red ribbon, 8¼" h 25.00

Lunch Box, steel, cone shape, illus of Snoopy laying on his back, "Have Lunch With Snoopy" on one side, "Go To School With Snoopy" on other side, American Thermos, 1968 .... 30.00

Magazine, *Newsweek*, Dec 27, 1971, Peanuts Gang cov, "Good Grief, $150 Million" article.................... 8.00

Model Kit, Snoopy and his Bugatti Race Car, Monogram/ Mattel, 1971 .... 100.00

Music Box, wood, Linus in pumpkin patch, plays "Who Can I Turn To?," Anri 120.00

Nodder, Charlie Brown, orange shirt, brown shoes, standing on black base, name on front, 6" h, 1959 ...... 75.00

Ornament, Snoopy carrying red and white striped candy cane, Determined, 1975 .... 8.00

Paint By Number Set, Snoopy Paint By Number Set, Craft House, 1980s 20.00

Pencil Holder, ceramic, Snoopy, figural doghouse, 1975..... 25.00

Plate, Woodstock's Christmas, Schmid, orig box, 1976 ...... 28..00

Punching Bag, Joe Cool, Ideal, 1976 .... 30.00

PEANUTS

In 1950 Charles M. Schulz launched Peanuts, a comic strip about kids and a beagle named Snoopy. Charlie Brown, Lucy, Linus, and the Peanuts gang have become a national institution. They have been featured in over sixty television specials, translated in over a dozen languages.

Charles M. Schulz Creative Associates and United Features Syndicate have pursued an aggressive licensing program. Almost no aspect of a child's life has escaped the licensing process.

Given this, why is the number of Peanuts collectors relatively small? The reason is that the strip's humor is targeted primarily toward adults. Children do not actively follow it during the formative years, i.e., ages seven to fourteen, that influence their adult collecting.

References: Jan Lindenberger, *The Unauthorized Guide to Snoopy Collectibles* (1997), *More Snoopy Collectibles* (1997), Schiffer Publishing.

Snoopy Astronaut, vinyl doll, fabric uniform, clear plastic helmet, ©1969, 7½" h, $50.00.

Snowdome, Snoopy, lying on doghouse, clear sides, yellow, green, and orange base 5.00

Spinning Top, Snoopy, Charlie Brown, Lucy, and Linus illus, Chein, 1960s 50.00

Squeeze Toy, vinyl, Linus, black and red striped shirt, black pants and shoes, 8¼" h, 1960s 25.00

Squeeze Toy, Pig Pen, smiling, blonde hair, blue shorts, black shoes, 9" h, 1960s 30.00

Suitcase, canvas, red, yellow trim, color illus of Snoopy as aviator, 12 x 18 x 4", 1970s 50.00

Toy, Push 'N Fly Snoopy, Romper Room/Hasbro, 1980 . . . . . . 15.00

Toy, Push and Play with the Peanuts Gang, Child Guidance, 1970s. 50.00

Toy, Snoopy's Fantastic Automatic Bubble Pipe, Chemtoy, 1970s 10.00

Toy, Talking Peanuts Bus, metal, Chein, 1967 . . . . 325.00

Vehicle, Woodstock in ice cream truck, friction, Aviva 10.00

Wristwatch, Snoopy dancing, Woodstock second hand, silver case, Determined, 1969 . . . . 110.00

PEDAL CARS

Pedal car is a generic term used to describe any pedal–driven toy. Automobiles were only one form. There are also pedal airplanes, fire engines, motorcycles, and tractors.

By the mid–1910s pedal cars resembling their full–sized counterparts were being made. Buick, Dodge, Overland, and Packard are just a few examples. American National, Garton, Gendron, Steelcraft, and Toledo Wheel were the five principal pedal car manufacturers in the 1920s and 30s. Ertl, Garton, and Murray made pedal cars in the post–1945 period. Many mail–order catalogs, e.g., Sears, Roebuck, sold pedal cars. Several television shows issued pedal car licenses during the mid–1950s and 60s.

Pedal car collecting is serious business in the 1990s. The $10,000 barrier has been broken. Many pedal cars are being stripped down and completely restored to look as though they just came off the assembly line. Some feel this emphasis, especially when it destroys surviving paint, goes too far.

References: *Evolution of the Pedal Car, Vol. 1* (1989, 1996 value update), *Vol. 2* (1990, 1997 value update), *Vol. 3* (1992), *Vol. 4* (1993, 1997 value update), L–W Book Sales; Andrew G. Gurka, *Pedal Car Restoration and Price Guide,* Krause Publications, 1996.

Newsletter: *The Wheel Goods Trader,* PO Box 435, Fraser, MI 48026.

Collectors' Club: National Pedal Vehicle Assoc, 1720 Rupert NE, Grand Rapids, MI 49505.

Atomic Missile, red, white and blue, Murray, 1961 . . . . . **$1,000.00**

Blue Streak, blue, white, trim, BMC, 1953 . . . . 400.00

BMC Special Racer, yellow, black trim, 1952. . . . . 1,000.00

Champion Fire Chief, red and white, attached bell on front with rope, Murray, 1950s. 600.00

Comet, Murray, 1949 . . . . 800.00

Convertible, Buick, Limited, opening trunk, 1949 . . . . 2,500.00

Custom Coca–Cola Truck, red and white, AMF, 1960s. 500.00

Dr Pepper Delivery Truck, white, green and red, AMF, 1962. . . . . 400.00

Earth Mover, yellow and black, Murray, 1960s. 1,000.00

Farmall 560 Tractor, red and white, 1960s 400.00

Fireball Racer, orig red and white paint, Murray, 1968 . . . . . 300.00

Mack Truck City Fire Dept, all orig, $1,375.00. Photo courtesy Gene Harris Antique Auction Center.

Fire Truck, red and white, plastic, AMF, 1980s 100.00

Flying Tiger, Murray, restored, 1945. . . . . 3,000.00

Ford 8000 Tractor, blue, white trim, 1968. . . . . 150.00

Garden Mark Tractor, green, white trim, AMF, 1963 . . . . . . 250.00

G–Man Radio Cruiser, orig light, Murray, 1958 . . . . 1,000.00

Good Humor Ice Cream Truck, white, blue and red, Murray, 1955. . . . . 350.00

GTO, red, 1970. . . . . 400.00

Hayseed Racing Car, Garton, 1960 . . . . 700.00

John Deere 730 Tractor, green and yellow, 1950s. 3,000.00

Jolly Roger Boat, blue and white, Murray, 1960s 1,500.00

Junior Chain Drive Wagon, orig gold and white paint, AMF, 1958 . . . . 550.00

Junior Trac, red, white trim, AMF, 1960s. 175.00

Kidillac, Garton, 1950s. 1,500.00

Lancer, orig trunk and trailer, Murray, 1950s 2,000.00

Mustang 535, AMF, 1969 . . . . 800.00

Official Astronauts Car, orig white paint, red and blue rocket dec on side, Murray, 1965 . . . . 800.00

Pacer, blue, AMF, 1968 . . . . 300.00

Plymouth Strato–Flite Auto, blue and white, 1957 . . . . . . 1,000.00

Police Radar Patrol, blue, red and white trim, Murray, 1955. . . . . 600.00

Pontiac, black, red trim, Murray, 1949. . . . . 1,500.00

Probe Jr, orig yellow paint and decals, AMF, 1960s. 400.00

Race Car, dark blue, yellow trim, Garton, 1950s. 650.00

Ranch Wagon, red and white, Murray, 1948. . . . . 700.00

Ranger, silver, black and white trim, Murray, 1967 . . . . 700.00

Safari Wagon, AMF, 1968 . . . . 500.00

Sand and Gravel Dump Truck, yellow, Murray, 1952 . . . . . 1,000.00

Silver Cup Special Thunderbolt, yellow, black trim, Murray, 1963. . . . . 300.00

Sport Crest Race Car, blue, red and white trim, Murray, 1962. . . . . 400.00

Station Wagon, red and white, Murray, 1950 . . . . 1,500.00

Studebaker, red, restored, Midwest Industries, 1953 . . . . . . 900.00

Taxi, yellow, black trim, AMC Roadmaster, 1959 . . . . 800.00

Tee Bird, blue and white, Murray, 1960s 800.00

Tin Lizzy, green, yellow trim, Garton, 1950s. 500.00

Torpedo, Murray, 1950s 1,000.00

Tote–All, red and white, AMF, 1970s 500.00

Tow Wrecker, black and white, AMF, 1955. . . . . 800.00

Trac Tractor, red, white trim, Turbo Drive, 1952 . . . . 400.00

PENNANTS

Felt pennants were popular souvenirs from the 1920s through the end of the 1950s. College sports pennants decorated the walls of dormitory rooms during this period. Pennants graced the radio antenna of hot rods and street rods. A pennant served as a pleasant reminder of a trip to the mountains, shore, or an historic site.

Most commercial pennants were stenciled. Once a pennant's paint cracks and peels, its value is gone. Handmade pennants, some exhibiting talented design and sewing work, are common.

Batman, color illus, black and white lettering, c1966, 29" l $25.00
Boston Yanks, football player illus, green, yellow lettering, c1950, 28" l 20.00
Boxing, Ali and Wepner 1975 heavyweight championship, blue, white lettering, Mar 24, 1975, 26½" l 28.00
Captain Marvel, blue, 1940s 85.00
Coolidge–Dawes, "Lincoln Tour 1924," blue, white lettering, 11 x 24" 75.00
Derby Day, red, white lettering, red and white design with pink accents, 1939, 18" l 15.00
Dizzy Dean, 1930s 35.00
Eisenhower–Nixon Inauguration, brown, white illus and lettering, white Capitol building scene, blue, yellow and green shading, 1953, 29" l 20.00
Elvis, red and green, center photo, 18" l 12.00
Humphrey, Hubert, "Unity With Humphrey," red, white, and blue, 1968, 30" l 30.00
New York Mets, blue, white and orange inscriptions and designs, late 1960s, 29½" l 18.00
Philadelphia Sixers, 1982–83 championship, red, white, and blue, 30" l 20.00
Playboy PMOC, gold, white lettering and crest, 1960s, 29" l 12.00
Ringling Bros Barnum & Bailey Circus, circus scenes, brown, white lettering, yellow trim and streamers, c1940, 24" l 25.00
Space, commemorative, 1st US orbital space flight, Feb 20, 1962, white, red and blue, 3' black and white John Glenn photo 40.00
Wallace, George, "Stand Up For America," red, white, and blue, 1968, 28" l 8.00

PENNSBURY POTTERY

In 1950 Henry Below, a ceramic engineer and mold maker, and Lee Below, a ceramic designer and modeler, founded Pennsbury Pottery. The pottery was located near Morrisville, Pennsylvania, the location of William Penn's estate, Pennsbury.

Henry and Lee Below previously worked for Stangl, explaining why so many forms, manufacturing techniques, and motifs are similar to those used at Stangl. A series of bird figurines were Pennsbury's first products.

Although Pennsbury is best known for its brown wash background, other background colors were used. In addition to Christmas plates (1960–70), commemorative pieces, and special order pieces, Pennsbury made several dinnerware lines, most reflecting the strong German heritage of eastern Pennsylvania.

The company employed local housewives and young ladies as decorators, many of whom initialed their work or added the initials of the designer. At its peak in 1963, Pennsbury had 46 employees.

Henry Below died on December 21, 1959; Lee Below on December 12, 1968. Attempts to continue operations proved unsuccessful. The company filed for bankruptcy in October 1970 and the property was auctioned in December. The pottery and its supporting buildings were destroyed by fire on May 18, 1971.

References: Harvey Duke, *The Official Price Guide to Pottery and Porcelain, Eighth Edition,* House of Collectibles, 1995; Lucile Henzke, *Pennsbury Pottery,* Schiffer Publishing, 1990; Dana Gehman Morykan and Harry L. Rinker, *Warman's Country Antiques & Collectibles, Third Edition,* Wallace–Homestead, Krause Publications, 1996; Mike Schneider, *Stangl and Pennsbury Birds: Identification and Price Guide,* Schiffer Publishing, 1994.

REPRODUCTION ALERT: Some Pennsbury pieces (many with Pennsbury markings) have been reproduced from original molds purchased by Lewis Brothers Pottery in Trenton, New Jersey. Glen View in Langhorne, Pennsylvania, marketed the 1970s' Angel Christmas plate with Pennsbury markings and continued the Christmas plate line into the 1970s. Lenape Products, a division of Pennington, bought Glen View in 1975 and continued making products with a Pennsbury feel.

Amish, ashtray, "Don't Be So Doppich," 5" d $25.00
Amish, ashtray, "Doylestown Trust" 12.00
Amish, ashtray, "The Solebury Naitonal Bank of New Hope PA," 5" d 30.00
Amish, ashtray, "What Giffs?" 18.00
Amish, salt and pepper shakers, pr. 35.00
Apple Tree, pie plate 90.00
Barber Shop Quarter, coffee mug, 3¼" h 35.00
Barber Shop Quarter, coffeepot, 8" h 90.00
Bell, Mother's Day, 1977 .... 35.00
Bird, Blue Bird, 4" h 150.00
Bird, Crested Chickadee, 4" h 150.00
Bird, Hen, yellow and brown, 10½" h 200.00
Bird, Wren, brown, 3" h 100.00
Bird, Wren, white, red comb 225.00
Black Rooster, butter dish, folk art 45.00
Black Rooster, casserole, cov, 10½ x 8¼" 100.00
Black Rooster, cup and saucer 15.00
Black Rooster, pie plate, 10" d 35.00
Eagle, beer mug, 5" h 30.00
Eagle, pitcher, 5¼" h 60.00
Eagle, pretzel bowl, 8 x 11" 55.00

Red Rooster, vegetable dish, divided, 9½" l, $35.00.

Hex, candy dish, 9" d **40.00**
Hex, cup and saucer **30.00**
Hex, dinner plate, 10" d **15.00**
Hex, luncheon plate, 10" d **15.00**
Kissing Over Cow, wall plaque **18.00**
Mother Serving Pie, plaque, sgd "K," 6" d **35.00**
Pennsylvania Hex, coffeepot **50.00**
Plaque, farm scene, 6" d **50.00**
Red Barn, pitcher, 6¼" h **100.00**
Red Rooster, chip and dip set **90.00**
Red Rooster, cup and saucer **18.00**
Red Rooster, dinner plate, 10" d. **20.00**
Red Rooster, eggcup, 4" h **22.00**
Red Rooster, salt and pepper shakers, pr, 2½" h **25.00**
Red Rooster, snack set, tray and cup **25.00**
Red Rooster, teapot **60.00**
Two Birds Over Heart, cake stand, 11" d **80.00**

PENS & PENCILS

Fountain pens are far more collectible than mechanical pencils. While a few individuals are beginning to collect ballpoint pens, most are valued by collectors more for their advertising than historical importance. Defects, e.g., dents, mechanical damage, missing parts, or scratches, cause a rapid decline in value. Surprisingly, engraved initials, a monogram, or name has little impact on value.

Lewis Waterman developed the fountain pen in the 1880s. Parker, Sheaffer, and Wahl–Eversharp refined the product. Conklin, Eversharp, Moore, Parker, Sheaffer, Wahl, and Waterman were leading manufacturers. Reynolds' introduction of the ballpoint pen in late 1945 signaled the end for the nib fountain pen.

Sampson Mordan patented the mechanical pencil in 1822. Early mechanical pencils used a slide action mechanism. It was eventually replaced by a spiral mechanism. Wahl–Eversharp developed the automatic "click" mechanism used on pens as well as pencils.

Fountain pen values rose dramatically from the late 1970s through the early 1990s. Many of these values were speculative. The speculative bubble burst in the mid–1990s. Today, prices are extremely stable with common fountain pens a very difficult sell.

References: George Fischler and Stuart Schneider, *Fountain Pens and Pencils*, Schiffer Publishing, 1990; Henry Gostony and Stuart Schneider, *The Incredible Ball Point Pen: A Comprehensive History & Price Guide*, Schiffer Publishing, 1998; Regina Martini, *Pens & Pencils: A Collector's Handbook, 2nd Edition*, Schiffer Publishing, 1998; Stuart Schneider and George Fischler, *The Illustrated Guide to Antique Writing Instruments, Second Edition*, Schiffer Publishing, 1997.

Periodical: *Pen World Magazine*, PO Box 6007, Kingwood, TX 77325.

Collectors' Clubs: American Pencil Collectors Society, RR North, Wilmore, KS 67155; Pen Collectors of America, PO Box 821449, Houston, TX 77282.

PENS

Conklin, Model 25P, lady's filigree cap ribbon, black,
   crescent filler **$60.00**
Conklin, Cushion Point, silver–pink stripes, gold filled
   trim, NOZAK filler, 1945 . . . . **75.00**

Dunn, black, red barren, gold plated trim **50.00**
Eversharp, ballpoint, CA model, black, gold filled cap,
   1946 . . . . **40.00**
Eversharp, Doric, desk, gold seal, green marble cov,
   lever fill, large adjustable nib **200.00**
Eversharp, Doric, lady's, Eversharp Gold Seal, gold marble color, 14K point, 12 sided cap and barrel, 1931 . . . . . **150.00**
Onoto, Ink Pencil Stylographic pen, black chased hard
   rubber, eyedropper, 1924 . . . . **55.00**
Parker, Blue–Diamond–Vacumatic, blue and black, gold
   plated trim, button filled, 1944 . . . . **100.00**
Parker, Lucky Curve, ring pen, black hard rubber, gold
   filled trim **150.00**
Parker, pen and pencil set, Duofold Deluxe, black and
   pearl, 3 narrow gold color bands on cap, push button
   fill, 1929 . . . . **450.00**
Reynolds, Model 2, orig ballpoint, 1945–46 . . . . **110.00**
Waterman, Taperlite, black, gold filled metal mounted
   cap, gold filled trim, lever filler, 1949 . . . . **100.00**

PENCILS

Advertising, mechanical, Secretary Pen Co, Elsie,
   ©Borden Co, 1930–40, 5" l **$60.00**
Advertising, Hudson–Essex, PA dealership, metal, bullet
   shape, "Shoot Straight For Triangle Motor Co," 1930s,
   4" l **30.00**
Character, Popeye, Eagle Pencil Co, mechanical, metal,
   silver–gray, black and dark red illus and text,
   1930–40, 10½" l **25.00**
Commemorative, "Remember Pearl Harbor, United We
   Stand, We Will Win," plastic, red, white, and blue,
   local business sponsor adv, 5" l **65.00**
Eversharp, repeating, dark blue, gold filled trim, 1941 . . . . . **50.00**
Eversharp, repeating, green marbelized base, upper half
   gold color metal cap, 1936 . . . . **100.00**
Sheaffer, Fineline 4000, novel point, platinum plating,
   1946 . . . . **40.00**
Wahl–Eversharp, ring top, gold filled case, 1923 . . . . **50.00**
Wahl–Eversharp, SS, engraved case, 1924 . . . . **175.00**

PEPSI–COLA

Caleb D. Bradham, a pharmacist and drugstore owner in New Bern, North Carolina, developed "Brad's Drink," a soda mix, in the mid–1890s. By 1898, Brad's Drink had become Pepsi–Cola. By 1902 Bradham was promoting Pepsi–Cola on a full–time basis. Two years later he sold his first franchise.

In 1910 the Pepsi–Cola network consisted of 250 bottlers in 24 states. Investing in the sugar market, Pepsi–Cola found itself in deep financial difficulties when the market collapsed immediately following World War I. Roy Megargel, a Wall Street financier, rescued and guided the company out of its difficulties. Pepsi–Cola survived a second bankruptcy in 1931.

In 1933 Pepsi–Cola's fortunes soared when the company doubled its bottle size and held its price to a nickel. Walter Mack (1938 to 1951) provided the leadership that enabled Pepsi to challenge Coca–Cola for the number one spot in the soda market. "Pepsi–Cola Hits The Spot, Twelve Full Ounces That's A Lot" was one of the most popular advertising jingles of the 1950s.

Pepsi Co., a division of Beatrice, enjoys a worldwide reputation, outselling Cola–Cola in a number of foreign countries. This is one reason why many foreign buyers have an interest in Pepsi–Cola memorabilia.

Beware of a wide range of Pepsi–Cola reproductions, copycats, fantasy items, and fakes. The 1970s Pepsi and Pete pillow, a Pepsi double bed quilt, and a 12" high ceramic statute of a woman holding a glass of Pepsi are a few examples.

Collectors place little secondary market value on contemporary licensed products.

References: James C. Ayers, *Pepsi–Cola Bottles Collectors Guide*, RJM Enterprises, 1995; Everette and Mary Lloyd, *Pepsi–Cola Collectibles*, Schiffer Publishing, 1993; Bill Vehling and Michael Hunt, *Pepsi–Cola Collectibles, Vol. 1* (1990, 1993 value update), *Vol. 2* (1990, 1992 value update), and *Vol. 3* (1993, 1995 value update), L–W Book Sales.

Collectors' Club: Pepsi–Cola Collectors Club, PO Box 1275, Covina, CA 91722.

Ashtray, glass, "Pepsi Beats The Others Cold!," 1960s, 4" sq **$25.00**
Bookmark, feather and bottle cap, 1940s, 3 x 12" **35.00**
Bottle, applied color label, c1960, 32 oz **25.00**
Bottle Carrier, cardboard, 6 bottle, c1960 . . . . **25.00**
Cookbook, Pepsi–Cola, soft cov, 1940 . . . . **15.00**
Cooler, metal, orig box, 24 x 18 x 14", c1960 . . . . **175.00**
Coupon, fold–over, "Pepsi–Cola Free Coupon Offer, Worth 25¢," 1940s, 6 x 7" **75.00**
Display, diecut cardboard, 3–dimensional stand–up, grocer holding 6 pack of bottles in 1 hand, offering soda bottle in other, late 1930s, 24" w, 68" h **675.00**
Fan, cardboard, wood handle, "McPherson Beverages, Inc, Bottlers of 7–Up & Pepsi–Cola," 1940s, 10 x 10" **75.00**
Fan, cardboard, wood handle, c1940, 10" sq **75.00**
Lighter, metal, bottle cap illus on side, 1950s, 4" l **150.00**
Magazine, *Pepsi World*, The Steele Years, 1959 . . . . **10.00**
Menu, 1 sheet, Pepsi glass and bottle cap, 1940s, 8 x 11" **50.00**
Napkin, cloth, c1940, 19" sq **25.00**
Napkin Dispenser, black and white, red, white, and blue bottle cap design on sides, c1940s **350.00**
Paperweight, glass, "Delicious Pepsi–Cola," c1940, 3 x 3" **75.00**
Pinback Button, celluloid and tin, "Pepsi Day For Crippled Children," 1970s, 1" d **25.00**

Playing Cards, Pepsi–Cola Bottling Co, Quincy, IL, orig yellow box, c1940 . . . . **100.00**
Poster, Counter Spy, Pepsi logo, 1940s, 8 x 19" **18.00**
Poster, premium, *Indiana Jones*, 18 x 32" **16.00**
Program, Evervess Convention, Atlantic City, Nov 12–15, 1947, 6 x 12" **75.00**
Radio, transistor, soda fountain cooler shape, complete with original leather carrying strap, 1930s **375.00**
Sign, cardboard, "Be Sociable, Have A Pepsi," trolley illus, 1950s, 28 x 11" **85.00**
Sign, celluloid and tin, "Ice Cold Pepsi–Cola Sold Here," 1930s, 9" d **275.00**
Sign, easel back, family enjoy picnic illus, "Pepsi–Cola, The Big Picnic Drink," 1940s, 18 x 27" **450.00**
Sign, plastic, light–up, bottle cap illus, "Take Home Pepsi," 1950s, 12 x 8" **150.00**
Stock Certificate, Pepsi–Cola Bottling Co of California, framed, 1936, 11 x 8½" **25.00**
Thermometer, "Bouncy To Ounce," 1950s, 26" d **160.00**
Ticket, Pepsi adv, Russel Bros Circus, 1930s **50.00**
Toy, truck, metal, Pepsi adv, Tonka, 1978, 7½" l **65.00**
Tray, "Have A Pepsi," 1950s, 13" d **75.00**
Tray, "Pepsi–Cola, Hits the Spot," 1940s **15.00**
Tray, rect, "Pepsi–Cola, Bigger and Better, Pepsi–Cola, Coast to Coast," red lettering on rim, titled soda bottle against blue and white US map background, 1939 . . . . . . **350.00**
Visor, "Say Pepsi Please," 1950s, 12" l **35.00**

PERFUME BOTTLES

Perfume manufacturers discovered that packaging is almost as important a selling factor for a perfume as its scent. Coty contracted with Lalique to produce exquisitely designed bottles for many of its perfumes. Many Czechoslovakian perfume bottles manufactured between the 1920s and 1960s are architectural miniatures reflecting the very best in design styles of the period.

A perfume bottle is a bottle with a stopper, often elongated, that serves as an applicator. A cologne bottle is usually larger than a perfume bottle. Its stopper also serves as an applicator. An atomizer is a bottle with a spray mechanism.

After a period of speculation and rapidly escalating prices in the 1980s and early 1990s, perfume bottle prices have stabilized, especially for common and middle range examples. Large countertop display bottles enjoyed a brief speculative price run in the early 1990s. They are tough sells today, largely because most collectors consider them overvalued.

References: Joanne Dubbs Ball and Dorothy Hehl Torem, *Commercial Fragrance Bottles*, Schiffer Publishing, 1993; Glinda Bowman, *Miniature Perfume Bottles*, Schiffer Publishing, 1994; Jacquelyne Jones–North, *Commercial Perfume Bottles, Third Edition*, Schiffer Publishing, 1996; Tirza True Latimer, *The Perfume Atomizer: An Object With Atmosphere*, Schiffer Publishing, 1991; Sue Mattioli, *Evening in Paris by Bourjois*, published by author, 1997; Beverly Nelson (comp.), *A Guide for the Collector of the Fragrances of the Bourjois Company*, published by author, 1996; Jeri Lyn Ringblum, *A Collector's Handbook of Miniature Perfume Bottles: Minis, Mates and More*, Schiffer Publishing, 1996.

Collectors' Clubs: International Perfume Bottle Assoc, PO Box 529, Vienna, VA 22180; Miniature Perfume Bottle Collectors, 28227 Paseo El Siena, Laguna Niguel, CA 92677.

Sign, cardboard in metal frame, 26½" h, 37¾" w, $82.50. Photo courtesy Collectors Auction Services.

Atomizer, Art Deco, opaque black ground, gold dec,
3" h **$65.00**

Atomizer, frosted, 4 molded panels of 4 seasons, Robj,
Paris, c1925, 6" h **600.00**

Atomizer, gold–blue Aurene, DeVilbiss, 8¾" h **795.00**

Atomizer, gold ground, enameled floral dec, clear blue
glass stemmed base, Czechoslovakian **125.00**

Atomizer, lavender transparent, Czechoslovakian,
3½" h **40.00**

Atomizer, orchid glass, long glass stopper, c1920,
6¼" h **75.00**

Atomizer, red, mottled colors, Czechoslovakian, 7½" h .. **65.00**

Atomizer, sapphire blue, gold flowers, leaves, and swirls,
melon ribbed body, orig gold top and bulb, Moser,
4½" h **250.00**

Atomizer, stippled gold, opaque jade, orig silk lined box,
Cambridge **135.00**

Cologne, amber, Czechoslovakian, 4¼" h.............. **55.00**

Cologne, blue transparent, Czechoslovakian, 3½" h **85.00**

Cologne, sapphire blue, white enameled young girl,
blue bubble stopper, Mary Gregory, 9½" h **215.00**

Cologne, SS overlay, clear ground **150.00**

Perfume, all over filigree florals and mesh, white enameled florals, blue mirrored faceted stones, jeweled
screw–on cap and dauber, Czechoslovakian, 2½" h **50.00**

Perfume, Amberina, orig yellow stopper, stamped
"Libbey," c1920................................... **295.00**

Perfume, Chaine D'Or, encased, beige tassled cardboard
box, imitation shagreen, c1926 .... **45.00**

Perfume, cranberry opalescent, Hobnail, flat stopper,
Fenton **90.00**

Perfume, cranberry, white enameled girl dec, clear ball
stopper, Mary Gregory, 4⅛" h..................... **165.00**

Perfume, crystal, brass and jewel ornamentation stopper,
Czechoslovakian, 2¼" h **75.00**

Perfume, figural Dutch girl, Goebel, c1935 .... **60.00**

Perfume, figural Queen Elizabeth, Crown Staffordshire,
England, 1930s **125.00**

Perfume, Langlois, inner glass stopper, metal cap, c1920 .... **45.00**

Perfume, Lionettes, frosted glass, brass top, 1923 .... **65.00**

Perfume, molded and frosted, gray, acid stamped
"Baccarat/France," mid–20th C, 6⅜" h **635.00**

Perfume, Olor de la Noche, 1940s................... **45.00**

Perfume, Sirenes, frosted mermaid with traces of gray
patina, molded signature on base, no cov, Rene
Lalique, 5½" h **250.00**

Perfume, Wildewood Toilet Water, frosted glass, molded
nude, c1920 .... **75.00**

Perfume, Wild Musk, Max Factor, figural acorn, chain,
celluloid box..................................... **50.00**

Scent, flattened globe shape, silver hinged rim and
screw cap mkd "Black, Starr & Frost," agate, 3" h **250.00**

Scent, glass, hobnail................................ **35.00**

Scent, ivory, carved, gourd shape, miniature, oriental,
1½" h **65.00**

Scent, multicolored jewels, enameled top, Czechoslovakian... **100.00**

PEZ

Eduard Haas, an Austrian food manufacturer, developed the PEZ formula in 1927. He added peppermint (Pfefferminz in German) oil to a candy formula, pressed it into small rectangular pellets, and sold it as an adult breath mint and cigarette substitute.

World War II halted the production of PEZ. When it reappeared in the late 1940s it was packaged in a rectangular dispenser. An initial foray into the United States market in 1952 was only modestly successful. Evaluating the situation, Haas added fruit flavors and novelty dispensers, thus enabling PEZ to make a major impact on the children's candy market.

Because the company carefully guards its design and production records, information regarding the first appearance of a particular dispenser and dispenser variations is open to interpretation. PEZ Candy, Inc., is located in Connecticut. A second, independent company with distribution rights to the rest of the world, including Canada, is located in Linz, Austria. Although the two cooperate, it is common for each company to issue dispensers with different heads or the same dispenser in different packaging.

There are three basic types of dispensers—generic, licensed, and seasonal. New dispensers appear regularly. Further, the company is quite willing to modify an existing design. The Mickey Mouse dispenser has gone through at least a dozen changes.

Pez has been made in Austria (current), Czechoslovakia (closed), Germany (closed), Hungary (current), Mexico (closed), United States (current), and Yugoslavia (current). Plants in Austria, China, Hong Kong, Hungary, and Slovenia make dispensers.

References: Richard Geary, *More PEZ For Collectors*, 2nd Edition, Schiffer Publishing, 1998; Richard Geary, *PEZ Collectibles*, Schiffer Publishing, 1994; David Welch, *Collecting Pez*, Bubba Scrubba Publications, 1994.

Newsletter: *PEZ Collector's News*, PO Box 124, Sea Cliff, NY 11579.

Note: Prices listed are for Pez containers in mint condition.

Annie, 1970s **$20.00**
Astronaut, blue helmet **85.00**
Baloo, with feet, blue head **20.00**
Bambi, with feet **25.00**
Barney Bear, 1980s.................................. **10.00**

Atomizer, amethyst glass, silver plated neck, $40.00.

Barney Rubble 2.00
Baseball Glove, brown glove, white ball. 120.00
Batgirl, blue mask, black hair. 75.00
Batman, blue mask 75.00
Betsy Ross, red stem, black hair, white bonnet 20.00
Blob Octopus, 1960s 70.00
Bouncer Beagle 6.00
Boy with Cap, white hair, blue cap 40.00
Bozo 100.00
Bride, white veil, brown, blond, or red hair 500.00
Brutus. 90.00
Bugs Bunny, with feet, 1979 . . . . 6.00
Bullwinkle, 1960s 150.00
Camel, brown face, red hat 35.00
Captain America, blue mask 20.00
Captain Pez 85.00
Casper 75.00
Cat, derby. 40.00
Charlie Brown, with feet, blue cap 20.00
Chick in Egg 12.00
Clown, with feet, green hat, Merry Melody Makers 5.00
Cockatoo, Kooky Zoo, 1970s. 30.00
Cool Cat. 40.00
Creature From the Black Lagoon, pearl green, 1965 . . . . 200.00
Crocodile, Kooky Zoo, 1970s 30.00
Daffy Duck. 15.00
Dalmatian 20.00
Daniel Boone, wearing coonskin cap. 95.00
Dead Head Dr Skull, 1960s. 1.00
Dino 3.00
Dog, Merry Melody Maker 20.00
Donald Duck 15.00
Droopy Dog 8.00
Dumbo. 25.00
Easter Bunny, color variation, entirely in pink, test mold
   bunny, 1990 . . . . 120.00
Elephant, aqua hair 170.00
Engineer, Pez Pal, 1969–70 . . . . 30.00
Fat Ears Rabbit 15.00
Fireman 30.00
Foghorn Leghorn. 20.00
Fozzie Bear, Sesame Street 1.00

Frankenstein 145.00
Frog, Merry Melody Makers 15.00
Garfield, with visor 3.00
Goofy, removable nose and teeth. 35.00
Gorilla, red stem, brown head 25.00
Green Hornet, black stem, green hat and mask. 200.00
Happy Bear, 1970s 10.00
Icee Bear, with feet 8.00
Incredible Hulk, Super Heroes, 1970s 5.00
Indian Brave, dark face 150.00
Indian Chief 55.00
Indian Squaw, 1976 . . . . 50.00
Jerry, 1980s. 10.00
Jiminy Cricket, green stem 25.00
Joker, soft head 70.00
Koala, Merry Melody Makers 20.00
Lamb, pink stem 10.00
Li'l Bad Wolf, Disney, 1960s 5.00
Lion's Club Lion, 1960s 800.00
Little Orphan Annie, red stem, golden brown hair 25.00
Maharaja, Pez Pal 60.00
Mama Giraffe, 1970s 20.00
Mary Poppins 385.00
Merlin Mouse 10.00
Miss Piggy 10.00
Monkey, Merry Melody Maker. 15.00
Moo Moo Cow, Kooky Zoo, 1960s 20.00
Mowgli, with feet 15.00
Mr. Ugly, blue stem, green face, black hair. 15.00
Nermal. 3.00
Octopus 40.00
Olive Oyl 145.00
Orange, crazy fruit, 1970s 40.00
Panda, Merry Melody Maker 5.00
Pebbles Flintstone 3.00
Penguin, soft head. 70.00
Peter Pan 80.00
Peter Pez 5.00
Pez Pal, Boy with Hat, 1969–70. . . . . 10.00
Pineapple, Crazy Fruit 200.00
Pinocchio, 1950s 12.00
Pistol, red, "Wild Cherry Dopple Pez Candy," instruc-
   tion card with German text, 5³/₄" l, 1960s 100.00
Policeman, blue stem, hat with black trim, separate plas-
   tic silver badge, 4" h 25.00
Pony, orange. 65.00
Popeye, removable pipe 45.00
Practical Pig, Disney, 1960s. 10.00
Raven, Kooky Zoo, 1970s 10.00
Rhino. 6.00
Ringmaster 25.00
Road Runner 5.00
Robot, blue, c1950, 3¹/₂" h 75.00
Rooster. 35.00
Rudolph the Red–Nosed Reindeer, 1960s. 5.00
Santa, off–white, red coat and hat, black boots, 3³/₄" h 200.00
Scrooge McDuck 20.00
Silly Clown, 1970s 25.00
Silver Glow. 10.00
Skull, with feet 3.00
Smurf, red stem. 10.00
Smurfette 8.00
Snoopy. 5.00
Snowman, 1976 Olympics 265.00

Left: Tom (Tom & Jerry), 4¹/₄" h, $10.00. Right: Puzzy Cat, black head, Austria, 4¹/₂" h, $10.00.

Snow White **60.00**
Space Gun, red, 1980s **55.00**
Speedy Gonzalez **10.00**
Spiderman **3.00**
Sylvester, white whiskers **2.00**
Thor, Super Heroes, 1970s. **60.00**
Tiger, whistle head **6.00**
Tinkerbell **120.00**
Truck, cab #1, single rear axle, 1960s **10.00**
Uncle Sam, blue–green stem, gray hat, contains 2 candy
    pkgs, "Pez Says Happy Birthday America" sticker,
    4³/₄" h, unopened. **80.00**
Whistle, 1980s **2.00**
Winnie the Pooh. **20.00**
Witch, 3 pc, no feet **10.00**
Wolfman **150.00**
Wonder Woman, MOC **145.00**
Zorro, with logo **50.00**

PFALTZGRAFF

The name Pfaltzgraff is derived from a famous Rhine River castle, still standing today, in the Pfalz region of Germany. In 1811 George Pfaltzgraff, a German immigrant potter, began producing salt–glazed stoneware in York, Pennsylvania.

The Pfaltzgraff Pottery Company initially produced stoneware storage crocks and jugs. When the demand for stoneware diminished, the company shifted its production to animal and poultry feeders and red clay flowerpots. The production focus changed again in the late 1940s and early 1950s as the company produced more and more household products, including its first dinnerware line, and giftwares.

In 1964 the company became The Pfaltzgraff Company. Over the next fifteen years, Pfaltzgraff expanded via construction of a new manufacturing plant and distribution center at Thomasville, North Carolina, the purchase of the Stangl Pottery of Trenton, New Jersey, and the acquisition of factories in Dover, Aspers, and Bendersville, Pennsylvania. Retail stores were opened in York County, Pennsylvania; Flemington, New Jersey; and Fairfax, Virginia.

References: Susan and Al Bagdade, *Warman's American Pottery and Porcelain,* Wallace–Homestead, Krause Publications, 1994; Harvey Duke, *The Official Price Guide to Pottery and Porcelain, Eighth Edition,* House of Collectibles, 1995; Harry L. Rinker, *Dinnerware of the 20th Century: The Top 500 Patterns,* House of Collectibles, 1997.

America, creamer and sugar, cov **$22.00**
America, cup and saucer. **6.00**
America, dinner plate **7.00**
America, gravy boat **20.00**
America, salad plate **4.00**
America, salt and pepper shakers, pr **15.00**
America, sherbet, 3" **5.00**
America, sugar canister **30.00**
America, sugar, cov. **15.00**
Christmas Heirloom, cup and saucer **8.00**
Christmas Heirloom, salt and pepper shakers, pr **12.00**
Gourmet, ashtray **5.00**
Gourmet, baker, oval, 10" **22.00**
Gourmet, casserole, cov, 12 oz, no lid **30.00**

Village, brown, dinner plate, $8.00.

Gourmet, chowder cup **2.50**
Gourmet, condiment set, 3 pcs **30.00**
Gourmet, cup and saucer **7.00**
Gourmet, dinner plate. **10.00**
Gourmet, flour canister **30.00**
Gourmet, gravy boat and underplate **12.00**
Gourmet, pie plate **20.00**
Gourmet, relish, 3 part **10.00**
Gourmet, soup bowl, 8⁵/₈" d **8.00**
Gourmet, vegetable bowl, oval, divided, 12³/₈" l **12.00**
Village, baker, rect, 14" **25.00**
Village, bread tray, 12¹/₂" **10.00**
Village, butter dish, cov, ¹/₄ lb **15.00**
Village, casserole, cov, round, 6³/₄" d **8.00**
Village, coffee canister, no lid, 6³/₄" h **6.50**
Village, creamer **10.00**
Village, gravy boat **20.00**
Village, pitcher, 6³/₈" h **15.00**
Village, salad plate, 7" d **3.00**
Village, sugar, cov. **12.00**
Village, tureen,cov **50.00**
Windsong, bread and butter plate **6.00**
Windsong, dinner plate. **12.00**
Yorktowne, baker, square. **25.00**
Yorktowne, bean pot, cov **35.00**
Yorktowne, bowl, 6" **7.50**
Yorktowne, bowl, 8¹/₂". **16.00**
Yorktowne, bread and butter plate, 6" d **4.00**
Yorktowne, casserole, cov, round, 8¹/₄" d **30.00**
Yorktowne, cookie jar, cov. **75.00**
Yorktowne, creamer **17.00**
Yorktowne, cup and saucer **10.00**
Yorktowne, grill plate **8.00**
Yorktowne, lazy susan bowls, 4 outer bowls only **10.00**
Yorktowne, salt shaker. **6.00**
Yorktowne, sherbet, ftd **8.00**
Yorktowne, tray, 3¹/₂ x 7¹/₂". **15.00**
Yorktowne, vegetable bowl, round, 8¹/₂" d **12.00**

PHOENIX BIRD CHINA

The Phoenix Bird pattern features a Phoenix Bird facing back over its left wing, its chest spotted and wings spread upward. Although produced predominantly in blue and white, pieces have been found in celedon (green).

There are a number of Phoenix Bird pattern variations: (1) Firebird with its downward tail, (2) Flying Dragon typified by six Chinese characters and a pinwheel–like design, (3) Flying Turkey with no spots on its chest and one wing only partially visible, (4) Howo with no feet and a peony–like flower, and (5) Twin Phoenix with two birds facing each other. Pieces with a cloud and mountain border are the most common. Pieces with a heart–like border are known as HO–O for identification purposes.

Phoenix Bird china was manufactured by a number of companies and made available in a wide variety of markets. Beginning in the 1970s many new pieces of Phoenix Bird arrived on the market. The shapes are more modern, the blues more brilliant, and most lack an identifying backstamp.

References: Joan Collett Oates, *Phoenix Bird Chinaware, Book 1* (1984), *Book II* (1985), *Book III* (1986), *Book IV* (1989), 1996 value update, published by author.

Collectors' Club: Phoenix Bird Collectors of America, 685 S Washington, Constantine, MI 49042.

Berry Bowl, HO–O, mkd "Made in Japan," 5½" d	**$25.00**
Bread and Butter Plate, 6" d	8.00
Buttermilk Pitcher, thumb–lug on handle, mkd "Japan," 6⅜" h	80.00
Butter Tub	48.00
Cake Plate, mkd "Japan," 9⅞" d	65.00
Cake Plate, Children's Playtime, mkd "made in Japan," 6¼" d	40.00
Cereal Bowl, 6" d	12.00
Chocolate Cup, handle	22.00
Cup and Saucer	8.00
Cup and Saucer, after dinner, unmkd, c1930s	18.00
Custard Cup	15.00
Dessert Plate, 7" d	12.00
Dinner Plate, 9¾" d	45.00
Eggcup, double	18.00
Fruit Dish, 5½" d	8.00
Hot Water Pot, #4, mark #17, 5¾" h	50.00
Luncheon Plate, 8½" d	20.00
Mustard Pot, cov	45.00
Pitcher, buttermilk, thumb–lug on handle, mkd "Japan," 6⅜" h	80.00
Platter, oval, 12" l	55.00
Platter, oval, 17" l	165.00
Rice Bowl, #1, int pattern, 4¾" d, 1⅞" h	12.00
Salt and Pepper Shakers, pr, #2, round	35.00
Salt and Pepper Shakers, pr, #7, bell shape	28.00
Soup Bowl, 7¼" d	35.00
Sugar, cov, #3	25.00
Teapot, cov, Q–shaped handle, mkd "M" and "Japan," 4" h, 8" w	70.00
Teapot, cov, thumb–lug on handle, mkd "Made in Japan," 4½" h, 9" w	70.00
Tile, round, 6" d	38.00
Vegetable Dish, oval, 7½" l	40.00
Vegetable Dish, oval, 10" l	45.00

PHOENIX GLASS

In 1880 Andrew Howard founded the Phoenix Glass Company in Phillipsburg (later Monaca), Pennsylvania, to manufacture glass tubes for the new electrical wires in houses. Phoenix bought J. A. Bergun, Charles Challinor's decorating business, in 1882. A year later Phoenix signed a contract with Joseph Webb to produce Victorian art glass. Phoenix began producing light bulbs in the early 1890s. In 1893 Phoenix and General Electric collaborated on an exhibit at the Columbian Exposition.

In 1933 the company introduced its Reuben and Sculptured lines. Phoenix acquired the Co–Operative Flint molds in 1937. Using these molds, Phoenix began manufacturing Early American, a pressed milk glass line in 1938.

In 1970 Anchor Hocking acquired Phoenix Glass. The construction of Phoenix's new plant coincided with the company's 100th anniversary in 1980. In 1987 Newell Corporation acquired Anchor Hocking.

Reference: Jack D. Wilson, *Phoenix & Consolidated Art Glass, 1926–1980,* Antique Publications, 1989.

Collectors' Club: Phoenix & Consolidated Glass Collectors Club, PO Box 3847, Edmond, OK 73083.

Bowl, swallows, purple wash	**$145.00**
Centerpiece Bowl, sculptured diving nudes, opaque white ground, 3 colors, 14" d	225.00
Creamer and Sugar, Catalonia, yellow	40.00
Dish, sculptured lotus blossoms and dragonflies, amber ground, oval, 8½" l	95.00
Floor Vase, bushberry, light green, 18" h	450.00
Ginger Jar, cov, bird finial, frosted ground	75.00
Planter, sculptured green lion, white ground	50.00
Plate, relief molded cherries, frosted and clear ground, 8½" d	50.00
Plate, relief molded dancing nudes, yellow ground, 8¼" d	65.00
Table Lamp, pine cone, brown, fixtures in top and base, 17½" h	165.00

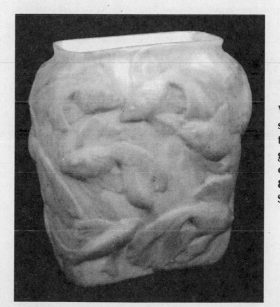

Vase, pillow shape, turquoise ground, peach colored carp, 8" w, 9" h, $115.00.

Umbrella Stand, thistle, white, orig paper label, 18" h. **425.00**
Vase, Bluebell, brown, 7" h **115.00**
Vase, clear and frosted, goldfish design, 9½" h **100.00**
Vase, clear and frosted, grasshoppers and reeds dec,
 8¾" h **125.00**
Vase, sculptured pink peonies, green leaves, white
 ground, 6¼" h **80.00**
Vase, philodendron, pink, paper sticker, 7½" h **95.00**
Vase, vine, custard ground, gilt highlights, 11" h **225.00**
Vase, wild geese, pearlized white birds, light green
 ground, 10" h **175.00**

PHOTOGRAPHS

In 1830 J. M. Daugerre of France patented a process of covering a copper plate with silver salts, sandwiching the plate between glass for protection, and exposing the plate to light and mercury vapors to imprint an image. The process produced Daguerreotypes. Fox Talbot of Britain patented the method for making paper negatives and prints (calotypes) in 1841. Frederick Scott Archer introduced the wet collodion process in 1851. Dr. Maddox developed dry plates in 1871. When George Eastman produced roll film in 1888, the photographic industry reached maturity.

Cartes de visite (calling card) photographs flourished from 1857 to 1910 and survived into the 1920s. In 1866 the cabinet card first appeared in England. The format quickly spread to the United States. It was the preferred form by the 1890s.

The family photo album was second only to the Bible in importance to late 19th–and early 20th–century families. The principal downfall of family albums is that the vast majority of their photographs are unidentified. Professional photographers produced and sold "art" folios. Two post–1945 developments produced profound changes. The 35 mm "slide" camera and home video equipment decreased the importance of the photographic print.

Before discarding family photos, check them carefully. A photograph showing a child playing with a toy or dressed in a costume or an adult at work, in military garb, or shopping in a store has modest value. Collectors prefer black and white over color prints, as the latter deteriorate over time.

References: Norman E. Martinus and Harry L. Rinker, *Warman's Paper*, Wallace–Homestead, Krause Publications, 1994; Susan Theran, *Prints, Posters & Photographs: Identification and Price Guide*, Avon Books, 1993; John S. Waldsmith, *Stereo Views: An Illustrated History and Price Guide*, Wallace–Homestead, Krause Publications, 1991.

Collectors' Clubs: American Photographic Historical Society, 1150 Avenue of the Americas, New York, NY 10036; National Stereoscopic Assoc, PO Box 14801, Columbus, OH 43214; The Photographic Historical Society, PO Box 39563, Rochester, NY 14604.

Note: See Wallace Nutting and Nutting–Like Photographs for additional listings.

Movie Still, black and white, Greta Garbo and Charles
 Bickford, *Anna Christie*, MGM, 1930 . . . . **$25.00**
Professional Photographer, Abbott, Bernice, 5th Avenue
 Theatre Interior, silver print, sgd and captioned in pencil on verso with photographer's handstamp, 1940s,
 9⅝ x 7¼" **575.00**

Movie Still, *Wizard of Oz*, autographed by Margaret Hamilton, 8½ x 11", $30.00.

Professional Photographer, Abbott, Bernice, St Luke's
 Church, Hudson Street, New York City, silver print,
 photographer's signature, in pencil, on mount recto,
 handstamp and title, in pencil, on mount verso,
 1930s, 9¼ x 7½" **920.00**
Professional Photographer, Allen, Albert Arthur, nude
 woman in chains, silver print, 1920s, 9 x 4" **150.00**
Professional Photographer, Blew, E W, Winter on the
 Creek, silver print, photographer's title and signature,
 in pencil, on mount recto, handstamp on mount
 verso, 1940s, 9½ x 12" **122.00**
Professional Photographer, Curtis, Edward S, At the Pool,
 animal dance—Cheyenne, on Van Gelder paper, photographer's credit, title, and copyright on recto, 1927,
 11½ x 15¼" **258.00**
Professional Photographer, Erwitt, Elliott, Yale's Oldest
 Living Graduate, silver print, sgd and editioned by
 photographer, in pencil, on verso, 1955, 7 x 9½" **690.00**
Professional Photographer, Gottscho, Samuel, Dogs, silver print, photographer's signature and copyright mark
 in negative, 1940s, 5½ x 13½" **488.00**
Professional Photographer, Habeberle, Ronald, Death at
 My–Lai, silver print, typed wire service caption on
 recto, 1968, 6¾ x 10¼" **805.00**
Professional Photographer, Halsman, Philippe, Winston
 Churchill, silver print, photographer's handstamp on
 verso, 1953, 9¾ x 7¾" **747.00**
Professional Photographer, Newman, Arnold, Sir Cecil
 Beaton, silver print, sgd, titled, and dated by photographer, in pencil, on recto, photographer's handstamp
 on verso, 1978, 13 x 10" **460.00**
Professional Photographer, Orkin, Ruth, American Girl
 in Italy, photographers stamp signature beneath image
 lower right, titled and dated in pencil on verso with
 estate stamp, 1952, 11 x 14" **575.00**
Snapshot, 2 black men, with liquor bottles, 1920s **8.00**
Snapshot, bride and bridesmaid, 1930, 9½ x 7" **20.00**
Snapshot, circus wagon pulled by ponies, black and
 white **8.00**

Snapshot, logging camp cooks, 1 holding large horn, black and white 8.00
Snapshot, small bark house on wagon in parade, decorated with flags, children looking out, 4½ x 8" 8.00
Snapshot, man with motorcycle, 1943 .... 8.00
Snapshot, woman sitting on motorcycle, c1920, 5 x 7" 35.00
Wire Service Photo, President Kennedy and Caroline, Jul 1963 .... 18.00

PICKARD CHINA

In 1894 Willard Pickard founded Pickard China in Chicago, Illinois. Until 1938, the company was a decorating firm; it did not manufacture the ceramics it decorated. Blanks were bought from foreign manufacturers, primarily French prior to World War I and German after the war.

Most of Pickard's early decorators were trained at Chicago's famed Art Institute. The company's reputation for quality soon attracted top ceramic painters from around the world. Many artists signed their work. Edward S. Challinor, noted for his bird, floral, fruit, and scenic designs, began working at Pickard in 1902 and remained with the company until his death in 1952. By 1908 Pickard offered more than 1,000 shapes and designs. In 1911 the company introduced gold–encrusted and gold–etched china.

In 1938 Pickard opened its own pottery in Antioch, Illinois. Pickard made china for the Navy during World War II. Decal patterns were introduced after the war. The company entered the limited edition bell and plate market in 1970 and introduced its first Christmas plate in 1976. In 1977 the U.S. Department of State selected Pickard to manufacture the official china services used at embassies and diplomatic missions around the world.

References: Susan and Al Bagdade, *Warman's American Pottery and Porcelain*, Wallace–Homestead, Krause Publications, 1994; Alan B. Reed, *Collector's Encyclopedia of Pickard China With Additional Section on Other Chicago China Studios*, Collector Books, 1995.

Collectors' Club: Pickard Collectors Club, 300 E Grove St, Bloomington, IL 61701.

Note: AOG stands for "all over gold."

Bonbon, pedestal base, Rose medallion on Morning Glory AOG, sgd "Marker," early 1920s, 6" d $250.00
Cake Plate, handled, Golden Pheasant, sgd "E. Challinor," early 1920s, 10" d 375.00
Dish, perforated handles, encrusted AOG, black border with flower sprays, sgd "Rean," late 1920s, 6¾" d 100.00
Flower Frog, figural scarf dancer, AOG, unsgd, 1930s, 6" h 160.00
Hatpin Holder, etched flowers AOG, c1925 .... 45.00
Limited Edition Plate, Alba Madonna, Christmas Series, Raphael, 1976 .... 90.00
Limited Edition Plate, At the Piano, Children of Renoir Series, Auguste Renoir, 1980 .... 75.00
Limited Edition Plate, Calliope With Gladioli, Gems of Nature Series, Bradford Exchange, 1990 .... 45.00
Limited Edition Plate, Precious Moment, Mother's Love Series, Irene Spencer, 1983 .... 140.00
Limited Edition Plate, White–Tailed Deer, Lockhart Wildlife Series, James Lockhart, 1975 .... 110.00

Cake Plate, Yosemite Valley, Nippon blank, E. Challinor artist, paper label "Pickard Studios, Chicago 13, Cake Tray, Yosemite Valley," maple leaf mark, 10½" d, $400.00.

Limited Edition Plate, Wild Irish Roses, Symphony of Roses Series, Irene Spencer, 1982 .... 95.00
Mayonnaise Dish, with underplate and ladle, flower shape, Rose and Daisy AOG, unsgd, 1930s, 6¼" d 140.00
Nut Dish, 3 part, center perforated handle, Rose and Daisy AOG, unsgd, 1930s, 6¼" d 40.00
Service Plate, scenic with gold scrolled border, sgd "C. Marker," late 1920s, 10¾" d 350.00
Vase, Pheasant medallion on white, sgd "E. Challinor," early 1920s 500.00
Vase, Rose medallion on Morning Glory AOG, sgd "C. Marker," early 1920s, 8" h 300.00

PICTURE FRAMES

Until the early 1990s most picture frames were sold at auction in boxed lots. This is no longer true. Collectors discovered that picture frames are an excellent indication of changing design styles and that the manufacturing quality of many picture frames, whether handmade or mass produced, was quite high.

Tabletop frames are the "hot" portion of the market in the late 1990s. Beware of placing too much credence in the prices on frames associated with a licensed movie or television character. Crossover collectors are the group forcing these values upward.

Beveled Glass, Art Deco, etched floral and leaf design, c1940, 14½ x 17" $85.00
Brass, Art Deco, half circle projection on 2 sides, easel back, 6 x 8" 80.00
Cast Iron, Art Nouveau, oval, gilded, folding stand, openwork scrolls and leaves, 10½ x 8" 50.00
Celluloid, 4–way easel back, 1950s, 8 x 10" 55.00
Folk Art, assorted soft woods, 14 x 17" 125.00
Gesso, pine framework, oval, acorns and leaves, gilded inner edge, mahogany stained 65.00

Glass, Art Deco, light blue tint, tin–plated corner
  mounts, 4 x 5" **22.00**
Golden Oak, molded, 14¼ x 17½" **20.00**
Mahogany, laminated, folk art pyramid dec, old varnish
  finish, 9 x 12¾" **45.00**
Oak, gilt liner, no glass, 19¾ x 26" **55.00**
Rosewood Veneer, beveled, 7⅝ x 8¾" **50.00**
Wood and Glass, Art Deco, black and white diagonal
  stripe design, Art Deco **75.00**

PIG COLLECTIBLES

Austrian, English, and German bisque and hand–painted glazed ceramic pig figurines and planters were popular souvenirs and fair prizes at the turn of the century. So many early banks were in the shape of a pig that "Piggy Bank" became a generic term for a child's bank in the early 20th century.

As an important food source, the pig was featured prominently in farm advertising. Warner Brothers' Porky Pig and Walt Disney's The Three Little Pigs are among the most recognized cartoon characters of the mid–20th century.

A pig collecting craze swept across America in the late 1970s and early 1980s, eventually displaced by cow mania.

Three German bisque pig figurines have been reproduced—a pig by an outhouse, a pig playing a piano, and a pig poking his head out of a large purse. Their darker green color distinguishes them from period pieces.

Collectors' Club: The Happy Pig Collectors Club, PO Box 17, Oneida, IL 61467.

Note: Shawnee Pottery produced Smiley Pig and Winnie Pig kitchen accessories, figural pigs with various decorative motifs.

Ashtray, pig artist painting, pig sketch on tablet **$95.00**
Ashtray, 2 pigs hugging, bisque, made in Germany **80.00**
Bank, pink pig alongside band, "Saving His Pennies To
  Make Pounds," 3½" h **50.00**
Bottle, amber, yellow ware **40.00**
Chocolate Mold, tin, 2 part **65.00**
Cutting Board, pig shape, wood, mkd "Arnold, Kent
  Feeds" **12.00**
Figurine, black pig jumping over green fence, bisque **5.00**
Figurine, carnival chalkware, 1950s, 7" h **45.00**
Figurine, mother pig rocking 2 baby piglets in cradle,
  "Hush a bye baby Don't you cry, You'll be sausage bye
  and bye" **80.00**
Figurine, pig chef, blue hat and jacket, standing by barrel **80.00**
Figurine, pig in cradle **60.00**
Figurine, pig poking head out of potty **50.00**
Figurine, pig pushing cart, "Porker Sausage Maker Are
  The Best Value," 2½" **65.00**
Figurine, pig sitting by green satchel **50.00**
Figurine, pig sitting in Dutch shoe **35.00**
Figurine, 3 piglets inside egg shape basin, "Triplets o
  fancy," mkd "Germany" **65.00**
Figurine, 3 pigs in front of fence, 2 orange mushrooms,
  4½" h **70.00**
Figurine, pink pig sitting by windmill, orange roof **80.00**
Grease Jar, figural pig, Old MacDonald pattern **195.00**
Jar, pig alongside, orange seal, 2¾" h **40.00**
Milk Pitcher, figural pig, brown, dressed in tie and tails,
  4" h **15.00**

Tape Measure, figural pig, silver plated, tail winds tape, unmkd, 36" tape, 2¼" l, $75.00.

Paperweight, figural pig, glass, "Best Pig Forceps, com-
  pliments J. Reimers, Davenport, IA" **100.00**
Pillow, pig shape, made from quilts **15.00**
Pin Dish, Good Luck horseshoe, yellow and green, pink
  pig, stamped "Made in Germany," 5" w **80.00**
Sculpture, sandstone, sgd "E Reed 1982," 18" l **425.00**
Toothpick Holder, souvenir, Watertown, NY, stamped
  "Made in Germany," 3" w **55.00**
Toy, stuffed, velvet, Steiff, 2½" **60.00**
Vase, 2 pigs poking out of large shoe, Germany **55.00**

PINBACK BUTTONS

In 1896 Whitehead & Hoag Company, Newark, New Jersey, obtained the first celluloid button patent. The celluloid buttons golden age stretched from 1896 through the early 1920s. Hundreds of manufacturers made thousands of buttons.

J. Lynch Company of Chicago introduced the first lithograph tin pinback buttons during World War I. Although lithograph buttons could be printed in multiple colors, the process did not produce the wide color range found in celluloid buttons. This mattered little. Lithograph tin buttons were much less costly to produce.

The lithograph tin pinback button played a major role in political campaigns from the early 1930s through the 1980s. Advertising buttons increased in size. Social cause buttons were dominant in the 1960s, colorful rock group buttons in the 1970s.

As the cost of lithograph tin pinback buttons rose, their popularity diminished. Today pinback buttons are sold primarily by greeting card manufacturers and retail gift shops.

Reference: William A. Sievert, *All For the Cause: Campaign Buttons For Social Change, 1960s–1990s,* Decoy Magazine, 1997.

American Air Races, Mechanic, red on cream, 1933,
  2½" d **$50.00**
Apollo II, 1969 . . . . **10.00**
Aristocrat Milk, red and white, 1930s **4.00**
Bartle's & Jaymes, Thank You For Your Support, multicol-
  ored, photo **8.00**
Big Chief White Bread, red, white, and blue, 1930s **20.00**
Blue Ribbon Cake, blue and white, 1930s **4.00**
Bowman Milk, Bud Bowman character, 1940s, 1" d **12.00**
Boycott Lettuce, United Farm Workers, red, white, and
  black, 1970s **10.00**
Buick, Looking Fine For 39 . . . . **45.00**

Creature of the Black Lagoon, litho metal, color illus, 1963 . . . . **35.00**

Dewey in 1948, white, dark blue elephant illus, 2½" d **25.00**

Disneyland 30th Year, multicolored, 1970s **10.00**

Dold Foods, red, white, and blue **5.00**

Eisenhower/Nixon, red, white, and blue, black and white photo, 3½" d **50.00**

Hudson, Ride The Green Lane Of Safety In A New 1939 Hudson, green, blue, black, and white **15.00**

Ice Capades, Donna Atwood photo, yellow ground, black lettering, late 1950s **12.00**

Join UWOC, black and white, 1960s **15.00**

Kennedy/Johnson, jugate, red, white, and blue, 3½" d **25.00**

Kingnut Spread, yellow, blue and white, 1930s **4.00**

Kodak, blue and white, 1940s, 1¼" d **75.00**

Krug's Bread, red and white, 1930s, 1" d **12.00**

Libby, McNeill & Libby Corned Beef, red, white, and blue, 1940 . . . . **5.00**

Make Love Not War, red, white, and blue, 3½" d **35.00**

Mazda Lamps, blue and white, 1930s **10.00**

Minneapolis–Moline Co, union member, 1944 . . . . **25.00**

Mint Julep Products, maroon and green, 1950s **3.00**

Munsing Wear, green and white, 1930s **5.00**

Nabisco Shredded Wheat, Top O' The Morning, red on white, c1940, 1¼" d **20.00**

New York Racing Assoc, Foolish Pleasure, horse race, "The Great Match," brown photo portrait, green lettering, 1965, 2¼" d **20.00**

Oscar Mayer Yellow Band Weiners, full color litho, 1930s, 1⅜" d **10.00**

Penn State, Orange Bowl, bowl of oranges, 2¼" d **18.00**

Pilgrim Bread and Cakes, blue, white, and orange, 1920–30 . . . . **15.00**

Pilsener Bread, brown and white, 1930s **5.00**

Quaker Rolled White Oats, full color, red rim, c1920, 2" d **75.00**

RCA Victor Television Is Million–Proof, yellow and red, 1950s, 1¼" d **15.00**

Red Cross Macaroni, red, white, and blue, 1930s **25.00**

Singer Sewing Machines, porcelain, red "S" logo, Dec 1939 . . . . **15.00**

Star Brand Shoes, hand holding red star, multicolored, white ground, blue lettering, 1920s, 7⅞" d **25.00**

Sugar Bowl, Fordham, New Orleans, LA, purple, 1942 . . . . . . **5.00**

Thank God I Am Not A Bolshevist, American flag furls in center, orig 3½ x 4½" white card with red and blue striping, patriotic verse, c1920, ½" d **75.00**

Young Americans For Freedom, red, white, blue, and black, 1970 . . . . **12.00**

PINBALL MACHINES

The introduction of Gottlieb's "Baffle Ball" in 1931 marked the beginning of the modern pinball machine era. Pre–1940 pinball machines typically had production runs of 25,000 to 50,000 machines. After 1945 production runs fell within the 500 to 2,000 range with an occasional machine reaching 10,000. Some scholars suggest that over 200 manufacturers made over 10,000 models, a result of a machine's high attrition rate. Several companies released a new model every three weeks during the 1950s.

The first electric machine appeared in 1933. Bumpers were added in 1936. Flippers arrived in 1947, kicking rubbers in 1950, score totalizers in 1950, multiple player machines in 1954, and solid state electronics in 1977. Machines by D. Gottlieb are considered the best of the pinballs, primarily because of their superior play and graphics.

The entire pinball machine was collected through the mid–1980s. More recently, collecting back glasses has become popular. Manufacturers were not concerned with longevity when making these glasses. Flaking paint is a restoration nightmare.

References: Richard M. Bueschel, *Collector's Guide to Vintage Coin Machines,* Schiffer Publishing, 1995; Richard M. Bueschel, *Encyclopedia of Pinball: Contact to Bumper, 1934–1936, Vol. 2,* Silverball Amusements, 1997; Heirbert Eiden and Jürgen Lukas, *Pinball Machines,* Schiffer Publishing, 1992, 1997 value update; Bill Kurtz, *Arcade Treasures,* Schiffer Publishing, 1994.

Periodicals: *Coin Drop International,* 5815 W 52nd Ave, Denver, CO 80212; *Coin–Op Classics,* 17844 Toiyabe St, Fountain Valley, CA 92708; *PinGame Journal,* 31937 Olde Franklin Dr, Farmington Hills, MI 48334, *Pinhead Classified,* 1945 "N" St, Ste 111, Newman, CA 95360.

Note: Prices are for machines in near mint to excellent condition.

American Amusement, Life, 1932 . . . . **$300.00**

Amusement Corp, Ski–Doo "23", 1932 . . . . **220.00**

Bally, Bally Bonus, 1936 . . . . **600.00**

Bally, Bazaar, 1966 . . . . **500.00**

Bally, Blue Bird, 1936 . . . . **600.00**

Bally, Champion, 1939 . . . . **900.00**

Bally, Golden Wheel, 1937 . . . . **950.00**

Bally, Midget Racer, 1946 . . . . **300.00**

Bally, New Improved Rocket, 1934 . . . . **1,000.00**

Bally, The President, 1932 . . . . **300.00**

Bally, Prospector, 1935 . . . . **950.00**

Bally, Screwy, 1932 . . . . **320.00**

Bally, Turf King, 1950 . . . . **850.00**

Beverator, Target, 1935 . . . . **385.00**

Chicago Coin, Shanghai, 1948 . . . . **400.00**

Pat (Nixon) for First Lady, pink and black, 3¼" d, $15.00.

Stoner Mfg, Ritz, $402.50. Photo courtesy James D. Julia.

Chicago Coin, Tit–For–Tat, 1935	375.00
Dudley Clark, Live Power, 1934	375.00
Exhibit Supply, Contact, 1939	450.00
Exhibit Supply, 1938 Lightning, 1938	400.00
Genco, Big Top, 1949	550.00
Genco, Criss Cross A–Lite, 1935	350.00
Genco, 42nd Street, 1933	400.00
Genco, Metro, 1940	500.00
Gottlieb, Caveman, 1981	500.00
Gottlieb, Charlie's Angels, 1978	400.00
Gottlieb, Ice Revue, 1965	700.00
Gottlieb, Keep 'Em Flying, 1942	500.00
Gottlieb, Sinbad, 1978	350.00
Gottlieb, Sing Along, 1967	700.00
Keeney, Repeater, 1936	600.00
Novelty Coin, O'Boy, 1939	350.00
Pacific, Major League, 1934	750.00
Peo, Daisy, 1932	260.00
Pierce, Totem, 1935	500.00
Premier, Chicago Cubs "Triple Play," 1985	550.00
Rock–Ola, World's Series, 1934	575.00
Western Equipment, Tiny, 1935	550.00
Williams, Magic City, 1967	700.00
Williams, Rainbow, 1948	450.00
Williams, Rancho, 1977	450.00
Williams, Show Girl, 1947	600.00

PIN–UP ART

The pin–up beauty owes her origin to 1920s' film magazines such as *Film Fun* and *Real Screen* whose front covers showed women with a fair amount of exposed skin. Artists such as Cardwell Higgins, George Petty, and Charles Sheldon continued to refine the concept through the 1930s. Petty's first gatefold appeared in *Esquire* in 1939.

Pin–up art reached its zenith in the 1940s. Joyce Ballantyne, Billy DeVorss, Gillete Elvgren, Earl Moran, and Alberto Vargas (the "s" was dropped at Esquire's request) were among the leading artists of the period. Their pin–up girls appeared everywhere—blotters, calendars, jigsaw puzzles, matchcovers, magazine covers, posters, punchboards, etc.

The reign of the pin–up girl ended in the early 1960s when the photograph replaced the artist sketch as the preferred illustration for magazines.

References: Denis C. Jackson, *The Price & ID Guide to Pin–Ups & Glamour Art*, TICN, 1996; Charles G. Martignette and Louis K. Meisel, *The Great American Pin–Up*, Taschen, 1996.

Newsletters: *Glamour Girls: Then and Now*, PO Box 34501, Washington, DC 20043; *The Illustrator Collector's News*, PO Box 1958, Sequim, WA 98382.

Blotter, Elvgren, "What A Deal," seated nude woman, surrounded by playing cards, Growers Exchange, Norfolk, VA, 1940s	**$8.00**
Blotter, Moran, Penn Securities, Jul–Sep 1948 calendar, 4 x 9"	12.00
Booklet, *World's Smallest Pin–Up Book*, fold–out, photos of nude nymphs, vinyl bound, 1955–60, 16 pp	5.00
Calendar, 1938, DeVorss, sample, "Do I Attract Your Attention?," 31 x 47"	250.00
Calendar, 1942, Petty, "A Good Number," 14 x 21½"	95.00
Calendar, 1944, MacPherson, artist sketch pad, poetry on each month, plastic spiral hanger, 9 x 14"	75.00
Calendar, 1945, Moran, Earl, Starlight, full color nude blonde, dark green drape, black ground	50.00
Calendar, 1945, Vargas, *Esquire*, orig envelope	90.00
Calendar, 1946, Armstrong, "It's A Date," Seattle Jeweler's date book, unused	25.00
Calendar, 1947, Petty, spiral bound, orig envelope, Fawcett Publications, 9 x 12"	70.00
Calendar, 1948, *Esquire*, Ladies of the Harem, full pad, 1948	15.00
Calendar, 1948, Moran, Earl, "Reflection," nude woman, full pad, 11 x 23"	110.00
Calendar, 1949, Elvgren, men working, desk top type, 12 sheets	15.00
Calendar, 1949, "Nursery Nifties," spiral bound, Brown & Bigelow, 8½ x 14½"	75.00
Calendar, 1949, Petty, "Come On Along," full color art, unused, 7½ x 16"	65.00
Calendar, 1950, Armstrong, "Irresistible," Brown & Bigelow, 11 x 23"	95.00
Calendar, 1955, Dec, "Stepping Out," 16 x 33"	85.00
Calendar, 1969, Elvgren, Curly Horse Ranch, cowgirl illus	45.00
Calendar, 1988, Chippendale Revue	8.00
Calendar Top, no pad, DeVorss, Daisy, nude woman, 22 x 30"	110.00
Candy Box, DeVorss, color image, 1930s, 11 x 16"	150.00
Card, set of 3, Earl Moran, red ground	22.00
Christmas Card, MacPherson, tan, red, black, and blue	25.00
Folder, Albine Calendar and Novelty Co, Chicago, IL, pin–up art tops, 12 illus, 1948	18.00
Folder, Sally of Hollywood & Vine, cardboard, sliding insert changing from dress to underwear to nude	40.00
Illusion Glass, set of 5, full color decal of pin–up wearing sheer clothing, clothing disappears when glass sweats, c1938, 5" h	100.00
Letter Opener, Elvgren, plastic, flatback, figural standing nude, holding adv disk overhead, 1940–50, 8½" h	18.00
Magazine, *Rascal*, Vol 1, #1, Camerarts Publishing, 1963	10.00
Matchcover, Petty, "Its In the Bag," Martins Tavern, Chicago, late 1940s	5.00

Calendar, Elvgren, "A Fair Shake," 1966, orig envelope, 5 x 10", $25.00.

Mirror, DeVorss, rect, full color, red haired woman holding gown tugged by puppy, 1940s, 2 x 3" **75.00**

Photograph, Marilyn Chambers, full color, blue marker signature, 1970s **50.00**

Playing Cards, Elvgren, Hats Off, double deck, seated brunette wearing green hat and red gloves on 1 deck, other with kneeling blonde wearing black hat and gloves, black and gold sliding titled box, unused, 1940s **60.00**

Postcard, woman, nude from waist up, arms folded over chest, divided back **10.00**

Poster, beautiful brunette, Raleigh Tobacco, full color, 1939–41 . . . . **15.00**

Poster, Lorna Maitland, nude, holding towel in front of her, black and white, 1964. **125.00**

Poster, woman in shorts walking dog, full color, Walt Otto, c1951, 17 x 33" **50.00**

Print, Elvgren, Adoration, woman on bed with scarf, 15 x 19" **60.00**

Print, *Esquire*, Phil Stack verse, WWII, matted, framed 11 x 14" **65.00**

Print, Seeman, The Enchanted Pool, 1930s, 15 x 20" **100.00**

Punchboard, Label, Elvgren, unused. **15.00**

Sticker, scantily clad cowgirl with guns, "Home on the Range," 1940s. **5.00**

PLANTERS PEANUTS

In 1906 Amedeo Obici, known as a peanut specialist, and Mario Peruzzi founded the Planters Nut and Chocolate Company, Wilkes–Barre, Pennsylvania. Initially, the company sold Spanish salted red skins priced at 10¢ a pound.

The Mr. Peanut trademark evolved from a 1916 contest. A young Italian boy submitted a rough sketch of a monocled Peanut figure. Hundreds of Mr. Peanut advertising and promotional items have been issued.

References: Jan Lindenberger, *Planters Peanut Collectibles Since 1961: A Handbook and Price Guide*, Schiffer Publishing, 1995; Mark Woodson, *Mr. Peanut Collectibles*, published by author, 1992.

Collectors' Club: Peanut Pals, PO Box 4465, Huntsville, AL 35815.

Ashtray, SP, figural, anniversary issue, 1906–1956. . . . . **$40.00**

Badge, employees, celluloid over metal, Planters Jamboree, Suffolk, VA, 1953 . . . . **210.00**

Bag, premium, Planter's Pennant Brand Salted Peanuts, translucent paper, red and blue printing, Mr Peanut holding red pennant, late 1920s, unused, 3 x 6" **12.00**

Book, *Soup to Nuts*, 1970 . . . . **5.00**

Booklet, *Seeing the USA with Mr Peanut*, 1950 . . . . **5.00**

Bookmark, cardboard, diecut, 1920–30 . . . . **20.00**

Bookmark, "Greetings from Mr Peanut," c1940, 7" h. **10.00**

Box, Planters Tavern Nuts, 1970s **10.00**

Can Holder, styrofoam, 1981. . . . . **5.00**

Charm, figural Mr Peanut, plastic, glow–in–the–dark, c1940s **15.00**

Chefs Apron and Cap, child's, cloth, Mr Peanut and Petey Planters image, unused, orig mailing envelope, c1950s **170.00**

Container, Planter's Peanut Oil, Ali D'Italia Oil of Peanuts brand, litho tin, flying airplanes, c1930s, 1 gal . . . **875.00**

Cookbook, *Cooking the Modern Way*, 1948, 40 pp. **22.50**

Desk Set, wooden, calculator, note pad, and pen, 1980s. **30.00**

Dish Set, child's, 3 pcs, Melmac, 1972. . . . . **15.00**

Dispenser, plastic, Honey Roast, 1986 . . . . **15.00**

Display, cardboard, diecut woman aviator, "My! These Planters Peanuts are Delicious," 9½ x 9¼ x 7" **425.00**

Earrings, plastic, Mr Peanut on yellow ground, clip–on, 1¼ x ⅞" **70.00**

Frisbee, plastic, white, Heritage logo **15.00**

Gift Pack, 4 unopened, sealed key wind Planters products, tin, orig cardboard box, dated 1944 . . . . **325.00**

Hat, plastic, hard hat type, Mr Peanut emblem **20.00**

Key Chain, brass, Munch 'N Go logo. **4.00**

Manual, Plant Rules, Planters Peanuts, Suffolk, VA, 1960s. . . . **8.00**

Mask, plastic, Mr Peanut with top hat, c1950, 11¼ x 7" **220.00**

Mug, plastic, yellow and white Mr Peanut illus, blue ground, white rim and handle, 1978 . . . . **5.00**

Nut Dish, plastic, figural top hat, 1993, 4 x 7" **8.00**

Oven Mitt, cotton, Mr Peanut illus, 1989 . . . . **7.00**

Paintbook, Seeing the USA, 48 states, 1950 . . . . **35.00**

Pin, figural Mr Peanut, blue plastic, 1950s, 1" h **8.00**

Pinback Button, Mr Peanut image, yellow ground, "Mr. Peanut" in red, c1940s, 1¼" d **15.00**

Puzzle, Between Meals Candy Bar, Hallmark/ Springbrok, 1977. . . . . **15.00**

Riding Toy, figural peanut, 1960s **80.00**

Toy, tractor trailer, plastic, 2 pc, red cab, yellow and blue trailer, Pyro, 1950s, 1¾" h, 5½" l, $264.00. Photo courtesy Wm. Morford Auctions.

Sign, Mr Peanut, paper, Mr Peanut pushing grocery cart,
"Planters Mr. Peanut Sale Stock up now and Save!,"
15 x 36" **175.00**
Tape Measure, Planter's 75th anniversary, 1906–1981 . . . . **6.00**
Watch, Mr Peanut's 75th anniversary, plastic strap **25.00**

AUCTION PRICES

Planters Peanut jars sold by James D. Julia, Inc., on November
14–16, 1997. Prices do not include the 15% buyer's premium.

Fishbowl shape, rect base, "Planters" emb on front,
glass lid with peanut finial, 12" h to top of finial,
rim chips, good condition. **$100.00**
Hexagonal, Mr Peanut painted on 3 panels,
"Planters" painted on alternating 3 panels, glass
lid with large knob finial, some chips to lid and
top of jar, 10" h to top of knob **100.00**
Octagonal, highly emb all 8 sides, alternating pan-
els with "Planters Peanuts" and Mr Peanut image,
glass lid with peanut finial, rim chips on lid and
jar, very good condition, 13" h to top of finial **200.00**
Peanut shape, highly emb, 4 corners emb with over-
sized peanut shell, 4 sides with "Planters" emb
vertically between peanut shell corners, glass lid
with peanut finial, some minor rim chips on lid
and jar, very good condition, 14" h to top of finial . . **300.00**
Slanted fishbowl shape, "Peanuts" emb on front, Mr
Peanut on threaded tin lid, scratch through Mr
Peanut image on lid, overall minor wear, 8½" h
to top of lid **80.00**
Square, emb "Planters" on sides, glass lid with
peanut finial, chips to rim of lid and jar, very
good condition, 9½" h to top of finial **150.00**

PLASTICS

There are hundreds of different natural, semisynthetic, and synthetic plastics known. Collectors focus on three basic types: celluloid, Bakelite, and melamine. Celluloid, made from cellulose
nitrate and camphor, is a thin, tough, flammable material. It was
used in the late 1880s and through the first four decades of the
20th century to make a wide range of objects from toilet articles to
toys. Celluloid's ability to mimic other materials, e.g., amber, ivory,
and tortoise shell, made it extremely popular.

In 1913 L. H. Baekeland invented Bakelite, a synthetic resinous
material made from formaldehyde and phenol. It proved to be a
viable substitute for celluloid and rubber. Easily died and molded,
Bakelite found multiple uses from radio cases to jewelry. Often it
was a secondary element, e.g., it was commonly used for handles.

Although injection molding was developed prior to World War
II, its major impact occurred during and after the war. Many new
plastics, e.g., melamine, were developed to take advantage of this
new technology. The 1950s through the 1960s was the golden age
of plastic. It was found everywhere, from the furniture in which
one sat to the dashboard of a car.

This is a catchall category. It includes objects made from plastic
that do not quite fit into other collecting categories.

References: Shirley Dunn, *Celluloid Collectibles Identification &
Value Guide*, Collector Books, 1996; Michael J. Goldberg,
Collectible Plastic Kitchenware and Dinnerware: 1935–1965,

Schiffer Publishing, 1995; Bill Hanlon, *Plastic Toys: Dimestore
Dreams of the '40s & '50s*, Schiffer Publishing, 1993; Jan
Lindenberger, *More Plastics for Collectors: A Handbook & Price
Guide*, Schiffer Publishing, 1996; Lyndi Stewart McNulty,
Wallace–Homestead Price Guide to Plastic Collectibles,
Wallace–Homestead, Krause Publications, 1987, 1992 value
update; Holly Wahlberg, *Everyday Elegance: 1950s Plastic Design*,
Schiffer Publishing, 1994.

Note: For additional listings see Costume Jewelry and Melmac.

Bakelite, adding machine, 1920, 7" h **$150.00**
Bakelite, bangle bracelet, narrow **8.00**
Bakelite, bar utensil set, 5 pcs, green handles **40.00**
Bakelite, beads, dark red, oval facet cut, graduated,
1920s, 27½" l **65.00**
Bakelite, bracelet, black and clear, on elastic, 1⅜" w **70.00**
Bakelite, brooch, black ship's wheel, carved, 1935,
1¾" d **45.00**
Bakelite, cigarette holder, tortoise shell, ivory and black **28.00**
Bakelite, clip, reverse carved, painted dec **45.00**
Bakelite, clock, Telechron, octagon, black **85.00**
Bakelite, corn cob holders, orig box **30.00**
Bakelite, desk light, revolving tin globe, stepped base,
stem, pen and paper clip holders **45.00**
Bakelite, flatware set, child's, knife, fork, and spoon, but-
terscotch handles **20.00**
Bakelite, flatware, 6 pcs, green handles **50.00**
Bakelite, hoop earrings, pr, yellow **25.00**
Bakelite, jewelry box, aqua **25.00**
Bakelite, lighter, dice shaped base, butterscotch, black
dots **60.00**
Bakelite, pencil sharpener, figural Joe Carioca **55.00**
Bakelite, pin, feather, red **18.00**
Bakelite, pin, USA, linked letters **145.00**
Bakelite, pin, vegetables, dangling **235.00**
Bakelite, pin, "V" shape, hand carved, brown **10.00**
Bakelite, poker chip caddy, brown, round **15.50**
Bakelite, radio/lamp, Lumitone, rocket shape, 1940s **160.00**
Bakelite, record player, Decca, 45 rpm, RCA Redhead
style, c1950 . . . . **85.00**
Bakelite, ring, carved, red **75.00**
Bakelite, salt and pepper shakers, pr, yellow and aqua **12.00**
Bakelite, thermometer, figural key, "Salisbury Beach,
Mass" **15.00**
Bakelite, tip tray, green **8.00**
Bakelite, transistor radio, Silverstone, black, leather
case, Sears, 1959 . . . . **30.00**
Bakelite, Tru–View viewer, 15 cards **35.00**
Catalin, alarm clock, GE, Catalin drapery, plastic case **55.00**
Catalin, radio, Crosley, brown **30.00**
Celluloid, badge, Official Gene Autry Club, center por-
trait, black, white, and orange, c1940 . . . . **65.00**
Celluloid, belt, orange, chain link, ivory illus cameo **150.00**
Celluloid, bill hook, round, Buster Brown and Tige illus,
"Buster Brown Vacation Days Carnival," ©1946 . . . . **40.00**
Celluloid, brush and comb set, pink, hp, flowers, orig
box, 1920s **40.00**
Celluloid, calculator, mechanical disk, calculates cost of
gasoline ranging from 34¢ to 44¢ per gallon,
American Art Works, c1940, 3" d **25.00**
Celluloid, card holder, 2 Mickey Mouse figures on black
base, "Walt Disney Enterprises Ltd/Japan" paper stick-
er, 1930s **90.00**

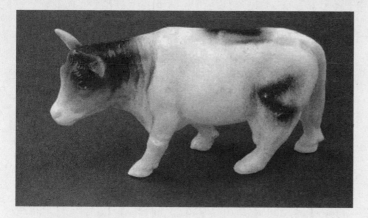

Celluloid, ox, black and white, Japan, 5¹/₂" l, 3" h, $30.00.

Celluloid, charm, Betty Boop, tinted colors, brass loop at
    top, 1930s..................................... 30.00
Celluloid, comb, pompadour, white.................. 30.00
Celluloid, cuticle cutter, ivory and cream.............. 3.00
Celluloid, doll, dressed in Welsh costume, 1950, 7" h...... 20.00
Celluloid, doll, windup, cloth outfit................... 35.00
Celluloid, eyeglasses, black........................ 30.00
Celluloid, figure, elephant, 4" l.................... 25.00
Celluloid, figure, hippo, 4" l...................... 20.00
Celluloid, manicure set, 6 pcs, travel, pink and white...... 20.00
Celluloid, nail file, figural lady's leg, painted high heel
    and garter...................................... 35.00
Celluloid, pin, fox............................... 40.00
Celluloid, rattle, duck shape...................... 12.00
Celluloid, recipe butler, Art Deco, red and blue.......... 60.00
Celluloid, statue, religious, Art Deco, metal medallion
    center, Milano, 1930s........................... 25.00
Celluloid, stickpin, pink, pearlized.................. 30.00
Celluloid, tape measure, black man.................. 150.00
Celluloid, toy, airship, hollow, red and blue, wood
    wheels, pull string, logo on tail fin, US Star Co, 1930s ... 100.00
Plastic, bowl, gray, multicolored speckles, mkd "Texas
    Ware"... 15.00
Plastic, butter, cov, yellow, molded colored fruit on lid....... 9.00
Plastic, candy dish, leaf shape, painted flamingo center,
    "Silver Springs, Fla"............................. 10.00
Plastic, coasters, set of 4, yellow, beige, red, and green,
    emb twig design................................. 9.00
Plastic, creamer and sugar, yellow Fido, black Fifi, F & F
    Mold and Die Works, Dayton, OH, Ken–L–Ration,
    c1950s.. 10.00
Plastic, dispenser, bowling ball shape, Catalin........... 100.00
Plastic, dresser set, 2 pcs, hand mirror and matching but-
    ton hook, orange, green rhinestones, butterfly motif...... 35.00
Plastic, flour sifter, handled, white swirl, red rose dec,
    red handle, 5 cup............................... 9.00
Plastic, plate, divided........................... 3.00
Plastic, roly poly, clown, orange and yellow............ 35.00
Plastic, salt and pepper shakers, pr, red, white lettering,
    Lustro–Ware.................................... 12.00
Plastic, sewing box, round, pink, clear lid, divided int...... 10.00
Plastic, spice shelf, pink, cut–out letters, repaired crack..... 25.00
Plastic, tea set, child's, pink teapot, creamer, sugar bowl,
    3 blue plates, 3 gray cups, 3 mustard saucers, and
    metal utensils, Ideal 1950s........................ 65.00

PLAYBOY

Hugh M. Hefner launched the first issue of *Playboy*, featuring the now famous calendar photograph of Marilyn Monroe, in December 1953. There was no cover date. Hefner was not certain the concept would work. *Playboy* grew at a phenomenal rate.

During the 1960s and 70s, Hefner opened a series of Playboy Clubs, launched several foreign editions, operated several gambling casinos, and organized a Hollywood production company. *Playboy* went public in 1971 and was listed on the New York and Pacific stock exchanges. *Oui* was launched in October 1972.

Christie Hefner became president of Playboy Enterprises in 1982. In the mid–1980s more than sixty companies were licensed to market products bearing the Playboy, Playmate, and Rabbit Head trademarks.

Reference: Denis C. Jackson, *The Price & ID Guide to Playboy Magazines, 3rd Edition*, TICN, 1997.

Collectors' Club: Playboy Collectors Assoc, PO Box 653, Phillipsburg, MO 65722.

Ashtray, Playboy Club adv, yellow glass, center Playmate
    holding key, 1960s, 4" sq........................ $20.00
Bar Set, 4 pcs, SS, box............................ 25.00
Beach Towel, early 1960s.......................... 20.00
Belt Buckle, gold, round, rabbit head................. 10.00
Book, *Twelfth Anniversary Playboy Reader*, hard cov,
    1966, 874 pp................................... 25.00
Calendar, 1961, Playmate, desk type, MIB.............. 45.00
Calendar, 1969, desk type, easel back, orig envelope,
    unused, 6 x 8"................................. 25.00
Candle, vase style, red, 1960s...................... 15.00
Car Air Freshener, Playboy logo, black and white.......... 2.00
Cigarette Lighter, chromium, black enameled panels,
    white rabbit logo, 2¹/₂" h......................... 45.00
Credit Card, Playboy Club International, gold, Jan 1979...... 6.00
Credit Card, Playboy Club International, membership
    card, Feb 1986................................. 5.00
Dinner Plate, china, Femlin with or without Playboy
    Club name..................................... 40.00
Dinner Plate, pewter, VIP, early 1960s, 10" d............ 50.00
Glass, VIP on the Rocks........................... 5.00
Key Card, plastic or metal, Playboy Club, gold or white,
    1960s.. 20.00
Key Chain, rabbit head, oval....................... 5.00
Magazine, 1953, Dec, Vol 1, #1, Marilyn Monroe cen-
    terfold and cov............................... 1,500.00
Magazine, 1955, Marilyn Monroe photos, black and
    white.. 300.00
Magazine, 1957................................. 5.00
Magazine, 1961, Jan–Dec, set of 12.................. 75.00
Magazine, 1966................................. 3.00
Magazine, 1971, 3 issues.......................... 5.00
Magazine, 1981, May, black cov features Crown Royal
    jigsaw puzzle ad................................ 4.00
Matchbook, 1961, unused.......................... 5.00
Matchbook, 1980, unused.......................... 3.00
Matchbook, Playboy Club, Atlanta.................... 2.00
Mug, clear glass, Playboy Club and city, 5¹/₂" h.......... 10.00
Mug, gray glass, emb rabbit head, 6 h................. 5.00
Plaque, "Caught Live at the Playboy Club," bunny tail,
    early 1960s................................... 75.00

Playing Cards, Playmate, open, complete, 1971–73 . . . . **20.00**
Puppet, hand, 1963. . . . . **100.00**
Puzzle, Annie Fanny **50.00**
Puzzle, blonde Playmate centerfold on white airbag
   cushion, red carpeting, cardboard canister, 1970 . . **28.00**
Shot Glass, weighted bottom, Playboy image, name
   repeated in black, c1960, 2³/₄" h **40.00**
Silverware, knife, fork or spoon, engraved rabbit head,
   early 1960s, price for each. **10.00**
Swizzle Stick, solid color. **5.00**

PLAYING CARDS

Playing cards came to America with the colonists. They were European in origin. The first American playing cards did not arrive on the scene until after the American Revolution. Caleb Bartlett (New York), Thomas Crehore (Dorchester, Massachusetts), David Felt (New York), the Ford (Foord) family (Milton, Massachusetts), and Amos and Daniel Whitney printed some of the first playing cards made in America. A. Dougherty, The New York Consolidated Card Company, and the United States Playing Card Company were the leading American manufacturers of playing cards. U.S. Playing Card introduced its Bicycle Brand in 1885. American card manufacturers are credited with introducing the classic joker, slick finish for shuffling, standard size, and upper corner indexes.

Card collectors specialize. Advertising, children's card games, miniature decks, novelty decks, and souvenir decks are just a few examples. Some collectors only collect one type of card, e.g., jokers. Although play is the primary focus of most playing cards, cards also have been used for fortune telling, instruction, e.g., World War II airplane spotting, and aiding travelers, e.g., a language set. These sets also appeal to collectors.

Always count the cards to make certain you are buying complete decks. American poker decks have 52 cards plus one or two jokers, pinochle decks have 48 cards, and Tarot decks 78 cards.

References: Everett Grist, *Advertising Playing Cards*, Collector Books, 1992, out of print; Norman E. Martinus and Harry L. Rinker, *Warman's Paper*, Wallace–Homestead, Krause Publication, 1994.

Collectors' Clubs: Chicago Playing Card Collectors, 1826 Mallard Lake Dr, Marietta, GA 30068; 52 Plus Joker, 204 Gorham Ave, Hamden, CT 06514; International Playing Card Society, 3570 Delaware Common, Indianapolis, IN 46220.

Note: Prices are for complete poker decks in mint condition.

Aircraft Spotter II, 1943 . . . . **$25.00**
Alaska, totem pole dec, 1926 . . . . **175.00**
AMC Pacer **5.00**
Avis **4.00**
Baltimore Storage Co **2.50**
Bannister Babies, double deck, 1954 . . . . **10.00**
Bataille De Nancy, Grimaud, France, 500th Anniversary,
   1977, 54 cards **12.00**
Bayer, red back with logo **20.00**
Belgium, Philips, 1972 . . . . **10.00**
Boomtown Wild West, red and white. **4.00**
Boron Motor Oil, can shape **5.00**
Bumble Bee Tuna **6.00**
California, Bullock's, Orange Grove, 1927 . . . . **50.00**

Camel Cigarettes. **4.00**
Cedarcrest Realty Company. **4.00**
Chicago Century of Progress, World's Fair, 1933, 54 dif-
   ferent views **15.00**
Clamcleats, sailors playing cards, 1986 . . . . **10.00**
Clavecin, Catel & Farcey, c1960 . . . . **15.00**
Coca–Cola, stewardess and Coke bottle with wings,
   1943. . . . . **50.00**
Cuba, flags on back, c1930 . . . . **30.00**
Dallas Cowboys Cheerleaders, 1982 . . . . **5.00**
Delta Air Lines, San Francisco **5.00**
Denmark, Handa, 1944. . . . . **25.00**
Diamond Salt, orig box **18.00**
Donegal, The Shirt You Live In, brown and white **4.00**
Dorney Park, Allentown, PA, Alfundo the clown illus **5.00**
Eureka Vacuum Cleaner Co, eagle, black, gold, and white **3.00**
Fairchild Semiconductor, electrical specifications on
   each card **5.00**
Fitzgeralds Casino, Reno, NV **5.00**
France, Salvidor Dali artist, 1969 . . . . **100.00**
Gatorade, red, white, and green **4.00**
GM Electro–Motive. **30.00**
Great Southwest, Indian and train photos, 1923 . . . . **80.00**
Hertz Rent–A–Car, dark green **8.00**
Hotel Fremont and Casino, Las Vegas, red and white,
   diamond design **5.00**
Kellogg's Frosties, 1978–80 . . . . **10.00**
Kennedy Kards, 1963 . . . . **15.00**
Kennedy Space Center, Florida **6.00**
Lone Star Beef **6.50**
Lottery Fortune **5.00**
Lover's Leap—Rock City, 1930s **4.00**
Mayflower, green and white **4.00**
Merit Cigarettes **4.50**
Mount Rushmore, SD **12.50**
New York World's Fair, trick deck, 1939, 48 cards. **50.00**
Norwalk 5 Ply Tire **5.50**
Ozark Airlines, 1984 World's Fair, sealed deck **2.00**
Paitnik, double deck, 1952 . . . . **25.00**
Pan American World Airways. **6.00**
Pillsbury Plus, cake box design **10.00**
Pin–Up, *Esquire*, blonde with black ground, double
   deck, 1943 . . . . **35.00**
Pin–Up, Vargas, 52 different backs, 1953 . . . . **115.00**
Queen High Equality, 1971 . . . . **30.00**

Tydol Flying A Gasoline, Tide Water Playing Cards, double deck, velvet cov case, unused, $75.00. Photo courtesy Wm. Morford Auctions.

Reynolds Wrap **20.00**
San Francisco, photos, Golden Gate Bridge back, 1950s **10.00**
Santa Fe Railroad, train in desert, 1952 . . . . **18.00**
Scania, photos of cars from 1891–1991 . . . . **8.00**
Sears Tower, Chicago, skyline **7.50**
Sea World, blue, black, and white, 1978 . . . . **7.50**
SS Milwaukee Clipper, ocean liner **10.00**
Swiss Air, red back, 1940s **8.00**
Tee–Up, golf cart on each card, orig box, c1950 . . . . **10.00**
Texas, views of Texas cities and people, 1920s **100.00**
Tydol Gasoline **30.00**
Vantage Cigarettes **4.00**
Vista Dome, 1950–60 . . . . **15.00**
Western Airlines **6.00**
Wild Animal Park, San Diego **5.00**
World Bridge, Modiano, Italy, 1953, 54 cards **28.00**
Yamaha **15.00**
Yellowstone, blue rays, white border, 1952 . . . . **25.00**

POCKETKNIVES

American manufacturers such as Samuel Mason and C. W. Platts of the Northfield Knife Company began making pocketknives in the 1840s. Numerous design, manufacturing, and marketing advances occurred. Collectors consider the period between the 1880s and 1940 as the pocketknife's golden age. American manufacturers received favorable tariff protection beginning in the 1890s. Before 1940, the best factory knives were handmade in a wide variety of designs and with the best material available.

The period between 1945 and the early 1960s is considered a dark age. Many pre–war manufacturers went out of business. A renaissance occurred in the 1970s as individual knife craftsmen began making pocketknives geared more for collecting and display than use. Bob Hayes, Jess Horn, Ron Lake, Jimmy Lile, Paul Pehlmann, Robert Ogg, and Barry Wood were leaders in the craftsman revival. Recently, collector and limited edition knives have flooded the market.

Pocketknives divide into three main groups: (1) utilitarian and functional knives, (2) advertising, character, and other promotional knives, and (3) craftsman knives. Alcas, Case, Colonial, Ka–Bar, Queen, Remington, Schrade, and Winchester are the best known manufacturers of the first group. Aerial Cutlery, Canton Cutlery, Golden Rule Cutlery, Imperial Knife Company, and Novelty Cutlery made many of the knives in the second group.

References: Jacob N. Jarrett, *Price Guide to Pocket Knives, 1890–1970*, L–W Books, 1993, 1995 value update; Bernard Levine, *Levine's Guide to Knives and Their Values*, 4th Edition, Krause Publications, 1997; C. Houston Price, *The Official Price Guide to Collector Knives, Eleventh Edition*, House of Collectibles, 1996; Roy Ritchie and Ron Stewart, *The Standard Knife Collector's Guide*, 3rd Edition, Collector Books, 1997; Jim Sargent, *Sargent's American Premium Guide to Pocket Knives & Razors, Identification and Values*, 4th Edition, Books Americana, Krause Publications, 1995; J. Bruce Voyles, *The International Blade Collectors Association Price Guide to Antique Knives, 2nd Edition*, Krause Publications, 1995.

Periodicals: *Blade Magazine*, 700 E State St, Iola, WI 54990; *Edges*, PO Box 22007, Chattanooga, TN 37422.

Note: Prices are for pocketknives in mint condition.

Champagne Knife, Kastor–cloisonné, $100.00.

Advertising, Champion Spark Plugs **$30.00**
Advertising, The Franklin Fire, Philadelphia, 1829–1929,
    metal, 3" l **75.00**
Advertising, Purina, 2 blade **15.00**
Bulldog, Gunstock Jack, pit bull etching, brown bone
    handle, 3½" l **100.00**
Bulldog, Serpentine Stockman, Oktoberfest etching, cel-
    luloid handle, beer stein shield, 3⅜" l **50.00**
Case, flyfisherman's knife, stamped "USA," 1965–69,
    3⅞" l **150.00**
Case, genuine pearl, long pull, stamped "XX,"
    1940–65, 3¼" l **225.00**
Case, leather handle, stamped "L," 1965–77, 3¼" l. **45.00**
Case, melon tester, 4200, white composition, serrated
    master blade, stamped "USA," 1965–70, 5½" l **125.00**
Case, Muskrat Hawbaker Special, bone handle, stamped
    "XX," 1940–60s, 3⅞" l **500.00**
Case, rigger's knife, 6246R, green bone, bail in handle,
    stamped "Tested XX," 1940–65, 4⅜" l **165.00**
Case, stag, 5265, saber ground, stamped "USA,"
    1965–70, 5¼" l **95.00**
Case, stag, Sidewinder, leather pouch and box, 1980–82 . . . **175.00**
Case, stag, Texas Lockhorn, leather pouch and box **145.00**
Case, white composition, handle mkd "Office
    Knife," 1940–65 . . . . **450.00**
Cattaraugus Cutlery, florist's, 10101, 1 blade **60.00**
Cattaraugus Cutlery, scout/utility, 2586, 2 blade **115.00**
Character, Hopalong Cassidy, riding Topper, blue, belt
    loop **40.00**
Character, Roy Rogers, black and white, chain, 3¼" l **32.00**
Commemorative, Case, Bobby Allison—1988 Dayton
    Winner **110.00**
Commemorative, Case, Elvis Presley, "Blue Elvis," blue
    jigged bone handle **100.00**
Commemorative, Case, NASA, 1972 . . . . **250.00**
Commemorative, Ka–Bar, Persian Gulf **55.00**
Commemorative, Ka–Bar, WWII, USMC, utility, walnut
    box with Marine Corps emblem **60.00**
Ka–Bar, fish, T–29, celluloid handle, 5" l **50.00**
Ka–Bar, lobster, 2307, stag handle **65.00**
Ka–Bar, dog's head, 61126L **875.00**
Ka–Bar, office, 42027S, imitation ivory handle, 3½" l **80.00**
Remington, Barlow, RC090, horn handle, 3⅜" l **125.00**
Remington, Jack, easy opener, R203, black handle, easy
    3⅝" l **150.00**
Remington, Jack, R173, brown bone, teardrop, 3¾" l **200.00**
Remington, Jack, R555, candy stripe scales, Remington
    circle UMC, 3¼" l **225.00**
Remington, Lockback, R1383, fish scaler, brown bone,
    4¼" l **450.00**
Remington, switchblade, R645, black handle, candy
    stripe, 4" l **160.00**

Remington, Scout, easy opener, bone, sheepfoot blade,
    scout hat shield on handle, 3½" l **700.00**
Schrade, Lobster Pen, 7604W, ivory celluloid handle,
    2¼" l **40.00**
Schrade, Senator, 744SSS, sterling handle **240.00**
Winchester, Senator Pen, 2059, celluloid handle, 3⅛" l **85.00**

POLITICAL & CAMPAIGN

Collectors prefer three–dimensional items. Material associated with winning candidates is more desirable than that associated with individuals who lost. While there are third party collectors, their number is small.

The period from the late 1890s through the mid–1960s is the golden age of political and campaign material. Today candidates spend most of their money on television advertising. The 1996 presidential election was noteworthy for its lack of political collectibles.

Political and campaign item collectors were one of the first specialty collector groups to organize. As a result, large hoards of post–1970 material exist. This is why most collectors concentrate on material dating prior to the 1970s.

Reference: Ted Hake, *Hake's Guide to Presidential Campaign Collectibles,* Wallace–Homestead, Krause Publications, 1992.

Newsletter: *The Political Bandwagon,* PO Box 348, Leola, PA 17540.

Collectors' Club: American Political Items Collectors, PO Box 340339, San Antonio, TX 78234.

REPRODUCTION ALERT: Campaign buttons have been widely reproduced. Examine the curl for evidence of modern identification marks having been scratched out. The backs of most early buttons were bare or had a paper label. Beware of any button with a painted back. Buttons made prior to 1896 were celluloid. Any lithograph button from an election earlier than 1896 is incorrect. Celluloid buttons need a collar since they are made in a sandwich fashion. Lithograph buttons have a one–piece construction.

Bush, George, box, bubble gum cigars, box of 24,
    "Bush/Dukakis Presidential Favorites," red, white, and
    blue, Philadelphia Chewing Gum Corp, unopened,
    c1988 . . . . **$10.00**
Bush, George, program, Republican National Conven-
    tion, New Orleans, Bush on cov, 1988, 22 pp **15.00**
Carter, James E, medal, bronze, raised bust, Presidential
    seal and inscription "39th President Of The United
    States Of America/Inaugurated January 20, 1977" on
    back, 2¾" d **20.00**
Carter, James E, poster, "Vote For Jimmy Carter," green
    and white, 1976, 14 x 22" **8.00**
Carter, James E, windup, "Jimmy The Walking Peanut,"
    plastic, painted features, orig box, late 1970s, 5" h **35.00**
Coolidge, Calvin, bell, brass, "Ring for Coolidge" **25.00**
Coolidge/Dawes, pinback button, jugate, black and
    white photos, black ground, Union bug stamp on
    reverse, Bastian **215.00**
Coolidge/Dawes, postcard, black and white photo,
    c1924 . . . . **20.00**
Cox, James E, pinback button, "Coxsure," litho, white
    letters, dark blue ground **50.00**

Dewey/Bricker, pinback button, jugate, litho, bluetone
    photos, red, white, and blue ground **35.00**
Dewey, Thomas E, ribbon, "Elect Dewey and
    Warren/Vote Republican," silvery white cotton fabric,
    black letters, 6" l **20.00**
Dewey, Thomas E, tie, dark brown fabric, white image,
    "Dewey In '48," orig tags inscribed "Rembrandt Paints
    Another Crosley Creation," 8" l **35.00**
Dukakis/Bentsen, cardboard, Texas Democratic Party,
    blue and white, 15 x 11" **8.00**
Eisenhower, Dwight D, matchbook, Inaugural, portraits,
    unused, 1953 . . . . **10.00**
Eisenhower, Dwight D, pinback button, "Make The
    White House The Dwight House," blue lettering,
    white ground. **8.00**
Eisenhower, Dwight D, plate, glazed china, black and
    white, "34th President Of The US/Inaugurated Jan 20,
    1953," "Decorated By Delano Studios/Setauket/NY"
    on reverse, 10½" d **30.00**
Eisenhower, Dwight D, salt and pepper shakers, pr,
    beige and tan, head lifts off for 1 shaker, body serves
    as other, c1952 . . . . **30.00**
Eisenhower, Dwight D, sheet music, *A March to
    Eisenhower,* 1953 Inauguration souvenir, red, white,
    and blue cov, 4 pp, 8 x 11" **10.00**
Eisenhower/Nixon, program, Inaugural Ball, Jan 1957 . . . . **20.00**
Goldwater, Barry M, fan, cardboard, portrait image,
    "Goldwater Fan Club," wood handle, 1964 . . . . **30.00**
Goldwater, Barry M, matchcover, "Goldwater for
    President," blue and white, 1964 . . . . **3.00**
Goldwater, Barry M, pen, brass, black inscriptions,
    1964, 5" l **10.00**
Goldwater, Barry M, poster, "A Choice...Not An Echo,"
    red, white, and blue, 1964, 14 x 21" **15.00**
Goldwater, Barry M, soda can, "Gold Water," "The Right
    Drink For The Conservative Taste," metallic green,
    gold, and white, unopened, 1964. . . . . **35.00**
Harding, Warren G, pinback button, "I'm For Harding,"
    black and white photo, black ground **38.00**
Hoover/Curtis, pinback button, celluloid, PA Keystone
    symbol, GOP elephant, red, white, and blue **12.00**
Hoover, Herbert, bandanna, sepia photo, red, white, and
    blue border, 14 x 18". **45.00**

Lyndon B. Johnson, flicker button, dark blue plastic ribbon, ©1964 Democratic National Committee, $15.00.

Hoover, Herbert, calendar, full color, glossy, 1930, 22 x 46" 50.00

Hoover, Herbert, license plate, cast aluminum, silver finish, c1928, 5 x 12" 100.00

Hoover, Herbert, pinback button, black and white photo, dark gray ground. 215.00

Humphrey, Hubert, letter opener, plastic, "Vote Demo! Hubert Humphrey For President," white, blue image, red lettering 8.00

Kennedy, John F, bandanna, color portrait, red, white, and blue flag border, white ground, ©1965 ta, 31" sq 15.00

Kennedy, John F, campaign hat, plastic, black "Kennedy for President" on red, white, and blue striped paper strip with stars and state abbreviations, 1960 .... 25.00

Kennedy, John F, book, *White House Nanny*, Maud Shaw, President and Mrs Kennedy and Caroline full color front cov, 1966, 128 pp 8.00

Kennedy, John F, calendar, memorial, black and white photo, 1967, 9 x 15" 25.00

Kennedy, John F, game, The Exciting New Game of the Kennedy's, Transco, 1962 .... 60.00

Kennedy, John F, magazine, *Time*, Election Extra, photos and summary of election, 1960, 16 pp 12.00

Kennedy, John F, pinback button, "God Bless Our President," bluetone photo, white ground, red rim and lettering, Capitol Dome and White House, mint 35.00

Kennedy, John F, plate, President and Mrs Kennedy full color photo, gold and white sunburst edge, red fabric thread hanger, tag "Arrow/Made In Japan," c1962, 6" d 25.00

Kennedy/Johnson, poster, "Democratic National Committee, Washington, DC," red, white, and blue,black and white jugate photo, 27 x 41" 75.00

Landon, Alfred M, poster, "Landon For President," paper, brown and white, 1936, 11 x 16" 25.00

McGovern, George, poster, red "I Believe Him," black and white photo, hand-written "McGovern/1972 Dem," 21 x 27" 12.00

Nixon, Richard M, Christmas card, family photo, full color, orig envelope postmarked 1967, New York return address, 4 x 6" 30.00

Nixon, Richard M, game, Who Can Beat Nixon?, Dynamic Design, 1970 .... 10.00

Nixon, Richard M, nodder, "Nixon for President," elephant head, orig box 125.00

Nixon, photograph, black and white, Richard Nixon shaking hands with Congressman George Bush. 12.00

Nixon, Richard M, postcard, black and white glossy photo, dated "Sept 29, 1952," 3½ x 5½" 10.00

Reagan/Bush, poster, "Reagan-Bush '84," multicolored, 16 x 22" 12.00

Reagan, Ronald, mug, white ceramic, "Republican National Convention August 20–23, 1984," blue portrait of Reagan and Bush, 5" h 12.00

Reagan, Ronald, paper dolls, First Family, President and Mrs Reagan, Dell 1981 .... 15.00

Roosevelt, Franklin D, cigar band, "Franklin D Roosevelt Hand Made," black, white, red, and gold, c1933, 3" l 10.00

Roosevelt, Franklin D, sheet music, *Nation's Prayer For the President/Dedicated to Franklin D Roosevelt*, black and white, ©1933, 9½ x 12½" 15.00

Roosevelt, Franklin D, thermometer, plaque, bright gold ground, black NRA symbol, portrait, "Together We Cannot Fail," brass frame, chain for hanging, 4 x 6" 35.00

Richard Nixon, bumper sticker, red, white, and blue, 9½ x 4", $8.00.

Roosevelt, Franklin D, ticket, 1937 Inauguration 40.00

Smith, Alfred E, banner, canvas, red, white, and blue, black and white illus, 1928, 3 x 4½" 400.00

Smith, Alfred E, key chain, silvered brass ring, black enamel donkey's head 35.00

Stevenson, Adlai E, pinback button, "Stevenson 1960," blue star, gold lettering 10.00

Stevenson, Adlai E, sheet music, *Believe in Stevenson*, blue and white cov, 1956 .... 15.00

Truman, Harry S, fan, *Philadelphia Evening Bulletin*, Democratic Nation Convention, Decker cartoon on 1 side, "Welcome Delegates" on other, 1948........... 28.00

Truman, Harry S, magazine, *Time*, Dec 31, 1945, Man of the Year issue 20.00

Truman, Harry S, menu, full color photo, 70th birthday dinner, May 1954 .... 15.00

Truman, Harry S, program, Inaugural Ball, National Guard Armory, portrait of President and Mrs Truman, Margaret, and Barkley, gold cov, blue binding cord, Jan 20, 1949 .... 35.00

Watergate, card game, The Watergate Scandal, 1973 .... 15.00

Watergate, puzzle, The Puzzle of Watergate, black and white cov, shrink-wrapped, ©1973 .... 20.00

Willkie, Wendell L, banner, "God Bless America/Wendell Willkie," fabric, red, white, and blue, 1940, 9 x 11½" 25.00

Willkie, Wendell L, license plate, orange, gold letters, dark blue outline, blue edge, 4 x 13½" 20.00

Willkie, Wendell L, sticker, diecut foil, "Willkie/The Hope of America," silver, blue and red, 3½ x 6" 10.00

PORCELIER PORCELAIN

The Porcelier Manufacturing Company was incorporated on October 14, 1926, with business offices in Pittsburgh, Pennsylvania, and a manufacturing plant in East Liverpool, Ohio. In 1930 Porcelier purchased the vacant plant of the American China Company in South Greensburg, Westmoreland County, Pennsylvania.

Initially, Porcelier produced light fixtures. Electrical kitchen appliances were added by the mid-1930s. Some credit Porcelier with making the first all-ceramic electrical appliances. In the course of its history, Porcelier made over 100 patterns of kitchenware and over 100 different light fixtures.

Sears, Roebuck and Company and Montgomery Ward were among Porcelier's biggest customers. Many products appear with brand names such as Heatmaster and Harmony House.

In March 1954 Pittsburgh Plate Glass Industries bought the Porcelier plant and adjacent land. The company was dissolved in the summer of 1954.

Reference: Susan E. Grindberg, *Collector's Guide to Porcelier China*, Collector Books, 1996.

Collectors' Club: Porcelier Collectors Club, 21 Tamarac Swamp Rd, Wallingford, CT 06492.

Appliance Coaster, set of 4, small	$24.00
Barock–Colonial, batter pitcher, gold	40.00
Barock–Colonial, sugar, cov, red	14.00
Basketweave Cameo, bean pot, individual	10.00
Basketweave Wild Flowers, sandwill grill	225.00
Black–Eyed Susan, pot, 6 cup, Colonial shape	45.00
Cattail, creamer	15.00
Country Life, sugar canister	35.00
Flower Pot, sugar, cov	12.00
French Drip #566, pot, 6 cup	35.00
Golden Fuchsia, creamer, platinum	20.00
Leaf and Shadow, pot, 4 cup, black trim	28.00
Nautical, creamer, gold trim	20.00
Ocean Waves, teapot, 2 cup	55.00
Orange Poppy, creamer	12.00
Pear, pot, 4 cup	25.00
Ribbed Betty, pot, 6 cup	35.00
Rope Bow, boiler, 6 cup	40.00
Scalloped Wild Flowers, sugar, cov	15.00
Scalloped Wild Flowers, percolator, electric	110.00
Scalloped Wild Flowers, pot, 6 cup	45.00
Serv–All Line, coffee canister, red/black	40.00
Serv–All Line, urn, electric, red/black	120.00
Silhouette, waffle iron, Colonial shape	185.00
Solid Color, pot, ribbed, 6 cup	30.00
Swordfish Mug	55.00

POSTCARDS

In 1869 the Austrian government introduced the first government–issued postcard. The postal card concept quickly spread across Europe, arriving in the United States in 1873.

The period from 1898 until 1918 is considered the golden age of postcards. English and German publishers produced most of the cards during the golden age. Detroit Publishing and John Winsch were leading American publishers.

The postcard collecting mania that engulfed Americans ended at the beginning of World War I. Although greeting cards replaced many postcards on sales racks, the postcard survived. Linen cards dominated the period between 1930 and the end of the 1940s. Chromolithograph cards were popular in the 1950s and 60s. Postcards experienced a brief renaissance in the 1970s and 80s with the introduction of the continental size format (4 x 6") and the use of contemporary designs.

Are the stamps on postcards valuable? The answer is no 99.9% of the time. If you have doubts, consult a philatelic price guide. A postcard's postmark may be an added value factor. There are individuals who collect obscure postmarks.

References: Diane Allmen, *The Official Price Guide to Postcards*, House of Collectibles, 1990; J. L. Mashburn, *Black Americana: A Century of History Preserved on Postcards*, Colonial House, 1996;

J. L. Mashburn, *Fantasy Postcards*, Colonial House, 1996; J. L. Mashburn, *The Artist–Signed Postcard Price Guide*, Colonial House, 1993; J. L. Mashburn, *The Postcard Price Guide: A Comprehensive Listing*, Third Edition, Colonial House, 1997; J. L. Mashburn, *The Super Rare Postcards of Harrison Fisher With Price Guide*, Colonial House, 1992; Susan Brown Nicholson, *The Encyclopedia of Antique Postcards*, Wallace–Homestead, Krause Publications, 1994; Robert Ward, *Investment Guide to North American Real Photo Postcards*, Antique Paper Guide, 1991; Jane Wood, *The Collectors' Guide to Post Cards*, L–W Books, 1984, 1997 value update.

Periodicals: *Barr's Post Card News*, 70 S Sixth St, Lansing, IA 52151; *Postcard Collector*, PO Box 1050, Dubuque, IA 52004.

Collectors' Clubs: Deltiologists of America, PO Box 8, Norwood, PA 19074; Postcard History Society, PO Box 1765, Manassas, VA 22110.

Note: *Barr's Post Card News* and the *Postcard Collector* publish lists of over fifty regional clubs in the United States and Canada. Prices listed are for postcards in excellent condition.

Advertising, Charteux Cooking Oil, French, Santa holding bottle, 1928	$50.00
Advertising, Fish Tires, boy and dog looking at sign, "Time to re–tire, Get a Fish," sgd Norman Rockwell, red, black, and white, 1924	150.00
Advertising, Fluorodont Toothpaste, woman wearing black lace veil, Chlorodont Co, Milan, Italy pub, sgd Ramos, used, 1951	6.00
Advertising, Harley–Davidson, new 1937 model, company issued, government postal card	75.00
Advertising, Helms Olympic Bread, building illus, "Official Olympic Games Bakers, 1932," linen, printed by Curt Teich	40.00
Advertising, Iron Horse Machine Silk, text on back, addressed to tailors, "The most reliable because it is the most flexible," PVP Belgium pub, unused, 1926	45.00
Advertising, Nelson's Radio & Television, Leesburg, FL, June Havoc illus, Radio Television Service using Sylvania Tubes adv, government postal card, c1951	25.00

Impala Custom Coupe by Chevrolet

Advertising, Chevrolet 1970 Impala Custom Coupe, unused, $5.00.

Advertising, Parker, "The Message on the Other Side was Written with the Amazing New Parker 51," linen, used, 1948 .... **48.00**

Advertising, Summer Suits, RB Clothing Co, Cincinnati, OH, fashionable men walking on boardwalk, used, 1929 .... **40.00**

Advertising, Voss Washing Machine, "More time for Self Improvement, when the Voss does the wash," woman reading book, Voss Brothers Mfg Co, Davenport, IA, 1921 .... **85.00**

Anti–Atomic War, skeleton talking into microphone while beating drum, "...we will be back after a brief intermission," issued for the Art Against Atomic War exposition, A Paul Weber, Germany, black and white, 1959 .... **50.00**

Black Saxophonists, humorous caricatures, sgd Adolf Jantzert, used, 1932 .... **50.00**

Commemorative, Atlantic crossing by Italian Air Force to the 1933 Chicago World's Fair, real photo, Italian **65.00**

Commemorative, 1933 Chicago World's Fair, set of 13, commemorating historic events of Baltimore and Ohio Railroad, orig envelope **100.00**

Commemorative, Stephen Darius' flight from Lithuania to New York City, Statue of Liberty and New York City skyline, real photo by J Skrinsko, 1933 .... **50.00**

Communist Leaders, drawing of Marx, Lenin, and Engels, monogrammed "M.C.," black and white, published in Russia, 1933 .... **30.00**

Congo, 2 native children holding New Year sign, writing on back, real photo, 1930 .... **65.00**

Drummer Boy, black boy playing drums, published by Ires, Italy, sgd Roy, used, Jul 1937 .... **40.00**

Eight Sokol Festival, Prague, Art Nouveau, printed by Jan Ziegloser, 1926 .... **200.00**

Figural, fish, wooden, printed in green ink, mailing tag tied on, used, Springfield, MA, 1943 .... **100.00**

French Red Cross, commemorative poster stamp and cancellation on back, sgd Christian Edward Rion, issued for The Liberation Festival, Dinard, France, 1948 .... **40.00**

Gimli, Canada, "Icelandic Jubilee," horse–drawn parade wagons, real photo, used, 1925 .... **60.00**

Ku Klux Klan, members in clan outfits wandering around grounds, "Scene at Pontiac, Mich, Labor Day, 1925," real photo **125.00**

"Let Freedom Ring," First Day of Issue cancellation, stamp for "Freedom of Speech and Religion, Want from Fear," brown, green, and white, Washington, DC, used, Feb 12, 1943 .... **6.00**

Maritime Art, International Exposition of Flemish Colonial Maritime Art, Antwerp, sgd Marfurt, 1930 .... **35.00**

Milic of Kromeriz, published by Neubert, Art Nouveau, from The Slav Epic set of 6, brown and white, 1928 ...... **50.00**

1952 Olympics, Helsinki, Finland, woman diving **60.00**

1964 USA Olympic cycling team in Japan, names listed on back, black and white **45.00**

Novelty, playable record, "Nixon's the One," 33¹/₃ rpm record with "excerpts from Nixon's nomination acceptance speech, August 8, 1968," published by United Citizens for Nixon–Agnew, Washington, DC, black and white, 7 x 7" **40.00**

Planet Mars, issued for "Brooklyn Institute Astronomy Round Table," with lecture on "Life on Other Worlds" by Dr I J LaFleur, real photo, 1940 .... **25.00**

Artist Signed, Mabel Lucie Attwell, "I'll Learn 'Em to Learn Me Music!," $7.00.

Radio Star, Paul Coleman of WSYR in hospital bed, real photo, Syracuse, NY, used, 1945 .... **30.00**

Skiing Competition, Czechoslovakia, sgd Dzian, 1935 ...... **75.00**

The Slavs in Their Country of Origin, published by Neubert, Art Nouveau, from The Slav Epic set of 6, brown and white, 1928 .... **50.00**

Stoney Indian Squaw, real photo, Harmon, Banff, Canada, used, 1951 .... **30.00**

Syracuse, NY, "Northern Terminal, South Bay," trolley station, real photo, used, 1921 .... **35.00**

Third International Aeronautics Show, Milan, Italy, sgd Manlio, 1939 .... **85.00**

28th International Eucharistic Congress, Chicago, Jun 20–24, 1926, flags, symbols, and the Pope **100.00**

White Star Line, bird's–eye view of London offices, Southampton Paquebot cancel, tan, black, and white, used, 1925 .... **40.00**

Willkie, Wendell, "Win With Willkie," real photo, Greyson Studios, New York City, 1940 .... **60.00**

Yugoslavia Communist Party, names listed on back, real photo, c1927 .... **50.00**

POSTERS

The full color poster arrived on the scene in the 1880s, the result of the lithographic printing revolution. Posters by Courier and Strobridge are considered some of the finest examples of American lithography ever printed. Philadelphia was the center of the poster printing industry in America prior to 1945.

Almost from its inception, collectors were fascinated with this colorful art form. Printers began overprinting their commercial runs and selling the extra posters through print dealers and galleries. Editions Sagot in Paris offered posters for sale featuring the art of Toulouse–Lautrec. Posters were an inexpensive advertising form and played a major role during World Wars I and II.

Scarce is a term that must be used very carefully when referring to posters. Print runs into the millions are known. Yet, most were destroyed. The poster collecting community was relatively small and heavily art focused until the 1970s.

Carefully check the date mark on movie posters. An "R," usually located in the lower right corner near the border in the white area, followed by slash and the date denotes a later release of a movie. These posters generally are not as valuable as posters associated with the initial release.

References: Tony Fusco, *Posters: Identification and Price Guide, Second Edition,* Avon Books, 1994; Janet Gleeson, *Miller's Collecting Prints and Posters,* Millers Publications, 1997; Susan Theran, *Prints, Posters & Photographs: Identification and Price Guide,* Avon Books, 1993; Jon R. Warren, *Warren's Movie Poster Price Guide, 4th Edition,* American Collectors Exchange, 1997.

Note: For additional listings see Movie Memorabilia.

Buy And Use Christmas Seals—Protect Your Home From Tuberculosis, Anon, children caroling on stamp design, full color, 1940, 11 x 15" **$45.00**

Dick Custer Cigars, "Dick Custer Holds You Up," cowboy desperado pointing 6–gun, c1920, 10 x 7" **20.00**

For Pictures Out Of This World—Argus C–3, full color, yellow–green man–in–the–moon focuses Argus telephoto lens against black ground, c1953, 22 x10" **100.00**

French National Railroads—Progress Power Precision, A Brenet, bright blue electric locomotive races past fiery factory setting, 1958, 24 x 39" **125.00**

Grape–Nuts, Anon, "With Every Spoonful There's a Reason—Right on the Tip of Your Tongue...," vignettes of cereal being made, served on the table, and as a healthy and epicurean element, 1929, 32 x 22" **45.00**

Hometies, Anon, mother with children portrait, multicolored, gray border, c1920, 20 x 30" **150.00**

Ireland Welcomes You, stylized shamrock and smiling sun, multicolored train at bottom, c1938, 24 x 39" **150.00**

Know Your Timber—It's Good Business, Earl B Winslow, Dept of Agriculture Forest Service, timber man measuring tree trunk, full color, 1945, 13 x 18" **75.00**

Norway—Land Of The Midnight Sun/Pan American World Airways, Anon, puffins and dolphins cavort under sun and purple mountains, full color, c1948, 24 x 37" **110.00**

Old Dutch Cleaner—Grande Economie, Anon, full color litho printed on cloth, c1920, 15 x 20" **95.00**

Progress Of Coffee, Anon, metal ribbed, scenes of plantation, ships, world map, and processing, 1932, 23 x 30" **100.00**

Rajaratnam Fireworks—Sivakaski, Anon, bright red and yellow sparkle letters against blue ground, c1965, 36 x 11" **75.00**

Special Excursion To Detroit, Anon, "Via Michigan Central Railway, Sunday May 19. $5.00 Round Trip from Buffalo," "Auspices The Railroad Enthusiasts, Inc...," Dreyfus' streamlined New Mercury and schedule, black and white illus, c1940, 8 x 14" **38.00**

Stop! Cross At The Corner, H Alonzo Keller, Keystone Automobile Club Public Safety Department, green and black printing, 1935, 17 x 22" **50.00**

35 Years Of Service—Your American Junior Red Cross 1917–1952, Joseph Binder, repetitive red cross and shield in airbrused red, white, and blue design, 1952, 11 x 14" **38.00**

All Hands On Deck, **Pat Boone, Buddy Hackett, Barbara Eden, 20th Century Fox, 1961, $115.00.**

AUCTION PRICES

Vintage movie posters sold by The Last Moving Picture Company on May 24, 1997. Prices include the 15% buyer's premium.

Adventures of Sherlock Holmes, The, 20th Century Fox, Basil Rathbone, linen, 1939, 27 x 41" **$3,450.00**

Back to Bataan, RKO Radio, John Wayne, linen, 1945, 41 x 81" **460.00**

Big Sleep, The, Warner Bros, Humphrey Bogart, Lauren Bacall, linen, 1946, 22 x 28" **431.25**

Brother Rat, Warner Bros, Ronald Reagen, Jane Wyman, 1938, 27 x 41" **201.25**

Goldfinger, United Artists, Sean Connery, linen, 1964, 41 x 81" **977.50**

Having a Wonderful Time, RKO Radio, Ginger Rogers, Douglas Fairbanks, Jr, linen, 1938, 72 x 41" **258.75**

House on Haunted Hill, Allied Artists, Vincent Price, 1958, 27 x 41" **690.00**

Little Colonel, The, Fox, Shirley Temple, Lionel Barrymore, 1935, 81 x 81" **1,955.00**

Little Orphan, The, Tom and Jerry, linen, 1949, 27 x 41" **920.00**

Popeye, Paramount, linen, 1939, 27 x 41" **3,737.50**

Prince and the Pauper, The, Warner Bros, Errol Flynn, linen, 1937, 27 x 41" **546.25**

Psycho, Paramount, Anthony Perkens, Janet Leigh, 1960, 27 x 41" **345.00**

Race for Life, A, Warner Bros, Rin–Tin–Tin, linen, 1928, 27 x 41" **431.25**

Sing, Bing, Sing, Paramount, Bing Crosby, linen, 1933, 27 x 41" **575.00**

Sleeping Beauty, Buena Vista, 1959, 22 x 28" **115.00**

Ten Commandments, The, Paramount, Charlton Heston, linen, 1946, 27 x 41" **316.25**

War and Peace, Paramount, Audrey Hepburn, Henry Fonda, linen, 1956, 27 x 41" **201.25**

Wild One, The, Columbia, Marlon Brando, linen, 1953, 41 x 81" **517.50**

Wizard of Oz, The, MGM, Judy Garland, borders expertly restored, 1939, 11 x 14" **4,312.50**

Yellow Submarine, Untied Artists, the Beatles, linen, 1968, 27 x 41" **632.50**

POTTERIES, REGIONAL

There were thousands of pottery factories scattered across the United States. Many existed only for a brief period of time.

Recent scholarship by individuals such as Phyllis and Tom Bess on the Oklahoma potteries, Carol and Jim Carlton on Colorado pottery, Jack Chipman on California pottery, and Darlene Dommel on the Dakota potteries have demonstrated how rich America's ceramic heritage is. This is only the tip of the iceberg.

This is a catchall category for all those companies that have not reached a strong enough collecting status to deserve their own category. Eventually, some will achieve this level. Collectors collect what they know. Thanks to today's scholarship, collectors are learning more about these obscure potteries.

References: California: Jack Chipman, *Collector's Encyclopedia of California Pottery, Second Edition,* Collector Books, 1998; Darlene Hurst Dommel, *Collector's Encyclopedia of Howard Pierce Porcelain,* Collector Books, 1997; Michael Schneider, *California Potteries: The Complete Book,* Schiffer Publishing, 1995; Bernice Stamper, *Vallona Starr Ceramics,* Schiffer Publishing, 1995.

Colorado: Carol and Jim Carlton, *Collector's Encyclopedia of Colorado Pottery: Identification and Values,* Collector Books, 1994; North Dakota: Darlene Hurst Dommel, *Collector's Encyclopedia of the Dakota Potteries: Identification & Values,* Collector Books, 1996; Oklahoma: Phyllis and Tom Bess, *Frankoma and Other Oklahoma Potteries,* Schiffer Publishing, 1995.

Periodical: *Collectors Express,* PO Box 221, Mayview, MO 64071.

Collectors' Clubs: Arkansas: Arkansas Pottery Collectors Society, PO Box 7617, Little Rock, AR 72217; Minnesota: Nemadji Pottery Collectors Club, 200 Old Co. Rd. 8, Moose Lake, MN 55767; North Dakota: North Dakota Pottery Collectors Society, PO Box 14, Beach, ND 58621.

California, Arcadia Ceramics, salt and pepper shakers, miniature **$52.00**

California, Ball Artware, figure, pheasant, 7½" h **30.00**

California, Cleminsons, spoon rest, gray, gold, and purple leaf design, 8½" l **5.00**

California, Cleminsons, wall pocket chef, 7¼" h **15.00**

California, De Lee Art, figure, Latino Dancer, female, hp dec, gold highlights, 11½" h **22.50**

California, Doranne of California, cookie jar, tortoise and hare, woodtone, c1970 . . . . **25.00**

California, Flintridge China, dinner plate, lavender ground, silver trim **18.00**

California, Freeman–McFarlin, figure, mermaid holding shell dish, pink bisque, c1957 . . . . **35.00**

California, Freeman–McFarlin, figure, owl, large eyes, 9" h **25.00**

California, Freeman–McFarlin, planter, stoneware, in–mold "Anthony" mark, 7 x 9" **20.00**

California, Hagan–Renaker, bank, pig, *Three Little Pigs,* 6¾" h **225.00**

California, Hagan–Renaker, figure, fox, flat face, black bisque, turquoise glaze **35.00**

California, Hagan–Renaker, figure, puppy, begging, "Carmencita," Pedigree Dogs Line, 2" h **50.00**

California, Haldeman, bowl, flared sides, Chinese style, blended glaze, 3½ x 10" **25.00**

California, Haldeman, dish, figural swan, sand lined with turquoise int, white ext, 5 x 7" **15.00**

California, Haldeman, figure, Caliente dancing lady, #403, 6½" h **25.00**

California, Haldeman, slave woman, 7" h. **60.00**

California, Haldeman, rose bowl, applied handmade flowers, 4¾" **25.00**

California, Haldeman, triple bud vase, white, 6½" h **20.00**

California, Keeler, figure, canary, tail down, 6" h **15.00**

California, Keeler, figure, seagull, wings up, mkd "Brad Keeler #29," 10½" **50.00**

California, Keeler, figure, Siamese Cat, #798 . . . . **25.00**

California, Manker, condiment tray, fish shape, 1,1¾ x 16¾" **100.00**

California, Manker, jar, cov, citron green, 6" h **75.00**

California, Manker, vase, cylinder, citron green and dove gray, 8" h **60.00**

California, Manker, vase, fluted, yellow, 6" h **50.00**

California, McCarty Brothers, planter, Mexican children playing musical instruments, price for pr **25.00**

California, Pacific, baby plate, divided, bunny design border, c1934, 9" d **45.00**

California, Pacific, baking dish, jade green, wood handle, 6¼" d **38.00**

California, Pacific, salad plate, spiral design **12.00**

California, Pacific, teapot, ftd, apricot. **75.00**

California, Pacific, teapot, individual, Apache red **38.00**

California, Pacific, vase, bird motif, c1939, 8¼" h. **25.00**

California, Padre, honey jar, bee hive shape, maroon **22.50**

California, Pierce, ashtray, stylized, light gray lava glaze ext, cobalt blue int **35.00**

California, Pierce, figure, monkey, 6" h **25.00**

California, Pierce, polar bear, brown on white, 4½" h **25.00**

California, Roselane, dealer sign, aqua, 3 x 12½" **100.00**

California, Roselane, figure, girl with bouquet, in–mold mark **8.00**

California, Roselane, figure, "Sparkler" deer, plastic, eyes, c1965, 4 x 3½" **9.00**

California, Santa Anita, dinner plate, Bird of Paradise, Flowers of Hawaii Line, 10½" d **6.00**

California, Weil, vase, sailor boy, hp dec, c1943, 10¾" h **22.50**

California, White, dish, handled, incised "Eugene White" **22.50**

California, Artistic California, planter, burgundy with gray specks, mkd "Artistic California 500" in script, 9¼" l, 4¾" h, $15.00.

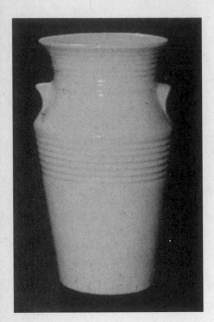

California, Pacific, vase, yellow, early 1930s, 7" h, $40.00.

California, Will–George/The Claysmiths, figure, bird on branch paper label, 2 x 5" **22.50**

California, Will–George/The Claysmiths, figure, child artist with model, incised mark, c1939, price for pr **60.00**

California, Will–George/The Claysmiths, figure, dachschund, stamp mark, 6½ x 9" **45.00**

California, Winfield, bowl, Primitive Pony 9 . . . . **30.00**

California, Winfield, dessert plate, hp Geranium pattern, 8½" d **51.00**

California, Winfield, salad plate, square, 7½" **10.00**

California, Ynez, figure, Jennifer, lace trim c1946, 5½" h **12.00**

Colorado, Broadmoor, figure, cowboy hat, black **45.00**

Colorado, Broadmoor, lamp base, cream, swirl design, sgd by Cecil Jones, 15" h **200.00**

Colorado, Broadmoor, planter, mouth open, red **65.00**

Colorado, Broadmoor, vase, applied handles, red, hand thrown **125.00**

Colorado, Denver White, cookie jar, cov, pine cone dec, figural squirrel finial, 8 x 6" **300.00**

Colorado, Denver White, cup and saucer, turquoise **35.00**

Colorado, Denver White, cabinet vase, turquoise **50.00**

Colorado, Johnson, wall plaque, train design, 8" **65.00**

Colorado, Lakewood, ashtray, blue, applied white cougar **55.00**

Colorado, Loveland, vase, floral design, 6" h **35.00**

Colorado, Rocky Mountain, condiment tray, applied center deer **10.00**

Colorado, Rocky Mountain, console tray, pine cone dec, 6" **15.00**

Colorado, Rocky Mountain, figure, poodle, 10" h **25.00**

North Dakota, Dickinson Clay Products, ashtray, figural cowboy hat, brown, "North Dakota" on rim, 4½ x 5" **45.00**

North Dakota, Dickinson Clay Products, ashtray, marine blue, white flowing overglaze, 4¼" d **35.00**

North Dakota, Dickinson Clay Products, bookends, pr, mountain sheep, green **350.00**

North Dakota, Dickinson Clay Products, creamer and sugar, bright orange ground, gold and black overglaze **35.00**

North Dakota, Dickinson Clay Products, paperweight, shield shape, red, 2¾" **35.00**

North Dakota, Dickinson Clay Products, salt and pepper shakers, pr, Cableware design, maroon red, 1½ x 2½" **30.00**

North Dakota, Dickinson Clay Products, vase, applied handles, metallic black, mkd "Dickota," 4¾" h **45.00**

North Dakota, Messer, ashtray, applied antelope on base . . . **350.00**

North Dakota, Messer, salt and pepper shakers, pr, figural grain elevator **100.00**

North Dakota, Pine Ridge, bowl, geometric motif, sgd "N. Firethunder" **300.00**

North Dakota, Pine Ridge, serving set, pitcher, 4 tumblers, geometric design, sgd "Ramona Wounded Knee" **600.00**

North Dakota, Pine Ridge, vase, cream colored sgraffito geometric motif, red ground **350.00**

North Dakota, Rushmore, dish, slip painted cattails, 11" l **75.00**

North Dakota, Rushmore, figure, molded cowboy boots, 3½" h **30.00**

North Dakota, Rushmore, pitcher, swirl design, uranium orange, 7" h **125.00**

North Dakota, Rushmore, trivet, Art Deco floral design, mint green, 5" **130.00**

North Dakota, University of North Dakota, ashtray, fish shape, mkd "UND Flossie MC" **85.00**

North Dakota, WPA Ceramics, figure, Peter Peter Pumpkin Eater, 5" h **700.00**

North Dakota, WPA Ceramics, plate, cobalt blue, Native American sgraffito design, 9" d **800.00**

North Dakota, WPA Ceramics, strawberry jar, hand thrown, turquoise **250.00**

North Dakota, WPA Ceramics, vase, green, wheat in relief, 8" h **300.00**

North Dakota, WPA Ceramics, vase, incised sgraffito wheat design, 5" h **350.00**

Oklahoma, Cherokee Pottery, figure, quail, dated "11–10–81,– 6" h **7.00**

Oklahoma, Creek Pottery, mug, Indian head, tomahawk handle, 4½" h **7.00**

Oklahoma, Creek Pottery, salt and pepper shakers, pr, figural teepee, 3" h **10.00**

Oklahoma, Gracetone Pottery, bowl, pedestal base, gunmetal, 6" h **20.00**

Oklahoma, Gracetone Pottery, scalloped edge, pink champagne, 6" d **10.00**

Oklahoma, Gracetone Pottery, figure, hound dog, cinnamon, 6" h **300.00**

Oklahoma, Hammat Originals, ashtray, banana leaf shape, 7" d **10.00**

Oklahoma, Hammat Originals, bowl, ftd, cabbage leaf shape, 9½" h **40.00**

Oklahoma, Hammat Originals, figure, "Chico" the monkey, 12" h **35.00**

Oklahoma, Hammat Originals, mug, coconut shape, 7 oz **5.00**

Oklahoma, National Youth Administration, pitcher, yellow ware, 20 oz **30.00**

Oklahoma, Sequoyah, ashtray, figural duck, mkd "'Evelyn Vann Sequoyah 1939," 8" l **100.00**

Oklahoma, Sequoyah, ashtray, figural turtle, mkd "Evelyn Van. 1939 Sequoyah #1," 5½" l **50.00**

Oklahoma, Sequoyah, pitcher, emb thunderbird, 3½" h **30.00**

Oklahoma, Sequoyah, vase, bulbous, applied frog handle, 5" h **80.00**

Oklahoma, Sequoyah Pottery, urn, reddish brown, mkd "Levide Going 1938 Sequoyah," 10" h, $160.00.

Oklahoma, Sequoyah, vase, straight neck, mkd "Winnie Simmer 1938–39 Sequoyah," 6¹⁄₂" h 50.00

Oklahoma, Synar Ceramics, basket, woodpine ext, aqua int, 7¹⁄₂" 15.00

Oklahoma, Synar Ceramics, vase, woodpine ext, aqua int, wheat design, 10" h 15.00

Oklahoma, Tamac, barbecue plate, butterscotch, 15" l 12.00

Oklahoma, Tamac, bud vase, frosty fudge glaze, 5¹⁄₂" h 10.00

Oklahoma, Tamac, chocolate pot, frost fudge glaze, 24 oz 70.00

Oklahoma, Tamac, spoon rest, foot shape, avocado, "For My Stirring Spoon" 10.00

Oklahoma, Tamac, wall vase, frost pine glaze 10.00

Oklahoma, Winart, pitcher, chartreuse with brown drip, 6" h 5.00

Oklahoma, Winart, planter, oblong, brown, frost, 15¹⁄₂" l 12.00

Oklahoma, Winart, salt and pepper shakers, pr, ball shape, pink ground, brown drip 8.00

Oklahoma, Winart, sip 'n smoke tray, 2–finger mug, persimmon with frost, 8 oz 10.00

Oklahoma, Winart, teapot, cov, individual, brown ground, frost, 12 oz 15.00

Oklahoma, Winart, tidbit tray, 2 tier, pink ground, frosty white rim, 10" d 25.00

PRECIOUS MOMENTS

During a visit to the Los Angeles Gift Show in 1978, Eugene Freeman, president of Enesco, saw some cards and posters featuring the drawings of Samuel J. Butcher. At first, Butcher and Bill Biel, his partner in Jonathan and David, were not thrilled with the idea of having Butcher's art transformed into three–dimensional form. However, after seeing a prototype sculpted by Yashei Fojioka of Japan, Butcher and Biel agreed.

Initially twenty–one pieces were made. Early figures are darker in color than those made today. Pieces produced between 1978 and 1984 and licensed by Jonathan & David Company have smaller heads than pieces relicensed by the Samuel J. Butcher Company and Precious Moments. Jonathan & David ceased operating in 1988.

The Enesco Precious Moments Club began in 1981. In 1989, Butcher opened the Precious Moments Chapel in Carthage, Missouri. In 1995 Goebel introduced hand–painted bronze miniatures. The year 1995 also saw Enesco launch its Century Circle Retailers, a group of 35 retailers selling a limited edition line of Precious Moments material.

References: Collectors Information Bureau, *Collectibles Market Guide & Price Index, 15th Edition,* Collector's Information Bureau, 1997, distributed by Krause Publications; Rosie Wells (ed.), *Rosie's Secondary Market Price Guide for Enesco's Precious Moments Collection, 15th Edition,* Rosie Wells Enterprises, 1997.

Periodical: *Precious Collectibles,* 22341 E Wells Rd, Canton, IL 61520.

Collectors' Club: Enesco Precious Moments Collectors' Club, PO Box 99, Itasca, IL 60143.

Bell, Love Is The Best Wish Of All, 1987 .... $35.00

Bell, May Your Christmas Be Merry, 1991 .... 35.00

Bell, The Lord Bless You And Keep You, 1982 .... 35.00

Bell, Time To Wish You A Merry Christmas, 1988 .... 40.00

Bell, Wishing You A Merry Christmas, 1984 .... 45.00

Bell, You're As Pretty As A Christmas Tree, 1994 .... 28.00

Doll, Aaron, 1985, 12" h 160.00

Doll, Angie The Angel Of Mercy, 1987 .... 275.00

Doll, Autumn's Praise, Jack–In–The–Boxes Series, 1990 .... 200.00

Doll, Bong Bong, 1986, 13" l 265.00

Doll, Katie Lynne, 1983, 16" h 185.00

Doll, May You Have An Old Fashioned Christmas, Jack–In–The–Boxes Series, 1991 .... 200.00

Doll, Mother Sew Dear, 1984, 18" h 350.00

Figurine, A Tub Full Of Love, 1987 .... 30.00

Figurine, Believe The Impossible, 1988 .... 55.00

Figurine, Birds Of A Feather Collect Together, Collectors Club Welcome Gift Series, 1986 .... 35.00

Figurine, Blessings From My House To Yours, 1983 .... 75.00

Figurine, Christmas Tree, Sugartown Series, 1992 .... 15.00

Figurine, 15 Happy Years Together: What A Tweet, 15th Anniversary Commemorative Edition, 1988 .... 150.00

Figurine, God Bless Our Years Together, 5th Anniversary Commemorative Edition Series, 1985 .... 250.00

Figurine, Grandma's Prayer, Special Edition Members' Only Series, 1986 .... 100.00

Figurine, Have A Beary Special Birthday, Birthday Club Inscribed Charter Membership Renewal Gift Series, 1989 .... 40.00

Figurine, Hello Lord, It's Me Again, Special Edition Members' Only Series, 1981 .... 375.00

Figurine, Join In On The Blessings, Collectors Club Welcome Gift Series, 1985 .... 55.00

Figurine, Let Us Call The Club To Order, Inscribed Charter Member Renewal Gift Series, 1983 .... 50.00

Figurine, Lord I'm Coming Home, 1986 .... 35.00

Figurine, Lord Keep My Life In Tune, Rejoice In The Lord Series, 1985 .... 110.00

Figurine, May You Have The Sweetest Christmas, Family Christmas Scene Series, 1985 .... 25.00

Figurine, Our Club Can't Be Beat, Birthday Club Welcome Gift Series, 1986 .... 75.00

Figurine, Where Would I Be Without You, Little Moments Series, 1996 .... 20.00

Limited Edition Plate, Enesco, Christmas Love Series, 1987, "My Peace I Give Unto Thee," $75.00.

Figurine, You Have Touched So Many Hearts, Musical
Figurines Series, 1988 . . . . **65.00**

Figurine, You're The Sweetest Cookie In The Batch,
Inscribed Charter Member Renewal Gift Series, 1995 . . . . . **35.00**

Figurine, You Are The End Of My Rainbow, Collectors
Club Welcome Gift Series, 1994 . . . . **35.00**

Ornament, Baby's First Christmas, 1981 . . . . **40.00**

Ornament, Blessed Are The Pure In Heart, 1984 . . . . **20.00**

Ornament, Dropping Over For Christmas, 1982 . . . . **50.00**

Ornament, Dr Sugar's Office, Sugartown Series, 1995 . . . . **18.00**

Ornament, 15 Years Tweet Music Together, 15th
Anniversary Commemorative Edition Series, 1993 . . . . **20.00**

Ornament, I'm Nuts About You, 1992 . . . . **25.00**

Ornament, O Come All Ye Faithful, 1983 . . . . **25.00**

Ornament, Serve With A Smile, 1986 . . . . **30.00**

Ornament, Waddle I Do Without You, 1987 . . . . **20.00**

Ornament, Your Are The End Of My Rainbow, Special
Edition Members' Only Series, 1994 . . . . **20.00**

Plate, Autumn's Praise, The Four Seasons Series, 1986 . . . . . . **45.00**

Plate, Blessings From Me To Thee, Christmas Blessings
Series, 1991 . . . . **50.00**

Plate, Christmastime Is For Sharing, Joy Of Christmas
Series, 1983 . . . . **40.00**

Plate, The Hand That Rocks The Future, Mother's Day
Series, 1983 . . . . **40.00**

Plate, He Covers The Earth With His Beauty, Beauty Of
Christmas Collection, 1995 . . . . **50.00**

Plate, Love Is Kind, Inspired Thoughts Series, 1984 . . . . **45.00**

Plate, Merry Christmas Deer, Christmas Love Series,
1988 . . . . **50.00**

Plate, Our First Christmas Together, Open Edition, 1982 . . . . . **45.00**

Plate, Wee Three Kings, Christmas Collection, 1983 . . . . **40.00**

PREMIUMS

A premium is an object given free or at a reduced value with the purchase of a product or service. Premiums divide into two groups: (1) point of purchase (you obtain your premium when you make the purchase) or (2) proof of purchase (you send proof of purchase, often box labels or seals, to a distribution point which then sends the premium to you).

Premiums are generational. The sixty– and seventy–something generations think of radio premiums. The fifty–, forty–, and older thirty–something generations identify with cereal and radio premiums. Younger generations collect fast–food premiums.

Collectors place a premium on three–dimensional premiums. However, many of these premiums arrived in paper containers and envelopes and contained paper instruction sheets. A premium is considered complete only if it has its period packaging and everything that came with it.

Ovaltine's offer of a "Little Orphan Annie" music sheet was one of the earliest radio premiums. Jack Armstrong, Lone Ranger, and Tom Mix premiums soon followed. By the middle of the 1930s every child eagerly awaited the phrase "Now, an important word from our sponsor" with pad in hand, ready to write down the address for the latest premium offer. Thousands of radio premiums were offered in the 1930s, 40s, and 50s.

Cereal manufacturers found that the inclusion of a premium in the box, even if it was unrelated to a specific radio or television show, was enough of an incentive to stimulate extra sales. Cereal premiums flourished in the post–1945 period. Although television premiums were offered, they never matched in numbers those offered over the radio.

The arrival of the fast–food restaurant and eventual competition between chains led to the use of premiums to attract customers. Many premiums were tied to television shows and movies. Although not a premium, fast–food packaging has also attracted the interest of collectors.

Not all premiums originated via cereal boxes, fast–food chains, radio, or television. Local and national food manufacturers and merchants used premiums to attract customers. Cracker Jack is the most obvious example.

References: Scott Bruce, *Cereal Box Bonanza: The 1950's*, Collector Books, 1995; *Hake's Price Guide to Character Toy Premiums: Including Comic, Cereal, TV, Movies, Radio & Related Store Bought Items*, Gemstone Publishing, 1996; Jim Harmon, *Radio & TV Premiums: Value and History From Tom Mix to Space Patrol*, Krause Publications, 1997; Robert M. Overstreet, *Overstreet Premium Ring Price Guide, Third Edition*, Gemstone Publishing, 1997; Tom Tumbusch, *Tomart's Price Guide to Radio Premiums and Cereal Box Collectibles*, Wallace–Homestead, Krause Publications, 1991.

Periodicals: *Box Top Bonanza*, 3403 46th Ave, Moline, IL 61265; *Premium Collectors Magazine*, 1125 Redman Ave, St Louis, MO 63138.

Newsletters: *The Premium Watch Watch*, 24 San Rafael Dr, Rochester, NY 14618; *The Toy Ring Journal*, PO Box 544, Birmingham, MI 48012.

Note: See Cracker Jack, Fast–Food Collectibles, and McDonald's for additional listings.

REPRODUCTION ALERT

Amos 'n' Andy, book, Rand McNally, hard cov, auto-
graphed, 128 pp, 1929, 6 x 8" **$250.00**

Boo Berry, poster and figural monster crayons, 1988 . . . . **20.00**

Borden, Fury's Western Roundup Party Kit, paper,
8 punch–out sheets, c1955 . . . . **25.00**

Caloric, paper dolls, two 12" h stand–up dolls, with blue and white pamphlet promoting Caloric give–away, 10 x 13" mailing envelope, unused, c1950s **15.00**

Cap'n Crunch, coloring book, Whitman, cover shows good guys tied up by Lafoote on ship, and Seadog hiding in barrel, 1968 . . . . **25.00**

Cap'n Crunch, comic book, Adventures of Quake and Quisp, 1965 . . . . **5.00**

Cap'n Crunch, figure, vinyl, 1971, 8" h **35.00**

Cap'n Crunch, puppet, plastic, 1960s. **25.00**

Cap'n Crunch, wall plaque, paper, Oath of Allegiance, color illus, unused, 1960s, 8 x 10" **25.00**

Carey Salt, ring, The Shadow, plastic, alligator, white day glow, black plastic insert, 1947 . . . . **575.00**

Chase & Sanborn, photo album, Eddie Cantor, 1932. . . . . **5.00**

Cheerios, comic book, Lone Ranger, 1954, 16 pp. **15.00**

Cheerios, mug, plastic, black and white, 3 different illus, 1950s **30.00**

Cheerios, postcard, Cheerios Kid and Donald Duck, Huey, Louie, and Disneyland, black and white, 1957 . . . . . **10.00**

Cheerios, Space Shuttle Adventure Kit, diecut styrofoam parts, black and white space shuttle iron–on transfer, peel–off sticker emblem, illus instruction card, full color 24–pp illus booklet, 1981 . . . . **25.00**

Cocoa Krispies, figure, Ogg, blonde hair, 1970. . . . . . . **28.00**

Cocoa Puffs, train, litho tin engine, 3 cars, "Cocoa Puffs Train" on top of cars, sides depict children eating Cocoa Puffs cereal, engine has windup key on side, missing smoke stack, Linemar, 12" l, c1959 . . . . **50.00**

Cocomalt, Big Little Book, *Buck Rogers in the 25th Century*, 1933 . . . . **40.00**

Cocomalt, Buck Rogers, child's helmet, stiff paper, multicolored, Cocomalt, c1933 . . . . **175.00**

Count Chocula, ring, plastic, orange frame, flicker inset of Count Chocula juggling **75.00**

Count Chocula, Spooky Shape Maker, 1970s **25.00**

Cream of Wheat, manual, Buck Rogers, *Solar Scout Manual*, 1935–36 . . . . **170.00**

Crest Toothpaste, book, *Around the World in 80 Days*, hard cov, 1978 . . . . **8.00**

Dari–Rich Chocolate Drinks, booklet, 1934, 24 pp. **8.00**

Dell Comics, ring, Gene Autry, gold plastic base, clear plastic cover over American flag, c1940s **65.00**

Dell Comics, ring, Lone Ranger, gold plastic base, clear plastic cover over American flag, c1940s **65.00**

Exxon, comic book, Mickey and Goofy Explore the Universe of Energy, 1985 . . . . **2.00**

Frito–Lay, Bandito eraser, yellow, figural Frito Bandito, 1½" h, 1960s **20.00**

Froot Loops, Toucan Sam, secret decoder, 1983 . . . . **5.00**

Frosted Flakes, radio, figural Tony the Tiger, plastic, 1970s, 8" h **20.00**

Frosted Flakes, spoon, sterling silver, 1983 . . . . **5.00**

Funny–Paste Toothpaste, astronaut mask, diecut cardboard, punch–out eyes, nose, and mouth, 1966, unused **50.00**

General Electric Light Bulbs, Mr Magoo, badge, metal **10.00**

General Foods/Jello, puppet, Mr Wiggle, soft vinyl, complete with 10 x 13" half–page Sunday newspaper advertisement for Mr Wiggle desserts and handpuppets, 1966 . . . . **175.00**

General Mills, card game, 2 decks with Cocoa Puffs, Franken Berry, Trix, Count Chocula, and Boo Berry characters, complete with mailer, 1981 . . . . **10.00**

Post Raisin Bran, badge, Hopalong Cassidy, litho tin, 1950s, $75.00.

Grape Nut Flakes, cardboard cutouts, West Point Cadet Uniforms, 2 squares cut from back of box, each have 2 West Point cadets in different uniforms, 1950s **10.00**

Grape Nut Flakes, pin, Roy Rogers, 1953. . . . . **5.00**

Green Giant, kite, plastic, 1960s, 42 x 48" **15.00**

Horlick's Malted Milk, decanter, Lum and Abner, c1936 . . . . . **45.00**

Kaboom, clown spoon hanger, plastic, 1969, 2" h **8.00**

Keds, ring, "U.S. Keds," silvered brass, c1962. . . . . **55.00**

Kellogg's, certificate, Tom Corbett Space Cadet, Space Academy, 1953 . . . . **35.00**

Kellogg's, Corvette, battery operated, plastic, red, silver and black accents, "2" sticker on both sides, gold foil "Corvette" name sticker, orig box with instruction sheet and photocopy of orig ad, Ideal, 1965 . . . . **100.00**

Kellogg's, eraser, Yogi Bear, 1960s, 2" h **20.00**

Kellogg's, Singing Lady Party Kit, masks, uncut, 1936 . . . . **60.00**

Kellogg's, snap together animals, set of 7, molded plastic, 3 dimensional, 1960s. **35.00**

Kellogg's, Space Satellite Launcher Set, 1956 . . . . **200.00**

King Vitamin, Royal King Coach, plastic, yellow, metal wheel, 3" l, 1970s **10.00**

Kix, Lone Ranger, ring, atom bomb, brass bands with lightning bolt design, bullet shaped top with red plastic end cap **80.00**

Kroger Food Stores, coloring book, Mickey Mouse Explorers, 1965 . . . . **10.00**

Lancaster PA Coal Company, blotter, The Shadow, Shadow silhouette, red, white, and blue, 4 x 9" **50.00**

Lone Ranger, ring, brass bands, plastic 6–gun, sparking, 1947. . . . . **75.00**

Lucky Charms, *Star Wars* character stick–ons, Lucky, 1977 . . . . **8.00**

Lum and Abner, family almanac, orig mailing envelope, Horlick's Malted Milk, 34 pp, 6 x 9". **40.00**

Mars Candy, Christmas card, Howdy Doody, set **45.00**

Mars Candy, Mickey Mouse Club Magic Manual, 1950s **12.00**

Maypo, figure with bowl, Arvin, molded rubber, depicts Marky Mayo sitting with legs out in front of him holding 5" d yellow hard plastic bowl, painted, red, blue, brown, and fleshtone, 1960s **90.00**

McCarthy, Charlie, game, Radio Party, orig mailing envelope, complete, 1938 . . . . **35.00**

Mix, Tom, National Chicle Gum, booklet, 1934, 8 pp **18.00**

Mix, Tom, premium catalog, folder, paper, 8¼ x 10¼" **25.00**

Mix, Tom, decoder, brass, revolving 6–guns, 1941 . . . . **85.00**

Nabisco, photo, Rin–Tin–Tin cast, 1954–56 . . . . **15.00**

Nabisco Honey Wheats, ring, Buggalo Bee, gray plastic base, color flicker picture, 1950s **20.00**

Nabisco Honey Wheats, ring, Chief Thunderthud, gray plastic base, color flicker picture, 1950s **25.00**

Nabisco Honey Wheats, flicker ring, Princess Summerfall Winterspring, gray plastic base, 1950s **30.00**

Ovaltine, iron–on transfer, Captain Midnight's Secret Squadron, orig envelope, c1948, 4" d **110.00**

Ovaltine, manual, Little Orphan Annie, Secret Society, password, signs, and signals, 1938, 8 pp **60.00**

Ovaltine, mug, Little Orphan Annie, ceramic, white, Annie and Sandy illus, 1932, 3" h **65.00**

Ovaltine, puzzle, Little Orphan Annie, Tucker County Horse Race, orig instruction sheet and mailing box, c1933, 9 x 12½" **70.00**

Ovaltine, ring, Little Orphan Annie, signet, brass base, silvered initials, 1937 . . . . **60.00**

Ovaltine, shake–up mug, plastic, orange, blue lid, Captain Midnight raised portrait, "Remember Your Secret Squadron Pledge," c1947, 5" h **90.00**

Pepsi–Cola, certificate, Counter–Spy Junior Agents Club, paper, c1950, 6 x 8½" **25.00**

Peter Pan Peanut Butter, coloring book, 1963 . . . . **8.00**

Pillsbury, Choo Choo Cherry, pillow, cloth, 1970 . . . . **15.00**

Pillsbury, Chug A Lug, mug, plastic, 1969 . . . . **12.00**

Pillsbury, Funny Face, set of 4 ramp walkers, plastic, orig shipping box, 1971 . . . . **200.00**

Pillsbury, Goofy Grape Pitcher and Cup Set, molded plastic, purple pitcher, 4 multicolored cups, Lefty Lemon, Jolly Ollie Orange, Brye Raspberry, and Goofy Grape cups, painted accents, 1973, 8½" h, 2 qt . . . **100.00**

Popsicle, ring, plastic, figural cowboy boot, 1951 . . . . **30.00**

Post Toasties Corn Flakes, ring, Casper, litho tin, ©1949 . . . . . **25.00**

Post Toasties Corn Flakes, ring, Henry, litho tin, unused, ©1949 . . . . **35.00**

Post Toasties Corn Flakes, ring, The Phantom, litho tin, unused, ©1949 . . . . **50.00**

Power House Candy, Roger Wilco, magni–ray ring, brass, paper insert under hinged cover, 1948 . . . . **35.00**

Pure Oil, Lone Ranger, bat–o–ball, 1938 . . . . **35.00**

Purvis, Melvin, badge, 2–toned brass, black and red enamel, "Roving Operative Melvin Purvis Junior G–Man Corps," 1936, 1½" h **25.00**

Purvis, Melvin, ring, brass, adjustable, eagle and shield design, 1936 . . . . **30.00**

Quaker Oats, book, Dick Tracy, c1939 . . . . **25.00**

Quaker Oats, Quake Explorers Kit, geologists metal tipped hammer, 4 ore specimens, geiger counter, dual–lens magnifying glass, tweezers, goggles, 4 exploration maps, instruction sheet, and mailing envelope, unused, 1960s **200.00**

Quaker Puffed Wheat & Rice, pinback button, Veronica Lake, 1948 . . . . **5.00**

Quisp, card game, Space Match, 1968 . . . . **25.00**

Quisp, clicker pistol, plastic, red, "Quisp" printed in raised letters on both sides, 1960s, 7" l **265.00**

Quisp, doll, cloth, 1965 . . . . **30.00**

Quisp, ring, Quisp Meteorite, 1960s **55.00**

Quisp, satellite launcher, plastic, rubber band powered launcher with emb "Quake" on each side, unused, 1960s, 2" d **40.00**

Ralston Wheat Chex, ring, Magic Pup, magnetized pup's head, 1951 . . . . **65.00**

Rice Krispies, doll, color fabric "Snap" cutout, mailing envelope with Snap illus on front and unused order form on back, uncut, 1948, 13 x 14" **100.00**

Rice Krispies, squeaker toy, Snap, Crackle, and Pop, 8" h, price for set of 3 . . . . **130.00**

Sears, book, *Tarzan of the Apes*, 1835 . . . . **25.00**

Sgt Preston, flashlight, black plastic, red and green color discs, facsimile signature, "Challenge of the Yukon," ©1949, 3" l **25.00**

Shredded Wheat, Train–O–Gram, Santa Fe Twin Unit Diesel, set of 3, unused, 1956, 4 x 7" **30.00**

Sky King, figure, set of 6, plastic, Sky King, Clipper, Penny, Sheriff, Songbird, and Yellow Fury, 1950s, 2½" h **150.00**

Star–Kist, Charlie the Tuna, Film Viewer, battery operated, plastic, 1971, 10" h **35.00**

Star–Kist, Charlie the Tuna, squeeze toy, vinyl, 1973, 7" h **30.00**

Sugar Crisp, comic book, Baseball Facts & Fun, 52 pp **30.00**

Sugar Crisp, paint–by–number set, 1954 . . . . **30.00**

Sugar Smacks, cereal bowl and mug, Digger Frog on bowl, figural mug, 1973 . . . . **20.00**

Sundial Shoes, ring, brass and plastic, 1950 . . . . **35.00**

Sunoco, blotter, Donald Duck, Donald driving car, 1942 . . . . **12.00**

Superman, ring, silvered brass, Superman Crusader, 1938–40 . . . . **160.00**

Tattoo Gum, Popeye, comic gum folder, 1933 . . . . **10.00**

Tip Top Bread, truck, punch–out, 11 x 9" card with 3 miniature punch–out loaves of bread to be assembled, unused, 1955 . . . . **35.00**

Trix, puppet, Trix Rabbit, cloth and vinyl, 1960s, 12" h **30.00**

Trix, Magic Whistle with Magnifying Glass, plastic whistle, built–in magnifying glass on top, raised image of Trix rabbit and "Trix Whistle," 1960s **10.00**

Trix, squeaker toy, Trix rabbit, vinyl, movable head, 1970s, 9" h **35.00**

Wheato–Nuts, Voodoo Eye Pendant, metal, envelope, 1930s **80.00**

Wonder Bread, hat, Howdy Doody **50.00**

Nabisco Shredded Wheat, skill puzzle, Rusty from Rin–Tin–Tin, $7.00.

PRESLEY, ELVIS

Elvis died on August 17, 1977. Or, did he? The first Elvis license material dates from the mid 1950s. Vintage Elvis dates prior to 1965.

Collectors divide Elvis material into two periods: items licensed prior to Elvis' death and those licensed by his estate, known to collectors as fantasy items. Some Elvis price guides refuse to cover fantasy pieces. Special items manufactured and marketed solely for Elvis fan club members are a third category of material and should not be overlooked.

References: Jerry Osborne, *The Official Price Guide to Elvis Presley: Records and Memorabilia*, House of Collectibles, 1994; Steve Templeton, *Elvis!: An Illustrated Guide to New and Vintage Collectibles*, Courage Books, Running Press, 1996.

Collectors' Club: Elvis Forever TCB Fan Club, PO Box 1066, Pinellas Park, FL 33281.

Album Slicks, 28 pcs, full color photos, unused, c1960–70 . . . . **$115.00**

Album, Official Elvis Presley Album, published by *Movie Teen Magazine*, 1956 . . . . **10.00**

Award, RIAA, gold album, *This Is Elvis*, commemorates sale of more than 500,000 copies, matted and framed, 21 x 17" **1,150.00**

Book, *Elvis Special 1964*, hard cov, World Distributors, Ltd, England, 108 pp, 7½ x 10" **10.00**

Booklet, *Elvis Presley—Man or Mouse*, privately printed by Chaw Mank, 1960 . . . . **15.00**

Charm Bracelet, gold colored metal, 4 metal charms, picture frame with black and white photo, guitar, hound dog, and heart, 1956, 6" l **60.00**

Christmas Card, Graceland scenes, sepia and blue tones, 1970s **30.00**

Fan Club Card, Elvis Presley Fan Club, sgd in blue pen and ink by president and secretary **575.00**

Hat, Army, "GI Blues," 1960 . . . . **35.00**

Letter, Tom Diskin of Col Tom Parker Management, concerning Elvis tour, 1973 . . . . **10.00**

Postcard, color photo, brown border, ©1987 Elvis Presley Ent., Inc., 4 x 6", $8.00.

Lobby Card, Flamingo Star, color illus, ©1960 20th Century Fox **12.50**

Mug, plastic, multicolored, "Elvis the King Lives On, 1935–1977" **5.00**

Photo Card, Elvis wearing red checkered jacket, late 1950s **10.00**

Photograph, glossy, black and white, sgd on back "yours Elvis Presley" in blue pen, c1955, 8 x 10" **575.00**

Pinback Button, color photo portrait, blue signature, 1956 Elvis Presley Enterprises copyright, 3" d **50.00**

Poster, *Girls! Girls! Girls!*, Paramount Pictures, 1960 . . . . **20.00**

Poster, "Give Elvis For Christmas," RCA adv, 1959. . . . . **40.00**

Record, *Loving You*, 45 rpm, orig sleeve, 1957 . . . . **20.00**

Schedule, tour dates, orig Thomas A Parker Management envelope, 1974 . . . . **10.00**

Sheet Music, *You Don't Know Me*, young Elvis photo cov, 1955 . . . . **10.00**

Tab, litho tin, blue and gold "I Love Elvis," metallic gold ground, 1970s, 2" d **10.00**

Tie Clip, handcuff design, includes photo of Elvis wearing tie clip and letter of authenticity **920.00**

Toy Guitar, brown plastic, circular framed photo of Elvis' face on top, raised plastic signature on body, cord strap with tassel ends, orig box with "Elvis Presley Guitar" label, 33" l **460.00**

Waste Basket, metal, various pictures of Elvis, c1977 . . . . **50.00**

PRINTS

Prints serve many purposes. They can be reproductions of an artist's paintings, drawings, or designs, original art forms, or developed for mass appeal as opposed to aesthetic statement. Much of the production of Currier & Ives fits this last category. Currier & Ives concentrated on genre, urban, patriotic, and nostalgic scenes.

Prints were inexpensive, meaning they could be changed every few years. Instead of throwing them out, they went into storage. Most prints were framed. In today's market, check the frame. It could be more valuable than the print.

References: Peter H. Falk (ed.), *Art Price Index, Fifth Edition*, Sound View Press, 1997; Janet Gleeson, *Miller's Collecting Prints and Posters*, Millers Publications, 1997; Martin Gordon, *Gordon's Print Price Annual*, Gordon & Larwrence Art Reference, published annually; Michael Ivankovich, *Collector's Value Guide to Early 20th Century American Prints*, Collector Books, 1998; Susan Theran, *Prints & Photographs: Identification and Price Guide*, Avon Books, 1993.

Periodicals: *Journal of the Print World*, 1008 Winona Rd, Meredith, NH 03253; *On Paper*, 39 E 78th St, #601, New York, NY 10021.

Newsletter: *The Illustrator Collector's News*, PO Box 1958, Sequim, WA 98382.

Note: For additional listings see Illustrators, Maxfield Parrish, and Norman Rockwell.

Barnet, Will, Child Reading—Red, color screenprint, edition of 100, sgd and titled in pencil lower margin, 1970, 20 x 10½" **$275.00**

Bishop, Isabel, Leaning on the Wall, etching, artist's proof, sgd in pencil lower right, 1927, 3⅞ x 2⅞" **373.00**

Roy Lichtenstein, "Flowers," color screenprint, #139/380, Ernst Beyeler publisher, full margins, 1973, 14³/₄ x 8¹/₂", $1,092.00. Photo courtesy Swann Galleries.

Kent, Rockwell, Canterbury Pilgrim, wood engraving printed in brown and black, sgd and dedicated "To E.C.T." in pencil lower right, 1931, 11 x 6⁷/₈" 373.00

Young, Mahonri M, Figures at the Shore of a Lake, color crayons on heavy cream wove paper, drawing of 2 crouching figures in color crayons verso, 11x 15" 258.00

PSYCHEDELIC COLLECTIBLES

Psychedelic collectibles describes a group of objects made during the 1960s and 70s that are highly innovative in their use of colors and design. American Indian tribal art, the artworks of Toulouse Lautrec and Alphonse Mucha, the color reversal approach of Joseph Albers, dancer Loie Fuller's diaphanous material, late 19th–century graphics, paisley fabrics, and quilts are just a few of the objects and techniques that are the roots of psychedelic design.

The period is marked by eclecticism, not unity—there were no limits on design. Psychedelic artists and manufacturers drew heavily on new technologies, e.g., inflatable plastic furniture. Coverings such as polyester and vinyl were heavily used.

Peter Max is the most famous designer associated with the psychedelic era. His artwork graced hundreds of objects. Although mass produced, some items are hard to find.

References: Eric King, *The Collector's Guide to Psychedelic Rock Concert Posters, Postcards and Handbills*, Svaha Press, 1996; Susanne White, *Psychedelic Collectibles of the 1960s & 1970s: An Illustrated Price Guide*, Wallace–Homestead, 1990, out of print.

Bloch, Julius, Tired Hitchhiker, litho, sgd, titled and numbered 39/40 in pencil lower margain, Library of Congress 3, c1930, 13³/₄ x 9¹/₄" 402.00

Bosman, Richard, Brooklyn Bridge, color woodcut, sgd and numbered 92/200 in pencil lower margin, 13³/₈ x 20" 400.00

Bosman, Richard, Poisoned, woodcut, sgd and numbered 27/50 in pencil lower margin, 1982, 15³/₄ x 9¹/₄" 460.00

Carroll, John, Reclining Woman (Sunbather), watercolor over pencil on tan wove paper, sgd in pencil, lower right, 10 x 14" 373.00

Dali, Salvador, The Merry Wives of Windsor, color drypoint on Japan paper, sgd and numbered 205/250 in pencil lower margin, printed by Ateliers Rigal, Fontenayaux Roses, published by Trans World Art, NY, from *Much Ado About Shakespeare*, 1970, 6⁷/₈ x 5" 258.00

Dehner, Dorothy, River Landscape #1, etching, sgd, titled, dated and numbered 5/35 in pencil lower margin, 1958, 4³/₈ x 17⁷/₈" 546.00

Diebenkorn, Richard, Untitled, offset litho, sgd in pencil lower right, edition of 100, published by Eric T Ledin, Mill Valley, CA, from the Drawings portfolio, 1948, 11¹/₈ x 8⁵/₈" 575.00

Dine, Jim, Heart for Film Forum, color woodcut on Mohawk paper, initialed and numbered 76/500 in pencil lower margin, printed by Joe Wilfer and Ruth Lingen at Spring Street Workshop, New York, published by artist and Pace Editions, NY, 1993, 15¹/₄ x 13¹/₄" 373.00

Dubuffet, Jean, Géométrie, litho, sgd, titled, dated and numbered 50/75 in pencil lower margin, from *Sites et Chaussés*, printed by artist, Paris, 1959, 20⁷/₈ x 15¹/₂" 546.00

Fulwider, Edwin L, Aerial View, Open Bridge, color litho, sgd and inscribed "75" in pencil lower margin, c1935, 10¹/₂ x 14³/₄" 172.00

Grooms, Red, Pierpont Morgan Library, color litho and offset color litho, sgd and numbered 158/300 in pencil lower margin, published by Marloborough Graphics, NY, 1982, 11³/₈ x 34³/₈" 431.00

Hoffman, Irwin D, Cigarette Underground, etching, sgd, titled and numbered 15/50 in pencil lower margin, c1940 . . . . 160.00

Beach Towel, Peter Max design, cotton, horizontal design, 2 fringed ends, white ground, blonde long–haired woman wearing hat and holding flower, sky filled with stars and planets, Citgo Oil Co premium, c1970, 34 x 52" **$75.00**

Belt, red, white, and blue stretch fabric, thick chromed metal buckle with glossy cardboard inset panel depicting pr of doves and rainbow, ©1970 Peter Max **140.00**

Flicker Sheet, Vari–Vue, 12 identical 3 x 3" sq psychedelic swirl designs, uncut, late 1960s, 9¹/₄ x 12¹/₂" **100.00**

Lamp, stiff black vinyl body, opening on front, attached to clear/black plastic sheet with repeated thin ray design, attached behind matching plastic disk, lights both white and green, second disk spins while front attachment is stationary and gives off psychedelic optical effect, orig electric cord, late 1960s, 10 x 10 x 2¹/₂" **25.00**

Magazine, *Life*, Sep 5, 1969, Peter Max cov article, brown–tone cov photo of Max on starry ground, 6–page article **9.00**

Mug, china, green ground, red, blue, yellow, and orange "Love" design, mkd "Genuine China By Iroquois" on bottom, ©Peter Max, c1970, 4¹/₄" h **70.00**

Paint, Hotmarx Psychedelic Paints For Cloth, bright pink blister card contains 5" l tube of fluorescent green paint, instruction on reverse, The American Crayon Co, early 1970s, 4¹/₂ x 8" **50.00**

Pillow, Peter Max design, inflatable, soft vinyl, clear, multicolored butterfly and human heads, white ground, black border, early 1970s, 15¹/₂" sq **35.00**

Pillow Cover, white cotton, multicolor profile portrait of female with stars, circles, and other designs, ©1970 Peter Max, 20 x 31" **75.00**

Poster, Bob Dylan, Columbia Records, Milton Glaser, previously folded to fit in album jacket, mounted on foam core, shrink wrapped, 33¹/₂ x 22¹/₂", $165.00. Photo courtesy David Rago Auctions.

Poster, "Drink Milk," man with long flowing hair and beard, spiral design on face with images hidden in eyes, beard, and hair, psychedelic border design, ©Eric Thono, c1970, 22 x 29" 100.00

Scarf, silk, green ground, black, white, gray, and purple butterfly, Peter Max, 21" sq 85.00

Serving Tray, litho tin, blue, smiling head against cloud background surrounded by birds, planets, and stars, Peter Max cat symbols at bottom, early 1970s, 13" d 55.00

Shaker Cup, Jell–O premium, yellow plastic, red and black planets and stars design, mural painter figure in foreground, ©1972 Peter Max Enterprises, Inc, 7¹/₄" h 40.00

Travel Bag, vinyl, zipper lid and attached carrying handles, psychedelic designs with repeated man portrait and full figure of woman surrounded by stars, c1970s, 8 x 18 x 10" 75.00

PUNCHBOARDS

Punchboards are self–contained games of chance that are made of pressed paper and contain holes with a coded ticket inside each hole. After paying an agreed upon amount, the player uses a "punch" to extract the ticket of his choice. Cost to play ranged from 1¢ to $1.00.

Animal and fruit symbols, cards, dominos, and words were used as well as numbers to indicate prizes. While some punchboards had no printing, most contained elaborate letters and/or pictures.

Punchboards initially paid the winner in cash. In an effort to appease the anti–gambling crowd, some punchboards paid off in cameras, candy, cigar, cigarettes, clocks, jewelry, radios, sporting goods, toys, etc.

The 1920s through the 1950s was the golden age of the punchboard. An endless variety were made. Many had catchy names or featured pin–up girls. Negative publicity resulting from the movie *The Flim Flam Man* hurt the punchboard industry.

Value rests with unpunched boards. Most boards sell for $15 to $30, although some have broken the $100 barrier.

Reference: Norman E. Martinus and Harry L. Rinker, *Warman's Paper*, Wallace–Homestead, Krause Publications, 1994.

Baseball Bucks, round, 10" $15.00
Bell Pots, slot symbols, $1.00 a punch 30.00
Big Game, fruit symbols 10.00
California or Bust, 11 x 12" 25.00
Canasta, 5¢ punch, removable score card 50.00
Chocolate Cherries, 12 x 13" 10.00
Cross Country Winner, seals, cash pay 20.00
Dime Joe, cash pay, 10¢ punch 15.00
Dollar Game, cash board 5.00
Forty Sawbucks, counter insert 25.00
Full of Tens, cash pay, 25¢ per punch 15.00
Glades Chocolates, set of 3 . . . . 25.00
Good As Gold, colorful, seals 20.00
Hi Yo Silver, cash board, 25¢ per punch 15.00
Junior Kitty, kitten picture, cash pay 30.00
Knee High, cash girlie board 15.00
National Winner 20.00
National Fins, 1,000 holes with seals 15.00
Odd Pennies Cigarettes 15.00
Pick A Cherry, cash pay, cherry seals 20.00
Planters Peanuts, 5¢ punch, peanut logo 30.00
Spend Your Pennies Here, 2¢ a Chance to Receive Cigarettes, c1920, 14 x 7¹/₂" 30.00
Take It Easy, colorful, nude 50.00
Ten Big Sawbucks, 20¢ cash board 20.00
Turkey Dinners, turkey illus, 10 x 12" 15.00
Worth Going For, 50¢ punch, girlie board 20.00
Yankee Trader 20.00

PURINTON POTTERY

Bernard Purinton founded Purinton Pottery, Wellsville, Ohio, in 1936. The company produced dinnerware and special order pieces. In 1940 Purinton moved to Shippenville, Pennsylvania.

Dorothy Purinton and William H. Blair, her brother, were the company's principal designers. Dorothy designed Maywood, Plaid, and several Pennsylvania German theme lines. Blair is responsible for Apple and Intaglio.

Purinton hand painted its wares. Because of this, variations within a pattern are common. Purinton made a complete dinnerware service including accessory pieces for each of its patterns.

The company utilized an open stock marketing approach. Purinton products were sold nationwide. Some were exported.

In 1958 the company ceased operations, reopened briefly, and then closed for good in 1959. Cheap foreign imports were the principal reason for the company's demise.

References: Jamie Bero–Johnson and Jamie Johnston, *Purinton Pottery*, Schiffer Publishing, 1997; Susan Morris, *Purinton Pottery: An Identification & Value Guide*, Collector Books, 1994.

Newsletter: *Purinton Pastimes*, PO Box 9394, Arlington, VA 22219.

Apple, baker $12.50
Apple, bean pot, metal warming stand 170.00
Apple, beer mug 90.00
Apple, canister set, 4 pcs, tall, oval 170.00
Apple, casserole, cov 80.00
Apple, coffee mug 50.00
Apple, creamer and sugar, miniature 30.00
Apple, Dutch jug, 2 pt 15.00
Apple, fruit bowl, green scalloped border 45.00

Apple, teapot, 2 cup, 6¹/₄" h, $25.00.

Apple, jug, 2 pt, 5³/₄"	40.00
Apple, Lazy Susan, 7 pcs	130.00
Apple, pickle dish	20.00
Apple, teapot, 6 cup, 6¹/₂"	45.00
Apple, tumbler, 12 oz	25.00
Brown Intaglio, bean pot, individual	30.00
Brown Intaglio, butter, cov	22.50
Brown Intaglio, chop plate	13.00
Brown Intaglio, planter, pinched ruffled top	75.00
Brown Intaglio, salt and pepper shakers, pr, stacking	30.00
Brown Intaglio, spaghetti bowl	70.00
Crescent, cocktail dish, Crescent Flower seahorse	220.00
Crescent, dinner plate	115.00
Crescent, marmalade jar, no lid	80.00
Crescent, pitcher, Crescent Flower bird	180.00
Fruits, creamer	15.00
Fruits, Dutch jug, 2 pt	25.00
Fruits, Kent jug, 1 pt	20.00
Fruits, Lazy Susan, 4 cov canisters	90.00
Fruits, salt and pepper shakers, pr, small jugs	18.00
Fruits, sugar, cov	8.00
Mountain Rose, baker	55.00
Mountain Rose, basket planter, 6¹/₄"	50.00
Mountain Rose, casserole, cov	85.00
Mountain Rose, fruit bowl	100.00
Mountain Rose, tea and toast set	20.00
Mountain Rose, wall pocket	90.00
Normandy Plaid, casserole, cov	22.50
Normandy Plaid, coffee mug	22.50
Normandy Plaid, vegetable bowl, open	13.00
Pennsylvania Dutch, cookie jar, wood lid	110.00
Pennsylvania Dutch, creamer and sugar	100.00
Provincial Fruit, meat platter	95.00
Provincial Fruit, tea and toast set	60.00
Saraband, canister set, 4 section, wedge, wood base, Cookies, Tea, Coffee, and Sugar	100.00
Tulip and Vase, coffee server	60.00
Tulip and Vase, tureen, cov	22.50
Windsong, honey jug	45.00

PUZZLES

Puzzles divide into two groups: (1) jigsaw and (2) mechanical. American and English collectors focus primarily on jigsaw puzzles. European collectors love mechanical puzzles.

The jigsaw puzzle first appeared in the mid–18th century in Europe. John Silbury, a London map maker, offered dissected map jigsaw puzzles for sale by the early 1760s. The first jigsaw puzzles in America were English and European imports and designed primarily for use by children.

Prior to the mid–1920s, the vast majority of jigsaw puzzles were cut from wood for the adult market and composition board for the children's market. In the 1920s the diecut, cardboard jigsaw puzzle evolved.

Avoid puzzles whose manufacturer cannot be determined, unless the puzzle has especially attractive graphics or craftsmanship. Diecut cardboard puzzles in excess of 500 pieces remain primarily garage sale items. Some collector interest exists for early Springbok puzzles.

References: *Dexterity Games and Other Hand–Held Puzzles,* L–W Books Sales, 1995; Norman E. Martinus and Harry L. Rinker, *Warman's Paper,* Wallace–Homestead, Krause Publications, 1994; Harry L. Rinker, *Antique Trader's Guide to Games & Puzzles,* Antique Trader Books, 1997; Anne D. Williams, *Jigsaw Puzzles: An Illustrated History and Price Guide,* Wallace–Homestead, 1990, out of print.

Collectors' Clubs: American Game Collectors Assoc, 49 Brooks Ave, Lewiston, ME 04240; National Puzzler's League, PO Box 82289, Portland, OR 97282.

Jigsaw, adult, diecut cardboard, Agate Mfg Co, Brockton, MA, Jiggers Weekly, The Grizzlies, 2 adult bears and cub approaching stream, 300 pcs, 10³/₄" x 13⁷/₈", period box, 8 x 8¹/₈ x 1¹/₈"	$20.00
Jigsaw, adult, diecut cardboard, Consolidated Paper Box Co, Perfect Double, Brookside Manor/Canal in Belgium, 280 pcs, 10¹/₄ x 15¹/₂"	10.00
Jigsaw, adult, diecut cardboard, Consolidated Paper Box, Perfect Picture Puzzle, Mountain Warfare, over 375 pcs, 19¹/₂ x 15¹/₂", 8 stars on box, c1943	25.00
Jigsaw, adult, diecut cardboard, Einson–Freeman, Long Island City, Radio Stars, Series #1, Eddie Cantor Jigaw Puzzle, over 200 pcs, 10 x 14³/₄", 1933	30.00
Jigsaw, adult, diecut cardboard, Hallmark Cards, Springbok, Super Bowl Sunday, over 500 pcs, 18 x 23¹/₂", period box	5.00
Jigsaw, adult, diecut cardboard, Milton Bradley, Dover Jig Picture Puzzle, #4728, The Circus, over 300 pcs, guide picture on box	20.00
Jigsaw, adult, diecut cardboard, Playboy Playmate Puzzle, AP115, Miss May Jennifer Liano, American Publishing, can container	12.50
Jigsaw, adult, diecut cardboard, Tichnor Bros, Cambridge, MA, See America First, #39, Natural Bridge, VA, over 300 pcs, period box	15.00
Jigsaw, adult, diecut cardboard, University Distributing Company, Cambridge, MA, Jig of the Week, #16, Between Two Fires, 20 x 15", paper insert, period box	12.00
Jigsaw, adult, diecut cardboard, Upson Co, TUCO, Peonies, 357 pcs, 14¹/₄ x 19", illus ©1937, guide picture on box	10.00

Jigsaw, adult, diecut cardboard, Pal O' Mine, 320 pcs, c1940, 19½ x 15", $15.00

Jigsaw, adv, diecut cardboard, Essolube, The Five Star Theater presents Foiled by Essolube: A Jig–Saw Melodrama, Dr Seuss illus, 150 pcs, 17 x 11¼", 1933, paper envelope 100.00

Jigsaw, adv, diecut cardboard, Proctor and Gamble, Adventures of Professor Oscar Quackenbush: Chasing Pink Elephants, 1 of series of 4, 9¾ x 7½", c1933, glassine envelope 15.00

Jigsaw, adv, diecut cardboard, Sharps the Word for Toffee, English, Festival of Britain 1951, aerial view of South Bank Exhibition, 204 pcs, 14 x 9½", period box, 6½ x 4⅞ x 1¼" 30.00

Jigsaw, adv, diecut cardboard, St. Onge's, Outfitters to Dad and Lad, Artic, RI, elderly sailor playing checkers with young boy, boy sitting on rowboat, 35 pcs, 4½ x 6⅜", paper envelope with instructions for "Puzzle Race," only adv on envelope, envelope 5 x 7" 10.00

Jigsaw, adv, uncut stiff board, Boston Sunday Globe supplement, 3 kittens among books stacked on back of desk or table, 34 pcs when cut, 6 x 8" 15.00

Jigsaw, children's, diecut cardboard, American Publishing Co, The Bionic Woman Jigsaw Puzzle, #1245, 204 pcs, 17¼ x 11", canister 20.00

Jigsaw, children's, diecut cardboard, C S Hammond, Brooklyn, NY, Little Folks Picture Puzzle: Happy Hour, set of 4, box 8 x 10", c1920 . . . . 40.00

Jigsaw, children's, diecut cardboard, Harter Publishing Co, H–110, 4–puzzle set, Cinderella, Fern Bisel Peat illus, 40 pcs, 7½ x 9½", cardboard box with 1 guide picture 40.00

Jigsaw, children's, diecut cardboard, Jaymar Specialty Co, Walt Disney's Interlocking Jigsaw Puzzle, Three Little Pigs, over 300 pcs, 22 x 14", late 1940s, guide picture on box. 25.00

Jigsaw, children's, diecut cardboard, Milton Bradley, frame tray, Cheyenne, 14 x 10", 1957. . . . . 25.00

Jigsaw, children's, diecut cardboard, Milton Bradley, Uncle Wiggley, 3–puzzle set, box 10 x 13", 1949 . . . . 65.00

Jigsaw, children's, diecut cardboard, Upson Co, Tuco Work Shops, Baby Huey the Baby Giant Puzzle, Huey floating on back while 2 ducks sit on his stomach and paddle, 10⅜ x 14⅜" 15.00

Jigsaw, children's, diecut cardboard, Whitman Publishing, frame tray, Hanna–Barbera Top Cat, #4457, policeman watching Top Cat in trash can sipping milk from bottle, 11⅜ x 14⅜", 1961 . . . . 20.00

Jigsaw, children's, wood, Sifo Co, St Paul, MN, Sammy Sun Tells the Days and Months, frame tray, clock with months and numbers in outer circle and days of week in inner circle, sun in center 15.00

Jigsaw, children's, wood, Parker Bros, United States Puzzle Map, cut on state lines, 8 x 13". 25.00

Jigsaw, multipurpose, game, diecut cardboard, Cadco–Ellis, Jingo: The Jigsaw Bingo Game, first player to fit 5 pcs vertically, horizontally, or diagonally into Jingo board wins round, box 13½ x 10 x 1", 1941. . . . . 35.00

Jigsaw, multipurpose, mystery, diecut cardboard, Janus Games, The Janus Mystery Puzzle, Ellery Queen The case of His Headless Highness, #3, 510 pcs, gun and dagger figurals, 21½ x 14¾", mystery story on back of box. 22.50

Jigsaw, wood, Falls Puzzles, Chagrin Falls, OH, Weaver of Dreams, St Clair portrait of young woman, 253 pcs, 39 figurals, 11 x 14", period box, 1930s 100.00

Jigsaw, wood, Gencraft, Sailing Off Block Island, yawl under full sail off Block Island Lighthouse, 512 pcs, 19 x 14", period box, 1960s. 25.00

Jigsaw, wood, Kingsbridge, Swedish, The Harbour, fishing and sailboats at dock, 197 pcs, 11 x 9", period tubular container with guide picture. 15.00

Jigsaw, wood, Parker Bros, Pastime Picture Puzzle, The Return of Old Ironsides, Colonial scene of captain and crew greeting villagers, 311 pcs, 40 figurals, 13 x 18", period box, 11/6/23. . . . . 75.00

Jigsaw, wood, F E Robie, MA, Reading Homer, Tedema (artist) print of Homer & scholars, 123 pcs, non–interlocking, color–line cutting, 9 x 6", period candy box. 30.00

Jigsaw, wood, Joseph K Straus, Calm of Night, Frederick D Ogden's moonlit scene of log cabin and mountain lake, 300 pieces, 12 x 16", period box, 1940s 15.00

Jigsaw, wood, unknown cutter, untitled, Hoover and colleagues meeting in White House, 406 pcs, 19 x 13", period packaging missing. 35.00

Jigsaw, children's, diecut cardboard, Whitman, frame tray, Fury, 4428;29, $20.00.

Skill, head and tail, Vess Mystery Puzzle, Whistle & Vess
    Beverages, St Louis, MO, 9 pcs, folded unseparated
    strip, 15$^1/_2$ x 1$^1/_4$", paper envelope, 2$^3/_8$ x 9" **5.00**
Skill, key chain, molded plastic, figural, Howdy Doody,
    blue, green, yellow, and red, orig selling price 10¢ **18.00**
Skill, sliced or dissected, Dickinson's Brands, 8 pcs, title
    pc and 7 product pcs including Globe Scratch Feed,
    Snowball Popcorn, Crescent Chick Feed, Evergreen
    Lawn Grass Seed, Santa Claus Popcorn, Dickinson's
    Lawn Seed, and Yankee Popcorn, colorful litho sketch-
    es, 9$^1/_2$ x 4$^3/_4$", paper envelope, 6$^7/_{16}$ x 3$^5/_8$" **45.00**
Skill, sliding block, Dad's Puzzler, imprinted with
    Standard Trailer Co, Cambridge Springs, PA, 1926. . . . . . . **15.00**

PYREX

The origins of Corning Glass begin with Amory Houghton and the
Bay State Glass Company, East Cambridge, Massachusetts, found-
ed in 1851. In 1854 Houghton established the Union Glass
Company, a leading producer of consumer and specialty glass, in
Sommerville, Massachusetts. In 1864 Houghton purchased the
Brooklyn Flint Glass Works and moved it to Sommerville. In 1868
Houghton moved his company to Corning, New York, and
renamed it the Corning Flint Glass Works. After an initial period
focused on producing tabletop glassware, the company's main
product became hand–blown glass light bulbs.

In 1908 Dr. Eugene C. Sullivan established a research laboratory at Corning. Dr. William C. Taylor joined Sullivan that same year.
In the early 1910s Sullivan and Taylor developed Nonex, a heat
resistant glass. Dr. Jesse T. Littleton joined Corning around 1912
and began experiments on glass suitable for baking vessels.

Corning Glass created a consumer products business in 1915,
launching a 12–piece Pyrex line. In 1920 Corning granted Fry
Glass Company, Rochester, Pennsylvania, a license to produce
Pyrex cooking glass under its Fry Oven Glass label. The 200–inch
glass disk for the Hale telescope at the California Institute of
Technology is one of the most famous uses for Pyrex.

Reference: Susan Tobier Rogove and Marcie Buan Steinhauer,
Pyrex By Corning: A Collector's Guide, Antique Publications,
1993, 1997–98 value update.

Baking dish, cov, clear, oval, 10" **$10.00**
Bean Pot, clear, 2 qt **10.00**
Beverage Server, etched, 4 cup **15.00**
Book, *Be a Better Cook with Pyrexware—Good*
    Things to Eat, 1947 . . . . **5.00**
Book, *Pyrex Ovenware For Baking and Serving,* 1931 . . . . **7.00**
Book, *Pyrex Recipes,* 1936 . . . . **7.00**
Bowl, delphite, 6" **13.00**
Bowl, delphite, 9" **17.00**
Buffet Server, Deluxe, red, with double warmer, 2$^1/_2$ qt **20.00**
Cake Dish, clear, round, 2 small handles, 8" d **8.00**
Casserole, cov, Butterprint, white on turquoise, 1 qt **10.00**
Casserole, cov, clear, oval, with mounter, 2 qt **18.00**
Casserole, cov, clear, round, 2 qt **12.00**
Casserole, cov, Deluxe Cinderella, 2$^1/_2$ qt **15.00**
Casserole, cov, Empire Scroll, oval, 2$^1/_2$ qt **20.00**
Casserole, cov, etched lid, clear, round, 1 qt. **12.00**
Casserole, cov, Golden Pine, 2 qt **15.00**
Casserole, cov, Golden Wreath, 2$^1/_2$ qt **20.00**
Casserole, cov, Holiday, 2 qt **15.00**

Nesting Bowl, Butterprint Cinderella, #443, turquoise on white,
$8.00.

Casserole, cov, Snowflake, 2$^1/_2$ qt **20.00**
Casserole, cov, Zodiac, 2$^1/_2$ qt **20.00**
Casserole, individual, clear, round, 8 oz. **4.00**
Chip and Dip Set, gold on white, 1961 . . . . **22.00**
Custard Cup, clear, 6 oz **3.00**
Dish, cov, divided, yellow, 1$^1/_2$ qt. **15.00**
Dish, divided, Town and Country, 1$^1/_2$ qt. **15.00**
Double Boiler, Flameware, 1$^1/_2$ qt **35.00**
Dry Measure Cup, clear, 1 cup, 1940 . . . . **5.00**
Fluted Pie Plate, clear, 6" d **6.00**
Freezer Server, Butterprint, turquoise on white, 1$^1/_4$ qt **10.00**
Loaf Pan, clear, 1$^1/_2$ qt **8.00**
Measuring Cup, clear, 2 spout, 1 cup, 1925 . . . . **8.00**
Measuring Cup, clear, red marking, 1 cup **4.00**
Measuring/Mixing Bowl, clear, 1$^1/_2$ pt. **4.00**
Mushroom Dish, bell shaped cov, clear **8.00**
Nesting Bowl, green, #403 . . . . **8.00**
Nesting Bowl, Orange Dot **6.00**
Nesting Bowl, Sandalwood Cinderella, #442 . . . . **7.00**
Nesting Bowls, Americana, set of 4 . . . . **28.00**
Nesting Bowls, clear, 1 qt, 1$^1/_2$ qt, 2$^1/_2$ qt. **20.00**
Nesting Bowls, Early America, #402 . . . . **5.00**
Nesting Bowls, Gooseberry Cinderella, #444, brown
    ground **12.00**
Percolator, Flameware, Deluxe, 4 cup **8.00**
Pie Plate, clear, 8" d **6.00**
Pie Plate, clear, 10". **8.00**
Pie Plate, clear, hexagonal, 9" **8.00**
Platter, clear, oval, 13". **8.00**
Platter, white, oval, 13" **8.00**
Refrigerator Dish, cov, blue opal, 1$^1/_2$ cup **5.00**
Refrigerator Dish, cov, clear, #510 . . . . **4.00**
Refrigerator Dish, cov, Daisy, #503, 1$^1/_2$ qt **10.00**
Refrigerator Set, cov, Gooseberry, set of 4. . . . . **22.00**
Roasting Pan, cov, aluminum bottom, clear glass top, 15" **30.00**
Saucepan, Flameware, 2 qt **15.00**
Serving Dish, Bluebelle, 1$^1/_2$ qt. **18.00**
Shirred Egg Dish, Flameware. **10.00**
Skillet, Flameware, 7" **10.00**
Teapot, clear, engraved, 4 cup **110.00**
Teapot, Flameware, thin handle **22.00**
Tile, square, etched initialed center, clear. **12.00**
Utility Dish, oblong, yellow, 1$^1/_2$ qt **6.00**
Vegetable Dish, divided, clear **10.00**

QUILTS

In the 18th century quilting was used for garments. Quilted curtains and bedcovers also enjoyed widespread popularity. Lap quilts and covers were common during the Victorian era. World War I had a negative effect on quilting as women worked in factories during wartime. A quilting revival occurred in the late 1920s and 1930s. World War II ended this quilting renaissance.

A quilt exhibition at the Cooper Hewitt Museum in New York in 1971 reawakened interest in historic quilts and revitalized the art of quilt making. Many of today's contemporary quilts are done as works of art, never intended to grace the top of a bed.

Beginning in the 1920s, most patchwork quilts were made using silk–screened fabrics. Cherry Basket, Dresden Plate, Grandmother's Flower Garden, Nursery Rhyme blocks, and Sunbonnet Babies were popular patterns of the 1920–30s period.

Reference: Liz Greenbacker and Kathleen Barach, *Quilts: Identification and Price Guide,* Avon Books, 1992.

Periodical: *Quilters Newsletter,* PO Box 4101, Golden, CO 80401.

Collectors' Club: American Quilter's Society, PO Box 3290, Paducah, KY 42001; The National Quilting Assoc, Inc, PO Box 393, Ellicott City, MD 21043.

Apple Trees, appliquéd, apple trees, birds, embroidered stems, brown, red, green, and yellow meandering border, 79 x 92" **$450.00**
Blocks, pieced, printed chintz, shades of brown and green on white, 1930–40, 35 x 41" **85.00**
Checkerboard, pieced, blue and white alternating squares, white squares embroidered with flowers and butterflies, blue binding, hand quilted, cotton batting, c1930s, 78 x 92" **375.00**
Crosses & Losses, pieced, white and lavender, blue–green ground, Amish, Mary Ann Miller, Holmes County, OH, c1935 . . . . **430.00**
Eagle, pieced and appliquéd, cotton, red, blue, white, brown, and yellow, center profile of eagle head in red,

blue, and white diamond surround, white ground, corner stars, red border, ocean waves and diamond quilting, c1940, 27 x 38" **2,300.00**
Flying Geese, pieced, orange and white, machine sewn, c1930–40, doll size, 21½ x 26" **70.00**
Friendly Cow, appliquéd, cotton and wool, red, brown, green, ocher, and beige, cow, apple tree, and scattered blossoms between 2 fences on white ground, flannel and cotton back, inscribed "The Friendly Cow, The friendly (sic) cow all red and white, I love with all my heart, She gives me cream with all her might, To eat with apple tart," c1928, 64 x 76½" **1,600.00**
Gingerbread Children, appliquéd, center gingerbread, appliquéd house surrounded by gingerbread boys and girls, white rick–rack braid detailing, white muslin ground, white backing with gingerbread binding, c1930, 36 x 48" **245.00**
Lightning Bolt, pieced, wool and corduroy, shades of blue, green, red, and black, Amish, Middlefield, OH, c1940, 80 x 80" **385.00**
Lone Star, pieced, bright colors on black ground, Amish, 1965, crib size, 43 x 43" **165.00**
Morning Glories, appliquéd, purple and green, embroidered name and date "Sylvia Harris 1936," 67 x 82" **200.00**
Old Maid's Puzzle, pieced, blue and light green, hand and machine sewn binding, Amish, c1950, 80 x 94" **75.00**
Sawtooth, pieced, blue calico and white muslin, allover quilting, cotton batting, "Made by the Ladies of Trinity Lutheran Church, Bowmanstown, Pennsylvania," c1935, crib size, 54 x 54" **225.00**
Sunbonnet Babies, appliquéd, colorful calico squares with appliquéd babies, white muslin squares with embroidered flowers, cotton batting, c1935, 68 x 86" **75.00**
Sunshine and Shadow, pieced, solid colors, machine sewn, hand quilted, Amish, Kokomo, IN, c1930s, 81 x 81" **410.00**

Diamond, pieced, multicolor, Amish, Lancaster County, PA, c1925, $875.00.

AUCTION PRICES

Quilts sold by Garth's Auctions on July 18–19, 1997. Prices include the 10% buyer's premium.

Baskets, pieced, 36 basket squares in multicolor and white alternating with gray–beige, overall wear and stains, 72 x 81" **$165.00**
Black Children, pieced, 12 diamonds with black children in multicolored prints, white, and beige, red border, embroidered faces, contemporary, stains, crib size, 24 x 32" **192.50**
Concentric Squares, pieced, multicolored postage stamp size squares, 88 x 92" **275.00**
Floral Medallions, appliquéd, 9 medallions with birds and matching vining border, puffed berries with embroidered stems, red and green, well quilted, minor stains and fading, edge binding frayed, 86 x 86" **1,320.00**
Grid, pieced, red and blue on white, some overall wear and small stains, good color, 82 x 91" **225.50**
Irish Chain, pieced, navy blue star print and white, some overall wear and stains, 74 x 74" **385.00**
Pinwheels, appliquéd, 18 red, blue, and teal green pinwheels, red and green border, overall wear and fading, large stitch quilting, small ink stain, 90 x 94" **330.00**

RADIO CHARACTERS & PERSONALITIES

Radio's golden age began in the 1920s and extended through the 1950s. Families gathered around the radio in the evening to listen to a favorite program. American Movie Classics' *Remember WENN* television show provides an accurate portrayal of the early days of radio.

Sponsors and manufacturers provided a wide variety of material ranging from cookbooks to photographs directed toward the adult audience. Magazines devoted exclusively to radio appeared on newsstand racks.

When collecting radio material, do not overlook objects relating to the shows themselves. Props, publicity kits, and scripts are a few examples. Many Big Little Book titles also focused on radio shows.

References: Jon D. Swartz and Robert C. Reinehr, *Handbook of Old–Time Radio: A Comprehensive Guide to Golden Age Radio Listening and Collecting,* Scarecrow Press, 1993.

Periodical: *Old Time Radio Digest,* 10280 Gunpowder Rd, Florence, KY 41042.

Newsletter: *Hello Again,* PO Box 4321, Hamden, CT 06514.

Collectors' Clubs: Friends of Vic & Sade, 7232 N Keystone Ave, Lincolnwood, IL 60646; National Lum 'n' Abner Society, #81 Sharon Blvd, Dora, AL 35062; North American Radio Archives, 134 Vincewood Dr, Nicholasville, KY 40356; Pow–Wow (Straight Arrow), PO Box 24751, Minneapolis, MN 55424; Radio Collectors of America, 8 Ardsley Circle, Brockton, MA 02402.

Note: For additional listings see Premiums.

Allen, Jimmie, bag, cloth, drawstring, white, red printing both sides, Cleo Cola log, bottle cap, and "Listen To The Air Adventures of Jimmie Allen Every Broadcast For Bulletins About Premiums," c1934, 4 x 6" **$150.00**

Allen, Jimmie, cast photo from *Sky Parade,* 1936 . . . . **40.00**

Amos 'n Andy, doll, wood, jointed, green jacket, yellow pants, black tie, orange hat, 1930s, 5³⁄₄" h **200.00**

Amos 'n Andy, greeting card, Get Well, black and white photo, Hall Brothers, 1931, 4¹⁄₂ x 5¹⁄₂" **30.00**

Amos 'n Andy, sheet music, *The Perfect Song/Musical Theme of the Pepsodent Hour,* ©1937, 8 pp, 9 x 12" **25.00**

Armstrong, Jack, magnetic tape reel, The All American Boy Radio Shows, 15–minute episodes, 1940–41, 7 pcs **70.00**

Armstrong, Jack, ring, Jack Armstrong Dragon's Eye, glow–in–the–dark, plastic, white, oval raised dark green stone, 1939 . . . . **700.00**

Benny, Jack, photo, black and white, glossy, sgd "Jello Again, Jack Benny," 1930s, 8 x 10" **45.00**

Benny, Jack, record set, 78 rpm, set of 4, comedy sketches, Top Ten Records, orig cov, 1947 . . . . **45.00**

Bergen, Edgar and Charlie McCarthy, handkerchief, linen–type fabric, white ground, bright red, blue, yellow, and black racehorse center, corner inscribed "Charlie McCarthy At The Races," 1930s, 9 x 9¹⁄₂" **30.00**

Bergen, Edgar and Charlie McCarthy, pencil sharpener, figural, diecut plastic, color decal, 1930s **70.00**

Bergen, Edgar and Charlie McCarthy, radio, plastic, ivory colored, figural, electric, Majestic, c1940, 6" h **800.00**

Bergen, Edgar and Charlie McCarthy, soap, figural, Kerk Gild, orig box, 1930–40, 4" h **75.00**

Mortimer Snerd, doll, composition and wire, Ideal, 13" h, $500.00.

Burns & Allen, coffee server, 1950s, complete set **120.00**

Cantor, Eddie, book, *Eddie Cantor in Laughland,* Goldsmith Publishing Co, 1934 . . . . **25.00**

Cantor, Eddie, pinback button, "For President Eddie Cantor Great in '48" **10.00**

Dragonette, Jessica, photo, black and white, glossy, white ink signature "For: S. H. Sweiber Your Appreciation Is Very Inspiring—Gratefully Yours, Jessica Dragonette," 1934, 8 x 10" **35.00**

Edwards, Ralph, book, *Radio's Truth or Consequences Party Book,* 1940. . . . . **8.00**

Fibber McGee and Molly, fan card, black and white, 1 large photo and 6 small photos below, 8 x 10" **50.00**

Fibber McGee and Molly, record set, 78 rpm, set of 4, live broadcasts, Fibber cov, 1947 . . . . **50.00**

Hope, Bob, figure, china, star shaped base, 1950s, 7¹⁄₄" h **250.00**

Linkletter, Art, game, Art Linkletter's Game of "People Are Funny," Whitman, 1954. . . . . **35.00**

Little Orphan Annie, book, *Little Orphan Annie and the Gila Monster Gang, #2302,* black and white illus, Whitman, ©1933, 248 pp, 5¹⁄₂ x 8" **20.00**

Little Orphan Annie, decoder, ROA, secret compartment, 1936, 1³⁄₄" h **15.00**

Little Orphan Annie, doll, cloth, stuffed, yarn hair, stitched oilcloth shoes, "American Needlecrafts/ B.B.B." neck tag, 1930s, 14" h **175.00**

Little Orphan Annie, map, ROA "Simmons Corners," Ovaltine premium, "Tucker County" community "Where Radio's Little Orphan Annie Has Had So Many Thrilling Adventures," c1937, 19 x 24" open **75.00**

Little Orphan Annie, pin, plastic, Orphan Annie Safety Guard Captain, glow–in–the–dark, inscribed "SG Captain 42," blue lettering, 1³⁄₄ x 2" **125.00**

Little Orphan Annie, salt and pepper shakers, Annie and Sandy, painted plaster, 1940s, 3" h **65.00**

McNeill, Don, Breakfast Club, album, Breakfast Club Family Album, Chicago, jokes and skits, c1941, 96 pp **18.00**

McNeill, Don, Breakfast Club, book, *The 1954 Breakfast Club Yearbook,* spiral bound **10.00**

Merman, Ethel, sign, cardboard, *Radio Star* magazine adv, 8¹⁄₂ x 12" **15.00**

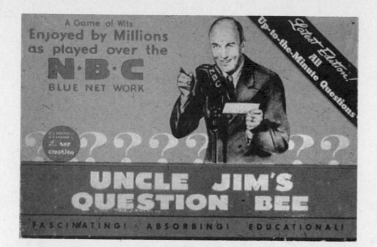

Uncle Jim, game, Uncle Jim's Question Bee, Lowell, 1938, $30.00.

Pearl, Jack, book, *Jack Pearl as Detective Baron Munchausen*, Goldsmith Co, 1934 . . . . 15.00

Pearl, Jack, game, The Baron Munchausen Game, Parker Brothers, 1933 . . . . 25.00

Penner, Joe, sheet music, *Don't Never Do-o-o That*, black and yellow cov, ©TB Harms Co, 1934 . . . . 20.00

Quiz Kids, game, Quiz Kids Electric Quizzer, #1000, "Approved and Endorsed by the Quiz Kids," Rapaport Bros, Inc, c1940 . . . . 40.00

Sgt Preston, book, *Sgt Preston and Yukon King*, ©Rand McNally & Co, 1955, 28 pp 30.00

Skelton, Red, postcard, radio show cast photo, matte finish, postmarked 1948 . . . . 20.00

Skippy, playing cards, 36 numbered cards, Poll Parrot Shoe sticker on lid, 1930s 60.00

Smith, Kate, pinback button, photo illus, black and red "Kate Smith's Philadelphia A & P Party, Nov 4, 1935, Hello Everybody," 2¼" d 25.00

The Shadow, game, 1 wood token, play money, colored discs, 4 wood black cap dice, dice shaker, 20" sq board, Toy Creations, 1940 . . . . 250.00

White, John, Death Valley Days, song folio, *Cowboy Songs in Death Valley*, 1934 . . . . 8.00

Winslow, Don, salt and pepper shakers, pr, Winslow and Red Pennington, 1940s 35.00

Wynn, Ed, game, Ed Wynn, The Fire Chief, Selchow & Righter, c1937 . . . . 25.00

RADIOS

Marconi, who designed and perfected the transmission and reception instruments that permitted the sending of electrical messages without the use of direct communication, is considered the father of radio. By the end of the 1890s, the Marconi "Wireless" was being used for ship–to–shore communications.

Significant technological developments took place rapidly. By the mid–1920s the cost and quality of radios had reached a point where they were within the budget of most American households. The radio was transformed from a black box with knobs, dials, and a messy battery to a piece of stylized console furniture. The table-top radio arrived on the scene in the 1930s.

Although the transistor was invented in 1927, it was not until the post–1945 period that it was used heavily in the production of radios. Today transistors are a major subcategory of radio collecting. The transistor also made possible the novelty radio, another popular collecting subcategory.

The value of any radio is directly related to its playability. If components, parts, or tubes are missing or if the radio needs repair, its value is lowered by 50% or more. Parts are readily available to restore radios. In fact, the collecting of radio accessories, ephemera, and parts is increasing.

References: John H. Bryant and Harold N. Cones, *The Zenith Trans–Oceanic: The Royalty of Radios*, Schiffer Publishing, 1995; Marty Bunis and Robert F. Breed, *Collector's Guide to Novelty Radios*, Collector Books, 1995; Marty and Sue Bunis, *Collector's Guide to Antique Radios, Fourth Edition*, Collector Books, 1997; Marty and Sue Bunis, *Collector's Guide to Transistor Radios, Second Edition*, Collector Books, 1996; Harold Cones and John Bryant, *Zenith Radio: The Early Years, 1919–1935*, Schiffer Publishing, 1997; Chuck Dachis, *Radios By Hallicrafters*, Schiffer Publishing, 1996.

David and Betty Johnson, *Guide to Old Radios: Pointers, Pictures, and Prices, Second Edition*, Wallace–Homestead, Krause Publications, 1995; Ken Jupp and Leslie Piña, *Genuine Plastic Radios of the Mid–Century*, Schiffer Publishing, 1998; David R. Lane and Robert A. Lane, *Transistor Radios: A Collector's Encyclopedia and Price Guide*, Wallace–Homestead, Krause Publications, 1994; Ron Ramirez, *Philco Radio: 1928–1942*, Schiffer Publishing, 1993; Norman R. Smith, *Zenith Transistor Radios*, Schiffer Publishing, 1998; Scott Wood (ed.), *Evolution of the Radio, Vol. 1* (1991, 1994 value update), *Vol. 2* (1993), L–W Books Sales; Eric Wrobbel, *Toy Crystal Radios*, published by author, 1997.

Periodicals: *Antique Radio Classified*, PO Box 802, Carlisle, MA 01741; *Radio Age*, PO Box 1362, Wahington Grove, MD 20880; *The Horn Speaker*, PO Box 1193, Mabank, TX 75147.

Newsletter: *Transistor Network*, 32 West Main St, Bradford, NH 03221.

Collectors' Clubs: Antique Radio Club of America, 300 Washington Trails, Washington, PA 15301; Antique Wireless Assoc, 59 Main St, Bloomfield, NY 14469.

Addison, Catalin, green or maroon body, ridges around body and left grill wrap over top in contrasting color, 1939 . . . . $700.00

Admiral, Bakelite tabletop, #4–A–27, elongated dial, 1947 . . . . 35.00

Admiral, Clipper, transistor, #8C2 . . . . 5.00

Admiral, Jupiter, transistor, #691, gray 20.00

Admiral, portable, #4E21, large "V" on front, side knobs, 1950s 35.00

Air King, portable, Royal Troubador, #A510, cloth covered, Bakelite grill and dial, 1947 . . . . 35.00

Airline, transistor, #GTM–1201, pocket size, wire handle, large dial below grill, 1960 . . . . 15.00

American Bosch, Cruiser, wooden tabletop, #35, 5 tubes, 3 knobs and dial on front, 1926 . . . . 75.00

Apex, #70, wide metal case, 2 knobs and dial, lid lifts to expose 9 tubes, 1929 . . . . 65.00

Arvin, radio/phono, #302, brown Bakelite, exposed turntable and arm, rounded front edge with grill and radio controls **50.00**

Bendix, brown Bakelite tabletop, #636–A, long AM dial, 1946. .... **25.00**

Crosley, brown plastic tabletop, #9–113, oversized speaker cloth, elongated dial, 1949 .... **15.00**

Crosley, #88CR, 8 tubes, 3 band, AM/FM radio, phono behind double doors, 1948 .... **25.00**

DeWald, tabletop, #500–A, brown or white painted Bakelite, rounded sides, elongated dial, 1946 .... **35.00**

DeWald, transistor, #K–702–B, leatherette cover. **50.00**

Emerson, Bakelite tabletop, #336, rounded corners, tall rect right dial, 1940. .... **15.00**

Farnsworth, brown cloth covered portable, #GP–350, front lifts to expose large circular right dial, 1947 ...... **35.00**

General Electric, Bakelite tabletop, #102, long louvers at top, elongated dial below, white, brown, or white, 1948. .... **15.00**

General Electric, plastic clock radio, #555, square clock face, round dial, 1953 .... **25.00**

General Electric, transistor, #P850, shirt pocket style, key ring top handle, 1962 .... **10.00**

Magnavox, Eton, wooden tabletop, large knob below dial window, 2 small knobs **100.00**

Magnavox, transistor, #IR1006, sub–miniature, black plastic, square, chrome trim, long dial across top **20.00**

Motorola, Bakelite tabletop, 50X1, rounded corners, square dial, 1941 .... **15.00**

Novelty, binoculars, figural, Bakelite **60.00**

Novelty, boat motor, figural, plastic, metal stand. **60.00**

Novelty, cow, figural, "Tune–A–Cow". **15.00**

Novelty, dollar bill, clear plastic block, bills inside **15.00**

Novelty, grand piano, lid opens, Japan **65.00**

Novelty, knight in armor, bust, lifting face plate, complete **35.00**

Novelty, lady's high heel shoe, figural **20.00**

Novelty, Ladybug, figural, wings open, complete **15.00**

Novelty, LOVE, plastic. **15.00**

Novelty, Miracle Whip, figural jar **30.00**

Novelty, pen, "Radibo," plastic, ballpoint pen with radio built into top. **25.00**

Novelty, Spiderman, head, oversized **45.00**

Philco, tabletop, #37–630T, 6 tubes, 3 bands, circular dial above tuning lever and 3 knobs, 1937 .... **75.00**

Philco, T–4, transistor, coat pocket style, large tuner dial at right, black and white, 1958. .... **60.00**

Pilot, Pilotone Universal, wooden tabletop, wide, large front dials, lid lifts to expose 5 tubes, 1926. .... **175.00**

RCA, transistor, #9–BT–9, plastic, logo across bottom, 1957. .... **75.00**

Stromberg–Carlson, #58–T, wooden tombstone, multi-band octagonal dial, 1936 .... **45.00**

Sylvania, Bakelite tabletop, #510H, horizontal front louvers, raised area on top, black, brown, or white, 1950 .... **35.00**

Westinghouse, console, #169, 4 band radio and phono behind doors, 1948 .... **15.00**

Zenith, Bakelite tabletop, #6D030, grill and dial form large semicircle, brown or white, 1946. .... **45.00**

RAILROADIANA

Canals and railroads competed head to head for right–of–ways in the 1830s. By the early 1840s, the railroad was the clear victor. The Civil War showed the importance and value of railroads. Immediately following the war, America went on a railroad building spree. The transcontinental railroad was completed. Robber barons such as Gould and Vanderbilt created huge financial fortunes from their railroad activities. A period of mergers occurred as the 19th century came to a close.

The period from the 1880s through the end of World War II is considered the golden age of railroads. The Interstate Highway system, a car in every garage, and the growing importance of air transportation ended the steel highway's dominance. Poor management and a bloated labor force added to its decline.

In the 1970s the federal government became actively involved in railroad management through Amtrak and Conrail. Thousands of miles of track were abandoned. Passenger service, except for a few key corridors, disappeared. Mergers continued into the 1990s. Even Conrail became a victim of consolidation.

References: Susan and Al Bagdade, *Warman's American Pottery and Porcelain*, Wallace–Homestead, Krause Publications, 1994; Stanley L. Baker, *Railroad Collectibles: An Illustrated Value Guide, 4th Edition*, Collector Books, 1990, 1996 value update; Richard C. Barrett, *The Illustrated Encyclopedia of Railroad Lighting, Volume 1: The Railroad Lantern*, Railroad Research Publications, 1994; Barbara J. Conroy, *Restaurant China: An Identification & Value Guide for Restaurant, Airline, Ship & Railroad Dinnerware, Vol. I*, Collector Books, 1998

Brad S. Lomazzi, *Railroad Timetables, Travel Brochures & Posters: A History and Guide for Collectors*, Golden Hills Press, 1995; Richard W. Luckin, *Butter Pat World: Transportation Collector's Guide Book*, RK Publishing, 1995; Richard W. Luckin, *Mimbres to Mimbreño: A Study of Santa Fe's Famous China Pattern*, RK Publishing, 1992; Richard W. Luckin, *Teapot Treasury and Related Items*, RK Publishing, 1987; Everett L. Maffet, *Silver Banquet II: A Compendium on Railroad Dining Car Silver Serving Pieces*, Silver Press, 1990; Douglas W. McIntyre, *The Official Guide to Railroad Dining Car China*, published by author, 1990.

Periodical: *The Main Line Journal*, PO Box 121, Steamwood, IL 60107.

Westinghouse, Jukebox Model 1, model 34X475, coin operated, white case, gold center panel, purple fabric speaker cover, 6 x 5¹/₂ x 9", carrying handle, $95.00.

Collectors' Clubs: Key, Lock and Lantern, Inc, 31 Sandle Dr, Fairport, NY 14450; Railroadiana Collectors Assoc, PO Box 4894, Diamond Bar, CA 91765; Railway and Locomotive Historical Society, PO Box 1418, Westford, MA 01886.

Almanac, *Every Man's Almanac,* MO Pacific Lines, 1927 . . . **$22.50**
Annual Report, Boston Elevated Railway, 1924 . . . . **8.00**
Bank, 2 pcs, pot metal, copper, General, W&ARR, Banthrico, Chicago, 1974, 11" l **15.00**
Blotter, Soo LIne, unused, 1920s **1.75**
Book, *C & NWRR Co, Rules... Operating Dept,* 1928 . . . . **5.00**
Book, *Pines Peak by Rail,* Hollenback, 1st ed, soft cov, 1962 . . . . **18.00**
Booklet, Lehigh Valley, *Claremont—The Great Terminal of the World's Great Port,* c1920 . . . . **18.00**
Booklet, *The Pacific Northwest and Alaska,* Union Pacific, black and white photos, 3 rail route maps, 1931, 48 pp **7.00**
Bowl, Illinois Central RR, Grecian Key mount on wide rim, ornate monogram, c1930, 7" d **45.00**
Brochure, Union Pacific Railroad, 1960 . . . . **10.00**
Calendar, Chesapeake & Ohio, 1938, complete **143.00**
Calendar, GN RR, Reiss painting **50.00**
Calendar, CNW RR, 1949 . . . . **35.00**
Calendar, Illinois Central Railroad, 1954 . . . . **75.00**
Calendar, Pennsylvania RR, 1929, "Harnessing the Plane to the Iron Horse," "Broadway LImited—Overnight to Chicago," and "The American—Overnight to St. Louis," locomotive and trimotor side by side, map with route below, full color, partial pad at bottom, metal ribs top and bottom, 29 x 29" **185.00**
Calendar, Pennsylvania RR, 1942, "Partners In Defense" **85.00**
Calendar, Pennsylvania RR, 1954, tri–month, complete **132.00**
Calendar, UP RR, 1960 . . . . **10.00**
Candy Box, cardboard, Pearson's Choo Choo 5 cents Salted Nut Roll Bars, speeding passenger train on lid, c1930 . . . . **6.00**
Chocolate Mold, 6–wheel locomotive, tin, hinged, 4½ x 6" **65.00**
Menu, Great Northern, 1944 . . . . **12.50**
Menu, Lehigh Valley Railroad, c1950 . . . . **3.75**

Menu, New York Central dining service, breakfast, red, white, and blue litho of the 20th Century Ltd and big "V," patriotic graphics, c1943, 4 pp, 6 x 9" **38.00**
Napkin, cloth, cotton, Northern Pacific Railway, logo woven in white on tan at center, 20 x 21" **15.00**
Plate, Atchison Topeka & Santa Fe, 10" d **275.00**
Plate, Baltimore & Ohio, diesel electric #51 1937 loco-motive in border, Shenango China, 9" d **65.00**
Plate, Canadian Pacific RR, North Staff's, Cobridge Pottery, England, Canadian Pacific Hotels, 1946, 7" d **45.00**
Platter, AT & SF, china, Griffon, 1924, 10" d **132.00**
Poster, French National Railroads/Progress Power Precision, A Brenet, blue electric locomotive racing past fiery factory setting, 1958, 24 x 39" **125.00**
Poster, Santa Fe System Line—Red Cliffs of Western New Mexico, multicolored, red and silver passenger train shooting through desert, Indian girls herd sheep under cottonwood tree in foreground, orig frame with silver plaque bottom center, c1950, 34 x 25" **150.00**
Poster, Special Excursion to Detroit, "Via Michigan Central Railway, Sunday May 19, $5.00 Round Trip from Buffalo," black and white, "Auspices The Railroad Enthusiasts, Inc...," Dreyfus' streamlined "New Mercury" and schedule, Detroit vs Boston base-ball game, c1940, 8 x 14" **38.00**
Soup Tureen, cov, Soo Line, round base, rounded han-dles, Soo Line dollar sign logo, 10 oz **125.00**
Stocks Certificate, Erie–Lackawanna Railroad Co, 1960s **7.50**
Stocks Certificate, Erie RR Co, 1950s **8.00**
Tablecloth, California Zephyr, dining car, white cotton damask, 12" woven center logo, 1930s, 45 x 42" **95.00**
Time Table, Burlington Northern, 1979 . . . . **4.00**
Time Table, Chesapeake & Ohio, 1957 . . . . **5.00**
Time Table, Illinois Central, 1961 . . . . **5.00**
Time Table, Lackawanna, New York City, Buffalo, Cleveland, Detroit, Chicago, 1947, 16 pp, 8 x 9" **8.00**
Time Table, New York Central, 1959 . . . . **6.00**
Time Table, Northern Pacific, April–May 1925 . . . . **81.00**
Time Table, Rutland, 1957 . . . . **5.00**
Time Table, Western Division, 1930 . . . . **15.00**
Token, B & O, brass, 1927 . . . . **20.00**
Token, Union Pacific, 1934 . . . . **5.00**
Towel, woven, white, blue stripe, "Pullman—Property Of the Pullman Company," 1929, 16 x 24" **15.00**
Tray, Illinois Central RR, oval, plain design, 1941, 9 x 12" **35.00**
View Book, Rocky Mountain Views on the Rio Grande Railroad from San Francisco to Salt Lake City, 1944 . . . . **8.00**

Badge, Penn Central RR Police/Sergeant, Ohio jurisdiction, lacquered brass, stamped 1969–1976, $75.00.

REAMERS

A reamer is a device used to extract juice from fruits. Reamers are collected primarily by composition, i.e., ceramic, glass, and metal. In an attempt to bring order to reamer collecting, Ken and Linda Ricketts and Mary Walker assigned reamers an identification num-ber. These numbers are used by most collectors.

There are two basic types of reamers: (1) hand operated and (2) mechanical. Reamers were extremely popular in the period between World War I and II. Only a few were made in the post–1945 period, a result of the popularity of frozen juice con-centrates and pre–packaged fruit juices.

In the early 1980s Edna Barnes reproduced a number of old reamers from molds belonging to the Jenkins Glass Company and

Imperial Glass Company. These reproductions are marked with a "B" in a circle.

Reference: Gene Florence, *Kitchen Glassware of the Depression Years, Fifth Edition*, Collector Books, 1995, 1997 value update.

Collectors' Club: National Reamer Collectors Assoc, 47 Midline Ct, Gaithersburg, MD 20878.

Anchor Hocking, glass, lime green, pouring spout,
6¼" d $22.00
Cambridge, glass, grapefruit, Seville yellow 275.00
Crisscross, glass, cobalt blue 245.00
Crisscross, glass, green, orange reamer 35.00
Crusscriss, glass, pink, lemon reamer 285.00
Crisscross, glass, pink, orange reamer 210.00
Czechoslovakia, ceramic, 2 pc, orange luster, pink flow-
ers, green leaves, 3¾" h 30.00
Federal, green transparent, pointed cone, tab handle 28.00
Fry, glass, clambroth 75.00
Hall, china, 1 pc, large, flat, green 155.00
Hazel Atlas, glass, small, cobalt blue, tab handle 225.00
Hocking, glass, clambroth, tab handle 88.00
Hong Kong, 2 pcs, stainless steel, flat, 2½" h 8.50
Japan, ceramic, 2 pcs, strawberry shape, red, green
leaves and handle, mkd "Occupied Japan," 3¾" h 65.00
Japan, ceramic, baby's orange, blue on white, 4½" h 28.00
Japan, ceramic, clown, light green and white, orange
hands and feet, 7½" h 40.00
Japan, ceramic, yellow, white flowers, green leaves,
lemon reamer, 4¾" h 65.00
Jeannette, glass, dark delphite, small 85.00
Jennnette, glass, green transparent, side pour, tab han-
dle, large, 5⅞" d 15.00
Jeannette, glass, jadeite, small, dark 40.00
Jeannette, glass, ultra marine, Jennyware 120.00
Jiffy Juicer, ceramic, large bowl with cone center, elon-
gated loop handle 60.00
Knapps Orange Juicer, aluminum, hinged, crank handle,
hand held 10.00
Kwicky Juicer, aluminum, pan style, Quan–Nichols Co 8.00

Limoges, ceramic, scalloped, orange and pearl luster,
brown handle, 5¼" d 115.00
McKee, glass, chalaine, emb "Sunkist" 185.00
McKee, glass, ftd base, white, emb "McK" 15.00
McKee, glass, green, 1948, 8" 18.00
McKee, glass, Seville yellow, emb "Sunkist" 40.00
McKee, glass, vaseline, green, emb "Sunkist" 185.00
Pearl, cast iron, wood insert, long handle 18.00
Presto Juicer, porcelain juicer, metal stand 60.00
Sealed Sweet, mechanical, metal, clamps to table, tilt
model 40.00
Sunkist, glass, chalaine blue 295.00
Sunkist, glass, medium jade 95.00
Sunkist, glass, pale jade 295.00
Sunkist, glass, white opalescent 35.00
Universal, Cambridge, china, 2 pcs, cream, lavender
lilies, green leaves, silver trim 155.00
US Glass, light pink, 2–cup pitcher set 35.00
Westmoreland, glass, baby, pink, 2 pc 195.00
White Milk Glass, Sunkist 145.00
Zippy, ceramic, hand–crank cone, Wolverine Products,
3¼" h, 6½" d 60.00

RECORDS

Thomas Edison is credited with the invention of the phonograph. In 1877 Edison demonstrated a phonograph he designed that played wax cylinder records. Although patenting his phonograph in 1878, Edison did not pursue the concept, preferring instead to concentrate on further development of the light bulb.

Alexander Graham Bell created the graphaphone, successfully marketing it by the end of the 1880s. Emile Berliner developed the flat disc phonograph in 1900. Discs replaced cylinders as the most popular record form by the end of the decade.

Initially records were played at a speed of 78 revolutions per minute (rpm). 45 rpm records became the dominant form in the late 1940s and 50s, eventually being replaced by the 33⅓ rpm format. Most phonographs, more frequently referred to as record players in the post–1945 period, could play 33⅓, 45, and 78 rpm records. The arrival of the compact disc in the early 1980s made the turntable obsolete.

Most records have relatively little value, especially those without their dust jackets or album covers. The more popular a song title, the less likely it is to have value. Many records were released in several pressings. Find out exactly which pressing you own. If a record is scratched or warped, its value disappears.

References: Perry Cox and Joe Lindsay, *The Official Price Guide to the Beatles: Records and Memorabilia*, House of Collectibles, 1995; Les Docks, *American Premium Record Guide, 1900–1965: Identification and Value Guide to 78s, 45s and LPs, Fifth Edition*, Books Americana, Krause Publications, 1997; Anthony J. Gribin and Matthew M. Schiff, *Doo–Wop: The Forgotten Third of Rock 'n' Roll*, Krause Publications, 1992; Fred Heggeness, *Goldmine Country Western Record & CD Price Guide*, Krause Publications, 1996; Fred Heggeness, *Goldmine's Promo Record & CD Price Guide*, Krause Publications, 1995; Ron Lofman, *Goldmine's Celebrity Vocals*, Krause Publications, 1994; Vito R. Marino and Anthony C. Furfero, *The Official Price Guide to Frank Sinatra Records and CDs*, House of Collectibles, 1993; R. Michael Murray, *The Golden Age of Walt Disney Records: 1933–1988*, Antique Trader Books, 1997.

Hazel Atlas, reamer and measure, transparent green, 2 cups, $35.00.

Tim Neely, *Goldmine Christmas Record Price Guide*, Krause Publications, 1997; Tim Neely, *Goldmine Price Guide to Alternative Records*, Krause Publications, 1996; Tim Neely (ed.), *Goldmine Price Guide to 45 RPM Records*, Krause Publications, 1996; Tim Neely and Dave Thompson, *Goldmine British Invasion Record Price Guide*, Krause Publications, 1997; Jerry Osborne, *Rockin' Records*, Antique Trader Books, 1998; Jerry Osborne, *The Official Guide to the Money Records*, House of Collectibles, 1998; Jerry Osborne, *The Official Price Guide to Country Music*, House of Collectibles, 1996; Jerry Osborne, *The Official Price Guide to Movie/TV Soudtracks & Original Cast Albums, Second Edition*, House of Collectibles, 1997; Jerry Osborne, *The Official Price Guide to Records, Twelfth Edition*, House of Collectibles, 1997.

Ronald L. Smith, *Goldmine's Comedy Record Price Guide*, Krause Publications, 1996; Charles Szabala, *Goldmine 45 RPM Picture Sleeve Price Guide*, Krause Publications, 1998; Neal Umphred, *Goldmine's Price Guide to Collectible Jazz Albums, 1949–1969, 2nd Edition*, Krause Publications, 1994; Neal Umphred, *Goldmine's Price Guide to Collectible Record Alburns, 5th Edition*, Krause Publications, 1996.

Periodicals: *DISCoveries Magazine*, PO Box 1050, Dubuque, IA 52004; *Goldmine*, 700 E State St, Iola, WI 54990.

Collectors' Clubs: Assoc of Independent Record Collectors, PO Box 222, Northford, CT 06472; International Assoc of Jazz Record Collectors, 15745 W Birchwood Ln, Libertyville, IL 60048.

Note: For additional listings see Beatles, Elvis Presley, and Rock 'n' Roll.

Ames Brothers, *I Couldn't Sleep a Wink Last Night*, 45 rpm, promo, RCA Victor, 1958 . . . . **$10.00**

Animals, *The Animals On Tour*, LP, yellow promo label, MGM, 1965 . . . . **125.00**

Anka, Paul, *Diana*, 45 rpm, white promo label, ABC Paramount, 1957 . . . . **25.00**

Annette, *I Can't Do the Sun*, 45 rpm, white promo label, Disneyland, 1957 . . . . **40.00**

Armstrong, Louis, *Cultural Exchange*, 45 rpm, promo, Columbia, 1959 . . . . **10.00**

Arnold, Eddy, *Christmas Is...*, LP, radio show, Diamond, 1960s **10.00**

Autograph, *King Biscuit Flower Hour*, 2 LP, live concert, Feb 1985 . . . . **30.00**

Autry, Gene, *Gene Autry's Greatest Hits*, LP, white promo label, Columbia, 1961 . . . . **25.00**

Avalon, Frankie, *Christmas Holiday*, 45 rpm, white promo label, Chancellor, 1958 . . . . **35.00**

Bachman Turner Overdrive, *Toyota Presents*, 2 LP, music and interview, RKO, 1970s **30.00**

Baez, Joan, *Radio Airplay Album*, LP, promo, A & M, 1976 . . . . **15.00**

Band, The, *The Last Waltz*, LP, promo, Warner, 1978 . . . . **15.00**

Bartholomew, Dave, *My Ding–A–Ling*, 45 rpm, promo colored vinyl version, King, 1952 . . . . **100.00**

Beach Boys, *Heroes & Villains*, 45 rpm, Brother, 1967 . . . . . . **30.00**

Beatles, *A Hard Day's Night*, 45 rpm, George Martin, white promo label, United Artists, 1964 . . . . **15.00**

Bee Gees, *Wouldn't I Be Someone*, 45 rpm, white and blue promo label, RSO, 1973 . . . . **10.00**

Benatar, Pat, *Retro Rock*, 2 LP, live show, Clayton Webster, Apr 1988 . . . . **30.00**

Berry, Chuck, *NBC Special*, 2 LP, music and interview, NBC Radio, Jan 1980 . . . . **30.00**

Big Bopper, *Chantilly Lace*, LP, white promo label, Mercury, 1957 . . . . **225.00**

Black Sabbath, *Paranoid*, LP, white promo label, Warner, 1972 . . . . **20.00**

Blanc, Mel, *I Taut I Taw a Record Dealer*, 45 rpm, yellow or white label, Capitol, 1951 . . . . **50.00**

Blood Sweat & Tears, *1974 Christmas Seals*, LP, AS, 1974 . . . . **25.00**

Blue Oyster Cult, *Innerview*, LP, music and interview, Show #18, 1970s **20.00**

Blues Brothers, *Neighbors*, LP, interviews, Belushi/ Aykroyd, promo, 1981 . . . . **25.00**

Bon Jovi, *The Bon Jovi Story*, 2 LP, music and interview, green, clear vinyl, United Stations, Sep 1989 . . . . **30.00**

Boone, Pat, *Watching the River Run*, 45 rpm, promo, disco, Warner, 1978 . . . . **10.00**

Boston, *What's It All About*, 45 rpm, public service show, interview with Tom Scholz, Bob Seger reverse, WIAA, Jan 1979 . . . . **25.00**

Bowie, David, *Heroes*, 12" promo single, RCA, 1973 . . . . **20.00**

Box of Frogs, *BBC Rock Hour*, LP, live concert, London Wavelength, Sep 1984 . . . . **30.00**

Britt, Elton, *The Wandering Cowboy*, LP, white promo label, ABC Paramount, 1959 . . . . **45.00**

Bruce, Lenny, *Lenny Bruce*, LP, promo, Fantasy, 1958 . . . . **75.00**

Buckinghams, *Susan*, 45 rpm, white promo label, Columbia, 1967 . . . . **18.00**

Budgie, *BBC Transcription Disc*, LP, live concert, BBC Transcription, 1973 . . . . **200.00**

Campbell, Archie, *Make Friends with Archie Campbell*, Starday, 1962 . . . . **8.00**

Campbell, Glen, *Big Bluegrass Special*, LP, Capitol, 1962 . . . . **55.00**

Checker, Chubby, *The Twist*, 45 rpm, red vinyl, issued during second hit run, Parkway, 1961 . . . . **200.00**

Chipmunks, *Come On–a–My–House*, 78 rpm, blue promo label, Coral, 1953 . . . . **30.00**

Gordon MacRae, Martha Wright, Franco Corelli, and Roberta Peters, *Firestone Presents Your Christmas Favorites, Volume 3*, FTP Records, NY, 33¹/₃ rpm, 1964, $5.00.

Clark, Petula, *Downtown*, 45 rpm, white promo label,
Warner, 1964 .... **10.00**

Clay, Cassius, *I Am the Greatest*, 45 rpm, promo, edited
version of stock copy, Columbia, 1962 .... **40.00**

Clooney, Rosemary, *Love, Look Away*, 45 rpm, USAF,
1958. . . .. **12.00**

Como, Perry, *Route 66*, 45 rpm, black promo label, RCA
Victor, c1958 .... **15.00**

Crewcuts, *Sh–Boom*, 45 rpm, white promo label,
Mercury, 1954. .... **25.00**

Deep Purple, *Woman From Tokyo*, 45 rpm, white promo
label, Warner, 1973. .... **18.00**

Dr Feelgood & The Interns, *Okeh*, OKM, 1962 .... **18.00**

Everly Brothers, *Two Yanks in London*, LP, white promo
label, Warner, 1966. .... **65.00**

Fabian, *Hey Roly Poly*, 45 rpm, white promo label,
Chancellor, 1957. .... **30.00**

Farm Aid, *Superstar Concert*, 3 LP, Westwood One,
1980s–90s **50.00**

Foley, Red, *Crazy Little Guitar Man*, 45 rpm, pink promo
label, Decca, 1958 .... **25.00**

Ford, Tennessee Ernie, *Ballad of Davy Crockett*, 45 rpm,
white promo label, Capitol, 1955. .... **10.00**

Francis, Connie, *My Happiness*, 45 rpm, yellow promo
label, MGM, 1958. .... **18.00**

Gates, David, *Swingin' Baby Doll*, 45 rpm, white promo
label, East West, 1959 .... **125.00**

Grand Funk Railroad, *We're an American Band*, 45 rpm,
gold vinyl promo, Capitol, 1973 .... **20.00**

Holly, Buddy, *True Love Ways*, 45 rpm, blue promo label,
Coral, 1960. .... **200.00**

Jackson, Michael, *Thriller*, 45 rpm, promo only, 5:11 version, Epic, 1982 .... **15.00**

Jagger, Mick, *Performance*, LP, white promo label,
Warner, 1970 .... **40.00**

James, Sonny, *Young Love*, 45 rpm, Groove, 1959. .... **25.00**

Jan & Dean, *Heart and Soul*, 45 rpm, white promo label,
Challenge, 1961 .... **50.00**

Jennings, Waylon, *Waylon Jennings at JDS*, LP, promo,
Sounds, 1964 .... **500.00**

Jethro Tull, *Bungle in the Jungle*, 45 rpm, green promo
label, Chrysalis, 1974 .... **20.00**

John, Elton, *Love Song*, 45 rpm, yellow promo label,
MCA, 1976. .... **25.00**

Joplin, Janis, *Retro Rock*, LP, music and interview,
Clayton Webster, 1982. .... **50.00**

Kiss, *Beth*, 45 rpm, stereo/mono version, Casablanca,
1976. .... **50.00**

Lennon, John, *Starting Over*, 45 rpm, Geffen, 1980. .... **15.00**

Little Anthony, *Tears On My Pillow*, 45 rpm, white promo
label, End, 1957 .... **25.00**

Lynyrd Skynyrd, *Gimme Back My Bullets*, 45 rpm,
promo, MCA, 1977 .... **25.00**

Mamas & The Papas, *California Dreamin'*, 45 rpm,
promo, picture sleeve, Dunhill, 1966 .... **75.00**

Martin, Dean, *Everybody Loves Somebody*, 45 rpm,
white promo label, Reprise, 1964. .... **12.00**

McLean, Don, *American Pie*, 45 rpm, brown promo
label with star, same song on both sides, United
Artists, 1972 .... **18.00**

Miller, Glenn, *Authentic Sound of Glenn Miller*, LP,
promo, RCA Victor, 1960. .... **40.00**

Miller, Mitch, *March From the River Kwai*, 45 rpm, yellow vinyl, stock picture sleeve, both sides same,
promo sticker on label, Columbia, 1969. .... **25.00**

Monkees, *Valleri*, 45 rpm, yellow promo label, Colgems,
1968. .... **40.00**

Monroe, Marilyn, *River of No Return*, 45 rpm, white
promo label, RCA Victor, 1951. .... **50.00**

Newton–John, Olivia, *If Not for You*, 45 rpm, multicolored promo label, UNI, 1971. .... **10.00**

Nilsson, Harry, *Me and My Arrow*, 45 rpm, yellow
promo label, RCA Victor, 1971. .... **10.00**

Penguins, *A Christmas Prayer*, 45 rpm, white promo
label, Mercury, 1955 .... **60.00**

Pink Floyd, *Off the Wall*, LP, edited for radio, promo cov,
Columbia, 1983 .... **100.00**

Presley, Elvis, *Elvis Is Back!*, LP, RCA Victor, 1960 .... **45.00**

Preston, Billy, *My Sweet Lord*, 45 rpm, star on label,
Apple, 1970 .... **10.00**

Quatro, Suzi, *Rolling Stone*, 45 rpm, radio statio copy,
RAK, 1972 .... **12.00**

Queen, *Queen*, LP, white promo label, gold emb
"Queen" on label, Elecktra, 1973. .... **50.00**

Rydell, Bobby, *Somebody Loves You*, EP, Capitol, 1965 ...... **15.00**

Sam the Sham, *Wooly Bully*, yellow promo copy, MGM,
1965. .... **12.00**

Simon & Garfunkel, *Bookends*, EP, blue and white label,
Columbia, 1968 .... **40.00**

Skyliners, *The Door Is Still Open*, 45 rpm, white promo
label, Colpix, 1961 .... **45.00**

Snow, Hank, *More Hank Snow Souvenirs*, EP, hard
cov, RCA Victor, 1964 .... **40.00**

Solitaires, *I Really Love You So*, 45 rpm, white promo
label, White Town, 1957 .... **50.00**

Sonny & Cher, *I Got You Babe*, 45 rpm, white promo
label, Atco, 1965. .... **10.00**

Soundtrack, *Auntie Mame*, Warner Bros, 1958 .... **50.00**

Soundtrack, *Barbarella*, Dyno Voice, 1968 .... **22.00**

Soundtrack, *Blue Hawaii*, RCA Victor, 1961 .... **35.00**

Soundtrack, *Camelot*, orig cast, Columbia, 1960. .... **25.00**

Soundtrack, *Dragnet*, RCA Victor, 1953 .... **55.00**

Annie Oakley Sings Ten Gallon Hat and I Gotta Crow From the
Broadway musical Peter Pan, **Little Golden Record #184, $8.00.**

Soundtrack, *Damn Yankees*, orig cast, RCA Victor, 1955 . . . . . **25.00**
Soundtrack, *Footloose*, Columbia, 1983 . . . . **8.00**
Soundtrack, *Gypsy*, orig cast, Columbia, 1959 . . . . **12.00**
Soundtrack, *Lady Sings the Blues*, Motown, 1972 . . . . **10.00**
Soundtrack, *Macbeth*, studio cast, RCA Victor, 1953 . . . . **45.00**
Soundtrack, *Magnificent Seven*, United Artists, 1960 . . . . **18.00**
Soundtrack, *Mary Poppins*, Sidewalk, 1968 . . . . **10.00**
Soundtrack, *No Way to Treat a Lady*, Dot, 1968 . . . . **8.00**
Soundtrack, *Patton*, 20th Century Fox, 1970 . . . . **10.00**
Soundtrack, *Pennies From Heaven*, Warner Bros, 1981 . . . . . **12.50**
Soundtrack, *Ragtime*, Electra, 1981 . . . . **8.50**
Soundtrack, *Sandhog*, Vanguard, 1954 . . . . **75.00**
Soundtrack, *Scarface*, MCA, 1984 . . . . **10.00**
Soundtrack, *Taste of Honey*, studio cast, Atlantic, 1960 . . . . . **20.00**
Soundtrack, *To Kill a Mockingbird*, Ava, 1962 . . . . **30.00**
Soundtrack, *The Voyage of Sinbad*, promo, Colpix, 1959 . . . . **75.00**
Soundtrack, *What's New Pussycat*, United Artists, 1965 . . . . . **15.00**
Sparks, *Wonder Girl*, 45 rpm, white promo label,
    Bearsville, 1972 . . . . **12.00**
Stevens, Ray, *Cat Pants*, 45 rpm, white promo label,
    Capitol, 1958 . . . . **25.00**
Supremes, *Buttered Popcorn*, 45 rpm, white promo
    label, Tamla, 1961 . . . . **60.00**
Temptations, *Dream Come True*, white promo label,
    Gordy, 1962 . . . . **40.00**
Tomlin, Lily, *Modern Scream*, 33 rpm, promo, picture
    sleeve, 7" record, Polydor, 1975 . . . . **10.00**
Travelers Insurance Co, *Triumph of Man*, New York
    World's Fair **8.50**
Turtles, *Guide For the Married Man*, 45 rpm, blue
    promo label, White Whale, 1967 . . . . **35.00**
Twitty, Conway, *Portrait of a Fool*, LP, yellow promo
    label, MGM, 1962 . . . . **50.00**
Vale, Jerry, *Mission Sunday*, EP, radio ads, SPF, 1974 . . . . . . **10.00**
Vinton, Bobby, *Satin Pillows*, red vinyl, white promo
    label, Epic, 1965 . . . . **25.00**
Welk, Lawrence, *On the Alamo*, 45 rpm, US Air Force,
    1957 . . . . **10.00**
Williams, Andy, *The Christmas Song*, green vinyl, white
    promo label, Columbia, 1963 . . . . **10.00**
Williams, Hank, *A Home in Heaven*, 45 rpm, yellow
    promo label, MGM, 1956 . . . . **18.00**
Wynette, Tammy, *White Christmas*, 45 rpm, promo, pic-
    ture sleeve, Epic, 1973 . . . . **10.00**

RED WING POTTERY

The Red Wing Stoneware Company, Minnesota Stoneware Company (1883–1906), and North Star Stoneware Company (1892–96) were located in Red Wing, Minnesota. David Hallem founded the Red Wing Stoneware Company in 1868. By the 1880s Red Wing was the largest American producer of stoneware storage vessels.

In 1894 the Union Stoneware Company was established as a selling agency for Minnesota, North Star, and Red Wing. Minnesota and Red Wing bought out North Star in 1896. In 1906 production was merged into one location and the Red Wing Union Stoneware Company created. The company made stoneware until introducing an art pottery line in the 1920s. During the 1930s Red Wing created several popular lines of hand–painted dinnerware that were sold through department stores, gift stamp redemption centers, and Sears.

In 1936 the company became Red Wing Potteries, Inc. Stoneware production ended in 1947. In the early 1960s the company began producing hotel and restaurant china. Financial difficulties that began in the 1950s continued. Red Wing ceased operations in 1967.

References: Dan and Gail DePasquale and Larry Peterson, *Red Wing Collectibles*, Collector Books, 1985, 1995 value update; B. L. Dollen, *Red Wing Art Pottery: Identification & Value Guide*, Collector Books, 1997; B. L. and R. L. Dollen, *Red Wing Art Pottery, Book II*, Collector Books, 1998; Ray Reiss, *Red Wing Art Pottery: Including Pottery Made for RumRill*, Property Publishing, 1996; Ray Reiss, *Red Wing Dinnerware: Price and Identification Guide*, Property Publishing, 1997.

Collectors' Clubs: Red Wing Collectors Society, 624 Jones St, Eveleth, MN 55734; The RumRill Society, PO Box 2161, Hudson, OH 44236.

Ash Receiver, pelican **$75.00**
Basket, white **25.00**
Blossom Time, bowl, 7½" **14.00**
Blossom Time, bread and butter plate, 6½" **6.00**
Blossom Time, cup **4.00**
Blossom Time, dinner plate, 10½" **10.00**
Blossom Time, fruit bowl, 5½" **7.00**
Blossom Time, saucer **5.00**
Bob White, beverage server, with stopper **85.00**
Bob White, bread and butter plate, 6½" **4.00**
Bob White, bread tray **80.00**
Bob White, butter warmer, cov, stick handle **80.00**
Bob White, casserole **48.00**
Bob White, cereal, 6½" d **15.00**
Bob White, cookie jar **45.00**
Bob White, cup and saucer **7.50**
Bob White, dinner plate **8.00**
Bob White, fruit bowl **7.50**
Bob White, hors d'oeuvre bird **50.00**
Bob White, Lazy Susan, with stand **90.00**
Bob White, pitcher, 6¾" **14.00**
Bob White, platter, 13" l **20.00**
Bob White, salt and pepper shakers, pr, bird shape **40.00**
Bob White, salt and pepper shakers, pr, hourglass shape **22.00**
Bob White, soup bowl **15.00**
Bob White, sugar, cov **25.00**
Bob White, vegetable bowl **25.00**
Capistrano, bread and butter plate **2.00**

Planter, slipper, rose, 9" l, $35.00.

Capistrano, butter dish, bottom only **20.00**
Capistrano, casserole, cov **45.00**
Capistrano, celery tray **28.00**
Capistrano, cup **2.00**
Capistrano, dinner plate **5.00**
Capistrano, platter, 13" **35.00**
Capistrano, salad plate **3.00**
Capistrano, salt and pepper shakers, pr **15.00**
Chevron, ashtray, 4" d **10.00**
Chevron, bud vase, kettle, 3" h **15.00**
Chevron, drip jar **25.00**
Chevron, dinner plate, 8" d **5.00**
Chevron, platter, oval, 12" l **12.00**
Chevron, saucer **3.00**
Chevron, sugar **20.00**
Console Set, #1365, 3 pcs, crackle glaze, royal blue,
    black candlesticks, Oriental woman carrying bamboo
    baskets on shoulders **160.00**
Cookie Jar, figural chef, brown **90.00**
Cookie Jar, figural dancing peasants **35.00**
Country Garden, dinner plate, 10½" d **20.00**
Country Garden, gravy boat **25.00**
Country Garden, salad plate, 8" d **15.00**
Country Garden, vegetable bowl, divided **25.00**
Figure, girl with flower, hp, 8½" h **140.00**
Figure, Oriental goddess, solid color **40.00**
Fondoso, bread and butter plate, 6½" d **5.00**
Fondoso, creamer, small **8.00**
Fondoso, mixing bowl, 8" d **20.00**
Fondoso, syrup jug **30.00**
Fruit Service, casserole, pineapple, large **35.00**
Fruit Service, marmalade, apple **25.00**
Fruit Service, salad bowl, individual, apple **10.00**
Fruit Service, salad bowl, pearl, large **20.00**
Iris, bowl, 5½" d **8.00**
Iris, creamer **8.00**
Iris, relish, 3 part **20.00**
Labriego, French casserole, oval, small **30.00**
Labriego, creamer **15.00**
Labriego, mug **20.00**
Labriego, sugar **25.00**
Labriego, water jug **30.00**
Lexington Rose, salad set, fork and spoon **35.00**
Lute Song, bowl, 8" d **12.00**
Lute Song, celery tray, 16" l **8.00**
Lute Song, vegetable bowl, divided **18.00**
Magnolia, cup and saucer **10.00**
Magnolia, salad plate, 7" d **4.00**
Magnolia, saucer **2.50**
Merrileaf, celery, 15" l **28.00**
Planter, banjo, black and white, 15" h **28.00**
Planter, rabbit **30.00**
Planter, swan **15.00**
Planter, violin, 14½" h **25.00**
Reed, ball jug, 16 oz **25.00**
Reed, casserole, 7½" d **30.00**
Reed, cup **15.00**
Reed, eggcup **25.00**
Reed, pie baker, 9" d **15.00**
Reed, platter, oval, 12" l **20.00**
Reed, tea cup **10.00**
Reed, teapot, 8 cup **55.00**
Round Up, creamer **40.00**
Round Up, dinner plate, chuckwagon, 10½" d **55.00**

Round Up, teapot **190.00**
Round Up, vegetable bowl, divided **65.00**
Smart Set, butter warmer, cov, stick handle **35.00**
Smart Set, cocktail tray **25.00**
Smart Set, cruet, pr, with stoppers and stand **55.00**
Smart Set, dinner plate, 7½" d **8.00**
Smart Set, jug, 60 oz **75.00**
Smart Set, Lazy Susan, 5 pcs **140.00**
Smart Set, pepper mill **90.00**
Smart Set, relish tray, 3 part **55.00**
Smart Set, salad bowl, 10½" d **80.00**
Tampico, beverage server, cov **75.00**
Tampico, cake plate, ruffled edge **35.00**
Tampico, cereal bowl **8.00**
Tampico, creamer **15.00**
Tampico, fruit dish **5.00**
Tampico, sugar, cov **15.00**
Town and Country, ashtray **8.00**
Town and Country, cruet, orig stopper **50.00**
Town and Country, dinner plate, 8" d **10.00**
Town and Country, teapot **150.00**
Village Green, casserole, 1 qt **15.00**
Village Green, marmite **8.00**
Village Green, mug **20.00**
Village Green, salad bowl, 12" d **35.00**
Village Green, sauce dish **12.00**
Village Green, shaker **15.00**
Village Green, casserole, large **28.00**

REGAL CHINA

Regal China Corporation, Antioch, Illinois, was established in 1938. In the 1940s, Regal was purchased by Royal China and Novelty Company, a distribution and sales organization. Royal used Regal to make the ceramic products that it sold.

Ruth Van Tellingen Bendel designed Snuggle Hugs in the shape of bears, bunnies, pigs, etc., in 1948. She also designed cookie jars, other figurines, and salt and pepper shaker sets.

Regal did large amounts of decorating for other firms, e.g., Hull's Red Riding Hood pieces. Regal has not sold to the retail trade since 1968, continuing to operate on a contract basis only. In 1976 it produced a cookie jar for Quaker Oat in 1976; 1983 products include a milk pitcher for Ovaltine and a ship decanter and coffee mugs for Old Spice. Regal currently is a wholly owned subsidiary of Jim Beam Distilleries.

Reference; Harvey Duke, *The Official Price Guide to Pottery and Porcelain, Eighth Edition*, House of Collectibles, 1995.

Butter, cov, Old MacDonald, cow head on lid, ¼ lb **$225.00**
Cansiter Set, Blue Willow, square jars, rounded covers,
    large flour, smaller sugar, tea, and coffee **180.00**
Cereal Canister, Old MacDonald, medium **200.00**
Cookie Jar, wolf, chip on ear **495.00**
Creamer, Alice in Wonderland, White Rabbit **400.00**
Creamer, Rooster **85.00**
Flour Canister, Old MacDonald, medium **200.00**
Grease Jar, pig **150.00**
Popcorn Canister, Old MacDonald, large **280.00**
Salt and Pepper Shakers, pr, Alice, white and gold **500.00**
Salt and Pepper Shakers, pr, A–Nod to Abe **350.00**
Salt and Pepper Shakers, pr, boy and girl **75.00**
Salt and Pepper Shakers, pr, milk churns **38.00**

Salt and Pepper Shakers, pr, pig, 1 pc. **95.00**
Shaker, Pee–A–Boo, white and red, small **250.00**
Snuggle Hugs, boy and dog, white. **65.00**
Snuggle Hugs, Mary and Lamb, yellow, black tail **45.00**
Tea Canister, Old MacDonald, medium **250.00**
Teapot, cov, duck head on lid **280.00**

ROBOTS

Robot toys of the late 1940s and early 1950s were friction or windup powered. Many of these lithographed tin beauties were made from recycled material. By the mid–1950s, most robots were battery powered. Japanese manufacturers produced several hundred models. Model variations are common, the result of manufacturers freely interchanging parts. Plastic replaced lithographed tin as the material of choice in the late 1960s.

Robot models responded to changing Space Age motifs. The Japanese Atomic Robot Man, made between 1948 and 1949, heralded the arrival of the Atomic age. Movies, such as *Destination Moon* (1950) and *Forbidden Planet* (1956), featuring Robbie the Robot, provided the inspiration for robot toys in the early and mid–1950s. S0pace theme television programs, e.g., *Lost in Space* (1965–1968), played a similar role in the 1960s. Ideal and Marx entered the toy robot market in the late 1960s.

Markings can be confusing. Many of the marks are those of importers and/or distributors, not manufacturers. Cragston is an importer, not a maker. Reproductions and fantasy items are a major problem in the late 1990s. Because of the high desirability and secondary market cost of robots such as Mr. Atomic ($10,000+), modern copies costing between $250 and $750 new are being made. Inexpensive Chinese and Taiwanese robots made in shapes that never existed historically are flooding the market.

Reference: Maxine A. Pinsky, *Marx Toys: Robots, Space, Comic & TV Characters,* Schiffer Publishing, 1996.

Periodicals: *Toy Shop,* 700 E State St, Iola, WI 54990; *Toy Trader,* PO Box 1050, Dubuque, IA 52003.

Action Planet Robot, Robbie style, black, red plastic hands, walks, sparks through face, red feet, clockwork mechanism, orig box, Yoshiya, 1965–70, 8³/₈" h **$485.00**
Answer Game Machine, battery operated, numbered buttons and levers with answer on screen on chest, clear plastic dome on head spins when total revealed, Japan, 1960s, 14¹/₂" h **400.00**
Astro Captain Robot, light tin face behind domed helmet, white plastic arms with claw hands, sparking torso, clockwork mechanism, Daiya, 1965–70, 6³/₄" h **285.00**
Atomic Robot, clockwork mechanism activates upper body to rise and twist revealing 2 facial expressions and creates a "cluck cluck" sound, plastic hinged arms, headlight on top of head, cardboard box, Yonezawa, 1965–70, 8¹/₂" h **745.00**
Atom Robot, silver, friction, bump–and–go action, hinged arms, skirt style body, litho details, orig box, Yonezawa, 1950s, 6¹/₂" h **800.00**
Blazer Superhero Robot, tin, red, yellow, black, and blue, plastic arms, windup, orig box, Bullmark, 1960s . . . **170.00**
Bulldozer Space Tractor, blue, red, orange, and yellow litho tin vehicle, driven by silver robot, battery operated, Marusan, 1960s **920.00**

Captain Robo, light blue and fluorescent pink tank style robot, friction driven, matching cream plastic trailer with pink bubble over drivers, orig box, Yonezawa, 1970s, 13" l **145.00**
Cragstan Astronaut, red litho, skirt style figure, domed helmet with plastic visor over astronaut face, crank wound, walking motion, clicking sound and arm movement, Yonezawa, 1950s, 9¹/₂" h **630.00**
Cragstan's Mr Robot, white finished skirt form body, red arms, lettered chest plate, domed plastic head with visible coils and antenna, battery operated, Japan, 1950s, 11" h **400.00**
Dalek, red plastic body, black base, battery operated, Marx, orig box, 6¹/₂" h **185.00**
Directional Robot, skirtform robot, light metallic blue, block head topped by red flashing light, head turns as robot goes in that direction, battery operated, orig box, Yonezawa, 1955–60, 11" h **1,840.00**
Earth Man, yellow version, litho tin, walks, lifts gun with lighting barrel and fires, wears oxygen tank with telescoping antenna, Normura, 1950s, 9¹/₂" h **975.00**
Engine Robot, gunmetal gray, block torso and head, torso with clear front panel revealing red and green gears, red feet, clockwork mechanism, key wind at left shoulder, cardboard box, Horikawa, 1965–70 . . . . **460.00**
Fighting Robot, plastic, brown, double firing machine guns in torso, battery operated, orig box, Japan, 1970s, 9¹/₂" h **200.00**
Fighting Spaceman, gray, battery operated, litho face behind helmet, rotating gun at chest, Horikawa, 1960–65, 11¹/₂" h **345.00**
Forbidden Planet Robby Robot, plastic, windup, metallic gray, clear plastic dome on head, silver face plate, antenna, Modern Toys, mkd "MGM/UA Entertainment Co" on box, 1984, 4¹/₄" h. **50.00**
Gear Robot, windup, plastic, built–in key, gold color body, yellow ear attachments, red arms and legs, black feet, tin litho eyes, chest panel under clear plastic cover, SH/Japan, 1970s **50.00**

Mighty 8 Robot, battery operated, dark gray, kaleidoscope window on torso lights up as robot walks forward, orig box, Masudaya, c1955–60, 11" h, $1,980.00. Photo courtesy James D. Julia.

Godaikin Sun Vultan Super Robot, Bandai, diecast metal, plastic, complete with accessories, carrying case with plastic handle, 1982, 10" h **100.00**

The Great Garloo, battery box remote control unit, fabric leopard skin skirt, plastic "Garloo" medallion around neck, metal link chain bracelet on wrist, cardboard box with red and black text and design, Marx, 1960s, 18" h **700.00**

Happy Harry the Hysterical Robot, plastic, bump and go action, movable arms, mouth, large white teeth, loud laugh, Straco/Japan, 1969, 13" h **400.00**

High Wheel Robot, metallic blue, clear panel in torso covers 6 plastic gears, remote battery control, light in head and chest, adjustable antenna, orig box, Yoshiya, 1960s, 8³/₄" h **1,265.00**

Jupiter Robot, red plastic Robbie style, black plastic arms, start/stop lever, clockwork mechanism, orig box, Yoshiya, 1960s, 7" h **415.00**

Lunar Spaceman, maroon plastic, plastic dome over plastic astronaut head, battery operated, hinged torso panels open to reveal firing gun, orig box, Japan, 1980s, 12" h **375.00**

Mars King, dark silver litho, TV screen in torso, battery powered, missing treads, orig box, Horikawa, 1960s, 9¹/₄" h **460.00**

Mechanical Space Man, light blue litho, 4–blade propeller on orange helmet, astronaut face, fixed arms, clockwork mechanism, Yoshiya, 1960s, 6" h **230.00**

Mechanical Television Spaceman, gray, clockwork mechanism, rotating antenna, TV screen in torso reveals rotating lithograph cylinder depicting outer space scene, orig box, Japan, 1965–70, 7³/₄" h **285.00**

Mechanical Walking Spaceman, metallic blue litho, flat arms, red feet, start/stop lever at front, clockwork mechanism, Yoshiya, 1960–65, 7¹/₂" h **430.00**

Mighty Robot, metallic green litho, sparking chamber, clockwork mechanism, Japan, 1960s, 5¹/₂" h **145.00**

Moon Doctor, windup, litho tin body, plastic glasses and arms, "X–25" on feet, orig box, Japan, 7" h, $1,785.00. Photo courtesy New England Auction Gallery.

Moon Explorer Spaceman, Robbie style, red, 4–blade propeller on head, astronaut face under plastic dome, friction powered, Yoshiya, 1950s, 7" h **485.00**

Mr Atom the Electronic Walking Robot, plastic, "Mr Atom" between eyes, lightning bolts, switches and dials on chest, clear plastic dome on top of head, dome eyes, instructions, boxed, The Advance Doll & Toy Co, 1950s **700.00**

Mr Mercury, light blue tin and plastic, remote battery control with walking, bending and picking up objects actions, control room at helmet visor, electric light on helmet, Yonezawa/Linemar, 1955–60s, 13" h **1,150.00**

Orange Bulldozer, orange, teal blue robot driver with light in head, battery operated, driver controls action of plow with side lever, Yoshiya, 1950s, 8¹/₂" l **575.00**

Pistol Action Robot, Robbie style, 3 moving lighted pistons visible under plastic dome maroon legs, battery operated, green remote control, Japan, 1950s, 8¹/₂" h **860.00**

Piston Robot, litho details, battery operated, 4 moving pistons at chest, hinged plastic arms, orig box, Japan, 1960s, 11" h **315.00**

R–35 Robot, cylindrical head, litho torso, light bulb eyes, litho battery box with robots on the move, forward and reverse motions, Masudaya, 1950s, 7⁵/₈" h **800.00**

Radar Robot, gunmetal gray torso, light gray litho legs and face with light bulb glass eyes, purple feet, adjustable rear radar screen with light bulb, claw hands with wrench in right hand, remote battery control in shape of robot face with push–button eyes, orig box, Normura, 1950s, 7⁷/₈" h **2,645.00**

Radar Scope Space Scout, gray, battery operated, TV screen torso displaying space scene, cardboard box, Horikawa, 1965–70, 9¹/₂" h **400.00**

Robbie the Roving Robot, gray, clockwork mechanism, hinged arms, antenna on head, Japan, 1950s, 7¹/₂" h **800.00**

Robert the Robot and His Remote Control Bulldozer, plastic, battery operated light, trigger gun with cranking directional controls, seated red and silver robot works gears, blue and yellow bulldozer with red treads, orig box, Ideal, 9" l **2,000.00**

Robodachi Robot, diecast metal, plastic, depicts baseball player, complete with unopened bag of accessories, instruction sheet, black and white comic booklet, color sheet picturing different robot figures from series, Japan, 3¹/₂" h, MIB **100.00**

Robot 2500, silver, battery operated, red light on torso, orig box, Durham Industries, Inc, 10" h **80.00**

Robot Commando, battery operated, plastic, blue body, red dome and accents, microphone shaped remote control box with joystick, voice activated, orig box, Ideal, 1961, 15" h **440.00**

Robotank–Z, gray, litho details, arms move, bump and go action, domed light at top of head, hinged plastic arms, orig box, Nomura, 1960s, 10¹/₂" h **400.00**

Rotate–O–Matic Super Astronaut, red, battery operated, astronaut walks forward, body rotates as guns fire from chest, orig box, Horikawa, 1980s, 11³/₄" h **175.00**

Roto Robot, gray, battery operated, hinged plastic arms, 3 guns on chest, walks, rotates while firing lit guns, Horikawa, 1965–70, 8³/₄" h **175.00**

Rototrac Bulldozer, red and yellow, battery operated, propulsion levers, light on head, bulldozer rolls forward and horn sounds when objects hit, orig box, Linemar, 1950, 9¹/₂" h **630.00**

Smoking Spaceman, gray body, red feet, battery compartments to legs, walks, breathes smoke, flashes eyes, cardboard box, Linemar, 1950s, 11⁷/₈" h 632.00

Space Dog, red, wobbly eyes, moving ears and lower jaw, spring tail, friction mechanism, Yoshiya, 1950s, 7¹/₂" l 400.00

Space Fighter, brown, battery operated, walks forward, hinged doors at chest reveal firing guns, orig box, Horikawa, 1965–70, 9" h 230.00

Sparky, windup, litho tin, built–in key, metallic green, black, red, yellow, and silver accents, Japan, 1960s, 5¹/₄" h 100.00

Star Strider, gray, battery operated, astronaut walks forward, body rotates as guns fire from chest, Japan, 1970s, 12¹/₂" h 172.00

Venus Robot, red and black plastic version, clockwork mechanism, Yoshiya, 1965–70, 5¹/₂" h 315.00

Venus Robot, red and black plastic, clockwork mechanism, Yoshiya, 1965–70, 5¹/₂" h 315.00

Video Robot, battery operated, plastic, litho tin, metallic blue, gold and silver accents, SH/Japan, 1970s, 9" h 100.00

ROCK 'N' ROLL

In spite of its outward appearance, the rock 'n' roll field tends to be traditionalist. Material from short–lived new wave or punk groups of the 1970s, e.g., The Damned and Generation X, do not appear to be attracting large numbers of collectors.

Collectors are specializing. Memorabilia from the girl groups of the late 1950s and early 1960s has become hot. The field is trendy. Autographs, guitars, and stage costumes are three categories that have gotten hot, cooled off, and show signs of resurgence. Hard Rock Cafés have spread around the world, creating an international interest in this topic. The top end of this market is documented by the values received at rock 'n' roll auctions held in London, Los Angeles, and New York.

References: Mark A. Baker, *Goldmine Price Guide to Rock 'N' Roll Memorabilia*, Krause Publications, 1997; David K. Henkel, *The Official Price Guide to Rock and Roll*, House of Collectibles, 1992; Eric King, *The Collector's Guide to Psychedelic Rock Concert Posters, Postcards and Handbills*, Svaha Press, 1996; Karen and John Lesniewski, *Kiss Collectibles: Identification and Price Guide*, Avon Books, 1993.

Collectors' Club: Kissaholics, PO Box 22334, Nashville, TN 37202.

REPRODUCTION ALERT: Records, picture sleeves, and album jackets, especially for the Beatles, have been counterfeited. Sound may be inferior. Printing on labels and picture jackets usually is inferior to the original. Many pieces of memorabilia also have been reproduced, often with some change in size, color, and design.

Note: See Beatles, Elvis Presley, Psychedelic, and Records for additional listings.

Allman Brothers, guitar, sgd, Session model, acoustic, sgd in black sharpie by Gregg Allman, Dickey Betts, "Jaimoe" Johanny Johanson, Butch Trucks, Warren Hayes, Allen Wood, Rick Danko, Garth Hudson, and Leum Helm $800.00

Bee Gees, radio, plastic, group sticker on front, retractable handle, AM, Vanity Fair, 1979 . . . . 40.00

Boone, Pat, pinback button, blue "Swoon With Pat Boone," white ground, red rim, 3¹/₂" d 5.00

Boy George, doll, hard plastic, soft vinyl head, hat, microphone and posing stand, orig box, LJN, 12" h 25.00

Byrds, lyrics, *So You Want to Be a Rock & Roll Star*, black marker handwritten lyrics on Chris Hillman's stationary, 3 verses, inscribed at bottom "Words & Music, Jim McGuinn–Chris Hillman Recorded by the–1966–BYRDS," sgd by Hillman, matted and framed with CD cov for Byrd's *Younger Than Yesterday*, 6 x 16" 1,150.00

Cassidy, David, concert poster, "David Cassidy of The Partridge Family," Curtis Hixon Hall, Tampa, Sun, Sept 26, 1971, 15 x 22¹/₂" 45.00

Cher, record jacket, Liberty, 1981 . . . . 8.00

Clark, Dick, cufflinks, pr, MIB 30.00

Clark, Dick, yearbook, Dick Clark Official American Bandstand Yearbook, color and black and white photos, 40 pp, c1950, 9 x 12" 25.00

Cochran, Eddie, and Gene Vincent, concert program, from ill–fated 1960 British tour, sgd by Cochran and Vincent on separate black and white portraits, inscribed "To Geoff & Ricky" 920.00

Cooke, Sam, and Clyde McPhatter, concert program, large fold–open pg from 1958 "Biggest Show of Stars" concert, sgd near images in ink and pencil by Sam Cooke, The Everly Brothers, and Clyde McPhatter, matted and framed, 16 x 20" 575.00

Cooper, Alice, poster, Cowtown Ballroom, red and yellow, 1970s 200.00

Dean, James, book, *James Dean*, biography by William Bast, paperback, Ballantine Books, 1956, 150 pp 15.00

Donovan, guitar, acoustic, Ibanez, sgd in black "Catch the Wind, Donovan '97," drawing of mountains beneath moon 460.00

Grateful Dead, autographed photo, black and white, felt–tip pen signatures by all band members, matted and framed, c1989, 11¹/₂" sq, $632.00. Photo courtesy Sotheby's.

Doors, poster, promotional, group photo, Elektra stereo tapes, blue, black, and white lettering, 36 x 24" **200.00**

Duran Duran, game, Duran Duran Into the Arena, Milton Bradley, 1985 . . . . **15.00**

Dylan, Bob, tour book, 28 pp, c1977, 10 x 14" **25.00**

Fleetwood Mac, poster, Jan 1970 concert, Deutsches Museum, Munich, West Germany, full color, 33 x 46" **30.00**

Freddy and the Dreamers, pinback button, black and white photos, red and white "I Love Freddy and the Dreamers," ©Premier Talent Associates, Inc, 1960s **22.00**

Garcia, Jerry, photograph, color, felt–tip pen signature **285.00**

Grateful Dead, picture, color print of band, sgd by Jerry Garcia, Bobby Weir, Bill Kreutzman, Mickey Hart, Phil Lesh, and Vince Welnick during 1955 tour, matted and framed, 14 x 18" **800.00**

Haley, Bill, and the Comets, sheet music, *Green Tree Boogie*, greentone photo on front, ©Myers music, 1955, 9 x 11" **20.00**

Hendrix, Jimi, handbill, Newport '69, Devonshire Downs **250.00**

Herman's Hermits, pinback button, 5 black and white photos, red and white, "I Love Herman's Hermits," ©Premier Talent Associates, Inc, late 1960s, 3$\frac{1}{2}$" d **15.00**

Holly, Buddy, contract, Elks Hall concert, 2–pp letter and envelope, Aug 3, c1950s **500.00**

Holly, Buddy, record label, black pen and ink signature on Coral record label for single *Heartbeat*, matted and framed with photograph of Buddy Holly & The Crickets, 13 x 17" **1,035.00**

Jackson, Michael, doll, poseable, American Music Awards outfit, red jacket, gold accents, black pants, sunglasses, microphone, glitter glove, and stand, LJN, ©MJJ Productions, orig box, 1984, 11" h **50.00**

Jefferson Airplane, poster, Fillmore concert, shiny silver Statue of Liberty illus, black ground, April 11–13, 1960s, 13 x 9" **50.00**

John, Elton, and Bernie Taupin, mirror, sgd, Rocket Record Co promotion, c1974 . . . . **350.00**

Kiss, colorforms, Rub n' Play Magic Transfer Set, 1979 . . . . . . **45.00**

Kiss, game, Kiss on Tour, American Publishing Corp, ©Aucoin Management, Inc, 1978 . . . . **45.00**

Kiss, program, World Tour, 1977–78, 11 x 17" **15.00**

Lennon, John, and Yoko Ono, autograph, "To Laura by John Lennon and Yoko Ono," color photograph, mounted and framed **575.00**

Lennon, John, and Yoko Ono, lithograph, chine colle on Japanese mino paper, artist proof, sgd lower left by artist, John Lennon's signature emb and stamped with red seal created by John Lennon, framed, 1986, 23$\frac{1}{2}$ x 20$\frac{1}{2}$" **460.00**

Mama Cass, contract, sgd, William Morris Agency, matted and framed with photo of Mama Cass, 18 x 17" **230.00**

McCartney, Paul, and George Martin, Abbey Road sign, metal, sgd, with cartoon face and inscription "wozere 3–8–95," 17 x 31" **800.00**

Michael, George, guitar, acoustic, sgd **350.00**

Monkees, thermos, metal, full color illus, ©Raybert Productions, Inc, 1967 . . . . **25.00**

Moody Blues, poster, Terrace Ballroom, Salt Lake City, UT, Apr 1, 1970, 18$\frac{1}{2}$ x 25$\frac{1}{2}$" **50.00**

Morrison, Jim, record, *Three Hour for Magic*, London Wavelength **350.00**

Nirvana, award, "Gold" album for *In Utero*, framed, 19$\frac{1}{2}$ x 15$\frac{1}{2}$" **575.00**

Peter, Paul, & Mary, ticket, Albany Armory, Albany, NY, Mon Feb 21, 1966 . . . . **35.00**

Presley, Elvis, ticket, San Antonio Convention Center Concert, Oct 8, 1974, unused **12.00**

Robbins, Marty, record jacket, *Rock'n Roll'n Robbins*, Columbia, 1956 . . . . **150.00**

Rolling Stones, electric guitar, Fender Squier Stratocaster, sgd on body and pickguard by all 4 current members in blue felt tip, "Pick It! Keith Richards, Mick Jagger, Charlie Watts, and Ronnie Wood," caricature drawing by Wood **2,875.00**

Rolling Stones, magazine, *Rolling Stones Monthly*, black pen ink signatures of Brian Jones, Mick Jagger, Keith Richards, Charlie Watts, and Bill Wyman on color cov featuring the Stones, matted and framed, c1964, 22 x 19$\frac{1}{2}$" **1,265.00**

Rolling Stones, picture, color group portrait, sgd by all members of band in bold felt tip, matted and framed, c1990, 11 x 14" **1,150.00**

Rolling Stones, poster, resembles old vaudeville sheet with pen and ink circus motif images, "Stones World Famous Traveling Movie The Only Big Coming This Season," Ziegfeld Theatre, NY City, Apr 15–30, printed on newspaper stock in black and red, matted and framed, 1970 . . . . **450.00**

Ross, Diana & The Supremes, ticket, Albany Armory, Albany, NY, Oct 4, 1969 . . . . **65.00**

Sex Pistols, Johnny Rotten, Paul Cook, Sid Vicious, and Steve autographs on photo from album sleeve, Jones, felt tip and black ballpoint ink, framed **450.00**

The Who, autograph, sgd by Pete Townshend, Roger Daltry, John Entwistle, and Keith Moon, May Day Whoot the Who Veeble Peeple May 1, c1965 . . . . **700.00**

The Who, sheet music, *Substitute*, bluetone group photo on cov, ©Fabulous Music Ltd, 1966 . . . . **12.50**

Woodstock, book, *Woodstock*, Joseph J Sia, Scholastic Book Services, 124 pp, 1970 . . . . **25.00**

Yard Birds, poster, Civic Auditorium, red, white, and blue, 1967, 14$\frac{1}{2}$ x 23$\frac{1}{2}$" **50.00**

Led Zeppelin, record, *Led Zeppelin III*, 33$\frac{1}{3}$ rpm, Atlantic, 1970, $10.00.

Zappa, Frank, contract, Today Show appearance, glossy
finish, 1990. . . . . **750.00**
Zappa, Frank, etching, "Mothers Segment" cover design,
sgd in pencil "F.Z. Frank Zappa," Dec 1967, 20 x 26" **975.00**

AUCTION PRICES

Rock 'n' Roll memorabilia sold by Sotheby's on December 20,
1997. Prices include the 15% buyer's premium.

Beach Boys, sgd electric guitar, Fender Squier
Stratocaster, sgd by Brian Wilson, Carl Wilson,
Mike Love, Al Jardine, and Bruce Johnston,
together with 2 laser photos of Mike Love and
Bruce Johnston with guitar after signing **$1,495.00**
Bob Dylan, Super Chromonica harmonica and
autograph, matted and framed with photo of Bob
Dylan, with letter of authenticity, 16 x 20" win-
dow opening size **2,587.00**
Bruce Springsteen, denim jacket, worn during Born
in the USA tour, Lee jacket, cut–off sleeves,
together with letter of authenticity and photo of
Springsteen wearing jacket **2,185.00**
Buddy Holly and the Crickets, autographs of all 3
band members in ballpoint pen on printed photo
of The Crickets, matted, 10$^1/_4$ x 8$^1/_4$" **1,150.00**
Janis Joplin, beaded purse, worn at 1968 Monterey
Pop Festival, together with letter of authenticity . . **2,070.00**
Jimi Hendrix, autograph, ink on paper, inscribed
"Stay free Jimi Hendrix," matted with printed
photo of Hendrix and gold record for *Purple
Haze*, autograph image size 1$^3/_4$ x 2$^3/_4$" **920.00**
Rolling Stones, promotional brochure, sgd by Mick
Jagger, Keith Richard, Charlie Watts, Bill Wyman,
Ian Stewart, and others, graphite on paper. **690.00**
The Doors, gold album award for *L.A. Woman*,
framed, 19$^1/_2$ x 15$^1/_2$" **920.00**

ROCKWELL, NORMAN

Norman Rockwell was born on February 3, 1894. His first professional drawing appeared in *Tell Me Why Stories*. Rockwell was
eighteen at the time. Rockwell is best known for his magazine covers, the most recognized appearing on *Boy's Life* and the *Saturday
Evening Post* (over 320 covers). Advertising, books, and calendars
are only a few of the additional media where his artwork
appeared. His artistic legacy includes more than 2,000 paintings.

Rockwell is one of America's foremost genre painters. He specialized in capturing a moment in the life of the average American.
His approach ranged from serious to humorous, from social com-
mentary to inspirational. He used those he knew for inspiration.
His subjects ranged from New England villagers to presidents.

Rockwell's artwork continues to be heavily reproduced. Do not
confuse contemporary with period pieces. His estate continues to
license the use of his images. Buy modern collectibles for display
and enjoyment. Their long–term value is minimal.

Reference: Denis C. Jackson, *The Norman Rockwell Identification
and Value Guide to Magazines, Posters, Calendars, Books, 2nd
Edition*, TICN, 1985.

Collectors' Club: Rockwell Society of America, PO Box 705,
Ardsley, NY 10502.

REPRODUCTION ALERT

Note: For additional listings see Limited Edition Collectibles.

Bell, Christmas, 1st ed, Dave Grossman, 1975 . . . . **$30.00**
Bell, Ben Franklin Bicentennial, Dave Grossman, 1976. . . . . . **28.00**
Book, *Tom Sawyer*, Heritage Press, 1936 . . . . **20.00**
Calendar, 1920, Painting the Kite, De Laval adv **325.00**
Calendar, 1950, Our Heritage, Boy Scout. **15.00**
Calendar, Top Value Stamp Catalog, 1967 . . . . **30.00**
Catalog, Montgomery Ward, 1925 . . . . **35.00**
Figurine, Bedtime, Rockwell Museum, 1978. . . . . **50.00**
Figurine, Exasperated Nanny, Dave Grossman, 1980. . . . . . . **125.00**
Figurine, Four Seasons, Childhood, Gorham Fine China,
1973, price for set of 4 . . . . **500.00**
Figurine, Jolly Coachman, Gorham, 1982. . . . . **50.00**
Figurine, Music Maker, Rockwell Museum, 1981 . . . . **90.00**
Figurine, No Swimming, Dave Grossman, 1973 . . . . **45.00**
Figurine, Painter, Rockwell Museum, 1983 . . . . **90.00**
Figurine, Saying Grace, Gorham, 1976. . . . . **150.00**
Figurine, Snow Queen, Lynell Studios, 1979. . . . . **85.00**
Figurine, Tom Sawyer, series #1, Grossman Designs, Inc,
1976. . . . . **100.00**
Figurine, Wrapping Christmas Presents, Rockwell
Museum, 1980 . . . . **120.00**
Ignot, *Saturday Evening Post* Covers, set of 12, 1975. . . . . . . **210.00**
Ignot, Tribute to Robert Frost, set of 12, Franklin Mint,
1974. . . . . **285.00**
Magazine, *American Artist*, Self–Portrait and article, Jul
1976. . . . . **18.00**
Magazine, *American Magazine*, illus cov, bound issue,
Jul–Dec 1940 . . . . **7.50**
Magazine, *Saturday Evening Post*, 250th ed, Rockwell
cov, illus, and portfolio, Aug 1977 . . . . **25.00**
Magazine Cover, *American Legion*, Jul 1978. . . . . **5.00**
Magazine Cover, *Boys Life*, Jun 1957 . . . . **42.50**
Magazine Cover, *Country Gentleman*, Mar 18, 1922 . . . . **45.00**
Magazine Cover, *McCall's*, Dec 1964. . . . . **12.00**
Magazine Cover, *Saturday Evening Post*, Feb 18, 1922 . . . . . **85.00**
Magazine Cover, *Saturday Evening Post*, Nov 16, 1946. . . . . . **25.00**
Magazine Cover, *Saturday Evening Post*, Aug 30, 1952 . . . . . **40.00**

Magazine, sgd,
*Saturday Evening
Post*, Dec 2, 1922,
11 x 14", **$135.00.**

Magazine Cover, *Saturday Evening Post*, Sep 7, 1957 . . . . . . **22.50**
Magazine Cover, *Scouting*, Feb 1934 . . . . **10.00**
Magazine Cover, *Scouting*, Oct 1953 . . . . **8.50**
Magazine Cover, *Yankee*, Aug 1972 . . . . **10.00**
Paperweight, River Shore **100.00**
Plate, A Mother's Love, Mother's Day Series, Rockwell
    Society, 1976 . . . . **120.00**
Plate, Boy Scout, Our Heritage, Christmas Series,
    Gorham, 1975 . . . . **60.00**
Plate, The Carolers, Christmas Series, Franklin Mint,
    1972 . . . . **165.00**
Plate, Faces of Christmas, Christmas Series, Dave
    Grossman, 1981 . . . . **75.00**
Plate, First Prom, American Family Series, Rockwell
    Museum, 1979 . . . . **30.00**
Plate, Leapfrog, Annual Series, Dave Grossman, 1979 . . . . . . **50.00**
Plate, Listening, Huckleberry Finn Series, Dave
    Grossman, 1980 . . . . **40.00**
Plate, Me & My Pal, Four Seasons Series, Gorham 1975,
    price for set of 4 . . . . **200.00**
Plate, Santa Plans His Visit, Christmas Series, Gorham,
    1981 . . . . **30.00**
Plate, Spring Flowers, River Shore, 1979 . . . . **120.00**
Plate, Surprises For All, Christmas Series, Lynell Studios,
    1980 . . . . **30.00**
Plate, Toy Maker, Heritage Series, Rockwell Society,
    1977 . . . . **260.00**
Playing Cards, Four Seasons, orig box, unopened **12.00**
Poster, Freedom of Speech, WWII, 1943 . . . . **35.00**
Print, "A Christmas Minuet," *Ladies Home Journal*, sub-
    scriber's gift, 1932 . . . . **25.00**
Registration Card, Official Boy Scout's, bi–fold,
    Rockwell illus front cov of Boy Scout, Cub Scout, and
    Sea Scout with flags, scouting trail banner bottom
    illus, orig envelope, dated Feb 1947, 5 x 4" **15.00**
Sheet Music, *Family Sing–a–Long with Mitch*, 1962 . . . . **15.00**
Stein, For a Good Boy, Rockwell Museum **95.00**

ROOKWOOD

In 1880 Cincinnatian Maria Longworth Nichols established Rookwood, a pottery named after her father's estate. She and a number of other Cincinnati society women designed and produced the first forms and decorative motifs.

Standard Ware was extremely popular in the 1880s and 90s. It was produced by applying an underglaze slip painting to a white or yellow clay body and then glazing the entire piece with a glossy, yellow–tinted glaze.

In 1904 Stanley Burt developed Vellum ware, a glaze that was a cross between high glaze and matte glaze. By 1905 a matte glaze replaced the company's high–glazed wares. Ombroso, a matte–glaze line, was introduced in 1910 to mark the company's 30th anniversary. In 1915 the company introduced a soft porcelain line featuring gloss and matte glazes.

By the early 1930s, the company was experiencing financial difficulties and filed for bankruptcy in 1941. A group of investors bought the company. A shortage of supplies during World War II forced ownership to be transferred to the Institution Divi Thomae Foundation of the Roman Catholic Archdiocese of Cincinnati in 1941. Sperti, Inc., operated the company for the Archdiocese. By the end of the 1940s the company was again experiencing financial difficulties.

In 1954 Edgar Heltman took over, shifting production to commercial ware and accessory pieces. Production ceased briefly in 1955. In 1956 James Smith bought the company from Sperti. Herschede Hall Clock Company bought Rookwood in 1959, moved its operations to Starksville, Missouri, and finally ceased operations for good in 1967.

Rookwood pieces are well marked. Many have five marking symbols: (1) clay or body mark, (2) size mark, (3) decorator mark, (4) date mark, and (5) factory mark.

References: Susan and Al Bagdade, *Warman's American Pottery and Porcelain*, Wallace–Homestead, Krause Publications, 1994; Anita J. Ellis, *Rookwood Pottery: The Glaze Lines*, Schiffer Publishing, 1995; Ralph and Terry Kovel, *Kovels' American Art Pottery: The Collector's Guide to Makers, Marks and Factory Histories*, Crown Publishers, 1993; L–W Book Sales (ed.), *A Price Guide to Rookwood*, L–W Book Sales, 1993.

Collectors' Club: American Art Pottery Assoc, PO Box 834, Westport, MA 02790-0697.

Ashtray, devil's head, black ext, green int, 2 handle–type
    ears, lion mark on bottom, 1930, 5½" w **$230.00**
Bookends, pr, elephants, shape #2444C, white glaze,
    5¾" h **285.00**
Bowl, porcelain, stylized red bellflowers and green
    leaves on oatmeal ground, Lorinda Epply, imp flame
    mark, "LE/XXVI/2287" **475.00**
Box, ftd, triangular, abstract molded dec, triangular
    finial, powder blue high gloss glaze, Louise Abel,
    1932, 5¼" h **225.00**
Bud Vase, tapered, blue flowers and green leaves on
    feathered pink ground, wax matte, Sallie Coyne, imp
    flame mark, "XXX/SEC/2307," 7¼ x 3¼" **500.00**
Inkwell, figural sphinx, molded pen tray, variegated
    straw colors, gray matte glaze, Louise Abel, 1920,
    8½" l, 9" h **25.00**
Paperweight, figural elephant, matte olive glaze, 4" h **250.00**
Rose Jar, powder pink, plum, blossoms around shoulder,
    E T Hurley, 5½" h **350.00**

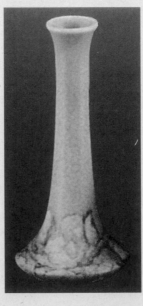

Bud Vase, wax matte, blue flowers, green leaves, feathered pink ground, imp flame mark, sgd "XXX/SEC/2307," Sally Coyne, 1930, 7¼" h, 3¼" w, $550.00. Photo courtesy David Rago Auctions.

Vase, porcelain, gray and blue geometric design on white ground, flame mark, sgd "LII/S/REM," Ruben Earl Menzel, 1952, 7³/₄" h, 4¹/₄" w, $495.00. Photo courtesy David Rago Auctions.

Trivet, southern bell, wearing hoop skirt, parasol, pastel
  colors, 5¹/₂" sq 225.00
Vase, baluster form, bleeding hearts, pale pink, blue and
  green, Edward Diers, 6³/₄" h 800.00
Vase, blue flowers and green leaves on blue and pink
  ground, wax matte, Margaret H McDonald, imp flame
  mark, "MHM/XXXI/915E," 6 x 4¹/₄" 700.00
Vase, blue gooseberries and amber leaves, purple to red
  to green ground, wax matte, Elizabeth Lincoln,
  imp flame mark, "XXVI/2900/LN," 1926, 9¹/₂ x 5¹/₂". 900.00
Vase, bulbous, 2 handles, slip painted blue thistle on
  one side, yellow lillies on other, mottled dark rose
  ground, wax matte, imp flame mark, "XXV/2784/X/
  ESM," 10¹/₄ x 8¹/₂" 700.00
Vase, bulbous, 4 sided, red and blue flowers on feath-
  ered blue ground, wax matte, E Abel, imp flame mark,
  "EA/XXIV/2762," 3³/₄ x 4" 425.00
Vase, bulbous, porcelain, flaring rim, brown on frothy
  cream and yellow ground, squeezebag dec, William
  Hentschel, imp flame mark, 5 x 4¹/₄". 650.00
Vase, coupe shape, porcelain, brown and blue squeeze-
  bag dec on lime green ground, W Rehm, imp flame
  mark, "WR/XLIV/2189," 6¹/₂ x 5¹/₄" 475.00
Vase, flared, blue flowers and green leaves on creamy
  yellow ground, wax matte, Sallie Coyne, imp flame
  mark, "XXXI/SEC/1369E," 7 x 4" 650.00
Vase, flared mouth, tapering toward foot, molded classical women, deep mauve ext, turquoise int, 13" h 200.00
Vase, olive green over red, pink, and yellow floral stylized dec, blue outline, lavender ground, Elizabeth
  Lincoln, 4³/₄" h 400.00
Vase, pink berries and green leaves on feathered blue
  ground, wax matte, imp flame mark, "XXVII/KJ/926E,"
  6¹/₄ x 3¹/₄" 450.00
Vase, red and yellow flowers against blue field on mus-
  tard ground, wax matte, Cora Crofton, imp flame
  mark, "XXIII/605," 5¹/₄ x 3¹/₂" 550.00
Vase, sprig of stylized white and yellow apple blossoms
  on light blue to pink ground, vellum, E T Hurley, imp
  flame mark, "XXVII/ETH/2721" 550.00
Vase, squat, bulbous, red and green flowers and leaves
  on feathered blue matte ground, Elizabeth Lincoln,
  imp flame mark, "LNL/XX/1110/V," 4 x 6". 650.00

Vase, red and yellow peony, green leaves, pink–blue
  ground, wax matte, shape #1369C, Elizabeth Lincoln,
  1928, 11¹/₄" h 1,000.00
Vase, teal green, deep rose, and brown, stylized floral
  dec, blue outline, deep rose rim, shoulder with mustard highlights, wax matte, WE Hentschel, 5¹/₄" h 450.00

ROSE BOWLS

A rose bowl is a small round or ovoid shaped bowl with a crimped, petaled, pinched, or scalloped opening at its top. It served as a container for fragrant potpourri or rose pedals.

Rose bowls are found in a wide variety of material with glass being the most common. A favorite giftware accessory, rose bowls often incorporate the best design qualities and materials of their era. Rose bowls are found in virtually every type of art glass.

The popularity of rose bowls extended from the second half of the Victorian era through the 1950s. The form is still made today.

Collectors' Club: Rose Bowl Collectors, PO Box 244, Danielsville, PA 18038.

Amberina, Hobnail, 6" h **$275.00**
Amethyst, fluted top, squatty, enameled dec 95.00
Amethyst, squatty, enameled dec, fluted top 100.00
Blue Opalescent, Opalescent Open, pedestal base 50.00
Burmese, hp roses, Fenton 70.00
Carnival, amethyst, Hobnail. 450.00
Cranberry, Arboresque, crimped top, opaque white
  design, crackle finish 125.00
Cranberry, lacy enamel dec, Baccarat. 150.00
Cranberry Opalescent, Coin Dot, large. 95.00
Cranberry Opalescent, Hobnail, Fenton 130.00
Cranberry Opalescent, enameled forget–me–nots 75.00
Crystal, gold enameling. 95.00
Crystal, Scalloped Six Points, George Duncan Sons & Co 50.00
Crystal, spherical, diagonal optics, Continental. 60.00
Crystal, Torpedo, Thompson. 85.00
Custard, Beaded Cable 65.00
Frosted Glass, Art Deco, enameled intertwining yellow
  and green design, 6¹/₂" h 55.00
Frosty Blue, opaque white overlay, cameo carved flow-
  ers and scrolling design, cut scalloped top 425.00
Green Opalescent, Beaded Drape 30.00
Green Opalescent, white opalescent swirl, collar 50.00
Green Satin, Shell and Seaweed, gold enameling 200.00
Multicolor Spatter 60.00
Olive Green Satin, molded roses, smooth rim. 85.00
Orange Iridescent, Honeycomb 350.00
Peach Satin, enameled and hp flowers, tall. 300.00
Pink and Yellow Spatter, tall 65.00
Pink Opalescent, pink and rose pansies, green leaves,
  cream ground, sgd, Smith Bros. 300.00
Pink Satin, Maize 140.00
Ruby Flashed, Heart with Thumbprint, Tarentum Glass 100.00
Ruby Flashed, Deer and Castle, clear and frosted,
  Bohemian 225.00
Ruby Flashed, Red Block 75.00
Sapphire Blue, 12–crimp top, MOP, shaded pink 250.00
Spangled, 8–crimp top, mica coral–like dec, cased deep
  rose, white int 110.00
Turquoise Satin 110.00
Yellow Satin, stenciled portrait, Victorian woman 125.00

ROSEMEADE

Rosemeade's origins began with Laura Taylor, a North Dakota studio potter who demonstrated her skills at the North Dakota Building at the 1939 New York World's Fair. Robert J. Hughes, president of the Greater North Dakota Association, saw Taylor's demonstration and organized the Wahpeton Pottery Company in 1940. Laura Taylor, a partner, was secretary/treasurer.

The company's products were marketed under the trade name Rosemeade in honor of Rosemeade Township, Taylor's birthplace. Vera Gethman and Taylor were the company's two principal designers. Glaze development fell under the watchful eyes of Howard Lewis and Taylor. The company produced a wide range of objects from commemorative and souvenir pieces to household and kitchenware.

In 1953 the company became Rosemeade Potteries. Howard Lewis left Rosemeade in 1956, replaced by Joe McLaughlin, who previously worked for Red Wing Potteries. McLaughlin began importing clay from Kentucky, introduced decal decoration, and incorporated the artistic designs of Les Kouba into the line.

Laura Taylor died in 1959. The company continued operating until 1961. Cheap Japanese copies made from molds cast from Rosemeade pieces and a new minimum wage law contributed to the company's closing. The salesroom remained open until 1964.

References: Darlene Hurst Dommel, *Collector's Encyclopedia of the Dakota Potteries: Identification & Values,* Collector Books, 1996; Harvey Duke, *The Official Price Guide to Pottery and Porcelain, Eighth Edition,* House of Collectibles, 1995.

Wall Pocket, 4–H Club, green, 4¼" h, $85.00.

Ashtray, applied dove, "North Dakota Peace Garden State"	**$165.00**
Ashtray, blue, round, white raised wheat dec	**40.00**
Ashtray, Minnesota State shape, "Minnesota Centennial"	**45.00**
Ashtray, pony, large	**110.00**
Bank, goldfish	**495.00**
Bank, rhinoceros	**285.00**
Bell, flamingo	**80.00**
Bookends, pr, Art Deco wolfhounds	**400.00**
Bookends, pr, bear, 4" h	**325.00**
Bowl, thrown, flared rim, pink, 7"	**45.00**
Bowl, Viking ship	**85.00**
Candle Holder, heart shape	**25.00**
Casserole, chicken	**185.00**
Cheese Dish, emb mouse in center, chartreuse, 6"	**50.00**
Cotton Dispenser, figural rabbit, white, hp pink ears int and eyes, 5" h	**135.00**
Cranberry Dish, spoon notch	**130.00**
Creamer and Sugar, blue petal	**50.00**
Creamer and Sugar, corn	**40.00**
Creamer and Sugar, turkey	**140.00**
Dish, cov, turkey	**65.00**
Dish, wheat design, 6¾" l	**75.00**
Figurine, blue button shoe	**45.00**
Figurine, Dutch shoe, 2 x 5½"	**45.00**
Figurine, elephant	**65.00**
Figurine, mountain goat, standing, on base	**155.00**
Figurine, pony, 4" h	**130.00**
Figurine, skunk, pr	**25.00**
Hors d'oeuvre Holder, figural fish	**65.00**
Incense Burner, log cabin	**65.00**
Jam Jar, barrel shape	**45.00**
Mug, brown, Minnesota Centennial, 3" h	**45.00**

Nut Cup, purple	25.00
Pin, mallard	375.00
Pin, prairie rose	375.00
Pitcher, braided handle, 3¾" h	50.00
Pitcher, raised cows dec, Elwood Dairy adv, 6" h	125.00
Planter, deer on log	55.00
Planter, dove, 4½ x 6"	140.00
Planter, grapes	30.00
Planter, peacock, 7½" h	175.00
Plate, mouse	40.00
Salt and Pepper Shakers, pr, chickens, 3¾" h	65.00
Salt and Pepper Shakers, pr, Chinese ring–necked pheasants	30.00
Salt and Pepper Shakers, pr, cucumbers	50.00
Salt and Pepper Shakers, pr, dog head	45.00
Salt and Pepper Shakers, pr, ducks, 3½" h	65.00
Salt and Pepper Shakers, pr, fish, pink	50.00
Salt and Pepper Shakers, pr, Fox Terriers	35.00
Salt and Pepper Shakers, pr, Greyhounds	35.00
Salt and Pepper Shakers, pr, leaping deer	60.00
Salt and Pepper Shakers, pr, quail, feather top knot, 2½" h	85.00
Salt and Pepper Shakers, pr, Scotties	35.00
Salt and Pepper Shakers, pr, turkeys	65.00
Spoon Rest, Minnesota Centennial	45.00
Spoon Rest, pansy	50.00
Spoon Rest, wild rose	55.00
Tea Bell, tulip shape, 3¾" h	130.00
Television Lamp, Palomino, standing, green foliage, 9½"	475.00
Tidbit Tray, pheasant	40.00
Tile, pheasant, wooden frame, Les Kouba, 8" d	85.00
Vase, 2 color swirl, top and bottom rim, mkd "North Dakota Rosemeade," 4" h	130.00
Vase, doe	35.00
Vase, pink, ruffled rim, 4" h	40.00
Wall Plaque, oval, applied fish, 3½ x 6"	175.00
Wall Pocket, deer, 5" h	65.00
Wall Vase, antique gray, bisque lining, raised Egyptian design, 5½" h	175.00

ROSEVILLE POTTERY

George Young purchased the J. B. Owens Pottery, renaming it the Roseville Pottery, in 1892. Cooking utensils, cuspidors, flowerpots, and umbrella stands were among the company's earliest products. Around the turn of the century, Roseville purchased the Midland Pottery plant in Roseville (1898), moved the company's main office to Zanesville, Ohio, bought Peters and Reed, and acquired the Muskingum Stoneware plant (1901).

Rozane, the company's first artware line, evolved into a general term used to describe all the company's art or prestige lines. John Herold established Roseville's commercial artware department in 1903. Artware, including dresser sets, juvenile ware, tea sets, and smoker sets dominated production until the late 1910s.

Roseville closed two of its factories in 1910. Fire destroyed another in 1917. In 1918 Russell Young replaced his father as manager; Frank Ferrel replaced Harry Rhead as art director. Ferrel shifted the company's production into industrial artware, resulting in the introduction of more than 80 new lines.

In 1932 the firm became Roseville Pottery, Inc. The company experienced a major slump in sales following World War II. New industrial artware lines failed to halt the decline. Mosaic Tile Company bought the Roseville plant in 1954. Production of Roseville ceased.

References: Virginia Buxton, *Roseville Pottery For Love…Or Money,* Tymbre Hill Publishing, 1996; Sharon and Bob Huxford, *The Collectors Encyclopedia of Roseville Pottery, First Series* (1976, 1997 value update), *Second Series* (1980, 1997 value update), Collector Books; Ralph and Terry Kovel, *Kovel's American Art Pottery: The Collector's Guide to Makers, Marks and Factory Histories,* Crown Publishers, 1993; Randall B. Monsen, *Collectors' Compendium of Roseville Pottery and Price Guide, Vol. 1,* Monsen and Baer, 1995.

Periodical: *Pottery Collectors Express,* PO Box 221, Mayview, MO 64071.

Collectors' Clubs: American Art Pottery Assoc, PO Box 834, Westport, MA 02790-0697; Roseville's of the Past, PO Box 656, Clarcona, FL 32710.

REPRODUCTION ALERT: Cheap reproduction Roseville pieces are surfacing at auctions and flea markets. Distinguishing characteristics include glaze colors and crude decorative techniques.

Ashtray, Pinecone, blue **$125.00**
Ashtray, Zephyr Lily, blue **75.00**
Basket, Blackberry, hanging, orig chains, 4¼ x 6¾" **1,400.00**
Basket, Bittersweet, green #810–10 . . . . **180.00**
Basket, Bushberry, hanging, pink **145.00**
Basket, Foxglove **90.00**
Basket, Freesia, hanging, green **235.00**
Basket, Fuschia, hanging, brown **200.00**
Basket, Magnolia, brown, #384–8 . . . . **80.00**
Basket, Mostique, hanging, 6½ x 6½" **350.00**
Basket, Peony, pink, #278–10 . . . . **140.00**
Basket, Pinecone, brown, raised mark **400.00**
Basket, Pinecone, hanging, blue, 5½ x 8" **700.00**
Basket, Snowberry, blue **150.00**
Basket, Tourist, hanging, no chains, 4½ x 7¼" **450.00**
Basket, Vista, hanging, 4¼ x 8" **350.00**
Basket, Zephyr Lily, brown **90.00**

Basket, Zephyr Lily, hanging, brown **210.00**
Bookends, pr, Apple Blossom, green, #326–6 . . . . **125.00**
Bookends, pr, Gardenia **165.00**
Bookends, pr, Pinecone, blue **145.00**
Bowl, Baneda, pink **175.00**
Bowl, Baneda, pink, 2 handles, 3¼ x 10½" **325.00**
Bowl, Clematis, brown, #485–10 . . . . **80.00**
Bowl, Earlham, 2 handles, 4 x 9¾" **300.00**
Bowl, Earlham, 4 sided, flaring, 2 handles, 4 x 9¾" **275.00**
Bowl, Ferrella, brown, oval, ftd, 5½" h **250.00**
Bowl, Florentine, 7" d **75.00**
Bowl, Imperial I, ftd **60.00**
Bowl, Imperial II, yellow and blue crystalline, 5 x 12½" **500.00**
Bowl, Montacello, oblong, 2 handles, black decal, 2¾ x 13" **250.00**
Bowl, Pinecone, blue, #179–9 . . . . **145.00**
Bowl, Pinecone, 3 ftd, blue, oval, 4¼ x 13" **750.00**
Bowl, Windsor, orange, 2 handles, 6¼" h **175.00**
Bud Vase, Pinecone, 7½ x 5" **375.00**
Bud Vase, Zephyr Lily, 7" h **90.00**
Candleholders, pr, Carnelian II **130.00**
Candleholders, pr, Clematis, brown, #1154–2 . . . . **50.00**
Candlesticks, pr, Dahlrose, 2 handles, 3½ x 5½" **175.00**
Candleholders, pr, Fuschia, green, #1133–5 . . . . **50.00**
Candleholders, pr, Lily, #1161–2 . . . . **45.00**
Candleholders, pr, Zephyr Lily, green, #1163 . . . . **80.00**
Candlesticks, pr, Freesia, brown, #1161 . . . . **135.00**
Candlesticks, set of 3, brown, 2 handles, 5 x 3¼" **250.00**
Centerpiece Bowl, oval, Topeo **100.00**
Centerpiece Bowl, Ferrella, attached frog, 5 x 9½" **150.00**
Compote, Florentine **35.00**
Console Bowl, Freesia, brown, #469-14, 16" **140.00**
Console Bowl, Teasel, beige, #345–12 . . . . **50.00**
Cornucopia, Columbine, 7" h **70.00**
Cornucopia, Foxglove, blue, #166–6 . . . . **50.00**
Cornucopia, Snowberry, 6" h **50.00**
Ewer, Foxglove, blue, #5–10 . . . . **150.00**
Ewer, Gardenia, tan, #618, 15" h **230.00**
Ewer, Pinecone, brown, 10 x 6½" **375.00**
Floor Vase, Bushberry, brown, 12½" h **230.00**

Basket, Magnolia, brown, 386–12, $100.00.

Floor Vase, Visa, 14¹/₂ x 7¹/₂"........................ **600.00**
Floor Vase, Wisteria, bottle shape, 2 handled, 15¹/₂ x 7"... **2,500.00**
Flowerpot and Saucer, Bushberry, 5" h............... **180.00**
Gravy Boat, Raymor, terra cotta.................... **20.00**
Jardiniere, Blackberry, small, foil label, 5¹/₄ x 6¹/₄"........ **550.00**
Jardiniere, Cherry Blossom, 2 handles, foil label, 8¹/₄ x
  12"... **1,400.00**
Jardiniere, Jonquil, 2 handles, black label, 8¹/₄ x 10³/₄"..... **450.00**
Jardiniere, Pinecone, blue, 2 handles, 8 x 10"........... **550.00**
Jardiniere, Sunflower, 6 x 8¹/₄"..................... **600.00**
Jardiniere and Pedestal, Columbine, blue, #655–4........ **70.00**
Jardiniere and Pedestal, Donatello, 22" h.............. **600.00**
Jardiniere and Pedestal, Futura, pink leaves on gray
  ground.. **900.00**
Jardiniere and Pedestal, Sunflower................... **80.00**
Lamp, Carnelian II, blue, 2 handles, molded hold in cen-
  ter of bottom, black label, 12¹/₄ x 8³/₄"............. **750.00**
Mugs, set of 4, Pinecone, single twig pattern, raised
  marks, 4¹/₄ x 4¹/₂"............................. **550.00**
Pitcher, Freesia, green, #20, 10".................... **215.00**
Pitcher, Holland, 6¹/₂" h......................... **225.00**
Pitcher, Magnolia, #388–6........................ **115.00**
Pitcher, Pinecone, blue, raised mark, 10¹/₄ x 7"........ **200.00**
Pitcher, Pinecone, bulbous, brown, imp mark, 8 x 8"..... **700.00**
Pitcher, Pinecone, bulbous, green, 8¹/₄" h............ **350.00**
Planter, Peony, #387, 8" l........................ **90.00**
Planter, Water Lily, hanging, brown................. **165.00**
Tray, double, Pinecone, green, 13".................. **265.00**
Urn, Baneda, foil label, 12¹/₂ x 9"................. **1,500.00**
Urn, Carnelian II, red, neoclassical, 2 handles, 15 x
  9¹/₂"... **1,700.00**
Urn, Falline, brown, foil label, 8¹/₄ x 6"............. **650.00**
Vase, Baneda, pink, 4¹/₂" h....................... **165.00**
Vase, Baneda, pink, pear shape, 2 handles, 6¹/₄ x 4"..... **250.00**
Vase, Blackberry, bulbous, 2 handles, black label, 5 x 5".. **300.00**
Vase, Blackberry, ovoid, 2 handles.................. **550.00**
Vase, Blackberry, squat base, 2 handles, stovepipe neck,
  black label, 5¹/₄ x 5"........................... **500.00**
Vase, Blackberry, pear shape, 5¹/₄ x 4¹/₄"............ **400.00**
Vase, Carnelian II, ovoid, pink and green, 14 x 7¹/₄"..... **1,100.00**
Vase, Carnelian II, red, 5" h...................... **100.00**
Vase, Cherry Blossom, pink, 2 handles, 8¹/₄ x 5¹/₄"...... **550.00**
Vase, Cherry Blossom, pink, squat, 2 handles, 5 x 5"..... **600.00**
Vase, Dahlrose, bulbous, 2 handles, 8¹/₄ x 7"......... **200.00**
Vase, Earlham, brown, 4 sided, closed in rim, square,
  9 x 6".. **500.00**
Vase, Earlham, bulbous, 2 handles, 7 x 8"............ **375.00**
Vase, Falline, brown, ovoid, 2 handles.............. **600.00**
Vase, Falline, ribbed, 2 handles, 9 x 7³/₄"............ **500.00**
Vase, ftd, Clemana, 2 handles, 6¹/₄ x 3¹/₄"........... **125.00**
Vase, ftd, Morning Glory, white, 2 handles, 8¹/₂ x 7".... **450.00**
Vase, Fuschia, blue, #895, 7" h.................... **120.00**
Vase, Futura, beehive shape, 2 handles, 7 x 5¹/₂"....... **1,100.00**
Vase, Futura, mottled blue–green glaze, squat base,
  ribbed middle, flaring neck, foil label, 10¹/₂ x 7¹/₄".... **1,000.00**
Vase, Imperial II, bulbous, blue and gold, 11¹/₄ x 6¹/₂".... **650.00**
Vase, Iris, #917–6............................. **80.00**
Vase, Jonquil, bulbous, 2 handles, black label, 9¹/₄ x
  6¹/₄"... **350.00**
Vase, Laurel, yellow............................. **5.00**
Vase, Luffa, barrel shape, green, 2 handles, 9¹/₂ x 7"..... **150.00**
Vase, Mayfair, 10" h............................ **70.00**
Vase, Pinecone, blue, #711–10.................... **430.00**
Vase, Pinecone, ftd, brown, 2 handles............... **500.00**

Dish, Water Lily, blue, 443–12, 12" l, $104.50. Photo courtesy Collectors Auction Services.

Vase, Pinecone, ftd, green, cylindrical, 2 handles, 8¹/₂
  x 3"... **275.00**
Vase, Savona, green, 12" h....................... **145.00**
Vase, Sunflower, bulbous, 8 x 6³/₄"................ **550.00**
Vase, Sunflower, flaring, 10 x 7¹/₂"................ **650.00**
Vase, Sunflower, squat, 2 handles, 5 x 5".......... **450.00**
Vase, Sunflower, tapered, 2 handles, 5 x 4¹/₄"........ **425.00**
Vase, Wincraft.................................. **30.00**
Vase, Windsor, bulbous, orange, 3" h.............. **175.00**
Vase, Wisteria, blue, conical, 2 handles, 9¹/₄ x 6¹/₂"..... **900.00**
Vase, Wisteria, brown, bulbous, 2 handles, 5 x 6¹/₂"..... **225.00**
Vase, Wisteria, conical, 2 handles, 8¹/₄ x 4¹/₂"........ **575.00**
Vessel, Baneda, green, squat, 2 handled, foil label,
  5 x 7".. **550.00**
Vessel, Ferrella, brown, squat, 2 handles, 6¹/₄" h....... **240.00**
Vessel, Futura, ftd, pink and green, 4 sided, 2 handles,
  8¹/₄ x 6¹/₄".................................. **650.00**
Vessel, Imperial II, conical, ridged, yellow and purple
  mottled glaze, 6 x 5³/₄"........................ **200.00**
Vessel, Laurel, persimmon, 2 handles, 6¹/₂ x 6³/₄"...... **300.00**
Vessel, Panel, brown, 4 x 7"..................... **175.00**
Vessel, Sunflower, 2 handles, 5 x 4".............. **425.00**
Vessel, Wisteria, 2 handles, foil label, 6 x 8¹/₂"....... **500.00**
Wall Pocket, Baneda, green, foil label, 8¹/₂ x 7³/₄"...... **1,200.00**
Wall Pocket, Cherry Blossom, 8 x 5¹/₄"............. **1,600.00**
Wall Pocket, Clematis, brown..................... **100.00**
Wall Pocket, Dahlrose, 10" h..................... **325.00**
Wall Pocket, Luffa, brown, 8¹/₄ x 6".............. **700.00**
Wall Pocket, Mostique, 10¹/₂" l.................. **150.00**
Wall Pocket, Wisteria, pear shape, 2 handles, 6 x 4¹/₂".... **350.00**
Wall Pocket, Wisteria, flaring, 8¹/₄ x 7"............ **1,400.00**

ROYAL CHINA

Although the Royal China Company purchased the former E. H. Sebring Company (Sebring, Ohio) plant in 1933, extensive renovation delayed production until 1934. Initially, Royal China produced mainly overglaze decal ware. Kenneth Doyle's underglaze stamping machine, developed for Royal China in 1948, revolutionized the industry, allowing for the inexpensive production of underglaze ware. By 1950 Royal China eliminated its decal ware.

The company produced a wide range of dinnerware lines. Colonial Homestead (early 1950s), Currier and Ives (1949/50), Old Curiosity Shop, and Willow Ware (1940s) are among the most popular. Royal Oven Ware was introduced in the 1940s.

In 1964 Royal China purchased the French–Saxon China Company, operating it as a wholly owned subsidiary. The Jeannette Corporation acquired Royal China in 1969. In 1970 fire destroyed the plant and Royal China's operations were moved to the French–Saxon plant, also located in Sebring, Ohio.

The company changed hands several times in the 1970s and 80s, being purchased by the Coca–Cola Bottling Company (1976), J. Corporation of Boston (1981), and Nordic Capitol of New York (1984). Each owner continued to manufacture ware under the Royal China brand name. Operations ceased in 1986.

References: Eldon R. Aupperle, *A Collector's Guide For Currier & Ives Dinnerware*, published by author, 1996; Susan and Al Bagdade, *Warman's American Pottery and Porcelain*, Wallace–Homestead, Krause Publications, 1994; Harvey Duke, *The Official Price Guide to Pottery and Porcelain, Eighth Edition*, House of Collectibles, 1995.

Collectors' Club: Currier & Ives Dinnerware Collectors Club, RD 2, Box 394, Hollidaysburg, PA 16648.

Blue Willow, berry bowl, 5½"	$4.50
Blue Willow, bread and butter plate	3.00
Blue Willow, cereal bowl, 6¼"	12.00
Blue Willow, creamer and sugar, cov	20.00
Blue Willow, platter, oval, 13" l	32.00
Blue Willow, platter, round, 12" d	25.00
Colonial Homestead, bread and butter plate, 6" d	2.50
Colonial Homestead, cup and saucer	5.00
Colonial Homestead, dinner plate	4.00
Colonial Homestead, salad plate, 7" d	2.50
Colonial Homestead, vegetable bowl, 9" d	8.00
Currier & Ives, ashtray, blue	10.00
Currier & Ives, baker	15.00
Currier & Ives, bread and butter plate, blue	5.00
Currier & Ives, bread and butter plate, blue, 6½"	3.00
Currier & Ives, cake plate, tab handle, blue	22.00
Currier & Ives, calendar plate, blue	28.00
Currier & Ives, candle lamp, base only, blue	85.00
Currier & Ives, casserole, cov, blue	90.00
Currier & Ives, cereal bowl, blue	14.00
Currier & Ives, coffee mug, blue	45.00
Currier & Ives, creamer, blue	5.00

Currier & Ives, creamer and sugar, cov, blue	24.00
Currier & Ives, cup and saucer, blue	4.00
Currier & Ives, custard, milk glass	5.00
Currier & Ives, dinner plate, blue, 10½" d	5.00
Currier & Ives, dinner plate, pink, 10½" d	15.00
Currier & Ives, fruit bowl, blue	4.00
Currier & Ives, gravy boat and liner, blue	20.00
Currier & Ives, iced tea tumbler	15.00
Currier & Ives, juice tumbler	12.00
Currier & Ives, mixing bowl, 6"	20.00
Currier & Ives, old fashion	10.00
Currier & Ives, pie plate, blue, 10"	20.00
Currier & Ives, platter, blue, 13"	28.00
Currier & Ives, salad plate, blue	9.00
Currier & Ives, salt and pepper shakers, pr, blue	25.00
Currier & Ives, soup bowl, blue	14.00
Currier & Ives, sugar, cov, blue	13.00
Currier & Ives, tumbler, milk glass	5.00
Currier & Ives, vegetable bowl, blue, 9" d	20.00
Currier & Ives, vegetable bowl, 2 part, blue	12.00
Currier & Ives, water tumbler	12.00
Memory Lane, berry bowl, pink, small	4.00
Memory Lane, bread and butter plate, pink	2.75
Memory Lane, butter, cov, pink, bottom crazed, ¼ lb	25.00
Memory Lane, cake plate, handled	15.00
Memory Lane, chowder mug, pink	12.00
Memory Lane, dinner plate, pink	5.00
Memory Lane, gravy and underplate	20.00
Memory Lane, luncheon plate, 9" d	7.00
Memory Lane, salad plate, 7" d	6.00
Memory Lane, soup bowl, pink	7.50
Memory Lane, vegetable bowl, cov, 10" d	25.00
Old Curiosity Shop, ashtray	8.00
Old Curiosity Shop, berry bowl	6.00
Old Curiosity Shop, bread and butter plate	3.00
Old Curiosity Shop, casserole, cov	65.00
Old Curiosity Shop, creamer	5.00
Old Curiosity Shop, cup	4.00
Old Curiosity Shop, dinner plate	10.00
Old Curiosity Shop, gravy boat	11.00
Old Curiosity Shop, place setting, 5 pcs	26.00
Old Curiosity Shop, plate, 12"	24.00
Old Curiosity Shop, platter, oval	24.00
Old Curiosity Shop, saucer	1.00
Old Curiosity Shop, soup	8.00
Old Curiosity Shop, sugar	9.00
Old Curiosity Shop, vegetable bowl, large	24.00

ROYAL COPENHAGEN

In the mid–18th century Europe's royal families competed with each other to see who would be the first to develop a porcelain formula. In 1772 Franz Heinrich Muller, a Danish pharmacist and chemist, discovered a formula for hard paste porcelain. Muller submitted his samples to the Queen Dowager. She was so delighted that she christened his firm "The Danish Porcelain Factory." Although founded privately in 1775, the Danish monarchy fully controlled the firm by 1779. Three wavy lines were chosen as the firm's trademark to symbolize the seafaring tradition of the Danes.

The company proved a drain on the Danish monarchy's finances. In 1867 A. Falch purchased the company under the condition that he be allowed to retain the use of "Royal" in the firm's title. Falch sold the company to Philip Schou in 1882.

Blue Willow, platter, round, 12¼" d, $25.00.

In 1885 Arnold Krog became art director of Royal Copenhagen and developed underglaze painting. Only one color is used. Shading is achieved by varying the thickness of the pigment layers and firing the painted plate at a temperature of 2,640 degrees Fahrenheit. Krog revitalized the company. In 1902 Dalgas became art director and introduced the blue and white Christmas Plate series in 1908.

Today the Royal Copenhagen Group also includes Bing and Grondahl. The firm is noted for its extensive dinnerware and gift-ware lines.

Reference: Robert J. Heritage, *Royal Copenhagen Porcelain: Animals and Figurines*, Schiffer Publishing, 1997.

Note: For additional references see Limited Edition Collectibles.

Figurine, Airedale, #1652 . . . . **$225.00**
Figurine, boy wearing raincoat, #3556 . . . . 225.00
Figurine, Brindle Boxer 225.00
Figurine, Bull Terrier, #3280 . . . . 195.00
Figurine, girl on rock 70.00
Figurine, girl with doll, #3539 . . . . 250.00
Figurine, girl with goose, #528 . . . . 200.00
Figurine, long–eared rabbit, #518 . . . . 165.00
Figurine, lovebirds, #402 . . . . 75.00
Figurine, man in Scandanavian dress selling produce,
    #12103 . . . . 300.00
Figurine, man on stump, #1738 . . . . 110.00
Figurine, man sitting on post, looking at rabbit, #456 . . . . . 255.00
Figurine, man with parrot. #752 . . . . 430.00
Figurine, nude on rock, #4027 . . . . 150.00
Figurine, otter, tan, #2936 . . . . 270.00
Figurine, parakeet on purple eggplant 65.00
Figurine, penguin, #3003 . . . . 50.00
Figurine, rabbit, #4705 . . . . 45.00
Figurine, reclining foal, #5691 . . . . 150.00
Figurine, sandman, #1145 . . . . 165.00
Figurine, snowman 95.00
Figurine, soldier and witch 450.00
Figurine, 2 Scandinavian women 25.00
Figurine, Wire Terrier, #3156 . . . . 175.00

Figurine, gray and cream colors, mkd "RC Denmark," dated 1925, 12" h, $750.00.

Plate, Admiring the Christmas Tree, 1981 . . . . **55.00**
Plate, Blackbird, 1966 . . . . 30.00
Plate, Bell Tower of Old Church in Jutland, 1942 . . . . 300.00
Plate, Boeslunde Church, Zealand, 1950 . . . . 175.00
Plate, Choosing the Christmas Tree, 1979 . . . . 60.00
Plate, Christmas Scene in Main Street, 1937 . . . . 135.00
Plate, Danish Watermill, 1976 . . . . 20.00
Plate, Fano Girl 185.00
Plate, Fishing Boats On the Way to the Harbor, 1930 . . . . . . 80.00
Plate, Flight of Holy Family to Egypt, 1943 . . . . 425.00
Plate, The Good Shepherd, 1940 . . . . 300.00
Plate, The Hermitage Castle, 1934 . . . . 115.00
Plate, Mother and Child, 1931 . . . . 90.00
Plate, Winter Twilight, 1974 . . . . 25.00
Plate, Zealand Village Church, 1946 . . . . 150.00
Vase, blue and white, lace pattern, 1926, 5¼" h 45.00
Vase, blue and white, lace pattern, 1935, 2¾" h 85.00

ROYAL COPLEY

Royal Copley and Royal Windsor are tradenames of the Spaulding China Company. Royal Copley, representing approximately 85% of all Spaulding production, was sold mostly through chain stores. Royal Windsor items were sold to the florist trade.

Spaulding China, Sebring, Ohio, began operations in 1942. The company chose names that had an English air, e.g., Royal Copley and Royal Windsor. Even marketing terms such as Crown Assortment and Oxford Assortment continued this theme.

Birds, piggy banks, Oriental boy and girl wall pockets, and roosters were among Royal Copley's biggest sellers. The small birds originally retailed for 25¢. Pieces were marked with a paper label.

Cheap Japanese imports and labor difficulties plagued Spaulding throughout the post–war period. In 1957 Morris Feinberg retired, contracting with nearby China Craft to fill Spaulding's remaining orders. Initially Spaudling was sold to a Mr. Shiffman, who made small sinks for mobile homes. After being closed for several years Eugene Meskil of Holiday Designs bought the plant. The company made kitchen ware. Richard C. Durstein of Pittsburgh bought the plant in 1982.

Reference: Mike Schneider, *Royal Copley: Identification and Price Guide*, Schiffer Publishing, 1995.

Newsletter: *The Copley Courier*, 1639 N Catalina St, Burbank, CA 91505.

Ashtray, Bow and Ribbon, 5¾" **$15.00**
Ashtray, straw hat and bow, 5" 10.00
Bank, farmer pig, paper label, 5½" h 30.00
Bank, pig with bow tie, 7½" h 40.00
Creamer, green leaf handle, rose and yellow body, raised
    letters on bottom, 3" h 10.00
Figurine, canary, paper label, 5½" h 25.00
Figurine, cockatoo, paper label, 7¼" h 30.00
Figurine, deer on sled, 6½" h 25.00
Figurine, finch, #2, paper label, 5" h 25.00
Figurine, parrot, yellow, 5" h 12.00
Figurine, sparrow, open beak, 5" h 10.00
Figurine, teddy bear, brown, 5½" h 35.00
Figurine, warbler, 5" h 12.00
Lamp, Colonial gentleman, orig shade 40.00
Lamp, pig, striped shirt, 6½" h 40.00
Lamp Base, deer and fawn on tree trunk, 11" h 30.00

Figurines, hen and rooster, No. 1, 5¹/₂" h hen, 6" h rooster, price for pair, $30.00.

Pitcher, daffodil, yellow and pink, 8" h	32.00
Planter, apple and finch, 6¹/₂" h	18.00
Planter, barefooted boy	18.00
Planter, Chinese boy with big hat, 7¹/₂"	18.00
Planter, coach, 3¹/₄"	12.00
Planter, dog and mailbox, 7³/₄" h	18.00
Planter, double spray, paper label	8.00
Planter, girl wearing hat with wide brim, 7¹/₂" h	30.00
Planter, hat with bow, wide brim, 5¹/₂" h	25.00
Planter, hummingbird, 5¹/₄" h	30.00
Planter, Joyce decal, gold stamp on bottom, 4" h	8.00
Planter, kitten with yarn ball, 8¹/₄" h	25.00
Planter, Linley decal, gold stamp on bottom, 4" h	8.00
Planter, nuthatch, 5¹/₂" h	10.00
Planter, Oriental boy, bamboo sides base, paper label, 7¹/₂" h	22.00
Planter, Oriental girl with wheelbarrow, paper label, 7" h	25.00
Planter, Princess Blackamoor, 8" h	25.00
Planter, pup in basket, 7"	15.00
Planter, reclining poodle, 6¹/₂"	28.00
Planter, rooster and wheelbarrow, paper label, 8" h	55.00
Planter, small rib, raised letters on bottom, 3¹/₂" h	6.00
Planter, teddy bear, black and white, 6¹/₄" h	35.00
Vase, Betty decal, gold stamp on bottom, 8" h	18.00
Vase, cylindrical, floral decal, 8" h	25.00
Vase, figural fish, red outline on fins, blue stripe, white ground, 6"	30.00
Vase, ftd, ivy dec, 8" h	8.00
Vase, sytlized leaf, paper label, 8¹/₂" h	8.00
Vase, trailing leaf and vine	15.00
Window Bow, black floral leaf and stem, paper label, 3¹/₂" l	10.00
Window Box, Harmony, paper label, 4¹/₄" l	8.00

ROYAL DOULTON

In 1815 John Doulton founded the Doulton Lambeth Pottery in Lambeth, London. Utilitarian salt glazed stoneware was the company's product. The firm was known as Doulton and Watts between 1820 and 1853. Henry Doulton, John's second son, joined the firm in 1835.

A connection was formed between the Lambeth School of Art and Doulton in the early 1870s. By 1885 over 250 artists, includ-

ing Arthur and Hannah Barlow and George Tinsworth, were working at Doulton. In 1887 Henry Doulton was knighted by Queen Victoria for his achievements in the ceramic arts.

Henry Doulton acquired the Niles Street pottery in Burslem, Staffordshire in 1877, changing the name to Doulton & Co. in 1882. This plant made high quality porcelain and inexpensive earthenware tableware. Charles Noke joined the firm in 1889, becoming one its most famous designers. Noke introduced Rouge Flambé. In 1901 King Edward VII granted the Royal Warrant of appointment to Doulton. "Royal" has appeared on the company's ware since that date.

Whereas production increased at the Burslem plant during the 20th century, it decreased at the Lambeth plant. By 1925 only twenty–four artists were employed, one of whom was Leslie Harradine, noted for his famed Dickens' characters. Commemorative wares were produced at Lambeth in the 1920s and 30s. Agnete Hoy, famous for her cat figures, worked at Lambeth between 1951 and 1956. Production at the Lambeth plant ended in 1956.

Although Royal Doulton made a full line of tabletop ware, it is best known for its figurines, character and toby jugs, and series ware. Almost all Doulton's figurines were made at Burslem. The HN numbers, named for Harry Nixon, were introduced in 1913. HN numbers were chronological until 1949 after which each modeler received a block of numbers. Noke introduced the first character jugs in 1934. Noke also created series ware, a line that utilizes a standard blank decorated with a wide range of scenes.

Today the Royal Doulton Group includes John Beswick, Colclough, Webb Corbett, Minton, Paragon, Ridgway, Royal Adderley, Royal Albert, and Royal Crown Derby. It is the largest manufacturer of ceramic products in the United Kingdom.

References: Susan and Al Bagdade, *Warman's English & Continental Pottery & Porcelain, 2nd Edition* Wallace–Homestead, Krause Publications, 1991; Jean Dale, *The Charlton Standard Catalogue of Royal Doulton Animals*, Charlton Press, 1994; Jean Dale, *The Charlton Standard Catalogue of Royal Doulton Beswick Figurines, Fifth Edition*, Charlton Press, 1996; Jean Dale, *The Charlton Standard Catalogue of Royal Doulton Beswick Storybook Figurines, Third Edition*, Charlton Press, 1996; Jean Dale, *The Charlton Standard Catalogue of Royal Doulton Beswick Jugs, Fourth Edition*, Charlton Press, 1997; Harry L. Rinker, *Dinnerware of the 20th Century: The Top 500 Patterns*, House of Collectibles, 1997.

Collectors' Clubs: Royal Doulton International Collectors Club, 701 Cottontail Ln, Somerset, NJ 08873; Royal Doulton International Collectors Club, 850 Progress Ave, Scarborough Ontario M1H 3C4 Canada.

Adrian, bell	**$20.00**
Adrian, cream soup and saucer	30.00
Adrian, cup and saucer, ftd, 2⁵/₈"	25.00
Adrian, dinner plate	25.00
Adrian, salad plate, 8¹/₈" d	15.00
Adrian, sugar, cov	50.00
Angelique, bread and butter plate, 6⁵/₈" d	12.00
Angelique, cake plate, handled, 10⁵/₈" d	35.00
Angelique, chop plate, 13¹/₄" d	120.00
Angelique, cup and saucer, flat, 2⁷/₈"	25.00
Angelique, dinner plate	22.00
Biscay, cup and saucer, flat, 3"	15.00

Biscay, dinner plate, 10⅝" **15.00**
Biscay, gravy boat, attached underplate **55.00**
Biscay, sugar, cov, ... **30.00**
Biscay, teapot, cov, oval. **100.00**
Biscay, vegetable bowl, oval, 9½" l **30.00**
Burgundy, bread and butter plate, 6⅝" d **6.50**
Burgundy, cup and saucer, ftd, 2¾" **15.00**
Burgundy, dinner plate **18.00**
Burgundy, gravy boat, attached underplate **55.00**
Burgundy, salad plate, 8" d **10.00**
Burgundy, sugar, cov **30.00**
Burgundy, teapot cov, no lid **60.00**
Burgundy, vegetable bowl, oval, 9½" l **30.00**
Cambridge, cereal bowl, 6⅞" d **20.00**
Cambridge, demitasse cup and saucer **25.00**
Cambridge, dinner plate, 10¾" d **20.00**
Camberidge, platter, oval, 13⅝" **60.00**
Cambridge, vegetable, oval, 10¾" **50.00**
Character Mug, Gone Away, D6545, 2½" **60.00**
Character Mug, John Doulton, D6656, 4½" h **70.00**
Character Mug, Sam Weller, 3⅜" h **50.00**
Character Mug, Tony Weller, 2¼" h **50.00**
Coronet, bread and butter plate, 6¼" d **12.00**
Coronet, cup and saucer, flat, 2⅛"h **25.00**
Coronet, dinner plate, 10⅜" d **25.00**
Coronet, platter, oval, 13⅛" l **85.00**
Coronet, salad plate, 8⅜" d **20.00**
Coronet, sugar, cov **50.00**
Coronet, vegetable bowl, oval, 9¾" **60.00**
Figure, Balloon Man, HN1954, 7¼" h **110.00**
Figure, Blue Belard, HN2105, 10" h. **350.00**
Figure, Captain, HN2260, 9⅜" h **300.00**
Figure, Helmsman, HN2499, 9½" h **175.00**
Figure, Lobster Man, HN2317, 7¼" h. **120.00**
Figure, Old Balloon Seller, HN1315, 7½" h **115.00**
Figure, Omar Khayyam, HN2247, 6¼" h **140.00**
Figure, Prized Possessions, HN2942, 7" h **345.00**
Figure, Rumpelstiltskin, HN3025, 8¼" h. **130.00**
Figure, Schoolmarm, HN2223, 6½" h **195.00**
Figure, Sleepy Darling, HN2953, 7¼" h **130.00**
Figure, Song of the Sea, HN2729, 7½" h **160.00**
Figure, St George, HN2051, 7⅜" h. **300.00**
Figure, Tuppence a Bag, HN2320, 5⅜" h **120.00**
Figure, Votes for Women, HN2816, 10" h. **200.00**
Figure, Wizard, HN2877, 9⅝" h **160.00**
Forsyth, cup and saucer, ftd, 3" h **15.00**

Forsyth, dinner plate, 10⅝" d **15.00**
Forsyth, fruit bowl, 5⅛" d **10.00**
Forsyth, salad plate, 8⅛" d **10.00**
Grantham, ashtray, 3⅝" d **10.00**
Grantham, bread and butter plate **6.00**
Grantham, cake plate, handled, 10" **40.00**
Grantham, cereal bowl, coupe, 6" d. **15.00**
Grantham, demitasse cup and saucer. **15.00**
Grantham, eggcup, 3½" h **12.00**
Grantham, fruit bowl, 5⅝" d **10.00**
Grantham, luncheon plate. **12.00**
Grantham, salad plate, square **15.00**
Grantham, sugar, cov **35.00**
Grantham, vegetable bowl, round, 8¼" d. **35.00**
Miramont, casserole, individual, 4⅜" d **40.00**
Miramont, creamer **35.00**
Miramont, demitasse cup and saucer **20.00**
Miramont, dinner plate **25.00**
Miramont, gravy boat **60.00**
Miramont, salad plate, 8" d **15.00**
Miramont, sugar, cov. **50.00**
Old Colony, bread and butter plate, 6⅝" d. **6.00**
Old Colony, cream soup and saucer **45.00**
Old Colony, dinner plate, 10⅝" d **25.00**
Old Colony, eggcup, 2" h **12.00**
Old Colony, salad plate, 8⅛" d **12.00**
Old Colony, sugar, cov **50.00**
Old Leeds Spray, bouillon cup and saucer **20.00**
Old Leeds Spray, cereal bowl, 6" d. **15.00**
Old Leeds Spray, cream soup and saucer **30.00**
Old Leeds Spray, demitasse cup and saucer **15.00**
Old Leeds Spray, dinner plate **18.00**
Old Leeds Spray, luncheon plate, 8⅝" d. **15.00**
Old Leeds Spray, platter, oval, 13¼" l **45.00**
Provencal, bread and butter plate, 6½" d **6.50**
Provencal, cake plate, handled, 10¾" **80.00**
Provencal, casserole, individual, 4⅜". **35.00**
Provencal, cream soup and saucer **25.00**
Provencal, cup and saucer, ftd, 2¾" h **15.00**
Provencal, dinner plate, 10¾" d. **20.00**
Provencal, gravy boat underplate **20.00**
Provencal, luncheon plate, 9¼" d **15.00**
Provencal, platter, oval, 13¼" l **50.00**
Provencal, sugar, cov **40.00**

SALEM CHINA

Biddam Smith, John McNichol, and Dan Cronin, formerly with Standard Pottery in East Liverpool, Ohio, founded the Salem China Company in Salem, Ohio, in 1898. Due to financial problems, it was sold to F. A. Sebring in 1918. Under the management of Frank McKee and Sebring's son, Frank Jr., the company became very successful through the sale of fine dinnerware, much of which was trimmed with 22K gold.

Viktor Schenckengost created many of Salem's shapes and designs during the 1930s and 40s. Salem China continued to manufacture dinnerware until 1967. Beginning in 1968, Salem was exclusively a distribution and sales business.

References: Susan and Al Bagdade, *Warman's American Pottery and Porcelain*, Wallace–Homestead, Krause Publications, 1994; Harvey Duke, *The Official Price Guide to Pottery and Porcelain*, *Eighth Edition*, House of Collectibles, 1995.

Figure, tiger, flambé glaze, printed mark, 14" l, $373.75. Photo courtesy Skinner's.

Bonjour, casserole.................................. $20.00
Bonjour, creamer 4.00
Bonjour, cup and saucer 5.00
Bonjour, dinner plate, 10" d....................... 10.00
Bonjour, dish, 5½" d 2.50
Bonjour, sugar 8.00
Century, bread and butter plate, 6" d 1.50
Century, casserole................................. 20.00
Century, creamer 5.00
Century, dinner plate, 10" d....................... 10.00
Century, fruit dish 2.50
Century, gravy boat 12.00
Century, soup bowl, 7" 10.00
Century, vegetable bowl, round, 8" d 12.00
English Village, cup and saucer, flat, 2⅞" 10.00
English Village, dinner plate, 9⅞" d 10.00
English Village, fruit bowl, 5¼" d 6.00
English Village, salad plate....................... 7.00
English Village, sugar, cov 15.00
Fish Set, plate, 9 x 10"........................... 12.00
Fish Set, platter, round, 16 x 14" 25.00
Free–Form, bowl, ftd 15.00
Free–Form, bread and butter plate, 6" d 1.50
Free–Form, casserole, 2 qt 20.00
Free–Form, cruet, ftd 15.00
Free–Form, dinner plate, 10" d 10.00
Free–Form, gravy boat 12.00
Free–Form, platter, square, 13"................... 12.00
Free–Form, soup bowl 8.00
Free–Form, teapot, ftd 35.00
Free–Form, vegetable bowl, divided 12.00
Heirloom, butter, cov 20.00
Heirloom, casserole 20.00
Heirloom, creamer 5.00
Heirloom, cup and saucer 12.00
Heirloom, dinner plate, 9" d 8.00
Heirloom, gravy boat 12.00
Hotco, butter, cov, 1 lb 25.00
Hotco, custard 4.00
Hotco, jug, small 10.00
Hotco, leftover, round, small 6.50

Hotco, pie baker.................................. 10.00
Lotus Bud, bread and butter plate, 6" d 1.50
Lotus Bud, casserole 20.00
Lotus Bud, creamer 5.00
Lotus Bud, dinner plate, 9" d 8.00
Lotus Bud, soup bowl, 8¼" d 10.00
Lotus Bud, sugar, cov 8.00
New Yorker, ashtray............................... 6.50
New Yorker, casserole 20.00
New Yorker, cup and saucer 5.00
New Yorker, dinner plate, 9" d 8.00
New Yorker, platter, 11½"......................... 10.00
Symphony, casserole 20.00
Symphony, creamer and sugar 5.00
Symphony, dinner plate, 9" d 8.00
Symphony, gravy boat 12.00
Symphony, sugar, cov, 3–point finial 8.50
Tricorne, casserole 30.00
Tricorne, cup and saucer 9.00
Tricorne, creamer................................. 8.00
Tricorne, nut dish, 3¼".......................... 12.00
Tricorne, party plate, 9" d 10.00
Victory, cake plate, 10"......................... 10.00
Victory, casserole 25.00
Victory, creamer................................. 4.00
Victory, cream soup saucer 6.00
Victory, mustache cup 15.00

SALT & PEPPER SHAKERS

The salt and pepper shaker emerged during the latter half of the Victorian era. Fine ceramic and glass shakers slowly replaced individual and master salts. These early shakers were documented by Arthur G. Peterson in *Glass Salt Shakers: 1,000 Patterns* (Wallace–Homestead, 1970).

Although pre–World War I figural salt shakers do exist, the figural salt and pepper shaker gained in popularity during the 1920s and 30s, and reached its zenith in the 1940s and 50s. By the 1960s, inexpensive plastic salt and pepper shakers had replaced their ceramic and glass counterparts.

Salt and pepper shaker collectors specialize. Salt and pepper shakers that included mechanical devices to loosen salt were popular in the 1960s and 70s. Depression era glass sets also enjoyed strong collector interest during that period. Currently, figural salt and pepper shakers are hot, having experienced a 100% price increase during the past five years.

References: Gideon Bosker and Lena Lencer, *Salt and Pepper Shakers: Identification and Price Guide*, Avon Books, 1994; Larry Carey and Sylvia Tompkins, *Salt and Pepper: Over 1001 Shakers*, Schiffer Publishing, 1994; Larry Carey and Sylvia Tompkins, *1002 Salt and Pepper Shakers*, Schiffer Publishing, 1995; Larry Carey and Sylvia Thompkins, *1003 Salt & Pepper Shakers*, Schiffer Publishing, 1997; Melva Davern, *The Collector's Encyclopedia of Salt & Pepper Shakers: Figural and Novelty*, Second Series, Collector Books, 1990, 1995 value update; Helene Guarnaccia, *Salt & Pepper Shakers*, Vol. 1 (1985, 1996 value update), *Vol. II* (1989, 1993 value update), *Vol. III* (1991, 1995 value update), *Vol. IV* (1993, 1997 value update), Collector Books; Mike Schneider, *The Complete Salt and Pepper Shaker Book*, Schiffer Publishing, 1993; Irene Thornburg, *Collecting Salt & Pepper Shaker Series*, Schiffer Publishing, 1998.

Century, Rose–Marie pattern, platter, 11⅜" l, $12.00.

Collectors' Club: Novelty Salt & Pepper Shakers Club, PO Box 3617, Lantana, FL 33465.

Note: All shakers listed are ceramic unless noted otherwise. Prices are for sets. For additional listings refer to Depression Glass and individual ceramics and glass manufacturer's categories.

Alligators, wearing shirts, "Florida"	**$10.00**
Apples, Kessler	**10.00**
Art Deco Woman, holding 2 hat boxes	**95.00**
Babies in Basket	**75.00**
Bananas, playing drums, dancing	**18.00**
Bed and Pillow, black and white	**15.00**
Begging Dog and Blue Bow	**15.00**
Bird on Basket	**8.00**
Bird on Stump	**18.00**
Birthday Cake	**12.00**
Black Boy and Dog, Van Telligen	**125.00**
Black Chef and Maid, chalkware, 2½" h	**40.00**
Black Children Leapfrogging	**75.00**
Black Head, White Gloves	**195.00**
Black Porter and Suitcase	**70.00**
Blossomtime, glass, amethyst, hp, 2–pc top	**145.00**
Bookcase, wood	**10.00**
Boot and Saddle	**12.00**
Bowlers	**12.00**
Boxer Dogs	**20.00**
Boy and Girl, carrying umbrellas, Napco	**12.00**
Boy and Girl, kneeling on chairs	**45.00**
Boy Davy Crockett	**75.00**
Bread People, Goebel	**20.00**
Bride and Groom, Sorcha Boru	**285.00**
Brown Derby Hat, "Hollywood, Calif."	**10.00**
Budweiser, plastic, 1970s	**165.00**
Bunny, green, Van Telligen	**35.00**
Bunny, yellow, Van Telligen	**35.00**
Burger Chef, plastic	**5.00**
Cactus, Arcadia Ceramics	**25.00**
Cactus, Rosemeade	**15.00**
Calves, bone china	**22.00**
Camels, brown, Ceramic Art Studio	**120.00**
Campbell Kids, range	**15.00**
Cat Head, Lefton	**25.00**
Cat, rhinestone eyes	**8.00**

Fish, one blue, one brown, Japan, 2⅝" h, $8.00.

Cat, sitting on block of ice	**12.00**
Cats, unmkd	**6.00**
Caveman and Cavewoman	**15.00**
Charlie Brown and Lucy, sitting on couch	**25.00**
Chinese Man and Woman, Ceramic Art Studio	**25.00**
Choir Boys	**12.00**
Christmas Snowman and Woman, man holding gift, woman holding wreath, both wearing hats, Napco sticker	**15.00**
Christmas Trees	**20.00**
Circus Horse and Wagon	**18.00**
Collies	**18.00**
Conestoga Wagons, brown and black, white tops	**10.00**
Cow Ladies, holding umbrellas	**18.00**
Cucumber and Corn, 1 pc	**10.00**
Dalmations	**22.00**
Danish Girls	**25.00**
Deer, nodders	**65.00**
Dick Tracy and Junior	**35.00**
Dinosaur	**15.00**
Dog, Art Deco, bright colors	**15.00**
Dog on Barstool, Enesco	**25.00**
Donkey and Elephant	**65.00**
Donkey and Tipped Cart	**15.00**
Dr Dog and Patient	**20.00**
Dutch Couple, large	**25.00**
Easter Bunny and Egg	**10.00**
Easter Eggs	**10.00**
Elephant, playing drums, fuzzy	**5.00**
Elf and Toadstool	**35.00**
Esso Pumps	**30.00**
Felix the Cat	**100.00**
Firestone Tires	**55.00**
Fish, black, white, and yellow, on tray	**18.00**
Fish, child's face, white ground, red dots	**12.00**
Flamingos	**15.00**
Florida Oranges, unmkd	**4.00**
Fred Flintstone and Barney Rubble	**55.00**
Garfield	**18.00**
Ghosts	**20.00**
Giraffe Heads	**10.00**
Girls, dressed in red and white hearts	**12.00**
Goldilocks, Regal	**150.00**
Greyhound Bus	**75.00**
Gun in Holster	**10.00**
Hearts, red	**10.00**
Hillbillies in Barrels	**15.00**
Horses, stylized	**6.00**
Ice Cream Cones	**8.00**
Jonah and the Whale, black	**85.00**
Kangaroos, mother and baby	**95.00**
Kellogg's Snap and Pop	**65.00**
King Cole and Fiddler	**35.00**
Latkes, fork and spoon arms	**18.00**
Laurel and Hardy, tray base, Dresden, 1930s	**100.00**
Lawn Mower, moving wheels and pistons, c1950s	**25.00**
Lions, Ceramic Art Studio	**100.00**
Lobster, red, claws held above head attached by springs, green base	**25.00**
Maid and Butler, Kessler	**10.00**
Mexican Man and Woman, stylized	**12.00**
Mermaids, "Long time no he, and Long time no she," Enesco	**15.00**
Mice and Cheese, plastic	**12.00**

Mickey and Minnie, on park bench	195.00
Milk Cans, Shawnee	45.00
Minehaha and Hiawatha	150.00
Mixmaster, plastic, 1950s	25.00
Mobilgas, shield shape	25.00
Monkey and Palm Tree	20.00
Monkey and Telephone	15.00
Moose	20.00
Mt Rainier, Washington	12.00
Mushrooms, black with spots, Japan sticker	12.00
Nude, nodder	30.00
Owls, Lefton	6.00
Pears	15.00
Pelicans, pink, Rosemeade	40.00
Penguins, black, white, and orange, 1930s	25.00
Pigs, fuzzy, "Florida"	10.00
Pillsbury Dough Boy	35.00
Pinocchio, Disney	165.00
Pixies, blue outfits, yellow hair	15.00
Poodle, head up, sitting on pillow	35.00
Poodles, wearing hats	10.00
Prairie Dogs, Rosemeade	40.00
Princess of Thumb	55.00
Rabbit and Carrot	10.00
Rabbits, on motorcycles	20.00
Rabbits, running, Rosemeade	35.00
Rabbits, playing accordion and drum	6.00
Rabbits, stylized, yellow	10.00
Rainbow Trout	12.00
Referees	18.00
Robin Hood and Marion, Twin Winton	125.00
Rocking Bears, 1 pc	12.00
Rotisserie, plastic	200.00
Sailor and Bo Peep, Shawnee	45.00
Sailor Boy and Girl, on wave, Sorcha Boru	75.00
Sandman	95.00
Santa and Mrs Claus, with tennis rackets	15.00
Santa and Reindeer	15.00
Schmoo	70.00
Scotties, black and white	8.00
Seagram's Seven, plastic	8.00

Sea Lions	15.00
Seals, New England Ceramics	10.00
Ship, St Lawrence Seaway	22.00
Skulls, nodders	90.00
Smokey Bear	100.00
Snails, blue and white	8.00
Space Creatures, black and white	12.00
Spanish Dancers, Ceramic Art Studio, 7½" h	100.00
Sports Players, Napco	15.00
Squirrel, brown	8.00
Sultan and Harem Girl	95.00
Surfer Girl and Surfboard	200.00
Swordfish	100.00
Telephone Directory, black phone, white book	15.00
Tomato, glass, yellow ground, hp pink and white rosebuds, Mt Washington	85.00
Turtles, polka dot and daisies shells, Japan sticker	15.00
TV Set, plastic, white viewing screen, brown and gold accents and legs, on/off switch raises shakers, orig box, 1950s, 3" h	65.00
Valentine Kids, black hair	235.00
Vegetable Heads, gold trim, Vallona Star	30.00
Washer and Dryer, plastic, Westinghouse adv	15.00
Watermelon Heads	8.00
Western Santa and Mrs Claus	22.00
Windmills	18.00
Winking Cat, Enesco	15.00
Woody Woodpecker, and girlfriend	45.00
Zebras	15.00

SAND PAILS

Pre–1900 tin sand pails were japanned, a technique involving layers of paint with a final lacquer coating. Lithographed tin pails arrived on the scene in the first two decades of the 20th century.

The golden age of lithographed tin sand pails began in the late 1930s and extended into the 1960s. After World War II, the four leading manufacturers were J. Chein & Co., T. Cohn, The Ohio Art Company, and U.S. Metal Toy Manufacturing. Character–licensed pails arrived on the scene in the late 1940s and early 1950s. By the mid–1960s, almost all sand pails were made of plastic.

Many sand pails were sold as sets. Sets could include sand molds, a sifter, spade, and/or sprinkling can.

Reference: Carole and Richard Smyth, *Sand Pails & Other Sand Toys*, published by authors, 1996.

Gas Pumps, Richfield Oil, plastic, yellow and blue, 2⅝" h, $132.00. Photo courtesy Collectors Auctions Services.

Advertising, Charms Pops, Hansel and Gretel and wicked witch scene, emb lobster on bottom, mkd "Charms Co., Bloomfield, N. J.," artist sgd "W.K.T.," 3" h	$150.00
Advertising, Safeguard Soap, children, zoo animals, flowers, and butterflies on sides, paper label reads "This Sandpail Free when you buy 2 bath or 3 complexion size bars of Safeguard," 5" h	80.00
Apex Tire and Rubber, Pawtucket, RI, rubber, splashed paint design on pail and handle, 4¼" h	50.00
J Chein, man selling balloons, smiling children, dog and cat, 5¼" h	75.00
J Chein, nursery rhymes, red, white, and blue, 5¼" h	85.00
J Chein, rabbit family at work, 4¼" h	130.00
J Chein, "Roundup," cowboys roping cattle, 7¼" h	125.00
T Cohn, baby animals and birds looking at baby, 4½" h	110.00

Safeguard Soap premium, litho tin, 5" h, $80.00.

T Cohn, children playing with garden sprinkler, 4¼" h **90.00**

T Cohn, children swimming and playing, 4½" h **120.00**

Kirchhof, Newark, NJ, children playing with Scottie dog,
4" h **130.00**

Ohio Art, calypso band around sides, metallic purple
ground, mkd "Ohio"in metallic pink circle in center **110.00**

Ohio Art, comical fishermen in boat, lighthouse, fish in
water, mkd "Ohio Art" with "Bryan, Ohio," and
"3F175," 5" h **65.00**

Overland Candy Co, Chicago, IL, Donald Duck, Huey,
Louie, and Dewey playing on beach, red
"Disneyland," ©1949 Walt Disney Productions, 3" h **220.00**

Unknown Manufacturer, safari scene, 5¼" h **75.00**

US Metal Toy Mfg Co, boy and girl playing with dogs,
lamb, and other animals, 4¼" h **80.00**

US Metal Toy Mfg Co, boy and girl water skiing, metal-
lic blue, silver, and yellow, 6½" h **60.00**

SCANDINAVIAN GLASS

Scandinavian Glass is a generic term for glassware made in
Denmark, Finland, and Sweden from the 1920s through the 1960s
and heavily exported to the United States. Collectors assign a high
aesthetic value to Scandinavian glass. Focus at the moment is on
key companies, e.g., Kosta Glasbruk and Orrefors, and designers
such as Edward Held, Nils Landberg, Vicke Lindstrand, Tyra
Lundgren, Ingeborg Lundin, Sven Palmqvist, Sven Erik Skawonius.

In the 1920s and '30s, Orrefors produced engraved crystal that
combined Modern abstractionism with classicism. In the 1940s
Orrefors' forms became heavier, decoration spare, and the inher-
ent refractive properties of glass were emphasized. Designers at
Kosta Glasbruk were moving in this direction in the 1930s. The
1950s saw an emphasis on simple light softly contoured forms.
Following a period of "Pop" influence in the 1960s, Orrefors'
pieces became sculptural in approach. It was also during this period that color entered the Scandinavian glass design vocabulary
and design links were established between Scandinavian and
Italian glass designers.

Currently, interest in Scandinavian glass is strongest in metropolitan regions in the Middle Atlantic States and West Coast. It is
now regularly featured in 20th Century Modern auction catalog
sales across the United States.

Finnish Nuutajarvi, vase, crystal, colorless with engraved
dec by Kaj Frank, mkd on base "Notsjoe FK," 5¼" h **$100.00**

Finnish Nuutajarvi, vase, heavy walled colorless vessel
with trapped tiny bubbles in symmetrical design,
engraved "G. Nyman/Nuutajarvi—57," 10½" h **400.00**

Kosta, decanter, figural bird bottle with head stopper,
engraved feathers, base mkd "Kosta 8218 – /V.
Lindstrand," 8¼" h, 8" l **400.00**

Kosta, oblique, solid wedge with two blue vitrified surfaces engraved with petroglyphs revealed through
polished front surface, base inscribed "Kosta 95689
Warff," 4¾" h **700.00**

Kosta, paperweight, attributed to Ann Warff, squared
colorless block, sky blue and yellow vitrified surface
sheared to reveal engraved petroglyphs at reverse,
base inscribed "Kosta 96736," 2¼" h **375.00**

Kosta, rose bowl, Art Deco, cut and polished, colorless
with etched surface and raised stylized floral panels,
incised "Kosta 1936 Came 4," 7" h **485.00**

Kosta, sculpture, elk, colorless glass oval block with flat
polished surface, vitrified yellow back, sky blue
engraved at edge with row of ten antlered elk reflected in base, inscribed "Kosta 967—Warff," 5¾" h,
9½" l **450.00**

Kosta, sculpture, shore bird, solid elongated figure, internally colored gray–green within colorless surround,
capped with bright red crest, lower edge engraved
"Kosta '84," raised on wooden block plinth, 15¼" h **175.00**

Kosta, vase, art glass, designed by Bertil Vallien, expanded oval fire dec with colorful shards and multi lines,
base inscribed "Kosta Boda/Artist Coll. B. Vallien
48280," 6¾" h **315.00**

Kosta, vase, bulbous base, long neck, internally dec with
vertical stripes, opal blue with aubergine, acid
stamped on base "Kosta/Lind/Strand," 11¾" h **400.00**

Kosta, vase, cased and wheel cut, heavy walled colorless
oval lined in bright emerald green, cut to clear on
interior in circles, base inscribed "Kosta B 2779,"
6¼" h **285.00**

Kosta, vase, cut glass, heavy walled bowl form, teal blue
surface dec cut to clear in polished oval and circular
facets, inscribed "Kosta 56693 Lindstrand," 4¼" h,
6½" d **575.00**

Kosta, vase, elongated bulbous body, internally dec with
vertical stripes in shaded blue, maroon coloration,
applied disk foot stamped "Lind/Strand/Kosta," 12¼" h . . . **750.00**

Kosta, vase, ventana veiled, attributed to Mona Morales–
Schild, colorless vessel with central cavities cased
blue, olive green, and orange, ext with concave panels to maximize optic illusory effect, base inscribed
"Kosta SS 122," 6⅞" h **700.00**

Leerdam Copier, vase, flared trumpet form, amber tinted
colorless glass, broad solid base stamped with
co–joined "LC," 7" h, 8½" d **115.00**

Leerdam Copier, vase, heavy green glass oval with wide
flattened rim, stamped on base with "C" in reverse
"L," AD Copier mark, 8½" h **285.00**

Orrefors, centerbowl, crystal, half round raised on heavy
solid glass pedestal, pen at center base with teardrop
aperture, labeled "Orrefors Sweden," unsgd, 6½" h,
12" d **350.00**

Orrefors, decanter, engraved crystal, sailors on shore leave obverse, sailor playing accordion reverse, Nils Landberg, inscribed on base "Orrefors Landberg, 1938, C IAD," 10¼" h, 6" w, $1,150.00. Photo courtesy Skinner, Inc.

Orrefors, cordial set, colorless squared decanter engraved with nude male diver underwater, orig stopper, accompanied by 5 glasses with different mermaid on each, decanter inscribed "Orrefors/Lindstrand 2983 B L.O.," glasses "2955," 12" h decanter, 2½" h glasses **175.00**

Orrefors, decanter, squared crystal bottle engraved with Romeo on one side, Juliet on other, labeled and inscribed "Orrefors/Lundberg 1880–111–F5," 11½" h **175.00**

Orrefors, vase, diminutive bowl of aubergine, bright blue, and colorless glass with vertical trapped air stripes, applied foot engraved "Orrefors/Ariel 246F/ Edvin Ohrstrom," 2¾" h, 4½" d **400.00**

Orrefors, vase, heavy walled colorless abstract cone form with internal blue spiral motif, base stamped "Lind/Strand/Kosta," 4" h **250.00**

Orrefors, vase, heavy walled colorless internally dec oval with central royal blue vertically lined network horizontally banded by pale peach colored divisions in perfect symmetrical alignment, base inscribed "Orrefors S. Graal No. 194 N Edward Hald," 7¾" h **2,075.00**

Orrefors, vase, heavy walled colorless oval vessel internally dec by vertical trapped air panels alternating with subtle gray feather panels, base inscribed "Orrefors Ariel No. 111F/Edvin Ohrstrom, 7½" h **2,525.00**

Orrefors, vase, heavy walled pale greenish crystal oval internally dec and colored in underwater scene with fish and aquatic plants, base inscribed "Orrefors Sweden/Graal N. 231D/Edward Hald," 5" h **975.00**

Orrefors, vase, octagonal faceted crystal with topaz engraved nude woman with scarf, base engraved "Orrefors/Lindstrand 1702.A4.9.," 1938, 10" h **230.00**

Orrefors, vase, portrait, titled "The Girl and the Dove," heavy walled amber tinted colorless and sapphire blue oval vessel internally air dec with framed bird and woman in profile amid blossom elements, engraved on base "Orrefors/Ariel Nr. 235N/Edvin Ohrstrom," 8" h **5,175.00**

Orrefors, vase, teardrop form, blue, amber, and colorless crystal internally dec with tiny controlled bubbles and netting, engraved "Orrefors/Kraka P N.349/Sven Palmqvist," 7" h **400.00**

Orrefors, vase/bucket, heavy walled cylinder transparent teal blue, notable clarity, base inscribed "Orrefors Expo. Pa. 245–62 Sven Palmqvist," 7" h, 6¾" d **175.00**

AUCTION PRICES

Scandinavian glass sold by Skinner's on January 24, 1998. Prices include the 15% buyer's premium.

Kosta, paperweight, by Ann or Goran Warff, mushroom shaped crystal with bubbled core, blue–green looping inclusions within base, inscribed "Kosta 97070 Warff," 5½" h **$258.75**

Kosta, vase, by Vicke Lindstrand, colorless crystal cylinder internally dec by teal blue amorphous element enhanced by cut and polished surface ovals, base engraved "Kosta 46693 V. lindstrand," 7⅛" h **517.50**

Kosta, vase, Trad I Autumn, designed by Vicke Lindstrand, heavy walled oval of colorless crystal internally dec by stylized black–brown trees with multicolored "leaves" falling and below in yellow, red, and orange, inscribed on base "Kosta LU 2011," shallow scratch at side, 7" h **2,645.00**

Orrefors, charger, Aqua Graal, by Edward Hald, broad colorless crystal platter with folded rim, internally dec by concentric rings of aubergine windows and gold–yellow swirls, all around central dark core, base inscribed "Aqua Graal No. 481P/Edward Hald/Orrefors '58," c1958, 14¼" d ... **805.00**

SCHOOP, HEDI

Hedi Schoop, born in Switzerland in 1906, was educated at Vienna's Kunstgewerbeschule and Berlin's Reimann Institute. In the early 1930s she and her husband, Frederick Hollander, a well–known composer, emigrated to America.

After arriving in Los Angeles, Schoop began making and marketing a line of plaster of Paris dolls dressed in contemporary fashions. Discovered by a representative of Barker Brothers, she was advised to scrap the textile clothing and do figures that were entirely ceramic.

Hedi's mother financed a plant in North Hollywood. Schoop employed many displaced European actors, dancers, and musicians as decorators. In 1942 the company became Hedi Schoop Art Creations. Business was strong in the late 1940s and early 1950s. The company introduced a line of TV lamps in the mid–1950s. A fire ended production in 1958. Schoop did not rebuild. Instead, she worked as a free–lance designer for several Los Angeles area firms. She retired permanently from the ceramics business in the 1960s, devoting her time after that to painting.

References: Jack Chipman, *Collector's Encyclopedia of California Pottery, Second Edition,* Collector Books, 1998; Mike Schneider, *California Potteries; The Complete Book,* Schiffer Publishing, 1995.

Ashtray, duck, green and gold, 5 x 6½" **$35.00**
Box, cov, boxer **150.00**
Cookie Jar, Darner Doll, blue and green **325.00**
Double Candle Holder, Fantasy **40.00**
Double Candle Holder, mermaid **125.00**

Figurine, peasant woman with basket and red scarf, stamped "Hedi Schoop Hollywood CA," 13" h, $165.00. Photo courtesy Jackson's Auctioneers & Appraisers.

Figures, pr, man and woman carrying urns, green and
gold, 12" h 75.00
Figurine, clown playin cello, 12½" h 55.00
Figurine, girl with basket and poodle, blue and gray,
stamped "Hedi Schoop Hollywood CA," 10" h 160.00
Figurine, Greek couple, 14" h 125.00
Figurine, Josephine, 13" h 40.00
Figurine, musicians, Art Deco, white and gold, 13" h 150.00
Figurine, peasant women, wearing red scarf, with bas-
ket, stamped "Hedi Schoop Hollywood, CA," 13" h. 165.00
Figurine, poodle, pink, black, and white, 12" l 125.00
Figurine, Repose 45.00
Figurine, rooster, crowing 125.00
Figurine, Siamese dancers 275.00
Flower Holder/Lamp Base, Colbert, 11½" h 40.00
Pencil Box, cov, teal and gray, painted feather on cov 65.00
Planter, woman reading book 60.00
Plate, apple, pr 65.00
Tray, King of Diamonds 30.00
Twin Vases, pr, large 125.00
Vase, crowing rooster, gold overglaze, 12" h 35.00

SEBASTIAN MINIATURES

Sebastian Miniatures, hand–painted, lightly glazed figurines, are the creation of Prescott W. Baston (1909–1984). He organized the Sebastian Miniature Company in 1940. Production initially was located in Marblehead, Massachusetts, eventually moving to Hudson, Massachusetts.

Sebastian Miniatures range in size from three to four inches. Production was limited. Baston also produced special commission advertising and souvenir figurines. Over 900 different figures have been documented. Pewter miniatures were introduced in 1969. In 1976, the Lance Corporation produced 100 of Baston's most popular designs for national distribution.

Prescott Baston died on May 25, 1984. His son, Woody, continued in his father's footsteps. The Sebastian Collectors Society plays a far greater role in determining secondary market pricing than normally expected from a collectors' club.

References: Collectors' Information Bureau, *Collectibles Market Guide & Price Index, 15th Edition,* Collectors' Information Bureau, 1997, distributed by Krause Publications; Glenn S. Johnson, *The Sebastian Miniature Collection: A Guide to Identifying, Understanding and Enjoying Sebastian Miniatures,* Lance Corp, 1982, out of print; Mary Sieber (ed.), *Price Guide to Limited Edition Collectibles,* Krause Publications, 1997.

Collectors' Clubs: The Sebastian Exchange Collector Assoc, PO Box 10905, Lancaster, PA 17605; Sebastian Miniatures Collectors Society, (company sponsored), 321 Central St, Hudson, MA 01749.

Accordion **$325.00**
Alden, John 42.00
Alden, Priscilla 42.00
Aunt B Trotwood 75.00
Barkis 75.00
Boston Tea Party 275.00
Buffalo Bill 100.00
Bunyan, Paul 200.00
Dickens, Charles 26.50
Dilemma, purple 275.00
Doctor 37.50
Family Sing 150.00
Family Feast 100.00
Fisherman's Wife 100.00
Girl on Diving Board 400.00
Grand Lodge of MA 30.00
Hancock, John 225.00
Harvard, John 140.00
Hawthorne, Nathaniel 150.00
Henry, Patrick 125.00
Houston, Margaret 100.00
Jack and Jill 75.00
Jefferson 75.00
Lincoln Memorial 48.00
Little Mother 37.50
Lobsterman 65.00
Manger 55.00
Masonic Bible 300.00
Mayflower, with clouds 200.00
Mr Beacon Hill 125.00
Mr Micawber 75.00
Mrs Cratchit 75.00
Peggoty 75.00
Penny Shop 65.00
Pilgrims 75.00
Pocahontas 125.00
Roosevelt, Franklin D 65.00
Satchel–Eye Dyer 125.00
Scrooge 75.00
Shaker Lady 70.00
Shepherds 55.00
Shoemaker 300.00
Slalom 175.00
Smith, John 125.00
Songs at Cratchits 75.00
St Joan of Arc 300.00
St Theresa Lisieux 225.00
Swedish Girl 200.00
Washington, George 38.00
Washington's Inauguration 250.00
Weller, Sam 75.00
White House, gold 125.00
Williamsburg Governor 55.00

SEWING COLLECTIBLES

The ability to sew and to sew well was considered a basic household skill in the 18th century, 19th century, and first two–thirds of the 20th century. In addition to utilitarian sewing, many individuals sewed for pleasure, producing work ranging from samplers to elaborately embroidered table coverings.

The number of sewing implements, some practical and some whimsical, multiplied during the Victorian era. Crochet hooks, pincushions, and tape measures were among the new forms. Metals, including gold and silver, were used. Thimbles were a popular courting and anniversary gift. Sewing birds attached to the edge of the table helped the sewer keep fabric taut.

As America became more mobile, the sewing industry responded. Many advertisers used needle threaders, tape measures, and sewing kits as premiums. A matchcover–like sewing kit became a popular feature in hotels and motels in the post–1945 era. While collectors eagerly seek sewing items made of celluloid, they have shown little interest thus far for post–1960 plastic sewing items.

References: *Advertising & Figural Tape Measures*, L–W Book Sales, 1995; Elizabeth Arbittier et al., *Collecting Figural Tape Measures*, Schiffer Publishing, 1995; Wade Laboissonniere, *Blueprints of Fashion: Home Sewing Patterns of the 1940s*, Schiffer Publishing, 1997; Sally C. Luscomb, *The Collector's Encyclopedia of Buttons*, Schiffer Publishing, 1997; Averil Mathias, *Antique and Collectible Thimbles and Accessories*, Collector Books, 1986, 1995 value update; Bridget McConnel, *The Story of Thimble: An Illustrated Guide for Collectors*, Schiffer Publishing, 1997.

Wayne Muller, *Darn It!, The History and Romance of Darners*, L–W Book Sales, 1995; Gay Ann Rogers, *An Illustrated History of Needlework Tools*, Needlework Unlimited, 1983, 1989 Price Guide; Glenda Thomas, *Toy and Miniature Sewing Machines* (1995), *Book II* (1997), Collector Books; Helen Lester Thompson, *Sewing Tools & Trinkets: Collector's Identification & Value Guide*, Collector Books, 1997; Estelle Zalkin, *Zalkin's Handbook Of Thimbles & Sewing Implements*, Warman Publishing Co, 1988, distributed by Krause Publications.

Collectors' Clubs: International Sewing Machine Collectors Society, 1000 E Charleston Blvd, Las Vegas, NV 89104; National Button Society, 2733 Juno Place, Apt 4, Akron, OH 44313; Toy Stitchers, 623 Santa Florita Ave, Millbrae, CA 94030.

Note: See Thimbles for additional listings.

Basket, round, wicker, beaded lid	$22.00
Button, celluloid, black, metal center strip, 1¼ x 2"	.35
Button, wood, brass rim, 1¼" d	.50
Button Box, round, wood shoe, boot label	22.50
Catalog, American Thread Co, New York, NY, 1921, 20 pp	19.00
Catalog, Clark's ONT J & P, Coats Edgings, 1945, 22 pp	12.00
Catalog, The Fashion World, NY, Spring and Summer Fashions, 1925, 42 pp	20.00
Catalog, Wilcox and Gibbs Sewing Machines, NY, 1921, 38 pp	15.00
Catalog, Youth's Companion, Boston, 1928, 20 pp	20.00
Glove Darner, double, wood, c1920	5.00
Mending Kit, Handy Pack, Art Deco	10.00
Mending Kit, Bakelite, purple, German	14.00
Mending Kit, plastic, bee with scissors	16.00
Needle Book, Elsie the cow, mounted needles, 4¾ x 5¼"	6.50

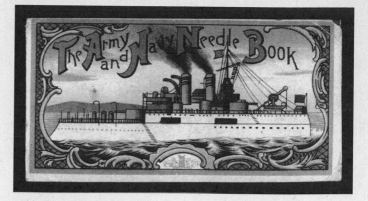

Needle Book, The Army and Navy Needle Book, Japan, 1930s, 5 x 2¾", $12.00.

Needle Book, Happy Home, paper, gold eye needles and threader, c1920	20.00
Needle Book, Lexington Ice Co, KY, c1920	5.00
Needle Case, celluloid, silver overlay design, c1920	12.00
Needle Sharpener, strawberry	6.00
Pincushion, blown glass, bird sitting on whale's tail, 1950s, 3 x 2"	40.00
Pincushion, figural camel	15.00
Pincushion, Lusterware, c1930	25.00
Pincushion, metal, heart, gold finish	5.00
Pincushion, metal, lady's slipper, feather, shell designs, Occupied Japan, c1937	35.00
Pincushion, satin, tomato	6.50
Pincushion, silk, hp, celluloid baby head in bonnet on top, green fabric leaves	55.00
Scissors, embroidery, polished steel, Germany, c1930, 3½" l	6.00
Scissors, SS, miniature, England	45.00
Sewing Kit, "Compliments of Hartsfield thru out California," tan leather, snap closure, painted metal ends, needle pocket for thread and thimble, c1940	25.00
Sewing Machine, Singer Automatic, black, gold geometric design, treadle base	135.00
Tape Measure, celluloid, fish	25.00
Tape Measure, celluloid, Indian boy head	30.00
Toy Sewing Machine, Baby Brother, metal body, gray–green metallic finish, battery operated motor on back, chain stitch, "Export Standard JIS S 8001, Labeled by Nippon Sewing Machine Mfg. Co. Ltd.," red sticker on bottom, Brother Sewing Machine Co, Ltd, 1960–70s, 6½ x 8¼"	80.00
Toy Sewing Machine, Bernina, white, light green, chain stitch, rubber feet, Steckborn, Switzerland, 1950–60s, 6¼ x 4¼ x 7¾"	150.00
Toy Sewing Machine, B/O Sewing Machine, Regular Stitch, battery operated, on/off switch, foot pedal, lockstitch, "Original Sewette Japan" stamped on sewing plate, Montgomery Ward, 1960s, 7½ x 8"	35.00
Toy Sewing Machine, Junior Miss, maroon enamel finish, wooden base, Artcraft Metal Products, Inc, West Haven, CT, 6¼ x 4 x 9"	100.00
Toy Sewing Machine, Sew Perfect, #9849, plastic and metal, battery operated, on/off switch, includes cassette with thread, bobbin with trim, 6 Simplicity projects, and fabric, Mattel, 1970–80s, 7 x 9¾"	5.00

Toy Sewing Machine, Signature Junior, electric, foot pedal, sewing light, die cast head, plastic base and carrying case, "Made in Japan" stamped on bottom, 1960s, 7½ x 11¼" 35.00

SHAWNEE POTTERY

Addis E. Hull, Jr., Robert C. Shilling, and a group of investors established the Shawnee Pottery Company, Zanesville, Ohio, in 1937. It was named for an Indian tribe that lived in the area.

Shawnee manufactured inexpensive, high–quality kitchen and utilitarian earthenware. The company perfected a bisque drying method that enabled decorating and glazing to be achieved in a single firing. In the late 1930s and early 1940s, Shawnee supplied products to large chain stores. Valencia, a dinnerware and kitchenware line, was created for Sears.

Robert Ganz joined Shawnee as a designer in 1938, creating some of the company's most popular cookie jars, e.g., Puss 'n Boots and Smiley. Designer Robert Heckman arrived in 1945 and was responsible for the King Corn line and numerous pieces featuring a Pennsylvania German motif.

Hull left Shawnee in 1950. In 1954 John Bonistall became president and shifted production from kitchenware to decorative accessories. He created the Kenwood Ceramics division to market the remaining kitchenware products. Chantilly, Cameo, Elegance, Fernwood, Petit Point, and Touché are several art lines introduced in the late 1950s. The company prospered in the late 1950s.

A decision was made to cease operations in 1961. Bonistall purchased Shawnee's molds and established Terrace Ceramics, Marietta, Ohio.

References: Pam Curran, *Shawnee Pottery*, Schiffer Publishing, 1995; Jim and Bev Mangus, *Shawnee Pottery: An Identification and Value Guide*, Collector Books, 1994, 1998 value update; Mark Supnick, *Collecting Shawnee Pottery: A Pictorial Reference and Price Guide*, L–W Book Sales, 1989, 1997 value update; Duane and Janice Vanderbilt, *The Collector's Guide to Shawnee Pottery*, Collector Books, 1992, 1996 value update.

Collectors' Club: Shawnee Pottery Collectors Club, PO Box 713, New Smyrna Beach, FL 32170.

Bank, Winnie, butterscotch	$500.00
Bookends, pr, cattails and ducks	65.00
Cookie Jar, basketweave, gold	95.00
Cookie Jar, Dutch Boy, stripes	195.00
Cookie Jar, Hamm's Bear	175.00
Cookie Jar, owl	130.00
Cookie Jar, Panda, with swirl	195.00
Cookie Jar, Smiley Pig, shamrock	295.00
Cookie Jar, winking pig	265.00
Creamer, cat, yellow and green	140.00
Creamer, elephant, red ears	42.00
Creamer, Smiley, yellow, blue bib	115.00
Creamer and Sugar, blue flower and fern	35.00
Figurine, puppy	90.00
Figurine, squirrel	60.00
Flower Bowl, Medallion	15.00
Grease Jar, fruit	40.00
Ice Bucket, elephant, pink	195.00
Ivy Planter, green, #3025	18.00
Ivy Planter, yellow, #3025	18.00

Milk Pitcher, Smiley Pig, pink and blue flowers, $192.50. Photo courtesy Gene Harris Antique Auction Center.

King Corn, casserole, cov, #74	85.00
King Corn, casserole, individual, #73	125.00
King Corn, cereal bowl, #94	55.00
King Corn, creamer, #70	30.00
King, Corn, lid, casserole, individual, #73	25.00
King Corn, mixing bowl, #5, 5"	40.00
King Corn, mixing bowl, #6, 6"	40.00
King Corn, mug, #69, 8 oz	45.00
King Corn, relish, #79	40.00
King Corn, salad plate, #93	40.00
King Corn, salt and pepper shakers, pr, large	48.00
King Corn, salt and pepper shakers, pr, #76, small	35.00
King Corn, salt and pepper shakers, pr, #77, large	35.00
King Corn, salt shaker, #76	18.00
King Corn, sugar, cov, #78	35.00
Pepper Shaker, owl	10.00
Pie Bird, pink, embroidered bib	50.00
Pitcher, Bo-Peep, green, blue, and yellow	125.00
Pitcher, Charlie Chicken	100.00
Pitcher, fern and flower	45.00
Pitcher, Smiley, blue flower	185.00
Pitcher, Smiley, cloverbud	250.00
Pitcher, Smiley, peach flower	195.00
Planter, alarm clock, USA 1262	25.00
Planter, Bo Peep, peach apron, mkd "USA"	125.00
Planter, boy and chicken, #645	35.00
Planter, car, 8 spoke	25.00
Planter, Chinese rickshaw boy	10.00
Planter, coolie with cart, pink, chartreuse, and dark green	10.00
Planter, cottage house, mkd "USA J543P"	40.00
Planter, elephant with basket on back, mkd "USA"	20.00
Planter, fawn, large	38.00
Planter, giraffe	50.00
Planter, girl standing at fence	8.00
Planter, globe, yellow base	30.00
Planter, Mexican boy and girl	24.00
Planter, Oriental and Bamboo, USA 702	18.00
Planter, Oriental old man, USA 617	24.00
Planter, Pixie, USA 536	18.00
Planter, Tony the peddler, USA 621	28.00
Planter, touring car, #506, 8 spoke, gold trim	20.00
Planter, 2 dogs, gold and gray	12.00

Planting Dish, emb flower, USA 182 . . . . 15.00
Queen Corn, butter, cov, #72 . . . . 29.00
Queen Corn, cookie jar, cov, #66 . . . . 143.00
Queen Corn, dinner plate, #68, 10½" d 9.00
Queen Corn, fruit bowl, #92, 6" d 11.00
Queen Corn, mixing bowl, #5, 5" d 15.00
Queen Corn, mixing bowl, #6, 6½" d 19.00
Queen Corn, mixing bowl, #8, 8" d 24.00
Queen Corn, mug, #69, 8 oz. 22.00
Queen Corn, pitcher, hot coffee, #7, 1 qt 48.00
Queen Corn, plate, 7¼" d 3.00
Queen Corn, platter, #96, 12" l 23.00
Queen Corn, shaker, #76, 3¼" h 3.75
Queen Corn, shaker, #77, 5¼" h 5.00
Queen Corn, teapot, cov, #75 . . . . 125.00
Queen Corn, vegetable bowl, #95, 9" l 27.00
Salt and Pepper Shakers, pr, chanticleer, small 45.00
Salt and Pepper Shakers, pr, Dutch boy and girl, large 75.00
Salt and Pepper Shakers, pr, farmer pigs 25.00
Salt and Pepper Shakers, pr, flowerpots 20.00
Salt and Pepper Shakers, pr, fruit, gold, small 40.00
Salt and Pepper Shakers, pr, milk cans, gold trim 50.00
Salt and Pepper Shakers, pr, owl, gold trim. 50.00
Salt and Pepper Shakers, pr, Puss 'n Boots 125.00
Salt and Pepper Shakers, pr, Smiley, blue, small 65.00
Salt and Pepper Shakers, pr, Smiley, green, large. 110.00
Salt and Pepper Shakers, pr, Smiley and Winnie, clover-
   bud, small. 65.00
Salt and Pepper Shakers, pr, watering cans 25.00
Salt and Pepper Shakers, pr, White Corn, large 150.00
Shaker, Mugsy, range. 110.00
Sock Darner, pink 90.00
Sugar Shaker, White Corn, gold 150.00
Teapot, emb rose, coral 50.00
Teapot, emb rose, 6 cup 30.00
Teapot, Granny Anne, peach and blue 145.00
Teapot, Granny Anne, purple apron 165.00
Teapot, snowflake, blue, 2 cup 50.00
Teapot, Tom Piper, gold trim, tiny spout repair 255.00
Vase, confetti globe, pink and black. 18.00
Vase, giraffe and baby, rust, #841 . . . . 60.00
Wall Pocket, wheat 35.00

AUCTION PRICES

Shawnee pottery sold at Gene Harris Antique Auction Center on January 14, 1998. Prices include the 10% buyer's premium.

Cookie Jar, Smiley, chrysanthemum. $192.50
Cookie Jar, Smiley, yellow bib, gold decals, hairline
   on neck. 99.00
Cookie Jar, Winnie, blue 253.00
Creamer, elephant 44.00
Milk Pitcher, Smiley, pink and blue flowers 192.50
Salt and Pepper Shakers, pr, blue Winnie, pink
   Smiley. 49.50
Salt and Pepper Shakers, pr, Smiley, pink, range size . . . 88.00
Salt and Pepper Shakers, pr, Smiley, red and blue,
   small size 16.50
Salt and Pepper Shakers, Smiley, yellow, gold trim,
   small size 55.00
Salt and Pepper Shakers, pr, Winnie and Smiley,
   pink heart, range size. 121.00

SHEET MUSIC

Sheet music is collected primarily for its cover art. The late 1880s through the early 1950s is considered the golden age of sheet music cover art. Every conceivable theme was illustrated. Leading illustrators lent their talents to sheet music covers.

Covers frequently featured a picture of the singer, group, or orchestra responsible for introducing the song to the public. Photographic covers followed the times. Radio stars, movie stars, and television stars appeared on sheet music covers to promote their show or latest screen epic.

Sheet music's popularity is closely related to the popularity of piano playing. When interest in piano playing declined in the 1950s, sheet music covers no longer exhibited the artistic and design creativity of former times. Collector interest in post–1960s sheet music, with the exception of TV show themes and rock 'n' roll sheets, is minimal.

Most sheet music is worth between $1.00 and $3.00, provided it is in near mint condition. In spite of this, many dealers ask an average $5.00 to $10.00 per sheet for mundane titles. Part of the reason for this discrepancy in pricing is the crossover influence of subject collectors. These collectors have little patience with the hunt. Not realizing how easy it is to find copies, they pay high prices and fuel the unrealistic expectations of the general dealer.

Further complicating the picture is the inaccurate, highly manipulative values in the Pafik and Guiheen price guide (Collector Books, 1995). The book has been roundly criticized, and rightly so, within the sheet music collecting community.

References: Debbie Dillon, *Collectors Guide to Sheet Music*, L–W Book Promotions, 1988, 1995 value update; Marion Short, *Covers of Gold: Collectible Sheet Music*, Schiffer Publishing, 1998; Marion Short, *The Gold in Your Piano Bench*, Schiffer Publishing, 1997.

Newsletter: *The Rag Times*, 15522 Ricky Ct, Grass Valley, CA 95949.

Collectors' Clubs: National Music Society, 1597 Fair Park Ave, Los Angeles, CA 90041; New York Sheet Music Society, PO Box 354, Hewlett, NY 11557; Remember That Song, 5623 N 64th Ave, Glendale, AZ 85301; Sonneck Society for American Music & Music in America, PO Box 476, Canton, MA 02021.

Advisor: Wayland Bunnell, 199 Tarrytown Rd, Manchester, NH 03103.

Alone and Blue, black and white interlocking decagon
   and triangle graphics, 1957 . . . . **$7.00**
And There You Are, Week End At the Waldorf, Ginger
   Rogers, Lana Turner, Walter Pidgeon, 1945. . . . . 8.00
*Ann Rutledge Theme, The Man Who Shot Liberty
   Valance*, photo of James Stewart and John Wayne,
   1962. . . . . 12.00
Brother Can You Spare a Dime, Warner Bros logo, white
   on turquoise blue, 1932 . . . . 6.00
Brotherhood Dance, The Brotherhood, Kirk Douglas giv-
   ing kiss of death to Alex Cord, 1968. . . . . 10.00
Bugle Call Rag, The Benny Goodman Story, drawing of
   Goodman, inset of Steve Allen and Donna Reed, 1951 . . . . . 8.00
Busy Doing Nothing, A Connecticut Yankee, Bing
   Crosby, Rhonda Fleming, 1948 . . . . 12.00

Cowboy, The, wide yellow borders, large drawing of western man on horse, 1933 . . . . **6.00**

Diamonds Are a Girl's Best Friend, Gentlemen Prefer Blondes, colorful Hirschfeld characters, 1949 . . . . **8.00**

Diga Diga Doo, Stormy Weather, Lena Horne, Bill Robinson, Cab Calloway, scenes, 1928. . . . . **12.00**

Doin the Ducky Wuck, Joe Penner, silhouette of duck in background, 1935 . . . . **5.00**

Fools Rush In, Tony Martin in record, 1940 . . . . **3.00**

For You For Me For Evermore, The Shocking Miss Pilgrim, Betty Grable, Dick Haymes, 1946 . . . . **3.00**

Frankie and Johnny, She Done Him Wrong, Starmer background of man and woman, large photo of Mae West, 1923 . . . . **85.00**

High Noon, Gary Cooper, Grace Kelly, 1952 . . . . **8.00**

If You Can Dream, Meet Me in Las Vegas, full page photo of Cyd Charisse, 1955 . . . . **12.00**

I'll Walk Along, Follow the Boys, Dinah Shore, 1944 . . . . **4.00**

I'm Getting So Now I Don't Care, picture of Rudolph Valentino, 1923 . . . . **8.00**

Impossible Dream, Man of La Mancha, drawing of Quixote, Dulcinia, and *Brigadoon*, 1968 . . . . **6.00**

I Was Lucky, Folies Bergere De Paris, caricature of Maurice Chevalier, 1935 . . . . **6.00**

Jimmy Rodgers' Album of Songs, 35 songs, small drawing of landscape, large inset of Rodgers, 1934 . . . . **15.00**

June in January, Here Is My Heart, Bing Crosby, Kitty Carlisle, 1934 . . . . **3.00**

Lonely, landscape background with large center inset of Fannie Ward, 1920 . . . . **10.00**

Look Out For Mister Stork, Dumbo, Disney, large drawing of Dumbo and mouse, 1941. . . . . **60.00**

Lovin Sam, Make It Snappy, full body photo of Cantor in blackface, 1922. . . . . **10.00**

Macho Man, large black and white photo of The Village People, 1978. . . . . **7.00**

Meet Me Tonight in Dreamland, In the Good Old Summertime, Judy Garland, Van Johnson, 1936 . . . . **20.00**

Memory, Cats, figures in large cat eyes at top, 1981 . . . . **3.00**

Mona Lisa, Captain Carey, U.S.A., Alan Ladd, Wanda Hendrix, teal blue and gray, 1949 . . . . **4.00**

My Defenses Are Down, Annie Get Your Gun, drawing of Betty Hutton shooting rifle, 1946 . . . . **12.00**

My Heart Sings, Anchors Aweigh, full page picture of Kathryn Grayson, 1943 . . . . **3.00**

Our Emblem March, large Veterans of Foreign Wars emblem, brown on dark blue, 1921 . . . . **8.00**

Our Love Affair, Strike Up the Band, Judy Garland, Mickey Rooney with snare drums, 1940. . . . . **15.00**

Page Miss Glory, photo of Marion Daivs wearing wide–brimmed hat, 1935. . . . . **10.00**

Ragtime Cowboy Joe, Incendiary Blonde, Betty Hutton, 1942. . . . . **6.00**

Rhythm On the River, Bing Crosby and Mary Martin with piano and guitar, 1940. . . . . **20.00**

Shadow of Your Smile, The Sandpiper, Elizabeth Taylor, Richard Burton, Academy Award credit, 1965. . . . . **3.00**

So Many Memories, silhouette scenes of courting man and woman, large inset of Rudy Vallee, 1937 . . . . **6.00**

Somewhere Along the Way, background of concentric circles and musical notes, large inset of Nat King Cole, 1952 . . . . **6.00**

There Goes My Heart, diagonal yellow lines on blue, inset of Doring Sisters, 1934 . . . . **5.00**

Three Coins in the Fountain, Webb, McGuire, Brazzi, Jourdan, Peters, and McNamara on coins, 1954 . . . . **5.00**

Trolley Song, Meet Me in St. Louis, large head photo of Judy Garland, 1944. . . . . **5.00**

Try a Little Tenderness, man and woman in heart, large inset of Ruth Etting, 1932. . . . . **7.00**

Tunes of Glory, drawing of Alec Guinness wearing kilt and dancing, 1961 . . . . **7.00**

Wake Up and Dream, geometric Art Deco design, 1929 . . . . . **12.00**

SHELLEY CHINA

Members of the Shelley family have manufactured ceramics in England's Staffordshire district since the mid–18th century. In 1872 Joseph Shelley and James Wileman formed Wileman & Co. Percy, Joseph's son, joined the firm in 1881. Percy hired designers and artists, significantly upgrading the company's product line.

Rowland Morris created Dainty White, the company's most successful popular dinnerware shape, around 1900. Frederick Rhead, trained at Minton, introduced Intarsio, Pastello, Primitif, Spano–Lustra, and Urbato series ware. Walter Slater, also trained at Minton, joined the firm. He adapted Intarsio to include Art Nouveau motifs, created Cloisello and Flamboyant ware, and introduced bone china production. Shelley dinnerware exported to America was well received. The company's mark consisted of the Shelley family name enclosed in a shield.

The company began making crest ware, miniature, and Parian busts following World War I. Fine china was known as "Eggshell." In 1925 Wileman & Co. became Shelley. Hild Cowham and Mabel Atwell's nursery ware proved highly popular in the 1920s and 30s. Tea wares added luster to Shelley's reputation. The Queen Anne octagonal shape is one of the best known.

Earthernware production ceased after World War II. Shelly concentrated on dinnerware. In 1966 Allied English Potteries acquired Shelley. It became part of the Doulton Group in 1971.

Reference: Robert Prescott Walker, *Collecting Shelley Pottery*, Francis Joseph Publications, 1997, distributed by Krause Publications.

Home on the Range, Ray Noble and His Orchestra, 1933, 9 x 12", $8.00.

Collectors' Club: National Shelley China Club, 5585 NW 164th Ave, Portland, OR 97229.

Bread and Butter Plate, Bridal Rose, 6" d	**$25.00**
Bread and Butter Plate, Dainty White, 6" d	32.00
Bread and Butter Plate, Forget–Me–Nots, 5" d	35.00
Bread and Butter Plate, Pansy, 5" d	35.00
Candy Dish, Crochet, white, blue trim 4½" d	35.00
Candy Dish, Pansy, 4" l	40.00
Candy Dish, Rose, 4" l	40.00
Creamer and Sugar, Begonia	40.00
Creamer and Sugar, Blue Rock, 6 flutes	52.00
Creamer and Sugar, Charm 5	60.00
Creamer and Sugar, Primrose, 6 flutes	45.00
Creamer and Sugar, Rock Garden	72.00
Cup and Saucer, Begonia	52.00
Cup and Saucer, Blue Rock	45.00
Cup and Saucer, Dainty White, gold, oversized	50.00
Cup and Saucer, Lily of the Valley, 14 flutes	45.00
Cup and Saucer, Pink Charm	45.00
Cup and Saucer, Wildflower	60.00
Demitasse Cup and Saucer, Pansy	65.00
Demitasse Cup and Saucer, Rose	65.00
Demitasse Cup and Saucer, Wildflower	70.00
Dinner Plate, Begonia, Westminster Abbey, 8" d	35.00
Dinner Plate, Crochet, 8" d	30.00
Dinner Plate, Charm 5	35.00
Eggcup, Dainty White, gold	35.00
Eggcup, Primrose, 6 flutes	62.00
Mug and Saucer, Dainty White	42.00
Nappy, 6 flutes, Begonia	38.00
Plate, Wildflower, 7" d	35.00
Snack Set, Blue Rock	55.00
Snack Set, Campanula	55.00
Sugar, individual, Lily of the Valley	28.00

SILVER, PLATED & STERLING

Sterling silver contains 925 parts of silver per 1,000. The remaining 75 parts consist of additional metals, primarily copper, that add strength and hardness to the silver. Silver plate, developed in England in the late 1860s, is achieved through electrolysis. A thin layer of silver is added to a base metal, usually britannia (an alloy of antimony, copper, and tin), copper, or white metal (an alloy of bismuth, copper, lead, and tin).

Silver plated ware achieved great popularity in the period between 1880 and 1915. Alvin, Gorham, International Silver Company (the result of a series of mergers), Oneida, Reed & Barton, William Rogers, and Wallace are among the principal manufacturers.

Silverware can be divided into three distinct categories: (1) flatware, (2) hollowware, and (3) giftware. This category includes hollowware and giftware. Currently silverware collecting is enjoying a number of renaissances. Plated pieces from the late Victorian era, especially small accessories such as napkin rings, benefited from the Victorian revival of the 1980s. The return to more formal dining has created renewed interest in tabletop accessory pieces.

References: Janet Drucker, *Georg Jensen: A Tradition of Splendid Silver,* Schiffer Publishing, 1997; Nancy Gluck, *The Grosvenor Pattern of Silverplate,* Silver Season, 1996; Tere Hagan, *Silverplated Flatware: An Identification & Value Guide, Revised 4th*

Edition, Collector Books, 1990, 1995 value update; Penny Chittim Morrill and Carole A. Berk, *Mexican Silver 20th Century Handwrought Jewelry & Metalwork,* Schiffer Publishing, 1994; Richard Osterberg, *Sterling Silver Flatware for Dining Elegance,* Schiffer Publishing, 1994; Dorothy T. Rainwater, *Encyclopedia of American Silver Manufacturers, 3rd Edition,* Schiffer Publishing, 1986; Harry L. Rinker, *Silverware of the 20th Century: The Top 250 Patterns,* House of Collectibles, 1997.

Note: See Flatware for additional silver listings.

SILVER

Box, cov, Continental, square form, repoussé with flowers and scrolls, 5" l, 17 oz	**$450.00**
Candelabrum, Continental, 5–light, knopped standard with floral bands, raised on domed base, 13" h, 42 oz	575.00
Candle Snuffer, profile of covered wagon attached to top of handle, 7¾" l	115.00
Citrus Squeezer, scissor style, spiked squeezing surface, 3¾" l	100.00
Dish, Continental, round, pierced leaf and flower motif, 9½" d, 7 oz	575.00
Fish Set, Continental, 9½" l octopus shaped fork, 10⅜" l skate shaped spatula, kelp handles	325.00
Inkwell, Birmingham, round hinged lid, front hinged compartment with gold wash int for stamps	250.00
Nut Dish, Gorham, round, openwork sides under beaded rim, ball feet	90.00
Spinning Game Top, Gorham, silver top with 6 sections engraved with various golf terms	115.00
Stamp Box, Napier & Co, hinged lid with engraved coat of arms, 3¾" l	85.00
Teapot, Continental, globular form, engraved with flowers and scrolls, raised on reticulated circular base, 7½" h, 25 oz	575.00
Tea Set, 3 pcs, Hermann Jacobsen, ovoid form, treen handle, 7" h teapot	425.00

Beverage Set, Tiffany, pitcher, 6 tumblers, and tray, acid etched bellflower swag and paterae dec, 106 ozs, 7¼" h pitcher, 3¾" h tumblers, 15" d tray, $5,175.00.

SILVER PLATED

Ashtray, Barbour, square, shell handle, match holder top,
   emb human figures **$15.00**

Brush and Mirror, Bristol, figural Art Nouveau motif,
   stamped, 8" l. **35.00**

Candle Snuffer, Meriden, emb floral design **12.00**

Child's Mug, Oneida, etched design. **7.00**

Cigar Box, unknown maker, lid has engraved cross set
   with agates, 8" sq **400.00**

Cigarette Holder, Graham Silver, champagne bottle,
   beaded trim, engraved "CIGARS," 10½" h **75.00**

Cigarette Lighter, ftd, Ronson, oval, Art Nouveau design **18.00**

Ice Bucket, Gorham, 2 handles, beaded rim, sq base **35.00**

Tea and Coffee Server, American Sheffield, 5–pc set,
   reeded base. **120.00**

Tea Tray, set of 4, 2 handles with folitate dec, 28" l **750.00**

Tray, Reed & Barton, Georgian style, scrolls and flowers
   relief design, inner rim ribbing. **32.00**

Vase, Christolfe, metal, short cylindrical neck, tapering
   shouldered body, flared cut–out foot with raised floral
   dec, stamped, 10¾" h **250.00**

STERLING SILVER

Basket, Watson Co, floral cut glass, sterling openwork
   rim and reeded swing handle, 4⅝" d **$260.00**

Center Bowl, Gorham, shallow, engraved with foliage,
   gadrooned border, 12½" d, 35 oz. **750.00**

Compote, George Jensen, bell shape, raised on stylized
   foliate standard continuing to ringed circular base,
   5½" d, 9 oz. **800.00**

Compote, Reed and Barton, scroll handles, monogram,
   6⅛" d **200.00**

Creamer, George Jensen, carved ivory handle flanked by
   squash blossoms, raised on spreading circular base,
   4½" h, 11 oz **2,075.00**

Sterling, serving tray, center with butterfly and pressed flowers between glass, sterling rim, mkd "W" in circle, stamped "Sterling 8860," engraved "9989," 11⅞" d, $150.00.

Flatware Service, Gorham, Buttercup pattern, 12 each
   dinner forks, salad forks, soup spoons, teaspoons,
   dinner knives, and butter spreaders, 70 oz **975.00**

Flatware Service, Wallace, Stradivarius pattern, 12 each
   dinner forks, salad forks, soup spoons, dinner knives,
   and butter spreaders, 24 teaspoons, 11 serving pcs,
   91 oz **700.00**

Fruit Bowl, Gorham, everted rim with reticulated foliate
   border, 12½" d, 32 oz. **1,265.00**

Iced Tea Spoons, set of 4, Tiffany & Co, incised leaf
   shape bowl, straw handle, 2 troy oz **150.00**

Punch Bowl, Dominick & Haff, ladle and 12 cups, reticulated rim, monogram, 11¾" d **2,645.00**

Salver, Tiffany & Co, swag dec border, 1" d. **460.00**

Sugar Caster, Tiffany & Co, flaring cylindrical form,
   leaves dec, 5½" h **400.00**

Trophy Cup, Gorham, goblet form, scrolling handles,
   10" h, 48 oz. **1,100.00**

Vase, Gorham, cylindrical, flaring, scrolls and flowers
   dec, lattice ground, 12" h, 20 oz **630.00**

Water Pitcher, Preisner, Hollowware, baluster form,
   scroll handle, 7¼" h **200.00**

SIZZLERS

Mattel produced Sizzlers between 1970 and 1978. Actually, Sizzlers disappeared during 1974, 1975, and 1977. George Soulakis and General Electric developed a nickel-cadmium rechargeable battery that could run for four to five minutes on a 90–second charge. Sizzlers had a hard plastic body and were painted in a variety of colors. Sizzler body types are divided into American cars, Grand Prix types, and exotics. Sizzler variants include Earthshakers, Hotline Trains, and Chopcycles.

Three different chargers were made: (1) a battery Juice Machine (resembling a 1970s gas pump), (2) a battery Goose Pump, revamped in 1978 as the Super Charger, and (3) the Power Pit, an AC charger (resembling a gasoline service station) that plugged into the wall.

Unrestored cars are worth between 20 and 25% of the value of the identical car in restored condition. Complete race sets and accessories still in period packaging are highly desirable.

Mattel failed to protect the Sizzler brand name. Contemporary Sizzlers are being manufactured by Playing Mantis of South Bend, Indiana.

Reference: Mike Grove, *A Pictorial Guide to Sizzlers*, published by author, 1995.

Note: Prices listed are for cars in unrestored condition.

#2354, Moon Ghost, 1978 . . . . **$10.00**
#4943, Fireworks, 1973. . . . . **50.00**
#4945, Ram Rocket, 1973. . . . . **50.00**
#4946, Hi–Way Hauler, 1973 . . . . **50.00**
#4947, Red Baron, 1973 . . . . **50.00**
#4948, Law Mill, 1973 . . . . **50.00**
#5630, Steering Trailer Set, 1973 . . . . **100.00**
#5661, Straight Scoop, 1971 . . . . **8.00**
#5879, Flat Out, 1972. . . . . **10.00**
#5885, Double Boiler, 1972 . . . . **10.00**
#6501, Angeleno M–70, 1970. . . . . **3.50**
#6502, Mustang Boss 302, 1970 . . . . **8.00**
#6504, Revvin/ Heaven, 1970 . . . . **3.50**

#6505, Hot Head, 1970 . . . . **3.00**
#6519, Sideburn,1971. . . . . **7.00**
#6520, Spoil Sport, 1971. . . . . **8.00**
#6538, Ferrari 512S, 1971 . . . . **10.00**
#6535, Mach F–F, 1971 . . . . **10.00**
#6552, Porsche, 1970 . . . . **55.00**
#9831, Live Wire II **3.00**
#9379, Boss Hoss II, 1976. . . . . **8.00**
#9380, Chevy Camaro II, 1976 . . . . **8.00**
#9382, Anteater II, 1976 . . . . **3.00**
#9383, Sideburn II, 1976. . . . . **3.00**
#9863, Lamborghini Countach, 1978. . . . . **15.00**
#9864, Corvette 4–Rotor, 1978 . . . . **20.00**
#9866, Long Count, 1978 . . . . **15.00**
#9865, Short Fuse, 1978 . . . . **15.00**
#9873, Vantom, 1976 . . . . **3.00**

SLOT CARS

Aurora Plastics Corporation, founded in March 1950, introduced a line of plastic model airplane kits in the fall of 1952. In December 1953, Aurora moved into a new plant in West Hempstead, Long Island, New York. Shortly thereafter Aurora began making a line of hobby craft products. In 1960 Aurora purchased K & B Allyn, a California manufacturer of gas–powered airplane motors.

Aurora launched the electric powered slot car in 1960. They were an overnight success. The slot car's golden age extends from 1962 through the mid–1970s. New models, scales, and track sets and accessories appeared on a regular basis. However, by the mid–1970s, many of the Aurora slot car innovators no longer worked for Aurora. The company changed hands several times during the 1970s and 80s. By the 1980s, Tyco assumed the leadership role in the slot car field.

References: John A. Clark, *HO Slot Car Identification and Price Guide*, L–W Book Sales, 1995; Thomas Graham, *Greenberg's Guide to Aurora Slot Cars*, Greenberg Books, 1995.

Periodical: *H.O. Cars*, PO Box 255, Monroe, CT 06468.

Newsletters: *H.O. USA Newsletter*, 435½ S Orange St, Orange, CA 92866; *Slot Car Trader*, PO Box 1868, Elyria, OH 44036.

Accessory, ATM, steerling wheel control unit **$30.00**
Accessory, Gilbert, Railway–Highway Crossing, MIB. **22.00**
Accessory, Strombecker, Deluxe Overpass Support Set **2.00**
Accessory, Strombecker, lap counter **22.00**
Car, AFX, '57 Nomad, lime green **40.00**
Car, AFX, Rebel Charger, orange **80.00**
Car, Aurora, AFX, Datsun Baja Pick–Up, yellow and blue **10.00**
Car, Aurora, AFX, Lola T260, white, red, and black. **10.00**
Car, Aurora, AFX, Matador Stock Car, white and blue **20.00**
Car, Aurora, AFX Magna–Traction, Dodge Charger Stock
    Car, yellow and red. **10.00**
Car, Aurora, AFX Magna–Traction, Jeep CJ7, 2–tone blue . . . **12.00**
Car, Aurora, Big Ryder, 40' Flatbed with Container, red,
    wine red, and white. **15.00**
Car, Aurora, Blazin Brakes, Corvette GT, white, red, yel–
    low, and orange **15.00**
Car, Aurora, Cats Eyes, GMC Blazer, white, red, orange,
    and yellow **20.00**
Car, Aurora, Cigarbox, Stingray, off–white. **15.00**
Car, Aurora, Cigarbox, Toronado, turquoise **15.00**

Aurora, Dino Ferrari 1381, blue and white, 1967–72, $35.00.

Car, Aurora, Flashback, Mako Shark, metallic orange, sil–
    ver stripe. **15.00**
Car, Aurora, Flashback, Toronado, metallic purple, silver
    stripe **15.00**
Car, Aurora, G–Plus, Candy Tyrell F1, red, blue, and
    white **30.00**
Car, Aurora, G–Plus, Ferrari Dayton Coupe, yellow,
    green, and black **15.00**
Car, Aurora, Lazer 2000, Odyssey 2000, white, dark
    pink, red–orange, orange, and pink **6.00**
Car, Aurora, Magna–Sonic, Baja Bug, red and white **20.00**
Car, Aurora, Scre–E–Echers, Rapid Rescue, yellow and
    red **5.00**
Car, Aurora, SP 1000, Atitali Capri, white, green, and red . . . **40.00**
Car, Aurora, Speed Shifter, BMW MI, white, blue, and
    red **20.00**
Car, Aurora, Speed Steer, Thunderbird Stock Car, blue,
    green, white, and yellow **20.00**
Car, Aurora, Super G–Plus, Dodge Magnum, white, blue,
    orange, and red **150.00**
Car, Aurora, Super Magna–Traction, Dodge Stock Car,
    gold chrome, blue, and red **15.00**
Car, Aurora, The Wild One, Wild Camaro, white and
    blue **40.00**
Car, Aurora, Thunderjet 500, Classic Lincoln Continen–
    tal, red **60.00**
Car, Aurora, Thunderjet 500, '63 Fairlane Hardtop, off–
    white **60.00**
Car, Aurora, Ultra 5, Shadow Can–Am, white, red,
    orange, and yellow **10.00**
Car, Aurora, Vibrator, Corvette Convertible, lemon **50.00**
Car, Aurora, Vibrator, Hot Rod Roadster, tan **45.00**
Car, Aurora, Xlerator, Chaparral 2F, orange and black **15.00**
Car, Cox, Ferrari, red **70.00**
Car, Eldon, Pontiac Bonneville, white. **20.00**
Car, Lionel, Corvette, tan, HO scale. **25.00**
Car, Marklin, Porsche Carrera Sportswagon, red **120.00**
Car, Revell, Ford Cobra Racer, burgundy **95.00**
Car, Strombecker, Cheetah. **28.00**
Car, Tyco, Blazer, black and red. **6.50**
Car, Tyco, Lambroghini, red. **8.00**
Car, Tyco, Z–28 Camaro #7, red, white, and blue **8.00**
Race Set, Aurora, Jackie Stewart Oval 8, HO scale, orig
    box **80.00**
Race Set, Elden, Power Pack 8 Race Set, 1/32 scale, orig
    box. **45.00**
Race Set, Marx, Grand Prix Race Set, 1/32 scale orig box **65.00**
Race Set, Strombecker, Indianapolis 5/1 Race Set, 1/32
    scale, orig box. **120.00**

SLOT MACHINES

In 1905 Charles Frey of San Francisco invented the first three–reel slot machine, known as the Liberty Bell. An example survives at the Liberty Bell Saloon, an establishment owned by Frey's grandson in Reno, Nevada.

Although the Mills Novelty Company copyrighted the famous fruit symbols in 1910, they were quickly copied by other manufacturers. They are still one of the most popular slot machine symbols. The jackpot was added in 1928.

Early slot machines featured wooden cabinets. Cast–iron cabinets appeared in the mid–1910s. Aluminum fronts arrived in the early 1920s. Mechanical improvements, such as variations in coin entry and detection of slugs, occurred during the 1930s. Additional security devices to prevent cheating and tampering were added in the 1940s. The 1950s marked the introduction of electricity, for operation as well as illumination.

The 1920s and 30s is the golden age of slot machines. Machines featured elaborate castings, ornate decoration, and numerous gimmicks. Caille, Jennings, Mill, Pace, and Watling are among the leading manufacturers.

References: Jerry Ayliff, *American Premium Guide to Jukeboxes and Slot Machines, Third Edition*, Books Americana, Krause Publications, 1991; Richard M. Bueschel, *Collector's Guide to Vintage Coin Machines*, Schiffer Publishing, 1995; Richard M. Bueschel, *Lemons, Cherries and Bell–Fruit–Gum: Illustrated History of Automatic Payout Slot Machines*, Royal Ben Books, 1995; Marshal Fey, *Slot Machines: A Pictorial History of the First 100 Years, Fourth Edition*, published by author.

Periodicals: *Antique Amusements, Slot Machines & Jukebox Gazette*, 909 26th St NW, Washington, DC 20037; *Coin Drop International*, 5815 W 52nd Ave, Denver, CO 80212; *Coin–Op Classics*, 17844 Toiyabe St, Fountain Valley, CA 92708; *Loose Change*, 1515 S Commerce St, Las Vegas, NV 89102.

A B T, Trip–L–Jax, 1930 . . . . **$1,200.00**

Baker, Baker's Pacers, 5¢, horse racing, floor model, wood case, 7 coin slots correspond to colors of racing horses, payoff drawer, 1930s, 40" w **1,600.00**

Buckley, Bones, countertop, spinning disks roll dice for craps, c1937 . . . . **3,500.00**

Buckley, Criss Cross, escalator coin entry, fancy casting around escalator and jackpot, c1948 . . . . **900.00**

Caille, Cadet, circular jackpot, c1938 . . . . **900.00**

Caille, Groetchen Columbia, club handle, small reels, coins travel in circle behind coin head, 1934 . . . . **250.00**

Caille, Superior Jackpot, 25¢, 4 reed, ornately emb, c1930, 15 x 24" **1,600.00**

Caille, Superior, nude woman on front, scroll work lower casting, coin entry in center above award card, c1928 . . . . **1,500.00**

Caille, Victory Mint, center pull handle, c1924 . . . . **2,750.00**

Jennings, Challenger Console, 5¢/25¢, silk–screened glass panels, c1946 . . . . **1,200.00**

Jennings, Duchess, 3 reel, front vendor, candy displayed behind windows flanking jackpot, c1934 . . . . . . **2,000.00**

Jennings, Four Star Chief, Indian carrying deer on front, large Indian chief above jackpot, 4 stars on top, 1936 . . **1,000.00**

Jennings, Governor, tic tac toe theme, Indian head above jackpot, 1948 . . . . **800.00**

Jennings, Little Duke, 1¢, 3 reel, painted cast aluminum Art Deco style case, c1935 . . . . **1,150.00**

Jennings, Rockola front, Sheffler strip, 1¢, 3 reel, 16 x 24", c1923 . . . . **1,350.00**

Jennings, Sportsman, golf ball vendor, pay card placed at angle, 1937 . . . . **2,500.00**

Jennings, Standard Chief, chrome finish, teardrop design on both sides of jackpot, flat Indian above jackpot, 1948 . . . . **800.00**

Jennings, Sun Chief, Indian bust, illuminated side panels, c1948 . . . . **1,750.00**

Jennings, Tic–Tac–Toe Chief, 10¢, chrome front, visible jackpot in oak cast, 16 x 27 x 16" **1,200.00**

Jennings, Victoria, 3 reel, 2 jackpots, fortune strips, c1932 . . . . **1,500.00**

Jennings, Wild Indian, 25¢, 3 reel, chrome front, oak cabinet, 17 x 18" **1,050.00**

Jennings, Wisecracker, 3 reel, anti–slugging window below coin chute, 1927 . . . . **2,400.00**

Keeney, Twin, 5¢/10¢, multiple denomination console model, electric, decorated wooden cabinet with silk–screened glass, 31 x 57 x 23" **100.00**

Mills, Black Cherry, escalator, painted silver with black case, 4 applied cherries, bib award card front, 1947 . . . . . **900.00**

Mills, C O K, 5¢, side vendor with future payout, c1930, 16 x 24" **1,450.00**

Mills, Diamond, 50¢, 3 reel, chrome front, c1950, 15 x 25" **950.00**

Mills, Eagle, gold coins, c1936 . . . . **2,200.00**

Mills, Fruit/1776 Spearmint, 5¢, 3 reel, emb, c1930, 16 x 24" **1,050.00**

Mills, High Top, strong player, light colors, 1946–62 . . . . . **1,000.00**

Mills, Horse Head Bonus, 5¢, Art Deco with "bonus" attachment, 16 x 26 x 16" **1,450.00**

Mills, Melon Bell, 3 reel, high top, melon on front, 1948 . . **1,200.00**

Mills, Poinsettia, gooseneck coin entry, flowers on lower casting, Liberty Bell under coin entry, c1930 . . . . **1,000.00**

Mills, Q T, 5¢, 3 reel, bell, brown cast front, cigarette symbols, win table, side handle, c1944, 18" h **1,600.00**

Mills Lion, 5¢, 3 reel, orig condition, c1931, 15 x 25", $1,380.00. Photo courtesy James D. Julia.

Mills, Silent Golden, 3 reel, Roman's head on front,
1932 . . . . **1,900.00**

Mills, Silent Mystery, 5¢, oak cabinet, metal castings,
gold award feature, 16 x 24 x 16" **1,100.00**

Mills, Silent Sales, 5¢, emb, side vendor, c1925,
19 x 24" **1,500.00**

Mills, Vest Pocket, 3 reel, box shape, plain design, 1938 . . . . **350.00**

Mills, Bantam, 3 reel, jackpot vendor front, 1932 . . . . **1,200.00**

Pace, All Star Comet, rotary escalator, stars and vertical
pointed stripes on front, 1936 . . . . **850.00**

Watling, Blue Seal, gooseneck, twin jackpot, 1930 . . . . **900.00**

Watling, Gumball Vendor, 1¢, gooseneck, ornate casting
around reels, gumball vendors on each side of twin
jackpot, c1921 . . . . **1,500.00**

Watling, Jack Pot, 5¢, style 50, "Blue Seal" front casting,
anti–slugging coin detector window under coin chute,
1929 . . . . **1,200.00**

Watling, Roll–A–Top, 5¢, counter model, ornate coin
front castings, oak cabinet, double jackpot, 1930s, 17
x 26 x 16" **2,600.00**

Watling, Treasury, 5¢, 3 reel, cast front, twin jackpot,
c1936, 24" **3,200.00**

SMURFS

Pierro "Peyo" Culliford, a Belgian cartoonist, created the Smurfs. Smurfs have a human appearance, are "three apples high," and blue in color. The name Smurf is a shortening of Schtroumpf, a French colloquialism meaning "watchamacallit." Over 100 Smurf characters are known.

The Smurfs first appeared as a comic strip. Soon the strips were collected into books and a line of toys licensed. In 1965 Schleich, a German firm, began marketing a line of two–inch high, PVC Smurf figures. A full collection numbers in the hundreds, the results of numerous decorating variations and discontinued markings. The first Smurf figures arrived in the United States in 1979.

After appearing in the movie *Smurfs and the Magic Flute* in 1975, Smurfs secured a permanent place in the collecting field when Hanna–Barbera launched its Smurf Saturday morning cartoon show in 1981.

References: Jan Lindenberger, *Smurf Collectibles: A Handbook & Price Guide* (1996), *More Smurf Collectibles* (1998), Schiffer Publishing.

Collectors' Club: Smurf Collectors Club International, 24 Cabot Rd W, Massapequa, NY 11758.

Ball Darts, velcro board and balls **$10.00**

Banner, plastic, "Happy Smurfday," Unique **3.00**

Book, *Astrosmurf, The,* soft cover, 1978 . . . . **5.00**

Book, *Baby Smurf's First Words,* soft cover, 1984 . . . . **2.00**

Book, *Smurf on the Grow,* Little Pops, 1982 . . . . **3.00**

Camera, plastic, Ilko Co, 1982 . . . . **8.00**

Car, Gargamel driver, metal, blue, Ertl, 1982 . . . . **18.00**

Costume, Smurfette, plastic **12.00**

Doll, Baby Smurf, outstretched arms, plush, cotton, 12" h **5.00**

Doll, Smurfette, rubber, synthetic hair, Hong Kong, 5" h **3.00**

Figure, Artist Smurf, #20045 . . . . **2.50**

Figure, Flower Smurf, #20019 . . . . **5.00**

Figure, Grandpa Smurf, #20226 . . . . **3.00**

Figure, Jonah Smurf, #20498 . . . . **3.00**

Figure, Postman Smurf, #20031 . . . . **3.00**

Figure, Singing Smurf, #20038 . . . . **3.00**

Figure, Smurfette, #20034 . . . . **3.00**

Game, The Smurf Card Game, Milton Bradley, 1983 . . . . **12.00**

Napkin, "Happy Smurfday," paper **3.00**

Pop–Up Book, *A Smurf Picnic,* Random House, 1982 . . . . **4.00**

Puzzle, Rhyming Match–Ups, Playskool, 1982 . . . . **8.00**

Puzzle, wood, Smurf carrying buckets, Playskool, 1982,
10 pcs **5.00**

Spinning Top, metal, 10" d **12.00**

Stocking, Christmas, "Have a Smurfette Christmas," felt,
17" l **3.00**

Tablecloth, Christmas theme, paper, Unique,
Philadelphia, PA, 1982 . . . . **3.00**

SNACK SETS

A snack set consists of two pieces, a cup and a matching underplate. Although glass was the most commonly used material, they also were made in ceramics and plastic. Dating back to the 1920s, the snack set achieved its greatest popularity in the 1950s and 60s. Snack sets were ideal for informal entertaining.

Most snack sets were sold in services consisting of four cups and four plates. Collectors pay a slight premium for a service of four sets in their period box. Some snack sets have become quite expensive, not because they are snack sets but because of their crossover value. Many chintz sets exceed $250.

Newsletter: *Snack Set Searchers,* PO Box 158, Hallock, MN 56728.

Note: Prices are sets consisting of one cup and one plate.

Anchor Hocking, Blue Mosaic **$6.50**

Anchor Hocking, Primrose **6.00**

Barker Bros, Lorna Doone **165.00**

Fostoria, Bouquet **34.00**

Germany, kidney shape, mother–of–pearl luster **15.00**

Gladstone, triple hearts, aqua and blue flowers with yel-
low center and green leaves **35.00**

Harker, Pate de Seur **15.00**

Hazel Atlas, Apple **25.00**

Hazel Atlas, Capri Colony, swirl blue **15.00**

Indiana, Sunburst, olive green **1.50**

Japan, Apple Blossoms, shell shape **15.00**

Lefton, Brown Heritage Floral **26.00**

Lefton, Holly Garland **22.00**

Lefton, Poinsettia **22.00**

Lefton, Violet Chintz **45.00**

Nelson, Black Beauty **125.00**

Federal, Yorktown, crystal, $3.00.

Noritake, stylized fish **50.00**
Pennsbury, Rooster **22.00**
Royal Albert, Gossamer **175.00**
Royal Albert, Tea Rose **25.00**
Royal Standard, Brown–Eyed Susan **25.00**
Royal Standard, Forget–Me–Not **25.00**
Royal Standard, Scot's Emblem **30.00**

SNOW BABIES

Snow babies, also known as sugar dolls, are small bisque figurines whose bodies are spattered with glitter sand, thus giving them the appearance of being coated in snow. Most are German or Japanese in origin and date between 1900 and 1940.

The exact origin of these figurines is unknown. The favored theory is that they were developed to honor Admiral Peary's daughter, Marie, born in Greenland on September 12, 1893. The Eskimos named the baby "Ah–Poo–Mickaninny," meaning snow baby. However, it is far more likely they were copied from traditional German sugar candy Christmas ornaments.

Babies, children at play, and Santa Claus are the most commonly found forms. Animal figures also are known. It is estimated that over 1,000 snow baby figurines were made. Many collections number in the hundreds. Do not overlook paper items—snow babies also appeared on postcards and in advertising.

Reference: Mary Morrison, *Snow Babies, Santas, and Elves: Collecting Christmas Bisque Figures,* Schiffer Publishing, 1993.

Angel, sitting, arms outstretched **$200.00**
Babies, carrying brown bear **185.00**
Babies, hugging, 1³/₄" h **145.00**
Babies, on red sled, Germany **85.00**
Babies, on wall, 2¹/₄" h **150.00**
Babies, pyramid form, yellow, red, and white **165.00**
Baby, holding ball **150.00**
Baby, holding baton **115.00**
Baby, inside igloo, polar bear on top **110.00**
Baby, in sleigh, sitting, arms raised, reindeer in front **150.00**
Baby, kneeling on 1 knee, 1" h **75.00**
Baby, lying on side, 1¹/₂" h **90.00**
Baby, on skis **150.00**
Baby, playing banjo **45.00**
Baby, playing fife, 2" h **125.00**
Baby, playing saxophone, Germany **80.00**
Baby, riding bear, red, white, and maroon, 1⁷/₈" h **150.00**
Baby, sitting, 2" h **195.00**
Baby, sitting in sled, pulled by reindeer **110.00**
Baby, sitting on box **125.00**
Baby, sledding, pulled by huskies, 2³/₄" h **90.00**
Baby, standing, holding tennis racket, Germany **135.00**
Baby, waving **160.00**
Baby, wearing bunny suit, Germany **150.00**
Baby, with club, 1¹/₂" h **110.00**
Baby, with umbrella, 1³/₄" h **100.00**
Bear, on 4 paws **95.00**
Bear, paws on sled **120.00**
Bear, playing hockey, 1¹/₂" h **70.00**
Bear, standing, 2¹/₂" h **115.00**
Boy, skier, carrying poles, 4" h **10.00**
Boy and Girl, ice skating, 2" h, price for pr **250.00**
Bunny, pulling cart, 2¹/₂" h **90.00**
Carolers, standing in snow, lantern, Germany, 2¹/₄" h **90.00**

Cat, on 4 feet **45.00**
Cat, pushing sled, 1³/₄" h **150.00**
Children, 2, with bell, 2" h **75.00**
Dwarf, kneeling, 1¹/₄" h **35.00**
Dwarf, long nosed, 1" h **45.00**
Dwarf, lying on side, 2" h **50.00**
Dwarf, sitting on stump, 1³/₄" h **50.00**
Elf, 1¹/₂" h **65.00**
Elf, sitting in doghouse **120.00**
Elf, with fairy, 2¹/₂" h **145.00**
Girl, astride sled, 1¹/₂" h **140.00**
Girl, carrying basket **375.00**
Girl, roller skating, 4³/₄" h **500.00**
Girl, seated on snowball, red skirt, arms raised **120.00**
Girl, striding, wearing winter coat, carrying leaf **12.00**
Girl, with ski poles, Japan **12.00**
Musicians, 3, 1³/₄" h **75.00**
Penguin, Germany, 4" l **70.00**
Penguins, walking, 1³/₄" h **30.00**
Polar Bear, 2¹/₂" h **115.00**
Santa, carrying stick, 2¹/₂" h **150.00**
Santa, on skis, 3¹/₂" h **400.00**
Santa, pushing cart, 1¹/₂" h **150.00**
Santa, with white cane, Germany **75.00**
Sheep, 2" h **70.00**
Snowman, dancing, 1³/₄" **5.00**
Snowman, playing banjo, 2¹/₄" h **50.00**

SNOW GLOBES

Snow globes originated in Europe in the mid–18th century. Manufacturing was primarily a cottage industry. Constantly gaining in popularity during the later decades of the Victorian era and the first three decades of the 20th century, the snow globe became extremely popular in the 1930s and early 1940s. Although the first American patent dates from the late 1920s, most globes sold in the 1930s were imported from Germany and Japan. They consisted primarily of a round ball on a ceramic or plastic base.

William M. Snyder founded Atlas Crystal Works, first located in Trenton, New Jersey, and later Covington, Tennessee, in the early 1940s to fill the snow globe void created by World War II. Driss Company of Chicago and Progressive Products of Union, New Jersey, were American firms making snow globes in the post–war period. Driss manufactured a series based on four popular characters (Davy Crockett, Frosty the Snowman, The Lone Ranger, and Rudoph the Red Nosed Reindeer); Progressive made advertising and award products.

The plastic domed snow globe arrived on the scene in the early 1950s. Initially German in origin, the concept was quickly copied by Japanese manufacturers. After a period of decline in the late 1960s and 70s, a snow globe renaissance occurred in the 1980s, the result of snow globes designed for the giftware market.

Reference: Nancy McMichael, *Snowdomes,* Abbeville Press, 1990.

Newsletter: *Roadside Attractions,* 7553 Norton Ave, Apt 4, Los Angeles, CA 90046.

Collectors' Club: Snowdome Collectors Club, PO Box 53262, Washington, DC 20009.

Note: Snow globes listed are plastic unless stated otherwise.

Skelly and Hood Tires, adv, red base, 143.00. Photo courtesy Wm. Morford Auctions.

Air Canada, dome, airplane above city buildings **$18.00**

Bart Simpson, pencil topper. **6.00**

California, calendar bank, globe mounted on red bank base with dial–type calendar in front, mkd "Made in Hong Kong/VN0355L," 4" h **10.00**

Child on Sled, bell shaped globe **8.00**

Cookie Monster, Sesame Street, dome, red base, mkd "Jim Henson Productions" **12.00**

Easter Egg, bunny inside egg shaped globe, 1980s **7.00**

Florida, salt and pepper shakers, pr, popsicle shaped domes, flamingos **20.00**

Frog, figural, mkd "VNO 614/Made in Hong Kong," 1980s, 4^{15}/$_{16}$" h **15.00**

Frog Prince, dome, mkd "3/1072/Ges.Gesch 1675631," 2^1/$_2$" h **12.00**

Glorieta Chapel, New Mexico, dome. **8.00**

Great Smokey Mts, salt and pepper shaker, rect TV set shape, top panel slides left or right for salt or pepper, mkd "Made in Hong Kong/No. V 3578," 1980s, 4" w, 2^3/$_4$" h **20.00**

Jack O' Lantern, dome **4.00**

Las Vegas, treasure chest shape, moving dice **12.00**

Los Angeles Raiders, dome, goal posts and helmet **8.00**

Louisiana, oval, lobster, sunken ship, and pelican, state map in background **12.00**

New York City, dome, Empire State Building, Statue of Liberty, World Trade Center, and skyline, 1980s **10.00**

Opera House, Sydney, Australia, dome, mkd "Made in Hong Kong/No. 352V," late 1980s, 2^1/$_4$" h **8.00**

Panama City Beach, figural dolphin above globe resting on waves **15.00**

Santa Claus, figural, mkd "Made in Hong Kong/No. 8824," 1980s, 5^5/$_8$" h **25.00**

Snoopy, on Dog House, dome, Willits, 1966 . . . . **20.00**

Snowman, figural, mkd "China," 1980s, 5^1/$_2$" h **18.00**

South of the Border, dome, large Mexican holding sign, 2 sleeping Mexicans on see–saw **12.00**

Star Trek, *U.S.S. Enterprise* suspended by lucite rod, glass ball, rotating hood, green glitter, limited edition from Willits Designs, made in China, 1992, 7" h **50.00**

Statue of Liberty, figural, snow dome is block in Statue's base **15.00**

Teenage Mutant Ninja Turtles, Raphael, dome, made in China, 1990 . . . . **15.00**

Turtle Back Zoo, bottle shaped, mkd "Made in Hong Kong, 1970s, 6^1/$_2$" l, 2^3/$_4$" h **12.00**

Wile E. Coyote, tall dome, "Feel Better" greeting on base **6.00**

SOAKIES

Soakies, plastic figural character bubble bath bottles, were developed to entice children into the bathtub. Soakies, now a generic term for all plastic bubble bath bottles, originates from "Soaky," a product of the Colgate Palmolive Company.

Colgate Palmolive licensed numerous popular characters, e.g., Rocky and Bullwinkle, Felix the Cat, and Universal Monsters. Colgate Palmolive's success was soon copied, e.g., Purex's Bubble Club. Purex licensed the popular Hanna–Barbera characters. Avon, DuCair Bioessence, Koscot, Lander Company, and Stephen Reiley are other companies who have produced Soakies.

Soakies arrived on the scene in the early 1960s and have remained in production since. Most are 10" high. Over a hundred different Soakies have been produced. Many are found in two or more variations, e.g., there are five versions of Bullwinkle.

Atom Ant **$20.00**
Augie Doggie **35.00**
Baby Louie **20.00**
Baloo **15.00**
Bambi **20.00**
Bamm–Bamm **30.00**
Batman. **50.00**
Blabber **12.00**
Bozo the Clown **25.00**
Breezly. **65.00**
Brutus. **30.00**
Bugs Bunny **15.00**
Cecil **35.00**
Cement Truck **25.00**
Cinderella. **15.00**
Creature From the Black Lagoon **60.00**
Deputy Dawg **25.00**
Dick Tracy **20.00**
Droop Along Coyote **12.00**
Elmer Fudd. **20.00**
Felix the Cat **32.00**
Fire Engine, hose gun **30.00**
Frankenstein **125.00**
Goofy. **15.00**
Huckleberry Hound **24.00**
Lippy the Lion. **20.00**
Mighty Mouse. **35.00**
Mr Jinx **30.00**
Mr Magoo **20.00**
Mummy **65.00**
Mushy Muskrat **25.00**
Pebbles Flintstone **30.00**
Peter Potamus **20.00**
Pinocchio. **15.00**
Pluto **15.00**
Popeye **20.00**
Punkin Puss **75.00**
Ricochet Rabbit **45.00**
Robin. **50.00**
Rocky Squirrel **25.00**
Santa **15.00**
Secret Squirrel **25.00**

Mr. Magoo, 1960s, $30.00.

Simon, Chipmunks	20.00
Smokey Bear	18.00
Snagglepuss	50.00
Snow White	25.00
Speedy Gonzales	18.00
Spouty Whale	35.00
Squiddly Diddly	20.00
Superman, Avon	10.00
Sylvester the Cat	20.00
Tennessee Tuxedo	30.00
Thumper	25.00
Top Cat	20.00
Touché Turtle	32.00
Tweety Bird	25.00
Wendy Witch	40.00
Winsome Witch	20.00
Woody Woodpecker	15.00
Yakki Doodle	25.00
Yogi Bear	25.00

SODA POP COLLECTIBLES

In addition to Coca–Cola, Pepsi, and Moxie, there are thousands of soda brands, ranging from regional to national, attracting collector interest. In the 1920s Americans became enamored with buying soda in a bottle to consume at their leisure. Tens of thousands of local bottling plants sprang up across America, producing flavors ranging from cream to sarsaparilla. Some brands achieved national popularity, e.g., Grapette and Hires.

Capitalizing on the increased consumption of soda pop during World War II, manufacturers launched a major advertising blitz in the late 1940s and early 1950s. From elaborate signs to promotional premiums, the soda industry was determined to make its influence felt. The soda bubble burst in the early 1970s. Most local and regional bottling plants ceased operations or were purchased by larger corporations. A few national brands survived and dominate the market.

References: Thomas E. Marsh, *The Official Guide to Collecting Applied Color Label Soda Bottles, Vol. II*, published by author, 1995; Tom Morrison, *Root Beer: Advertising and Collectibles* (1992), *More Root Beer: Advertising and Collectibles* (1997), Schiffer Publishing; Allan Petretti, *Petretti's Soda Pop Collectibles Price Guide*, Antique Trader Books, 1996; Jeff Walters, *The Complete Guide to Collectible Picnic Coolers & Ice Chests*, Memory Lane, 1994.

Periodical: *Club Soda*, PO Box 489, Troy, ID 83871.

Collectors' Clubs: Dr. Pepper 10–2–4 Collectors Club, 3508 Mockingbird, Dallas, TX 75205; Grapette Collectors Club, 2240 Hwy 27N, Nashville, AR 71852; National Pop Can Collectors, PO Box 7862, Rockford, IL 61126; Painted Soda Bottle Collectors Assoc, 9418 Hilmer Dr, La Mesa, CA 91942; Root Beer Float, PO Box 571, Lake Geneva, WI 53147.

Note: For additional listings see Coca–Cola, Moxie, and Pepsi–Cola.

Belt Buckle, Dr Pepper, enamel, 1930s	$200.00
Beverage Set, Old Kentucky Root Beer, pitcher and 4 mugs, ceramic, 1930s	335.00
Blackboard, Frostie Root Beer, tin	65.00
Blackboard, Grapette	150.00
Book, Hire's Root Beer, *1940 Rootbeer Book*, rules and schedules, 40 pp	28.00
Bottle, Double Cola, 1952	85.00
Bottle, Dr Pepper, Colorado	17.50
Bottle, NuGrape, 1955	65.00
Bottle, Orange Crush, light green, 9" h	3.50
Bottle Carrier, Barq's, cardboard, 1950s	10.00
Bottle Carrier, Brownie, cardboard, 1950s	10.00
Bottle Carrier, Cherry Blossoms, tin, 1930s	100.00
Bottle Carrier, Cleo Cola, cardboard, 1930s	35.00
Bottle Carrier, Dr Pepper, tin, 1930s	165.00
Bottle Carrier, Frostie, cardboard, 1950s	8.50
Bottle Opener, Canada Dry, metal, wall mount, gray and red raised lettering, Starr X Brown Co, 3¼" h	50.00
Bottle Opener, Dr Pepper, metal, wall mount, 1950–60s	15.00
Bottle Opener, 7–Up, wood handle, 1950s	25.00
Calendar, Chero Cola, woman holding bottle, 1921	600.00
Calendar, Chero Cola, woman at beach sitting on lifeboat, 1927	245.00
Calendar, Dr Pepper, 1929	700.00
Calendar, Dr Pepper, Earl Moran illus, 1937	450.00
Calendar, Dr Pepper, woman in yellow gown, 1938	250.00
Calendar, Dr Pepper, girl with half mask, 1950	55.00
Calendar, Grapette, 1955	100.00
Calendar, Mission Orange Soda, 1953	65.00
Calendar, Nehi, girl's portrait and historical events noted, 1936	180.00
Calendar, Nehi, woman leaning on boat at beach, 1927	325.00
Calendar, NuGrape, 1929	235.00
Calendar, Orange Crush, girl in swimsuit, 1932	75.00
Calendar, Royal Crown Cola, with Arlene Dahl, 1953	150.00
Calendar, 7–Up, 1961	30.00
Calendar, Squirt, 1941	150.00
Calendar, Sun Crest Soda, 1953	45.00
Can, Hire's Root Beer, steel, flat top	45.00
Can, Lucky Strike Root Beer, steel, cone top	50.00
Can, Nehi, steel, flat top	25.00
Can, Old Fashioned Ma's Root Beer, steel, cone top	40.00
Can, Orange Crush, steel, flat top	25.00
Can, Shasta, steel flat top	8.00
Can, Sprite, aluminum, pull tab	25.00

Cookbook, *7–Up Goes to a Party!*, 1961, 15 pp, $5^3/_8$ x $8^1/_4$", $10.00.

Can, Tab, aluminum, pull tab........................30.00
Carrying Case, Uncle Joe's Soda, 1929.................75.00
Clock, Dr Pepper, plastic and metal, illuminated, bottle cap shape, white ground, black hands and numerals, red Dr Pepper label and numerals 10, 2, and 4, $11^1/_2$" d...135.00
Clock, Frostie Root Beer, Frostie swinging on pendulum, cuckoo...125.00
Cooler, Dr Pepper, aluminum, emb red lettering, textured surface, side carry handles, 28–bottle capacity, Progress Aluminum #1, late 1950s–60s, 18" l, 13" w, 17" h...40.00
Cooler, Hires Root Beer, aluminum emb blue, red, and black lettering, sandwich tray, side drain, 38–bottle capacity, Cronstroms #13, 1950s, 22" l, 13" w, 13" h.....25.00
Cooler, Royal Crown Cola, yellow, emb red lettering, galvanized sandwich tray and liner, front drain, built–in bottle opener on side, 32–bottle capacity, Progress A1, late 1940s–50s, 19" l, 13" w, 19" h.........55.00
Cup, paper, Hires Root Beer, striped 3.00
Cup, plastic, Yoo–Hoo, Yogi Berra 15.00
Dispenser, Buckeye Root Beer, 1940s...................650.00
Dispenser, Cherry Smash, glass and Bakelite, 1930s.......160.00
Dispenser, countertop, Hire's Root Beer, soda fountain type, 4 metal taps, 1 on each side, c1940s, 12 x 16 x 22"...300.00
Dispenser, Foster's Beverages, glass and Bakelite, 1930s....100.00
Dispenser, Grape Shrub, glass, 1930s...................325.00
Dispenser, Hire's Root Beer, wood barrel, 1940s.........385.00
Dispenser, Orange Crush, glass, 1930s...................400.00
Dispenser, Trufruit Root Beer, ceramic, 1930s............300.00
Display, glass, iceberg shape, green 7–Up bottle inside iceberg, c1940–50s, 8 x 7 x 9"......................375.00
Door Decal, Mission Orange, 1940s 15.00
Figure, Fresh Up Freddie, soft vinyl rooster, tan body, red head and tail feathers, white, shirt, dark green trousers, replica bottle in hand, ©1959, 9" h..........195.00
Glass, Canada Dry, 1939 World's Fair, orig box, price for set of 6..50.00
Glass, Dr Pepper, applied color label...................60.00
Glass, Fanta, applied color label 15.00

Glass, Nehi, Golden Anniversary, "Nehi Royal Crown Cola Par–T–Pak," 1955........................25.00
Glass, Orange Crush, applied color label...............40.00
Label, Grape Smash 10.00
Lighter, 7–Up, logo, 1950s.............................25.00
Magazine Tear Sheet, Orange–Crush, 1930s............10.00
Matchbook, Nehi, woman aviator 18.00
Match Holder, Dr Pepper, tin, 1940s...................100.00
Menu Board, Orange Kist, smiling orange face, "Smile/Refresh With A Smile," 19 x 27".............900.00
Menu Board, 7–Up, c1940s, 9 x 23"...................225.00
Miniature Bottle, A–Treat, paper label 8.00
Miniature Bottle, Canada Dry, c1950, $3^1/_2$" h...........5.00
Miniature Bottle, Dr Pepper, emb....................35.00
Miniature Bottle, Hire's Root Beer, applied color label 18.00
Mug, A & W Root Beer, applied color label, logo inside United States map.................................8.00
Needle Case, Nu Grape, 1930s.........................45.00
Pencil Clip, Orange Crush............................18.00
Pinback Button, 7–Up, Fresh Up Freddie, litho, cartoon bird illus, 1950s, $1^3/_8$" d.........................15.00
Pitcher, ceramic, Orange Crush, 1940s.................200.00
Postcard, Royal Crown Cola, 1950s.....................4.00
Poster, Grapette, 1972, 9 x 23".........................8.00
Poster, 7–Up, 1960s, 5 x 15"...........................12.00
Puzzle, Cleo Cola, 1930s..............................45.00
Radio, Royal Crown, figural can, 1970s.................35.00
Ruler, 7–Up, Fresh Up Freddie, plastic, clear, yellow strip, color Freddie illus, black, white, and red 7–Up logo, bicycle riding safety rules text, 1950s, 2 x $6^1/_4$"......20.00
Sign, Canada Dry, light–up, frosted glass, "Authorized Fountain Canada Dry 5¢ a glass," orig box, 1930s, 14 x 5 x $6^1/_2$"....................................400.00
Sign, Capital Club Soda, cardboard, 1940s, 6 x 9"...10.00
Sign, Cheer Up, tin, wide–eyed owl illus, c1940–50s, 19 x 19"...550.00
Sign, Chocolate Soldier, 1950s, 9 x 27"...............100.00
Sign, Dee–Light, tin, promoting grape, c1930, 6 x 18".....200.00
Sign, Dr Pepper, cardboard, girl in convertible, 1940 .....350.00
Sign, Dr Pepper, porcelain, 1930–40s, $10^1/_2$ x $26^1/_2$".......275.00
Sign, Grapette, porcelain, oval, 10 x 7"...............350.00
Sign, Grape Ola, tin, 1920s, 20 x 28".................300.00
Sign, Hire's Root Beer, tin over cardboard, c1950s, 6 x $8^1/_2$"...150.00
Sign, Lime Cola, tin, 1920–30s, 10 x 28".............110.00
Sign, Mt Cabin, tin, bellhop holding sign, c1940, 12 x 18"...100.00
Sign, Natural Chilean Soda, flange, rect, painted metal, black man's face, "Yassuh!–Uncle Natchel," 15" h, 22" w..150.00
Sign, Nehi, tin, "Curb Service/Nehi Sold Here Ice Cold," 1950s, 20 x 28".................................160.00
Sign, Niagara Punch, tin, bottle illus, yellow ground, "Drink Niagara Punch," c1920s, 9 x 20"............150.00
Sign, Orange Crush, "Ask For Crush," 3 x 27".........145.00
Sign, Pal, diecut cardboard, easel back, 1940s, 11 x 20"....110.00
Sign, 7–Up, rect, "Drink 7Up, The Friendly Fresh Up Drink," c1930s, 4 x 10".............................275.00
Sign, Sun Drop Cola, tin, emb, 1954, 30"d.............400.00
Syrup Jug, Dr Pepper, paper label, 1930s..............125.00
Syrup Jug, Teem, paper label.........................25.00
Thermometer, Dr Pepper, tin, 1960s, 20" h...........50.00
Thermometer, Old Dutch Root Beer, 1940, 27" h.....65.00

Sign, Squirt, emb tin, self–framed, red, yellow, and blue flag, yellow ground, 13⅝" h, 20" w, $192.50. Photo courtesy Collectors Auction Services.

Thermometer, Orange Crush, porcelain, ribbed bottle
 illus, c1930–40s, 6 x 15" **325.00**
Thermometer, Wishing Well Orange, tin, self–framed,
 bottle shape, "Drink Wishing Well Orange," c1961,
 40½" h, 10½" w **195.00**
Tray, Frank's, flamingos in water, 1950s, 13 x 18" **40.00**
Tray, Orange Crush, 1940s, 13 x 18" **50.00**
Tray, Squirt, 1950s, 12" d. **85.00**

SOUVENIRS

Novelty souvenirs featuring historical or natural landmarks with identifying names were popular keepsakes prior to World War I. Commemorative pieces include plates issued during anniversary celebrations and store premiums, many of which featured calendars. Souvenirs tend to be from carnivals, fairs, popular tourist attractions and hotels, and world's fairs.

The souvenir spoon arrived on the scene in the late 1880s. In the 1920s the demitasse spoon replaced the teaspoon as the favored size. The souvenir spoon craze finally ended in the 1950s, albeit the form can still be found today.

Plastic souvenir items dominate the post–World War II period. Many pieces were generic with only the name of the town, site, or state changed from one piece to another. In the late 1960s ceramic commemorative plates enjoyed a renaissance.

The vast majority of items sold in today's souvenir shops have nothing on them to indicate their origin. Souvenir shops are gift shops, designed to appeal to the universal taste of the buyer.

References: Pamela E. Apkarian–Russell, *A Collector's Guide to Salem Witchcraft & Souvenirs,* Schiffer Publishing, 1998; Wayne Bednersh, *Collectible Souvenir Spoons,* Collector Books, 1998; Dorothy T. Rainwater and Donna H. Felger, *American Spoons, Souvenir and Historical,* Everybodys Press, Schiffer Publishing, 1977; Dorothy T. Rainwater and Donna H. Felger, *Spoons From Around the World,* Schiffer Publishing, 1992.

Periodical: *Souvenir Building Collectors Society,* PO Box 70, Nellysford, VA 22958.

Newsletter: *Antique Souvenir Collector,* Box 562, Great Barrington, MA 01230.

Collectors' Clubs: American Spoon Collectors, 7408 Englewood Ln, Kansas City, MO 64133; The Scoop Club, 84 Oak Ave, Shelton, CT 06484; Statue of Liberty Collectors' Club, 26601 Bernwood Rd, Cleveland, OH 44122.

Note: See Advertising, British Royal Commemoratives, Patriotic, Postcards, and World's Fair for additional listings.

Ashtray, Florida shape, brass, emb **$12.00**
Ashtray, Leaning Tower of Pisa, silver **32.00**
Ashtray, Niagara Falls, jasperware, blue and white, mkd
 "Occupied Japan" **25.00**
Bank, Dollar Savings Bank, Pittsburgh, PA, silvered lead **85.00**
Bank, Easton National Bank, Easton, PA, copper. **65.00**
Blotter, Yellowstone Park, metal **35.00**
Book, *Walt Disney's Guide to Disneyland,* full color,
 1960, 28 pp **30.00**
Booklet, Yosemite Visitor's Guide, color, 32 pp **8.00**
Bowl, South Boone, Terre, MO, Cemetry ME Church,
 scalloped edge, blue tint **12.00**
Building, Arc de Triomphe, Paris, copper **5.00**
Building, Arc de Triomphe, Paris, copper **5.00**
Building, Bunker Hill Monument, Boston, MA, copper **5.00**
Building, Cologne Cathedral, Germany, antique pewter
 or silver **75.00**
Building, Eiffel Tower, Paris, copper, antique brass. **35.00**
Building, Field Museum of Natural History, Chicago, IL,
 silver or copper **30.00**
Building, Jefferson Memorial, Washington DC, copper **15.00**
Building, Rockefeller Center, NY City, copper, 2⅝ x
 2 x 1" **25.00**
Building, Statue of Liberty, NY City, 6" h **7.00**
Building, Washington DC Capitol **5.00**
Card Folder, Yellowstone National Park, 1928. . . . . **5.00**
Clock, 1933 Chicago World's Fair, alarm, black enamel,
 windup, plastic over illus "A Section Of The Hall Of
 Science," tree, shrubs, and lawn illus **95.00**
Coloring Book, 1964–65 New York World's Fair, Spertus
 Publishing Co, 80 pp. **25.00**
Compact, Empire State Building, Art Deco **35.00**
Compact, Hawaii, Elgin. **30.00**
Creamer, St James, MN **25.00**
Cup, New Orleans **12.00**
Dresser Tray, Portland Hotel, milk glass **30.00**
Fur Clip, Beckman Bros, Great Falls, MT **25.00**
Hat, Disneyland, Mousketeers, stiff black felt, large
 black plastic ears, white, blue, and orange,
 "Disneyland/Mickey Mouse" patch, c1960 . . . . **25.00**
Matchbox, Niagara Falls, sterling **100.00**
Mug, Joilet High School, Joilet, IL, china **17.50**
Paperweight, glass, Old South Church, Boston, MA,
 brown tone photo scene **35.00**
Paperweight, glass, round, New Salem State Park **30.00**
Paperweight, Mt St Helens, dated 1988 . . . . **25.00**
Pencil Box, Alaska, pyrography of Eskimo totem pole,
 snap closure **13.00**
Pennant, Coney Island, felt, c1930. **20.00**
Pennant, Hershey Park, felt, brown and white, c1950 . . . . **25.00**
Pinback Button, Detroit, multicolored lighthouse scene,
 red "Where Life Is Worth Living" **45.00**
Pinback Button, 2nd Annual North Country Speed
 Skating Championship/Watertown Winter Carnival,
 January 17–18, 1942, dark red on gray. **15.00**
Pinback Button, Sled Dog Exhibit, Camden, ME, 1940 . . . . . . **15.00**

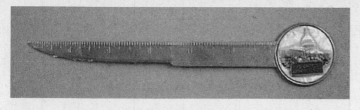

Letter Opener/Ruler, US Capitol, Washington, DC, metal blade, pearlized plastic medallion with Capitol bldg, 7⁵/₈" l, $5.00.

Pitcher, Statue of Liberty	35.00
Plate, Idaho	6.00
Plate, Wildwood, NJ, Ocean Pier & Fun Chase, pierced border	8.00
Playing Cards, Disneyland, white ground, castle illus	5.00
Playing Cards, 1939 New York World's Fair, double deck	135.00
Playing Cards, Pro Football Hall of Fame, Canton, OH, building illus	7.50
Playing Cards, Vista Dome, 1950–60	15.00
Postcard, Georgian Hotel, Athens	2.00
Postcard, Touraline Hotel, Boston, hotel view	4.00
Program, Rose Bowl Parade, 1940	20.00
Spoon, Algiers, sterling	20.00
Spoon, Capri, Italy, sterling, enameled classical urn top, emb bowl	45.00
Spoon, Colorado, sterling	20.00
Spoon, Honolulu, sterling	25.00
Spoon, New Year's, sterling	18.00
Spoon, San Francisco, sterling	18.00
Spoon, Washington DC, sterling	15.00
Tea Set, Niagara Falls, hp, scenic transfers, Stadler	120.00
Tray, Alabama, metal	28.00
Tray, Florida, metal	28.00
Tray, Fort William Henry, metal	7.00
Tray, Indiana, metal	28.00
Tray, Mexico, metal	28.00
Tray, New York, metal	7.00
Tray, Pennsylvania, metal	28.00
Tray, Washington DC, metal	28.00
Tray, Williamsburg, VA, metal	8.00
Tumbler, Pearl Harbor	10.00
Visor, 1980 Olympics, fabric, elastic headband, Winter Games symbol	25.00
Wall Pocket, Hamburg, Germany, heart shape, hp, scenic, orig labels	30.00

SPACE ADVENTURERS, FICTIONAL

Philip Francis Nowland and John F. Dille launched *Buck Rogers 2429 A.D.* in January 1929. The late 1930s was the golden age of this famous space explorer. Buck Rogers in the 25th Century, a television program airing between September 1979 and April 1981, created a renewed interest in Buck.

Flash Gordon was Buck Rogers' main rival in the 1930s. The 1940s was Flash's golden age. A second generation became hooked on Flash when the movie serials were repeated dozens of times on television in the late 1940s and 50s.

Americans were enamored by space in the early 1950s. Television responded with Captain Video and His Video Rangers, Flash Gordon, Rocky Jones Space Ranger, Space Patrol, and Tom Corbett, Space Cadet. A second generation of space adventure

series, e.g., Lost in Space and Star Trek, was launched in the 1960s and 70s. Spinoffs such as Deep Space Nine and Babylon 5 have kept the legend of the space adventurer alive on television.

Collectors' Club: Galaxy Patrol, 22 Colton St, Worcester, MA 01610.

Note: See Star Trek and Star Wars for additional listings.

Alien, Astro Base, Ideal, motorized, plastic, orig box, 20" h	$75.00
Alien, Blaster Target Game, HG Toys, pistol, cardboard target	165.00
Alien, Glow Putty, Laramie, MOC	25.00
Alien, Halloween costume, Ben Cooper	25.00
Battlestar Galactica, action figure, Colonial Warrior, Mattel, MIB	40.00
Battlestar Galactica, action figure, Imperious Leader	5.00
Battlestar Galactica, Halloween costume, Cylon Warrior, 1978, boxed	15.00
Battlestar Galactica, Cylon Radio, plastic, figural head of Cylon warrior, Vanity Fair, 1978, MIB	75.00
Battlestar Galactica, Lasermatic Pistol, Mattel, 1978	30.00
Battlestar Galactica, Poster Art Set, Craft Master, 1978, MIB	15.00
Battlestar Galactica, Space Station Kit, General Mills premium, when assembled becomes complete cockpit for colonial viper, contains space operations manual, communicator headset, activator card, colonial warrior patch, 11 space mission cards, 20 x 28" poster, and 4 iron-on patches, unused	115.00
Black Hole, action figure, Dr Durant	20.00
Black Hole, stamp activity book	8.00
Black Hole, wristwatch	25.00
Buck Rogers, Interplanetary Space Fleet Kit, Buck Rogers Co, John Dille, balsa wood kit with paint vials, sandpaper, and instruction sheet featuring rockets to be built to complete space fleet, orig box mkd "Super-Dreadnought #4," 1945	2,275.00
Buck Rogers, Liquid Helium Water Pistol, Daisy, lihto metal pistol, 7" l	625.00
Buck Rogers, Paint By Numbers Set, Craft Master, 1980s	10.00
Buck Rogers, Printing Set, Cosmic Conquests, Stamperkraft/J Dille, litho box features Buck, Wilma, and Dr Huer, 22 rubber stamps, used paper, orig box	250.00
Buck Rogers, Satellite Pioneers Map of Solar System, 1958	40.00
Buck Rogers, Sonic Ray Flashlight Gun, plastic, black, green, yellow, code signal screw, Norton-Honer, 1950s, 7¼" l	120.00
Buck Rogers, Starfighter, metal, plastic, complete with accessories, Corgi, 6" l, MIB	55.00
Buck Rogers, Super Foto Camera, Norton-Honer, 1955	70.00
Buck Rogers, Super Scope Telescope, plastic, 9" l, 1955	70.00
Buck Rogers, 25th Century Electronic Communications Outfit, Remco, J Dille, 2 plastic phones, secret decoder, electric wire, box insert featuring Buck inside TV-like screen, Buck Rogers featured on box	100.00
Buck Rogers, wristwatch, GLJ Toys, 1978	15.00
Captain Marvel, greeting card, Third Eye, psychedelic day-glo colors, Captain Marvel comic book illus, blank inside, unused with orig envelope, 1971, 6 x 9"	6.00
Captain Marvel, jigsaw puzzle, Fawcett, "Captain Marvel Rides the Engine of Doom," c1941, orig box	75.00

Tom Corbett, book, *Tom Corbett: A Trip to the Moon*, Wonder Books #713, Marcia Martin author, Frank Vaughn illus, 1953, $8.00.

Captain Marvel, Punch–Out Book, Samuel Lowe, unused, c1942, 8 x 12" 275.00

Captain Marvel, sneaker box, mkd "Nat's Periodical Publ – 1976, The World's Mightiest Sneaker," litho box with flying Captain Marvel, box for size 10 royal blue sneakers 150.00

Captain Video, flying saucer ring 200.00

Captain Video, goggles 50.00

Captain Video, Rite–O–Lite Flashlight Gun, 1950s 40.00

Captain Video, Rocket Launcher, Lido, plastic, includes rocket launcher and missiles, box reverse has 2 unpunched Video Ranger figures 235.00

Captain Video, Space Vehicle, Lido, plastic, 4" l, 1950s...... 25.00

Captain Video, Troop Transport Ship, Lido, MIB 150.00

Close Encounters of the Third Kind, UFO sighting map, Skywatchers Club premium 5.00

E T, Action Figure, LJN, plastic, poseable arms, "Speak & Spell," 3¹/₂" h, MOC 25.00

E T, Doll, felt, stuffed, fleshtone, printed design on both sides, blue plastic eyes, c1982 .... 20.00

E T, Stunt Spaceship, LJN, windup, plastic, silver and green, 2" h, MOC 25.00

Flash Gordon, Dart Gun, Ja–Ru, 5³/₄" l, plastic, blue, yellow accents, orange darts, 1981................... 20.00

Lost in Space, comic book, Gold Key................... 20.00

Mike Mercury, lunch box and thermos, Independent Television Corp, litho tin, "Mike Mercury's Supercar Orbital Food Container," old store stock, 1960s......... 135.00

Planet of the Apes, bank, Play Pal, figural Dr Zaius, vinyl, 11" h, 1960s 25.00

Planet of the Apes, lunch box, Aladdin, steel, emb, 1974 .... 50.00

Planet of the Apes, Vehicle, prison wagon, AHI, friction 45.00

Rocky Jones Space Ranger, coloring book, Whitman, unused, 1951, 32 pp, 11 x 15".................... 60.00

Space: 1999, coloring book, Saalfield, #C1881, space ship orbiting moon cov 15.00

Space: 1999, Eagle Transport, Dinky, #360, diecast, 1975 .... 35.00

Space: 1999, Moon Car, Ahi, plastic, yellow, 3 tires on each side with silver wheel covers, 2 astronaut figures in orange outfits in vehicle seat, "Space:1999" paper sticker, 1976, MOC............................. 65.00

Space: 1999, Space Expedition Dart Set, 1976, MOC 15.00

Space: 1999, utility belt, Remco, 1976.................. 25.00

Space Patrol, binoculars, plastic, black, 1950s 100.00

Space Patrol, Cosmic Smoke Gun, 6" l, plastic, metallic green, 1950s..................................... 100.00

Space Patrol, Rocket Lite Flashlight, Rayovac, MIB 325.00

Space Patrol, Space–O–Phone, Ralston Purina Company mailer, pr of 3"–l yellow and blue plastic space phones, attached string, instruction sheet with order blank, 1950s.................................. 100.00

Space Patrol, Space Patrol Commander Thunderbirds, Gun, Lone Star, plastic, red, blue plastic front sight, fires spring–loaded darts, 8¹/₂" l, 1965................. 60.00

Tom Corbett Space Cadet, coloring book, Saalfield, 1952.. 40.00

Tom Corbett Space Cadet, Official Space Academy Set, Marx, #7012, plastic and tin litho pcs, orig 14 x 23 x 4¹/₂" box 425.00

Tom Corbett Space Cadet, playsuit, girl's, cloth, gray top and skirt with polka dots around neck and cuff, yellow felt section around chest and back area with red and blue logo 85.00

Tom Corbett Space Cadet, Atomic Pistol Flashlight, Marx, 8" l, plastic, red, orig red, white, blue, and yellow box 100.00

Tom Corbett Space Cadet, wrist compass 45.00

Tom Corbett Space Cadet, thermos bottle, Aladdin, c1952, 6¹/₄" h 35.00

SPACE EXPLORATION

Collector interest in artifacts relating to the manned space program began in the early 1980s. After a brief fascination with autographed material, collectors moved to three–dimensional objects.

The collapse of the Soviet Union coupled with Russia's and several cosmonauts' need for capital has resulted in the sale of space memorabilia by several leading auction houses around the world. Everything from capsules to space suits are available for purchase.

This category focuses primarily on material associated with manned space flight. Collector interest in material from unmanned flights is extremely limited.

Reference: Stuart Schneider, *Collecting the Space Race*, Schiffer Publishing, 1993.

Newsletter: *Space Autograph News*, 862 Thomas Ave, San Diego, CA 92109.

Apollo–X Moon Challenger, plastic body, litho tin plates, blinking lights, TN, Japan, 1960s............. $100.00

Bank, Apollo 11, lunar landing commemorative, plastic, white rocket shape, blue launch pad base, inscriptions of astronauts names, landing phrase, title and location of "Manned Spacecraft Center," 8¹/₂" h 20.00

Booklet, *Cape Kennedy Air Force Station*, c1962, 5 x 8" 15.00

Key Fob, Project Mercury, acrylic bar holding encased 4¢ "U.S. Man In Space" commemorative postage stamp, 1960s................................... 20.00

Mug, white ceramic, "First In Space TV," Westinghouse logo and small NASA emblem, astronaut near Eagle landing module with transmitter scene, early 1970s, 3³/₄" h 50.00

Paint By Number Set, Space Traveler Paint–By–Number Set, Standard Toykraft, 1950s 100.00

Pinback Button, Apollo XI, July 1969, Armstrong, Collins, and Aldrin, red, white, and blue, $30.00.

Paperback Book, *American Space Digest*, Schick Safety Razor premium, full color illus and photos, 1963, 3³/₄ x 5³/₄" 20.00

Pinback Button, moon landing commemorative, astronaut legs striding from landing module, black, white, and red 20.00

Pinback Button, "Sputnik Spotter," pink, black and white, "Official Watcher," 1950s 20.00

Plate, Armstrong setting foot on lunar surface, landing phrase and date in silver, iridescent gold, silver, and blue, "Hand Painted By Count Agazzi," 10" d 20.00

Record, *Lunar Landing/Man On the Moon*, 33¹/₃ rpm, audio highlights of Apollo 11 mission, 6³/₄ x 20¹/₂" color fold–out "Lunar Landing Mission Profile" map of mission travel, Metropolitan Life premium, orig paper slipcase envelope, 1969 . . . . 15.00

Space Shuttle Adventures Kit, Cheerios premium, includes 24–pp full color illus booklet, space shuttle iron–on transfer, 4¹/₂ x 5" peel–off emblem sticker sheet, unopened package of styrofoam shuttle flying model with instructions for assembly, orig 8¹/₂ x 10¹/₂" mailing envelope, 1981 . . . . 20.00

Space Shuttle Ring and Patch, bright silver luster metallic expansion ring with miniature replica of space shuttle on top, fabric patch, orig box, Avon, 1982 . . . . 20.00

Tumblers, set of 2, clear glass, Command Module shape, red, white, and blue, "Moonshot" pictorial and "Apollo11/Man On The Moon, 6" h 20.00

View–Master, America's Man in Space, 3 full color reels and booklet, orig 4¹/₂ x 4¹/₂" envelope 20.00

View–Master, Moon Rockets and Guide Missiles, 3 reels, Cape Canaveral and the Navaho, Atlas and Titan, and Moon Rockets, orig 4¹/₂ x 4¹/₂" envelope, 1959 . . . . 20.00

Wristwatch, animated, metal bezel, 2 astronauts and landing module on lunar surface against space sky with Earth in partial eclipse, command module rotating every 60 seconds, brown vinyl band with brown plastic buckle, Swiss, 1969 . . . . 100.00

SPACE TOYS

Space toys divide into three basic groups: (1) astronauts and spacemen, (2) spacecraft (capsules, flying saucers, rockets, and satellites), and (3) tanks and vehicles. Robots are excluded. They have reached the level of independent collecting status.

The toy industry, especially the Japanese, responded quickly to the growing worldwide interest in manned space flight. The first lithographed tin toys arrived on the market in the late 1940s. Toys became increasingly sophisticated during the 1950s. The number of parts that lit up or made sounds increased.

Plastic became the principal construction material by the early 1970s. Production shifted from Japan to China and Taiwan, a move that collectors view as having cheapened the toys. The decline in public interest in the space program in the mid–1970s also led to a decline in the production of space toys. Most collectors focus on space toys made prior to 1970.

The period box is an essential component of value, often adding 25% to 40% to the toy's value. The artwork on the box often is more impressive than the toy itself. Further, the box may contain information about the name of the toy, manufacturer, and/or distributor not found on the toy itself.

References: Dennis Way Nicholson (comp.), *The Gerry Anderson Memorabilia Guide*, Cooee Concepts Pty (Australia), 1994; Maxine A. Pinsky, *Marx Toys: Robots, Space, Comic, Disney & TV Characters*, Schiffer Publishing, 1996; Stuart Schneider, *Collecting the Space Race*, Schiffer Publishing, 1993.

Periodicals: *Toy Shop*, 700 E State St, Iola, WI 54990; *Toy Trader*, PO Box 1050, Dubuque, IA 52003.

Note: For additional listings see Robots, Space Adventurers, Star Trek, and Star Wars.

Adventure with Stars, Capitol Publishing Co, includes sighting instrument, star finder, observer's log, sky map, and 112 pp adventure book of stars, c1958, 15 x 10¹/₄" box $50.00

Aero Jet Range Rocket, Ranger Steel Products, plastic rocket operates on energy pellets, flies 200–300' in air, orig box 85.00

Airport Saucer, MT, Japan, battery operated, litho tin and plastic, saucer spinning around airport with flashing control tower, orig box, 8" d 235.00

Atomic Disintegrator Cap Pistol, Hubley, metal and plastic, repeating cap pistol, mkd "Atomic Disintegrator" both sides, orig box, 7¹/₂" l 650.00

Atomic Flash Gun, Chein, litho tin, needs flint, orig box, 7¹/₂" l 120.00

Baby Space Gun, Japan, friction, litho tin, "Space Rescue" missile lithoed on stock, siren sound, 6" l 130.00

Cosmic Ray Gun, Ranger Steel, litho tin gun with emb details, sparking action, 6¹/₂" l 250.00

Cragstan Rocket Ship XX2, TN, Japan, friction, litho tin and plastic, sparking tail spinner, new old stock, orig box, 1950s, 13¹/₂" l 250.00

Electronic Astro Jack, Stanzel, Schulenburg, TX, battery operated, flying spaceboy and space station, 4" h spaceboy 85.00

Flashing Rocket Ship Space Pistol, Irwin, rocket shaped pistol with moving pilot and rockets, click trigger for flash and interplanetary signals, 1950s, 7¹/₂" l, MOC 270.00

Two–Stage Rocket Launching Pad, Normura, battery operated, litho tin, Jupiter silo and technician at control panel, TV screen lights up and broadcasts rocket launch, orig box, 1950s, 7½" h, $375.00.

Floating Satellite, SH, Japan, battery operated, target game, bowl floats and stays in air, aim and shoot it down 175.00

Flying Saucer Men, Industrial Die Cutting Co, litho cardboard catapult set with spacemen images, complete with 5 different 3" d spacemen disks, unused, orig box, 1950s 75.00

Flying Saucer with Space Pilot, Cragston, battery operated, orig box, 1950s 250.00

Jetson's Turnover Tank, China, windup, litho tin, unauthorized, Judy Jetson lithoed on turret, 1960s, 5" l 135.00

King Flying Saucer, KO, Japan, battery operated, litho tin body, plastic base, turning motion, space sound, rotating lights, orig box with inserts, 7½" d 175.00

Kuzan's Astro Zapper, Kuzan, plastic, with ammo 85.00

Mechanical Orbiting Missile, GNK, Germany, windup, plastic and litho tin, rotating globe on base, satellite attached to globe by wire travels around globe, orig box, 4½" h 225.00

Mystery Space Explorer Tank, AHI, Japan, litho tin, bump–and–go action, fires lighted gun, figure moves, radar antenna revolves, orig box, 8" l 450.00

Mystery Space Ship, Marx, plastic, complete with 7¼" d saucer, 11" h platform, rocket launcher, moon men, astronauts, and manual with more than 50 tricks and hints, hand–cranked gyro powered, defies gravity, new old store stock 100.00

New Flash Gun, SH, Japan, battery operated, lihto tin, light and sound, orig box with Robbie the Robot image, 9½" l 225.00

Planet Special Rocket, Great Britain, friction, litho tin rocket with pilots and passengers, orig box, 1950s, 6½" l 350.00

PN 130 Space Satellite, West Germany, half–globe base, satellite and rocket projecting from opposite sides extend to 15", 3" d globe 175.00

Robert the Robot and His Remote Control Bulldozer, Ideal, battery operated, plastic, trigger gun with cranking directional controls, seated red and silver robot works gears, blue and yellow bulldozer with red treads, orig box, 9" l 2,000.00

Rocket Dart Pistol, Daisy, 1950s 65.00

Rocket Satellite Action Game, Tarco Toy, electronic, remote control, joy stick with attached magnet moves spaceships through course, Buck Rogers type graphics on orig box 100.00

Rocket Ship SV–3, Linemar, Japan, friction, litho tin, small dent one side, orig box, 6½" l 150.00

Rocket Shot Pinball, Lindstrom, bagatelle, Art Deco graphics, red, yellow, and black, orig box, 24 x 12" 75.00

Satellite Explorers, WS/NY #73, 6 Archer style plastic spacemen with clear helmets in orig unopened bag, 1 red, 1 blue, 2 yellow, 2 green 125.00

Sky View Observatory, Bellevue Mfg Co, complete with 20x telescope, compasss, flashlight, instructions, and Zodiac cards, 16" h 125.00

SP–1 Space Car, Linemar, Japan, friction, tin, travels with engine noise and sparks, needs flint, orig box, 6" l 550.00

Space Age Erector Set #3 18000, Gilbert, plastic parts, builds rocket ships, space missiles, jet fighters, or ICBM's 125.00

Space Beetle, Y, Japan, 21 Century Space Series, battery operated, plastic, crawls on 4 caterpillar treads, tread angle can be changed to elevate crawler, 9" l 65.00

Space Bus, Usagayi, Japan, friction, litho tin, astronauts, capsules, planets, rockets, and comets dec, destination plate reads "Space," Robbie robot image on roof, clear plastic windows, orig box, 14½" l 1,500.00

Space Flying Jeep, Linemar, Japan, friction, litho tin, moves forward propelling colorful turbo spinner, orig box, 6½" l 215.00

Space Helmet with Radar Goggles, Banner Plastics, copper metallic swirled plastic with day–glo orange trim, helmet top shaped as rocketship, yellow and green goggles, orig box with inserts, 1950s 650.00

Spacemen, Marx, hp plastic spacemen with detachable equipment, 3" h men, on 8 x 11" space card, complete set of 7 .... 70.00

Space 1999 Colorforms, orig 8 x 12" boxed set with booklet, 1976 .... 50.00

Space Patrol Capsule, TT, Japan, windup, litho tin capsule, raised design engines, lithoed walking space astronaut at rear, half–figure pilot sitting under clear plastic dome, 5" d 180.00

Space Patrol Round Rocket, Asahitoy, Japan, windup, litho tin, raised pilot's helmet in cockpit, orig box, 5½" l 200.00

Space Pilot Super Sonic Gun, Merit, England, battery operated, plastic, orig box, 1953, 9" l 225.00

Space Target Game, Knickerbocker Plastic, includes super atomic pistol, 3 rubber darts, spinning and flashing friction sparkler, and space ship, orig box, 19 x 14" 125.00

Super Cycle, Japan, friction, litho tin motorcycle, red, mkd "Atom" and "S" inside Superman type shield, 12" l 1,100.00

Super Robot Tank, SH, Japan, friction, litho tin, tank with coil–headed robot driver at wheel, dual firing barrels with pom–pom retracting motion, unpainted metal on barrels shows some corrosion, 9" l 350.00

Super Sonic Gun, Japan, friction, litho tin, siren sound, 7½" l 275.00

USA NASA Apollo Spacecraft with Astronaut, MT, Japan, battery operated, lihto tin spacecraft, celluloid astronauts, 1 astronaut driver, other suspended above 9½" l spacecraft, orig box 225.00

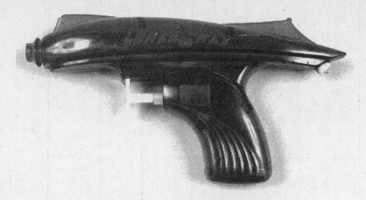

Lunar Ray Water Pistol, red plastic, 7¼" l, $20.00.

US Command Space Satellite Moon Radio 3640, Educational Electronics Co, Command Space Satellite Mark II, intercepts local broadcasts, 8 x 7 x 3½" orig box **175.00**

Whistling Space Top Set, Linemar, Japan, set includes activator and pr of 2" d litho tin automatic whistling tops with colorful space graphics, orig box **140.00**

X–Ray Gun, TN, Japan, battery operated, litho tin with emb details, pom–pom action, flashing light, complete with tripod, orig box, 16" l **300.00**

X–7 Space Explorer Ship, MT, Japan, battery operated, litho tin, bump–and–go action, flashing lights, orig box, 8" l **180.00**

Z–26 Space Capsule, KO, Japan, friction, litho tin capsule, half–figure astronaut sitting at controls under clear plastic dome, 6" d **135.00**

AUCTION PRICES

Space Toys sold by New England Auction Gallery in November, 1997. Prices include a 5% buyer's premium.

Atomic "5" Pistol, Newell #149, red plastic, spring firing action uses table tennis balls, 1950s, 9½" l . . **$168.00**

Bump 'N Go Space Explorer, KO, Japan, windup, litho tin, X–8 tank, bump–and–go motion, figural astronaut revolves under plastic dome, 6" l **131.25**

Jetson's Hopping Elroy, Marx/HB, windup, litho tin, replaced plastic antenna with 2 discs, orig box missing top flaps, 1963, 4" h **764.40**

Moon Rocket, MT, Japan, friction, litho tin, mkd "3", astronaut at controls lithoed in center, 7" l **189.00**

Orbit Explorer with Airborne Satellite, KO, Japan, windup, litho tin tank, center plastic spout blows air as styrofoam ball hovers above, litho tin astronaut with TV camera rotates inside dome, aerial spins, 6¼" l **808.50**

Rex Mar's Space Target Game, Marx, litho tin, 5 figural targets, complete with 11½" l plastic space rifle and ammo, 6 x 14" l **437.85**

Rocket Ship, possibly Wyandotte, pressed steel, red rocket with white rubber tires, 1930s, 6½" l **111.30**

Stratoblaster, Fenwal, plastic, repeating cap rifle with telescopic sight to 3x magnification, missiles and rockets emb on grips, 27" l, box missing sides **322.35**

SPORTING COLLECTIBLES

This category includes memorabilia from sports that do not have separate categories, e.g., baseball, basketball, football, and hockey. The listings include amateur and professional material.

Sports memorabilia has attracted collector interest for two reasons. First, collectors grew tired of two–dimensional trading cards. They wanted three–dimensional material, especially items used to play the sport. Second, decorators began creating sports theme restaurants and bars in the 1980s. Collectors were amazed at the variety of material available.

When buying any game–related object, obtain a written provenance. Beware of sports autographs. The FBI reports that forgeries are as high as 70% and more in some sports categories. The only way to make certain the signature is authentic is to see the person sign it. One hot area in the late 1990s is trophies.

References: Mark Allen Baker, *Sports Collectors Digest Complete Guide to Boxing Collectibles*, Krause Publications, 1995; Roderick A. Malloy, *Malloy's Sports Collectibles Value Guide, Up–to–Date Prices For Noncard Sports Memorabilia*, Attic Books, Wallace–Homestead, Krause Publications, 1994.

Periodical: *Boxing Collectors News*, 3316 Luallen Dr, Carrollton, TX 75007.

Collectors' Clubs: Boxiana & Pugilistica Collectors International, PO Box 83135, Portland, OR 97203; Olympic Pin Collector's Club, 1386 5th St, Schenectady, NY 12303.

Note: For additional listings see Auto & Drag Racing, Baseball Cards, Baseball Memorabilia, Basketball Cards, Basketball Memorabilia, Football Cards, Football Memorabilia, Golf Collectibles, Hockey Cards, Hockey Memorabilia, Horse Racing, Hunting, and Tennis Collectibles.

Boating, pinback button, speedboat races, Devil's Lake Regatta, blue and white, Jul 1934 . . . . **$12.00**
Bowling, game, Bowl–A–Strike, ES Lowe, 1962 . . . . **10.00**
Bowling, game Bowlem, Parker Bros, 1930s **20.00**

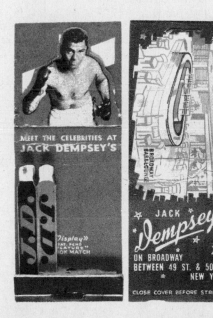

Boxing, matchcover, Jack Dempsey's on Broadway adv, Feature, Lion Match, $15.00.

Bowling, game, Donald Duck Pins and Bowling Game, Pressman, 1950s **45.00**

Bowling, nodder, composition, yellow shirt and shoes, blue trousers, holding bowling ball, mounted on wood block base, inscribed "You're Right Down My Alley," 6" h **45.00**

Boxing, book, *Joe Louis: American,* Margery Miller, dust jacket inscribed "To Phillip Kaplan from Joe Louis Dec. 17/46," **345.00**

Boxing, newspaper adv, Max Baer, endorsing premium physical development set from Quaker Wheat Crackels, from Sunday comic strip page, 10½ x 15½" **12.00**

Boxing, poster, Cassius Clay vs Jim Robinson, Miami Beach Convention Hall, Tue, Feb 7, 1961, 14 x 22". **207.00**

Boxing, ticket, Cassius Clay vs Alejandro Lavorante, Los Angeles Memorial Sports Arena, orchestra ringside, Fri, Jul 20, 1962, 8:30 pm **253.00**

Dog Race, game, Toy Creations, #1213, 1937 .... **30.00**

Gymnastics, autograph, Olga Korbut **8.00**

Ice Skating, autograph, Brian Boitano, PS, 8 x 10" **30.00**

Ice Skating, doll, Sonja Henie, The Skating Doll, composition, sleep eyes, mkd "R&B," 17" h **350.00**

Ice Skating, pinback button, Ice Capades, Donna Atwood portrait, black lettering on yellow ground, late 1950s. **12.00**

Olympics, book, *Olympische Spiel 1964,* German text, summary of Innsbruck, Austria Winter Olympics and Tokyo Summer Olympics, 384 pp **30.00**

Olympics, coin, 1980 Winter, oval, rolled, pine tree, Olympic rings, stamped "Lake Placid, NY," 1½" l **8.50**

Olympics, flask, white china, Olympic logo, inscribed "XVII Olympiade Rom 1960," issued by Lufthansa Airlines, 5½" h **15.00**

Olympics, pinback button, Olympic Team Support, red, white, and blue, 1970s **8.00**

Olympics, program, 1936 Summer Olympics, Berlin, 96 pp **75.00**

Pool, game, Lazy Pool, Dashound, 1965 .... **5.00**

Sailing, magazine cover, *Sports Illustrated,* Sep 6, 1954 ..... **10.00**

Skiing, program, 1932 Winter Olympics, Lake Placid, NY. ... **45.00**

Swimming, autograph, Gertrude Ederly, printed black and white drawing, 6½ x 8" sheet, blue ink inscription "Hold Strongly to 'Faith' in All You Do!, Best Always,

Swimmingly Yours, Gertrude Trudy Ederly, New York, Successful Channel Swim, August 6, 1926, 35 miles in 40½ Hrs, Cape Gris Nez to Kingdown," dated 1969 ...... **22.00**

Track and Field, comic book, True Comics, Track & Field, Parents' Magazine Press, Apr 1941 .... **65.00**

Wrestling, comic book, WWF Battlemania, WWF Action, Valiant **1.50**

Wrestling, game, WWF Wrestling Stars Game, Milton Bradley, 1985 .... **12.00**

AUCTION PRICES

Muhammad Ali boxing memorabilia sold by Chistie's Los Angeles on October 19, 1997. Prices include a 15% buyer's premium.

Banner, Cassius Clay vs Joe Frazier, Fight I, Mar 8, 1971, cloth, "Battle of Champions, Tickets Now On Sale, Cassius Clay vs Joe Fazier, Mon. Mar 8," blue, black, red, and yellow on white ground, gold fringe, 135 x 22" **$2,530.00**

Pennant, Cassius Clay vs Sonny Liston, Fight I, Feb 25, 1964, Miami Beach, blue ground, gold lettering "I Was There" and fighters' names and images, some light fading **1,955.00**

Pennant, Muhammad Ali vs Joe Frazier, Fight III, Thrilla in Manila, Oct 1, 1975, fighters' faces in orange, white, blue, and orange lettering on blue and white ground, 9½ x 7½" **863.00**

Poster, Muhammad Ali vs Henry Cooper, Fight II, London, May 21, 1966, red, white, and blue cardboard site poster featuring photographic images of Ali and Cooper, 14 x 21" **1,495.00**

Poster, Muhammad Ali vs Joe Frazier, Fight II, Madison Square Garden, Jan 28, 1974, black and yellow cardboard site poster, depicts both fighters in full fight poses, 24 x 28". **4,600.00**

Program, Cassius Clay vs Sonny Liston, Fight I, Feb 25, 1964, Miami Beach, 14 pp, 9 x 12" **1,610.00**

Wirephotos, Muhammad Ali vs Floyd Patterson, Fight I, scenes from Heavyweight Championship bout, 8 x 10", group of 26 .... **1,265.00**

STAMPS

Stamp collecting as a hobby was extremely popular throughout the middle decades of the 20th century. After a speculation period in the 1960s and 70s, when stamps became an investment commodity, the bubble burst in the 1980s. Middle– and low–end stamps experienced major price declines. To its credit, Scott Publishing adjusted the prices within its guides to reflect true market sales. Since this meant reducing the value for many stamps, the results sent shock waves through the market.

Stamp collecting is still in a period of recovery. Many question whether stamp collecting will ever recover its former popularity. Today's market is almost exclusively adult–driven. Investment continues to be the dominant collecting motivation. The overall feeling within the market is positive. Attendance is up at stamp shows. Modestly priced stamps are selling strongly. Interest in foreign issues is rising.

Condition, scarcity, and desirability (popularity) are the three pricing keys. Before researching the value of any stamps, carefully read the front matter of the book you are using, especially infor-

Softball, Double Header #212, J DeBeer & Son, Albany, NY, orig box, minor scuffs on ball and box, $99.00. Photo courtesy Past Tyme Pleasures.

mation relating to catalog values, grade, and condition. Make certain you understand the condition grade being used for pricing. Most stamp collectors want examples graded at very fine or above.

Book values are retail value. Valuable stamps are far easier to sell than lesser valued stamps. Expect to have to discount commonly found stamps by 60% to 70% when selling them. It may make far more sense to use recently issued United States stamps for postage than to try to sell them on the secondary market.

Most catalogs provide unused and used (canceled) values. In some cases, the postmark and/or cancellation may have more value than the stamp.

The five–volume *Scott 1998 Standard Postage Stamp Catalogue* (Scott Publishing Co., 911 Vandemark Road, Sidney, OH 45365) is the basic reference used by most collectors to determine values. Volume 1 contains information about United States stamps. If the collection you are evaluating only contains United States stamps, also consult Marc Hudgeons' *The Official 1997 Blackbook Price Guide of United States Postage Stamps, Nineteenth Edition* (House of Collectibles, 1996).

Over the past few years, numerous advertisements from the International Collectors Society have appeared in newspapers and magazines offering stamps featuring prominent personalities issued by countries such as Grenada. These stamps are being printed specifically for sale to unknowledgeable collectors who believe they are purchasing a bargain and long–term collectible. Nothing is further from the truth. They are not the "Hot New Collectible" claimed by the International Collectors Society. Both philatelic and regular collectors are shunning these stamps now and will do so in the future.

Periodicals: *Linn's Stamp News,* PO Box 29, Sidney, OH 45365; *Scott Stamp Monthly,* Box 828, Sidney, OH 45365; *Stamp Collector,* 700 E State St, Iola, WI 54990; *Stamps,* 85 Canisteo St, Hornell, NY 14843.

Collectors' Clubs: American Philatelic Society, PO Box 8000, State College, PA 16803; International Stamp Collectors Society, PO Box 854, Van Nuys, CA 91408.

Note: David J. Maloney, Jr.'s *Maloney's Antique & Collectibles Resource Directory* (found at your local library) contains the names of many specialized collectors' clubs.

STANGL

Johann Martin Stangl became the president of the Fulper pottery located in Flemington, New Jersey, in 1928. In 1929 he purchased Fulper. Stangl continued to produce some pieces under the Fulper trademark until around 1955. Stangl made inexpensive artware, dinnerware, and utilitarian ware.

In 1940 Stangl introduced a line of bird figurines, inspired by images from Audubon prints. Auguste Jacob designed and created the models for the birds. Initially, twelve birds were produced. A few out–of–production birds were reissued between 1972 and 1977. These are clearly dated on the bottom. When production ceased in 1978, over a hundred different shapes and varieties had been made. In addition, more than fifty dinnerware patterns were introduced between 1942 and 1968.

Johann Martin Stangl died in 1972. Frank Wheaton, Jr., bought Stangl and sold it to Pfaltzgraff Pottery in 1978. Pfaltzgraff ended production.

References: Susan and Al Bagdade, *Warman's American Pottery and Porcelain,* Wallace–Homestead, Krause Publications, 1994; Harvey Duke, *The Official Identification and Price Guide to Pottery and Porcelain, Eighth Edition,* House of Collectibles, 1995; Harvey Duke, *Stangl Pottery,* Wallace–Homestead, Krause Publications, 1992; Mike Schneider, *Stangl and Pennsbury Birds,* Schiffer Publishing, 1994.

Collectors' Club: Stangl/Fulper Collectors Club, PO Box 538, Flemington, NJ 08822.

Amber Glo, butter dish **$25.00**
Americana, chop plate, 12" d **25.00**
Americana, creamer **6.00**
Americana, cream soup saucer **4.00**
Americana, dinner plate, 9" d **7.00**
Americana, salad bowl, 10" **30.00**
Americana, teapot, 6 cup **35.00**
Antique Gold, ashtray **7.00**
Antique Gold, pitcher, #4055 . . . . **17.00**
Apple Delight, bread and butter plate **4.00**
Apple Delight, creamer **8.00**
Apple Delight, lug soup **12.00**
Apple Delight, luncheon plate **5.00**
Apple Delight, saucer **3.00**
Ashtray, pheasant **30.00**
Bird, #3250A, Standing Duck, 3¼" h **125.00**
Bird, #3250F, Quacking Duck, 1⅜" h **125.00**
Bird, #3275, Turkey, 3⅜" h **375.00**
Bird, #3276D, Bluebirds, 1978, 8¼" h **200.00**
Bird, #3407, Owl, terra rose blue finish, 4½" h **200.00**
Bird, #3444, Cardinal, matte finish, 6¾" h **130.00**
Bird, #3450, Passenger Pigeon, 9¼ x 19¼" **1,100.00**
Bird, #3453, Mountain Bluebird, 6⅜" h **1,100.00**
Bird, #3490D, Redstarts, 9½" h **210.00**
Bird, #3518D, White–Crowned Pigeons, 7⅞ x 12½" **600.00**
Bird, #3581, Chickadees, group, black and white, orig price tag, 5¾ x 8¼" **350.00**
Bird, #3599D, Hummingbirds, 1973, orig price tag, 8¾" h **375.00**
Bird, #3628, Rieffers Hummingbird, 1972, orig price tag, 4⅞" h **80.00**

#3586, Della Ware Pheasant, natural colors, 15½" l, 9" h, $450.00.

Fruit, sandwich plate, center handle, 12" d, $12.00.

Bird, #3715, Bluejay, with peanut, antique gold, repaired beak, 10¼" h 95.00
Bird, #3749S, Western Tanager, 5" h 325.00
Bird, #3752D, Red Headed Woodpeckers, gloss finish, 7¾" h 325.00
Bird, #3755, Audubon Warbler, orig price tag, 4½" h 425.00
Bird, #3853, Golden Crowned Kinglets, group, 5½" h 600.00
Bird, #3923, Vermillion Flycatcher, 5¾" h 850.00
Caribbean, candy dish 30.00
Caribbean, relish, #3857, 3 part 35.00
Caribbean, vase, #2041, 9" h 50.00
Children's Dish Set, 2 pcs, Bunny Lunch 300.00
Children's Dish Set, 2 pcs, Ducky Dinner 200.00
Children's Dish Set, 2 pcs, Kitten Capers 190.00
Children's Dish Set, 2 pcs, Playful Pups 190.00
Children's Dish Set, 3 pcs, Carousel, blue border 350.00
Children's Dish Set, 3 pcs, Circus Clown 300.00
Children's Dish Set, 3 pcs, Ginger Girl, 1957 .... 450.00
Children's Dish Set, 3 pcs, Humpty Dumpty, pink border ... 300.00
Children's Dish Set, 3 pcs, Little Bo Peep 200.00
Children's Dish Set, 3 pcs, Peter Rabbit 450.00
Colonial, bean pot, handled, 7" h 45.00
Colonial, console bowl, oval, 12 x 8" 25.00
Colonial, creamer 10.00
Colonial, eggcup 8.00
Colonial, vegetable, cov, oval, 10" l 15.00
Country Garden, creamer 10.00
Country Garden, cup 13.00
Country Garden, plate, 10" d 16.00
Country Garden, salt and pepper shakers, pr 20.00
Country Garden, saucer 5.00
Country Garden, server 10.00
Dessert Mold, fruit center, brown 22.00
First Love, cup and saucer 10.00
First Love, plate, 6" 6.00
First Love, plate, 8" 10.00
First Love, plate, 10" 16.00
Fruits and Flowers, salt shaker 12.00
Fruits and Flowers, vegetable bowl, 8" 35.00
Golden Blossom, bread and butter plate, 6" 5.00
Golden Blossom, cereal bowl 12.00

Golden Blossom, cup 10.00
Golden Blossom, dinner plate, 10" 15.00
Golden Blossom, salad plate, 8" 10.00
Golden Blossom, salt and pepper shakers, pr 20.00
Golden Blossom, saucer 3.00
Golden Blossom, snack plate, handled, 12" 15.00
Gloden Blossom, vegetable bowl, divided 25.00
Golden Harvest, bowl, 5¾" 18.00
Golden Harvest, chop plate, 12½" 35.00
Golden Harvest, creamer and sugar, cov 24.00
Golden Harvest, vegetable, oval, divided, 10¼" 40.00
Lyric Casual, sugar 22.00
Magnolia, salt and pepper shakers, pr 20.00
Orchard Song, berry bowl 5.00
Orchard Song, bowl, 8" 7.50
Orchard Song, bread and butter plate, 6" 5.00
Orchard Song, butter dish 35.00
Orchard Song, creamer 8.00
Orchard Song, cup 10.00
Orchard Song, cup and saucer 10.00
Orchard Song, dinner plate, 10" 10.00
Orchard Song, eggcup 10.00
Orchard Song, fruit bowl 10.00
Orchard Song, platter, oval 35.00
Orchard Song, salad plate, 8" 10.00
Orchard Song, salt and pepper shakers, pr 20.00
Orchard Song, saucer 3.00
Orchard Song, server 7.00
Orchard Song, sugar 12.00
Pink Lady, plate, 5" 8.00
Pink Lady, plate, 9" 16.00
Prelude, cup and saucer 10.00
Prelude, plate, 6½" 6.00
Prelude, plate, 10" 16.00
Starflower, dinner plate, 10" 13.00
Thistle, bread and butter plate, 6" 4.00
Thistle, cup 5.00
Thistle, dinner plate, 10" 10.00
Thistle, luncheon plate, 9" 8.50

Candy Dish, Morning Blue, center handle, 6" d, $7.00.

Thistle, salad plate, 8" 7.50
Thistle, saucer. 2.50
Town & Country, salt and pepper shakers, pr, cylinders,
    honey glaze 25.00
Town & Country, toothbrush holder, green 45.00
Tulip, casserole, 8" d. 40.00
Tulip, salad bowl, 11" d. 45.00
Wild Rose, chowder bowl, 5" 18.00
Wild Rose, cup and saucer 10.00
Wild Rose, plate, 8" 10.00
Wild Rose, plate, 10" 16.00
Wild Rose, salad bowl, 12" d. 50.00

AUCTION PRICES

Stangl birds auctioned by The Stangl/Fulper Collectors Club on June 7, 1997. Prices include a 10% buyer's premium.

3250C, Feeding Duck, 1³/₈" h $75.00
3273, Rooster, hollow base, orig label, glued tail,
    5³/₄" h 275.00
3275, Bluebird, 5¹/₈" h 70.00
3405D, Cockatoos, revised, 9¹/₂" h 120.00
3443, Flying Duck, teal, 9" h 225.00
3446, Hen, yellow, 7¹/₂" h 185.00
3451, Willow Ptarmigan, 11" h 2,500.00
3454, Key West Quail Dove, both wings raised, 9" h . . 800.00
3491 & 3492, Hen Pheasant and Cock Pheasant,
    6⁵/₈" h hen, 6¹/₈" h cock, price for pr 275.00
3580, Cockatoo, 8³/₄" h 110.00
3582D, Parakeets, green, 7¹/₂" h 250.00
3627, Rivoli Hummingbird, 6¹/₈" h 175.00
3635, Goldfinch, grouping, 4¹/₂ x 12¹/₂". 250.00
3717D, Bluejays, 13" h 3,700.00
3750D, Western Tanagers, 8" h 4225.00
3754D, White Wing Crossbills, matte finish, factory
    repaired base flaw crack, 8⁵/₈" h 400.00
3852, Cliff Swallow, 3¹/₂" h. 185.00
3868, Summer Tanager, 3⁷/₈" h 425.00
3934, Yellow–Throated Warbler, 5³/₄" h 350.00

STAR TREK

Gene Roddenberry's Star Trek appeared on TV beginning in September 1966 and ending on June 3, 1969. The show's initial success was modest. NBC reversed a decision to cancel the show in 1968 when fans rose in protest. A move to Friday evenings in its final season spelled doom for the show in the ratings war.

NBC syndicated Star Trek. By 1978 it had been translated in 42 languages and shown in 51 countries. Over 125 stations carried it in the United States. There were more than 350 local fan clubs.

The first Star Trek convention was held in 1972, drawing 3,000 fans. A dispute between the professional and fan managers of the convention resulted in two separate conventions in 1974. Before long, dozens of individuals were organizing Star Trek conventions around the country.

In 1979 Paramount released *Star Trek: The Motion Picture*. Its success led to additional films and television series starring the crew of the *Enterprise*. In September 1987 *Star Trek: The Next Generation* was launched. *Deep Space Nine* and *Star Trek: Voyager* followed. The *Generations* movie appeared in 1994 and *First Contact* in 1996.

References: Ursula Augustin, *Star Trek Collectibles: Classic Series, Next Generation, Deep Space Nine, Voyager*, Schiffer Publishing, 1997; Sue Cornwell and Mike Kott, *Star Trek Collectibles, Fourth Edition*, House of Collectibles, 1996; Christine Gentry and Sally Gibson–Downs, *Greenberg's Guide to Star Trek Collectibles, Vol. 1* (1991), *Vol. 2* (1992), *Vol. 3* (1992), Greenberg Books, Kalmbach Publishing; Jerry B. Snyder, *A Trekker's Guide to Collectibles With Values*, Schiffer Publishing, 1996.

Collectors' Clubs: International Federation of Trekkers, PO Box 84, Groveport, OH 43125; Starfleet, 200 Hiawatha Blvd, Oakland, NJ 07436; Star Trek: The Official Fan Club, PO Box 111000, Aurora, CO 80042.

Action Figure, Deep Space Nine, Playmates, Dukat, 1st
    series, Playmates, MOC $20.00
Action Figure, Deep Space Nine, Playmates, Odo, 1st
    series, Playmates, MOC 20.00
Action Figure, Deep Space Nine, Playmates, Quark, 1st
    series, MOC 20.00
Action Figure, Next Generation, Galoob, Ferengi, MOC 85.00
Action Figure, Next Generation, Galoob, Selay, MOC. 65.00
Action Figure, Next Generation, Galoob, Tasha Yar,
    MOC 30.00
Action Figure, Next Generation, Playmates, Admiral
    McCoy, 2nd series, MOC. 15.00
Action Figure, Next Generation, Playmates, Ambassador
    Sarek, 4th series, MOC 15.00
Action Figure, Next Generation, Playmates, Commander
    Riker, 1st series, MOC 20.00
Action Figure, Next Generation, Playmates, Worf, 1st
    series, loose 10.00
Action Figure, Voyager, Playmates, Captain Janeway, 1st
    series, MOC 15.00
Action Figure, Voyager, Playmates, Tukok, 1st series,
    MOC 15.00
Bank, Captain Kirk, hard vinyl, Play Pal, Inc, ©Paramount Pictures Corp, 1975, 11" h 75.00
Book, *Making of Star Trek, The*, Stephen Whitfield and
    Gene Roddenberry, Ballantine, 1st ed. 15.00

Limited Edition Collector Plate, Mr. Spock, 1984, $95.00.

Book, *Making of Star Trek: The Motion Picture*, Susan Sackett and Gene Rodenberry, paperback, Wallaby, 1980. . . . . **30.00**

Book, *Making of the Trek Conventions, The*, Joan Winston, Doubleday, 1977 . . . . **45.00**

Book, *Planet of Judgment*, Joe Haldeman, Bantam, 1977 . . . . . **5.00**

Book, *Trouble with Tribbles*, David Gerrold, Ballantine, 1973. . . . . **10.00**

Book, *Vulcan*, Kathleen Sky, Bantam, 1978. . . . . **15.00**

Bumper Sticker, Beam Me Up Mr Spock, Aviva, 1979. . . . . **2.00**

Bumper Sticker, I Am A Trekkie, Aviva, 1979 . . . . **2.00**

Bumper Sticker, I Grok Spock, Lincoln Enterprises **1.00**

Bumper Sticker, My Other Vehicle Is a Romulan Warbird, Creation **2.00**

Bumper Sticker, *USS Enterprise* NCC–1701, Creation **2.00**

Cake Decorator, 10–pc set, original TV show, scenes of *Enterprise* on centerpiece, Tuttle, 1976 . . . . **10.00**

Calendar, 1973, color photos from orig television show, Lincoln Enterprises, 1973. . . . . **10.00**

Calendar, 1977, cloth, hanging, vertical printed design, Franco **30.00**

Candy Dish, Pfaltzgraff, white and blue, *Star Trek VI*, movie version command insignia shape, blue and yellow USS Enterprise NCC–1701–A insignia emblem in bottom of dish, orig box, 9½". **30.00**

Cereal Bowl and Mug, plastic, "The Motion Picture," 1979. . . . . **20.00**

Clock, wall, white, red 20th anniversary logo on face, 1986. . . . . **25.00**

Coloring Book, Spock and Kirk cover, Saalfield, 1975. . . . . . . **10.00**

Costume, Mr Spock, Paramount Pictures, 1975. . . . . **75.00**

Decanter, Grenadier, full figure standing Spock, gold metallic glaze, 1979, 13" h **700.00**

Door Hanger, plastic, rect, color photo on front, "Warning, Entering Unexplored Territory, Do Not Disturb" on back, Antioch, 1992–95 . . . . **2.00**

Drinking Glass, Star Trek Animated Series, set of 4, Dr Pepper promo, 1976 . . . . **150.00**

Drinking Glass, *Star Trek: The Motion Picture*, set of 3, Coca–Cola promo, 1979 . . . . **75.00**

Drinking Glass, *Star Trek III: The Search for Spock*, set of 4, Taco Bell promo, 1984. . . . . **35.00**

Flashlight, gun shape, red and white, blister pack with battery on header card and photos from *Star Trek: The Motion Picture*, Larami, 1979. . . . . **25.00**

Greeting Card, "I was going to shoot you with a phaser...But it seemed so unromantic," Kirk with bow and arrow illus, California Dreamers, 1st series, 1985 . . . . **2.50**

Hat, corduroy, *Star Trek IV*, embroidered movie log, Official Star Trek Fan Club, 1986 . . . . **12.00**

Magazine, *US*, Dec 1979, Spock and *Star Trek: The Motion Picture* cov **5.00**

Mobile, *Enterprise*, paper, orig envelope. **35.00**

Model, *Enterprise*, 3–pc set, Ertl, 1989 . . . . **15.00**

Napkins, set of 8, paper, Kirk, Spock, McCoy, and *Enterprise* in red, white, and blue on white ground, Tuttle, 1976. . . . . **10.00**

Paint By Number Set, Star Trek Paint By Number Set, Hasbro, 1972 . . . . **30.00**

Pajamas, child's, 2 pc, color photos from *Star Trek: The Motion Picture*, orig package, Pajama Corp of America, 1979 . . . . **35.00**

Pennant, *Star Trek II* logo, triangle shape, Spock in Vulcan robes, "Spock Lives," Image Products, 1982, 12 x 30" **8.00**

Pinback Button, Kirk, in gray uniform, *Star Trek: The Motion Picture*, Aviva, 1979, 2¼" d **2.00**

Pinback Button, "Paramount Pictures Star Trek Adventure" above *Enterprise* color photo, Universal Studios, 1989 . . . . **3.00**

Pinback Button, *Star Trek III: The Search for Spock*, blue and yellow, Taco Bell promo, 3" d **2.00**

Pinball Machine, *Star Trek: The Motion Picture* theme, Bally, 1979 . . . . **400.00**

Plaque, Star Trek: The Next Generation, Jason Palmer, 1994. . . . . **75.00**

Playing Cards, *Star Trek II: The Wrath of Khan*, orig box, 1982. . . . . **20.00**

Pocketknife, Swiss army style, ivory handle with *Enterprise* and logo, Taylor Cutlery, 1978 . . . . **75.00**

Poster, black light flocked, Dynamic Publishing Co, 1976. . . . . **15.00**

Poster, crew and transporter, Langley Associates, 1976, 20 x 24" **4.00**

Sheet Music, original TV show, Bruin Music,1970 . . . . **3.00**

Sheet Music, *Star Trek IV: The Voyage Home*, Famous Music, 1986 . . . . **3.00**

Tie, clip–on, *Enterprise* ship, "Star Trek," and "NCC 1701" repeated in diagonal stripes, Lee, 1976 . . . . **35.00**

Tray, metal, collapsible legs, color photo, ©1979 Paramount Pictures Corp and Marsh Allan Products, Inc, orig sealed plastic bag, 12½ x 17" **75.00**

Wallet, blue plastic, snap closure, *Star Trek: The Motion Picture* motif, Larami, 1979 . . . . **25.00**

Waste Basket, metal, *Star Trek:: The Motion Picture*, Chein, 1979, 13" h **75.00**

Windbreaker, nylon, 20th anniversary, patch showing *Enterprise* and "Star Trek—20th Anniversary, "*U.S.S. Enterprise*" on back, Lincoln Enterprises, 1986 . . . . **30.00**

Wristwatch, limited edition, William Shatner, DeForrest Kelly, and Leonard Nimoy color photo on face, Star Trek logo below, blue imitation leather bands, unused, 1980s. **35.00**

Vulcan Ears, 20th anniversary promotional giveaway, Pocket Books, 1986, $20.00.

STAR WARS

Star Wars: A New Hope, George Lucas' 1977 movie epic, changed the history of film making. Luke Skywalker, Princess Leia, Hans Solo, Chewbacca, Ben (Obi–Wan) Kenobi, Darth Vadar, R2–D2, and C–3PO have become cultural icons. Their adventures in the *Star Wars* trilogy were eagerly followed.

Much of the success of the *Star Wars* trilogy is credited to the special effects created by Lucas' Industrial Light and Magic Company. John Williams' score and Ben Burtt's sound effects also contributed. Twentieth Century Fox granted a broad license to the Kenner Toy Company. Approximately 80% of *Star Wars* merchandise sold in Canada and the United States is made by Kenner. Almost every Kenner product was available in England, Europe, and other English–speaking countries through Palitoy of London.

The logo on the box is a good dating tool. Licensing rights associated with the release of *Star Wars* were retained by Twentieth Century Fox. Lucasfilm Ltd. owns the licensing rights to the sequels and regained the right to the *Stars War* name before releasing *The Empire Strikes Back.*

References: John Kellerman, *Star Wars Vintage Action Figures: Reference & Price Guide,* Krause Publications, 1998; Stephen J. Sansweet, *Star Wars: From Concept to Screen to Collectible,* Chronicle Books, 1992; Stuart W. Wells III, *Star Wars Collectibles Price Guide,* Antique Trader Books, 1998.

Newsletter: *The Star Wars Collector,* 20982 Homecrest Ct, Ashburn, VA 22011.

Collectors' Club: Official Star Wars Fan Club, PO Box 111000, Aurora, CO 80042.

Accessory, tri–pol laser cannon, Empire Strikes Back, MIP . . . **$10.00**
Accessory, radar laser cannon, Return of the Jedi, MIP **8.00**
Action Figure, Empire Strikes Back, Kenner, Chewbacca,
  MOC **65.00**
Action Figure, Empire Strikes Back, Kenner, Dengar, MOC . . . **55.00**
Action Figure, Empire Strikes Back, Kenner, Lando
  Calrissian, MOC **45.00**

Action Figure, *Return of the Jedi,* Admiral Ackbar, No. 70310, Kenner, $20.00.

Action Figure, Empire Strikes Back, Kenner, Yoda, orange
  snake, MOC **35.00**
Action Figure, Power of the Force, Kenner, Boba Fett, loose. . . **25.00**
Action Figure, Power of the Force, Kenner, Imperial
  Gunner, MOC **110.00**
Action Figure, Power of the Force, Kenner, R2–D2,
  pop–up light saber, loose **55.00**
Action Figure, Power of the Force, Kenner, Teebo, MOC **125.00**
Action Figure, Power of the Force, Kenner, Wicket
  Warrick, loose **25.00**
Action Figure, Return of the Jedi, Ben Kenobi, loose **15.00**
Action Figure, Return of the Jedi, C–3PO, removable
  limbs, MIB **30.00**
Action Figure, Return of the Jedi, Darth Vader, MIB. **45.00**
Action Figure, Return of the Jedi, Rebel Soldier, MIB. **35.00**
Action Figure, Return of the Jedi, Squidhead, MIB. **45.00**
Activity Book, Empire Strikes Back Mis or Match
  Storybook **8.00**
Activity Book, Return of the Jedi, How to Draw Star Wars
  Heroes, Creatures, Spaceships, and other
  Fantastic Things **8.00**
Activity Book, Star Wars, Darth Vader's Activity Book **8.00**
Backpack, Empire Strikes Back, Darth and Stormtrooper,
  black, Factories, Inc. **15.00**
Bathrobe, May the Force Be With You, Wilker Bros **10.00**
Belt, leather, tan, Empire Strikes Back, logo on enameled
  brass buckle **15.00**
Belt Buckle, Darth Vader, boxed. **20.00**
Book, *Empire Strikes Back Pop–Up Book,* Random
  House, 1978 . . . . **10.00**
Book, *Hans Solo Revenge,* Ballantine, 1979 . . . . **5.00**
Book, *Making of Return of the Jedi.* **10.00**
Book, *The Star Wars Album,* Ballantine, 1977. . . . . **10.00**
Book Cover, Return of the Jedi, speeder bikers backed
  with Jabba **2.00**
Bookmark, Empire's Royal Guard. **6.00**
Bookmark, Luke **6.00**
Bottle, Star Wars Luke Skywalker Shampoo, soft plastic
  body, hard plastic head, story booklet, orig contents,
  sealed, Omni Cosmetics Corp, ©1983 Lucasfilm Ltd **25.00**
Bubble Bath, Star Wars, figural Leia, Omni Cosmetics. **10.00**
Bumper Sticker, Star Wars 10th Anniversary Convention,
  gold foil **1.50**
Cake Decorating Kit, R2–D2, Wilton **15.00**
Cake Decorations, Darth Vader and Stormtrooper, plastic **5.00**
Cake Decorations, Star Wars, C3–P0 and R2–D2 . . . . **4.00**
Cake Pan, Boba Fett, Wilton **15.00**
Cake Pan, C–3PO, Wilton **12.00**
Calendar, 1978, Star Wars **10.00**
Candle, Chewbacca, Wilton **4.00**
Candy Mold, Return of the Jedi/Star Wars I, Darth, Boba
  Fett, Stormtrooper, Wilton **4.00**
Card Game, Ewoks Paw Pals, Parker Brothers **4.00**
Cereal Bowl, Return of the Jedi, 20 oz **5.00**
Charm Bracelet, Stormtrooper, Chewbacca. **15.00**
Clock/Radio, Return of the Jedi, AM/FM, Bradley **25.00**
Coloring Book, Empire Strikes Back, Yoda **3.00**
Comic Book, Star Wars Annual, #1, Marvel, 1979 . . . . **2.50**
Cookie Jar, ceramic, C3–PO, Roman Ceramics **65.00**
Cookie Jar, ceramic, R2–D2, Roman Ceramics **95.00**
Cork Board, Empire Strikes Back, Yoda **15.00**
Cup, Empire Strikes Back, Yoda, 10 oz **5.00**
Darth Vader Glow–in–the–Dark Paint Set **10.00**
Diary, My Jedi Journal, Ballantine **8.00**

Dinner Plates, paper, Star Wars, 9" d, package **10.00**
Dinnerware Set, Wicket, 3 pcs **4.00**
Doll, stuffed, plush, Chewbacca **35.00**
Doll, stuffed, plush, Princess Kneesaa **15.00**
Duffle Bag, Return of the Jedi, Yoda **10.00**
Earmuffs, Return of the Jedi **5.00**
Eraser, Jabba, figural, carded **3.00**
Figurine, Luke Skywalker, Sigma **20.00**
Game, Yoda the Jedi Master, Kenner, 1981 . . . . **25.00**
Gift Wrap, Happy Birthday, Star Wars, roll **5.00**
Greeting Card, Stormtrooper, Drawing Board Greeting
    Cards, Inc **4.00**
Gun, Han Solo Laser Pistol, 1977 . . . . **40.00**
Gun, Return of the Jedi Electronic Laser Rifle **40.00**
Ice Skates, Darth Vader and Royal Guards, Brookfield **35.00**
Iron–On, Chewbacca, Han Solo, Star Wars **5.00**
Iron–On, Princess Leia, Star Wars **5.00**
Iron–On, R2–D2, Empire Strikes Back **5.00**
Jewelry, earrings, clip–on, C3–PO **8.00**
Key Chain, Empire Strikes Back, Darth Vader, plastic **3.00**
Key Chain, Return of the Jedi, Millennium Falcon, brass **3.00**
Key Chain, Star Wars, Darth Vader, metal **5.00**
Kite, Darth Vader, Spectra Star **10.00**
Kite, Ewoks on hang gliders **10.00**
Latchhook Kit, Chewbacca rug, Lee Wards **35.00**
Latchhook Kit, R2–D2, pillow, Lee Wards **35.00**
Mask, plastic, Chewbacca, Ben Cooper **5.00**
Mask, rubber, Wicket, Ben Cooper **18.00**
Mask, rubber, Yoda, Ben Cooper **15.00**
Model, Return of the Jedi X–Wing Fighter, MPC **10.00**
Music Box, Wicket and Kneesaa, Sigma **45.00**
Necklace, Empire Strikes Back, enameled Chewbacca
    pendant **10.00**
Notebook, spiral, Star Wars, Mead **6.00**
Notepad, Wookiee Doodle Pad **5.00**
Pajamas, Boba Fett and Darth Vader, long sleeve **10.00**
Patch, cloth, Brotherhood of Jedi Knights, 3½" d **10.00**
Patch, cloth, Official Star Wars Fan Club, yellow and red
    on black circle **5.00**
Pen, Return of the Jedi, blue ink, ballpoint, logo and
    characters, 2 pack **4.00**
Pencil Case, vinyl, pouch style, zipper, Luke and Vader
    dueling, Butterfly Originals **5.00**
Pin, Empire Strikes Back, Chewbacca **10.00**
Play–Doh Set, Attack the Death Star, Kenner **30.00**
Play–Doh Set, Ice Planet Hoth **25.00**
Play–Doh Set, Wicket the Ewok **20.00**
Playset, Creature Cantina, Star Wars, MIP **85.00**
Playset, Death Star Space Station, complete, Kenner, MIP . . . **65.00**
Playset, Droid Factory, MIP **75.00**
Playset, Hoth Ice Planet, Empire Strikes Back, MIP **65.00**
Playset, Jabba the Hutt Dungeon, Return of the Jedi,
    Sears, MIP **90.00**
Playset, Land of the Jawas, Star Wars, MIP **75.00**
Playset, Rebel Command Set, Empire Strikes Back, Sears,
    MIP **100.00**
Postcard, Star Wars droids, "Greetings, Earthling!,"
    20 pack **10.00**
Poster, Cincinnati Pops, John Williams Star Wars Festival,
    co–sponsored by Kenner, watercolor of Darth Vader
    conducting with lightsaber, 18 x 28" **35.00**
Poster, Empire Strikes Back, Darth Vader with crossed
    lightsabers, 18 x 24" **10.00**

Puzzle, Battle on Endor, Return of the Jedi, Craft Master,
    170 pcs **5.00**
Puzzle, Space Battle, Star Wars, series #1, Kenner,
    500 pcs **5.00**
Puzzle, Vader and Kenobi Duel, Star Wars, series #2,
    Kenner, 500 pcs **5.00**
Record, *Star Wars and Other Space Themes*, LP, Geolff
    Love **10.00**
Record, *The Story of Star Wars*, LP, 16–pp booklet,
    Buena Vista **10.00**
Roller Skates, child's, Return of the Jedi, Darth Vader, red
    trim, laces, and wheels, Darth Vader and royal guard
    illus, orig box, Brookfield Athletic Shoe Co,
    ©Lucasfilm Ltd, 1983 . . . . **25.00**
Ruler, lenticular, Return of the Jedi, logo and battle
    scenes, 6" **5.00**
Sewing Kit, Return of the Jedi, Wicket and Friends Sew
    'N Show Cards, Craft Master **10.00**
Sharpener, plastic, Return of the Jedi, baby Ewoks **3.00**
Skateboard, Luke Skywalker and Darth Vader dueling,
    Brookfield **75.00**
Sneakers, child's, Star wars shoelaces, Darth Vader illus,
    orig illus box and punch–out sheet, Stride Rite, ©1982
    Lucasfilm Ltd, size 5½ **12.00**
Socks, Return of the Jedi, Darth Vader, Charleston
    Hosiery Mills **5.00**
Stamp Kit, Star Wars, boxed, H E Harris & Co **10.00**
Storage Case, Empire Strikes Back, vinyl **30.00**
Storage Case, Star Wars, vinyl **30.00**
Storage Case, Return of the Jedi, vinyl **50.00**
Suitcase, Darth Vader and Royal Guard **15.00**
Suncatcher, Millennium Falcon **8.00**
Soup Bowl, Empire Strikes Back, 14 oz **5.00**
Switch Plate Cover, Switcheroo, Darth Vader, Kenner **20.00**
Toothbrush, Empire Strikes Back, battery operated, Kenner . . . **30.00**
Underwear, boy's, Darth Vader, Underoos, thermal **15.00**
Vehicle, All Terrain Armored Transport, Empire Strikes
    Back, MIP **90.00**
Vehicle, Captivator, Return of the Jedi, MIP **8.00**
Vehicle, Darth Vader SSP Van, Kenner, 1978 . . . . **50.00**

Model, Luke Skywalker's Snowspeeder, *Empire Strikes Back*, ©Lucas Film Ltd, 1980 trademark, MPC, 8" l, $30.00.

Vehicle, Ewok Battle Wagon, Power of the Force, MIP 85.00
Vehicle, Imperial Shuttle, Return of the Jedi, MIP 100.00
Vehicle, Imperial Troop Transporter, Star Wars, MIP 75.00
Vehicle, Land Speeder, Star Wars, MIP 45.00
Vehicle, Mobile Laser Cannon, Empire Strikes Back, MIP 10.00
Vehicle, Scout Walker, Empire Strikes Back, MIP 55.00
Vehicle, Speeder Bike, Return of the Jedi, MIP 25.00
Vehicle, TIE Interceptor, Return of the Jedi, MIP 65.00
Vehicle, Twin–Pod Cloud Car, Empire Strikes Back, MIP 45.00
Wallet, vinyl, Droids 10.00
Wallet, vinyl, Return of the Jedi, color Yoda illus, orig
    blister card, Adam Joseph Industries 25.00
Watch, digital, C3–PO and R2–D2, X–wings on wide
    oval face, black plastic band, Bradley 45.00
Watch, digital, Star Wars logo in black, silver face plate,
    black vinyl band, R2–D2 and Darth Vader on each
    side, Texas Instruments 50.00
Watch, Darth Vader with saber, white Star Wars logo on
    gray face, black vinyl band, Bradley 50.00

STEIFF

Giegen on the Benz, Bad Wurtemburg, Germany, is the birthplace and home of Steiff. In the 1880s, Margarette Steiff, a clothing manufacturer, made animal–theme pincushions for her nephews and their friends. Fritz, Margarette's brother, took some to a county fair and sold them all. In 1893 an agent representing Steiff appeared at the Leipzig Toy Fair.

Margarette's nephew, Richard, suggested making a small bear with movable head and joints. It appeared for the first time in Steiff's 1903 catalog. The bear was an instant success. An American buyer placed an order for 3,000. It was first called the "teddy" bear in the 1908 catalog.

In 1905 the famous "button in the ear" was added to Steiff toys. The first buttons were small tin circles with the name in raised block letters. The familiar script logo was introduced in 1932, about the same time a shiny, possibly chrome, button was first used. Brass ear buttons date after 1980.

The earliest Steiff toys were made entirely of felt. Mohair plush was not used until 1903. When fabrics were in scarce supply during World War I and World War II, other materials were used. None proved successful.

By 1903–04 the Steiff catalog included several character dolls. The speedway monkey on wooden wheels appeared in the 1913 catalog. Character dolls were discontinued in the mid–1910s. Cardboard tags were added in the late 1920s. Teddy Babies were introduced in 1929.

Steiff's popularity increased tremendously following World War II. A line of miniatures was introduced. After a period of uncertainty in the 1970s, due in part to currency fluctuation, Steiff enjoyed a renaissance when it introduced its 1980 Limited Edition "Papa" Centennial Bear. More than 5,000 were sold in the United States. Steiff collectors organized. A series of other limited edition pieces followed. Many credit the sale of the "Papa" Bear with creating the teddy bear craze that swept America in the 1980s.

References: Jürgen and Marianne Cieslik, *Button in Ear: The History of Teddy Bear and His Friends*, distributed by Theriault's, 1989; Jürgen and Marianne Cieslik, *Steiff Teddy Bears*, Steiff USA, 1994; Margaret Fox Mandel, *Teddy Bears and Steiff Animals* (1984, 1997 value update), *Second Series* (1987, 1996 value update), Collector Books; Margaret Fox Mandel, *Teddy Bears, Annalee*

Animals & Steiff Animals, Third Series, Collector Books, 1990, 1996 value update; Linda Mullins, *Teddy Bear & Friends Price Guide, Fourth Edition*, Hobby House Press, 1993; Christel and Rolf Pistorius, *Steiff: Sensational Teddy Bear, Animals & Dolls*, Hobby House Press, 1991.

Collectors' Clubs: Steiff Club USA (company sponsored), 225 Fifth Ave, Ste 1033, New York, NY 10010; Steiff Collectors Club, PO Box 798, Holland, OH 43528.

Anniversary Bear, #3026, yellow mohair, peach felt
    pads, black eyes, embroidered features and claws,
    with certificate, orig box, 1980s, 16" h $250.00
Badger, Diggy, mohair, chest tag, glass eyes, c1975,
    6³⁄₈" l 120.00
Chimpanzee, tan mohair, ear button, black plastic eyes,
    felt face and feet, fully jointed, 1950s–60s, 4¼" h 50.00
Guinea Pig, Swinny, synthetic fur, ear button and chest
    tag, plastic eyes, felt feet, c1965, 4½" l 80.00
Kitten, gray mohair, ear button, glass eyes, 3¾" h 50.00
Micki, mohair, cloth, and rubber, orig tag, button, and
    bracelet, 1950s, 10" h 40.00
Mouse, tan mohair body, black glass bead eyes, button
    nose, nylon whiskers, white diecut felt ears and paws,
    white felt tail, orig tag, 1950s, 3½" h 70.00
Nimrod Teddy Bear Hunters, boxed set of 3, #1024,
    #0210/22, beige, white, and yellow, all orig and tied
    in box, 7³⁄₈" h, 15½" w, 10³⁄₁₆" d box 150.00
Pony, orange synthetic fur, chest tag, glass eyes, soft
    stuffing, c1960, 10" l 30.00
Poodle, gray mohair, fully jointed, glass eyes, button and
    tag missing, c1960, 16" l 40.00
Teddy Bear, blonde mohair, ear button, chest tag, glass
    eyes, fully jointed, c1980, 9¾" h 50.00
Teddy Bear, blonde mohair, ear button missing, glass
    eyes, fully jointed, excelsior stuffing, embroidered
    nose, mouth, and claws, 1950s, 13" h 300.00
Teddy Bear, golden plush, button and yellow tag in ear,
    "Made in U.S. Zone Germany" label attached to side

Kitten, ear button, glass eyes, embroidered pink nose, mouth, and claws, c1920–30, $175.00.

seam, brown and black glass eyes, black stitched
nose, swivel head and joints, growler, excelsior stuff-
ing, c1945, 29" h **2,875.00**

Teddy Bear, light brown plush, button in ear and remains
of yellow tag, brown stitched nose, brown and black
glass eyes, swivel joints, excelsior stuffing, tan felt
pads, c1950, 11½" h **350.00**

Teddy Bear, Molly Bear, synthetic fur, ear button, chest
tag, unjointed, sitting position, c1980 . . . . **45.00**

Teddy Bear, tan mohair, ear button, chest tag, fully joint-
ed, c1980, 13" h **65.00**

Teddy Bear on Irish Mail Cart, blonde mohair bear, ear
button, black steel eyes, moveable head, embroidered
nose, mouth, and claws, felt pads, steel frame, solid
wood wheels, fabric bellows damaged, c1920, 10" h,
9" l vehicle **2,415.00**

Weasel, Wiggy, synthetic white winter fur, ear button
and chest tag, black plastic eyes, embroidered nose
and mouth, felt pads, 1970s, 7⅝" l **260.00**

Welsh Terrier, beige and gray mohair, ear button, glass
eyes, embroidered nose, mouth, and claws, red collar,
moveable head, 1950s, 9½" l **70.00**

STEMWARE

There are two basic types of stemware: (1) soda–based glass and (2) lead– or flint–based glass, also known as crystal. Early glass was made from a soda–based formula, which was costly and therefore available only to the rich. In the mid–19th century, a soda–lime glass was perfected, which was lighter and less expensive, but lacked the clarity and brilliance of crystal glass. This advance made glassware available to the common man.

The pricipal ingredients of crystal are silica (sand), litharge (a fused lead monoxide), and potash or potassium carbonate. The exact formula differs from manufacturer to manufacturer and is a closely guarded secret. Crystal can be plain or decorated, hand blown or machine made. Its association with quality is assumed.

There are three basic methods used to make glass—free blown, mold blown, or pressed. Furthermore, stemware can be decorated in a variety of ways. It may be cut or etched, or the bowl, stem or both may be made of colored glass. The varieties are as endless as the manufacturers. Notable manufacturers include Baccarat, Fostoria, Lenox, Orrefors, and Waterford.

References: Gene Florence, *Stemware Identification: Featuring Cordials With Values, 1920s–1960s,* Collector Books, 1997; Bob Page and Dale Frederiksen, *Crystal Stemware Identification Guide,* Collector Books, 1998; Harry L. Rinker, *Stemware of the 20th Century: The Top 200 Patterns,* House of Collectibles, 1997.

Note: See individual manufacturers' categories for additional listings.

Baccarat, Harmonie, highball, 5½" h **$35.00**
Baccarat, Harmonie, iced tea **40.00**
Baccarat, Harmonie, water goblet **35.00**
Baccarat, Montaigne, cordial, 3⅛" h **25.00**
Baccarat, Montaigne, fluted champagne, 6⅞" h **25.00**
Baccarat, Montaigne, tumbler, 3⅛" h **25.00**
Baccarat, Montaigne, water goblet, 6⅜" h **25.00**
Cambridge, Chantilly, champagne, 6" h **15.00**
Cambridge, Chantilly, claret **15.00**

Lenox, Antique, water goblet, blue, $15.00.

Cambridge, Chantilly, cocktail, 5⅝" h **15.00**
Cambridge, Chantilly, iced tea, ftd, 7¾" h **20.00**
Cambridge, Chantilly, juice, ftd, 5⅜" h **15.00**
Cambridge, Chantilly, tumbler **15.00**
Cambridge, Chantilly, water goblet **15.00**
Cambridge, Rose Point, champagne, 6½" h **20.00**
Cambridge, Rose Point, cocktail **22.00**
Cambridge, Rose Point, iced tea, ftd **25.00**
Cambridge, Rose Point, tumbler **20.00**
Cambridge, Rose Point, wine **45.00**
Duncan & Miller, Chantilly, champagne, 5½" h **30.00**
Duncan & Miller, Chantilly, cocktail, 5⅛" h **16.00**
Duncan & Miller, Chantilly, iced tea, ftd **20.00**
Duncan & Miller, Chantilly, water goblet **17.00**
Duncan & Miller, First Love, champagne, 5" h **20.00**
Duncan & Miller, First Love, cocktail 4½" h **20.00**
Duncan & Miller, First Love, cordial, 3½" h **40.00**
Duncan & Miller, First Love, iced tea, 6½" h **20.00**
Duncan & Miller, First Love, wine **32.00**
Duncan & Miller, Willow, champagne **13.00**
Duncan & Miller, Willow, cocktail **13.00**
Duncan & Miller, Willow, highball **16.00**
Duncan & Miller, Willow, juice, ftd **13.00**
Duncan & Miller, Willow, old fashioned **18.00**
Duncan & Miller, Willow, water goblet **16.00**
Duncan & Miller, Willow, wine **22.00**
Gorham, Bamberg, champagne **30.00**
Gorham, Bamberg, claret **40.00**
Gorham, Bamberg, cordial **35.00**
Gorham, Bamberg, iced tea **42.00**
Gorham, Bamberg, juice **30.00**
Gorham, Bamberg, water goblet **42.00**
Gorham, Bamberg, wine **40.00**
Gorham, Crown Point, cocktail **22.00**
Gorham, Crown Point, fluted champagne **22.00**
Gorham, Crown Point, iced tea, ftd **24.00**
Gorham, Crown Point, juice **22.00**
Gorham, Crown Point, water goblet **25.00**
Gorham, Crown Point, wine **25.00**
Gorham, Florentine, champagne, 5⅛" h **22.00**
Gorham, Florentine, iced tea, ftd **25.00**
Gorham, Florentine, water goblet **25.00**
Gorham, Gentry, fluted champagne **12.00**

Gorham, Gentry, cocktail **12.00**
Gorham, Gentry, juice **12.00**
Gorham, Lady Anne, champagne, 5⅝" h **10.00**
Gorham, Lady Anne, highball, 6" h **7.00**
Gorham, Lady Anne, old fashioned, double **7.00**
Gorham, Lady Anne, water goblet **12.00**
Gorham, Rosewood, champagne **35.00**
Gorham, Rosewood, cocktail **35.00**
Gorham, Rosewood, cordial **40.00**
Gorham, Rosewood, iced tea, ftd **36.00**
Gorham, Rosewood, wine **40.00**
Lenox, Antique, champagne, blue, 5" h **12.00**
Lenox, Antique, highball, crystal, 5" h **12.00**
Lenox, Antique, iced tea, blue, 6⅝" h **15.00**
Lenox, Antique, juice, crystal, 6" h **20.00**
Lenox, Antique, old fashioned, crystal, 3⅜" h **12.00**
Lenox, Antique, wine, blue, 5" h **15.00**
Lenox, Ariel, champagne, 5⅝" h **22.00**
Lenox, Ariel, iced tea, 8¼" h **22.00**
Lenox, Ariel, wine, 7¾" h **22.00**
Lenox, Atrium, champagne, 5⅝" h **17.00**
Lenox, Atrium, iced tea **20.00**
Lenox, Atrium, wine **22.00**
Lenox, Charleston, brandy, 5" h **22.00**
Lenox, Charleston, champagne **16.00**
Lenox, Charleston, highball, 5⅞" h **7.00**
Lenox, Charleston, old fashioned, double, 4" h **7.00**
Lenox, Charleston, water goblet **16.00**
Lenox, Green Mist, champagne, 5" h **25.00**
Lenox, Green Mist, iced tea **15.00**
Lenox, Green Mist, water goblet, 7⅛" h **15.00**
Lenox, Green Mist, wine, 6¼" h **16.00**
Lenox, Madison, champagne **15.00**
Lenox, Madison, iced tea **16.00**
Lenox, Madison, water goblet, 8½" h **15.00**
Lenox, McKinley, fluted champagne, 8" h **25.00**
Lenox, McKinley, water goblet **25.00**
Lenox, McKinley, wine **25.00**
Lenox, Wheat, fluted champagne **17.00**
Lenox, Wheat, iced tea **17.00**
Lenox, Wheat, water goblet **17.00**

Lenox, Wheat, wine **17.00**
Mikasa, Arctic Lights, brandy, 5¾" h **12.00**
Mikasa, Arctic Lights, champagne, 6½" h **12.00**
Mikasa, Arctic Lights, cordial, 7" h **12.00**
Mikasa, Arctic Lights, iced tea, 8½" h **12.00**
Mikasa, Arctic Lights, wine **12.00**
Mikasa, Olympus, fluted champagne **10.00**
Mikasa, Olympus, highball **7.00**
Mikasa, Olympus, water goblet, 9" h **10.00**
Mikasa, Olympus, wine **10.00**
Orrefors, Coronation, fluted champagne **20.00**
Orrefors, Coronation, claret **20.00**
Orrefors, Coronation, cocktail, "V" shape, 4½" h **22.00**
Orrefors, Coronation, cordial, 2⅝" h **22.00**
Orrefors, Coronation, iced tea **22.00**
Orrefors, Coronation, oyster cocktail **22.00**
Orrefors, Coronation, tumbler **20.00**
Orrefors, Coronation, water goblet, 6" h **22.00**
Orrefors, Prelude, champagne, 5¼" h **17.00**
Orrefors, Prelude, claret, 7⅜" h **22.00**
Orrefors, Prelude, cordial, 5¼" h **20.00**
Orrefors, Prelude, martini **20.00**
Orrefors, Prelude, schnapps **17.00**
Orrefors, Prelude, sherry **17.00**
Orrefors, Prelude, tumbler, 5½" h **22.00**
Orrefors, Prelude, water goblet, 8¼" h **22.00**
Orrefors, Prelude, wine **22.00**
Sasaki, Wings, cocktail, 4⅛" h **25.00**
Sasaki, Wings, iced tea, 6⅜" h **25.00**
Sasaki, Wings, juice, 3⅞" h **20.00**
Sasaki, Wings, port, 4⅞" h **25.00**
Sasaki, Wings, sherbet, 4" h **25.00**
Sasaki, Wings, sherry, 4⅞" h **28.00**
Sasaki, Wings, water goblet **20.00**
Stuart Crystal, Hampshire, champagne, 4½" h **30.00**
Stuart Crystal, Hampshire, claret **30.00**
Stuart Crystal, Hampshire, cordial **30.00**
Stuart Crystal, Hampshire, iced tea, ftd **44.00**
Stuart Crystal, Hampshire, old fashioned **40.00**
Stuart Crystal, Hampshire, sherry **30.00**
Stuart Crystal, Hampshire, tumbler **35.00**
Stuart Crystal, Hampshire, water goblet **40.00**

Sasaki, Wings, left to right: Wine, $25.00; Champagne, 4½" h, $20.00; and Fluted Champagne, $25.00.

STEUBEN GLASS

Frederick Carder and Thomas Hawkes founded the Steuben Glass Works in 1903. Initially Steuben made blanks for Hawkes. The company also made Art Nouveau ornamental and colored glass. Steuben Glass had trouble securing raw materials during World War I. In 1918 Corning purchased Steuben Glass from Carder and Hawkes. Carder became art director at Corning.

Steuben experienced numerous financial difficulties in the 1920s, reorganizing several times. When Corning threatened to close its Steuben division, Arthur Houghton, Jr., led the move to save it. Steuben Glass Incorporated was established. All earlier glass formulas were abandoned. The company concentrated on producing crystal products.

In 1937 Steuben produced the first in a series of crystal pieces featuring engraved designs from famous artists. Depsite production cutbacks during World War II, Steuben emerged in the post–war period as a major manufacturer of crystal products. The company's first crystal animals were introduced in 1949. Special series, incorporating the works of Asian and British painters, and a group of 31 Collector's pieces, each an interpretation of a poem commissioned by Steuben, were produced during the 1950s and 60s.

Reference: Kenneth Wilson, *American Glass 1760–1930: The Toledo Museum of Art*, 2 vols., Hudson Hills Press and The Toledo Museum of Art, 1994.

Bowl, Aurene, gold, oval, iridescent, Carder, 3" h, 6" d **$450.00**
Bowl, Aurene, gold, shallow, silvery transparent
    lustre, Carder, 1³/₄" h, 9³/₄" d **250.00**
Bowl, flared bell body raised on slender integrated base,
    engraved "Steuben," D Pollard, 3³/₄" h, 5¹/₈" d **120.00**
Bowl, oval, Roseline cut to alabaster in Grapes pattern,
    raised applied handles at each end, Carder, 12¹/₂" l **230.00**
Bowl, Verre de Soie, shallow, 3 applied prunt feet,
    Carder **145.00**
Candlesticks, pr, Blue Aurene, ropetwist shaft, Carder,
    10" h **1,840.00**
Center Bowl, Aurene, gold, angular shallow round bowl,
    orange tone iridescent lustre, Carder, 2" h, 14" d **400.00**
Center Bowl, blue and topaz, ribbed Celeste blue
    bulbed bowl raised on cupped transparent topaz
    amber pedestal foot, Carder, 5¹/₂" h, 12" d **285.00**
Center Bowl, Verre de Soie, 8 pinched apertures around
    rim of flower arrangement, Carder, 3" h, 8" d **285.00**
Champagne Goblet, Aurene gold, iridescent, inscribed
    base, 5³/₄"h **460.00**
Cocktail/Lemonade Pitcher, applied strap handle, rose
    reeding and conforming cover, Carder, 10¹/₂" h **210.00**
Compote, Aurene on calcite, flared deep bowl raised on
    spiral ribbed calcite shaft and round foot, 7" h **925.00**
Compote, Aurene on calcite, gold, low cupped pedestal
    foot on flared bowl with fine lustrous iridescent gold,
    Carder, 2³/₄" h, 10" d **460.00**
Figure, chick, inscribed "Steuben," G Thompson, 4" h **200.00**
Figure, frog, applied eyes and feet, inscribed "Steuben,"
    L Atkins design, 4³/₄" l **400.00**
Figure, kitten under mouse, inscribed "Steuben,"
    L Atkins design, 3³/₄" l **485.00**

Figure, owl, facing right, frosted eyes, inscribed
    "Steuben," D Pollard design, 5¹/₂" h **230.00**
Figure, porpoise, diving pose, L Atkins, 12" l **860.00**
Figure, songbird, inscribed "Steuben," Madigan, 3" h **200.00**
Lamp Base, Grape pattern, elongated flared neck over
    bulbous base, acid etched pattern, spiraled leaves and
    vines around neck, mounted to unsigned gilt metal
    base and 2–socket shaft, 26" h **925.00**
Lamp Shade, Aurene, gold, 10–rib bell form, iridescent,
    fleur–de–lis marks at rim, Carder, 6¹/₂" h **185.00**
Paperweight, spiraled, central teardrop, inscribed
    "Steuben," G Tompson design, 3¹/₂" d **345.00**
Plate, wild turkey audubon, base engraved "Steuben,"
    10" d **345.00**
Sculpture, Thistle Rock, cut and polished glass rock sup-
    porting golden thistle, base inscribed "Steuben," vel-
    vet lined red leather case, Vermeil, 7" h **2,185.00**
Table Glass Set, set of 16, service for 4 of sherbets with
    undertrays, cream soups and 8¹/₄" plates, each
    engraved with elk emblems, bases mkd "S" **375.00**
Vase, Aurene, blue, flared rim on cobalt blue iridized
    body, base inscribed "Steuben," 8" h **860.00**
Vase, Celeste blue, fleur–de–lis mark on round applied
    disk foot, Carder, 8³/₄" h **287.50**
Vase, ivory, oval, raised flared rim, Carder, 8¹/₄" h **517.50**
Vase, transparent, Pomona green, spiral swirled rib
    molded form, black glass pedestal, Carder, 10" h **345.00**
Vase, transparent, sea green, ribbed, flared, and footed
    oval with folded rim and foot, stamped "Steuben" on
    base, 7¹/₂" h **140.00**
Vase, trumpet shape, light amethyst with fleur–de–lis
    mark on round polished base, inserted into wrought–
    iron leaf form base painted white, Carder, 11¹/₂" h vase . . . **230.00**
Vase, swirled rect rib molded jade polished at top rim,
    9¹/₂" h, 5³/₄" d, 3¹/₄" w **290.00**

STEUBENVILLE POTTERY

The Steubenville Pottery Company, Steubenville, Ohio, operated from 1879 to 1959. The company manufactured household utilitarian wares ranging from dinnerware to toilet sets.

In 1939 Steubenville began the production of Russel Wright's American Modern shape line. Woodfield Leaf with its distinctive leaf pattern on the body and leaf finials on covered pieces was another of the company's popular shape lines. Other body shapes include Antique Adam, Contempora (designed by Ben Seibel), Monticello (distributed by Herman Kupper), and Olivia.

Barium Chemicals, parent company of Canonsburg Pottery, bought Steubenville in 1959 and moved the company's molds and equipment to Canonsburg. Canonsburg Pottery continued to use the Steubenville name during much of the 1960s.

Reference: Harvey Duke, *The Official Price Guide to Pottery and Porcelain, Eighth Edition*, House of Collectibles, 1995.

Note: See Russell Wright for American Modern dinnerware by Steubenville.

Adam Antique, cup and saucer **$12.00**
Adam Antique, dinner plate **10.00**
Adam Antique, eggcup **10.00**
Adam Antique, fruit bowl **2.00**
Adam Antique, gravy boat **20.00**

Cluthra Vase, double "M" handles, blue, engraved signature "Steuben, F Carder," small base edge repair, 10" h, $1,320.00. Photo courtesy Jackson's Auctioneers & Appraisers.

Adam Antique, creamer and cov sugar, price for set, $12.00.

Adam Antique, jug, 1 qt **15.00**
Adam Antique, plate, 6" sq **3.00**
Adam Antique, platter, 11" l **10.00**
Adam Antique, salad plate **5.00**
Adam Antique, teapot **30.00**
Adam Antique, vegetable dish **25.00**
Betty Pepper, casserole **20.00**
Betty Pepper, creamer and sugar **12.00**
Betty Pepper, plate, 9" d **5.00**
Betty Pepper, teapot, 2 cup **15.00**
Contempora, cup and saucer **12.00**
Contempora, fruit dish, 6" d **5.00**
Contempora, plate, 8¼" d **6.00**
Contempora, platter, oval, 14½" l **15.00**
Contempora, salad bowl, 11" d **50.00**
Monticello, casserole **20.00**
Monticello, cup and saucer **5.00**
Olivia, butter dish **20.00**
Olivia, casserole **20.00**
Olivia, gravy boat **12.00**
Shalimar, casserole **20.00**
Shalimar, cup and saucer **3.00**
Shalimar, plate, 9" d **5.00**
Woodfield, bowl, cov **20.00**
Woodfield, chop plate, golden fawn **15.00**
Woodfield, gravy, stick handle, jungle green **15.00**
Woodfield, relish, 2 part, 9½" l **30.00**

STOCKS & BONDS

A stock certificate is a financial document that shows the amount of capital on a per share basis that the owner has invested in a company. Gain is achieved through dividends and an increase in unit value. A bond is an interest bearing certificate of public or private indebtedness. The interest is generally paid on a fixed schedule with the principal being repaid when the bond is due.

Joint stock companies were used to finance world exploration in the 16th, 17th, and 18th centuries. Several American colonies received financial backing from joint stock companies. Bonds and stocks help spread financial risk. The New York Stock Exchange was founded in the late 18th century.

In the middle of the 19th century, engraving firms such as the American Bank Note Company and Rawdon, Wright & Hatch created a wide variety of financial instruments ranging from bank notes to stock certificates. Most featured one or more ornately engraved vignettes. While some generic vignettes were used repeatedly, vignettes often provided a detailed picture of a manufacturing facility or product associated with the company.

Stocks and bonds are collected primarily for their subject matter, e.g., automobile, mining, railroad, public utilities, etc. Date is a value factor. Pre–1850 stocks and bonds command the highest price provided they have nice vignettes. Stocks and bonds issued between 1850 and 1915 tend to be more valuable than those issued after 1920.

Before paying top dollar attempt to ascertain how many examples of the certificate you are buying have survived. The survival rate is higher than most realize. Unused stock and bond certificates are less desirable than issued certificates. Finally, check the signatures on all pre–1915 stocks. Many important personages served as company presidents.

References: Norman E. Martinus and Harry L. Rinker, *Warman's Paper*, Wallace–Homestead, Krause Publications, 1994; Gene Utz, *Collecting Paper: A Collector's Identification & Value Guide*, Books Americana, Krause Publications, 1993.

Periodical: *Bank Note Reporter*, 700 E State St, Iola, WI 54990.

Collectors' Clubs: Bond and Share Society, 26 Broadway at Bowling Green, Rm 200, New York, NY 10004; Old Certificates Collector's Club, 4761 W Waterbuck Dr, Tucson, AZ 85742.

STOCKS

Alaska Treadwell Gold Mining Co, blue, 2 miners and mountains vignette, ornate, 1931 . . . . **$15.00**
Atwood Grapefruit Co, grapefruit, 1941–51 . . . . **10.00**
Cincinnati, New Orleans & Texas Pacific RR, gray and white, steam train vignette, issued, 1930s **15.00**
Commercial Farms Co, Davidson Co, deer vignette, unissued, 1922 . . . . **6.00**
Fruit of the Loom, Inc, fractional share of common stock, script, green, black, and white, 1938 . . . . **5.00**
Gulf Mobile & Ohio Railroad Company, green, locomotive and women vignette, 1943 . . . . **5.00**
Hornell Airways, Inc, 2 women and sun rising over mountains vignette, issued and canceled, 1920s **75.00**
Jantzen Knitting Mills, engraved, woman diving into water vignette, issued, 1930s **35.00**
Kaiser–Frazer Corp, blue, issued, 1940s **6.00**
Lincoln Motor Co, orange, sgd by WC Leland, issued, 1920s **20.00**
Lincoln Printing Co, engraved Abe Lincoln vignette, 1962–65 . . . . **5.00**
New York Central RR, brown, Commodore Vanderbuilt vignette, issued, 1940s **12.00**
Northampton Brewery Corp, PA, orange, engraved, woman, ship, and city skyline vignette, issued, 1930s **15.00**
Palmer Union Oil Co of Santa Barbara, CA, oil wells vignette, ornate design, canceled, 1928, 7½ x 11" **12.50**
Penn National Bank & Trust Co of Reading, gray, colonial man vignette, issued but not canceled, 1930 . . . . **15.00**
Piggly Wiggly Western States Co, orange, early Piggly Wiggly store photo vignette, issued, 1920s **10.00**
Pittsburgh Tin Plate & Steel Corp, eagle over city vignette, canceled, 1920 . . . . **15.00**
Sentinel Radio Corp, green, goddess and 2 radio towers vignette, issued, 1956 . . . . **5.00**
Verde Mines Milling Co, State of AZ, 1929 . . . . **6.00**

BONDS

City of Fort Wayne, Paul Baer Field Aviation, $1,000, high wing radial engine plane vignette, brown border, coupons, issued, 1929 . . . . **$45.00**

Consolidted Edison Co, NY, $1,000, blue, tower, Brooklyn Bridge, and New York City background vignette, issued, 1949 . . . . **7.50**

Delaware & Hudson Railroad Co, $1,000, 2 women and farm scene vignette, 1963 . . . . **5.00**

Erie Railroad Co, $1,000, man, woman, and logo vignette, red border, 1945 . . . . **8.00**

Ford International Capital Corp, $1,000, blue, black, and white, 1968 . . . . **12.00**

General Motors Corp, $1,000, streamlined car, truck, locomotive, 3 heads, and factory building vignette, coupons, issued, 1954 . . . . **15.00**

Gulf Mobile & Ohio, $1,000, diesel locomotive, vignette, orange border, 1957 . . . . **6.00**

Southern Bell Telephone & Telegraph, $1,000, person speaking on telephone and city and rural landscapes vignette, coupons, issued, 1947 . . . . **15.00**

United Air Lines, $100 share, olive, 1970s **6.00**

STUFFED TOYS

The bear is only one of dozens of animals that have been made into stuffed toys. In fact, Margarette Steiff's first stuffed toy was not a bear but an elephant. The stuffed toy animal was a toy/department store fixture by the early 1920s.

Many companies, e.g., Ideal and Knickerbocker, competed with Steiff for market share. Following World War II, stuffed toys became a favorite prize of carnival games of chance. Most of these toys were inexpensive imports from China and Taiwan.

Many characters from Disney animated cartoons, e.g., *Jungle Book* and *The Lion King*, appear as stuffed toys. A major collection could be assembled focusing solely on Disney–licensed products. The 1970s stuffed toys of R. Dakin Company, San Francisco, are a modern favorite among collectors.

The current Beanie Baby craze has focused interest on the miniature stuffed toy. As with any fad, the market already is flooded with imitations. The Beanie Baby market is highly speculative. Expect a major price collapse in a relatively short period of time.

References: Dee Hockenberry, *Collectible German Animals Value Guide: 1948–1968*, Hobby House Press, 1988; Carol J. Smith, *Identification & Price Guide to Winnie the Pooh Collectibles, I* (1994), *II* (1996), Hobby House Press.

Periodical: *Soft Dolls & Animals*, 30595 Eight Mile, Livonia, MI 48152.

Note: See Steiff and Teddy Bears for additional listings.

Alligator, vinyl, green and brown, glass eyes, c1950, 9½" **$35.00**

Bambi, plush, Gund, 1953, 15" **60.00**

Beagle, plush, glass eyes, 9" **25.00**

Big Boy, cloth, pillow type, litho, name on shirt, 14" **5.00**

Boa Constrictor, plush, multicolored, felt eyes and tongue, c1958 . . . . **12.00**

Bunny, Dakin, bean bag, glass eyes, 1977 . . . . **25.00**

Camel, tan plush, 1 hump, glass eyes, c1950, 8" **65.00**

Woody Woodpecker, talking, vinyl head, stuffed corduroy body, felt hands and feet, orig box, Mattel, 1960s, 18" h, $200.00.

Cat, Siamese, mohair, sitting, c1950, 9" **100.00**

Coca–Cola Santa, plush, plastic face, holding miniature Coke bottle, 1950, 16" h **75.00**

Collie, long and short mohair, glass eyes, sewn nose, felt mouth **125.00**

Dinosaur, multi–mohair, glass eyes, felt fins, 1960, 14" **100.00**

Dopey, cloth body, Gund, 12" **45.00**

Elephant, sitting, musical, gray and white, 1960, 14½" **30.00**

Elf, felt body, mohair beard, glass eyes, 1930s, 10" **100.00**

Elsie the Cow, plush, c1986 . . . . **80.00**

Floppy Robby Seal, soft stuffing, sewn eyes, c1950, 6" **65.00**

Frog, green, velvet top, white satin bottom, c1960, 9" **12.00**

Giraffe, mohair, gold and orange, felt ears, glass eyes, 1950s, 11" **70.00**

Grasshopper, mohair, felt clothes, glass eyes, 1950s, 18" **100.00**

Hamster, mohair, gold, jointed head, glass eyes, felt paws and mouth, 5" **48.00**

Kliban Cat **35.00**

Lamb, curly black, glass eyes, embroidered features, ribbon at neck, 10" **110.00**

Leo the Lion, mohair, reclining, orig tag, c1955, 45" **600.00**

Lobster, felt, orange, glass eyes, 7" **45.00**

Mickey & Mecky Hedgehog, vinyl swivel heads, pressed mask face, tan, squinting eyes, smiling mouths, bristly hair, felt bodies, sewn–on clothes, checkered costumes, c1950, price for pr **475.00**

Monkey, mohair, glass eyes, velvet astronaut uniform, rocket, Dakin, 1961 . . . . **100.00**

Monkey, mohair, jointed, glass eyes, felt clothes, 1953, 8" **90.00**

Mule, "One of the Twenty Mule Team" collar inscription, Boraxo promo, 1980s **15.00**

Ocelot, mohair, gold and black, sewn nose and mouth, 1955, 6½ x 13" **95.00**

Penguin, black and white, black plastic wings, c1960, 10" **10.00**

Pig, mohair, pink, felt mouth and tail, cord on neck, 6½" **85.00**

Polar Bear, champagne plush, straw fill, movable arms and legs, long snout, black button eyes, stitch face, leather collar, c1920, 16" **300.00**

Poodle, plush, c1960, 10" **125.00**
Poodle, standing, curly, gray, 1960, 12" **15.00**
Ronald McDonald, printed cloth, red, yellow, black, and
    white, 16½" **7.50**
Ruth the Rabbit, standing, plush, gold, jointed, purple
    bead eyes, long lashes, sheer organdy over flowered
    print costume, cloth tag, c1934, 19" **525.00**
Sambo, cloth, red jack, turban, crimson shoes, holding
    closed umbrella in 1 hand, plate of felt pancakes in
    other, mkd "Dream Doll/R. Dakin & Co/Japan," 10" **12.00**
Scottie, cotton, plaid, embroidered collar and features,
    hand made, c1950, 4½" **5.00**
Terrier, plush, white, black spots, swivel head, white
    muzzle, yellow glass eyes, embroidered features, red
    ribbon, c1960, 12" **15.00**
Tom Cat, black velvet body, mohair tail, glass eyes,
    sewn nose and mouth, c1960, 5" **85.00**
Tony, Esso tiger, orange and black, felt trim, 8" **45.00**
Vulture, felt and fabric, black yarn hair, Walt Disney,
    1966 copyright tag, 5" **40.00**
Walrus, mohair, plastic tusks, 1950s, 4" **50.00**
Zebra, mohair, black and white, 1950s, 8" **70.00**

SUPER HEROES

Early super heroes such as Batman and Superman were individuals who possessed extraordinary strength and/or cunning, yet led normal lives as private citizens. They dominated the world of comic books, movie serials, newspaper cartoon strips, radio, and television from the late 1930s through the end of the 1950s. Captain Marvel, Captain Midnight, The Green Lantern, and Wonder Woman are other leading examples of the genre.

The 1960s introduced a new form of super hero, the mutant. The Fantastic Four (Mr. Fantastic, The Human Torch, The Invisible Girl, and The Thing) initiated an era that included a host of characters ranging from Spiderman to The Teenage Mutant Ninja Turtles. Most mutant super heroes are found only in comic books. A few achieved fame on television and the big screen.

In the 1990s comic book storytellers and movie directors began blurring the line between these two distinct groups of super heroes. The death of Superman and his resurrection as a person more attune with the mutant super heroes and the dark approach of the Batman movies are two classic examples.

Collectors prefer three-dimensional objects over two-dimensional material. Carefully research an object's date. Age as a value factor plays a greater role in this category than it does in other collectibles categories.

Reference: Bill Bruegman, *Superhero Collectibles: A Pictorial Price Guide,* Toy Scouts, 1996.

Newsletter: *The Adventures Continue* (Superman), 935 Fruitsville Pike, #105, Lancaster, PA 17601.

Collectors' Clubs: Air Heroes Fan Club (Captain Midnight), 19205 Seneca Ridge Club, Gaithersburg, MD 20879; Batman TV Series Fan Club, PO Box 107, Venice, CA 90291; Rocketeer Fan Club, 10 Halick Ct, East Brunswick, NJ 08816.

Note: For additional listings see Action Figures, Comic Books, and Model Kits.

Batman, Batmobile, Taiwan, battery operated, plastic, red with green windshields, 1970s, 10" l, $150.00.

Batman, Batmobile, AHI, Japan, battery operated, plastic, forward, reverse, and turning action, operating dome light, radio controlled, complete with power transmitter and orig box, 1977, 8" l **$450.00**
Batman, Batmobile, Simms, Inc, Aurora, IL, plastic, Batman and Robin figures inside clear plastic shell, on card with Batman punching Joker illus, 1966, 8" l **150.00**
Batman, Batmobile and Batboat with Trailer, AHI, Japan, friction, plastic vehicles with figural Batman and Robin, on lithoed 6 x 12" l case with header card and plastic bubble **165.00**
Batman, bread wrapper, New Century Bread Co, plastic wrapper with running Batman and Robin, Batmobile, Batplane, Penguin, Riddler, Bat logos, and collage of villains including Caveman, Calendarman, Vulture, Shark, Cluemaster, Fox, and Mr Zero, unused, 1966 . . . . . . **18.00**
Batman, Colorforms, complete with booklet, 1966, 8 x 12" box. **40.00**
Batman, coloring book, Batman Meets Blockbuster, Whitman, neatly colored, 40 pp, 1966, 8 x 11 . . . . **8.00**
Batman, coloring book, Whitman, unused, 80 pp, 1967, 8 x 11" **20.00**
Batman, figure, Clementoni, Italy, 1967, 13" h, MOC **200.00**
Batman, pinback button, Batman & Robin Society, Button World, Dynamic Duo image, "Charter Member—Batman 7 Robin Society," 1966, 3" d **8.00**
Captain America, Captain America in relief against green ground, ©1967 Marvel Comics Group, Louis Marx & Co, Japan, 2¼ x 4" **28.00**
Captain America, car, Corgi, rocket shaped vehicle with Captain America driver, orig box, ©1979 Marvel Comics Group, 6" l **55.00**
Captain Midnight, shoulder patch **40.00**
Captain Midnight, stamp album, Air Heroes, Skelly Oil premium. **25.00**
Captain Midnight, whistle, plastic, dark blue, logo, code wheel, "Captain Midnight's SS 1946" **75.00**
Falcon, action figure, Mego, 7½" h, ©1974 Marvel Comics. **45.00**

Fantastic Four, drinking glass, 7–Eleven promotional, 1977, 5½" h **10.00**

Green Hornet, Secret Service Car, ASC, Japan, battery operated, tin, Black Beauty car with Green Hornet image on roof, Hornet logo on hood, and vinyl half – figure driver behind wheel, bump–and–go action, machine guns make noise and light up, unauthorized **600.00**

Incredible Hulk, gum card pack, Topps, unopened, 7 TV photo cards, 1 sticker, and 1 pc gum, photo of Lou Ferrigno as Hulk on wrapper, unopened, 1979 . . . . **6.00**

Incredible Hulk, sticker wrapper, Philadelphia Gum Corp, empty wrapper with Hulk illus originally contained 5 gum card size stickers, 1966 . . . . **12.00**

Phantom, coloring book, Ottenheimer, 1965 . . . . **45.00**

Phantom, Halloween costume, Collegeville, 1956 . . . . **200.00**

Spider–Man, Halloween costume, Ben Cooper, vinyl plastic 1–pc bodysuit, 1972, orig box **35.00**

Spider–Man, Halloween bucket, Renzi, red hard plastic, molded as Spider–Man's head, 1979, 10" h **12.00**

Spider–Woman, Halloween costume, Ben Cooper, vinyl plastic 1–pc bodysuit, orig box illus with Batgirl, Wonder Woman, and Supergirl, early 1970s, 8 x 10" window display box **20.00**

Spider–Woman, Under–oos, Union Underwear, 11 x 11" pkg with 2–pc stretch polyester underwear, sealed pkg, 1979 . . . . **15.00**

Super Friends, lunch box, Aladdin, litho tin, Wonder Woman surrounded by Superman, Batman, and Robin, Batgirl in center back panel surrounded by Flash and Green Arrow, ©1976 DC Comics **18.00**

Superman, Colorforms Adventure Set, #630, ©1978 DC Comics **18.00**

Superman, hair brush, wooden, tan colored, curved top, black and brown bristles, flying Superman carrying banner reading "Superman American" against gold ground, 2¼ x 4 x 1½" **90.00**

Superman, jigsaw puzzle, American Publishing Corp, Superman battling shark underwater as girl is dragged to bottom chained to cement block, canister container, ©1974 National Periodical Pub **15.00**

Superman, Junior Quoit Set, 8 pcs, orig box **60.00**

Superman, label, Superman Brand Safety Matches, features full figure flying Superman, 1940s, 1½ x 2⁴/4" **275.00**

Catalog, The Superhero Merchandise Catalog, Superhero Enterprises, Inc, color cov, 1975, 6⁵/₈ x 10³/₁₆", $9.00.

Superman, labels, Superman Socks, Sport–Wear Hosiery, Nat'l Comics Pub, 3–pc printer's proof set with front label and 2 side labels, 1949, 8 x 10" front label, 2 x 10" side labels **925.00**

Superman, membership certificate, Action Comics premium, #295834, early 1960s, 8½ x 11" **60.00**

Superman, movie viewer, Chemtoy Co, Chicago, complete with 2¾" viewer and 2 boxed films, ©1965, MOC **25.00**

Superman, paperback book, *Superboy & the Legion of Superheroes*, Tempo Books, 160 pp, 1977 . . . . **7.00**

Superman, play suit, Ben Cooper, shirt, pants, and cape, shirt lithoed with images of Superman and Superboy and "Remember—This suit won't make you fly, only Superman can," large size 12–14, orig box **275.00**

Wonder Woman, record and story album set, Peter Pan Records, 33⅓ rpm, *Wonder Woman vs The War God* and *Amazon From Space*, 16–pp color comic book, illus by Neal Adams, 1977 . . . . **8.00**

Captain Action, Green Hornet outfit, green overcoat with gold linen lining, mask, hat, white shirt, black pants, shoes, stinger cane, gas pistol, shoulder holster, wristwatch message receiver, TV radar scanner with phone adapter, and gas mask, orig box, $3,300.00. Photo courtesy Toy Scouts, Inc.

AUCTION PRICES

Batman items sold by Toy Scouts, Catalog #31, closing date September 19, 1997.

Bat–Chute, CDC, 1966, unused **$40.00**
Batmobile and Boat Set, Corgi Jr, 1979, MOC **70.00**
Bat–Scope, Kellogg's premium, 1966 . . . . **40.00**
Cape, B&K, 1966, MIP **25.00**
Drinking Glass, Batgirl, Pepsi Super Series, 1976 . . . . . . **10.00**
Drinking Glass, Batman, Pepsi Super Series, 1976 . . . . . . **5.00**
Drinking Glass, Robin, Pepsi Super Series, 1976 . . . . . . **10.00**
Film, 8 mm, Columbia Films, 1960s **25.00**
Frame Tray Puzzle, Watkins–Strathmore, 1966 . . . . **10.00**
Halloween Costume, Batgirl, Ben Cooper, 1977 . . . . . . **25.00**
License Plate, Groff Signs **30.00**
Night Light, Sanpit, 1966, MOC **25.00**
Periscope, Winner Promotions, 1974 . . . . **45.00**
Puppet, Ideal, 1966 . . . . **25.00**
Record, Picture Disc, RCA, 1988, unused **25.00**
Wristwatch, c1950–53, unused **20.00**

SWANKYSWIGS

A Swankyswig is a decorated glass container used as packaging for Kraft Cheese which doubled as a juice glass once the cheese was consumed. The earliest Swankyswigs date from the 1930s. They proved extremely popular during the Depression.

Initial designs were hand stenciled. Eventually machines were developed to apply the decoration. Kraft test marketed designs. As a result, some designs are very difficult to find. Unfortunately, Kraft does not have a list of all the designs it produced.

Production was discontinued briefly during World War II when the paint used for decoration was needed for the war effort. Bicentennial Tulip (1975) was the last Swankyswig pattern.

Beware of Swankyswig imitators from the 1970s and early 1980s. These come from other companies, including at least one Canadian firm. Cherry, Diamond over Triangle, Rooster's Head, Sportsman series, and Wildlife series are a few of the later themes. In order to be considered a true Swankyswig, the glass has to be a Kraft product.

References: Gene Florence, *Collectible Glassware From the 40's, 50's, 60's: An Illustrated Value Guide, Third Edition,* Collector Books, 1996; Jan Warner, *Swankyswigs, A Pattern Guide Checklist, Revised,* The Daze, 1988, 1992 value update.

Collectors' Club: Swankyswig's Unlimited, 201 Alvena, Wichita, KS 67203.

Kiddie Cup, ducks and ponies, 3³/₄" h, $3.00.

Antique, blue, 3³/₄" h	**$4.00**
Antique, brown, 3³/₄" h	**4.00**
Antique, green, 3³/₄" h	**4.00**
Antique, orange, 3³/₄" h	**4.00**
Antique, red, 3³/₄" h	**4.00**
Atlantic City, cobalt, 5" h	**25.00**
Band #1, red and black, 3³/₈" h	**3.00**
Band #1, red and blue, 3³/₈" h	**4.00**
Band #1, blue, 3³/₈" h	**5.00**
Band #2, red and black, 3³/₈" h	**4.00**
Band #2, red and black, 4³/₄" h	**6.00**
Band #3, blue and white, 3³/₈" h	**4.00**
Bicentennial, yellow, tulip type	**8.00**
Bustling Betsy, brown, 3³/₄" h	**4.00**
Bustling Betsy, orange, 3³/₄" h	**4.00**
Bustling Betsy, yellow, 3³/₄"	**4.00**
Carnival, fired on orange	**5.00**
Carnival, yellow	**10.00**
Checkerboard, blue and red, 3¹/₂" h	**25.00**
Checkerboard, green, 3¹/₂" h	**28.00**
Circle and Dot, blue, 4³/₄" h	**10.00**
Circle and Dot, blue, 3¹/₂" h	**6.00**
Circle and Dot, black, 3¹/₂" h	**6.00**
Circle and Dot, red, 4³/₄" h	**8.00**
Coin, clear, 3³/₄" h	**2.00**
Cornflower, #2, dark blue, 3¹/₂" h	**3.00**
Cornflower #1, light blue, 3¹/₂" h	**5.00**
Cornflower #2, red, 3¹/₂" h	**4.00**
Daisy, red, white, and green, 3¹/₄" h	**3.00**
Daisy, red, white, and green, 4¹/₂" h	**15.00**
Dots and Diamonds, red, 3¹/₂" h	**8.00**
Forget–Me–Not, dark blue, 3¹/₂" h	**3.00**
Forget–Me–Not, light blue, 3¹/₂" h	**3.50**
Forge–Me–Not, red, 3¹/₂" h	**3.00**
Forget–Me–Not, yellow	**3.00**

Jonquil, yellow, 3¹/₂" h	**3.00**
Kiddie Cup, bird and elephant, red	**2.00**
Kiddie Cup, duck and horse, black	**6.00**
Kiddie Cup, pig and bear, blue	**2.00**
Lattice and Vine, white and blue, 3¹/₂" h	**8.00**
Lily of the Valley, red and black	**10.00**
Posy, jonquil	**4.00**
Posy, violet, 3¹/₂" h	**5.00**
Red Fox, Sportsmen Series, black, 4⁵/₈" h	**5.00**
Red Tulip, #1, special issue, Del Monte, 3¹/₂" h	**40.00**
Sailboat, blue, 3¹/₂" h	**10.00**
Sailboat, red and white, round rack, 5" h, price for set	**60.00**
Star, black	**5.00**
Star, blue, 4³/₄" h	**7.00**
Star, blue, red, green, and black, 3¹/₂" h	**4.00**
Star, cobalt, white stars, 4³/₄" h	**18.00**
Texas Centennial, black, blue, green, and red	**20.00**
Tulip #1, black, 3¹/₂" h	**4.00**
Tulip #1, red, 3¹/₂" h	**4.00**
Tulip #2, red, green, and black, 3¹/₂" h	**28.00**
Tulip #3, blue, 3³/₄" h	**3.50**
Tulip #3, red, 3³/₄" h	**3.00**
West Virginia Centennial, cobalt, 4³/₄" h	**25.00**

SWAROVSKI CRYSTAL

Daniel Swarovski founded D. Swarovski & Co. in Georgenthal, Bohemia, in 1895. Initially the company produced high quality abrasives, crystal stones for the costume jewelry industry, and optical items. The company continues to produce several accessory and jewelry lines including the inexpensive Savvy line and the high-end Daniel Swarovski boutique collection.

In 1977 Swarovski introduced a line of collectible figurines and desk items. A crystal mouse and a spiny hedgehog were the first two figurines. Swarovski figurines have a 30% or more lead content. In 1987 the International Swarovski Collectors Society was formed. Swarovski produces an annual figurine available only to Society members. Every three years a new theme is introduced, e.g., "Mother and Child," three annual figures featuring a mother sea mammal and her offspring.

Initially Swarovski crystal figurines were marked with a block-style SC. In 1989 Swarovski began using a mark that included a swan. Swarovski was included in the mark on larger pieces. Pieces made for the Swarovski Collectors Society are marked with an SCS logo, the initials of the designer, and the year. The first SCS logo included an edelweiss flower above the SCS.

Regional issues are common. Some items were produced in two versions, one for Europe and one for the United States. Many items with metal trim are available in rhodium (white metal) or gold.

A Swarovski figurine is considered incomplete on the secondary market if it does not include its period box, product identification sticker, and any period paper work. Society items should be accompanied by a certificate of authenticity.

Today the Daniel Swarovski Corporation is headquartered in Zurich, Switzerland. Production and design is based in Wattens, Austria. Swarovski has manufacturing facilities in 11 countries, including a plant in Cranston, Rhode Island. The company employs more than 8,000 people worldwide.

Be alert to Swarovski imitations with a lower lead content which often contain flaws in the crystal and lack the Swarovski logo.

References: Jane Warner, *Warner's Blue Ribbon Book on Swarovski: Beyond Silver Crystal*, published by author, 1997; Tom and Jane Warner, *Warner's Blue Ribbon Book on Swarovski Silver Crystal, Fourth Edition*, published by authors, 1997.

Periodical: *Swan Seekers News*, 9740 Campo Rd, Ste 134, Spring Valley, CA 91977.

Newsletter: *The Crystal Report*, 1322 N Barron St, Eaton, OH 45320.

Collectors' Club: Swarovski Collectors Society (company sponsored), 2 Slater Rd, Cranston, RI 02920.

Ashtray, #7641nr100, sculpted crystal, SC or swan logo, 3³/₈" d **$225.00**
Bear, #7636nr112, SC mark only, USA only, SC logo, 4¹/₂" h **1,300.00**
Bell, #7467nr071000, SC or swan logo, 5³/₄" h **125.00**
Bunny, #7652nr45, ears flat on top of head, SC logo, 1¹/₂" h **180.00**
Butterfly, #7671nr30, metal antennae, no base, USA only, SC logo, 1" h **85.00**
Cactus, 2 flowers, SCS eidelweiss mark, Collectors Society renewal gift, 1988 . . . . **200.00**
Candle Holder, #7600nr131, small, prickets, SC logo, ¹⁵/₁₆", price for set of 6 . . . . **350.00**
Cat, #7634nr52, flexible metal tail, SC logo, 2" h **375.00**
Cigarette Holder, #7463nr062, sculpted crystal, SC or swan logo, 2³/₈" **110.00**
Dachshund, #7641nr75, metal tail, rigid, limp, or gently arched, SC or swan logo **90.00**
Duck, #7653nr45, silver beak, SC logo, 1⁷/₈" l **80.00**
Elephant, #7640nr40, frosted tail, swan logo, 2" h **100.00**
Falcon Head, #7645nr45, SC or swan logo, 1³/₄" h **130.00**
Frog, #7642nr48, black eyes and clear crown, SC or swan logo **90.00**
Hedgehog, #7630nr50, silver whiskers, 50 mm body, SC logo, 2" h including spines **130.00**
Hummingbird, #7552nr100, crystal and gold metal, green stones on wings, feeding in crystal lotus flower, SC logo, 4" w **900.00**

Key Chain, 15 mm crystal ball, SCS swan logo on rhodium chain, Collectors Society renewal gift, 1989 . . . . **50.00**
Lighter, #7462nr062, chrome, crystal base, SC or swan logo, 3¹/₂" h **275.00**
Limited Edition Figurine, Armour, Turtledoves, #do1x891, 2 doves on arch shaped tree branch, SCS swan mark, 1989 . . . . **700.00**
Limited Edition Figurine, Care For Me, Seals, #do1x911, mother and baby harp seal on ice floe, no whiskers, SCS swan mark, 1991 . . . . **360.00**
Limited Edition Figurine, Save Me, Whales, #do1x921, mother and baby whales breaching the surf, noses in air, SCS swan mark, 1992 . . . . **330.00**
Mallard, #7647nr80, frosted beak, SC or swan logo, 3¹/₂" l **135.00**
Ornament, snowflake, hexagonal metal trim ring and neck chain, hexagonal ring stamped "SC" at top on back side, orig blue velour pouch, silver logo box, 1981 . . . . **350.00**
Paperweight, cone, bermuda blue, #7452nr600, facets spiral around cone, color shades from dark to light blue, SC or swan logo, 3¹/₈" h **275.00**
Picture Frame, oval, #7505nr75G, gold trim, SC or swan logo, 3" h **275.00**
Pig, #7638nr65, crystal "J" shaped tail, SC logo, 1³/₄" l **200.00**
Salt and Pepper Shakers, pr, #7508nr068034, rhodium screw-off tops, SC logo, 3¹/₈" h **300.00**
Schnapps Glass, #7468nr39000, USA, price for set of 6 . . . . **275.00**
Sparrow, #7650nr32, silver metal open beak, SC logo, 1¹/₄" h **140.00**
Swan, #7658nr27, SC logo, 1" h **125.00**
Treasure Box, cov, #7465nr52/100, butterfly on removable lid, SC or swan logo **175.00**
Treasure Box, oval, #7466nr063000, flowers on removable lid, SC or swan logo **225.00**

SYRACUSE CHINA

Syracuse China traces its origins to W. H. Farrar, who established a pottery in Syracuse, New York, in 1841. The plant moved from Genessee Street to Fayette Street in 1855 and operated as the Empire Pottery. The Empire Pottery became the Onondaga Pottery Company after a reorganization in 1871, retaining that name until 1966 when the company became the Syracuse China Company. Few noticed the change because Onondaga Pottery had marketed its dinnerware under a Syracuse China brand name since as early as 1879.

Onondaga introduced a high-fired, semi-vitreous ware in the mid-1880s that was guaranteed against crackling and crazing. In 1888 James Pass introduced Imperial Geddo, a translucent, vitrified china. By the early 1890s, the company offered a full line of fine china ware.

Onondaga made commercial as well as household china. In 1921 a new plant, devoted exclusively to commercial production, was opened. In 1959 Onondaga Pottery acquired Vandesca-Syracuse, Joliette, Quebec, Canada, a producer of vitrified hotel china. In 1984 Syracuse China absorbed the Mayer China Company.

After manufacturing fine dinnerware for 99 years, Syracuse China discontinued its household china line in 1970, devoting its production efforts exclusively to airline, commercial, hotel, and restaurant china.

References: Cleota Reed and Stan Skoczen, *Syracuse China*, Syracuse University Press, 1997; Harry L. Rinker, *Dinnerware of the 20th Century: The Top 500 Patterns*, House of Collectibles, 1997.

Briarcliff, cream soup and saucer	$25.00
Briarcliff, dinner plate, 10" d	15.00
Briarcliff, fruit bowl, 5¹/₈"	12.00
Briarcliff, salad bowl, 8" d	12.00
Corelbel, fruit bowl	20.00
Corelbel, place setting	100.00
Corelbel, soup bowl	28.00
Meadow Breeze, cup and saucer, ftd	15.00
Meadow Breeze, dinner plate, 10³/₄" d	20.00
Nimbus Platinum, fruit bowl	18.00
Nimbus Platinum, place setting	80.00
Radcliffe, fruit bowl	18.00
Radcliffe, place setting	95.00
Rosalie, fruit bowl	20.00
Rosalie, place setting	100.00
Sharon, fruit bowl	20.00
Sharon, place setting	90.00
Sharon, soup bowl	32.00
Sherwood, demitasse cup and saucer	15.00
Sherwood, dinner plate, 9³/₄" d	10.00
Sherwood, salad plate, 8" d	12.00
Sherwood, sugar, cov	30.00
Stansbury, bread and butter plate, 6¹/₂" d	6.00
Stansbury, fruit bowl, 5¹/₈" d	8.00
Stansbury, platter, oval, 14¹/₈" l	40.00
Stansbury, salad plate, 8" d	8.00
Stansbury, vegetable, oval, 9¹/₄" l	30.00
Suzanne, cup and saucer, ftd	20.00
Suzanne, dinner plate, 10" d	15.00
Suzanne, salad plate, 8" d	12.00
Suzanne, platter, oval, 12¹/₈" l	45.00
Sweetheart, creamer	35.00
Sweetheart, cup and saucer, ftd	30.00
Sweetheart, dinner plate, 10¹/₂" d	20.00

Stansbury, dinner plate, 10³/₈" d, $15.00.

Sweetheart, salad plate, 8¹/₄" d	15.00
Wayne, cereal bowl	32.00
Wayne, fruit bowl	28.00
Wayne, place setting	140.00
Wayne, soup bowl	36.00
Wayside, butter, cov, ¹/₄ lb	32.00
Wayside, creamer	20.00
Wayside, cup and saucer	14.00
Wayside, dinner plate, 10¹/₈" d	16.00
Wayside, salad plate, 8" d	10.00
Wayside, sugar, cov	25.00

TAYLOR, SMITH & TAYLOR

Around 1900 Joseph G. Lee, W. L. Smith, John N. Taylor, W. L. Taylor, and Homer J. Taylor founded the firm that eventually became Taylor, Smith & Taylor. The Taylors purchased Lee's interests in 1903, only to sell their interests to the Smiths in 1906. The company's plant was located in Chester, West Virginia, the corporate offices in East Liverpool, Ohio.

Taylor, Smith & Taylor made a wide range of plain and painted semi–porcelain wares, e.g., dinnerware, hotel and restaurant ware, and toilet sets. Lu–Ray (introduced in 1930), Pebbleford, and Vistosa are three of the company's most popular dinnerware shapes. In the 1960s a line of cooking and oven ware was produced. Special commission work ranged from dinnerware premiums for Mother's Oats to Gigi and Holly Hobbie plates for American Greetings Corp.

Anchor Hocking purchased Taylor, Smith & Taylor in 1973. The plant closed in January 1982.

References: Susan and Al Bagdade, *Warman's American Pottery and Porcelain*, Wallace–Homestead, 1994; Harvey Duke, *The Official Identification and Price Guide to Pottery and Porcelain*, Eighth Edition, House of Collectibles, 1995; Kathy and Bill Meehan, *Collector's Guide to Lu–Ray Pastels: Identification and Values*, Collector Books, 1995.

Beverly, cup and saucer	$5.00
Beverly, gravy boat	12.00
Beverly, platter, oval, 11¹/₂" l	10.00
Beverly, sugar, cov	8.00
Delphian, creamer and sugar, cov	12.00
Delphian, cup and saucer	5.00
Delphian, plate, 9¹/₄" d	8.00
Empire, bowl, 36s	8.00
Empire, butter dish	20.00
Empire, creamer	4.00
Empire, plate, 8¹/₄" d	4.00
Empire, plate, 10" d	10.00
Empire, platter, oval, 11¹/₂" l	10.00
Empire, soup bowl	10.00
Ever Yours, Golden Button, creamer	2.50
Ever Yours, Golden Button, platter, oval	3.00
Ever Yours, Golden Button, salt and pepper shakers, pr	8.00
Fairway, casserole	20.00
Fairway, eggcup	10.00
Fairway, plate, 7¹/₄" d	4.00
Fairway, 9¹/₄" d	8.00
Garland, cup and saucer	7.00
Garland, plate, 7" d	4.00
Laurel, cake plate, round, 10³/₄" d	10.00

Laurel, casserole. 20.00
Laurel, creamer and sugar 12.00
Laurel, cream soup cup. 12.00
Laurel, plate, 10" d 10.00
Lu–Ray, bowl, 36s, green. 45.00
Lu–Ray, cream soup, blue 75.00
Lu–Ray, creamer, blue 10.00
Lu–Ray, creamer, pink 10.00
Lu–Ray, lug soup, blue 21.00
Lu–Ray, lug soup, pink 21.00
Lu–Ray, mixing bowl, large, blue 140.00
Lu–Ray, plate, 9" d, blue 11.00
Lu–Ray, plate, 9" d, cream. 11.00
Lu–Ray, plate, 9" d, green. 11.00
Lu–Ray, plate, 9" d, pink 11.00
Lu–Ray, platter, 13½" l, blue 14.00
Lu–Ray, platter, 13½" l, green 14.00
Lu–Ray, relish, 4 part, blue 135.00
Lu–Ray, salt and pepper shakers, pr, blue 16.00
Lu–Ray, salt and sepper shakers, pr, pink 16.00
Lu–Ray, saucer, green 1.50
Lu–Ray, saucer, pink 1.50
Lu–Ray, saucer, yellow 1.50
Lu–Ray, sugar, cov, blue 12.00
Lu–Ray, sugar, cov, cream 12.00
Lu–Ray, tea cup and saucer, blue. 12.00
Lu–Ray, tea cup and saucer, cream 12.00
Lu–Ray, tea cup and saucer, green 12.00
Lu–Ray, tea cup and saucer, pink. 12.00
Lu–Ray, vegetable, oblong, pink. 10.00
Marvel, bread and butter plate, 7" d. 4.00
Marvel, cup and saucer. 5.00
Marvel, dinner plate, 9" d 8.00
Marvel, eggcup. 10.00
Marvel, gravy boat 12.00
Marvel, platter, 11½" l. 10.00
Marvel, salad bowl 15.00
Marvel, soup bowl 10.00
Marvel, teapot 20.00
Paramount, batter jug 35.00

Paramount, butter dish. 20.00
Paramount, casserole, ftd, rattan handle 20.00
Paramount, creamer 5.00
Paramount, gravy boat. 12.00
Pastoral, cup and saucer 5.00
Pastoral, plate, 6½" d 2.00
Pebbleford, casserole. 20.00
Pebbleford, coffeepot 35.00
Pebbleford, creamer 5.00
Pebbleford, gravy boat. 12.00
Pebbleford, plate, 10" d 10.00
Pebbleford, platter, 13" l 12.00
Plymouth, chop plate, lug handle, 11¼" d 10.00
Plymouth, creamer 4.00
Plymouth, sugar, cov. 8.00
Versatile, wheat pattern, bread and butter plate 3.00
Versatile, wheat pattern, cup and saucer 6.00
Versatile, wheat pattern, fruit bowl. 3.00
Versatile, wheat pattern, lug soup 5.00
Versatile, wheat pattern, luncheon plate. 3.50
Versatile, wheat pattern, salad plate 3.50
Versatile, wheat pattern, platter, 13" l 8.00
Versatile, salt and pepper shakers, pr 5.00
Versatile, sauce boat 8.00
Versatile, wheat pattern, vegetable, oval. 7.00
Vistosa, creamer, red. 10.00
Vistosa, eggcup, yellow 10.00
Vistosa, 9" d, cobalt blue. 8.00
Vistosa, salad bowl, ftd, red 130.00
Vogue, cream soup cup. 12.00
Vogue, cup and saucer 5.00
Vogue, eggcup 10.00
Vogue, gravy boat 12.00

TEAPOTS

Collecting by form was extremely popular in the 1940s and 1950s. It fell completely out of favor in the 1970s and 1980s. A small but dedicated group of teapot collectors kept collecting interest alive. Today, the teapot is enjoying a collecting renaissance.

Tea drinking was firmly established in England and its American colonies by the middle of the 18th century. The earliest teapots were modeled after their Far Eastern ancestors. Teapot shapes and decorative motifs kept pace with the ceramic and new design styles of the 19th century. The whimsical, figural teapot was around from the start.

Teapots were a common product of American ceramic, glass, and metal manufacturers. The "Rebekah at the Well" teapot appeared in the mid–1850s. Hall China of East Liverpool, Ohio, was one of the leading teapot manufacturers of the 1920s and 30s. Figural teapots were extremely popular in the 1930s. The first etched Pyrex teapot was made in the late 1930s.

Shape, followed by decoration, then manufacturer and/or country of origin are the value keys.

References: Tina M. Carter, *Teapots: The Collectors' Guide to Selecting, Identifying and Displaying New and Vintage Teapots*, Running Press, Courage Books, 1995; Garth Clark, *The Eccentric Teapot: 400 Years of Invention*, Abbeville Press, 1989.

Periodical: *Tea Talk*, PO Box 860, Sausalito, CA 94966.

Versatile, wheat pattern, dinner plate, platinum trim, $4.00.

Note: All teapots listed are ceramic.

Arabia of Finland, Anemone, blue bands, S shape. **$60.00**

Commemorative, Dartmouth Potteries, England, Queen Elizabeth coronation, raised profile on dark brown ground, raised arms on reverse, crown finial, 5" h, 8½" l **125.00**

Cortendorf, Germany, cat, beckoning pose, black and white, green eyes and ribbon, 6 cup. **50.00**

Czechoslovakia, Blue Onion, 4" h, 6½" w **20.00**

Czeckoslovakia, figural Dutch girl, holding basket of flowers, hp, blue dress. **95.00**

Czechoslovakia, tea set, 3¾" h teapot, creamer, and sugar, Art Deco style, panel with blue leaved trees, blue clouds, yellow sky, green and pink ground, circular design in same colors on reverse, burnt orange ground **110.00**

England, black transfer of 2 women with baby on ground, polychrome enamel accents, "H.&S." mark, 6¾" h **70.00**

England, porcelain, red and blue sprigs, 6" h **100.00**

Graniteware, cream and green, gooseneck spout **75.00**

Hall, Albany, brown with gold. **70.00**

Hall, Basketball, Chinese red. **850.00**

Hall, Benjamin, Celedon green **80.00**

Hall, Birdcage, maroon with gold, 6 cup **200.00**

Hall, Boston, Addison gray **20.00**

Hall, Coverlet, canary. **50.00**

Hall, Doughnut, cobalt blue **160.00**

Hall, French, Chinese red, white lid. **110.00**

Hall, French, Monterrey green, gold flowers, 8 cup. **45.00**

Hall, Globe, light green and gold, dripless, 6 cup. **200.00**

Hall, Liptons, Camillia. **30.00**

Hall, Los Angeles, cobalt with gold, 6 cup **190.00**

Hall, Manhattan, blue **65.00**

Hall, Melody, Chinese red **180.00**

Hall, Murphy, light blue **35.00**

Hall, Newport, pink, floral decal, 5 cup. **50.00**

Hall, Ohio, black with gold, 6 cup. **150.00**

Hall, Philadelphia, green with gold, 4 cup **25.00**

Hall, Plume, pink **20.00**

Hall, Royal, ivory **150.00**

Hall, Streamline, canary with platinum **40.00**

Hall, Sundial, canary with gold **125.00**

Hall, tea set, 3 pcs, Hollywood, mauve with gold. **90.00**

Hall, Windshield, mustard yellow, floral decal, 6 cup **90.00**

Haviland, pine cone design, gold trim, 10½" h. **25.00**

Japan, musical, oval, 6 cup **10.00**

Japan, whimsical man, nose is spout, pastel pink, blue, and yellow, c1930. . . . . **25.00**

Occupied Japan, colonial couple dec **20.00**

Occupied Japan, Dragonware, raised dragon and coralene dec, gold trim, 6 cup **30.00**

Prince Kensington, England, Cottage Ware, Ye Olde Cottage. **35.00**

Royal Canadian Art Potter, Hamilton, Canada, dripless, brown, hp flowers **30.00**

Royal Copenhagen, blue and white flowers and leaves design, acorn finial, 10" h **65.00**

Royal Doulton, Gold Lace, H4989, 9½" h **100.00**

Sessions, Clock, plastic **45.00**

Shawnee, Flower, blue, gold trim. **30.00**

Shelley China, Wildflower, 4½" h. **125.00**

Souvenir, Clarice Cliff, "Greetings from Canada," teepee shape, spout is Indian, handle is totem pole, c1950, 5⅞" h **150.00**

Souvenir, Germany, US Capitol, Washington, DC, square, scenic, gold trim, 4½" h. **20.00**

Souvenir, Japan, Victoria Ceramics, souvenir, tea set, teapot, cup and saucer, hp, California Redwoods, Chandelier Drive–Thru Tree, c1940, 2" h **18.00**

Stangl, Town and Country, blue **75.00**

Taylor, Smith & Taylor, Vistosa, sharon pink **50.00**

Torquay, "Take a Cup of Tea Its Very Refreshing," sailboat scene, 4½" h. **95.00**

US Zone, Germany, figural cat, black, ivory, and gray, tail handle, paw spout, 9" h. **50.00**

William Adams & Sons, Ltd, Express White, Empress shape **50.00**

TEDDY BEARS

The teddy bear, named for President Theodore Roosevelt, arrived on the scene in late 1902 or early 1903. The Ideal Toy Corporation (American) and Margarette Steiff (German) are among the earliest firms to include a bear in their stuffed toy lines.

Early teddy bears are identified by the humps in their backs, elongated muzzles, jointed limbs, mohair bodies (some exceptions), and glass, pinback, or black shoe button eyes. Stuffing materials include excelsior, the most popular, kapok, and wood–wool. Elongated limbs, oversized feet, felt paws, and a black embroidered nose and mouth are other indicators of a quality early bear.

Teddy bear manufacturers closely copied each other. Once the manufacturer's identification label or marking is lost it is impossible to tell one maker's bear from another.

America went teddy bear crazy in the 1980s. A strong secondary market for older bears developed. Many stuffed (plush) toy manufacturers reintroduced teddy bears to their line. Dozens of teddy bear artisans marketed their hand–crafted creations. Some examples sold in the hundreds of dollars.

The speculative fever of the 1980s has subsided. Sale of the hand–crafted artisan bears on the secondary market has met with mixed results. While the market is still strong enough to support its own literature, magazines, and show circuit, the number of collectors has diminished. Those that remain are extremely passionate about their favorite collectible.

Hall, Victorian style, Connie, green, $60.00. Photo courtesy Gene Harris Auctioneers & Appraisers.

References: Pauline Cockrill, *Teddy Bear Encyclopedia*, Dorling Kindersley, 1993, distributed by Hobby House Press; Ann Gehlbach, *Muffy VanderBear: Identification & Price Guide*, Hobby House Press, 1997; Dee Hockenberry, *The Big Bear Book*, Schiffer Publishing, 1996; Margaret Fox Mandel, *Teddy Bears and Steiff Animals* (1984, 1997 value update), *Second Series* (1987, 1996 value update), Collector Books; Margaret Fox Mandel, *Teddy Bears, Annalee Animals & Steiff Animals, Third Series*, Collector Books, 1990, 1996 value update; Linda Mullins, *American Teddy Bear Encyclopedia*, Hobby House Press, 1995; Linda Mullins, *Teddy Bear & Friends Price Guide, 4th Edition*, Hobby House Press, 1993; Linda Mullins, *Teddy Bears Past & Present, Vol. II*, Hobby House Press, 1992; Jesse Murray, *Teddy Bear Figurines Price Guide*, Hobby House Press, 1996; Cynthia Powell, *Collector's Guide to Miniature Teddy Bears: Identification & Values*, Collector Books, 1994; Carol J. Smith, *Identification & Price Guide to Winnie the Pooh Collectibles, I* (1994), *II* (1996), Hobby House Press, 1994.

Periodicals: *National Doll & Teddy Bear Collector*, PO Box 4032, Portland, OR 97208; *Teddy Bear & Friends*, PO Box 420235, II Commerce Blvd, Palm Coast, FL, 32142; *Teddy Bear Review*, 170 Fifth Ave, 12th Flr, New York, NY 10010.

Collectors' Clubs: Good Bears of the World, PO Box 13097, Toledo, OH 43613; Teddy Bear Boosters Club, 19750 SW Peavine Mtn Rd, McMinnville, OR 97128.

Note: See Steiff and Stuffed Toys for additional listings.

Character Novelty Co, cinnamon synthetic plush, plastic eyes, label sewn into ear, c1960, 15" h **$60.00**
Clemens, gold mohair, glass eyes, fully jointed, brown embroidered nose and mouth, excelsior stuffing, c1940, 17" h **285.00**
Cosy Orsi, 8" h **95.00**
Crisly, beige mohair, fully jointed, kapok stuffing, glass eyes, paper tag attached to chest, c1960, 22" h **325.00**
Eden, rattle, orig tags, 1970s **25.00**
England, cinnamon mohair, glass eyes, squeaker, full jointed, short oval body, straight arms and legs, velveteen pads, embroidered nose and mouth, 12½" h **85.00**
England, long yellow mohair, fully jointed, kapok stuffing, glass eyes, embroidered nose and mouth, felt pads, blue and white knitted overalls, 17" h **200.00**
German, Bellhop, mohair, 11" **275.00**
German, blonde mohair, fully jointed, excelsior stuffing, glass eyes, embroidered nose, mouth, and claw felt pads, 9½" h **400.00**
Gund, Cubbie Bear, dark brown plush, molded vinyl face, painted eyes, wearing dress, shoes, and removable apron, label sewn in leg seam, c1950, 13" h **85.00**
Herman, golden mohair, shoe button eyes, fully jointed, fabric nose, embroidered mouth, excelsior stuffing, 19" h **172.00**
Herman, light yellow mohair, shoe button eyes, fully jointed, excelsior stuffing, 19" h **143.00**
Ideal Toy Co, Musical Clown Bear, cinnamon synthetic plush, molded soft vinyl face, plastic eyes, white pants with brown and yellow spots, yellow felt hat, label sewn in shoulder seam, c1950, 15" h **135.00**
Ideal Toy Co, brown plush, cream paws, plastic eyes, molded nose and mouth, tail squeaks, orig label, 17" **40.00**

Ideal Toy Co, The Original Teddy Bear, 75th anniversary commemorative, brown plush, label, special edition box, 1978, 16" h **50.00**
Knickerbocker, brown mohair, fully jointed, 21" **250.00**
Knickerbocker, Pouting Bear, brown plush, foam stuffing, molded face, 1950s, 6" h **10.00**
Knickerbocker, Smokey, plush, stuffed, 24" h **75.00**
Mattel, Gentle Ben, black plush, plastic eyes, pink mouth, red felt tongue, pull string, 1967, 16" h **35.00**
North American Bear Co, Very Important Bear, William Shakesbear, 1981–88 . . . . **400.00**
Schuco Toy Co, Acrobat Bear, short mohair, pale beige over metal body, jointed arms and legs, black metal eyes, c1960, 5½" h **750.00**
Schuco Toy Co, Yes/No Bear, yellow mohair, black steel eyes and eyeglasses, fully jointed, 4¾" h **430.00**
Unidentified Maker, blonde plush mohair, fully jointed, excelsior stuffing, glass eyes, long pointed nose, embroidered features and claws, long bullet–shaped body, curved arms, straight legs with large feet, 20½" h **115.00**
Unidentified Maker, curly brown mohair, glass eyes, embroidered nose, mouth, and claws, brown felt pads, excelsior stuffing, unjointed, 9½" h **1,380.00**
Unidentified Maker, gold mohair, windup, glass eyes, felt and flannel outfit, red metal tricycle with white wheels, 6¾" h **460.00**
Unidentified Maker, long cinnamon mohair, fully jointed, excelsior and kapok stuffing, glass eyes, flannel pads, embroidered nose and mouth, oval body, straight arms and legs, 14½" h **115.00**
Unidentified Maker, mohair, jointed at shoulders and hips, excelsior stuffing, shoe button eyes, 8½" h **85.00**
Unidentified Maker, orange mohair, Roosevelt type, fully jointed, glass eyes, mouth opens to reveal white glass teeth, long oval body, straight short arms and legs, 1 broken tooth, 16½" h **460.00**
Unidentified Maker, yellow mohair, fully jointed excelsior stuffing, glass eyes, embroidered nose and mouth, long oval body, short curved arms, straight legs, pink and white knitted sweater **315.00**
WDP, Winnie the Pooh, plush, stuffed, c1960s, 6" h **75.00**

American, gold mohair, fully jointed, black and diamond button eyes, front body seam, early 20th C, 27" h, $325.00. Photo courtesy Collectors Auction Services.

TELEPHONES & RELATED MEMORABILIA

Until the mid–1990s, telephone collecting centered primarily on candlestick telephones and single, double, and triple wall–mounted, oak case telephones. Avant–garde collectors concentrated on colored, rotary–dial telephones from the Art Deco period. The Automatic Telephone Company (General Telephone) and Western Electric (Bell System) were the two principal manufacturers of this later group. Kellogg, Leich, and Stromberg Carlson also made colored case telephones.

Recently collector interest has increased in three new areas: (1) the desk sets of the late 1930s and 40s, typified by Western Electric Model 302 A–G dial cradle telephone (1937–1954 and designated the "Perry Mason" phone by collectors), (2) colored plastic phones of the 1950s and 60s, e.g., the Princess, and (3) figural telephones, popular in the late 1970s and throughout the 1980s.

References: James David Davis, *Collectible Novelty Phones*, Schiffer Publishing, 1998; Kate Dooner, *Telephones: Antique to Modern, 2nd Edition*, Schiffer Publishing, 1998; Kate Dooner, *Telephone Collecting: Seven Decades of Design*, Schiffer Publishing, 1993; Richard D. Mountjoy, *One Hundred Years of Bell Telephone*, Schiffer Publishing, 1995.

Collectors' Clubs: Antique Telephone Collectors Assoc, PO Box 94, Abilene, KS 67410; Mini–Phone Exchange, 5412 Tilden Rd, Bladensburg, MD 20710; Telephone Collectors International, 19 N Cherry Dr, Oswego, IL 60543.

TELEPHONES

Advertising, Crest Toothpaste, Sparkle, 10½" h	**$40.00**
Advertising, Pizza Hut, Pizza Pete, 1980s	**50.00**
Automatic Electric, model 35A, wall, all position transmitter, 1930s	**25.00**
Automatic Electric, monophone, Art Deco style, Bakelite, gold trim, c1928, 5 x 9"	**150.00**
Automatic Electric, monophone, c1928, 5½ x 9"	**75.00**
Automatic Electric, ringer inside, round base, late 1930s	**150.00**
Connecticut Telephone & Electric Co, desk, Model TP–6–A, metal, 6 x 8"	**50.00**
Federal Tel & Tel Co, Grab–a–phone, 8 x 10"	**150.00**
Gray Manufacturing Co, Gray Telephone Pay Station Co, Hartford, payphone, Model 23J, metal, 10½ x 6"	**100.00**
GTE Automatic Electric, payphone, Model 120–A, "semi post pay," 21 x 6"	**125.00**
Kellogg, Masterphone, desk, rotary dial	**45.00**
Leich Electric, desk, orange Bakelite, c1935, 5¾ x 9"	**50.00**
Leich Electric, desk/wall, Beehive, crank, Bakelite, c1930s, 10 x 5½"	**125.00**
Novelty, Banana Splits Talking Telephone, plastic, battery operated, payphone style, interchangeable records, Hasbro, 1969	**75.00**
Novelty, Beetle Bailey	**65.00**
Novelty, Garfield, 1980s	**35.00**
Stromberg–Carlson, magneto desk set, black Bakelite, crank or dial option, 8 x 8"	**50.00**
Western Electric, desk, black, lucite buttons, c1960s	**50.00**
Western Electric, desk, ivory, Model 304, c1950s	**75.00**
Western Electric, desk, Model 500, clear plastic	**55.00**
Western Electric, Trimline, c1968	**40.00**

RELATED

Almanac, Bell Systems Telephone, 58th anniversary issue, 1934	**$14.00**
Booklet, Bell Telephone, Alexander Graham Bell, Bell portrait cov, 1951, 32 pp	**6.00**
Bottle, candlestick telephone shape, Avon	**5.00**
Journal, Canadian Telephone Journal, phone illus, cov with black and white hockey player, Jan 1938	**6.00**
Magazine, *General Telephone Co of Wisconsin News Lines*, Jul 1856	**8.00**
Magazine, *Telephony*, 1955	**2.00**
Paperweight, figural glass bell, dark blue, gold lettering, Bell System, NY Telephone Co, 3¼" h	**70.00**
Pin, service award, New England Telephone & Telegraph, octagonal, 10K gold, raised Bell System logo above faux ruby, 1930s, ½" d	**15.00**
Playing Cards, Telephone Pioneers of America, Bell logo, dark blue and white	**3.00**
Sign, porcelain enamel, Indiana Telephone Corporation, Local & Distance Service, 2 sided, black and white, late 1940s, 18 x 18"	**65.00**
Telephone Card, ACMI, Birthday Card	**12.00**
Telephone Card, Ameritech, Snowflake, $2.00 value, 1st ed	**5.00**
Telephone Card, AT&T, Golden Gate Bridge, 10 units	**17.00**
Telephone Card, FTI Telecom, Magic Minutes	**8.00**
Telephone Card, NYNEX, Holiday Peace Card, $5.00 value	**8.00**
Telephone Card, Sprint, Popsicle Pup	**40.00**

TELEVISION CHARACTERS & PERSONALITIES

Television programming is only fifty years old. Prior to World War II, television viewing was largely centered in the New York market. In 1946 the first network was established, linking WNBT, NBC's New York station, with Schenectady and Philadelphia.

Networks were organized, and programming ordered. By 1949 Americans were purchasing televisions at the rate of 100,000 units a week. In 1955 one–third of all American homes had a television. In the mid–1980s virtually every home included one or more sets.

The 1950s and 60s are the golden age of television licensing. Many early space and western programs licensed over fifty different products. The vast majority of the licensed products were directed toward the infant and juvenile markets.

Television licensing fell off significantly in the 1970s and 80s, the result of increased adult programming, higher fees, and demands by stars for a portion of the licensing fees. Most television shows have no licensed products.

References: Paul Anderson, *The Davy Crockett Craze: A Look at the 1950's Phenomenon and Davy Crockett Collectibles*, R & G Productions, 1996; Tim Brooks and Earle Marsh, *The Complete Directory to Prime Time Network and Cable TV Shows: 1946 – Present, Sixth Edition*, Ballantine Books, 1995; Dana Cain, *Film & TV Animal Star Collectibles*, Antique Trader Books, 1998; Greg Davis and Bill Morgan, *Collector's Guide to TV Memorabilia: 1960s & 1970s*, Collector Books, 1996; Ted Hake, *Hake's Guide to TV Collectibles*, Wallace–Homestead, Krause Publications, 1990; Jack Koch, *Howdy Doody: Collector's Reference and Trivia Guide*,

Collector Books, 1996; Cynthia Boris Liljeblad, *TV Toys and the Shows That Inspired Them,* Krause Publications, 1996.

Norman E. Martinus and Harry L. Rinker, *Warman's Paper,* Wallace–Homestead, Krause Publications, 1994; Kurt Peer, *TV Tie–Ins: A Bibliography of American TV Tie–In Paperbacks,* Neptune Publishing, 1997; Christopher Sausville, *Planet of the Apes Collectibles,* Schiffer Publishing, 1998; Vincent Terrace, *Encyclopedia of Television—Series, Pilots, and Specials, 1937–1973,* 3 Vol, Zoetrope, 1986; Ric Wyman, *For the Love of Lucy: The Complete Guide For Collectors and Fans,* Chronicle Books, 1995; Dian Zillner, *Collectible Television Memorabilia,* Schiffer Publishing, 1996.

Periodicals: *Big Reel,* PO Box 1050, Dubuque, IA 52004; *Television Chronicles,* 10061 Riverside Dr #171, North Hollywood, CA 91602; *The TV Collector,* PO Box 1088, Easton, MA 02334.

Note: For additional listings see Autographs, Cartoon Characters, Coloring Books, Comic Books, Cowboy Heroes, Hanna–Barbera, Games, Little Golden Books, Lunch Boxes, Movie Memorabilia, Pez, Smurfs, Space Adventurers, Star Trek, Super Heroes, TV Guide, Warner Bros., and Whitman TV Books.

Addams Family, record, theme song, 45 rpm, Vic Mizzy **$25.00**

Alfred Hitchcock Presents, record, theme song, 45 rpm, 1950s, 7" **20.00**

A–Team, Colorforms Adventure Set, 1983. . . . . **21.00**

All in the Family, doll, Joey Stivic, MIB. **80.00**

Andy Griffith Show, coloring book, #5644, "Ronny Howard of the Andy Griffith Show Pictures to Color," cover shows Ron Howard sitting with hand under chin, 3 inset pictures of show characters, Saalfield, 1962. . . . . **130.00**

Andy Griffith Show, postcard, color photo of Griffith promoting his appearance at Nevada casino. **10.00**

Bachelor Father, color studio postcard of John Forsythe. **10.00**

Ben Casey, costume, white, embroidered "Ben Casey M. D.," above pocket, complete plastic and rubber stethoscope, MIB. **45.00**

Ben Casey, Play Hospital Set, plastic medicine chest, supplies, instruments, medical bag, certificate, charts, and doctor's cap, Transogram, 1962, MIB **45.00**

Ben Casey, record, theme song, 45 rpm, 7" **10.00**

Beretta, game, Beretta The Street Detective Game, Milton Bradley, 1976. . . . . **25.00**

Berle, Milton, Milton Berle Car, windup, tin litho, orig box, Marx, 1950s, 5½" l **320.00**

Beverly Hillbillies, car, plastic, spring wound motor, plastic removable character figures, complete with accessories, orig box, Ideal, 1963. . . . . **500.00**

Beverly Hillbillies, photo, press release, Buddy Ebsen and Jed from "The Hollywood Palace," 1964 . . . . **12.00**

Bewitched, doll, Samantha, Ideal, 1967, 12½" h. **350.00**

Big Valley, studio cast photo, black and white. **10.00**

Bozo the Clown, coloring set, box contains 12 pre–numbered sketches, 10 colored pencils, and sharpener, Hasbro, 1968 . . . . **25.00**

Bozo the Clown, orig Bozo personal appearance contract, Larry Harmon Pictures Corp, 3 pp **20.00**

Bozo the Clown, pocket watch, made in Japan, plastic, Bozo illus in center, movable metal hands, stem, MOC **15.00**

Brady Bunch, costume, Collegeville, 1970s **75.00**

Brady Bunch, doll, Kitty Karry–All, Remco, 1969 . . . . **150.00**

Buffalo Bill Jr, belt buckle **5.00**

Candid Camera, record, 33 rpm, *Kids' I Love You Songs,* "To Be Telecast on CC 1/10/65," 7". **10.00**

Captain Kangaroo, doll, talking, Mattel, 1967, 20" h **35.00**

Captain Kangaroo, finger paint set, paper sheets, wooden spoons, 4 jars of finger paint, and instructions, Hasbro, 1956, orig 8 x 12" box **25.00**

Carol Burnett, card game, Carol Burnett's Card Game Spoof, Milton Bradley, 1964. . . . . **25.00**

Car 54 Where Are You?, car, friction, litho metal, green and white, rubber tires, "54" on both doors and hood, "High Way Patrol" on rear fender, 1960s, 2½ x 7". **80.00**

Car 54 Where Are You?, coloring book, #1157, Whitman, 1962. . . . . **45.00**

Charlie's Angels, van, #434, pink, Corgi, 1978, MIB **30.00**

CHIPS, Highway Patrol Van, Empire, 1980, MIB **225.00**

Columbo, game, The Columbo Detective Game, Milton Bradley, 1973 . . . . **12.00**

Courtship of Eddie's Father, photo, press release, Bill Bixby on Mike Douglas show, 1972. . . . . **6.00**

Danny Thomas Show, frame tray puzzle, Angela Cartwright, America's Little Darling on Nationwide TV, ©Saalfield, 1962, 10½ x 14", 27 pcs **30.00**

Dennis the Menace, coloring book, #1135, Whitman, 1961. . . . . **40.00**

Dick Van Dyke, game, The Dick Van Dyke Game, Standard Toykraft, 1962–64 . . . . **90.00**

Ding Dong School, Scrapbook, Whitman, unused, 1953. . . . . **15.00**

Dobie Gillis, bobbing head, composition, 7" h **110.00**

Doc Savage, jigsaw puzzle, #4610, diecut cardboard, Doc with clenched fists, Whitman Publishing Co, 14 x 18", 100 pcs **10.00**

Dragnet, badge 714, bronze finish, yellow box with Jack Webb illus, ID card on bottom, Knickerbocker, 1955 . . . . . **25.00**

Dragnet, Badge 714 Target Game, Knickerbocker, 1955 . . . . . **50.00**

Dragnet, Crime Lab Kit, plastic battery operated pistol, badge, handcuffs, microscope, magnifying glass, test tube, fingerprint kit, wallet with ID card, "Case

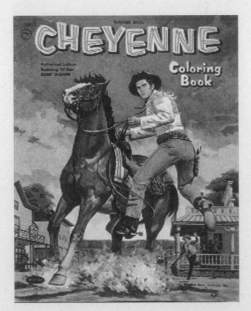

Cheyenne, coloring book, Whitman #1169, unused, ©1958, 8½ x 11", $35.00.

Dukes of Hazzard, board game, Ideal, 1981, $10.00.

Closed" stamp, attaché case shaped cardboard container with brass carrying handle and clasp, Transogram, 1955 .... 90.00

Dragnet, sheet music, theme song, ©Schumann Music Co, 1953 .... 22.00

Dragnet, Talking Police Car, battery operated, plastic, tin base plate, searchlight unit on removable dome, foil "Badge 714" sticker on side, metal crank activates talking device, complete with plastic accessory pcs, Ideal, 1954 .... 200.00

Dr Kildare, activity book, Golden Funtime, punch–out, 1962 .... 20.00

Dr Kildare, jigsaw puzzle, 4318, #2, includes 14 x 12" color portrait for framing, ©Milton Bradley, 1962, over 600 pcs 20.00

Duke, Patty, photo, press release, John Astin and Patty Duke 6.00

Dukes of Hazzard, backpack, blue denim, front has Rebel flag at top and General Lee at bottom, Remco, 1981 .... 39.00

Dukes of Hazzard, poster, full color, cast members on General Lee car, Weekly Reader Book Club premium, late 1970s–80s, 24 x 18" 18.00

Dynasty, Christmas card, cast photo, "The 12 Dynasty Days of Christmas" on back 15.00

Emergency, paramedic truck, red, "Emergency 51 Rescue Squad" decal on each door and rear, Dinky, 1978, 2 x 5 x 9" box, 1978 .... 50.00

Emergency, playset, Rescue Squad with Fire House, plastic vehicles, cardboard fire house, MOC 15.00

Fall Guy, stunt plane with action figure, #4225, plastic, orange and yellow, stunt ladder, clear plastic "Fall Guy Air Show" banner, 3½" h pilot action figure wearing blue pants, orange shirt, brown gloves, boots, and aviator cap, orig box, Tonka, 1983 .... 25.00

Family Affair, coloring book, Whitman, 1968 .... 10.00

Family Affair, doll, Mrs. Beasley, talking, Mattel, 1967 ...... 70.00

Flipper, costume, Collegeville, 1964 .... 65.00

Flipper, music box, litho metal, vinyl/fabric pop–out Flipper figure, Mattel, 1966, 5¼ x 5¼ x 5½", 1966 ...... 60.00

F Troop, coloring book, #9560, Saalfield 20.00

General Hospital, jigsaw puzzle, #8857, diecut cardboard, Tuco, Upson, 15 x 11", over 300 pcs 8.00

Get Smart, coloring book, #4519, "Get Smart! (Maxwell Smart, That Is), Saalfield, 1965 .... 65.00

Get Smart, Get Smart/Secret Agent 86/Pen–Radio, orig box, Multiple Toy Makers, 1966 .... 45.00

Gilligan's Island, coloring book, Whitman, 1965 .... 50.00

Girl From U N C L E, book, paperback, *Blazing Affair*, 1966 .... 8.00

Girl From U N C L E, costume, dress type costume, transparent mask, Halco, 1960s 100.00

Gobel, George, game, I'm George Gobel, and Here's The Game, Schaper, 1955 .... 45.00

Godfrey, Arthur, Flamingo Ukelele, plastic, complete with 16 pg instruction booklet, and brown cardboard carrying case, Emenee, 1950s 75.00

Good Times, doll, JJ Fun Pal, stuffed body, vinyl head, red long johns, black and yellow Dyn–O–Mite design on chest with cloud and lightning bolt, denim cap, Shindana Toys, 1975, 15" h, MIB 50.00

Green Acres, coloring book, Eva Gabor and Eddie Albert standing by fence with cow, Whitman, 1967 .... 35.00

Griffin, Merv, game, Merv Griffin's Word For Word Game, Mattel, 1963 .... 15.00

Grizzly Adams, action figure, Grizzly and Nakoma, Mattel, MIB, price for pr 125.00

Happy Days, doll, Fonzie, Mego 80.00

Happy Days, radio, plastic, figural, full color paper sticker showing Fonzie standing by jukebox, orig box, 9" h 20.00

Hardy Boys, doll, Kenner, 1979, 12" h 40.00

Highway Patrol, car, friction, litho tin, litho image of Broderick Crawford in passenger seat and policeman driver, makes siren sound when pushed, mkd "SM–Made In Japan," 8" l 135.00

Highway Patrol, Highway Patrol Official Dan Mathews Holster Revolver & Badge Set, plastic cap pistol and shoulder strap, Highway Patrol insignia on holster, 2" litho tin button inscribed "Highway Patrol Chief," England, orig box 110.00

Hogan's Heroes, record, *Hogan's Heroes Sing the Best of World War II*, 33 rpm, 1960s 15.00

Honeymooners, bus, pressed steel, wood wheels, red, white, and blue, fleshtone faces of Honeymooner show characters depicted at windows, metal drive mechanism on rear axle, Wolverine, 1955, 14" l 425.00

Honeymooners, uniform, bus driver, includes cap, coin changer, coins, bus tickets, and ticket puncher, VIP, orig box, 1956 .... 395.00

Howdy Doody, Air–O–Doodle Circus Train, plastic train, boat, and plane, cut–out character passengers, Plasticraft/Kagran, 1950s 65.00

Howdy Doody, bank, Clarabell, plastic, 1970s, 9" h 45.00

Howdy Doody, bubble pipe, Lido, 1950s, 4" l 65.00

Howdy Doody, Christmas light, plastic, emb, 1950s 125.00

Howdy Doody, Cosmic Scout Nightlight, plastic, figural Howdy wearing bubble space helmet, bulb in stomach, wood base, orig box, Alden Corp, 7" h 200.00

Howdy Doody Crayon Set, Milton Bradley, Kagran, orig box 145.00

Howdy Doody, doll, Princess Summerfall Winterspring, Beehler Arts, plastic, braided black hair, 1950s, 8" h 220.00

Howdy Doody, Electric Carnival Game, Harett–Gilmar, 1950s 100.00

Howdy Doody, football, Kagran, white pebble grained rubber, ivory white vinyl lacing, Howdy image, Kagran, 1950s 75.00

Howdy Doody, hat, western style, woven tan straw, red and silver fabric sticker on crown front, red vinyl piping trim, adjustable chin strap, "Tex–Straw" paper tag, Arlington Hat Co, 1950s 75.00

Howdy Doody, push puppet, Kohner Products #180, $25.00.

Howdy Doody, ice cream wrapper, Howdy Doody Fudge Bar, 1950s................................. 3.00

I Dream of Jeannie, costume, brown and yellow jump-suit, mask, Ben Cooper, 1960s.................... 130.00

I Dream of Jeannie, Jeannie Jade Jewelry, plastic, green necklace, 3 charms, 1975, 6 x 9½" card.............. 35.00

I Love Lucy, Desi's Conga Drum, cardboard, vinyl strap, red, black and white graphics on sides with picture of Desi playing drum, orig 4 pp booklet, 19" h.......... 190.00

I Love Lucy, doll, Lucy, stuffed, cloth, molded plastic face, yellow yarn hair, red and white cloth outfit, 27" h, 1950s...................................... 165.00

Ironside, game, Ideal, 1967.......................... 90.00

Julia, coloring book, #9523, Saalfield, 1968............. 25.00

Julia, doll, vinyl, bendable, white nurse's uniform, white hat and shoes, Mattel, 1968, 11½" h, MIB........... 150.00

Knight Rider, action figure, Michael Knight, Kenner, 6" h..... 25.00

Knight Rider, press photo, David Hasselhoff, detailed description on bottom, black and white, glossy, 1980s, 8 x 10"................................... 10.00

Knight Rider, Self–Inking Stamp Set, Larami, 1982......... 27.00

Kojak, action figure, cloth outfit, miniature glasses, lol-lipops, cigar, and holster with revolver, Excel Toy Corp, 8" h, MOC.................................. 45.00

Kojak, car, Buick, Corgi, diecast metal, metallic copper, gold int, 1977, 2¾" l, MOC........................ 25.00

Kojak, record, LP, cover with closeup illus of Telly Savalas with lollipop, contains 4 "Super Dynamic Detective Stories," 1977........................... 25.00

Kung Fu, lunch box, steel, plastic thermos, King–Seeley Thermos Co, 1974............................... 50.00

Land of the Giants, book, *Flight of Fear*, Carl Henry Rathjen, Whitman, #1516, hard cov, 1969, 212 pp....... 17.50

Lassie, figure, plastic, orig cardboard tag inscribed "Lassie—Wonder Dog of TV," orig box, 1955.......... 65.00

Lassie, Lassie & Timmy Erasable Pix, 4 black and white pictures, crayon slate, 5 crayon markers, Standard Toykraft, Standard Toykraft, 1950s, orig 15 x 18" box..... 40.00

Laugh–In, lunch box, emb steel, Aladdin, 1970.......... 45.00

Laugh–In, record, *Why Won't You Come Home?*, Jo Ann Worley, 45 rpm................................ 10.00

Laugh–In, playing cards, George Schlatter/Ed Friendly Productions and Romart, 1969.................... 15.00

Laverne and Shirley, jigsaw puzzle, #425–01, diecut cardboard, H G Toys, 10 x 14", 150 pcs.............. 12.00

Leave It to Beaver, coloring book, Beaver and Wally holding skis cov, Whitman, 1958.................. 65.00

Little House On the Prairie, doll, Laura, vinyl head, stuffed cloth body, cloth outfit, 1978, 12" h........... 40.00

Love Boat, action figures, set of 6, plastic, Mego, 1981, 3½" h....................................... 75.00

Man From U N C L E, apparel set, bullet–proof vest, 3 targets, shells, binoculars, and bazooka, Gilbert, 1965... 100.00

Man From U N C L E, cigarette lighter gun, silver colored lighter, red decal, 3 x 4" black plastic case, Ideal, 1966.. 50.00

Man From U N C L E, costume, Illya Kuryakin, painted mask, rayon costume, illus window box, Halco, 1967..... 90.00

Marx, Groucho, cocktail napkin set, 36 napkins, series #1, "That's Me, Groucho," paper, cartoon illus, orig box, monogram of California, 1954................. 45.00

Marx, Groucho, game, You Bet Your Life, Groucho's, Lowell, 1955.................................. 55.00

Mary Hartman, Mary Hartman, game, Reiss, 1970s........ 25.00

M*A*S*H, costume, Cpl Klinger, Ben Cooper, orig box, 1981.. 40.00

M*A*S*H, key chain, lucite, rect, color photo of cast member on front, helicopter and emblem on back........ 8.00

McHale's Navy, model kit, PT 73, Revell, 1965.......... 85.00

Monkees, Clever Finger Dolls, Davy and Mickey, plastic, vinyl, elastic loops, jointed arms, cloth outfits, vinyl boots, rooted hair, Remco, 1970, 5" h........... 70.00

Monkees, guitar, plastic, diecut litho paper label, Monkees illus with musical notes in background, black neck, red underside, Mattel, 1966, 20" h......... 90.00

Monkees, Monkeemobile, diecast, metal, Monkees logo on each side, figures seated in front, Corgi, 1960s, 4¾" l....................................... 75.00

Mork and Mindy, Shrinky Dinks, Colorforms, 1979....... 21.00

Mr Ed, coloring book, cover shows Mr Ed wearing flow-ered hat and glasses, Whitman, 1963................ 45.00

Mr Ed, hand puppet, Mattel, 1962.................... 60.00

Mr Peepers, Mr Peepers School Bag and Game Kit, 9 x 13" vinyl school bag and accessories, orig box, Pressman, 1955................................. 50.00

My Favorite Martian, coloring book, "Uncle Martin the Martian," Golden Press, 1964..................... 45.00

My Favorite Martian, Martian Magic–Tricks Kit, contains instructions for 16 tricks, Gilbert, 1960s, MIB.......... 45.00

My Favorite Martian, skullcap, red felt, molded, metal wire spring attached to each side, Ray Walston illus on fabric patch attached to front, 1963.............. 60.00

Nanny and the Professor, press photo, Juliet Mills, black and white, glossy, 1969, 7 x 9".................... 24.00

Ozzie and Harriet, coloring book, Saalfield, 1973, 32 pp, unused................................. 30.00

Partridge Family, doll, Laurie, Remco, 1973, 20' h........ 100.00

Partridge Family, magazine, *Life*, David Cassidy color cov photo, Oct 29, 1971........................... 29.00

Petticoat Junction, game, Standard Toykraft, 1964........ 45.00

Pee Wee Herman, doll, Miss Yvonne, 5" h............. 10.00

Pee Wee Herman, doll, Pee Wee, 15" h............... 15.00

Pee Wee Herman, figure, Pee Wee, scooter and helmet, Matchbox, 6" h............................... 40.00

Pee Wee Herman, playset, Pee Wee's Playhouse, c1980s, MIB **88.00**

Pinky Lee, coloring book, "Pinky Lee's Health and Safety Cut–Out Coloring Book," Pocket Books, 1955. . . . . **25.00**

Pinky Lee, doll, Juro Celebrity Doll series, stuffed cloth body, vinyl head, black and white checkered cloth suit, red bow tie, "Pinky Lee NBC–TV" cloth label stitched to chest of jacket, complete with orig picture folder with words to "Yoo–Hoo It's Me," 1950s, orig 4½ x 9 x 26" box. **200.00**

Policewoman, doll, Angie Dickinson, Sergeant Pepper, 1976, 9" h, MIB **40.00**

Punky Brewster, doll, stuffed, vinyl hands and head, brown hair, purple jacket with plastic heart shaped button, blue and red shirts, blue jeans, red bandanna tied around one knee, plastic key around neck, Galoob, 18" h, 1980s, 18" h, MIB **60.00**

Rat Patrol, Midget Motors Jeep, plastic body, rubber wheels, machine gun on swivel base, "Rat Patrol" sticker on side, orig box, Remco, 1966. . . . . **80.00**

Real McCoys, Whitman TV Book, cover illus of family in car, 1961 . . . . **20.00**

Rifleman, frame tray puzzle, #4427, Al Andersen cartoon drawing of Lucas and Mark hiding behind rocks, Indians on horseback approaching in distance, 1960, 18 pcs **25.00**

Saturday Night Live, book, *A Really Wild and Crazzzy Book!*, scripts and notes from the show, Avon, 1977, 123 pp **24.00**

Saturday Night Live, book, *SNL: The First 20 Years*, photos, 1994 . . . . **15.00**

Sea Hunt, Adventure Set, mini life boat and 3 divers, 6 x 12" photo of new Sea Hunt series star Ron Ely, Jaru, 1987 . . . . **18.00**

Shari Lewis Show, doll, Charlie Horse, Ideal. **45.00**

Shari Lewis Show, doll, Lamb Chop **60.00**

Shari Lewis Show, Halloween costume, Hush Puppy, Halco, 1961, MIB **45.00**

Shari Lewis Show, Shari Lewis & Her Friends Printer Set, 6 wooden handled plastic character stamps, black ink pad, and stamp sheets, orig box, Colorforms, 1962 . . . . **30.00**

Silvers, Phil, game, Phil Silvers, Sgt Bilko—CBS Television's "You'll Never Get Rich" Game, Gardner, 1955 . . . . **50.00**

Six Million Dollar Man, activity book, cover shows closeup illus of Steve Austin's face, 1976 . . . . **25.00**

Six Million Dollar Man, Bionic Mission Vehicle **140.00**

Six Million Dollar Man, Bionic Transport and Repair Station, MIB **45.00**

Soupy Sales, game, Soupy Sez Go–Go–Go!, Milton Bradley, 1961 . . . . **65.00**

Soupy Sales, pinback button, black and white Soupy photo, 1960s **18.00**

Starsky and Hutch, .357 Magnum Water Pistol, plastic, black, header card with color photos of show's stars, Fleetwood Toys, 1976, 6½" l **20.00**

Starsky and Hutch, car, battery operated, plastic, red, white racing stripes, light, siren, 1976, 15½" l. **50.00**

Starsky and Hutch, Shoot–Out Target Game, Berwick, 1970s **50.00**

Steve Canyon, costume, Halco, synthetic fabric, jumpsuit style, molded plastic mask, Halco, 1959, orig 9 x 11 x 3" box **30.00**

Steve Canyon, lunch box, steel, black and white printed pictures of jets inside box lid, complete with matching steel thermos, Aladdin, 1959 . . . . **225.00**

SWAT, puzzle, canister container with illus of cast member's heads and action scene background, 1976 . . . . **21.00**

Tarzan, figure set, 3" h Tarzan, chimp, serpent, gorilla, lion, tiger, goat, zebra, and crocodile, 1967, MOC **75.00**

Tarzan, Paint 'N Wear Kit, Avalon, 1976. . . . . **15.00**

That Girl, paper dolls, Saalfield, 1967, MIB **60.00**

Today Show, doll, J Fred Muggs, Ideal, stuffed body, rubber head and hands, brown hair, striped shirt, yellow pants, tag with name on both sides and "Famous Chimp Featured On NBC Today Show," 1955, orig 6 x 8 x 10" box, 14" h **75.00**

Tonight Show, balloon, yellow, "Goo–Goo Steve Allen— Star Of NBC–TV Tonight," blue inscription with sketch of Allen, 6½" l **15.00**

The Untouchables, Eliot Ness and the Untouchables Sawed–Off Shotgun, Transogram, ©Desilu, gun with 2 red and 2 green plastic shells and bullets, orig 9 x 24" box with Robert Stack photo on front **220.00**

The Untouchables, The Official Untouchables Detective Set, 6" l snub nose–cap revolver, vinyl holster, belt, 16 bullets, badge, and ID wallet, orig cardboard display frame box, 1961 . . . . **185.00**

The Untouchables, game, The Official Untouchables Mechanical Arcade Target Game, Marx, orig box, 1960s **165.00**

Vegas, puzzle, cover shows Bob Urich leaning on money wheel with Las Vegas in background, 1978 . . . . **21.00**

Voyage to the Bottom of the Sea, Seaview Submarine, complete with 1 torpedo, Remco, 15" l **250.00**

Welcome Back Kotter, doll, John Travolta, blue sweater, blue jeans, Chemtoy, 1977, 12" h, MIB. **85.00**

Welcome Back Kotter, photograph, black and white, glossy, ABC press release, Gabe Kaplan, Ron Palillo, and John Travolta in black leather jackets and boots, from "Sweatside Story" episode, Apr 21, 1977, 8 x 10" **15.00**

Munsters, lunch box and thermos, King–Seeley, $187.00. Photo courtesy Collectors Auction Services.

TELEVISION LAMPS

"You will go blind if you watch television in the dark" was a common warning in the early 1950s. American lamp manufacturers responded by creating lamps designed to sit atop the television set and provide the correct amount of indirect lighting necessary to preserve the viewer's eyesight.

The need was simple. The solutions were imaginative and of questionable taste in more than a few cases. Most television lamps were ceramic and back–lit. Motifs ranged from leaping gazelles to a prancing horse with a clock in the middle of his body graced by a red Venetian blind, pagoda–like shade.

Reference: Leland and Crystal Payton, *Turned On: Decorative Lamps of the Fifties*, Abbeville Press, 1989.

Art Deco Deer, 2 deer, 1 leaping, 1 grazing, mauve,
  Haeger, #5473, 14" h. **$45.00**
Bucking Bronco, gray, Haeger, #6105, 11½" l. **40.00**
Buffalo, standing on rocky base **45.00**
Chuck Wagon, wagon made from cactus wood **50.00**
Crowing Rooster, perched on picket fence, Lane, 13" h. **55.00**
Drama Masks, comedy and tragedy, black masks, white
  shade, Haeger, 9" h **40.00**
Flamingos, pink and black, Lane **50.00**
Flying Mallards, Maddux **45.00**
Gazelle, chalkware, red and gold **35.00**
Leaf, stylistic, green. **25.00**
Mosaic Horses, molded plastic **50.00**
Owl, brown, green int, glowing eyes, Kron. **50.00**
Planter, rect, chartreuse, 10¾" l, 4" h **20.00**
Poodle, Haeger, #R-1140, 10¼" h **35.00**
Racing Greyhound, #6202, green, Haeger, 13" l **50.00**
Reclining Horse, rust colored, black mane, 14" l, 9" h **30.00**
Seashells, grouping with plastic palm trees and flamingo . . . **25.00**
Spanish Galleon, bronze colored **35.00**
Two–Masted Ship, yellow ship, tin sails, gold trim, sea
  wave base **60.00**
Vase, brass, Tower **10.00**

Gazelle, Haeger, green and white, unmkd, 10½" h, 13½" w, $71.50. Photo courtesy Collectors Auction Services.

TELEVISIONS

Television sets are divided into three groups: (1) mechanical era sets, 1925 to 1932, (2) pre–World War II sets, 1938–1941, and (3) post–1946 sets. Mechanical era sets, also known as radiovisors, were used in conjunction with the radio. Reception was limited to the Chicago and New York area.

The electronic picture tube was introduced in 1938. The smaller the tube, the older the set is a good general rule. Early electric sets provided for a maximum of five channels, 1 through 5. Many sets made prior to 1941 combined the television with a multiband radio. Fewer than 20,000 sets were produced. Many of the sets were sold in kit form.

Production of television sets significantly increased following World War II. Channels 6 to 13 were added between 1946 and 1948. Channel 1 was dropped in 1949, replaced with V.H.F. channels 2 through 13. The U.H.F. band was added in 1953.

Collectors focus primarily on the black and white sets from the 1940s and 1950s. There is some interest in color sets made prior to 1955. Brand and model numbers are essential to researching value. Cabinet condition also is critical to value, sometimes more important than whether or not the set is operational. Sets made after 1960 have more reuse than collectible value.

References: Harry Poster, *Poster's Radio & Television Price Guide: 1920–1990, Second Edition*, Wallace–Homestead, 1994, out of print; Scott Wood (ed.), *Classic TVs With Price Guide: Pre–War Thru 1950s*, L–W Book Sales, 1992, 1997 value update.

Periodical: *Antique Radio Classified*, PO Box 802, Carlisle, MA 01741.

Collectors' Club: Antique Wireless Assoc, 59 Main St, Holcomb, NY 14469.

Admiral, F2817, console, double doors, 1954, 27" tube **$20.00**
Admiral, 24R12, console, Bakelite, rect screen with
  square block grille, 1953, 14" screen **35.00**
Air King, A–1001, console, screen slightly forward of
  wooden cabinet, 1949, 10" screen **100.00**
Andrea, C–VK12, console, continuous tuner to right of
  screen, 12" screen **100.00**
Arvin, 4080T, tabletop, metal, slightly rounded top,
  cabinet painted green, 1950, 8" screen **110.00**
Capehart/Farnsworth, GV–260, tabletop, controls beside
  and below screen, rounded front top, mesh grille,
  1947, 10" screen **200.00**
CBS–Columbia, 20C, console, wooden, 1950, 20"
  screen. **20.00**
CBS–Columbia, 20M, tabletop, metal, 1950, 20" screen **15.00**
Crosley, 348–CP, DeLuxe Spectator, Swing–A–View picture tube above tilt–out controls and radio, pull–out
  phono, 1948, 10" screen **175.00**
Crosley, 9–409M, console, double doors, controls to left
  and right of screen, 1949, 12" screen **35.00**
DuMont, RA–105, console, square lines, c1949, 15" **35.00**
DuMont, RA–119, Royal Sovereign, console, double
  doors, 1952, 30" screen **400.00**
Emerson, 545, tabletop, screen centered and slightly forward of cabinet, 6 knobs, 13–channel tuner below,
  1947, 10" screen **150.00**
Emerson, 614, tabletop, Bakelite, porthole–look screen,
  ribs across front and sides, 1950, 10" screen **75.00**

Emerson, 669, console, double doors conceal screen, 1950, 19" screen **10.00**

FADA, 925, tabletop, screen trim slightly out at front and top, 1949, 16" screen **65.00**

General Electric, 10T1, tabletop, Bakelite, streamlined with sloping side and 4 knobs below screen, 1949, 10" screen **100.00**

General Electric, 801, console, small double doors conceal large dial AM radio and screen, 1947, 10" screen . . . **125.00**

General Electric, 901, console, mahogany cabinet, projection set with AM–FM radio and phone, 1947, 18 x 24" screen **200.00**

Hallicrafters, T–506, tabletop, wooden, 12–channel push–button tuner, 1949, 7" screen **150.00**

Hallicrafters, 818, tabletop, porthole–look screen, 1950, 16" screen **50.00**

Meck, XL–750, tabletop, wooden, screen at front left, 1949, 10" screen **100.00**

Motorola, 17P5, portable, painted metal, handle on top, controls on right, 1959, 17" screen **35.00**

Motorola, VT–71, tabletop, wooden, 1948, 7" screen **75.00**

Motorola, 21K16, console on 4 spindle legs, sliding board covers front, 1954, 21" screen **45.00**

Muntz, 17PS, portable, painted metal, handle and tuner on top, 1959, 17" screen **25.00**

National, TV–10W, tabletop, wooden, 1949, 10" screen **150.00**

Olympic, TV–928, console, mirror–in–lid TV on left, radio and pull–out phono behind right door, 10" screen **100.00**

Philco, 48–700, tabletop, wooden, picture tube at right of center, 1948, 7" screen **175.00**

Philco, 48–2500, buffet style, mirror in lid, 1948, 25" screen **30.00**

Philco, 51–T1601, tabletop, metal, rounded top, screen over 4 knobs, 1951, 16" screen **15.00**

RCA, TCS, console, tube in center, tambour doors, 1946, 10" screen **750.00**

RCA, 8T270, tabletop, 1949, 16" screen **50.00**

RCA, 9PC41, buffet style, projection set, channel 1 tuner, 1949 . . . . **45.00**

RCA, TT5, tabletop, 5–channel tuner, vision only, 1939, 5" screen **3,500.00**

Silvertone, 101, tabletop, square–lined cabinet, 1950, 12" screen **35.00**

Silvertone, 133, console, wooden, pull–out phono beneath screen, 1949, 12" screen **50.00**

Sentinel, 406TVM, tabletop, wooden, cabinet stepped at top and bottom, 1949, 12" screen **85.00**

Sparton, 4931, console, 5 knobs below screen, 1949, 10" screen **75.00**

Stewart–Warner, AVC–1, console, mirror in lid, 1948, 10" screen **100.00**

Stromberg–Carlson, TC–10, console, porthole–look screen, perforated front, picture expander in large tuner control at right, 1949, 10" screen **125.00**

Sylvania, 21C529, Sylouette, Halolight with plastic–corered light in front of screen, 1959, 21" screen **200.00**

Sylvania, 245, console, simple styling, 4 knobs below screen, 1950, 12" screen **35.00**

Tele–King, KC–42, console, 1953, 24" screen **10.00**

Tele–Tone, TV–208, portable, porthole–look screen, handle on top, 1948, 7" screen **75.00**

Westinghouse, 21T206, tabletop, controls above screen, 1959, 21" screen **10.00**

Westinghouse, H–181, highboy, double doors conceal screen and controls, 4 tall legs, 1948, 10" screen **125.00**

Westinghouse, H–610, tabletop, 4 knobs to right of masked screen, 1948, 10" screen **65.00**

Zenith, C–2225, portable, metal, tuner at upper right, 1959, 21" screen **10.00**

Zenith, G2322, tabletop, brown Bakelite, 1950, 12" screen **65.00**

HMV 900, English, horiz mirror set, 1937, $4,000.00.

TEMPLE, SHIRLEY

Born on April 23, 1928, in Santa Monica, California, Shirley Temple was the most successful child movie star of all time. She was discovered while attending dance class at the Meglin Dance Studios in Los Angeles. Fox Film's *Stand Up and Cheer* (1934) was her first starring role. She made a total of twelve pictures that year.

Gertrude George, Shirley's mother, played a major role in creating Shirley's image and directing her licensing program. Requests for endorsements and licenses were immediate. Hundreds of products were marketed.

By 1935 Temple was the number one box office star, a spot she retained through 1938. In 1940 Temple starred in *The Blue Bird* and *Young People*, her last films for Fox. She immediately signed a $100,000 a year contract with MGM and starred in *Kathleen* in 1941, her first teenage/adult movie role. Shirley married for the first time in 1945. She retired from films in 1950, the same year she divorced her husband and married Charles Black.

In 1957 Shirley was host of the *Shirley Temple Storybook*. In the 1960s Shirley Temple Black became active in Republican politics. After serving as a U.S. Delegate to the United Nations and Ambassador to Ghana, she became Chief of Protocol in Washington. Her final government service was as Ambassador to Czechoslovakia in 1989.

References: Edward R. Pardella, *Shirley Temple Dolls and Fashion: A Collector's Guide to the World's Darling*, Schiffer Publishing, 1992; Dian Zillner, *Hollywood Collectibles: The Sequel*, Schiffer Publishing, 1994.

Limited Edition Plate, "Bright Eyes," Shirley Temple Classic Collection, Norman Rockwell Museum, 1984, $30.00.

Book, *The Little Colonel*, black and white scenes from
movie, Saalfield, c1935, 4³/₄ x 5¹/₄". **$50.00**
Book, *Shirley Temple, Her Life in Pictures*, Saalfield,
©1938, softcover, glossy stiff paper, sepia photos,
32 pp, 7¹/₂ x 9¹/₄". **20.00**
Cereal Bowl, cobalt blue glass, 1930s **45.00**
Creamer, cobalt blue glass, 1930s, 4¹/₂" h **30.00**
Doll, vinyl, fully jointed, painted open mouth and eye-
brows, fixed brown glass eyes with artificial upper
lashes, rooted hair, fabric dress, back of neck mkd
"ST–14–H–213" Ideal, ©1972, 17" h **75.00**
Home Movie, *Glad Rags to Riches*, 8 mm black and
white silent film, plastic reel, original box, 1950s **15.00**
Magazine, *Hollywood*, Feb 1937, color portrait of
Temple on cover, 8¹/₂ x 11" **75.00**
Paper Dolls, unpunched 9¹/₂" h stand–up doll, 4 pp of
clothing, Whitman, ©1976, 10 x 13" **15.00**
Paper Dolls, Saalfield #1770, Shirley Temple Christmas
Book, 1937. . . . . **55.00**
Photograph, glossy, teenage, early 1940s, 8 x 10". **20.00**
Photograph, glossy, Temple in Santa outfit, fleshtone tint
face and hair, dark blue and bluish white tint outfit
trim and snow, printed Christmas greeting and facsim-
ile signature at bottom, c1936, 8 x 10". **25.00**
Pinback Button, beaded brass frame, celluloid over
black and white photo, "New Theatre–WFBR/Shirley
Temple Club," 1930s, 1¹/₄" d **100.00**
Pitcher, glass, transparent blue, frosted white portrait and
facsimile signature, Wheaties premium, c1938,
4¹/₂" h, 3" d **40.00**
Playing Cards, boxed double deck, United States Playing
Card Co, c1936–37, ³/₄ x 3³/₄ x 4³/₄" **100.00**
Postcard, *Captain January*, sepia, unused, 1936, 3¹/₂ x
5¹/₂" **15.00**
Ring, celluloid, green base, diecut black and white flat
celluloid sheet with black and white photo, "Made in
Japan," 1930s **90.00**

Sewing Cards, 9 stiff paper cards with picture of Temple's
doll house, drum, musical top, beach pail, etc, miniature Shirley Temple wax crayons, Saalfield, ©1936,
4¹/₄ x 6¹/₂" cards, 1 x 4¹/₂ x 6³/₄" box **150.00**
Sheet Music, *Curly Top* title song, purple tone closeup
photo, smaller seated photo in sepia, purple on white
artwork, c1935, 9¹/₂ x 12¹/₄" **20.00**
Sheet Music, *The Right Somebody to Love*, ©1936,
black and white photo of Temple on yellow, blue, and
green nautical art background, 9¹/₄ x 12¹/₄" **12.00**

TENNIS COLLECTIBLES

Tennis came to America in the mid–1870s. After a tennis craze in the 1880s, the sport went into a decline. International play led to a revival in the early 1900s. The period from 1919 to 1940 is viewed by many tennis scholars as the sport's golden age.

Tennis collectibles are divided into two periods: (1) pre–1945 and (2) post–1945. There is little collector interest in post–1945 material. There are three basic groups of collectibles: (1) items associated with play such as tennis balls, ball cans, rackets, and fashions, (2) paper ephemera ranging from books to photographs, and (3) objects decorated with a tennis image or in a tennis shape. Because tennis collecting is in its infancy, some areas remain high-ly affordable (rackets) while others (tennis ball cans) already are in the middle of a price run.

Reference: Jeanne Cherry, *Tennis Antiques & Collectibles*, Amaryllis Press, 1995.

Collectors' Club: The Tennis Collectors Society, Guildhall Orchard, Great Bromley, Colchester, CO7 7TU U.K.

Autographed Tennis Book, William T Tilden **$50.00**
Ball Can, Bancroft Winner, black, gold, and white **25.00**
Ball Can, D & M, blue and red, flat lid. **75.00**
Ball Can, Dunlop Vinnie Richards, red, white, and black,
flat lid. **45.00**
Ball Can, MacGregor, red and white plaid and black **25.00**

Ball Cans, Chernold, Tony Rocheson and Italian flag on red ground, $30.00; D & M Championship, blue and red, $75.00.

Ball Can, Spalding, Pancho Gonzales, blue	**20.00**
Ball Can, Wilson Ellsworth Vines, blue and green, dome lid	**60.00**
Ball Can, Wilson, Jack Kramer, red and white	**40.00**
Ball Can, Wright & Ditson, red and white	**30.00**
Cigarette Cards, famous 1930s tennis players, green, set of 50.	**25.00**
Magazine, *American Lawn Tennis*, 1920s	**5.00**
Playing Cards, Arzy's Tennis Shop, Beverly Hills, white ground, gold and red border	**6.00**
Program, USLTA, Forest Hills, 1936	**15.00**
Program, Wimbledon, All England Lawn Tennis Club, 1950s	**5.00**
Racquet, Dayton, wood handle, steel head, wire strings, diamond trademark decal, 1930s	**15.00**
Racquet, Hazell's Streamline, England, 3–shaft construction, 1930s	**100.00**
Racquet, Prince Classic, aluminum, green throat pc, 1960s	**8.00**
Racquet, Don Budge, Famous Player Series, Wilson, 1940s	**10.00**
Racquet, Winchester, wood handle, trademark decal, 1930s	**40.00**

THIMBLES

By the middle of the 19th century, the American thimble industry was able to produce finely worked thimbles. Gold and silver thimbles were restricted to the upper class. Utilitarian thimbles were made of brass or steel. In 1880 William Halsey patented a process to make celluloid thimbles. Aluminum thimbles made their appearance in the second quarter of the 20th century.

A thimble was one of the few gifts considered appropriate for an unmarried man to give to a lady. Many of these fancy thimbles show little wear, possibly a result of both inappropriate sizing and the desire to preseve the memento.

Advertising thimbles were popular between 1920 and the mid–1950s. Early examples were made from celluloid or aluminum. Plastic was the popular post–war medium. The first political thimbles appeared shortly after ratification of the nineteenth amendment. They proved to be popular campaign giveaways through the early 1960s.

References: Averil Mathis, *Antique and Collectible Thimbles and Accessories*, Collector Books, 1986, 1995 value update; Gay Ann Rogers, *Price Guide Keyed to American Silver Thimbles*, Needlework Unlimited, 1989; Estelle Zalkin, *Zalkin's Handbook of Thimbles & Sewing Implements*, Warman Publishing, 1988, distributed by Krause Publications.

Newsletter: *Thimbletter*, 93 Walnut Hill Rd, Newton Highlands, MA 02161.

Collectors' Clubs: The Thimble Guild, PO Box 381807, Duncanville, TX 75138; Thimble Collectors International, 8289 Northgate Dr, Rome, NY 13440.

Note: For additional sewing listings refer to Sewing Items.

Aluminum, "Coca Cola," USA	**$3.00**
Aluminum, "White Sewing Machine," USA	**2.00**
Bone China, glazed, "The Names project" blue transfer	**10.00**
Brass, cloisonné design, China, c1980	**15.00**

Silver, Cupid and swags, Simons, $90.00.

Brass, nickel plated, England	**10.00**
Brass, "Use Hudson Soap," England	**35.00**
Bronze, "Collector Circle Member," USA, 1981	**4.00**
Copper, blue stone top, Germany, c1920	**50.00**
Glass, scalloped edge, etched grapes, USA.	**10.00**
Gold, 10K, village scene, unmkd, c1920	**100.00**
Plastic, green, "Singer Sewing Machines," USA	**2.50**
Plastic, pink, "First Federal, Decatur, Ill," USA	**1.50**
Plastic, white, plain, USA	**.50**
Plastic, white, "Jimmy Carter For President In '76," USA	**1.00**
Sterling Silver, abalone and mother–of–pearl inlay, Mexico, c1980	**17.00**
Sterling Silver, limited edition, American Quilter's Society, Paducah, Kenturcky, Simons Brothers Co, USA, 1986	**65.00**
Sterling Silver, Chester, England, c1920	**50.00**
Sterling Silver, enameled, bluebird dec, West Germany	**45.00**
Sterling Silver, "James Walker wishes you luck," Birmingham, England, c1924	**60.00**
Sterling Silver, niello style, souvenir, mkd "900," Russia, c1980	**35.00**
Sterling Silver, set with spider turquoise stone, Navajo, USA, 1994	**25.00**
Sterling Silver, size 4, USA, c1920	**30.00**

TIFFANY

Charles L. Tiffany and John B. Young founded Tiffany & Young, a stationery and gift store, in 1837. In 1841 Tiffany & Young became Tiffany, Young & Ellis. The name was changed to Tiffany & Company in 1853.

In 1852 Tiffany insisted that its silver comply with the English sterling silver standard of 925/1000. Charles Lewis Tiffany was one of the leaders in the fight that resulted in the federal government adopting this standard, passing a 1906 statute that set 925/1000 as the minimum requirement for articles marked "sterling."

During the 1850s Tiffany & Company produced some electroplated wares. Production increased significantly following the Civil War. The manufacture of electroplated ware ended in 1931.

Tiffany incorporated as Tiffany & Co., Inc., in 1868, the same year the company acquired the Moore silverware factory. Tiffany's silver studio became America's first school of design. Beginning in 1868, Tiffany silverware was marked with "Tiffany & Co." and the letter "M" for Edward C. Moore, head of the studio. The company continued to mark its silverware with the initial of its incumbent president until the practice was discontinued in 1965.

Tiffany's jewelry, especially its botanical brooches and use of semi–precious gemstones, captured the world's attention at the Paris Exposition Universelle in 1878. Louis Comfort Tiffany, son of Charles Tiffany, became the company's first Design Director. Under his leadership, the company manufactured a wealth of Art Nouveau objects, especially jewelry and lamps.

Recognized as one of the world's most respected sources of diamonds and other jewelry, Tiffany craftsmanship extends to a broad range of items including fine china, clocks, flatware, leather goods, perfume, scarves, silver, stationery, and watches. Tiffany opened its New York Corporate Division 1960. The Vince Lombardi Trophy for the National Football League Super Bowl Championship is one of its most famous commissions.

References: John A. Shuman III, *The Collector's Encyclopedia of American Art Glass*, Collector Books, 1988, 1996 value update; Moise S. Steeg, Jr., *Tiffany Favrile Art Glass*, Schiffer Publishing, 1997; Kenneth Wilson, *American Glass 1760–1930: The Toledo Museum of Art*, 2 vols., Hudson Hills Press and The Toledo Museum of Art, 1994.

REPRODUCTION ALERT: Brass belt buckles and badges marked "Tiffany" have been widely reproduced.

BRONZE

Desk Set, gilt–bronze, Bookmark pattern, pair of bookends, pad holder, cigarette box, rect box, calendar, letter rack, thermometer, clock, inkwell, letter opener, stamp box, pair blotter ends, pen tray, rocker blotter, and magnifying glass, each stamped "Tiffany Studios New York" and variously numbered, 19½" l blotter ends, price for set **$4,000.00**

Desk Set, gilt–bronze, Venetian pattern, blotter ends, letter rack, pen tray, memo pad, picture frame, paper clip, paperweight, brush wipe, stamp box, and double inkwell, each stamped "Tiffany Studios New York" and model number, 6½" h letter rack, price for set **3,150.00**

Desk Set, gilt–bronze, Zodiac pattern, blotter ends, letter rack, inkwell, pen tray, and cigarette box, each stamped "Tiffany Studios New York," 9½" l letter rack, price for set **1,100.00**

Cigarette Box, caramel slag panels, brass frame, mkd "809 Tiffany Studios New York," c1920, 6⅝" l, 4⅛" w, 2" h, $175.00.

Heraldic Lamp, 12 paneled mottled green favrile glass shaded with alternating heraldic panels, stamped "Tiffany Studios N.Y.," strapwork motif base stamped "Tiffany Studios New York 690," 18" h, 9" d shade, $1,400.00. Photo courtesy Wm. Doyle Galleries.

Picture Frame, gilt–bronze, Abalone pattern, stylized floral and linear dec border, red and green enamel with abalone shell disks, stamped "Tiffany Studios New York 1145," 12" h, 9½" w **2,200.00**

Picture Frame, gilt–bronze, interlacing motif border, stamped "Tiffany Studios New York 921," 11" h, 9" w . . . **1,250.00**

Picture Frame, gilt–bronze, scroll border, stamped "Tiffany Studios New York 2019," 10¼" h, 8¼" w **1,150.00**

Picture Frame, gilt–bronze and enamel, geometric border with black and red details, sgd "Tiffany Studios New York 2076," 10¾" h, 8¾" w **2,300.00**

GLASS

Basket, gold iridescent favrile glass, pedestaled parfait base, folded flared rim, applied ambergris transparent handle, inscribed "L.C.T. Favrile 1849," 10" h **$1,900.00**

Bowl, low, blue iridescent favrile glass, undulating edge, ribbed sides, sgd "L.C.T. Favrile," 6" d **975.00**

Bowl, gold favrile glass, 10 ribs, sgd "L.C. Tiffany," 2¾" h, 7" d **275.00**

Bowl and Underplate, purple iridescent favrile glass, sgd, 4" d bowl, 6" d plate **625.00**

Candlestick, amber iridescent favrile glass, twisted standard, circular base, sgd, 7" h **750.00**

Candlesticks, favrile glass, white overlaid with gold iridescence, knopped standard, spreading circular base, sgd, 8½" h **800.00**

Compote, gold iridescent, stretch border sgd "L.C. Tiffany Favrile" **450.00**

Compote, pastel gold opalescent, molded diamond quilted pattern, flared bowl with opal ext, dark golden amber int with stretched iridescent luster tinted pink, ftd pedestal base sgd "L.C. Tiffany Inc. Favrile 156L," 2¾" h, 9¼" d **650.00**

Compote, purple, blue, and gold iridescent favrile glass, ruffled, sgd "L.C.T. 1944B," orig paper Tiffany label, 4" h, 5" d **800.00**

Flower Holders, favrile glass, cylinder form, applied double band with 8 apertures, sgd, 3" h, price for pair **450.00**

Tumbler, gold iridescent favrile glass, threaded, sgd, 4" h . . . **300.00**

Vase, amber iridescrnt favrile glass, globular, tall cylindrical neck, sgd "L.C. Tiffany Favrile," 7" h **550.00**

Vase, gold iridescent favrile glass, floriform, sgd, 11½" h . . **1,700.00**

Vasc, gold iridescent favrile glass, slender flattened oval, 8–ribbed body, integrated tooled handles, sgd "L.C.T. Favrile," 8" h **900.00**

Vase, miniature, iridescent oyster white glass, 2 pulled handles, sgd "L.C.T. 9773B," 3½" h, 2" w **800.00**

Vase, paperweight, aquamarine favrile glass cased to bright iridescent red–orange, baluster form, int dec with 6 red–centered white blossoms and green leaves, sgd "L.C. Tiffany Favrile 5779C," 7" h **5,500.00**

LAMPS

Floor Lamp, gilt bronze, dome shaped metal shade with glass border with pierced foliate overlay, fluted column supported by 3 arms, stamped mark, 61" h, 10" d shade **$8,600.00**

Floor Lamp, 12–paneled white and amber favrile glass shade, stamped "Tiffany Studios N.Y. 1963," knopped standard with counterbalance spreading circular base, stamped "Tiffany Studios New York 619," 54" h, 9" d shade. **5,700.00**

Lamp, Dragonfly, dome shaped favrile glass shade set with 6 dragonflies, each with blue body and wings, white and amber ground set with cabochon "jewels," stamped "Tiffany Studios N.Y. 585," twisted gilt–bronze standard with base of flattened leaves, stamped "Tiffany Studios New York 697," 19" h, 14" d shade. **6,900.00**

Lamp, green favrile glass shade with heraldic motif, stamped "Tiffany Studios N.Y. 1914," knopped square bronze standard with figural relief and circular base with strapwork motifs, stamped "Tiffany Studios New York 557," 26" h, 20" d **11,500.00**

Lamp, Lily, 3–light, gold iridescent favrile glass shades, signed "L.C.T.," gilt–bronze circular base molded with flat leaves, stamped "Tiffany Studios New York 320," 9" h **4,600.00**

Lamp Base, gilt–bronze, cylindrical standard, spreading circular base, scrolling feet, stamped mark, 62" h **5,400.00**

STERLING SILVER

Bowl, handled, ftd base, openwork band below reeded rim, approx 16 troy oz, 8⅞" d **$225.00**

Bowl, reticulated border, #18187C makers 3706," approx 5 troy oz, 6¼" h **80.00**

Candlewick Lamp, ebony handle, #18157/4467, 2½" h **175.00**

Card Tray, oval shaped, 4 ball feet, monogrammed, approx 3 troy oz, 5¼" l **100.00**

Chocolate Pot, chased repoussé motif, #4755 maker's 4210, monogrammed base, approx 11 troy oz, 7" h **1,500.00**

Cream Jug, engraved border, #16741 maker's 4314, approx 4 troy oz, 3" h **100.00**

Cup, ftd, beaded border, #13258 maker's 4531, approx 4 troy oz, 4" h **100.00**

Pill Box, gold plated, floral design, cov with topaz colored Egyptian face set with 11 rose diamonds, monogrammed, 1½" d **1,600.00**

Turkish Coffee Service, Persian pattern, stylized foliate motif, coffeepot, cov sugar, and creamer, approx 34 troy oz, 10" h coffeepot **3,200.00**

Silver Porringer, enameled pink and red rose sprays, matching small plate, c1960, $1,000.00.

Vase, gilt–bronze, ovoid form, horizontal banded design, stamped "Tiffany Studios New York 1862," 7" h **350.00**

Water Pitcher, lobed ovoid form, undulating horizontal ribs with cartouches, approx 34 troy oz, 10½" h **2,500.00**

TIFFIN GLASS

J. Beatty and Sons built a large glass works in Tiffin, Ohio, in 1888. In 1892 Tiffin Glass Company became part of the U.S. Glass Company, a combine based in Pittsburgh, Pennsylvania.

During the Depression, Tiffin made hundreds of patterns, its output twice that of Cambridge and A. H. Heisey. Tiffin purchased Heisey blanks to meet its production requirements. The company's famed "Lady Stems" were made between 1939 and 1956.

Tiffin's profits carried many other plants in the U.S. Glass Company. Several plants making inexpensive glassware were closed or sold during the Depression. By 1951 Tiffin was the only U.S. Glass plant remaining in operation. U.S. Glass Company purchased Duncan & Miller in 1955. In 1962 U.S. Glass declared bankruptcy and closed the Tiffin factory.

Production resumed under the name "Tiffin Art Glass Corporation," a firm created by former Tiffin employees. Tiffin Art Glass produced high quality, etched stemware and glass accent pieces. The company also offered a pattern matching program, annually manufacturing retired patterns.

Tiffin purchased the molds and equipment of the T. G. Hawkes Cut Glass Company, Corning, New York, in 1964. Continental Can purchased the Tiffin factory in 1966, selling it in 1968 to the Interpace Corporation, a holding company of Franciscan china. Tiffin was sold once again in 1980, this time to Towle Silversmiths. Towle began importing blanks from Eastern Europe. In 1984 Towle closed the Tiffin factory and donated the land and buildings to the city of Tiffin. Jim Maxwell, a former Tiffin glass cutter, bought the Tiffin molds and equipment. The Tiffin trademark is now a registered trademark of Maxwell Crystal, Inc. In 1992 Maxwell placed four Hawkes and Tiffin patterns back into production.

References: Fred Bickenheuser, *Tiffin Glassmasters, Book I* (1979, 1994–95 value update), *Book II* (1981, 1994–95 value update), *Book III* (1985), Glassmasters Publications; Bob Page and Dale Fredericksen, *Tiffin Is Forever, A Stemware Identification Guide*, Page–Fredericksen, 1994; Ruth Hemminger, Ed Goshe and Leslie Piña, *Tiffin Modern: Mid–Century Art Glass*, Schiffer Publishing, 1997; Leslie Piña, *Tiffin Glass: 1914–1940*, Schiffer Publishing,

1997; Harry L. Rinker, *Stemware of the 20th Century: The Top 200 Patterns,* House of Collectibles, 1997.

Collectors' Club: Tiffin Glass Collectors' Club, PO Box 554, Tiffin, OH 44883.

Athens Diana, champagne $25.00
Athens Diana, cocktail 18.00
Athens Diana, cup and saucer 22.00
Athens Diana, jug, #128 . . . . 260.00
Athens Diana, oyster cocktail 18.00
Byzantine, cocktail, #15048, crystal 20.00
Byzantine, cocktail, #15048, yellow 15.00
Byzantine, iced tea, ftd, 6½" 15.00
Byzantine, juice tumbler, ftd, crystal 18.00
Byzantine, plate, crystal, 8½" 7.50
Byzantine, plate, yellow, 7½" d 15.00
Byzantine, platter, yellow, 12¾" l 35.00
Byzantine, sherbet, low, crystal 12.00
Byzantine, water goblet, ftd, crystal 20.00
Byzantine, wine, crystal 22.00
Cadena, cordial, topaz 80.00
Cadena, sherbet, low, topaz 15.00
Cadena, wine, topaz 35.00
Cerice, comport, #5831, crystal, 6" h 27.50
Cerice, cordial, #15071, crystal 40.00
Cerice, wine, crystal 30.00
Cherokee Rose, bud vase, 8" 45.00
Cherokee Rose, candlesticks, pr, #5902, 2 lite 160.00
Cherokee Rose, claret, #17403, 4 oz, 6" 50.00
Cherokee Rose, cocktail, #17399, 3½ oz 20.00
Cherokee Rose, cocktail, #17403, 3½ oz 20.00
Cherokee Rose, cordial, #17399 . . . . 50.00
Cherokee Rose, cordial, #17378 . . . . 55.00
Cherokee Rose, creamer 22.00
Cherokee Rose, creamer and sugar, beaded 60.00
Cherokee Rose, iced tea, #17399, 10½ oz 35.00
Cherokee Rose, pitcher, #194, ftd 695.00
Cherokee Rose, relish, #5902, 3 part, 6½" 40.00
Cherokee Rose, sherbet, #17403, champagne stem 20.00
Cherokee Rose, sherbet, #17399, tall 20.00
Cherokee Rose, water goblet, #17399, 9 oz 25.00
Cherokee Rose, water goblet, #17403, 9 oz 25.00
Cherokee Rose, wine, #17399, 3½ oz, 6" 35.00
Cordelia, cocktail, crystal 10.00
Cordelia, sherbet, crystal, 3¾" 8.00
Flanders, bread and butter plate, pink, 6" d 16.00
Flanders, candlesticks, pr, crystal 95.00
Flanders, champagne, crystal 15.00
Flanders, cocktail, yellow 30.00
Flanders, cordial, #196, crystal 55.00
Flanders, cordial, #196, yellow 75.00
Flanders, cordial, pink 150.00
Flanders, creamer and sugar, flat, pink 265.00
Flanders, creamer and sugar, flat, yellow 225.00
Flanders, cup and saucer, yellow 100.00
Flanders, dinner plate, pink 185.00
Flanders, finger bowl, crystal 39.00
Flanders, iced tea, ftd, pink 75.00
Flanders, pitcher, cov, #194, pink 595.00
Flanders, salad plate, crystal 9.00
Flanders, sherbet, crystal, 4⅜" 15.00
Flanders, tumbler, #020, crystal, 9 oz 17.00
Flanders, tumbler, #020, crystal, 12 oz 24.00

Flanders, tumbler, ftd, crystal, 4⅞" 20.00
Flanders, tumbler, ftd, pink, 12 oz 60.00
Flanders, vase, flared top, ftd, pink, 8" 895.00
Flanders, whiskey, ftd, 4 oz 80.00
Flanders, wine, crystal 45.00
Flanders, wine, pink 85.00
Fuchsia, bud vase, #14185, crystal, large, 8¼" h 38.00
Fuchsia, bud vase, #14185, crystal, small, 6½" h 30.00
Fuchsia, bud vase, crystal, 10½" h 45.00
Fuchsia, candle holders, pr, #5902, 2 light, crystal, 5⅜" . . . 175.00
Fuchsia, candlesticks, pr, duo, ball center, crystal 150.00
Fuchsia, champagne, crystal 18.00
Fuchsia, cocktail, crystal 20.00
Fuchsia, cordial, #15083, crystal 40.00
Fuchsia, creamer and sugar, #5902, crystal 52.00
Fuchsia, iced tea, #15083, ftd, crystal 30.00
Fuchsia, juice tumbler, #15083, ftd, crystal 18.00
Fuchsia, luncheon plate, crystal 22.00
Fuchsia, old fashion tumbler, flat, crystal, 3⅜" 48.00
Fuchsia, parfait, crystal, 5¹⁵⁄₁₆" 32.00
Fuchsia, plate, #5902, crystal, 14½" d 65.00
Fuchsia, relish, 3 part, crystal, 6⅜" 30.00
Fuchsia, sherbet, #15083, high, crystal, 5⅜" 15.00
Fuchsia, sherbet, #15083, low, crystal, 4⅛" 12.00
Fuchsia, water goblet, #15083, crystal, 7½" 25.00
Fuchsia, wine, #15083, crystal, 5¹⁄₁₆" 35.00
June Night, bread and butter plate, crystal, 6" d 16.00
June Night, bud vase, crystal, 10½" 45.00
June Night, champagne, #17358, crystal 18.00
June Night, champagne, #17392, crystal, 5½ oz 16.00
June Night, claret, #17471, crystal, 4 oz 30.00
June Night, cocktail, #17358, crystal, 3½ oz 20.00
June Night, cocktail, #17392, crystal 14.00
June Night, cordial, #17392, crystal 35.00
June Night, cordial, #17471, crystal 33.00
June Night, creamer and sugar 55.00
June Night, iced tea, #17394, ftd, crystal 22.00
June Night, iced tea, #17403, crystal 32.00
June Night, juice tumbler, #17392, ftd, crystal 17.00
June Night, juice tumbler, #17471, crystal 14.00
June Night, mayonnaise set, #5902, crystal, 3 pcs 48.00

King's Crown, water goblet, cranberry flashed, 5⅝" h, $10.00.

June Night, nut bowl, #5902, crystal, 6" d **45.00**
June Night, plate, #5902, crystal, 14" d **24.00**
June Night, salad plate, crystal, 8" d. **8.00**
June Night, sherbet, #17471, crystal. **12.00**
June Night, sugar, crystal **28.00**
June Night, tumbler, crystal, 10½ oz **24.00**
June Night, water goblet, #17403, 9 oz **25.00**
June Night, water goblet, #17471, 9 oz **20.00**
June Night, wine, #17392, crystal, 3½ oz. **20.00**
June Night, wine, #17403, crystal, 3½ oz. **35.00**
June Night, wine, #17471, crystal, 3½ oz. **22.00**
King's Crown, bud vase, cranberry flashed, 9" h **20.00**
King's Crown, candy dish, cov, ftd, cranberry flashed **20.00**
King's Crown, claret, cranberry flashed, 4⅜" h **12.00**
King's Crown, cocktail, cranberry flashed, 4" h **8.00**
King's Crown, iced tea, cranberry flashed **8.00**
King's Crown, oyster cocktail, cranberry flashed **10.00**
King's Crown, wine, cranberry flashed **10.00**
Persian Pheasant, champagne, #17358, crystal **25.00**
Persian Pheasant, claret, #17358, crystal, 4½ oz **40.00**
Persian Pheasant, cocktail, #17358, ribbed stem, crystal **18.00**
Persian Pheasant, saucer champagne, #17358, ribbed
    stem, crystal **25.00**
Persian Pheasant, water goblet, #17358, ribbed stem,
    crystal **30.00**
Rose Point, basket, #3500/55, square, 2 handled, 6". **65.00**
Rose Point, bowl, #3400, ftd, 12" d **95.00**
Rose Point, celery, #3400/64, 12". **100.00**
Rose Point, comport, #3400/7, 5½" **45.00**
Rose Point, cracker plate, #3400/6, 10¾". **35.00**
Rose Point, relish, #3500/64, 3 part, 4 ft, 10" **40.00**

TONKA

Mound Metalcraft, located on the banks of Lake Minnetonka in Mound, Minnesota, was incorporated in September 1946 to manufacture garden tools and household products. Absorbing the toy business of L. E. Streeter Company, Tonka introduced two pressed steel toys at the 1947 New York Toy Fair. By 1949 the line included fourteen different products including a doll hospital bed.

In 1956 Mound Metalcraft changed its name to Tonka and introduced its line of Hi–Way trucks. Tonka gained a reputation for producing nicely designed, realistic–looking vehicles.

In 1961 Tonka purchased a plastics company and began producing plastic accessories for its vehicles. Tonka acquired Kenner in 1988. Hasbro purchased the combined company in 1991.

The year 1963 is the major divider between younger and older Tonka collectors. Restoration of early examples is common and often unreported by the seller. Beware.

References: Don and Barb DeSalle, *Tonka Trucks: 1947–1963*, L–W Book Sales, 1996; Richard O'Brien, *Collecting Toys: Identification and Value Guide, 8th Edition*, Krause Publications, 1997.

Note: Prices listed are for vehicles in mint condition.

Aerial Ladder, #48. . . . . **$275.00**
Aerial Ladder, #700, 32½" l. **420.00**
Aerial Ladder, #998. . . . . **100.00**
Aerial Sand Loader Set, #992, loader and dump truck. **180.00**
Airlines Luggage Service, #420, 16⅝" l **215.00**
Airport Service Set, #2100. . . . . **275.00**

Allied Van Lines, #400, 23½" l. **300.00**
Allied Van Lines, #739 . . . . **175.00**
Back Hoe, #422, 17⅛" l **160.00**
Big Mike Dual Hydraulic Dump Truck, 14" l. **760.00**
Boat Transport, #41, 38" l **255.00**
Bulldozer, #100, 8⅞" l **75.00**
Bulldozer, #300 . . . . **145.00**
Camper, #530, 14" l **185.00**
Car Carrier, #40 . . . . **150.00**
Carnation Milk Step Van, #750, 11¾" l. **335.00**
Cement Mixer, #120, 15½" l **210.00**
Cement Mixer, #620 . . . . **170.00**
Crane and Clam, #150, 24" l **175.00**
Deluxe Fisherman, #130 . . . . **350.00**
Deluxe Sportsman, #22 . . . . **300.00**
Dragline, #514 . . . . **120.00**
Dump Truck, #06 . . . . **200.00**
Dump Truck, #180, 13" l **225.00**
Dump Truck and Sand Loader, #616 . . . . **180.00**
Farm Stake and Horse Trailer, #35 . . . . **200.00**
Farm Stake Truck, #04 . . . . **385.00**
Ford Falcon. **100.00**
Freighter **275.00**
Gasoline Truck, #33 . . . . **645.00**
Giant Dozer, #118, 12½" l **100.00**
Grain Hauler Semi, #550, 22¼" l. **275.00**
Green Giant Semi Reefer. **400.00**
Green Giant Transport Semi, #650, 22¼" l **310.00**
Hi–Way Dump Truck, #980, 13" l **240.00**
Hook and Ladder **330.00**
Houseboat Set, #136, 29" l **500.00**
Hydraulic Aerial Ladder, #48. . . . . **270.00**
Hydraulic Dump Truck, #20 . . . . **400.00**
Hydraulic Dump Truck, #520 . . . . **210.00**
Hydraulic Land Rover, #42, 15" l **700.00**
Jeep Commander, #304, canvas top, 10½" l **60.00**
Jeep Dispatcher, #200, 9¾" l **80.00**
Jeep Pumper, #425, 10¾" l **210.00**
Jeep Surrey, #350 . . . . **120.00**
Jeep Universal, #249. . . . . **75.00**
Jolly Green Giant, white, green stake racks. **300.00**
Loader, #352. . . . . **80.00**
Logger, #08. . . . . **220.00**
Logger Semi, #575, wood flat bed **250.00**
Lumber Truck, #998, 183¾" l. **160.00**
Mighty Tonka Dump Truck, #900 . . . . **130.00**
Military Jeep Universal, #251, 10½" l **100.00**
Military Tractor, #250 . . . . **145.00**
Mini Camper, #70, 9⅝" l. **150.00**
Mini Stake Truck, #56, 9¼" l **70.00**
Mini Tonka Mixer, #77 . . . . **100.00**
Mini Tonka Livestock Van, #90, 16" l **100.00**
Minute Maid Delivery Van, #725, 14½" l **550.00**
Mobile Clam, #942. . . . . **175.00**
Mobile Dragline, #135 . . . . **170.00**
Nationwide Moving Van, #39, 24½" l **370.00**
Parcel Delivery Van, 12" l **260.00**
Pickup and Trailer, #28 . . . . **290.00**
Pickup Truck, #580 . . . . **250.00**
Pickup Truck, #880, 13¾" l **310.00**
Power Boom Loader, #115, 18½" l **550.00**
Pumper Truck, #926 . . . . **165.00**
Ramp Hoist, #640, 19¼" l **400.00**
Rescue Squad, #105, 13¾" l **280.00**

Rescue Van **360.00**
Road Grader, #12 . . . . **195.00**
Sanitary Truck, #140 . . . . **600.00**
Service Truck, #01 . . . . **235.00**
Shovel and Carry All, #120, 33" l **250.00**
Sportsman, #05 . . . . **190.00**
Stake Pickup, #308, 12⅝" l **150.00**
Steam Shovel Deluxe, #100, 22" l **165.00**
Steel Carrier Semi, #145, 22" l **350.00**
Stock Rack Truck, with animals, 16¼" l **450.00**
Suburban Pumper, #990, 17" l **350.00**
Tandem Air Express, with trailer, #36, 24¾" l **450.00**
Tanker, #145 . . . . **400.00**
Terminal Train, #720, 33⅝" l **210.00**
Thunderbird Express Semi, 24" l **400.00**
Tractor and Carry–All Trailer, #170, with #150 crane and
    clam **400.00**
Tractor and Carry–All Trailer, #125, with #100 steam
    shovel **350.00**
Trencher, #534, 18¼" l **110.00**
Troop Carrier, #380, 14" l **145.00**
Utility Truck, #03 . . . . **300.00**
Wrecker, #18, white sidewalls **150.00**

TOOLS

From the 1920s through the end of the 1950s, the basement workshop was a standard fixture in many homes. Manufacturers quickly developed hand and machine tools for this specific market. The do–it–yourself, fix–it–yourself attitude of the late 1940s through the 1960s resulted in strong tool sales.

Tool collectors collect primarily by brand or tool type. Most focus on tools made before 1940. Quality is critical. Most collectors want nothing to do with cheap foreign imports. Interest is building in power tools and some specialized tool groups, e.g., Snap–on–Tools.

References: Ronald S. Barlow, *The Anique Tool Collector's Guide to Value, Third Edition,* Windmill Publishing, 1991; *The Catalogue of Antique Tools, 1997 Edition,* Martin J. Donnelly Antique Tools, 1997; Terri Clemens, *American Family Farm Antiques,* Wallace–Homestead, Krause Publications, 1994; Herbert P. Kean and Emil S. Pollak, *A Price Guide to Antique Tools,* Astragal Press, 1992; Herbert P. Kean and Emil S. Pollak, *Collecting Antique Tools,* Astragal Press, 1990; Kathryn McNerney, *Antique Tools, Our American Heritage,* Collector Books, 1979, 1996 value update; Emil and Martyl Pollak, *A Guide to American Wooden Planes and Their Makers, Third Edition* The Astragal Press, 1994; R. A. Salaman, *Dictionary of Tools,* Charles Scribner's Sons, 1974; John Walter, *Antique & Collectible Stanley Tools: A Guide to Identity and Value, Second Edition,* Tool Merchants, 1996; Jack P. Wood, *Early 20th Century Stanley Tools,* catalog reprint, L–W Book Sales, 1996 value update; Jack P. Wood, *Town–Country Old Tools and Locks, Keys and Closures,* L–W Books, 1990, 1997 value update.

Collectors' Clubs: Early American Industries Assoc, 167 Bakersville Rd, South Dartmouth, MA 02748; Tool Group of Canada, 7 Tottenham Rd, Ontario MC3 2J3 Canada.

Auger Bit, Stanley, #49, depth stop, nickel plated **$8.00**
Axe, Winchester, diamond edge broad axe **60.00**
Axe, Winchester, hunting style **35.00**

Bead Saw, Stanley, steel blade, hardwood handle,
    orange enamel finish, 10" l **25.00**
Bench Clamp, Stanley, #203, black japanned triangle
    frame, wing nut screw **18.00**
Block Plane, Stanley, #S18, steel, type "AA," S & W Hart
    trademark, "W.N." stamped on both sides, c1925 . . . . **135.00**
Boxwood Rule, Stanley, #136½, caliper slide and brass
    tips, 5" l **15.00**
Breast Drill, Stanley, cast iron, steel, built–in level,
    2 speed, 16" l **20.00**
Butt Chisel, Stanley, #60, plastic handle, ¾" **5.00**
Caliper, handwrought, double end figure 8, 12" bow tie,
    brass washer **35.00**
Carpenter's Bead Saw, H Disston & Sons, Philadelphia,
    PA, c1935, 17" l **145.00**
Carpenter's Brace, 8" **60.00**
Carpenter's Brace, Millers Falls **10.00**
Carpenter's Rule, Stanley, hardwood, steel trim, painted
    finish, 4 fold, 2 ft. **20.00**
Chisel, Millers Falls, hobby carving set, 5 small lino chisels with palm grip handles, orig wooden box, c1950 . . . . . **15.00**
Chisel, Stanley, #25, Everlasting chisel, steel shank, hickory handle, lacquered finish **15.00**
Claw Hammer, Winchester **35.00**
Corner Brace, Unknown Manufacturer, modern, triangular frame, 2 wooden wrists, wooden pad **20.00**
Double Claw Hammer, Double Claw Hammer Co, 12" l . . . **275.00**
Dowel Jig, Stanley, cast iron, nickel plated finish **20.00**
Felling Axe, Keen Kutter, modern style, 3½" edge **22.00**
Fore Plane, Stanley, #6C, type "20," blue finish, 1962–67 . . . . **45.00**
Hammer, Keen Kutter **25.00**
Hammer, Stanley, #100, velvet lined box, presentation
    plaque, "Golden Hammer of Merit" **130.00**
Hand Drill, Stanley, cast iron frame, hardwood handles,
    japanned finish, 12" l **20.00**
Level, Chapins Stephens Co, Pine Meadow, CT, aluminum, 3 portholes, brass center plane, 30" l **30.00**
Level, C S Co, Pine Meadow, CT, hardwood, brass ends,
    large round dial marked off in degrees, 28" l **75.00**
Level, Edward Preston & Sons, pocket level, brass, 3" l **35.00**
Level, Unknown Manufacturer, lignum vitae and brass,
    unusual rotating brass cov protects level's vial, 12" l **12.50**

Whetstone, Humble Oil Co adv, celluloid, 1⅝ x 2⅞", $121.00.
Photo courtesy Wm. Morford Auctions.

Machinist's Bench Rule and Level, Stanley, #38½, "Sweetheart" trademark, 4" l **65.00**

Machinist's Hammer, Millers Falls Co, brass, 7" l **45.00**

Machinist's Level, Stanley, cast iron, 6" l **20.00**

Mallet, Stanley, hickory handle, 10½" l **10.00**

Mason's Level, Stanley, softwood, brass, adjustable, 42" l **25.00**

Miter Box, Stanley, cast iron, 20" l **50.00**

Monkey Wrench, Bay State Tool Co, wooden grips **15.00**

Monkey Wrench, Handee Wrench Co, New Bedford, MA, slotted steel handle **25.00**

Oil Burner Level, Stanley, #38, cast iron, doorstop shape, flat bottom, bowed top, orange lacquer finish, 6" l **10.00**

Pattern Maker's Block, Stanley, #9, "AA" mark on iron, late adjuster, replaced side handle, S & W Hart, 1923–25 .... **950.00**

Pipe Wrench, Craftsman Tool Co, wheel shaped lower jaw, 12" l **20.00**

Pipe Wrench, H & E Wrench Co, New Bedford, MA, metal **45.00**

Plumb Bob, C L Berger & Sons, Boston, MA, brass, surveyor's, 3" l **55.00**

Pocket Wrench, Keen Kutter, #93, 4" l **12.00**

Ratchet Brace, Stanley, #965, nickel plated, alligator jaws **14.00**

Rule, Esborn Lumber Corp, New York, NY, advertising hook rule, with lumber scales, reverse imprinted with company advertising, 24" l **65.00**

Saw, James Howarth, Sheffield, pad saw with turned ebony handle, long brass ferrule **65.00**

Saw, Spear & Jackson, Sheffield, brass backed, closed handle **35.00**

Screwdriver, Stanley, ratchet, steel, hardwood, 6" l **20.00**

Screwdriver, Winchester, #7160, 1½" l **35.00**

Scroll Saw, American Boy Scroll Saw, Delta Specialty Co, Milwaukee, hand–crank, 8 x 11" **80.00**

Shank Bits, set of 15, P M Co, Forstner pattern, round, in mahogany rack **195.00**

Sheetmetal Shears, with lever linkage, Bartlet Mfg Co, Detroit **22.00**

Smooth Plane, Stanley, #1, type "AA" mark on plane and box, S & W Hart, orig box, 1922–35 .... **2,300.00**

Smooth Plane, Stanley, #2, type "BB" mark on iron, 1936 .... **175.00**

Smooth Plane, Stanley, #3, type "15," 1931–32 .... **45.00**

Smooth Plane, Stanley, #4, type "18," 1946–47 .... **15.00**

Socket Chisel, Stanley, steel shank, hickory handle, lacquered finish **10.00**

Tape Measure, Stanley, steel, black finish, 6" l **15.00**

Tongue and Groove Plane, Stanley, cast iron, rosewood, 10½" l **35.00**

Tool Box, Stanley, walnut, 22" l **50.00**

Tool Cabinet, Stanley, oak, 29" l **50.00**

Tool Chest, Stanley, hard wood, enamel, blue and yellow, 20" **50.00**

Tool Tray, pine, sq nail construction, cutout handle, well worn, refinished, 29½" l, 12" w, 8½" h **45.00**

Victor Smooth Plane, Stanley, #1104, gray frame, red frog, stained red handle and knob, orig box **100.00**

Watchmaker's Caliper, double, figure 8 shape, 3½" **12.00**

Wrench, The Victor, adjustable alligator jaw, 7" l **10.00**

Yard Stick, Hazelton, Contoocook, NH, brass tipped, calibrated in ⅛ yard increments **65.00**

Yard Stick, Stanley, maple, brass, 36" l **20.00**

TOOTHPICK HOLDERS

Toothpick holders were popular household accessories through the end of the 1950s. They still are a common fixture on restaurant checkout counters. In fact, restaurant and individual silver–plated toothpicks are two underappreciated subcategories.

When is a toothpick holder not a toothpick holder? When it is a match holder, miniature spoon holder for a toy table setting, a salt shaker with a ground off top, a small rose bowl, shot glass, an individual open sugar, a vase, or a whimsy. A toothpick is designed to hold toothpicks. Toothpicks have a flat bottom and allow enough of the toothpick to extend above the top so one can be extracted with no problem. If the toothpicks do not extend above the top or stand erect, chances are the object is not a toothpick holder.

References: Neila and Tom Bredehoft, *Findlay Toothpick Holders*, Cherry Hill Publications, 1995; William Heacock, *Encyclopedia of Victorian Colored Pattern Glass, Book 1, Toothpick Holders From A to Z, Second Edition*, Antique Publications, 1976, 1992 value update; National Toothpick Holders Collectors Society, *Toothpick Holders: China, Glass, and Metal*, Antique Publications, 1992.

Collector's Club: National Toothpick Holders Collectors Society, Red Arrow Hwy, PO Box 246, Sawyer, MI 49125.

Art Glass, purple slag, figural boot **$50.00**

Bisque, figural cat, wearing coachman's outfit, barrel holder **55.00**

Bisque, figural dwarf, 4½" h **25.00**

Bisque, Geisha, blue rim, 2½" h **15.00**

Brass, souvenir, "I'm From Missouri" **25.00**

Brass, top hat and umbrella **20.00**

Ceramic, blue faced dog, multicolored glaze, Japan, 3¼" h **20.00**

Ceramic, top hat, sunset hunting dog scene, green and cream ground, cobalt blue band **40.00**

China, Bavarian, hp florals **40.00**

China, boot, floral dec, Occupied Japan, 2¾" h **10.00**

China, Majolica, sunflower **90.00**

Blue Carnival Glass, Aurora Jewels, Imperial, 1950s–80s, $25.00.

Custard Glass, Argonaut Shell **375.00**
Custard Glass, Ring Band, flower bud **165.00**
Custard Glass, souvenir, Belvedere, IL **35.00**
Glass, Fancy Loop, green, gold dec, Heisey **165.00**
Glass, figural, cat on cushion. **45.00**
Glass, figural, horse pulling cart, amber **75.00**
Glass, figural, trough, Heisey. **48.00**
Glass, Sunbeam, clear. **30.00**
Milk Glass, Button & Bulge, hp florals **35.00**
Milk Glass, figural barrel, metal hoops. **25.00**
Milk Glass, Tramp's Shoe. **30.00**
Opalescent Glass, blue, reverse swirl **85.00**
Opalescent Glass, cranberry, ribbed lattice. **240.00**
Pattern Glass, Beatty Honeycomb, blue **50.00**
Pattern Glass, Bohemian, green, gold dec. **265.00**
Pattern Glass, Colonial, cobalt, Cambridge. **25.00**
Pattern Glass, Croesus, amethyst, gold dec **150.00**
Pattern Glass, Daisy & Button, blue, V ornament. **50.00**
Pattern Glass, Elephant Toe, rose stain **80.00**
Pattern Glass, Fancy Loop, green, gold dec, Heisey. **165.00**
Pattern Glass, Gonterman Swirl, blue. **225.00**
Pattern Glass, Heart, pink opaque **60.00**
Pattern Glass, Hobnail, Frances Ware. **50.00**
Pattern Glass, King's Crown, ruby stained **38.00**
Pattern Glass, Leaf Umbrella, mauve, cased **365.00**
Pattern Glass, Pineapple & Fan, green **185.00**
Pattern Glass, Punty & Diamond Point, Heisey **260.00**
Pattern Glass, Ribbed Pillar, pink **85.00**
Pattern Glass, Royal Ivy, clear **160.00**
Pattern Glass, Royal Ivy, frosted rubina. **165.00**
Pattern Glass, Royal Oak, frosted rubina. **125.00**
Pattern Glass, Texas Star, clear **130.00**
Pattern Glass, 3 dolphins, amber **45.00**
Pattern Glass, Vermont, opaque ivory **125.00**
Plastic, white log, red woodpecker with pronged bead
    picks up toothpicks, 4¹/₂" l, 2¹/₂" h. **10.00**
Ruby Stained, Diamond Peg **25.00**
Ruby Stained, souvenir, Button Arches, "Mother 1947". **20.00**
Silver Plate, cat and bucket **65.00**
Silver Plate, chick, half egg and wishbone **30.00**
Silver Plate, owl, seated on branch, 2" h. **75.00**
Silver Plate, rabbit, beside egg **25.00**
Silver Plate, rooster, engraved "Picks," 2" h. **48.00**
Wood, figural beaver, painted features, broad tail, hol-
    lowed out tree trunk **5.00**

TORQUAY POTTERY

Pottery manufacturing came to the Torquay district of South Devon, England, in the 1870s following G. J. Allen's discovery of a red terra–cotta potting clay in 1869. Allen organized the Watcombe Pottery, producing a wealth of art pottery terra–cotta products.

In 1875 Dr. Gillow founded the Torquay Terra–Cotta Company. Its products were similar to those of Watcombe Pottery. It closed in 1905, only to be reopened by Enoch Staddon in 1908. Staddon produced pottery rather than terra–cotta ware.

John Philips established the Aller Vale Pottery in 1881. The company specialized in souvenir pieces. Designs were painted on pieces with a thick colored slip that contrasted with the color of the ground slip coat. This "motto" ware achieved widespread popularity by 1900. In 1902 Aller Vale and Watcombe merged and became Royal Aller Vale and Watcombe Art Potteries. The new company produced commemorative and motto ware.

Burton, Daison, and Longpark pottery are examples of numerous small companies that sprang up in the Torquay District and made wares similar to those produced by Aller Vale and Watcombe. Longpark, the last of these companies, closed in 1957. When Royal Aller Vale and Watcombe closed in 1962, the era of red pottery production in Torquay ended.

Reference: Susan and Al Bagdade, *Warman's English & Continental Pottery & Porcelain, Second Edition,* Wallace–Homestead, Krause Publications, 1991.

Collectors' Clubs: North American Torquay Society, 12 Stanton, Madison, CT 06443; Torquay Pottery Collectors Society, 23 holland Ave, Cheam, Sutton, Surrey SM2 6HW U.K.

Candlestick, scandy, "Be the Day Weary or Be the Day
    Long at Last It Ringeth to Evensong," imp Watcombe
    mark, 7¹/₂" h **$145.00**
Chamberstick, black cockerel, "Snore and You Sleep
    Alone," stamped "Longpark Torquay," 4" h **80.00**
Chamberstick, colored cockerel, "Many Are Called But
    Few Get Up," Longpark Torquay mark, 4¹/₂" h **110.00**
Coffeepot, cottage, "May the Hinges of Friendship Never
    Go Rusty," Watcombe Torquay mark, 7" h. **100.00**
Compote, ftd, "Do Not Stain Todays Blue Sky With
    Tomorrows Clouds," 5" h **115.00**
Creamer, cottage, "Wookey Hole, Help Yourself to the
    Cream," Royal Watcombe Torquay mark, 1³/₄" h **38.00**
Creamer, black cockerel, "Straight From the Cow,"
    Longpark Torquay mark, 2¹/₄" h. **40.00**
Creamer, colored cockerel, "Be Aisy With Tha Crain,"
    Longpark Torquay mark, 2³/₄" h. **40.00**
Dish, scandy, "There's More in the Kitchen," 7" d **90.00**
Eggcup, cottage, "Fresh Today," Longpark Torquay mark,
    1³/₄" h. **32.00**
Inkwell, scandy, "Wa'al Us Be Main Glas Tu Zee'e,"
    Aller Vale mark, 2" h **35.00**
Jam Jar, sailboat scene, "Southsea, Be Aisy With Tha
    Jam," stamped "Longpark Torquay, England," 4³/₄" h. **50.00**
Mug, 2 handles, scandy, "A Stitch in Time Saves Nine,"
    imp "Watcombe Pottery" mark, 3" h **70.00**
Pen Tray, sandy, "The Pen is Mightier Than the Sword,"
    stamped "Longpark Torquay," 9" l. **40.00**
Pitcher, colored cockerel, "There Would Be No Shadows
    if the Sun Were Not Shining," Longpark Torquay mark,
    6" h **150.00**
Pitcher, cottage, "Fairest Gems Lie Deepest," Watcombe
    Torquay mark, 3" h **30.00**
Plate, black cockerel, "From Durham Tis Deeds Alone
    Must Win the Prize," Longpark Torquay mark, 5" d **60.00**
Plate, cottage, "Better To Sit Still Than Rise To Fall,"
    Watcombe Torquay mark, 6¹/₂" d **50.00**
Sugar Bowl, snow cottage, "Take a Little Sugar,"
    Watcombe Torquay mark, 1³/₄" h **45.00**
Sugar Dish, colored cockerel, "Be Aisy With Tha Sugar,"
    stamped "Longpark Torquay," 1³/₄" h. **45.00**
Tea Stand, cottage, "He Also Serves Who Stands and
    Waits," stamped "Longpark Torquay," 5¹/₂" d **50.00**
Tray, "A Reminder of a Visit to the English Lake District,"
    Coronation year 1937, stamped "Watcombe Torquay
    England," 5" l, 3" w. **70.00**

TOYS

Toys drive the 20th–century collectibles market. The standards for condition, scarcity, and desirability established by the toy community are now being applied throughout the antiques marketplace.

The toy market of the 1990s is highly sophisticated. In fact, some question if there is a single toy market any longer. Many categories within the toy market have broken away and become independent collecting categories. This category covers manufacturers and toy types still located within the general toy category.

Currently, the post–1945 period is the hot period among toy collectors. Prices for pre–1920 cast–iron and penny toys are stable and, in some cases, in decline. Pressed steel dominates vehicle collecting with a small cadre of collectors beginning to look at plastic. Diecast toys, the darlings of the 1970s and 80s, have lost some of their luster. Vehicles remain the toy of choice among collectors aged thirty–five and above. Young collectors focus on action figures and licensed toys.

With so many toys of the post–1945 era of Far Eastern origin, the national collecting prejudice for toys made in one's own country has diminished. What it is rather than where it was made is the key today. One result is a lowering of quality standards for more recently issued toys. The pre–1960s toy market remains heavily quality–driven.

The contemporary toy market is cursed by two groups of individuals—toy speculators and toy scalpers—whose activities badly distort pricing reality. Toy speculators hoard toys, thus upsetting the traditional supply and demand cycle. Toy scalpers created artificial shortages for modern toys. They accept no financial or moral responsibility for their actions when the speculative bubble they created bursts. And, it always does.

References: General: Sharon and Bob Huxford (eds.), *Schroeder's Collectible Toys: Antique to Modern Price Guide, Fourth Edition*, Collector Books, 1998; Sharon Korbeck (ed.), *Toys & Prices, 5th Edition*, Krause Publications, 1997; Richard O'Brien, *Collecting Toys: Identification and Value Guide, 8th Edition*, Krause Publications, 1997.

Generational: Bill Bruegman, *Toys of the Sixties*, Cap'n Penny Productions, 1991; Tom Frey, *Toy Bop: Kid Classics of the 50's & 60's*, Fuzzy Dice Productions, 1994; Robin Sommer, *I Had One of Those: Toys of Our Generation*, Crescent Books, 1992; Carol Turpen, *Baby Boomer Toys and Collectibles*, Schiffer Publishing, 1993.

Juvenile: Joe Johnson and Dana McGuinn, *Toys That Talk: Over 300 Pullstring Dolls & Toys—1960s to Today*, Firefly Publishing, 1992; *Price Guide to Pull Toys*, L–W Book Sales, 1996; *Tops and Yo–Yos and Other Spinning Toys*, L–W Book Sales, 1995.

Lithograph Tin: Alan Jaffe, *J. Chein & Co.: A Collector's Guide to an American Toymaker*, Schiffer Publishing, 1997; Lisa Kerr, *American Tin–Litho Toys*, Collectors Press, 1995; Maxine A. Pinsky, *Greenberg's Guide to Marx Toys, Vol. I* (1988) and *Vol. II* (1990), Greenberg Publishing.

Miscellaneous: Raymond V. Brandes, *Big Bang Cannons*, Ray–Vin Publishing, 1993; Christopher Cook, *Collectible American Yo–Yos, 1920s–1970s: Historical Reference & Value Guide*, Collector Books, 1997; David Gould and Donna Crevar–Donaldson, *Occupied Japan Toys With Prices*, L–W Book Sales, 1993; Morton A. Hirschberg, *Steamtoys: A Symphony in Motion*, Schiffer Publishing, 1996; Jay Horowitz, *Marx Western Playsets: The Authorized Guide*, Greenberg Publishing, 1992.

Don Hultzman, *Collector's Guide to Battery Toys: Identification & Values*, Collector Books, 1998; Anthony Marsella, *Toys From Occupied Japan*, Schiffer Publishing, 1995; Jack Matthews, *Toys Go to War: World War II Military Toys, Games, Puzzles & Books*, Pictorial Histories Publishing, 1994; Albert W. McCollough, *The New Book of Buddy "L" Toys, Vol. I* (1991), *Vol. II* (1991), Greenberg Publishing; Harry A. and Joyce A. Whitworth, *G–Men and FBI Toys and Collectibles: Identification & Values*, Collector Books, 1998.

Plastic: Bill Hanlon, *Plastic Toys: Dimestore Dreams of the '40s & '50s*, Schiffer Publishing, 1993.

Vehicles: Don and Barb DeSalle, *The DeSalle Collection of Smith–Miller & Doepke Trucks*, L–W Book Sales, 1997; Charles F. Donovan, Jr., *Renwal, World's Finest Toys: Vol. 2, Transportation Toys & Accessories*, published by author, 1996; Edward Force, *Corgi Toys*, Schiffer Publishing, 1984, 1997 value update; Edward Force, *Dinky Toys*, Schiffer Publishing, 1988, 1992 value update; Edward Force, *Solido Toys*, Schiffer Publishing, 1993; Joe and Sharon Freed, *Collector's Guide to American Transportation Toys, 1895–1941*, Freedom Press, 1995; Sally Gibson–Downs and Christine Gentry, *Motorcycle Toys: Antique and Contemporary*, Collector Books, 1995; Jeffrey C. Gurski, *Greenberg's Guide to Cadillac Models and Toys*, Greenberg Publishing, 1992.

Ken Hutchison and Greg Johnson, *The Golden Age of Automotive Toys: 1925–1941*, Collector Books, 1996; Dana Johnson, *Collector's Guide to Diecast Toys & Scale Models, 2nd Edition*, Collector Books, 1998; Douglas P. Kelley, *The Die Cast Price Guide Post–War: 1946 to Present*, Antique Trader Books, 1997; Raymond R. Klein, *Greenberg's Guide to Tootsietoys, 1945–1969*, Greenberg Publishing, 1993; Richard O'Brien, *Toy Cars & Trucks: Identification and Value Guide, 2nd Edition*, Krause Publications, 1997; R & B Collectibles & Marketing, *Texaco Collectors 1997 Price Guide*, published by authors, 1997.

John Ramsay's Catalogue of British Diecast Model Toys, Sixth Edition, Swapmeet Publications, 1995; Mike and Sue Richardson, *Diecast Toy Aircraft: An International Guide*, New Cavendish, 1998; David Richter, *Collector's Guide to Tootsietoys, Second Edition*, Collector Books, 1996; Ron Smith, *Collecting Toy Airplanes: An Identification & Value Guide*, Books Americana, Krause Publications, 1995; Gerhard G. Walter, *Tin Dream Machines: German Tin Toy Cars and Motorcycles of the 1950s and 1960s*, New Cavendish, 1998.

Periodicals: *Antique Toy World*, PO Box 34509, Chicago, IL 60634; *Model and Toy Collector Magazine*, PO Box 347240, Cleveland, OH 44134; *Toy Farmer*, 7496 106th Ave, SE, Lamoure, ND 58458; *Toy Shop*, 700 E State St, Iola, WI 54490; *Toy Trader*, PO Box 1050, Dubuque, IA 52003.

Collectors' Clubs: Antique Toy Collectors of America, Two Wall St, 13th Flr, New York, NY 10005; Canadian Toy Collectors Society, 67 Alpine Ave, Hamilton, Ontario L9A1A7 Canada.

Maloney's Antiques & Collectibles Resource Directory by David J. Maloney, Jr., lists many collectors' clubs for specific types of toys. Check your local library for the most recent edition.

Note: For additional toy listings see Action Figures, Barbie, Bicycles, Breyer Horses, Cap Guns, Cartoon Characters, Coloring Books, Construction Toys, Cowboy Heroes, Disneyana, Dolls, Ertl, Fisher–Price, Games, GI Joe, Hanna–Barbera, Hess Trucks, Hot Wheels, Matchbox, Model Kits, Monsters, Occupied Japan, Paint

By Number Sets, Paper Dolls, Pedal Cars, Premiums, Puzzles, Radio Characters and Personalities, Robots, Sand Pails, Sizzlers, Slot Cars, Space Adventurers, Space Toys, Star Trek, Star Wars, Steiff, Stuffed Toys, Super Heroes, Teddy Bears, Television Characters & Personalities, Tonka, Toy Soldiers, Toy Train Accessories, Toy Trains, View–Master, and Warner Bros.

AHI, Japan, Ben Hur Trotter, windup, litho tin, rocking horse with rubber ears pulling cart with gladiator holding metal whip, orig box, 7" l $300.00

AJ Renzi Corp, Leominster, MA, Monster Car, plastic convertible with visible pistons, Dracula and Wolfman in front seats, Frankenstein and other monster in rear seats, spoked wheels mkd "Renzi," c1964, 17" l 925.00

All Metal Products (Wyandotte), Fleet–Line Truck Set #8000, litho tin and plastic, includes 9" l auto transport, 4 plastic cars, trailer truck, stake truck, 8" l moving van, wrecker truck, and extra cab, orig box 735.00

Alps, Japan, Happy Fiddler Clown, battery operated, litho tin, cloth, and plastic, seated clown plays fiddle, animated arms, moves body, turns head, loud screeching sound, orig box, 10" h 375.00

Alps, Japan, Happy Santa with Lighted Eyes, battery operated, litho tin and vinyl, drumming Santa with animated arms, swaying head, and lighted eyes, orig box, 10" h 365.00

Aoshin, Japan, Acrobat Cycle, battery operated, plastic, GT2000 cycle with full figure rider, orig box, 9" l 145.00

Arnold, West Germany, Sabena Airlines Piccola Helicopter, litho tin, remote controller spins plastic prop while copter travels in circle, orig box, 6" l helicopter 70.00

Auburn Rubber, Garrison's Gorillas' Gear, plastic accessories include mess kit, belt with attachments, and knife in sheath, orig box, ©ABC 1968, 9 x 14" box 95.00

Auburn Rubber, Train Set #525, rubber–like vinyl, includes 10" l engine and tender, coal car, gondola, caboose, conductor, engineer, and flag man, orig box 110.00

Bandai, Japan, Ford panel Delivery Truck, friction, litho tin, "Flowers, for gracious living" on panels, elephant on door plate, Ford hubs, fold–down rear gate, 11½" l . . . 775.00

Corgi, Simon Snorkel Fire Engine #1126–B1, 1977–81, $40.00.

Bandai, Japan, Isetta 700, friction, tin, red and white vehicle with detailed litho tin int and opening front door, 6½" l 250.00

Bandai, Japan, Lotus Racer, battery operated, tin, #16 racer, controllable speed, steerable front wheels, engine sound, plastic driver, Goodyear black rubber tires, orig box, 9½" l 325.00

Bandai, Japan, Porsche with 2 Openable Doors, battery operated, tin, white body, litho tin int, plastic driver, bump-and-go action, doors open and close when vehicle stops, motor sound, visible rear engine, orig box, 10" l 200.00

Bandai, Japan, Volkswagen Sedan, battery operated, tin, black rubber tires, VW hubs, vinyl driver, bump–and–go action, clear plastic cover reveals lighted rear working engine, orig box, 10" l 250.00

BS, West Germany, Momentum Sand Toy, litho tin, uses marble as weight, orig box, 7" h 165.00

Buddy L, Telephone Maintenance Repair Truck and Trailer #450, metal truck with black rubber tires, 2 side decals, ladder, rope, and 10" l trailer, orig box, 16" l truck 450.00

Chein, Clown with Umbrella, windup, litho tin, clown balances spinning umbrella on nose while moving with vibrating motion, 6½" h 275.00

Chein, Popeye Shadow Boxer, windup, litho tin, vibrating motion, swinging arms, ©King Features Syndicate, 7" h 1,750.00

Chein, Santa Walker, gift version, windup, litho tin, 6" h 735.00

Conway Custom Cars, Mech Packard Convertible, windup, plastic, red convertible with litho tin int, windscreen, and hood ornament, battery operated headlights, twist steering wheel for sounding horn, orig box, c1940s, 11" l 525.00

Corgi, James Bond Aston Martin D.B.5 #261, diecast, Bond driver, retractable machine guns, opening roof, ejector seat, orig box, 3½" l 185.00

Corgi/Glidrose, James Bond Aston Martin D.B.5 #270, diecast, scale model, ejector seat, bullet screen telescopic over–riders, retractable machine guns, revolving number plates, orig box, 4" l 95.00

Cortland, Checker Cab, windup, litho tin, green and yellow, orig box and guarantee slip, 7" l 250.00

Empire, Popeye Hat and Pipe, tin kazoo pipe, vinyl hat, ©King Features Syndicate, MOC 160.00

Biller, Germany, Slugger Champions, windup, litho tin 1950s, 3½" sq base, $175.00.

England, Funfair Flyer, windup, litho tin, carnival toy with Big Top, circus train, and rides, litho tin car travels on carnival track, 11" l 525.00

Excel, Three Stooges Jolly Theatre, 9 x 8" projector and film, uncut cardboard sheet with movie tickets and characters including 5" h Stooges figures, instructions, orig box depicts Stooges and other characters, 1947 . . . . . 210.00

France, Shell Service Station with Autos, plastic, with trees, pumps, Shell sign, and 3 autos, orig box, 9 x 6 x 15" l station 200.00

Gardner, Donald Duck Tricky Toe, litho cardboard, Donald kicks football with animated foot, complete with paper field, cardboard stadium, and store display sign, unused in orig box, ©Walt Disney Productions 80.00

Gong Bell Co, Healthy Milk Co Delivery Truck #123, litho wood truck, pressed steel wheels, boy delivering milk and Elsie-like cow on sides, cardboard milk case contains 3 milk bottles, opening side door, 12½" l 265.00

Gund, Popeye's Swea Pea Hand Puppet, vinyl face, orig box 85.00

Halsam, Mickey Mouse Safety Blocks, 15 sq wooden blocks, orig box, ©Walt Disney Enterprises, orig litho box with pie-eyed Mickey and Minnie, large size blocks 260.00

Hasbro, Transformers, Blitzwing 55.00
Hasbro, Transformers, Bombshell 25.00
Hasbro, Transformers, Crosshairs 65.00
Hasbro, Transformers, Devastator 250.00
Hasbro, Transformers, Horribull 50.00
Hasbro, Transformers, Megatron 250.00
Hasbro, Transformers, Red Alert 100.00
Hasbro, Transformers, Submaurader 45.00
Hasbro, Transformers, Trypticon 225.00

Hubley, Ford Powermaster Tractor #961, metal, scale model Ford, black rubber tires, power steering, 1/12th scale, 3–point hitch can be lowered or raised, orig box, 11" l 195.00

Hubley, Mighty-Metal Helicopter, diecast, orig box, 1969, 9" l 70.00

Hubley, Navy Fighter Bomber, #1495, diecast metal, bomber plane, orig box, 9" l, 12" wingspan 80.00

Hubley, P–38 Fighter #1881, diecast metal, fighter plane, orig box, 9" l, 12" wingspan 170.00

Hubley, Panther Pistol, diecast, plastic grip, complete with litho cardboard attached arm and hand, orig box . . . 250.00

Hubley, School Bus #1821, diecast, orig box, 1969, 9" l 75.00

Husky, Man From U N C L E Missile Firing Car, diecast, Solo and Kuryakin figures, ©MGM 1966, MOC 215.00

Ichiko, Japan, Alitalia Service Jeep, battery operated, litho tin, full figure plastic driver, advances, flashing rear light, 7½" l 215.00

Ichiko, Japan, Renault Floride, friction, tin, red body, black roof, detailed litho tin int, black rubber tires, orig box, 8" l 160.00

Ideal, Flight Patrol Airplane Set, 8 plastic planes with manually spinning props, orig box, 1950s 115.00

Irwin, Barney Rubble pull toy, plastic, Barney driving green turtle shell car with red wheels, 11" l 1,125.00

Irwin, Mechanical See–Saw, #609, windup, plastic, 2 girl riders, hp features, orig box 110.00

Irwin, Waltzing Royal Couple, windup, plastic, hp features, orig box, 5" h 150.00

Itako, Occupied Japan, Peaceful Pigeon, windup, litho tin, orig box, 8" l 800.00

Japan, Boeing 727 Astro Jet, friction, litho tin, American airlines jet, orig box, 10" l, 11" wingspan 70.00

Japan, Broderick Crawford Highway Patrol Car, friction, litho tin car with extended guns, orig box, 6" l 200.00

Japan, Elephant Circus, friction, litho tin, convertible with elephant juggling globe from trunk, orig box, 7" l . . . 275.00

Japan, Friction Convertible Vessel, friction, litho tin, boat with center section that flips over to convert to cruise ship, orig box, 11" l 165.00

Japan, Groolies Monster Car, windup, litho tin, Universal Monsters at each window, diecut bloodshot eyes for headlights, skull above grille, orig box, 4½" l 200.00

Japan, Liberty Ferry, windup, litho tin, orig box, 26" l base 400.00

Japan, MG Car II, friction, tin, convertible, detailed litho tin int, black rubber tires, mounted rear spare, hubs mkd "MG," orig box, 8" l 275.00

Japan, Musical Jackal, battery operated, litho tin and plush, monkey plays xylophone, animated arms, turning head, swaying body, lighted eyes, orig box, 10" h 515.00

Japan, Packard 52, friction, tin, red sedan, blue tin wheels, orig box, 7" l 185.00

Japan, Royal Cub, battery operated, litho tin and plush, Mama bear walking with crying baby bear in carriage, baby cries and drinks her milk by lifting arms, lighted flower inside carriage, orig box, 8" h, 8" l 315.00

Japan, Self–Loading & Unloading Dump Car with Track, windup, litho tin, with orig key and 3 balls, orig box, 7 x 28" l track 175.00

Japan, Superior Go-Kart, litho tin and plastic, full figure plastic driver advances with low and high speeds, full turning action, real engine sound, orig box, 9" l 130.00

IRCO, Japan, Ford Convertible, friction, tin, litho tin int, 7" l, $302.50. Photo courtesy Collectors Auction Services.

Japan, Chevrolet Impala, friction, tin, litho tin int, 11¼" l, $165.00. Photo courtesy Collectors Auction Services.

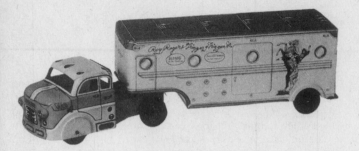

Marx, Roy Rogers Hauler and Van Trailer, litho tin, 15" l, $203.50.
Photo courtesy Collectors Auction Services.

Japan, United 727 Jet Liner, friction, litho tin, Boeing
727 mkd "United" on tail fin, orig box, 16" l **85.00**

Joustra, France, Bimbo Clown Car, windup, litho tin, figural Bimbo driver, circular motion, 4½" l **265.00**

K, Japan, Zoom Boat, battery operated, litho tin, F–570
speedboat with visible rear engine and half figure
litho tin pilot, remote control operation, forward/
reverse motion, orig box, 10" l **110.00**

Katz Toys, Spirit of St Louis Plane #117, litho tin, plane
mkd "NX211" on wing, 12" l, 12" wingspan **285.00**

KND, Occupied Japan, Acrobat Car, windup, tin, red tin
car with helmeted and goggled drivers with emb
details, "No. 1" and "No. 2" on opposite sides, lever
makes car perform acrobatic rollover turns, orig box,
5" l **470.00**

KO, Japan, Circus Car, friction, litho tin, clown on roof
and in back window, advances while balancing
Styrofoam ball above stream of air, orig box, 5" l, 5" h . . . **110.00**

KO, Japan, Hot Rod Racer, friction, litho tin, exposed
pistons, orig box, 6½" l **315.00**

Kosuge, Japan, Dreamland, windup, litho tin, 3" l
Dreamland vehicle navigates 19" l track, orig box **285.00**

Lakeside Toys, Stingray Aquaphibian Terror Fish, friction,
litho tin, advances with moving eyes, mouth, and
tail, Lakeside Toys, ©AP Films 1966, orig box, 9" l **325.00**

Lincoln Lines, City Transit Lines Trolley #45, windup,
plastic, green, complete decals featuring passengers at
each window, recoil motor, advances with clanging
trolley noise, orig box, 13½" l **130.00**

Lindstrom, Skeeter Duck, litho tin, advances in figure 8
motion with shaking head, orig box, 9½" l **80.00**

Linemar, Disney Express Train, windup, litho tin, train
filled with Disney characters, orig box, ©Walt Disney
Productions, 12" l **225.00**

Linemar, Japan, Goofy on High Wheel Bike, windup,
litho tin, rubber ears, Goofy rider pedals with animated leg action while bell lithoed with Pluto and Minnie
rings, ©Walt Disney Productions, 7" h **980.00**

Linemar, Japan, Mechanical Fred Flintstone on Dino,
windup, litho tin, Dino advances in waddling motion
with sound, orig box, ©Hanna-Barbera, 8" l **775.00**

Linemar, Japan, Mickey Mouse Skater, windup, litho tin,
felt pants, skating motion, orig box, 7" h **825.00**

Linemar, Japan, Pluto Disney Convertible, friction, tin
convertible with litho tin int, celluloid Pluto driver
with hp details, orig cartoon box with Mickey driving
convertible, other character on end flaps, ©Walt
Disney Productions, 6" l **750.00**

Linemar, Mickey Mouse Trike, windup, litho tin tricycle
with ringing bell, celluloid Mickey with hp details,
©Walt Disney Productions, 4" h **450.00**

Linemar/HB, Wilma Flintstone on Trike, windup, litho tin
trike, full figure celluloid Wilma, bell rings, 4" h **365.00**

Marx, Babyland Nursery Playset #3379, litho tin building, plastic accessories in orig bags including nurse,
babies, and cribs, orig box **485.00**

Marx, Battleground Playset #4754, plastic pcs in orig
bags with instructions, orig box **380.00**

Marx, Dairy Delivery Truck, litho tin, orig box, 10½" l **325.00**

Marx, Dick Tracy Police Car with Siren, friction, plastic,
half figure Tracy behind wheel, siren sound, orig box,
10" l **340.00**

Marx, Donald Duck and His Nephews, plastic, hp
details, Donald pulling nephews attached by metal
rod, orig box, 11" l **600.00**

Marx, Fix-All Tractor, litho tin, complete with parts in
orig bags and instructions, orig box **110.00**

Marx, Great Britain, Speed Cop, 8 curved litho tin race
track sections, 2 straight sections, police car, and
speeding car, 9" l curved track, 4" l cars, orig box **180.00**

Marx, Jetspeed Racer, battery operated, tin, Indy type
racer, orig box, 17" l **900.00**

Marx, Popeye Pirate Pistol, litho tin, clicker gun, orig
box, ©KFS 1935, 10" l **850.00**

Marx, Ring-A-Ling Circus, windup, litho tin, orig box,
1925, 7" d **2,300.00**

Marx, Speed King Racer, windup, litho tin, 16" l **325.00**

Marx, The Big Parade, windup, litho tin, soldiers, marching band, and ambulance circle track while airplane
spins overhead, orig box, 1930s, 24" l **1,150.00**

Marx, Toy Town Express Van lines, litho tin, truck mkd
"Dodge," orig box, 11" l **400.00**

Marx, Tri-City Express Service Truck, litho tin, truck car-
ries adv boxes, 14" l **300.00**

Minic, Ford Light Van, windup, diecast, orig box, c1936,
3½" l **120.00**

MT, Japan, Donald Duck Piston Race Car, battery operated, litho tin, open wheel racer, plastic Donald driver, advances with sound, flashing, and moving pis-
tons, run and spin action, orig box, 9½" l **175.00**

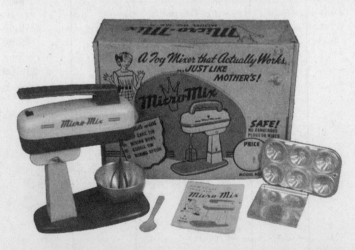

**Micromatic Tool & Mfg Co, Milwaukee, WI, Micro–Mixer #MX48,
battery operated, tin, red and white, aluminum accessories, orig
box, 10¼" h mixer, $150.00.**

Mirror Aluminum Toys, Like Mother's, aluminum bakeware, includes cake pan, pie pan, angel food pan, muffin tin, cov double boiler, potato masher, mixing bowl, cookie sheet, spatula, slotted spoon, measuring spoons, and 6 cookie cutters, orig box, $25.00

MT, Japan, Magic Fire Car, friction, litho tin, fire car with vinyl headed animal driver, advances with bell ringing sound and extended front bumper, orig box, 7" l **75.00**

Nosco, Cop–Cycle, friction, plastic, full figure helmeted and goggled driver and half figure passenger in side car, orig box, 1950s, 5½" l **525.00**

Nosco, Mechanical Fast Freight, windup, plastic, 6–unit train including coal car and tender, orig box, 17" l **150.00**

Nosco, Mechanical Playtoys #6321, windup, plastic, City of Los Angeles streamlined 4–unit train, bus, and station wagon, orig box, 4" l station wagon **185.00**

Occupied Japan, Ice Cream Cart, windup, litho tin, pedaled by celluloid man in uniform with hp features, 3½" l **190.00**

Occupied Japan, Skier, windup, celluloid boy skier with hp features, tin skis, orig box **400.00**

Ohio Art, Davy Crockett Sand Pail, litho tin, Davy with rifle and horse, Indian village, fort, bail handle, dated 1955, 8" h **135.00**

Ohio Art, Mickey Mouse Wash Tub, lihto tin, Mickey and Minnie around sides, 1930s, 5¼" d, 2¼" h **85.00**

Pelham Puppets, Huckleberry Hound Marionette, composition with hp details and fabric hat and jumpsuit, with handles and instructions, orig box, 9½" h **475.00**

PN, West Germany, Mystery Car and Garage #900, litho tin, car exits garage, circles around and enters other door, 2 x 3 x 5" garage, 4" l car **210.00**

Pressman, Little Orphan Annie Bubble Set, pipe, bubble, and tray, ©Harold Gray, 5 x 8" litho box **65.00**

Pride Products, Heidi Doody Hand Puppet, vinyl face with hp details and moving eyes, Howdy and other series' characters on cartoon box, ©Kagran, 8" h **575.00**

Regal Toy, Yogi Bear Speedboat, blue plastic speedboat with Yogi driver, ©Screen Gems, Inc, 1960s, 17½" l **175.00**

Renwal, Little Hospital Nursery Set #279, includes 5 vinyl babies in cribs, weighing scale, and pans, unused in orig box, 1950s **320.00**

RK, Inc, Rootie Kazootie Tool Box, litho tin, TV characters and "Fix–A–Rootie" on lid, 3 x 6 x 14" l **185.00**

Rubbertone Corp, Hopalong Cassidy Drum, cardboard, drum heads with Hoppy photos, ©Wm Boyd 1950, 5" d **550.00**

S&E, Japan, Snapping Alligator, windup, litho tin, alligator twists and turns and snaps jaws trying to catch bee, orig box, 12" l **120.00**

S, Japan, Betty Boop Tambourine, litho tin, features dancing Betty surrounded by musical notes, 6" d **210.00**

Salco/Banner, Tarzan Jungle Animals, 8 detailed plastic animals, firing white man, Tarzan figure with bow, orig box, 1966 . . . . **215.00**

Saunders, Super Catapult Plane Carrier #38, plastic, complete with 5 planes in orig pkging and instructions, shoot planes from landing deck using catapult with rubber band, orig box, 12" l **145.00**

Saunders, Super Motor Bus, gyro motor, plastic, black rubber tires, forward and reverse motion, orig box, 13" l **150.00**

Schuco, Ford FK 1000 #1049, windup, diecast, Micro Racer series, lever controls wheel direction, on/off switch, gray rubber wheels, detachable rear gate, orig box, 4½" l **130.00**

Schuco, Motodrill #1006, windup, litho tin, full figure rider on cycle, orig key and box, 5" l **465.00**

Schuco, US Zone Germany, Flotano 3009, plastic, girl water skier with hp details, pull string attached, orig box, 5" l **160.00**

Schuco, US Zone Germany, Flic Traffic Regulator #4520, windup, policeman standing on base rotates as he lifts right arm in simulated traffic signals while lights change on base, orig box, 5" h **285.00**

Schuco, West Germany, Mercedes 190SL, #2095, windup, tin, convertible, plastic int, Schuco tires, Mercedes hubs, orig key, steering wheel, cable, and pylons, orig box, 8½" l **485.00**

Sears, Roebuck & Co, Arctic Explorer Sled, battery operated, futuristic 12" l vehicle with plastic props and

Nomura, Japan, Roaring Gorilla Shooting Gallery, battery operated tin gorilla, tin cork–firing pistol, fold–out target box, 1950s, $175.00.

radar screen advances with flashing lights and revolving propellers, with smaller independent friction scout sled, orig box **900.00**

Seymour Products, Brenda Starr Cub Reporter Camera, real camera, ©Chicago Tribune, orig box **335.00**

Spain, Coca–Cola Delivery Truck, yellow cab, red bed mkd "Beba Coca–Cola," with 6 cases and bottles, 8" l **250.00**

Spain, Magilla Gorilla squeeze toy, vinyl, hp features, holding cane, ©Hanna–Barbera/Screen Gems 1967, 8" h **320.00**

SSS, Japan, Auto Transporter, friction, litho tin, 12½" l transport truck carries four 4" l passenger cars, orig box **210.00**

Structo, Army Cub Jeep #200, pressed steel, orig box, 10½" l **70.00**

Structo, Fix It Tow Truck #910, pressed steel, implements in sealed bag, with instructions, orig box, 11" l **180.00**

T Cohn, Roadside Steel Service Station #624, litho tin station, plastic accessories including truck, car, and attendants, unused in orig 8 x 12" box **415.00**

Thomas Toys, Airport Traffic Control Set, plastic, includes 13" l Super Constellation, mobile radar transmitter, signal light flasher, and remote control unit, orig 13 x 17" box **250.00**

Thomas Toys, Battle Stations Sea & Air Combat Action Set, plastic, includes exploding battleship, 7 x 9" l atom bomber with bombs, and 10" l submarine with torpedoes, orig box **250.00**

TPS, Japan, Fishing Monkey on Whale, windup, litho tin, monkey on back of whale with fishing rod in hand attached to 2 fish, toy travels back and forth with rocking motion as fish move and flap fins, orig box, 9" l **390.00**

TPS, Japan, Girl with Chickens, windup, litho tin, girl wearing dress and apron raises and lowers her hand in feeding motion and nods her head, 2 chickens attached to rod move back and forth as they peck at ground, orig box, 5½" h **450.00**

TPS, Japan, Happy the Violinist, windup, litho tin, clown violinist, orig box, 9½" h **485.00**

TPS, Japan, Helicopter on Airfield, windup, litho tin, airfield base, windup litho tin copter follows track, orig box, 6 x 9" base **135.00**

Schuco, US Zone Germany, Mirakocar 1001, 1 wheel replaced, orig box, 4½" l, $100.00. Photo courtesy Collectors Auction Services.

Sutcliffe, England, *Nautilus* Submarine, windup, tin, mid–1950s, 6" l, $250.00.

TPS, Japan, Pat the Pup, windup, litho tin, pat dog on nose and he moves and twirls rubber tail while barking, with orig heart shaped illus instruction tag and orig box, 5" h **145.00**

TPS, Japan, Skip Rope Animals, windup, litho tin, animals playing jump rope, orig box, 9" l **275.00**

Unique Art, Finnegan, windup, litho tin, baggage handler advances with cart that moves with erratic motions, orig box, 13" l **280.00**

Unknown Mfg, Howdy Doody Ready–to–Make Toy Kit, Clarabell, complete, orig box, 1950s **100.00**

Unknown Mfg, Kart Super Veloce, battery operated, plastic, full figure driver on go–cart, orig box, 7½" l **125.00**

Unknown Mfg, Keystone Service Station #143, station with plastic pump and rubber hose, plastic passenger car, orig box, 6 x 10" station **400.00**

Unknown Mfg, Keystone Wood Block Village #706, litho wood buildings including railroad station, houses, and drugstore, complete with trees, orig litho box **200.00**

Unknown Mfg, Olive Oyl figure, wood, jointed, hp facial details, ©KFS, 5" h **90.00**

Unknown Mfg, Pluto pull toy, wooden, litho Pluto with fabric ears and rope tail, 1940s, 12" l **140.00**

Unknown Mfg, Police Motorcycle, friction, litho tin, helmeted and goggled policeman riding motorcycle, mkd on each with "J.F.," luggage rack in rear, simulated front headlight, 1950s, 8" l **225.00**

Unknown Mfg, Superior Service Station, litho tin station with plastic accessories and "Cola Drinking Station," car wash, and 2 passenger cars, 1950s, 24" l, 18" d, 10" h **365.00**

Usagai, Japan, Fiat Convertible, friction, litho tin, black rubber tires, litho tin rear spare, orig box, 6¼" l **185.00**

Usagai, Japan, Fiat Sedan, friction, litho tin, black rubber tires, litho tin rear spare, orig box, 6¼" l **185.00**

West Germany, Motorcycle Cop & Car, windup, litho tin, 4" l cycle attached to 5½" l passenger car by rod, cycle moves around car as if trying to pull it over, orig box **625.00**

West Germany, Shunting Train, windup, litho tin, 3 unit train navigates track on 3–part fold–out 42" l base, orig box, 1950s **210.00**

West Germany, Sky Rider #700, litho tin and celluloid, 2 airplanes with celluloid props circle above litho tin hangar, orig box, 4 x 4" planes, 8½" h **165.00**

Wolverine, Action Ski Jumper #32A, litho tin, 26" l sloped track mkd "Sun Valley Ski Jumper," litho card-

Wolverine, car and trailer, friction, litho tin, red, white, and blue, wooden wheels, 14" l car, 14⅛" l trailer, $330.00. Photo courtesy Collectors Auction Services.

board 4½" h diecut jumper rolls down track, spring lever at end propels jumper into air as he somersaults over litho tin obstacle and lands on his feet, orig box, 1930s 500.00

Wyandotte, Easter Bunny Delivery, litho tin, bunny wearing helmet riding motorcycle with sidecar, 9" l 300.00

Wyandotte, Nationwide Air Rail Service Truck, litho tin, black rubber tires, 12" l 125.00

Wyandotte, Nationwide Air Rail Service Truck, litho tin, black rubber tires, 12" l 200.00

Wyandotte, Rocket Ship, pressed steel, white rubber tires, 1930s, 6½" l 110.00

Y, Japan, Circus Jeep, friction, litho tin, figural clown driver, orig box, 6" l 315.00

Yone, Japan, Copter on Parade, windup, litho tin and plastic, 3 helicopters attached by rod, advance with spinning plastic props and litho tin saucer umbrella tops, orig box, 7" l 240.00

Yonezawa, Japan, Trolley Bus, windup, litho tin, trolley scoots around 2 litho structures using metal track as guide, orig box, 1950s, 4" l trolley 650.00

TOY SOLDIERS

Toy soldier is a generic term. The category includes animal, civilian, holiday, and western figures in addition to military figures. Military figures are preferred.

The earliest toy soldiers were two–dimensional paper soldiers, often printed in sheets that were cut apart for play. Hilperts of Nuremberg, Germany, introduced the first three–dimensional toy soldiers near the end of the 18th century.

Britains and Mignot are the leading manufacturers of 20th–century toy soldiers. Mignot offered models of more than 20,000 different soldiers in the 1950s. Britains introduced its first hollow–cast figures in 1893. Many figures had movable arms. Britains quality is the standard by which collectors judge all other mass–produced figures.

The American dime store soldier arrived on the scene in the 1930s and remained popular through the early 1950s. Barclay and Manoil dominated the market primarily because of their realistic castings and originality of poses. Pre–1941 Barclay soldiers have helmets that are glued or clipped on.

Recently adult collectors have been speculating heavily in limited production toy soldiers made by a small group of toy soldier craftsman. Others are buying unpainted castings and painting them. The result is an increased variety of material on the market. Make certain you know exactly what you are buying.

Toy soldier collectors place a premium of 20% to 40% on set boxes. Beware of repainted pieces. Undocumented touch–up is a major problem in the market.

References: Norman Joplin, *The Great Book of Hollow–Cast Figures*, New Cavendish Books, 1992; Norman Joplin, *Toy Soldiers*, Running Press, Courage Books, 1994; Henry I. Kurtz and Burtt R. Ehrlich, *The Art of the Toy Soldier*, Abbeville Press, 1987; Richard O'Brien, *Collecting American–Made Toy Soldiers: Identification and Value Guide, No. 3*, Books Americana, Krause Publications, 1997; Richard O'Brien, *Collecting Foreign–Made Toy Soldiers: Identification and Value Guide*, Krause Publications, 1997; James Opie, *Collecting Toy Soldiers*, Pincushion Press, 1992; James Opie, *The Great Book of Britains*, New Cavendish, 1993; Edward Ryan, *Paper Soldiers: The Illustrated History of Printed Paper Armies of the 18th, 19th & 20th Centuries*, Golden Age Editions, 1995, distributed by P.E.I. International; Joe Wallis, *Armies of the World, Britains Ltd. Lead Soldiers 1925–1941*, published by author, 1993.

Periodicals: *Military Trader*, PO Box 1050, Dubuque, IA 52004; *Plastic Warrior*, 815 North 12th St, Allentown, PA 18102; *Toy Soldier Review*, 127 74th St, North Bergen, NJ 07047.

Collectors' Clubs: American Model Soldier Society, 1528 El Camino Real, San Carlos, CA 94070; Miniature Figure Collectors of America, 102 St. Paul's Rd, Ardmore, PA 19003; Toy Soldier Collectors of America, 5340 40th Ave N, St Petersburg, FL 33710.

All–Nu Paper Soldiers, flag bearer, WWI helmet, c1942, 5" h $5.00

All–Nu Paper Soldiers, General MacArthur, c1942, 5" h 8.00

All–Nu Paper Soldiers, ski trooper, c1942, 5" h. 6.00

All–Nu Paper Soldiers, soldier throwing grenade, WWI helmet, c1942, 5" h. 3.00

Auburn Rubber, #202, bugler, US Infantry 19.00

Auburn Rubber, #208, wounded soldier 39.00

Auburn Rubber, #214, Foreign Legion Private 24.00

Auburn Rubber, #222, sniper, crawling 50.00

Auburn Rubber, #236, signalman 60.00

Auburn Rubber, #238, charging soldier with tommy gun 17.00

Auburn Rubber, #240, motorcycle soldier with sidecar 50.00

Auburn Rubber, firing soldier 44.00

Auburn Rubber, tank defender 48.00

Barclay, #701, flagbearer, pre–WWII 26.00

Barclay, #702, machine gunner, kneeling, pre–WWII 16.00

Barclay, #704, soldier on parade, short stride, pre–WWII 19.00

Barclay, #705, soldier at attention, pre–WWII 22.00

Barclay, #706, charging soldier, pre–World War II. 25.00

Barclay, #708, officer with sword, pre–WWII 24.00

Barclay, #709, bugler, long stride, tin helmet, pre–World War II 21.00

Barclay, #711, drum major, short stride, pre–World War II 25.00

Barclay, #718, West Point Cadet, with rifle, pre–WWII 20.00

Barclay, #719, sailor, white uniform, long stride, post–1934 .... 23.00

Barclay, #721, naval officer, short stride, pre–World War II 24.00

Barclay, #723, marine officer, blue, pre–WWII 32.00

Barclay, #727, Italian officer, c1935–36 .... 150.00

Barclay, #728, machine gunner, lying flat, cast helmet, pre–WWII 20.00

Barclay, #746, army doctor, pre–World War II 23.00

Barclay, #757, sailor, with signal flags, pre–WWII 26.00

Barclay, #2003, Paint Your Own Army Set, orig box, c1934 .... 240.00

Britains, Argentine Cavalry #217, orig box, c1947, $225.00.

Barclay, sniper, kneeling, firing, short stride, pre–WWII **21.00**

Blenheim, #B17, Royal Marines, marching at the slope, officer, sword at carrry, orig box, 1923 . . . . **75.00**

Blenheim, #B63, Royal Company of Archers Colors, 2 color bearers, escort of 4 privates, orig box **90.00**

Blenheim, US Naval Academy, Color Guard, 4 standard bearers, escort of 2 midshipmen, orig box **100.00**

Britains, #33, 16th/5th Lancers, mounted at the half in review order with officer turned in the saddle, orig box **170.00**

Britains, #117, Egyptain Infantry, at attention in review order, orig Whisstock box, c1935 . . . . **180.00**

Britains, #122, The Black Watch, standing firing in tropical service dress with officer holding binoculars, orig Whisstock box, c1940 . . . . **300.00**

Britains, #167, Turkish Infantry, standing on guard in review order, orig Whisstock box, c1935 . . . . **130.00**

Britain, #1632, The Royal Canadian Regiment, marching at the slope with officer, orig "Soldiers of the British Empire" box, c1940 . . . . **1,100.00**

Britains, #1835, Argentine Naval Cadets, marching at the slope in review order with officer, orig box, 1948–49 . . . . **1,800.00**

Built–Rite, #14, Front Line Trench and Soldier Set, trench and 6 WWII soldiers **60.00**

Built–Rite, #20, Army Battery Set **145.00**

Built–Rite, #25, Fort and Soldier Set, WWII soldiers, 2 sandbag foxholes and fiberboard pistol **175.00**

Built–Rite, #60, Navy Battle Fleet and Coast Artilley Gun **75.00**

Built–Rite, #201, 26–pc Guardsman Set, 2 trenches, artillery base, cannon, pistol, and WWII soldiers **120.00**

Crescent, #11, infantry prone with bren gun, WWII **6.00**

Crescent, #19, US Marine **7.00**

Crescent, #68, Senegalese marching at slope **15.00**

Crescent, #74, mounted lancer charging **12.00**

Crescent, #103, RAF infantry **10.00**

Elastolin, #8838, Norman swinging dword down **12.00**

Elastolin, #9172, Union drummer boy **10.00**

Elastolin, #9185, Confederate officer mounted **20.00**

Elastolin, #9800, Howitzer **35.00**

Elastolin/Lineol, kneeling nurse attending wounded, holds foot of soldier sitting on keg **40.00**

Grey Iron, #2, cadet **28.00**

Grey Iron, #4/6, US Doughboy with bayonet **26.00**

Grey Iron, #6AF, Foreign Legion Officer **38.00**

Grey Iron, #8MA, US Cavalry Officer **40.00**

Grey Iron, #14, US Sailor, in blue **19.00**

Grey Iron, #14AW, US Naval Officer, in white **20.00**

Grey Iron, #23, Red Cross Nurse **20.00**

Grey Iron, Greyklip Armies, Set 5/Aviator Corps, pilot and plane, detachable wings, price for set **142.00**

Grey Iron, Greyklip Armies, Set 2/Company B, marching, bugler, officer, flagbearer, drummer, and rifleman, price for each **4.50**

Grey Iron, Uncle Sam's Defenders, charging rifleman, machine gunner, charging officer, rifleman at attention, flagbearer, and officer saluting, price for each **6.00**

Heyde, French Ambulance Unit, horse–drawn ambulance, 2–horse team, rider with whip, stretcher bearers, stretchers and casualties, mounted and foot medical officers, and medical orderly, orig box **275.00**

Heyde, Hessian Infantry, marching at the slope, officers, standard bearer, 4 mounted dragoons, movable reins on horses **375.00**

Manoil, #7, flag bearer, pre–WWII **26.00**

Manoil, #7, flag bearer, pre–WWII **26.00**

Manoil, #10, bugler, hollow base, pre–WWII **80.00**

Manoil, #12, machine gunner, flat base, pre–WWII **28.00**

Manoil, #14, sailor, hollow base, pre–WWII **55.00**

Manoil, #16, Ensign, pre–WWII **24.00**

Manoil, #23, machine gunner, sitting, pre–WWII **26.00**

Manoil, #27, tommy gunner, bloated version, pre–WWII **42.00**

Manoil, #29, wounded soldier, walking, pre–WWII **25.00**

Manoil, #31, bomb thrower, 3 grenades in pouch, pre–WWII **28.00**

Manoil, #42, crawling field doctor, pre–WWII **60.00**

Manoil, #45/9, combat, post–WWII **29.00**

Manoil, #45/12, sniper, post–WWII **38.00**

Manoil, #45/14, soldier with shell for bazooka, post–WWII **35.00**

Manoil, #46, anti–aircraft gunner, pre–WWII **23.00**

Manoil, #48, Navy gunner, pre–WWII **27.00**

Manoil, #53, sitting soldier without gun, pre–WWII **40.00**

Manoil, #58, parachute jumper, pre–WWII **30.00**

Manoil, #525, aviator holding bomb, post–WWII **34.00**

Manoil, #527, aircraft spotter, post–WWII **38.00**

Manoil, flag bearer, post–WWII **29.00**

Manoil, prone machine gunner, post–WWII **53.00**

Manoil, tommy gunner, post–WWII **32.00**

Marx, Mickey Mouse Soldier Set, 1930s **175.00**

McLoughlin, Playtime Soldiers on Parade, 175 pcs, 1937 . . . . **95.00**

Mignot, Ancient Greek Cavalry, mounted with swords, spears, and shields, orig box **250.00**

Mignot, Austrian Cavalry, mounted in review order, with officer, trumpeter, and standard bearer, orig box **200.00**

Mignot, Drum Majors of the Empire, drum majors of French Napoleonic regiments including Orphans of the Guard, Marines of the Guard, St Cyr Academy, and various line infantry regiments, special limited edition, orig boxes **475.00**

Mignot, French Musketeers Period of King Louis XIII, marching with muskets at shoulder arms, with officer and standard bearer, orig box, c1960 . . . . **275.00**

Mignot, French Napoleonic Horse Artillery Escort, mounted with sabers, with trumpeter and officer carrying standard, c1950 . . . . **467.00**

Mignot, French Navy Sailors, marching at the slope in summer white uniforms, with officer, bugler, and standard bearer, orig box, c1950 . . . . **522.00**

Mignot, French Volunteer Infantry, marching at the slope in blue and white uniforms, bicorne hats and tricolor pants, orig box, c1950 . . . . **220.00**

Crescent, #91, infantry throwing grenade, WWII, $6.00.

Mignot, Russian Imperial Guard, mounted in review order with sabers, trumpeter and officer carrying standard, c1950 . . . . **410.00**

Milton Bradley, #4518, Soldiers Five with Pistol, 1920s. **80.00**

Nostalgia, 1st Gurkha Light Infantry, 1800, red and blue uniforms, marching with slung rifles, officer with sword at the carry, orig box **80.00**

Nostalgia, New South Wales Lancers, 1900, marching carrying lances on the shoulder, khaki uniforms, trimmed in red and plumed campaign hats, officer holding swager stick, orig box **85.00**

J Pressman and Co, NY, #1551, Soldier Set, set of 5, 4½" cardboard soldiers, marbles, c1940 . . . . **40.00**

SAE, #1761, French Cuirassiers, mounted at the walk, orig box **50.00**

Whitman, #999, 100 Soldiers Punch–Out Book, 1943 . . . . . . **55.00**

TOY TRAIN ACCESSORIES

Toy train accessories and boxed train sets are two of the hottest toy train collecting categories in the 1990s. Toy train accessories divide into two main groups: (1) those made by toy train manufacturers and (2) those made by others. Many of the latter were in kit form.

As with toy trains, toy train accessories are sized by gauge. An HO building on a Lionel train platform appears very much out of place. O and S gauge accessories are the most desired. The period box adds 15% to 25% to the value.

Bachmann Brothers, a manufacturer of eyeglasses, produced its first plastic train accessory, a picket fence, in 1949. A log cabin followed in 1950. By the mid–1950s Bachmann's Plasticville O/S gauge buildings were found on the vast majority of America's toy train platforms. An HO line was introduced in 1955, an N gauge line in 1968. Plasticville houses are marked with a "BB" on a banner in a circle.

Bachmann ended a challenge to its market supremacy by Unlimited Plastics' Littletown when it acquired the company in 1956. Bachmann carefully stores its Plasticville dies, giving it the ability to put any model back into production when sufficient demand occurs.

References: Frank C. Hare, *Plasticville, 3rd Edition*, Kalmbach Publishing, 1993; Alan Stewart, *Greenberg's Guide to Lionel Trains, 1945–1969, Vol VI: Accessories*, Kalmbach Publishing, 1994.

Accessory Set, Ives, 4 telegraph poles, 1 clock, 1 crossing sign, 1 semaphore, orig box, 1932 . . . . **$80.00**
Airport Hangar, Plasticville **35.00**
Autumn Trees, Plasticville **50.00**
Barn, Plasticville **25.00**
Barnyard Animal Set, 18 pcs, Plasticville **45.00**
Bell Danger Signal, American Flyer, S gauge, #584, 1946–47 . . . . **17.50**
Billboard, American Flyer, S gauge, #566, whistling, 1951–55 . . . . **18.00**
Billboard, Lionel, O gauge, 310 . . . . **4.00**
Billboard, Plasticville **2.50**
Brakeman with lantern, American Flyer, S gauge **125.00**
Bridge Approach Signal, Ives, O gauge, diecast base, painted round post with arm and chairs, 1931–32 . . . . **90.00**
Bridge, Dorfan, O gauge, #410 . . . . **170.00**
Bridge, Ives, arch base, 2 sections, 21" l **275.00**
Bridge, Ives, O gauge, #91 . . . . **20.00**
Bridge, trestle, American Flyer, S gauge, 750 . . . . **12.50**
Bungalow, Plasticville **20.00**
Catalog, Lionel Trains, Lionel Corporation, New York, NY, color illus, 1937, 48 pp **85.00**
Cathedral, Plasticville **65.00**
Cattle Loading Pen, Plasticville **15.00**
Church, American Flyer, S gauge, illuminated, 1953 . . . . . . **400.00**
Circuit Breaker, Lionel, illuminated, 1931–32 . . . . **60.00**
Clock, Ives, sq post, diamond shaped face, movable hands, 1932 . . . . **8.00**
Coal Loader, Lionel, O gauge, scoop and drawer, shoot action **150.00**
Colonial Church, Plasticville **30.00**
Control Tower, Unique, 2 story, litho tin, 3 x 2 x 4" **15.00**
Country Church, Plasticville **30.00**
Crossing Gate, American Flyer, S gauge **3.00**
Crossing Gate, Ives, litho, painted base, 1932 . . . . **16.00**
Crossing Gate, Marx, plastic . . . . **.15**
Crossing Sign, Ives, 1931–32 . . . . **8.00**
Crossing Warning Bell, Marx **10.00**
Curved Track, Buddy L, dark green, 1 section **20.00**
Diner Kit, Plasticville **55.00**
Eureka Diner, American Flyer, S gauge, #275, 1952–53 . . . . **220.00**
Fire House Kit, Plasticville **20.00**
Floodlight Tower, Marx, stamped steel, 2 bulbs, red, black or silver **15.00**
Freight Shed, Lionel, terra–cotta roof, maroon base, green piers, illuminated, 1931–32 . . . . **360.00**
Freight Station, Plasticville **38.00**
Frosty Bar, Plasticville **40.00**
Greenhouse, Plasticville **62.00**
Imitation Grass, American Flyer, 1949–56, full bag, 1/2 lb . . . **23.00**
Lamp Post, Marx, plastic, 6" . . . . **.15**
Lamp Post, Marx, stamped steel **10.00**
Lamp Post Set, Marx, lighted, Boulevard **9.00**
Lighting Set, Lionel, O gauge, #27 . . . . **18.00**
Log Cabin, rustic fence and tree, Plasticville **25.00**
Log Loader, Lionel, O gauge, crane and hook **90.00**
Manual, Lionel Trains, extra sheets, 1949, 56 pp **15.00**
Mobile Home, Plasticville **50.00**
Motel, Plasticville **20.00**

Outhouse, Plasticville **12.00**
Passenger Station, Ives, 113 . . . . **200.00**
Railroad Accessories, Plasticville **40.00**
Railroad Signal Bridge, Plasticville **11.00**
Railroad Signs, set of 8, American Flyer, white **160.00**
Railroad Switch Tower, Plasticville **15.00**
Railroad Water Tank, Plasticville **10.00**
Railroad Work Car, Plasticville **50.00**
Railway Figure Set, American Flyer, S gauge, 25 pcs,
   1953 . . . . **325.00**
Road Signs, Plasticville **45.00**
Roadside Stand, Plasticville . . . . . . : **20.00**
Semaphone, Ives, double arm, 107D **80.00**
Semaphore, Marx, plastic . . . . **.15**
Signal Set, Marx, plastic, 3 pcs **3.00**
Smoke Cartridge, American Flyer, S gauge, 25 . . . . **3.00**
Station Platform, American Flyer, S gauge, non–illumi-
   nated, 1953 . . . . **300.00**
Street Accessories, 15 pcs, Plasticville **45.00**
Supermarket, large, Plasticville **35.00**
Telegraph Post, Ives, red and white, 1932 . . . . **6.00**
Telephone Booth, Plasticville **10.00**
Telephone Pole, Marx, plastic, 7" . . . . **.15**
Town Hall, American Flyer, S gauge, illuminated, 1953 . . . . . **320.00**
Transformer, American Flyer, S gauge, 250 watt,
   1946–52 . . . . **135.00**
Truss Bridge, American Flyer, S gauge, #571, 1955–56 . . . . . . **5.00**
Tunnel, American Flyer, S gauge, orig box, 11½" l **17.00**
Tunnel, Ives, mountain style, 11" l **120.00**
Tunnel, Ives, O gauge, papier–mâché, 16" l **30.00**
Twin Crossing Gate, Marx, 6" . . . . **.15**
Well, Plasticville **10.00**
Whistle Stop Set, American Flyer, S gauge, 1952–53 . . . . . . **200.00**

TOY TRAINS

The mid–1920s through the late 1950s is the golden age of toy trains. American Flyer, Ives, and Lionel produced electric model trains that featured highly detailed castings and markings. A slow conversion to plastic occurred within the industry in the late 1950s and early 1960s. Most collectors shun plastic like the plague.

Trains are collected first by company and second by gauge. Lionel is king of the hill, followed by American Flyer. As a result, O, O27, and S are the three most popular gauges among collectors. Collector interest in HO gauge trains has increased significantly in the past five years. Many toy train auctions now include HO trains among their offerings. Interest is minimal in N gauge.

The 1990s witnessed several major shifts in collecting emphasis. First, post–World War II replaced pre–World War II trains as the hot chronological collecting period. Pre–1945 prices have stabilized. In the case of cast–iron trains, some decline has been noted. Second, accessories and sets are the hot post–1945 collecting areas. Prices on most engines and rolling stock have stabilized.

Third, the speculative bubble in mass–produced trains of the 1970s and 1980s has burst. With some exceptions, most of these trains are selling below their initial retail cost on the secondary market. Fourth, adult collectors currently are investing heavily in limited edition reproductions and special model issues. These pieces have not been strongly tested on the secondary market. Fifth, there are initial signs of a growing collector interest in HO material, primarily the better grade German trains, and inexpensive lithographed tin windup trains.

References: General: *Greenberg's Pocket Price Guide, Lionel Trains, 1901–1998*, Kalmbach Publishing, 1997; *Greenberg's Pocket Price Guide: Marx Trains, 6th Edition*, Kalmbach Publishing, 1996; *Greenberg's Pocket Price Guide, American Flyer S Gauge, 14th Edition*, Kalmbach Publishing, 1997; Richard O'Brien, *Collecting Toy Trains: Identification and Value Guide, No. 4*, Krause Publishing, 1997; Bob Roth, *Greenberg's Pocket Price Guide, LGB, 1968–1996, Third Edition*, Kalmbach Publishing, 1996.

American Flyer: Greenberg Books, three–volume set.

Lionel: Greenberg Books, four volumes dealing with Lionel trains made between 1901 and 1942, seven volumes covering the 1945 to 1969 period, and two volumes for the 1970 to 1991 period. Also check Lionel Book Committee, Train Collectors Association, *Lionel Trains: Standard of the World, 1900–1943, Second Edition*, Train Collectors Association, 1989.

Miscellaneous: Greenberg Books has one or more price guides for Athearn, Kusan, Ives, Marx, and Varney.

Note: For a complete list of toy train titles from Greenberg Books, a division of Kalmbach Publishing Co., write PO Box 1612, Waukesha, WI 53187, and request a copy of their latest catalog. If you are a serious collector, ask to be put on their mailing list.

Periodicals: *Classic Toy Trains*, PO Box 1612, Waukesha, WI 53187; *LGB Telegram*, 1573 Landvater, Hummelstown, PA 17036; *Lionel Collector Series Marketmaker*, Trainmaster, 3224 NW 47th Terrace, Gainesville, FL 32606.

Collectors' Clubs: American Flyer Collectors Club, PO Box 13269, Pittsburgh, PA 15234; LGB Model Railroad Club, 1854 Erin Dr, Altoona, PA 16602; Lionel Collectors Club of America, PO Box 479, LaSalle, IL 61301; Marklin Club—North America, PO Box 51559, New Berlin, WI 53151; The National Model Railroad Assoc, 4121 Cromwell Rd, Chattanooga, TN 37421; Toy Train Operating Society, 25 W Walnut St, Ste 308, Pasadena, CA 91103; Train Collectors Assoc, PO Box 248, Strasburg, PA 17579.

Ajin, HO scale, locomotive, #1, New Haven 4–6–4
   Hudson, painted black and silver, with tender, Korean,
   1986, 9" l **$920.00**

Top: Tenshodo, HO scale, locomotive and tender, Great Northern 4–8–4 Class S–1 Northern #2553, factory painted "Glacier Park," with box, Japanese Crown, 1960, 15" l, $1,725.00.
Bottom: Ajin, HO scale, engine #0753, New Haven DL–109, Korean, 1982, 10½" l, $400.00. Photos courtesy Sothebys.

Ajin, HO scale, locomotive, #4503, Frisco 4–8–4, painted black with meatball emblem, with box and tender, Korean, 1976, 9" l **635.00**

American Flyer, S gauge, boxcar, #623, Illinois Central, 1953 . . . . **10.00**

American Flyer, S gauge, caboose, #24526, 1957 . . . . **12.00**

American Flyer, S gauge, engine, #405, Silver Streak, Alco Pa, 1952 . . . . **80.00**

American Flyer, S gauge, engine, #499, New Haven, GE Electric, 1956–57 . . . . **150.00**

American Flyer, S gauge, engine, #21234, Chesapeake and Ohio, GP–7, 1961–62 . . . . **110.00**

American Flyer, S gauge, engine, #21551, Northern Pacific, Alco Pa, 1958 . . . . **100.00**

American Flyer, S gauge, engine, #21918/21918–2, Seaboard, Baldwin, 1958 . . . . **175.00**

American Flyer, S gauge, hopper, #921, CB&O, 1953–57 . . . . **30.00**

American Flyer, S gauge, hopper and dump car, #719, CB&Q, 1950–54 . . . . **30.00**

American Flyer, S gauge, operating baggage car, #732, unpainted red plastic shell, 1951–54 . . . . **18.00**

American Flyer, S gauge, passenger car, #662, Vista Dome, 1950–52 . . . . **24.00**

American Flyer, S gauge, steam locomotive, #320, Hudson, 4–6–4, 1946–47 . . . . **60.00**

American Flyer, S gauge, steam locomotive, #345, Pacific, 4–6–2, 1954 . . . . **50.00**

American Flyer, S gauge, steam locomotive, #958, Mobilgas, 1957 . . . . **10.00**

American Flyer, S gauge, steam locomotive, #21130, 62–63, 1959–60 . . . . **110.00**

American Flyer, S gauge, tank car, #24313, Gulf, 1957–60 . . . . **20.00**

American Flyer, S gauge, tank car, #24330, Baker's Chocolate, 1961–72 . . . . **25.00**

Atlas, steam locomotive, #6415, Milwaukee Road 4–6–4 Baltic, painted black and red, with box and tender, Japanese, 1979, 9" l **632.00**

Auburn Rubber, train set, #525, vinyl, loco–tender, coal car, gondola, caboose, and 3 trainmen **80.00**

Auburn Rubber, Western Train Set, #922, vinyl, 8" l locomotive, tender, passenger car, 1950s **50.00**

Buddy L, boxcar, red, 1921–31 . . . . **1,000.00**

Buddy L, gondola, black, 1921–31 . . . . **1,000.00**

Buddy L, hopper, black, 1928–31 . . . . **1,500.00**

Buddy L, locomotive and tender, black, 1921–31 . . . . **2,200.00**

Buddy L, stockcar, red, 1921–31 . . . . **750.00**

Dorfan, narrow gauge, caboose, #607 . . . . **90.00**

Dorfan, narrow gauge, gondola, #600 . . . . **65.00**

Dorfan, O gauge, baggage car, #120, green, maroon, brass trim **120.00**

Dorfan, O gauge, boxcar, orange, brown **54.00**

Dorfan, O gauge, coach, Boston, red, brass trim **180.00**

Dorfan, O gauge, engine, #51, 0–4–0 . . . . **120.00**

Dorfan, O gauge, engine, 0–4–0, red **360.00**

Dorfan, O gauge, tender, #160 . . . . **70.00**

Dorfan, wide gauge, engine, 0–4–0, red **1,080.00**

Fujiyama, HO scale, locomotive, #844, Union Pacific 4–8–4 Class FEF 2 Northern, painted 2–tone gray and silver, with tender and box, Japanese Crown, 1967, 16" l **2,185.00**

Ives, O gauge, baggage car, #50 . . . . **75.00**

Ives, O gauge, caboose, #70 . . . . **4.00**

Ives, O gauge, chair car, #551 . . . . **110.00**

Ives, O gauge, gondola, #1677 . . . . **50.00**

Ives, O gauge, gravel car, #563 . . . . **70.00**

Ives, O gauge, locomotive and tender, #1100, 0–4–0 . . . . **190.00**

Ives, O gauge, lumber car, #559 . . . . **40.00**

Ives, O gauge, parlor car, #552 . . . . **110.00**

Ives, O gauge, pullman, #1504 . . . . **90.00**

Ives, O gauge, steam locomotive, #258, 2–4–0 . . . . **255.00**

Ives, O gauge, stock car, #65 . . . . **35.00**

Ives, standard gauge, observation, #186 . . . . **65.00**

Ives, standard gauge, pullman, #339 . . . . **95.00**

Ives, standard gauge, steam locomotive, #10, electric **260.00**

Ives, standard gauge, steam locomotive, #1760, 4–4–2 . . . . **700.00**

Ives, standard gauge, tank car, #1775 . . . . **65.00**

Katsumi, HO scale, locomotive, #7029, Union Pacific 4–8–2 Mountain, painted greyhound and yellow, with tender, Japanese, 1977, 28" l **550.00**

Lionel, O gauge, baggage car, #1813 . . . . **18.00**

Lionel, O gauge, boxcar, #2954, 1940–42 . . . . **145.00**

Lionel, O gauge, boxcar, #3366, circus car, 1959–62 . . . . . **65.00**

Lionel, O gauge, boxcar, #6464–735, New Haven, 1969 . . . . **15.00**

Lionel, O gauge, caboose, #1007, Lionel Lines, SP Die 3, 1948–52 . . . . **1.50**

Lionel, O gauge, caboose, #0017, NYC, 1939–42 . . . . **50.00**

Lionel, O gauge, caboose, #6119–50, DL&W, brown and white, 1957–59 . . . . **20.00**

Lionel, O gauge, caboose, #6417–50, Lehigh Valley, N5C, gray, 1954 . . . . **32.00**

Lionel, O gauge, coach, #637, 1936–39 . . . . **55.00**

Lionel, O gauge, engine, #60, Lionelville, trolley type, aluminized paper reflector, 1955–58 . . . . **175.00**

Lionel, O gauge, engine, #153, electric, 0–4–0 . . . . **50.00**

Lionel, O gauge, engine, #204, Santa Fe, Alco AA units, 1957 . . . . **60.00**

Lionel, O gauge, engine, #212, US Marine Corps, Alco A, 1958–59 . . . . **48.00**

Lionel, O gauge, engine, #1700E, Erie, Alco AA units, 1952–54 . . . . **115.00**

Lionel, O gauge, engine, #3927, Lionel Lines, 1956–60 . . . . **60.00**

Lionel, O gauge, flatcar, #1887, fence and horses, 1959 . . . . **120.00**

Lionel, O gauge, gondola, #2452, Pennsylvania, 1945 . . . . . . **4.50**

Lionel, O gauge, gondola, #2812, 1938–42 . . . . **30.00**

Lionel, O gauge, gondola, #3444, Eric, 1957–59 . . . . **30.00**

Lionel, O gauge, gondola, #4452, Pennsylvania, 1946–48 . . . . **48.00**

Lionel, O gauge, handcar, #1100, Mickey Mouse, 1935–37 . . . . **600.00**

Lionel, O gauge, hopper and dump car, #816, 1927–42 . . . . **55.00**

Lionel, O gauge, hopper and dump car, #0016, South Pacific, 1938–42 . . . . **60.00**

Lionel, O gauge, hopper and dump car, #3456, N&W, 1951–55 . . . . **20.00**

Lionel, O gauge, log dump, #3364, 1960s **20.00**

Lionel, O gauge, Mercury Project, #6413, 1962–63 . . . . **18.00**

Lionel, O gauge, observation, #530, 1926–32 . . . . **16.00**

Lionel, O gauge, observation, #604, 1920–25 . . . . **20.00**

Lionel, O gauge, observation, #2631, 1938–42 . . . . **25.00**

Lionel, O gauge, Operating Radar Car, #3540, 1959–60 . . . . **60.00**

Lionel, O gauge, pullman, #600, 1933–42 . . . . **75.00**

Lionel, O gauge, pullman, #605, 1925–32 . . . . **65.00**

Lionel, O gauge, satellite car, #3519, 1961–64 . . . . **18.00**

Lionel, O gauge, steam locomotive, #203, 0–6–0, 1940–42 . . . . **325.00**

Lionel, O gauge, steam locomotive, #665, 4–6–4, 1954–59 . . . . **75.00**

Ives, The Ives Railway Lines #691, motor #3235, orig box, $400.00.

Lionel, O gauge, steam locomotive, #1062, 1963–64 . . . . **18.00**
Lionel, O gauge, tank car, #0045, Shell, 1939–42 . . . . **50.00**
Lionel, O gauge, tank car, #1515, 1933–37 . . . . **25.00**
Lionel, O gauge, tank car, #2555, Sunoco, 1946–48 . . . . **30.00**
Lionel, O gauge, tank car, Gulf, #6065, 1956–57 . . . . **8.00**
Lionel, O gauge, tank car, #6365, Lionel Lines, 1958–59 . . . . . **5.00**
Lionel, O gauge, tank car, #6463, rocket fuel, 1962–63 . . . . . **12.00**
Lionel, O gauge, tank car, #6465, Lionel Lines, 1958–59 . . . . . **5.00**
Lionel, O gauge, timber car, #6361, 1960s **20.00**
Lionel, O gauge, transformer car, #2461, 1947–48 . . . . **20.00**
Lionel, O gauge, United States Mail, #3428, 1959 . . . . **25.00**
Marx, baggage car, tin, St Paul & Pacific, 7" l **30.00**
Marx, caboose, plastic, brown and white "45" **15.00**
Marx, coach, tin, The Joy Line Coach, green body, yel-
    low round roof, blue frame **150.00**
Marx, gondola, tin, Joy Line, Venice Gondola, blue body
    and frame **80.00**
Marx, hopper, plastic HO, red and white "Huron
    Portland Cement" **6.00**
Marx, locomotive, diesel, plastic, black and white "Rock
    Island," powered "A" unit **50.00**
Marx, locomotive, diesel, plastic, orange and black
    "Allstate," 8–wheel powered "A" unit **80.00**
Marx, locomotive, 0–4–0, black and orange "NH" **9.00**
Marx, Old Time Western Set, plastic, Marlines, battery
    operated, 0–27 2–rail track, black locomotive and ten-
    der, yellow gondola, and red caboose **100.00**
Marx, steam locomotive, litho tin, Sumar Lines, 1–pc
    engine and tender **60.00**
Marx, tank car, plastic, white and red "Rocket Fuel" **15.00**
Micro Cast, HO scale, locomotive, #92, Great Northern
    0–6–0 Switcher, custom painted "Glacier Park," with
    tender and box, Korean, 1969, 8" l **747.00**
Revell/Rapido, N gauge, hopper, Boston & Maine, #2543 . . . . **10.00**
Revell/Rapido, N gauge, tank car, Sinclair, #0484R **8.00**
Revell/Rapido, N gauge, steam locomotive, Baltimore
    and Ohio, yellow lettering **75.00**
Samhongsa, HO scale, steam locomotive, #710, Texas
    and Pacific 4–6–2, painted blue, black, and silver,
    with box and tender, Korean, 1990, 9" l **920.00**
Samhongsa, HO scale, steam locomotive, #3009, New
    Haven 2–8–2, black and silver finish, with box and
    tender, Korean, 1979, 6½" l **460.00**

Samhongsa, HO scale, steam locomotive, #3314, New
    Haven 4–8–2, black and silver finish, Korean, orig
    box, 1983, 8" l **500.00**
Tenshodo, HO scale, locomotive, #821, Great Northern
    0–8–0, painted black and silver, with tender and box,
    Japanese, 1979, 6" l **632.00**
Toby, HO scale, locomotive, #1518, St Louis–San
    Francisco Railway 4–8–2 Class Mountain, painted
    blue, black, silver, gold, and oxide, with box,
    Japanese Crown, 1968, 13" l **1,725.00**
Tootsietoy, Akana Fast Freight, boxed set, 1929 . . . . **375.00**
Tootsietoy, baggage car, 1921 . . . . **30.00**
Tootsietoy, caboose, 1939 . . . . **22.00**
Tootsietoy, Freight Train, boxed set, 1933 . . . . **150.00**
Tootsietoy, gondola flatcar, 1921 . . . . **30.00**
Tootsietoy, Midnight Flyer, boxed set, 1931 . . . . **200.00**
Tootsietoy, Pennsylvania RR, Passenger Train, boxed set,
    1940 . . . . **275.00**
Tootsietoy, Southern Boxcar, 1939 . . . . **22.00**
Tootsietoy, tank car, Borden's Milk, 1939 . . . . **30.00**
Tootsietoy, Zephyr Railcar, 1935 . . . . **75.00**
Unique, boxcar, tin, Unique Lines and 3509 . . . . **20.00**
Unique, circus car, tin, Unique U Circus, 7½" l **120.00**
Unique, engine, tin, Unique Lines, with tender, 10" l **60.00**
Unique, passenger car, tin, Garden City **100.00**
United, HO scale, locomotive, #201, Denver and Salt
    Lake 2–6–6–0, painted black and white, with tender
    and box, Japanese, 1976, 7½" l **747.00**
Van Hobbies, HO scale, locomotive, #2860, Canadian
    Pacific 4–6–4 Hudson, painted maroon, silver and
    black, with tender, Korean, 1987, 9" l **1,495.00**
Van Hobbies, HO scale, locomotive, #2910, Canadian
    Pacific Railroad 4–4–4 Jubilee, painted maroon and
    gray, orig box, Japanese, 9" l **1,380.00**

TRANSPORTATION

America is a highly mobile society. America's expansion and growth is linked to its transportation system, whether road, canal, rail, or sky. Few communities have escaped the impact of one or more transportation systems. As a result, transportation memorabilia has a strong regional collecting base.

Further, collectors are fascinated with anything relating to transportation vehicles and systems. This is a catchall category for those transportation categories, e.g., bus, canal, and trolley, not found elsewhere in the book.

References: Barbara J. Conroy, *Restaurant China: Identification & Value Guide for Restaurant, Airline, Ship & Railroad Dinnerware, Vol. I,* Collector Books, 1998; Alex Roggero and Tony Beadle, *Greyhound: A Pictorial Tribute to an American Icon,* Motorbooks International, 1995.

Collectors' Clubs: Bus History Assoc, 965 McEwan, Windsor, Ontario N9B 2G1 Canada; Central Electric Railfans' Assoc, PO Box 503, Chicago, IL 60690; International Bus Collectors Club, 1518 "C" Trailee Dr, Charleston, SC 29407; National Assoc of Timetable Collectors, 125 American Inn Rd, Villa Ridge, MO 63089.

Note: For additional listings see Automobiles, Automobilia, Aviation Collectibles, Bicycles, Ocean Liner Collectibles, and Railroad Collectibles.

Badge, Canal Days, Manayunk, PA, May 17, 1980, blue ground, photo of canal passing under railroad bridge, 3¹/₈ x 2¹/₈" **$4.00**

Blotter, Southern Steamship Company, Philadelphia, PA, Christmas motif, coaching scene, 1922 calendar, 7³/₄ x 22". **18.00**

Bond, Arkansas Highway Bond, $10,000, State House vignette, green border, 1931 . . . . **12.00**

Bond, New York City Rapid Transit, $1,000, State House vignette, green border, 1931 . . . . **12.00**

Book, *Galley Guide, The: A Purely Humanitarian Work, Planned Out of Consideration For the Digestive Apparatus of Those Who Cruise–The Thing, After All, Upon Which Success or Failure Largely Depends*, Alex W Moffat, Motor Boat Publishing, NY, 1923, 145 pp. **22.00**

Book, *High–Water Cargo*, Doran, Edith M, New Brunswick, NJ, Rutgers University Press, illus by Forrest Orr, novel about life along the Delaware and Raritan Canal in the 1850s, hardcover, orig dj, 1950 and 1965, 224 pp. **20.00**

Book, *Motorbus Transportation*, 4–vol set, illus, 1930 . . . . . . **20.00**

Book, *Old Towpaths: The Story of the American Canal Era*, Harlow, Alvin F, D Appleton and Company, 1926, 401 pp **50.00**

Book, *Sandy and Beaver Canal, The*, Gard, Max R and William H Vodrey Jr, East Liverpool, OH, East Liverpool Historical Society, softcover, map insert, 210 pp, 1952 . . . . **40.00**

Booklet, *Boston*, published by Convention Bureau of the Chamber of Commerce, 64 pp, 7 x 10" **9.00**

Brochure, Cruising With Safety, sailboat and motorboat photos, glossy stiff cov, 3rd ed, 1947, 76 pp **10.50**

Calendar, Greyhound Lines, 1938, Greyhound bus passing foreground scene of touring interest, 20 x 32" **45.00**

Calendar, Rapid Transit, 1949, Moses King, photos **22.00**

Game, Around the World in 80 Days, Transogram, 1957 . . . **35.00**

Game, Blizzard of '77, CP Marino, cover shows bus and walking man in blizzard scene, 1977 . . . . **12.00**

Game, On the Buses, Denys Fisher, 1973 . . . . **25.00**

Hat Badge, Diamond Cab, silvered brass, inscribed serial number and title in black lettering, c1930s **45.00**

Operator's Badge, Penn Transit, silvered and enameled brass, c1930s **45.00**

Pin, The Greyhound Lines Star Driver, metal, bronze luster, inverted star, center inscription, stylized floral pattern on each star tip, orig presentation box, c1940s. **20.00**

Pinback Button, Pennsylvania Boatmen's Reunion, Rolling Green Park, Aug 1929, black and white photo of Pennsylvania Main Line canal boat crossing aqueduct, 1¹/₄" **20.00**

Poster, Trolleybus to Kingston, double–decker bus and cityscape image, Greg Brown, c1930, 20 x 20". **150.00**

Salt and Pepper Shakers, pr, Greyhound Lines, diecast metal, painted, silver, black, and white Greyhound bus replicas, black hard rubber wheels, mkd "Japan," c1950s **70.00**

Schedule, Travel by Motor Coach Richmond, Fredericksburg, Washington, blue and white, 1927 . . . . **8.50**

Sheet Music, *Travelin' Man*, Jerry Fuller, 1961. . . . . **5.50**

Stock Certificate, Boston Elevated Railway Co, 1929. . . . . . . **8.50**

Ticket, Chicago Rapid Transit Co, weekly pass, 1933 . . . . . . **2.00**

Ticket, Mt Vernon Transit, 1946 . . . . **4.00**

Ticket, Sturgeon Bay Transit, 1946 . . . . **5.00**

Ticket, Two Rivers Transit, 1946 . . . . **4.00**

Toy, Greyhound Bus, litho tin, friction, Greyhound name repeated 3 times with dog illus on each side, bus driver depiction on front window, mkd "Made in Japan," 1960s **45.00**

Toy, 1964–65 NYWF Greyhound Glide–A–Ride, tin, friction, 2 pcs, cab and passenger trailer shuttle bus, orig box. **95.00**

Trolley Sign, Ivory Soap, blue and red lettering, cream ground, framed, sgd "Dorothy Hope Smith," 12¹/₂ x 22¹/₂". **30.00**

Trolley Sign, Lifebuoy Health Soap, man using product illus, black and orange lettering, yellow ground, framed, 12¹/₂ x 22¹/₂" **15.00**

Trolley Sign, Sunkist Lemons, teapot, cup and saucer, and lemons, yellow, blue, green, orange, and red, framed, 12³/₄ x 22³/₄" **55.00**

Trolley Sign, Sunkist Oranges, red, orange, blue, white, and yellow, framed, 11³/₄ x 22" **95.00**

TROLLS

Trolls originated in Scandinavian folklore. In the late 1950s Helena and Martii Kuuskoski, a Finnish couple, began marketing cloth troll dolls. Thomas Dam, a Danish woodcarver, also started selling troll figurines. A troll craze developed. By the early 1960s, Dam–designed trolls were being produced in Denmark, New Zealand, and the United States (Hialeah, Florida).

Dozens of manufacturers, many failing to permanently mark their products, hopped aboard the troll bandwagon. Dam filed a copyright infringement suit against Scandia House Enterprises, a division of Royalty Designs of Florida. The court ruled that the troll image was in the public domain. Eventually Dam signed an agreement with Scandia House to distribute his designs in America. Troll collectors take a negative approach to cheap foreign troll imports from Hong Kong and Japan.

A second major troll craze occurred in the early 1990s. Thomas Dam trolls were distributed by EFS Marketing Associates during this period under the Norfin trademark. Ace Novelty, Applause Toys, Russ Berrie & Company, and Uneeda Doll Company also

Bus, cigarette lighter, porcelain enameled metal, Chevrolet School Bus, 1⁷/₈" h, 2¹/₈" w, $15.00. Photo courtesy Collectors Auction Services.

manufactured troll lines. China and Korea replaced Hong Kong and Japan as the source for inexpensive, often unmarked trolls.

References: Debra Clark, *Trolls: Identification & Price Guide*, Hobby House Press, 1993; Pat Peterson, *Collector's Guide to Trolls: Identification & Values*, Collector Books, 1995.

Newsletters: *Troll Monthly*, 216 Washington St, Canton, MA 02021; *Trollin'*, PO Box 601292, Sacramento, CA 95860.

Activity Book, Hobnobbins Paint with Water, Golden **$1.50**

Bank, girl wearing yellow raincoat, red hair, blue eyes, mkd "Made in Denmark Thomas Dam," 7" h **30.00**

Brochure, Dam Things, front shows orig sales brochure featuring Dam Things dolls, back lists prices and order information **15.00**

Cookie Cutter, aluminum, mail–in offer, 3½" h **20.00**

Doll, Dam, cheerleader, white hair, vinyl painted body, 2½" h **15.00**

Doll, Dam, donkey, seated, blonde mohair hair, amber eyes, 1964, 3" h **25.00**

Doll, Dam, horse, light gold mane and tail, amber eyes, 1964, 3" **35.00**

Doll, Dam, hula girl, plastic lei, fringe skirt, 6" h **10.00**

Doll, Dam, Indian, black hair, amber eyes, brown cotton garment with yellow zig–zag design, 3" h **12.00**

Doll, Dam, Playboy Bunny, yellow hair, blue eyes, felt costume, 5½" h **35.00**

Doll, Dam, tartan girl, black hair, red and green plaid shirt, matching hair ribbons, green skirt, 12" h **120.00**

Doll, L Khem, moon troll, maroon long braided hair and eyes, orange cheeks and eyebrows, 1964, 3" h **25.00**

Doll, Norwegian, A/S NyForm, girl with accordion, brown and gray hair, amber eyes, molded and paint- ed red and white clothing, 6" h **45.00**

Doll, Norwegian, Gleek, Stiky Vik, pale green vinyl body covered with dark green dyed rabbit fur, 3 toed feet, 3 fingered hands, round nose, 1 molded shield hand, other hand holding spiked ball, 3" h **5.00**

Doll, Norwegian, Ressler, tailed troll, red hair, blue eyes, glued rabbit fur costume, tail with tufted tip, 3½" h **35.00**

Doll, Norwegian, unmarked, red wooden body, painted eyes, plaid cap, white mohair beard, black felt feet, 2½" h **3.00**

Doll, Norwegian, Viking, wooden, carrying club–like weapon, metal helmet, legs wrapped with cord, 3" h **5.00**

Doll, Russ, Roman Soldier, red hair, brown eyes, tan and orange outfit, gold helmet and sword, 4" h **8.50**

Doll, Uneeda Wishnik, groom, white hair, gray eyes, orig outfit **25.00**

Doll, Uneeda Wishnik, Here Come the Judge, light orange hair, gold eyes, black gown with white letter- ing, 6" h **45.00**

Doll, Uneeda Wishnik, Laugh–In, Sock–It–To–Me cos- tume, white hair, red eyes, 6" h **50.00**

Doll, Uneeda Wishnik, Poppa–He–Nik, green caveman costume, glued felt "H" on front, 5" h **20.00**

Doll, Uneeda Wishnik, Rock–Nik, black hair, amber eyes, 1–pc red and blue costume with sequins dec, guitar glued to costume, 6" h **15.00**

Marionette, Knickerbocker, Terry Troll, stuffed body, vinyl head, painted features, peach hair, 1964, 11" h **50.00**

Nodder, Japan, Lucky Nik, bright red hair, brown eyes, oversized ears, standing on green pedestal base with white lettering, 1967, 5" h **30.00**

Nodder, Japan, Lucky Shnook, black hair, attached round tag, "Lucky Schnook. Rub me every day I'll bring you good luck," 4½" h **30.00**

Pencil Topper, S.H.E., yellow hair, green eyes, green felt dress, green hair bow, 1964 . . . . **10.00**

Playset, Marx, Troll Party, scenic playground **45.00**

TV GUIDE

TV Guide first appeared as *Tele–Vision Guide* on June 14, 1948. Its title was shortened to *TV Guide* on March 18, 1950. Published in New York, *Tele–Vision Guide* was one of a number of regional weekly, digest–sized TV log magazines.

Walter Annenberg bought *TV Guide* near the end of 1952 and went national with the April 3, 1953, issue whose cover featured a picture of Lucy Ricardo (Lucille Ball) and baby Ricky.

Value rests primarily with cover images. Issues #26 (9/25 to 10/1,1953) with George Reeves as Superman and #179 (9/1-7/56) with Elvis are two of the most sought–after issues. Occasionally an inside story is the key. The April 19–25, 1969, issue includes a story of the Beatles. Early fall premier issues command a small pre- mium. Condition is critical. The survival rate is high. Collecting emphasis rests primarily with issues pre–dating 1980.

Reference: Ron Barlow and Ray Reynolds, *The Insider's Guide to Old Books, Magazines, Newspapers, Trade Catalogs*, Windmill Publishing, 1995.

Periodical: *PCM (Paper Collectors' Marketplace)*, PO Box 128, Scandinavia, WI 54977.

1948, Nov 6, Howdy Doody **$75.00**
1950, Mar 18, Marilyn Monroe **500.00**
1950, May 6, Hopalong Cassidy **150.00**
1953, Apr 3, first issue, Lucille Ball and newborn Desi Arnaz IV, Chicago edition **400.00**

1964, Jun 27–Jul 3, Johnny Carson and wife, $5.00.

1953, Sep 18, Fall Preview	150.00
1953, Sep 25, Superman star George Reeves	315.00
1953, Dec 11, Jack Webb cov, Dragnet, Ramar, Howdy Doody Color Carnival contest Peanut Gallery Guest entry form	12.00
1954, May 21, Wally Cox cov	12.00
1957, Sep 14, Fall Preview, 1957–58	40.00
1958, Sep 14, Fall Preview, 1958–59	50.00
1962, Nov 10, Beverly Hillbillies cov, Car 54 article	8.00
1963, May 11, Andy Griffith cov, The Outer Limits article	15.00
1963, Sep 14, Fall Preview, 1963–64	40.00
1963, Dec 28, Patty Duke, Farmer's Daughter article	25.00
1964, Feb 22, The Fugitive, Robert Vaughn/Outer Limits article	13.00
1964, Sep 19, Fall Preview, 1964–65	40.00
1965, Mar 6, The Fugitive cov, The Three Stooges article	20.00
1965, May 29, Bewitched cov, Alfred Hitchcock article	20.00
1965, Jul 10, The Munsters cov, My Living Doll article	25.00
1965, Sep 11, Fall Preview 1965–66	50.00
1965, Nov 6, Lost in Space cov, Wackiest Ship article	30.00
1965, Nov 27, Hogan's Heroes cov, Liza Minelli article	10.00
1966, Feb 5, I Dream of Jeannie cov, 12 O'Clock High article	10.00
1966, May 21, Wild, Wild West cov, Dick Van Dyke article	10.00
1966, Sep 10, Fall Preview, 1966–67	45.00
1966, Oct 8, Jim Nabors cov, Arthur Miller article	12.00
1966, Dec 31, Girl From U N C L E (Stephanie Powers) cov, Larry Hagman article	8.00
1967, Mar 25, I Spy cov, Batman's Burt Ward article	10.00
1967, May 13, Bewitched cov, Mission Impossible article	25.00
1967, Jul 22, Bonanza cov, Lost in Space article	35.00
1967, Sep 15, Fall Preview, 1967–68	25.00
1967, Sep 23, The Monkees cov, General Custer article	25.00
1968, May 21, Wild, Wild West, Dick Van Dyke article	10.00
1968, Jan 6, Wild, Wild West cov, Your Child and TV article	15.00
1969, Nov 22, I Dream of Jeannie	10.00

TYPEWRITERS

E. Remington & Son's Sholes & Glidden typewriter, introduced in 1874, was the first commercially produced typewriter in the United States. The keyboard consisted only of capital letters.

The earliest typewriters are known as blind models, i.e., the carriage had to be lifted away from the machine to see what had been written. Five major manufacturers joined forces in 1893 to form the Union Typewriter Company. Their monopoly was soon challenged by L. C. Smith & Brothers and the Underwood Typewriter Company. These companies led the field in typewriter innovation in the pre–1940 period.

Electric typewriters appeared briefly in the 1900s. It was not until the 1930s that IBM introduced the first commercially successful electric typewriter. The electric typewriter replaced the manual typewriter by the late 1960s, only to lose its market position to the home computer in the late 1980s.

Advanced typewriter collectors focus primarily on pre–1920 models. Post–1920 typewriters with unusual features are the exception. The keyboard is a good barometer. If the letter placement, i.e., QWERTY, is the same as a modern typewriter or computer keyboard, chances are strong the machine has little value.

Europe, particularly Germany, is the center of typewriter collecting. The number of American collectors remains small.

References: Michael Adler, *Antique Typewriters: From Creed to QWERTY*, Schiffer Publishing, 1997; Darryl Rehr, *Antique Typewriters & Office Collectibles*, Collector Books, 1997.

Newsletters: *Ribbon Tin News,* 28 The Green, Watertown, CT 06795; *The Typewriter Exchange,* 2125 Mount Vernon St, Philadelphia, PA 19130.

Collectors' Club: Early Typewriter Collectors Assoc, 2591 Military Ave, Los Angeles, CA 90064.

Bar–Let, 3–row, frontstrike, black	$35.00
Bar–Let, 3–row, frontstrike, red, blue, maroon, or green	50.00
Barr, 4–row, frontstrike, 1930s	30.00
Bing, 4–row, oblique frontstrike, ink pad	35.00
Bing, Student, 4–row, oblique frontstrike	35.00
Burroughs Electric	50.00
Burroughs, 4–row, frontstrike	10.00
Carissima, Bakelite housing and lid, 1934	200.00
Corona, animal keyboard, 1931	100.00
Corona, Corona Special, 3–row, folding, black	30.00
Corona, folding, with tripod stand	100.00
Corona, Special, red, blue, or green	50.00
Corona, Gorham sterling silver body, 1932	1,000.00
Dayton, portable, 4–row, frontstrike	75.00
Demountable, 4–row, frontstrike	50.00
Ellis, frontstrike, full function adding machine, beveled glass sides, 1920s	100.00
Geniatus, c1928	50.00
IBM Selectric	50.00
Keaton Music Typewriter	300.00
Macy's Portable, 4–row	20.00
Masspro, 1932	50.00
Mercedes, 4–row, frontstrike	30.00
Remington Electric, 1925	150.00
Remington Noiseless	30.00
Rheinmetall, 4–row, frontstrike, ordinary design	20.00
Underwood, portable	15.00
Woodstock Electrite, 1924	10.00

UNIVERSAL POTTERY

In 1926 the Atlas China Company (Niles, Ohio) and the Globe Pottery Company (Cambridge, Ohio), both owned by A. O. C. Ahrendts, were consolidated and renamed the Atlas Globe China Company. Financial pressures resulted in another reorganization in the early 1930s. The factory in Niles closed. Globe was liquidated, its assets becoming part of the Oxford Pottery, also owned by Ahrendts.

In 1934 the company became Universal Pottery. Universal made baking dishes, a fine grade of semi–porcelain dinnerware, and utilitarian kitchenware. Tile manufacturing was introduced in 1956, and the company became The Oxford Tile Company. It continued to make dinnerware until 1960. Universal Promotions distributed Universal. It subcontracted with Hull, Homer Laughlin, and Taylor, Smith & Taylor to continue manufacturing Universal patterned pieces with a Universal backstamp into the 1960s.

References: Susan and Al Bagdade, *Warman's American Pottery and Porcelain,* Wallace–Homestead, Krause Publications, 1994; Harvey Duke, *The Official Identification and Price Guide to Pottery and Porcelain, Eighth Edition,* House of Collectibles, 1995.

Ballerina, platter, burgundy, 11¹/₂" d, $12.00.

Ballerina, creamer, chartreuse $10.00
Ballerina, cup, burgundy 4.00
Ballerina, dinner plate, chartreuse 7.00
Ballerina, eggcup, burgundy 15.00
Ballerina, gravy boat, burgundy 12.00
Ballerina, luncheon plate, chartreuse 4.00
Ballerina, serving bowl, burgundy 10.00
Ballerina, shaker, burgundy 5.00
Ballerina, sugar, cov, burgundy 12.00
Calico Fruit, creamer 10.00
Calico Fruit, cup 8.00
Calico Fruit, custard cup, 5 oz 3.00
Calico Fruit, dinner plate, 9" d 6.00
Calico Fruit, luncheon plate, 7" d 4.00
Calico Fruit, mixing bowl, 9¹/₈" d 17.00
Calico Fruit, platter, 13" d 30.00
Calico Fruit, refrigerator jar, cov, 4" d 10.00
Calico Fruit, refrigerator jar, cov, 5" d 15.00
Calico Fruit, refrigerator jar, cov, 6" d 20.00
Calico Fruit, saucer 3.00
Calico Fruit, serving bowl, tab handles 20.00
Calico Fruit, sugar, cov 18.00
Calico Fruit, utility shakers, pr 15.00
Cattail, batter jug 65.00
Cattail, canteen jug 20.00
Cattail, creamer 12.00
Cattail, jug 25.00
Cattail, platter 25.00
Cattail, salad set, 3 pcs 60.00
Cattail, stack set, cov 20.00
Cattail, tumbler 35.00
Circus, bowl, 5¹/₄" d 6.00
Circus, bread and butter plate, 6¹/₈" d 4.00
Circus, cup 8.00
Circus, dinner plate, 9¹/₈" d 9.00
Circus, platter, 13¹/₂" d 25.00
Circus, saucer 3.00
Circus, soup bowl, 7³/₄" d 10.00
Fruit and Flowers, platter 15.00

Holland Rose, bowl, small 4.00
Holland Rose, bread and butter plate 3.00
Hollyhocks, salad bowl 15.00
Iris, canteen jug 15.00
Iris, casserole, cov 15.00
Iris, dinner plate 5.00
Iris, jug 15.00
Iris, pie baker 12.00
Iris, stack set, cov 25.00
Rambler Rose, bread and butter plate 3.00
Rambler Rose, dinner plate, 9" d 6.00
Rambler Rose, gravy boat 7.00
Rambler Rose, utility shaker 5.00
Red and White Kitchenware, ball jug 30.00
Red and White Kitchenware, bean pot, cov 30.00
Red and White Kitchenware, shaker 10.00
Red and White Kitchenware, syrup 35.00
Red and White Kitchenware, teapot, 6 cup 40.00
Red Poppy, bread and butter plate 3.00
Red Poppy, platter, 11¹/₂" d 10.00
Refrigerator ware, blue and white, canteen jug 20.00
Refrigerator ware, blue and white, refrigerator set, cov 30.00
Woodvine, bread and butter plate, 6" d 3.00
Woodvine, cup and saucer 7.00
Woodvine, dinner plate, 9" d 5.00
Woodvine, gravy boat and underplate 20.00
Woodvine, luncheon plate 4.00
Woodvine, platter 12.00
Woodvine, salt and pepper shakers, pr 10.00
Woodvine, soup bowl, flat 4.00
Woodvine, utility jar, cov 17.00
Woodvine, vegetable bowl, oval 7.00

U.S. GLASS

United States Glass resulted from the merger of eighteen different glass companies in 1891. The company's headquarters were in Pittsburgh. Plants were scattered throughout Indiana, Ohio, Pennsylvania, and West Virginia.

Most plants continued to manufacture the same products that they made before the merger. Older trademarks and pattern names were retained. Some new shapes and patterns used a U.S. Glass trademark. New plants were built in Gas City, Indiana, and Tiffin, Ohio. The Gas City plant made machine–made dinnerware, kitchenware, and tabletop items in colors that included amber, black, canary, green, and pink. The Tiffin plant made delicate pressed dinnerware and blown stemware in crystal and a host of other colors. U.S. Glass' main decorating facility was in Pittsburgh.

During the first three decades of the 20th century, several plants closed, the result of strikes, organizational mismanagement, and/or economic difficulties. In 1938, following the appointment of C. W. Carlson, Sr., as president, the corporate headquarters moved from Pittsburgh to Tiffin. Only the Pittsburgh and Tiffin plants were still operating. Carlson, along with C. W. Carlson, Jr., his son, revived the company by adding several new shapes and colors to the line. The company prospered until the late 1950s.

By 1951 all production was located in Tiffin. U.S. Glass bought the Duncan and Miller molds in 1955. Some former Duncan and Miller employees moved to Tiffin. U.S. Glass created a Duncan and Miller Division.

C. W. Carlson, Sr., retired in 1959. U.S. Glass profits declined. In 1962 U.S. Glass was in bankruptcy. Production resumed when

C. W. Carlson, Jr. and some former Tiffin workers founded Tiffin Art Glass Corporation.

Reference: Gene Florence, *Collector's Encyclopedia of Depression Glass, Thirteenth Edition,* Collector Books, 1998.

Aunt Polly, berry bowl, 4³/₄" h, blue $17.50
Aunt Polly, butter, cov, blue 210.00
Aunt Polly, candy dish, cov, 2 handled, green. 75.00
Aunt Polly, luncheon plate, 8" d, blue 20.00
Aunt Polly, pickle bowl, handled, oval, 7¹/₄", blue 40.00
Aunt Polly, pitcher, blue, 48 oz, 8" h 175.00
Aunt Polly, salt and pepper shakers, pr, blue. 225.00
Aunt Polly, sherbet, green 10.00
Aunt Polly, sugar, cov, green 25.00
Cherryberry, berry bowl, 4" d, pink 8.50
Cherryberry, butter, cov, green 175.00
Cherryberry, creamer, pink 20.00
Cherryberry, olive dish, handled, 5", green 18.00
Cherryberry, salad bowl, 6¹/₂" d, crystal 16.00
Cherryberry, salad plate, 7¹/₂" d, green 18.00
Cherryberry, sherbet plate, 6" d, crystal 6.50
Cherryberry, tumbler, 9 oz, 3⁵/₈", pink. 35.00
Floral and Diamond Band, berry bowl, 4¹/₂" d, green 9.00
Floral and Diamond Band, butter, cov, green 130.00
Floral and Diamond Band, compote, 5¹/₂" h, pink. 17.00
Floral and Diamond Band, creamer, 4³/₄", green 19.00
Floral and Diamond Band, iced tea tumbler, 5" h, pink. 40.00
Floral and Diamond Band, luncheon plate, 8" d, pink. 42.50
Floral and Diamond Band, nappy, handled, 5³/₄", pink 12.00
Floral and Diamond Band, water tumbler, 4" h, green. 25.00
Flower Garden With Butterflies, ashtray, amber. 165.00
Flower Garden With Butterflies, bonbon, cov, 6⁵/₈" d,
    black 250.00
Flower Garden With Butterflies, candlesticks, pr, 8" h,
    pink 135.00
Flower Garden With Butterflies, candy dish, cov, flat, 6",
    crystal. 130.00
Flower Garden With Butterflies, comport, 4¹/₂ x 4³/₄",
    blue 50.00
Flower Garden With Butterflies, cup, green 65.00
Flower Garden With Butterflies, plate, 8" d, canary
    yellow 25.00
Flower Garden With Butterflies, powder jar, ftd, 7¹/₂" h,
    pink 145.00

Flower Garden With Butterflies, sandwich server, center
    handle, black 125.00
Flower Garden With Butterflies, tumbler, 7¹/₂" h, amber. 175.00
Primo, bowl, 7³/₄" d, yellow. 30.00
Primo, cake plate, 3 ftd, 10", green 30.00
Primo, creamer, yellow 12.00
Primo, dinner plate, 10" d, green 22.00
Primo, grill plate, 10" d, yellow 15.00
Primo, saucer, yellow 3.00
Primo, sherbet, green 14.00
Primo, tumbler, 5³/₄" h, yellow 22.00
Strawberry, berry bowl, 4" d, pink 9.00
Strawberry, butter, cov, crystal 135.00
Strawberry, creamer, pink 20.00
Strawberry, olive dish, handled, 5", green. 17.00
Strawberry, salad plate, 7¹/₂" d, crystal 12.00
Strawberry, sugar, cov, green 55.00
US Swirl, berry bowl, 4³/₈" d, pink 6.00
US Swirl, comport, pink 18.00
US Swirl, pitcher, 8" h, green. 55.00
US Swirl, sugar, cov, pink 32.00

VALENTINES

The valentine experienced several major changes in the early decades of the 20th century. Fold or pull out, lithograph novelty, mechanical action, and postcard valentines replaced lacy valentines as the preferred form. Diecut cards became common. Chromolithography brightened the color scheme.

The candy, card, flower, and giftware industry hopped aboard the valentine bandwagon big time following 1920. Elementary schools introduced valentine exchanges when inexpensive mass-produced valentine packs became available. Companies and stars licensed their images for valentine use.

Valentine collectors specialize. Many 20th–century valentines, especially post–1945 examples, are purchased by crossover collectors more interested in the card's subject matter than the fact that it is a valentine. Valentine survival rate is high. Never assume any post–1920 valentine is in short supply.

References: Robert Brenner, *Valentine Treasury: A Century of Valentine Cards,* Schiffer Publishing, 1997; Dan and Pauline Campanelli, *Romantic Valentines,* L–W Book Sales, 1996.

Collectors' Club: National Valentine Collectors Assoc, PO Box 1404, Santa Ana, CA 92702.

Measure,
green,
3 spout,
$30.00.

Greeting Card, Art Deco, folder, fancy, orig lined envelope . . $14.00
Greeting Card, "Best Valentine Wishes," woman wearing
    winter clothing reading valentine card, c1920 . . . . 1.50
Greeting Card, boxed set, Fun to Make Hallmark
    Valentines, material and envelopes to make 16 valen-
    tines, unused, 5¹/₂ x 10¹/₂" 20.00
Greeting Card, Burger King image, sheet of 6, 1977 . . . . 4.00
Greeting Card, diecut heart, 3 x 3". 8.00
Greeting Card, diecut heart, girl with real feather in hat,
    hp, 5¹/₂" l. 10.00
Greeting Card, emb hearts, scrollwork, matching enve-
    lope, 1920s, 5³/₄ x 5³/₄" 30.00
Greeting Card, figural cat, eyes and tongue move. 8.00
Greeting Card, fold–out, lace dec, cartouche of woman,
    1940. . . . . 15.00

Greeting Card, German, "To My Sweetheart," boy wearing golf shirt, swing golf club, c1920 . . . . **4.00**

Greeting Card, heart shape, cupid dec, musical instruments **2.00**

Greeting Card, honeycomb, Beistle, red, 1926, 6" h **5.00**

Greeting Card, honeycomb, Beistle, light red, 1927, 10" h **8.00**

Greeting Card, honeycomb, Beistle, "Wheel of Love," 1930s, 6½ x 9½" **55.00**

Greeting Card, honeycomb, Carrington Card Co, Germany, "Hello! Be My Valentine?," boy and girl talking on phone, c1930 . . . . **15.00**

Greeting Card, honeycomb, "Cupid's Temple of Love," c1928 . . . . **15.00**

Greeting Card, honeycomb, Germany, sailboat, zeppelin, 1920–30s, 6 x 11" **25.00**

Greeting Card, mechanical, automobile, 1923, 8 x 12" **35.00**

Greeting Card, mechanical, Bettie Boop, diecut, movable feather in hair moves eyes and changes message from "Don't Keep Me Waiting For Your Love, Valentine" to "Or I'll Start Looking Around, Valentine," 1940 . . . . **30.00**

Greeting Card, mechanical, cupids and flowers, 1925, 5 x 8" **10.00**

Greeting Card, mechanical, girl stirring kettle, 1930s, 4 x 6" **6.50**

Greeting Card, mechanical, German, "I Hope I Can Catch Your Heart, Dear Valentine," girl sitting on ground, boy standing with arms up looking at 2 squirrels in tree, 1930s **25.00**

Greeting Card, mechanical, Goofy holding net, movable arm, 1939, 3 x 5" **28.00**

Greeting Card, mechanical, seaplane, 1930, 8 x 12" **35.00**

Greeting Card, mechanical, stand–up, German, diecut, Puss 'N Boots, hat swivels to change eyes **15.00**

Greeting Card, mechanical, stand–up, Walt Disney Productions, Pinocchio and Jimminy Cricket in Coachman's Cab to Pleasure Island, 1939, 6 x 7" **20.00**

Greeting Card, mechanical, "Such Is Married Life," c1950 . . . . **45.00**

Greeting Card, Paramount Pictures, Gulliver with his captors, mechanical, 1939, 4 x 6" **25.00**

Greeting Card, pop–up, "You're the one FORE me Valentine," 1940–50 . . . . **30.00**

Greeting Card, Seven Dwarfs at doorway, mechanical, Dopey's head moves, ©WDE 1938, 4¾ x 5" **30.00**

Greeting Card, stand–up, rocking horse with cowboy, 1920s–30s, 4 x 4¼" **12.00**

Greeting Card, "To My Sweetheart," boy playing rugby, wearing striped shirt, c1920 . . . . **3.50**

Greeting Card, Valland Co, Raggedy Andy, stand–up, 1921, 4 x 7" **20.00**

Greeting Card, Walt Disney Productions, Gepetto, Cleo, and Figaro, mechanical, 1939, 5" **20.00**

Greeting Card, Whitney, heart shape, folder, children, 1925, 5 x 5" **3.00**

Greeting Card, "Will You Be My Valentine," boy wearing sailor suit and duck, c1920 . . . . **2.00**

Postcard, Clapsaddle, Ellen H, "Love's Greeting," boy and girl, sgd, 1922 . . . . **5.00**

Postcard, Clapsaddle, Ellen H, "St. Valentine's Greetings," girl and boy, sgd **5.00**

Postcard, Whitney, "Be My Valentine," girl wearing purple dress, holding bouquet of roses, gold heart and verse background, 1930s **1.25**

VAN BRIGGLE POTTERY

Artus Van Briggle established the Van Briggle Pottery Company in 1900. His pottery won numerous awards including one from the 1903 Paris Exhibition.

Following Van Briggle's death in 1904, his wife, Anne, became president of the company, reorganized, and built a new plant. Van Briggle produced a wide range of products including art pottery, garden pottery, novelty items, and utilitarian ware. Artware produced between 1901 and 1912 is recognized for its high quality of design and glaze. Van Briggle's Lorelei vase is a classic.

A reorganization in 1910 produced the Van Briggle Pottery and Tile Company. By 1912 the pottery was leased to Edwin DeForest Curtis who in turn sold it to Charles B. Lansing in 1915. Lansing sold the company to I. F. and J. H. Lewis in 1920, who renamed the company Van Briggle Art Pottery. Kenneth Stevenson acquired the company in 1969. He continued the production of art pottery, introducing some new designs and glazes. Upon his death in 1990, Bertha (his wife) and Craig (his son) continued production.

The Stevensons use a mark similar to the interlocking "AA" mark used by Artus and Anne. Because they also make the same shapes and glazes, novice collectors frequently confuse newly made ware for older pieces. Because the Stevensons only selectively release their wholesale list, discovering which older shapes and glazes are in current production is difficult.

Prior to 1907 all pieces had the "AA" mark and "Van Briggle." These marks also were used occasionally during the 1910s and 20s. "Colorado Springs" or an abbreviation often appears on pieces made after 1920. Some early pieces were dated. Value rises considerably when a date mark is present.

References: Susan and Al Bagdade, *Warman's American Pottery and Porcelain*, Wallace–Homestead, Krause Publications, 1994; Richard Sasicki and Josie Fania, *Collector's Encyclopedia of Van Briggle Art Pottery*, Collector Books, 1993, 1998 value update.

Collectors' Club: American Art Pottery Assoc, PO Box 834, Westport, MA 02790-0697.

Greeting Card, Chiclets Gum adv, with 4 gum wrappers, 1930s, 10¼ x 5½", $175.00. Photo courtesy Past Tyme Pleasures.

REPRODUCTION ALERT: Van Briggle pottery is still being produced today. Modern glazes include Midnight (black), Moonglo (off–white), Russet, and Turquoise Ming.

Bookends, figural squirrels, turquoise, incised "Van Briggle," 1940s, 7" h **$225.00**

Bowl, emb stylized leaves, Persian rose glaze, shape #776, imp logo and "Van Briggle/20/776," 1920, 6¼" d 130.00

Bowl, leaves around shoulder, pierced rim, turquoise, 1930s, 4" h 50.00

Bowl, low, dragonflies, mulberry with blue overspray, incised logo and "Van Briggle/U.S.A.," 1923–26, 9" d **175.00**

Bowl, low, floral band molded in relief, high gloss cobalt glaze, incised logo and "Van Briggle Art Pottery/Colorado Springs CO," c1980, 10½" d 90.00

Bowl, spade shaped leaves, deep mulberry with blue overspray, incised logo and "Van Briggle/U.S.A," 1923–26, 10½" l 325.00

Bowl, stylized leaves, mulberry and blue matte glaze, shape #510, incised logo and "Van Briggle/U.S.A.," 1923–26, 8" d 150.00

Bowl, stylized leaves, Persian rose glaze, incised "Van Briggle," 1940s, 6" h 70.00

Bud Vase, medium and dark mulberry, incised logo and "20," 1920s, 7" h 190.00

Candlestick, blue with turquoise, incised logo and "Van Briggle," 1920–23, 4" h 100.00

Figurine, elephant, brown with green and purple over–spray, incised logo, 1940s, 9" l 100.00

Figurine, elephant, turquoise blue, incised logo, c1950...... 90.00

Figurine, Indian maiden grinding corn, turquoise, incised logo and "Van Briggle/Colo Spgs Colo," 1940s, 5½" h 80.00

Flower Frog, 3 frog figures, dark blue mottled glaze, 1920s, 4½" d 55.00

Flower Frog, turtle figure, turquoise and blue, 1930s, 6" d 50.00

Lamp, ftd, bulbous shape, 3 handles, turquoise, original shade, incised logo, 1940s, 12" h 160.00

Paperweight, figural elephant, turquoise blue, 1930s, 3½" l 55.00

Planter, emb figure of swan on obverse, leaves on reverse, brown and green, incised logo and "Van Briggle/Colo Spgs," 1930s, 9½" l 275.00

Plaques, pr, Big Buffalo and Little Star, turquoise blue, artist's initials "MC," 1950s, 6" h 80.00

Vase, 4 handles, emb florals, mulberry glaze, 1930s, 3¾" h 70.00

Vase, butterfly, turquoise and blue, incised logo and "Van Briggle/Colo Springs," 1940s, 3" h 40.00

Vase, emb florals, Persian rose, 1950s, 5" h 60.00

Vase, emb florals, turquoise, incised logo and "Van Briggle/Colo Springs," 1960s, 5½" h................. 40.00

Vase, flowers and leaves, light green and blue, shape #503, incised logo and "Van Briggle/USA," c1923-26, 10" h 275.00

Vase, mulberry, shape #838, incised logo and "Van Briggle/20," c1920, 6" h........................... 160.00

Vase, pinched rim with twisted panels, turquoise blue,1940s, 5" h 60.00

Vase, stylized florals, turquoise blue, imp logo, "Van Briggle/Colorado Springs," 1930s, 9½" h 65.00

Vase, stylized iris, deep mulberry and blue glaze, shape #503, incised logo and "Van Briggle, Colo Sprgs," 1920s, 10" h 140.00

Vase, stylized leaves, Persian rose, shape #863, incised logo and "Van Briggle/Colo Spgs," 1940s, 8" h 100.00

Vase, stylized leaves around shoulder, handles, deep mulberry matte glaze, bluish green overspray, shape #780, incised logo and "Van Briggle/Colo Spgs," 1920s, 7½" h... 325.00

Vase, tulip shaped, turquoise blue, 1940s, 4" h........... 35.00

Vase, turquoise shading to dark blue, incised logo and "Van Briggle/Colo Spgs," 1920s 90.00

Vase, yucca leaves, turquoise blue, 1930s, 4½" h......... 75.00

VENDING MACHINES

Vending machines were silent salesmen. They worked 24 hours a day. Thomas Adams of Adams Gum is created with popularizing the vending machine. In 1888 his Tutti–Frutti gum machines were placed on elevated train platforms in New York City. The wedding of the gumball and vending machine occurred around 1910.

Leading vending machine manufacturers from its golden age, 1920 through the end of the 1950s, include Ad–Lee Novelty, Bluebird Products, Columbus Vending, Northwestern, Pulver, Volkmann, Stollwerck and Co., and Victor Vending. Figural machines and those incorporating unusual mechanical action are among the most desirable.

Today's vending machine collectors collect either globe–type machines or lithograph tin counter top models dating prior to 1960. While period paint is considered an added value factor, retention of period decals and labels and workability are the main value keys. Since the average life of many vending machines is measured in decades, collectors expect machines to be touched up or repainted.

Vending machines are collected either by type or by material dispensed. Crossover collectors can skew pricing.

Vase, yucca leaves, turquoise blue, 1930s, 4½" h, $77.00. Photo courtesy Jackson's Auctioneers & Appraisers.

References: Richard M. Bueschel, *Collector's Guide to Vintage Coin Machines*, Schiffer Publishing, 1995; Richard M. Bueschel, *Guide to Vintage Trade Stimulators & Counter Games*, Schiffer Publishing, 1997; Bill Enes, *Silent Salesmen: An Encyclopedia of Collectible Gum, Candy & Nut Machines*, published by author, 1987; Bill Enes, *Silent Salesman Too: The Encyclopedia of Collectible Vending Machines*, published by author, 1995.

Newsletter: *Around the Vending Wheel*, 5417 Castana Ave, Lakewood, CA 90712.

Candy, Candy Univender, Stoner, front mirror, 1957 . . . . . . **$180.00**
Candy and Snacks, U–Select–It, Model 74–AP, Coan Manufacturing Co, 1958 . . . . **180.00**
Cigarette, Deluxe, Rowe Vending Machine Co, Los Angeles, CA, 1928 . . . . **450.00**
Cigarette, Lucky Strike, Wilson Mfg, 1¢, dispenses single cigarettes, c1931 . . . . **800.00**
Condom, Harmon Mfg, 25¢, c1962 . . . . **75.00**
Gum, Adams Gum, A H DuGrenier, 1951 . . . . **60.00**
Gum, Dietz Self–Service, Toledo, OH, 1926 . . . . **850.00**
Gum, Too Choos and Joy Mint, Pulver, red porcelain case, c1930. . . . . **400.00**
Gumball, Ace, Operators Vending Supply Co, aluminum, Art Deco motif, orig "Ace" decal, c1930, 16½" h **650.00**
Gumball, Ad–Le Novelty Co, Model D, cast iron, profit sharing mechanism, orig paint, c1920, 16" h **350.00**
Gumball, Baseball Gum Vendor, Ekhom Manufacturing Co, aluminum, baseball motif, 7 slots, orig paint, c1930, 14" h **500.00**
Gumball, Columbus, Model JMJ, aluminum, orig paint, c1950, 14½" h **900.00**
Gumball, Columbus, Model 34, porcelain–coated cast iron, globe with large "4," orig barrel locks, c1936, 14" h **300.00**
Gumball, Empire Vendor, D Robbins, Co, Brooklyn, NY, aluminum, front and lid, Empire State Building emb on front and shoot cov, c1932, 16½" h **300.00**

Coca–Cola, Vendorlater Mfg, Model VMC 44, restored, 56" h, 16" w, 16" d, $2,070.00. Photo courtesy Sotheby's.

Gumball, Fortune Gum, Yu–Chu Gum Co, nickel plated, "1¢ Fortune Gum" cut into base, orig decals, c1930, 15½" h **300.00**
Gumball, Simpson, R D, Aristocrat, cast iron, brass, chrome plated, orig "Superior" decal, c1935, 13" h **300.00**
Gumball, Simpson, RD, Double Commander, brushed aluminum, two 5–sided irregular shaped globes, c1941, 14" h **900.00**
Gumball, Vendex Gumball Machine, cast iron, jar shaped globe, c1930, 12" h **150.00**
Match, Match Vender, Krema Manufacturing Co, Chicago, 1922. . . . . **350.00**
Peanut, Hot Nuts, C D Stover, flashing red glass bullseye in base, c1933, 16" h **350.00**
Peanut, Penny Back Peanut, Model 33, Northwestern, 1937. . . . . **550.00**
Peanut, Stanley Hot Nut, Silent Sales Vending Co, Philadelphia, PA, 1925 . . . . **1,750.00**
Pencil, Automatic Pencil Vender, Charles M Weeks Co, Walden, NY, imprints and personalizes pencils for a nickel, 1925 . . . . **500.00**
Postage Stamp, American Postmaster, Dillon Manufacturing Co, Washington, DC, 1950 . . . . **100.00**
Postage Stamp, Postage Stamp Machine Co, 5¢ and 10¢, c1948. . . . . **45.00**
Radio, Rol–A–Coin, Robert–Lawrence Electronics Corp, Minneapolis, MN, 1946. . . . . **120.00**
Soda, Coca–Cola, Model C–51, Cavalier Corp of Chattanooga, TN, 1958 . . . . **600.00**

VENETIAN GLASS

Italian glass is a generic term for glassware made in Italy from the 1920s into the early 1960s and heavily exported to the United States. Pieces range from vases with multicolored internal thick and thin filigree threads to figural clowns and fish.

The glass was made in Murano, the center of Italy's glass blowing industry. Beginning in the 1920s many firms hired art directors and engaged the services of internationally known artists and designers. The 1950s was a second golden age following the flurry of high–style pieces made from the mid–1920s through the mid–1930s.

Reference: Rosa Barovier Mentasti, *Venetian Glass: 1890–1990*, Arsenale Editirce, 1992, distributed by Antique Collectors' Club.

Newsletter: *Vertri: Italian Glass News*, PO Box 191, Fort Lee, NJ 07024.

Alfred Barbini, vase, cordonato oro, flared baluster form of colorless glass with prominent vertical cords cased to aqua–blue with controlled bubble and gold fleck dec fused between, 15½" h **$925.00**
Alfred Barbini, vase, intarsio, Ercole Barovier design, fused transparent red and green glass squares checkered with colorless segments with symmetrically controlled bubbles, 8½" h, 5¾" d **4,600.00**
Alfred Barbini, vase, perfect sphere blown of opal glass with 2 colorless spirals formed in execution, inscribed "Barbini Murano 33," 9¼" h **175.00**
Alfred Barbini, vase, vaso a canne, flattened oval composed of fused blue, green, black–aubergine, and

aventurine stripes swirled to right with optical illusory effect, engraved 3–line mark on base "Barovier/& Toso/Murano," 15¼" h **2,300.00**

Aureliano Toso, bowl, Dino Martens, oriente, tricorn dish of colorless glass with enclosed white, red, yellow, blue, black, and green squares and gold aventurine sections, 2½" h, 6¼" w **450.00**

Aureliano Toso, leaf dish, attributed to Dino Martens, oriente, fused sections of orange–yellow, aubergine, white, turquoise, and aventurine with transparent red, green, and blue, all within colorless surround clipped and folded in leaf form, 2½" h, 7½" l **425.00**

Barovier & Toso, bowl, rugiada, designed by Ercole Barovier for 1940 Biennale, colorless glass in elongated oval with open handes and overshot rough textured surface over gold foil inclusions, 4¼" h, 13" l **925.00**

Barovier & Toso, vase, graffito, Ercole Barovier, 1969, tapered colorless glass cylinder with combed lattimo white outlines on air trap windows accented by gold aventurine inclusions overall, 11" h **1,375.00**

Barovier & Toso, vase, saturneo, Ercole Barovier 1951 design, free–blown bottle form, colorless glass internally dec by 5 double rows of teal–green–aqua bull's–eye murrine separated by lattimo white filligrana vertical rods highlighted by aventurine accents throughout, 11½" h.......................... **9,200.00**

Cenedese, clown lamp, figural glass lamppost with inebriated clown chased by fantasy dog, base inscribed "Cenedese Murano 1973," small fracture at dog's foot, 24" h **350.00**

Cenedese, Sculpture, humpback whale, vetreria corroso, heavy aquamarine glass with turquoise blue lips and eyes, etched overall and splotched with metallic oxides to produce corroded effect, base incised "Cenedese Murano 97V" and "Talberto," 15" l **1,375.00**

IVR Mazzega Studio, sculpture, Miro portrait, Jean Miro design, execution attributed to Ermanno Nason, red glass with applied blue eye and ear, raised upon colorless columnar "found" candlestick body base, etched and painted with polka–dot skirt, stockings, and black pumps, engraved on base "Miro/Mezzega IVR Murano," chip on back corner base, 13½" h **2,300.00**

IVR Mazzega Studio, sculpture, woman, designed by Pablo Picasso, hands on hips in angry stance, black on white glass, mkd "Picasso" at lower side, engraved on base "Picasso IVR Mazzega Murano," rigaree chip, 13¾" h................................... **2,500.00**

Lino Tagliapietra, platter, fused glass, shallow oval tray of blue–aquamarine transparent glass with central oval composed of rose–red murrine, inscribed on reverse "Lino Tagliapietra 88," 17" l, 12½" w **450.00**

Lino Tagliapietra, vase, executed with Marina Angelin, folded double rim on conical turquoise blue glass oval with medial encalmo band of perfectly aligned black vertical stripes, base inscribed "Tagliapietra/ Angelin by Murano 10/100 1984," 9" h, 13" d **1,375.00**

Murano Studio, block aquarium, attributed to Gino Cenedese, 2 thick green and colorless glass rect blocks encasing a silver fish with red striped fins and tail among green water grasses, 4¾" h, 6¼" l **575.00**

Murano Studio, bowl, iridescent, heavy walled half–round internally dec with colored powder between colorless surround, 6" d **65.00**

Murano Studio, bowl, jardiniere form with applied black handles, prunts, and body wraps, 4½" h **225.00**

Murano Studio, console set, 3 pc, attributed to Salviati Co, Venetian Revival style, colorless glass, center compote and matching sottile pedestaled vases, all with applied ruby–red rigaree, 5½" h compote, 8¾" h vases... **350.00**

Murano Studio, fruit bowl, design by Ercole Barovier for 1934 Biennale, black aubergine with oro antico aventurine, centerbowl and 5 pcs of fruit, 11" d bowl **315.00**

Murano Studio, sculpture, hat, full size, mottled dark navy blue dec with white hat band and symmetrical red threading on curved brim, 5" h, 13" l **350.00**

Murano Studio, sculpture, walrus, attributed to Salviati, solid lattimo white in topaz shaded to colorless overall surround, applied tusks, eyes, and ears, 5¾" h, 10½" l.. **175.00**

Murano Studio, vase, attributed to Ercole Barovier, colorless oval body with 12 gold enhanced leaves suspended within as in Rilievi Aurati, 7½" h **975.00**

Murano Studio, vase, A V E M, red cased and silver speckled bulbous body dec by multicolored latticinio and millifiore canes with colorless rim wrap and medial rigaree, 12½" h **250.00**

Murano Studio, vase, bianca nero, Dino Martens technique, parallel groups of spiraled white and black filagrana separated by d'oro aventurine threads in colorless glass surround, 9¼" h...................... **375.00**

Murano Studio, vase, zanfirico, possibly A V E M, elliptical colorless body internally dec by spiraled polchrome rods and glass canes, 10" h **200.00**

Seguso, bowl, fantasy patchwork, folded rim on round bowl comprising panels of stepped window squares

Lino Tagliapietra, Tesuto bowl, closed–in rim, tapering base, layers of green, black, and white caning, clear ground, engraved "Lino Tagliapietra Effetra International Murano ITALY," 8½ x 11½", $935.00. Photo courtesy David Rago Auctions.

in brilliant yellow and red outlined in white sutured at each corner with black–aubergine dots, "Archimede Seguso/Made in Italy/Murano" label, 4" h, 9" d **700.00**

Seguso, vase, fantasy patchwork, design attributed to Archimede Seguso, intricate stepped window squares of brilliant yellow and red outlined in white sutured with black–aubergine at each corner, 7" h **575.00**

Seguso, vase, fantasy spiral, oval glass body composed of netted white and amethyst square windows arranged in progressive diagonal pattern, Archimede Seguso paper label, 11" h **550.00**

Venini, ceiling lamp, studio glass, Massimo Vignelli design, fused fasce in green, yellow, gray, and white, cased lattimo white within, mounted to single socket light fixture, 19½" h shade **1,050.00**

Venini, ceiling lamp, studio glass, Massimo Vignelli 1954 design, lattimo white glass fused to transparent horizontal fasce of blue, green, red, blue, aubergine, and colorless stripes, mounted to socket fixture, 19½" h shade **800.00**

Venini, centerbowl, studio glass, pre–war design, heavy walled colorless glass with symmetrically arranged internal bolla bubbles, edges folded into rect form, applied ring foot stamped "Venini Murano," 4¼" h, 14½" l, 11½" w **225.00**

Venini, leaf bowl, studio glass, Trya Lundgren, white on colorless filligrana internal design in figurative medial pattern, stamped on base "Venini Murano Italia," 9¼" l **350.00**

Venini, sculpture, chicken, 1950 Fulvio Bianconi design, Gallina of lattimo white swirled body with yellow beak and feet, red comb, black eyes, wings, and disk foot stamped "Venini Murano Italia," 6½" h **1,375.00**

Venini, sculpture, obelisk, obelischi a canne de zanfiri-co, designed by Paolo Venini, exhibited at Biennale 1954, solid colorless glass with core of spiraled multicolored glass threads, base stamped "Venini Murano Italia," 6" h **375.00**

Venini, vase, fasce orizzontali, Fulvio Bianconi 1953 design, flared oval transparent body with brilliant stripes of red, blue, green, and aubergine alternating with colorless, base stamped "Venini Murano Italia," minor water stain at base only, 17" h **12,650.00**

Venini, vase, "Istanbul," Fulvio Bianconi 1952 design, flared, purple, gray, colorless, and pale yellow patch-work squares, stamped "Venini Murano Italia," 8" h **7,000.00**

Venini, vase, spirali vaso a canna, 1983 production of Bianconi fused transparent green and red alternating colorless diagonally striped filligrana, labeled and incised "Venini italia '83," 11" h **200.00**

Venini, vase, studio glass, double incalmo, design by Riccardo Licata, 1953–56, medial band of black and red on white murrine, brilliant transparent green above, blue below, stamped on base "Venini Murano Italia," 9½" h **7,500.00**

Venini, vase, studio glass, fazzoletto, camichato slumped handkerchief bowl of lattimo white cased to cornflower blue, base stamped "Venini/Murano/Italia," 4½" h **315.00**

Venini, vase, studio glass, fasce verticali, Fulvio Bianconi 1952 design, fused stripes of alternating red, blue, and green transparent glass free–blown and shaped in elliptical form, unsgd, 10½" h **4,150.00**

Venini, vase, studio glass, design attributed to Napoleone Martinuzzi, broad sphere of transparent teal blue–green color with applied angular handles at raised folded rim in traditional Venetian style, stamped on base "Venini Murano Italia," 8¼" h **975.00**

Venini, vase, studio glass, occhi, Tobia Scarpa 1960–61 design, bulbous barrel shape, colorless and dark purple–aubergine patchwork in overall "window" grid–work, base stamped "Venini Murano Italia," 9" h **3,750.00**

VERNON KILNS

In 1912 George Poxon established Poxon China in Vernon, California. Initially the company made tiles. Following World War I production shifted to earthenware dishes and hotel and restaurant ware. In 1928 George Poxon turned the company over to his wife Judith and her brother James Furlong. The company was renamed Vernon China.

In 1931 Faye G. Bennison bought Vernon China and changed the name to Vernon Kilns. Initially the company produced decal ware utilizing older Vernon China/Paxon shapes. An earthquake in 1933 shattered most of the company's inventory and did extensive damage to the kilns. This proved a blessing in disguise as Vernon Kilns introduced numerous new shapes and pattern lines. Art ware also was introduced, remaining in production until 1937.

In 1940 Vernon Kilns signed a contract with Walt Disney Productions to make figures of the characters from *Dumbo, Fantasia,* and *The Reluctant Dragon.* Specialty transfer print ware was introduced in the 1930s. The late 1940s and early 1950s saw the production of hundreds of commemorative patterns and series such as Moby Dick and Our America.

The Coronada shape line was introduced in 1938, Melinda in 1942, San Marino in the mid–1940s, and Anytime in 1955. Hand–painted Organdie and Brown–Eyed Susan were popular patterns.

In January 1958 a decision was made to close the company. Metlox Potteries, Manhattan Beach, California, bought the molds, modified some, and continued production of Anytime, Barkwood, Brown–Eyed Susan, Organdie, Sherwood, and Tickled Pink for a year. Although the Vernon Kilns plant closed, the corporation remained alive until it was legally dissolved in 1969.

Possibly Salviati, compote, white latticino and green swirls, c1930, 5 x 11½", $192.50. Photo courtesy David Rago Auctions.

References: Susan and Al Bagdade, *Warman's American Pottery and Porcelain,* Wallace–Homestead, Krause Publications, 1994; Harvey Duke, *The Official Price Guide to Pottery and Porcelain, Eighth Edition,* House of Collectibles, 1995; Maxine Feek Nelson, *Collectible Vernon Kilns,* Collector Books, 1994, out of print.

Newsletter: *Vernon Views,* PO Box 945, Scottsdale, AZ 85252.

Brown–Eyed Susan, bread and butter plate $3.00
Brown–Eyed Susan, cup and saucer 10.00
Brown–Eyed Susan, dinner plate, 9¾" d 8.00
Brown–Eyed Susan, salad plate 5.00
Brown–Eyed Susan, salt and pepper shakers, pr 12.00
Calico, chop plate, 12" d 15.00
Calico, dinner plate 10.00
Calico, tidbit, 2 tier 30.00
Gingham, butter, cov 45.00
Gingham, casserole, cov 50.00
Gingham, chicken pot pie, cov 35.00
Gingham, chop plate, 12" d 15.00
Gingham, chowder 12.00
Gingham, coaster, set of 6 . . . . 32.00
Gingham, dinner plate, 9¾" d 12.00
Gingham, eggcup 25.00
Gingham, flat soup 12.00
Gingham, gravy, round 15.00
Gingham, jug, bulbous, 1 pt 35.00
Gingham, pitcher, streamline, 2 qt 45.00
Gingham, platter, oval, 14¼" l 20.00
Gingham, salad plate, 7½" d 6.00
Gingham, teapot, cov 60.00
Gingham, teapot, individual 50.00
Gingham, tumbler 30.00
Hawaiian Flowers, fruit bowl, maroon 12.00
Hawaiian Flowers, salt and pepper shakers, pr, maroon 45.00
Homespun, bread and butter plate 6.00
Homespun, butter, cov 50.00
Homespun, butter pat 32.00
Homespun, chicken pie, cov 35.00
Homespun, chop plate, 12½" d 18.00
Homespun, chowder 12.00
Homespun, coaster, set of 6 . . . . 32.00
Homespun, coffee carafe 45.00
Homespun, cup and saucer 12.00
Homespun, dinner plate, 9½" d 10.00

Homespun, eggcup 25.00
Homespun, flat soup 12.00
Homespun, gravy 25.00
Homespun, jug, bulbous, 1 pt 35.00
Homespun, jug, bulbous, 1 qt 45.00
Homespun, juice tumbler, ftd, pink 7.00
Homespun, lug soup 10.00
Homespun, pitcher, streamline, 2 qt 40.00
Homespun, platter, oval, 10½" l 15.00
Homespun, platter, 13" 17.00
Homespun, salt and pepper shakers, pr 20.00
Homespun, syrup 60.00
Homespun, teapot 60.00
Homespun, tumbler 8.00
Homespun, vegetable bowl, 7½" d 18.00
Moby Dick, cup, blue ultra 40.00
Moby Dick, dinner plate, blue ultra 45.00
Moby Dick, fruit bowl, blue ultra 25.00
Moby Dick, lug soup, brown 35.00
Moby Dick, salad plate, blue ultra, 7" 25.00
Moby Dick, sugar, open, blue ultra 30.00
Organdie, bread and butter plate 3.00
Organdie, butter, cov 50.00
Organdie, casserole, cov, round 45.00
Organdie, chicken pot pie, cov 35.00
Organdie, chowder, lug handle 9.00
Organdie, coasters, set of 6 . . . . 30.00
Organdie, coffee carafe 48.00
Organdie, creamer and cov sugar 25.00
Organdie, cup and saucer 3.00
Organdie, dinner plate, 10½" 16.00
Organdie, eggcup 28.00
Organdie, flat soup 15.00
Organdie, flower pot, 5" 25.00
Organdie, fruit bowl, 5½" 2.50
Organdie, jug, bulbous, 1 pt 30.00
Organdie, jug, bulbous, 1 qt 40.00
Organdie, luncheon plate, 9½" 5.00
Organdie, pitcher, streamline, 2 qt 40.00
Organdie, salad plate 4.00
Organdie, salt and pepper shakers, pr, large 18.00
Organdie, spoon holder 22.00
Organdie, syrup 60.00
Organdie, teapot 60.00
Organdie, teapot, individual 45.00
Organdie, tidbit, 2 tier 45.00
Organdie, tumbler, straight side 25.00
Organdie, vegetable bowl, 7½" d 25.00
Organdie, vegetable bowl, oval, divided 35.00
Samilla, dinner plate 160.00
Souvenir Plate, Chicago Fair 28.00
Souvenir Plate, State of Louisana 22.00
Souvenir Plate, Texas "The Lone Star State" 22.00
Souvenir Plate, University of Chicago 22.00
Tam O' Shanter, butter, cov 50.00
Tam O' Shanter, butter pat 32.00
Tam O' Shanter, casserole, cov 50.00
Tam O' Shanter, chicken pot pie, cov 35.00
Tam O' Shanter, chop plate, 14" d 18.00
Tam O' Shanter, coaster, set of 6 . . . . 32.00
Tam O' Shanter, coffee carafe 50.00
Tam O' Shanter, cup and saucer 4.50
Tam O' Shanter, eggcup 18.00
Tam O' Shanter, flat soup 15.00

Gingham, salt and pepper shakers, pr, small, $15.00.

Tam O' Shanter, fruit bowl **4.00**
Tam O' Shanter, gravy **25.00**
Tam O' Shanter, salad bowl, individual **10.00**
Tam O' Shanter, teapot **60.00**
Tam O' Shanter, tumbler **25.00**
Tweed, eggcup **25.00**
Tweed, vegetable bowl, 8⅞" d **28.00**
Tweed, platter, oval, 12½" l **20.00**

VIETNAM WAR

The Vietnam War divided America. As a result, there are two distinct groups of collectibles: anti–war demonstration and military.

Destabilization followed the withdrawal of the French from Indo–China. In the early 1960s American military advisors were in South Vietnam assisting the country's military. In May 1962 President Kennedy sent 1,800 U.S. Marines to Thailand to protect it from a possible invasion by communist forces from Laos. On June 16, 1962 two U.S. Army officers were killed north of Saigon. On November 1, 1963, the government of President Diem was overthrown by South Vietnamese armed forces. America recognized the new government on November 7, 1963.

America increased its military and economic aide to South Vietnam in 1964. Mounting casualties during 1965 spurred protests. By the end of 1966, the United States had 400,000 troops in South Vietnam. The casualty count was over 6,600 killed and 37,500 wounded. Nguyen Van Thieu was elected president in 1967 amid charges of election fraud. Dissent continued to mount, reaching a fever pitch in the late 1960s and 70s. North Vietnam launched the Tet offensive on January 30, 1968.

Although Nixon reduced the U.S. troop commitment in 1969, major anti–war demonstrations took place in October and November. America continued to disengage from Vietnam. By December 1971 American troop strength dropped to 184,000. On March 30, 1972, North Vietnam crossed the DMZ and entered South Vietnam from Cambodia.

A peace agreement was signed on January 22, 1973. It proved ineffective. The South Vietnamese government fell to the North in 1975. America's presence in Vietnam ended. President Ford offered amnesty to deserters and draft evaders in September 1974. A general pardon was issued in 1977.

References: Richard J. Austin, *The Official Price Guide to Military Collectibles, Sixth Edition,* House of Collectibles, 1998; Ray Bows, *Vietnam Military Lore 1959–1973... Another Way to Remember, Vol. I,* Bows & Sons, 1988; Ron Manion, *American Military Collectibles,* Antique Trader Books, 1995.

Newsletter: *Vietnam Insignia Collectors Newsletter,* 501 West 5th Ave, Covington, LA 07433.

Ashtray, souvenir, 2 pc, green ceramic, "Embassy Hotel
    Saigon" and bird logo **$48.00**
Book, *Frontline—The Commands of Wm. Chase,* autobi-
    ographed 1st ed, 1975, 228 pp **38.00**
Bracelet, POW, names **25.00**
Cloth Insignia, United States Air Force, green B–52 in
    center, "Peace Hell/Bomb Hanoi" on border, 4" d **21.00**
Hand Grenade, practice, Viet Cong, wooden handle,
    canister, olive green, 9" **25.00**
Hat, baseball style, blue, Bob Hope USO Tour, large
    "3AD" embroidered to front, palm tress with "3390

S.W. 4133 BW," and palm trees to 1 side, "Anderson
    AFG Guam, 1969," "Sheryle Uliman" sewn to rear,
    caricature of Bob Hope with "Bob Hope Show 1969
    Escort" clipped to side and encased in plastic **36.00**
Helmet Carrying Bag, nylon, dark olive drab, quilted lin-
    ing, zipper and dual grip handles, dated 1974 . . . . **48.00**
Jungle Hammock, mesh and cotton, rubberized con-
    struction, dark olive drab, with rigging lines **28.00**
Leaflet, South Vietnamese Propoganda, dated Apr, 1969,
    5 x 7" **5.00**
Lighter, Super–Ace, Japan, brused silver flip–top case,
    enameled *USS Endurance* patch design appliqué on 1
    side, engraved "Trawler Killers' A Wooden Ship With
    Iron Man, Vietnam, 1970" on other **52.00**
Lighter, Zenith, brushed silver flip–top case, 1 side
    engraved bamboo shoot design and "1962 NSAPAC" **25.00**
Manual, Blue Book of Coastal Vessels South Vietnam,
    illus, hardback, 556 pp, 1967 . . . . **87.00**
Medal, Technical Service, on 1st class ribbon with
    French style pins **24.00**
Medical Kit, nylon pouch, plastic container with con-
    tents, belt clips on back **40.00**
Newspaper Headline, "Vietnam Peace Pacts Signed," 1973 . . . **12.00**
Patch, Navy Far East Cruise, embroidered with 6–flag
    design ground, 5 x 3½" **30.00**
Pinback Button, "Cease Fire Now!," red and white litho,
    center stop sign design **10.00**
Pinback Button, "Demonstrate Against The War/Out
    Now Nov. 6th," yellow lettering, blue and yellow
    design against bright red ground **10.00**
Pinback Button, "Nixon/Vietnam," "Nixon You Liar/Sign
    The Treaty/Nov. 4 Coalition," white on brown ground **10.00**
Pinback Button, "Nov. 6, 1971" green lettering on white
    peace dove against purple, blue, and green circles,
    New York address and "Make Contributions NPAC" **10.00**
Pinback Button, "Uncle Sam Bleeds You," red, white,
    blue, and black, caricature of Uncle Sam in military
    uniform holding money bag **20.00**
Pinback Button, "War Is Not Healthy For Children And
    Other Living Things," stylized green flower with pink
    and orange petals, black inscription **20.00**
Pinback Button, "Viet Nam Peace Parade Comm" with
    New York City phone number, white stylized peace
    dove superimposed over dark blue shape of United
    States against light blue ground **10.00**
Poster, "Out Now, Stop the Bombing, March Against the
    War," Student Mobilization Committee, Berkeley, CA,
    1970, 22 x 14" **50.00**
Record, *Dick Gregory at Kent State,* 2–record set, May 4,
    1970 Kent State shooting account, Poppy, 1970 . . . . **50.00**
Ring, SS, 3–dimensional hand on top with fingers form-
    ing peace symbol, c1970 . . . . **20.00**
Service Award, gold luster metal pendant, with green
    and white enamel, accented by center red flame sym-
    bol on green and white fabric ribbon, inscribed
    "Viet–Nam," "Chien–Dic," and "Boi–Tinm" **20.00**
Stickpin, metal, red, white, and blue painted furling flag
    at half staff and Peace sign, "Vietnam 1961–," card-
    board box with clear plastic top window inscribed
    "Wear This Pin For Peace," Pace Emblem Co,
    New York, NY, c1970s, 1¾" h **20.00**
Sun Hat, Army, reversible from dark olive drab to orange
    poplin with stiched brim, soft crown, adjustable head-
    band **30.00**

VIEW–MASTER

William Gruber, a Portland, Oregon, piano tuner, and Harold Graves, president of Sawyer's, a Portland photo–finishing and post-card company, were the two principals behind View–Master. On January 20, 1939, a patent was filed for a special stereoscope utilizing a card with seven pairs of views. Sawyer, Inc., manufactured and sold View–Master products.

The Model A viewer, with its flip front opening and straight viewing barrels, was introduced in 1939. It was replaced by an improved Model B viewer in 1943. The more familiar Model C square viewer arrived in 1946 and remained in production for eleven years.

By 1941 there were more than 1,000 View–Master sales outlets. During World War II, View–Master made special training reels for the United States Navy and Army Air Corps. View–Master's golden years were 1945 to 1960. Hundreds of new reels appeared. The three–pack set was introduced.

In 1966 General Aniline and Film Corporation (GAF) purchased Sawyer's. GAF introduced new projects and the 3–D talking View–Master. Arnold Thaler purchased View–Master in 1980, only to sell it to Ideal. When Tyco acquired Ideal, View–Master was part of the purchase. Today, the View–Master brand name is owned by Mattel, the result of its purchase of Tyco in 1997.

References: Sharon Korbeck (ed.), *Toys & Prices, 5th Edition,* Krause Publications, 1997; John Waldsmith, *Stereo Views: An Illustrated History and Price Guide,* Wallace–Homestead, Krause Publications, 1991.

Collectors' Club: National Stereoscopic Assoc, PO Box 14801, Columbus, OH 43214.

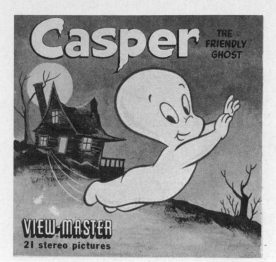

Reel, Casper the Friendly Ghost, B–533, $6.00.

Camera, Mark II, film cutter, made in Europe	$200.00
Camera, Personal 3–D, custom film cutter	175.00
Projector, S–1, brown metal, single lens, carrying case	50.00
Projector, Sawyer's, plastic, single lens	10.00
Projector, Stereomatic 500, 3–D, 2 lenses, carrying case	250.00
Reel, Buddhist Temples of Bangkok, Siam, #4820, 1949	2.00
Reel, Carlsbad Caverns National Park	5.00
Reel, Colonial Williamsburg, VA	10.00
Reel, Death Valley National Monument, #284	5.00
Reel, Grand Coulee Dam, Washington, #196, 1949	2.00
Reel, Hawaiian Hula Dancers, #62	3.00
Reel, Hot Springs National Park, AR, #299	1.00
Reel, Island of Kuai, Hawaii, #72	6.00
Reel, Kings Canyon National Park, CA, #118	2.00
Reel, Lucerne, Switzerland, #2014, 1948	1.00
Reel, Mardi Gras, New Orleans, LA, #332, 1949	3.00
Reel, Marine Studios, St Augustine	5.00
Reel, Mexico City and Vicinity, #501	3.00
Reel, Movie Stars, Hollywood III, #742	15.00
Reel, People of the Nile Valley, Egypt, #3308, 1950	3.00
Reel, Prehistoric Cliff Dwellers of Mesa Verde, CO, #9055, 1959	5.00
Reel, Reno, Biggest Little City in the World, #14	8.00
Reel, Rocky Mountain National Park, CO, #101	2.00
Reel, Roosevelt's Little White House, Warm Springs, GA, #343, 1949	1.00
Reel, Washington, DC, #137	3.00
Reel, Wilderness of Judea, Palestine, #4017, 1949	2.00
Reel Set, ABC Circus, Sawyers, 1950s	40.00
Reel Set, Alice in Wonderland, GAF, 1964, 1952 reissue	15.00

Reel Set, Alpine Wild Flowers, Sawyer's	12.00
Reel Set, Amazing Spider Man, GAF, #H–1	15.00
Reel Set, Balance of Nature, Ecology, GAF, #B–686	25.00
Reel Set, Batman, GAF, #B–492	20.00
Reel Set, Brady Bunch, 1974	45.00
Reel Set, Buck Rogers, GAF, #L–15	20.00
Reel Set, Buckaroo Banzai, GAF, #4056	5.00
Reel Set, Bugs Bunny, Sawyers, 1959	10.00
Reel Set, Butterflies of North America, GAF, #B–610	10.00
Reel Set, Captain Kangaroo, "Bunny Rabbit Hunt," "Bunny Rabbit Paints A Picture," and "The Pie Machine," 1957	20.00
Reel Set, Cowboy Star Adventures, #946, 951, 956, Roy Rogers in "The Holdup," Gene Autry in "The Kidnapping," Hopalong Cassidy in "The Cattle Rustler," 1953	25.00
Reel Set, Cowboy Stars, #950, 955, and 960, Gene Autry and his Wonder Horse Champion, Hopalong Cassidy and Topper, Cisco Kid and Pancho, 1950	30.00
Reel Set, Daktari, GAF, 1968	20.00
Reel Set, Dark Shadows, GAF, 1960s	80.00
Reel Set, Disneyland Sets, 1960s or early 1970s, Fantasyland, Frontierland, Tomorrowland, price for each	18.00
Reel Set, Donald Duck, Sawyers, 1957	20.00
Reel Set, Dracula Set, 1976	20.00
Reel Set, Dr Shrinker and the Wonderbug Set, Kroft Supershow #1	30.00
Reel Set, Eight Is Enough Set, 1980	20.00
Reel Set, Family Affair, 1969	50.00
Reel Set, Frankenstein Set, 1976	20.00
Reel Set, Grimm's Fairy Tales, Sawyers, 1960	20.00
Reel Set, Grizzly Adams Set, 1976, MIP	25.00
Reel Set, Hans Christian Andersen's Fairy Tales, Sawyers, 1958	10.00
Reel Set, Happy Days Set, The Not Making of a President, 1974, MIP	20.00
Reel Set, Harlem Globetrotters Set, 1977, MIP	25.00
Reel Set, Heidi, Sawyers, 1950s	10.00
Reel Set, Instructional Swimming with Don Schollander, 1972	10.00
Reel Set, James Bond Moonraker Set, 1979	30.00
Reel Set, Jetsons Set, 1980s	20.00
Reel Set, Johnny Mocassin, ©1957	25.00
Reel Set, Korg 70,000 B. C., ©Hanna–Barbera	15.00

Stereoscope Light Attachment, orig box, instructions, and reel list, c1950, 5⅝" h, $20.00.

Reel Set, Lancelot Link Secret Chimp, 1970 . . . . 15.00
Reel Set, Lassie, Look Homeward, Sawyer, #B–480 . . . . 25.00
Reel Set, Laugh–In, GAF, #B–497 . . . . 25.00
Reel Set, Lone Ranger, GAF reissue 40.00
Reel Set, Lost in Space, "The Condemned Of Space,"
   1967 . . . . 65.00
Reel Set, Man On the Moon, 1964 NASA Apollo project,
   complete with keyed story booklet, 1969 . . . . 25.00
Reel Set, M*A*S*H, 1978 . . . . 25.00
Reel Set, Mighty Mouse, GAF, 1968 . . . . 15.00
Reel Set, Mission Impossible, 1968 . . . . 20.00
Reel Set, Mod Squad, "Bad Man On Campus," 1968 . . . . 25.00
Reel Set, Mork and Mindy Set, orig story booklet, 1979 . . . . . 20.00
Reel Set, Peter Pan, Sawyers, 1957 . . . . 20.00
Reel Set, Prehistoric Animals, Sawyers, 1950s 15.00
Reel Set, Puss N Boots, GAF, #B–320 . . . . 20.00
Reel Set, Secret From Space Starring Tom Corbett,
   ©Rockhill Radio, 1954 . . . . 50.00
Reel Set, Seven Wonders of the World, Sawyer,
   #B–901 . . . . 12.00
Reel Set, Shaggy DA, GAF, 1976 . . . . 8.00
Reel Set, Six Million Dollar Man Set, 1974 . . . . 30.00
Reel Set, Sleeping Beauty, Sawyers, 1959 . . . . 8.00
Reel Set, Snoopy and The Red Baron, GAF, 1969 . . . . 20.00
Reel Set, Snow White, Sawyers, 1950 . . . . 20.00
Reel Set, Space: 1999, 1975 . . . . 8.00
Reel Set, Tarzan of the Apes, B–444, edition A 30.00
Reel Set, Time Tunnel, 16 pp booklet, 1967 . . . . 50.00
Reel Set, Tom Corbett Space Cadet 45.00
Reel Set, Iop Cat, B5131–"Medal For Meddling," 5132–
   "Zoo Operation," and 5133–"No Cat Fishing," 1962 . . . . . . 30.00
Reel Set, TV Stars, includes Ed Sullivan, Groucho Marx,
   Jack Benny, Pinkie Lee, Danny Thomas, Ozzie &
   Harriet, Charlie McCarthy and Edgar Bergen, ©1955 . . . . . . 45.00
Reel Set, Voyage to the Bottom Of the Sea, 1966 . . . . 15.00
Reel Set, Wild Bill Hickok & Jingles, B4731–"The Wells
   Fargo Robbery," ©1953, B4732–"The Proud Old
   Soldier" and B4733–"The Sindlers," ©1956 . . . . 25.00
Viewer, Model C, black Bakelite, light attachment,
   1946–56 . . . . 25.00
Viewer, Model D, focus, orig box 85.00
Viewer, Model F, illuminated, plastic, dark brown 20.00
Viewer, Model H, illuminated, GAF logo, 1967–81 . . . . 15.00

WADE CERAMICS

In 1958 A. J. Wade, George Wade and Son, Wade Heath & Co., and Wade (Ulster) combined, formed The Wade Group of Potteries, and went public.

George Wade and Son, located at the Manchester Pottery in Burslem, is the best known of the group. Prior to World War I, the company made industrial ceramics, concentrating heavily on the needs of the textile industry. After the war, the company made insulators for the electrical industry.

A. J. Wade, George's brother, established a firm to market glazed tiles and faience fireplace surrounds. A. J. Wade became a partner in Wade, Heath & Co., a manufacturer of Rockingham jugs, teapots, etc. In 1935 Colonel G. A. Wade, a son of George Wade, gained control of A. J. Wade's two companies. Previously, in 1926/28, Col. Wade assumed control of George Wade and Son.

In the late 1920s, George Wade and Son introduced a line of moderately priced figurines. They did so well the company added a line of animals. Production of these figurines ceased during World War II when the company shifted to wartime production.

In 1938 Wade, Heath & Co. acquired the Royal Victoria Pottery. A line of tableware was introduced. A license was acquired from Disney to produce character figurines. Although heavily devoted to wartime production in the early 1940s, the company did manufacture a line of utilitarian dinnerware and tea ware.

In 1950 Wade (Ulster) was established. Located in Portadown, Northern Ireland, the company produced industrial ceramics.

The ceramic giftware industry went into decline in the 1960s. The Wade Group focused on industrial production. When the giftware industry revived in the 1970s, The Wade Group returned to the market. Wade Heath & Co. devotes its efforts to commission and special contract orders, serving a large number of clients ranging from breweries to tobacco companies. In 1969 Wade (PDM) was established within The Wade Group to deal with the design and marketing of promotional items. This new group works with glass, plastic, and tin, in addition to ceramics.

Wade is best known in the United States through its Red Rose Tea premiums. These are made by George Wade & Son. Different sets are made for the American and Canadian market. Some figures are based on figures in the "Whimsies" line. Do not confuse the two. Whimsies are slightly larger.

References: Pat Murray, *The Charlton Standard Catalogue of Wade, Vol. One: General Issues, Second Edition* (1996), *Vol. Two: Decorative Ware, Second Edition* (1996), *Vol. Three: Tableware, Second Edition* (1998), Charlton Press; Pat Murray, *The Charlton Standard Catalogue of Wade Whimsical Collectables, Fourth Edition*, Charlton Press, 1998; Ian Warner and Mike Posgay, *The World of Wade, Collectable Porcelain and Pottery* (1988, 1993 value update), *Book 2* (1995) Antique Publications.

Collectors' Clubs: The Official International Wade Collectors Club, Royal Works, Westport Rd, Burslem, Stoke–on–Trent, ST6 4AP England; Wade Watch, 8199 Pierson Ct, Arvada, CO 80005.

Ashtray, Art Deco shape, applied rabbit **$120.00**
Ashtray, primrose, pink, yellow flowers **20.00**
Bowl, Chelsea, black, ribbed foot **40.00**
Candle Holder, baby seal, light gray, black holder **38.00**
Candle Holder, badger, gray, black, and white, blue
   holder **38.00**

Cigarette Box, shape 242, white, light blue stylized flowers, gray leaves 40.00
Dish, ballerina 10.00
Dish, British Ford 10.00
Dish, mare and colt, light brown, black dish 60.00
Dish, Scotsmen 10.00
Dish, squirrel, green 25.00
Figure, donkey, cheerful Charlie 220.00
Figure, duckling, beige 120.00
Figure, Hiawatha, red trousers, yellow feather 350.00
Figure, kissing bunnies, white and gray 110.00
Figure, pongo, mauve 75.00
Figure, Sammy Seal, orange, black eyes and nose 300.00
Flower Pot, Bella Donna, white ground, green and yellow leaves, red berries, yellow int 10.00
Ginger Jar, white ground, red and black enamelled floral design 30.00
Jug, Art Deco, pyramid shape, white ground, blue spout and handle, blue and gold center panel 160.00
Jug, Harmony Ware, white ground, multicolored stars 50.00
Jug, horse's head 50.00
Jug, souvenir, Nova Scotia map, white ground, multicolored map, violet flowers, gold rim 25.00
Jug, squat, yellow and black stripes 70.00
Jug, swirling tree branches design, woodpecker handle 150.00
Lamp, barrel shape, amber, silver bands 50.00
Lighter, table, urn shape, band of shamrocks around middle, gray and blue 35.00
Lucky Leprechaun, figure, cobbler, brown face, dark green hat, gray coat and boots, blue trousers, paper label, 1950s 30.00
Lucky Leprechaun, figure, Crock O'Gold, flesh colored face, blue hat and coat, light gray trousers, brown boots, 1970s 15.00
Lucky Leprechaun, plaque, shamrock shape, white and green, black lettering 200.00
Lucky Leprechaun, figure, tailor, flesh colored face, green hat, white coat, light blue trousers, gray boot, 1960s 20.00
Minikins, cat standing, brown, black eyes and nose 30.00
Minikins, mouse, white, yellow ears, black eyes, orange nose, orange daisy front, orange and blue musical notes back 30.00
Minikins, rabbit sitting, brown, turquoise ears, black eyes and nose 30.00
Minikins, pelican, white, black/blue eyes, yellow wings and feet, blue waistcoat, red bow-tie 30.00
Night Light, rabbit, 2 pc, orange, green burrow and tray, yellow and orange flowers 250.00
Nut Bowl, Black Forest, black, white flowers, gold rim 8.00
Oil Jug, miniature, African animal transfer print 25.00
Pin Tray, shamrock shape, emb shamrocks int, gray-blue 8.00
Planter, Rose Trellis, white ground, dark pink and green print 20.00
Red Rose Tea Premium, Corgi, honey brown, black nose 9.00
Red Rose Tea Premium, frog, yellow 7.00
Red Rose Tea Premium, lion 6.00
Red Rose Tea Premium, Little Red Riding Hood, beige dress, red cape, green base 6.00
Red Rose Tea Premium, Mother Goose, brown hat, honey brown dress 10.00
Red Rose Tea Premium, Little Jack Horner, beige, pink cushion, blue plum 6.00
Red Rose Tea Premium, otter, beige, blue base 7.00

Red Rose Tea Premium, poodle, white 10.00
Red Rose Tea Premium, Puss in Boots, blue hat, coat, brown trousers 15.00
Red Rose Tea Premium, Queen of Hearts, 2 small hearts, beige dress, pink dress 15.00
Red Rose Tea Premium, rabbit, beige, ears open 8.00
Red Rose Tea Premium, Wild Board, brown, green on base 15.00
Salt and Pepper Shakers, pr, Mr and Mrs Penguin, light green 360.00
Salt and Pepper Shakers, pr, Mr and Mrs Rabbit 90.00
Wall Plaque, figural seagull, white, black wing tips, yellow beak and feet 90.00
Wall Plaque, figural yacht, green hull, blue roof, beige and mauve sails 50.00
Wall Plate, Regency and Romance 30.00
Whimsie, badger, gray, black and white face 35.00
Whimsie, Cocker Spaniel with ball, white and gray 30.00
Whimsie, crocodile, green and brown 70.00
Whimsie, leaping fawn, white, green base 45.00
Whimsie, lion, light brown 50.00
Whimsie, mare, white, brown mane, tail, and hooves, green base 45.00
Whimsie, panda, small, black and white, black band on chest 35.00
Whimsie, pig, pink, green base 75.00
Whimsie, swan, yellow beak, black tip 195.00
Whimtray, bactrian camel, light brown, black, blue, or yellow tray 30.00
Whimtray, cockatoo, black, blue, pink, or yellow tray 30.00

WAGNER WARE

In 1891 Milton M. and Bernard P. Wagner established the Wagner Manufacturing Company in Sidney, Ohio. William, a third brother, soon joined the company. In order to add a line of skillets, Milton and Bernard purchased the Sidney Hollow Ware Foundry in 1903, placing William in charge. Finding the two companies in direct competition, Sidney Hollow Ware was sold and William bought into the main company as a partner. Louis, a fourth brother, joined the company a short time later.

Wagner Manufacturing made brass casting and cast-iron hollow ware, some of which was nickel plated. Wagner was one of the first companies to make aluminum cookware. The line included cake and ice cream molds, coffeepots, percolators, pitchers, scoops, spoons, and teapots. The company won numerous awards for its aluminum products between 1900 and 1940.

Several generations of Wagners were involved in the company management as individuals died and passed stock interests to their sons. In 1953 Philip Wagner, one of Milton Wagner's sons, was serving as president. He made it known he wanted to sell the company. Cable Wagner, William Wagner's son, purchased the Wagner Hotel Company. Randall Company of Cincinnati, Ohio, purchased the balance.

In 1957 Randall's Wagner Division purchased the Griswold Cookware line from McGraw Edison. Textron of Providence, Rhode Island, acquired the Randall Company in 1959. Textron's Wagner Division acquired the Durham Manufacturing Company of Muncie, Indiana, a manufacturer of casual leisure furniture for household use. In 1969, Textron sold its household line to General Housewares Corporation, a holding company. The sale included all patent and trademark rights for Griswold and Wagner.

Reference: David G. Smith and Charles Wafford, *The Book of Griswold & Wagner: Favorite Piqua, Sidney Hollow Ware, Wapak,* Schiffer Publishing, 1995.

Newsletter: *Kettles 'n Cookware,* Drawer B, Perrysburg, NY 14129.

Bread Stick Pan, divided	$60.00
Breakfast Skillet, aluminum, wood handle	40.00
Bundt Pan	160.00
Cake Griddle	300.00
Chef Skillet, #1286D	20.00
Corn Bread Stick Pan	50.00
Deep Fat Fryer, cov	110.00
Double Skillet, hinged	85.00
Dutch Oven, #10, flat top	80.00
Dutch Oven, #247	24.00
Griddle, #6, handled, stylized logo	110.00
Griddle, handled	10.00
Juicer, #453, aluminum	35.00
Lard Ladle	20.00
Lid, Dutch Oven, #7	24.00
Lid, Dutch Oven, #10	40.00
Little Slam Bridge Pan, #1340, black iron	125.00
Omelet Pan, #821, wood handles	30.00
Pie Pan, aluminum, 9" d	50.00
Pot, 1 qt	20.00
Pot, 2 qt, #1265, bail handle	20.00
Roaster, #3, oval	130.00
Roaster with Trivet, #7, oval, aluminum	55.00
Roaster with Trivet, #8, oval, aluminum	48.00
Roaster with Trivet and Book, #8, Magnalite	35.00
Scoop, #902	25.00
Scoop, #912	25.00
Skillet, #2, stylized logo	120.00
Skillet, #4, stylized logo	50.00
Skillet, #7, stylized logo	25.00
Skillet, #8, stylized logo	25.00
Skillet, #9, stylized logo	30.00
Skillet, #11	120.00
Vienna Roll Pan	125.00
Waffle Iron, square	125.00
Warm Over Pan	100.00

WALLACE CHINA

The Wallace China Company, Vernon, California, was founded around 1931. The company made vitrified, plain and transfer printed wares for the hotel, institution, and restaurant markets. Willow ware in blue, brown, green, and red transfers was produced during the 1930s and 1940s.

Wallace China is best known for its Westward Ho houseware line, the result of a 1943 commission from the M. C. Wentz Company of Pasadena. Wentz wanted restaurant barbecue ware. Till Goodan, a well–known western artist, created three patterns: Boots and Saddles, Pioneer Trails, and Rodeo. His name is incorporated in most designs. A three–piece Little Buckaroo Chuck set for children and the El Rancho and Longhorn dinnerware patterns also were designed by Goodan.

In 1959 Shenango China Company acquired Wallace China. Wallace China operated as a wholly owned subsidiary until 1964 when all production ceased.

References: Jack Chipman, *Collector's Encyclopedia of California Pottery, Second Edition,* Collector Books, 1998; Harvey Duke, *The Official Price Guide to Pottery and Porcelain, Eighth Edition,* House of Collectibles, 1995.

Boots and Saddle, cup	$35.00
Boots and Saddle, fruit dish, 5" d	50.00
Boots and Saddle, mixing bowl, 6" d	50.00
Boots and Saddle, napkin ring	50.00
Boots and Saddle, salad bowl	400.00
Boots and Saddle, soup bowl, 5¾" d	55.00
Boots and Saddle, sugar, open	55.00
Boots and Saddle, vegetable bowl, 8" d	175.00
Chuckwagon, bowl, 6¾" d	12.00
Chuckwagon, plate, 6¼" d	35.00
Davy Crockett, ashtray	45.00
Desert Ware, dinner plate, 9" d	10.00
El Rancho, bowl, 4¾" d	20.00
El Rancho, jam jar, cov, undertray	80.00
El Rancho, plate, 9½" d	70.00
Hibiscus, dinner plate	8.00
Kit Carson, ashtray	45.00
Kit Carson, cereal bowl	20.00
Longhorn, creamer, ftd	75.00
Longhorn, cup and saucer	45.00
Longhorn, dish, 6½" d	35.00
Longhorn, platter, oval, 15½" l	175.00
Pioneer Trails, ashtray, 5½" d	45.00
Pioneer Trails, cup and saucer	55.00
Pioneer Trails, dinner plate	60.00
Pioneer Trails, shaker, 5¼" h	125.00
Pioneer Trails, soup bowl, rim, 8" d	150.00
Rodeo, chili bowl	50.00
Rodeo, cup and saucer	50.00
Rodeo, plate, 7¼"	45.00
Sam Houston, ashtray	45.00

Pioneer Trails, chop plate, 13" d, $175.00.

WALL POCKETS

The earliest American wall pockets were made by folk potters in Virginia's Shenandoah Valley. The flower wall pocket became a standard household form in the 1920s and remained popular through the end of the 1940s.

When the post–war Modern design styles became popular, wall pockets were out. The wall pocket regained some of its former popularity in the 1960s and 1970s. Import companies, such as ENESCO, included wall pockets in their catalogs. These new examples stimulated interest in collecting older ones.

References: Marvin and Joy Gibson, *Collectors Guide to Wall Pockets: Affordable & Others,* L–W Book Sales, 1994; Joy and Marvin Gibson, *Collector's Guide to Wall Pockets: Book II,* L–W Book Sales, 1997; Betty and Bill Newbound, *Collector's Encyclopedia of Wall Pockets: Identification and Values,* Collector Books, 1996, 1998 value update; Fredda Perkins, *Wall Pockets of the Past,* Collector Books, 1996.

Collectors' Club: Wall Pocket Collectors Club, 1356 Tahiti, St. Louis, MO 63128.

Abingdon, acanthus leaf, 8³/₄ x 8" **$25.00**
Brush, flying duck **45.00**
Camark, cat, climbing wall, 10" h **35.00**
Camark, scoop, emb floral dec, 8" h **10.00**
Ceramicraft, champagne glass, 5¹/₂" **12.00**
Cleminson, black kettle, "...the Kitchen is the Heart of
  the Home!" **20.00**
Czechoslovakian, bird and berry, 8" **40.00**
Czechoslovakian, bird with nest, 5" h **35.00**
Czechoslovakian, crested bird, 7" h **45.00**
Czechoslovakian, owl on castle, 5¹/₂" h **40.00**
Czechoslovakian, parrot, 7" h **35.00**
Czechoslovakian, toucan, 7¹/₂" h **40.00**
Dugan/Diamond Glass Co, bird with grapes, clear, 7³/₄
  x 7¹/₂" **40.00**
Dugan/Diamond Glass Co, woodpecker design, 8¹/₂ x
  1³/₄" **50.00**
Germany, bird at nest hole, 6⁷/₈" h **18.00**
Hull, flying goose, 8" **45.00**
Hull, pitcher, Sunglow, 5¹/₂" h **50.00**
Hull, whisk broom, Sunglow, 8¹/₂" l **50.00**
Hull, Woodland, shell, 7¹/₂" **75.00**
Imperial Glass Co, whisk broom shape, white milk glass,
  7¹/₂" h **30.00**
Japan, cone shape, Geisha girl dec, 8³/₄" h **20.00**
Japan, daffodils, 4" h **10.00**
Japan, dancing lady, 8¹/₂" h **45.00**
Japan, Dutch girl, 6" h **15.00**
Japan, Dutch girl with basket, 6¹/₂" h **12.00**
Japan, fish, 9¹/₂ x 7³/₄" **30.00**
Japan, girl devil, red, 4³/₄" h **8.00**
Japan, girl with pink hat, 5¹/₂" h **15.00**
Japan, grapes, 6⁵/₈" h **12.00**
Japan, Holly Hobbie, 7³/₄" h **10.00**
Japan, horse head and horseshoe, 8¹/₂" **20.00**
Japan, lady in empire dress, 6¹/₄" h **15.00**
Japan, Oriental woman, yellow basket, 8" h **20.00**
Japan, pink flower, green stem, imp "Made in Japan,"
  6" h **10.00**
Japan, winking white cat, climbing wall, 7" h **8.00**

Jeannette Glass Co, clear, 6¹/₂ x 3¹/₂" **15.00**
Lefton, hp, floral dec, gold trim, 6 x 8" **20.00**
Maddux of California, white sunburst, #691, 8¹/₂" **12.00**
McCoy, apple and leaves, 7 x 6" **35.00**
McCoy, bellows with bird handle, 7" h **25.00**
McCoy, Dutch shoes, 7¹/₂" h **15.00**
NcCoy, flower, rustic colors, 1946 . . . . **15.00**
McCoy, lily shape, 6" h **12.00**
McCoy, lovebirds on trivet, 8" h **45.00**
McCoy, mailbox, blue, 1951 . . . . **50.00**
Metlox, Homestead Provincial **45.00**
Metlox, Poppytrail Rooster, 7³/₄" h **25.00**
Morton, lovebirds on nest, 6¹/₂" h **15.00**
Morton, peacock, 6¹/₂" h **20.00**
Occupied Japan, red flower, black stamp mark, 5¹/₂" h **20.00**
Peasant Art Industry, made in Czechoslovakia, multicol-
  ored florals, mkd "J Mrazek," 13" h **60.00**
Pennsbury, house, "God Bless our mortgaged home,"
  6" sq **30.00**
Pennsbury, tulip, 6" sq **30.00**
Red Wing, violin, 13¹/₂" h **20.00**
Roseville, Apple Blossom, 8" h **125.00**
Roseville, Corinthian, 8" h **95.00**
Roseville, Florane, 9" h **80.00**
Roseville, Freesia, 8" h **150.00**
Roseville, Wincroft, mkd "USA 267–5" **110.00**
Royal Copley, bonnet with flowers, 5" h **25.00**
Royal Copley, Chinese boy with hat, 7¹/₂" h **25.00**
Royal Copley, hen and rooster, 6³/₄" d, price for pr **65.00**
Royal Copley, pigtail girl, 6³/₄" h **25.00**
Shawnee, birdhouse, mkd "USA 830," 6" **20.00**
Shawnee, ribbon bow **12.00**
Shawnee, Scottie dog, 9 x 5" **30.00**
Shawnee, teapot with apple, 6¹/₂" **20.00**
Stangl, Cosmo, green matte glaze, 1937 . . . . **45.00**
Tiffin Glass Co, shiny opaque black, applied gold bands **50.00**
Treasure Craft, elf on bucket, 5⁵/₈" **12.00**
Treasure Craft, elf leaning on well, 5" h, paper label **25.00**
Weller, Floral, 9¹/₂" h **75.00**
Weller, Marvo, 6³/₄" h **100.00**
Weller, Wild Rose **75.00**

Italy, raised design, 8" h, price for pr, $18.00.

WARNER BROTHERS

The Warner Brothers Animation Studio, located initially in a bungalow dubbed Termite Terrace, produced over 1,000 six– and seven–minute theatrical cartoons between 1930 and 1969. Cartoon Hall of Fame characters who appeared in these select shorts included Bugs Bunny, Daffy Duck, Elmer Fudd, Porky Pig, the Road Runner, Sylvester, the Tasmanian Devil, Tweety, Wile E. Coyote, and Yosemite Sam. Creative artists include Tex Avery, Bob Clampett, Friz Freleng, Chuck Jones, and Bob McKimson. The voice of Mel Blanc gave a distinct personality to characters such as Bug Bunny and Daffy Duck.

During the 1940s and 50s Warner Bros. characters appeared on movie screens and in comic books and newspapers. The launching of The Bugs Bunny Show on ABC in 1960 introduced them to a new audience. In the 1970s and 80s the Warner cartoons were shown at film festivals and made available on video cassette and laser disc.

Warner found it owned a licensing goldmine. Warner Bros. stores appeared in shopping malls in the early 1990s. Warner Bros. continues to pursue a vigorous licensing program.

Although third in popularity behind Disney and Hanna–Barbera in cartoon collectibles, Warner Bros. collectibles have established a strong collecting niche. Collectors are advised to look beyond the superstars at characters such as Bosco, Foghorn Leghorn, Pepé Le Pew, and Speedy Gonzales.

Reference: Bill Bruegman, *Cartoon Friends of the Baby Boom Era: A Pictorial Price Guide*, Cap'n Penny Productions, 1993.

Activity Book, Bugs Bunny Magic Paint Book, Kool–Aid
  premium, 32 pp, Whitman Publishing Co, ©1961–62
  Warner Bros, Inc, 8¼ x 11¼" **$40.00**
Alarm Clock, Sylvester dressed for dinner with mouth
  open holding fork and knife, Tweety flying above as
  seconds tick away, Bayard, ©Warner Bros, Inc, 1974,
  made in France, 4½" d, 5" h...................... **175.00**
Alarm Clock, blue, smiling full figure Bugs Bunny holding carrot, orange minute hands and gold accent sec-
  ond hand, clear plastic window, Seth Thomas Electric,
  ©Warner Bros, Inc, 1970, 3½ x 3½ x 3¾" **45.00**
Backscratcher, Tasmanian Devil, Great America, 1973 ...... **15.00**
Bank, Bugs Bunny, basket of carrots, Dakin **50.00**
Bank, emb full color Bugs Bunny and Elmer Fudd, talk-
  ing mechanism, plastic, Janex, 1977................... **55.00**
Bank, Sniffles the Mouse, standing beside barrel, metal,
  1940s, 5" h...................................... **125.00**
Bank, Tasmanian Devil, ©Warner Brothers, Inc, 1977,
  5½" h.. **45.00**
Bank, Yosemite Sam, Dakin, 1971, 7¼" h................ **40.00**
Book, *Bugs Bunny's Birthday Surprise*, 1970s **5.00**
Bookends, pr, Bugs Bunny, pushing yellow stroller with
  smiling and waving full figure bunny, Holiday Fair,
  ©Warner Bros, 1970s, 3½ x 4 x 6½" h, 5¾" w **40.00**
Candle Holder, Bugs Bunny, ceramic................... **15.00**
Card, tan, brown line drawing imprint of Road Runner,
  sgd in black ink by Chuck Jones, black printed text on
  both sides, funny Latin definitions of Road Runner,
  Jones' signature above "Original Road Runner" at bottom, 2¼ x 3¾" **60.00**
Carnival Statue, Porky Pig, pink, black accents, wearing
  blue jacket with silver glitter accents on pink accent
  base, early 1940s, 7" h **40.00**

Drinking Glass, Tweety, Warner Brothers Collector Series, Pepsi, 1973, 16 oz, $5.00.

Cereal Bowl, Porky Pig body shape, plastic, smiling
  figural head with flicker eyes, Eagle, 1950s............. **40.00**
Colorforms, Bugs Bunny and Friends Cartoon Kit,
  Colorforms,1962 .... **40.00**
Coloring Book, Bugs Bunny, Private Eye, Whitman,
  1957, unused **15.00**
Coloring Book, Dangerous Desert Featuring Yosemite
  Sam, Watkins–Strathmore, 1963..................... **10.00**
Coloring Book, Elmer Fudd, Elmer pushing Bugs in
  wheelbarrow cov, Watkins–Strathmore, 1964 .... **10.00**
Coloring Book, Porky Pig, Porky as artist at easel with
  palette cov, 16 pp, Saalfield, 1938, 10¾ x 15¼" **75.00**
Coloring Book, Sylvester and Tweety, Whitman, 1955....... **20.00**
Comic Book, The Road Runner March of Comics
  Give–Away, #347, Child Life Shoe premium, 1970 .... **10.00**
Cookie Jar, *Spacejam*, Michael Jordan and Bugs Bunny,
  MIB **150.00**
Costume, Bugs and Tweety, synthetic fabric, plastic
  mask, orig 3 x 8½" display box, 1960s **20.00**
Doll, Sylvester, Mighty Star Dolls, 1971, 17" h **15.00**
Doll, Tweety, yellow, orange accent beak and feet, blue
  and black eyes, pull–string talker, Mattel, ©Mattel,
  1976, 6¾" h **20.00**
Figure, Bugs Bunny, holding carrot, Dakin, ©1971
  Warner Bros, Inc, orig paper label, 10¾" h.............. **40.00**
Figure, Bugs Bunny, Tyco, 1994....................... **3.00**
Figure, Bugs Bunny, standing on star shaped pedestal,
  ceramic, Great America............................. **80.00**
Figure, Daffy Duck, with hunting sign, bisque, 1980s **50.00**
Figure, Elmer Fudd, hard plastic, movable head, full
  color, Dakin, 1968, 7" h **55.00**
Figure, Foghorn Leghorn, ©Warner Bros, Inc, 1970, 6" h..... **60.00**
Figure, Marvin the Martian, pewter, Rawcliffe............. **28.00**
Figure, Pepe Le Pew, standing atop gray marble accent
  base, black "California Western Railroad Fort Bragg–
  Willits, California" on base, 1960s, 7½" h **40.00**
Figure, Speedy Gonzales, vinyl, movable head, arms,
  and legs, yellow sombrero, green fabric shirt, red
  shoulder sash, white trousers, Dakin, 1970, 7½" h **35.00**
Figure, Tweety, innertube around waist, ceramic, 1975...... **35.00**
Figure, Tweety, pewter, miniature..................... **15.00**

Soakie, Speedy Gonzalez, Colgate–Palmolive, 1960s, $35.00.

Figure, Yosemite Sam, ceramic, 1985 . . . . **39.00**
Finger Puppet, Tweety, vinyl head, Great America, 1978 . . . . . **25.00**
Game, Bugs Bunny Adventure Game, Milton Bradley,
  1961 . . . . **32.00**
Game, Looney Tunes, Milton Bradley, 1968 . . . . **35.00**
Glass, Daffy, stewing over fire, Pepsi premium **40.00**
Hand Puppet, Elmer Fudd, 1950s **35.00**
Hand Puppet, Wile E Coyote, 1969, 8" h **20.00**
Iron–On, 2–pack, Wile E Coyote and Road Runner,
  sealed package **12.00**
Lamp, Road Runner and Wile E Coyote, figural, colorful
  illus shade, blue night light in back, ©Warner Bros,
  1977, made in Hong Kong **60.00**
Lunch Box, metal, Looney Tunes, American Thermos,
  1959 . . . . **100.00**
Lunch Box, metal, Porky's Lunch Wagon, dome shape,
  ©1959 Warner Bros Pictures Inc **175.00**
Lunch Box, metal, Road Runner, King–Seeley Thermos,
  1970s **55.00**
Lunch Box, vinyl, Yosemite Sam, holding gun in each
  hand, King–Seeley Thermos, 1971 . . . . **40.00**
Mirror, Tweety, full color, framed, c1980 . . . . **30.00**
Mug, white ceramic, colorful Road Runner design, from
  Marriott's Great America theme park, ©1975 Warner
  Bros, Inc **20.00**
Music Box, Daffy, Elmer and Bugs Bunny caroling, MIB **145.00**
Music Box, Elmer, plays *Over the Rainbow* **95.00**
Ornament, Speedy Gonzales, 1978, loose **20.00**
Ornament, Porky Pig, 1979, MIB **30.00**
Ornament, Wile E Coyote, 1978, MIB **20.00**
Pillow, Sniffles the Mouse shape, stuffed, 1960s **20.00**
Planter, figural Tweety standing next to well, "1977
  Warner Bros. Inc." stamped on base, 4 x 6¼ x 5¼" **40.00**
Plate, Looney Tunes, Mother's Day, 1977, MIB **15.00**
Puzzle, frame tray, Bugs Bunny and Friends in Elmer's
  Garden, Jaymar, c1948, 11 x 14" **15.00**
Record, *Bugs Bunny Meets Hiawatha*, 78 rpm, 10 x 10"
  paper sleeve, Capitol, 1958 . . . . **15.00**
Salt and Pepper Shakers, pr, ceramic, figural Porky Pig
  and long brown boot, Shoemaker, Japan, 1950s, 4" h **90.00**
Squeeze Toy, Bugs Bunny, rubber, Dell **30.00**

Stuffed Toy, Wile E Coyote, brown and tan cloth,
  ©Warner Bros Inc, 1971, 15½" h **20.00**
Thermos, metal, Yosemite Sam, Bugs Bunny, and Elmer
  Fudd against different color backgrounds, red cup,
  #2815, ©1971 Warner Bros, Inc, 6½" h **60.00**
Tie, child's, smiling Bugs Bunny eating carrot, yellow,
  white, and orange accents, c1940, 2¾" w, 10½" l **40.00**
Wall Plaque, plaster, smiling figural Bugs Bunny, blue,
  pink, and gray accents, late 1940s, 7" h **90.00**
Watch, smiling full figure Porky Pig with arms as hour
  and minute hands, orig red vinyl on leather child's
  band, Ingraham, 1949 . . . . **75.00**

WATCHES

Watches divide into three main collecting categories: (1) character licensed, (2) pocket, and (3) wrist. Character licensed watches arrived on the scene in the late 1930s. Although some character pocket watches are known, the vast majority are wristwatches. Collectors divide character watches into two types: (a) stem wound and (b) battery operated. Because they are relatively inexpensive to make, battery–operated licensed watches are frequently used as premiums by fast–food companies.

Pocket watches are collected by size (18/0 to 20), number of jewels in the movement, open or closed (hunter) face, case decoration, and case composition. Railroad watches generally are 16 to 18 in size, have a minimum of 17 jewels, and adjust to at least five positions. Double–check to make certain the movement is period and has not been switched, a common practice.

The wristwatch achieved mass popularity in the 1920s. Hundreds of American, German, and Swiss companies entered the market. Quality ranged from Rolex to Timex. Again, collectors divide the category into two groups: (a) stem wound and (b) battery operated.

In the early 1990s a speculative Swatch watch collecting craze occurred. The bubble burst in the late 1990s. Prices have fallen sharply. The craze had a strong international flavor.

Watch collecting as a whole enjoys one of the strongest international markets. On this level, brand name is the name of the game. Watches are bought primarily as investments, not for use.

References: Howard S. Brenner, *Collecting Comic Character Clocks and Watches*, Books Americana, 1987, out of print; Hy Brown with Nancy Thomas, *Comic Character Timepieces: Seven Decades of Memories*, Schiffer Publishing, 1992; Gisbert L. Brunner and Christian Pfeiffer–Belli, *Wristwatches*, Schiffer Publishing, 1993, 1997 value update; Edward Faber and Stewart Unger, *American Wristwatches: Five Decades of Style and Design*, Revised, Schiffer Publishing, 1997; Heinz Hample, *Automatic Wristwatches from Germany, England, France, Japan, Russia and the USA*, Schiffer Publishing, 1997; Robert Heide and John Gilman, *The Mickey Mouse Watch: From the Beginning of Time*, Hyperion, 1997; Helmut Kahlert, Richard Mühe, and Gisbert L. Brunner, *Wristwatches: History of a Century's Development*, Schiffer Publishing, 1986; Cooksey Shugart, Richard E. Gilbert, and Tom Engle, *Complete Price Guide to Watches, 18th Edition*, Collector Books, 1998; *W.B.S. Collector's Guide for Swatch Watches*, W.B.S. Marketing, n.d.

Periodical: *International Wrist Watch*, PO Box 110204, Stamford, CT 06911.

Newsletter: *The Premium Watch Watch,* 24 San Rafael Dr, Rochester NY 14618.

Collectors' Club: National Assoc of Watch & Clock Collectors, 514 Poplar St, Columbia, PA 17512.

Advertising, Chicken of the Sea, gold luster finish, mermaid image, gold luster metal expansion band strap, 1970s **$65.00**

Advertising, Cracker Jack, red hard plastic case with clear plastic crystal, red, white, and blue dial, blue vinyl band with red plastic buckle, orig instruction and warranty slip, c1990s **15.00**

Advertising, Gulf Oil, gold luster metal, dark blue translucent dial, animated blue, white, and orange logo, black leather bands, 1960s **75.00**

Advertising, Hawaiian Punch, red, white, and blue dial, Punchy holding juice can, black fabric strap with silvered metal buckle, with 3" d "Punchy For President" pinback button, late 1970s. **60.00**

Advertising, Keebler, chrome luster, Ernie the Keebler Elf, textured black leather bands, 1980s **40.00**

Advertising, McDonald's, digital, Ronald McDonald images, charcoal plastic case with matching vinyl band, ©1984 with text for Ronald McDonald House program "Children's Charities Established In Memory Of Ray A. Kroc," MOC **10.00**

Advertising, Reddy Kilowatt, Ballanda Corp, Los Angeles, orig warranty paper and 1 x 2 x 9½" black plastic display case, c1970–80s **175.00**

Character, Alice in Wonderland, US Time, Alice image, blue ground, missing straps, 1951 . . . . **40.00**

Character, Babe Ruth, 1 x 1¼" silvered metal Art Deco style case, facsimilie signature on dial, movement mkd "7 Jewels B.K. Co," inside back of case has jeweler's mark and "33" **175.00**

Character, Barbie, Bradley Time, Barbie profile, blue border, silver numerals, light blue leather straps, orig red plastic display case, ©1971 Mattel **100.00**

Character, Batman, ©NPPI 1966, Swiss, Luna Watch Service guarantee sheet, bat logos on band, on 4 x 9" Batman illus litho card, Batman's face on 1" d dial **775.00**

Character, Cinderella, Timex, storybook box, simulated glass slipper watch holder, instruction sheet, ©Walt Disney Productions, ¾" d dial **500.00**

Character, Cool Cat, Sheraton, gold metal case, white face, black hands, smiling Cool Cat image, simulated red leather band with gold accent metal clasp, c1970 . . . . **175.00**

Character, Davy Crockett, Bradley, Crockett image, blue and white sky ground, yellow rim with numerals depicted as arrowheads, missing minute hand, winding mechanism is frozen, 1956 . . . . **40.00**

Character, Dick Tracy, New Haven Clock & Watch Co, chrome plated metal, Tracy image, tan leather straps, complete with box insert display platform, orig price tag, warranty slip, and guarantee paper, c1947 . . . . **175.00**

Character, Disneyland Canoe Races, employee watch, blue velvet pouch with gold colored metal corn tips on front flap, text and simulated ribbon design for "30th Annual Disneyland Canoe Races 1963–1993," sun and blue water design, black hands, Disney characters in canoe between crystal and watch face, with clear liquid which moves back and forth, edition number on case reverse **195.00**

Swatch, Seospeed, Flumotions, GN 102, gentlemen's 3rd model, navy blue case, 3 hands, 1988, $190.00.

Character, Donald Duck, Bradley, replaced band, 1970s **35.00**

Character, Elvis, Koral, goldtone metal, Elvis stamp on blue ground, gold border, black vinyl strap with gold music notes, attached cardboard tag with stamp reproduction, orig plastic display case, ©1992 United States Postal Service. **40.00**

Character, Flipper, ITF, MGM, chromed metal, green image and name, black ground, glow–in–the–dark numerals, chromed metal expansion band, 1960s **75.00**

Character, Garfield, Nelsonic Industries, NY, 1" d brass colored watch, clear plastic oval shaped case with red Garfield name on front, blue strap with graphics of Garfield reclining on moon with "The Cat Jumped Over The Moon" in word balloon, 1980s **25.00**

Character, Howdy Doody, silvered metal bezel, dial face pictures Howdy at 12, 3, 6, and 9 o'clock, orig ½ x 2 x 10" case with "40th Anniversary Edition" engraved on reverse, Hour Classic Collectibles distributed by Three Cheers From Applause, Inc, 1987 . . . . **65.00**

Character, Louie, US Time, 1⅛ x 1½" chromed metal case, Louie wearing green shirt and hat with red hands and numerals, silvery white ground, replaced plastic straps, 1950s **100.00**

Character, Mickey Mantle, Roger Maris, Willie Mays, All Star Watch, 1¼" chrome luster metal bezel, clear crystal baseball image with facsimile signatures of all 3 centering dial face, early 1960s. **100.00**

Character, Mickey Mouse, Bradley, 1⅜" d chromed metal case, Mickey image with orange hands pointing at black numerals, white ground, black leather band, 1978. . . . . **65.00**

Character, Mickey Mouse, Helbros, 1¼ x 1½" chromed metal case, matching metal expansion band, Mickey with hands pointing to silver lines, bright silver ground, 1960s. **65.00**

Character, Nightmare Before Christmas, Timex, 1" d black and purple case and crystal designed like window with bars, dial with full color Lock, Shock, and Barrel illus, black plastic band, card reverse has incised logo with Jack portrait, attached to clear plastic display stand with Timex/Nightmare sticker on base, orig box, 1993 . . . . **45.00**

Character, Ren & Stimpy, Nickelodian Bigtime Enterprises, brown band, flicker image on dial reads "Happy Happy!," and "Joy Joy!," laughing Ren and Stimpy images, orig illus warranty and case, ©1992 . . . . . . **50.00**

Character, Roy Rogers, Ingraham, chrome luster metal, Roy on Trigger, black signature, red numerals, black leather straps with silver western symbols, 1951 . . . . **65.00**

Character, Smokey Bear, Bradley, replaced band. **45.00**

Character, Snow White, US Time, chromed metal case, silver dial with name, purple numerals and hands, c1958 . . . . **45.00**

Character, Space Mouse, Webster Luna, 1960s, MIB **65.00**

Character, Speedy Gonzalez, 1" d chrome accent metal case, smiling Speedy image, yellow glove watch hands, red soft vinyl band with gold accent metal clasp, Hong Kong, c1970s **90.00**

Character, Three Little Pigs, Lorus, Three Pigs image, yellow ground, black numerals, second hand disk spins as seconds tick and depicts Big Bad Wolf huffing and puffing, orig 3³/₄" h plastic case with gold Mickey Mouse image and orig price sticker, c1990 . . . . **50.00**

Character, Uncle Scrooge, Lorus, Uncle Scrooge with hands holding coins dial illus, orig black vinyl straps, c1990 . . . . **75.00**

Character, Wonder Woman, Dabs, orig box, 1972 . . . . **245.00**

Character, Woody Woodpecker, Endura, 1972 . . . . **65.00**

Character, Zorro, ⁷/₈" d chromed metal case, black and white dial, name in red, orig black leather straps with simulated tooled leather silver and yellow design, c1957 . . . . **65.00**

Commemorative, Disneyland 35 Years, Lorus, 1¹/₄" d black plastic case with white dial including text and castle outline in green, red, purple, orig black vinyl straps **20.00**

Commemorative, Epcot Center 10th Anniversary, 2¹/₂ x 5¹/₂ x ³/₄" litho tin container and "Company D" cardboard slipcase, back of tin mkd "1982 The Dawn Of A New Disney Era/The Continuation Of a Dream 1992," purple cardboard insert complete with illus warranty card mkd "One of 3000," silver and gray metal watch case and bands, silver face with raised silvered metal triangle at 10 o'clock, 10th anniversary design on reverse of case **100.00**

Pocket Watch, character, Betty Boop, Ingraham, 1934, MIB **500.00**

Pocket Watch, character, Charlie McCarthy, Gilbert, 1938, MIB **500.00**

Pocket Watch, Graf Zeppelin, 2" d silvered brass bezel, clear replacement over dial face with "Zep" art over upper half of world globe, engraved art of "Graf Zeppelin" airship above image of early world sailing vessels, "Trail Blazers/Around The World" title and inscription "1929 Time 21 Days," 1930s **375.00**

Pocket Watch, character, Roy Rogers, Bradley, 1959, MIB **250.00**

Pocket Watch, adv, Sundial Shoes, New Haven Clock Co, silvered metal case and bezel, clear plexiglas over gold luster on black dial face, central design of tiny Scotch boy figure symbol to right of "Time will tell—wear Sundial Shoes," sweep second hand, c1930s **90.00**

Swatch, Bongo/African graffiti, #SE1514–LN, 9 hole band, orig box. **55.00**

Swatch, Compass/World Tour, #SE1722–LV, 9 hole band, orig box **55.00**

Swatch, Exotica/Flower Basket, #SE1696–LR, 8 hole band, orig box. **65.00**

Swatch, Frozen Dreams/Modern Fears, #SE1234–LB, 8 hole band, orig box. **75.00**

Swatch, Passion Flower/Tropical Fiesta, #SE1504—GN, 8 hole band, orig box **80.00**

Swatch, pink mermaid/snorkeling, #SE1530–LN, 8 hole band, orig box. **55.00**

Swatch, Rising Sun/Aqua Fun, #SE1860–LK, 9 hole band, orig box. **40.00**

Swatch, Robin/Comic Heroes, #SE1490–GJ, 8 hole band, orig box. **80.00**

Wristwatch, Gruen Geneve Airways, employee's watch, manual wind, 1932, $198.00. Photo courtesy Collectors Auction Services.

Swatch, Short Wave/Radio Days, #SE1588–LF, 8 hole band, orig box. **55.00**

Wristwatch, Alpha, 17 jewels, chronograph, stainless steel, c1950s. **150.00**

Wristwatch, Elgin, 17 jewels, gold filled, curved. **60.00**

Wristwatch, Hamilton, electric, Titan II, gold filled **115.00**

Wristwatch, Longines, 17 jewels, gold jewel settings, flared case, c1950 . . . . **150.00**

Wristwatch, Rolex, Air King, 25 jewels, stainless steel, c1962 . . . . **400.00**

Wristwatch, Zenith, 36 jewels, chronograph, auto wind, stainless steel, c1969 . . . . **200.00**

WATERFORD CRYSTAL

Waterford Crystal, Waterford, County Waterford, Ireland, traces its lineage to a crystal manufacturing business established by George and William Penrose in 1783. Although this initial effort to manufacture crystal and other glassware in Waterford only lasted sixty–eight years, the items produced enjoyed an unequaled reputation.

The end of flint glass production in Dublin around 1893 marked the demise of almost three centuries of glassmaking in Ireland. In 1902 sand from Muckish in Donegal was brought to the Cork Exhibition where London glass blowers used a small furnace and and made drinking glasses cut in an "early Waterford style." This attempt to create an interest in reviving glassmaking in Ireland failed.

In 1947, almost fifty years later, a small glass factory was established in Ballytuckle, a suburb of Waterford, located approximately one–and–one–half miles from the site of the Penrose glasshouse on the western edge of the city. Apprentices were trained by immigrant European craftsmen displaced by World War II.

The management of Waterford Crystal dedicated its efforts to matching the purity of color, inspired design, and the highest quality levels of 18th– and 19th–century Waterford glass. Capturing the brilliance of the traditional, deeply incised cutting patterns of earlier Waterford pieces provided an additional challenge.

Waterford Crystal continued to grow and prosper, eventually moving to a forty–acre site in Johnstown, near the center of Waterford. In the early 1980s computer technology improved the accuracy of the raw materials mix, known in the crystal industry as the batch. Improvements in furnace design and diamond cutting wheels enabled Waterford craftsmen to create exciting new intricate glass patterns. Two additional plants in County Waterford helped the company meet its manufacturing requirements.

Waterford Crystal stemware consists of essentially twelve stem shapes with a variety of cutting patterns which expand the range to over thirty suites. Many popular patterns have been adapted for giftware, providing an opportunity to acquire matching bowls, vases, and other accessories. In addition to producing stemware, giftware, and lighting, Waterford Crystal also executes hundreds of commissioned pieces. All Waterford Crystal can be identified by the distinctive "Waterford" signature on the base.

References: Bob Page and Dale Frederiksen, *Crystal Stemware Identification Guide*, Collector Books, 1998; Harry L. Rinker, *Stemware of the 20th Century: The Top 200 Patterns*, House of Collectibles, 1997.

Claria, water goblet, 8¹/₂" h, $10.00.

Avalon, fluted champagne, 8⁷/₈" h	$20.00
Avalon, iced tea	25.00
Avalon, water goblet, 8¹/₂" h	20.00
Avalon, wine galss	20.00
Avoca, cocktail	30.00
Avoca, cordial	30.00
Avoca, fluted champagne, 7³/₈" h	30.00
Avoca, iced tea	37.00
Avoca, juice	32.00
Avoca, old fashioned	27.00
Avoca, saucer champagne, 5¹/₄" h	30.00
Avoca, tumbler	35.00
Avoca, water goblet, 7" h	25.00
Ballymore, cordial	20.00
Ballymore, fluted champagne, 8¹/₄" h	22.00
Ballymore, iced tea	25.00
Ballymore, old fashioned	22.00
Ballymore, water goblet	22.00
Ballyshannon, cordial	20.00
Ballyshannon, double old fashioned	22.00
Ballyshannon, fluted champagne	22.00
Ballyshannon, iced tea, ftd	30.00
Ballyshannon, old fashioned	22.00
Ballyshannon, water goblet	22.00
Carina, brandy	22.00
Carina, cordial, 4⁵/₈" h	17.00
Carina, cordial, 5¹/₄" h	17.00
Carina, double old fashioned	22.00
Carina, fluted champagne, 8¹/₂" h	22.00
Carina, iced tea, ftd	30.00
Carina, old fashioned, 3⁵/₈" h	22.00
Carina, water goblet, 8" h	22.00
Claria, fluted champagne, 9" h	12.00
Claria, iced tea, 8" h	15.00
Claria, wine glass, 8" h	12.00
Hanover, brandy, 5¹/₄" h	17.00
Hanover, bud vase, 4" h	20.00
Hanover, decanter, 12¹/₄" h	75.00
Hanover, double old fashioned, 4" h	12.00
Hanover, fluted champagne, 8³/₄" h	15.00
Hanover, iced tea	20.00
Hanover, water goblet, 8¹/₂" h	15.00
Hanover, wine glass, 7⁵/₈" h	15.00
Kinsale, cocktail, 4³/₄" h	32.00
Kinsale, cordial, 3⁷/₈" h	30.00
Kinsale, decanter	150.00

Kinsale, finger bowl	40.00
Kinsale, fluted champagne	35.00
Kinsale, iced tea	45.00
Kinsale, jug	90.00
Kinsale, juice	32.00
Kinsale, old fashioned, 3⁵/₈" h	37.00
Kinsale, plate, 6" d	22.00
Kinsale, plate, 8" d	25.00
Kinsale, saucer champagne, 4³/₄" h	35.00
Kinsale, tumbler, 5" h	37.00
Kinsale, water goblet, 6³/₄" h	45.00
Kinsale, wine glass	40.00
Laurent, fluted champagne, 8¹/₂" h	15.00
Laurent, iced tea, 7⁵/₈" h	17.00
Laurent, water goblet, 7⁵/₈" h	15.00
Laurent, wine glass, 7¹/₈" h	15.00
Maeve, brandy	25.00
Maeve, cocktail	22.00
Maeve, cordial	20.00
Maeve, fluted champagne	22.00
Maeve, highball glass	25.00
Maeve, iced tea, ftd	30.00
Maeve, juice	20.00
Maeve, saucer champagne	22.00
Maeve, tumbler, flat, 5" h	22.00
Maeve, water goblet	22.00
Maeve, wine glass	20.00
Sheila, cocktail, 4¹/₈" h	30.00
Sheila, cordial, 3⁷/₈" h	22.00
Sheila, decanter, 12³/₄" h	175.00
Sheila, finger bowl	35.00
Sheila, fluted champagne, 7¹/₈" h	35.00
Sheila, iced tea	40.00
Sheila, jug, 6³/₄" h	80.00
Sheila, juice, flat, 3⁵/₈" h	30.00
Sheila, old fashioned, 3¹/₂" h	30.00
Sheila, plate, 6" d	20.00
Sheila, plate, 8" d	22.00
Sheila, saucer champagne, 4³/₄" h	27.00
Sheila, tumbler, flat, 5" h	30.00
Sheila, water goblet, 7" h	32.00
Sheila, wine glass	32.00

WATT POTTERY

In 1886 W. J. Watt founded the Brilliant Stoneware Company in Rose Farm, Ohio. The company made salt–glazed utilitarian stoneware. Watt sold his business in 1897. Between 1903 and 1921 Watt worked for the Ransbottom Brothers Pottery in Ironspot, Ohio. The Ransbottoms were Watt's brothers–in–law.

In 1921 Watt purchased the Globe Stoneware Company in Crooksville, Ohio, renaming it the Watt Pottery Company. Watt made stoneware containers between 1922 and 1935.

In the 1930s Watt introduced a line of kitchenware designed to withstand high oven temperatures. Pieces were rather plain with decoration limited to a white and/or blue band. The mid–1940s' Kla–Ham'rd series featured pieces dipped in a brown glaze.

Watt's Wild Rose pattern, known to collectors as Raised Pansy, was introduced in 1950. Production difficulties resulted in a second pattern design, marketed as Rio Rose but called Cut Leaf Pansy by collectors.

Watt introduced new patterns each year during the 1950s. Although Watt sold patterns under specific pattern names, collectors group them in a single category, e.g., Starflower covers Moonflower and Silhouette. Watt introduced its Apple series in 1952, producing pieces for approximately ten years. Several variations were produced. The Tulip and Cherry series appeared in the mid–1950s. Rooster was introduced in 1955. The Morning Glory series arrived in the late 1950s followed by the Autumn Foliage in 1959. Lines introduced in the 1960s met with limited success.

Watt also made advertising and special commission ware. Pieces marked Esmond, Heirloom, Orchard Ware, Peedeeco, and R–F Spaghetti may have Watt backstamps. Watt was not evenly distributed—50% of the company's products were sold in New York and New England, 25% in the greater Chicago area, a small amount distributed by Safeway in the southern and western states, and the balance throughout the midwest and northeast.

On October 4, 1965, fire destroyed the Watt Pottery Company factory and warehouse. Production never resumed.

References: Sue and Dave Morris, *Watt Pottery: An Identification and Value Guide*, Collector Books, 1993, 1996 value update; Dennis Thompson and W. Bryce Watt, *Watt Pottery: A Collector's Reference with Price Guide*, Schiffer Publishing, 1994.

Collectors' Club: Watt Pottery Collectors USA, Box 26067, Fairview Park, OH 44126.

Apple, bowl, #74, 3 leaf	$25.00
Apple, casserole, cov, #18, French handle, blade knob	100.00
Apple, cookie jar, cov, #503, 3 leaf	325.00
Apple, creamer, #15, 3 leaf	75.00
Apple, creamer, #62, 3 leaf, Lennox, SD adv	55.00
Apple, dinner plate, #29	180.00
Apple, grease jar, #01	70.00
Apple, mixing bowl, #07, ribbed, 3 leaf, Rock Rapids adv	60.00
Apple, mixing bowl, #600, 3 leaf	20.00
Apple, nappy, #04, 3 leaf	35.00
Apple, pie plate, #33	150.00
Apple, pitcher, #15	50.00
Apple, pitcher, #16, 3 leaf	140.00
Apple, pitcher, #17, 3 leaf, ice lip	225.00
Apple, refrigerator pitcher, #69, 3 leaf, ice lip	140.00
Apple, salt and pepper shakers, pr, #45 and #46, barrel	325.00
Apple, salt and pepper shakers, pr, #117 and #118, hourglass, raised "S" and "P"	225.00
Apple, salt and pepper shakers, pr, #117 and #118, hourglass, "S" and "P" holes	200.00
Apple, spaghetti, #25, 3 leaf	300.00
Basket Weave, cookie jar, #101, pink	175.00
Basket Weave, mixing bowl, #9, blue	25.00
Basket Weave, salad bowl, #100, yellow	25.00
Bleeding Heart, bean pot	130.00
Bleeding Heart, pitcher, #15	55.00
Cherry, baker, cov, #54	125.00
Cherry, bowl, #4	30.00
Cherry, mixing bowl, #8	50.00
Cherry, platter, #31	125.00
Cherry, spaghetti bowl, #25	150.00
Dutch Tulip, baker, cov, #66	225.00
Dutch Tulip, canister set, #8182	550.00
Dutch Tulip, creamer, #62	350.00
Dutch Tulip, pitcher, #16	175.00
Dutch Tulip, salad bowl, #73	300.00
Kitch–N–Queen, baker, cov, #67	90.00
Kitch–N–Queen, ice bucket, #59	150.00
Kitch–N–Queen, mixing bowl, #7	20.00
Kitch–N–Queen, mixing bowl, #12	30.00
Kitch–N–Queen, mixing bowl, #65	40.00
Kitch–N–Queen, pie baker, #33	75.00
Kitch–N–Queen, pitcher, #17, ice lip	175.00
Kitch–N–Queen, salt and pepper shakers, pr, #117 and #118, hourglass	200.00
Open Apple, mixing bowl, #7	100.00
Open Apple, nappy, #05	150.00
Open Apple, salad bowl, #73	175.00
Pansy, mixing bowl, #7	25.00
Pumpkin, casserole, #8, loops	40.00
Rio Rose, casserole, cov, #18, grooved handle	100.00
Rio Rose, chop plate, #49	55.00
Rio Rose, cookie jar, #21	150.00
Rio Rose, cup and saucer, #40 and #41	90.00
Rio Rose, pitcher, #15	150.00
Rio Rose, plate, #42	35.00

Apple, mug, #121, price for pair, $33.00. Photo courtesy Gene Harris Auctioneers & Appraisers.

Rooster, pitcher,
6¹/₄" h, $125.00.

WEDGWOOD

In 1759 Josiah Wedgwood established a pottery near Stoke–on–Trent at the former Ivy House works in Burslem, England. By 1761, Wedgwood had perfected a superior quality inexpensive clear–glazed creamware which proved to be very successful.

Wedgwood moved his pottery from the Ivy House to the larger Brick House works in Burslem in 1764. In 1766, upon being appointed "Potter to Her Majesty" by Queen Charlotte, Wedgwood named his creamware "Queen's ware." The Brick House works remained in production until 1772.

Wedgwood built a new factory in Etruria in 1769, the same year he formed a partnership with Thomas Bentley. Wedgwood's most famous set of Queen's ware, the 1,000–piece "Frog" Service created for Catherine the Great, Empress of Russia, was produced at the Etruria factory in 1774.

By the late 1700s, the Wedgwood product line included black basalt, creamware, jasper, pearlware, and redware. Moonlight luster was made from 1805 to 1815. Bone China was produced from 1812 to 1822, and revived in 1878. Fairyland luster was introduced in 1915. The last luster pieces were made in 1932.

In 1906 Wedgwood established a museum at its Etruria pottery. A new factory was built at nearby Barlaston in 1940. The museum was moved to Barlaston and expanded. The Etruria works was closed in 1950.

During the 1960s and 1970s Wedgwood acquired many English potteries, including William Adams & Sons, Coalport, Susie Cooper, Crown Staffordshire, Johnson Brothers, Mason's Ironstone, J. & G. Meakin, Midwinter Companies, Precision Studios and Royal Tuscan. In 1969 Wedgwood acquired King's Lynn Glass, renaming it Wedgwood Glass. The acquisition of Galway Crystal Company of Galway, Erie, followed in 1974.

In 1986 Waterford and Wedgwood merged. The Wedgwood Group, now a division of Waterford Wedgwood, consists of six major divisions: Wedgwood, Coalport, Johnson Brothers, Mason's Ironstone, Wedgwood Hotelware, and Wedgwood Jewellery. The Wedgwood Group is one of the largest tabletop manufacturers in the world. It is a public company comprising eight factories and employing 5,500 people in the United Kingdom and overseas.

References: Susan and Al Bagdade, *Warman's English & Continental Pottery & Porcelain, Second Edition,* Wallace–Homestead, Krause Publications, 1991; Robin Reilly, *Wedgwood: The New Illustrated Dictionary, Revised,* Antique Collectors' Club, 1995; Harry L. Rinker, *Dinnerware of the 20th Century: The Top 500 Patterns,* House of Collectibles, 1997; Harry L. Rinker, *Stemware of the 20th Century: The Top 200 Patterns,* House of Collectibles, 1997.

Collectors' Club: The Wedgwood Society, The Roman Villa, Rockbourne, Fordingbridge, Hants, SP6 3PG, U.K.

CRYSTAL

Rio Rose, platter, #31	80.00
Rio Rose, roaster, cov, #20	100.00
Rio Rose, saucer, #27	17.00
Rooster, bowl, #73	80.00
Rooster, bowl, cov, #05, PA Dutch Days adv	400.00
Rooster, casserole, cov, #18, French handle	200.00
Rooster, creamer and sugar, cov, #62 and #98	250.00
Rooster, mixing bowl, #7	35.00
Rooster, mixing bowl, #63	90.00
Rooster, nappy, cov, #05	200.00
Starflower, baker, cov, #67, 5 petal	100.00
Starflower, bean pot, #76, handled	95.00
Starflower, cookie jar, #21, 5 petal	225.00
Starflower, grease jar, #47	400.00
Starflower, mixing bowl, #64, 4 petal	50.00
Starflower, mug, #501, 4 petal	85.00
Starflower, pitcher, #16	85.00
Starflower, platter, #31	150.00
Starflower, refrigerator pitcher, #69, 5 petal	500.00
Starflower, salt and pepper shakers, pr, #45 and #46, barrel, 5 petal	100.00
Swirl, casserole, cov, #7, rose	70.00
Swirl, mixing bowl, #5, yellow	30.00
Swirl, mixing bowl, #8, green	45.00
Swirl, pie plate, #9, blue	50.00
Tear Drop, bean pot, dec cov, #76	175.00
Tear Drop, bowl, #66	50.00
Tear Drop, cheese crock, #80	275.00
Tear Drop, mixing bowl, #5	40.00
Tear Drop, mixing bowl, #9	50.00
Tear Drop, nappy, #06	35.00
Tear Drop, pitcher, #15	50.00
Tear Drop, pitcher, #16	80.00
Tear Drop, salad bowl, #74	35.00
Tear Drop, salt and pepper shakers, pr, #117 and #118, hourglass, raised "S" and "P"	300.00
Tulip, baker, #604, ribbed	200.00
Tulip, cookie jar, #503	400.00
Tulip, creamer, #62	250.00
Tulip, mixing bowl, #65	100.00
Tulip, pitcher, #17, ice lip	250.00
Tulip, salad bowl, #73	275.00

Dynasty, brandy	$20.00
Dynasty, cordial	27.00
Dynasty, double old fashioned	30.00
Dynasty, fluted champagne	30.00
Dynasty, iced tea	35.00
Dynasty, water goblet	35.00
Dynasty, wine glass	30.00
Monarch, brandy	17.00

Monarch, cordial 22.00
Monarch, double old fashioned 25.00
Monarch, fluted champagne 25.00
Monarch, iced tea 30.00
Monarch, water goblet 30.00
Monarch, wine glass 25.00

DINNERWARE

American Clipper, bread and butter plate, 6" d $10.00
American Clipper, cream soup 37.00
American Clipper, cup and saucer, flat 25.00
American Clipper, demitasse cup and saucer 22.00
American Clipper, dinner plate 25.00
American Clipper, gravy boat and attached underplate 80.00
American Clipper, salad plate 15.00
American Clipper, vegetable bowl, cov, octagonal 125.00
American Clipper, vegetable bowl, oval, 9½" l 50.00
Amherst, bread and butter plate, 6" d 6.00
Amherst, cereal bowl, coupe, 6⅛" d 15.00
Amherst, chop plate, 13½" d 65.00
Amherst, coffeepot, cov, 7" h 75.00
Amherst, cream soup and saucer 40.00
Amherst, creamer 22.00
Amherst, cup and saucer, ftd 20.00
Amherst, demitasse cup and saucer 17.00
Amherst, dessert plate, 7" d 7.00
Amherst, dinner plate, 10¾" d 17.00
Amherst, fruit bowl, 5⅛" d 16.00
Amherst, luncheon plate, 9" d 15.00
Amherst, platter, oval, 14⅛" l 60.00
Amherst, platter, oval, 17¼" l 100.00
Amherst, salad plate, 8⅛" d 9.00
Amherst, soup bowl, flat, 9" d 20.00
Amherst, soup tureen, cov 200.00
Amherst, sugar, cov 37.00
Amherst, teapot, cov 75.00
Amherst, vegetable bowl, oval, 10⅞" l 55.00
Charnwood, ashtray, 4½" d 12.00
Charnwood, bread and butter plate, 6" d 10.00

Charnwood, bud vase, 5¼" h 35.00
Charnwood, cake plate, sq, handled, 10⅞" d 75.00
Charnwood, coaster, 4" d 12.00
Charnwood, coffeepot, cov 125.00
Charnwood, cream soup and saucer 50.00
Charnwood, creamer 35.00
Charnwood, cup and saucer, ftd 27.00
Charnwood, demitasse cup and saucer 25.00
Charnwood, dinner plate 37.00
Charnwood, fruit bowl, 5" d 17.00
Charnwood, gravy boat and underplate 100.00
Charnwood, luncheon plate, 9" d 25.00
Charnwood, platter, 14¼" l 100.00
Charnwood, salad plate, 8⅛" d 17.00
Charnwood, soup bowl, flat, 8" d 37.00
Charnwood, sugar, cov 45.00
Charnwood, teapot, cov 125.00
Charnwood, vegetable bowl, cov, round 150.00
Charnwood, vegetable bowl, oval, 10" l 70.00
Conway, bread and butter plate 8.00
Conway, cup and saucer, ftd 17.00
Conway, dinner plate, 10½" d 17.00
Conway, salad plate, 8⅛" d 10.00
Conway, soup bowl, flat, 8⅛" d 20.00
Countryside, bread and butter plate, 5⅞" d 7.00
Countryside, cup and saucer 10.00
Countryside, dinner plate, 10" d 12.00
Countryside, salad plate, 7" d 8.00
Florentine Turquoise, ashtray, 4½" d 25.00
Florentine Turquoise, bread and butter plate, 6" d 12.00
Florentine Turquoise, cereal bowl, 6⅛" d 30.00
Florentine Turquoise, chop plate, 13⅜" d 100.00
Florentine Turquoise, coffeepot, cov, 8" h 125.00
Florentine Turquoise, creamer 45.00
Florentine Turquoise, cup and saucer, ftd 30.00
Florentine Turquoise, dinner plate, 10¾" d 32.00
Florentine Turquoise, fruit bowl, 5" d 25.00
Florentine Turquoise, luncheon plate, 9" d 32.00
Florentine Turquoise, platter, oval, 14¼" 100.00
Florentine Turquoise, salad plate, 8" d 17.00
Florentine Turquoise, soup bowl, flat, 8" d 37.00
Florentine Turquoise, sugar, cov 55.00
Florentine Turquoise, teapot, cov 125.00
Florentine Turquoise, vegetable bowl, oval, 10⅝" l 75.00
Napolean Ivy, bread and butter plate, 5¾" d 7.00
Napolean Ivy, cup and saucer 20.00
Napolean Ivy, dinner plate, 10" d 17.00
Napolean Ivy, salad plate 8.00
Quince, bread and butter plate, 6⅜" d 8.00
Quince, casserole, individual 30.00
Quince, creamer, 4" h 22.00
Quince, coffeepot, cov, 8" h 80.00
Quince, cup and saucer 20.00
Quince, dinner plate 22.00
Quince, gravy boat and underplate 60.00
Quince, salad plate 13.00
Quince, salt and pepper shakers, pr 50.00
Quince, soup bowl, 7⅜" d 25.00
Quince, sugar, cov 30.00
Quince, vegetable bowl, oval, 9⅜" l 45.00
Wild Oats, bread and butter plate, 6" d 8.00
Wild Oats, cup and saucer 17.00
Wild Oats, dinner plate, 10¼" d 20.00
Wild Oats, salad plate, 8" d 12.00

Florentine Turquoise, dinner plate, 10¾" d, $32.00.

WELLER

Samuel Augutus Weller established the Weller Pottery Company in Fultonham, Ohio, in 1872. In 1888, Weller moved operations to Zanesville. By 1890 a new plant was built.

During a visit to the 1893 Columbian Exposition in Chicago, Weller saw Lonhuda ware. He bought the Lonhuda Pottery and brought William Long, its owner, to Zanesville to supervise production at Weller. When Long resigned in 1896, Weller introduced Louwelsa Weller, based on Long's glaze formula.

Weller purchased the American Encaustic Tiling Company plant in 1899. By 1900 Weller enjoyed a virtual monopoly on mass–produced art pottery. Soon Weller was exporting large amounts of pottery to England, Germany, and Russia.

In the 1910s Japanese potteries made almost exact copies of Weller products that sold in the American market for half the cost. Weller increased its production of ware for the floral and garden industries to offset the financial losses.

Weller purchased the Zanesville Art Pottery in 1920 and incorporated. Several new lines were introduced in the late 1920s. Weller's son–in–law became president in 1932. Divorce from his wife forced him to leave the company. The divorce settlement entitled him to reproduced Zona dinnerware, which he took to Gladding, McBean.

In 1945 Essex Wire Corporation leased space in the Weller factory. By 1947 Essex Wire bought the controlling stock of the company. The factory closed in 1948.

References: Sharon and Bob Huxford, *The Collectors Encyclopedia of Weller Pottery,* Collector Books, 1979, 1998 value update; Ralph and Terry Kovel, *Kovels' American Art Pottery: The Collector's Guide to Makers, Marks and Factory Histories,* Crown Publishers, 1993; Ann Gilbert McDonald, *All About Weller,* Antique Publications, 1989, out of print.

Collectors' Club: American Art Pottery Assoc, PO Box 834, Westport, MA 02790-0697.

Baby Plate, Zona, rolled edge, duckling dec, 7" d	$80.00
Bowl, Patra, 2 handled, script sgd "Weller," 4" h	70.00
Bowl, Woodcraft, emb squirrel, Weller circle stamp mark, 6" d	80.00
Bud Vase, double, Roma, die imp mark, 8½" h	80.00
Candlesticks, pr, Coppertone, figural turtle on lily pad, half kiln mark, 3 x 5"	650.00
Console Bowl, Wild Rose, green, 6 x 18"	70.00
Cookie Jar, Mammy, incised "Weller," 11" h	1,800.00
Dish, Coppertone, lily pad shape with frog, Weller half kiln mark, 4 x 15 x 10"	850.00
Flower Frog, Ardsley, polychrome kingfisher, black glaze kiln stamp, 8½ x 6"	450.00
Jardiniere, Muskota, continuous raised frieze of children walking in woods, 7¼" h	600.00
Jardiniere, Zona, die imp mark, 9" d	55.00
Planter, Coppertone, frog grasping lilypad bowl, script sgd "Weller," 4½" h	190.00
Planter, Klyro, green die imp mark, 3½" h	50.00
Syrup Pitcher, Mammy, incised "Weller," 6¼" h	700.00
Umbrella Stand, Ardsley, 19" h	550.00
Umbrella Stand, Zona, 20" h	800.00
Umbrella Stand, Zona, Weller kiln stamp, 19¾" h	425.00
Urn, Sabrinian, ftd, shell shaped body, 2 seahorse handles, ink stamped, 12" h	300.00

Vase, blue dec, multicolored floral dec, 8–sided paneled body, cobalt blue matte ground, imp "Weller," 7½" h	300.00
Vase, Cameo, blue, 8" h	60.00
Vase, Chase, fan shaped, white horseback hunter and dog on cobalt blue ground, incised "Weller Pottery," 8½" h	250.00
Vase, Coppertone, 2–handled, green, incised "Weller Hand Made," 7 x 8¾"	425.00
Vase, Coppertone, 4 ftd, imp "Weller," 4½" h	70.00
Vase, Coppertone, classic shape, stepped base, burst bubbles, 8¾" h	100.00
Vase, Coppertone, flaring, black, 6½" h	100.00
Vase, Coppertone, flaring, incised "Weller Pottery," 13 x 5¾"	650.00
Vase, Coppertone, flaring with squat base, green glaze, incised "597/JA," 12¼ x 7¾"	850.00
Vase, Glendale, ovoid, die stamp, 8¼ x 4½"	550.00
Vase, Hudson, 2–handled, berry branch and flowers on shaded pink to green ground, ink mark, 6½" h	475.00
Vase, angular handles, jonquils on shaded blue ground, Mae Timberlake, incised "Weller Pottery" and signature, 9¾" h	650.00
Vase, Hudson, classic shape, pink and blue irises on shaded green to pink ground, Mae Timberlake, ink stamp, signature, 14¾" h	1,900.00
Vase, Hudson, floral dec on shaded gray, pale green, and ivory ground, imp "Weller," 9¼" h	300.00
Vase, Hudson, gourd shaped, 2–handled, clover dec on shaded blue ground, McLaughlin, half kiln stamp and signature, 6½" h	500.00
Vase, Hudson, gourd shaped, 2–handled, dogwood blossoms on shaded blue ground, Mae Timberlake, script sgd "Weller Pottery" and signature, 6¾" h	500.00
Vase, Hudson, lily–of–the–valley on light blue ground, 9" h	110.00
Vase, Hudson, ovoid, blue irises on blue ground, Hester Pillsbury, Weller ink kiln stamp, sgd by artist, 7" h	750.00
Vase, Hudson, tapering, white and dec, irises, 11¾" h	100.00

Double Cornucopia Vase, Blossom, pastel blue ground, 1927–30, 6½" h, $50.00.

Vase, Hudson, thistle blossoms on thorned stems with leaves, lavender and gray matte ground, imp "Weller/400," 12" h 500.00

Vase, Hudson, white and dec, white roses, stamped "Weller," 14½" h 500.00

Vase, Hudson, wide band of pastel roses, imp "Weller," 13" h 600.00

Vase, Hudson Perfecto, ovoid, mauve nasturtium and green leaves on shaded mauve ground, die stamp, 7 x 4¼" 375.00

Vase, Hudson Perfecto, pink blossoms and green leaves on pink to gray ground, Dorothy England, sgd by artist, 6½ x 5½" 400.00

Vase, Klyro, green with red florals, 9" h 70.00

Vase, LaSa, classic shape, tree and landscape dec, sgd "Weller," Weller Ware paper label, 8½" h 325.00

Vase, LaSa, ovoid, trees in landscape, nacreous glaze, 8½" h 400.00

Vase, LeMar, opaque black pines and mountains on glazed fuchsia ground, kiln ink stamp, 9½" h 550.00

Vase, Malverne, floral buds and leaves on rim, script sgd "Weller," 5" h 70.00

Vase, Malverne, imp "Weller Pottery," 9" h 50.00

Vase, Roma, die imp mark, 9" h 90.00

Vase, Silvertone, emb iris, lavender, circle ink mark, partial paper label, 6" h 120.00

Vase, Stellar, bulbous and squat, white stars on blue matte ground, Hester Pillsbury, sgd "HP" in white, incised "Weller Pottery," 4 x 6¼" h 750.00

Vase, Stellar, script incised "Weller," 4½" d 300.00

Vase, Tutone, ovoid body with 3 buttressed handles on inverted pedestal, flower, berry, and leaf on green, peach, and brown matte ground, Charles Fouts, artist's cipher and Weller kiln ink stamp, 7½" h 125.00

Vase, Velva, handled, light brown, script sgd "Weller Pottery," 6" h 75.00

Vase, Zona, die imp mark, 8" h 60.00

Vessel, Coppertone, beaker shaped, incised "Weller Handmade," 6 x 5" 350.00

Wall Pocket, Ardsley, green, Weller circle stamp, 12" h 350.00

AUCTION PRICES

Weller vases sold by Dave Rago Auctions on June 29, 1997. Prices include a 10% buyer's premium.

Chase, fan shaped, white mounted hunter and dog, blue ground, incised "Weller Pottery," 8½" h **$275.00**

Hudson, bulbous, lotus flower on white and gray ground, stamped "Weller," 10" h 165.00

Hudson, corseted, daisies on shaded pink to green ground, sgd "M. Ansel," ink stamp, 8¾" h 495.00

Hudson, cylindrical, pink roses on blue ground, stamped "Weller," 13½" h 522.50

LaSa, ovoid, landscape, nacreous glaze, 8½" h 247.50

Hudson, ovoid, lily–of–the–valley on shaded blue ground, Sara Timberlake, stamp mark and signature, 9" h 550.00

Hudson, tapering, white and dec, hp swans and lake, stamped "Weller," 6¼" h 3,190.00

Hudson, ovoid, pink flowers and leaves on shaded gray to pink ground, incised "Weller" and artist's cipher, 7" h 490.00

Woodcraft, cylindrical, squirrel and tree limb handles, stamped "Weller," 17¾" h 1,650.00

WESTERN COLLECTIBLES

This category divides into three parts: (1) items associated with working cowboys and cowgirls such as horse tack, wagon trail memorabilia, everyday work clothes, dress duds, and rodeo memorabilia; (2) material related to the western dude ranch, and (3) objects shaped like or portraying images associated with the American West. It does not include items associated with literary, movie, and television characters.

Americans went western crazy in the 1950s, partially the result of the TV western. Western maple furniture was found in living rooms, dens, and children's bedrooms. Western motifs from riders on bucking horses to Mexicans taking siestas beneath cactus decorated everything from dinnerware to linens. The western revival of the early 1990s reawakened collector interest in this western motif material from the 1950s. As the decade ends, the craze seems to be abating, largely the result of high prices asked by dealers for commonly found items.

References: Judy Crandall, *Cowgirls: Early Images and Collectibles,* Schiffer Publishing, 1994; Michael Friedman, *Cowboy Culture: The Last Frontier of American Antiques,* Schiffer Publishing, 1992; Dan and Sebie Hutchins, *Old Cowboy Saddles & Spurs: Identifying The Craftsmen Who Made Them, Sixth Annual,* Horse Feathers Publishing, 1996; William Manns and Elizabeth Clair Flood, *Cowboys: The Trappings of the Old West,* Zon International, 1997; Joice Overton, *Cowboy Equipment,* Schiffer Publishing, 1998; Jeffrey B. Snyder, *Stetson Hats and the John B. Stetson Company, 1865–1970,* Schiffer Publishing, 1997.

Periodical: *American Cowboy,* PO Box 6630, Sheridan, WY 82801.

Newsletter: *Cowboy Guide,* PO Box 6459, Santa Fe, NM 87502.

Collectors' Club: National Bit, Spur & Saddle Collectors Assoc, PO Box 3098, Colorado Springs, CO 80934.

Lamp, chalkware, cowboy on bucking bronco, orig glass shade, repair to front leg, c1930s, 15½" h, 15½" w, $176.00. Photo courtesy Collectors Auction Services.

Bandanna, cotton, blue, white cowboys and horses **$20.00**

Book, *The American Cowboy: The Myth & The Reality,* Frantz, Joe and Julian Choate, 1st ed, illus, 232 pp, 1955, dj **25.00**

Book, *Boots & Saddles OR, Life in Dakota With General Custer,* Custer, Elizabeth, map and illus, Western Frontier Library series, 280 pp, 1961 . . . . **15.00**

Book, *Lives & Legends of Buffalo Bill,* Russell, Don, 1st ed, maps and illus, 514 pp, 1960 . . . . **50.00**

Book, *My Home On the Range: Frontier Life in the Bad Lands,* Johnston, Harry V, photos and illus, inscribed by author, 313 pp, 1942, dj **75.00**

Bootjack, cast iron, V–shape, ornate **45.00**

Boots, leather, tooled design, 1940s **325.00**

Branding Iron, set of 3, "T.H.C.," "T.S.," and "U.J." **125.00**

Bull Whip, leather, with leather lariat **145.00**

Calendar, 1926, "John Krabania, The Fashio, Kingman, Ariz," cowgirl wearing big hat and red scarf **150.00**

Catalog, Visalia Saddle Company, 1935, 128 pp **75.00**

Cowboy Hat, Plainsman type, tan suede leather, silk band, woven fabric tie strings **70.00**

Cowboy Hat, Texas 1836–1936 Centennial **295.00**

Cowboy Hat, Tom Mix style, tan suede, silk band **150.00**

Cowgirl Outfit, child's, split cowhide riding skirt and vest, red suede trim **175.00**

Game, Buckaroo The Cowboy Roundup Game, Milton Bradley, 1947 . . . . **35.00**

Game, Legend of Jesse James, The, Milton Bradley, 1966 . . . . **90.00**

Game, Rodeo, The Wild West Game, Whitman, 1957 . . . . . . **30.00**

Gun Belt, leather, double buckles, brass stud dec, $2^3/_4$ x 36" **60.00**

Horse Bridle, loom beaded, multicolored, against white ground, 8–point star and arrow motif, rosette on each side, red yarn tassels across forehead and nose piece, red hem tape trim **925.00**

Map, Nevada Pony Express Map, 1960–1960, published by the Nevada Pony Express Centennial Committee, chromolithograph, 22 x 17", framed **250.00**

Mittens, cowhide, 15" l **35.00**

Moccasins, pr, Iroquois baby's, leaf motif on black cloth vamp, white beadwork on black cuff trimmed with red hem tape **165.00**

Moccasins, pr, Woodland, embroidered buckskin, bright colored floral embroidered vamp against hide ground **200.00**

Photograph, horse–drawn train of ore cars, Colorado, treated paper, c1920–30, 7 x 5" **70.00**

Pin, enameled, rope circled horse rider, 1920s **32.50**

Pin, figural Texas, Sam Houston, ribbon, 1936 . . . . **90.00**

Pinback Button, "Ride 'Em Cowboy," cowboy riding bucking horse illus, c1930 . . . . **75.00**

Pipe Bag, Navajo, opaque and translucent glass beads against hide ground, crosses and geometric elements, 2 stylized 10 x 4" pipes **520.00**

Program, Chicago Rodeo, Soldiers' Field, Grant Park, Aug 14–22, 1926, $11^1/_4$ x $8^1/_4$" **45.00**

Program, Second Annual Roundup, Aug 5, 6, 7, 1920, Bozeman Montana, $8^1/_2$ x $5^1/_2$" **25.00**

Ribbon, Texas Cowboy Reunion, Stamford, attached fob, 1938 . . . . **75.00**

Saddle, brown leather, hand tooled **258.00**

Saddle, tooled brown leather, mkd "American Indian Trading Co" **632.00**

Spoon and Fork Set, Navajo, SS, hand–stamped finial of human profile, arrow, geometric, and figural motifs, c1940s **375.00**

Spurs, pr, Art Deco style, aluminum **50.00**

Spurs, pr, brass **60.00**

Spurs, pr, Mexican **60.00**

Spurs, pr, nickel plated **55.00**

Sticker, "Cheyenne Frontier Days," comical cowboy shooting guns, $3^1/_2$" d **75.00**

Wall Hanging, 4 pcs, pressed cardboard, covered wagon, singing cowboy playing guitar, howling dog, campfire scene, 1950s **50.00**

WESTMORELAND

Westmoreland, Jeannette, Pennsylvania, traces its history to the East Liverpool Specialty Glass Company and the influence of Major George Irwin. Irwin was instrumental in moving the company from East Liverpool, Ohio, to Jeannette, Pennsylvania, to take advantage of the large natural gas reserves in the area. Specialty Glass, a new Pennsylvania Company, was established in 1888. When the company ran out of money in 1889, Charles H. and George R. West put up $40,000 for 53% of the company's stock. The name was changed to Westmoreland Specialty Company.

Initially Westmoreland made candy containers and a number of other glass containers. In 1910 the company introduced its Keystone line of tableware. Charles West had opposed the move into tableware production, and the brothers split in 1920. George West continued with the Westmoreland Specialty Company, changing its name in 1924 to the Westmoreland Glass Company.

Westmoreland made decorative wares and Colonial–era reproductions, e.g., dolphin pedestal forms, in the 1920s. Color, introduced to the tableware lines in the early 1930s, was virtually gone by the mid–1930s. Amber, black, and ruby were introduced in the 1950s in an attempt to bolster the line.

In 1937 Charles West retired and J. H. Brainard assumed the company's helm. Phillip and Walter Brainard, J. H.'s two sons, joined the firm in 1940. In an effort to cut costs, all cutting and engraving work was eliminated in the 1940s. Grinding and pol-

Sign, Lee Riders, 2 sided, tin, light scratching on 1 side, c1960, $17^1/_2$" d, $220.00. Photo courtesy Wm. Morford Auctions.

ishing of glass ceased in 1957. No new molds were made until the milk glass surge in the early and mid–1950s.

The milk glass boom was over by 1958. While continuing to produce large quantities of milk glass in the 1960s, Westmoreland expanded its product line to include crystal tableware and colored items. The effort was unsuccessful. Attempts to introduce color into the milk glass line also proved disappointing. The company kept its doors open, albeit barely, by appealing to the bridal trade.

In the search for capital, an on–site gift shop was opened on April 12, 1962. The shop produced a steady cash flow. Shortly after the shop opened, Westmoreland began selling seconds. Another valuable source of cash was found.

By 1980 J. H. Brainard was searching for a buyer for the company. After turning down a proposal from a group of company employees, Brainard sold Westmoreland to David Grossman, a St. Louis–based distributor and importer, best known for his Norman Rockwell Collectibles series. Operations ceased on January 8, 1984. Most of the molds, glass, historic information, catalogs, and furniture were sold at auction.

References: Lorraine Kovar, *Westmoreland Glass, 1950–1984* (1991), *Vol. II* (1991), *Vol. III: 1888–1940* (1998), Antique Publications; Chas West Wilson, *Westmoreland Glass*, Collector Books, 1996, 1998 value update.

Collectors' Clubs: National Westmoreland Glass Collectors Club, PO Box 625, Irwin, PA 15692; Westmoreland Glass Society, PO Box 2883, iowa City, IA 52244.

Note: All items are white milk glass unless noted otherwise.

Beaded Grape, ashtray, 4"	**$8.00**
Beaded Grape, bowl, #1884, flared, ftd, 9"	**35.00**
Beaded Grape, bowl, cov, #1884, flared, ftd, 5" sq	**25.00**
Beaded Grape, bowl, cov, #1884, high ft, 7" sq	**40.00**
Beaded Grape, candlesticks, pr, #1884	**22.50**
Beaded Grape, candy box, cov	**28.00**
Beaded Grape, creamer and sugar	**18.00**
Beaded Grape, honey pot, cov, #1884, gold grapes, 5"	**50.00**
Beaded Grape, honey pot, cov, hp roses	**65.00**
Beaded Grape, powder jar, cov, square	**40.00**
Beaded Grape, salt and pepper shakers, pr, ftd	**22.00**
Beaded Grape, sugar, #1884	**15.00**
Beaded Grape, water goblet	**18.00**
Dolphin, shell compote, 8"	**25.00**
English Hobnail, goblet, round ftd, crystal	**10.00**
English Hobnail, plate, 8", crystal	**10.00**
English Hobnail, sherbet, sq ftd, crystal	**8.00**
English Hobnail, sugar, sq ftd, crystal	**8.00**
English Hobnail, wine, round ftd, crystal, 2 oz	**10.00**
Flute, butter, cov, red	**35.00**
Flute, custard, owl, red	**35.00**
Flute, eggcup, chick, red	**15.00**
Fruits, creamer and sugar	**15.00**
Hobnail, ashtray, 8" sq	**10.00**
Hobnail, bowl, handled, ftd	**20.00**
Old Quilt, creamer, large	**28.00**
Old Quilt, creamer, small	**10.00**
Old Quilt, fruit bowl, #43, crimped, ftd, 9"	**45.00**
Old Quilt, oil cruet, orig stopper	**20.00**
Old Quilt, salt and pepper shakers, pr, flat	**25.00**
Old Quilt, sugar, large	**28.00**
Old Quilt, sugar, small	**10.00**

Old Quilt, water pitcher	**45.00**
Paneled Grape, appetizer set, 3 pcs	**65.00**
Paneled Grape, basket, oval, handled, 6"	**24.00**
Paneled Grape, basket, oval, split handle	**30.00**
Paneled Grape, bowl, #1881, crimped, ruby stained, 10"	**60.00**
Paneled Grape, bowl, #1881, crimped, ruby stained, 8"	**45.00**
Paneled Grape, bowl, cupped, ftd, 9"	**115.00**
Paneled Grape, bowl, ftd, 9½"	**45.00**
Paneled Grape, bowl, gold grapes and leaves, orig label, 10½" d	**125.00**
Paneled Grape, bowl, oval, cupped, ftd, 6"	**24.00**
Paneled Grape, bowl, shallow, ftd, 8¾"	**55.00**
Paneled Grape, bud vase, 9"	**18.00**
Paneled Grape, bud vase, 15"	**28.00**
Paneled Grape, bud vase, 18"	**50.00**
Paneled Grape, butter, cov, ¼ lb	**30.00**
Paneled Grape, cake stand, #1881, skirted, 11"	**70.00**
Paneled Grape, candle holder, Colonial handle	**28.00**
Paneled Grape, candlesticks, pr, #1881, 4"	**25.00**
Paneled Grape, candy dish, cov	**45.00**
Paneled Grape, celery vase	**32.00**
Paneled Grape, chocolate box, cov, round	**45.00**
Paneled Grape, cologne bottle, gold dec	**28.00**
Paneled Grape, compote, #1881, crimped, 4½"	**30.00**
Paneled Grape, compote, cov, ftd, #1881, 7"	**40.00**
Paneled Grape, creamer and sugar, #1881, individual, ftd	**20.00**
Paneled Grape, creamer and sugar, lacy edge, large	**38.00**
Paneled Grape, cruet	**20.00**
Paneled Grape, cup and saucer	**14.00**
Paneled Grape, egg tray, center handle	**52.00**
Paneled Grape, flowerpot	**50.00**
Paneled Grape, gravy boat and liner	**70.00**
Paneled Grape, iced tea tumbler	**18.00**
Paneled Grape, jardiniere, #1881, ftd, 5"	**25.00**
Paneled Grape, jardiniere, 6½"	**35.00**
Paneled Grape, juice tumbler	**20.00**
Paneled Grape, pickle dish, oval	**16.00**
Paneled Grape, pitcher, 1 pt	**45.00**
Paneled Grape, pitcher, 1 qt	**40.00**

Paneled Grape, parfait, $20.00.

Paneled Grape, pitcher, 32 oz **32.00**
Paneled Grape, planter, square **38.00**
Paneled Grape, platter, 6 x 9" **35.00**
Paneled Grape, punch cup **10.00**
Paneled Grape, punch ladle, plain **38.00**
Paneled Grape, relish, 3 part **25.00**
Paneled Grape, salt and pepper set, 2 flat shakers and tray . . . **45.00**
Paneled Grape, salt and pepper shakers, pr, #1881, ftd **20.00**
Paneled Grape, salt and pepper shakers, pr, flat **35.00**
Paneled Grape, sauce boat and liner **50.00**
Paneled Grape, sherbet, #1881, ftd **16.00**
Paneled Grape, tidbit, 2 tier. **45.00**
Paneled Grape, toothpick holder **18.00**
Paneled Grape, vase, bell shape, ftd, 6" **25.00**
Paneled Grape, vase, bell shape, ftd, 9" **40.00**
Paneled Grape, water goblet, 8 oz **18.00**
Paneled Grape, window planter, #1881, 5 x 9" **25.00**
Paneled Grape, wine goblet. **22.50**

WHISKEY BOTTLES, COLLECTIBLE

This market has fallen on hard times. The speculative bubble burst in the mid–1980s. Prices did not stabilize, they totally collapsed for most examples. Most manufacturers, distributors, and collectors' clubs have disappeared. Today more bottles are purchased for their crossover theme than they are for their importance as collectors' special editions whiskey bottles. Although often priced higher by sellers, the vast majority of bottles sell for less than $10, if a buyer can be found at all.

The Jim Beam Distillery offered its first set of novelty (collectors' special edition) bottles during the 1953 Christmas season. Over a hundred other distillers followed suit.

The early 1970s was the golden age of collectors' special edition whiskey bottles. Several distillers offered miniature series. By the late 1970s the market was saturated. Most distillers returned to the basic bottle package.

The argument still rages as to whether or not a bottle is worth more with its seal unbroken. Check the liquor laws in your state. Most states strictly prohibit selling liquor without a license. Value has always centered on the theme of the bottle. The liquor inside has never affected value. As a result, an empty bottle has the same value as a full one.

References: Ralph and Terry Kovel, *The Kovels' Bottle Price List, Tenth Edition,* Crown Publishers, 1996; Jim Megura, *The Official Price Guide to Bottles, Twelfth Edition,* House of Collectibles, 1997; Michael Polak, *Bottles: Identification and Price Guide, Second Edition,* Avon Books, 1997.

Collectors' Clubs: Jim Beam Bottle & Specialties Club, 2015 Burlington Ave, Kewanee, IL 61443; National Ski Country Bottle Club, 1224 Washington Ave, Golden, CO 80401.

Ezra Brooks, Baltimore Oriole Wildlife, 1979 . . . . **$25.00**
Ezra Brooks, Baseball Hall of Fame, 1973 . . . . **20.00**
Ezra Brooks, Christmas Decanter, 1966 . . . . **7.00**
Ezra Brooks, Gold Prospector, 1969. . . . . **8.00**
Ezra Brooks, Keystone Kops, 1980 . . . . **35.00**
Ezra Brooks, Military Tank, 1971 . . . . **17.00**
Garnier, Apollo, 1969 . . . . **20.00**
Garnier, Eiffel Tower, 1951, 12½" h **15.00**
Garnier, Harlequin with Mandolin, 1958 . . . . **35.00**

Lionstone, Fire Fighters Fight Fires and Save Lives, 1974, $60.00.

Garnier, Paris Taxis, 1960 . . . . **25.00**
Jim Beam, Akron Rubber Capital, 1973 . . . . **17.00**
Jim Beam, Antique Coffee Grinder, 1979 . . . . **12.00**
Jim Beam, Arizona, 1968 . . . . **5.00**
Jim Beam, Bobby Unser Olsonite Eagle, 1975 . . . . **45.00**
Jim Beam, Charlie McCarthy, 1976 . . . . **25.00**
Jim Beam, Great Dane, 1976. . . . . **8.00**
Jim Beam, Kansas, 1960 . . . . **40.00**
Jim Beam, Light Bulb, 1979. . . . . **15.00**
Jim Beam, Seattle World's Fair, 1962 . . . . **10.00**
Jim Beam, Walleye Pike, 1987. . . . . **20.00**
J.W. Dant, Boeing 747 . . . . **7.00**
J.W. Dant, California Quail **8.00**
J.W. Dant, Wrong–Way Charlie **17.00**
Kentucky Gentlemen, Confederate Infantry. **10.00**
Kentucky Gentlemen, Kentucky Gentlemen, 1969 . . . . **12.00**
Kentucky Gentlemen, Revolutionary War Officer **15.00**
Lionstone, Bartender **20.00**
Lionstone, Canadian Goose. **50.00**
Lionstone, Giraffe–Necked Lady, miniature, Circus series **12.00**
Lionstone, Jesse James. **20.00**
Lionstone, Mourning Doves, Bird series **60.00**
Lionstone, Saturday Night Bath, Bicentennial Westerns **60.00**
Lionstone, The Perfesser. **40.00**
Lionstone, Wells Fargo Man. **10.00**
Luxardo, Cherry Basket, 1960 . . . . **17.00**
Luxardo, Dolphin, 1959 . . . . **50.00**
Luxardo, Sir Lancelot, 1962. . . . . **15.00**
Luxardo, Tower of Fruit, 1968 . . . . **20.00**
McCormic, Bat Masterson, Gunfighter series **25.00**
McCormic, Elvis '55, 1979, Elvis Presley series. **45.00**
McCormic, Jeb Stuart, Confederate series **30.00**
McCormic, Passenger Car, 1970, Train series **40.00**
McCormic, Pocahontas, Famous American Portrait series **35.00**
McCormic, The Pony Express, Car series. **20.00**
McCormic, Thomas Jefferson, 1975, The Patriots **15.00**
McCormic, Wood Duck, 1980, Bird series **30.00**
Old Commonwealth, Alabama Crimson Tide, 1981 . . . . **25.00**
Old Commonwealth, Kentucky Thoroughbreds, 1976 . . . . **35.00**
Old Commonwealth, South Carolina Tricentennial, 1970 . . . . **15.00**
Old Fitzgerald, Blarney Castle, 1970 . . . . **15.00**
Old Fitzgerald, Gold Coast Decanter, 1954 . . . . **12.00**

Old Fitzgerald, Memphis Commemorative, 1969 . . . . **10.00**
Ski Country, Barrel Racer, standard, Rodeo **60.00**
Ski Country, Peace Dove, miniature, Birds **25.00**
Ski Country, Skunk Family, standard, Animals **45.00**

WHITMAN TV BOOKS

The Whitman Publishing Company is a subsidiary of the Western Printing & Lithographing Company. Organized initially to bail out a failed business customer, the Whitman Publishing Company produced 200 items by 1929 in quantities consisting of 14 million books and 1.5 million games. By 1957 sales had reached $80 million. The company had plants in Hannibal (Missouri), Mount Morris (Illinois), Poughkeepsie (New York), Racine (Wisconsin), and St. Louis (Missouri).

This category is devoted to 8" books designated as 50¢ juveniles and specifically those authorized versions associated with television shows from the 1950s to the 1970s. Although laminated photographic covers became the norm in the mid–1950s, it is possible to find some titles with a plain cover. Be alert to later printings with different cover artwork.

Peeling lamination, split spines, darkened paper, and faded cover colors are common condition problems. Finding examples in excellent condition or better is difficult.

Whitman's success spawned imitators. A. L. Burt Company, M. A. Donahue & Company, Goldsmith Publishing, Grosset & Dunlap, Saalfied Publishing, and Triangle Books are just a few.

Reference: David and Virginia Brown, *Whitman Juvenile Books: Reference & Value Guide*, Collector Books, 1997.

Newsletter: *The Authorized Edition Newsletter*, RR1, Box 73, Machias, ME 04654.

Bat Masterson, #1550, Wayne C Lee, 282 pp, 1960 . . . . **$15.00**
Beverly Hillbillies, The Saga of Wildcat Creek, Doris
   Schroeder, 212 pp, 1963 . . . . **15.00**
Bonanza, Killer Lion, #1568, Steve Frazee, 212 pp, 1966 . . . . **17.00**
Circus Boy, War On Wheels, #1578, Dorothea J Snow,
   282 pp, 1958 . . . . **25.00**

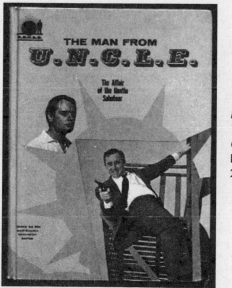

Man From U N C L E, The Affair of The Gentle Saboteur, Brandon Keith, 1966, 210 pp, $10.00.

Combat, The Counterattack, #1520, Franklin M Davis, Jr,
   210 pp, 1964 . . . . **15.00**
Dragnet, Case Stories, #1527, Richard Deming, 282 pp,
   1957 . . . . **20.00**
Dr. Kildare, The Magic Key, #1519, William Johnston,
   210 pp, 1964 . . . . **10.00**
Family Affair, Buffy Finds a Star, #1567, Gladys Baker
   Bond, 140 pp, 1970 . . . . **15.00**
F Troop, The Great Indian Uprising, #1544, William
   Johnston, 214 pp, 1967 . . . . **17.00**
Fury and The Lone Pine Mystery, #1537, William Fenton,
   282 pp, 1957 . . . . **25.00**
Gilligan's Island, #1566, William Johnston, 212 pp, 1966 . . . . **18.00**
Green Hornet, The Case of the Disappearing Doctor,
   #1570, Brandon Keith, 212 pp, 1966 . . . . **35.00**
Have Gun, Will Travel, #1568, Barlow Meyers, 282 pp,
   1959 . . . . **25.00**
Hawaii Five–O, The Octopus Caper, #1553, Leo R Ellis,
   212 pp, 1971 . . . . **12.00**
Ironside, The Picture Frame Frame–Up, #1521, William
   Johnston, 212 pp, 1969 . . . . **10.00**
I Spy, Message From Moscow, #1542, Brandon Keith,
   210 pp, 1966 . . . . **25.00**
Leave It to Beaver, #1526, Cole Fannin, 210 pp, 1962 . . . . . . **30.00**
Lucy and The Madcap Mystery, #1505, Cole Fannin,
   210 pp, 1963 . . . . **25.00**
Maverick, #1566, Charles I Coombs, 282 pp, 1959 . . . . **20.00**
Mission: Impossible, The Priceless Particle, #1515,
   Talmage Powell, 212 pp, 1969 . . . . **15.00**
Patty Duke and The Adventure of the Chinese Junk,
   #2334, Doris Schroeder, 190 pp, 1966 . . . . **17.00**
Star Trek, Mission to Horatius, #1549, Mack Reynolds,
   210 pp, 1968 . . . . **45.00**
The Waltons, Up She Rises!, #1539, Gladys Baker Bond,
   138 pp, 1975 . . . . **5.00**
Voyage to the Bottom Of the Sea, #1517, Raymond F
   Jones, 212 pp, 1965 . . . . **20.00**

WICKER

Wicker is a generic term used to describe woven objects made from cane, fiber, dried grasses, rattan, reed, rush, or willow. Wicker as a term was not used until the early 20th century. While most individuals think of wicker primarily in terms of furniture, it was used for a wide range of materials from baskets to window boxes.

Wakefield and Heywood were fierce competitors in the wicker furniture market through the 1870s, 80s, and 90s. In 1897 the two firms merged, creating the Heywood Brothers and Wakefield Company. The company had a virtual monopoly on the wicker furniture market until the 1920s.

In 1917 Marshall B. Lloyd of Menominee, Michigan, invented a machine that twisted chemically treated paper that in turn could be woven by his Lloyd loom. Lloyd's art fiber furniture featuring a closely woven style gained rapid acceptance. In 1921 Heywood Brothers and Wakefield Company, now officially Heywood–Wakefield, purchased Lloyd Manufacturing.

Collectors have little interest in post–1930 wicker. Its only value is as secondhand furniture. Use form (coffee tables and end tables) and weave (loosely woven) to identify post–1930 wicker.

Reference: Tim Scott, *Fine Wicker Furniture: 1870–1930*, Schiffer Publishing, 1990.

Bird Cage, painted white, $200.00.
Photo courtesy Gene Harris
Auctioneers & Appraisers.

Armchair and Ottoman Set, Art Deco style, close weave
design, cutout leaf pattern on back, painted yellow **$600.00**
Armchair, serpentine arms, back, and legs, cane seat,
ball legs, painted white **400.00**
Armchair, tight weave design, diamond patterns on
back and skirt, cushion with inner springs, natural **300.00**
Armchair, tight weave design, upholstery across back,
wrapped legs, floral cushion, natural **350.00**
Chair, barrel back, flat arms, round seat, skirt extends to
ground with alternating closely woven panels and
open oval rings, painted white **50.00**
Chaise Lounge, Art Deco style, close weave design,
green and red patterns in back and on sides, natural **900.00**
Chest, 4 drawers, close weave design, painted green **600.00**
Corner Chair, photographer's, scrolled backrest, 3 spin-
dles, sq seat, scrolled apron, painted white **300.00**
Crib, open weave design, fancywork on headboard and
footboard, wrapped legs, painted white **650.00**
Desk, close weave design, oak top, woven shelf,
wrapped legs, painted dark brown **450.00**
Desk, 3 wooden drawers and top, wrapped feet, painted
white **550.00**
Desk, with gallery, close weave design, 1 drawer, wood-
en top, wrapped legs, painted white **550.00**
End Table, stained oak top, open weave skirt, woven
shelf, wrapped legs, painted white **260.00**
Fainting Couch, sleigh back, straight skirt, upholstered,
painted white **150.00**
Floor Lamp, open weave base, silk–lined shade with dia-
mond patterns, painted green **700.00**
Lingerie Chest, 6 drawers, tight weave design, cane and
gesso, natural **655.00**
Lounge Chair, tight weave design, flat woven arms with
spaces for drinks and magazines, adjustable ottoman
with footrest, natural **500.00**
Loveseat, open weave design, floral cushions and back
rest, ball feet, painted white **450.00**
Planter, elongated hourglass shape, woven green top,
rattan **150.00**
Planter, open weave arch, tight weave side plant holders
and shelf, diamond patterns on sides, painted white **550.00**

Rocker, child's, Lloyd Manufacturing Co, wing design on
back, diamond pattern on skirt, painted white **200.00**
Rocker, tight weave design, open weave work by arms,
diamond pattern on back and skirt, white cush-
ion, painted orange **350.00**
Rocker, spider–web back with oval above lyre,
scrolled arms, spindled skirt, painted white **300.00**
Rocker, wingback, floral back upholstery and cushion,
natural **350.00**
Settee, serpentine arms and back with open weave and
tight weave design, inverted triangles on back, paint-
ed cane seat, painted white **500.00**
Sewing Box/Seat, hinged lid, fabric on backrest and lid,
front green diamond pattern, red trim, natural **175.00**
Sewing Table, tight weave design, bottom shelf, ball
feet, painted orange **200.00**
Sofa, Art Deco style, diamond pattern in back and skirt,
natural **600.00**
Sofa, Bar Harbor, inverted triangle designs in back, floral
cushions, painted white **500.00**
Sofa, close weave design, diamond patterns on back
and skirt, painted orange **700.00**
Stand, 3 tiers, natural oak oval top, wicker base with
gate legs and open work panels, painted white **550.00**
Table, circular stained oak top, open weave skirt and
woven shelf, painted white **250.00**
Table, circular woven top, metal legs, painted white **150.00**
Table, oval, wooden top, tight weave skirt, painted white . . . **250.00**
Table, rect, woven top and shelf, braided edge, ball feet,
painted white **350.00**
Table Lamp, open weave shade, painted white **250.00**
Tea Cart, top shelf with openwork skirt, base shelf with
straight skirt, spoked wheels, painted white **140.00**
Telephone Chair, tight weave design, oak side shelf, bot-
tom storage shelf, natural **355.00**
Towel Rack, woven base, wrapped column, natural **200.00**
Washstand, child's, porcelain enamel accessories, old
white repaint, 12½ x 22" top, 31½" h **225.00**
Work Table, rect top, medial and base shelves, painted
white **250.00**

Fishing Creel, Turtle trademark, $260.00. Photo courtesy Lang's
Sporting Collectables.

WILLOW WARE

Willow ware is a pattern based upon a Chinese legend. A wealthy father wished his daughter to marry a man he had chosen. Instead, she ran off with a young lover. The couple was pursued by a group of assassins (or the father or jilted bridegroom–to–be, depending on who you believe). They escaped to a pagoda on an island. The gods took pity and turned them into a pair of turtle doves so they could be together forever. This story provides the key decorative elements of the Willow pattern—a willow tree, two pagodas (one for the father, the other on the island for the lovers), a fence, three individuals crossing a bridge to the island, and two birds.

As early as the 1830s, over 200 British pottery manufacturers made pieces featuring a variation of the Willow pattern. By 1900 American, Dutch, French, German, Irish, and Swedish ceramic manufacturers had copied the pattern. The Japanese also copied the Willow pattern. It was one of the most popular patterns made during the "Occupied Japan" period.

Although found primarily in blue, Willow ware also was produced in black, brown, green, mulberry, pink, red, and polychrome. Collectors prefer blue. As a result, harder–to–find colors often sell for less. Manufacturer is the key to value. Collectors place a premium on ware made by manufacturers with a reputation for quality.

References: Leslie Bockol, *Willow Ware*, Schiffer Publishing, 1995; Mary Frank Gaston, *Blue Willow: An Identification & Value Guide, Revised Second Edition*, Collector Books, 1990, 1996 value update.

Newsletter: *The Willow Word*, PO Box 13382, Arlington, TX 76094.

Collectors' Club: International Willow Collectors, PO Box 13382, Arlington, TX 76094.

REPRODUCTION ALERT: The Scio Pottery, located in Scio, Ohio, is currently producing a Willow pattern. These poor–quality pieces are unmarked. A wall plaque (plate) made in China is also being produced. It is marked "BLUE WILLOW" and impressed "Made in China."

Note: Pieces listed are blue unless noted otherwise.

Buffalo, platter, oval	**$25.00**
Churchill China, butter dish, cov, 1/4 lb	15.00
Churchill China, casserole, cov, 6" d	30.00
Churchill China, chop plate, 12³/₄" d	12.00
Churchill China, clock, plate	45.00
Churchill China, cup and saucer, flat, 2⁷/₈"	7.00
Churchill China, gravy boat	15.00
Churchill China, platter, oval, 14¹/₂" l	25.00
Churchill China, salad plate, 8" d	5.00
Churchill China, salt and pepper shakers, pr	10.00
Homer Laughlin, cup, 3¹/₄"	15.00
Homer Laughlin, nappy, 8¹/₄"	45.00
Japan, berry bowl, small	5.00
Japan, bread and butter plate	4.00
Japan, bread and butter plate, 6" d	5.00
Japan, child's grill plate, 4¹/₄"	60.00
Japan, child's tea set, 4 cups and saucers, 4 plates, cov teapot, cov sugar, creamer, orig box, 17 pcs	20.00
Japan, creamer, round	15.00

Churchill, dinner plate, 10³/₈" d, $6.00.

Japan, cruets, pr, oil and vinegar, orig stoppers	90.00
Japan, cup and saucer, decal	10.00
Japan, dinner plate	10.00
Japan, kerosene lamp reflector	50.00
Japan, mug	12.00
Japan, vegetable bowl, open, oval, 10¹/₂"	35.00
Johnson Brothers, baker, 10³/₄"	30.00
Johnson Brothers, butter dish, cov, 1/4 lb	25.00
Johnson Brothers, cake plate	15.00
Johnson Brothers, cake server	20.00
Johnson Brothers, cereal bowl, coupe, 6¹/₈" d	5.00
Johnson Brothers, cup and saucer	8.00
Johnson Brothers, dinner plate, 10¹/₄" d	8.00
Johnson Brothers, gravy boat and underplate	25.00
Johnson Brothers, luncheon plate, 8³/₄" d	10.00
Johnson Brothers, platter, oval, 12" l	18.00
Johnson Brothers, salad plate, 7⁷/₈" d	7.50
Johnson Brothers, salt and pepper shakers, pr	20.00
Johnson Brothers, teapot, cov	45.00
Maastricht, bread and butter plate, 6" d	10.00
Occupied Japan, child's cup, 1³/₄"	15.00
Occupied Japan, child's plate, 3³/₄"	12.00
Occupied Japan, child's plate, 4³/₄"	20.00
Occupied Japan, child's platter, oval	50.00
Occupied Japan, child's saucer, 3¹/₄"	8.00
Ridgway, flat soup	25.00
Ridgway, grill plate	25.00
Ridgway, plate, 7"	15.00
Royal China, ashtray, 5¹/₂" d	8.00
Royal China, bread and butter plate, 6¹/₄" d	4.00
Royal China, chop plate, 12" d	12.00
Royal China, creamer	10.00
Royal China, cup and saucer	10.00
Royal China, dinner plate, 9³/₄" d	10.00
Royal China, fruit bowl, 5¹/₂" d	4.00
Royal China, sugar	12.00
Royal China, teapot	40.00
Royal China, tidbit, 3 tier	35.00
Royal China, vegetable bowl, nick under rim, 10" d	18.00

Royal Doulton, cake plate, 11" d **35.00**
Royal Doulton, coffeepot, cov **85.00**
Royal Doulton, demitasse cup and saucer **25.00**
Royal Doulton, mug, 3½" h **30.00**
Sadler, creamer and sugar **60.00**
Unmarked, batter bowl, int dec **75.00**
Unmarked, bowl, 5¼" **4.00**
Unmarked, child's creamer, 2" h **20.00**
Unmarked, child's cup, 2¼" **12.00**
Unmarked, child's plate, 4½" d **10.00**
Unmarked, child's platter, oval, 6½ x 3¾" **35.00**
Unmarked, child's sugar, cov, 3½" h **25.00**
Unmarked, child's teapot, cov, 4" h **50.00**
Unmarked, dresser box, cov **90.00**
Unmarked, pie plate **40.00**
Unmarked, salad plate **5.00**
Unmarked, sauce tureen, cov, with ladle, int pattern **225.00**
Unmarked, sugar, cov, open handles slanted upward, large . . . **40.00**
Unmarked, water tumbler **20.00**
USA, snack cup **3.00**

WORLD'S FAIRS & EXPOSITIONS

The 1851 London Crystal Palace Exhibition is considered the first modern World's Fair. America's first was the 1853 New York Crystal Palace Exhibition featuring 4,685 exhibitions, approximately half of which were from the United States. Several World's Fairs were held each decade during the 19th century. In 1928 an international convention was called to regulate the scheduling and method of conducting World's Fairs. Thirty–nine nations signed a Paris agreement creating the Bureau of International Expositions to limit the frequency of World's Fairs and define the rights and obligations of organizers and participants. The Bureau meets biannually.

World's Fairs divide into two basic types: (1) universal and (2) special category. The 1939/40 New York World's Fair and the 1967 Montreal Expo are examples of universal World's Fairs. Spokane's 1974 Expo and Transpo '86 in Vancouver were special category World's Fairs. BIF rules stipulate that one universal fair can be held every ten years, special category fairs can be held every two years but in different countries.

Most World's Fair material pictures a building, logo, or mascot. Often the name of the fair is missing. Manufacturers assume individuals will recognize the image. Collectors should familiarize themselves with the main buildings and special features of each World's Fair and Exposition.

References: Howard M. Rossen, *World's Fair Collectibles: Chicago, 1933 and New York, 1939,* Schiffer Publishing, 1998; Larry Zim, Mel Lerner and Herbert Rolfes, *The World of Tomorrow: The 1939 New York World's Fiar,* Main Street Press, Harper & Row, 1988, out of print.

Periodical: *World's Fair,* PO Box 339, Corte Madera, CA 94976.

Collectors' Club: World's Fair Collectors' Society, PO Box 20806, Sarasota, FL 34276.

1926 Sesquicentennial, compact, nickel case, brass
    medallion inset, 2¼" d **$25.00**
1926 Sesquicentennial, program and ticket, "Official
    Sesqui Centennial Daily Program and Guide," Sep 19,
    32 pp, Wed ticket, 1³/₁₆ x 2" ticket **12.00**

1933 **Century of Progress, cigar cutter, green enameled dec, Byrd's Polar Ship on reverse, 4⅛" l, $35.00.**

1933 Century of Progress, ashtray, fountain in center surrounded by Fair buildings, round, nickel plated bronze, 4⅝" d **1.00**
1933 Century of Progress, bookmark, logo and Fort, gilt, 4½" l **2.00**
1933 Century of Progress, bracelet, 1–pc construction, nickel, black and silver logo in center, 2¼" d **17.50**
1933 Century of Progress, bracelet, enameled nickel, belt buckle clasp with logo overlay, 2¼" d **22.00**
1933 Century of Progress, brush, ceramic doll handle, pink dress, pink bristles, gold cord around waist, orig display card, 3¾" **45.00**
1933 Century of Progress, dexterity puzzle, Sky Ride image, tin frame, rect, 3¼ x 4¼" **70.00**
1933 Century of Progress, guide book, 192 pp **2.00**
1933 Century of Progress, hot plate pad, Communications and Electrical Group below Fair name, octagonal, foil cov, 5" w **2.00**
1933 Century of Progress, letter opener, logo on 1 side of handle, building on other, bronze plated, 7½" l **2.00**
1933 Century of Progress, paperweight, bust of Lincoln on obverse, log cabin birthplace on reverse, gilt white metal, round, 76 mm **40.00**
1933 Century of Progress, pin, triangular frame, Fair name on overlay, clip backing, nickel plated, 1" w **8.00**
1933 Century of Progress, plate, Ford Rotunda, dark green and white, Shenango China, 9" d **48.00**
1933 Century of Progress, pocket mirror, brass back with color litho view of Lama Temple, 2¼" d **38.00**
1933 Century of Progress, ring, logo on top, sterling **7.00**
1933 Century of Progress, sheet music, *World's Exposition March,* simple drawing of grounds, inset of Eddy Hanson and Grace Wilson at piano, 1933 . . . . **15.00**
1933 Century of Progress, souvenir booklet, "Official Pictures in Color," 60+ pp, 8½ x 11" **8.00**
1933 Century of Progress, souvenir ticket book, Sky Ride, Lagoon Watercraft, Wings of a Century, Lincoln Group, Ft Dearborn, Alligator Wrestling, Lion Motordrome, Streets of Paris, Hollywood, Indian Village, and Art Institute, 4 stubs removed, 2½ x 6½" **55.00**

1933 Century of Progress, souvenir token, Hoover Exhibit, goddess and woman, Fair building, round, bronze, 30 mm **2.00**

1933 Century of Progress, stereoscope and cards, 42 photos, metal viewer, orig box with order slips **75.00**

1939 New York, change purse, leather, Trylon and Perisphere in raised silver oval on side, zipper closure, 3 x 4" **28.00**

1939 New York, club pin, Children's World Restaurant, member "Abie" the Clown Club, litho, orange and blue on white ground, 1½" d **65.00**

1939 New York, folding seat, metal cane with fold–out seat, Trylon and Perisphere and manufacturer's logo on handle, Fair Seat, Trans–American Specialties **75.00**

1939 New York, giant mechanical pencil, painted wood, blue and orange Trylon and Perisphere on gold ground, 11" l **28.00**

1939 New York, giant pen, wood handle, brass nib, color Trylon and Perisphere decal on side, 12" l **28.00**

1939 New York, key chain, license tag, enameled brass, black and orange, "New York World's Fair 1940" and tag number on front, emb Goodrich Tires and Batteries adv on back, 18 x 45 mm **60.00**

1939 New York, map, includes routes and bridges and tunnels to Fair, 4–minute crossings, and event dates, heavy paper **12.00**

1939 New York, music box, enameled, Trylon and Perisphere and Fair name on lid, 4½" h **60.00**

1939 New York, nail file, bronze handle with Trylon and Perisphere and Fair name, 4" l **18.00**

1939 New York, pennant, felt, white Trylon and Perisphere and lettering, green ground, 12" l **22.00**

1939 New York, plaque, sirocco wood, Trylon and Perisphere and "New York World's Fair 1939," 5 x 7" **25.00**

1939 New York, plate, blue and white, Food Building, by Spode for Abraham Strauss, 10½" d **125.00**

1939 New York, plate, blue and white, Hall of Production, by Spode for Abraham Strauss, 10½" d **95.00**

1939 New York, plate, blue and white, Trylon and Perisphere center, Fair views around, J & G Meakin, England, 10½" d **70.00**

1939 New York, plate, tan ground, relief picture of potter at work, "Joint Exhibit of Capital and Labor…" on bottom, 7" d **32.00**

1939 New York, postcard folder, Russian Pavilion, sepia cards, blue and black cov with statue of worker in front of Pavilion **55.00**

1939 New York, salt and pepper shakers, pr, plastic, Trylon and Perisphere, blue and orange, "New York World's Fair" on base, 4" h **15.00**

1939 New York, shirt, man's, linen, Trylon and Perisphere and "1939 World's Fair" in red and blue repeating design, Van Huesen, faded **135.00**

1939 New York, silhouette, bust of lady, black paper pasted to card, "Silhouette – Portrait Cut At the New York World's Fair 1940" at top, 4 x 6" **40.00**

1939 New York, souvenir booklet, Billy Rose Aquacade, starring Johnny Weissmuller and Eleanor Holm, dated 1939, 32 pp, 11½ x 9½" **15.00**

1939 New York, thermometer, syroco wood, Trylon and Perisphere images, 2¾" sq **10.00**

1939 New York, tie clasp, brass, 2 pc with hanging Trylon and Perisphere charm, orig box **45.00**

1964 New York, ashtray, figural Unisphere, painted hollow bisque, silvered metal wire orbital rings, "1964–New York World's Fair–1965" decal on 3½" d base, 4½" h **40.00**

1964 New York, badge, "Frederick County Days…," black and yellow ribbon, souvenir half dollar, 3" h **15.00**

1964 New York, card game, Official 1964–65 New York World's Fair Children's Card Game, 36 cards with multicolor Fair attraction images, orig box, ©1964 Ed–U–Cards, 3¾ x 4¾ x ½" box **18.00**

1964 New York, coffee cup, oversized, ceramic, cartoon dog and inscription "I Was A Coffee Hound at the New York World's Fair 1964–1965," Japan foil sticker, 4½" d, 3¾" h **45.00**

1964 New York, key chain, Billy Graham Pavilion, Bible verses on flip–out pages inside, view of Pavilion on cov, 1¼ x 1¾" **25.00**

1964 New York, plate, Unisphere and other attractions in center, gilt dec border, 10¼" d **5.00**

1964 New York, program, Sea Hunt performance at Underwater Grotto Theatre in Transportation and Travel Pavilion, 20 pp, 8¼ x 11" **15.00**

1939 New York, bank, emb Esso adv "New York World's Fair 1939," and Fair logo, chip to lip of coin slot, 5¾" sq, $165.00. Photo courtesy Collectors Auction Services.

WORLD WAR II

World War II collectibles are divided into two basic groups, Allied versus Axis and military versus home front. During the recent 50th World War II anniversary celebrations, home front material received as much attention as military material.

By the late 1930s the European nations were engaged in a massive arms race. Using the Depression as a spring board, Adolph Hitler and the National Socialists gained political power in Germany in the mid–1930s. Bitter over the peace terms of World War I, Hitler developed a concept of a Third Reich and began an aggressive unification and expansion program.

The roots of the Second World War are found in the Far East, not Europe. Japan's invasions of China and Korea and the world's failure to react encouraged Hitler. In 1939 Germany launched a blitzkrieg invasion of Poland. Although technically remaining neutral, America provided as much support as it could to the Allies.

America entered the war on December 7, 1941, following the Japanese attack on Pearl Harbor. There were four main theaters—Western, Eastern, Mediterranean, and Pacific. The entire world, either directly or indirectly, was involved in World War II in the period between 1942 and 1945. Neutral countries faced tremendous pressure from both sides.

The tide of battle turned in the Pacific with the Battle of Midway and the invasion of Guadalcanal in 1942. In 1943 the surrender of General von Arnim in Tunisia and the invasion of Italy put Allied forces in command in the Mediterranean theater. The year 1943 also marked the end of the siege of Stalingrad and the recapture of Kiev. Allied forces regained the offensive in the Western theater on June 6, 1944, D–Day. Germany surrendered on May 7, 1945. After atomic bombs were dropped on Hiroshima (August 6) and Nagasaki (August 9), Japan surrendered on August 14, 1945.

It is incorrect to assume military collectibles are war–driven. Many armed forces fighting in 1939, 1940, and 1941 used equipment left over from World War I. During the Korean Conflict, many military units used large quantities of World War II equipment. This is why provenance (ownership) plays a critical role in determining the value of a military collectible. Further, beware of the large quantity of Russian material that is flooding the collecting market now that the Iron Curtain has fallen. Much of this material is of recent production and hastily made.

References: Richard J. Austin, *The Official Price Guide to Military Collectibles, Sixth Edition,* House of Collectibles, 1998; Stan Cohen, *V For Victory: America's Home Front During World War II,* Pictorial Histories Publishing, 1991; Stanley Cohen, *To Win the War: Home Front Memorabilia of World War II,* Mortorbooks International, 1995; Robert Heide and John Gilman, *Home Front America: Popular Culture of the World War II Era,* Chronicle Books, 1995; Jon A. Maguire, *Silver Wings, Pinks & Greens: Uniforms, Wings, & Insignia of USAAF Airmen in World War II,* Schiffer Publishing, 1994; Ron Manion, *American Military Collectibles Price Guide,* Antique Trader Books, 1995; Jack Matthews, *Toys Go to War: World War II Military Toys, Games, Puzzles & Books,* Pictorial Histories Publishing, 1994; Sydney B. Vernon, *Vernon's Collector's Guide to Orders, Medals, and Decorations, 3rd Revised Edition,* published by author, 1995.

Periodicals: *Military Collectors' News,* PO Box 702073, Tulsa, OK 74170; *Military Trader,* PO Box 1050, Dubuque, IA 52004; *World War II,* 741 Miller Dr, SE, Ste D2, Harrisburg, PA 20175; *WWII Military Journal,* PO Box 28906, San Diego, CA 92198.

Collectors' Clubs: American Society of Military Insignia Collectors, 526 Lafayette Ave, Palmerton, PA 18701; Orders and Medals Society of America, PO Box 484, Glassboro, NJ 08028.

Note: For additional listings see Nazi Items.

Atlas, *Global Atlas of the World At War,* Mathews–
   Northup, 1944 .... $12.00
Bank, bisque, brown, 6" h figural bullet with "V" in
   relief, white bisque base, orig 25 stamp mark 65.00
Blotter, National Wartime Nutrition Program adv 8.00
Blotter, "The Schmidt Family Has Gone To War," B–24
   Liberator bomber illus, 4 x 9¼", unused 13.00
Book, *A Photographic Record of All the Theaters of
   Action Chronologically Arranged,* Wm G Wise & Co,
   Inc, NY, pictorial history, 1944, 7 x 10" 125.00

Bracelet, souvenir, Army Air Forces, nickel plated brass
   band with center incised short wing 8th Air Force
   patch design, inscribed "With Love" **48.00**
Broadside, Civil Defense, What to Do in Blackouts,
   black and white, 1942, 28 x 43" **75.00**
Compact, souvenir, enlisted visor cap shape, painted
   metal **75.00**
Fan, blonde WAC, Pledge of Allegiance, pull–out sides
   with tank and battleship, reverse commemorates 20th
   anniversary of a dance school, 10½" w opened **15.00**
Flight Suit, Navy, tan cotton, woven spec label, matching belt, zipper front, several pockets, USN mkd
   below spec label, size 36–S **70.00**
Footlocker, Army Air Forces, GI's, plywood, olive drab
   finish, mkd "U.S." outside, maker mkd and dated
   1942 inside lid, metal fittings **40.00**
Game, Bomber Attack/Fight the Enemy, Advance
   Games, Inc, ©1942 .... **90.00**
Gardening Set, Plant For Victory, Vaughan's Seed Store
   seed packets attached to box insert, illus garden book,
   blueprints for planting seeds, wooden garden stakes,
   row planting tool, canning labels, 16 x 33 x 2" box,
   unused **200.00**
Handkerchief, souvenir, silk, color trim, printed airborne
   wing in corner with "11th Airborne Division/188th/
   paraglider infantry/the Philippines/1945" **20.00**
Identification Bracelet, Army nurse, curved sterling body,
   hand–engraved "Lt. Florence A. Blair / N–721310" **52.00**
Identification Card, Army officer's, tri–fold, center mug
   shot photo, fingerprints on 1 side, data on other, serial number printed on outside, issued to 2nd
   Lieutenant in signal corps, Nov 20, 1942, official emb
   seal over lapping photo **20.00**
Lapel Pin, metal, pinback, "Remember," and "Pearl
   Harbor" with mounted pearl between **22.00**
Letterhead, air base illus, black and white **4.00**

Matchcovers. Top: Bond Bread Navy Plane Set, Wildcat Fighter, Lion Match, $8.00. Bottom: Greater New York Fund, full length, National Match, $9.00.

Mae West Life Preserver, Army Air Forces, yellow fabric over rubber bladders with straps, type B–4, dated 1942... 60.00

Magazine, *All Hands,* Sep 1945, Navy, End of War edition, atomic photos.. 18.00

Manual, *Recognition Pictorial Manual,* Bureau of Aeronautics, Navy Department, Washington, DC, silhouettes and technical information on Allied and Axis aircraft, black and white, 80 pp, Jun 1943, 6 x 10"....... 75.00

Map, World–Wide News Map, Richfield Oil Co, Europe and North Africa 1 side, reverse has smaller world, Southwest Pacific, and Polar maps, lists major war events from 1931 through early 1943, folder opens to 21 x 28".. 25.00

Model, "Allied Sport" aircraft, Victory Series, American Modelcraft, Chicago, balsa ribs, 2 pre–printed balsa sheets, partially assembled, orig box with "Save This Carton—Cardboard Is Needed To Help Win The War" on bottom panel, mid–1940s.......................... 32.00

Newspaper, *San Francisco Chronicle,* Dec 8, 1941, Pearl Harbor attack.. 55.00

Patch, American War Mothers, red, white, and blue stiff felt, 4" d.. 25.00

Patch, Army 101st Airborne, embroidered screaming eagle with white tongue and airborne tab............. 60.00

Pencil Sharpener, catalin plastic, marbled tan and black, decal slogan and aircraft wing symbols on upper wing, pencil inserts into nose of aircraft, steel sharpener blade in bottom.. 40.00

Periodical, *Prisoners of War Bulletin,* 3 issues, dated 1944 and 1945, reports on Japanese and German camps, published by American National Red Cross....... 55.00

Pillow Cover, glossy fabric, single star service flag above woven inscription "Berlin Or Bust, In God We Trust, Serving In U.S. Army," fringed edges, 15½ x 16½"....... 35.00

Pin, brass, diecut fighter plane.......................... 15.00

Pin, GOC United States Air Force Observer, Ass't Chief, wings, blue and white enameled symbol for Ground Observer Corps volunteer worker, mkd "sterling silver"... 12.00

Pinback Button, celluloid, Air Raid Warden, red, white, and blue, white luminous film, back paper inscription reads "Buy War Bonds At Minnesota Federal Savings & Loan Association"... 35.00

Pinback Button, "I'm Housing A War Hero," Hospitality House building with "Welcome" awning, red, white, and blue.. 12.00

Pinback Button, "Pound 'Em For Pearl," black on white, red checkered rim... 15.00

Pinback Button, "U.S. Defense Agent," red, white, and blue.. 15.00

Plaque, Army Quartermaster, brass, wheel with 13 stars, crossed sword and key above hub, spread winged Eagle at top, 12" d.. 40.00

Playing Cards, International Aircraft Silhouettes, US Playing Card Co, boxed, complete with instruction card and generic Joker, aircraft silhouette views, 1940s, used... 40.00

Pocket Mirror, multicolored, transport aircraft in flight against sunset sky under rippling flag................. 40.00

Postcard, Victory Series, #V1, soldier, civilian worker, and sailor, Tichnor Bros, 1941, unused................. 20.00

Postcard, Vultee P–66, Keep Them Flying, Longshaw........ 7.00

Poster, "Budget To Buy Victory Bonds & Build Your Bank Account," attractive woman working on household expenses, 21 x 31"..................................... 45.00

Poster, "Buy US Defense Bonds," full color, shows worker and "I'm Buying Bonds Are You?," published by Bethlehem Steel Co, 15½ x 17"................... 35.00

Poster, "If You Tell Where He's Going...He May Never Get There!," sailor image, white lettering on red block, Government printing #556153, 1943, 10 x 14"......... 65.00

Poster, "Mine Eyes Have Seen The Glory," shadow profiles of GI's in combat with woman in Army uniform looking up, Women's Army Corps and emblem on both sides, 20 x 30", framed........................ 94.00

Poster, "We'll Take Care of the Rising Sun—You Take Care of Rising Prices," ration rules appeal, full color, 16 x 23".. 65.00

Punchboard, Remember Pearl Harbor, Hula Jackpot, Coconut Jackpot, war bond purchase symbols, 11½ x 8", unused.. 175.00

Ration Book, 2 sets of coupons....................... 10.00

Ring, Army Air Forces, SS, emblem on crest............. 56.00

Savings Bond Sales Award, aluminum, replica bond certificate issued Jan 1946, "Appreciation of Volunteer Service in Financing World War II Through Sales of United States Bonds to 85,000,000 Americans," issued by War Finance Committee, 1¾ x 3¼"......... 15.00

Sewing Kit, Army Air Forces, cotton, olive drab, roll–up pouch, contains thread and safety pins............... 25.00

Stamp Album, Sky Heroes, Sinclair Oil premium, 24 pp, 4 x 8¾", unused.................................... 10.00

Streamer, white silk, black embroidered "Combat Infantry Regiment," 4' l................................. 25.00

Sweetheart Bracelet, Airborne wings on crest with "love, Joe" on back.. 28.00

Sweetheart Locket, heart shape, gold finish, Eagle, globe, and anchor device on front, chain loop......... 20.00

Sweetheart Pin, gilt and enamel ferry command patch chain, linked to USA pin.............................. 20.00

Pillow Cover, silk, "Army Air Forces, Traux Army Air Field, Madison, Wis," flocked planes and banner, dark blue ground, red fringe, 17½" sq, $25.00.

Sweetheart Pin, Marine's, brown leather, dark blue diecut battleship image between "My Man Is In The Marines," and "No Trespassing," mounted on blue leather dart with vertical bar in fastener glued on rear **25.00**

Tumbler, set of 8, decaled "V" for victory, red, white, and blue, gold band at top, pin–up in "V," job title at bottom **45.00**

Valentine, Army Sweetheart, red, white, and blue folder, emb eagle, flag, and heart on front, Victory symbol and flag inside with sentimental verse to soldier, Gibson Greeting Card Co, 5 x 6", unused **10.00**

Window Sign, cardboard, red, white, and blue Navy Department symbol upper left, serial number lower right, facsimile signature of Naval officer, 8 x 10½" **25.00**

WRIGHT, RUSSEL

Russel Wright (1904–1976) is one of the most important industrial designers of the 20th century. In 1931 Wright began selling aluminum and pewter objects from a small studio on East 53rd Street in New York City. It was also during this period that he introduced his Circus Animals series. Suffering financially in 1933 and 1934, Wright's life changed for the better when Americans fell in love with aluminum.

In 1936 Wright, his wife Mary, and Irving Richards formed the Raymor Company. Wright designed exclusively for Raymor for five years, after which time he sold his interests to Richards and formed Russel Wright Associates. In 1951 Wright spelled out his design philosophy in his book, *Guide to Easier Living.*

Wright designs appeared in a wide range of mediums from wood to metal. Acme Lamps Company, American Cyanide (plastic dinnerware), Chase Brass and Copper, Conant Ball (furniture), General Electric, Heywood–Wakefield (a sixty–piece furniture line), Hull Cutlery (flatware), Imperial Glass, Klise Woodworking Company, National Silver (flatware), Mutual Sunset Lamp Company, Old Hickory Furniture, Old Morgantown, and the Stratton Furniture Company are some of the companies that made products based upon Wright's designs.

Russel Wright designed several major dinnerware lines: American Modern for Steubenville (1939–1959), Iroquois Casual for Iroquois China (1946–1960s), Highlight for Paden City (1948), a solid color institutional line for Sterling China (1949), White Clover for Harker (1951), and the oriental–inspired Esquire shape for Knowles (1955). He also designed an art pottery line for Bauer.

References: Susan and Al Bagdade, *Warman's American Pottery and Porcelain,* Wallace–Homestead, Krause Publications, 1994; Ann Kerr, *The Collector's Encyclopedia of Russel Wright Designs, Second Edition,* Collector Books, 1997.

Note: See Edwin Knowles (Esquire) and Paden City Pottery (Highlight) for additional listings.

ALUMINUM

Bun Warmer **$65.00**
Cheese Knife **85.00**
Gravy Boat **100.00**
Ice Bucket **60.00**
Pitcher, round handle **125.00**
Tidbit, 2 tier **125.00**
Vase, round **100.00**

CHINA

American Modern, after dinner cup and saucer, cedar **$25.00**
American Modern, bread and butter plate, granite, 6" d **5.00**
American Modern, casserole, cov, white **50.00**
American Modern, chop plate, seafoam **35.00**
American Modern, coaster, seafoam **15.00**
American Modern, creamer, granite **12.00**
American Modern, creamer, seafoam **15.00**
American Modern, cup and saucer, granite **12.00**
American Modern, dinner plate, chartreuse, 10" d **12.00**
American Modern, dinner plate, coral **8.00**
American Modern, pitcher, coral **40.00**
American Modern, pitcher, seafoam **50.00**
American Modern, platter, chartreuse, 13½" l **30.00**
American Modern, salad bowl, chartreuse **80.00**
American Modern, salad plate, seafoam, 8" d **15.00**
American Modern, salt and pepper shakers, pr, granite **20.00**
American Modern, sauce boat, chartreuse **40.00**
American Modern, sugar, cov, chartreuse **18.00**
American Modern, sugar cov, granite **12.00**
American Modern, tumbler, gray **80.00**
American Modern, vegetable, cov, white **75.00**
Highlight, cereal bowl, snow glaze **15.00**
Highlight, creamer, blueberry **18.00**
Highlight, cup and saucer, blueberry **18.00**
Highlight, cup and saucer, citron **18.00**
Highlight, fruit bowl, nutmeg, small **12.00**
Highlight, platter, oval, large, dark green **40.00**
Highlight, sugar bowl, black pepper **20.00**
Highlight, vegetable bowl, oval, blueberry **45.00**
Iroquois Casual, bread and butter plate, ice blue, 6½" d **5.00**
Iroquois Casual, butter dish, pink sherbet, ½ lb **75.00**
Iroquois Casual, casserole, lettuce, 2 qt **30.00**
Iroquois Casual, cereal bowl, ice blue, 5" d **10.00**
Iroquois Casual, chop plate, ice blue, 14" d **35.00**
Iroquois Casual, coffeepot, cov, ice blue **125.00**
Iroquois Casual, cup and saucer, lettuce **18.00**
Iroquois Casual, dinner plate, lettuce, 10" d **12.00**
Iroquois Casual, fruit bowl, ice blue, 5½" d **10.00**
Iroquois Casual, gravy bowl, ice blue, 5¼" **15.00**
Iroquois Casual, pitcher, cov, lemon, 1½ qt **125.00**
Iroquois Casual, salad plate, ice blue, 7½" d **10.00**
Iroquois Casual, salt and pepper shakers, pr, stacking, lettuce **25.00**
Iroquois Casual, vegetable, cov, 2 part, avocado **30.00**
Iroquois Casual, vegetable, divided, pink sherbet, 10" **35.00**
Iroquois Casual Redesigned, cereal bowl, ice blue, 5" d **12.00**

American Modern, creamer, coral, $12.00.

Iroquois Casual Redesigned, creamer, ice blue **15.00**
Iroquois Casual Redesigned, fruit bowl, 5³/₄" d **12.00**
Iroquois Casual Redesigned, mug, ice blue. **75.00**
Iroquois Casual Redesigned, pitcher, oyster **175.00**
Iroquois Casual Redesigned, salt shaker, pink sherbet **110.00**
Iroquois Casual Redesigned, teapot, ice blue **180.00**
White Clover, bread and butter plate, coral, 6" d **8.00**
White Clover, casserole, cov, green, 2 qt **35.00**
White Clover, cereal bowl, coral **10.00**
White Clover, creamer, coral **15.00**
White Clover, dinner plate, green, 9¹/₂" d **18.00**
White Clover, fruit bowl, charcoal **8.00**
White Clover, grill plate, charcoal, 11" d **20.00**
White Clover, pitcher, cov, green, 2 qt **40.00**
White Clover, platter, coral, 13¹/₂" l **25.00**
White Clover, salt and pepper shakers, pr, charcoal **40.00**
White Clover, teacup and saucer, green **15.00**
White Clover, vegetable bowl, cov, coral, 8¹/₂" d **50.00**

GLASS

American Modern, cocktail, chartreuse, 3 oz, 2¹/₂" **$25.00**
American Modern, cordial, smoke, 2 oz, 2" **30.00**
American Modern, dessert dish, smoke, 4" d **30.00**
American Modern, iced tea, coral, 15 oz, 5¹/₄" h **25.00**
American Modern, pilsner, seafoam, 7" h **125.00**
American Modern, sherbet, seafoam, 5 oz, 2³/₄" **25.00**
American Modern, water goblet, seafoam, 11 oz, 4¹/₂" **35.00**
American Modern, wine, coral, 4 oz, 3" **25.00**
Flair, iced tea, crystal, 14 oz **45.00**
Flair, juice tumbler, crystal, 6 oz **40.00**
Flair, water goblet, crystal, 11 oz **45.00**
Twist, iced tea, crystal **35.00**
Twist, juice tumbler, crystal **25.00**
Twist, water goblet, crystal. **30.00**

PLASTIC DINNERWARE

Flair, Ming Lace, cup and saucer **$7.00**
Flair, Ming Lace, dinner plate **8.00**
Flair, Ming Lace, salad plate **8.00**
Flair, Ming Lace, sugar, cov **10.00**
Meladur, bread and butter plate, 5³/₄" d **3.00**
Meladur, cereal bowl **6.00**
Meladur, cup and saucer. **7.00**
Meladur, dinner plate, 9" d **6.00**
Residential, cup and saucer. **5.00**
Residential, dinner plate **7.00**
Residential, tumbler **10.00**

YARD–LONGS

Yard–long is a generic term used to refer to photographs and prints that measure approximately 36 inches in length. The format can be horizontal or vertical.

The yard–long print arrived on the scene in the first quarter of the 20th century, experiencing a period of popularity in the late 1910s and early 1920s. Most were premiums, issued by such diverse companies as Pompeian Beauty and Pabst Brewing's Malt Extract. Some came with calendars and were distributed by a wide range of merchants. Some had titles such as "A Yard of Kittens" or "A Yard of Roses." Always check the back. Many yard–long prints have elaborately printed advertisements on their back.

Yard–long prints are one of the many forms that show the amazing capabilities of American lithographers. Brett Litho, Jos. Hoover & Sons, J. Ottmann, and The Osborne Company are a few of the American lithographers who produced yard–long prints.

Yard–long photographs also were popular in the 1910s and 20s. The form survived until the early 1950s. Graduation pictures, especially military units, banquet photographs, and touring groups are the most commonly found. Many have faded from their original black and white to a sepia tone. Unless stopped, this fading will continue until the picture is lost.

Reference: Keagy and Rhoden, *Yard–Long Prints, Book III*, published by authors, 1995.

Calendar, woman wearing black gown and red wrap
    with black fur trim, Selz Good Shoes, sgd Gene
    Pressler, Geo Peterman's Shoe Store, Belle Plaine,
    Iowa adv, 1924 . . . . **$300.00**
Calendar, woman wearing pink gown and slippers and
    sheer white wrap, sgd Haskell Coffin, EA Mayne,
    General Merchandise, Sanborn, Iowa adv, 1920 . . . . **225.00**
Calendar, woman wearing sleeveless red gown and
    fringed shawl, Selz Good Shoes, sgd Earl Chambers,
    Hughes Clothing Co, Sabetha, Kansas adv, 1929. . . . . . . **275.00**
Calendar, woman wearing sleeveless red gown, Selz
    Good Shoes, Murray's, Rensselaer, Indiana adv, 1923 . . . . **325.00**
Calendar, woman wearing tassel–hemmed dress   and
    gold robe with blue lining, Selz Good Shoes, by
    McClelland Barclay, Peterman's Shoe Store, Belle
    Plaine, Iowa adv, 1927 . . . . **250.00**
Photograph, choral society **35.00**
Photograph, civic organization banquet **35.00**
Photograph, family reunion **30.00**
Photograph, military company grouping. **60.00**
Photograph, military graduation. **35.00**
Photograph, scenic, panoramic, Niagara Falls. **35.00**
Photograph, school graduation class **20.00**
Photograph, theater group **45.00**
Photograph, tourist group **30.00**
Print, Battle of the Chicks, Ben Austrian,©1920 . . . . **200.00**

Left: Calendar, 1930, Selz Good Shoes, sgd "Earl Christy," calendar pad removed, $400.00. Right: Print, Butterick Pattern Lady, Butterick transfers adv, 1930, $425.00.

Print, Foot Rest Hosiery lady, Ruebel's Variety Store,
    Eldore, Iowa adv, 1920 . . . . **275.00**
Print, Honeymooning in the Alps, sgd Gene Pressler,
    Pompeian Beauty adv, 1923 . . . . **150.00**
Print, woman wearing sleeveless gown and sheer wrap
    holding peacock feather fan and sitting on bench,
    1921 . . . . **225.00**

YELLOW WARE

Because it was made from a finer clay, yellow ware is sturdier than redware and less dense than stoneware. Most pieces are fired twice, the second firing necessary to harden the alkaline–based glaze of flint, kaolin, and white lead.

The greatest period of yellow ware production occurred in the last half of the 19th century. By 1900 Americans favored white bodied ware over yellow ware. Although no longer playing a major role in the utilitarian household ceramic market, some yellow ware forms, such as mixing bowls and cake molds, were made into the 1950s by firms such as J. A. Bauer, Brush Pottery, Morton Pottery, Pfaltzgraff Pottery, Red Wing, and Weller.

Reference: Lisa S. McAllister, *Collecting Yellow Ware, An Identification & Value Guide: Book II*, Collector Books, 1997.

Baking Dish, oval, applied game birds and vines, glazed
    int, 10" l **$50.00**
Beater Jar, Morton Pottery, sponged glaze **165.00**
Beater Jar, Robinson–Ransbottom Pottery, Roseville, OH,
    brown sponging on yellow ground, stamp mark,
    6½" h **35.00**
Beater Jug, Brush–McCoy, plain yellow, 5½" h **175.00**
Bowl, blue stripes, 10" d **35.00**
Bowl, brown and blue bands, 12" d **30.00**
Bowl, brown center band, 8" d **35.00**
Bowl, molded slip dec blue bands, 8¼" d **50.00**
Bowl, molded slip dec blue stripe, 6" d **38.00**
Butter Crock, brown and white stripes, ribbed base,
    7¼" d **125.00**
Candlestick, Jugtown Pottery, North Carolina, 7¼" d **150.00**
Canister, Brush–McCoy, bluebirds dec, thin white bands **275.00**
Chamber Pot, white band, dark brown stripes, 1⅞" h **45.00**
Child's Feeding Dish, Weller, shallow, brown bands, 7" d . . . **175.00**
Cookie Jar, emb dec, combination yellow ware and
    stoneware **125.00**
Creamer, molded tavern scenes and vining, brown drip
    glaze, 4¼" h **15.00**
Cruet, Ohio, Rockingham glaze, orig stopper, 10" h **400.00**
Custard Cup, Rockingham glaze **20.00**

Bowls, brown bands, minor edge wear and chipping, 9½" d and 10½" d, price for pair, $35.00. Photo courtesy Collectors Auction Services.

Custard Cup, Weller, brown bands, imp mark **25.00**
Dish, brown Rockingham sponging, 5¾" d **50.00**
Figure, bust of Franklin, brown runny glaze, 6" h **35.00**
Match Safe, Brush–McCoy, Kolor–Kraft line, 6¼" h **600.00**
Match Safe, plain yellow, 6⅜" h **500.00**
Miniature Jug, Pearl China and Pottery Co, Ohio, plain
    yellow, orig paper label **150.00**
Mold, ear of corn, 3¾" l **82.00**
Mug, white center band, 2 brown bands, 3¾" h **115.00**
Pie Plate, Morton Pottery, mottled green and brown **200.00**
Pie Plate, Wedgwood, brown flowers and bird transfer
    dec, 9" d **75.00**
Pitcher, Brush–McCoy, Nurock line, emb neck **150.00**
Pitcher, Hull, Zane Grey, blue banded, 1 pt **125.00**
Pitcher, figural man's head with tricorne, cobalt drip on
    yellow ware body, 6½" h **60.00**
Pitcher, Robinson–Ransbottom Pottery, Roseville, OH,
    raised yellow waffle pattern on sides, light yellow
    ground, mkd, 6" h **20.00**
Planter, Robinson–Ransbottom Pottery, Roseville, OH,
    bowl shape, blue green mottled glaze, 3½" h **20.00**
Plate, Wedgwood, pink lustre, grape vine and leaf
    design, "Made in England" imp mark **200.00**
Pudding Dish, slip dot flower dec **75.00**
Rolling Pin, wood handles, 15" l **190.00**
Salt Box, hanging, blue "Salt" stamped on thick white
    center band, thin white band above and below, wood-
    en lid **250.00**
Spice Shakers, pr, Morton Pottery, Amish line, plain yel-
    low **250.00**
Tankard, Morton Pottery, emb dec, 5" h **150.00**
Utility Bowls, Utility, set of 6, Morton Pottery, Daisy,
    green stamped flower dec **400.00**
Water Pitcher, Red Wing, molded body swirls, yellow
    glaze, imp "Red Wing U.S.A. #735" mark, 7½" h **35.00**

BEANIE BABIES – EXCLUSIVE REPORT

Please read my comments about Beanie Babies on Page 31 before consulting the list below. The values are highly conservative and far more realistic than those found in many Beanie Baby price guides. They reflect the market. They **DO NOT** prop the market. With a few exceptions, e.g., the very first Beanie Babies, most are selling at one–half to one–third of book—the more recent the example, the greater the discount. The Beanie Baby market collapse is at hand. A year from now, sellers will thank their lucky stars if they can get these prices.

All items are priced each. Beanie Babies without tags have little or no value. New Tag = hang tag with star; Old Tag = hang tag without star; R = retired; D = discontinued.

	New Tag	Old Tag		New Tag	Old Tag
Ally the Alligator, R 10/1/97	$15	$40	Digger the Crab, orange, R 7/1/95	$XX	$325
Ants the Anteater	5	XX	Digger the Crab, red, R 5/11/97	20	50
Baldy the Eagle, R 5/1/98	8	XX	Doby the Doberman	5	XX
Batty the Bat	5	XX	Doodle the Rooster, R 7/1/97	18	XX
Bernie the St. Bernard	5	XX	Dotty the Dalmatian	5	XX
Bessie the Cow, R 9/30/97	15	40	Early the Robin	5	XX
Blackie the Bear	5	25	Ears the Bunny, R 5/1/98	8	30
Blizzard the Snow Tiger, R 5/1/98	8	XX	Echo the Dolphin, R 5/1/98	8	XX
Bones the Dog, R 5/1/98	8	55	Fetch the Golden Retriever	5	XX
Bongo the Monkey, body colored tail, R 12/31/97	10	35	Flash the Dolphin, R 5/11/97	20	50
Bongo the Monkey, face colored tail, R 12/31/97	10	40	Fleece the Lamb	5	XX
Britannia the Bear, European release	75	XX	Flip the Cat, R 10/1/97	12	35
Bronty the Brontosaurus, R 6/1/96	XX	300	Floppity the Bunny, lavender, R 5/1/98	8	XX
Brownie the Bear R 7/1/93	XX	600	Flutter the Butterfly, R 6/1/96	XX	300
Bruno the Terrier	5	XX	Fortune the Panda	5	XX
Bubbles the Fish, R 5/11/97	25	60	Freckles the Leopard	5	XX
Bucky the Beaver, R 5/11/97	20	45	Garcia the Bear, tie-dyed, R 10/1/97	75	120
Bumble the Bee, R 6/1/96	125	300	Gigi the Poodle	5	XX
Caw the Crow, R 6/1/96	XX	300	Glory the Bear	5	XX
Chilly the Polar Bear, R 12/31/94	XX	750	Gobbles the Turkey	5	XX
Chip the Calico Cat	5	XX	Goldie the Goldfish, R 12/31/97	10	35
Chocolate the Moose	5	50	Gracie the Swan, R 5/1/98	8	XX
Chops the Lamb, R 1/1/97	25	60	Grunt the Razorback, R, 5/11/97	30	75
Claude the Tie-Dyed Crab	5	XX	Happy the Hippo, gray, D 1/1/95	XX	300
Congo the Gorilla	5	XX	Happy the Hippo, lavender, R 5/1/98	8	45
Coral the Fish, R 1/1/97	25	60	Hippity the Bunny, mint green, R 5/1/98	8	XX
Crunch the Shark	5	XX	Hissy the Snake	5	XX
Cubbie the Bear, R 12/31/97	10	35	Hoot the Owl, R 10/1/97	15	40
Cubbie the Bear, Chicago Cubs promo, May	65	XX	Hoppity the Bunny, pink, R 5/1/98	8	XX
Cubbie the Bear, Chicago Cubs promo, Sept	50	XX	Humphrey the Camel, R 12/31/95	XX	800
Curly the Bear	5	XX	Iggy the Iguana	5	XX
Daisy the Cow	5	30	Inch the Worm, felt antennae, D 6/1/96	35	80
Derby the Horse, coarse yarn, R 12/15/97	10	30	Inch the Worm, yarn antennae, R 5/1/98	8	XX
Derby the Horse, fine yarn, R 1995	XX	1,500	Inky the Octopus, pink, R 5/1/98	8	35
Derby the Horse, white dot on forehead	5	XX	Inky the Octopus, tan, with mouth, D 7/1/95	XX	300
			Inky the Octopus, tan, without mouth, D 7/1/94	XX	400
			Jake the Mallard Duck	5	XX
			Jobber the Parrot	5	XX
			Jolly the Walrus, R 5/1/98	8	XX
			Kiwi the Toucan, R 12/31/96	40	75
			Kuku the Cockatoo	5	XX
			Lefty the Donkey, R 12/31/96	100	XX
			Legs the Frog, R 10/1/97	15	50
			Libearty the Bear, R 12/31/96	100	XX
			Lizzy the Lizard, blue and yellow, R 12/31/97	10	100
			Lizzy the Lizard, tie-dyed, R 1/1/95	XX	350
			Lucky the Ladybug, 7 glued–on dots, D 12/31/96	XX	125
			Lucky the Ladybug, 11 printed spots, R 5/1/98	8	XX
			Lucky the Ladybug, 21 printed spots, D	100	XX

Fleece the Lamb, new tag, $5.

	New Tag	Old Tag
Magic the Dragon, hot pink stitching, R 12/31/97 . . .	$40	$XX
Magic the Dragon, light pink stitching, R 12/31/97 . .	10	35
Manny the Manatee, R 5/11/97	30	665
Maple the Bear, Canadian exclusive	75	XX
McDonald's Teenie Beanie Babies, 1997, R 4/97	5	XX
McDonald's Teenie Beanie Babies, 1998, R 6/97	3	XX
Mel the Koala	5	XX
Mystic the Unicorn, coarse yarn, gold horn, R 11/1/97	10	30
Mystic the Unicorn, fine yarn, D 7/1/95	XX	130
Mystic the Unicorn, coarse yarn, iridescent horn. . . .	5	XX
Nana the Monkey, tan tail, R 7/1/95	XX	1,000
Nanook the Husky.	5	XX
Nip the Cat, gold with pink ears, R 7/1/95	XX	350
Nip the Cat, white face and belly, R 7/1/95.	XX	225
Nip the Cat, white paws, R 12/31/97	10	XX
Nuts the Squirrel	5	XX
Patti the Platypus, deep fuchsia, R 7/1/94	XX	600
Patti the Platypus, fuchsia, R 5/1/98	8	25
Patti the Platypus, magenta, R 7/1/96	XX	275
Patti the Platypus, raspberry, R 7/1/94.	XX	400
Peace the Tie-Dyed Bear	20	XX
Peanut the Elephant, dark blue, D 12/31/95	XX	2,000
Peanut the Elephant, light blue, R 5/1/98	8	125
Peking the Panda, R 1/1/95	XX	700
Pinchers the Lobster, R 5/1/98	8	40
Pinky the Flamingo	5	30
Pouch the Kangaroo	5	XX
Pounce the Cat	5	XX
Prance the Cat.	5	XX
Pride the Bear, Canadian exclusive, D	100	XX
Princess the Bear, Princess Diana commemorative . .	50	XX
Puffer the Puffin.	5	XX
Pugsly the Pug Dog	5	XX
Punchers the Lobster, D 7/1/93.	XX	1,250
Quackers the Duck, with wings, R 5/1/98	8	30
Quackers the Duck, without wings, D 7/1/95	XX	1,100
Radar the Bat, R 5/11/97	40	100
Rainbow the Chameleon	5	XX
Rex the Tyrannosaurus, R 7/1/96.	XX	325
Righty the Elephant, R 1/1/97.	100	XX
Ringo the Raccoon	5	30
Roary the Lion.	5	XX
Rocket the Bluejay.	5	XX
Rover the Dog, R 5/1/98	8	XX
Scoop the Pelican	5	XX
Scottie the Terrier, R 5/1/98	8	XX
Seamore the Seal, R 10/1/97	60	120
Seaweed the Otter	5	20
Slither the Snake, R 12/31/95.	XX	800
Sly the Fox, brown belly, D 7/1/96	50	XX
Sly the Fox, white belly, R	8	XX
Smoochy the Frog	5	XX
Snip the Siamese Cat	5	XX
Snort the Bull, white feet	5	XX
Snowball the Snowman, R 12/31/97.	10	XX
Sparky the Dalmatian, R 5/11/97	30	XX
Speedy the Turtle, R 10/1/97.	15	60
Spike the Rhino.	5	XX
Spinner the Spider	5	XX
Splash the Whale, R 5/11/97	25	100
Spook the Ghost, not "Spooky," R 12/31/97	XX	125

	New Tag	Old Tag
Spooky the Ghost, R 12/31/97	$12	$35
Spot the Dog, with spot, R 10/1/97.	15	35
Spot the Dog, without spot, R 7/1/94	XX	850
Spunky the Cocker Spaniel.	5	XX
Squealer the Pig, R 5/1/98	8	35
Steg the Stegosaurus, R 12/1/96	XX	300
Sting the Manta Ray, R 1/1/97	40	125
Stinger the Scorpion	5	XX
Stinky the Skunk	5	20
Stretch the Ostrich.	5	XX
Stripes the Tiger, gold, fewer stripes, R 5/1/98	12	XX
Stripes the Tiger, orange, D 7/1/96	XX	150
Stripes the Tiger, orange, fuzzy belly, D.	XX	300
Strut the Rooster	5	XX
Tabasco the Bull, red feet, R 1/1/97	65	90
Tank the Armadillo, 7 ridges, R 7/1/96	80	95
Tank the Armadillo, 9 ridges, no shell, R 7/1/96	80	XX
Tank the Armadillo, 9 ridges, with shell, R 10/1/97 . .	35	XX
Teddy the 1997 Holiday Bear, R 12/31/97.	20	XX
Teddy the Bear, brown, new face, R 10/1/97	20	75
Teddy the Bear, brown, old face, R 7/1/95	XX	900
Teddy the Cranberry Bear, new face, R 7/1/95.	XX	500
Teddy the Cranberry Bear, old face, R 7/1/95	XX	600
Teddy the Jade Bear, new or old face, R 7/1/95	XX	375
Teddy the Magenta Bear, new or old face, R 7/1/95. .	XX	500
Teddy the Teal Bear, new or old face, R 7/1/95	XX	550
Teddy the Violet Bear, new or old face, R 7/1/95	XX	600
Tracker the Basset Hound.	5	XX
Trap the Mouse, R 7/1/95.	XX	400
Tuffy the Terrier	5	XX
Tusk (Tuck) the Walrus, R 1/1/97	40	80
Twigs the Giraffe, R 5/1/98	8	25
Valentino the Bear.	12	25
Velvet the Panther, R 10/1/97	15	40
Waddle the Penguin, R 5/1/98	8	20
Waves the Whale, R 5/1/98	8	XX
Web the Spider, R 7/1/95.	XX	400
Weenie the Dachshund, R 5/1/98.	8	20
Whisper the Deer	5	XX
Wise the Owl	5	XX
Wrinkles the Bulldog.	5	XX
Ziggy the Zebra, R 5/1/98	8	25
Zip the Cat, all black, D 7/1/95	XX	750
Zip the Cat, white face and belly, D 1995.	XX	200
Zip the Cat, white paws, R 5/1/98	8	30

Puffer the Puffin, new tag, $5.

INDEX